ASPEN PUBLISHERS

The Complete Guide to Human Resources and the Law
2007 Edition

by Dana Shilling

The Complete Guide to Human Resources and the Law is an invaluable tool for the HR professional who needs to place legal principles and developments in the context of the practical problems he or she faces every day. The law as it relates to human resources issues is an ever-growing, ever-changing body of information that involves not just court cases but also statutes and the regulations of adminis-trative agencies. *The Complete Guide to Human Resources and the Law* brings you the most up-to-date information as well as practical tips and checklists in a well-organized, easy-to-use resource.

Highlights of the 2007 Edition

The 2007 Edition provides new and expanded coverage of issues such as:

* The Supreme Court resolved the wage-and-hour treatment of "donning and doffing" time for safety gear in *IBP, Inc. v. Alvarez* [126 S. Ct. 514 (2005)], and ruled early in 2006 that the 15-employee minimum for Title VII claims is a substantive element of the claim and not a jurisdictional prerequisite; hence, the issue can be waived if it is not raised in a timely manner. [*Arbaugh v. Y&H Corp.,* 126 S. Ct. 1235 (Feb. 26, 2006)] The court also made it clear that disparate impact claims are cognizable in the ADEA context. [*Smith v. City of Jackson,* 544 U.S. 228 (2005)]

* DOL issued a Final Rule under the Uniformed Services Employment and Reemployment Rights Act (USERRA) [*see* 70 Fed. Reg. 75313 (Dec. 19, 2005)] and drafted a new form for the notice employers must give employees about their rights to resume employment after an active duty commitment.

Wolters Kluwer
Law & Business

- Final IRS Regulations were issued explaining allocation of compensation income between work performed inside and away from the United States. [T.D. 9212, 70 Fed. Reg. 40,663 (July 14, 2005)]

- The Gulf Opportunity Zone Act of 2005 [P.L. 109-35] made changes in the definition of "dependent" for tax purposes, affecting Health Savings Accounts and dependent care benefits.

- The IRS continued to move toward an all-electronic system for filing and paying employment-related taxes.

- Both statutes [the Katrina Emergency Tax Relief Act of 2005, P.L. 109, 73; and the Gulf Zone Opportunity Act, P.L. 109-135] and rulemaking addressed the effect of the 2005 hurricanes on pension and benefit plans (for example, by waiving penalties when hurricane victims take plan distributions). Presumably these rules will offer a template if there are catastrophic storms in 2006.

- For 2006, the definition of "highly compensated employee" changed to one who earns $100,000 or more per year, and a "key employee" is now defined as one who earns over $140,000 a year.

- The Deficit Reduction Act of 2005 [P.L. 109-171] increased the PBGC premium for single-employer plans from $19 per employee per year to $30 per employee per year, and also imposed a one-time $1,250 per participant premium for 2006–2010 for certain plan terminations.

- Regulations were issued under Code § 402A, explaining the treatment of Roth 401(k) plans. [T.D. 9237, 2006-6 I.R.B. 394] Regulations were also proposed covering distributions from Roth 401(k) plans. [71 Fed. Reg. 4320 (Jan. 26, 2006)]

- The IRS greatly expanded the information available about administration of nonqualified benefit plans under Code § 409A by publishing more than 200 pages of regulations on October 4, 2005 [70 Fed. Reg. 58,930], although to accommodate the anticipated volume of comments, the IRS announced that the proposal probably would not be finalized until the Fall of 2006.

10/06

For questions concerning this shipment, billing, or other customer service matters, call our Customer Service Department at 1-800-234-1660.

For toll-free ordering, please call 1-800-638-8437.

THE COMPLETE GUIDE TO HUMAN RESOURCES AND THE LAW

ASPEN PUBLISHERS

THE COMPLETE GUIDE TO HUMAN RESOURCES AND THE LAW

2007 Edition

Dana Shilling

Wolters Kluwer
Law & Business

AUSTIN   BOSTON   CHICAGO   NEW YORK   THE NETHERLANDS

This publication is designed to provide accurate and authoritative information in regard to the subject matter covered. It is sold with the understanding that the publisher is not engaged in rendering legal, accounting, or other professional services. If legal advice or other professional assistance is required, the services of a competent professional person should be sought.

—From a *Declaration of Principles* jointly adopted
by a Committee of the American Bar Association
and a Committee of Publishers and Associations

Printed in the United States of America

ISBN 0-7355-5995-3

1 2 3 4 5 6 7 8 9 0

About Wolters Kluwer Law & Business

Wolters Kluwer Law & Business is a leading provider of research information and workflow solutions in key specialty areas. The strength of the individual brands of Aspen Publishers, CCH, Kluwer Law International and Loislaw are aligned within Wolters Kluwer Law & Business to provide comprehensive, in-depth solutions and expert-authored content for the legal, professional and education markets.

CCH was founded in 1913 and has served more than four generations of business professionals and their clients. The CCH products in the Wolters Kluwer Law & Business group are highly regarded electronic and print resources for legal, securities, antitrust and trade regulation, government contracting, banking, pensions, payroll, employment and labor, and healthcare reimbursement and compliance professionals.

Aspen Publishers is a leading information provider for attorneys, business professionals and law students. Written by preeminent authorities, Aspen products offer analytical and practical information in a range of specialty practice areas from securities law and intellectual property to mergers and acquisitions and pension/benefits. Aspen's trusted legal education resources provide professors and students with high-quality, up-to-date and effective resources for successful instruction and study in all areas of the law.

Kluwer Law International supplies the global business community with comprehensive English-language international legal information. Legal practitioners, corporate counsel and business executives around the world rely on the Kluwer Law International journals, loose-leafs, books and electronic products for authoritative information in many areas of international legal practice.

Loislaw is a premier provider of digitized legal content to small law firm practitioners of various specializations. Loislaw provides attorneys with the ability to quickly and efficiently find the necessary legal information they need, when and where they need it, by facilitating access to primary law as well as state-specific law, records, forms and treatises.

Wolters Kluwer Law & Business, a unit of Wolters Kluwer, is headquartered in New York and Riverwoods, Illinois. Wolters Kluwer is a leading multinational publisher and information services company.

ASPEN PUBLISHERS SUBSCRIPTION NOTICE

This Aspen Publishers product is updated on a periodic basis with supplements to reflect important changes in the subject matter. If you purchased this product directly from Aspen Publishers, we have already recorded your subscription for the update service.

If, however, you purchased this product from a bookstore and wish to receive future updates and revised or related volumes billed separately with a 30-day examination review, please contact our Customer Service Department at 1-800-234-1660, or send your name, company name (if applicable), address, and the title of the product to:

ASPEN PUBLISHERS
7201 McKinney Circle
Frederick, MD 21704

Important Aspen Publishers Contact Information

- To order any Aspen Publishers title, go to *www.aspenpublishers. com* or call 1-800-638-8437.

- To reinstate your manual update service, call 1-800-638-8437.

- To contact Customer Care, e-mail *customer.care@ aspenpublishers.com,* call 1-800-234-1660, fax 1-800-901-9075, or mail correspondence to Order Department, Aspen Publishers, PO Box 990, Frederick, MD 21705.

- To review your account history or pay an invoice online, visit *www.aspenpublishers.com/payinvoices.*

CONTENTS

*A complete table of contents for each chapter
appears at the beginning of the chapter.*

CONTENTS

Chapter 19
HEALTH INSURANCE CONTINUATION AND PORTABILITY (COBRA AND HIPAA)

Chapter 20
DISABILITY PLANS

Chapter 21
INSURANCE FRINGE BENEFITS

CONTENTS

PREFACE

This book, initially published in 1998, has been supplemented and revised several times to deal with changes in the law as they reflect and create changes in the economic climate. In its current incarnation, this book is published in revised form annually.

Over time, the HR function has become more difficult because laws usually get longer and more elaborate (and even things passed as simplification measures are generally full employment programs for lawyers and accountants).

The 2005–2006 period was a crucial one for the pension system, and private pensions are more critical than ever in light of the financial troubles of the Social Security system. The long-lasting trend away from the defined benefit plan, which had once been the predominant pension form, continued, in favor of hybrid plans such as cash balance plans and defined contribution plans. The PBGC's deficit deepened as it took over a number of major pension plans, and the PBGC faced the prospect of shouldering many more in light of financial difficulties in the airline and manufacturing sectors. The Deficit Reduction Act of 2005, P.L. 109-171, enacted significant increases in the PBGC premium.

Clearly, some legal response was required to the looming pension crisis, and in 2005, both Houses passed pension reform legislation. The intention was to have a conference bill ready for President Bush's signature in March 2006. That deadline passed, as did goals of having the bill signed by April 15, 2006, and before the 2006 Easter recess. Finally, just before Congress adjourned for the summer in August 2006, the Pension Protection Act of 2006 (PPA; H.R. 4) was passed by both Houses and a conference agreement was obtained. By that point, this book had already been set in type, so it was impossible to revise the text to reflect the new provisions. We have, however, provided a separate insert supplement discussing the PPA.

In addition to the transition from defined benefit to defined contribution pension plans, other established trends continued. Health care costs continued to rise. Although the rate of increase slowed somewhat, employers' insurance premiums still rose significantly, and the cost of prescription drugs was still a major cost driver. Employers responded, once again, by raising employees' share of the cost. The proportion of retirees receiving work-related health benefits continued to decline, and here too, employers engaged in additional rounds of cost-shifting.

The 2007 Edition is divided into 43 chapters, in eight parts:

- Part I: Pay Planning, including compensation planning, bonuses, severance pay, and tax issues.

- Part II: Pension Law, comprising basic pension concepts, defined benefit plans, and the transition from the predominance of defined benefit plans to the rise of defined contribution and 401(k) plans; cash balance plans; nonqualified plans; and plans for early retirement and retiree health benefits.

- Part III: Pension Plan Administration, going from the adoption of a plan to disclosures to plan participants, handling claims and appeals, amending the plan, complying with ERISA and tax rules, handling plans in the context of corporate transitions such as mergers and acquisitions, and terminating a plan.

- Part IV: Benefit Plans, such as health plans, continuation coverage and portability requirements for health insurance, plans that provide insurance coverage, and disability plans.

- Part V: The HR Function, including hiring and recruitment, HR computing, recordkeeping, corporate communications, employee privacy rights, diversity issues, and work-family issues.

- Part VI: Employee Relations, not only the major topic of labor law but also occupational safety and health, unemployment insurance, and worker's compensation.

- Part VII: Substantive Laws Against Discrimination, focusing on Title VII (and sexual harassment, which is considered a form of sex discrimination), age discrimination, disability discrimination, the Family and Medical Leave Act, and wrongful termination suits.

- Part VIII: Procedure for Handling Discrimination Charges, not only in the context of lawsuits brought by the EEOC, by state regulators, or by private individuals, but by using arbitration and other alternative dispute resolution methods to resolve problems without going to court.

NOTE ON WEB SOURCES: American Lawyer Media's excellent Web site, http://www.law.com, uses very long URLs that are hard to cite; so does PlanSponsor.com. Therefore, for convenience, citations to cases and articles appearing there are simply cited to law.com; do a search for the name of the article if you'd like to retrieve it.

Unfortunately, items on the Web, and Web sites themselves, can "go out of print." In some instances, by the time the current edition of this book was ready for print, items that I had read or downloaded in the past and mentioned in the text are no longer available online or are not available to the general public. In those cases, the item is cited as "Posted to [name of cite] on [date]."

PART I

PAY PLANNING

CHAPTER 1

PAY PLANNING

§ 1.01   INTRODUCTION

When the first edition of this book was published in 1998, many employers—especially those in industries involving media or e-commerce—found themselves in a seller's market. Dot-coms were absorbing many workers, often at salaries and benefit packages so lavish that other employers found it difficult to compete.

Since then, the collapse of the dot-coms, serious stock market declines, the September 11 attack, war in Iraq, and an overall economic downturn have changed the picture. Employers have the luxury of getting many excellent resumes for every job opening—and of holding the line on compensation and benefits instead of having to "pump up the volume" to attract and retain good employees. Until mid-2000, it was often assumed that stock prices follow one inevitable trend: upward. This was not, of course, a rational assumption. Many businesses experienced "underwater" stock options (the price at which the employee can purchase shares is actually higher than the market price of the shares).

In many businesses (especially service businesses), payroll is one of the largest—or even *the* largest—corporate expense. So increasing the payroll will have tremendous bottom-line impact.

Although salary is an important element of compensation, it must be considered not only in the context of an entire compensation package, but in the context of noncompensation considerations such as work-family issues or whether the company is a good place to build a career.

[A]   SEC Proposal

At the beginning of 2006, the Securities and Exchange and Commission (SEC) voted to increase the amount of disclosure that public corporations must make about the pay packages of top management. Under the proposal, the total compensation (including perquisites, stock options, and retirement benefits) of the CEO, CFO, three other highest-paid officers, and all directors would have to be disclosed. (The determination of who is highest paid requires consideration of all forms of compensation, not merely salary and bonus.) The SEC does not intend to impose limits on the actual compensation, only to make it more transparent to stockholders and potential stockholders. The proposed disclosure format calls for disclosure of salary, bonus, equity-based awards, long-term incentives, other compensation, and total compensation of all kinds. Under prior law, perquisites had to be disclosed if they exceeded $50,000; the proposal reduces the disclosure trigger to $10,000. [Rel. Nos. 33-8655, 34-53185, and IC-27218; *see* Stephen Labaton, *SEC to Require More Disclosure of Executive Pay*, New York Times, Jan. 18, 2006, at p. A1; Sutherland Asbill & Brennan LLP, *Legal Alert: The SEC Proposes Changes to the Executive and Director Compensation Disclosure Rules,* <http://www.sablaw.com/files/tbl_s10News/FileUpload44/15095/LegalAlertSECProposes> (Jan. 27, 2006)]

The SEC followed up on this by issuing interpretive guidance concerning what constitutes a perquisite. Items that are directly, integrally related to the performance of an executive's duties are not perquisites, whereas items that offer personal benefits, and are not uniformly available to all employees, are perquisites. The SEC stated that the determination does not depend on whether the item is tax deductible as an ordinary and necessary business expense. For example, offices, even luxurious ones, are not perquisites, nor is business travel, business entertainment, or an itemized expense account that can only be used for business purposes. However, commuter transportation, management of the employee's personal investments, housing, and club memberships (unless used exclusively for business entertainment) constitute perquisites. [Powell Goldstein LLP, *SEC Provides Guidance on Definition of "Perquisites,"* <http://www.pogolaw.com/attachments/414.pdf> (Mar. 2, 2006)]

The SEC finalized the proposal on July 26, 2006. The Final Rule requires publication of both tables of top management compensation and narrative disclosure. Public companies must use the Compensation Discussion and Analysis (which will be filed with the SEC, so the CEO and CFO must certify it) to disclose the compensation for top management. Compensation disclosure extends three years back. The value of equity-based awards such as stock options must be disclosed, and the SEC has drafted the rule to provide information about the timing of option grants, as part of a drive against back-dating. Salary and bonuses of top management must be disclosed, and so must retirement plans, and post-employment benefits (e.g., golden parachutes). A similar disclosure format is required for compensation of directors. The final rule, like the proposal, increases the size of related-person transactions that must be disclosed ($120,000 rather than the prior rule of $60,000). Public companies must disclose the extent to which directors are independent, and must reveal more about officers' and directors' holdings of the company's own stock. [SEC Press Release, *SEC Votes to Adopt Changes to Disclosure Requirements Concerning Executive Compensation and Related Matters*, <http://www.sec.gov/news/press/2006/2006-123.htm> (July 26, 2006)]

§ 1.02 DECISION FACTORS IN SETTING COMPENSATION

A business's compensation policies reflect many factors:

- What the business can afford to pay;
- Competitive factors (other local companies competing for workers, prevailing wages, unemployment rates);
- Impact on cash flow (until recently, cash-poor companies with bright prospects often relied heavily on stock options and/or the potential for an IPO as elements of compensation);
- Effect on future financing (venture capitalists who expect one-third of the shares in a new business, or a business receiving later rounds of funding, will not want too many of the shares to be assigned to employees);
- The compensation package favored by the kind of workers the employer wants to attract. If the objective is to minimize turnover, for instance, workers with

families will place a high value on health benefits, whereas more mobile younger workers will tend to favor higher cash compensation and pension portability;

• Tax factors for both employer and employee; the objective is for the employer to get the highest permissible deduction, and for the employee to retain as much as possible after taxes.

In the 2004 bonus season, bonuses represented 10% of payroll; it had been only 8.8% a year earlier. Most bonuses were performance-based, which can create problems for productive employees in below-average corporate divisions. The trend was to increase the use of bonuses (a one-time cost) in lieu of salary increases, which become fixed costs. Hewitt Associates reported typical raises for 2004 and 2005 at a well-below-average range of 3.4 to 3.7%. Mercer HR Consulting's conclusion was that in companies where all employees are eligible for bonuses, clerical and support staff bonuses usually come in at about 3 to 5% of annual salary; middle managers 10 to 15%; upper managers 15 to 25%; and top executives 30 to 50% of pay. [Jeff D. Opdyke, *Getting a Bonus Instead of a Raise*, Wall Street Journal, Dec. 29, 2004, at p. D1]

Before the dot-com stock market crash of 2001, the average raise was about 4%. In contrast, CEOs who had been in office for at least two years got an average 7.2% increase in salary and bonus in 2003, reaching a median of $2.12 million. Because inflation in general was low, the impact of small salary increases was somewhat blunted. However, employees were expected to shoulder a larger percentage of ever-increasing health care costs. [Erin White and Chris Maher, *Please, Sir, A Bit More?* Wall Street Journal, Oct. 26, 2004, at p. B1; Michael S. Derby, *Sorry, You're Only Getting a 3.5% Raise Again,* Wall Street Journal, June 24, 2004, at p. D2]

According to the Department of Labor, the inflation-adjusted cost of wages in the private sector actually fell in both 2004 and 2005, although the cost of benefits increased by about 0.7% in 2005, lower than the rate of increase in earlier years. Over a period of 20 years, the real (inflation-adjusted) wages of blue collar workers went up only 1.1%, although the increase in benefit costs means that their overall compensation increased 10% in this period. For service workers, the overall rise in compensation costs was 9.1%, including a 1.4% average wage increase. Total compensation of white collar workers went up 18.1% overall, and wages by 11.1%, with executives gaining the most (total compensation up 18.3%, salary up by 14.4%). [Floyd Norris, *When It Comes to Pay, It Helps to Be the One Signing the Checks*, New York Times, Feb. 4, 2006, at p. C3] The Department of Labor reported a surprisingly large increase at the end of 2004: weekly salaries (including commissions and end-of-year bonuses) were 5.7% higher than the fourth quarter of 2003. The nationwide weekly average wage in Q4 2004 was $812. [Rafael Gerena-Morales, *Weekly Salaries Rise an Average of 5.7% in U.S.*, Wall Street Journal, July 20, 2005, at p. A2]

The Government Accountability Office (GAO) concluded that, between 2001 and 2005, increases in benefit costs outpaced total increases in wages. Until 2005, the cost of paid leave was the largest benefit cost; in that year, health insurance became the largest cost. In 2005, the cost of health insurance equaled the cost of paid leave for the first time. Between 1991 and 2005, the cost of paid leave rose 5%, whereas the cost of health insurance went up 28%. [The report is available at http://www.gao.gov/cgi-bin/getrpt?GAO-06-285; see Fred Schneyer, *GAO: Benefit Cost Hikes in Front of Wage Increases,* PlanSponsor.com (Feb. 24, 2005) and Allison Bell, *GAO: Benefits Cost Increases Squeeze Out Wages,* National Underwriter Online News Service (Feb. 24, 2006)]

In mid-2003, the Wall Street Journal reported a trend toward dismissing employees not because they were poor performers or hard to work with—but simply because they were at the top of the company's pay scale and therefore could be replaced by lower-cost, perhaps less experienced workers. This was one of the factors behind the noticeable decline in the median weekly pay of full-time workers between 2002 and 2003. (Median earnings fell from over $610 to about $600 a week.) For example, Circuit City replaced many commissioned sales-persons with salaried workers to cut costs. [Carlos Tejada and Gary McWilliams, *New Recipe for Cost Savings: Replace Expensive Workers*, Wall Street Journal, June 11, 2003, at p. A1]

In 2004, average earnings for women were 80% of average earnings for men; 25 years earlier, women had earned an average of only 62% as much as men. The BLS reported that the median weekly pay for men in late 2004 was $693; women's was $560. However, the narrowed gap reflected better opportunities for women, with men standing still or losing ground. Most of the jobs added to the economy were low-paying service jobs. Men are more vulnerable to layoffs than women are, because men are more likely to work in manufacturing and other cyclical industries. [Louis Uchitelle, *Gaining Ground on the Wage Front*, New York Times, Dec. 31, 2004, at p. C1]

In July 2005, the Bureau of Labor Statistics announced that it would stop collecting monthly payroll data about women workers. However, there was high demand for the information, so in January 2006 the agency announced that it would resume data collection, either in July 2006 or January 2007. [*BLS to Reinstate Data on Women Workers in Payroll Survey by Early 2007, Officials Say,* 74 L.W. 2412]

The Ninth Circuit held that projected pay of $37 million for two Gemstar-TV International executives was extraordinary. The compensation packages for the two were placed into escrow pursuant to the Sarbanes-Oxley Act when the SEC investigated whether or not the executives had overstated revenues and deceived stockholders. The Ninth is the first circuit to attempt to define "extraordinary" compensation in this context. Because it treats the rationale for the legislation as protection of creditors and investors, an extraordinary payment is defined as one that would not typically be made by the company in its customary course of business. There is no single litmus test, but relevant factors include the purpose and size of the payment and the circumstances under which it was made. Here, the severance packages were five to six times base salary, and the bonuses apparently reflected the reported amounts that were allegedly fraudulent. [*SEC v. Gemstar-TV Guide Int'l Inc.*, 05 401 F.3d 1031 (9th Cir. 2005), discussed in Pam Smith, *9th Circuit Defines "Extraordinary" Executive Pay*, The Recorder (Mar. 24, 2005) (law.com)]

§ 1.03   BENEFITS AS AN ELEMENT OF COMPENSATION

The accepted rule of thumb is that the cost of benefits adds about one-third to the employee's stated salary.

The size of the benefit package is often directly related to the size of the company. Generally, for any particular benefit, the percentage of companies offering that benefit increases with the size of the workforce, and it is also often true that larger companies offer a more generous benefit package.

In general, unionized workers have access to more benefits than non-unionized workers, and pay and benefits tend to be lower in the South than in other regions.

Data released by the BLS in the summer of 2005 showed that the average employee compensation was $24.17 an hour, of which $17.15 represented wages and $7.02 benefit costs (a ratio of approximately 70:30). The cost of providing legally mandated benefits such as FICA taxes, Worker's Compensation, and unemployment insurance averaged $2.10 an hour. The employer's cost of providing health, life, and disability insurance averaged $1.76 an hour, paid leave cost $1.54, retirement and savings $0.90. In 2003, 57% of private-sector workers had access to retirement benefits; 60% had access to health care benefits; 50% had access to life insurance benefits; 39% had access to short-term disability benefits other than paid sick leave; and 30% had access to long-term disability benefits.

The most important determinant in benefit access was full-time status; full-timers were five times as likely as part-timers to have access to life insurance and dental care. Workers who earned $15 an hour or more had much greater benefit access than lower-paid workers, and benefits were more generous in goods-producing than in service industries. [BLS Monthly Labor Review Editor's Desk (June 22, 2005), <http://www.bls.gov/opub/ted/2005/jun/wk3/art03.htm>]

The predominant story in 2005–2006 was the reduction of pension and benefit availability, led by, but not limited to, bankrupt or reorganized companies. Once large companies in financial trouble began to terminate or freeze pensions, reduce or eliminate retiree health benefits, and increase employee copayment responsibilities for health plans, other companies tended to fall into line so that their costs and therefore their prices would remain competitive. [Eduardo Porter and Mary Williams Walsh, *Benefits Go the Way of Pensions,* New York Times, Feb. 9, 2006, at p. C1]

§ 1.04   AVOIDING DISCRIMINATION

The Equal Employment Opportunity Commission (EEOC) Compliance Manual contains a section dealing with compensation issues in the context of various antidiscrimination statutes. The EEOC's position is that antidiscrimination laws apply to all aspects of compensation, including salary, overtime, bonuses, options, profit sharing, fringe benefits, and expense accounts. The agency says that employers are never justified in taking race, color, sex, national origin, religion, age, or disability into account in setting compensation.

The EEOC says that equal severance benefits are required for all similarly situated employees, regardless of age. Employers may not deny severance because the employee is eligible for a pension, although sometimes pension benefits can be offset against the severance pay. Denying recall rights to older workers operates as involuntary retirement. Because the cost of providing severance pay does not rise with the employees' ages, employers are not allowed to assert an equal cost defense.

However, retiree health benefits can legitimately be offset against severance if the retiree is eligible for an immediate pension; if he actually receives health benefit coverage; and the retiree benefits are at least comparable to Medicare in type and value. If the retiree is over 65, benefits must be at least comparable to one-fourth the value of Medicare benefits. The offset itself must be reduced by any percentage by which the pension is reduced for retirement before normal retirement age, and by any percentage of the premium that the retiree has to pay for retiree health coverage.

The Compliance Manual says that "if the employer provides additional pension benefits that are enough, or are higher than those necessary to bring an employee up to the level of an unreduced pension, the employer can offset the full amount of those benefits. On the other hand, if the employer offers benefits that are insufficient to raise the employee to an unreduced pension, the employer cannot claim any offset at all."

§ 1.05 VARIABLE PAY

A variable pay system makes part of the compensation dependent on meeting goals or targets. Because these plans are supposed to create incentives for better work, communication is key. Formal annual review explaining how the award was calculated is useful to pinpoint areas in which employees succeeded and those in which more work is necessary. The most effective plans had "moderate stretch" (i.e., they asked employees to achieve targets that were not impossible, but were not comfortably in view either).

In general, corporate profits rose in 2005, but the trend was to award raises based on individual or group performance rather than granting across-the-board raises reflecting the corporation's performance. A corporation taking this tack might give raises of 3 to 5% for top performers, 2 to 3% for average employees, and 1.5% or less to those whose performance was sub-par. Hewitt Associates found in 2004 that top performers got raises of close to 10%, whereas average employees received raises of about 3.6% and poor performers got flat salaries or raises in the 1.3% average range. At one time, pay for performance measures were limited to top management; they are now being used throughout the organization. The rationale is to attract and retain top performers in a low-unemployment environment, without raising the compensation budget high enough to impair the organization's ability to compete. In 2004, close to half of companies said they had a retention program, whereas only about a third had one in 2003. [Erin White, *The Best vs. the Rest*, Wall Street Journal, Jan. 30, 2006, at p. B1; Kaja Whitehouse, *More Companies Offer Packages Linking Pay Plans to Performance*, Wall Street Journal, Dec. 13, 2005, at p. B6]

§ 1.06   WAGE AND HOUR ISSUES

The HR department's many and varied responsibilities probably include handling (or outsourcing and supervising) payroll matters, including paying employees subject to the appropriate deductions.

The Fair Labor Standards Act (FLSA) [29 U.S.C. §§ 201–219 and 251–262] regulates wages and hour matters. The FLSA forbids sex discrimination in compensation, sets a minimum wage, requires extra pay when a "non-exempt" worker puts in overtime hours, and sets standards for record keeping and record retention. The Department of Labor's Wage and Hour Division is responsible for administering the FLSA.

Buy-back premiums for firefighters (75% of regular hourly pay for any of their 10 sick days that were not used) constituted remuneration to be included in the regular rate of pay that was used to calculate overtime. According to the Eighth Circuit, all remuneration, unless otherwise excluded by the FLSA, has to be included in the regular rate of pay. [*Acton v. Columbia*, 436 F.3d 969 (8th Cir. 2006)]

State laws that do not conflict with the FLSA, and that provide additional protection for employees, are not preempted by the federal law. Therefore, you should check your state law to see if it covers employees who are not covered by the FLSA, or if the law imposes additional compliance burdens. The FLSA says that suit may be maintained in either state or federal court. In mid-2003, the Supreme Court interpreted this to mean that an FLSA suit for unpaid wages, liquidated damages, interest, and attorney's fees can be removed by the defendant employer from state to federal court. Just because the suit may be maintained in either system doesn't prevent removal, or require a case to remain in the same system from beginning to end. [*Breuer v. Jim's Concrete of Brevard Inc.*, 538 U.S. 691 (2003)]

On another question of balancing federal and state law, a stagehand sued his employer in California state court, under California's Labor Code, for failure to pay overtime. The defendant removed the case to federal court, claiming that it was preempted by the Labor Management Relations Act (LMRA) § 301. [*See* § 30.02[D] for more discussion of § 301 preemption] However, the Ninth Circuit ruled that the case should have stayed in the state court system, because the only question is whether the plaintiff's work on different TV and movie productions should have been aggregated to determine his overtime wages. It was not necessary to interpret a Collective Bargaining Agreement to make the determination. [*Gregory v. SCIE, LLC*, 317 F.3d 1050 (9th Cir. 2003)]

The Fourth Circuit denied damages under state wage and hour law in a case in which the plaintiff alleged that his employer refused to let him exercise stock options. There was no unconditional promise of options as part of his compensation package as a salaried employee, so the options were not recoverable as remuneration for work. [*Varghese v. Honeywell Int'l*, 424 F.3d 411 (4th Cir. 2005)]

Employees have a private right of action (that is, they can sue their employers) for unpaid minimum wages and/or overtime, plus liquidated damages, attorneys' fees, and court costs. Courts have the power to order legal and equitable relief against employers who fire employees, or otherwise discriminate or retaliate against them for making an FLSA complaint or participating in a Wage and Hour Division proceeding. [29 U.S.C. § 216]

Not only can employees sue their employers, the Secretary of Labor has the power to sue for unpaid minimum wages and overtime. The funds go directly to the employees who should have received them, not to the Department of Labor (DOL). The court can enjoin the employer against committing any further violations. Willful violations of the FLSA are criminal rather than civil in nature, so prosecution by the federal Attorney General's office is possible, in addition to DOL actions or civil suits by the employees.

The Wage and Hour Division of the Employment Standards Administration (part of DOL) announced that in fiscal 2005 it collected $166 million in back wages for more than 241,000 employees. More than 219,000 employees received $134.2 million in minimum wage and overtime back wages to redress FLSA violations— $119.4 million for overtime violations, $14.8 million for minimum wage violations. Nearly $1.8 million in back wages was collected for Family and Medical Leave Act violations, although the number of FMLA cases fell 10% between 2004 and 2005. The Wage and Hour Division also reduced its processing time significantly, taking an average of 85 days rather than the 139 days it took to handle a case in 2001. [*DoL Collects $166 Million in Back Wages in 2005*, PlanSponsor.com (Feb. 8, 2006)]

The FLSA allows the pay of hourly (but not salaried) workers to be docked for absenteeism. DOL Opinion Letter No. 89 [discussed in Employment Alert, March 5, 1998 at p. 11] says that a deduction to reflect unpaid leave under the Family and Medical Leave Act (FMLA) does not convert an otherwise exempt person into a nonexempt hourly worker. However, this relief provision is limited to FMLA leave, where both the worker and the employer company come under the FMLA's provisions.

Courts differ as to whether FLSA punitive damages are available. The Seventh Circuit and Eastern District of Pennsylvania said yes, because it is a form of relief provided in egregious cases; the Eleventh said no, because the FLSA statute doesn't specifically allow punitive damages. [*See* Shannon P. Duffy, *Punitive Damages Available Under FLSA, Federal Judge Rules,* The Legal Intelligencer (Oct. 15, 2001) (law.com); *Travis v. Gary Community Mental Health Center,* 921 F.2d 108 (7th Cir. 1990); *Snapp v. Unlimited Concepts Inc.,* 208 F.3d 928 (11th Cir. 2000)]

A California jury awarded $172 million to 116,000 current and former Wal-Mart employees for illegal denial of meal breaks: $57 million in general damages and $115 million in punitive damages. This was the first of 40 cases filed to go to trial. (California Labor Code § 226.7 requires a 30-minute meal break for every five hours worked.) [David Kravets, *Jury Awards $172M to Wal-Mart Employees*, <http://www.verizon.net> (Dec. 22, 2005)]

California's Court of Appeals has decided several cases about the status of payments under California Labor Code § 226.7. The appellate districts are split as to whether the payments are "wages" or "penalties." If the payments are wages, the statute of limitations is longer (four years, under California Business & Professions Code § 17200 vs. only one year for penalties). The First and Second Districts have characterized the amounts as penalties, while the Fourth District has characterized them as wages. [*Mills v. Superior Court* (2d Dist.); *National Steel & Shipbuilding v. Superior Court* (Godinez) (4th Dist.); *Murphy v. Kenneth Cole Productions* (1st Dist.); *see* Marie-Anne Hogarth, *Calif. Appeal Courts at Odds over Meal Breaks*, The Recorder (Jan. 31, 2006) (law.com)]

[A] FLSA Litigation

A mid-2003 Supreme Court decision involved an FLSA suit in Florida state court for unpaid wages, liquidated damages, prejudgment interest, and attorneys' fees. The defendant removed the case to federal court. The plaintiff tried to get the case returned to state court. Two federal laws were in conflict. The FLSA itself says that a suit can be maintained in any state or federal court, whereas 28 USC § 1441(a) gives general rules for removing a case to federal court. The Supreme Court says that the case was properly removed to federal court. The FLSA provision doesn't forbid removal, and the case could have been commenced in federal court, so it was proper to remove it there. [*Breuer v. Jim's Concrete of Brevard, Inc.*, 538 U.S. 691 (2003)]

Employers face not only class actions from groups of dissatisfied employees, but also a special kind of "collective action lawsuit" authorized by FLSA § 216. Employees are entitled to benefits under these lawsuits only if they file a written consent statement opting into the action and agreeing to be bound by its settlement or judgment. The plaintiffs' attorney has to convince the court that this is an appropriate procedure, because the potential plaintiffs are similarly situated and there is a reasonable basis for going forward with the case. Usually, 15–30% of the possible plaintiffs decide to opt in. The percentage gets higher if, for example, a union gets involved in recruiting possible plaintiffs.

Late in 2003, the Eleventh Circuit held that once a named plaintiff in an FLSA collective action settles his own claims, he will not be allowed to continue the action and notify other class members of a potential case. The Eleventh Circuit distinguished between the FLSA collective action form and the Rule 23 class action, where class members can opt out and the representative plaintiff has the status of a private Attorney General to pursue grievances. In this case, a group of nurses charged their employer with failure to pay overtime. Three of them agreed to have their claims dismissed in return for a payment of overtime. The district court did not find evidence that there were others who wanted to opt in, and therefore denied permission to notify possible plaintiffs. Finally, the fourth plaintiff settled and asked leave to appeal the rejection of notification. The Eleventh Circuit refused, finding that continuing the case would mean that the last settling plaintiff, who no longer had a financial interest in the case might end up litigating an action that had no other plaintiffs. [*Cameron-Grant v. Maxim Healthcare Servs. Inc.,* 347 F.3d 1240 (11th Cir. 2003)]

Another Eleventh Circuit case rules that if an additional claim is added to an FLSA collective action for overtime pay, workers who opted in initially are not required to opt in again, because it cannot be concluded that they agreed only to the specific claims initially asserted. [*Prickett v. DeKalb County,* 349 F.3d 1294 (11th Cir. 2003)]

In the First Circuit view, it was not protected activity under the FLSA for a safety engineer to tell his supervisors about potential overtime violations affecting the security guards the engineer supervised. It was just part of his job, so firing him for pointing out possible violations could not be forbidden retaliation. [*Claudio-Gotay v. Becton Dickinson Caribe Ltd.,* 375 F.3d 99 (1st Cir. 2004)]

In 2003, the Third Circuit ruled that it was an abuse of judgment for the district court to exercise supplemental jurisdiction over a state wage payment claim. The Third Circuit decided that state claims substantially predominated over the federal ones, because the state issues affected far more plaintiffs than the FLSA claims in the same case. There were complex and novel state-law issues to be resolved, the state plaintiffs had to opt out whereas the federal FLSA plaintiffs had to opt in, and there were individual fact issues in the state case that did not arise under the FLSA. [*DeAsencio v. Tyson Foods Inc.,* 342 F.3d 301 (3d Cir. 2003)]

Once a group action begins, the defendant employer has a strong incentive to settle the case because of the expense of proceeding with discovery. For example, the District Court for the District of Minnesota upheld a magistrate judge's order compelling discovery of the names and addresses of potential plaintiffs. Discovery was ordered over the employer's objections that it was inappropriate until the employer's motion to compel arbitration was resolved; that the judge had to find that all the persons whose names were sought were similarly situated; and that the discovery order violated employee privacy. [*Bailey v. Ameriquest,* 2002 WL 100388 (D. Minn. Jan. 23, 2002)] A group of unskilled delivery workers supplied by labor agents to supermarkets and drug stores filed suit, charging that they were denied payment of the minimum wage, overtime, and other benefits. A class of unskilled delivery workers identified as independent contractors was certified. The Southern District of New York ruled that it had supplemental jurisdiction over the state-law wage and hour claims—even for workers who did not join in the federal FLSA collective action. [*Ansoumana v. Gristede's Operating Corp.,* 201 F.R.D. 81 (S.D.N.Y. 2001)]

The Ninth Circuit made it clear in early 2004 that one thing you don't have to worry about is RICO. A plaintiff charged his former employer and its managers with racketeering offenses, charging them with mail fraud for underpaying him and misrepresenting his entitlement to overtime pay. (The alleged wire fraud came in because his paychecks and W-2 forms were mailed, and employees could arrange for direct deposit of their wages.) The Ninth Circuit refused to expand RICO to allow what were essentially basic state contract claims to be brought in federal court. Furthermore, there was no predicate (underlying) RICO offense, because misrepresenting legal consequences, such as entitlement to overtime, does not constitute fraud. [*Miller v. Yokohama Tire Corp.*, 358 F.3d 616 (9th Cir. 2004)]

The City of Chattanooga hired three housing code inspectors on the same day; the white female earned significantly more than the two black males. Various employment practices gave rise to complaints by employees, and eventually the defendant, the city's housing administrator, decided to fire all three of them. The white female inspector quit, the two black males were fired, and one of them became the plaintiff in this case, asserting FLSA retaliation claims. The jury found in his favor, awarding back pay and damages for mental and emotional distress. The Sixth Circuit upheld the award, finding that there was adequate evidence of retaliation to support the award. The plaintiff asked to have the damages doubled as liquidated damages, but the Sixth Circuit refused, finding that the issue was not properly raised on appeal.

The FLSA allows "such legal or equitable relief as may be appropriate to effectuate" the statutory scheme, so the Sixth Circuit concluded this was broad enough to justify damages for emotional injury as compensation for harm suffered: the plaintiff provided evidence of the distress he suffered when he lost his job and was worried about being able to support his family. The Sixth Circuit considered that the $40,000 award for this purpose (in conjunction with $10,232 in back pay) might be on the high side, but did not reflect the jury's passion, bias or prejudice, and was not excessive enough to shock the conscience. [*Moore v. Freeman*, 355 F.3d 558 (6th Cir. 2004)]

For a full discussion of the issues involved in awards of liquidated (i.e., double) damages under the FLSA, see Aashish Y. Desai's article, *Federal Class Action Overtime Cases—Can You Really Get Double Damages?* [72 L.W. 2195 (Oct. 14, 2003)]. Desai concludes that there is a strong presumption that winning FLSA plaintiffs will get double damages, unless the employer can assert a defense of good faith and reasonable belief that the action did not violate the FLSA.

In mid-2004, the Second Circuit ruled that 29 C.F.R. § 522.109(a), an FLSA exemption, is invalid. The rule, which exempts providers of companionship services for the elderly and infirm if they are employed by an agency or other employer other than the family using the services, was deemed invalid and not entitled to deference because it violates the Congressional intent to provide minimum wage and overtime protection for persons such as these home care workers. [*Coke v. Long Island Care at Home Ltd.*, 376 F.3d 118 (2d Cir. 2004)]

Although the heading for this discussion is "FLSA litigation," arbitration is also a possible means of resolving wage and hour disputes. In 2004, the Fifth Circuit confirmed that FLSA claims can be the subject of a compulsory predispute arbitration agreement: there is nothing in the FLSA that requires the court system rather than arbitration to resolve disputes. The limitations on discovery in arbitration do not deprive plaintiffs of substantive rights under the FLSA. The Fifth Circuit interpreted the arbitration agreement to mean that the arbitrator would award attorneys' fees to the plaintiffs if they prevailed and applicable state or federal law called for a fee award—so they were not deprived of rights in this respect either. The District Court did agree with one argument raised by the plaintiffs: that the agreement imposed excessive costs on employees who wanted to arbitrate a dispute. The Fifth Circuit found that it was unnecessary to decide whether the invalid provisions could be severed, and the rest of the agreement enforced, because the employer eventually agreed to pay all of the costs of arbitration itself (other than a $125 filing fee). Thus, the employees could not be deprived of their rights to assert claims by fear of prohibitive costs, because their cost exposure was limited. The Fifth Circuit rejected the plaintiffs' arguments that the arbitration agreement was unconscionable under Texas law. [*Carter v. Countrywide Credit Indus. Inc.,* 362 F.3d 294 (5th Cir. 2004); *see also Adkins v. Labor Ready Inc.,* 303 F.3d 496 (4th Cir. 2002) (there is no inherent conflict between the FLSA and the Federal Arbitration Act, and FLSA claims can be subject to mandatory arbitration because the FLSA's statutory language is similar to that of the ADEA, and ADEA claims are subject to mandatory arbitration)]

§ 1.07   MINIMUM WAGE

The minimum wage is $5.15 per hour. One Eighth Circuit case allowed payment of less than minimum wage under the facts of the case.

"On-call" time, when employees had to be able to report to the hospital within 20 minutes, had to be reachable by telephone, cell phone, or pager, and had to abstain from drugs and alcohol, was not "work" time because of the limited restrictions on employees' activities. Therefore, it was acceptable to pay less than the minimum wage for this time. [*Reimer v. Champion Healthcare Corp.,* 258 F.3d 720 (8th Cir. 2001)]

The Department of Labor permits unpaid internships for trainees, so the trainees can acquire usable job skills. The criteria for an acceptable internship program include the following conditions:

- Even though the employer's facilities are used, the training is similar to the curriculum of a vocational school;
- The real benefit of the training goes to the trainee, not the employer (in fact, the employer's operations may even be slowed down by the actions of the novices);
- Trainees are closely supervised, but do not replace regular employees;
- The trainee explicitly agrees to work without pay;
- There is no guarantee that the trainee will be hired for a paid job.

Since 1997, efforts have been made to get Congress to raise the minimum wage, but the efforts have not been successful. The Bureau of Labor Statistics reports that in 2004, about 2 million workers (2.7% of the total) earned the federal minimum wage or less. Typically, they were under age 25 and lacked a high school diploma; however, many of them were tipped employees of restaurants or bars, so the stated wage was only a part of their compensation. In two states (Ohio and

Kansas) it is permissible to pay certain farm workers and small business employees less than the federal minimum wage. Almost one half of the civilian labor force lives in states where the minimum wage is higher than the federal minimum wage. The states of Washington, Oregon, California, Alaska, Hawaii, Minnesota, Wisconsin, Illinois, Florida, Delaware, Maryland, New Jersey, Connecticut, Rhode Island, New York, Massachusetts, Vermont, Maine, and the District of Columbia set a minimum wage higher than the federal requirement.

More than 100 cities and counties have been the site of "living wage" campaigns that sought to require government contractors to pay a wage high enough for workers to live on—generally much higher than the stated minimum wage. There also is increasing attention to the question of the effect of health benefits on compensation. [Joi Preciphs, *States Take on Minimum Wage,* Wall Street Journal, Mar. 14, 2006, at p. A4; John M. Broder, *States Take Lead in Push to Raise Minimum Wages,* New York Times, Jan. 2, 2006, at p. A1]

§ 1.08 DETERMINING WHO IS AN "EMPLOYEE"

There are many reasons why it becomes necessary to determine if a particular person who performs services is an independent contractor or an employee of the company for which the services are performed. For example, employment status is involved in determining who is allowed to participate in pension and benefit plans; who is entitled to overtime; who is entitled to unemployment benefits and Worker's Compensation; and who can sue under antidiscrimination laws. Although similar factors are used in analyses for different purposes, it is possible that someone will be considered an employee for some purposes but not for others.

If the individual is an employee, the employer will be responsible for paying FUTA taxes and its own share of FICA, and will have to withhold income taxes. In contrast, independent contractors are responsible for their own tax compliance.

Clearly, the company saves money if it can characterize workers as independent contractors, because it saves on taxes and benefits (even if the cash compensation is the same). To prevent abuses, this is an area where the IRS and other regulators are active in determining whether the so-called independent contractor is really an employee.

The Internal Revenue Code specifically identifies some groups as statutory employees, and others as statutory non-employees. [I.R.C. §§ 3121, 3401, 3306, 3508] The categories of statutory employees are:

- Agents or commission drivers who deliver food products, laundry, or dry cleaning;
- Full-time traveling salespersons who solicit orders for merchandise to be delivered later;
- Full-time life insurance salespersons;
- Corporate officers;
- People who work in their own homes, but under the supervision of someone who supplies the materials to be used in work (e.g., assembling clothing components).

However, a licensed real estate agent who is not paid on the basis of hours worked, and who has a written contract identifying him or her as an independent contractor, will not be considered an employee. Neither will a "direct seller" who sells consumer products outside of a permanent resale establishment, who is paid on the basis of output, and who has a written contract as an independent contractor. According to the Tax Court, an attorney exercised enough control over two people who worked in the lawyer's office to make them employees of the practice rather than independent contractors. Two secretaries were allowed to set their own hours, but the lawyer required them to log hours of work and paid dues for membership in a legal secretaries' organization. The lawyer neither paid employment taxes nor filed Form 1099s for them: he reported their compensation on his own Schedule C as "negative receipts," not identifying the expenses as payment for secretarial services. The Tax Court focused on the extent of control and noted that the attorney provided office space and supplies. The secretaries were neither at risk of loss nor able to profit by his legal practice. [*Kumpel v. Commissioner,* TC Memo 2003-265]

Under I.R.C. § 414(n), a long-term leased employee may have to be counted in testing pension and benefit plans for discrimination. A safe harbor is permitted when a company gets less than 20% of its non-highly-compensated employees through leasing services, and if those services provide adequate pension coverage for their employees.

Bronk v. Mountain States Telephone & Telegraph Inc. [140 F.3d 1335 (10th Cir. 1998)] holds that, although the Employment Retirement Income Security Act (ERISA) [29 U.S.C. § 1001 *et seq.*] forbids excluding employees from the plan once they have satisfied minimum age and service requirements, it is permissible to draft the plan to deny participation to leased employees, even if they are common-law employees of the sponsor company. The Tenth Circuit position is that I.R.C. § 414(n)(1)(A) merely requires that leased employees be treated as employees; it doesn't require them to be offered plan participation.

An IRS determination that someone who did recruitment and management work for a company, pursuant to a contract, was an employee is not determinative with respect to the FLSA or minimum wage law, because there was no evidence that the IRS actually litigated the question of employee status. [*Morrison v. International Programs Consortium Inc.,* 253 F.3d 5 (D.C. Cir. 2001)] The IRS classified the officer and sole shareholder of a corporation as an employee, resulting in FICA tax liability. The Tax Court and the Third Circuit agreed with the IRS on this issue. Instead of receiving a salary, the sole shareholder received the net income of his home repair company. He reported the funds on Schedule E, as non-passive income, but did not pay FICA on these sums. The Third Circuit pointed to Internal Revenue Code sections and regulations (§§ 3121(b); 3306(c); Reg. § 31.3121(d)-1(b)) explicitly stating that a corporate officer who performs services for the corporation is an employee. The corporation also asked for relief under § 530, but this was denied because the corporation did not have reasonable legal authority supporting its position. [*Nu-Look Design, Inc. v. CIR,* 356 F.3d 290 (3rd Cir. 2004)]

The Fifth Circuit ruled that people who performed services for Mobil Corporation while they were on the payroll of other companies were not "regular employees" of Mobil, and therefore could not get retroactive ERISA-type employment benefits from Mobil (e.g., severance, retirement, medical, disability). The plan administrator reasonably treated them as not being regular employees. [*MacLachlan v. Exxon Mobil Corp.*, 350 F.3d 472 (5th Cir. 2003)]

Independent contractors can be considered "beneficiaries" under ERISA plans and therefore a suit by a commodities trader that made state insurance and tort law claims about the denial of disability benefits was preempted by ERISA. [*Shyman v. Unum Life Ins. Co.*, 427 F.3d 452 (7th Cir. 2005); *see Ruttenberg v. U.S. Life Ins. Co.*, 413 F.3d 652 (7th Cir. 2005) (another case involving floor traders, for the proposition that independent contractors can be beneficiaries of ERISA plans)]

In December 2005 the Los Angeles County Superior Court ordered FedEx to pay $5.3 million to a group of drivers who were improperly classified as independent contractors. The company was ordered to classify the drivers properly and distribute copies of the December 19 court order. Drivers were forced to shoulder expenses that should have been borne by the company, such as fuel, oil, tires, repairs, and liability insurance. Payments to the 200 class members ranged from a few hundred dollars to a peak of $98,000, and $12.3 million in attorneys' fees also was awarded. An additional 32 cases involving FedEx drivers in 25 states have been consolidated for trial in Indiana. [*Estrada v. FedExGround*, No. BC 210130 (L.A. County Super. Ct. Dec. 19, 2005); *see* Petra Pasternak, *Judge Delivers Order to FedEx: Pay Misclassified Drivers,* The Recorder (Dec. 30, 2005) (law.com)]

§1.09 STAFFING ARRANGEMENTS

The U.S. workforce can no longer be divided simply into full-time and part-time workers, or permanent workers and "temps." Many other arrangements have evolved, although, as noted above, the employer's characterization of the arrangement is not always accepted for tax and other legal purposes. Some of the possibilities are:

- Workers who are actually employed by a temporary agency that recruits, trains, and sends workers to companies that are clients of the agency;
- Long-term temporary assignments—where the temporary worker stays at one location for weeks or months, instead of being hired on a daily basis;
- Payrolling—a company wants to hire a specific person, and therefore arranges for a temporary agency to hire that person and be responsible for payment, taxes, and other employment-related matters;
- Part-time workers;
- Independent contractors—who are genuinely self-directed; have clients rather than employers who control their work; and are responsible for their own tax compliance;

- Contract workers—an arrangement usually made with technical workers who are formally employed by a technical services firm. This arrangement is often used for long-range projects, including those that require the contract worker to relocate to the employer's site;
- Leased employees—who are paid by the leasing company, which also handles administrative tasks like tax and Worker's Compensation compliance;
- Outsourcing—delegating a function such as payroll processing, guarding a worksite, or operating an employee cafeteria to a company that specializes in that function.

§ 1.10 SIZE OF THE CONTINGENT WORKFORCE

Clearly, many ways to work have evolved.

The BLS uses more than one definition for "contingent workers," the broadest of which is workers "who do not expect their current job to last."

The BLS also collects information about "alternative" work arrangements (employment can be both contingent and alternative at the same time).

The Department of Labor said that of the 1.2 million jobs added to the workforce in 2004, more than 1 million (i.e., nearly all) of these were part-time jobs; 18% of the overall job market in 2004 consisted of part-time jobs—the highest proportion since 1997. The Bureau of Labor Statistics reported that only 1.44 million of the part-time workforce said they wanted to work full-time; this was less than 10% of the total, but still more than one-third higher than the proportion of part-time workers who wanted full-time work in 2000. According to the Employee Benefits Research Institute, in 2003, 19% of the 25 million part-time workers had health benefits, and a further 37% were covered as dependents of someone else, but 44% did not have health insurance. [David Koeppel, *When "Job" Means Part Time, Life Becomes Very Different*, New York Times, Oct. 10, 2004, at § 10 p. 1]

In July 2004, the BLS reported that the labor force was 131.2 million people, of whom 2.4 million (9% higher than the year before) worked for temporary agencies. The size of the labor force increased only 1% in the same period. Part-time employees must be allowed to participate in qualified plans (if they meet the other requirements) once they reach 1,000 hours of service. Plans using the elapsed time method of crediting service automatically include part-time employees even without the 1,000 hour threshold. Failing to include part-timers with over 1,000 hours of service can result in a need to correct the plan terms: *see, e.g.*, Rev. Proc. 2003-44, 2003-25 I.R.B. 1051, which compels employers to make up for contributions or accruals that should have been made previously. In a 401(k) plan, the employer has to make the contributions on behalf of the employee and make up for lost matches plus amounts that would have been earned if timely contributions had been made. The IRS position is that employees who were denied the opportunity to make contributions should not be forced to do so when the employer corrects the plan deficiencies.

The American Staffing Association and the BLS estimate that in 1999, the percentage of temporary workers had stabilized at about 2.2% of the nonfarm workforce (about twice as high as the 1990 level).

The question is how to interpret these trends. One argument is that workers like and benefit by greater flexibility (especially if they have to combine work and family obligations). The contrary point of view is that career-level full-time jobs with benefits are eroding, and many people are forced to work shorter hours or for less money and fewer benefits with less security than they would prefer.

§ 1.11   CO-EMPLOYERS

It's not always possible to say that one company is the employer and the other has no responsibility. Sometimes two companies (such as a leasing company and the company where the individual actually performs services) will be jointly liable—e.g., if the individual is injured at the workplace or harms someone else.

In 2000, the NLRB ruled that temporary workers could be included in the same bargaining unit as permanent employees, provided that the characteristics of the jobs were similar. But in 2004, the NLRB overturned this decision and ruled that the consent of both the agency supplying the workers and the company where the services are performed is required before temporary workers can be made part of the bargaining unit. [M.B. Sturgis Inc., 331 N.L.R.B. 173 (Aug. 25, 2000), overruled 343 N.L.R.B. 76 (Nov. 19, 2004)]

For FLSA purposes, the First Circuit ruled that a staffing company and its client companies do not become co-employers. The staffing company is the FLSA employer, because it hires and controls the workers, assigns them to job sites, and controls their schedules. [*Baystate Alternative Staffing Inc. v. Herman,* 163 F.3d 668 (1st Cir. 1998)]

In contrast, the Occupational Safety and Health Review Commission (OSHRC) decided that an employee-leasing company was not subject to the Occupational Safety and Health Act, because the workers were not their employees. In this reading, employees work in the employer's "business," and here the leased workers were assigned to a factory where the leasing company did not exercise significant control over them. [*Secretary of Labor v. Team Am. Corp.,* 1998 WL 733708 (OSHRC 1998)]

Early in 2006, the Northern District of California held that workers paid through a staffing agency were not common-law employees of the company to which they were leased. Thus, they were not entitled to employee benefits such as pension, life and health insurance, disability benefits, or severance pay. The plaintiffs had been informed that they were not eligible for benefits, and the plan documents excluded leased employees, contract workers, and independent contractors. The court rejected the argument that the company had to classify them in writing as ineligible because the evidence showed that they were classified as ineligible in practice. [*Curry v. CTB McGraw-Hill LLC,* 2006 U.S. Dist. LEXIS 5920 (N.D. Cal. Jan. 30, 2006)]

In a late 2002 Third Circuit case, a utility company hired an independent contractor to repair damaged telephone lines. An employee of the independent contractor company was seriously injured during the repairs. The Third Circuit ruled that an injured worker is allowed to sue anyone who might be liable for his or her injury—except for the employer named on a Worker's Compensation insurance certificate. [*See* § 33.03 for more discussion of Worker's Compensation exclusivity] As a general rule, the injured employees of an independent contractor do not have a tort cause of action against the hirer of the independent contractor. However, the Restatement (Second) of Torts does provide some exceptions, when the hiring company is negligent in giving orders or directions to the independent contractor, or when it retains some control over the job and exercises that control in a negligent manner. However, the injured person was not permitted to sue his own employer, because there was no evidence that it made a deliberate attempt to injure him, so Worker's Compensation exclusivity applied. [*Gass v. Virgin Islands Tel. Corp.,* 311 F.3d 237 (3d Cir. 2002). *See also Figueroa v. HOVIC,* 198 F. Supp. 2d 632 (D.V.I. 2002); *Hooker v. Department of Transp.,* 27 Cal. 4th 198 (2002)]

After the merger of two home health agencies, the question arose of whether a person's work for the two agencies should be aggregated in determining if overtime had been worked. The determination hinged on whether they were a single enterprise—where related activities were performed through unified operations or with common control or common business purpose. Both agencies provided home health services (although they did handle patients with different levels of care and different Medicare eligibility), so they were related. The Ninth Circuit looked to practical operations, not formal corporate structure, to determine if they were related, and treated the two agencies as a common enterprise subject to the FLSA, and required aggregation of work done for the two. [*Chao v. A-One Medical Servs., Inc.,* 346 F.3d 908 (9th Cir. 2003)] In a case involving a garment factory with six subcontractors, the Second Circuit applied six factors to determine whether a company that is alleged to be a joint employer "suffers or permits" work to be done on its behalf (those factors were not exclusive; the Second Circuit allowed District Courts to consider any other factors that it finds relevant to the determination):

- Whose premises and equipment were used to perform the work?
- Did garment contractors shift work among the potential joint employers?
- Did the plaintiffs engage in a separate job that was essential to the alleged employer's production process?
- Could contractual responsibility shift to another subcontractor without material changes?
- What was the degree of supervision of the work by the alleged employer or its agents?
- Did the plaintiffs work exclusively or predominantly for the defendant?

[*Zheng v. Liberty Apparel Co.,* 355 F.3d 61 (2d Cir. 2003)]

§ 1.12   APPLICABLE TESTS

[A]   The 20-Factor Test

Determining employee status is not a simple matter. The internal IRS documents used to train tax auditors set out 20 factors to be used to determine if income tax withholding is required:

1. If the employer gives instructions that the employee has to follow;
2. If the employer trains the employee;

Tip: Don't assign independent contractors to take training sessions with employees!

---

3. If the person renders services that are specific to him or her and can't be delegated to someone else;
4. If the employer provides whatever assistants are needed for the work (someone who provides his own assistants is more likely to be an independent contractor);
5. Whether the services are integrated into the employer's ordinary work, or are separate;
6. If the work relationship continues over time;

Tip: Independent contractors should not be asked to be on call.

---

7. If the worker is subject to a shift system or other established, structured work hours or work schedule;
8. If the employer demands the worker's full-time commitment;
9. If the worker works for other companies at the same time (if the answer is "yes," it tends to imply independent contractor status, although part-time common-law employees may hold more than one job);
10. If work is done on the employer's premises;
11. If the employer determines the order or sequence of tasks to be done to accomplish the overall task;
12. If the worker has to submit regular oral or written reports;
13. If payment is by time (hour, week, or month) rather than project;
14. If the employer supplies tools and materials;
15. If the worker has to make a significant financial investment to accomplish the tasks;
16. If the employer pays business and travel expenses;
17. If the worker has a profit-and-loss interest in the underlying business of the employer;
18. If the worker gets paid by the employer's customers;

19. The employer's right to fire the worker (as distinct from carrying out the termination provisions of a contract, or refusing to renew the contract) tends to imply employee status;
20. The possibility of the worker's becoming liable to the employer if he or she quits suggests independent contractor status, because this is consistent with remedies for breach of contract.

At a minimum, if the IRS examines records and determines that common-law employees were incorrectly treated as independent contractors, the employer will have to make up the employment taxes that should have been paid but were not. Additional penalties may also be imposed. If the employer filed the required information returns (W-2s and 1099s) and did not intentionally misclassify the worker, then the penalty will be limited to 1.5% of the employee's wages, plus 20% of the FICA taxes that went unpaid because of the incorrect classification.

Those penalties are doubled if the information returns were not filed (unless there was no willful neglect, and there was reasonable cause for failure to file). Even heavier penalties are assessed if the employer not merely was mistaken about filing responsibilities, but deliberately attempted to avoid taxation.

[B] Safe Harbor Treatment

In 1979, Congress passed a safe harbor provision, Section 530 of the Revenue Act of 1978. Under this provision, if an employer treats someone as an independent contractor, the IRS will not be able to reclassify that person as an employee (and will not be able to assess back taxes and penalties) as long as the employer made the characterization reasonably and in good faith. Employers can also apply for a refund of penalties that they believe were improperly assessed.

There are three safe harbor tests for reasonableness:

1. The court system or the IRS has created published authority (e.g., decisions, IRS rulings, or IRS Technical Advice Memorandums) that justifies independent contractor treatment in similar situations;
2. The IRS has already audited the employer, and the audit did not uncover any problems of worker characterization;
3. There is an established practice, within a significant segment of the employer's industry, of treating people who do similar work as independent contractors.

To use the safe harbor, the employer must have treated the person consistently as an independent contractor, including filing Form 1099 as necessary. If the person was treated as a common-law employee at any time after December 31, 1977, the safe harbor will not be available.

IRS Notice 2002-5 (2002-3 I.R.B. 320) creates a retroactive expansion (effective for assessments made on or after August 5, 1997) of the Tax Court's jurisdiction in employment status proceedings. The expanded jurisdiction implements § 314(f) of the Community Renewal Tax Relief Act of 2000. [Pub. L. No.106-554] Notice 2002-5 explains the IRS's procedure for issuing a Notice of Determination of Worker Classification, and how taxpayers can petition the Tax Court, under Code § 7436, for review of such a determination. (The Tax Court has jurisdiction under § 7436 to review an IRS determination that someone is an employee or a determination that the taxpayer fails to qualify for the safe harbor, and has the power to determine the proper amount of employment tax resulting from such a determination.)

Notice 2002-5 says that IRS will issue a Notice of Determination of Worker Classification if, and only if, it has determined that the safe harbor doesn't apply, and if misclassified persons are performing services for the employer. An employer cannot go to the Tax Court for review without the Notice. Only the employer, not the employees, can use the review procedure, and it is not available to third parties whom the IRS has not named as employers of the workers in question. Late in 2002, the Tax Court ruled [*Evans Publishing, Inc. v. Commissioner,* 119 T.C. 242 (2002)] that it has jurisdiction over persons that the IRS classified as employees, even though the IRS did not originally raise those issues at trial. In this case, the IRS issued a Notice of Determination to Evans Publishing, saying that sales personnel and graphics workers should have been treated as employees for the years 1993–1995, and assessing employment taxes. The company went to the Tax Court seeking redetermination of this classification. The Tax Court ruled that Code § 7476(a) gives the Tax Court jurisdiction over an IRS determination of employee status and the appropriate amount of related employment taxes. Code § 6214(a) lets the Tax Court redetermine the correct amount of a deficiency, including additional amounts claimed by IRS before a hearing or rehearing.

[C] Other Tests of Employee Status

The fundamental test is ability to control work behavior, both as to methods and as to results. This is the test used to determine employee status for ERISA purposes.

State unemployment insurance coverage typically depends either on the common-law right of control, or supplying a worker with a workplace, tools, and materials in addition to control. Most states use an "ABC test": someone who performs services is an employee, and the employer must pay unemployment insurance premiums for that person, unless:

- the person is customarily engaged in an independent trade, business, profession, or occupation;
- no direction or control is given in performing the services;
- the services are not performed in the usual course of the employer's business, or are not performed within any regular business location of the employer.

The employer must pay unemployment insurance plus penalties and interest for misclassified workers.

The FLSA test is based on economic reality. In other words, someone who is not economically dependent on a company, and is not an integral part of its operations, would not be an employee. Factors in the decision include:

- The worker's investment in facilities or equipment;
- Presence or absence of opportunity to earn profits or suffer losses due to managerial or special skills;
- Degree of control others have over the person's work;
- Permanence of the work relationship;
- Skill required to perform the services.

In this case, misclassification can lead to a duty to pay any unpaid minimum wages and overtime, plus liquidated damages, attorneys' fees, and court costs.

§ 1.13   BENEFITS FOR CONTINGENT WORKERS

This issue came to prominence in connection with Microsoft "perma-temps" who were characterized by the company as freelancers and independent contractors, paid through invoices submitted to the accounts payable department rather than through the payroll process. The IRS ruled that these people were really common-law employees. They sued to be held eligible to participate in Microsoft's savings and employee stock ownership plans.

The Ninth Circuit ruled that eligibility for participation depends on being a common-law employee; the form in which payment is rendered is not relevant. The court also rejected the agreement signed by the workers, characterizing them as ineligible for plan participation, on the grounds that an agreement of this type cannot alter employee status. [*Vizcaino v. Microsoft Corp.*, 97 F.3d 1187 (9th Cir.1996), *aff'd*, 120 F.3d 1006 (9th Cir. 1997), *cert. denied*, 522 U.S. 1088 (1998)]

The case was sent back to the district court to sort out the rights of individual plaintiffs. The district court narrowed down the plaintiff class to certain employees of temporary agencies and workers who were reclassified as common-law employees by the IRS.

The Ninth Circuit ruled on the case again in May 1999 [173 F.3d 713 (9th Cir.1999)], holding that temporary agency workers who also satisfy the common-law control test can be considered Microsoft employees entitled to participate in the stock plan. The case went back to the district court yet again [142 F. Supp. 2d 1299 (W.D. Wash. 2001)], and on January 9, 2000, the Supreme Court again refused to hear an appeal of the decision. [*cert. denied*, 522 U.S. 109 (2000)]

In December 2000, Microsoft agreed to pay $96.9 million to settle the *Vizcaino* case and another pending case. However, two of the class members appealed the settlement in May 2001. More than 2,500 members of the class filed claims against the fund, but damages and attorneys' fees cannot be paid out until the appeal of the settlement is resolved. [The settlement agreement can be found at <http://www.bs-s.com/vizcaino/mssettle.pdf>]

In March 2003, the Third Circuit decided an important case, holding that to draft a benefits plan to exclude hourly employees does not violate ERISA. [*Bauer v. Summit Bancorp.*, 325 F.3d 155 (3d Cir. 2003)] In this analysis, ERISA allows the employer to deny participation for any reason, as long as ERISA's age and length of service requirements are respected. Of course, if the employer wishes to draft the plan to cover hourly as well as salaried workers, this is permissible.

The trustees of a multi-employer pension plan sued one of the participating employers under ERISA, charging the company with failure to make contributions that the trustees claimed were due under the CBA. At issue were 25 people employed at various times in the period 1992–2000. The employer called them "casual employees," not entitled to pension and welfare benefits; the trustees characterized them as regular employees. Additional issues were raised by the two people in this group who worked after the expiration of the CBA. The Seventh Circuit ruled that the employer was not permitted to hire a casual worker for a specific project, then retain the worker after the project but still consider him or her a casual worker. Therefore, until the expiration of the CBA, the employer had an obligation to make benefit contributions for so-called "casual" workers who were actually assigned to the same work as regular employees. However, for those who worked after the expiration of the CBA, there was no contractual obligation to make plan contributions. [*Dugan v. RJ Corman R.R. Co.*, 344 F.3d 662 (7th Cir. 2003)]

§ 1.14   WORK SCHEDULING

[A]   Overview

To an ever-increasing extent, new (and usually longer) schedules are replacing the conventional nine-to-five or eight-to-four workday. Sometimes, the operation has to be open around the clock to accommodate emergencies. Many retail and service businesses add longer hours to accommodate customers who work long hours themselves and need to do business on weekends, evenings, and holidays. Demand for a factory's products might be so high that the only way to cope is to schedule two or even three shifts a day. Demand might be high but unpredictable, or predictably seasonal, so that the plant runs at full steam for several months, then layoffs and terminations are required on the off season.

For all these reasons, some employees will have to work overtime and weekend hours occasionally. Some will have to work unconventional hours as a long-range or permanent condition of employment. As business becomes more international, it becomes necessary to be able to deal with customers during their work week—which may occur on a very different schedule from the traditions of the U.S. workplace.

The 40-hour work week is only conventional, not sacred. The five-day week is also a fairly recent innovation: the six-day schedule prevailed for part of the 20th century. In some environments, a 40-hour week over just four days works well, because employees like having the extra day off, and are sometimes more productive in the longer day than in more, shorter work days.

The Current Population Survey (a joint venture between the Bureau of Labor Statistics and the Bureau of the Census) found that in 2002, about 40% of U.S. employees were assigned to evening, weekend, overnight, or rotating shifts, leaving only 30% working the so-called "standard" work week of Monday to Friday, 9 A.M. to 5 P.M. [Teresa Rivas, *Atypical Workdays Becoming Routine*, Wall Street Journal, Apr. 4, 2006, at p. A19]

"Flextime" is a schedule under which employees commit to working at least a certain number of hours per day, week, or month, and also agree to be present at certain agreed-upon times (e.g., for the weekly staff meeting or when customer demand is highest). Otherwise, they can work any schedule that suits their needs and allows them to complete their work tasks. Flextime can work for employees who have work-family problems (e.g., caring for children or elderly relatives). Flextime can be an Americans with Disabilities Act (ADA) "reasonable accommodation" and can also be used by employees taking FMLA leave.

In mid-2005, more than a quarter of all full-time workers could work a flexible schedule, but only 10.7% were covered by a formal, employer-sponsored flextime program. Formal flextime programs were rarest in the production/transportation industry (5.9%) and natural resources, construction, and maintenance sectors (6.4%), whereas 14.2% of management/professional employees were covered by a formal program. Flexible scheduling reached its highest level in May 2001, when 28.6% of workers had formal or informal access to flexible schedules. [Monthly Labor Review, *Formal Flextime Programs Not Common*, (July 7, 2005) <http://www.bls.gov/opub/ted/2005/jul/wk1/art03.htm>; Monthly Labor Review, *Flexible Work Schedules in 2004*, (July 2, 2005) <http://www.bls.gov/opub/ted/2005/jul/wk1/art01.htm>]

The availability of flextime can cause conflict if workers perceive that executives or favored rank-and-file workers are given special treatment—or if employees believe that "flexibility" means that they will be required to work longer hours with no additional compensation. To combat this, some employers allow all employees to apply for flexible schedules; review their flextime system frequently; set up a scheduling team; and stress the value of cross-training so employees can cover for one another when they exercise flextime options. [Sue Shellenbarger, *Fairer Flextime: Employers Try New Policies for Alternative Schedules,* Wall Street Journal, Nov. 17, 2005, at p. D1]

The BOLD Initiative, a project involving a number of large employers (e.g., PepsiCo, Johnson & Johnson, and Prudential Financial), reported productivity increases of 5 to 10% as a result of workplace flexibility programs like telework, flextime, and compressed work weeks. (To avoid conflicts with collective bargaining agreements, such plans typically exclude unionized workers.) The gains were obtained through reduction in overtime and unscheduled absences, and improved efficiency and productivity when employees were at work. After Chubb Corp. implemented its plan, unscheduled absences dropped 50%, and overtime per employee fell 40% at the claims service center. The number of claims handled increased by 18% with no reduction in quality, and the number of customer calls handled by claims representatives increased 7%. Pitney Bowes reduced overtime costs at its call center by 80% by implementing flexible scheduling. [Leah Carlson, *Flexibility Proves Profitable for Large Firms*, Employee Benefit News (Sep. 15, 2005) (benefitnews.com)]

There is a basic division between hourly workers, who get more pay if they put in longer hours, and salaried workers, whose compensation does not vary with the number of hours worked. A time clock or other system must be used to track the hours of hourly workers. Salaried workers may have to keep track of time if their time is billed out to clients, or if management wants to analyze task and time performance.

It is customary, although not legally required, for hourly employees to clock out when they leave the workplace (e.g., for lunch breaks or to do personal errands). They are not normally paid for this nonwork time. Salaried employees are usually not charged for such nonwork time, although personal time is sometimes charged against their sick leave. In a unionized workplace, the Collective Bargaining Agreement (CBA) determines issues like scheduling of meal breaks and when employees have to punch in and punch out.

The Second Circuit says that, if the employer requires employees to stay on the job site during their lunch breaks (in this case, for security purposes at an outdoor site), then the employees are working and must be compensated for this time. [*Reich v. Southern New England Telecommunications Corp.*, 121 F.3d 58 (2d Cir. 1997)]

Although some states have laws requiring meal breaks during a work shift, California is one of the few to impose fines. The California law allows employees required to work over five hours without a meal break to sue to recover one hour's pay per missed meal; the statute of limitations is three years. (There is no corresponding federal requirement.) Approximately 100 California suits are pending on this issue, but only a handful of class actions have been certified, e.g., *Savaglio v. Wal-Mart Stores*, No. 83587 (Alameda County Superior Court). [Pamela A. MacLean, *Meal-Break Lawsuits Simmer, Then Boil*, Nat'l Law Journal, Jan. 31, 2005 (law.com)]

In addition to Wal-Mart's wrangles as to whether it must provide health insurance for its employees (*see* Chapter 18), the retailer has been ordered to pay $172 million by a California jury in a class action involving 200,000 employees who were deprived of meal and rest breaks. Of that verdict, $115 million constituted punitive damages. A class of Pennsylvania employees was certified at the beginning of 2006, alleging a seven-year pattern of deprivation of breaks. Wal-Mart was in the difficult-to-maintain position of claiming that its business records about wages and hours were too unreliable to be introduced in court. [*Hummel v. Wal-Mart Stores Inc.*, discussed in Asher Hawkins, *Wal-Mart Employees Who Missed Breaks Certified as a Class,* The Legal Intelligencer (Jan. 4, 2006) (law.com); *Savaglio v. Wal-Mart Stores*, No. C-835687 (Alameda County Superior

Court 2005), discussed in Justin Scheck, *Wal-Mart Stuck with $172M Lunch Tab*, The Recorder (Feb. 23, 2005) (law.com)]

Also note that the IRS issued a Quality Assurance Bulletin (i.e., an internal staff document) in early 2006 taking the position that if a defined contribution plan includes improper clauses dealing with part-time employees, the plan can be disqualified, even if it has received a determination letter dated after July 1, 2001. (An earlier letter will protect the plan against retroactive disqualification). As 401(k) plans become more popular, employees are more and more reluctant to wait one year before participating. In response, many employers have amended their plans to allow immediate participation—but other employers do not want to eliminate the tenure requirement because that could open the door to coverage of part-timers. Labor Regulations § 1.410(a)-3 says that a clause excluding part-time employees who customarily work no more than 20 hours per week is not permissible because the employee may actually work more than 1,000 hours in a year. That would make the part-time exclusion a service requirement that violates the rules. The plan would therefore be disqualified by this possibility, even if in practice no part-time employee actually works more than 1,000 hours in a year. Effective February 1, 2006, IRS document specialists have been ordered to challenge plans that include possibly improper exclusions, but not to challenge classifications that do not relate to hours of service. Under the Quality Assurance Bulletin, part-time employees may still be excluded from the plan as long as there is no possibility that there will be an indirect hours-of-service requirement that violates § 410(a)(1). The plan can have a fail-safe by allowing immediate participation for full-time employees and entry after one year for part-timers, but with any part-time worker who actually works more than 1,000 hours becoming a participant on the first plan entry date after the computation period ends. Plans that do not have a fail-safe clause to ensure compliance with § 410(a) should consider using Voluntary Correction Program (VCP) to correct the failure. [SunGard Corbel News: Pension Technical Updates, *IRS Provides Guidance on Part-Time Employee Exclusions*, <http://www.corbel.com/news/technicalupdates.asp?ID=333&T=P> (Mar. 16, 2006)]

[B]   Telecommuting

To an increasing extent, employees are working from home or from other remote locations by "telecommuting," working on a computer and dealing with other employees and clients or customers by telephone or e-mail.

Telecommuting can be useful for employees who are recovering from an injury or illness; those who have family responsibilities; part-timers and project workers; and those who would otherwise have to relocate or face a long commute each day. Telecommuting also reduces the size of the office that the employer has to maintain.

By 2004, acceptance of telecommuting had spread from lower-level and technical employees to senior management, fueled by greater availability of broadband connections and also a post-9/11 desire to decentralize operations.

According to Gartner Inc., in 2005, 82.5 million workers throughout the world worked at home at least one day a month—twice as many as in 2000. The company projects that the figure will reach 100 million by 2008. In the United States, 12% of workers put in at least one at-home workday per month in 2000, rising to 23% in 2005, in part because the security measures for protecting sensitive business data have improved. WorldatWork's Telework Advisory Group says that 9.9 million people who are not self-employed work at home full-time or part-time. [Christopher Rhoads and Sara Silver, *Working at Home Gets Easier*, Wall Street Journal, Dec. 29, 2005, at p. B4; Tom Herman and Rachel Emma Silverman, *Telecommuters May Face New Taxes*, Wall Street Journal, Nov. 1, 2005, at p. D1]

However, telecommuting is not a panacea. Some people find it very hard to be productive in light of the greater distractions available outside the workplace. It can be difficult to maintain lines of communication or to coordinate the efforts of workers at different locations.

In many organizations, the limiting factor is management's unwillingness to adopt or expand telework programs. Some supervisors demand to see their employees working; some managers don't understand the business case for telecommuting; and others are more interested in increasing their power base by increasing the number of visible employees in the office reporting to them.

There are many practical steps that a company can take to make the arrangement smoother and more productive. The "teleworkers" should sign written agreements clarifying whether they are independent contractors or common-law employees; who they will report to; whether the telework assignment is expected to be temporary or permanent; how often they will be expected to go to the office; how many hours they will work; their work schedule; and promotion possibilities.

A project that is suitable for telecommuting is one that can be handled by one person, with limited input from others, with input that has to be effective via telephone or computer, rather than in person. The project should be clearly defined and easily measured, so the supervisor will be able to assess if milestones are being met and the teleworker's performance is adequate.

Personality characteristics of successful telecommuters include being comfortable working essentially alone, without office social contacts; being able to schedule tasks and hold to a schedule; being able to get the job done despite distractions and family needs; and having the discipline to perform away from the supervisor's eyes.

Telecommuting relies heavily on electronics, so it's important to safeguard hardware and data. If possible, the telecommuter should have back-up equipment (perhaps a laptop that can be used while traveling or when the desktop computer is out of order). Telecommuters should be required to back up their data frequently, to have a high-quality uninterruptable power source to give them time to save work before the computer goes down, and they should be required to keep backup disks and other media in a safe location (such as a fireproof safe or a safe deposit box)—preferably somewhere outside the home. It's also possible to "deliver" data to an Internet storage site.

Make sure the telecommuter has homeowner's insurance (if necessary, in the form of a rider or a separate policy) that covers the computer equipment against theft and damage. This is especially important if the employer supplies the equipment. A "consequential damages" provision that covers lost data and business opportunities is hard to find, but a valuable addition to the policy.

A CFO.com article from 2004 cites potential savings of $3,000 per employee per year, with productivity going up 4–12%, and major real estate savings, in connection with telework (those figures come from Cigna, a strong advocate of telework), which points out that employees generally channel what otherwise would have been commuting time into extra effort on work—about 1.8 extra work hours for every 3 hours of travel time they didn't have to put in. Microsoft UK's finance director pointed out that workers who have flexible hours are often the ones who have the best time-management skills.

In mid-2003, New York's highest court, the Court of Appeals, decided an important question by ruling that a former telecommuter who lived in Florida and submitted work to a Long Island company over telephone lines was not entitled to New York unemployment benefits when the arrangement ended and the employer was no longer willing to allow her to work from home. The court's theory was that benefits are provided where the person works, and in this case "work" took place in her Florida home, not the physical location of the employer company. The system is supposed to encourage the recipient of the benefits to get another job, and he or she is more likely to look for work near home. The applicant applied for benefits in Florida ($275 a week) but was turned down for having quit her job in New York voluntarily to move to Florida. She was told that she might qualify for interstate benefits of $365 a week in New York, so she applied, was granted benefits, but was subsequently found ineligible and ordered to repay the benefits she received, an order that she appealed all through New York's court system. [*Allen v. Comm'r of Labor,* 100 N.Y.2d 282 (N.Y. App. 2003)]

New York found that 100% of the earnings of a computer programmer who lives in Tennessee and spends only a quarter of his time in New York were taxable in New York, because he worked at home for his own convenience and not that of his employer. [*Matter of Huckaby v. State Div. of Tax Appeals,* 4 N.Y.3d 427, *cert. denied,* 126 S. Ct. 546 (2005)]

Telework can also be a lifeline for disabled workers, and it is an important part of the Bush administration's New Freedom initiative, a plan for integration of people with disabilities into the stream of ordinary life. See http://www.eeoc.gov for the EEOC's fact sheet on using telework to promote full employment opportunity for people with disabilities; how to supervise telecommuters; and the extent to which offering telework options is a reasonable accommodation to disability.

On the related question of whether the employer is required to provide reasonable accommodation when the question is the employee's ability to commute to the workplace, it has generally been held that the employer does not have such an obligation, because the employer's duty of accommodation is conceived of as relating to the workplace rather than the difficulty of getting from home to the workplace. [Paul W. Cane Jr., *"I Want to Work at Home": Telecommuting As a Reasonable Accommodation* (special to law.com Mar. 28, 2005), citing cases such as *Raffaele v. City of New York*, 2004 WL 1969869 (E.D.N.Y. Sept. 7, 2004); *Dicino v. Aetna U.S. Healthcare*, 2003 WL 21501818 (D. N.J. June 23, 2003)]

[C] Integrated Time Off

An integrated time-off system is an attendance policy that gives the worker the right to take a certain number of days off per year, no matter what the reason for being away from work. The value to the employer is that it keeps people at work because they no longer have an incentive to take sick days for every minor illness just because otherwise they would lose the time. A common system is to provide a certain amount of paid vacation (e.g., one to three weeks a year), six to eight paid holidays, and six sick days a year. Employers vary as to whether they allow unused sick days to be carried over from year to year, or impose a "use it or lose it" rule. A PTO (Paid Time Off) program integrates vacation and sick days. An Integrated Disability Program (also known as "24-hour coverage") adds disability benefits to the mix. For example, an integrated time-off plan might give the worker 100% pay for days 1–3 of any illness (from the PTO bank), 75% of pay for days 4–90 of the illness from the short-term disability plan, and 66% of pay from the long-term disability plan for an illness lasting over 90 days (as long as the employee satisfies the LTD plan's requirements, of course).

Employers moving to a PTO plan can convert already accrued sick days to PTO time, although that probably means that employees will be entitled to be paid for unused PTO days when their employment ends, even though unused sick days under a conventional plan usually do not have to be paid for. If your state requires payment of accrued days off, it probably makes more sense to define the PTO as accruing on a monthly or weekly basis rather than awarded as a lump at the beginning of the year. That way, employees who leave partway through the year will have accrued fewer days that must be paid for.

In response to the perception that employees rate free time as one of their prime goals (28% of respondents to a Yankelovich Monitor survey said they would take a pay cut to get more time off), more and more companies are using extra paid time off as a performance reward. Part of this trend is to centralize all time off (vacation, sick leave, personal days, holidays, volunteer leave) into a single bank that is easier to monitor. A CCH survey found that two thirds of respondents had adopted a PTO bank, whereas only one sixth did in 1991. In fact, some companies have an electronic system that tracks time-off usage and recommends that workers who don't use all of their allotment should take a mental health day to relax! Although only 8% of employers have written disaster compensation policies, most companies do informally continue compensation when a natural disaster prevents employees from getting to work, perhaps by charging it as vacation time. [Sue Shellenbarger, *Companies Retool Time-Off Policies to Prevent Burnout, Reward Performance*, Wall Street Journal, Jan. 5, 2006, at p. D1]

Integrating disability cases into the plan requires a procedure for evaluating and managing short-term disability cases and coordinating the disabled person's return to work, which may require an interval in a light-duty job.

There is no uniform standard measure of absenteeism, and no standard measure of the effectiveness of prevention programs, but probably 40–50% of lost work days occur in "incidental absences" of one to five days. After that, it's likely that the employee will qualify for short-term disability, but STD programs are sometimes defined in terms of calendar days, sometimes by lost work days, and employer's calculations of lost days sometimes include the five-day waiting period, sometimes don't.

In many instances, employees call in sick when actually they need personal time for other reasons. This is one reason why HR professionals find work-life programs to be an effective tool. Employees will be more likely to give notice of absence in advance, allowing the employer to "cover" the employee's tasks, instead of waiting until the last minute. According to IOMA's Report on Managing Benefit Plans, the average number of work-life programs has gone from 3.4 per organization in 2000 to 7.3 in 2002. [Carlos Tejada, *Working at a Fever Pitch,* Wall Street Journal, Mar. 20, 2003, at p. D1]

A CareerBuilder.com poll found that, in 2005, 43% of employees called in sick just because they wanted time off—whereas only 35% admitted doing this in 2004. Of those who claimed sick days inappropriately, 23% said they needed to catch up on their sleep; 17% didn't feel like going to work; 16% had a doctor's appointment, and 9% used the day to catch up on housework and errands. More than one third (38%) said they considered sick days equivalent to vacation days (and, in fact, more and more employers are moving toward an integrated time-off system). Wednesday was the most popular fake sick day, with 27% calling in, while 26% took inappropriate sick days on Monday and 14% on Friday. Almost two thirds of hiring managers said they were suspicious about self-made three-day weekends, and almost one quarter of hiring managers have fired someone for taking time off improperly. [News Articles, *Poll: More Employees Lying about Being Ill,* PlanSponsor.com, Jan. 26, 2006]

At the other end of the scale, LifeCare Inc. found that about one third of poll respondents said they sometimes went to work when they actually were sick because it would have been too risky to claim a sick day. One quarter of respondents came in to work when they were sick because they didn't want to let down co-workers who depended on them; 12% said they were too busy to miss a day at work; 5% said they saved their sick days to add to their vacation allotment; and 9% used sick days for child care, and 3% for elder care. [Rebecca Moore, *Survey: A Third of Workers Will Not "Risk" Taking a Sick Day,* PlanSponsor.com, Mar. 21, 2006]

[D] Coping With Absenteeism

The Society for Human Resource Management reported that, in 2004, unscheduled absenteeism was 2.4%, the highest level in five years (versus only

1.9% in 2003). The survey showed that many employees called in at the last minute even when they knew in advance that time off would be required. The average cost of absenteeism was estimated at $610 per employee—which doesn't include lost productivity, overtime work by other employees who had to pick up the slack, or utilization of temporary workers as substitutes. The SHRM concluded that only 38% of unscheduled absences are caused by the employee's illness; 23% are taken because of family issues, 18% for personal needs, 11% for stress, and 10% reflecting an "entitlement mentality." Companies with poor or fair morale were found to have 35% unscheduled absenteeism versus only 1.9% at companies with good or very good morale. The trend was to allow fewer sick days (an average of 7.6 in 2003, 6.9% in 2004); fewer employers permitted unused sick days to carry over from year to year (51% in 2000, 37% in 2004). [Kathy Gurchiek, *Unscheduled Absenteeism Soars; Reasons and Solutions Vary,* SHRM Home (Society for Human Resource Management), Nov. 2, 2004, <http://www.shrm.org/hrnews_published/archives/CMS_01076.asp>]

The other side of the coin, however, is "presenteeism"—sick employees who insist on coming in to work when they should be recuperating. They are unlikely to be productive in that situation, and the worst case scenario is that they trigger endless rounds of colds and flu "going around the office." Harvard Medical School professor Ronald Kessler estimates that presenteeism is responsible for two-thirds of the productivity losses occurring at work. [Denise DeFulco, *When Employees Are Sick, Absenteeism Can Be a Virtue,* New York Times, Sept. 26, 2004, § 10 at p. 1] The pendulum has swung, and many companies encourage employees to get treatment (especially over-the-counter drugs that are not covered by the employer's plan) to avoid unproductive days at work and infecting other employees. [Sarah Rubenstein, *Nursing Employees Back to Health*, Wall Street Journal, Jan. 18, 2005, at p. D5]

In 2005, the International Foundation of Employee Benefit Plans surveyed a group of HR professionals. Nearly all (84%) of the respondents said they would offer reduced hours to a worker who was seriously ill (e.g., suffering from breast cancer), 70% would offer flexible schedules, and 62% would offer extra breaks or rest periods. More than a quarter (28%) would allow job-sharing. More than one half of the respondents (56%) said that their companies had actual experience of employees with breast cancer. A third of those employees asked for adjustments to their work load. Nearly all (96%) needed periodic time off; 82% needed a modified work schedule; and two thirds required leaves of absence. [*Survey: Most Large Employers Bend Rules for Sick Workers*, NU Online News Service, Oct. 24, 2005]

§ 1.15   OVERTIME AND OVERTIME PLANNING

[A]   Generally

One of the major functions of the FLSA is to require "time and a half for overtime" to be paid to all nonexempt hourly employees who work more than

40 hours in a work week. They must receive 150% of their normal pay rate for the additional hours.

According to the D.C. Circuit, the FLSA does not require employers to pay overtime when a worker puts in more than eight hours in a particular day, as long as his or her hours for the week as a whole do not exceed 40. The plaintiff alleged that her CBA required payment of overtime, but even if that is true, the court ruled that it did not have federal subject matter jurisdiction over a contract interpretation claim. [*Fernandez v. Centerplate/NBSE*, 441 F.3d 1006 (D.C. Cir. 2006)]

> **Tip:** The Workers Economic Opportunity Act [Pub. L. No. 106-202 (May 18, 2000)] amends the FLSA to make it clear that stock options are not part of the "regular rate of pay" for FLSA purposes. The statute explains the wage-and-hour consequences of stock option and stock appreciation rights plans. Although the FLSA does not require it, many companies offer "comp time"—additional time off—if an hourly employee puts in more than his or her normal schedule, but less than 40 hours, during a work week.

Certain categories of employees are exempt from the FLSA's minimum wage and overtime provisions. [29 U.S.C. § 213(a)(1)] The major exempt categories are executives, administrators, professionals, and outside salespersons. Whether a person is exempt depends on the actual duties of the job, not the job title. Exemption is based on "primary duties"—what the person does for 50% or more of the work time.

Exempt workers do not have to be paid for weeks in which they do not work at all, but otherwise 29 C.F.R. § 541.118(a) provides that their salary cannot be reduced based on the number of hours worked or the number of hours of absences. The employer cannot reduce the wages of exempt employees for absences that were caused by the employer or the operating requirements of its business. Nor can the employer take deductions to penalize an exempt worker for work place infractions, other than violations of major safety rules.

Specifically, docking a worker's pay for "variations in quantity or quality of work" is appropriate for hourly workers who are entitled to overtime, but not for exempt workers. The real test, however, is whether reductions are ever taken. In 1997, the Supreme Court ruled that police officers were exempt salaried employees, even though the employee manual said that pay could be docked for various disciplinary infractions: the mere possibility didn't make them nonexempt. [*Auer v. Robbins*, 519 U.S. 452 (1997)]

All Detroit Edison employees, whether classified as hourly or exempt-salaried, are paid under the same payroll system, and everyone is paid on the basis of reported hours. Salaried employees must report at least 40 hours per week to receive an unreduced salary, but pay is not reduced for absences of less than a full day. Sometimes salaried employees are scheduled to work only 36 hours in one week (and 48 hours in the next); they are instructed to report 40 hours in the

36-hour weeks. Sometimes they forget to report the extra hours; sometimes they report under 40 hours because they take personal days or end work in the middle of the week. A group of plaintiffs sued the company, seeking overtime. Initially the District Court ruled that reducing employees' pay for under-reporting hours represented unlawful docking of their compensation. Then, after the DOL issued an opinion letter permitting docking pay for under-reporting of hours, the District Court reversed itself and dismissed the case. On appeal, the Sixth Circuit affirmed the second District Court opinion. The employees in question were exempt as salary-based administrative employees. Employees never lost pay for times when they were ready, willing, and able to work, but there was no work for them. Adjustments within the payroll system do not convert an exempt salaried worker to an hourly employee entitled to overtime. [*Acs v. Detroit Edison Co.*, 2006 U.S. App. LEXIS 9281 (6th Cir. 2006); DOL Op. Letter, 2003 DOLWH LEXIS 3 at *7 (July 9, 2003)]

Tip: If an exempt employee is absent for less than one day for sickness, disability, or personal reasons, the employer is not permitted to reduce the employee's paycheck, although some court cases say that it's permissible for the employer to reduce the amount of leave available to the employee.

[B] Categories of Exempt Employees

The FLSA defines executives, professionals, and other categories of workers, based on their main responsibilities. However, the statute left many important questions unresolved, and furthermore the existing regulations expressed obsolete concepts about the workplace and the economy. On April 23, 2004, DOL published a 150-page Final Rule amending 29 C.F.R. Part 541, explicating changes in the FLSA § 13(a) overtime exemption for executive, administrative, professional, outside sales, and computer employees: 69 Fed. Reg. 22122 *et seq.* For guidance in somewhat more concise form, see the Wage and Hour Division's FairPay Fact Sheets at <http://www.dol.gov/esa/regs/compliance/whd/fairpay/fact_exemption.htm>.

The Department of Labor's Fair Pay Overtime Initiative site is at <http://www.dol.gov/esa/regs/compliance/whd/fairpay/main.htm>. Additional FLSA information is available at <http://www.wagehour.dol.gov>.

Until this Final Rule was promulgated, the minimum salary test for the white-collar exemption under the FLSA had remained pegged at $155 a week since 1976. The Final Rule nearly triples this, to $455 a week. DOL also believed that changes in work categories were necessary because of shifts in the composition of the workforce since 1949—the last time the categories were changed!

The Final Rule (effective August 23, 2004) provides for both a minimum salary (anyone who earns less than $23,660 a year is automatically entitled to overtime) and a maximum. Highly compensated white-collar workers earning $100,000 or more a year are automatically exempt from overtime as long as their salary is at least $455 a week, and as long as they regularly perform at least one duty as an exempt executive, professional, or administrative worker.

The Final Rule applies only to white-collar workers. Blue-collar workers "who perform work involving repetitive operations with their hands, physical skill and energy" (69 Fed. Reg. 22122) are entitled to overtime pay.

In response to criticisms of chain stores and other operations charged with giving low-level personnel "management" titles (to preclude them from overtime eligibility), the amended version of 29 C.F.R. § 541.2 provides that "a job title alone is insufficient to establish the exempt status of an employee. The exempt or nonexempt status of any particular employee must be determined on the basis of whether the employee's salary and duties meet the requirements of the regulations in this part."

The exemptions discussed here all require that the person be compensated on a salary rather than hourly basis, and that the person must earn at least $455 a week. A person is considered to be paid on a salary basis if the set compensation for the pay unit (e.g., week or month) is not subject to reductions based on variations in how much work the person does, or how well the work is performed.

The general rule is that as long as a salaried worker does any work in a pay period, he or she must be paid for the entire period, and deductions must not be taken for time when the employee is ready, willing, and able to work but there is no work for him or her to do. However, employers of salaried workers are permitted to make deductions for full days away from work that the employee takes as personal days; sick days taken under a bona fide plan; unpaid FMLA leave; or when the employee is suspended for violating a major safety rule or for other workplace infractions. Deductions can also be made if the last week a salaried employee works is a partial week.

An individual can also be paid on a fee basis for administrative, professional, or computer-oriented work while remaining exempt from overtime entitlement. The minimum salary test is applied to work done on a fee basis by comparing the compensation and the time spent to complete the assignment with the standard $455 weekly salary.

Tip: Even if they do not satisfy the salary test, outside salespersons, teachers, lawyers, and doctors are exempt from overtime. *See* <http://www.dol.gov/esa/regs/compliance/whd/fairpay/fs17g_salary.htm> for discussion of issues about salaried employees. *See also*, Snell & Wilmer's Overtime Compliance Guide and Audit, <http://www.swlaw.com/publications/files/Overtime_Guide_and_Audit_Web.pdf> for flow charts for determining which employees are entitled to overtime.

A worker will be considered an executive—and therefore not entitled to overtime pay because of executive status—if:

- The person's primary duty is management either of the entire enterprise that employs him or her, or a recognized subdivision or department of the enterprise.
- He or she "customarily and regularly" directs the work of two or more fellow employees (or two full-time equivalents in an enterprise that has some part-time workers).
- He or she has hiring and firing authority, or can make suggestions that "are given particular weight" with respect to (29 C.F.R. §§ 541.100, 541.102).

The C.F.R. defines "management" as activities such as hiring and training employees, appraising their work performance, assigning tasks, budgeting, and complying with legal requirements. § 541.106 explicates the concept of "concurrent duties" (the issue involved when there is controversy about whether a person is a manager or a rank-and-file worker). If a person otherwise qualifies as an executive, he or she remains exempt despite the performance of concurrent duties (nonexempt work such as waiting on customers, stocking shelves, or cleaning business premises, undertaken by a person whose primary duty is management). However, a person such as a factory supervisor whose main duties are nonexempt does not become an executive merely because he or she occasionally has to make discretionary decisions.

A "business owner" (29 C.F.R. § 541.101) owns a bona fide equity interest of 20% or more in the business that employs him or her, and who is actively employed in the management of the business. A business owner is considered a manager and therefore is not entitled to overtime, even if he or she earns less than $455 a week.

An exempt administrative worker is primarily engaged in "work directly related to the management or general business operations" of the employer company or its customers. See 29 C.F.R. § 541.201—work in "functional areas" such as purchasing, marketing, HR, public relations, etc. The employee must be required to exercise discretion and independent judgment on significant matters.

29 C.F.R. § 541.203 provides examples of this exemption, e.g., insurance claims adjusters; financial services employees who collect and analyze information about customers' income, assets, and investments; and executive assistants and administrative assistants. There is a specific provision (§ 541.203(e)) clarifying that personnel clerks are typically not exempt from overtime, but human resources managers "who formulate, interpret or implement employment policies" are exempt.

Yet another overtime exemption applies to those employed in "a bona fide professional capacity," defined by 29 C.F.R. § 541.300 either as work requiring advanced knowledge acquired by formal education, or "requiring invention, imagination, originality or talent in a recognized field of artistic or creative endeavor." In addition to the traditional "learned professions" (e.g., medicine, law, engineering, teaching, pharmacy), registered nurses, registered or certified medical technicians, and physician's assistants, and dental hygienists are considered to be professionals. Not entirely reassuringly, the Ninth Circuit pointed out that the FLSA does not distinguish between treatment of human beings and that of animals, with the result that veterinarians at an animal clinic are considered physicians and thus are professionals with advanced degrees who are not eligible for overtime. [*Clark v. United Emergency Animal Clinic*, 390 F.3d 1124 (9th Cir. 2004)] 29 C.F.R. § 541.302 defines creative professionals as those whose primary work requires creativity and artistry, e.g., in music, writing, acting, or graphic arts— work that cannot be done by a person with only general "manual or intellectual ability and training."

The Fifth Circuit agreed that nurse practitioners and physician's assistants are not exempt and are entitled to be paid overtime. The Department of Labor issued an opinion letter and stated in an operations handbook that these health workers are not exempt. The Fifth Circuit ruled that, under *Auer v. Robbins*, 519 U.S. 452 (1997), the DOL was interpreting an ambiguous regulation, and therefore its interpretation was controlling because it was not inconsistent with the regulation or clearly erroneous. Although 29 C.F.R. § 541.3(d) specifically calls physician's assistants, nurses, and technologists "learned professionals" who are exempt under the duty requirement, they are not listed as one of the professions that fall outside the "salary basis" exception. The physician's assistants and nurse practioners are paid on an hourly basis rather than receiving a salary, so the Fifth Circuit deemed the relevant question to be whether they are licensed to practice "medicine or any of its branches." Because they are not licensed to practice medicine and because their work is similar to that of registered nurses who are eligible for overtime, the Fifth Circuit ruled in favor of overtime eligibility. [*Belt v. Emcare, Inc.* 444 F.3d 403 (5th Cir. 2006); *see* 69 Fed. Reg. 22,122 (Apr. 23, 2004) for the § 541.3(e) Regulation]

According to a late-2005 DOL Wage & Hour Opinion Letter, social workers were a "learned profession" exempt from overtime because the job requires a graduate degree, whereas caseworkers, who merely have to show a bachelor's degree in any social science and do not have specialized academic training, were not exempt and thus were entitled to overtime. [Wage & Hour Op. Letter FLSA 2005-50 (Nov. 15, 2005); *see* 74 L.W. 2332]

Systems analysts, computer programmers, software engineers (or people doing the same kind of work, even if their title changes to respond to this fast-moving field) are exempt from overtime under 29 C.F.R. § 541.400. There is an alternative test for computer professionals: a person who earns either the ordinary $455/week salary test, or an hourly rate of $27.63/hour or more, is not entitled to overtime. The Final Rule exempts computer professionals from overtime, but the exemption refers to those who, e.g., design and develop hardware and software, not to people who assemble or repair computers.

According to the Sixth Circuit, a computer help desk employee who does troubleshooting, maintenance, and support is not a "computer professional" exempt under the FLSA, because the work is not analytical enough; programming, software engineering, and systems analysis were not involved, and his work was completely directed by others, not performed with individual initiative. [*Martin v. Indiana Michigan Power Co.,* 381 F.3d 574 (6th Cir. 2004). See <http://www.dol. gov/esa/regs/compliance/whd/fairpay/fs17e_computer.htm> for the Department of Labor's fact sheet on classification of IT workers]

The final white-collar exemption, for Outside Sales staff, is defined by § 541.500 as workers whose primary duty is making sales or getting orders or contracts. The mainstay of such an employee's work is performed outside the employer's place of business. This category does not include mail, telephone, or online sales unless these media are only used to set up a personal appointment. When it comes to "drivers who sell," (§ 541.504) the test is whether sales predominates over delivery (thus making the person exempt) or whether delivery predominates (making him or her eligible for overtime).

A 2006 DOL opinion letter states that workers compensated on the basis of commissions can be exempt from the overtime requirement as sales personnel if they are paid a percentage of what is charged to customers (in this case, personal trainers, aerobics instructors, and tennis pros in health and athletic clubs) but not if they are paid a flat fee. The exemption requires the employee to work for a retail or service establishment, to have a regular rate of pay at least one and a half times minimum wage, and to receive at least half of their earnings from commissions in a representative period. [Fred Schneyer, *DOL: FLSA Exemption Depends on Pay Scheme,* PlanSponsor.com, (Apr. 4, 2006)]

The Final Rule does not affect the eligibility of blue-collar workers for overtime pay. The Final Rule's examples of blue collar workers are construction workers, carpenters, electricians, plumbers, laborers, etc. (69 Fed. Reg. 22122; 29 C.F.R. § 541.3). Public safety workers (e.g., police officers, firefighters, paramedics, Emergency Medical Technicians) are also entitled to overtime. Employers continue to be bound by whatever overtime arrangements they have entered into under Collective Bargaining Agreements, and state laws that are more protective of workers are not preempted by the Final Rule (29 C.F.R. § 541.4).

For information about state wage and hour laws (the FLSA does not preempt state laws that offer greater protection to the employee) see DOL's links to state Labor Departments. [<http://www.dol.gov/esa/contacts/state_of.htm>] According to attorney Camille Olson, there are 18 states with laws that supplement the federal protection: Alaska, Arkansas, California, Colorado, Connecticut, Hawaii, Illinois, Kentucky, Maryland, Minnesota, Montana, NewJersey, North Dakota, Oregon, Pennsylvania, Washington, West Virginia, and Wisconsin. [See (no by-line) "DOL's Overtime Final Rule Is Not Final Word on Eligibility in 18 States," 72 L.W. 2739 (June 8, 2004)]

[C] Payment of Overtime

Nonexempt hourly employees must be paid time-and-a-half (150% of their normal pay rate, including commissions) when they work more than 40 hours in any work week. Work time is all the time when the employer controls the employee's actions, including times the employee is required to be on duty or at a prescribed place. However, bona fide meal periods are not considered work time. Ordinary commuting to work is not work time, Work-related travel, such as an assignment to deliver something or go to a meeting at a client's office, is work time.

These are some items that may require compensation or overtime:

- Rest breaks under 20 minutes;
- Down time or on-call time that prevents the employee from carrying out personal business;
- Preparation before shift or clean-up after shift;
- Mandatory classes, meetings, or conventions;
- Travel time other than normal commuting.

As long as the entire work week is under 40 hours, 29 C.F.R. § 778.602(a) does not require the employer to pay overtime if a particular workday exceeds eight hours, or if weekend work is required. (However, in a unionized workplace, the CBA often requires extra payment in these situations.) Employees who lived with their families in company housing at a dam/powerhouse complex sought overtime pay for on-call time during their 24-hour duty shifts (they also worked 10-hour maintenance shifts, but did not seek overtime for those). During the duty shift, employees could do whatever they wanted, as long as they remained ready to be called out as necessary. They were paid 10 hours' wages for six hours' work on the shifts, with double-time for any callout that lasted more than 15 minutes. The issue was the FLSA status of the 14 hours of the 24-hour shift when the employee might be called out. The Ninth Circuit ruled that it was a close case, but on balance the workers were "waiting to be engaged" (i.e., the time was not compensable) and not "engaged to wait" for work. They were free to engage in personal activities (although they had to remain within close range of the work site); they were seldom called out (although they were only called out to do critical safety maintenance) and the employees were aware of the pay practice yet continued to work. [*Brigham v. Eugene Water & Electric Board,* 357 F.3d 931 (9th Cir. 2004)]

The general rule is that overtime must be paid in cash, on the regular payday for the pay period in which the overtime is worked. Allowing 1½ hours off for every overtime hour worked is permissible, as long as the comp time is given in the same period and is not carried over. FLSA § 207(o)(5) provides that state and local government employees are entitled to use their comp time within a reasonable time of requesting the time off, as long as this is not unduly burdensome to the agency that employs them. However, the employer is not obligated to grant the specific time requested by the employee. [*Mortensen v. Sacramento County, California,*

368 F.3d 1082 (9th Cir. 2004); *Houston Police Officers Union v. Houston,* 330 F.3d 298 (5th Cir. 2003)]

The work week doesn't have to be Monday–Friday, 9–5: it can be defined as any 168 consecutive hours, starting any time. It doesn't have to be the same as the payroll period. Different work groups or individuals can have different work weeks. Usually, once an employer sets a work week, it has to abide by it—but a permanent change that is not a subterfuge to evade the FLSA's overtime requirements is permitted. [*See* 29 C.F.R. § 778.104, averaging a long and a short week to see if overtime is payable is not allowed]

If the premium rate (such as differentials for Sunday or holiday work) is at least 150% of the nonpremium rate, the premium rate is not included in the calculation of the regular rate. A "clock pattern" premium (which is required by many CBAs) for working past basic hours is not included in the basic rate if it meets the 150% test. However, a shift differential, such as additional payment for working the night shift, is included in determining the rate to which overtime is applied. Under a 2002 Sixth Circuit decision, the FLSA requires calculation of overtime pay based on all employee pay rates, including bonuses. Premium pay can be credited against overtime, but only if the overtime and the premium-pay hours occur in the same work week. [*Herman v. Fabri-Centers of America Inc.,* 308 F.3d 580 (6th Cir. 2002)]

[D] Case Law on Overtime

In a shaky economy, FLSA litigation (and employment discrimination litigation) predictably increases, because many potential plaintiffs are no longer employed and do not fear that filing suit will lead to their discharge. Employers often take the position that the FLSA rules are outdated, and fail to represent the current realities of the workplace, because the statutory categories represent outmoded categories.

Issues often raised in litigation include misclassification of workers as exempt and demands that workers (especially in the retail and restaurant industries) work "off the clock."

Certain occupational groups are especially vulnerable to wage and hour violations. The New York Times reported in 2005 that labor law violations, such as failure to pay overtime, classifying common-law employees as independent contractors, and locking workers in the job location, were very common among the 2.3 million janitors in the country. The problem was complicated by the immigration status of many such workers—even persons legally within this country might not be legal workers; language problems and fear of management prevent many workers from making complaints. In March 2005, Wal-Mart settled with the Justice Department, agreeing to pay $11 million for employing illegal workers. Target settled with the DOL for $1.9 million in August 2004 for non-payment of overtime to 775 maintenance workers in five states. [Steven Greenhouse, *Among Janitors, Labor Violations Go with the Job*, New York Times, July 13, 2005, at p. A1]

The world's largest retailer, Wal-Mart, was required to defend allegations of overtime infractions in 28 states. In December 2002, a Portland, Oregon federal jury found that Wal-Mart had forced employees to work overtime without pay in the 1994–1999 period. This was the first of 40 cases to go to trial. It was not a class action, but one of many suits involving individual plaintiffs. Wal-Mart reportedly settled a case in 2000 involving 69,000 workers in Colorado, with a settlement of $50 million. [Steven Greenhouse, *U.S. Jury Cites Unpaid Work at Wal-Mart,* New York Times, Dec. 20, 2002, at p. A36]

Several recent cases stress that it is the actual duties of the job, not the title, that determine whether overtime is payable. Class actions were brought in California, involving major corporations, and some were settled based on claims that ordinary hourly workers were given meaningless "assistant manager" titles to avoid the obligation to pay overtime. This practice has been alleged against large retailers (especially for night workers), restaurants, insurers, and financial services companies. [Ann Zimmerman, *Big Retailers Face Overtime Suits As Bosses Do More "Hourly" Work,* Wall Street Journal, May 26, 2004, at p. A1]

Other major settlements and verdicts include:

- Up to $18 million under settlement of two class actions about routine misclassification of Starbucks "managers" and "assistant managers" as exempt. [*Shields v. Starbucks Corp.,* No. 01-06446 FNC (MANx) settlement filed in the Central District of California, Apr. 19, 2002]
- In late 2005, Electronic Arts settled a lawsuit, agreeing to pay $15.6 million in claims, attorneys' fees, and costs to a class of employees who charged that they worked overtime but were not paid for it. The case was significant because the traditional assumption was that employees in the software/Internet sector were willing to work extremely long hours as long as they received stock options, but decline in the value of options has led to a renewed interest in conventional compensation, including overtime. [Nick Wingfield, *Electronic Arts Settles Lawsuit, Will Pay Overtime for Some Jobs,* Wall Street Journal, Oct. 5, 2005, at p. B5]
- Family Dollar Stores was found liable for misclassifying rank-and-file workers as store managers in a bid to avoid paying overtime. The initial jury award was more than $19 million in back pay and unpaid overtime to 1,424 current and former employees, but it was reduced to $16.6 million. However, that award was then doubled on the grounds that the violation was willful. [Rebecca Moore, *Family Dollar Ordered to Pay $33M in Overtime,* PlanSponsor.com, Apr. 11, 2006]
- UBS AG settled several federal class actions involving overtime pay, agreeing to pay up to $89 million for all state and federal claims that financial advisers and trainee financial advisers were improperly classified as exempt from earning overtime. About three quarters of the settlement goes to the affected employees, the rest to legal and administrative costs. [News item, *UBS Settles Employee Overtime Compensation Suits for $89 Million* (AP) (Feb. 10, 2006) (law.com)]

- The Pepsi Cola Company was ordered by the New Jersey Supreme Court to pay overtime to the people who deliver Pepsi products and stock shelves with the products. These workers are not outside salespeople exempt from overtime. [*New Jersey Dep't of Labor v. Pepsi-Cola Co.,* No. C-1028-01 (N.J. May 2, 2002)]
- The Northern District of California granted final approval of a $35 million settlement for 1,500 current and former Pacific Bell engineers. The engineers alleged that they routinely worked more than 50 hours a week. Pacific Bell claimed a professional exemption, but very few of the workers in this group had professional engineering degrees. [*Kelly v. Pacific Telesis Group,* No. 97-CV-02729 (N.D. Cal.) settlement approved Mar. 15, 2002]
- Sanderson Farms agreed to pay over $450,000 back wages and interest to over 500 workers in poultry processing plants. [*Sanderson Farms Inc. v. DOL,* No. 2:99-CV-148-GR (S.D. Miss.) settlement filed Mar. 19, 2002]

In November 2005, the U.S. Supreme Court resolved the proper treatment of time spent "donning and doffing" (putting on and removing) safety gear required for the job and time spent walking from the locker room to the production area. [*IBP, Inc. v. Alvarez,* 126 S. Ct. 514 (2005)] Under the Portal-to-Portal Act, the FLSA applies to the employee's "workweek," the time when he or she is engaged in the principal activity(ies) of the job. Walking within the place of business is not considered work time; neither are "preliminary or postliminary" activities. However, the Supreme Court ruled that putting on and taking off gear that is integral to work is compensable as part of the work day, as is walking between the production area and the area where protective clothing is put on and removed. However, the time employees spend waiting to put on their protective gear is not compensable because it is not closely enough related to the principal activities of the job.

Early in 2006, Toyota offered $4.5 million to a group of about 1,000 current and past employees to settle disputes about donning time and time to walk to the assembly line. The settlement includes payments of about $1,000 per year of work, capped at $5,000, plus retroactive pension contributions. [*Toyota Offering $4.5M to Workers for Changing Clothes,* PlanSponsor.com (Feb. 17, 2006)]

The largest overtime pay class action ever to be tried was settled in September 2004 for over $200 million, resolving claims that Farmers Insurance Exchange wrongfully deprived approximately 2,400 Californian claims adjusters of overtime pay. At trial, the jury awarded more than $90 million, and the First District affirmed and the state Supreme Court denied review. The defendant settled for the full judgment plus attorneys' fees and accumulated interest, and agreed to pay overtime to all class members—including another $40 million for overtime worked since the case began. A separate multidistrict case covering claims adjusters nationwide in the District Court for the District of Oregon resulted in a $53 million judgment for the plaintiffs. [*Bell v. Farmers Insurance Exchange,* No. 774013-0 (Alameda County Superior Court), discussed in Mike McKee, *Huge Settlement Ends Record-Setting Overtime Class Action,* The Recorder, Sept. 7, 2004 (law.com); *In re Farmers Insurance Exchange Claims Representatives' Overtime Pay Litigation,* MDL No. 1439 (D. Ore. 2004), discussed in *Insurer Loses to Adjusters on Overtime,* New York Times, May 4, 2005, at p. C6, and Tresa Baldas, *New Overtime Rules Bring Suits,* Nat'l Law Journal, Mar. 17, 2005 (law.com)]

In 18 states, including Alaska, California, Colorado, Connecticut, Illinois, and New Jersey, the state labor laws are more protective of employees than the FLSA, so another future litigation area will be determining the applicability of state or federal rules in a given situation.

It's important to note that not all employee overtime claims result in victory.

The Middle District of Alabama rejected a proposed overtime class action that managers and assistant managers of a drugstore chain sought to bring, on the grounds that the would-be class plaintiffs did not prove that they had enough in common to be similarly situated for FLSA purposes. There was evidence to back up the employer's contention that the bulk of their work was supervisory even though they did some non-exempt work. [*Holt v. Rite Aid Corp.,* No. 2:03cv748-A (M.D. Ala. Aug. 23, 2004)] Yet, a few days later, the California Supreme Court found class certification appropriate for wage and hour suits, such as one brought by over 600 Sav-on Drug Stores employees who charged that they were misclassified as managers to avoid overtime obligations. The court approved class treatment because there was "substantial, if disputed" evidence that the misclassification occurred pursuant to a policy. The defendant's position was that overtime cases are inappropriate for class actions because they must be proven on a person-by-person basis, but the California Supreme Court held that individual issues do not preclude class certification if they are manageable, even if class members have to itemize their damages. [Mike McKee, *Calif. Supremes Approve Wage-and-Hour Suit,* The Recorder, Aug. 27, 2004 (law.com)]

29 C.F.R. § 541.3 defines a professional as a person who satisfies a duties test and is paid on a salaried basis. Early in 2005, the Tenth Circuit ruled against a class of Wal-Mart pharmacists who alleged that Wal-Mart's prospective reduction in their salaries when their workload was expected to decrease made them hourly workers entitled to overtime. The plaintiffs admitted that the written compensation policy called them salaried employees, but charged that the policy as actually applied prospectively reduced their base hours and salary when store sales declined. The Tenth Circuit remanded the case for further factual determinations, because it did not believe that Wal-Mart changed pharmacists' salaries often enough to convert them to hourly employees. The Tenth Circuit held that it is permissible to reduce salary to accommodate business needs. Furthermore, Wal-Mart conformed to DOL opinion letters allowing reduction in salaried employees' work schedules and pay in response to economic slowdown. [*In re Wal-Mart Stores Inc. FLSA Litigation,* 395 F.3d 1177 (10th Cir. 2005)]

An auto dealer's office manager was held not to be an exempt "executive," although she could be deemed an exempt "administrator" because she did office work and supervised four other people. [*Lott v. Howard Wilson Chrysler-Plymouth,* 203 F.3d 326 (5th Cir. 2000)]

The Middle District of Florida ruled in 2002 that life insurance agents are not entitled to overtime, because their work is not production-oriented. [*Hogan v. Allstate Ins. Co.,* 210 F. Supp. 2d 1312 (M.D. Fla. 2002)]

Early in 2003, the Fourth Circuit held that plaintiffs who sued for overtime payments for work done during two five-week periods in 1997 and 1999 were not entitled to prevail. Even though they did some nonexempt work, they were nonetheless exempt administrative employees. The plaintiffs, 17 salaried employees earning between $52,000 and $65,000 a year, were pressed into service to help with the extra work mandated by regularly scheduled maintenance shutdowns of the power plant where they worked. The plaintiffs were exempt because they were salaried rather than earning hourly wages, and because they fell within the administrative/professional/executive test. According to the Fourth Circuit, an employee's primary duties are assessed using the totality of the circumstances, and exceptional circumstances occurring for five or six weeks on an 18-month cycle don't change the underlying nature of the job. [*Counts v. South Carolina Elec. & Gas Co.,* 317 F.3d 453 (4th Cir. 2003)]

The FLSA does not require overtime to be paid for time spent completing OSHA's 10-hour general construction safety course that was a pre-requisite of employment. In this case, the employees had to take four two-and-a-half-hour training sessions in the evening, outside normal working hours. In the Sixth Circuit view, the employer was helping the employees—it could have deferred hiring them and putting them on the payroll until after they had completed the course; they were better off being able to earn a paycheck while learning, even without overtime. [*Chao v. Tradesmen Int'l Inc.,* 310 F.3d 904 (6th Cir. 2002)] Nor did the First Circuit require payment of overtime for the time campus police officers spent getting certified as Emergency Medical Technicians, even though they had to get the certification to maintain their jobs, because emergency rescue was not an integral and indispensable part of their principal job duties. [*Bienkowski v. Northeastern Univ.,* 285 F.3d 138 (1st Cir. 2002)]

The Seventh Circuit ruled that time spent attending counseling sessions mandated by the employer—including travel time—was work time compensable under the FLSA. [*Sehie v. City of Aurora*, 432 F.3d 749 (7th Cir. 2005)] The plaintiff left work without permission after becoming infuriated by being ordered to work a double shift. Her employer required a fitness-for-duty examination. The doctor performing this examination recommended six months of weekly therapy appointments as condition of retaining her job. The employer ordered the plaintiff to be treated by the city's psychotherapist, not one of her own choosing. The plaintiff attended 16 one-hour sessions, each involving two hours of travel time, before quitting her job. She sued the city for compensation for the sessions. Because the purpose of counseling was to improve her work ability, it was for the employer's benefit and hence compensable. If the employee's comfort was the objective, the court said, she would have been permitted to select her own therapist.

In a suit for the recovery of unpaid overtime, the California Supreme Court ruled that individual officers, directors, and shareholders were not personally liable. Sometimes California's Department of Labor Standards and Employment imposes individual liability on the basis of economic reality, but the court ruled that this policy is not entitled to deference because it was never promulgated under the Administrative Procedures Act. Corporate directors can be jointly liable with the corporation if they personally direct or participate in tortious conduct, but the court declined to impose personal liability in *Reynolds v. Bement* because failure to comply with statutory overtime requirements is not tortious, and there was no allegation that the officers or directors retained the unpaid overtime compensation for their own benefit. [*Reynolds v. Bement*, 36 Cal. 4th 1075 (Cal. Sup. 2005)]

The First Circuit (like the Sixth, Eighth, Tenth, and Eleventh, but unlike the Second, Fourth, and Ninth) takes the position that a letter within an organization can constitute protected activity, so retaliation on the basis of such a letter is illegal. The Second, Fourth, and Ninth Circuits only allow retaliation claims if the employee brought a suit or made a formal agency complaint. [*See, e.g., Ball v. Memphis Bar-B-Q Co.,* 228 F.3d 360 (4th Cir. 2000)] According to the Eleventh Circuit, punitive damages are not available for violation of the antiretaliation provision. [*Snapp v. Unlimited Concepts, Inc.,* 208 F.3d 928 (11th Cir. 2000)]

Cintas Corp. filed petitions in 70 federal courts against nearly 1,800 current and former employees, seeking to have all of the employees' claims for overtime arbitrated individually rather than as a class. The suit was filed in March 2003 and about 2,400 employees joined. In February 2006, a California District Court ruled that 483 of the claims could be pursued by litigation, but the other claimants were covered by mandatory arbitration clauses. Cintas' litigating posture was that arbitration must be held in the county in which the claimant was employed by Cintas. The company's unusual strategy was to split up the cases, not only in the hope that many employees would drop small claims as not worth pursuing, but to avoid the bottom-line and stock market impact of a large judgment or settlement. (An earlier California lawsuit against Cintas was settled for $10 million in 2003.) [Theo Francis, *Cintas Seeks Separate Claims in Overtime Spat,* Wall Street Journal, Mar. 29, 2006, at p. B5]

[E] Scheduling Workers for Overtime

Sometimes, the employer will have to provide additional incentives, such as meal vouchers or free meals in the employee cafeteria or transportation home, for overtime work. But it is more common for employees to compete to be able to put in extra hours at the higher overtime rate. It is legitimate to assign overtime in order of seniority: to let employees bid for overtime work, with priority to the most senior.

In a unionized workplace, the CBA determines how much notice the company must give when overtime will be required; the extent to which overtime is assigned and when it is voluntary; who gets to bid on it; maximum overtime hours; and meal and rest breaks during overtime. If the employer assigns overtime, the disciplinary procedure should be drafted to specify that refusal to work mandatory overtime is a legitimate subject for discipline.

The FLSA allows employers to maintain a policy under which overtime work must be authorized. (Otherwise, employees would have an incentive to goof off during the day and catch up during better-paid overtime hours). But overtime pay is required if the employer permits or even is aware that nonexempt employees are working more than 40 hours a week.

Tip: The amount of overtime can be reduced by

- Planning further in advance;
- Being more realistic about deadlines;
- Coordinating tasks better, so materials and intermediate products are available when the production cycle requires them;
- Coordinating vacation and leave schedules so there will be enough employees available and it won't be necessary for a few workers to put in extra hours to cover for those who are absent.

---

§ 1.16   VACATIONS AND VACATION PAY

Some degree of paid vacation time, including major holidays and two to four weeks of vacation time, is almost universal in U.S. corporations. (European entitlement to vacation time is both greater and more formal—it's usually a matter of labor law, not left up to the employer's discretion.)

In March 2005, the BLS reported that 77% of employees in the private sector were entitled to paid holidays and vacations. [Bureau of Labor Statistics, *National Compensation Survey: Employee Benefits in Private Industry in the United States, March 2005*, <http://www.dol.gov/ebsa0003.pdf> (Aug. 2005)]

The theoretical availability of time off doesn't always predict actual usage patterns. Expedia.com's "vacation deprivation" survey showed that in 2006, employees were projected to have an average of three unused vacation days apiece. In effect, they would be giving employers back close to $54 billion in value. In 2005, 421 million vacation days were waived. Almost one third of survey respondents said they do not use all of their vacation days. [*Americans Return Compensation to Employers Via Lost Vacation*, PlanSponsor.com (Jan. 5, 2006)]

> **Tip:** Audit requirements may actually require employees with access to the firm's cash and books to take at least two consecutive weeks of vacation. An employee who never uses his or her full allotment of vacation time could be a conscientious person who wants to cope with a backlog, a workaholic who really needs to "get a life" outside the office, a sub-par employee who needs extra time to make up for incompetence, or an embezzler who has to hang around to prevent crooked schemes from unraveling!

The federal Davis-Bacon Act requires government contractors to pay for unused vacation days when an employee terminates but there is no general FLSA provision covering other situations. Most of the states impose a similar requirement for state government employees, but not in the private sector. Some states, however, have rules about this. In California, any employer that offers paid vacations must pay for unused time when an employee leaves. However, it is permissible for the employer to cap the number of days, weeks, or months of vacation that can be accumulated in a year. In Oklahoma, unused vacation time is payable on termination only if this is agreed on in an established policy. In New Hampshire, vacation, sick, and personal days are wages if the benefits are a matter of employment practice or policy. The Massachusetts statute defines wages to include holiday or vacation pay due under any written or even oral agreement, and Wyoming requires employers to pay for unused vacation time accrued under the employer's vacation policy. [No by-line, *Pay for Unused Vacation? Depends on Where You Live,* BLR (Business and Legal Reports) HR e-Lert! Oct. 1, 2002]

A query posted to Workindex.com asked if an employer with locations in Texas and Georgia can change its paid time-off policy so that accrued PTO would no longer be paid when the employee terminates. The answer was that the change would be permissible if the employee handbook discloses the policy, and it is applied fairly to all employees, in a non-discriminatory fashion. There is no Georgia statute on point; however, *Shannon v. Huntley's Jiffy Stores,* 174 Ga. App. 125 (Ga. App. 1985), upholds a "use it or lose it" handbook provision that denies accrued PTO to terminating employees. Texas Labor Code § 61.014 requires "wages" to be paid in full at termination, but that is defined to mean compensation for vacation, holidays, sick days, parental leave, and severance under a written agreement or the employer's written policy. Therefore, payment will not be due for accrued, but unpaid, vacation days if the Texas employer's policy is to deny payment. [Workindex.com, Legal Archive Article (benefitslink.com)]

IRS Private Letter Ruling 9635002 allows the employer to add the value of any unused vacation days to an employee's 401(k) plan account. Payroll taxes do not have to be paid or withheld on such amounts, and income tax on the value of the vacation days is deferred until the 401(k) account is accessed. The value of the vacation days does not reduce the amount of cash compensation that the employee can defer.

The "group emergency pool" technique can be used to maintain the paycheck of a sick employee who would not otherwise be entitled to pay. It works especially well in smaller companies that cannot afford a short-term disability plan. Employees donate unused vacation days, and the donor's salary for those days is contributed to the sick employee. The company can allow pooling of vacation time only, sick leave only, or both. Usually, the maximum donation is 80 hours, so that donor employees can take at least some vacation. The donation can be accounted for on an hour-for-hour basis, or a dollar-for-dollar basis if participants have widely varying salaries.

IRS Notice 2005-68, 2005-40 I.R.B. 622, includes information about the tax consequences of leave-based donation programs. That is, employees agree to give up some of their vacation, sick, or personal leave days in exchange for cash that the employer donates to a nonprofit organization for Hurricane Katrina relief. Such donations, made before January 1, 2007, are not included in the gross income of the employee who makes the donation. This notice was promulgated based on similar programs for donations made after September 11, 2001, and presumably the IRS will issue additional rulings if there are additional disasters of similar magnitude.

§ 1.17 GARNISHMENTS AND DEDUCTIONS FOR SUPPORT ORDERS

[A] Assignments versus Garnishments

There may be instances in which the HR department is asked to apply some of an employee's wages to a debt, such as consumer debts, student loan debt, and the obligation to support children, and/or an ex-spouse.

An "assignment" is an action undertaken by an individual to direct some of his or her future compensation to creditors. A "garnishment" is a deduction from wages made pursuant to a court order. Federal law doesn't say anything about wage assignments, although many states limit the amount or percentage of each paycheck that can be assigned, permit assignments only for certain classes of debts, or require the spouse's consent to the assignment.

Pensions cannot be assigned before they are received (except through a Qualified Domestic Relations Order (QDRO) *see* § 12.08). Once a pension payment is made, the recipient can do whatever he or she wants with it, but the "anti-alienation" rules of ERISA prevent advance assignment.

The federal Consumer Credit Protection Act (CCPA) [15 U.S.C. § 1671 *et seq.*] puts limits on garnishment. Generally, the maximum permitted garnishment will be 25% of the employee's "disposable" earnings, with stricter limits on garnishments for very low-income workers. "Disposable earnings" is defined as approximately equal to gross income minus Social Security taxes and withheld income taxes. Health insurance premiums and spousal and child support are not deducted, even if the support is ordered by a court. Thus, serious problems can occur if the same individual is subject to garnishment both for consumer debt and support payments.

Garnishment for support rather than consumer debt can be higher [15 U.S.C. § 1673]:

- 50%, if the employee is supporting a spouse or child other than the subject of the order, and the garnishment order covers less than 12 weeks' worth of arrears;
- 55%, if conditions are the same but more than 12 weeks of arrears are involved;
- 60%, if the employee does not have a new family to support, and arrears are 12 weeks or less;
- 65%, if there is no second family and arrears exceed 12 weeks.

There is no limit on garnishments that respond to an order issued by a Chapter 11 or Chapter 13 bankruptcy court, or on a debt due for any state or federal tax. The general rule against alienation of plan benefits doesn't prevent the IRS from garnishing a taxpayer's (or rather, nontaxpayer's) vested interest in qualified benefits when the agency has a judgment for unpaid taxes.

The CCPA says that, if state law limits garnishment more than the federal law does, employees are entitled to the protection of the stricter state-law limits. In other words, the garnishment is limited to what is permitted by state law. Under the CCPA, it's illegal to fire an employee for having one garnishment, but it's lawful to fire if additional garnishments are imposed. [16 U.S.C. § 1674] Willful violation of this provision can be punished by a $1,000 fine and/or one year's imprisonment.

It should be noted that qualified plan benefits can be garnished to collect a criminal restitution order under the Mandatory Victims Restitution Act of 1996, which provides restitution for property losses. Restitution orders have the same status as tax liens, for which plan benefits can also be garnished. [*U.S. v. Novak*, 441 F.3d 819 (9th Cir. 2006)]

Under Maryland and Colorado law, cash tips received from customers are considered "remuneration" that has to be included in the garnishment calculations. [*United Guaranteed Res. Ins. Co. v. Demmick*, 916 P.2d 638 (Colo. App. 1996); *Shanks v. Lowe*, 774 A.2d 411 (Md. 2001)]

The federal Fair Debt Collection Practices Act (FDCPA) [28 U.S.C. § 3001] lets the federal government collect its judgments by garnishing property held by a third party on the basis of the debtor's "substantial non-exempt interest" in the property. According to the Sixth Circuit, tax levies do not violate ERISA's anti-alienation provisions. [*U.S. v. Sawaf*, 74 F.3d 119 (6th Cir. 1996)]

[B] Student Loan Garnishments

There are separate federal rules at 20 U.S.C. § 1095a with respect to garnishment to repay student loans. Up to 10% of disposable earnings can be garnished to repay those loans. The employee can sign a document agreeing to a higher garnishment level. Before the garnishment order is submitted to the employer, the employee has the right to contest the garnishment and suggest a voluntary repayment schedule. If a person is fired or laid off from a job, and is rehired (by the original employer or someone else) within 12 months after termination, student loan garnishment is deferred until the person has been back in the workforce for 12 months.

The federal provisions do not require employers to change or depart from their normal payment mechanisms to comply with student loan garnishment orders, but if they fail to comply with the order entirely, employers can be penalized by the amount that should have been withheld to satisfy the garnishment, plus costs, fees, and punitive damages.

Federal law forbids an employer to discharge, refuse to hire, or discipline a person because he or she is subject to a student loan garnishment. Employers that violate this rule can be ordered to reinstate the affected employee with back pay, and can also be ordered to pay punitive damages and attorneys' fees.

[C] Child Support Collection

State governments are heavily involved in child support enforcement, to prevent children from becoming welfare recipients because their parents do not support them. The federal government also requires state governments to take this enforcement role. Under a federal statute, the Child Support Enforcement Amendments of 1984 [P.L. 98-378], states can lose federal funding if they do not enact laws requiring wage withholding for support arrears. States must also have a procedure for Qualified Medical Child Support Orders (QMCSOs) under which parents who are covered by an Employee Group Health Plan (EGHP) are required to take steps to enroll their children under the plan.

Federal law also requires state-court child support orders to contain a withholding provision, so a withholding order can be issued as soon as a parent falls behind on support, with no need for separate court proceedings. The state child support enforcement agency notifies the employer that a particular employee has child support arrears. The employer is obligated to impose withholding as of the first pay period after 14 days of the date the agency mailed its notice. Once withholding begins, the employer has an obligation to notify the child support agency promptly if the employee quits or gets fired. The notice should give the termination date, the employee's last known address, and the address of the new employer (if known).

The CCPA percentage limits discussed above apply to child support orders. Depending on circumstances, up to 65% of disposable income may be subject to withholding for support. The Child Support Enforcement Amendments allow states to impose a late payment fee of 3 to 6% of the overdue support. Support withholding takes priority over other legal processes (e.g., for consumer debts or student loans) applying to the same income.

Employers must also submit data about newly hired employees to the state unemployment insurance agency within 20 days of hiring. The information is aggregated into a National Directory of New Hires that is used to track down "deadbeat parents" who fail to pay child support.

The basic federal report (which can be made by mail or magnetic tape; state support enforcement agencies can accept telephoned, faxed, and e-mailed reports) consists of:

- Employer's name, address, and Taxpayer Identification Number;
- Employee's name;
- Employee's address;
- Employee's Social Security number.

States may impose additional requirements, such as telephone numbers, driver's license number, and information about the group health plan (to be used in conjunction with a (QMCSO). The employer also has to make a quarterly report of wages paid, for use in instituting withholding orders. Failure to make a required report can be penalized by $25 per employee, or $500 for conspiracy with an employee to avoid the requirement.

§ 1.18   USERRA

Under the Uniformed Services Employment and Reemployment Rights Act [38 U.S.C. § 4301 *et seq.*] (USERRA), employers have obligations toward their employees who temporarily leave employment to fulfill a military commitment. After the reservist or National Guardsman or -woman returns to civilian life, the employer is obligated to re-employ the person. In this context, uniformed services means the Armed Forces (the Coast Guard is included), the National Guard, and the various service Reserves. According to employment litigator Sam Samaro, USERRA probably offers the broadest protection to employees of any anti-discrimination statute. For one thing, it puts the burden of proof on the employers. Department of Labor staffer Gordon Berg said that in fiscal 2002, 1,200 USERRA cases were filed—much higher than the average of 900 per year for the preceding four years. Such cases can be a public relations nightmare for the defendant company.

USERRA requires the employee to give the employer advance written or verbal notice of leave, unless this would be impossible, unreasonable, or precluded by military necessity. The statute requires the employer to reinstate the service member after discharge, in the job he or she would have achieved but for the period of military service, applying the "escalator principle" to seniority, status, compensation, and other seniority-related rights. The statute is not clear what re-employment rights apply if the person would have been laid off even absent active military duty. Furthermore, the employer is not obligated to offer the returned service member a job at the same location, and federal law does not require the employer to pay the service member during military leave. The employee can elect to use accrued vacation or other paid leave while he or she is serving, but employers are not allowed to require the service member to use accrued paid leave.

The employer is obligated to make a reasonable effort to provide training to refresh or upgrade the returning service member's skills. Employees who cannot qualify for their former job must be placed in an alternative position. However, re-employment is not required if circumstances have changed so much that it would be impossible, unreasonable, or impose an undue hardship to do it. When active duty lasted 181 days or more, the re-employed person can be fired only for cause during the first year of reinstatement (and only for cause in the first six months after re-employment following service of 30 to 180 days).

If the service member was on active duty for 30 days or less, USERRA requires him or her to report back to work after active duty on the next regular work day. If the military commitment was 31 to 180 days, the general rule is that USERRA requires the employee to apply for re-employment within 14 days of finishing the military commitment. The period to re-apply stretches to 90 days if the service member was on active duty for over 180 days.

Under USERRA, the employer must treat a period of military duty as active service with the employer for eligibility, vesting, and benefit accrual purposes. However, once the service member returns to work, he or she is entitled to benefits attributable to employee contributions only to the extent that he or she actually made such contributions. The employer is not obligated to make contributions to a 401(k) plan while the employee is on active service, but when the service member is re-employed, the employer must make whatever employer contributions would have been made if the service member had continued at work.

For plans that require or accept employee contributions, USERRA gives the employee a period of time equal to the shorter of five years or three times the duration of military service to make the contributions. Once these contributions are made, the employer must make any matching contributions that the plan calls for. However, the employer is not obligated to make contributions that include earnings or forfeitures that would have been allocated to the employee if the contributions had been made during the term of military service. At the end of 2003, the Ser-vicemembers Civil Relief Act (SCRA) [Pub. L. No. 108-189] was signed to clarify the protection available to persons serving in the military. SCRA specifies that the 6% interest rate ceiling covers only obligations and liabilities incurred by the service member (or jointly with his or her spouse) before entering military service. (Therefore, a plan loan made to a plan participant who is already on military duty can charge the plan's normal interest rate.) But interest over and above the permitted 6% level must be forgiven, not merely postponed until the service-member returns.

For this purpose, "interest" includes charges associated with the loan such as fees and service charges, but the cost of bona fide insurance is not included.

The statute also makes it clear that service in the National Guard lasting over 30 days is military service. To get relief under SCRA, the servicemember must give the creditor written notice and a copy of the call-up order no later than 180 days after the servicemember is terminated or released from service. Once the notice is given, it reduces the interest rate retroactively to the date of the callup.

The creditor can petition the court for relief, which will be granted if the court deems that military service does not restrict the servicemember's ability to repay at a higher interest rate. [*See, e.g.,* DOL guidelines, <http://www.dol.gov/ebsa/faqs/faq_911_2.html>]

Creditors—including pension plans, if the service members have outstanding plan loans—are legally obligated under USERRA to reduce interest rates to 6% or less on debts owed by those entering military service. The statute allows plan fiduciaries to petition the relevant court to maintain a higher interest rate, based on a showing of the service member's ability to pay. USERRA also allows (but does not obligate) the plan to suspend the obligation to make regular payments of plan loans during the term of military service.

Under federal law, USERRA leave does not have to be paid leave (although some state laws do impose a requirement of a period of paid leave). The federal statute allows employees, at their option, to use accrued vacation or other paid leave while they are on active duty, but the employer is not permitted to force them to do so if they prefer unpaid leave and preservation of their leave accrual.

There is no requirement that employers provide pay supplements to prevent service members from suffering a loss of income when they lose their civilian paychecks and get military pay (often much lower). However, some employers elect to do so as a patriotic statement of support for the troops. The time periods vary from three months to several years. The GAO studied past military operations, and concluded that 41% of reservists lost income when called up for active duty, 30% experienced no change, and 29% actually had higher income post-call-up.

Tip: EBIA Weekly's Question of the Week for November 20, 2003, deals with a former employee who resigned, elected COBRA coverage, and then was called for active duty. EBIA noted that he was not eligible for continuation coverage under USERRA because he resigned prior to his active-duty call up; active duty was not the reason why he left that employment. It's unclear whether COBRA coverage can be terminated on the basis of alternate health coverage under the military system, but it would probably not be permitted. IRS Notice 90-58 says that COBRA coverage cannot be terminated, because the military health system, Tri-Care, is not an EGHP for COBRA purposes. Reg. § 54.4980B-7 Q&A 2, however, implies that the IRS thinks termination is permissible. The Department of Labor, in its FAQ for reservists called to active duty, says that COBRA coverage cannot be terminated. [EBIA Weekly Questions of the Week (Nov. 20, 2003); the DOL FAQ is at <http://www.dol.gov/ebsa/faqs/faq_911_2.html>]

Reservists don't get much notice before being deployed, and they can be called up for an uncertain period of anywhere from weeks to years, leaving employers to scramble to fill those positions. It is often prudent to cross-train other employees to cover for absent service members.

Health care for service members and their families raises difficult questions. If the active duty deployment lasts 30 days or more, the service member and family become entitled to coverage under TRICARE, the military health care system. However, this can create difficulties for family members, because it can be difficult to locate a TRICARE (military medical system) provider—many doctors refuse to participate in the system, because its reimbursement rates are low. Only about 40% of hospitals and 30% of doctors regularly participate in TRICARE, but some providers will do so on a case-by-case basis.

Being called for active service is also a COBRA event, requiring notice and giving the service member and family the option of continuing coverage in the employer's plan for up to 24 months by making premium payments. After a service member is deactivated, he or she and family members can also do a kind of reverse-COBRA election by choosing to remain within the TRICARE system for a period of time. [GAO-03-549T, *Military Personnel: Preliminary Observations Related to Income, Benefits, and Employer Support for Reservists During Mobilizations* (Mar. 19, 2003) <http://www.gao.gov/cgi-bin/getrpt?GAO-03-549T>]

The Fifth Circuit decided a USERRA suit for declaratory, injunctive and equitable relief, back pay and benefits, and liquidated damages at the end of 2004. The 15 plaintiffs are firefighters and Emergency Medical Technicians who are Reservists or in the National Guard. They charged the City of San Antonio with violating USERRA § 4321(a)(2) by denying them employment benefits (pay, overtime, opportunities to bid on overtime and promotions and to earn extra vacation time) when they were on active duty. The plaintiffs took the position that USERRA requires them to be treated as constructively present when they're on active duty. The City relied on USERRA § 4316(b)(1), which gives military absentees only the same entitlement to non-seniority rights and benefits as employees who are on leave for non-military reasons.

There is no legal obligation for employers to have a seniority system at all, but if they do, a returning servicemember must be reinstated at an "escalator" position comparable to the level he or she would have achieved by remaining at work rather than being called to duty. For non-seniority rights and benefits, the escalator principle does not apply. The Fifth Circuit held that USERRA § 4316 applies to inactive duty (drilling and training) as well as active service, and granted summary judgment for the city on issues of straight-time pay, overtime opportunities, and loss of chances to upgrade because there is no form of non-military leave that would provide such opportunities to a person who was absent from work. The issues of bonus day leave, perfect attendance leave, and the cap on overtime hours that could be worked were remanded for further proceedings because it was unclear whether military and non-military leave should be treated equally. USERRA § 4323 does not provide a statute of limitations (although it says that state statutes of limitations do not apply), so the Fifth Circuit applied the four-year statute of limitations provided by 28 U.S.C. § 1658. [*Rogers v. City of San Antonio*, 392 F.3d 758 (5th Cir. 2004)]

The returning servicemember has an obligation to notify his or her employer of the intent to return to work, but this does not create a statutory right to an eight-hour rest period before returning to work. The Third Circuit ruled in 2004 that the mother of a deceased servicemember, who claimed that the car accident that killed her son was due to his employer's refusal to grant a rest period, did not have a cause of action under USERRA. [*Gordon v. Wawa Inc.*, 388 F.3d 78 (3d Cir. 2004)]

According to BNA's Daily Labor Report (August 18, 2004), since the 9/11 attack, one out of every 74 servicemembers has filed a USERRA complaint. A 2005 New York case denied summary judgment for the employer in a case in which an Army reservist was terminated after returning from an active duty mission that occurred during a critical point in the negotiation of a significant deal. The stated reason for his termination was that the plaintiff left a voicemail message for a co-worker, saying he was going to "hunt her down and kill her," so he was terminated for violation of the zero-tolerance anti-violence policy. He said later that the message was a joke. The court agreed that a reasonable jury could conclude that the stated rationale for discharge was pretextual because a reasonable jury would have treated the message as a joke; it was overreaction to dismiss an eight-year employee with a good record just for one incident. [*Warren v. IBM*, No. 03 Civ. 3340 (N.Y. 2005), discussed in Victoria M. Phipps, *What Employers Need to Know About "Citizen Soldiers,"* special to Law.com, Mar. 21, 2005]

In 2005 the New York Times reported on reservists who felt their careers had been "downsized" after their military experience, including an Air Force reservist who had been earning $200,000 a year as a stockbroker when he was called up. When he returned, his company had merged and reassigned his clients and was unwilling to offer him employment other than cold-calling in return for a $2,000 monthly draw. About one third of the 500,000 reservists that were called up are professionals, including lawyers who feel they have missed partnership opportunities. The Department of Defense said that it received 6,242 USERRA complaints in 2004. [Stacey Stowe, *After Uniform, White-Collar Blues,* New York Times, Oct. 28, 2005, at p. B1]

The Seventh Circuit, stating that it was reluctant to do so but that the statutes compelled the result, affirmed summary judgment for the employer when a Vietnam veteran suffering from a skin disorder resulting from exposure to Agent Orange disease sued under USERRA and the Veterans Reemployment Act of 1974. The USERRA claims accrued before the statute was enacted, and USERRA, including the governance of re-employment, is not retroactive. The Veterans Reemployment Act does not create re-employment rights after disability leave has been granted, only upon return from active duty. Therefore, the plaintiff was not entitled to have the years he was on disability for a military-connected condition, included when calculating his pension. [*Bowlds v. General Motors*, 411 F.3d 808 (7th Cir. 2005)]

An Air Force reserve non-commissioned officer worked for a military contractor. When he was called to active duty, his employer lost the Air Force contract and became a subcontractor to the company that received the contract. After his honorable discharge from the Air Force Reserve, Coffman applied to return to his old job; however, his replacement had been hired on a permanent basis, so Coffman was hired in a different capacity. He subsequently brought suit against the new contractor under USERRA. The Eleventh Circuit affirmed the district court's grant of summary judgment to the defendant (the new contractor). At issue in this case of first impression was whether the new contractor. Chugach Support Services could be considered Coffman's former employer for USERRA purposes. The district court looked to prior interpretations of "successor in interest." USERRA defines "employer" to include a "successor in interest" to the previous employer, but does not define successor in interest. [38 U.S.C. § 4303(4)(A)(iv)] The Eleventh Circuit agreed that the contractor was not a successor in interest to the original employer. Although the plaintiff was one of only three persons not hired by the contractor, and the only one who had served in the military, the Eleventh Circuit ruled that there was no merger or transfer of assets between the two companies; one lost the military contract and the other one won it.

In the Eleventh Circuit's view, discriminatory motivation under USERRA can be inferred from factors such as the close proximity in time between military activity and an adverse employment action; inconsistencies between the employer's actions and the explanations offered for them; expressed hostility toward military personnel; or disparate treatment of employees with similar work records based on their military experience. In this case, the court ruled that the plaintiff failed to present either direct or circumstantial evidence that his military status entered into any employment decision. [*Coffman v. Chugach Support Servs. Inc.*, 411 F.3d 1231 (11th Cir. 2005)]

[A] Regulations

Although USERRA is a 1994 statute, the first proposed regulations were not issued until September 20, 2004, by the Department of Labor's Veterans' Employment and Training Service (VETS). A few months later, on December 10, 2004, President Bush signed the Veterans Benefits Improvement Act of 2004, P.L. 108-454, amending USERRA Title 38 § 4317 to provide continuation of health coverage for up to 18 months at the servicemember's expense. Under the VBIA, for elections made after December 10, 2004, the servicemember can elect 24 months of continuation coverage.

The statute also requires all employers (there is no minimum number of employees for coverage) to give all employees (not just those whom the employer knows to have military commitments) a notice of USERRA rights, benefits, and obligations. The statute required the DOL to draft the necessary form, which it did, at the last minute: in an Interim Final Rule dated March 10, 2005. The official text can be found at <http://www.dol.gov/vets/programs/userra/poster.pdf>. The notice of USERRA rights can either be posted, like the mandatory postings dealing with topics such as equal employment opportunity and minimum wages, or be provided to each employee by hand delivery, mail, or e-mail.

Regulations were proposed on September 20, 2004. State laws are preempted only if they offer less protection than the federal rule: 20 C.F.R. § 1002.7.

The proposed regulations (20 C.F.R. § 1002.266) entitle the servicemember to pension accruals or employer contributions if he or she is re-employed by the original employer or by another employer covered by the same multi-employer pension plan. (This requirement is not found in the statute, and was added by the proposed regulation.) Health plan administrators must set reasonable requirements for elections for continued coverage (20 C.F.R. § 1002.165). The Department of Labor sought comments as to whether there should be a specific date for electing continuation coverage, and also about the timing for the employer's pension contributions when a servicemember is re-employed (a subject that is not addressed by USERRA). Section 1002.262 of the proposal sets a 30-day deadline for this purpose.

Under USERRA, military service is not a break in service when it comes to participation, vesting, or benefit accruals. For either a defined benefit or a defined contribution plan, pension calculations must be based on the pay rate the employee would have received if he or she had not been deployed. If the pay rate is uncertain (for example, it depends on sales commissions) the employer must use the average rate of compensation during the 12-month period prior to military service.

The proposal requires 401(k) plans to include the period of uniformed service in calculations of vesting and benefit accrual. Returning servicemembers must be permitted to make up the elective deferrals that they could have made if they had not been on active duty. They have the choice of making up all or any part of the missed contributions, and cannot be charged interest. They can take up to three times the length of military service (but not more than five years) to make up the contributions.

The employer is required to match only to the extent the servicemember makes the contributions within a specified time frame. The USERRA statute does not set a timetable for the employer contributions. The regulations require the employer contributions to be made within 30 days after re-employment if the employee can't or doesn't have to contribute (e.g., profit-sharing plans). Employer matches based on elective deferrals must satisfy the plan's general timing requirements for matching contributions.

Applying for military service (rather than just performance of military service) is a protected right, so employers are forbidden to discriminate or retaliate on this basis (20 C.F.R. §§ 1002.18–.20). Joint employers are covered by USERRA, and so are a company's successor in interest, even if unaware of the servicemember's re-employment claims (20 C.F.R. §§ 1002.35–.37). The proposals make it clear that USERRA does not just protect full-time permanent workers. Job applicants, temporary, part-time, probationary, and seasonal employees; employees who have been laid off; strikers; employees on leave of absence—but not independent contractors—are covered by USERRA (20 C.F.R. § 1002.40–.44). The employer must treat the employee on active service as if he or she were on furlough or leave of absence; if the employer offers more than one type of non-military leave, military leave must provide the same benefits as the most generous of those (20 C.F.R. § 1002.149). If employees request, they must be allowed to apply their accrued vacation, annual, or similar paid leave (but not unpaid leave) to their period of active duty, but the employer can't force an employee to use up paid leave while on active duty (20 C.F.R. § 1002.151–.153).

The employer must be prompt about re-employing a returned service member. Unless there are unusual circumstances, re-employment should occur within two weeks of the application, and for weekend National Guard duty, it should occur on the next regularly scheduled work period (20 C.F.R. § 1002.180–.181).

One acceptable alternative is for the employer to use the "escalator principle" and grant the re-employed employee the raises and benefit increases that were reasonably certain to have occurred if he or she had not been called to duty. However, the regulations permit other alternatives, such as returning the employee to the position held before deployment; giving him or her a comparable position to the pre-service or elevator position; or making the nearest possible approximation to one of those. If the person would have been laid off if he or she had remained at work, re-employment to layoff status is permitted (20 C.F.R. § 1002.194).

The appropriate placement of the employee depends on factors such as length of service, the employee's qualifications, and any extent to which military service caused or aggravated an existing disability (20 C.F.R. § 1002.196–.197). Sections 225 and 226 require the employer to make reasonable efforts to accommodate disability of persons seeking re-employment and to help the applicant become qualified to perform the duties of the offered job. [Ballard Spahr Andrews & Ingersoll, LLP, *Department of Labor Proposes New Regulations Under USERRA for Military Leave Rights* (Jan. 4, 2005); Lisa N. Bleed and Charles A. Storke, *USERRA Update,* Trucker Huss ERISA and Employee Benefits Attorneys; Faegre & Benson LLP: *Department of Labor Publishes USERRA Notice Just Before the Deadline,* Mar. 11, 2005 (law.com)]

In 2005, DOL issued a Final Rule [Notice of Rights and Duties under the Uniformed Services Employment and Reemployment Rights Act, RIN 1293-AA14, 70 Fed. Reg. 75313 (Dec. 19, 2005)] instructing employers to use their best judgment about how to give notice. The Final Rule clarifies that USERRA's anti-retaliation provision also applies to non-servicemembers, such as spouses and dependents who assist servicemembers in vindicating their rights under USERRA. The Final Rule extends the employer's obligation to make up for omitted pension plan contributions to 90 days or when the contribution would otherwise be made for the year when the employee was on active duty—whichever is later. The previous rule gave employers only 30 days for this purpose. Health coverage must be restored retroactively whenever an employee is deployed in such a way that it is impossible for him or her to meet the requirement of notifying the employer of the intention to continue coverage—even if the active duty employee failed to satisfy the insurer's exclusions or waiting periods.

CHAPTER 2
TAX ASPECTS OF PAY PLANNING

§ 2.01   INTRODUCTION

One reason why corporations adopt pension and benefit plans is that, under appropriate circumstances, the employer will get a tax deduction, and the employee will receive valuable benefits—but the employee will not have immediately taxable income as a result of the benefits (or only part of the benefit will generate taxable income).

Therefore, an important part of pay planning is determining what portion of each employee's compensation is taxable, and performing tax withholding, depositing taxes, issuing information returns, and maintaining tax records.

The basic tax rule is that everything received is taxable income, unless there is a specific exclusion. Therefore, the tax definition of "wages" includes vacation pay, commissions, bonuses, and some fringe benefits, not just straight salary. Severance pay is considered taxable wages, but payments for cancellation of an employment contract are not wages.

These items have been granted exclusions from taxable income:

- Worker's Compensation benefits;
- The employer's contributions to qualified pension plans (but the employee's pretax deferrals placed into 401(k) plans are FUTA and FICA wages);
- Up to $50,000 in § 79 group-term life insurance coverage. Additional coverage is taxable income that must be reported on the W-2 form, but income tax withholding is not required. The excess coverage is not subject to FUTA, but is subject to both the employer and employee share of FICA;
- Certain fringe benefits, e.g., employee discounts, working condition and de minimis fringes, qualified transportation fringes, qualified dependent care assistance within limits, etc.

When a new employee is hired the employer must use Form I-9 to verify immigration status and that the person can lawfully work within the United States. [*See* § 23.11 for more information about immigration issues in hiring]

In 2003, the Tax Court ruled that a corporate officer (she and her husband were the corporation's sole shareholders) was an employee. Therefore, amounts that the corporation paid for two years and identified as "royalties" were actually wages subject to FICA tax. Although the corporate officer had an employment agreement calling for this characterization, the Tax Court did not feel bound by this self-serving, non-arm's-length document. The taxpayer characterized the company as a small start-up business, but the Tax Court noted that she had operated it profitably for several years before incorporating, and that the company had enough funds to pay "rent" and "royalties" to her. The Tax Court also found that the § 530 safe harbor (*see* § 1.12[B]) was unavailable, because the corporation did not act reasonably in making the characterization. [*Charlotte's Office Boutique, Inc. v. Commissioner*, 121 T.C. 89 (2003); the Ninth Circuit affirmed, 425 F.3d 1203 (9th Cir. 2005), holding that the tax court had jurisdiction to hear the case.]

Rev. Rul. 2004-98, 2004-42 I.R.B. 664, makes it clear that an employer's attempt to structure qualified transportation fringe benefits fails to satisfy Reg. § 1.132-9(b). The stratagem purported to reduce cash compensation in exchange for parking; the employer then made so-called "reimbursement" payments so that net after-tax pay was the same as if there had been no reduction in compensation. Employment taxes were paid only on the reduced amount. The example in the ruling is $1,500 gross income and a $100 reduction to pay for parking, $105 FICA, and $73 tax withholding; the employer pays the employee an extra $79.75 as parking reimbursement, yielding net pay of $1,301.45—precisely what the employee would receive if he or she earned $1,500 minus withholding. The IRS says that this is unacceptable, because an employee is only permitted to exclude from gross income reimbursements of parking expenses that were actually incurred. When an employee gets a choice between cash and an employer benefit, or an employer unilaterally reduces cash compensation to provide a non-taxable benefit, the benefit is considered to be provided by the employer, not purchased by the employee. In the example, the employee has no true expense that the employer can reimburse. The "reimbursement" payments must be included in income (and are subject to FICA, FUTA, and withholding), whether or not the reduction in gross income is mandatory or elective, and whether or not the employer originally provided free parking and then purported to impose a charge and then instituted this payroll arrangement.

Also with regard to schemes to reduce taxable income improperly, the Department of Justice announced in April 2004 that it had filed suit against two individuals and their businesses. The DOJ charged a fraudulent employee benefit scheme that reduced reported wages twice on account of health insurance premiums paid by the employer, resulting in unlawful under-reporting. (In addition to paying premiums that were properly excluded from employees' gross income, the employer also "reimbursed" the employees for premiums actually paid by the employer, and/or made payments to employees as "advance reimbursement" of future medical expenses. [*United States v. Zanfel*, Civ. No. 04-CV-2703 (N.D. Ill. filed 4/15/04); the agency's press release on the case was posted at <http://www.justice.gov/opa/pr/2004/April/04_tax_239.htm>]

Rev. Rul. 2004-55, 2004-26 I.R.B. 1081, addresses the tax status of long-term disability (LTD) benefits provided through a group insurance policy issued by a third-party carrier. The employer paid the entire premium, which was not included in the employee's gross income. The employer amended the plan to provide that it would continue to pay for LTD on a pre-tax basis for eligible employees, but also allowed eligible employees to make an irrevocable election to be taxed currently on the premiums so that the employer would pay the premiums on an after-tax basis. The election must be made for the entire series of premiums; it cannot be made for only part of it. If the employee elects after-tax treatment, then the employer allocates a proportion of the group premium to that employee, includes it in gross income, and reports it on Form W-2. An employee can make a new irrevocable election for each plan year before the beginning of that plan year;

a newly hired person can make an irrevocable prospective election for the rest of that plan year. Reg. § 1.105-1(d)(2) applies a three-year lookback rule: if net premiums for coverage for a period of at least three policy years are known at the beginning of a calendar year, then the portion of that amount received by an employee that is attributable to employer contributions is the ratio of the part contributed by the employer for the last three policy years to the total. The ruling says that when a plan is amended, the amended plan is considered a new plan when employer and employee contributions are calculated. The IRS did not apply the three-year lookback rule to this plan because the employer and employee never shared contributions to the coverage. Thus, benefits received by employees who elect employer coverage are attributable solely to after-tax employer contributions and are excludable, but benefits received after the employer provided the benefits on a pre-tax basis are including in the recipient's income. This ruling also says that if the employer offers both STD and LTD and permits employees to elect a separate payment method for each, the two need not be aggregated for tax purposes.

§ 2.02   THE COMPENSATION DEDUCTION

Internal Revenue Code § 162 allows a corporation to deduct its ordinary and necessary business expenses, including reasonable salaries in exchange for personal services rendered to the corporation. Salaries are only reasonable if the person hired is qualified to perform the services, and actually performs them. If vacation pay is treated as deferred compensation, it is not deductible until the year it is actually paid. [*See* I.R.C. § 404(a)(5)]

In mid-2004, District Courts in Michigan clashed as to whether early retirement incentive payments offered to teachers in exchange for tenure rights were wages. The Western District said that such payments are wages for FICA purposes; two weeks later, the Eastern District said that because the payments were not wages, the retired teachers could get a refund of FICA withheld on the payments. [Compare *Klender v. United States* 328 F. Supp. 2d 754 (E.D. Mich. 2004) with *Appoloni v. United States*, 73 L.W. 1094 (W.D. Mich. July 21, 2004); *but see North Dakota State Univ. v. United States*, 255 F.3d 599 (8th Cir. 2001)] The Sixth Circuit resolved the split in mid-2006 by ruling that the payments were FICA wages because "compensation" should be defined broadly, and because eligibility for the payments depended on at least a minimum tenure with the employer, showing that payments were made for services, not for relinquishments of tenure rights. [*Appoloni v. United States/Klender v. U.S.*, Nos. 04-2068, 05-1049 (6th Cir. June 7, 2006); the Federal Circuit earlier ruled that severance payments to retiring employees, reflecting past work, are FICA wages: *Abrahamsen*, 228 F.3d 1360 (Fed. Cir. 2000)]

The Working Families Tax Relief Act of 2004 (WFTRA) amended § 152(c) to define a "qualifying child" as one who satisfies relationship, residency, and age tests, and who does not provide more than half of his or her own support. The qualifying child must be either under 19 as of the close of the calendar year, a student under 24 at the end of the calendar year, or be permanently and totally disabled at any time during the year. The current version of § 152(d)(1) defines a "qualifying relative" as a relative other than the taxpayer's child (e.g., a dependent parent) who has income below the exemption amount and receives at least half of his or her support from the taxpayer. When it comes to determining the tax impact of employer-provided health coverage, status as a dependent under § 105(b) is determined without regard to § 152(b) and (d). The IRS will revise the regulations under § 106 so that the same definition of dependent will be used throughout. If the employer provides health coverage for someone who is not a qualifying child or a qualifying relative, the value of that coverage will be taxable income for the employee. Domestic partners and same-sex spouses fall into this category (*see* § 18.06). [Notice 2004-79, 2004-49 I.R.B. 898]

In September 2004, the IRS announced its Tip Rate Determination and Education Program, a voluntary compliance tool for the hospitality industry, had succeeded in its pilot and would be extended indefinitely. The program allows employers to choose among several methods of complying with tip reporting: Tip Rate Determination Agreement; Tip Reporting Alternative Commitment; and Tip Reporting Alternative Commitment Designated by Employer. The IRS intends these methods to be non-burdensome on employers. [<http://www.irs.gov/newsroom/article/0,,id=129379,00.html>; Publication 1875 is the IRS' food and beverage industry tip guide]

When the Tax Court decided the case of *Exacto Spring Corp. v. C.I.R.* [196 F.3d 833 (7th Cir. 1999)] it used a seven-factor test to determine the reasonableness of executive compensation, using factors such as the difficulty of finding qualified employees, the employee's contribution to the business, his or her qualifications and earnings history, and what comparable executives earned in other companies.

When the case was appealed, the Seventh Circuit held that the seven-factor test was not valid. It didn't explain how to weight the various factors; some of the factors were vague; and some of them didn't relate to I.R.C. § 162's objective of preventing corporations from disguising dividends paid to stockholders (which are not deductible by the corporation) as compensation to employees. Although the Seventh Circuit considered the compensation at issue here ($1.1 million in one year, $1.3 million in another) to be somewhat higher than reasonable, most of it was deductible because it rewarded the CEO for his unusually great success in increasing stockholders' return on their investment.

The Second Circuit said that the test of reasonableness is whether a hypothetical independent investor in the company would be willing to approve that level of compensation. Consideration should also be given to whether comparable companies paid extra to CEOs who also acted as CFO and treasurer. [*Doxsil Corp.,* T.C. Memo 1999-155] The Sixth Circuit treated $4.4 million paid to a company's president and sole shareholder as all reasonable and deductible.

Much of the company's profits were directly attributable to him, and it was fair to compensate him highly when the company had funds to make up for underpayment in earlier years. [*Alpha Medical Inc.,* 172 F.3d 942 (6th Cir. 1999)]

Internal Revenue Code § 162(m) provides that a public corporation (i.e., one whose stock is traded on public markets, unlike closely held private companies) is not allowed to deduct any portion of any employee's compensation that exceed $1 million. In this context, compensation means salary plus benefits, but does not include qualified retirement plans. Furthermore, compensation over $1 million can be deducted if:

- It represents commissions paid on sales;
- It is paid under a contract that was already in effect on February 17, 1993 (the effective date of § 162(m)), and has not been materially modified after that date and before the compensation was paid;
- The compensation is based on performance measured by objective goals set by a Board of Directors compensation committee. The performance-based arrangement must be disclosed to the stockholders, and must be ratified by a majority vote. The money can't be paid until the compensation committee certifies that the performance goals have been met.

Another trend in executive compensation is the "tax gross-up"—companies that reimburse their top management for the income tax they encounter on perks such as restricted stock and country club fees. Home Depot's CEO, for example, received a $2 million base salary and $3.3 million in reimbursement of the tax generated by his perks. The advantage of tax gross-ups is that they are buried in the fine print of financial statements and attract little attention. The golden parachutes offered to management when there is a change of control frequently include a gross-up. According to the compensation research firm Equilar Inc., in 2000, 38% of corporations offered gross-ups to at least one top executive, a proportion that rose to 52% in 2004. Of course, the gross-ups themselves are taxable, requiring further grossing up! [Mark Maremont, *Latest Twist in Corporate Pay: Tax-Free Income for Executives,* Wall Street Journal, Dec. 22, 2005, at p. A1]

§ 2.03   INCOME TAX WITHHOLDING

[A] Calculation

At the time of hiring, the employer must also have the employee submit Form W-4 (Employee's Withholding Allowance Certificate) to indicate the filing status (married filing a joint return, married filing a separate return, single, head of household) and the number of withholding allowances that he or she claims. The more withholding allowances, the less that will be withheld from the employee's paycheck.

Although there are other methods, the amount of income tax to be withheld is usually calculated under either the percentage method or the wage bracket method. (The calculations will be done by the payroll preparation contractor, if the employer outsources this function.)

Under the percentage method, the IRS tables are used. The number of allowances claimed is multiplied by the amount from the allowance table; the result is subtracted from the employee's wages. The wage rate table gives the actual dollar amount to be withheld.

Under the wage bracket method, tables are used to compute withholding per weekly, semiweekly, or other pay period, based on wage level, marital status, and number of claimed exemptions.

See T.D. 9212, 70 Fed. Reg. 40663 (July 14, 2005) for final regulations explaining how to allocate between work performed inside and outside the United States. Generally speaking, compensation (other than certain fringe benefits) is allocated on the basis of time spent working in the United States vs. working outside the country. Fringe benefits (e.g., housing, education, local transportation, moving expenses, hardship pay), however, are generally allocated on a geographic basis. [The Regulations were proposed as REG-136481-04, 69 Fed. Reg. 47816 (Aug. 6, 2004)]

Rev. Rul. 2004-109, 2004-50 I.R.B. 958, says that payments made to employees under employment contracts are wages for employment tax purposes if they are not independent of the employer-employee relationship, so the taxes are due and must be withheld on bonuses that are paid in return for signing an employment contract and that are not contingent on future performance of services. Rev. Rul. 2004-110, 2004-50 I.R.B 960, says that a payment made when a contract is canceled before its anticipated end date is also treated as wages, because the employee does not provide clear, separate, adequate consideration for the employer's payment that is separate from the terms and conditions of the employment relationship that was severed.

For income tax purposes, "supplemental wages" means compensation other than, or in addition to, ordinary cash compensation. Bonuses, commissions, overtime pay, severance pay, back pay, taxable fringe benefits, and payments for accumulated sick leave are all supplemental wages.

If the supplemental wages are combined with ordinary compensation in a paycheck, with no allocation between the two, withholding should be done as if the supplemental wages were ordinary compensation. However, if the supplemental amount is paid in a separate check, or as part of the regular paycheck but with an explicit allocation, then either the supplemental and regular wages can be treated and withheld as a single payment (with a credit for amounts already withheld) or a 28% flat rate can be applied to the supplemental wages.

For payments made after 2004, once a person's supplemental wage income exceeds $1 million, the employer must withhold on the supplemental income at the highest income tax rate (currently, 35%). Employers have an obligation to keep a cumulative record of this income so that they will be aware when the $1 million threshold is crossed.

Regulations were proposed in January 2005, setting out flat rates of withholding for supplemental wages. The employer withholds at a 25% rate for supplemental wages up to $1 million and 35% on any balance paid by the employer or any member of its I.R.C. § 52 controlled group. (The 25% rate is scheduled to rise to 28% in 2011.) A payment made by a third party acting as the employer's agent is deemed made by the employer, even if the designation of the agent does not satisfy the I.R.C. § 3504 rules.

Because this two-step procedure can be burdensome, commentators expected the IRS to build in more flexibility when the proposal is finalized. Regular wages are those paid for a current payroll period at a regular periodic rate such as hourly or daily, or a predetermined fixed amount. Any compensation payment other than regular wages constitutes supplemental wages: including but not limited to bonuses, overtime, back pay, tips, commissions, expense reimbursement, fringe benefits that are not cash, sick pay received from a third-party agent of the employer, income from exercise of nonqualified stock options, and nonqualified deferred compensation covered by I.R.C. § 409A. For an employee whose only compensation in a calendar year is in the form of commissions, bonuses, or tips, withholding is performed as if they were regular wages—although the compensation would be supplemental wages for someone who received a salary or hourly wages. The proposal doesn't tackle the question of what to do if someone receives no regular wages but more than one type of supplemental wages. [70 Fed. Reg. 767, 2005-6 I.R.B. 484, REG-152945-04, RIN 1545-BD96, Notice of Proposed Rulemaking Flat Rate Supplemental Wage Withholding <http://www.irs.gov/pub/irs-regs/15294504.pdf> (Jan. 5, 2005)]

The withholding system must distinguish between compensation paid to the employee and reimbursement of legitimate business expenses that the employee incurred on the employer's behalf (reimbursement is not taxable income). For tax purposes, expense accounts are either "accountable" or "non-accountable" plans. Amounts paid under an accountable plan are not wages for the employee, and therefore are not subject to FICA or FUTA. Withholding is not required. Employees must meet two tests under an accountable plan:

- They paid or incurred deductible expenses in the course of employment;
- They are required to provide adequate accounts of the expenses within a reasonable time of incurring them.

If they receive any amount over and above the expenses, they have an obligation to return it within a reasonable time. The general tax rule is that it is reasonable for employees to be reimbursed within 30 days of spending money; to provide an expense account within 60 days of spending the money; and to return excess amounts within 120 days of the initial advance.

Accounting for a per diem or a fixed allowance (e.g., X cents per mile for business travel) is considered adequate as long as the payment is no higher than the government per diem rates for meals and lodging [*see* IRS Publication 1542] and the standard mileage rate for travel. [IRS Publication 553]

If these tests are not met, the money is treated as if it were paid under a nonaccountable plan (one which does not require documentation of expenses). Expenses reimbursed under a nonaccountable plan are considered wages, included in income and subject to withholding in the first payroll period after there has been an reasonable time to return any excess funds.

Rev. Proc. 2004-29, 2004-20 I.R.B. 918, allows the use of statistical sampling methods to establish the amount of substantiated fully deductible meal and entertainment expenses. Expenses in this category are those that are fully deductible because they satisfy an exception, e.g., supper or supper money occasionally provided as a *de minimis* fringe so that employees can work overtime; meals furnished on the employer's premises for the employer's convenience; and in-house meals furnished to employees who are required to remain on the premises. A taxpayer filing an original return or a taxpayer who is under examination, involved in litigation, or applying for a refund can use statistical sampling; but sampling cannot be used to substantiate I.R.C. § 274(d) meal and entertainment expenses, to determine employment tax liability, or to determine whether an amount is excludable from the employee's gross income. Rev. Proc. 2004-29 is effective for tax years ending after May 2, 2004.

All of the employee's taxable income is subject to income tax withholding, except to the degree that a withholding exemption is available. FICA (Social Security) taxes are imposed on the employee's taxable income, up to a certain amount (the amount is $94,200 for 2006; each year's wage base must be published in the Federal Register no later than November 1 of the preceding year). The employer and employee are each taxed at a rate of 6.2% on income up to the limit, and Medicare taxes are imposed on all compensation.

AJCA § 251, affecting I.R.C. §§ 3121(a), 421(b), 423(c), provides that for FICA and FUTA purposes, the definition of "wages" does not include remuneration from exercising an ISO or option to buy stock under an employee stock purchase plan. The spread (fair market value of the stock minus its option price) is not income at time of exercise, but constitutes capital gain when the stock is disposed of (as long as the statutory holding period is satisfied). Such remuneration is not taken into account in determining Social Security benefits. These provisions are effective with respect to stock acquired through options exercised after the AJCA date of enactment.

Effective January 1, 2005, when interests in nonstatutory stock options and/or nonqualified deferred compensation are transferred from the employee to the non-employee ex-spouse incident to a divorce, the transfer does not constitute "wages" for FICA/FUTA purposes. However, FICA and FUTA are triggered when the options are exercised or the deferred compensation is paid or made available; for employment tax purposes, the non-employee spouse is treated as if the employee spouse had received the funds. Non-statutory stock options are subject to FICA and FUTA when the recipient exercises them. The income the non-employee spouse realizes on exercise of NSOs and amounts distributed are wages subject to withholding on the payments to the non-employee spouse. But the employee spouse's employer provides a Form 1099-MISC (and reports the withholding on Form 945) rather than issuing a Form W-2. [Rev. Rul. 2004-60, 2004-24 I.R.B. 1051]

Payments made to employees under a Reduction in Force program that qualify as Supplementary Unemployment Benefits (SUB) under Code § 3402(o) are not FICA wages (and are not subject to FUTA), although they are subject to income tax withholding. The Court of Federal Claims decided in 2002 that the employees' termination under this program was involuntary and complete. They ceased to perform services for the employer. Code § 3402(o) defines SUB payments as payments includible in gross income for income tax purposes, made on account of involuntary separation from employment.

In contrast, payments made to employees who did not participate in the RIF program, and who stayed on standby subject to active recall, were wages, because such employees remained on the corporate payroll and did not completely sever their connection to the company. Lump sums elected by terminated employees in consideration for surrender of all employment-related rights were also FICA wages, because the individuals chose to participate in the program and did not undergo involuntary separation from employment. In short, severance paid in connection with involuntary separation is not subject to FICA or FUTA if paid in connection with a RIF or similar situation, but severance for voluntary separation is liable to FICA and FUTA. [*CSX Corp., Inc.,* 52 Fed. Cl. 208 (Fed. Cl. 2002)] Late in 2003, the Court of Federal Claims affirmed its earlier ruling [*CSX Corp. v. U.S.,* No. 95-858T (Fed. Cl. Oct. 31, 2003)], holding that CSX was not deprived of a benefit that was available to similarly situated taxpayers when the IRS revoked a Private Letter Ruling it had issued benefiting CSX.

In a contemporary case on a similar issue, the Court of Federal Claims ruled [*Kraft Foods North America Inc. v. U.S.,* No. 02-342T (Fed. Cl. Nov. 14, 2003)] that certain severance payments could not be treated as nonqualified deferred compensation under Code § 3121(v)(2), even under transition rules that gave employers discretion to adopt reasonable good-faith interpretations of the rules for deferred compensation. (Kraft had applied for refunds of FICA taxes, on the grounds that it was at least reasonable to treat the benefits as nonqualified deferred compensation.) According to the court, the payments were not compensation for specific services and thus were not deferred compensation.

The November 2003 issue of the Journal of Accountancy discusses the accounting implications of the *CSX* decision. Severance payments made to employees who have been laid off or terminated, and that constitute SUBs and not wages subject to payroll taxes, may entitle the payor company to refunds of Social Security, Medicare, and FUTA taxes. The payments must have been made under a Reduction in Force (RIF) plan that is evidenced by documents such as employment contracts or the employee handbook. The refund is limited to three years' worth (because the statute of limitations for making refund claims is three years), and is claimed by filing an amended payroll tax return (Form 941C, with a correct Form 941 for each of the quarters involved).

To document the SUB status of the payments, payroll records and company policies must be reviewed. SUBs paid after the employee reached the FICA base for the relevant year are not subject to Social Security tax, but are subject to Medicare tax. Furthermore, there might be SUBs for the same person in two or even three tax years. Severance is often paid in annuity form, so there might be payments over all of the three years for which refunds can be claimed.

If the company wishes to apply for the employee portion of the overpayment, a written authorization from the employees in question is needed to request records on their behalf. Once a refund is obtained, it should be placed into escrow in case the IRS audits the amended return and demands part or all of the money back. When refunds are distributed to former employees, the employer must issue a W-2C and a 1099-INT for each recipient, showing the change to the original submission of the W-2 and the interest paid by the IRS. If the process lasts more than a single tax year, a 1099-INT must be filed for each year. [Douglas Letsch, *In the Money?* Journal of Accountancy (November, 2003) <http://www.aicpa.org/pubs/jofa/nov2003/letsch.htm>]

In addition, all of the employee's taxable income is subject to Medicare tax, paid at the rate of 1.45% each by employer and employee. Income tax, Social Security, and Medicare taxes are reported by the employer on Form 941 (Employer's Quarterly Federal Tax Return).

Under IRS Notice 2004-10, [2004–6 I.R.B. 433], a sponsor of a retirement or Archer MSA plan that furnishes Form 1099 or Form 5498 to payees can deliver the payee statement in electronic form for 2003 and later years—even though the 2003 Form 1099 and W-2G instructions say this is not permitted.

Electronic payee statements are permitted for all 1099s, 1098s, and 5498s. The forms that were called Form 1099-MSA and 5498-MSA have been renamed SA so that they can be used for Health Savings Accounts as well as MSAs.

[B] Withholding on Pensions

The general rule is that income tax withholding is required when a plan makes payments to retired employees. There are circumstances under which the retirees can elect to waive withholding, but there are other circumstances in which withholding is mandatory.

For ordinary pension payments in annuity form, the plan can use its regular withholding procedures, based on the number of withholding exemptions on the retiree's Form W-4P. If no W-4P is submitted, the plan should withhold as if the retiree were married and claimed three withholding allowances.

However, if the distribution is a lump sum or other nonperiodic payment and not an annuity, the question is whether it is an "eligible rollover distribution." If it is not, the basic requirement is to withhold at a 10% rate, although the person receiving the lump sum can use the W-4P to claim exemption from withholding. If the recipient of the lump sum expects to be in a high tax bracket, the person can ask for withholding at a rate higher than 10%.

An eligible rollover distribution is an amount that could be placed in the retiree's IRA, Roth IRA, or transferred to another qualified plan. Any such amount that is not rolled over is subject to withholding at a rate of at least 20%. The recipient of the distribution can increase the withholding rate, but cannot lower it below 20% or claim a withholding exemption. *See* Code § 3405 and the instructions for Form 1099-R.

One effect of the Economic Growth and Tax Relief Reconciliation Act of 2001 (EGTRRA) [Pub. L. No. 107-16] is to broaden the category of amounts that can be rolled over, and therefore that may be subject to withholding on this basis— although EGTRRA also lowers income tax rates, so 20% may in fact be higher than the retiree's actual tax rate.

Withholding from lump-sum pension distributions is not reported on Form 941. Instead, Form 945 (Annual Return of Withheld Federal Income Tax) is used. The pension withholding amounts should be combined with the other Form 945 amounts, but for nonpayroll withholding only, not payroll taxes. [*See* Form 945 instructions] The recipient of the distribution receives a Form 1099-R (Distributions from Pensions, Annuities, Retirement or Profit-Sharing Plans). [*See* Chapter 12 for further information on distributions from qualified plans]

Depending on the jurisdiction, there also may be state law requirements, including tax withholding on pensions and other retirement income. Internal Revenue Code § 114 says that states do not have jurisdiction to tax the retirement income of non-residents. To qualify for the exemption, the income must be paid under a retirement plan that gives the payee a legally enforceable right to compensation that cannot be unilaterally reduced or terminated. Furthermore, payment must be made over a period of at least 10 years, in substantially equal periodic payments. A retired law firm partner—not coincidentally, a tax lawyer—received a favorable determination from a New York state administrative law judge (ALJ). The retired partner was entitled to receive post-retirement payments calculated as a share of the firm's profits. The ALJ accepted the ex-partner's argument that the payments constituted retirement payments, even though the New York taxing authorities said that because profit-based payments fluctuate, they could not be substantially equal. [*Matter of McDermott*, No. 820099 (N.Y. Division of Tax Appeals 2006), discussed in John Caher, *Ruling Forecloses State Taxes on Ex-Partner's Profits*, New York Law Journal, Mar. 23, 2006, law.com]

§ 2.04   FUTA TAX

FUTA (federal unemployment) taxes are paid entirely by the employer, on the first $7,000 of the employee's wages that are subject to FUTA. The short-form FUTA return is the Form 940-EZ; the long form is Form 940. The net tax rate is

0.8%. The states have their own taxable wage bases, ranging from $7,000 in several states to $34,000 (Hawaii (2006)).

IRS Final Regulations issued January 29, 1999, affecting I.R.C. § 3121 deal with the status of nonqualified deferred compensation for FICA and FUTA purposes. Wages are subject to FUTA (and FICA) when they are paid, or considered constructively paid. Welfare plan benefits and severance pay are not considered deferred compensation. Window benefits (early retirement incentives that are available only for a limited time) are not deferred compensation if paid after January 1, 2000. Nonqualified deferred compensation counts for FICA and FUTA either when the work giving rise to the compensation is done or when the right to collect the deferred amounts is no longer subject to a substantial risk of forfeiture—whichever comes later. The Code has "nonduplication" rules to make sure the same amount is not subject to FICA and FUTA both when the work is done and when the funds are paid out.

Before filing electronically, the employer must apply to the IRS, which has 45 days to either accept or reject the application. Once accepted, the employer will have to send a successful test transmittal before the IRS finalizes permission to file electronically. Due dates for electronic filing are the same as for paper forms: the first day of the first calendar month after the year for which the return is made; or, if tax deposits have been made as they come due, the tenth day of the second calendar month after the end of the year.

The Supreme Court seldom tackles employment tax issues, but see its 2001 decision in *United States v. Cleveland Indians Baseball Co.* [532 U.S. 200 (2001)] If an employee settles an employment case and receives back pay, for FICA and FUTA purposes the money is taxed in the year in which the wages were actually paid and not the year in which they were earned—whether the tax rates in the year of payment were higher or lower than the rates for the year in which the money was earned.

§ 2.05   TRUST FUND TAX COMPLIANCE
AND THE 100% PENALTY

The FICA tax withheld from employees' salary (both the OASDI and the Medicare components) is called a "trust fund tax." (Although the employer must pay its FICA share, and must pay FUTA, these are not trust fund taxes).

Frequently, the employer will collect employee FICA tax from each payroll, but will not have to deposit the tax until the end of the quarter. A cash-strapped company's temptation to "borrow" that money for its own immediate needs is strong. To reduce the temptation, I.R.C. § 6672 imposes a 100% penalty that cannot be discharged in bankruptcy on "responsible persons" who willfully fail to submit the withheld trust fund taxes to the government. The 100% penalty means that the penalty is as large as the amount of taxes that were not properly paid. Furthermore, all of the personal assets of the responsible party can be attached to satisfy the debt.

Tax law creates a very large class of responsible persons, including the corporation's officers, shareholders, and directors, based on their level of responsibility within the corporation. The factors include authority to hire and fire; to decide which creditors will be paid and in what order, control over payroll, and power to deposit federal tax amounts. Top managers will probably be liable because of their degree of control over corporate financial managers. Lower-level managers probably will not be liable unless their duties include actually writing checks (and thus actual knowledge of amounts disbursed or not disbursed). Even parties outside the corporation, such as its bankers and its accountants, can be liable if they have the real control over corporate funds.

When a penalty is due, the government can either collect all of it from one responsible person or divide it among several. To avoid liability, an individual has to prove that he or she was incorrectly characterized as a responsible person, or that the failure to pay over the money was not willful. In this context, "willfulness" only means knowledge that the taxes were not submitted, and a failure to correct the situation. If a responsible person finds out that a payment was missed in one quarter, that creates a duty to investigate to find out if other payments were missed as well.

The responsible person's duty is to use all of the corporations "unencumbered funds" to pay trust fund taxes. Unencumbered funds are those not already assigned to a debt that existed before the tax liability arose.

Tip: To protect yourself, get your corporate board of directors to adopt a policy that allocates funds to the trust taxes first. In fact, if the company owes money to the IRS under several tax provisions, make sure that the tax payments are allocated first to the trust fund taxes, because the other penalties are lower than 100%. Without clear instructions from the taxpayer, the IRS will apply the taxes that yield the highest penalties, not the lowest. Furthermore, employees can indicate the allocation when they make voluntary payments—but once the IRS starts collection activities, it won't take instructions about how to apportion the funds.

Thanks to the Taxpayer Bill of Rights 2 [Pub. L. No. 104-168] a responsible person is entitled to notice before the IRS imposes the 100% penalty. The notice must also give the names of other responsible persons, the IRS' collection efforts against them, and the success of those efforts. (The other responsible parties who actually pay the IRS can sue other responsible parties to make them pay their fair share.) The recipient of the notice can pay the penalty and sue for a refund, or contest the penalty in federal court. Collection efforts will be suspended until the case is resolved.

For a case involving the power under Code § 6672 to collect taxes from a corporate officer, *see In the Matter of Prescription Home Health Care, Debtor; United States v. Prescription Home Health Care.* [316 F.3d 542 (5th Cir. 2002)]

A home health care provider company filed for bankruptcy protection under Chapter 11, owing over $600,000 in unpaid taxes, interest, and penalties. Avoiding IRS collection efforts was the major reason inspiring the filing. The IRS's claim against the company included a priority claim of approximately $400,000 in unemployment and payroll taxes and $250,000 in trust fund taxes that had been withheld but not remitted. The corporation filed a reorganization plan, providing that the company's president would retain his interest in the debtor company. The plan also called for payment of the priority portion of the IRS claim over a six-year period, with payment of general unsecured claims over a ten-year period. The IRS would receive about half of the general unsecured portion of the claim. Confirmation of this plan would enjoin the creditors from collecting from the company's management and employees (which, of course, would prevent the IRS from using its power against responsible persons).

In mid-2004, the Middle District of Florida reversed the Bankruptcy Court, which held that a debtor was not a "responsible person" potentially liable for trust fund tax penalty. The district court found that, although the defendant only agreed to be named as president and sole shareholder of her lover's business as an accommodation to him (he had credit problems that kept him from wanting to serve as a corporate officer), she was nevertheless a responsible person. Because she willfully failed to pay the company's employment taxes, she was personally liable. The court's test was power, duty, and authority—not knowledge of day-to-day business operations. There can be more than one responsible person in a business. It was not necessary that the IRS provide written notice for the defendant to be aware of the company's financial problems; clearly she knew about the cash flow problems, because she invested some of her own money in the business and helped it to get a loan. It was reckless disregard to ignore the risk posed by failure to pay the taxes. [*In re Marino*, 311 B.R. 111 (M.D. Fla. 2004)]

IRS policy is to avoid assessing the § 6672 penalty against a responsible person as long as a corporate debtor complies with the terms of its bankruptcy payment plan. However, the IRS might depart from this policy close to the end of the statute of limitations, when failure to enforce might make the debt uncollectable.

The IRS objected to confirmation of the bankruptcy plan. One reason for its objection was that the statute of limitations for collecting trust fund taxes from the company president as responsible person would expire while the reorganization plan was still in force, putting the IRS at risk of non-collection.

The Bankruptcy Court, as affirmed by the District Court, enjoined the IRS from assessing and collecting taxes from the company's president, on the theory that such relief would allow him to concentrate on reorganizing the corporate debtor, making it able to repay the IRS. The Fifth Circuit, however, vacated the injunction and sent the case back to the District Court. The Fifth Circuit ruled that bankruptcy courts have jurisdiction over a suit between non-debtors (in this case, the IRS's suit against the company president, who was not a bankruptcy debtor) only if the suit is related to the bankruptcy. Usually, this is defined to mean that the outcome of the proceeding could have an effect on the bankruptcy estate.

Underpaying taxes creates an obligation to catch up on the payments, plus interest. Penalties may also be assessed for, e.g., failure to file, late filing, or serious understatement of the amount of tax. Furthermore, criminal liability can be imposed in five situations:

- Willful failure to collect or pay over federal tax (the penalty is up to $10,000 and/or five years in prison, plus the costs of prosecution);
- Willful failure to pay tax, make a return, keep records, or provide mandated information to the IRS is a misdemeanor (not a felony); the penalty is up to a year in jail and/or a $25,000 fine for an individual, or a $100,000 fine (corporation), plus prosecution costs;
- Willful furnishing of a false or fraudulent tax statement, or willful refusal to furnish a required statement, carries a penalty of up to $1,000 and/or one year's imprisonment per violation;
- Willful tax evasion can be punished by up to five years in prison and/or $100,000 (for an individual) or $500,000 (for a corporation);
- It is perjury to willfully sign a return or other tax document that the signer knows to be false or inaccurate. The penalty can be up to three years' imprisonment and/or $100,000 (individual) or $500,000 (corporation).

Although these penalties are heavy, in practice the IRS often attempts to collect civil penalties instead of criminal ones, because it's easy to prove that taxes were not paid as required, but hard to prove the state of mind of the person or organization who was supposed to make the payment.

On a related issue, late in 2002 the Ninth Circuit ruled that the plaintiff was not entitled to abatement of interest (Code § 6404(e)) on employment taxes. The taxpayer owned a beauty salon and leased out individual spaces to beauticians whom she treated as independent contractors. In 1988, however, she signed the IRS Form 2504 (Agreement to Assessment and Collection of Additional Tax and Acceptance of Overassessment), agreeing that the IRS was entitled to collect about $32,000 in taxes and penalties. She made the payment as agreed, but the IRS applied the payment to the taxes, penalties, and interest for the relevant years, and took the position that she still owed about $10,000 in additional taxes and penalties. In 1993, she was notified of the remaining liabilities. The IRS refused to abate interest on the grounds that § 6404(e) is inapplicable to employment taxes [*see Woodral v. Commissioner*, 112 T.C. 19 (1999)], and the Tax Court and Ninth Circuit agreed with the agency. [*Miller v. Commissioner of Internal Revenue*, 310 F.3d 640 (9th Cir. 2002)]

A manufacturing company did not file timely employment tax returns for 1998 or 1999, nor did it deposit or pay its tax liability for those years. In 2000, it filed the overdue returns and paid the taxes and interest. The IRS assessed penalties for failure to file, failure to make timely deposits, and late payment of taxes. The company sought a refund and abatement of penalties, claiming that its noncompliance should have been excused because of financial difficulties it suffered because of the loss of a major customer (one that historically provided 80% of its revenues). The IRS denied the request. The plaintiff sued for a refund of penalties already paid and abatement of those still unpaid, stating that it would go out of business if it had to pay FICA and FUTA taxes. The Seventh Circuit granted summary judgment for the IRS. The company paid its other creditors (although some of them late), increased officers' salaries, and repaid a loan to an insider. I.R.C. §§ 6651(a) and 6656(a) impose a mandatory penalty for failure to deposit and pay FICA and FUTA unless the taxpayer can show the failure was due to reasonable cause, not willful neglect. There is no statutory definition of reasonable cause. Under the regulations, the taxpayer must show that it either was unable to pay the tax or would suffer undue hardship by paying the tax when due—despite the exercise of ordinary business care and prudence. The regulations impose a higher standard for trust fund taxes than for corporate income taxes. In this case, the Seventh Circuit found that there was no reason to abate the penalties. The company had paid taxes when its revenue was at its lowest ebb, and stopped when the financial situation improved somewhat; and the corporate officers should not have given themselves raises when the company's finances were so perilous. They obtained additional credit as soon as they determined to return to tax compliance, showing that they could have borrowed money to make timely payments. [*Diamond Plating Co. v. United States*, 390 F.3d 1035 (7th Cir. 2004)] The Bankruptcy Abuse Prevention and Consumer Protection Act of 2005 (BAPCA; P.L. 109-8) extends the avoidance period (i.e., makes it easier for the bankruptcy trustee to reverse payments) with respect to transfers made to insiders—including certain transfers made under employment contracts that are not in the ordinary course of business.

In 2004, the Sixth Circuit held that an officer of a bankrupt corporation was a responsible person. He was the CEO and majority shareholder and controlled the corporation's financial affairs. He was aware of the tax deficiencies, and nevertheless chose to pay other creditors rather than satisfying the tax obligation. The Sixth Circuit rejected the taxpayer's argument that he did not have control over the funds as a result of lock-box arrangements with lenders. The court ruled that corporate funds can only be considered encumbered by legal obligations imposed by statutes and regulations, not by contractual agreements voluntarily accepted. [*Bell v. U.S.*, 355 F.3d 387 (6th Cir. 2004)]

§ 2.06   W-2 FORMS

The W-2 form, used to report employee compensation, is a multipart form. Forms are sent to the IRS and to state tax authorities (and city authorities, in cities that impose their own income tax). The employer must also furnish the employee with copies that the employees can use to prepare their tax returns. Of course, the fact that the employer submits the same information to the taxing authorities makes it harder for employees to omit employment income from their tax returns.

EGTRRA, the 2001 tax bill, made many dramatic changes, some of which are reflected on the W-2 form. [*See* Announcement 2001-93, 2001-44 I.R.B. 416, for an explanation of how to report I.R.C. § 414(v) catch-up contributions made by plan participants over age 50] The W-2 form now has a new Code W for employers' contributions to HSAs. Copies B, C and 2 of W-2 can be furnished electronically if employee consents. The employer can create online "fill-in" versions of W-2 and -3 forms and print them out for distribution. [*See* <http://www.socialsecurity.gov/employer> and click "Business Services Online"]

The Gulf Opportunity Zone Act of 2005, Pub. L. No. 109-135, 119 Stat. 2577, includes technical corrections to WFTRA, affecting Code § 21(b)(1) (dependent care benefits) and § 223 (health savings accounts), increasing the number of people who can be considered qualifying relatives (e.g., certain married persons who file joint returns can now be claimed as dependents on other taxpayers' returns). Employers should review their payroll software to make sure that W-2 forms are correct. Notice 2005-61 [2005-39 I.R.B. 607] explains how to report dependent care expenses on the W-2 if the employer has amended its cafeteria plan to offer a special grace period for dependent care assistance. It also may be necessary to have a special enrollment period for dependent care spending accounts to reflect the changed definition, and to have forms so that divorced custodial parents can waive the right to claim their children as dependents.

The 2006 tax bill, the Tax Increase Prevention and Reconciliation Act (TIPRA), P.L. 109-222, did not include significant provisions affecting employment taxes.

§ 2.07 TAX DEPOSITS

Employment taxes (withheld income taxes, FICA) are usually remitted by the employer either once a month or every other week. The schedule for reporting depends on the size of the employer's tax obligation for the previous year; the IRS notifies employers every November which category they will fall into for the next year. [*See* Treas. Reg. § 31.6302-1]

If the employer had a total of $50,000 or less in employment taxes during the previous year, then the employer will probably have to make a deposit once a month, no later than the fifteenth of the month following the month that the taxes relate to. [*See* 68 Fed. Reg. 43329 (July 17, 2003) for Proposed Regulations about exceptions to the deposit requirements for de minimis amounts of accumulated FICA taxes]

In late 2004, the threshold for FUTA deposits was raised. Quarterly deposits are required only if the accumulated tax reaches $500 (rather than the previous level of $100). Because the maximum amount is $56 per employee per year, employers with eight or fewer employees are therefore relieved of the deposit requirement. [T.D. 9162, 2004-51 I.R.B. 987, 69 Fed. Reg. 69819 (Dec. 1, 2004)]

Employers who had a larger employment tax roll for the previous year usually have to make semiweekly deposits, on the Wednesday after payday (if payday is Wednesday, Thursday, or Friday; on the Friday after payday if payday is Saturday,

Sunday, Monday, or Tuesday). The purpose of these schedules is to give employers at least three business days after payday to deposit the funds.

There is also a "one-day rule" under I.R.C. § 6302(g): if the tax liability for a period reaches $100,000, the tax money must be deposited on the first banking day after the $100,000 level is reached.

The basic reporting form is the quarterly Form 941, but income tax and back-up withholding on nonpayroll amounts are reported once a year on Form 945—Annual Return of Withheld Federal Income Tax.

§ 2.08   TRANSITION TO ELECTRONIC FILING

For many years, the IRS has been developing rules for electronic filing of tax forms. According to the agency, more than eight million business returns were electronically filed in 2005, with a 99% accuracy rate. By 2006, most business and employment tax returns (including information returns) could be filed electronically. (The TeleFile program, which allowed some forms to be filed over the telephone, was discontinued in mid-2005.)

Business taxpayers can pay all of their federal taxes online or by phone using the Electronic Federal Tax Payment System (EFTPS). EFTPS is set up to facilitate transmission and processing of tax information submitted by corporations. EFTPS is a highly secure site, using the highest available level of encryption. Users have to enroll, and need a Taxpayer ID, a PIN, and an Internet password to log on. EFTPS users go online or make a phone call at least one calendar day before the due date of a return to input the tax information for their accounts; then the taxpayer directs movement of funds from an approved bank account to the U.S. Treasury account. (Payments can be scheduled in advance.) [*see* IRS Publications 4132, 966, 4169, 4321, 4130, 4276, and 4048]

Mid-size and large corporations (assets of $50 million or more; at least 250 returns—including income tax returns, employment tax returns, and information returns—filed per year) are required to file their Forms 1120 and 1120-S electronically for tax years ending on or after December 31, 2005. The following year, corporations filing 250 returns must file electronically if their assets are $10 million or more. The IRS has revamped its corporate electronic filing system, known as Modernized e-file (MeF). Large corporations must either register with the IRS as a "Large Taxpayer" that prepares their returns in-house or work with an e-file service provider approved by the IRS; there is a directory of approved providers at <http://www.irs.gov>.

W-2 forms can be submitted electronically, although the Social Security Administration rather than the IRS site is the proper place of filing.

Certain types of return cannot be e-filed:

- Amended returns (until January 2007);
- Specialized 1120-series forms (e.g., for real estate investment trusts and life insurance companies);

- Returns with pre-computed penalties and interests; and
- Requests that corporate overpayments be applied to another account.

Implementation of a coordinated system of federal and state corporate tax filing is scheduled for 2006.

§ 2.09   BANKRUPTCY ISSUES

In April 2005 the Supreme Court decided that IRA balances are exempt from creditor claims in bankruptcy because the right to receive IRA funds is "on account of age." Although IRA funds can be withdrawn at any age, there is a substantial penalty on withdrawals prior to age 59½ unless another exemption is available. The Supreme Court resolved a circuit split under which the Second, Fifth, Sixth, and Ninth Circuits took the position eventually adopted by the Supreme Court, but the Eighth Circuit deemed IRA account holders to have unlimited access to their funds, so creditors should be able to reach the funds. (It is likely that the Supreme Court accepted the policy argument that IRAs often receive rollovers from qualified pension plans.) [*Rousey v. Jacoway*, 544 U.S. 320 (2005)]

A 2004 Ninth Circuit case involves a Chapter 11 bankruptcy case that was converted to Chapter 13, raising the question of what priority should be awarded to administrative expense claims arising after the petition but before the conversion. The Ninth Circuit read 11 USC § 348(d) to permit federal employment taxes to retain their administrative-expense priority. The Ninth Circuit treated post-petition tax debt as an administrative expense as long as it relates to taxes incurred by the estate. 11 USC § 1322(a)(2) requires the Chapter 13 plan to provide full payment of administrative expenses (including penalties and interest) as first-priority claims. Pre-petition, unsecured tax debt generally takes eighth priority, and is paid over the life of the plan without interest. The Ninth Circuit cited cases from other circuits preserving the administrative expense status of tax debt when Chapter 11 cases are converted to Chapter 7, and saw no reason to treat Chapter 11 to Chapter 13 conversions differently. [*In re Fowler*, 394 F.3d 1208 (9th Cir. 2005)]

Although the primary impact of BAPCA (The Bankruptcy Abuse Prevention and Consumer Protection Act of 2005; P.L. 109-8) is on individual filings, this legislation has some provisions that affect employment tax planning:

- Clarification that a broad range of retirement savings vehicles will be excluded from the individual debtor's bankruptcy estate—not just government plans and private employer plans subject to ERISA Title I, but also tax-deferred annuities under 403(b) plans, health insurance plans regulated by state law, IRAs (including education IRAs), and funds placed in a § 529 (tuition savings program) a year or more before the bankruptcy filing. In general, the IRA exemption is limited to $1 million, but qualified rollovers into the IRA are not counted for this purpose. Furthermore, protection is granted to employee contributions even before they are deposited into the plan. This wide scope of protection applies even if the debtor is an insider of the employer corporation, and whether the debtor elects the state or federal exemption scheme.

- BAPCA alters the previous treatment of plan loans. It is not a violation of the automatic stay to withhold a debtor-employee's wages to repay a plan loan from a qualified plan.
- Pre-BAPCA, wages, salaries, and commissions for services rendered filing of the bankruptcy petition generally could be paid and claimed as administrative expenses. BAPCA strictly limits payments of retention bonuses and severance payments to corporate insiders.

§ 2.10   2005 PROPOSED REGULATIONS

In May 2005 the IRS proposed new Regulations covering Code § 415 (the previous regulations were published in 1981!). *See* 70 Fed. Reg. 31214 (May 31, 2005). One of the areas covered by these regulations is the issue of post-separation payments.

The general tax rule is that payments made after an employee's separation from service are not compensation for § 415 purposes. The practical effect is that after an employee is terminated, he or she can no longer defer funds (e.g., severance benefits) paid by the ex-employer by depositing them in a 401(k) or 403(b) or 457 account. However, under the Proposed Regulations, a payment made within the 2½-month period after separation can be deferred in two situations. Either the payment would have been made anyway, even if employment had not terminated, or the payment relates to bona fide vacation, sick leave, or other leave the employee would have had access to if employment had continued.

The IRS proposes that this provision take effect for limitation years that begin on or after January 1, 2005, and taxpayers are permitted to rely on this part of the proposal until Final Regulations are issued.

Code § 409A provision governing non-qualified plans also has implications for the taxation of post-severance compensation (*see* § 8.09[D] for a more detailed discussion).

CHAPTER 3

BONUSES AND SEVERANCE PAY

§ 3.01 INTRODUCTION

Although regular compensation and benefits are the main focus of compensation planning, there are two important types of nonrecurring compensation that also play an important role: bonuses and severance pay. In a booming economy, bonuses often seem more significant, as a means of recruiting and retention in a competitive environment, and as a means of "sharing the wealth" within the enterprise. However, in an economic downturn, many employers will be motivated to offer bonuses rather than salary increases, because salary increases are a fixed cost and bonuses have a greater discretionary component and can be reduced or eliminated in years when corporate profits dip. In the 2003 bonus season, bonuses constituted 8.8% of payroll, a percentage that rose to 10% in 2004, whereas, according to the consulting firm Hewitt Associates, the typical raises for 2004 and 2005 were in the 3.4 to 3.7% range (lower than in previous years). Research by Mercer HR Consulting shows that at companies where all employees are eligible for bonuses, clerical and support staff bonuses usually range between 3 and 5% of annual salary; middle managers get 10 to 15%, upper managers 15 to 25%, and top executives 30 to 50%. [Jeff D. Opdyke, *Getting a Bonus Instead of a Raise*, Wall Street Journal, Dec. 28, 2004, at p. D1]

During the bull market years, many executives received large or even multi-million-dollar annual bonuses. Even after the boom ended, a number of companies continued to pay very large bonuses even though corporate results were much less positive. In many instances, plans were amended mid-year to safeguard bonuses of executives who failed to meet the targets originally required to trigger the payments. [Jesse Drucker, *As CEOs Miss Bonus Goals, Goalposts Move*, Wall Street Journal, July 7, 2004, at p. C1]

A 2005 WorldatWork/Aon Corporation survey showed that many employers anticipated layoffs in 2006—but had no severance pay plans. More than a quarter (28%) expected layoffs; 26% were unsure whether a reduction in force would be necessary; 30% had no formal severance plan; 63% had not reviewed their severance plan in the preceding year; and 12% had *never* reviewed their severance plan. Among survey respondents who provide severance pay, nearly all (85%) define it based on the number of years worked, while 32% provide one week of severance pay per year worked and 23% pay two weeks per year of tenure. [*Survey Uncovers Layoff Planning Weakness*, NU Online News Service (Dec. 14, 2005)]

Also see §8.02[D] for a discussion of taxation of nonqualified deferred compensation under I.R.C. §409A. Although many commenters asked to have severance plans exempted from the reach of §409A, Regulations proposed in October, 2005 reflect the Treasury's and IRS's belief that any attempt at tax planning by manipulating the timing of compensation—including compensation paid after a voluntary or involuntary separation from service—should be tested to see if §409A applies. [REG-158090-04, RIN 1545-BE 79, 70 Fed. Reg. 57930 (Oct. 4, 2005)]

The 2005 bankruptcy reform act (P.L. 109-8) limits the ability of a company that is a Chapter 11 debtor to offer retention bonuses and/or severance pay and then claim these payments as an administrative expense in the bankruptcy case. A retention bonus or severance payment to a director, officer, partner, or control person is allowed only if the fact and amount of the payment are both reasonable.

A retention bonus to an insider is allowed only if the insider has, in fact, received a bona fide job offer elsewhere paying at least as much as the insider's job, preventing the insider from taking the offer is essential to the business's survival, and the amount of the bonus is limited to either 10 times the average retention payment made to rank-and-file employees or 25% of any similar payment made to or on behalf of the insider in the previous calendar year.

Severance payments to insiders are allowed only as part of a program covering all full-time employees, and insiders must not receive severance that exceeds 10 times the average severance payment to the rank and file.

§ 3.02   BONUSES

New York State's highest court, the Court of Appeals, decided in October 2000 that discretionary bonuses used by investment banks and law firms are not "wages" that are protected by state labor law. The bonus is not considered a wage, even if part of it is based on the firm's performance. [*Truelove v. Northeast Capital & Advisory Inc.*, 95 N.Y.2d 220 (2000)]

The plaintiff in *Schara v. Commercial Envelope Mfg. Co. Inc.* [321 F.3d 240 (1st Cir. 2003)] sued his former employer for what he claimed were three years of bonuses owed to him. He alleged that his original employment contract called for him to receive a 1% bonus on accounts other than house accounts. The former employer revised the employment agreement to make the bonus payable on all accounts after it failed to provide him with the life insurance coverage stipulated in the employment contract. (The plaintiff had already had two heart attacks when he took the job at issue, so he was very concerned with protection for his survivors.)

The former employer said that it signed neither the original nor the revised employment contract, and therefore the Statute of Frauds forbids enforcement of these claims. The trial judge refused to instruct the jury on the Statute of Frauds issue. The jury awarded the plaintiff damages of over $220,000, representing bonus payments on all accounts. The First Circuit affirmed the jury award.

The Statute of Frauds is sometimes not applied to contracts that could end in less than a year—especially if the employer has the right to terminate employment. In this case, the plaintiff signed the original and amended contracts, and was told that the employer had signed (although he did not receive copies). The employer's failure to sign was not the employee's fault, and was not held against him.

§ 3.03   SEVERANCE PAY

[A]   Generally

There is no federal law requiring that employees receive severance pay, but nevertheless it is very common for employers to provide this type of compensation (unless the employee was fired for misconduct). Severance pay is often defined as a certain number of days or weeks of pay for every year of service with the employer.

The most important characteristic of severance pay is that it is over and above the normal salary or wages earned for past services. Severance payments are by and large discretionary, unlike payment for past services, which must be made when employment terminates. If the employer enters into an express or implied contract to provide severance benefits, that contract can be enforced. However, employers typically retain the right to alter their severance pay plans, and this is sometimes done just before a major layoff. Employers may also provide benefits to only certain persons affected by a mass layoff, claiming that the others were terminated for poor performance.

A common rule of thumb is to provide two weeks' severance for every year of service by a rank-and-file employee, a month per year for senior managers. In response to an international survey performed by Right Management Consultant, 57% of U.S. respondents said that they cap severance payments for senior executives.

Employees of companies in bankruptcy are at especially high risk of losing severance. Severance payments by bankrupt companies require court approval (and 2005's bankruptcy reform legislation limits payments to insiders), and must compete with other creditor claims.

It can be good business to use severance packages to reduce the impact of layoffs, because when the economy recovers, your company may need to recruit. There is also a trend toward emphasizing noncash benefits, such as continuing health insurance outside of COBRA.

Tip: It may also be necessary to offer a lump-sum bonus for employees who stay on until a project or division is wound up in an orderly fashion instead of leaving as soon as they know their job is endangered.

[B]   Severance Arrangements as ERISA "Plans"

ERISA is not involved in an employer's one-time decision to grant or enhance severance benefits. Nor is there an ERISA component to an employer's payroll practices or payments of extra money for active workers' overtime or holiday work. However, ERISA does come into play if severance payments are made in connection with a "plan," and even an unwritten or informal arrangement might constitute a plan.

Once the severance payment comes within the ambit of ERISA, the degree and nature of regulation depend on whether the plan is characterized as a pension plan or a welfare benefit plan. The arrangement will not be a pension plan (and therefore will not be subject to the stringent rules imposed on pension plans) if:

- Payments are not contingent on the recipient's retirement—i.e., the recipient can retain the payments even if he or she gets another job;

- The total payments do not exceed twice the recipient's compensation for the year just before the termination;
- The payments are completed within 24 months of the termination. If the termination is part of a "limited program of terminations" then payments can be completed within 24 months of the time the recipient reaches normal retirement age, if that is later.

[*See* DOL Reg. 29 C.F.R. §§ 2510.3-2(b) and 2510.3-1(a)]

The Third Circuit ruled in mid-2003 that a person who quit a company that had a severance program to which he was not entitled was not a "participant" in the severance plan. He was not laid off, so he would not have been eligible for the benefits in any event. His resignation prevented him from becoming eligible for severance in the future. Therefore, he had no standing to bring an ERISA suit about denial of the benefit. [*Miller v. Rite Aid Corp.,* 334 F.3d 335 (3d Cir. 2003)]

An early 2004 case from the Third Circuit holds that employees did not have a vested right to benefits under severance and several other plans that the company terminated in 1993. Although the plan documents stated an intent to "confer vested rights" on participants, the court ruled that because the plan sponsor also reserved the right to amend or terminate the plan, there was no legal commitment to make the benefits unalterable or irrevocable. [*Lettrich v. J.C. Penney Co.,* 213 F.3d 765 (3d Cir. 2004)]

In a 2002 case from the Seventh Circuit, many employees were terminated when their employer transferred a business division to another company. The workers were re-employed by the purchaser company, but sought severance pay under two ERISA welfare benefit plans. The plan implemented in 1992 specified severance payments if the employer reduces the workforce for business reasons. The 1993 plan specified development and implementation of an appropriate severance program if business and economic conditions required a Reduction in Force (RIF). The Seventh Circuit ruled in favor of the defendant employer, because the plaintiffs were not laid off; they were re-employed by the new owner of the division. The 1993 plan did not create a legally enforceable promise to provide severance pay, because it was too vague to be enforceable. The Seventh Circuit saw no reason to depart from the normal rule, that severance pay is discretionary with the employer unless there is an enforceable written plan. [*Brines v. XTRA Corp.,* 304 F.3d 699 (7th Cir. 2002)]

Also in 2002, the Sixth Circuit ruled that employees who took substantially similar jobs with the purchasing corporation had not been "released" from employment, and therefore were not entitled to severance benefits. The plan defined release as permanent separation initiated by the company because of a factor such as lack of work, a RIF, or unsatisfactory performance by the employee. The plaintiff employees here did not face a threat of unemployment and thus had no economic injury to be redressed through severance pay. [*Cassidy v. Akzo Nobel Salt Inc.,* 308 F.3d 613 (6th Cir. 2002)]

A more complex situation arose in *Beaver v. Earthgrains Baking Companies Inc.* [216 F. Supp. 2d 920 (N.D. Iowa 2002)] The plaintiff's employer was acquired by another company. The plaintiff was offered about 18 months of continued employment with the acquiror company. She received a letter saying she would receive severance benefits under the first employer's policy at the end of this retention period.

A few days later, the acquiror company sent the plaintiff an e-mail saying that employees who rejected the retention offer, or who accepted it and voluntarily resigned during the retention period, would be eligible for severance under the acquiree company's plan. Less than a week after that, the acquiror company announced that it had misinterpreted its predecessor's policy; severance would be available only to persons either released from employment or required to work more than 50 miles away from the current work location. At that point, the plaintiff, who had accepted the retention offer, resigned and applied for severance benefits. The acquiror company refused to pay the benefits.

The plaintiff sued, alleging vested rights to receive the benefits. She lost, on the grounds that severance benefits are welfare benefits that do not vest and therefore can be modified unilaterally by the potential payor unless there is a contractual obligation to the contrary. In this case, the predecessor company that established the severance plan retained the right to modify the plan, and severance was payable on a case-by-case basis as dictated by circumstances. The input of several officers and directors was required, showing that the severance award was discretionary. The court did not accept the plaintiff's argument that the communications from the successor company either amended the plan or established a new severance plan that did not impose the same limitations.

In an unpublished 2005 decision, the District Court for the District of New Jersey holds that an employee could not get severance pay from her former employer, an acquired company, because she was offered a new job with the acquiring company. The acquired corporation's severance plan called for payment of benefits based on corporate sale only if the employee was not offered a job, or was offered a job located more than 50 miles from the employee's office. The plaintiff said that she was not offered a job, only invited to apply for one, and it was too far away for her to be interested in it. However, the court said that it was reasonable to calculate the 50-mile limitation on the basis of map distance rather than normal commuter mileage. [*Way v. Ohio Cas. Ins. Co.*, D.N.J., No. 04-4418 (JBS) (unpublished) (Dec. 16, 2005); *see Employee Offered Work with New Employer Cannot Get Severance*, PlanSponsor.com (Jan. 6, 2006)]

It was not an illegal interference with an employee's right to benefits to fire him for misuse of a company cell phone, when termination occurred only a month before he would have been eligible for almost $200,000 in severance pay. The fact that his supervisors were aware of this potential payment doesn't prove specific intent to impair accrual of the severance payment; nor did the fact that other employees were caught misusing company phones but were not terminated. [*Koons v. Avantis Pharmaceuticals Inc.*, 367 F.3d 768 (8th Cir. 2004)]

It was not an abuse of discretion for a severance plan administrator to deny severance benefits to a person fired for cause (she accessed company computer files without authorization). The plan defined termination for cause and gross and willful misconduct to include all violations of company policy. [*Johnson v. U.S. Bancorp Broad-Based Change in Control Severance Pay Program,* 424 F.3d 734 (8th Cir. 2005)]

In *Hamilton Sundstrand Corp. v. Healey* [2001 U.S. Dist. LEXIS 16415 (N.D. Ill. Oct. 12, 2001)] terminated employees complained to the state Department of Labor that their former employer had not made the severance payment promised when they were terminated as a result of the employer's outsourcing certain functions. The employees were hired by the outsourcing firm so, although nominally their employer changed, they did not have a period of unemployment. The employer didn't make the severance payments because, before the terminations, the plan documents had been amended to eliminate severance pay when outsourcing occurred. The employer was able to get a federal declaratory judgment that the employees' claims were preempted by ERISA, leaving the state DOL no jurisdiction to investigate. The District Court accepted the argument that the severance plan was an ERISA plan because it involved ongoing administration.

In another case involving a change of control, the plaintiff left his job when his employer company was acquired. He sued for severance benefits under the company's plan, which covered employees suffering a loss of employment within a year after a change in control. He said he was entitled to benefits even though he quit, because the plan covered resignations due to cuts in authority, duties, responsibilities, or status. The court agreed with him on this point, but disagreed with his contention that the plan was not subject to ERISA (because the plan involved discretion as to coverage plus ongoing administration). So he received severance benefits, but not a supplemental bonus. He was also entitled to an award of attorneys' fees, because the terms of the plan called for fee awards to eligible employees seeking to enforce benefits under the plan. [*Bowles v. Quantum Chem. Co.,* 266 F.3d 622 (7th Cir. 2001)]

The Ninth Circuit ruled early in 2003 that benefits were offered neither under an amendment to an existing ERISA plan nor under a new plan. [*Winterrowd v. American General Annuity Ins. Co.,* 321 F.3d 933 (9th Cir. 2003)] This case involved a group of commissioned salespersons for an insurance company that was acquired by another insurer. The acquiror decided to shut down the acquired company and terminate its workforce. Salaried employees of the acquired company were eligible for a Job Security Plan, which provided a variety of termination benefits including severance pay. The plaintiffs in this case were non-salaried workers and were not eligible under the Job Security Plan. However, they were offered a special severance package in return for agreeing to stay at work during a transition period. They were offered lump sums based on average sales commissions for a ten-month period. After they accepted the packages they were told that the lump sums had been recalculated based on six-month average commissions, reducing the lump sums they were entitled to from a range of $99,000 to

$200,000 to a range of $48,000 to $117,000. They received the smaller sums at the end of the transition period.

They filed suit for breach of contract, but lost at the district court level. The district court ruled that ERISA preempted the state claims. The Ninth Circuit, however, ruled that the change in policy that reduced the severance package could not be treated as a plan amendment (because the acquiring corporation did not formally amend the plan until the suit had been filed) or the creation of a new plan. A plan requires an ongoing administrative structure and a formula for determining who is entitled to receive benefits, and in what amounts. The Ninth Circuit remanded the case for determination of the breach of contract claims under state law.

The plaintiff was laid off and then terminated; between the two events, the employer adopted a new, less favorable severance plan. The plaintiff claimed that he was entitled to benefits under the old plan. The employer said that he could receive benefits under the new plan, but only if he waived his claim for benefits under the old plan. He refused to do so. He sued in state court for breach of contract. The case was removed to federal court because the severance plan was an ERISA plan. The Eighth Circuit held that it was an ERISA plan because there was ongoing administration of continuing benefits. The Eighth Circuit also held that the employer could lawfully condition access to benefits under the new plan on waiver of claims to benefits under the old plan. [*Petersen v. E.F. Johnson Co.*, 366 F.3d 676 (8th Cir. 2004)]

[C]   Case Law on Other Severance Pay Issues

Yochum v. Barnett Banks [234 F.3d 541 (11th Cir. 2000)] involves an employee who worked for a bank that was sold to NationsBank. The first employer's severance plan denied severance benefits to anyone who rejected a written offer of comparable employment. The plaintiff was offered a job that would result in forfeiture of his stock options, and would reduce the duration of his salary guarantee from two years to one year. He did not accept the job; he went to work for a competitor. Based on his rejection of a "comparable" job, the plan's administrative committee denied severance benefits. The Eleventh Circuit did not require de novo review (because the plan had reserved discretion). But, because the committee had a conflict of interest and made its decision based on "false and incomplete" information, a heightened arbitrary and capricious standard of review was applied. The committee failed to examine the employment contract, and did not realize that the salary guarantee had been reduced.

An ex-executive received $4.5 million in parachute payments, then sued the new owners of the company that had employed him to collect the $10 million he would have earned in the three years remaining on his employment contract. Unsurprisingly, he lost, on the grounds that a person who resigns in order to collect severance cannot collect future salary as well. [*Gerow v. Rohm & Haas Co.*, 308 F.3d 721 (7th Cir. 2002)]

The plaintiff was also unsuccessful (with regard to ADEA claims and claims that converting a defined benefit to a cash balance plan violated ERISA, as well as claims involving the severance plan) in *Campbell v. BankBoston, N.A.* [327 F.3d 1 (1st Cir. 2003)] The predecessor corporation of the defendant adopted a Separation Pay Plan, providing benefits for those terminated under a RIF or job elimination—but not those who quit voluntarily or those who failed to explore comparable job opportunities within the organization. The administrator of the severance plan was given sole discretion to interpret the plan, set rules under the plan, determine eligibility, or modify or terminate the plan at any time.

BankBoston sold part of its business to Investors Bank and Trust (IBT). BankBoston took the position that refusing to accept a job with IBT was a voluntary resignation, precluding the availability of severance benefits. On the last day of employment for a group of affected employees, the plan was amended to exclude severance for those refusing an offer from an employer acquiring any assets or operations of a BankBoston company. The plaintiff was offered a job, but not the same job as his old one because he had a specialized job that was not required by the acquiring company. In the First Circuit's analysis, the amendment to the plan ended the plaintiff's entitlement to severance unless he could prove that the amendment was invalid. The plaintiff claimed that the amendment was a violation of fiduciary duty—an argument that, according to the First Circuit, was ruled out by the Supreme Court's decisions in *Curtis-Wright v. Schoonejongen* [514 U.S. 73 (1995)] and *Lockheed v. Spink* [517 U.S. 882 (1996)] that the act of amending a plan is not a fiduciary act. In this reading, a severance plan is a welfare benefit plan, so benefits do not vest until they are paid.

According to the Eighth Circuit, a settlement award to a laid-off employee, reflecting his age, years of service, and earnings impairment, constitute "wages" for income and FICA tax purposes. [*Mayberry v. U.S.,* 151 F.3d 855 (8th Cir. 1998)] The court did not accept the employee's contention that the money was a nontaxable personal injury award. The funds replaced wages and did not come from settling tort claims, so they should be taxed as wages.

In *Bock v. Computer Associates International* [257 F.3d 700 (7th Cir. 2001)], the plaintiff was covered by a severance pay program that provided severance pay equal to the "bonus amount" plus twice the highest base salary plus 12 months' worth of "incentive compensation." The plaintiff was terminated and received severance of twice his base salary. (He was a sales executive who received large commissions but did not get an annual bonus.)

The suit arose because he said his $675,000 in commission income should have been included in the calculation. The question is whether commissions or only annual bonuses are considered "incentive compensation." The Seventh Circuit remanded the case to see whether the plaintiff knew or had reason to know how the employer defined "incentive compensation." If he knew that commissions were not counted, the ex-employer might be able to avoid using them in calculating his severance. Otherwise, the plain meaning of the term "incentive" does include commissions. The plaintiff couldn't raise an estoppel argument, because he didn't rely on the employer's representations to his detriment. On remand [2001 U.S. Dist. LEXIS 16381 (N.D. Ill. Oct. 9, 2001], the District Court found that the plaintiff suffered detrimental reliance because he gave up other ways to protect his future income. Therefore, the District Court reaffirmed its earlier decision for the plaintiff.

The Fourth Circuit ruled on the question of whether a corporation, in its role as administrator of the severance pay plan, abused its discretion in awarding benefits. The plaintiff charged that his benefits should have been calculated based on his initial hiring by the company; the employer said that the relevant date was 17 years later, after he was rehired after working somewhere else in the interim. (The difference was receiving four rather than 38 weeks of severance pay.) The Fourth Circuit found the plan language to be somewhat ambiguous, but because the plan gave the administrator discretion, the plan's interpretation was entitled to deference. [*Colucci v. AGFA Corp. Severance Pay Plan*, 431 F.3d 170 (4th Cir. 2005)]

Abramowicz v. Rohm and Haas Co. [2001 U.S. Dist. LEXIS 17693 (E.D. Pa. Oct. 30, 2001)] is yet another change-of-control case. Rohm and Haas made a job offer to the plaintiff to induce him to go to work for a joint venture in which Rohm and Haas was participating. The plaintiff took the job. When ownership of the joint venture changed, he refused to work for either the original employer or the new owner of the joint venture.

His job offer said that he would be entitled to severance if the joint venture discontinued operations within two years and the employee could not return to his present position. However, the severance plan was amended in the interim, eliminating his entitlement. The court applied *Sprague v. General Motors* [133 F.3d 388 (6th Cir. 1998)], which says that in the absence of fraud, an informal, nonplan document cannot amend a plan. Therefore, the job offer did not amend the severance plan, and the plaintiff was not entitled to severance benefits.

Just before a merger, the welfare benefit plan was amended, and a number of employees lost eligibility for severance payments. The matter went to arbitration. The arbitrator awarded about $1.5 million on the grounds that the plan sponsor violated its fiduciary duties by denying severance claims. The defendant—despite having removed the plaintiffs' state court case to federal court and petitioning the district court to compel arbitration—returned to the district court seeking to have the award vacated. The district court vacated the award, finding that the arbitrator had exceeded his powers, misread the contract, and applied the wrong legal standard for reviewing the compensation committee's decision to deny severance. The Fifth Circuit reversed the district court and reinstated the $1.5 million award, holding that the arbitrator did not show a manifest disregard for the law, so even if he misunderstood the law or misinterpreted the contract, his award must be upheld. [*Kergosien v. Ocean Energy Inc.,* 390 F.3d 346 (5th Cir. 2004)].

A late 2004 Eighth Circuit case involved two plaintiffs who were covered by a Change in Control Severance Pay Program, which provided severance if they resigned for "good reason," defined as the occurrence, within 24 months after a change in control, of a 10% or greater reduction in the employee's base compensation, unless base compensation was replaced by other guaranteed compensation. The plaintiffs' employer merged with another corporation, resulting in a partial change in control for severance plan purposes. The plaintiffs resigned and filed claims for severance benefits. When the claims were denied, they sued under ERISA and state law for breach of contract and late payment of earned commissions. The Eighth Circuit upheld the district court's ruling for the defendant. Before the plaintiffs resigned, they received an addendum to the new plan, providing guaranteed non-recoverable draws equal to their previous guaranteed base salary. This guaranteed compensation was the reason for the severance committee to hold that there had not been an occurrence triggering entitlement to severance pay—a decision sustained by the Eighth Circuit. The state law claims were dismissed because ERISA's civil enforcement provisions are the exclusive remedy for benefits under an ERISA plan. [*Johnson v. U.S. Bancorp*, 387 F.3d 939 (8th Cir. 2004)]

In 2005, the Fourth Circuit ruled that a release of all employment-related claims, signed by an employee released due to RIF as a condition of receiving severance benefits, did not preclude her suit under the Family and Medical Leave Act (FMLA), because the FMLA regulations [29 C.F.R. § 825.220(d)] do not permit releases of FMLA claims unless the release is approved either by the Department of Labor or by a court. [*Taylor v. Progress Energy,* 415 F.3d 364 (4th Cir 2005); *but see Faris v. Williams WPC-I, Inc.*, 332 F.3d 316 (5th Cir. 2005), holding that public policy favors the enforcement of releases, including FMLA releases]

At her termination interview, an employee scheduled for RIF was given 45 days to decide whether to accept a severance package, including payment of COBRA premiums. The severance package was conditioned on signing a release of all employment-related claims. Before she signed the release, she received a COBRA information packet from the employer and other COBRA materials from the employer's third-party administrator (TPA). The employee accepted most of the severance payments, then sued the employer, alleging employment discrimination. The plaintiff charged that the release was invalid because it was obtained under duress; she said she was threatened with loss of COBRA benefits if she did not release her claims. The Washington Court of Appeals was not persuaded because there was insufficient evidence that she had been misled about COBRA rights, and she had been given correctly phrased COBRA materials before she signed the release. The court accordingly dismissed her discrimination claims. [*Goh v. American President Lines, Ltd.,* 127 Wash. App. 1016 (Wash. App. 2005)]

The Northern District of Illinois awarded a statutory penalty of $20 per day for 511 days to an employee whose employer did not respond to his request for a copy of the severance plan document (SPD). After the plaintiff's position was eliminated, he was given a copy of the SPD and offered nine weeks' severance if he signed a waiver and release. He received only half of the promised severance, because the employer alleged that he had refused to return his company-provided laptop. He requested a copy of the actual severance plan, but did not receive one until he brought suit. The employer argued that it was not obligated to provide the document, because the employee had received an SPD. The severance plan and the SPD were almost identical, but the SPD stated that it was merely a general summary and employees should not rely on it. The court was not persuaded by this argument, but did order penalties much lower than the possible $110 per day because it did not believe that there had been intentional concealment. [*Reddy v. ABN AMRO N. Am., Inc.,* 2006 U.S. Dist. LEXIS 16713 (N.D. Ill. 2006); *see* Rebecca Moore, *Failure to Provide Plan Document Proves Costly*, PlanSponsor. com (Mar. 13, 2006)]

West Virginia found unemployment insurance benefits to be available to someone who participates in a voluntary severance program initiated by the employer if the claimant's separation from service is the result of lack of work and termination occurred under a workforce reduction plan. [*Baldwin*, Unempl. Ins. Rep. (CCH) ¶ 8787 (W.Va. 2005)]

[D] Parachute Payment Law and Regulations

A specialized form of severance, the "parachute" payment comes into play in the course of a hostile takeover or takeover attempt. The best-known form is the "golden parachute" for executives—the counterpart of the "golden handcuff" compensation packages that are supposed to keep top managers from leaving companies that depend on their services. A golden parachute arrangement is supposed to deter unwanted takeover attempts, because so much cash severance (and other benefits, such as stock, enhanced pension benefits, and insurance) is owed to the top managers that the acquisition becomes even more expensive—perhaps prohibitively so. A few states mandate the payment of "tin parachutes" to rank-and-file employees when they lose their jobs during a corporate transition.

A "single-trigger" golden parachute agreement gives the executive the right to additional compensation whenever the employer company merges or is acquired. A "double-trigger" agreement doesn't become effective until there has not only been a corporate transition, but the executive has been demoted or terminated and therefore has a real economic injury.

Internal Revenue Code §§ 280G(b) and 4999 impose a 20% excise tax on excess parachute payments—and, furthermore, the payor corporation cannot deduct whatever portion of the payment is not reasonable and therefore does not constitute an ordinary and necessary business expense. (Payments from a qualified pension plan are not considered parachute payments, so they do not affect the excess calculation.)

An excess parachute payment is an amount that:

- Is not reasonable compensation for work done either before the change in ownership and control, or is scheduled to be done after the change; and
- Exceeds three times the "base amount."

A parachute payment is a payment contingent on change in the corporation's ownership or control, or the ownership or control of a significant portion of the corporation's assets. If the executive and corporation entered into a compensation agreement within the year before a change in ownership or control, the payments are presumed to be parachute payments unless there is clear and convincing evidence of a different motivation for the payments.

The base amount is the executive's average annual compensation for the five years just before the change in ownership or control. Bonuses, fringe benefits, pensions, and severance pay as well as cash compensation are used in the calculation.

On August 4, 2003, the IRS issued Final Regulations dealing with golden parachutes. [68 Fed. Reg. 45745, August 4, 2003; also see the technical corrections made by T.D. 9083, RIN 1545-AH49m, 68 Fed. Reg. 59114 (Oct. 14, 2003), and the explanations provided in Rev. Proc. 2003-68, 2003 34 I.R.B. 398] A corporation is exempt from the rules about excess parachute payments if, just before control of the corporation changed, the corporation was not publicly traded and holders of at least 75% of the voting power of the corporation approved the payment. Furthermore, only one change in ownership or control will be deemed to have occurred with respect to any transaction, even if the language might make it appear that there were multiple changes.

The Final Regulations also clarify that a corporation that qualifies as a Subchapter S corporation but fails to make the election nevertheless is exempt from the rules about excess parachute payments. However, foreign corporations cannot qualify for the small-business exemption.

The final rule takes the position that accelerating the vesting of a stock option creates value that counts toward determining whether there has been a parachute payment.

The excise tax on excess parachute payments can be prepaid either in the year of the change in control or any later year—as long as the amount, form, and commencement date of the payments is already known and is reasonably ascertainable under the Code § 3121(v) rules on FICA taxation of nonqualified deferred compensation. However, the excise tax cannot be prepaid on any part of an excess parachute payment that is attributable to continuing to provide health benefits to the recipient of the parachute payment.

[E] Parachute Payment Cases

In 2003, the Tax Court found that lump sum payments to corporate executives under agreements entered into after a change in control were excess parachute payments, and were not deductible to the extent that they exceeded reasonable compensation for the executive. Proposed Regulation § 1.280G-1, Q&A 22 (which was later finalized more or less intact) states that a payment is contingent on a change in control if it would not have been made if there had never been a change in control. So that probably would not cover agreements made after the change in control has occurred. However, Q&A 23 of the same regulation says that an agreement will be treated as having been made before the change in control if it was signed after the change—based on a legally enforceable agreement made before the change.

In this case, 18 executives got employment agreements when their employer was worried about possible hostile takeovers. The company was, in fact, acquired a year later. Seven executives quit and received parachute payments. The acquiring company negotiated agreements with the remaining executives to replace the golden parachute agreements. Eleven executives were awarded close to $15 million in retention payments and supplemental retirement benefits, in addition to major salary increases. The acquiring company deducted $10.4 million of this amount. The IRS, as affirmed by the Tax Court, disallowed $7.6 million as excess parachute payments. The Tax Court defined reasonable compensation as the 90th percentile for comparable executives at comparable companies (i.e., the top 10% in earnings). [*Square D Co.,* 121 T.C. No. 11 (2003)]

Golden parachute agreements involve large sums of money that are potentially payable to sophisticated executives—a group who, not surprisingly, often litigate disputes about the payments.

Eligibility to participate in the plan providing parachute payments was the issue in *Habets v. Waste Management, Inc.* [363 F.3d 378 (5th Cir. 2004)] The Fifth Circuit ruled that once the company's Board of Directors exercised its discretion to decide who was a participant in the parachute plan by removing the plaintiff from the list of eligible persons (after he lost his officer status in a corporate restructuring), the plaintiff was no longer entitled to receive parachute payments. Under the plain language of the agreement, only corporate officers were entitled to parachute payments, so termination of his officer status also terminated eligibility for the payments.

An Eighth Circuit case from late 2003 was brought by an executive who, mistakenly believing that she was entitled to severance under a golden parachute agreement, gave her employer a "notice of termination." The defendant's employer entered into a joint venture that would eliminate the plaintiff's job. She took another job within the employer's organization. Although the second job paid $15,000 more a year than the first, the plaintiff believed it was a demotion because it carried lesser responsibilities.

In the plaintiff's view, she had good cause to quit, and the parachute was triggered because she was offered a lesser position. The employer corporation's position—which the courts upheld—was that there had been no change in control, and therefore the parachute payment had not been triggered. The employer also treated the "notice of termination" letter as a resignation under the terms of the company's standard employment agreement. The plaintiff argued that she did not resign, she merely sought to collect benefits she was entitled to under an ERISA plan, and that the defendant company terminated her illegally for seeking to enforce her ERISA rights.

The plaintiff filed discrimination charges with the EEOC (charging race and sex discrimination as well as interference with ERISA rights) and brought suit in state court. The defendant corporation removed the case to federal court. The plaintiff charged that she was the victim of race and sex discrimination because a white male was named as CEO of a joint venture the defendant corporation was involved in. This claim was dismissed as time-barred, because she did not file the charge for over a year, and the statute of limitations was 300 days. The plaintiff said that she filed on time, because the statute of limitations should be measured from FTC approval of the joint venture. The Eighth Circuit refused to accept this argument: in employment cases, the statute of limitations begins when a decision is made and communicated to the employee.

The Eighth Circuit ruled that the plaintiff had no reasonable basis for believing that she was entitled to severance. She resigned, and therefore was not subject to any adverse employment action. The plaintiff accepted the Vice Presidency she was offered. An earlier Eighth Circuit case, *Jones v. Reliant Energy-ARKLA* [336 F.3d 689 (8th Cir. 2003)] had already established the principle that it is not an adverse job action to offer an employee a new job instead of severance pay. In this case, the plaintiff did not suffer a reduction in pay or benefits, which further weakened her position. [*Curby v. Solutia, Inc.,* 351 F.3d 868 (8th Cir. 2003)]

In an early 2004 Seventh Circuit case, the plaintiff sued his ex-employer for unpaid parachute payments under a change of control provision. He also sought a bonus that he said was compensation that he had earned. However, the courts not only granted summary judgment for the employer, but ordered the plaintiff to pay more than a quarter of a million dollars of the defendant's attorneys' fees. (The plaintiff, a corporate executive, could reasonably be expected to have an extra quarter of a million dollars tucked away someplace.)

The plaintiff had served as vice president for the defendant since 1990. In 2000, however, he lost the confidence of top management and was relieved of his job responsibilities. A separation agreement was drafted calling for payment of six months of base salary, plus a $500,000 lump sum, but with no bonuses payable for 2000 or 2001. Then, based on allegations of misconduct on the plaintiff's part, the offer was withdrawn. At the beginning of January, 2001, the plaintiff announced that his employment had been constructively terminated. He retained counsel who negotiated with the defendant, but no agreement was reached.

Without exhausting his administrative remedies within the corporate organization (he claimed that exhaustion of remedies would have been futile), the plaintiff sued in District Court for severance pay and bonuses under the change in control provision. Although there was some restructuring within the corporate group that employed the plaintiff, the Seventh Circuit did not find that there was a change in control triggering this provision. The Seventh Circuit found no reason why exhaustion of administrative remedies could not have occurred. The plaintiff was required to pay the prevailing defendant's attorneys' fees because the court did not believe that the plaintiff had litigated in good faith with substantial justification for his position. [*Stark v. PPM America, Inc.,* 354 F.3d 666 (7th Cir. 2004)]

PART II

PENSION LAW

CHAPTER 4
BASIC PENSION CONCEPTS

§ 4.01   INTRODUCTION

This chapter provides a summary and overview of the major ERISA and tax issues that help shape plan design. Many of these subjects are taken up in greater detail in the other chapters in this Part of the volume.

Also note that at press time, in August 2006, Congress was attempting to agree on a conference version of a major pension reform bill that, if passed and signed by the President, would make important changes (summarized in the Preface) to many aspects of pension law.

The conventional wisdom is that, although saving for retirement is a good thing, few people would have the resources or the wisdom or self-discipline to save enough on their own to provide for comfortable retirement. Therefore, the federal government collects FICA (Social Security) taxes from employers and employees, and dispenses Social Security benefits to retired and disabled workers and their families. In the private sector, employers make part of the employee's compensation available immediately in cash.

The employee's total compensation package also includes benefits such as health insurance and fringe benefits, plus deferred compensation that will eventually provide a lump sum or income at the time of the employee's normal, disability, or early or late retirement.

Although the conventional rule of thumb is that benefit cost is approximately one third as high as base compensation, in 2006 the U.S. Chamber of Commerce concluded that 40% is now a more accurate figure. (Benefit costs as a percentage of payroll have gone up almost 1% per year since 2000.) Between 2003 and 2004, the cost of providing retirement and savings plans went from 6.7% of payroll to 8%. Another 10.5% of payroll went to pay for vacation and holidays, and medical expenses represented 11.9% of payroll. In 2004, the average cost of all benefits was $18,358 per employee, and this figure was $20,158 in 2005. [Press release, *U.S. Chamber Study Finds Employee Benefit Costs Consume 40 Percent of Payroll Expenses,* <http://www.uschamber.com/press/releases/2006/April/06-72.htm>; the full survey can be purchased from <http://www.uschamber.com/research/benefits>]

The subject of pensions and benefits is an important one. Because of the high risk of improprieties or mistakes in handling the funds that the employees rely on for future security, pension plans are administered by fiduciaries. A fiduciary is an individual or institution that takes care of the property of others, and therefore must be held to the highest standards of ethics and prudence. [*See* Chapter 15 for further discussion of the obligations of plan fiduciaries, and penalties that can be imposed for misconduct or failure]

In 1974, Congress, concerned about potential abuses of pension plans, passed the Employee Retirement Income Security Act (ERISA). ERISA provides very detailed rules for how pension plans must be administered; how they must accumulate funds for later benefit payments; who qualifies for various kinds of benefits; how those benefits are to be distributed; and how the plan must keep records and communicate with its participants and beneficiaries. ERISA governs not only how ongoing plans operate, but how they can be created and how they can change form by merging with other plans or undergoing termination.

Furthermore, ERISA establishes pensions and benefits as an entirely and inherently federal area of jurisdiction. States are forbidden to legislate in this area, so the question of whether "ERISA preemption" has occurred is an important one.

The bulk of ERISA deals with pension plans, although the statute has less extensive provisions dealing with other types of plan, including profit-sharing plans, stock bonus plans, and welfare benefit plans such as health plans, vacation plans, and cafeteria plans.

The legal definition of a pension plan describes it as a plan established and maintained primarily to pay definitely determinable benefits to participants— usually monthly for the rest of the retiree's life, although lump sum payouts and annuities for a term of years are also permissible. Unlike profit-sharing plans, pension plans normally make distributions only on the basis of retirement, death, disability, or term of employment; hardship distributions are usually not available.

The management of a pension plan is complex, time-consuming, and expensive. On one level, employers have an incentive to do this because it makes it easier to recruit and retain quality employees in a competitive market. On another level, employers are motivated to maintain a plan that satisfies Internal Revenue Code requirements because the employer will be entitled to get a tax deduction for its contributions to, and administrative costs of running, a plan that satisfies the Code's numerous requirements for "qualified" plans.

> **Tip:** In March, 2004, the Supreme Court ruled that for the purposes of ERISA Title I, the sole shareholder/president of a Professional Corporation is an employee. As long as there is at least one other plan participant other than the business owner and spouse, then ERISA's anti-alienation provision applies, and the shareholder's creditors cannot reach his or her interest in the pension plan. [*Raymond B. Yates, M.D., P.C. Profit Sharing Plan v. Hendon*, 541 U.S. 1 (2004)]

As a general rule, the employer's tax deduction is taken on a cash basis—for the year in which money was contributed to a qualified plan. Employers that maintain nonqualified plans instead of, or in addition to, qualified plans do not get a deduction until the employee receives benefits from the nonqualified plan and includes them in income.

One of the most important criteria for plan qualification is that the plan must not discriminate in favor of highly compensated employees (HCEs). For 2001, HCEs are those who earn $85,000 a year or more; for 2002–4, the HCE figure is $90,000 or more; for 2005 it is $95,000; and for 2006 it is $100,000. Yet many companies identify a need for additional benefits to stay competitive in the executive recruiting stakes. It is legal to maintain nonqualified plans limited to, or offering superior benefits for, HCEs [*see* Chapter 8 for more discussion], but the expenses associated with these plans will not be federally tax deductible.

Tip: In February 2003, the Department of Labor changed the name of the sub-agency formerly known as the Pension and Welfare Benefits Administration (PWBA) to the Employee Benefits Security Administration (EBSA). [*See* 68 Fed. Reg. 5374 (Feb. 3, 2003)]

---

§ 4.02   EXTENT OF COVERAGE

In the more than 30 years since ERISA took effect, the pension sector of the economy has grown mightily, but has changed its characteristics very significantly. There has been a tremendous shift from plans in which the employer makes the contributions, decides how contributions will be invested, and takes the investment risk to plans in which employees bear a far greater burden of making both contributions and decisions.

In 1975, for example, there were 311,094 pension plans in the United States. The number of plans peaked in 1987, and then declined to 730,031 in 1998.

The defined benefit plan, sometimes referred to as the "traditional" pension plan, has lost its dominance in favor of defined contribution plans, especially 401(k) plans. In fact, by 1999, only 11% of all plan contributions were made to defined benefit plans. Defined benefit plans themselves have evolved. Some of them now offer lump sums in addition to the traditional annuity. Also *see* Chapter 7 for a discussion of the cash balance plan, a defined benefit variant.

According to the Investment Company Institute, total U.S. retirement assets were $14.3 trillion at the end of 2005—$1 trillion higher than the total in 2004. About half of the overall assets ($7.3 trillion) were in defined contribution plans and individual retirement accounts. [*Retirement Savings Rose to $14.3 Trillion in U.S. During 2005*, Wall Street Journal, May 10, 2006, at p. D3]

Aon Consulting reported that defined contribution plans were nearly ubiquitous in both public and private workplaces that they surveyed, with 90% having a 401(k), 403(b), or 457 plan. Less than a quarter (23%) had defined benefit plans, 12% had profit-sharing plans, 12% had nonqualified plans, and 8% had ESOPs. [Aon Consulting, *2006 National Employee Benefits Trend Survey*, <http://www.aon.com/about/publications/pdf/issues/may_06_article3.pdf> (April, 2006)] Watson Wyatt research showed that in 1985, almost 90% of the Fortune 500 companies provided defined benefit plans to new hires—a proportion that dropped to 50% in 2003, 42% in 2004, and 37% in 2005. In 2003, only 17% of the Fortune 100 offered defined contribution plans, a percentage rising to 25% in 2004 and 36% in 2005. Hybrid pension plans (e.g., cash balance and pension equity plans) declined greatly in popularity: These plans were on the upswing of popularity until 2002 when they became mired in legal questions. In 2004, one third of the Fortune

100 had hybrid plans vs. only 27% in 2005. [Fred Schneyer, *Study: DB Plans Continued Vanishing in 2005*, PlanSponsor.com (May 3, 2006)]

BLS data confirmed the trends. In 2005, only 60% of workers had access to some kind of retirement plan, and 85% of those with access participated in the plan. Forty-two percent participated in a defined contribution plan, and 21% participated in a defined benefit plan. Although 401(k) plans are the predominant defined contribution form, they are not the only form. In 2003, 70% of those participating in a defined contribution plan participated in a thrift/savings plan, 21% in a profit-sharing plan, and 11% in a money purchase plan. The most common match formula was 50% of employee deferrals up to 6% of salary. [Rebecca Moore, *BLS Data Shows Changing Landscape in Retirement Plan Coverage,* PlanSponsor.com (Mar. 6, 2006)]

Nevertheless, close to half the workers in the private sector (45%; about 48 million people) will not have pensions when they retire (if they ever can afford to retire!). This group is expected to grow as the number of pension plans shrinks. Most of these people work in wholesale/retail trade, manufacturing, or personal services. Small businesses are especially likely to be maintained without pension plans. [Joi Preciphs, *Congress May Focus on Retirement Funds*, Wall Street Journal, Jan. 4, 2006, at p. A4]

The Congressional Research Service looked at earlier pension trends, for the period 1998–2003 and concluded that during this period, the percentage of workers in the private sector whose company sponsored a pension plan rose slightly, from 62% to 64.8%, and the percentage of workers participating rose from 43.1% to 46.8%. In 1998 52.3% of private-sector workers worked for an employer that sponsored a defined contribution plan, a figure that rose to 56.4% in 2003. In 1998, 35.4% of workers participated in a defined contribution plan, which rose to 41% in 2003 (a 72.6% participation rate for those who had access to a plan). The employees most likely to participate in a defined contribution plan were male, over 35, married, working full time, and had a college degree, owned a home, and had access to employer contributions to the plan. However, most participants did not defer very much into the plan. In 2003, the average was $1,896 a year. Nearly all employees (85%) deferred less than $500 per month, and a mere 3% deferred $1,000 a month (the maximum deferral allowed in 2003). In 2003, the mean deferred compensation plan balance was $34,757 (i.e., the total amount in all plans divided by the number of participants) and the median (the point at which half the balances were larger and half smaller) was $15,000. [Patrick Purcell (CRS), *Retirement Plan Participation and Contributions: Trends from 1998 to 2003*, <http://www.opencrs.ctd.org/getfile.php?rid = 43309> (Oct. 12, 2005)]

§ 4.03   EFFECT OF DEMOGRAPHICS ON PLANS

The Baby Boom, people born after World War II, are the largest age cohort in U.S. history. The oldest boomers are already 55 years old—and perhaps eligible for early retirement.

That means that soon, employers will not only face the challenge of paying pensions to a very large group of retirees—they will have a smaller group of active workers to generate corporate income and profits. Furthermore, retirees may take priceless and irreplaceable skills and work ethics with them when they leave the workforce.

The population is aging. In 2001, senior citizens made up 12.4% of the population. The fastest-growing demographic group was the "oldest old": people over 85. Senior citizens consume more health services than younger people, so retiree health benefits [*see* Chapter 9] and the Medicare system will be severely strained.

It may be necessary to amend ERISA and the Internal Revenue Code to facilitate phased retirement; many companies may find it desirable to keep older employees on the payroll at least part-time, while making limited pension payments to them. The AARP found there are significant differences between those who take phased retirement and others. Phased retirees and those who work part-time after retirement are better educated, have higher household income and wealth, and are more likely to be managers in skilled positions than retirees and full-time older workers. Phased retirees are more likely to work for its own sake, rather than just for money, and are less likely to ever fully retire than those who did not take phased retirement. [*Retirees Continue Working but Not for the Reason You Think*, PlanSponsor.com (Feb. 24, 2006)]

Chapter 9 discusses programs and incentives for early retirement; however, labor force participation by older workers has increased. Between 1965 and 1974, as Medicare entered the picture, and the supply of workers was large, early retirement incentives were created, and the average retirement age for men fell to 63, where it has remained ever since. Now, however, factors such as recession, the shift away from defined benefit pension plans, threats to pension stability and Social Security, and declines in availability of retiree health benefits have reversed the trend toward earlier retirement. Many of these senior workers are in "bridge" jobs (part-time or seasonal work forming a bridge between their earlier careers and full-scale retirement).

Various bills have been introduced in Congress that require defined benefit plan sponsors to change the mortality assumptions used to value plan liabilities. Watson Wyatt Worldwide analyzed what would happen if those changes were implemented. Actuaries are required to use the Group Annuity Mortality table (GAM-83), published by the Society of Actuaries in 1983. Watson Wyatt's research showed that in 2004, 70% of firms used GAM-83 for both current and projected liability. The bills introduced in Congress would require the use of a more current Society of Actuaries table, the Retired Pensioners Mortality Table (RP-2000), which reflects mortality experience in the period from 1990 to 1994. The bills require the Department of the Treasury to revise mortality tables every 10 years, but companies may use different assumptions if they can prove that RP-2000 does not adequately reflect their mortality experience. Unlike GAM-83, RP-2000 is a "generational mortality table" that is not static and predicts continuing improvements in life expectancy. Watson Wyatt concluded that if adopted, the new rules would somewhat increase liabilities for most sponsors, especially plans that cover more men than women. The higher the life expectancy, the greater the estimated cost of a life annuity and therefore the higher the pension liability. The RP-2000 increases life expectancies for men, but shortens them for women vis-à-vis the GAM-83, so the net effect depends on the composition of the plan population. For Watson Wyatt's two hypothetical plans, shifting to RP-2000 in 2006 would raise one plan's liabilities by 0.5% and the other plan's liabilities by 1.75%. [Watson Wyatt—Insider *Retirement Income: WW Research How Would the Proposed Changes to Mortality Standards Affect Plan Sponsors?* <http://www.watsonwyatt.com/us/pubs/insider/showarticle.asp?ArticleID = 15435>]

§ 4.04   INVESTMENT FACTORS

For many years, the strong investment climate allowed plans to reduce or even suspend their contributions to defined benefit plans, because the plans were ample to satisfy the obligation to make future payments.

Then, in 2000 and 2001, plans suffered multiple blows. The collapse of the dot-com bubble gravely damaged the stock market. The September 11 attack and the Enron scandal subjected the market—and therefore plan investments—to additional stresses.

In the 1990s, many companies found that their investment experience was so favorable that they were able to suspend contributions to their plans, because the plan was already fully funded. This trend later reversed. In 2000, for example, the total of unfunded liabilities for all private pension plans was $26 billion, a seemingly large amount that rose to $111 billion in 2001. However, these figures were calculated by the PBGC, which points out that it uses a low interest rate to project future liabilities. (Some commentators also suggest that the PBGC is exaggerating the gravity of the situation as part of a campaign to raise premiums.) [John D. McKinnon, *Warning of Pension-Plan Shortfall Raises Pressure for Financial Fix,* Wall Street Journal, Sept. 5, 2003, at p. A1]

Under FAS 87, a company must record a charge against equity if the plan is underfunded by more than a certain amount. To avoid this, some major corporations contributed cash and stock to their pension plans, even though the plans were adequately funded to meet current liabilities and did not violate ERISA obligations. (Correction of underfunding can also reduce the PBGC premium that the company must pay. [*See* § 5.08[B], *supra*])

Corporations have an incentive to use different measures to claim to employees that the pension obligation is large (e.g., by using a 4% interest crediting rate) while simultaneously assuring investors that it is small (e.g., by using a 6% rate). It is lawful to do so, although FASB is considering whether the two standards should be brought closer together. FASB's research into cash balance plans shows that cash balance plans were marketed to employers because the use of different interest rates can make them look cheaper than they prove to be in practice. [Mary Williams Walsh, *Talk of Changing Pension Math Raises Concern on Benefit Cuts*, New York Times, Jan. 20, 2005, at p. A1]

As long as the assumptions are reasonable, plans are also given significant discretion in setting assumptions about when workers will retire and how interest rates will move. Companies can greatly reduce the amount of contributions they make to the plan by tailoring favorable assumptions. [Ellen E. Schultz and Theo Francis, *For Pension Plans, Risky Is Fine*, Wall Street Journal, Dec. 10, 2003, at p. C1; Mary Williams Walsh, *Failed Pensions: A Painful Lesson in Assumptions*, New York Times, Nov. 12, 2003, at p. C1]

According to the GAO, more than half of the largest corporations were able to run their pension plans in the late 1990s without making any additions to their pension plans, as a result of legal loopholes and successful investment performance. Some of those corporations (e.g., United Airlines) now have catastrophic shortfalls between their pension assets and future liabilities, which will probably be passed along to the PBGC. The GAO criticized a number of practices that would permit a company to, in effect, misrepresent the true state of its pension plan without violating the law—such as using unrealistic valuation assumptions and not adjusting the value of assets after a decline in value. [Mary Williams Walsh, *Some Big Companies Failed to Add to Pensions in 1990's,* New York Times, June 1, 2005, at p. C11]

§ 4.05   DEFINED BENEFIT/DEFINED CONTRIBUTION

The traditional kind of pension plan, the one usually in effect when ERISA was passed, is the defined benefit plan. In a plan of this type, the employer agrees to provide benefits according to a formula. A typical formula would set the pension level as $x\%$ times the number of years the employee worked before retirement times the employee's average pay for his or her last five years working for the employer—or perhaps the average of the three years in which he or she earned the most.

The employer's contributions for all employees go into a single account or trust for the entire plan. However, there must be a separate account balance for each participant who makes voluntary contributions. [I.R.C. § 411(b)(2)(A)]

In some ways, this arrangement is problematic both from the employer's and the employee's point of view. When employees retire, they receive a fixed pension that will probably not be inflation-indexed and will not offer cost of living adjustments. In a highly inflationary environment, they will find that their pension buys less and less over time. Nor will their pension increase if the investment climate is favorable.

From the employer's point of view, defined benefit plans carry heavy burdens, including uncertainty. The employer's commitment is to contribute enough to the plan each year to ensure that the participants will receive the promised level of benefits. Not only does this require elaborate (and expensive) actuarial calculations, it places the investment risk on the employer, who will have to make larger contributions in years in which the value of the plan's securities portfolio declines.

> **Tip:** The qualified plan rules do not allow the employer to have discretion over the actuarial assumptions used by a defined benefit plan.

Defined benefit plans are required to maintain liquid assets of at least three times the amount paid out in the previous 12 months. Failure to maintain this amount is called "liquidity shortfall," and plans in this category are required to make quarterly payments to increase the assets and eliminate the shortfall. There is a 10% excise tax for failure to make the payment—and a 100% excise tax if the shortfall continues for five consecutive quarters. However, for plan years in and after 1994, the IRS can waive part or all of the excise tax if the employer had reasonable cause for the shortfall, there was no willful neglect, and the employer is taking reasonable measures to eliminate the shortfall. [I.R.C. § 4971(f)(4)]

Defined benefit plans are also subject to full funding limitations. [*See* § 5.05[E]]

A defined contribution plan is a different, and much simpler, structure. The employer establishes a separate account for each employee who has satisfied the criteria for plan participation. If the plan requires or accepts employee contributions, there will usually be separate subaccounts for employer and employee contributions, but this is not a legal requirement.

The employer's commitment is to contribute the amount required by the plan formula—generally a simple percentage of compensation. ERISA § 404(c) permits the plan to give control over the assets to the participant. If this is done, the plan's fiduciaries will not be liable for losses that result from the control exercised by the participants.

There is no limit on the number of plans a particular employer can maintain, and it is not uncommon for an employer to maintain both defined benefit and defined contribution plans. Under prior law, § 415(e) imposed a limit on benefits from a combination of defined benefit and defined contribution plans, but that limitation was repealed for limitation years beginning on or after January 1, 2000. [*See* IRS Notice 99-44, 1999-35 I.R.B. 326 for implications of repeal]

ERISA § 404(c) requires the plan to give participants adequate information about the investment options they have for their accounts. The plan must offer at least three diversified investment types, with materially different characteristics with respect to risk and return.

In a sense, the Social Security system is a kind of pension plan. Both employers and employees pay FICA taxes to fund retirement benefits. Although all earned income is subject to Medicare taxes, the FICA tax phases out at a figure that changes every year. (For 2006, only the first $94,200 of earned income is subject to FICA tax.) The employer makes FICA contributions on all or nearly all of rank-and-file workers' pay, but only on a smaller proportion of the compensation of top earners.

The Internal Revenue Code contains "permitted disparity" rules for "integrating" a qualified plan with Social Security (disparities are not permitted in 401(k) plans). Within limits, the employer can reduce its plan contributions on behalf of rank-and-file employees to compensate for the employer's FICA contributions. As long as the permitted disparity rules are satisfied, the plan will remain qualified, and will not be considered discriminatory—even though the practical effect is to cut down on contributions and lower the pension the rank-and-file employees will eventually receive.

§ 4.06   OTHER PLAN TYPES

[A]   Money Purchase Plan

A money purchase plan provides definitely determinable benefits, funded by fixed employer contributions made in accordance with a single allocation formula for all participants. Money purchase plans are subject to the I.R.C. § 412 minimum funding standard. The plan must offer QJSAs and QPSAs. [See §§ 12.05, 12.06] Money purchase plans can accept employee contributions and make plan loans to participants.

[B]   Profit-Sharing Plan

A profit-sharing plan must have a definite formula, set in advance, for allocating the employer's total contribution among the various plan participants, and for distributing the account money to participants. Distributions can be made after the funds have been in the account for a certain length of time (ERISA requires this to be at least two years), attainment of a stated age (which does not have to be retirement age) or an event such as retirement, termination, illness, or disability. Profit-sharing plans have to have formulas for allocating and distributing employer contributions, but the corporation's Board of Directors can legitimately be given discretion to set the level of contributions each year. Since 1986, it has not been necessary for the contributions to be made from corporate profits, or only in a year in which there are profits. The maximum contribution that the employer can deduct is 15% of the participant's contribution for the year. Profit-sharing plans are allowed to make plan loans. *See* Rev. Rul. 2005-55, 2005-33 IRB 284, for an explanation of why a profit-sharing plan's health benefit feature violated the minimum vesting requirement.

[C]   Target-Benefit Plan

A target-benefit plan is a money purchase plan (and therefore subject to the defined contribution rules), but contributions are calculated to fund a specified level of retirement benefits at normal retirement age. The participant receives the aggregate of all contributions plus their earnings, although the actual benefit may be either higher or lower than the target, depending on investment results.

[D] Floor-Offset Plan

A floor-offset plan is a hybrid plan, where the defined benefit portion of the plan guarantees a minimum level of benefits, offset by the annuity the retiree could purchase at retirement with the balance in the defined contribution portion of the plan. *Lunn v. Montgomery Ward & Co. Retirement Security Plan* [166 F.3d 880 (7th Cir. 1999)] holds that an employee who retired four years after normal retirement age was not entitled to additional retirement benefits to make up for the reduced duration of benefits. The court upheld the idea of floor-offset plans, finding that this type of plan does not violate ERISA benefit accrual requirements or antiforfeiture provisions.

[E] New Comparability Plan

A new comparability plan is a special type of defined contribution plan (or combination of defined contribution and defined benefit plan) that can increase the allocation for HCEs without violating the antidiscrimination rules. *See* § 4.22.

An article in the January 2005 issue of the *Journal of Accountancy* discusses new comparability plans as a way to reduce pension costs while increasing benefits for key employees. However, small businesses such as medical practices can also use new comparability plans as a flexible means of accommodating the differing planning objectives of employee-shareholders: say, a young doctor who wants a higher degree of current compensation while an older colleague wants to concentrate on retirement accruals. These "class-based" plans do not work well for small businesses when all the employees are co-owners, and they all want the same treatment, or in companies in which the owners and key employees are much younger than the other employees.

The plan document can define the classes used to group the employees in various ways, although a plan amendment is required to change the number or definition of classes, and this cannot be done retroactively. A class could be specified, for example, as all employees born before a certain date, those hired after a certain date, those with a certain number of years of service, those working in a particular department, those with a stated title or type of job, or those assigned to a named region. The IRS and DOL have not issued technical guidance, but if every employee is placed in a separate class, the agencies might rule that the plan has become a deemed 401(k). For example, a medical practice could have three classes: owners, managers, and other employees. To reward productivity, the plan could have different classes for offices depending on their revenue streams and productivity levels. [Mark Papalia, *Class-Based Pensions: A Cost-Saving Alternative for Companies of All Sizes,* Journal of Accountancy (January 2005) <https://www.aicpa.org/PUBS/JOFA/jan2005/papalia.html>]

[F] SEP

A SEP (Simplified Employer Pension) is an IRA sponsored by the employer, under a written plan whose contribution formula does not discriminate in favor of HCEs.

[G] SIMPLE

A Savings Incentive Match Plan for Employees (SIMPLE) plan, available only to companies with 100 or fewer employees, involves employer contributions to employees' own IRAs.

§ 4.07   IRA/QUALIFIED PLAN INTERFACE

As the name suggests, an Individual Retirement Arrangement (IRA) is maintained by an individual on his or her own behalf, not by a corporation. However, the two types of plan interact when an IRA is used as a "conduit" for a transfer of funds between two qualified plans, or when distributions from a qualified plan are sheltered from immediate taxation by being rolled over to an IRA.

Employers can maintain a program under which employees authorize payroll deductions to be invested in either regular or Roth IRAs. Such arrangements do not constitute ERISA plans (and therefore do not subject the employer to regulation or potential supervision) if:

- The employer doesn't make any contributions;
- Employee participation in the arrangement is completely voluntary;
- The employer's sole involvement is letting employees participate (without endorsing participation), making the payroll deductions, and forwarding the amounts to the IRA sponsor.

The employer can collect reasonable reimbursement for its services in connection with the employees' IRAs, but no other compensation. The employer can provide educational materials about IRAs and the value of saving for retirement, but must make it clear that the employer's role is purely administrative and does not involve contributions to the plan. It's also permissible for the employer to distribute literature prepared by the IRA sponsor, and even to display its own logo on the materials.

Either the employer can choose a single IRA sponsor or inform employees of criteria for choosing a sponsor. However, it is not permitted for the employer to negotiate special terms for its own employees that are not available to everyone who buys IRAs through that sponsor. The employer should inform employees that there are other ways to fund IRAs; that IRAs are not a suitable investment for everybody; and that IRAs work the same way whether the employee authorizes a payroll deduction or submits the contribution directly to the IRA sponsor. [*See* IRS Announcement 99-2, 1999-2 I.R.B. 44, 29 C.F.R. § 2510.3-2(d), and DOL Interpretive Bulletin 99-1, 64 Fed. Reg. 32999-33003 (June 18, 1999)]

EGTRRA increases the maximum amount that can be contributed to an IRA (especially by persons over 50) and institutes a tax credit for low-income IRA investors, so IRA options will be more attractive than ever before.

EGTRRA also creates another option, the "deemed IRA," for plan years beginning after December 31, 2002. A qualified plan can permit employees to contribute to a separate account within a qualified plan. If the separate account meets the criteria for being either a conventional or a Roth IRA, it is treated as an IRA and not a qualified plan—and the employer's qualified plan won't lose its qualified status just because of the IRA subaccounts. The difference between a deemed IRA and the payroll deduction plan described above is that the employer, not the employee, sets up the account, although deemed IRAs can take payroll deductions.

Deemed IRAs are considered IRAs rather than qualified plans, so it is not necessary to satisfy ERISA's coverage and nondiscrimination rules. However, deemed IRAs are subject to ERISA's fiduciary and enforcement provisions, including the requirements for processing claims. Each deemed IRA must be held in a separate account or separate annuity under the plan, and the plan must provide separate accounting for the IRS contributions and earnings.

In 2003, the IRS provided guidance for implementation of the deemed IRA, in Rev. Proc. 2003-13, 2003-4 I.R.B. 317. The Revenue Procedure sets out the plan amendments necessary for this purpose. The plan documents must be amended to provide for deemed IRAs no later than the date the plan accepts its first deemed IRA contribution. (There's a transition provision for plan years beginning between December 31, 2002, and January 1, 2004: The amendment can be delayed until the end of the plan year.)

The employer must use a good faith EGTRRA plan amendment for this purpose. The Revenue Procedure contains a model amendment that can be used to comply. The amendment must also contain language satisfying the requirements of Code § 408 or § 408A; sample language can be found in the Listing of Required Modifications at www.irs.gov/ep.

Deemed IRA regulations were proposed at 68 Fed. Reg. 27493 (May 20, 2003) and finalized effective July 22, 2004, for accounts or annuities established under § 408(q) on or after August 1, 2003. Under the final rule, the deemed IRA account must satisfy the rules for either a traditional or Roth IRA. SEP and SIMPLE IRAs cannot be used as deemed IRAs. Because the employer's qualified plan and the deemed IRA are treated as separate entities, rules such as the minimum distribution requirements must be satisfied separately for each. If the qualified plan and deemed IRAs are maintained in separate trusts, the failure of one to qualify will not disqualify the other—but commingling of assets in separate trusts is permitted for investment purposes. It is permissible to hold all of the employer corporation's deemed IRAs in a single trust—it is not necessary to have a separate trust for each employee. Furthermore, it is acceptable to place the deemed IRAs into a trust that includes an employer plan that includes life insurance contracts, as long as none of the insurance contracts are included in the deemed IRAs. The plan document must be amended to cover deemed IRAs no later than the date the first deemed IRA contributions are accepted. Revenue Procedure 2003-13, 2003-4 I.R.B. 317, has a sample plan amendment with language that is acceptable for this purpose.

Another IRA-coordination provision is in effect for plan years beginning after December 31, 2005; under it, employers will be allowed to make contributions similar to Roth IRAs to qualified plans. That is, the contributions will not be deductible when made, but can be withdrawn from the account post-retirement free of tax. Roth-type contributions are subject to all the rules governing qualified plans.

See T.D. 9220, 2005-20 I.R.B. 596, for Temporary Regulations governing Roth IRA conversions in which an annuity contract is distributed from a traditional IRA on or after August 19, 2005. The IRS adopted concepts similar to those used in gift tax to determine the fair market value (FMV) of the annuity contract on the date of the conversion. (The FMV of the annuity contract is the amount deemed distributed as a result of the conversion.) If the conversion occurs close to the time the annuity contract was purchased, the premiums paid set the FMV. For older contracts that were fully paid at the time of conversion, the FMV depends on the price of comparable contracts. If further premiums must be paid, valuation is based on premium payments adjusted for interpolated terminal reserve. The IRS adopted this approach to deter the use of springing cash value annuities to reduce the taxable income resulting from a Roth IRA conversion. (Valuation is an issue for Roth IRAs but not for traditional IRAs because the distribution of an annuity contract from a traditional IRA usually is not taxable because the annuity is subject to the minimum distribution requirements of § 401(a)(9).) [These Regulations are discussed in Sutherland Asbill & Brennan LLP, *Legal Alert: Valuing IRA Annuities in Roth IRA Conversions* (benefitslink.com) (Aug. 22, 2005)]

Roth 401(k) plans (i.e., plans that do not give rise to tax benefits at the time funds are deferred, but from which funds can be withdrawn tax-free at retirement) are another option. [*See* § 6.04[E]]

§ 4.08   INCIDENTAL BENEFITS

A qualified plan is permitted to offer incidental benefits such as disability, Social Security supplements for early retirees, lump-sum death benefits, incidental death benefits, or 401(h) retiree health benefits. Life insurance can be provided as an incidental benefit as long as the death benefit does not exceed 100 times the estimated monthly retirement benefit under the qualified plan it supplements. However, offering other benefits, such as other medical benefits or layoff benefits, is forbidden, and can lead to loss of plan qualification.

§ 4.09 STRUCTURE OF ERISA

ERISA is not an easy statute to understand. A vast variety of plan provisions can legally be embodied in qualified plans, and many of these provisions depend on complex mathematical formulas. Furthermore, ERISA is both a labor law and a comprehensive and difficult piece of tax legislation.

Title I of ERISA, also referred to as the labor title, covers issues such as plan structure, fiduciary conduct, and prohibited transactions. Title II is the tax title, covering the requirements for plan qualification and tax deductions. The Title II provisions are duplicated in the Internal Revenue Code. There is some overlap between the two titles. For instance, prohibited transactions are defined in Title I, but the excise tax penalty is imposed under Title II.

Many of the provisions that are most significant for plan administration are found in Title I, Subtitle B. This subtitle is divided into six parts:

- Part 1: Reporting and disclosure;
- Part 2: Participation and vesting standards;
- Part 3: Funding standards;
- Part 4: Fiduciary responsibility;
- Part 5: Administration and enforcement;
- Part 6: Continuation coverage for health insurance.

Although there are some exceptions, the safest way to operate is just to assume that all benefit plans will be subject to at least some ERISA requirements. For example, a welfare plan (one that provides nonpension benefits such as health insurance or severance pay) is subject to most of the rules on reporting and disclosure, and the fiduciary, administration, and enforcement rules of Parts 4 and 5, but does not have to satisfy the participation, vesting, or funding standards.

§ 4.10 REQUIRED PROVISIONS FOR ALL QUALIFIED PLANS

Although within these confines a tremendous number of variations can be created, ERISA and the I.R.C. impose certain obligations on all qualified pension plans:

- The plan must be in writing [ERISA § 402(a)(1)];
- The employer must intend the plan to be permanent (although mergers and terminations are permitted under appropriate circumstances) [Reg. § 1.401-1(b)(2). Annuity, profit-sharing, and stock bonus plans are also subject to this requirement];
- The plan must provide a procedure for amendments and must indicate who has the authority to amend the plan [ERISA § 402(a)(1)];
- Plan funds must be managed through use of a trust [ERISA § 403(a), I.R.C. § 401(a)], unless they are held in a custodial account that is invested and

managed by someone other than the account custodian. Defined contribution plans can allow participants to direct the investment of the assets allocated to their accounts, but the participants cannot actually hold the assets [Rev. Rul. 89-52, 1989-1 CB 110];

- The plan must be operated for the exclusive benefit of its participants and their beneficiaries. [I.R.C. § 401(a)(2)] If the employer attempts to violate this rule by obtaining reversions of plan assets, an excise tax will be imposed under I.R.C. § 4980 unless an exception to the general rule applies. Even on termination, defined contribution plans generally cannot return any assets to the employer. Independent contractors must not be allowed to participate, because they are not considered employees;

- The plan must have a published funding policy [ERISA § 402(b)(1)]; (*See* Rev. Rul. 2003-83, 2003-30 I.R.B. 128, holding that the aggregate entry age normal funding method will no longer be considered a reasonable funding method under Code § 412(c)(3), and explaining how to change to an acceptable funding method, and Rev. Rul. 2003-88, 2003-32 I.R.B. 292, explaining the statute of limitations for excise taxes imposed under Code § 4971 on failure to satisfy the minimum funding standard.);

- Contributions made to the plan, or benefits received under the plan, are subject to the limitations of the I.R.C.;

- Benefits must not be decreased when Social Security benefits increase;

- Employees must be permitted to participate in the plan as soon as they satisfy the plan's minimum participation standards [I.R.C. §§ 401(a)(3), 410];

- The plan must satisfy minimum coverage requirements, and defined benefit plans must satisfy a minimum participation rule;

- Employee contributions and salary deferrals intended for 401(k) plans must be deposited into the plan as soon as possible, always within 90 days [DOL Reg. § 2510.3-102];

- The plan must not discriminate in favor of highly compensated employees (HCEs);

- The plan's vesting schedule must satisfy federal standards—and if the plan is top-heavy (concentrates its benefits on the highest-paid group) it must vest even faster than the basic rule [I.R.C. §§ 401(a)(7), 404(a)(2), 411(b)] EGTRRA, the 2001 tax law, also increased the speed with which employer matching contributions must vest;

- Benefits must be distributed only to participants and their beneficiaries (including "alternate payees" under Qualified Domestic Relations Orders). This is known as the "anti-alienation" rule. In particular, creditors cannot reach pension benefits before they have been distributed;

- Pension benefits must start within 60 days of the end of the plan year in which the individual reaches the plan's normal retirement age (NRA), reaches age 65, terminates service or has 10 years of service—whichever occurs last;

- The plan must furnish Summary Plan Descriptions (SPDs), Summaries of Material Modifications (SMMs) and other disclosure documents [*see* Chapter 11];

- The plan must designate at least one fiduciary who is responsible for management. Named fiduciaries are allowed to delegate certain plan responsibilities to other people, such as investment managers—but only if the plan specifically permits such delegation;
- The plan must have a procedure for making claims and appealing denials of applications. The claims procedure must be disclosed in the Summary Plan Description [*see* §§ 10.05, 11.02] but need not be included in the plan document itself;
- Defined benefit plans must pay premiums to the Pension Benefits Guaranty Corporation (PBGC);
- Transfers of assets between plans, and mergers and terminations of plans, are also regulated. [*See* I.R.C. § 411(d)(3)]

One additional risk of plans that offer a lump-sum payout is the equivalent of a "run on the bank." That is, participants who fear that their plan will be taken over by the PBGC (perhaps after pension assets have been diverted in favor of special plans for top management) often opt for early retirement and a lump-sum payout while funds are still available. Of course, this hastens the financial deterioration of the plan.

§ 4.11   NORMAL RETIREMENT AGE

Many ERISA and tax rules depend on the concept of drawing a pension at, before, or after the plan's Normal Retirement Age (NRA). The standard NRA remains 65, although perhaps this will change not only as life expectancies increase, but as the Social Security system phases in a higher age for receiving unreduced benefits. (The basic Social Security retirement age is gradually being increased from 65 to 67.)

However, a plan can set the NRA either higher or lower than 65. The plan can choose an NRA lower than 65 if this is customary for the company or for its industry—as long as this choice is not a device to accelerate funding. If the NRA is very low—below 55—I.R.C. § 415(b) requires that maximum pension payable under the plan be reduced, in light of the large number of payments that will be made. However, a profit-sharing plan is allowed to have an NRA lower than 55, even if this is below the industry average.

> **Tip:** If the plan does not specify an NRA, the NRA will be deemed to be the age at which accrued benefits no longer increase solely on account of age or service.

If the plan sets the NRA above 65, or if there is no definition in the plan, then each participant will have an individual NRA. It will be either his or her 65th birthday or the fifth anniversary of plan participation, whichever comes later.

§4.12 NORMAL RETIREMENT BENEFIT

The NRB, or Normal Retirement Benefit, is a related concept. It is either the benefit commencing at the NRA or the early retirement benefit (if the plan provides one)—whichever is greater. The early retirement benefit is not adjusted actuarially for this purpose, even though it will be paid for more years than if benefits had commenced at the NRA. Early retirement subsidies are not counted if they continue only until the retiree becomes eligible for Social Security, and if they do not exceed the Social Security benefit.

Not everyone retires on the anniversary of plan participation. If benefits depend on average compensation for, e.g., three or five years, then Treas. Reg. § 1.411(a)-7(c)(5) mandates treatment of the last partial year of service as a full year.

Although there is growing interest in "phased retirement" (a diminishing work schedule creating a transition between full-time employment and full retirement), tax law still has little flexibility in this area. In mid-2004, the Supreme Court ruled that the "anti-cutback" rule of ERISA § 204(g) prohibits a plan from being amended in a way that suspends payments of early retirement benefits the individual has already accrued. In this case, the suit was brought by workers who took early retirement at a time that their pension plan called for suspension of pension payments if they took another job as construction workers. Instead, they worked as construction supervisors. Later, the plan was amended to suspend the benefit payments to anyone who worked in the construction industry at all. The Supreme Court found the amendment improper because workers are entitled to rely on the terms of their pension plan in making career-planning decisions. [*Central Laborers' Pension Fund v. Heinz*, 541 U.S. 739 (2004)]

§4.13 PARTICIPATION AND COVERAGE

Both defined benefit and defined contribution plans are subject to "minimum coverage" rules under I.R.C. § 410(b). Remember, one of the main motives in passing ERISA was to prevent plans from concentrating unduly on providing benefits to stockholders and managers. However, it can be difficult to satisfy the various tests in a small company [*see* § 4.14[A] for top-heavy plan rules] or in a company where there is a great disparity between managers' pay and rank-and-file pay, or where there is a stable group of HCEs but heavy turnover in rank-and-file employees.

To satisfy the minimum coverage rules, the plan must either cover a percentage of the rank and file that is at least 70% of the percentage of highly compensated employees covered by the plan; or the plan must cover a reasonable classification of employees that is not discriminatory. Furthermore, the contributions made on behalf of, or the benefits provided to, the rank-and-file must equal at least 70% of those made or provided to the highly compensated.

Defined benefit plans are subject to a minimum participation rule. On each day of the plan year, the plan must benefit either 40% of all the company's work force, or 50 people, whichever is less. However, plans that are not top-heavy and do not benefit any highly compensated employee or former employee are exempt from the minimum participation rule.

A 2003 Third Circuit decision holds that a "salaried-only" pension plan that excludes hourly workers is acceptable under ERISA, and does not violate the minimum participation rule. [*Bauer v. Summit Bancorp*, 325 F.3d 155 (3d Cir. 2003)]

The I.R.C. does not require qualified plans to cover all employees from the time of hiring. It is permissible for a plan to require employees to be at least 21 years old and to have completed one year of service before being eligible for participation. Part-time employees must be covered if they can work 1,000 hours within a 12-month period. If plan benefits become 100% vested after only two years, a qualified plan (other than a 401(k) plan) can require two years of service for participation.

§ 4.14   VESTING

[A]   Generally

Participation in a plan is only the first step toward eventually receiving a pension. Vesting is the process of the benefits becoming nonforfeitable. ERISA includes detailed vesting rules to prevent earlier abuses, under which plans were often drafted so that so many years of service were required to achieve a pension that many rank-and-file employees would end up forfeiting their pensions (with the forfeitures going to swell the accounts of highly compensated executives and stockholders).

The normal benefit must always be nonforfeitable at the normal retirement age. It is not required that employees immediately gain 100% ownership of their defined contribution accounts, or the amounts contributed on their behalf to a defined benefit plan. Vesting is the process of moving toward 100% ownership. The Code prescribes minimum funding schedules; employers are always permitted to give employees faster vesting.

There are only two basic vesting schedules allowed by I.R.C. § 411(a):

- Five-year cliff vesting: participants are not vested at all for the first five years of service, but then they are immediately 100% vested as to employer contributions;
- Three-to-seven graded vesting: no vesting at all for three years, but full vesting by seven years of service, increasing proportionately in years 4, 5, and 6.

Top-heavy plans must provide even faster vesting—three-year cliff or six-year graded—but plans with a lot of participants usually are not top-heavy.

For example, if a participant leaves employment at a time when he or she is 60% vested, then a participant in a defined contribution plan will be entitled to $60 of every $100 in his or her individual account. A participant in a defined benefit plan will be entitled to an annuity of $60/month for every $100/month that would have been payable if he or she had remained at work until becoming 100% vested.

EGTRRA, the 2001 tax legislation, provides even faster vesting for employer matching contributions (as distinct from the employer's own contributions). Vesting for matching contributions must be either three-year cliff vesting or graded vesting over two to six years (20% in the second year of service, 40% in the third year, etc.).

Pre-ERISA years of service earned when the employee was younger than 22 can be excluded when applying ERISA's vesting standards. The plaintiff in a Seventh Circuit case was hired in 1967, at age 18, and worked until 1978. Under the pre-ERISA version of the plan, he would not have been vested because the plan had 10-year cliff vesting, and years served before age 22 were not counted. The Seventh Circuit rejected the plaintiff's argument that Congress did not intend for pre-ERISA service credits to be lost, on the grounds that congressional intention is not relevant when a statute is unambiguous. Accrual and vesting are related but different concepts, and although amendments cannot reduce accrued benefits, changes in the way an employee becomes vested are acceptable. [*Silvernail v. Ameritech Pension Plan,* 439 F.3d 355 (7th Cir. 2006)]

Rev. Rul. 2005-55, 2005-33 I.R.B. 284, rules that a profit-sharing plan fails to satisfy the § 411 vesting requirement, and therefore fails to satisfy § 401(a)(7), if it devotes part of the employer's annual contributions to providing a medical reimbursement account for each participant that can only be accessed to reimburse his or her health care expenses. Profit-sharing plans are subject to the incidental benefit rule: That is, they must primarily be devoted to deferred compensation, but incidental life, accident, or health insurance can be provided, up to 25% of the funds allocated to the account. Because the plan says that the medical reimbursement account can only be distributed to reimburse medical expenses, the plan violates the rule requiring profit-sharing account balances to be non-forfeitable. The IRS ruled that this problem can be avoided by making the medical expense reimbursement account distributable on the same terms as the deferred compensation account (e.g., when the employee severs employment with the plan sponsor).

[B] Vesting on Termination

All qualified plans must provide that, if the plan is completely or partially terminated, all affected participants immediately become 100% vested. [I.R.C. § 411(d)(3)] For plans that are not subject to the minimum funding standard of I.R.C. § 412 (for instance, profit-sharing and stock bonus plans), 100% vesting must also occur when the employer completely ceases to make contributions to the plan. A profit-sharing or stock bonus plan is deemed terminated on the day when the plan administrator notifies the IRS of the cessation of contributions.

Under Rev. Rul. 2003-65 [2003-25 I.R.B. 1035], freezing of accruals under a plan is not a "termination" with respect to the decision of whether vesting service can be disregarded if accruals resume. Therefore, all years of service for the sponsor since the establishment of the plan count toward vesting. This is also true if a frozen plan is merged into a new plan of the same employer, with accruals resuming after the plans merge.

The Sixth Circuit ruled that a group of former employees of the defendant, who became employees of a larger corporation because of a corporate sale, were not entitled to immediate vested benefits under the seller's pension plan. They immediately became employees of the buyer corporation, so there was no layoff triggering immediate vesting under the seller's plan. [*Morgan v. SKF USA Inc.*, 385 F.3d 989 (6th Cir. 2004)]

[C] Vesting and Service

For vesting purposes, a year of service is a period of 12 consecutive months during which the employee performs at least 1,000 hours of service. Plans are not required to provide fractional years of service credit—i.e., if someone works only 500 hours, the employer does not have to credit half a year of service.

Tip: For the purposes of vesting or participation for accrual purposes, a year of service can be any period of 12 consecutive months that the employer designates. But a year of service for plan eligibility purposes must start on the first day of employment. A plan can have more than one vesting year. If the plan selects a single vesting year for convenience, it doesn't have to be the same as the plan year.

Early in 2004, the Ninth Circuit upheld IRS Reg. § 1.410(a)-7(a)(1)(ii), which allows calculation of vesting under an "elapsed time" method. The plan participant-plaintiffs charged that the Regulation violated ERISA because it did not require counting of each hour of service, but the Ninth joined three other Circuits that held that the IRS was entitled to deference in issuing the Regulation because one of the primary goals of ERISA is to reduce the burden of compliance. [*Johnson v. Buckley*, 356 F.3d 1057 (9th Cir. 2004)]

§ 4.15 BREAK-IN-SERVICE RULES

For some pension-related purposes, it makes a big difference whether the individual has been continuously employed by the employer sponsoring the plan, or whether employment has been interrupted: whether the person has been laid off and then recalled, for instance. Interruption of continuous employment is called a "break in service"—a concept that has many implications.

A one-year break in service has occurred when a person renders 501 or fewer hours of service for the employer in a particular year. If someone works more than 501 but less than 1000 hours for the employer in a given year the employer does not have to credit a year of service, but cannot penalize the employee for the break in service.

After someone has had a one-year break, the employer can disregard service before the break for vesting purposes until the employee has come back to work and completed a year of service. After there have been five consecutive one-year breaks in service, a defined contribution plan, or some insured defined benefit plans, can treat the vested benefits as forfeited, and allocate them to other participants.

If the participant was 0% vested before the break in service, the "Rule of Parity" requires the plan to add up the number of years of service before the break. If the number of consecutive one-year breaks is at least five, or is greater than or equal to the aggregate number of pre-break years of service (whichever is greater), the rule allows the pre-break years to be disregarded for vesting purposes, even if the participant is later rehired.

However, under the Retirement Equity Act of 1984 [Pub. L. No. 98-397], a break in service that is caused by parenting leave probably cannot be counted against the employee. A reservist who is called to active military duty does not have a break in service during the active-duty period. [*See* § 1.18, *infra,* for more about the employment law implications of call-ups of reservists and members of the National Guard]

In 2006, the Ninth Circuit ruled that pregnancy leave taken before the 1979 effective date of the Pregnancy Discrimination Act (*see* § 34.06[B]) need not be taken into account for crediting service in current benefit determinations. Before the PDA took effect, employees on pregnancy leave of absence did not get service credits, even though employees with other temporary disabilities did. [*Hulteen v. AT&T Corp.*, 441 F.3d 653 (9th Cir. 2006)]

The Third Circuit joined the Second Circuit in 2005, ruling that a multi-employer plan violated ERISA by failing to include, for benefit accrual purposes, 10.5 years of service before a break in service that occurred before ERISA's effective date. The Third Circuit ruled that ERISA § 203 does allow pre-ERISA breaks in service to be disregarded for vesting purposes, but the service must be considered for benefit accrual. [*DiGiacomo v. Teamsters Pension Trust Fund of Philadelphia*, 420 F.3d 220 (3d Cir. 2005); the Second Circuit case is *McDonald v. Pension of the NYSA-ILA Pension Trust Fund*, 320 F.3d 151 (2d Cir. 2003)] The Fifth and Seventh Circuits disagree. [*Mello v. Sara Lee Corp.*, 431 F.3d 440 (5th Cir. 2005); *McClain v. Retail Food Employers Joint Pension Plan*, 413 F.3d 582 (7th Cir. 2005)]

§ 4.16 PLAN LIMITS

One of the basic purposes of ERISA is to prevent plans from unduly favoring executives, managers, and other highly paid employees. One of the ways ERISA furthers this objective is by placing limits on the amount that can be contributed each year to a defined contribution plan, deferred in a 401(k) plan, or provided as a benefit under a defined benefit plan.

The underlying principle is that plan limits are adjusted annually. The adjustment reflects changes in the Consumer Price Index. Starting in 2003, the changes will be rounded down in $5,000 increments; until then, changes are adjusted in $10,000 increments.

Before 2000, I.R.C. § 415(e) imposed a combined limitation on the allocations to defined contribution plans plus accrued benefits from defined benefit plans. However, as of 2000, plans are permitted to—but not obligated to—impose a combined limitation with respect to employees who participate in both types of plans. Defined benefit plans are allowed to increase benefits (for retirees as well as active employees) to reflect repeal of the combined limitation.

The breakdown below contains the limitations applicable to various amounts applicable to pension administration for the years 2001–2006. The figures reflect statutory changes imposed by EGTRRA as well as the process of adopting cost-of-living increases and making adjustments for inflation. *See* IR-2005-120 (Oct. 14, 2005) <http://www.irs.gov/newsroom/article/0,id=149631,00.html>.

There were few changes between 2002 and 2004, because in most cases the comparatively tame rate of inflation did not trigger an adjustment.

1. Maximum annual benefit under a defined benefit plan (§ 415(b)(1)(A)): $140,000/$160,000/$160,000/$165,000/$170,000/$175,000; the maximum amount is reduced for benefits that begin before age 62, but increased for benefits beginning after age 65. But see the Job Creation and Worker Assistance Act of 2002 for relief provisions for employers that do not want to adopt EGTRRA's automatic increases in plan limits.

2. Maximum contribution to a defined contribution plan (§ 415(c)(1)(a)): $35,000 and 25% of compensation/$40,000 and 100% of compensation/ $40,000 and 100% of compensation/$41,000 and 100% of compensation/$42,000 and 100% of compensation/$44,000 and 100% of compensation.

3. Definition of a "highly compensated employee" under § 414(q)(1)(B): $85,000 a year/$90,000 a year/$90,000 a year/$90,000 a year/$95,000/ $100,000.

4. Limit on annual compensation that can be taken into account in making calculations, as prescribed by §§ 401(a)(17), 404(l): $170,000/$200,000/$200,000/$205,000/$210,000/$220,000.

5. Maximum 401(k) deferral: $10,500/$11,000 plus catch-up contributions for persons over 50/ $12,000 plus catch-up contributions/$13,000 plus catch-up contributions/$14,000 plus catch-up contributions/$15,000 plus catch-up contributions.

Regulations proposed by the IRS in May of 2005 (70 Fed. Reg. 31214, May 31, 2005) may require your plan to be amended to cope with changes in the rules under § 415. The proposals affect, e.g., calculating how multiple plan distributions relate to the maximum amount that an employee can receive in a given year, calculation of the Qualified Joint and Survivor Annuity for married participants who also receive a partial lump sum distribution, and whether payments are made under

§ 415 (and therefore can be deferred in a 401(k) plan) when they are made after the employee's separation from service. A payment made within 2½ months after separation counts under 415 as long as it would have been made if the participant had stayed employed, and/or if it constitutes bona fide sick leave or vacation leave.

§ 4.17   EMPLOYEE CONTRIBUTIONS

Although 401(k) plans get their basic funding from employees' deferred salary (and may get matching contributions from the employer), pension plans work the other way around. They get their basic funding from the employer, but some plans require and other plans permit employees to make additional contributions to the plan. Internal Revenue Code § 411(c)(2) characterizes employee contributions as mandatory if making the contribution is a precondition of the employer match.

> **Tip:** The Bankruptcy Abuse Prevention and Consumer Protection Act of 2005 (BAPCA; P.L. 109-8) gives employees additional protection against their contributions being seized by their employer's creditors, when the employee has made the contribution but the employer has not yet deposited it into the plan.

Employee contributions are also important in determining whether or not a plan discriminates in favor of highly compensated employees. I.R.C. § 414(g) contains the formula for testing whether the employer's aggregate contributions to the plan on behalf of HCEs are too high. If the plan fails to satisfy the requirements of this section, it will be disqualified, unless the excess contributions made on behalf of the HCEs, plus the earnings on the excess contributions, are returned to the company's employees by the end of the plan year after the year of the excess contribution. A 10% excise also applies to excess employee contributions (e.g., made by HCEs) that are not distributed within two and a half months of the end of the plan year.

Benefits attributable to employer contributions cannot be assigned or anticipated before they are received, except in the form of a QDRO. But employees can withdraw some or all of their voluntary contributions while continuing to be employed and to participate in the plan. Employees must always have the right to withdraw their own voluntary contributions to the plan at any time, without the accrued benefits attributable to employer contributions becoming forfeitable. [I.R.C. § 401(a)(19)] However, if the plan mandates employee contributions, I.R.C. § 411(a)(3)(D) allows the plan to provide that employer contributions will be forfeited if a participant withdraws any mandatory employee contributions at a time when he or she is less than 50% vested. If the benefits are repaid within five years after the withdrawal, or two years after the employee returns to participation under the plan (whichever comes first), the benefits must be restored.

Employees are always 100% vested in their own voluntary contributions to a pension plan. When an employer matches these voluntary contributions, EGTRRA requires vesting in the employer's matching contributions to occur either on a three-year cliff schedule, or a six-year graded schedule, beginning with 20% vesting in the second year of the employee's service.

The significant Supreme Court case of *Hughes Aircraft Co. v. Jacobson* [525 U.S. 432 (1999)] involved a defined benefit plan that mandated employee contributions (most defined benefit plans do not). A large part of the plan was attributable to employee contributions. The Hughes plan operated at a surplus. The employer suspended its contributions in light of the surplus. It also amended the plan to provide for early retirement benefits and to add a new benefit structure for new participants. Under the new structure, employee contributions were no longer required, because the plan was funded by the surplus from the older plan.

The Supreme Court did not accept the contention of the employee plaintiffs that the employer had an obligation to share the plan surplus with the employees who contributed to it, rather than using the surplus to reduce the employer's future obligations. In the Supreme Court's view, in a defined benefit plan, the employer assumes and also controls the risks. Any surplus can properly be used for other obligations—because the employer is always obligated to provide the vested benefits provided by the plan. In this analysis, Hughes did not violate ERISA, because it did not stop providing the vested benefits defined by the plan.

Nor did the Supreme Court accept the argument that Hughes had improperly terminated the old plan. Instead, the court permitted an amendment creating a new benefit structure (and did not treat it as the creation of a second plan) if only one pool of assets funds both obligations. Benefits continued to be paid to longer-serving employees on the basis of the original plan, so the old plan was not terminated merely because the additional benefit structure was added.

§ 4.18   PLAN LOANS

Under the right circumstances, plans are permitted to make loans to participants. These loans can be a useful resource if, for instance, a plan participant wishes to buy a house or pay a child's tuition. Loans to rank-and-file participants are usually permitted. However, a direct or indirect loan to a "party in interest" or a "disqualified person" is a prohibited transaction, unless a prohibited transaction exemption is available to justify the loan.

Under I.R.C. § 72(p), the general rule is that plan loans are treated as distributions—in other words, taxable income to the recipient. But there are certain exceptions. A loan will not be treated as a distribution if it does not exceed $50,000 or half the present value of the employee's nonforfeitable accrued benefit under the plan (whichever is less). (The employee can borrow up to $10,000, even if this amount is more than half the value of the accrued benefit.) Where the participant's account balance is the only security, the loan is theoretically not permitted to exceed half the pledged amount. The DOL Regulations dealing with plan loans do not forbid participants from borrowing funds from their accounts, pledging 50% of the account, and then taking hardship withdrawals, even though these steps have the effect of reducing the security below 50% of the account. [*See* Reg. § 2550.408-1(f)(2)]

The agreement to take a loan from the plan must call for repayment within five years, in payments made at least quarterly, with level amortization. Plans are permitted to impose variable interest rates on plan loans.

> **Tip:** BAPCA (P.L. 109-8), the 2005 bankruptcy reform statute, makes it clear that when an employee files for bankruptcy protection (even a Chapter 13 wage-earner plan), it is not a violation of the automatic stay for the employer to withhold from the employee's wages in order to repay a plan loan from a qualified plan. Plan loans do not qualify for the automatic discharge provision of Bankruptcy Code § 523, and bankruptcy plans are not permitted to materially alter the terms of a plan loan. However, amounts that an employee uses to repay plan loans are not considered "disposable income" and therefore cannot be reached by the employee's other creditors.

For reservists and National Guard members on active duty, federal law limits interest rates on all loans to the service member (including plan loans) to 6%. However, plan fiduciaries have the right to petition the relevant court to permit a higher interest rate. Under USERRA [*see* § 1.18, *infra*], a pension plan is allowed— but not obligated—to suspend the obligation to make regular repayments of plan loans during active military service.

Publicly traded companies must also be aware of the Sarbanes-Oxley Act [Pub. L. No. 107-204] ban on loans made by such companies to their directors and executive officers; this prohibition took effect on July 30, 2002, although loan arrangements already in effect on that date are exempt as long as their terms are not materially modified after July 30, 2002.

Plan loans made to parties in interest are likely also to constitute prohibited transactions for ERISA fiduciary purpose, subject to a 15% excise tax. *See* Rev. Rul. 2002-43, 2002-28 I.R.B. 85 for calculation of the excise tax if the loans are outstanding for more than one year (therefore constituting multiple prohibited transactions) and overlap the transition period when the excise tax was raised from 5% to 15%.

§4.19 EMPLOYER'S DEDUCTION

An employer that maintains a qualified defined benefit plan is entitled to deduct the greatest of these three amounts:

- The minimum funding standard as provided by I.R.C. § 412;

- The amount necessary to fund the cost of covering all the employees for their projected future service;
- The amount necessary to fund present and future costs, which may include liabilities stemming from service performed before the plan was established.

Code § 404(a)(6) permits a grace period for making pension contributions on account of a prior tax year, as long as the payment is made before the return is filed. In 2003, the Court of Federal Claims joined the Ninth and Tenth Circuits in holding that the contributions must relate to work done in the year in which the return is filed, not work done after year-end. [*Vons Co.'s Inc.*, 55 Fed. Cl. 709 (2003)]

§ 4.20   REVERSIONS

If there were no statutory ban, unscrupulous employers might raid pension assets when they needed cash, or might terminate plans merely to recoup assets or excess assets. To prevent this, defined contribution plans (including profit-sharing and stock bonus plans) usually cannot return any assets to the employer under any circumstances. Even forfeitures (amounts contributed on behalf of employees whose employment terminates before they become vested) are to be allocated to other participants in the plan.

Under appropriate circumstances, employers can receive reversions from a defined benefit plan after satisfaction of all obligations under the plan to employees. Nor may the employer lawfully transfer assets from an overfunded plan to an underfunded plan.

Internal Revenue Code § 4980 imposes an excise tax on the amount of assets reverting to an employer from a qualified plan. The tax rate, for reversions occurring after September 30, 1990, is at least 20%. The rate rises to 50% unless the employer either transfers 25% of the assets in question to a qualified replacement plan, or increases the benefits under the terminating plan to the extent of 20% of the previous benefits to participants. A qualified replacement plan covers at least 95% of the active employees from the terminated plan who continue to be employed.

§ 4.21   FORFEITURES

Depending on the plan, at least some employees—and perhaps the vast majority of the rank-and-file workforce—will terminate employment before they become vested. The contributions made on account of such employees are known as forfeitures.

Under I.R.C. §§ 401(a)(8) and 404(a)(2), defined benefit plans are required to provide that forfeitures will not be applied to increase the benefits any employee would otherwise receive. Instead, favorable plan experience when it comes to forfeitures (or mortality or employee turnover) reduces the amount the employer has to contribute to the plan. In contrast, defined contribution plans are allowed to—and usually do—allocate forfeitures to the accounts of other participants.

If someone leaves employment, and is later rehired by the same company, the eventual retirement benefit must be adjusted actuarially to reflect both periods of employment (unless the break-in-service rules make this unnecessary). Another option is for the plan to give timely notice of its provisions for suspension of benefits, so there is no forfeiture. [Treas. Reg. § 2520.203-3(b)(4)]

When an employee dies, the plan can impose forfeiture of his or her unvested benefits, except if a Qualified Preretirement Survivor Annuity (QPSA) is required. [See § 12.06]

§ 4.22   DISCRIMINATION TESTING

One of the most basic plan concepts is that a plan must be operated for the exclusive benefit of its participants and beneficiaries. Furthermore, one of the main reasons for the creation of ERISA, and its elaborate structure of rules, is to prevent plans from being administered so that company owners, or major executives, get generous benefits while rank-and-file workers get little or nothing. A qualified plan must be "tested" for "discrimination." In this context, discrimination does not mean discrimination on the basis of sex, race, nationality, and so forth; it means allowing a disproportionate share of plan benefits to go to Highly Compensated Employees (HCEs).

A pension, annuity, profit-sharing, or stock bonus plan can lawfully favor HCEs in terms of contributions or benefits, but not both. [See I.R.C. §§ 401(a)(4), 404(a)(2)] Internal Revenue Code § 414(q) says that, for plan years after 1996, an HCE is defined as someone who owned 5% or more of the employer company's stock in either the current or the preceding year—or someone whose compensation for the preceding year was at least $80,000, as adjusted for inflation. For 2002–2004, the applicable figure is $90,000; for 2005, it is $95,000; for 2006, it is $100,000.

The employer has the right to choose to use an alternative definition, under which HCEs are those who not only earn more than the amount of $80,000 as adjusted, but are also in the top 20% of earners in the company.

The Code used to contain rules called "family aggregation rules" (nicknamed "aggravation rules" because of their complexity) under which the compensation of several members of the family owning a family business had to be combined for purposes including discrimination testing. However, effective for plan years beginning on and after January 1, 1997, the family aggregation rules were abolished by the Small Business Job Protection Act (SBJPA) of 1996. [Pub. L. No. 104-188]

It does not violate the antidiscrimination rules for a plan to be "integrated" with Social Security within limits set by the "permitted disparity" rules of Code § 401(l). In effect, the employer can treat the employee's Social Security benefit (which was partially funded by the employer's FICA contributions) as part of the pension, or the employer can treat its FICA contributions as pension contributions.

The subject of discrimination testing is too complex to be fully laid out in this book. However, it should be noted that the Code includes "safe harbor" provisions for discrimination testing. Plans are not obligated to follow the safe harbor rules; they can set their own formulas. But if they do follow the safe harbor rules, they are sure not to be challenged by the IRS on this issue.

§ 4.23   LEASED EMPLOYEES

Leased employees (hired by a company from an agency that supplies workers) play a significant role in the economy. However, it is often the case that the treatment of a particular individual varies depending on the context. It is simplistic to say that a person is just an employee or a non-employee. Internal Revenue Code § 414(n) requires some people to be treated as employees eligible for plan participation even though they are formally employed by a leasing company rather than by the company for whom they perform services each day.

Section 414(n) refers to "leased employees," who are nominally employed by a "leasing organization" (e.g., an organization that furnishes temporary and contingent workers) but who "perform services" for a "service recipient." Instead of paying the leased employees directly, the service recipient pays the employees' wages (and an agency commission) to the leasing organization, which handles payroll functions including tax withholding.

However, the leased employees will be treated as employees of the service recipient when it comes to determining whether the service recipient's pension plans discriminate in favor of highly compensated employees. If the leasing organization maintains a pension plan for the employees it leases out, its contributions or benefits are treated as if they came from the service recipient for the service recipient's discrimination tests. The leasing organization's plan must count all service by leased employees for the leasing organization (even when they're leased out to a service recipient) with respect to coverage, vesting, contributions, and benefits under its own plan.

Service recipients have to count leased employees when they test their plans under the minimum participation, age and service, vesting, and top-heavy rules. They must be taken into account when computing limits on compensation and benefits and whether contributions to the plan are deductible. Furthermore, the leased employee will be treated as an employee under the Code's rules for fringe benefits such as group term life insurance, accident and health insurance, cafeteria plans, and dependent care assistance. Leased employees also have COBRA rights (they can elect continuation of health coverage).

For I.R.C. § 414(n) purposes, leased employees are those who provide services that last more than a year to a service recipient in conformity with the service recipient's agreement with the leasing organization. As a result of amendments made by the Small Business Job Protection Act of 1996, the test for 1997 and later years is whether the service recipient provides the primary direction or control for the work. (Service for related companies, such as the service recipient's controlled group of corporations, is aggregated with service for the service recipient.)

These rules relate to "substantially full-time service," which is defined as 1,500 hours of service in a 12-month period, or a job that is equivalent to 75% of the hours that the service recipient's actual employees put in during a 12-month period. In other words, after a year of the recipient's full-time work, the leased employee is treated as the service recipient's employee for pension testing purposes. However, if the worker is a common-law employee for other purposes, this safe harbor cannot apply.

Even if leased employees have to be counted in determining whether the service recipient's pension plans are discriminatory, they do not have to be offered participation in the plan until they satisfy any conditions for plan participation lawfully imposed by the plan (e.g., if the employer imposes an age-21 minimum for participation, and a leased employee starts working for the employer at age 19, completing a year of service at age 20, participation can be delayed until the leased employee reaches 21).

To qualify for the safe harbor, the service recipient must get 20% or less of its rank-and-file workforce (that is, workers who are not HCEs) through leasing—and the leasing organization must have its own qualified pension plan that fits particularly stringent criteria. The leasing organization's plan must be a money purchase plan. It must not be integrated with Social Security. The leasing organization's employees must be able to participate as soon as they are hired by the organization. They must be fully vested immediately. Furthermore, the leasing organization must contribute at least 10% of compensation for each plan participant.

Although it is good practice to have individuals you believe to be independent contractors sign waivers agreeing that they are not entitled to participate in pension and benefit plans, these waivers are not sufficient if, under otherwise applicable legal principles, they really are common-law employees. The IRS will issue determination letters as to whether contingent employees are leased employees and, if so, how it affects the plan's qualification.

Bronk v. Mountain States Telephone & Telegraph Inc. [140 F.3d 1335 (10th Cir. 1998)] holds that employees must be permitted to participate in the plan of the company that leases them, once they have satisfied the plan's age and service requirement.

However, it does not violate ERISA to draft the plan to exclude leased employees (even leased employees who count as common-law employees) from all participation. [*See* IRS Notice 84-11, Q&A 14: "[I.R.C.] § 414(n)(1)(A) requires only that a leased employee be treated as an employee; it does not require that a leased employee be a participant in the recipient's qualified plan."]

Similarly, in the view of the Eleventh Circuit [*Wolf v. Coca-Cola Co.*, 200 F.3d 1337 (11th Cir. 2000)] it is legitimate to draft a plan to exclude certain categories of employees, even if the leased employees fit the definition of common-law employees. The Eleventh Circuit didn't find it necessary to follow *Vizcaino v. Microsoft* [159 F.3d 388 (9th Cir. 1998)], because Microsoft's plan purported to cover all common-law employees. As the *Wolf* court reads it, standing to sue under ERISA requires eligibility under the plan, not just common-law employee status.

In April 2000, the IRS released a Technical Advice Memorandum (TAM) (informational memorandum that does not have the full force of a formal regulation) about workers who claim that they were inappropriately treated as independent contractors or as employees of a leasing company or professional employer organization.

As long as plan participation is limited to employees on the payroll record, coming under specified job codes or work status codes, and as long as contingent workers are fully informed that they are not entitled to plan participation, the IRS did not see any violation of I.R.C. § 410 or Treas. Reg. § 1.401(a)-3(d), even though certain workers were excluded. The plan was not ambiguous and did not give the employer inappropriate discretion to exclude workers. The IRS inquired as to whether the job categories served an independent business purpose, and found them valid. The IRS also approved a plan provision that said that workers would not be retroactively admitted to plan participation even if an administrative agency or court treated them as employees rather than contractors. The IRS treated this provision as improving the stability and predictability of the plan.

§ 4.24 COMMUNICATING WITH EMPLOYEES

The subject of communications and notification to employees rates a chapter of its own [*see* Chapter 11], so here it will merely be noted that the plan administrator is responsible for reporting and disclosure, and can be held liable if appropriate disclosures are not made.

ERISA permits three methods of communication:

- Giving each employee a copy of the plan itself;
- Giving each employee a booklet containing the Summary Plan Description (SPD), describing the features of the plan in understandable language;
- Posting a notice on the bulletin board to inform employees that the company has adopted a plan, and where copies of the plan documents can be consulted.

Nearly all plans adopt the second alternative. The actual plan document is a lengthy, highly technical legal document, and doesn't do much to inform the average employee about rights and obligations under the plan.

§ 4.25 FIDUCIARY DUTY

A fiduciary is anyone who has charge of someone else's property or finances. Fiduciaries have legal duties to act honestly, prudently, and in the best interests of the owner of the assets. Pension plan fiduciaries have a duty to invest intelligently, selecting a diversified portfolio of appropriate investments that do not involve an excessive degree of risk.

ERISA obligates fiduciaries to administer the plan exclusively in the interests of plan participants and their beneficiaries. Specifically, if there is a situation in which one strategy would be most beneficial to the participants and another strategy would be most beneficial to the corporation sponsoring the plan, the fiduciaries must choose the first course of action, not the second.

If the plan has more than one named fiduciary, they are jointly and severally liable. Someone who alleges fiduciary impropriety can sue any one fiduciary, all of them, or any combination, and can collect the entire amount of liability from each one or from any combination of fiduciaries—no matter which fiduciary was actually at fault. The harshness of this high standard is relieved somewhat by the fact that fiduciaries who are sued can bring fiduciaries who weren't sued into the lawsuit, and can make them pay their fair share.

§ 4.26 BANKRUPTCY EFFECTS

Confusion may arise because the Bankruptcy Code uses the term "plan" to refer to the reorganization plan resolving creditors' claims, and not to ERISA plans. A Chapter 11 filing, in which the debtor continues to do business while reorganizing, sometimes affects ERISA plans, and sometimes does not; it is common for employers to modify or terminate ERISA plans as part of the reorganization process. Employee benefit claims against a bankrupt employer may include unpaid wages, vacation pay, severance pay, Worker's Compensation, insurance, and retirement benefits. Claims against the bankruptcy estate for wages and pension or welfare benefits are unsecured claims, and are paid according to the Bankruptcy Code's system of priorities. First priority is given to administrative claims, including wages, salaries, and commissions for services performed after the bankruptcy filing.

Before the 2005 bankruptcy reform legislation was passed, each employee was entitled to a third priority claim of up to $4,925 for wages, salaries, commissions, vacation, sick leave, and severance pay relating to the period 90 days before the bankruptcy filing or 90 days before the cessation of the employer's business— whichever came first. The Bankruptcy Abuse Prevention and Consumer Protection Act of 2005 (BAPCPA), P.L. 109-8, increased the amount to $10,000 and the period to 180 days before the filing or cessation of business.

Defined benefit plans, including 401(k) plans, are treated the same way as other employee benefits when priorities are set, based on whether the contributions relate to pre- or post-petition services. However, to motivate employees, employers often petition the bankruptcy court for permission to make contributions that were pending at the time of filing such as deferrals withheld from paychecks but not yet deposited into the 401(k) plan trust.

Bankruptcy Code § 1114 provides special protection for retirees' non-pension benefits (health coverage, life insurance, disability insurance). In effect, they become super-priority administrative expenses and a court order is required for the debtor or bankruptcy trustee to modify them. [Kenni B. Merritt, *Employee Benefits in Bankruptcy: The Employer's Perspective and the Employee's Perspective*, Oklahoma Bar J. (January 2005) (via benefitslink.com)]

There are two kinds of bankruptcy that may have an effect on pension plans: the employer's or an employee's. If the employer is one who seeks bankruptcy protection, an argument could be made under Bankruptcy Code § 547 that the employer's contributions to a qualified plan during the 90 days before the bankruptcy filing are "preferential transfers," and therefore should be returned to the bankruptcy estate and preserved so that creditors can make claims on them.

When it comes to the employee's bankruptcy, a highly relevant case is *Patterson v. Shumate* [504 U.S. 753 (1992)], which provides that ERISA plan law constitutes "applicable non-bankruptcy law" that will permit amounts in the plan to be excluded from the bankruptcy estate. The Supreme Court also held, in its 2005 *Rousey v. Jacoway* decision (544 U.S. 320), that IRAs are more akin to qualified plans than bank accounts from which withdrawals may be freely made. Therefore, the Supreme Court extended the exemption of qualified plans from the bankruptcy estate to IRAs. BAPCA contains a number of provisions affecting both employer and employee bankruptcies:

- Makes the employee's interest in qualified plans and IRAs exempt from the bankruptcy estate. The IRA exemption (which includes both conventional and Roth IRAs) is limited to $1 million—but the $1 million figure does not include amounts rolled over into an IRA from a qualified plan
- As noted above, limits severance and retention payments to corporate insiders and makes it easier for the business' bankruptcy trustee to set aside preferential payments made to insiders
- Increases the employer's ability to continue to collect repayments of plan loans from employees who have sought bankruptcy protection
- Gives the bankruptcy court the power to cancel the employer's modifications of its retiree health benefits made during 180 days before filing of a bankruptcy petition, although if the court is persuaded that the balance of equities favors leaving the modifications in place, they can be affirmed.

Internal Revenue Code § 401(a)(33) forbids certain plan amendments if the plan is covered by ERISA § 4021. Plan benefits may not be increased while the plan sponsor is a bankruptcy debtor. The plan cannot be amended to increase the plan's liabilities because of an increase in benefits, any change in the accrual of benefits, or any change in the rate at which benefits become nonforfeitable. The ban applies only if the amendments in question take effect before the effective date of the employer's plan of reorganization.

The restrictions do not apply if the plan would otherwise have a funded current liability percentage of at least 100%; if the IRS determines that the amendment is reasonable and increases benefits only slightly; or if the amendment is actually required to conform to changes in tax law.

§ 4.27   FACTORS IN CHOOSING A PLAN FORM

In deciding which form of plan to adopt, or whether to convert a plan or terminate an old plan and adopt a new one, the employer must balance many considerations, including financial and tax factors and the expected effect of a plan in motivating employee behavior (including retiring at the time most convenient for the employer).

Participants in a defined benefit plan know what their eventual pension will be if they stay with the plan until normal retirement age. If they terminate employment earlier, the vesting rules also control the size of the pension that will be paid later on, when they reach retirement age. This degree of certainty is valuable, but retirees have the problems caused by having a fixed income that does not reflect investment results.

In contrast, defined contribution plan participants know how large their account is at any given time. They can make projections of how large it will grow, based on predictions about interest rates and stock market trends. Market risk shifts from the employer to the employee and future retiree. Defined contribution plans also offer more portability: the contents of the employee's account from Plan A can simply be rolled over to Plan B when the employee stops being a Company A employee and is hired by Company B.

Defined benefit, but not defined contribution plans, are covered by the Pension Benefit Guaranty Corporation (PBGC)'s insurance program. The PBGC insures that employees will receive their pension benefits, at least the part that does not exceed a maximum figure. In exchange, employers must pay insurance premiums to the PBGC. If an underfunded defined benefit plan is terminated, the PBGC takes over part of the obligation to pay benefits. Some participants lose their pensions in this situation; some receive less than the normal amount.

In 2006, the federal Department of Energy announced that it would reimburse its contractors for the cost of maintaining defined contribution plans, but would no longer pay for defined benefit plan costs. Nearly 100,000 companies are DoE contractors. The agency's rationale is that defined benefit plans are more costly, so supporting defined contribution plans would reduce the cost of the work to the taxpayers. [Rebecca Moore, *Energy Dep't Cuts Contractor Pension Cost Coverage*, PlanSponsor.com (May 4, 2006)] In mid-2006, however, the agency suspended the enforcement of the policy for a year, with the reversal taking effect immediately. [Rebecca Moore, *Energy Department Reverses Decision to Cut Pension Benefits*, PlanSponsor.com June 20, 2006]

§ 4.28   STRATEGIES FOR REDUCING PENSION COSTS

Large companies have devised strategies for reducing pension obligations by reducing future accruals without unlawfully reducing benefits that have already accrued. For instance, if a plan is frozen, additional service does not increase the benefit. Freezing can make an underfunded plan compliant, or even overfunded.

Companies interested in reducing pension costs can cap the number of years of service that will be counted toward a pension. The benefit can be based on high-five, last-five, last-10, or career-average compensation instead of high-three, which tends to result in a larger pension obligation. Plans can reduce the "multiplier" (i.e., set the pension as x% rather than x.5% of the chosen compensation figure, per year of service). [*See also* Chapter 7 for a discussion of cash balance plans, which tend to have the same effect as using a career average computation, thereby reducing the employer's obligation. *See also* Ellen S. Schultz, *Pension Cuts 101: Companies Find Host of Subtle Ways to Pare Retirement Payouts*, Wall Street Journal, July 27, 2000, at p. A1]

A number of companies, not necessarily those in financial trouble, froze their pension plans (i.e., ceased making contributions); "grandfathered" in current workers, but announced that new hires would not be covered by the pension plan; or excluded workers under 40 from plan participation. (Workers over 40 can sue under the ADEA, so they were generally spared.) Pension freezes are not a "reportable event" that must be disclosed to the PBGC, so there are no official figures on the prevalence of this tactic. Unless the freeze violates a collective bargaining agreement, employers are free to take this step at their discretion. For accounting purposes, a freeze reduces the amount that must be carried on the books as liability for future payments, so it gives rise to accounting gains that are treated as income. The amount increases when (as is now true) interest rates are low because low interest rates require maintenance of large reserves to satisfy future obligations. *See* § 5.05[L] for more discussion of plan freezes.

For example, Hewlett-Packard announced that it would freeze pension benefits based on age and tenure in 2007. Benefits would remain intact for those whose age plus years of service added up to 62 or more. For everyone else, they would keep their existing balances, but there would be no further accruals. Sears announced a freeze in 2006 that applied to all employees. Previously, companies that froze their pension plans often did so in conjunction with the adoption of a cash balance plan, but given the current uncertainty about the legal status of the cash balance plan, some companies are moving to a defined contribution plan, eliminating future accruals altogether. [Ellen E. Schultz, Charles Forelle, and Theo Francis, *Forecast: More Pension Freezes,* Wall Street Journal, Jan. 12, 2006, at p. C1; Kaja Whitehouse, *Companies Lock Younger Workers Out of Pensions*, Wall Street Journal, July 26, 2005, at p. D2]

CHAPTER 5

DEFINED BENEFIT PLANS

§5.01   INTRODUCTION

This chapter deals, in detail, with issues that are specific to defined benefit plans. *See* Chapter 4 for background issues on pensions, Chapter 6 for defined contribution plans and 401(k) plans, and Chapter 7 for cash balance plans.

The PBGC publishes its Data Book in late March each year. The Data Book explains the agency's operations, financial condition, and who is entitled to receive benefits from the PBGC, which now covers about 34.6 million workers and retirees in close to 30,000 defined benefit plans. Single copies of the Data Book can be ordered from PBGC Data Book, Suite 240, 1200 K Street NW, Washington, D.C. 20005-4026.

IRS Announcement 2005-80, 2005-46 I.R.B. 967, lists § 412(i) defined benefit plans and 20 other tax-saving devices. The IRS wants some users of these devices to contact the agency, surrender the improper tax benefits, and in some cases pay penalties. The devices in question include some Roth IRA transactions, Charitable Remainder Trust distributions, and ESOPs. Section 412(i) plans often use annuity contracts or life insurance policies with a guaranteed return to fund defined benefit plans because the guaranteed return simplifies reporting. Furthermore, because in many cases the guaranteed rate of return is under 3%, older business owners with high incomes can deduct very large annual contributions. The IRS says that 412(i) programs targeted for settlement are those in which the accumulated plan assets are greater than the benefits payable; if the death benefits from the life insurance policies in the plan are greater than the benefits specified in the plan documents; or if participants have greatly unequal rights to buy life insurance contracts under the plan. The IRS intends to impose 5% or 10% penalties on the improper vehicles, but penalties will be waived for taxpayers who relied on a favorable written opinion from an independent tax advisor who was not involved in the marketing of the shelter. [<http://www.irs.gov/pub/irs-drop/a-05-80.pdf>; discussed in Allison Bell, *Settlement Offer Could Affect Small DB Pension Plans,* NU Online News Service (Oct. 28, 2005)]

§5.02   BENEFIT LIMITS

The limit on the maximum benefit that anyone can receive from a qualified defined benefit plan in a year is set by I.R.C. § 415(b)(1). At first, the limit was set at $90,000 a year, with provision for inflation adjustment. EGTRRA raised the annual benefit limit to $160,000, to be indexed for inflation in minimum increments of $5,000. This amount did not change in 2003, but rose to $165,000 for 2004, $170,000 for 2005, and $175,000 for 2006. No matter how much a person earns, only $220,000 per year in compensation (2006 amount) can be taken into account when calculating the benefit under a defined benefit plan. For 2006, a "highly compensated employee" under § 414(q)(1) is one who earns $100,000 or more, and a "key employee" in a top-heavy plan is one who earns more than $140,000. [IR-2005-120 (Oct. 14, 2005)]

However, EGTRRA—like many complex pieces of legislation—had some unintended effects. "Technical corrections" are laws adopted to clarify difficult points or remove such unintended effects. In defined benefit plans that incorporate the legal limitations by reference, the effect of EGTRRA could be to increase the benefit automatically, even if this was not what the employer wanted to do. [*See* Rev. Rul. 2001-51, 2001-45 I.R.B. 427]

A bill signed into federal law on March 9, 2002, the Job Creation and Worker Assistance Act of 2002 (JCWAA) [Pub. L. No. 107-147] makes it clear that amendments adopted before June 30, 2002, to "freeze" the defined benefit at its pre-EGTRRA level, will be legitimate and will not be considered a forbidden cutback in benefit levels. The JCWAA also provides that if an employer has both a defined benefit plan and a 401(k) plan containing only elective deferrals (no employer matches), the limitation on benefits under overlapping plans. I.R.C. § 404(a)(7)) does not apply. [For more information about the JCWAA, *see, e.g.,* <http://www.cyberisa.com/erisa_new_current.htm> and <http://benefitsattorney. com/child/stimulus1.html> (no www)]

§ 5.03   BENEFIT FORMS FOR DEFINED BENEFIT PLANS

All pension plans must provide the basic payment form: a life annuity for single participants, and a QJSA (qualified joint and survivor annuity) for married participants. The basic form of QJSA provides a certain level of benefits while both the former employee and spouse are still alive. When one of them dies, the payment is cut in half, because only one person remains to be supported. Although employers are allowed to offer 50% survivor annuities, they are also allowed to subsidize the survivor annuity so that it is more than 50% of the initial payment, or even so that the payment does not decline when one payee dies.

Internal Revenue Code § 401(a)(25) says that a plan that provides for alternative benefit forms (annuity, installment, lump sum, early retirement) must specify, in a definite form that precludes employer discretion, what actuarial assumptions (such as interest rates and mortality assumptions) are used to calculate equivalencies among different benefit forms. This disclosure obligation does not, however, extend to the plan's funding assumptions.

In a flat benefit plan, the pension is defined as a certain number of dollars per month, or a percentage of average annual compensation or average compensation for the "high three" years. A unit benefit plan defines the pension as compensation times years of participation times a percentage rate. Some plans of this type increase the accrual rate in later years, or are calculated using a "high five" or "final average pay" (the average of the last three years of work, when presumably earnings will be at their peak).

Tip: Rev. Rul. 2002-84, 2002-50 I.R.B. 953 provides instruction for retiree taxpayers who receive a mistaken overpayment from a defined benefit plan, when the overpayment is recouped by the plan in later years.

See 69 Fed. Reg. 13769 (Mar. 24, 2004) for procedures for reducing the number of benefit forms (e.g., when the plan offers redundant benefits forms or numerous forms, some of which are seldom elected and are hard to administer), provided that the core benefit forms remain available to participants.

Final Regulations were published under § 411(d)(6) on August 11, 2005, further explaining the benefits and payment forms that can be eliminated from defined benefit plans. The IRS also published proposals in the same document, allowing elimination of benefits that fail a utilization test. The Final Regulations largely reflect the Proposed Regulations.

Under the Final Regulations, the sponsor of a defined benefit plan can eliminate an optional benefit after 90 days if the benefit is redundant. Any benefit outside the core options can be eliminated after four years. The core options are defined as the straight life annuity; the 75% joint and contingent annuity; the 50%/100% joint and contingent annuity; the 10-year certain and life annuity; and an option such as a lump sum or a survivor annuity that would be valuable for a participant with a short life expectancy. A benefit is redundant if an option in the same benefit family is retained and the participant's rights with respect to the retained benefit are not subject to materially greater restrictions than the restrictions that applied to the benefits that were eliminated. There are six benefit "families" describing different types of payments (e.g., a 50% joint and contingent annuity; level installment payments lasting 10 years or less). Core benefits are benefits such as lump sums that do not fit into any of the families.

The Final Regulations limit the elimination of options where the retained benefit, or any core benefit under the core benefit rule, has a different annuity starting date or a lower actuarial present value than the benefits that were eliminated—the plan sponsor must show that administering the eliminated benefit was unduly burdensome, and its elimination has no effect, or only a de minimis effect. As an anti-abuse measure, the Final Rule forbids multiple amendments (i.e., a series of amendments that, construed together, reduce or eliminate a protected benefit in a forbidden manner). The Proposed Regulations would allow elimination of any benefit that is not a core option and was never elected by anyone even though it was available to at least 100 participants in a two-year look-back period. For smaller plans, the look-back period might have to be extended to three or five years. [T.D. 9219, 2005-38 I.R.B. 538]

IRS Regulations proposed at 70 Fed. Reg. 31214 (May 31, 2005) unify and systematize the § 415 rules, explaining how to calculate the maximum permitted benefit when a retiree has multiple annuity start dates and how to calculate qualified joint and survivor annuities when the benefit is partly taken as a lump sum and partly in annuity form.

In response to comments, the IRS somewhat modified the rules about required minimum distributions from defined benefit plans (and defined contribution plans that handle distributions by purchasing annuities): 69 Fed. Reg. 33288 (June 15, 2004). These Final Regulations explain the types of increases in benefits (e.g., COLAs, benefit increases pursuant to plan amendments; return of employee contributions when the employee dies) that will be permitted. The form of the distribution can be changed for annuities that do not have a life contingency; and an employee who marries can change to a QJSA. When a plan terminates, or when an employee actually retires, the form of distribution can be changed prospectively— even if another form of payment was used pre-retirement or before the plan terminated. *See* Chapter 12 for more detailed discussion of plan distribution issues.

§ 5.04   MORTALITY TABLES

Before 2002, the IRS required defined benefit plans to use the 1983 Group Annuity Mortality (83GAM) table for making the actuarial calculations for the value of accrued benefits. [I.R.C. § 417(e)] The mortality tables must be used to make sure that the value of a lump sum benefit is at least as great as the predicted value of an annuity.

Defined benefit plans also have to calculate adjustments of the plan limitations, as required by I.R.C. § 415(b), when the benefit under the plan is paid in any form other than a QJSA, or when the employee retires before age 62 or after age 65.

However, Rev. Rul. 2001-62, 2001-53 I.R.B. 632 requires plans to switch to the 1994 Group Annuity Reserving (94GAR) table no later than for distributions with an annuity starting date on or after December 31, 2002. For nearly all participants, the new mortality table will require greater benefits for employees. The Ruling contains two model plan amendments that can be used to bring the plan into conformity.

Legislation has been introduced in Congress to require defined benefit plans to change their mortality assumptions, using the Society of Actuaries' Retired Pensioners Mortality Table 2 (RP-2000), which reflects mortality experience from the years 1990 to 1994. The proposal would also require the Treasury to update the table every 10 years. RP-2000, unlike the static GAM83, is a "generational mortality table" that assumes that life expectancy will continue to increase. Greater life expectancies make life annuities more expensive and therefore increase plans' pension liabilities.

See also RIN 1212-AA55, the PBGC's mortality rates for determining the present value of annuities purchased to fund employee benefits in involuntary or distress termination of a single-employer plan in 2006. The figures reflect the adoption of the 1994 Group Annuity Mortality Tables to replace the 1983 tables previously used by the PBGC. [<http://www.pbgc.gov/practitioners/Mortality-Table/content/page15511.html>]

§ 5.05   FUNDING THE DEFINED BENEFIT PLAN

[A]   Minimum Funding Standard

The process of funding a defined contribution plan is quite simple. The employer simply determines a percentage of compensation, and as long as the contribution does not exceed the Code maximum, then there are no further problems. No discretion is involved.

In contrast, funding a defined benefit plan requires subtle decisions about long-range economic and employment trends in order to deposit enough money to yield the correct stream of future benefits to plan participants and their beneficiaries.

Defined benefit, money purchase, and target benefit plans (but not profit-sharing plans, stock bonus plans, or plans under I.R.C. § 412(i) that are exclusively funded by the purchase of individual insurance or annuity contracts) are subject to a "minimum funding" requirement under I.R.C. § 412.

The IRS proposed regulations, affecting Code § 411(d)(6), at 69 Fed. Reg. 13769 (Mar. 24, 2004). This Code provision contains the "anti-cutback rule" forbidding elimination or reduction of accrued benefits. However, de minimis changes, such as elimination of minor and seldom-elected benefit forms, is permissible. Under this proposal, there are six basic families of optional benefit forms. Within a family, redundant methods can be eliminated, as long as some core options are retained, and as long as the changes do not affect annuity starting dates within 90 days after the amendment is adopted. As long as the core options designated by the IRS are retained, and the amendment does not take effect for start dates within four years of the adoption of the amendment, it is permissible to amend the plan to eliminate an optional form of benefits.

For this purpose, the core options are the straight life annuity, the 75% joint and survivor annuity, the annuity for life or 10 years certain, and the most valuable option that the plan provides for a participant with a short life expectancy.

> **Tip:** As a general rule, this procedure cannot be used to eliminate a lump-sum optional benefit.

An excise tax of 10% is imposed by I.R.C. § 4971 for failure to meet the minimum funding standard. The excise tax rises to 100% of any deficiency that remains uncorrected a reasonable time after the plan receives notice of deficiency from the IRS.

Rev. Rul. 2003-88, 2003-32 I.R.B. 192, provides that if Form 5330 or a statement attached to it discloses an accumulated funding deficiency or an unpaid liquidity shortfall, the statute of limitations for imposing the § 4971 excise tax is three years from the filing of the Form 5330. If disclosure is not made, the statute of limitations is six years. Either statute of limitations can be extended by agreement of the taxpayer. The statute of limitations is determined without reference to whether or not the accumulated funding deficiency or unpaid liquidity shortfall is disclosed on the plan's Form 5500.

According to the Supreme Court case, *United States v. Reorganized CF&I Fabricators of Utah Inc.* [518 U.S. 213 (1996)], the 100% assessment is a penalty (and therefore an ordinary unsecured claim) and not an excise tax entitled to seventh priority, if the company subject to it files for bankruptcy protection.

Underfunding has other implications. If the plan is covered by PBGC insurance, the PBGC must be notified whenever the minimum funding standard is not met. If the plan is terminated [*see* Chapter 17], then underfunding can make the plan liable to the PBGC for accumulated funding deficiencies.

However, complying with the minimum funding standard doesn't solve all of the employer's problems, because I.R.C. § 4972 also imposes an excise tax on excess contributions to a defined benefit plan.

Therefore, the employer should make sure that its contributions to the defined benefit plan fall within the acceptable range. Contributions should not be small enough to constitute underfunding—especially not small enough to trigger PBGC termination of the plan. But the employer will not want to contribute more than can be deducted, and will particularly want to avoid the excise tax on excess contributions.

For plan years 2004–2005 only, the Pension Funding Equity Act of 2004, Pub. L. 108-218, adopts the approach of using a weighted corporate bond average instead of the 30-year Treasury rates in funding calculations.

Underfunding is intimately related to plan "freezes," where employers amend the plan to alter future accruals. There is no single statutory definition of the term. In commonly used parlance, in a "soft freeze," accruals are terminated based on years of service, so benefits continue to increase based on increases in participants' compensation. A "hard freeze," however, stops all benefit accruals. Plan sponsors also have the option of freezing the plan only as to certain groups of workers, or closing the plan to new participants while maintaining it for those who are "grandfathered in." PBGC guidelines about voluntary terminations identify a freeze as an acceptable alternative to termination under certain circumstances—for instance, where the plan is not fully funded and the sponsor can no longer afford the full cost, but cannot perform a voluntary termination for lack of assets to cover all the liabilities. Plans may also be frozen when termination at a later time is planned. *See* § 5.05[L].

[B] Deduction Limit

The funding standard serves another purpose: it sets an upper limit on the amount that the employer can deduct under I.R.C. § 404. If the employer overstates its pension liabilities by 200% or more, and therefore takes too large a deduction, with the result that its income taxes are underpaid by 20% or more, then a 20% accuracy-related underpayment penalty can be imposed under I.R.C. § 6662. The penalty will be suspended if the pension overstatement was less than $1,000, or if the plan relied on substantial authority such as Revenue Rulings or IRS Notices.

EGTRRA, the tax law passed in 2001, allows all defined benefit plans to deduct contributions to the plan that do not exceed the plan's unfunded current liability—even if they are greater than the FFL. Before EGTRRA, this provision was limited to plans with more than 100 participants; EGTRRA § 652(a) extended it to all defined benefit plans, adding § 404(a)(1)(D)(i) to the Code for this purpose. In order to encourage adequate funding of plans, EGTRRA § 653(a) allows the employer to make nondeductible contributions that do not exceed the accrued liability full-funding limitation for the plan.

Pensions are a form of deferred compensation, and any form of compensation is deductible only if it is reasonable and constitutes an ordinary and necessary business expense. Part of the compensation of particularly highly-paid employees may have to be disregarded for certain tax-related purposes.

For example, under I.R.C. § 401(a)(17) only $200,000 of compensation (adjusted for inflation in increments of $5,000) can be taken into account. EGTRRA increased this amount from $150,000 (adjusted for inflation; and it rose to $210,000 in 2005 and $220,000 in 2006). Even legitimate compensation may have to be deducted over a span of several years, not all at once. Employee compensation (including benefits and retirement plan costs) must be capitalized under I.R.C. § 263A if it is incurred in connection with production or purchase for resale of either real property or tangible personal property.

There are further requirements under I.R.C. § 404, a section included in the Code to distinguish pension and annuity plans from profit-sharing and stock bonus plans. Under I.R.C. § 404(a), the plan must have been in existence by the end of the employer's tax year for the employer to be able to deduct the contribution in the year it was made. Note that not only are plan sponsors subject to excise tax penalties if they fail to contribute enough to the plan, they are also subject to excise tax, under I.R.C. § 4972, for excess contributions.

[C] Calculating the Contribution

To set the employer's contribution level, the actuary for a defined benefit plan can use either of two basic methods (each of which has variations).

The accrued benefit method, which is also called the unit credit cost method, defines the plan liabilities on the basis of benefits that accrue in that particular year. The projected benefit cost method calculates benefits on the assumption that benefits accrue as long as a person remains a participant in the plan. ERISA § 3(31) defines variations on the projected cost method, including the entry age normal method, aggregate cost method, attained age normal cost method, and frozen initial liability cost method.

The contribution for each participant has two aspects: normal cost and supplemental liability. The normal cost for each participant is the actuarial value of the benefit units assigned for that year. The supplemental liability covers benefits for service before adoption of the plan, or between the time the plan was adopted and the time it is amended to increase coverage.

[D] Minimum Funding Standard Account

A "minimum funding standard account" must be maintained in all plan years until the end of the year in which the plan terminates. [*See* I.R.C. § 412(b) and ERISA § 302(b)] The minimum funding standard is met when there is no accumulated funding deficiency at the end of the year. There is no deficiency if, for all plan years, the credits to the funding standard account are at least equal to the total charges.

The minimum funding standard account consists of charges for normal costs, past service liabilities, experience losses in investments, and funding deficiencies. The general rule is that experience losses and funding deficiencies have to be amortized, not deducted currently. The charges to the account are offset by credits for, e.g., the employer's contributions to the plan, investment experience gains, and funding deficiencies that are waived by the IRS.

Internal Revenue Code § 412(l) imposes additional obligations on single-employer plans with 100 or more participants whose "funded current liability" percentage falls below 80% for the current year when it was below 90% for the preceding year. The funded current liability percentage equals the value of the plan assets divided by current liabilities. The underfunded plans are obligated to notify their participants and beneficiaries of the funding deficiency, and must pay an additional PBGC premium. In egregious cases, the PBGC may be able to bring a civil suit against the plan.*

> **Tip:** If assets and liabilities of one plan are spun off to another plan, a separate funding standard account should be maintained for each plan, and adjustments will have to be made with respect to the spun-off assets and liabilities.

[E] Full Funding Limitation

An excise tax might be imposed whenever the employer's contribution falls below the plan's "full funding limitation" (FFL). The excise tax will not be imposed if the contribution is greater than the FFL, even if the funding standard account shows a deficit for the year. The employer's income tax deduction for plan contributions can never be more than the FFL. At all times, the FFL must be at least equal to 90% of the plan's current liability.

The FFL is a formula that can be expressed as A–B. A is the lower of the accrued liability or a percentage of the current liability. B is either the fair market value of the plan assets or the value of the assets calculated based on the I.R.C. § 412(c)(2) fixed debt obligation, whichever is lower. The "current liability" means all liabilities to participants and beneficiaries. However, "unpredictable contingent events" can be left out of the calculation.

The percentage used to calculate factor A was set at 150% for plan years beginning before 1998. The Taxpayer Relief Act of 1997 set up a new schedule.

For plan years that begin within the calendar years 1999 or 2000, the limit is 155%, rising to 160% for plan years beginning within calendar 2001. Then EGTRRA made further changes. The applicable percentage is 165% in 2002 and 170% in 2003. Between 2004 and 2010 (the year in which all EGTRRA provisions expire unless Congress renews them), the percentage test is abolished. At that point, the FFL will be the difference between the plan's accrued liability (including normal cost) and the value of the plan's assets.

[F] Funding Procedures

Actual funding of the plan is done by the employer's contributing cash, non-cash property, or its own securities. The valuation of cash is simple; for property and securities, it can be difficult. The prohibited transaction rules [*see* 8.03] must be consulted to make sure that contributions do not violate these rules. Wherever possible, transactions should be structured so that the plan trust will not have Unrelated Business Taxable Income (UBTI). In general, plan trusts are not subject to income tax—unless they have unrelated income.

Wherever possible, the employer should avoid contributing depreciated property to the plan. That's because I.R.C. § 267(b)(4) provides that the employer will have taxable gain (capital or ordinary, depending on the facts) if it contributes appreciated property to the plan. But losses on contributions of depreciated property are not recognized, because there is a transfer between the trust grantor and the trust's fiduciary.

Tip: An employer that wants to use depreciated property in funding can sell the property to a third party, recognize the tax loss, then contribute the cash proceeds of the sale.

The plan will have to make quarterly payments to fund plan liability. [*See* I.R.C. § 412 and ERISA § 302] For a calendar-year plan, the due dates are April 15, July 15, October 15, and January 15 of the following year. Note that these are not the same dates as the corporation's estimated income tax payments.

Fiscal year plans modify this schedule. For instance, the dates are advanced by three months for a plan with a fiscal year ending March 31 (three months after the end of a calendar year).

Quarterly payments will be excused if the funded current liability percentage for the prior plan year was 100% or more. The purpose of the quarterly payments is to make sure that the employer contributes at least 90% of the I.R.C. § 412 funding limit for the year, or 100% of the funding liability for the preceding year (whichever is less).

If the funded current liability percentage fell below 100% in the preceding year, failure to pay a quarterly installment on time will obligate the sponsor to pay interest to the plan. Plans with more than 100 participants must include any liquidity shortfall in the quarterly payment, even if this increases the size of the payment that would otherwise have to be made.

The liquidity shortfall equals the base amount minus the plan's liquid assets on the last day of the quarter. The base amount, in turn, equals three times the adjusted disbursements from the plan for the 12 months ending on the last day of the quarter. There is also a 10% excise tax on liquidity shortfall that is not paid for any quarter as it comes due, rising to 100% of the unpaid amount if the shortfall is not paid for any quarter followed by the next four consecutive quarters. The IRS has the power to waive part or all of this I.R.C. § 4971(f)(4) excise tax if the sponsor had reasonable cause to miss the payment, was not guilty of willful neglect, and has taken appropriate steps to remedy the shortfall.

The I.R.C. § 412(e) amortization period (the time to amortize the unfunded liability) can be extended by the Secretary of Labor for a period of up to 10 years. Rev. Proc. 2004-44, 2004-31 I.R.B. 134, details the procedure for a sponsor or plan administrator to get the extension. The request must be signed by the taxpayer maintaining the plan, or an authorized representative such as an enrolled actuary. IRS Form 2848 (power of attorney) must be filed if the authorized representative signs. The request for the extension is considered a request for a ruling, and so must satisfy the requirements for getting a ruling. The applicant must document why the extension is necessary to continue the plan or prevent a substantial cutback in the levels of employee compensation or pension benefits. Information must be provided, e.g., financial reports and other basic information about the plan; how long an extension is sought; and the size of the unfunded liability. Extension requests should be submitted by the last day of the plan year for which the extension is supposed to take effect, although later applications can be considered if good cause is shown to excuse the delay.

Because it can be difficult to provide enough evidence in support of a request before the plan year has ended, Rev. Proc. 2004-44 suggests that requests generally should not be made more than 180 days before the end of the plan year for which the extension is requested. The Revenue Procedure has two appendixes: a Model Notice informing unions and the participants, beneficiaries, and alternate payees of the plan that an extension application has been made, informing them that they can send relevant information to the IRS; and a checklist for determining whether the submission to the IRS is complete.

On March 31, 2006, FASB released an Exposure Draft, *Employers' Accounting for Defined Benefit and Other Postretirement Plans*, No. 1025-300, amending FASB Statements Nos. 87, 88, 106, and 132(R). If the proposal is adopted, the funding status of a defined benefit pension plan would be the difference between the fair market value of the plan's assets and the projected benefit obligation; for a retiree health plan, the relevant figure would be the accumulated postretirement benefit obligation. Thus, an overfunded plan would be recorded as an asset, while an underfunded plan would be recorded as a liability.

FASB announced the proposal out of a concern that current reporting mechanisms make it possible for corporations to understate the true extent of their future responsibilities for defined benefit pensions and for retiree health benefits. The date for calculating pension fund values would be the same as the date for calculating other corporate obligations, such as the employer's statement of financial position (current rules allow a gap of up to three months, which can result in better results for the pension plan if the market turns up in the interval). The proposal was immediately criticized on the grounds that it would require such large expenses to be disclosed in the balance sheet (rather than, as under current rules, in the notes to the financial statement) and that many corporations would have no balance-sheet net worth for reporting purposes. However, most corporations would not experience changes in their pension and retiree health expenses on the income statement. The proposal applies to both public and closely held corporations. FASB said that because the necessary information must already be collected to draft the notes in the financial statement, the cost of compliance would be minor. [<http://www.fasb.org/draft/ed_pension&postretirement_plans. pdf>; *see, e.g.,* Aon Consulting Alert, *FASB to Change Employers' Balance Sheet for Pensions and Retiree Health Benefits in 2006,* <http://www.aon.com/ alert_4_5_06.pdf> (Apr. 5, 2006); Mary Williams Walsh, *Shocks Seen in New Math for Pensions,* New York Times, Mar. 31, 2006, at p. C1; Rebecca Moore, *FASB Issues Proposed Accounting Changes for Pensions and OPEB,* PlanSponsor.com (Mar. 31, 2006)]

[G] Liens Based on Funding Failures

Under I.R.C. § 412(n), a lien can be imposed against the employer, and in favor of the plan subject to PBGC jurisdiction, if the employer fails to make a required contribution to the plan when it is due.

> **Tip:** The person responsible for making the payment that was missed has an obligation to inform the PBGC within 10 days of the due date that the payment was missed.

The lien covers all of the employer's real and personal property. The lien can be imposed if the plan's funded current liability percentage fell below 100% and the unpaid balance, plus interest, was more than $1 million. It starts on the date the payment should have been made, and runs to the end of the plan year in which the liabilities go over the $1 million mark.

The PBGC can sue in federal district court under ERISA § 4003(e)(1) to enforce the lien against the employer. This power can be exercised at any time until three years after the PBGC knew or should have known of the failure to make the necessary payment (extended to six years if the employer committed fraud or concealment), or for six years after the due date from the payment.

[H] Plan Valuation Issues

An actuarial valuation must be performed at least once a year to determine the assets, liabilities, and contribution level for plans subject to I.R.C. § 412. (EGTRRA gives the Treasury the power to adopt regulations that call for even more frequent valuations.) The information is also used to prepare the Schedule B for the 5500-series form.

The basic factors in setting assumptions include:

- Employee compensation;
- Early retirement rate;
- Employee turnover;
- Disability and mortality rates (both before and after retirement);
- (For QJSAs) Life expectancy of employees' spouses;
- Expected percentage return on the plan's investments (interest assumptions may have to be adjusted in the future to reflect the plan's investment record);
- Administrative expenses, defined either as dollars per participant or a reduction in the plan's rate of return.

Within the limits set by I.R.C. § 412 and other relevant provisions, the size of the contribution can be increased or decreased somewhat based on corporate needs. However, the plan's actuarial assumptions must always be reasonable—each individual assumption, not just the aggregate. Courts have the power to overturn a plan's actuarial assumptions, even if the assumptions are not unreasonable. This is especially likely to happen if the plan has applied its own assumptions inconsistently.

Tip: In general, the valuation date has to be within the plan year for which the assets are being valued, or within a month before the start of the plan year—but EGTRRA § 661(a) creates an exception under which the valuation date can sometimes be in the previous year. This exception can only be used if the plan assets, valued as of the prior plan year's date, is at least 125% of the plan's current liability.

ERISA § 302(c) provides that a plan covered by PBGC termination insurance requires IRS approval to change its actuarial assumptions, if the aggregated unfunded vested benefits of all underfunded plans maintained by the employer, or members of the same controlled group, exceed $50 million. Approval for the change is also required if the change in the assumptions raises the unfunded cumulative liability for the current plan year by more than $50 million, or more than $5 million, if this is 5% or more of the current liability.

[I] Interest Rates

Internal Revenue Code § 412(l)(7)(C)(i) sets the parameters for the interest rates used to determine the employer's contributions and the plan's current liability.

The Department of the Treasury has the power to issue Regulations that lower the permissible range [*see* I.R.C. § 412(b)(5)] but it is not allowed to fall beneath 80% of the weighted 30-year average Treasury rate.

Factors in the interest rate assumption include:

- The economic components of interest rates;
- Current long-term interest rates;
- The plan's individual actuarial and investment factors;
- Long-range economic trends, especially in the money supply and interest rates throughout the economy. For plan years 2004 and 2005, the Pension Funding Equity Act of 2004 (Pub. L. 108-218) provides that the permissible range is between 90% and 100% of the weighted average rate of interest on investment-grade corporate bonds; the Treasury Department will calculate and publish the relevant rates.

[J] Funding Changes

Rev. Procs. 2000-40 and -41, 2000-42 I.R.B. 357 and 371, provide the procedures under which the sponsor or administrator of a defined benefit plan subject to I.R.C. § 412 or ERISA § 302 can get the Secretary of the Treasury to approve a change in the plan's funding method under I.R.C. § 412(c)(5)(A):

- A shift from the entry age normal method to the unit credit method of complying with the minimum funding obligation;
- Setting the normal cost level as a dollar amount instead of a level percentage of compensation under the aggregate method;
- Changing the method of valuing assets;
- Changing the valuation date from the first day of the plan year to the last day;
- Changing the plan year (which has the incidental effect of changing the valuation date);
- Changing the software used to perform valuation, if this changes the actual computations;
- Changing the method of determining the cost of ancillary benefits.

The IRS has jurisdiction to review the appropriateness of any change that significantly affects the plan's minimum funding requirement or full funding limitation. The agency will approve a change in funding method only if the proposed new method and the form of the transition are both acceptable.

Requests for change should be directed to the IRS Commissioner, TE/GE Attention: T:EP:RA P.O. Box 27063 McPherson Station, Washington, D.C. 20038. The due date is the end of the plan year in which the change will be effective. The IRS has discretion to extend the due date by up to two and a half months if the plan submits a statement giving adequate reason for the delay.

[K] Minimum Funding Waivers

What can a company do if it is unable to satisfy its funding obligations and meet other business debts? ERISA and the Code give the employer various options. It may be possible to amend the plan retroactively to reduce the accrued benefits. [*See* I.R.C. § 412(c)(8)] DOL and the IRS might grant a variance from the minimum funding standards. The amortization periods used in the funding standard account can be extended. The funding method can be changed.

Internal Revenue Code § 412(d) allows employers to apply for a waiver of the minimum funding standard in any year. The due date for the application is the fifteenth day of the third month after the end of the plan year for which the waiver is requested. To get a waiver, the employer must show that meeting the standard would create "temporary substantial business hardship." The IRS considers factors such as conditions in the employer's industry, if the employer has an operating loss, and whether the plan can continue without a waiver.

A retroactive plan amendment can be adopted within two and a half months after the close of the plan year, with the effect of reducing benefits that accrued during the plan year for which the amendment is effective. [I.R.C. § 412(c)(8)] Notice must be given to the IRS and to the plan's interested parties. The IRS has a 90-day period to review the proposed plan amendment. If the IRS does not disapprove, then the amendment takes effect at the end of the 90-day period.

If the application is granted, the IRS will waive part or all of the funding deficiency for the year. The employer may have to provide security if the amount in question is substantial. But the IRS does not have the power to waive amortization of funding deficiencies that were waived in earlier years.

The IRS can grant up to ten additional years to amortize items such as unfunded past service liability and net experience losses. The IRS can grant this relief only if it concludes that the extension serves the purposes of ERISA and protected participants and beneficiaries in the long run by making the plan more stable.

ERISA § 302(c) requires that a defined benefit plan that is subject to PBGC termination insurance must get IRS approval to change its actuarial assumptions if all of the employer's plans (including all plans within its controlled group of corporations) have an aggregate unfunded benefit in excess of $50 million, or if the proposed change in assumptions decreases the unfunded current liability by $50 million or more for the current plan year—or by more than $5 million, representing more than 5% of the current liability.

Plans can't have it both ways. If they are granted minimum funding relief (other than a change of funding methods), as long as the relief continues, the plan is limited in its ability to adopt plan changes that increase benefits, change benefit accrual, or change the rates at which benefits become nonforfeitable. [*See* I.R.C. § 412(f)] However, amendments will be permitted if the IRS agrees that they are reasonable and increase plan liabilities only by a minimal amount, if they are actually required for the plan to remain qualified, or if the amendment merely repeals one that would have retroactively decreased accrued benefits under the plan.

Rev. Proc. 2004-15 [2004-7 I.R.B. 490] explains how to apply for a waiver of the minimum funding standard. Requests must be directed to Employee Plans, IRS, Commissioner, TE/GE Attention: SE:T:EP:RA, PO Box 27063, McPherson Station, Washington, DC 20038. The requester must pay a user fee as provided by Rev. Proc. 2004-8, [2004-1 I.R.B. 240]. The waiver application provides information about the employer, its financial condition, executive compensation, the nature and extent of the business hardship justifying the waiver, the structure of the pension plan, and other relevant information. The request form must be signed by the taxpayer, its authorized representative, or by an enrolled actuary. Furthermore, the statements in the form are made under penalty of perjury, and must be signed by an officer of the corporation, not merely someone holding a Durable Power of Attorney.

[L]   Pension Freezes

The Center for Retirement Research at Boston College examined a trend of the mid-2000s: pension freezes by companies that were financially sound. They identified 17 such companies, including Coca-Cola, IBM, and Hewlett-Packard. The researchers noted that, traditionally, it was very rare for a company to freeze a defined benefit plan, and this event was generally associated with a bankruptcy or severe financial problems. They attributed the acceptability of freezes to a combination of four factors:

1. Reducing workers' compensation to be able to compete in the global market.
2. Cutting back pensions because health costs had soared.
3. Financial risks (such as stock market exposure) that made funding defined benefit plans unattractive.
4. Upper management's lack of interest in rank-and-file pensions because so much of their compensation came from nonqualified plans.

The researchers identified three forms of plan freezes:

1. Closing the plan to new hires;
2. A partial freeze that covers new hires and some current employees; or
3. A total freeze that affects all employees.

Usually, the freeze is accompanied by creation of a 401(k) plan, which reduces the employer's responsibility to making any matching contribution it promises. The report cites the example of a defined benefit plan that provided 1.5% of final salary per year of service. An employee with 10 years of service would be entitled to a pension of 15% of salary at the time of the freeze. A hypothetical 50-year-old with a salary of $48,000 would be entitled to $7,200 a year at age 62, whereas if the plan had not been frozen and he had worked to age 62, earning $58,000 at that time, his pension would have been $8,700 a year.

Pension plan freezes also provide a cosmetic gloss to the company's financial statements. Freezing a pension means that future payment liabilities are eliminated or greatly reduced, resulting in an accounting gain that is considered income for the corporation. Furthermore, if interest rates are low, the discounted present value of future benefits is high (because the role account earnings have in providing future benefits is comparatively small, more money must be set aside at the outset), creating an even more dramatic effect on the corporate bottom line. [Alicia H. Munnell, Francesca Golub-Sass, Mauricio Soto, and Francis Vitagliano, *Why Are Healthy Employers Freezing Their Pensions?* Center for Retirement Research Brief No. 44, <http://www.bc.edu/centers/crr/issues/ib_44.pdf> (Mar. 2006)]

EBRI released a study in 2006 of the amount of additional savings that a worker would need to make up for lost accruals after a pension freeze. For example, a high-salaried worker who accrued pension benefits until retirement at 65 and would get a pension of $70,960 a year under a defined benefit plan would get a retirement benefit of only $42,988 a year if his pension were frozen at age 45 and he then invested in a 401(k) plan. A mid-range earner who would have had a defined benefit pension of $53,220 a year would get $36,740 a year under the freeze-at-age-45 scenario; and a worker with a $35,480 defined benefit pension would get $28,387 a year under the freeze scenario. The older the worker, the more negative the effect of a pension freeze, because these workers have less time to deposit additional funds in their accounts to make up for the loss of defined benefit accruals. Persons close to retirement age (60–64) might have to save an additional 20% to make up for the losses.

Assuming an 8% rate of return, contributions to the 401(k) or other replacement plan would have to rise by 6.6% to replace a career-average defined benefit plan, or by 8.1% to replace a final-salary defined benefit plan. Extra contributions of 2.7% would be needed to replace cash balance plans. Even more savings would be needed to make up for benefits lost to freezes if a lower rate is assumed: at a 4% rate of return, for example, an 11.6% contribution indemnification rate would be needed for those covered by a career-average plan, and 13.5% for a final-salary plan.

EBRI also noted that the makeup of compensation has shifted. In 1970, for example, wages and salaries accounted for 89.4% of total compensation. Retirement benefits made up 6.5% (2.6% of which went to Social Security), while health benefits accounted for 2.4% (of which 2.0% went to the group health plan and 0.4% to Medicare taxes), with 1.8% being "other benefits." In 2004, however, wages and salaries were down to 80.6% of total compensation, with retirement benefits at 9.1% (Social Security 4.0%), health benefits up to 8.4% (1.2% Medicare taxes, 7.2% group health), and other benefits fairly stable at 1.9%. Furthermore, although the funding shortfall for defined benefit plans has been frequently reported and could become the subject of federal legislation, the shortfall in funding retiree health benefits is more than three times as great. In 2004, the defined benefit shortfall for Fortune 500 companies was $98 billion—vs. $335 billion for retiree health benefits. The defined benefit shortfall is dropping because of stock market conditions and changes in employer practices, but the retiree health shortfall's upward trend is continuing. [EBRI Issue Brief, <http://www.ebri.org/pdf/briefspdf/EBRI_IB_03-20063.pdf>; *see* Rebecca Moore, *EBRI Studies What Workers Will Need to Offset Pension Freezes*, PlanSponsor.com (Mar. 9, 2006); Mary Williams Walsh, *When Your Pension Is Frozen*, New York Times, Jan. 22, 2006, News of the Week in Review, at p. 3]

§ 5.06   BENEFIT ACCRUALS

Another issue in plan administration and compliance is the schedule on which benefits are contributed on the individual's behalf, being added to the pension account so that eventually the participant will receive his or her defined benefit. Vesting is a separate but related concept. Vesting determines the extent to which employees will be entitled to receive the accrued benefit when they retire or employment otherwise terminates.

Defined benefit plans must accrue benefits using one of the three permitted mechanisms:

1. The 3% rule: at all times, the accrued benefit must be at least 3% of the maximum benefit calculated under the plan's formula, multiplied by the number of years of participation.
2. The 133.5% test: the accrued benefit payable at Normal Retirement Age equals the normal retirement benefit, and accrual in any plan year does not exceed 133.5% of the accrual for any prior year. In other words, benefits must accrue in a fairly level manner in each year.
3. The fractional rule: the annual benefit an employee has accrued at the time of separation from service must be proportionate to what he or she would have received by remaining employed until normal retirement age.

Under § 412(i), insured plans whose accrued benefit is always at least equal to the cash surrender value of the insurance are exempt from the minimum funding rules.

The Second Circuit ruled in early 2006 that Xerox unlawfully reduced the pension benefits of persons who left the company and were rehired. Xerox used a "phantom account offset" system under which the lump sum received when the individual left the company for the first time was used to cut the benefits at eventual retirement. The Second Circuit ruled that a plan amendment occurs not when the plan administrator changes the way the plan operates, but when the employees are properly informed of the change. The court ruled that proper information was not provided until 1998, so applying it to anyone who was rehired before that date would be a violation of the anti-cutback rule. [*Frommert v. Conkright,* 74 LW 1448 2d Cir. (Jan. 6, 2006), 04-4609-cv]

§ 5.07   NOTICES OF REDUCTION OF BENEFIT ACCRUALS

Defined benefit plans (and other plans subject to the I.R.C. § 412 full funding rules) have an obligation under ERISA § 204(h) and I.R.C. § 4980F (a new provision added by EGTRRA) to provide notice of plan amendments that significantly reduce future benefit accruals. The notice must contain the text or a summary of the plan amendment, and the effective date of the amendment. Notice must be given at least 15 days before the effective date of the plan amendment. [*See* the JCWAA § 411(u) for technical corrections to this provision]

Not only is an excise tax ($100 per day) imposed on the failure, but in "egregious" cases (where the employer intentionally refused to give notice, or failed very badly to disclose the needed information) the plan amendment will not be given effect. Therefore, participants will be entitled to the unreduced benefit that was in effect before the plan was amended.

In April 2002, the IRS issued a Notice of Proposed Rulemaking [NPRM-Reg-136193-01], applicable to defined benefit plans and to individual account plans subject to the Code § 412 and corresponding ERISA § 302 funding standards. The NPRM was finalized, with only minor changes, as T.D. 9052, RIN-1545-BA08 2003-19 I.R.B. 879 in the spring of 2003. The plan is required to provide notice to plan participants when the rate of future accrual is significantly reduced, or when an early retirement subsidy is modified in a way that operates as a reduction in the rate of future benefit accruals.

The objective of these rules is to strike a balance between allowing the employer reasonable flexibility in plan design and administration, and providing adequate notice to participants. In general, the notice must be given at least 45 days before the effective date of the change, but the notice can be as short as 15 days before the effective date for certain merger and acquisition-related transactions of small plans. Also in connection with mergers and acquisitions, where there is a plan-to-plan transfer or merger that affects only the early retirement benefit or subsidy, notice can be given after the effective date of the amendment, but no more than 30 days later.

The notice must be given in a form that is understandable to the average plan participant, providing enough information to understand the effect of the amendment. Excise tax penalties are imposed under ERISA § 204(h)(6) for failure to provide the required notice. *See also* T.D. 9219, 2005-38 I.R.B. 538.

The Pension Funding Equity Act of 2004, P.L. 108-218, provides that certain employers who are required to make additional contributions under I.R.C. § 412(l) can elect instead to make lower "alternative deficit reduction contributions" for certain plan years. This relief is available to commercial passenger airlines, steel mills, and 501(c)(5) organizations. § 412(l)(12)(B) forbids amendments that increase the plan's liabilities by increasing benefits, changing the accrual of benefits, or changing the rate at which benefits become nonforfeitable, except to the extent that the amendment is required by a CBA that was in effect on April 10, 2004, or unless an actuary certifies that the amendment has the effect of increasing contributions more than the increase in annual charges to the funding standard account. Guidance on such issues is provided by Announcement 2004-38, 2004-18 I.R.B. 878, Announcement 2004-43, 2004-21 I.R.B. 955 (as corrected by Announcement 2004-51, 2004-23 I.R.B. 1041), and Notice 2004-59, 2004-36 I.R.B. 447.

§ 5.08 PBGC COMPLIANCE

[A] PBGC Organization

Formally speaking, the Pension Benefit Guarantee Corporation (PBGC) is organized as a corporation, but it's really a quasi-governmental agency that draws its powers from ERISA § 4002. The PBGC's Board of Directors consists of the Secretaries of Labor, Treasury, and Commerce. The federal court system gives the agency special deference, by giving its cases the earliest possible calendar dates. Employers sued by the PBGC in connection with a plan termination can be required to pay part or all of the agency's litigation costs.

The main task of the PBGC is to guarantee that participants in defined benefit plans will receive a basic benefit even if their plan is insufficiently funded, or if it is terminated.

[B] PBGC Premiums

The PBGC stays afloat by charging a premium to employers who maintain defined benefit plans. The Deficit Reduction Act of 2005 (DRA '05), P.L. 109-171, increased the PBGC premium for single-employer plans from $19 per employee per year to $30, and also called for annual inflation indexing of the premium, which had been fixed at $19 for many years. Furthermore, DRA '05 also imposes a special $1,250 per participant premium for the years 2006 through 2010 when a single-employer plan is terminated under ERISA §§ 4041(c)(2)(B) or 4042. If the plan is terminated while the sponsor's Chapter 11 bankruptcy case is pending, the special premium is not due until the sponsor's bankruptcy discharge or until the bankruptcy case is dismissed. The bankruptcy rules do not apply to cases filed before October 18, 2005.

> **Tip:** If a plan has fewer than 500 participants, it can submit a certificate from an enrolled actuary stating that there are no unfunded vested benefits. Nor is it necessary to calculate unfunded vested benefits if the plan is fully insured, or if the plan was fully funded in the year before the year in question. When a plan terminates, the PBGC premium is payable until the plan assets have been distributed, or until a trustee is appointed (whichever comes first). When the business of winding up the plan is completed, the PBGC refunds any unearned part of the premium.

The premium is charged for each participant, terminated vested participant, and beneficiary already receiving benefits, other than "lost" beneficiaries (the plan knows they may be entitled to benefits, but can't find them) for whom an insurance company has an irrevocable commitment to pay all the benefits. All defined benefit plans that are subject to PBGC insurance must file Form PBGC-1 each year as a combined annual report and declaration of premium payments.

The premium is paid with Form 1-ES (if the plan has more than 500 participants) or with Form 10-SP (short form for smaller plans). The contributing sponsor and the plan administrator are both liable for the PBGC premium. If the premium is not paid on time, interest runs from the due date, plus a late charge of 5% per month (capped at 100% of the original unpaid premium). The PBGC is also empowered to collect unpaid premiums from what would otherwise be the employer's federal tax refund. If the employer is a federal contractor, the PBGC can seize federal contract payments.

> **Tip:** The forms are available online as PDF files. [*See* <http://www.pbgc. gov/practitioners/premium-filings/content/page1142.html>]

A PBGC Final Rule appearing in the Federal Register of December 14, 1998 [63 Fed. Reg. 68684], amends 29 C.F.R. Part 4007 to provide that the final filing due date for a calendar-year plan's premium declaration will be October 15. In other words, the date is the same for the declaration as the extended date for the Form 5500. The Final Rule makes corresponding changes in the treatment of the declaration for fiscal-year plans. It is now due the fifteenth day of the tenth full calendar month of the premium payment year. (Adjustments are made if the plan changes its plan year, or if it is a new or newly covered plan.) [*See also* 65 Fed. Reg. 75160 (Dec. 1, 2000), which simplifies administration of premium payments.]

The administrator can pay a prorated premium for a short plan year, instead of paying the full premium and getting a refund or claiming a credit against future premium payments. A short plan year might occur during a plan's first, partial year; in the year of termination; or when a trustee is appointed under ERISA § 4042. The December 2000 rule also changes the definition of "participant."

The plan can exclude from the count—and therefore not pay premiums for—a person who has no accrued benefits and to whom the plan has no other benefit liabilities. The bottom line is that a new plan doesn't have to pay premiums for its first year unless it credits service before the beginning of the plan.

[C] Accounting Issues

On the fifteenth of every month, the PBGC updates its Web site [<http://www.pbgc.gov/practitioners/interest-rates/content/index.html>] to give the interest rates that should be used in that month for:

- Valuation of lump-sum payments made by the plan;
- Variable rate premiums;
- Valuation of annuity benefits;
- PBGC charges imposed with respect to employer liability, unpaid contributions, and unpaid premiums.

PBGC staff can be reached by e-mail to answer compliance questions about:

- Premium calculations and payments: premiums@pbgc.gov;
- Coverage and standard terminations: standard@pbgc.gov;
- Distress terminations: distress.term@pbgc.gov;
- Early warning program: advance.report@pbgc.gov;
- ERISA § 4010 reporting: EISA.4010@pbgc.gov;
- Reportable events: post-event.report@pbgc.gov;
- General legal questions: AskOGC@pbgc.gov;
- Problem resolution officer: practitioner.pro@pbgc.gov;
- Other: Ask.PBGC@pbgc.gov.

§ 5.09 REPORTABLE EVENTS

The PBGC doesn't want to be caught by surprise when a plan fails. To this end, plan administrators have a duty to report unusual events to the PBGC that might eventually require the agency to take over payment of pensions. Depending on the seriousness of the event, the PBGC might merely maintain a watchful attitude; or it might seek the appointment of a temporary trustee to manage the plan, or even go to the appropriate federal District Court to seek authority to terminate the plan.

The PBGC Regulations list 17 reportable events. Some of them must be reported 30 days before the event is scheduled to occur; others may be reported after the fact:

- The plan's bankruptcy or insolvency;
- The sponsoring employer's bankruptcy or insolvency;

- The sponsoring employer's liquidation under the Bankruptcy Code or any similar law (or that of a member of its controlled group of corporations);
- Notice from the IRS that the plan has ceased to be a qualified retirement plan;
- IRS determination that the plan has terminated or partially terminated;
- Failure to meet the minimum funding standard;
- Receiving a minimum funding waiver from the IRS;
- Inability to pay benefits as they come due;
- DOL determination that the plan fails to comply with ERISA Title I;
- Adoption of a plan amendment that decreases any participant's retirement benefit (except for certain decreases relating to integration with Social Security);
- A reduction in the number of active participants in the plan, to the extent that the number is less than 80% of the census at the beginning of the year or 75% of the number of active participants at the beginning of the preceding plan year;
- Distributing $10,000 or more to a participant who is a "substantial owner" (a definition roughly equal to 10% shareholder in the employer corporation) if the plan has any unfunded, nonforfeitable benefits after the distribution. Distributions made on account of the death of the substantial owner are not counted for this purpose;
- Merger or consolidation of the plan, or transfer of its assets;
- DOL requirement of an alternative method of compliance under ERISA § 110;
- A change of plan sponsor (or the same plan sponsor leaving a controlled group of corporations), if the plan has $1 million or more in unfunded nonforfeitable benefits;
- A "person" involved with the plan leaving a controlled group of corporations;
- The controlling sponsor, or a member of its controlled group, engages in a highly unusual transaction, such as declaring an extraordinary dividend or redeeming 10% or more of its stock;
- Transfer of a total of 3% or more of the plan's benefit liabilities outside the sponsor's controlled group within a 12-month period (whether or not the transferee is another plan).

At one time, the sponsoring employer had a duty to report the events to the plan administrator, but now it is only required that the events be reported to the PBGC. ERISA § 4043 requires advance notice of liquidating bankruptcy, extraordinary dividends, transfer of 3% of plan liabilities, or leaving a controlled group of corporations.

In March 2005, the PBGC issued a new set of final ERISA § 4010 regulations, under which electronic reporting is mandated when the total unfunded vested benefits for a controlled group of corporations exceed $50 million. (The rules apply whether or not the corporations are publicly traded.) Filing under § 4010 is also required if any plan maintained by a member of the controlled group misses contributions of $1 million or more, or if any group member has received a funding waiver from the IRS of $1 million or more. A corporation required to file under this provision must provide the PBGC with separate liability calculations for active, retired, terminated, and vested participants (and the number of people in each category); current liability and projected increases in current liability or payments; disclosure of benefit liability assumptions; and additional information about other pension plans in the same controlled group of corporations. *See* the PBGC Web site for requirements for plans that formerly were subject to § 4010 annual reporting but are not subject for the current year. [<http://www.pbgc.gov/practitioners/reporting-and-disclosure/content/page14529.html>]

In addition to the required report to the PBGC, whenever a defined benefit plan fails to satisfy the minimum funding standard, and there has been no waiver of minimum funding granted, then participants must be notified. Form 200 must be filed with the PBGC within 10 days of the time a failure to meet the minimum funding standard involves $1 million or more.

CHAPTER 6

DEFINED CONTRIBUTION AND 401(k) PLANS

§ 6.01   INTRODUCTION

As explored in Chapters 4 and 5, the defined benefit plan not only places the investment risk on the employer (because the employer must adjust its contributions to provide the promised level of benefits—and if the value of the plan's assets declines, and its investment return goes down, the employer must supply additional funds) but also subjects the employer to complex and expensive administrative requirements.

In the 1990s, therefore, the trend was to shift from defined benefit to defined contribution or 401(k) plans. The 401(k) plan form grew fast, because (although employer matches are permitted) the predominant form of funding for these plans is deferral of employee compensation.

The 2005 BLS National Compensation Survey found that 53% of all workers in private industry are potential participants in at least one defined contribution retirement plan. However, workers earning $15 an hour or less were much less likely (41%) to have access to such a plan than higher-paid workers (69%). Sixty-two percent of full-time, but only 23% of part-time, workers had access. Nearly two thirds of white-collar workers, half of blue-collar workers, but only about a quarter (28%) of service-sector workers had access to a defined benefit plan. Sixty-nine percent of workers in workplaces with more than 100 employees had access, but only 40% of those in smaller workplaces did. Access, of course, is not the same as participation; some workers can't afford to participate, others simply choose not to. [Elizabeth Dietz, *Access to Defined Contribution Retirement Plans Among Workers in Private Industry, 2005*, <http://www.bls.gov/opub/cwc/print/cm20060425ch01.htm> (Apr. 26, 2006)]

Researcher Alicia Munnell (with Steven A. Sass) was involved in subsequent research on the question of the impact of 401(k) plans on female retirees. The portability feature is favorable for women, who tend to change jobs more often than men. However, women's longer life expectancy means that they have to make their money stretch further. If they invest their plan balances in annuities at retirement, they will receive a lower annuity benefit than a man would (because of the differences in life expectancy), whereas a defined benefit plan pays male and female workers the same if they had the same income and tenure. With respect to married women's post-retirement income, defined benefit plans require both spouses to consent to payment in any form other than a QJSA; this is not true of 401(k) plans. In most couples, the wife is younger than the husband, so if the husband spends the entire 401(k) balance, the wife will have financial problems in widowhood. [Alicia S. Munnell and Steven A. Sass, *401(k) Plans and Women: A "Good News/Bad News" Story*, Center for Retirement Research at Boston College, Just the Facts on Retirement Issues #13 (Jan. 2005), <http://www.bc.edu/crr/>]

§ 6.02   DEFINED CONTRIBUTION PLANS

At one time, the defined benefit plan was the standard form of pension plan, but it has been replaced in this role by the defined contribution plan. In 2006, the maximum contribution that an employer may make to such a plan is $44,000 (up from $42,000 in 2005).

The defined contribution plan has comparatively few administrative requirements and offers greater portability than a defined benefit plan, because there is a separate account for each participant. Once a person becomes eligible for participation, the employer merely makes contributions, using a simple formula based on compensation, to each employee's account. Although defined contribution plans are legally required to offer QJSA payments, it is more typical for employees to elect payment of their balances as a lump sum at retirement.

The accrued benefit for a participant in a defined contribution plan equals the balance in the account. The balance, in turn, consists of employer contributions, any mandatory employee contributions that the plan requires, plus any voluntary contributions that the plan permits and the employee chooses to make. Defined contribution plans usually maintain separate subaccounts for the employer and employee component of each employee's account, but this is not a legal requirement.

The IRS issued Final Rules applying to loans made on or after January 1, 2004, from qualified defined contribution plans, including loans made to participants who are on military leave (*see* § 1.18), refinanced loans, and exceptions to the ban on new loans to participants whose earlier loans are in default. A participant who suspends loan repayment during military service and then returns to work must repay the entire loan and its interest in substantially level installments by the end of the original loan term plus the period of military service. If the loan was not a mortgage on the principal residence, repayment must occur within five years plus the period of service, if the original loan term was less than five years. A new loan can be made despite a default based on an enforceable agreement to repay by payroll withholding, or if the plan receives security for the loan in addition to the participant's account balance. [CIGNA's Pension Analyst, *IRS Issues Additional Loan Rules* (September 2003) <http://www.cigna.com/professional/pdf/loanCPA2003.pdf>]

ERISA § 404(c) allows the participant to control the assets in a defined contribution account, including directing the investment of the account. If the participant assumes control, the plan's fiduciaries will not be liable for losses that result from participant control over the funds. Section 404(c) requires the plan to disclose adequate information about their investment alternatives. The plan must offer at least three diversified investment types, with materially different risk and return characteristics.

However, it should be noted that selecting an annuity provider who will distribute plan benefits is a fiduciary act. Therefore, it must be undertaken prudently and in the sole interest of plan participants and their beneficiaries. The basic legal document on this issue is DOL's Interpretive Bulletin 95-1, 29 C.F.R. § 2509.95-1, which requires selection of the safest available annuity provider. Typically, the annuity provider will be an insurance company.

The DOL issued Advisory Opinion 2002-14A on December 18, 2002, to clarify the principles of this bulletin. The fiduciary must select the best provider based on factors such as the quality and diversification of the insurer's portfolio; its size as compared to the size of the contract; the insurer's capital and surplus levels; and the strength of any guarantee programs backing the annuity. The fiduciary has a duty to consult an expert independent of the annuity provider, unless the fiduciary has the qualifications necessary to make the assessment. In some circumstances, it may be acceptable for a fiduciary to select a product that is slightly less safe than a competing product, if there is a very large price differential between the two. However, it is never prudent to select an annuity product that, objectively speaking, is risky.

If a state guaranty association is in the picture, the Advisory Opinion says that the fiduciary should consider whether the annuity provider and the annuity product are covered; the extent of the guarantee; and how likely the guaranty association is to be able to continue to meet its obligations. [The Advisory Opinion was posted online at <http://www.dol.gov/pwba/regs/aos/ao2002-14a.html>]

Also in connection with annuities, *see* 69 Fed. Reg. 33288 (June 15, 2004), discussed further in § 12.07[D], for minimum distribution requirements for annuity contracts purchased with the account balance from a defined contribution plan.

[A] 2005 Proposed Regulations

In mid-2005, the IRS issued Proposed Regulations on maximum benefits and contributions reflecting the many statutory changes made since the previous set of regulations, which were published in 1981. The limitation for defined contribution plans under Code § 415(c) (limitations that also apply to mandatory employee contributions required under certain defined benefit plans) applies to the annual additions allocated to the plan participant for the limitation year: employer contributions, pre-tax employee contributions, after-tax employee contributions, and forfeitures. However, the limit does not apply to earnings on participants' accounts, amounts transferred or rolled over from another plan, or elective deferrals that exceeded the maximum, but were removed in time to correct the error. The IRS has the power to recharacterize (as annual additions) gains to a participant's account from other sources. For example, a sale of employer stock to a plan for less than fair market value (FMV) could make the bargain element an annual addition.

To be treated as annual additions for a limitation year, employer contributions must be made within 30 days of the due date (as extended) of the employer's federal income tax return. A contribution can be an annual addition if made by the 15th day of the 10th month after the end of the tax year. Employee contributions must actually be made to the plan within 30 days of the close of the limitation year. Forfeitures are annual additions for the year that contains the date in which the forfeitures are allocated to the participants' accounts.

Catch-up contributions by a person over 50 are not annual additions. Repayments of plan loans, rollovers, and plan-to-plan transfers, and repayments of previously cashed-out balances to restore prior years of service also are not annual additions.

Restorative payments made by a plan to cover its losses from assets that are likely to lead to a suit for fiduciary breach or other remedial actions (a DOL order, a court settlement, or participation in the Voluntary Fiduciary Correction Program) are likewise not annual additions. The Proposed Regulations say that a payment is a restorative payment only if it is made to all similarly situated participants affected by the breach.

The Proposed Regulations define compensation to include wages, salaries, professional fees, commissions, tips, bonuses, fringe benefits, reimbursements under non-accountable expense accounts, employer-provided health care coverage, moving expense reimbursement that is included in gross income, gains recognized under a § 83(b) election, and the value of nonqualified options that are taxable when granted. The Proposed Regulations also define certain items as not being compensation: the employer's contributions to qualified plans; distributions from either qualified or nonqualified plans; gains on the exercise of nonqualified options or the vesting of restricted property; gains on the disposition of stock by exercising a statutory stock option; and other tax-favored items, such as the premiums an employer pays on group-term life insurance that are not included in taxable income.

Certain items of elective deferral or salary reduction contributions are considered compensation for § 415 purposes even though they are not taxable income for the recipient (e.g., 401(k) deferrals, SEP, SIMPLE, 403(b) and 457(b) plan contributions, cafeteria plan elections, and qualified transportation fringes).

As a safe harbor, a plan can use either wages on the W-2 or wages subject to income tax withholding as a definition of § 415 compensation. It is also permissible to use a simplified definition limited to wages, salaries, fees, and amounts received for personal services, excluding all other items. Under the Proposed Regulations, the definition of "compensation" for the § 415 limits cannot include compensation over the § 401(a)(17) limit ($220,000 for 2006). Therefore, in a 401(k) plan, a participant who reaches $220,000 in compensation for the year must stop making deferrals even if he or she has not deferred the maximum amount.

Under the Proposed Regulations, a defined contribution plan can impute § 415 compensation to a permanently and totally disabled participant, and make contributions on his or her behalf, as if they were still paid at the rate applicable immediately before disability ensued. However, HCEs are not entitled to post-disability imputed compensation, unless the plan provides for contributions for all disabled participants for a fixed and determinable period. Imputed compensation contributions are always fully vested. Generally, under the proposal, § 415 compensation does not include payments made after termination of employment, but regular compensation, commissions, bonuses, overtime, shift differentials and cashouts of accrued leave that could have been used if the person had continued to be employed are § 415 compensation.

Payments within two and a half months of severance from employment can be considered § 415 compensation, but severance pay is not. Post-termination payments can be electively deferred under § 401(k) if they are § 415 compensation. If they are, the deferral is permitted even if payment is made after the year of termination. [Prop. Reg., 70 Fed. Reg. 31213 (May 31, 2005). *See* Deloitte's

Washington Bulletin, *Updated 415 Regulations—An In-Depth Review* (June 20, 2005) (benefitslink.com)]

§6.03   NEW COMPARABILITY PLANS

On October 6, 2000, the IRS published Proposed Regulations at 65 Fed. Reg. 59774-59780 setting the nondiscrimination requirements for "new comparability plans." These are defined contribution plans that are allowed to perform cross-testing and demonstrate nondiscrimination under Treas. Reg. § 1.401(a)(4)-(8) by reference to their benefits rather than the employer's contributions, although they must satisfy a "gateway" requirement preserving at least a minimum rate of accrual for non-HCEs. In practice, this is usually done by finding a defined benefit equivalent for the allocations and then arranging them in rate groups.

Some employers find new comparability plans attractive because these plans allow a much higher allocation rate for highly compensated employees than for other employees. For example, a medical group might use three allocation rates in its new comparability plan: the highest for doctors who are also shareholders in the group, the lowest for nonphysician employees, and one in the middle for physicians who are not shareholders in the practice. [The Regulations were finalized by T.D. 8954, R.I.N. 1545-AY36, 66 Fed. Reg. 34535–34545 (June 29, 2001). *See also* Notice 2000-14, 2000-10 I.R.B. 737 (Feb. 24, 2000) for the IRS opinions on issues raised by new comparability plans]

The plan document can specify the classes in many ways—by age, hiring date, length of service, type of job, or the location in which they work, for example. The number or definition of classes can only be changed via plan amendment, and the changes must be prospective only, not retroactive. It has been suggested that the IRS and the DOL might treat the plan as a deemed 401(k) plan rather than a new comparability plan if this process were extended to the point that every employee is in a separate class, but the agencies have not issued technical guidance on this point. [Mark Papalia *Class-Based Pensions: A Cost-Saving Alternative for Companies of All Sizes,* Journal of Accountancy (January 2005)(via benefitslink.com)]

On December 12, 2002, the IRS issued Proposed Regulations dealing with cash balance plans. [67 Fed. Reg. 76123] This proposal included rules under Code § 401(a)(4) under which cash balance plans could use a modified version of the new comparability rules to perform nondiscrimination testing. However, in April 2003, the IRS responded to concerns raised by commenters, and issued Announcement 2003-22, 2003-17 I.R.B. 846 (April 7, 2003) withdrawing the proposals relating to cross-testing and new comparability plans.

§6.04   401(k) PLANS

[A]   Overview

The Cash or Deferred Arrangement (CODA), also known as the 401(k) plan, has achieved prominence as one of the leading forms of plans for providing post-retirement income. Such plans were authorized by a 1978 amendment to the Internal Revenue Code and first became available in 1981.

Almost two thirds of large employers considered their 401(k) plan their primary retirement vehicle in 2005. Only 35% considered the 401(k) their primary plan in 1995. Large-scale employers such as Hewlett-Packard, IBM, Motorola, and Sears phased out defined benefit plans in favor of 401(k)s. In 1997, only 4% of employers with 401(k)s had automatic enrollment, a percentage that rose to 19% in 2005. In 2001, only 35% allowed new hires to participate without a waiting period, while 43% did so in 2005. The level of pre-tax employee contributions remained fairly stable (in the 6.5–7% range) from 1999 to 2005. [Jerry Geisel, *401(k) Is Main Retirement Plan for Most Big Firms,* Business Insurance, Sept. 27, 2005, <http://www.businessinsurance.com/cgi-bin/news.pl?newsId=6403>]

Hewitt Associates surveyed more than 2.5 million employees who were eligible for 401(k) plan participation. The survey found that plan participation increased from 68.1% in 2002 to 70.3% in 2004. The average 2004 plan balance was $69,000. Less than half of workers under 30 participated (46%), and 23% of participants had a balance of $5,000 or less. In 2004, close to 80% of employees who made 401(k) contributions contributed enough to get an employer match. The average 401(k) portfolio was invested 40% in equities and 27% of accounts were half or more invested in employer stock. The average 401(k) participant was 43, had worked for the employer for 10 years, and earned about $58,000, whereas the average nonparticipant was 39, earned only $33,000, and had been with the company only 5.4 years. Of those participants, 23% had an outstanding plan loan. [Daily Business Journal, *Employees Still Eschewing 401(k) Plans,* benefits-link.com (Aug. 30, 2005)]

Although 401(k) plans are subject to the rules for defined contribution plans, strictly speaking 401(k)s are not conventional pension plans. In a 401(k) plan, the employee agrees to have part of his or her salary, up to the limitation provided by the plan (which, in turn, is subject to limitations under the Tax Code) deferred and placed into an individual account instead of being paid in cash as it is earned. The advantage to the employee (apart from the forced savings aspect) is that the appreciation in value of the account is not taxed until withdrawals begin.

Many 401(k) plans feature an "employer match" (the employer contributes a percentage of what the employee contributes) but this is not a mandatory feature of this type of plan.

Tip: Employers have an incentive to "match" if it increases deferrals by non-HCEs, because the increased deferrals make it easier to satisfy the ADP test. Some plans also allow employees to make after-tax contributions to their accounts, subject to the § 401(m)(2) limits.

The Third Circuit allowed a group of 401(k) participants to seek money damages for losses resulting from alleged breaches of fiduciary duty, even though the alleged breach affected only a sub-group of plan participants. The plaintiffs charged that the benefits and investment committees, and the individual committee members, continued to offer company stock as an investment option after they knew the price of the stock was unlawfully inflated. The District Court dismissed the case on the grounds that the plaintiffs sought relief for their individual losses, not on behalf of the plan as a whole. The Third Circuit reversed, however, holding that the relief sought was an allocation among the individual accounts proportional to their losses. The Third Circuit construed the claim as dependent on losses to the whole plan, and the assets were aggregated and held in trust at all times. [*In re Schering-Plough Corp. ERISA Litigation*, 420 F.3d 231 (3d Cir. 2005). The Northern District of Illinois also permitted suit by the subset of participants who were harmed: *Rogers v. Baxter Int'l Inc.*, 74 LW 1544 (N.D. Ill. Feb. 22, 2006). The Sixth and Eighth Circuits also have permitted suits by a subset of the participants under 502(a)(2). The Fifth Circuit has ruled to the contrary (in a case that it has agreed to rehear)]

In September 2004, the Department of Labor proposed regulations covering the rights of servicemembers returning from active service (*see* § 1.18) that also affect 401(k) plans. Periods of uniformed service must be counted with respect to 401(k) plan vesting and benefit accrual. Returning servicemembers must be permitted to catch up with voluntary contributions such as elective deferrals that could have been made if they had not been in the military. The proposal clarifies that the employer must let the employee make up all or any part of the missed contributions. If the contributions can't be made up as elective deferrals because the returned servicemember no longer works for the original employer, the plan sponsors must give the servicemember the opportunity to receive the maximum match of after-tax contributions that would be available under the plan through matching of after-tax contributions. The employer's obligation to make matching contributions depends on the servicemember's making the contributions within specified time frames. The Regulations require the employer contributions to be made within 30 days after reemployment for profit-sharing and other contributions for which the employee is not required to participate. Matching contributions when the employees make up elective deferrals must follow the plan's normal schedule for employer matches. [EBIA Weekly, *Proposed USERRA Regulations Address Elective Deferrals, Timing of Employer Contributions* (law.com)]

[B] Deferral Limits

Thanks to EGTRRA, the amount that employees can defer will increase greatly between 2001 and 2006. EGTRRA also includes other novel 401(k) provisions. Participants in 401(k) plans who are over 50 are permitted to make additional "catch-up" contributions, and low-income plan participants are allowed to take a tax credit and not a mere deduction in connection with part of their 401(k) deferrals.

For 2006, the maximum elective deferral in a 401(k) plan is $15,000. Between 2007 and 2010 (the entire EGTRRA statute is scheduled to sunset on

January 1, 2011, unless Congress makes it permanent in whole or in part) the $15,000 amount will be indexed for inflation, but only when changes in the index mandate increases in $500 increments. In 2005, 401(k) participants aged 50 or older could make additional catch-up contributions of up to $2,000; this amount rose to $2,500 in 2006.

The limitation on deferrals is applied on the basis of the individual employee's tax year (and not the plan year). Furthermore, it applies to all CODAs in which the individual participates, not merely those relating to corporations in the same controlled group as the employer. However, the Job Creation and Worker Assistance Act of 2002 (JCWAA) [Pub. L. No. 107-147] provides that if the employer has a 401(k) plan with elective deferrals only (no employer match) and also a defined benefit plan, the I.R.C. § 404(a)(7) "overlapping limitation" does not apply.

Participants in 401(k) plans are always 100% vested in their deferrals at all times. Employees must be allowed to participate in the cash or deferred part of the plan starting with the first entry date after they have one year of service with the employer. Participants must be re-admitted to the plan immediately if they terminate their jobs but are re-employed at the same company before they have undergone a one-year break in service.

[C] Catch-Up Contributions

EGTRRA added a new I.R.C. § 414(v), which allows employees who are age 50 or older to order additional deferrals, over and above the normal limits. These additional amounts are referred to as catch-up contributions. The intent is to make sure that older employees will come closer to getting the same benefit from the enhanced opportunities for deferrals over the course of their careers as younger employees who can make the greater deferrals for a greater number of years. Catch-up contributions can be made for taxable years beginning after December 31, 2001.

The maximum catch-up contribution is $5,000 in 2006. Between 2007 and the time EGTRRA sunsets, the $5,000 catch-up amount will be indexed in increments of $500.

EGTRRA § 631 provides that, if all employees who have reached age 50 are permitted to make catch-up contributions, the amount of the catch-up contributions will not be used in calculating the contribution limits. Nor will the catch-up amounts be used in nondiscrimination testing.

A plan participant is eligible to make catch-up contributions as of January 1 of the calendar year in which he or she reaches age 50—irrespective of the plan year.

Final Regulations for catch-up contributions, effective July 8, 2003, applicable to contributions in taxable years beginning on or after January 1, 2004, appear in T.D. 9072, 4830-01-p, RIN-1545-BA24. (The Final Rule adopts, with some changes, the proposals published at 66 Fed. Reg. 53555 (Oct. 23, 2001)).

An employee can make catch-up contributions after exceeding the other limits set by statute, discrimination testing, or the provisions of the plan. The limit on catch-up contributions is applied across all of the plans of a single employer, and across the plans sponsored by related employers.

Code § 414(v)(3) provides that these additional elective deferrals are free from some otherwise applicable limitations on elective deferrals, and are also exempt from certain nondiscrimination tests. Nevertheless, catch-up contributions generally must be made available to all eligible individuals in any plan of the employer's that permits elective deferrals. There is no requirement that an employer permit catch-up contributions in any of its plans—but if any plan allows them, all plans that permit elective deferrals must give this option to employees who have reached the age of 50.

Employees described in § 410(b)(3), such as unionized employees covered by a collective bargaining agreement are disregarded in determining whether the plan satisfies the universal availability requirement. However, the IRS decided not to adopt comments on the proposed regulations, and therefore plan participants who have not met the minimum age and service requirements cannot be excluded for this purpose. Nor can participants in different qualified separate lines of business be excluded.

It is acceptable for a plan to impose different limits on catch-up contributions for different groups of employees (including HCEs and non-HCEs) as long as each limit is nondiscriminatory for benefits, rights, and features (*see* Code § 401(a)(4)).

These regulations explain how to calculate the limits for catch-up contributions either on the basis of the plan's calendar year or plan year or on a payroll-by-payroll basis. It is acceptable for a plan to impose a "cash availability limit" (restricting the elective deferrals to amounts available after applicable taxes have been withheld from pay). In a merger or acquisition situation, if the plan satisfied the universal availability requirement before the corporate transaction, it will be treated as satisfying this requirement until the end of the plan year after the plan year of the transaction.

[D] Other EGTRRA 401(k) Changes

Low-income 401(k) plan participants are entitled to a tax credit for their deferrals, for tax years beginning after December 31, 2001, and before January 1, 2007. For this purpose, a low-income employee is one whose income is below $50,000 for a joint return, $25,000 for a single person's return. The maximum credit is $1,000 (50% of the first $2,000 deferred under the 401(k) plan).

Under current law, a small (under $5,000) balance can be "cashed out"—i.e., even if the employee wants the money to remain within the plan, the employer has the right to close out the account and send such small, hard-to-administer sums to the account owner's last known address. (Tax should be withheld, and an early distribution penalty should be taken if the person is under age 59½.)

As a result of EGTRRA, there is an automatic rollover of 401(k) cashouts between $1,000 and $5,000 to an IRA if the participant neither directs a different rollover nor elects to receive the distribution. However, EGTRRA also provides that such transfers need not be made until the Department of Labor issues final regulations, and sets a deadline of June 7, 2004, for issuance of the final regulations. *See* 69 Fed. Reg. 9900 (Mar. 2, 2004) for a Proposed Rule with a safe harbor protecting fiduciaries who process automatic rollovers by transferring rollovers in the range between $1,000 and $5,000 to an IRA. The plan's SPD (and, if necessary, an SMM) must inform participants of the conditions for these rollovers. The Regulations were finalized at 69 Fed. Reg. 58017 (Sept. 28, 2004). *See* § 12.02 for more about automatic rollovers.

[E]   Roth 401(k)s

Yet another EGTRRA legacy is I.R.C. § 402A, which authorizes "qualified plus contribution programs"—in effect, 401(k) accounts that operate like Roth IRAs. Employees' elective salary deferrals are taxed when they are placed in the account, but can be withdrawn tax-free as long as they have remained in the account for five years and the person withdrawing is at least 59½ or disabled (or the withdrawal is made by the estate of a deceased account holder).

A person who cannot contribute to a Roth IRA because of excess income (over $110,000 for a single person, or $160,000 for a joint return) can nevertheless contribute to a Roth 401(k). Furthermore, the maximum contribution to a Roth 401(k) is the normal 401(k) maximum, which is much higher than the Roth IRA maximum contribution. For 2006, the 401(k) limit is $15,000 plus $5,000 in catch-up contributions for employees over 50, whereas the Roth IRA limit is $4,000 plus a $1,000 catch-up contribution. Roth 401(k) plans are subject to the minimum distribution rules. No provisions are made for converting an existing conventional 401(k) account to a Roth 401(k).

Because Roth 401(k)s were authorized by EGTRRA, it is possible that they will expire in 2010, the sunset date for any EGTRRA provisions not re-enacted by Congress. In that case, new contributions to Roth 401(k) accounts will no longer be permitted, but funds can remain within the plan or be rolled over to a conventional IRA. [Jane J. Kim, *New Roth 401(k) Plans Target High-Income Earners*, Wall Street Journal, Mar. 30, 2005, at p. D2]

In 2006, Roth 401(k)s were adopted by some major corporations, making it more likely that smaller companies would emulate these market leaders. According to the brokerage firm A.G. Edwards, 5.5% of its employees signed up for Roth 401(k)s, and Vanguard reported 15% of its employees. However, Hewitt Associates reported that only 6% of its large corporate clients adopted Roth 401(k) plans. [Jeff D. Opdyke, *A New Kind of 401(k) Picks Up Steam*, Wall Street Journal, Mar. 2, 2006, at p. D1]

In 2006, the IRS issued final regulations, covering Roth 401(k) plans, under Code § 402A, applicable to plan years beginning on or after January 1, 2006.

The final regulations largely reflect the March 2005 proposals. Traditional IRAs can be converted to Roth IRAs, but traditional pension accounts cannot be converted to Roth form. To receive Roth treatment, the contributions must be irrevocably designated as Roth contributions; the employer must treat the contributions as wages subject to withholding; and the contribution and its allocable share of earnings and losses must be maintained in a separate plan account. Roth contributions are included when the plan is tested for discrimination. Employers are not permitted to offer a 401(k) plan that accepts only designated Roth contributions: contributing employees must be given a choice between making pre-tax elective contributions and designated Roth contributions.

Roth IRA contributions are subject to income limits, but Roth 401(k)s are not subject to income limits. Under the final regulations, employers must credit and debit designated Roth contributions and withdrawals to a Roth account designated for the employee. Gains, losses, and other credits and charges must be separately allocated to each account on a reasonable and consistent basis. Forfeitures cannot be allocated to Roth accounts. Designated employee contributions and certain rollovers are the only permissible contributions to an employer-sponsored Roth account: Employer matches are not permitted, although employers can use automatic enrollment in a Roth 401(k) plan. Designated Roth contributions can be treated as catch-up contributions, and can be collateral for plan loans to participants. Roth 401(k) plans can have automatic enrollment, but the plan must disclose the extent to which default contributions are Roth contributions. It is permissible, but not mandatory, for the plan to allow HCEs who make both pre-tax and Roth contributions in a year to decide whether the excess contributions will be taken from the pre-tax or the Roth account. [T.D. 9237, RIN 1545-BE05, 4830-01-p, 2006-6 I.R.B. 394; *see* Allison Bell, *Feds Release Final Roth Regs,* NU (National Underwriter) Online News Service, <http://www.NUCO.com> (Jan. 3, 2006); CCH Pension and Benefits News Story, *Roth 401(k) Requirements Clarified in Final Regs* (Jan. 9, 2006); *Final Regulations on Roth 401(k)s Issued,* Watson Wyatt—Insider, January 2006 (benefitslink.com)]

The IRS also addressed Roth 401(k) distributions in 2006 in Proposed Regulations. [71 Fed. Reg. 4320 (Jan. 26, 2006)] Distributions that have been in an account for at least five years can be withdrawn penalty-free and used tax-free for certain purposes, such as the purchase of a first home. The IRS ruled that when 401(k) assets are rolled over into a Roth IRA, the time the assets were in the 401(k) plan cannot be counted toward the five-year Roth IRA requirement.

§ 6.05   401(k) ANTIDISCRIMINATION RULES

Understandably, highly compensated employees are in a better position to bypass immediate receipt of part of their salaries than rank-and-file employees. Therefore, the Internal Revenue Code includes detailed provisions for determining whether the plan is excessively unbalanced in favor of deferrals by HCEs.

There are two antidiscrimination tests: the ADP test (Actual Deferral Percentage) and the ACP test (Aggregate Contribution Percentage). A full discussion is beyond the scope of this book; you should just be aware that the 401(k) plan will be scrutinized for compliance with at least one of these tests.

According to Treas. Reg. § 1.401(k)-1(f)(6), if the plan fails both those tests for a plan year, the excess contribution percentage must be corrected within the first two and a half months after the end of the plan year. Failure to correct makes the employer liable to a 10% excise tax on the amount of excess deferral that is not corrected. [I.R.C. § 4979] If the failure continues for 12 months, the plan will be disqualified.

The employer can correct the situation in three ways:

- Distributing the excess contributions (and the income allocated to them) out of the plan before the end of the following plan year;
- Recharacterizing the excess contributions as after-tax contributions;
- Making qualified nonelective or qualified matching contributions.

Given the complexity of these rules, the IRS has recognized various safe harbor mechanisms that employers can use to simplify compliance. [*See* EGTRRA §§ 663 and 666 for provisions making it somewhat easier to benefit HCEs without rendering the plan discriminatory]

Companies that use the safe harbor are required to give plan participants notice that is accurate and comprehensive enough to inform them of their rights. The notice must be given a reasonable period (30–90 days) before the beginning of the plan year. Therefore, in a calendar year plan, notice is required on or before December 1 of the previous year.

Another option for employers who do not want to commit to using the safe harbor, but who want to make non-elective contributions, is to give notice, again by December 1 of the preceding year, that the plan may be amended in the next calendar year to provide for safe harbor non-elective contributions, and that the employees will receive a further notice explaining their rights if such an amendment is adopted.

At the end of 2004, the IRS finalized regulations under I.R.C. §§ 401(k) and 401(m): 69 Fed. Reg. 78143 (Dec. 29, 2004). In general, the Final Regulations apply to plan years that begin on or after January 1, 2006, but plan sponsors can apply the Final Regulations to any plan year that ends after December 29, 2004, as long as they do it consistently. Under the new rules, all CODAs within a plan are considered a single plan for testing purposes, but employers are not permitted to aggregate plans that have inconsistent ADP testing methods. Excess contributions that are returned to highly compensated employees must be credited with gain or loss for the "gap" period between the end of the plan year and the time of the actual distribution, to the extent gain or loss would have been credited on a total distribution.

The general rule, preserved by the Final Regulations, is that contributions cannot be pre-funded. That is, they cannot be made before the employee has performed services. However, there are three exceptions—contributions made for unusual bona fide administrative contributions; forfeitures allocated as matching contributions; and matching allocations of shares for a required payment under the terms of an ESOP loan. Even if they are permitted, pre-funded deferrals and contributions are not deductible, cannot be treated as elective contributions or matching contributions, and cannot be used in discrimination testing.

The Final Regulations ban making repeated changes in discrimination testing procedures or other plan provisions if the motivation is to distort the results of non-discrimination testing. The IRS has placed accelerated 401(k) deductions on its list of abusive tax transactions.

The mandatory written notice that must be given to employees describing their rights and obligations under a safe harbor plan can be provided electronically, rather than on paper. [The IRS press release is available at <http://www.treasury.gov/press/releases/js2171.htm>]

Participants in 401(k) plans are required to be given an effective opportunity to make or change their deferral elections at least once a year. Whether the mechanism is effective depends on factors such as the adequacy of notice of the availability of the election, the time frame in which it can be made, and the extent of conditions placed on the election.

The Final Regulations permit plans to utilize automatic enrollment, that is, to have a default of enrolling newly eligible employees even without an affirmative election from them. But the Final Regulation adopts the Department of Labor's position that a plan sponsor is a fiduciary as to investment of automatic enrollment contributions unless the participant affirmatively elects an investment option other than the default option.

§6.06 DISTRIBUTIONS FROM THE 401(k) PLAN

[A] General Rule

Pre-tax deferrals from a 401(k) plan cannot be distributed to the participant until:

- Retirement,
- Death,
- Disability,
- Separation from service [see below for the abolition of the "same desk" rule],
- Hardship,
- The participant reaches age 59½.

Although profit-sharing plans can make distributions purely because of the number of years the participant has worked for the employer, or the number of years the funds have remained in the account, these are not acceptable rationales for distributions from a 401(k) plan. [I.R.C. § 401(k)(2)(B)(ii)]

In July, 2003, the IRS proposed regulations to simplify the process of amending defined contribution plans (including 401(k) plans) when alternate benefit forms are restricted or eliminated. The IRS proposed to eliminate the requirement that 90 days advance notice be given. The proposal will not become effective until Final Regulations are published, so any plan amendment changing benefit forms that is adopted before finalization will have to comply with the advance notice requirements. [REG-112309-03, RIN 1545-BC35, 68 Fed. Reg. 40581 (July 8, 2003); *see also* 69 Fed. Reg. 13769 (Mar. 24, 2004), further explicating the revised anti-cutback rule, although predominantly with regard to defined benefit plans]

The IRS returned to this subject yet again in T.D. 9176, 4830-01-p, RIN 1545-BC35. This Final Regulation on elimination of forms of distribution under defined contribution plans took effect January 25, 2005. The Final Regulation adopts, with some revisions, the Notice of Proposed Rulemaking at 68 Fed. Reg. 40581 (July 8, 2003). The general rule of I.R.C. § 411(d)(6)(A) is that a plan will fail to satisfy § 411 if a plan amendment decreases any participant's accrued benefit. T.D. 8900 provided some exceptions to the rule.

EGTRRA enacted § 411(d)(6)(E), providing that the accrued benefit is not reduced by elimination of a form of distribution—if the participant can receive a single-sum distribution at the same time as the eliminated form of distribution, and the single-sum distribution is based on at least as great a portion of the account as the form of distribution that was eliminated. A plan amendment under the Final Regulation can apply only to distributions whose annuity starting date occurs after the adoption of the amendment, not to distributions that have already commenced.

The Eastern District of Kentucky awarded 401(k) benefits to a deceased participant's parents because his beneficiary designation of his then-wife was revoked by their subsequent divorce. He did not have a new spouse or surviving children, so his estate, for which his parents were the beneficiaries, was the appropriate recipient. [*Dudley v. NiSource Corp. Servs. Co.,* No. 5:05-217-JMH (E.D. Ky. 4/18/06), discussed in Fred Schneyer, *Participant's Parents to Get 401(k) Proceeds,* PlanSponsor.com (Apr. 28, 2006)]

[B] Hardship Distributions

Treas. Reg. § 1.401(k)-1(d)(2)(i) defines hardship as an immediate and heavy financial need that cannot be satisfied by reasonable access to the participant's other assets. The hardship withdrawal from the plan must not exceed the amount of the need plus any taxes and penalties that the participant can reasonably expect to incur.

Certain categories have been identified as automatically satisfying the financial needs test:

- Medical expenses of the employee, spouse, and dependent children;
- Purchase of a principal residence (but not routine mortgage payments);
- Staving off eviction or foreclosure of the mortgage on the principal residence;

- Tuition, room, board, and related expenses for the next 12 months for post-secondary education of the employee, spouse, or dependents.

Employees are expected to seek insurance reimbursement wherever it is available to cope with financial hardship; to liquidate their other assets to the extent this is reasonable; to cease further elective contributions to pension plans; to seek other distributions and nontaxable loans from employer plans; and to engage in commercial borrowing on reasonable terms, before they take hardship distributions from their 401(k) plans.

Under the Final Regulations, 69 Fed. Reg. 78143 (Dec. 29, 2004), a hardship distribution must satisfy both the "events test" (the participant has an immediate and heavy financial need) and a "needs test" (the distribution must be necessary to satisfy the need). A hardship distribution for medical expenses is limited to expenses that would be deductible as medical care under I.R.C. § 213(d), although the 7.5% of AGI limit does not apply. So, only prescription drugs and insulin count for this purpose. When post-secondary education expenses are taken as a hardship distribution, the pre-2005 definition of "dependent" rather than the Working Families Tax Relief Act definition can be used until final WFTRA regulations have been issued. If the criteria of I.R.C. § 152(e) are satisfied, a non-custodial parent who pays a child's medical expenses can take a hardship distribution to pay the medical bills. The Final Regulations add two new grounds for distributions: funeral or burial expenses within the immediate family, and expenses for repairs to the principal residence.

The tragic hurricane season of 2005 created the need for new law on hardship withdrawals in response to natural disasters. *See* the Katrina Emergency Tax Relief Act of 2005, P.L. 109-73, and the Gulf Opportunity Zone Act of 2005, P.L. 109-135, Notice 2005-92, 2005-51 I.R.B. 1165, and IRS Publication 4492, *Information for Taxpayers Affected by Hurricanes Katrina, Rita and Wilma,* for information about "qualified Hurricane Katrina distributions" of up to $100,000 from qualified plans. These distributions may be taken by an eligible person from August 25, 2005, to January 1, 2007, if he or she was a resident in the disaster area and suffered a hurricane-related loss.

[C] Elimination of "Same Desk" Rule

One basis on which employees can get distributions from a 401(k) plan is separation from service—i.e., ceasing to be an employee. Before EGTRRA was passed, the "same desk" rule was applied. Under this rule, a person would not be considered separated from service if the original employer had gone through a merger, consolidation, or liquidation, but the employee continued to carry out the same job for the successor company, and thus would not be entitled to a distribution from the plan.

EGTRRA provides, for distributions made after December 31, 2001, that if a corporation sells "substantially all" (defined as 85% or more) of its business assets to an unrelated company, or sells a subsidiary to an unrelated person or company, the selling company's employees have separated from service even if, in practice, they carry out the same tasks for the new employer. [This provision is subject to the EGTRRA sunset date of January 1, 2011. *See also* Rev. Proc. 2000-27, 2000-21 I.R.B. 1016]

[D] "Orphan" Plans

In addition to plan freezes (*see* § 5.05[L]), problems arise because of "orphan" or "abandoned" plans—plans in which the sponsor went out of business, without making arrangements to terminate the plan and distribute benefits. DOL estimates that roughly 1,650 401(k) plans are abandoned each year (about 2% of the total), affecting approximately 33,000 workers and balances of about $850 million. One advantage of a defined contribution plan over a defined benefit plan is that defined contribution plans are designed to be portable. But participants in these "orphan" plans, although they retain ownership of their accounts, often have difficulty in accessing them, because under previous law, if there was no representative of the sponsor company available, the financial institution could not release funds until DOL appoints an independent fiduciary to supervise the distribution. DOL issued rules in April 2006 so that financial institutions holding assets from the defunct plans of bankrupt companies will be able to roll over the 401(k) balances, giving the account holders access to the funds without the prior-law requirement of court approval. The new rules apply starting in late 2006.

The April 2006 document comprises three rules: one describing the procedure to be used by a financial institution to terminate the plan and distribute benefits to the plan's participants; another creating a safe harbor for fiduciaries who make distributions to participants and beneficiaries of "orphaned" plans when there is no election on file covering the method of distribution; and the third creating a procedure for filing a simple terminal report for an abandoned plan. [71 Fed. Reg. 20820 (Apr. 21, 2006); *see* Rebecca Moore, *DoL Issues Final Rules Regarding Abandoned Plans,* PlanSponsor.com (Apr. 20, 2006); Robert Guy Matthews, *When Access Is Denied to Your 401(k),* Wall Street Journal, Feb. 14, 2006, at p. D1]

§ 6.07   ADMINISTRATION OF THE 401(k) PLAN

In 2000, the IRS gave its blessing for 401(k) plans to operate by automatically enrolling eligible workers rather than by permitting participation only by those workers who took steps to opt in: Rev. Rul. 2000-8, 2000-7 I.R.B. 617.

An automatic plan sets a default savings rate such as 2% to 3% of pay and establishes a default investment, such as a money market or stable value fund. Usually only about 4% of eligible opt out; Hewitt Associates estimates that in a plan where opting in is required, 30% of eligible workers never join. A step-up program gets the employee's advance consent to increasing his or her contributions as income increases.

The employer has an obligation to deposit deferrals and after-tax employee contributions into the plan no later than the fifteenth business day of the second month after the funds were withheld from payroll or turned over to the employer.

Through the early 2000s, about one seventh of large companies had automatic 401(k) enrollment, a proportion that had increased to one fifth by mid-decade. In an automatic enrollment plan, workers' 401(k) deferrals are invested in a pre-set mix of stocks, bonds, and cash that is rebalanced each year. Such plans can also automatically increase each employee's contributions each year until the employee directs otherwise. Companies with automatic enrollment typically set the default rate low. That reduces the number of employees who opt out, but it also means that many employees will face retirement with limited savings. Equity funds have gained in popularity as a default option, and lifecycle funds are becoming more common. To cope, some companies draft their plans so that the default investment rate automatically goes up when an employee gets a raise.

One problem with automatic enrollment, however, is that employers often institute match programs to make enrollment in the plan more attractive—but incentives are not needed if enrollment is automatic, and a significant increase in enrollment (and consequent expansion in the matching obligation) could place a strain on the employer's willingness or ability to maintain the plan. However, if rank-and-file participation rates fall too far, the employer's ability to make contributions on behalf of HCEs will become limited. [Carla Fried, *How to Make Employees Take Their 401(k) Medicine*, New York Times, Nov. 13, 2005, Business, at p. 7; Jeff D. Opdyke, *Retirement Plans Go Automatic*, Wall Street Journal, July 20, 2005, at p. D1; Kaja Whitehouse, *Automatic 401(k) Enrollments Face Drawback*, Wall Street Journal, July 17, 2005, at p. B8]

There are some unresolved legal questions that make many employers wary of setting up automatic enrollment features. Most states (Alaska, Arizona, California, Connecticut, Delaware, Hawaii, Idaho, Illinois, Indiana, Kansas, Kentucky, Maryland, Michigan, Minnesota, Nebraska, Nevada, New Hampshire, New Jersey, New York, North Carolina, North Dakota, Oklahoma, Oregon, Pennsylvania, Puerto Rico, Rhode Island, Texas, Utah, Vermont, Virginia, Washington, West Virginia) have anti-garnishment statutes that impose a requirement that employees give written consent before wage deductions are made and it is not clear if ERISA preempts such laws. Federal legislation has been introduced to make it clear that ERISA does preempt them. [Tom Anderson, *Legal Questions, Cost Inhibit Automatic Enrollment*, Employee Benefit News, <http://www.benefitnews.com/pfv.cfm?id=7530> (June 1, 2005)]

New language was added to the Form 5500 instructions in 2003. Form 5500 requires the plan's auditors to review deposits of participants' elective deferrals. The auditor must confirm that the employer made timely deposits. The DOL's rationale for the new requirements was that enlisting the help of auditors puts pressure on the employers to make timely deposits.

A late 2003 article noted the rare, but increasing, reports of companies that fail to forward payroll contributions to the appropriate retirement accounts, fail to make required matches, or both. The DOL said that it closed 962 criminal cases dealing with retirement plans in 1999—and almost 50% more (1,459) in the fiscal year that ended September 30, 2003. Plan assets recovered as a result of DOL investigations rose from $24.7 million (1999) to more than $137 million (2003). Government investigators credited the greater scrutiny arising from the accounting scandals as well as overall growth in the size of the 401(k) market for the increase in recoveries. [Ian McDonald, *Is Money Missing from Your 401(k)?*, Wall Street Journal, Dec. 18, 2003, at p. D1] The Northern District of New York imposed liability on both a father and a son for failing to deposit nearly $43,000 in employee deferrals into the company's 401(k) plan after the funds were deducted from employees' paychecks. (DOL brought suit for fiduciary breach after the company went out of business.) The father argued that he was retired, but he continued to receive a paycheck and worked at the office on most days, and his negligence made it easier for his son to misappropriate the funds. Both men were held to be trustees who exercised control over plan contributions. [*Chao v. James C. Docster Inc.*, No. 3:01-CV-827, 2006 U.S. Dist. LEXIS 33216 (N.D.N.Y. Mar. 31, 2006)]

Rev. Rul. 2004-10 [2004-7 I.R.B. 484], reassures plan administrators that a defined contribution plan does not fail to satisfy the requirements of Code § 411(a)(11) if the accounts of ex-employees are charged a pro rata share of the plan's administrative expenses such as investment management fees, while the accounts of current employees are not charged. This result obtains if the expenses are proper for ERISA purposes, reasonable in amount, and the allocation is reasonable. The charge does not constitute a "significant detriment" to the ex-employees [Reg. § 1.411(a)—11(c)(2)(i)], because analogous fees would be charged in the investment market outside the pension context. *See* EBSA's Field Assistance Bulletin 2003-3 for guidelines on how to allocate expenses among the various plan participants. Because the allocation of expenses is a right or feature of the plan, it must be nondiscriminatory as defined by Code § 401(a)(4).

A May 2003 EBSA Field Assistance Bulletin notes that Department of Labor policy has changed. Employers are permitted to bill couples who divorce for the legal and accounting cost of dividing a retirement plan and processing a QDRO. Under the earlier policy, the employer had to either absorb such costs as a cost of plan administration, or divide it among all the plan's participants. Many companies outsource QDRO processing; a standard fee might be $300, or more if the standard Web-based form has to be adapted for individual needs. The IRS ruled that shifting that cost to employees does not violate the Internal Revenue Code, although the SPD must be amended to disclose the change. [Jennifer Saranow, *Cost of Divorce Just Went Up—In Your 401(k)*, Wall Street Journal, Nov. 9, 2004, at p. D3]

Many employees, including some who can easily afford the deferral, are not making large enough 401(k) contributions to trigger employer matches. Non-participation is motivated by, e.g., desire to consume rather than save; lack of knowledge; procrastination; a heavy debt burden for student loans, consumer goods, or health care; lack of belief in financial markets. [Tara Siegel Bernard, *Workers Could Be Saving More in 401(k)s, Study Says*, Wall Street Journal, Feb. 23, 2005, at p. D3]

The Vanguard Center for Retirement Research reported that, in 2004, only 13% of workers eligible to make catch-up contributions to their 401(k) plans did so. The average catch-up contribution from employees who made one (typically the more affluent) was $2,207. Close to one third of those with household income of more than $150,000 made catch-up contributions in 2004 vs. only 5% of those with household income of less than $50,000. (Using a different sample of respondents, the Profit Sharing/401k Council of America (PSCA) reported that close to 24% of eligible workers made catch-up contributions in 2003.) Accounts including catch-up contributions averaged $253,244 vs. a balance of only $89,060 for those who did not make the extra contributions. [Spencer Benefit Reports, *Only 13% of Those Age 50 and Older Made Catch-Up Contributions in 2004, According to Vanguard,* <http://www.newslettersonline.com/user/user.fas/s=583/fp=4/tp=41?T=open-article,899017&P=article> (Sept. 6, 2005)]

Over the last 30 years, fee structures for qualified plans have developed, sometimes in ways that artificially inflate fees and/or make it difficult to understand the real cost of such plans. The legally mandated disclosures are often confusing to participants, especially the financially unsophisticated. Plan administrators should be aware of the potential for hidden fees such as, for example, "soft-dollar" commissions paid to brokerages under SEC Rule 28(e); fees to sub-transfer agents for servicing accounts; 12b-1 fees for account distributions and account servicing; or unitized variable annuity wrap fees. Small companies usually pay higher fees for their 401(k) plans than do larger companies, in part because the former often use group annuities that impose high fees and redemption charges. Plans with fewer than 50 employees pay an average of 1.4% of assets per year in fees—$14/$1,000 invested, versus 1.17% for plans with more than 1,000 participants. When investment returns are low, fees can wipe out the entire appreciation for the year. [Matthew D. Hutcheson, *Uncovering and Understanding Hidden Fees in Qualified Retirement Plans,* <http://www.401khelpcenter.com> (Jan. 27, 2005); Christopher Oster and Karen Damato, *Big Fees Hit Small Plans,* Wall Street Journal, Oct. 21, 2004, at p. D1]

Generally, mutual funds set their fees ("expense ratio") as a percentage, such as 0.5 to 2%, of the funds invested. In 2004, many employers responded to the history of bear market losses by reducing their tolerance of high fees that were accepted during the bull market. Because the 401(k) market is very competitive, employers often can achieve significant fee reductions (and thus enhance workers' accounts without contributing more to them themselves) by insisting on reductions and threatening to move their accounts. [Ken Brown and Christopher Oster, *As Returns Sag, Employers Turn Up Heat on 401(k) Fees,* Wall Street Journal, Sept. 14, 2004, at p. A1]

§ 6.08   INVESTMENT ADVICE FOR PARTICIPANTS

PWBA Advisory Opinion 2001-09A [(Dec. 14, 2001) <http://www.dol.gov/ebsa/programs/ori/advisory2001/2001-09A.htm>] says that it would not be a prohibited transaction for a company that provides financial services to retain an independent professional to use computer modeling and modern portfolio theory to offer discretionary asset allocation services and recommended asset allocation services in connection with individual account plans—i.e., 401(k) plans. Participants will be given advice about how to allocate assets within their accounts, but would be permitted to either accept or reject the advice.

The company upon which the Advisory Opinion is based, SunAmerica Retirement Markets Inc., stated that the fiduciary for the 401(k) plan would be given detailed information about the independent financial expert's role in developing model portfolios to be recommended to plan participants—and how the expert's involvement will affect the fee structure that SunAmerica charges for its services. The financial expert's compensation is not affected by participant's decisions about how to allocate the assets in their accounts (although SunAmerica's earnings from the 401(k) plan can increase based on these choices). SunAmerica will pay fees to the financial expert, but to preserve the expert's independence, the fee from SunAmerica will not be more than 5% of the expert's annual gross income.

SunAmerica applied for a prohibited transaction exemption. EBSA went one further by issuing an Advisory Opinion. The difference is that only SunAmerica would have been able to use an exemption, whereas the advisory opinion can be relied on by others. [*See* Tom Lauricella, *Decision Allows 401(k) Investors to Have Pros Call the Shots,* Wall Street Journal, Dec. 26, 2001, at p. C1]

Although the ability to offer financial advice makes it much easier for employers to provide financial education for employees, some commentators are skeptical about whether 401(k) participants, other than those who are already highly financially sophisticated, are interested in, or will make optimal use of, full-service brokerage accounts. In 1997, only 5% of the largest companies (those with over 5,000 employees) offered brokerage accounts in their 401(k)s. This number increased to 11% by 2002, and financial consultants Cerulli Associates estimate that one-third of plans will provide self-directed accounts by 2006.

Although in practical terms, higher-paid employees are much more likely to be interested in investment advice than their lower-paid co-workers, the antidiscrimination rules require that if a plan includes this feature, it must be made available to all. The fees for maintaining self-directed accounts usually fall somewhere between $50 and $250 a year, plus commissions on trades. [Donna Rosato, *New 401(k) Tool, But Who Needs It?* New York Times, Feb. 2, 2003, at p. B9]

§ 6.09   401(k) PLANS RESPOND TO THE ECONOMY

[A]   Market Effects

In the 1990s, 401(k) plans rose to prominence. Balances in 401(k) plans grew during the bull market—and 401(k) plan participants were often first-time or novice stock market investors, so they brought a new group of investors to the market. At the peak, there were 42 million 401(k) plan participants, with a total of $1.8 trillion invested in their accounts.

Unfortunately, however, when the stock market declined in March 2001, and when the attack of September 11, 2001, made the economy's problems worse, 401(k) plans were also adversely affected. The average plan balance peaked at $47,000 in 1999, and declined for the first time in 2000 to $42,000. In 1997, close to 79% of eligible employees participated in their company's 401(k) plan—dropping to 75% in late 2001.

In late 2005, more than $2 trillion was invested in 401(k)s, but 30% of eligible employees did not participate in their company's plan—and, often, these people lacked any other kind of savings. Interest in automatic enrollment has been growing and companies are taking a more active role—in part because 401(k) options have gotten so complicated that employees need a lot of hand-holding.

Traditionally, GICs and other stable value products were the dominant investment vehicles for 401(k)s—sometimes capturing an 80% market share. GICs lost favor during the 1990s mutual fund boom, but still represent more than 20% of the assets in larger defined contribution programs. As Baby Boomers age, many of them become more conservative in their investing style, so stable value funds could gain popularity. Some investors are confused because stable value funds go by so many names (guaranteed annuity option; fixed fund; fixed income fund; capital preservation fund). According to Hewitt's 401(k) index, 21.92% of 401(k) assets were placed in stable value funds (more than $460 billion), making stable value funds the second most popular investment option (employer stock was the most popular). About two thirds of the largest 401(k) plans offer a stable value option, whereas only one third of smaller plans do. [*401(k) Plans: Stable Values*, PlanSponsor.com magazine articles (February 2006)]

Although there are many reasons why so few employees take full advantage of their 401(k) plans, one obstacle is that many employees perceive making investment decisions as too difficult and time-consuming. Early in 2006, the Wall Street Journal reported that many 401(k) plans reduced the size and complexity of their investment menus. Some did this by turning back to "collective investment funds," a low-cost alternative that invests in stocks and bonds on behalf of 401(k) plans and other qualified retirement plans. These funds were popular in the 1980s, then lost out to mutual funds. Mutual funds still dominate the 401(k) investment landscape, but collective funds are making a comeback. Collective investment funds operate much like mutual funds—but are not subject to the SEC regulation of mutual funds and are not required to issue prospectuses or shareholder reports. The disclosure of fees and portfolios also is not required. Collective investment funds are subject to federal and state banking regulations and are covered by ERISA. In addition, collective funds generally have lower fees due to their generally staid investment techniques, like concentrating on stable value investments, and lack of solicitation of retail customers. [Eleanor Laise, *Firms Revive Low-Cost 401(k) Option*, Wall Street Journal, Jan. 28–29, 2006, at p. B3]

Perhaps as an equal and opposite reaction, the trend toward simplification was countered by many large companies that offered "brokerage" and "mutual fund" windows. The percentage of companies offering brokerage windows rose from 12% in 2001 to 16% in 2005. The windows work like a brokerage account funded by transfers from the 401(k) plan, with investment choices either screened by the employer or at the will of the account holder. Some employers with window plans tackle liability concerns by limiting the amount of the account that can be invested in brokerage windows or by screening the investment options offered to reduce risk. Window plans were most prevalent in industries with a large proportion of affluent and financially sophisticated employees who already understood basic investing concepts. [Jane J. Kim, *New Choices for 401(k) Plans*, Wall Street Journal, Oct. 11, 2005, at p. D1]

In the bear market of 2000 to 2002, both qualified plans and 401(k)s lost money, but the qualified plans—with professional management—performed somewhat better, because professional managers have fiduciary duties that require frequent re-balancing of portfolios. Individual investors often cling for too long to unsuccessful investments. [Jane J. Kim, *Pensions Outperformed 401(k) Plans in Bear Market*, Wall Street Journal, Nov. 23, 2004, at p. D2]

When 401(k) plans first emerged, many companies imposed a one-year waiting period before newly hired employees could participate in the plan. The current trend, however, is to allow participation by new hires. According to the Profit Sharing/401(k) Council of America's latest survey, about 60% of 401(k) plan sponsors now permit eligibility within three months of being hired. Less than half of plans permitted this in 1998, and about half did in 2003. Companies consider earlier potential participation a benefit in recruiting employees. Since 1998, employers have been allowed to perform discrimination testing eliminating first-year workers participating in the plan, so they have less fear that low participation rates by new employees would endanger the plan's qualification. However, waiting periods do serve some useful functions. Plans are at risk of failing anti-discrimination testing if too few low-paid workers participate, so a waiting period can screen out transitory workers and preserve the plan's qualification. Paperwork costs for transient employees can also be a burden on a plan. [(No by-line), *Eligibility Grows for 401(k) Plans As Firms Ease Rules*, Wall Street Journal, Jan. 12, 2005, at p. D2]

[B] Enron Effects

Enron, a Texas energy trading firm, filed for bankruptcy protection on December 2, 2001, triggering not only a huge scandal (because of faked audit reports and document destruction) but also a broader appraisal of the role of company stock in 401(k) plans, and indeed in retirement saving in general.

During the bull market, publicly traded companies had very strong incentives to use their own stock to compensate employees. Not only could they save cash by offering stock or stock options, but distributing stock to employees reduces the risk of unfriendly takeovers, increases employees' stake in the company and therefore at least theoretically their loyalty, and gives employees the chance to benefit from increases in the value of the stock. The problem is that, in a bear market, employees suffer correspondingly as a result of decreases in the value of the stock.

Although the general rule is that corporations do not get a tax deduction for dividends they pay to their stockholders, sometimes a dividend deduction is available in connection with stock ownership by employees. Technical tax rules sometimes also allow companies to use Employee Stock Ownership Plans (ESOPs) as a vehicle for low-cost borrowing. [Ellen E. Schultz and Theo Francis, *Companies' Hot Tax Break: 401(k)s,* Wall Street Journal, Jan. 31, 2002, at p. C1]

> **Tip:** If employers provide proper disclosure, they can set their own rules about diversification and limitations on resale of stock, because these are considered business decisions by management that are not subject to fiduciary duty. However, there is a fiduciary duty to offer prudent investment options to employees (whether or not they choose to take advantage of them!).

Nearly all 401(k) plans offer several investment options, and some plans offer more than a dozen options; the most popular number of options is somewhere between eight and twelve. Nevertheless, despite the availability of diversification, most 401(k) investors do not diversify their accounts.

Many employees hold a belief that their company's stock is more likely to prosper or at least offer stable value than the stock market at large. Others may hold a large position in employer stock because they're afraid that selling their shares and re-investing will be viewed as a lack of confidence in the employer. It's common for employer matches to be made in company stock rather than cash, and to forbid employees to sell such stock before reaching age 50, or until they have been with the company for a certain number of years, which also encourages build-up of company stock in 401(k) accounts.

However, diversification is not necessarily the cure to all 401(k) planning ills. It should be noted that in a broad stock market decline, like the one that marked late 2001 and early 2002, even a diversified portfolio is likely to suffer losses in many of its components.

Congress responded with the introduction of many pieces of legislation taking differing approaches to protecting retirement savings, such as limitations on concentration in employer stock and limitations on the length of time employees could be compelled to hold matching stock contributions in their accounts.

[C] Blackout Periods

In certain instances, often associated with corporate mergers and acquisitions, or with the release of corporate earnings and other financial statements, a "blackout period" is imposed, and ordinary activities in connection with plan accounts are suspended. Because of concerns that rank-and-file employees are at risk of losing money during blackouts, the Sarbanes-Oxley Act [Pub. L. No. 107-204] not only limits the trading activities of corporate insiders, but also obligates the corporation to provide notice of future blackout periods to the employees at large.

A blackout period, according to § 306(a)(4) of the Act, means a period that lasts more than three consecutive business days, during which at least 50% of the plan's participants or beneficiaries' ability to trade in the employer company's stock is affected. Blackout periods can be attractive from the corporate point of view, because if too many employees want to sell their stock at once, the price of shares is likely to decline.

An "individual account plan" means a retirement plan that has more than one participant, and where each participant has his or her own separate account. For instance, a 401(k) plan is an individual account plan, but a defined benefit pension plan is not, because the whole plan has only one account from which benefits are paid.

Certain events that affect trading are not considered blackout periods, so the notice requirement doesn't apply. Under the legal definition, blackout periods are only temporary, so if rights are permanently amended or eliminated, this does not constitute a blackout period, and notice will not be required.

Furthermore, if the plan imposes regularly scheduled blackouts—for instance, every quarter at the time that earnings figures are released—and if the scheduled blackouts have been disclosed to participants and beneficiaries in the Summary Plan Description (SPD) or other plan communications, notice will not be required.

Finally, an event is not a blackout period if it is imposed just because someone becomes—or ceases to be—a participant or beneficiary in an individual account plan because of a corporate merger, acquisition, or divestiture. Limitations on just one person's account (relating to a divorce-related court order or a tax levy, for instance) are not considered blackout periods either, because a blackout period is a mass rather than an individual event.

In 2003, the Eastern District of New York upheld an SPD provision stating that transfer limitations can be imposed in situations such as excessive trading, and the plan's Administrative Committee has the discretion to refuse to implement participants' trading instructions if the committee finds them inappropriate. The committee issued a policy barring overly frequent market timing trades in amounts over $75,000. The plaintiffs sued under ERISA § 510, alleging that they were discriminated against for exercising their rights under the plan. Although the court agreed that former as well as current participants could bring a § 510 action (a point on which not all courts are agreed), nevertheless the court ruled that the SPD reserved the right to restrict trading, and the actual restrictions were a mere rule modification and not an impermissible retroactive plan amendment. ERISA does not provide plan participants with a right to unlimited trading of their accounts. [*Straus v. Prudential Employee Sav. Plan,* 253 F. Supp. 2d 438 (E.D.N.Y. 2003)]

CHAPTER 7

CASH BALANCE PLANS

§ 7.01   INTRODUCTION

A cash balance plan is a hybrid pension plan that shares features of a conventional defined benefit plan with characteristics more like a profit-sharing or 401(k) plan. Cash balance plans are subject to the defined benefit plan rules.

The IRS's definition of a cash balance plan, found at 64 Fed. Reg. 56579, is "a defined benefit pension plan that typically defines an employee's retirement benefit by reference to the amount of a hypothetical account balance." In a typical cash balance plan, this account is credited with hypothetical allocations and interest that are determined under a formula set out in the plan.

The plan is drafted so that the corporation's books reflect an individual account for each participant. The employer funds the plan each year, based on a percentage of pay, and subject to the I.R.C. § 415 limit on employer contributions. The pension the employee will eventually receive reflects two elements: an annual benefit credit (a percentage of pay) and annual interest credited at the rate specified by the plan. Because cash balance plans provide individual accounts, the plans are more portable than ordinary defined benefit plans.

At retirement, the employee's retirement annuity is based on the vested account balance. In practice, although in most defined benefit plans accrual is greatest in the later years of employment, in cash balance plans accrual is greatest in the early years. Defined benefit plans often provide early retirement subsidies; cash balance plans seldom do.

Changing an existing defined benefit plan to a cash balance plan, via plan amendments, is called a conversion. Generally, the new cash balance benefit formula applies to new employees, and may also apply to employees who had already earned benefits under the plan before the conversion.

Although plan amendments cannot reduce benefits earned before the conversion, some conversions have the effect that employees who already earned benefits do not earn additional retirement benefits for varying periods of time after the conversion. This effect, often referred to as "wearaway" or "benefit plateau," continues until the employee's benefit under the ongoing cash balance formula catches up with the employee's protected benefit.

A report from the ERISA Advisory Council defines wearaway as an effect of plan transitions. The employee can get either the frozen benefit under the old plan formula or the total benefit under the cash balance plan—whichever is greater. But for employees who are close to early retirement age, the frozen benefit may be so much larger than the accruals under the new cash balance formula that, in effect, little or nothing will be accrued for a long time, until the benefit under the old rules is "worn away."

Despite the legal uncertainty surrounding these plans, many of them have been adopted. Over 700 cash balance plans were adopted in the 1990s, and many requests for determination letters were filed, although the IRS imposed a moratorium on granting such requests. According to the IRS, there were 1,231 cash balance plans in 2000, a figure that grew 60%, reaching 1,965 at the end of 2002.

(Some employers have more than one cash balance plan.) PBGC figures released in 2004 show that there were about 29,000 small pension plans (under 1,000 people, including retirees and former employees, covered by the plan). Of those small plans, only about 2% (675 plans) were cash balance plans. Among the plans covering 1,000 to 9,999 people, 12% (386 plans) were cash-balance plans, and 26% of plans covering 10,000 or more people (170 plans) were of the cash balance type. Overall, the 1,231 cash balance plans represented 4% of all plans. [Ellen E. Schultz, *Cash-Balance Conversions Spread*, Wall Street Journal, Oct. 5, 2004, at p. D2]

According to the AARP Public Policy Institute, by late 2005 more than a quarter of participants in single-employer defined benefit plans were in plans using cash balance formulas. However, analysis of the Form 5500 reports filed in 2003 showed that 23 out of the 25 largest plans that converted had transition provisions to lessen the impact of the conversion on their existing workforce, and about 45% of workers affected by these conversions received transition relief. The most common strategy was to grandfather in older workers under the previous plan formula or to pay them a pension calculated under either the old or the new formula, whichever yielded a larger pension. Some companies granted supplemental credits based on pay to some or all of the employees who had participated in the old defined benefit plan, but that was the least common transition strategy. Out of the 23 plans with transition provisions studied, seven granted transition relief to everyone in the defined benefit plan at the time of the conversion. The others specified criteria (e.g., minimum age, minimum service, combination age/service formula) for transition relief. Eight of the plans limited the scope of transition provisions to a term of years; the rest made them available throughout the life of the grandfathered-in staff. [Daniel J. Beller, *Transition Provisions in Large Converted Cash Balance Plans*, AARP Public Policy Institute #2005-13, <http://www.aarp.org/research/work/benefits/2005_13_pension.pdf> (Oct. 2005)]

The Congressional Research Service pressed home the potential consequences of cash balance conversions by informing legislators what would happen in the (very unlikely) case that Congress switched to cash balance plans. For example, the Chairman of the Senate Finance Committee, Republican Charles E. Grassley of Iowa, would be entitled to a pension worth $508,266 at age 70 under the existing system if he remained in office long enough to accumulate 18 years' service. The same tenure would result in a pension worth only $161,623 under a cash balance plan. [Mary Williams Walsh, *What If a Pension Shift Hit Lawmakers, Too?* New York Times, Mar. 9, 2003, at p. B1]

§ 7.02   CASH BALANCE PLANS: PROS AND CONS

Cash balance plans are authorized by a sentence in the preamble of IRS Proposed Regulations that were published on September 11, 1991, creating a safe harbor. Under this proposal, changing the accrual pattern of a defined benefit plan "will not cause a cash balance plan to fail to satisfy the requirement of I.R.C. § 411(b)(1)(H)." This proposal was never finalized, but the IRS has permitted many cash balance conversions, including some involving major corporations. [For the history of cash balance plans, *see* Ellen E. Schultz, *Inquiry Sought into History of Pension Rule*, Wall Street Journal, Jan. 14, 2000, at p. A4, and *How a Single Sentence from IRS Paved Way to Cash Balance Plans*, Wall Street Journal, Dec. 28, 1999, at p. A1]

Cash balance plans are attractive to employers because the employer can retain any difference between the plan's actual investment return and the rate of return promised to employees. The plan can become self-funded if the gap is large enough so that the employer will not have to make further contributions.

Responding to a congressional inquiry, the GAO published a report in late 2005 that concluded cash balance conversions usually result in lower benefits for employees. The GAO studied 31 conversions made by large corporations and 102 conversions by smaller companies and found that most workers—of all ages— were entitled to lower pensions under the new form. The median monthly benefit that a 30-year-old worker would receive at age 68 would be $750 per month ($59 less than under a defined benefit plan), while a 40-year-old worker would receive $891 under a cash balance plan—$188 a month less than his or her defined benefit plan pension. A 50-year-old worker would receive $238 a month less than under the defined benefit plan it replaced. However, the GAO did not find the situation to be entirely negative. For instance, a cash balance conversion is better for all employees than if the defined benefit plan was terminated. In addition, some workers, including 27% of 50-year-old workers, would get a larger pension under the cash balance plan than under the defined benefit plan, and 70% of employers offered some grandfathering protection against the worst impact of a conversion. [The report is available online at <http://www.gao.gov/new. items/d0642.pdf>; *see* Allison Bell, *Researchers Say Typical Pension Shifts Hit Benefits*, NU Online News Service, Nov. 7, 2005; Marcy Gordon (AP), *GAO: Pension Switch Hurts Employees*, <http://kevxml2adsl.verizon.net/_1_ 29VUTO102PGKZKI[. . .]>, Nov. 4, 2005]

Cashpensions.com published a report in 2005, "Cash Balance Legislation: Myth Versus Fact," [<http://www.cashpensions.com/CB-Myths-Facts&208-16-05.pdf>, Aug. 16, 2005)] in which the organization's reasons for opposing cash balance conversions were outlined, including:

- Although some employers protect employees from negative impact, older workers usually lose a lot of pension income.
- Employers are well aware of the disparate impact of the conversion on older workers.
- Cash balance conversions create a risk that even more liabilities will be dumped on the PBGC—which is already hard-pressed financially.
- Employers can recruit and retain good workers without offering younger, mobile workers cash balance pensions.
- Cash balance plans are not easier for employees to understand than defined benefit plans, and they are not better appreciated by employees (although naïve

stockholders may be pleased if the conversion creates the impression that the corporation's bottom line is healthier because of accounting changes).

- More than half of employers who convert expect to cut their pension costs.
- It is not inevitable that employers who maintain hybrid plans will have to freeze or terminate their plans if they are not allowed to convert them to cash balance plans.

A study by the AARP Public Policy Institute concluded that employers often favor cash balance conversion (rather than terminating a defined benefit plan and creating a defined contribution plan) because terminating an overfunded plan could give rise to excise taxes on reversions to the employer.

The BLS found that in 1991, 3% of employees of medium-sized and large businesses who were covered by a defined benefit plan were covered by a cash balance plan—a proportion that rose to 23% in 2000. In 2003, about 26% of participants in single-employer defined benefit plans were in cash balance plans. [Jules H. Lichtenstein and John Turner, AARP Public Policy Institute, *Cash Balance Plans and Older Workers,* <http://www.aarp.org/ppi>]

In mid-2004, a trend away from cash balance plans was noted (especially after the IBM settlement), and many companies froze or terminated their cash balance plans or ceased providing any pension plans other than 401(k)s. An EEOC spokesperson said that 950 complaints about cash balance plans had been filed with the agency. [Michelle V. Rafter, *In Just a Year, Cash-Balance Plans Go From Panacea to Pariah,* Workforce Management, June 2004, <http://www.workforce.com/section/02/feature/23/73/92/>]

§ 7.03   "WHIPSAW" AND FINANCIAL FACTORS

The "whipsaw" issue arises because I.R.C. § 417 specifies the interest and mortality assumptions that must be used in converting from annuity to lump sum payment. When a worker covered by a defined benefit plan terminates employment, the sponsor must calculate the present value of any lump sum distribution.

This is done by projecting the account balance that would be available at normal retirement age, using PBGC-authorized interest rate assumptions. The next step is to find the value of the annuity that could be purchased with that sum. Finally, the PBGC interest rate assumptions are used again, to reconvert the annuity to a lump sum that represents the present value of the participant's account.

Applying this so-called whipsaw calculation to some cash balance plans increases the lump sum available to some plan participants. The participants who benefit naturally argue that the calculation has to be applied—and plan sponsors want to argue that they can bypass the whipsaw calculation. The higher the interest rates used, the less likely participants are to complain. Therefore, the whipsaw problem is most acute for disputes about plan actions taken before 1995, because in 1994 the PBGC raised its interest rate assumptions significantly.

The District Court for the District of Ohio required the whipsaw calculation to be performed for early retirement benefits payable as an immediate lump sum, producing a payout larger than the hypothetical account balance under the plan. The plaintiff brought a class action alleging that the lump sums as calculated were too small. The court accepted the plaintiff's contention that the present value calculation should have used the ERISA § 205(g)(3) valuation rules. The District Court ruled that the ERISA valuation rules are valid, so cash balance plans must follow them even if whipsaw results. [*West v. AK Steel Corp. Retirement Accumulation Pension Plan,* 318 F. Supp. 2d 579 (D. Ohio 2004)]

§ 7.04   CASE LAW ON CASH BALANCE PLANS

According to *Eaton v. Onan Corp.* [117 F. Supp. 2d 812 (S.D. Ind. 2000)], converting a defined benefit plan to a cash balance plan does not violate either the ADEA or ERISA's ban on age discrimination in benefit accruals. The court said that the ERISA provisions do not apply to employees younger than the plan's "normal retirement age."

Late in 2001, the company and the plaintiffs reached a settlement of that case, and of a companion tax court case, *Arndt v. Commissioner* [Docket No. 334-9912 (Tax Ct. 2001). *See* Lee A. Sheppard, *Settlement Reached in Cash Balance Plan Case,* 2001 Tax Notes (Oct. 1, 2001) (law.com)] Under the settlement, Onan Corp. agreed to compensate 1500 early retirees and over-40 employees for their losses stemming from the conversion to a cash balance plan. Onan did not admit to age discrimination, but did agree to make changes in plan design favorable to older employees. All participants can elect to receive a lump sum that is equal to the present value of the minimum annuity they would receive at the plan's normal retirement age—even if this is greater than their cash balance account.

Esden v. Bank of Boston [229 F.3d 154 (2d Cir. 2000)], a class action against a pension plan, tackles some important issues. The plaintiffs alleged that the plan's calculation of lump sum distributions violated the ERISA antiforfeiture rule.

The plan projected cash balances that would be taken as lump sums using a 4% interest rate, well below the 5.5% rate used to accrue interest credits. When the projection was discounted back to present value, participants received less than the actuarial equivalent of the normal balance. Part of the benefit was also contingent on the distribution option chosen, which was alleged to violate ERISA § 203(a) and I.R.C. § 411(a)(2).

The Second Circuit agreed with the view expressed by the IRS in Notice 96-8, 1996-1 C.B. 359, that "whipsaw," the result of projecting the account value using a rate below the guaranteed rate, violates ERISA because the participant is entitled to the present value of the accrued benefit. The Second Circuit view is that a variable interest rate is permissible as long as it is definitely determinable and does not grant discretion to the employer to set the amount after establishing the plan.

Lyons v. Georgia-Pacific Corp. [221 F.3d 1235 (11th Cir. 2000)], holds that the lump sum benefit under a defined benefit plan must be calculated by using the

PBGC discount rate to discount the normal retirement benefit to present value. Although the district court treated the IRS Regulations about the discount rate [Treas. Reg. § 1.411(a)-11] as "unreasonable," the Eleventh Circuit upheld the validity of the regulations.

In *Berger v. Xerox Corp. Retirement Income Guarantee Plan* [231 F. Supp. 2d 804 (S.D. Ill. 2001)], the judge says that improper interest rate calculations were used to arrive at the pre-retirement lump sum payments for terminated vested participants. Therefore, the court ordered recalculation for everyone who received such a distribution since January 1, 1990. Like *Esden* and *Lyons*, the *Berger* court required the use of the interest crediting rate in effect as of the date of the disposition. In August 2003, the Seventh Circuit ruled once again for the plaintiffs [*Berger v. Xerox Corp. Retirement Income Guarantee Plan*, 338 F.3d, 755 (7th Cir. 2003), *cert. denied* (Oct. 7, 2003)] stating harshly that Xerox violated ERISA by inducing ex-employees "to sell their pension entitlement back to the company cheap" (opinion at p. 9). The Seventh Circuit rejected Xerox's argument that its plan was a hybrid cash balance plan, ruling instead that Xerox violated ERISA's rules for calculation of lump-sum pension entitlements. By and large, the Seventh Circuit affirmed the District Court, but modified the judgment to provide somewhat higher damages for plaintiffs with small (under $25,000) cash balance lump sums.

In late 2003, the parties reached a proposed settlement (contingent on court approval) under which $239 million would be paid to thousands of workers who retired in the period 1990–1999. The payments would come from the pension plan for salaried employees, but Xerox would not be required to make additional contributions to cover the distributions until 2005 or later years. [Mary Williams Walsh, *Xerox Reaches Settlement With Retirees on Pension Suit,* New York Times, Nov. 15, 2003, at p. C2] The Ninth Circuit held in mid-2006 that Xerox's method of accounting for prior distributions when calculating retirement benefits violated ERISA by placing too high a value on the prior distributions and reducing the benefits accordingly. The Ninth Circuit remanded the case to the District Court for further proceedings, directing that the cash balance plan, as a hybrid plan, must satisfy both defined benefit and defined contribution rules. [*Miller v. Xerox Corp.,* Nos. 04-55582, 55583 (9th Cir. May 8, 2006)]

The 2003 First Circuit case of *Campbell v. BankBoston, N.A.* [327 F.3d (1st Cir. 2003)] raised important issues about age discrimination allegations in both the cash balance plan and severance context (discussed in Chapter 3). The unsuccessful plaintiff raised ERISA and ADEA claims, but summary judgment was granted for the employer. BankBoston employed the plaintiff for 37 years. BankBoston converted its defined benefit plan to a cash balance plan. The practical effect of the change was to reduce the plaintiff's retirement benefits by about $3,000 a year.

On January 1, 1989, the defendant employer adopted a cash balance plan. The plan included a safeguard minimum benefit for long-term employees, to make sure they got at least as much as they would have received under the prior defined benefit plan, with continued accrual of benefits. In 1995, the defendant realized that grandfathering-in those employees would be very expensive. On January 1,

1997, the cash balance plan was amended to eliminate continued accrual under the plan after December 31, 1996. This amendment had the effect of ending the plaintiff's pension accrual entirely.

The First Circuit did not accept the plaintiff's argument that the application of wearaway was a forfeiture of an accrued pension benefit. The court's interpretation was that accrued benefits were not reduced, only expected benefits, and an employer has the right to modify or eliminate expected benefits. ERISA was not violated because the reduction involved only future expected accruals.

Grandfathering was also at issue in a 2004 Third Circuit case. According to the Third Circuit, the doctrine of ratification cannot be used to make retroactive changes to a pension plan that would have the effect of reducing accrued benefits. The plaintiff in this case went to work for *Cigna* in 1983, when it had a defined benefit plan. In 1997, amendments were proposed transferring younger, shorter-term employees to a cash balance plan, with long-term employees grandfathered into the defined benefit plans. The plan amendments included a "rehire rule" under which long-term employees who were rehired after December 31, 1997, after leaving the company would be covered by the new cash balance plan rather than the old plan. However, the document adopting this amendment was not signed by the CEO until December 31, 1998. The plaintiff left CIGNA at the beginning of 1998 and was rehired on December 9, 1998 (i.e., before the formal adoption), so his suit contended that he was entitled to be grandfathered into the defined benefit plan. CIGNA's position was that the CEO's signature was purely a formality, providing retroactive ratification of plan changes that had already occurred. The district court agreed with the employer, but the Third Circuit reversed on the grounds that an amendment cannot be ratified subsequently if it affects intervening rights of plan participants and other third parties. [*Depenbrock v. CIGNA Corp.,* 389 F.3d 78 (3d Cir. 2004), discussed in Shannon P. Duffy, *In Big Win for ERISA Plaintiffs, 3rd Circuit Ruling Protects Worker's Accrued Benefits*, Legal Intelligencer, Nov. 15, 2004 (law.com)]

The Southern District of Illinois issued an extremely controversial ruling that IBM's cash balance plan conversion and amendments to the cash balance plan violated ERISA. [*Cooper v. IBM Personal Pension Plan and IBM*, 2003-2 USTC ¶ 50,596 (S.D. Ill. 2003)] (IBM announced plans for an immediate appeal.) The decision, widely interpreted as an attack on all cash balance plans, held that the IBM pension credit formula was invalid because it reduced accrued benefits because of increases in age or service. According to Judge G. Patrick Murphy, IBM could have achieved its objectives of saving costs and providing pensions in a form more attractive to its younger workforce by terminating its defined benefit plan and adopting a defined contribution plan instead, but the plan amendments that IBM actually adopted were not acceptable under ERISA. This decision was rendered on various motions, rather than after a full trial, and some issues were still unsettled, so the case proceeded on the issue of what relief the plaintiffs should be granted.

On February 12, 2004, Judge Murphy ruled against IBM once again (although the case was far from over). IBM argued that it would be inappropriate to grant retroactive relief to the class of plaintiffs, because IBM was suddenly confronted with a drastic change in the law (i.e., the earlier decision in this case that IBM discriminated against older employees). Judge Murphy did not find this argument at all persuasive; he ruled that the only thing that changed was IBM's strategy for evading unwelcome pension rules. [*Cooper v. IBM Personal Pension Plan and IBM Corp.*, Memo and Order Civil No. 99-829-GPM (Feb. 12, 2004), discussed in BenefitsBlog (B. Janell Grenier, Esq.): *Cooper v. IBM Cash Balance Plan Developments* (Feb. 13, 2004), <http://www.benefitscounsel.com/archives/000911.html>]

In September 2004, a partial settlement for about $300 million was reached with respect to the termination claim involving several thousand employees who were not vested at the time of termination. Age discrimination and other claims were not included in this settlement, although the parties agreed to cap further damages at $1.4 billion. The settlement had little cash flow impact on IBM, because the company in effect paid out funds that had already been placed into the pension plan, and compensatory and punitive damages are not available in such cases. [David Cay Johnston, *I.B.M. Employees Get $320 Million in Pension Suit*, New York Times, Sept. 30, 2004, at p. A1; Ellen E. Schultz, Theo Francis, and William M. Bulkeley, *IBM Sets Accord on Pension Plan for $300 Million*, Wall Street Journal, Sept. 30, 2004, at p. A3; Ellen E. Schultz, *IBM Settles Small Part of Pension Suit*, Wall Street Journal, Sept. 17, 2004, at p. A3]

In mid-June 2004, the trend of anti-cash-balance decisions was halted by Judge Catherine Blake's decision that cash balance plans are not inherently guilty of age discrimination. In Judge Blake's view, ERISA does not mandate the annuity payable at age 65 as the sole test of the value of the accrued benefit; it would be more sensible to value the cash balance plan balance using ERISA's defined contribution tests. In this case, the contribution credits increased with the plan participant's age, leading Judge Blake to conclude that the plan did not discriminate against older participants. [*Tootle v. A/RINC Inc.*, 222 F.R.D. 88 (D. Md. 2004), discussed in Jerry Geisel, *Cash Balance Design Not Age Biased: Judge*, Business Insurance, June 15, 2004, <http://www.businessinsurance.com/cgi-bin/news.pl?newsId=3994>]

The Eastern District of Pennsylvania dismissed age discrimination claims against PNC Financial Service's Group cash balance conversion. PNC's plan was similar to the IBM plan that was held discriminatory in 2003. The Eastern District ruled that ERISA § 204(b)(1)(H)'s requirement that the rate of accrual cannot be reduced does not require that the annuity payable at normal retirement age (NRA) be considered the only measurement of the rate, so it was not persuaded by the IBM decision's reasoning. The Eastern District treated the accrual rate as the change in the employee's cash balance account each year. [*Register v. PNC Financial Servs. Group, Inc.*, 2005 U.S. Dist. LEXIS 29678 (E.D. Pa. Nov. 21, 2005)]

Late in 2004, the Sixth Circuit overruled the district court, which had held that a pre-retirement mortality discount should not be used to compute the lump-sum distribution of accrued benefits payable on death of a cash balance plan participant. The Sixth Circuit ruling was based on procedural grounds rather than the appropriateness of the plan's pre-retirement mortality assumptions. The Sixth Circuit ruled that the plaintiff did not ask for appropriate equitable relief, because he had already been paid more than the plan terms required. Asking for a recalculation therefore was not appropriate equitable relief under ERISA § 502(a)(3), and he could not have a constructive trust imposed because there had been no unjust enrichment to reverse and plan assets had not been wrongfully conveyed to a third party. [*Crosby v. Bowater Inc. Ret. Plan,* 382 F.3d 587 (6th Cir. 2004)]

Some claims involving FleetBoston's cash balance conversion were allowed to proceed by the District Court for the District of Connecticut, and class certification was granted on the surviving claims. Age discrimination and ERISA § 204(b)(1) claims survived, as did claims that participants were not given the required 15 days' notice of decrease in the rate of benefit accrual and claims that the SPD was inadequate. The court dismissed the claim that the nonforfeitability requirement (ERISA § 203(a)) was violated by making cash balance benefits dependent on waiving early retirement benefits, because the District Court found that there was no requirement of making a choice; participants always received the greater of the cash balance account benefit or the benefit accrued under the predecessor defined benefit plan.

A claim that the plan violated ERISA § 204(b)(1)(B) (the provision that forbids back-loading), however, failed because if calculations were made on the basis of the cash balance plan having been in effect for all plan years, employees would always have accrued benefits under the cash balance plan and never under the defined benefit plan. [*Richards v. FleetBoston Fin. Corp.,* No. 3:04-cv-1638 (JCH), (D. Conn. Mar. 31, 2006); *see* Rebecca Moore, *FleetBoston Cash Balance Suit Moves Forward,* PlanSponsor.com (Apr. 5, 2006)]

Suit was filed in July 2005, charging that Southern California Gas Company's cash balance conversion had a disparate impact on older workers, although the plan permitted "grandfathered-in" workers to use the defined benefit plan's formula for five years after the conversion. This case also involved allegations of wearaway. [Ellen E. Schultz, *Sempra Unit Workers Sue Over Converting Pension,* Wall Street Journal, July 11, 2005, at p. A4; Mary Williams Walsh, *California Utility Workers Claim Bias in Pension Changes,* New York Times, July 11, 2005, at p. C2]

§ 7.05   THE CONVERSION PROCESS

At least 15 days' notice must be given in advance of adoption of a plan amendment that significantly reduces the rate of benefit accruals in the future. [*See* § 11.05 for a discussion of EGTRRA rules increasing the amount of disclosure that participants are entitled to in this situation] The plan may also have to issue a revised SPD and/or a Summary of Material Modification in connection with the conversion.

The PWBA (now called EBSA) published a cash balance plan FAQ. [<http://www.dol.gov/ebsa/faqs/faq_consumer_cashbalanceplans.html>] Question 11 says that neither ERISA nor the Tax Code obligates employers who convert to a cash balance plan to give employees the option of remaining in the old plan. The employer can simply replace the old formula with the new formula for all participants, as long as the benefits already accrued as of the date of the conversion are not reduced. Or the employer can keep current employees under the old plan formula, applying the new formula only to those hired after the change. Another option is for some employees to be "grandfathered in," or allowed to receive their pensions under the old formula.

> **Tip:** If the converted plan does offer choices to participants, and if they have to sign a waiver as part of the option process, make sure that the waiver conforms to the standards of the Older Workers Benefit Protection Act. [29 U.S.C. § 621 *et seq.*]

The District Court for the District of New Jersey, in an unpublished 2006 decision, ruled that AT&T was not required to provide 15 days' notice of conversion of its defined benefit plan to cash balance form. The amount of future benefits was not reduced, so notice was not required. The plaintiffs' argument that notification of reduction in the "rate of future benefits" was required was unsuccessful. The court ruled that although AT&T described the effects of the transaction in favorable terms, it did not engage in a level of active concealment that would give rise to remedies for the participants. [*Engers v. AT&T*, No. 9803660 (JLL) (unpublished) (D.N.J. Mar. 31, 2006); discussed in Fred Schneyer, *AT&T Cleared in Cash Balance Notification Suit,* PlanSponsor.com (Apr. 4, 2006)]

§ 7.06   DECEMBER 2002 REGULATIONS: PROPOSAL AND WITHDRAWAL

[A]   Terms of Proposal

In December 2002, the IRS published a set of Proposed Regulations, REG-209500-86, at 67 Fed. Reg. 76123 (Dec. 11, 2002). The purpose was to give guidance to plan sponsors, although the Treasury Department left the moratorium on cash-balance plan conversions in effect.

The proposal created the concept of an "eligible cash balance plan," for which the rate of benefit accrual can properly be defined as the additions to the plan participant's hypothetical account for the plan year. Previously accrued interest credits are not included in the rate of accrual. In an eligible cash balance plan, the normal form of benefit for accruals in the current plan year is immediate payment of the balance in the hypothetical account. The participant accrues the right to future interest credits without regard to future service at the same time as the accrual of additions to the hypothetical account. The calculation must use a reasonable rate of interest, and the interest rate must not decrease based on reaching

65 (or any other specific age). Interest credits must be provided for all future periods, including those occurring after normal retirement age (NRA).

The Proposed Regulations stated that merely converting a defined benefit plan to cash balance form would not make the plan fail under Code § 411(b)(1)(H), provided that the converted plan became an eligible cash balance plan, and also provided that the play did not create wearaway (the opening account balance for each participant would at least equal the actuarial present value of the prior accrued benefit, using reasonable actuarial assumptions).

The Proposed Regulations' approach to avoiding age discrimination was to forbid plans to stop or reduce accruals after NRA on the basis of age (whether the participant is older, younger, or at the NRA). The mandate of continued accrual of benefits post-NRA is satisfied to the extent that the benefits are distributed to the participant, or are increased actuarially to account for delayed distribution.

Plans that explicitly called for a higher accrual or allocation rate for younger participants would violate the Proposed Regulations. An indirect reduction would occur on account of a characteristic that (after all facts and circumstances are considered) is a proxy for age. However, the Proposed Regulations permitted plans to "cap" the number of years of service or participation that could be taken into account for accruals.

The Proposed Regulations defined it as a violation of § 411(b) to fail to provide optional forms of benefits, ancillary benefits, or other rights or features with respect to benefits or allocations because of attainment of any age—or to provide these things on a less favorable basis because of attainment of the stated age. However, age-based variance in the subsidized portion of an early retirement benefit, qualified disability benefit, or supplement to the Social Security benefit would not violate the Proposed Regulations.

[B] Withdrawal

Although initially the Department of the Treasury announced in September 2003 that it was reviewing information with a view to finalizing the December 2002 proposals, in October it was reported that the Treasury had decided to refrain from proceeding, waiting until Congress passed cash balance legislation. [Compare Ellen E. Schultz and Theo Francis, *Treasury to Issue Guides on Cash-Balance Payouts*, Wall Street Journal, Sept. 16, 2003, at p. D5, with their article, *Treasury May Delay Pension Rules*, Wall Street Journal, Oct. 16, 2003, at p. A6.]

The proposal became politically controversial and unpopular enough to impel Congress to include a provision in the Consolidated Appropriations Act of 2004, Pub. L. 108-199 (the federal funding bill for fiscal 2004) forbidding the Treasury to use any of the funds appropriated for its use to implement the 2002 Proposed Regulations.

On June 15, 2004, the Treasury issued Announcement 2004-57, 2004-27 IRB 15 withdrawing the December 2002 Proposed Regulations. The agency cited thousands of comment letters received, both from employees claiming adverse effects from cash balance conversions and from employers concerned that traditionally accepted defined benefit provisions would be deemed age-discriminatory. The Treasury said that the Proposed Regulations were withdrawn to give Congress a chance to adopt legislation—and also said that neither it nor the IRS would issue guidance on age discrimination issues in cash balance plans or conversions until Congress acted. Pending technical advice cases (applications for determination letters) will not be processed as long as the tax issues remain under consideration by Congress.

[C] Other 2004 Developments

The Consolidated Appropriations Act of 2004 mandated that the Treasury draft language to address the risks of age discrimination and wearaway caused by cash balance conversions, and to provide relief for older and long-service employees. The Treasury complied by issuing Release JS-1132 on February 2, 2004. [*Preserving Cash Balance Plans for Workers: Treasury Proposes Legislation to Protect Defined Benefit Plans and Ensure Fair Treatment of Older Workers in Cash Balance Conversions*, <http://www.treas.gov/press/releases/js1132.htm>]

Release JS-1132 calls for a five-year hold-harmless period after a cash balance conversion, during which the benefits earned by any participant would have to be at least as valuable as the benefits that would have been earned under the prior plan if the conversion had not occurred. The five-year period was chosen to be both attractive enough to employers to deter plan freezes, and adequately protective of employees' expectations for retirement security. Under the Release, plans would be subject to a 100% excise tax on the shortfall between required and actual benefits, if the employer failed to provide the required level of benefits, or if wearaway occurred. The excise tax would be waived if current workers are grandfathered in, or if workers are given a choice between the traditional and the cash balance plan. The excise tax would also be limited to the greater of the plan sponsor's taxable income or the plan's surplus assets at the time of the conversion (because some employers favor cash balance conversions because they are in financial difficulties).

Release JS-1132's approach to age parity is a requirement that plans provide pay credits for older and longer-service employees that are not less than the pay credits for younger employees. Interest credits must not be discriminatory. To eliminate whipsaw, the release permits cash balance plans to distribute employees' account balances as single sums, but interest must not be credited at an unrealistic, above-market rate.

In March 2004, FASB issued an interpretation of its Statement No. 87 (*Employers' Accounting For Pensions*) discussing appropriate accounting for cash balance plans for periods of service in plans using market-related variable formulas, or formulas other than salary times years of service. [FASB Project Summary (March 10, 2004), <http://www.fasb.org/project/interpretation_st87.shtml>]

CHAPTER 8
NONQUALIFIED PLANS

§8.01 INTRODUCTION

[A] Generally

One of the most important aspects of maintaining a qualified plan (and therefore obtaining a tax deduction for related costs) is satisfying the Internal Revenue Code's tests for nondiscrimination. It is not illegal for an employer to set up a discriminatory plan, and in fact many types of nonqualified plans have evolved for companies that want to recruit, retain, or motivate senior management and/or persons who own significant amounts of stock in the corporation. Nonqualified plans are also used to provide post-retirement income higher than the levels that can be generated through a qualified plan.

In contrast with the elaborate rules required to get a current deduction for contributions to a qualified plan, the rules for nonqualified plans are much simpler. The employer is allowed to discriminate in both contributions and benefits in favor of highly compensated employees (HCEs). The plan does not have to be operated through a trust.

In fact, the employer doesn't even have to fund the plan in advance. Payments can be made as they come due, out of the employer's general assets instead of from a special trust. Insurance policies can also be used to fund nonqualified plan benefits. The ERISA funding requirements don't apply to nonqualified plans, so promises and forms of securities can be used for funding a nonqualified plan even if they would not be acceptable in a qualified plan.

In a qualified plan, a "bad boy" clause (one that removes entitlement to benefits) is allowed only for fraud or abuse of fiduciary duty. In a nonqualified plan, benefits can be forfeited by an executive who leaves the company.

Under a qualified plan, the employer gets a current deduction each year as it makes contributions to the plan. The employer's deduction for nonqualified plan expenses is not available until the year in which the participant receives money from the plan and includes it in income. The corporation's general creditors are entitled to make claims against reserves set aside to pay nonqualified plan benefits, but the qualified plan trust is protected against creditors' claims.

For many years, the subject of nonqualified plans was a backwater, with little of note occurring. That was altered in 2004 by the enactment of the American Jobs Creation Act (AJCA), P.L. 108-357, creating new I.R.C § 409A.

The statute gave the IRS 60 days to issue guidance, which was supposed to be similar to but more restrictive than the golden parachute rules under I.R.C. § 280G. The IRS satisfied this requirement by issuing Notice 2005-1, 2005-2 I.R.B. 274, a set of questions and answers, although some issues remain to be resolved. [*See* §8.02[D]]

At the end of 2004, the First Circuit decided a case about an insurance company's nonqualified deferred compensation plan for general agents. The plaintiffs charged the company with violating the terms of the plan as well as committing unfair and deceptive trade practices and breaking the implied covenant of good faith and fair dealing. The plaintiffs alleged that the defendant unlawfully imposed a tax charge on the general agents to offset the tax cost of operating the plan. The defendant admitted that it imposed the charge, but stated that the charge was a reasonable one and permitted by the plan terms. The district court, as affirmed by the First Circuit, granted summary judgment for the defendant, finding that the contract provided enough discretion to impose such a charge.

Because the general agents are not employees, the plan had to be a non-qualified plan. Taxes were imposed at the corporate level. The plan documents give the defendant sole discretion to determine the amount of net earnings to be credited to each general agent's account; "net" means net of expenses and taxes.

With respect to the covenant of good faith claim, the First Circuit ruled that the clear terms of the plan documents gave the defendant discretion to make deductions. The breach of fiduciary duty claim failed, because the First Circuit found that fiduciary duty required exercising discretionary power in good faith, prudently, and after serious consideration of the alternatives—standards that the defendant satisfied. [*McAdams v. Massachusetts Mutual Life Ins. Co.*, 391 F.3d 287 (1st Cir. 2004)]

[B] Structures for Nonqualified Plans

Various structures have evolved for providing nonqualified plan benefits to executives, managers, and other favored corporate employees.

[1] SERP

A Supplemental Executive Retirement Plan (SERP), also known as an excess-benefit plan, can be used to defer amounts that exceed the qualified plan limits.

[2] QSERP

A Qualified Supplemental Executive Retirement Plan (QSERP) is a qualified plan used to enhance retirement benefits for executives. The plan must satisfy nondiscrimination requirements and is subject to the I.R.C. § 415 limits. However, the employer's contributions can be integrated with Social Security, reducing the amount the employer has to contribute on behalf of lower-paid employees. To adopt a QSERP, the employer corporation can simply amend the plan documents to include an annual list of people or job titles entitled to additional benefits of $X/year. Usually, QSERP amounts are subtracted from the amounts that would otherwise be payable under nonqualified plans. Because the QSERP is a qualified plan, the employer gets a current deduction, and the employee is not taxed until benefits are actually paid (and the employee has some certainty that they will be paid because of prefunding). If the QSERP is a defined contribution plan, it is subject to the overall limitation on contributions to all defined contribution plans; if the employer is already making close to the maximum contribution under other qualified plans there is little leeway for the QSERP.

[3] Rabbi Trust

A rabbi trust (so-called because the first one was created by a synagogue for its clergyman) sets aside assets in an irrevocable trust to pay the benefits, although the corporation's creditors can reach the assets. The assets in the trust cannot revert to the employer until all of the obligations to pay deferred compensation have been satisfied. Executives are not taxed until they receive benefits from the trust, because of the risk that creditor claims will prevent benefit payments. A "springing" rabbi trust is set up with only minimal funding. However, if the control of the corporation changes (for instance, because of a merger or acquisition), then the trust provides for funding for payment of benefits. The rabbi trust will not be considered "funded" for ERISA purposes just because it has a spring provision.

One of the effects of the AJCA (*see* § 8.02[D]) is to ban offshore rabbi trusts.

The Gulf Opportunity Zone Act of 2005 (GOZA), P.L. 109-137, clarifies the AJCA by imposing a January 1, 2005, effective date for the applicability of I.R.C. § 409A to nonqualified plans that use offshore rabbi trusts or protect benefits against the risk of decline in the company's financial health. GOZA provides that this rule applies to amounts set aside or restricted with respect to deferral of compensation vested on or before December 31, 2004.

However, the harshness of this requirement is ameliorated by transition relief provided by Notice 2006-33, 2006-15 I.R.B. 754, so that nonqualified deferred compensation plans can come into compliance with § 409A if they use offshore trusts or protect nonqualified benefits against risk of decline in the company's financial health. One of the criteria of § 409A compliance is that off-shore rabbi trusts and protective provisions with "financial distress" triggers are forbidden. Notice 2006-33 gives the comparatively small group of plans that use these techniques to avoid penalties by amending the plan to meet the § 409A requirements no later than December 31, 2007. Failure to do so means that amounts deferred under the plan will be included in the plan participant's gross income, as well as a 20% penalty and an interest penalty.

[4] Secular Trust

A secular trust is an irrevocable trust whose assets cannot be reached by the employer's creditors, including its bankruptcy creditors. It offers more protection to the executive's right to receive deferred compensation than a rabbi trust, but has less favorable tax consequences. The price of increased protection for the employee is that the employee has taxable income (taxed using the I.R.C. § 72 annuity rules) equal to the employer contributions to the trust on the employee's behalf. The employer can deduct its contributions to the trust, to the extent they are ordinary and necessary business expenses, in the tax year in which the contributions become taxable income for the employee.

[5] Top Hat Plan

A top hat plan is an unfunded deferred compensation plan limited to managers and/or HCEs. Top hat plans that are pension plans must file a brief notice each year with the Department of Labor, although less disclosure is required than for a qualified plan. An unfunded top hat pension plan is not subject to the ERISA participation, vesting, funding, or fiduciary responsibility rules. The plan must have a claims procedure. Top hat plans that are not pension plans are probably exempt from ERISA Title I. The modest role that ERISA plays in regulating top hat plans is probably enough to preempt state law, so suits cannot be brought in state court involving claims against top hat plans.

For example, the Eleventh Circuit held that survivor benefits under a top hat plan's joint and survivor annuity provision were not payable to a wife whose husband began receiving benefits when married to his first wife. The retiree received reduced benefits from a joint and survivor annuity when married to his first wife. After her death, he continued to receive the reduced benefit, and remarried one year later. Five years after that, his former employer was acquired, and the acquiring company decided to accelerate payments under the plan by offering lump sum payouts based on a single life annuity for the retiree's life without consideration of the current spouse's life expectancy. The original plan sponsor had explicitly reserved the right to amend the plan, so the Eleventh Circuit held that the lump sum distribution was permissible. There was no evidence that the lump sum was worth less than the full equivalent of the value of future benefits, so there was no benefit reduction. Top hat plans are not subject to ERISA's participation and vesting rules. Even if the QJSA rules had applied, a survivor annuity would be available only to the person who was married to the employee when benefits commenced, not to later spouses. There could not have been a fiduciary violation because the top hat plan was not subject to the fiduciary rules. [*Holloman v. Mail-Well Corp.*, 443 F.3d 832 (11th Cir. 2006)]

[6] Excess Benefit Plan

An excess benefit plan exists simply to provide benefits greater than I.R.C. § 415 would allow under a qualified plan. Unfunded excess benefit plans are exempt from ERISA Title I—but this means that they are vulnerable to regulation by the states.

[7] Integrated Plan

An integrated plan provides additional benefits over and above the 401(k) plan, but subject to the same employer match provisions and offering the same investment options. The participant directs the deferral percentage. First, transfers (of both elective deferrals and employer matches) are made to the qualified plan, then to the nonqualified plan.

[8] Tandem Plan

Tandem plans combine with qualified plans to generate larger retirement accruals; they generally offer different investment choices and features from the regular qualified plan.

[9] Wrap Plan

Wrap plans accumulate funds on behalf of top executives throughout the year, then make an annual transfer to the qualified plan of the maximum amount that can be accrued for those executives without violating the nondiscrimination rules. [*See New Options in Nonqualified Retirement Plans,* <http://institutional. vanguard.com/cgi-bin/INewsPrint/101179341> (no www)]

§8.02 TAXATION OF NONQUALIFIED PLANS

[A] General Considerations

Nonqualified plans can create some subtle tax problems for plan participants. The mere fact that the employer promises to pay benefits in the future doesn't create income for the plan participants, until plan benefits are either actually or constructively received. Constructive receipt is a tax concept roughly equivalent to deliberately turning down money that the taxpayer is entitled to.

Employees are taxed on benefits from nonqualified plans as they are distributed. To the extent that the employee already had to pay tax on amounts not yet distributed, employees are entitled to compute an exclusion ratio (percentage of a distribution that has already been taxed and will not be taxed again).

Nonqualified plan participants are taxed in the year in which rights to property become transferable, or the substantial risk of forfeiture ends, whichever comes first. Sometimes, property rights depend, directly or indirectly, on the plan participant continuing to perform services for the employer. If there is a covenant not to compete, however, property rights might depend on not performing services! Under the IRS Regulations, the facts of each case must be examined to determine whether there is a substantial risk of forfeiture because of a requirement of continued employment or noncompetition.

As for the trust income, there are complex factors (centering around the extent of the employer's contributions and degree of control) that determine ownership of the trust, and therefore whether the employer, the employee, or the trust itself should be taxed on income earned by a secular trust arrangement.

> **Tip:** If the employer is concerned about having to pay income tax, funding could be done with no-income or low-income assets such as zero-coupon bonds or insurance policies.

Effective January 1, 2005, transfers of interests in nonqualified deferred compensation and nonstatutory stock options from employee spouse to non-employee spouse incident to a divorce are not "wages" for FICA/FUTA purposes. FICA and FUTA come into play, however, when the options are exercised or the deferred compensation is paid or made available. Nonstatutory options are subject to FICA and FUTA when exercised by the spouse who received them in the divorce. The employee spouse is liable for FICA taxes on the exercise, because the payments relate to the employee spouse's employment. The income the non-employee spouse realizes on exercise of options constitutes wages subject to withholding; the withheld taxes must be deducted from payments to the non-employee spouse. Because the non-employee spouse is by definition not an employee, W-2 reporting is not required. Instead, the employer's obligation is to issue a Form 1099-MISC to the non-employee spouse, and to report the wage withholding on Form 945. [Rev. Rul. 2004-60, 2004-24 I.R.B. 1051. (*See* § 22.02 and § 22.08 for further discussion of stock options.)]

For the calendar year 2005, Notice 2005-94, 2005-52 I.R.B. 1208, suspended the employers' and payers' reporting and wage withholding obligations for § 409A deferrals of compensation. Wages for § 3401(a) purposes do not include § 409A amounts that the employee has neither actually nor constructively received during the calendar year. However, if the unreported amounts must be included in gross income, the IRS may publish additional guidance requiring corrected payee statements and information returns. For CY 2005, the IRS will not impose penalties under §§ 6651(a), 6654, or 6662 for amounts includable in gross income under § 409A, as long as the service provider reports and pays any taxes due under the future guidance.

Notice 2006-4, 2006-3 I.R.B. 307, eases the valuation requirements for stock rights (options and stock appreciation rights) granted before January 1, 2005. Any good faith attempt to set the exercise price at or above fair market value is acceptable. Stock rights issued between January 1, 2005, and January 1, 2007, must satisfy the § 409A "reasonable valuation" requirements as clarified by Notice 2005-1. Stock rights after January 1, 2007, will be subject to the provisions of the Final Regulations under § 409A, in which the IRS intends to provide detailed valuation procedures.

[B] I.R.C. § 83 Issues

Tax planning for nonqualified plan participants also requires a look at I.R.C. § 83, which sometimes requires employees to include in income amounts that have not been distributed from the nonqualified plan. Section 83 provides that whenever property is transferred to anyone except the employer for the provision of services, the employee's taxable income includes the fair market value of the transferred property, minus any amount paid for the property.

Section 83 doesn't apply to transfers to qualified plan trusts, or to a deferred compensation arrangement that gives the employee a mere contractual right to receive compensation in the future. Many stock option transactions are also exempt from this section. However, § 83 does apply to assets set aside in trusts, escrows, or similar arrangements that are not subject to the claims of the corporation's general creditors.

Where § 83 applies, the employee's tax is based on the value of the employee's income on the plan trust at the time of taxation, and not on the fair market value of the employer's contributions from the trust.

In 1996, the Tax Court decided that § 83(a) requires inclusion in income as soon as vacation and severance pay benefits are secured with a letter of credit, on the theory that the employee should be deemed to have received those amounts. [*Schmidt Baking Co. v. Commissioner*, 107 T.C. 271 (1996)]

Congress passed legislation to overturn that result: Internal Revenue Service Restructuring and Reform Act of 1998 (IRSRRA) [Pub. L. No. 105-206 § 7001], which adds a new I.R.C. § 404(a)(11). This section makes it clear that deeming is not proper. Amounts secured in this way must not be included in taxable income until they are actually received. IRS Notice 99-16, 1999-13 I.R.B. 10 provides information about accounting changes required to conform to the IRSRRA requirements.

[C] Employer's Tax Deduction (Pre-AJCA)

The employer gets a tax deduction for contributions made to a secular trust (as long as they are ordinary and necessary business expenses) in the year in which the contributions are taken into the employee's taxable income. Internal Revenue Code § 404(a)(5) gives the rules for deferred compensation plans for employees. Similar rules are found for the deferred compensation of independent contractors in I.R.C. § 404(d)(2).

Employer contributions to a plan that provides deferred compensation for shareholders who are not employees or independent contractors are not deductible. Treasury Regulation § 1.404(a)-12(b)(1) provides that the employer deducts only the amount of the actual contribution, even if employees have to include a larger sum in income (because of appreciation on amounts within the plan).

When deferred compensation is paid directly to the employee under an unfunded arrangement, the employer gets the deduction in the year of the payment—not the year of the contribution, which would be the rule in a qualified plan. If the deferred compensation obligations are merely contractual, and not funded or otherwise secured, then the employer doesn't get a deduction until the employee actually receives the compensation. If the deferred compensation exceeds the reasonable amount that would constitute an ordinary and necessary business expense, the excess is not deductible.

The employer cannot receive a deduction unless it maintains a separate account for each employee covered by a funded deferred compensation arrangement that is not a qualified plan.

Most employers use accrual-basis accounting (whereas nearly all employees use the cash method). If an accrual-basis employer defers payment of compensation to a year other than the year in which it was earned, the deduction must be delayed until the year of actual payment, unless the company is financially unable to pay, or unless it is impossible to determine the correct amount to be paid until after the year ends. [*See* Treas. Reg. §§ 1.404(a)-1(c), 1.404(b)-1]

Distributions from nonqualified plans (unless the distributions are made on account of death, sickness, accident, disability, or disability retirement) are considered wages for FICA and FUTA purposes. Internal Revenue Code § 3121(v)(2) provides that, for the purposes of paying the employer's share and withholding the employee's share of FICA and Medicare tax, amounts deferred under a nonqualified deferred compensation plan are taken into account only once. This is either the time when the services are performed or when there is no longer a substantial risk of forfeiture—whichever occurs later.

In general, income taxes must be withheld at a rate of 10% of the lump sum or benefits paid from the nonqualified deferred compensation arrangement. However, I.R.C. § 3405 gives the payee of the benefits the option of telling the plan not to withhold.

Tip: Many nonqualified plans contain a provision that benefits become payable as soon as the corporation undergoes a change in control (e.g., merger or sale of the corporation's assets or stock). Deferred compensation that becomes due at this time could be an "excess parachute payment" subject to a 20% excise tax. So the value of a provision of this type in providing reassurance (and therefore motivation) for senior management must be balanced against the risk of greater corporate excise tax liability.

[D] AJCA and § 409A

The American Jobs Creation Act of 2004 (AJCA), P.L. 108-357, adds new I.R.C. § 409A to the Internal Revenue Code. It is effective for amounts deferred after 2004. There is no requirement of common-law employment, so deferred payments to independent contractors and outside directors are also subject to these rules. The I.R.C. § 409A rules supplement those already in place governing economic benefit and constructive receipt of deferred compensation. In effect, amounts deferred under a nonqualified plan are included in the recipient's gross income unless they were previously included in his or her income, or unless they are subject to a substantial risk of forfeiture. Compensation is taxed when I.R.C. § 409A is triggered, or the previous rules apply—whichever comes first.

Compliance with I.R.C. § 409A is critical because the AJCA carries a big stick: unless its requirements are satisfied, all compensation deferred under the nonqualified plan for all taxable years is included in the participant's gross income for the current year, plus interest and a penalty of 20% of the compensation included in gross income. Penalties are also imposed if plan assets are placed into a trust outside of the United States, whether or not the assets are available to satisfy the claims of creditors. Another creditor protection measure applies the penalties if plan assets are placed in a domestic trust triggered by the employer's financial condition.

A plan is considered a nonqualified deferred compensation plan if it is not a qualified pension or welfare benefit (e.g., vacation, sick leave, disability pay, death benefit plan, HSA, HRA, medical reimbursement plan). For 2005, transition relief is available: severance plans for non-key employees, or employees covered by a CBA, are not subject to I.R.C. § 409A, as long as the plan is amended by December 31, 2005. A distribution made in 2005 under a qualified plan that triggers a distribution under a SERP excess benefit plan will not violate I.R.C. § 409A.

Whether an option plan is subject to I.R.C. § 409A depends on the terms of the arrangement. If the exercise price for the option is at least as high as the underlying stock's fair market value on the date of the grant, then the option is not considered deferred compensation unless it includes some deferral feature over and above the ability to exercise the option in the future. There is a statutory exemption for ISOs and employee stock purchase plans. By and large, Stock Appreciation Rights (SARs) will be subject to I.R.C. § 409A, although a SAR, that has a fixed payment date, or a non-discounted publicly traded SAR, will be exempt.

I.R.C. § 409A requires elections to defer compensation to be made on or before the end of the taxable year before the year in which the compensation will be earned. For performance-based compensation (e.g., sales commissions) based on services rendered over a period of 12 months or more, the election can be made within the six months before the end of the service period.

Distributions to key employees cannot be made earlier than six months after separation from service, or upon the key employee's death. A key employee is one covered by I.R.C. § 416(I)(l)(c)—that means up to 50 officers of a corporation who earn over $130,000 a year; owners of 5% of the employer corporation's stock; and 1% owners who are paid over $150,000 a year by the employer corporation.

The AJCA forbids acceleration of distributions. Distributions from a deferred compensation plan can be made only when the person earning the money is separated from service, dies, when a specified time is reached (or when a specified schedule begins), when the corporation changes control, the participant becomes disabled (unable to engage in substantial gainful activity as a result of a condition expected to result in death or last for at least 12 months; or receives income replacement benefits for at least three months under an Accident & Health plan on account of total disability), or there is an unforeseeable emergency (e.g., severe financial hardship to a participant because of illness or accident to the participant or close family member; casualty loss to the participant's property; or results of other events beyond the participant's control; otherwise, elective withdrawals are forbidden, even with a penalty). Even if an unforeseeable emergency has occurred, the amount of the distribution must not exceed the amount needed to cope with the emergency and pay the taxes on the premature distribution. Nor can distributions be made if the hardship could be handled through insurance reimbursement or liquidation of the participant's other assets.

Changes in the form of distribution that have the effect of accelerating payment of deferred compensation are forbidden to the same extent as acceleration of the distribution. However, I.R.C. § 409A is not violated merely because a plan provides a choice between cash and taxable property, if the same amount of income is included in income in the same year irrespective of the participant's election. Therefore, the plan can provide for a choice of a lump sum or a fully taxable annuity contract without falling afoul of I.R.C. § 409A.

The initial election to defer must specify the form of any payment that is supposed to be received at a specified time or on a specified schedule. Exceptions are made to this general rule for payments under a QDRO, payments made to comply with federal conflict of interest requirements, amounts needed to pay FICA taxes, and amounts withheld when there has been an I.R.C. § 457(f) vesting event. A lump sum payment of up to $10,000 is also permitted to a terminated employee.

To prevent an error in one participant's plan from affecting the other participants, the general rule is that all account balance plans for a given employee are considered a single plan, and all non-account-balance plans for him or her are considered a single plan, and any other plans are aggregated into another single plan. The plan aggregation rules are not applied in determining if a payment exceeds $10,000.

If an election is made to defer distribution past its original date, the election must be made 12 months before the scheduled distribution date, and must defer payment for an additional five years.

Amounts deferred before December 31, 2004—and earnings on such amounts—are not subject to I.R.C. § 409A. Furthermore, if a plan was in existence on October 3, 2004, and was not materially modified, there is transition relief and the plan can continue to use its existing provisions for deferrals before January 1, 2005, although the IRS can still raise a challenge based on the deferral failing to satisfy the requirements of pre-AJCA law. A material modification occurs if the employer adds new benefits or enhances any right or benefit that was in existence on October 3, 2004. Under the grandfather rule, an employer's exercise of discretion as to the time and form of distribution that was permitted by the plan terms as of October 3, 2004, will not be considered a material modification of the plan that will trigger application of the I.R.C. § 409A rules. An amendment adopted to comply with § 409A will only be considered material if it adds or increases benefits; an amendment that eliminates future deferrals is not considered a material modification.

For an account balance plan, the amount that can be grandfathered is the earned and vested account balance as of December 31, 2004, plus subsequent earnings (as long as the right to the earnings was vested on that date). For a non-account-balance plan, the value of the grandfathered benefit is the present value of the earned and vested benefit that would have been paid at the earliest possible date if the plan participant had voluntarily separated from service on December 31, 2004. Therefore, early retirement subsidies are not grandfathered if they were not payable as of that date, but post-2004 benefits that accrued solely by passage of time are included when the present value of the grandfathered benefit is determined. The employer can use the plan's actuarial assumptions for valuation, as long as the assumptions are reasonable.

The 2005 version of Form W-2 provides a new Code Y in Box 12, for reporting deferrals under an I.R.C. § 409A nonqualified deferred compensation plan. The AJCA said that withholding would not be required until December 31, 2005; Notice 2005-1 (see below) extends this for an additional year, until January 1, 2006. However, the employer need not report if an individual's aggregate deferrals for the year under all nonqualified plans are $600 or less. Reporting can be delayed until the amount deferred under a non-account-balance arrangement can be ascertained. Deferrals for non-employees (e.g., divorced ex-spouses of employees) are reported on Box 15a of the Form 1099-MISC. *See* Announcement 2004-96, 2004-47 I.R.B. 872. (Deferrals are reported even if there is no taxable income, so that the IRS can collect the information for enforcement purposes.)

Notice 2005-1 fleshes out the requirements, although further guidance is required on distributions, how to document the plan, and penalties for non-compliance. (The IRS planned to issue further guidance in 2005, based on reactions to Notice 2005-1.) The IRS announced that employers can rely on this Notice until the further guidance is provided, and that if the final version is more restrictive, it will operate prospectively only. For the benefit of companies that grant stock options, but whose stock is not publicly traded, the relatively flexible valuation rules that apply to Incentive Stock Options can also be used in this context. Furthermore, although in general, plans will have to operate in compliance with I.R.C. § 409A no later than January 1, 2005, plan amendments can be held off until December 31, 2005.

Notice 2005-1 Q&A 19 says that an employer is in compliance to the extent its deferred compensation arrangements are in conformity with the notice or a reasonable, good faith interpretation of the statute as to any issue not addressed in the notice. The Notice clarifies that it is not a violation of I.R.C. § 409A for an employer to amend a plan that was adopted before December 31, 2005, to permit a participant to terminate participation or cancel a previous election to defer compensation.

A payment (e.g., a bonus) is not subject to I.R.C. § 409A as long as the employer makes the payment no later than the next taxable year after the amount ceases to be subject to a substantial risk of forfeiture. The payment must be made within two and a half months after the end of the employer's tax year or the end of the employee's tax year in which the condition lapses—whichever is later.

I.R.C. § 409A does not apply to payments when all the taxpayers involved use the accrual method. Nor does it apply to payments made to someone who is actively engaged in providing non-employee or non-director services to two or more unrelated recipients. An entity is deemed related if the service provider owns at least a 20% interest in it. Property (such as restricted stock) that is subject to I.R.C. § 83 is not subject to I.R.C. § 409A, but a service provider's enforceable right to receive property in a later year (e.g., under a restricted stock unit plan) can be subject to I.R.C. § 409A.

Q&A 9 of Notice 2005-1 says that all plans of the same type (account balance, non-account-balance, or other) are considered a single plan when calculating the amounts subject to the 20% penalty on deferral of non-grandfathered amounts. As a general rule, defined contribution plans are account balance plans and defined benefit plans are non-account-balance plans; determinations are made under the FICA tax rules found at I.R.C. § 3121(v)(2).

Notice 2005-1 says that deferred compensation is subject to a substantial risk of forfeiture if it is conditional on substantial future services or the occurrence of a condition related to the compensation, and the possibility is substantial. Extensions of time during which the risk applies, or additional substantial risks that take effect after the beginning of the service period, will be disregarded when the determination is made.

A possibility is considered to be substantial for an employee-owner based on factors such as the owner's relationship to other shareholders and the extent of their control, the employee-owner's position in the corporation and the extent to which he or she is subordinate to other employees, relationship to the corporation's officers and directors, who has the authority to fire the employee-owner, and whether or not the substantial risk of forfeiture has ever been enforced in the past. In effect, the test is the extent of the employee-owner's control over the corporation. Notice 2005-1 says that refraining from rendering substantial services pursuant to a non-compete agreement is not considered a substantial risk of forfeiture (although it might be under I.R.C. § 83 or I.R.C. § 457, because the Notice 2005-1 definition is quite narrow).

It does not constitute prohibited acceleration for a company to waive or accelerate the satisfaction of a condition that is a substantial risk of forfeiture, as long as the other conditions of I.R.C. § 409A are satisfied. For example, if a plan will pay a lump sum upon separation from service after at least 10 years, changing the requirement to five years will not violate I.R.C. § 409A. Plans can be amended to allow cashout of up to $10,000. Plans can also be amended so that the entire interest under a future deferral will be distributed in a lump sum whenever the participant's interest in the plan falls below the *de minimis* amount specified by a plan when a distribution event occurs. It is also permissible to accelerate distributions to someone other than the participant to satisfy a QDRO; to the participant to pay FICA and income taxes under § 3121(v); or to a participant to the extent required to pay income taxes generated by a § 457(f) plan's vesting event.

Deferred compensation payments can be accelerated in connection with a change in control (change in ownership or effective control of the company); the change-in-control event must be objectively determinable.

The general rule is that employers cannot use the termination of a non-qualified plan as a means of accelerating distributions. However, on or before December 31, 2005, the employer can terminate the plan and make distributions without the IRS treating the termination as a material modification. A 12-month transition period is allowed for after a change-of-control event, so that the surviving company can figure out what to do about nonqualified plans. Q&A numbers 11 through 14 provide that "change in control" is defined similarly to the I.R.C. § 280G golden parachute rules.

A valuation method that would be acceptable for valuing property in a decedent's estate will be accepted as an I.R.C. § 409A valuation method. The exercise price or base value of non-grandfathered stock options or discounted SARs can be reformed, by means of an amendment adopted by December 31, 2005, to reset the price or value to the fair market value of the stock on the original grant date. [These rules are discussed in, e.g., [Haynes & Boone § 409A News Alert, *§ 409A Stock Valuation Guidance for Privately-Held Companies,* benefits-link.com (Jan. 23, 2006)]

In 2005, the IRS sought comments on the treatment of older split-dollar insurance plans when drafting new rules under § 409A. Many people within the financial services industry hoped that the Proposed Regulations at 70 Fed. Reg. 57930 (Oct. 4, 2005) would include a blanket exemption from § 409A for all split-dollar plans, but the IRS did not include this provision in the proposal because the agency says that some split-dollar plans are deferred compensation (e.g., endorsement method plans, employers' irrevocable promises to pay future premiums), although the agency concedes that § 409A should not apply to arrangements limited to the provision of death benefits, or to employer loans to pay for split-dollar plans. Most of the provisions of the Proposed Regulations are slated to take effect January 7, 2007, but some provisions might be applied in 2006 to taxpayers who appear to be acting in bad faith. [Allison Bell, *Feds Propose Regs for Nonqualified Deferred Comp Plans*, NU Online News Service (Sept. 29, 2005)]

[E] 2005 Proposed Regulations

The IRS proposed a massive set of regulations (200+ pages!) under § 409A, 70 Fed. Reg. 58930 (Oct. 4, 2005), with an intended effective date of January 1, 2007. [*See, e.g.,* Groom Law Group, *Proposed IRS Regulations Provide*

Reasonable Framework for Redesign of Nonqualified Programs, benefitslink.com, Oct. 11, 2005)] Because of the volume of comments, the IRS announced that the Regulations probably would not be finalized until Fall 2006. [Fred Schneyer, *409(a) Rules Not Expected Until Fall,* PlanSponsor.com, Mar. 28, 2006)]

The October 2005 proposals cover many aspects of nonqualified plans: valuation; severance pay plans; initial elections to defer compensation; performance-based compensation; commissions; and rules for distributing deferred compensation, including relief for certain delays in distribution.

The basic rule is that a nonqualified stock option is not subject to § 409A if it is granted for at least the FMV of the stock on the date of the grant; it is taxable under § 83; and the option does not have the effect of deferring compensation. Generally speaking, stock appreciation rights (SARs) are treated like stock options.

Severance pay plans are exempt from § 409A if they are collectively bargained; if they are broad-based (i.e., not limited to key employees); or if payments are made within two years after the year of termination of employment. Payments under the third exemption must not exceed the smaller of two years' compensation for the employee or twice the § 401(a)(17) limit. (For 2006, the 401(a)(17) limit is $220,000.) There is a special exception for severance payments that would not otherwise be exempt, but are made within 2½ months of the end of the year of termination of an employee who was involuntarily terminated. An initial election to defer severance resulting from involuntary separation from service can be made at any time before the employee has a legally binding right to the payment, as long as the severance pay is the subject of bona fide arm's-length negotiations. For severance payments under a window program, the initial election to defer the payment can be made until participation in the program becomes irrevocable.

The Proposed Regulations expand on the § 409A statutory language requiring deferred compensation to be paid on a fixed schedule, no earlier than a fixed date, or on the basis of an event (death, disability, change in corporate control, separation from service, or unforeseeable emergency). The Proposed Regulation gives rules for determining when separation from service has occurred (for an employee or an independent contractor). Distributions made to a key employee of a public corporation cannot be made because of separation from service until at least six months have elapsed since the separation.

The plan must have a schedule for making the distribution (e.g., three months after the participant becomes disabled). The Proposed Regulations permit a payment to be treated as made on the designated date as long as it is made by the end of the year including the designated date or the 15th day of the third month after the designated date, whichever is later. It is permissible for a plan to call for different forms of distribution depending on the nature of the triggering event. Distributions can be made later than the date that would otherwise be mandated if making a timely payment would jeopardize the employer corporation's solvency or if the delay is beyond the employer's control.

Employees must make their initial election to defer compensation under a nonqualified plan by the end of the year preceding the year in which the compensation subject to deferral is earned. The election must be irrevocable and must give the time and form of payment. If the election is to defer "performance-based compensation," it can be made up to six months before the end of the period against which performance is measured. Newly hired employees have up to 30 days after they first become eligible to participate in the plan to make their deferral election.

Under the Proposed Regulations, the employer can terminate the nonqualified plan and distribute its benefits without violating the rule against acceleration of benefits, as long as the employer terminates all of its plans of the same type (the proposal gives the example of all account balance plans) with respect to all participants. Within 12 months of the plan termination, no payments can be made unless they would have been made even if the plan had not terminated. Payments must be completed within 24 months of the termination. The Proposed Regulations also permit termination of plans in connection with liquidation, change in control, or in bankruptcy with court approval. The IRS may issue guidance with additional circumstances under which plan terminations will be permitted. There is a five-year embargo on the employer's adoption of another plan of the same type.

Employers and participants have until the end of 2006 to change the distribution provisions for § 409A amounts. Piggyback elections (provisions that make distributions under qualified plans control distributions under nonqualified plans) are still permitted. Plans are given until the end of 2006 to replace options or SARs that are subject to § 409A (e.g., discounted options) with exempt options or SARs. However, the ability to cancel a deferral election or terminate participation in the plan and receive the deferred amounts was not extended from 2005 to 2006.

Although Notice 2005-1 required plans to be amended by December 31, 2005, to satisfy § 409A, these Proposed Regulations extend that deadline to December 31, 2006. Compliance with the Proposed Regulations is permitted, but not required, during 2006 for a plan to satisfy the requirement of operating in good faith.

§ 8.03   PROHIBITED TRANSACTIONS

ERISA § 502(i) gives the DOL power to assess a civil penalty against a "party in interest" who engages in a prohibited transaction with a nonqualified plan. The penalty, which is usually assessed in connection with top hat plans, is 5% for every year or partial year in which the prohibited transaction continues in effect. There is an additional 100% penalty if DOL issues a notice of violation, but the violation is not corrected within 90 days (or whatever extension of time DOL grants).

CHAPTER 9

EARLY RETIREMENT AND RETIREE HEALTH BENEFITS

§ 9.01   INTRODUCTION

One goal of the legal system is to permit employers and employees to work out arrangements under which their mutual economic needs are met. Employers are not allowed to mandate retirement purely on the basis of age (except in a few safety-related occupations), and must accommodate employee's wishes to continue working after normal retirement age, if the employees are still capable of tackling the job.

However, although some individuals have personal reasons for wanting to stay at work, and others would prefer to retire but are financially unable to do so, there is a large group of employees who, on the contrary, prefer to retire before normal retirement age (NRA). The employer may also wish to reduce its payroll, without dismissals or layoffs. One way to do so is by offering incentives for voluntary early retirement.

According to BLS's National Compensation Survey (released in 2005; covering 2002–2003), in 2002, 83% of defined benefit plans included an early retirement option, although only 3% of such plans allowed early retirement with no age requirements, and only 11% allowed retirement before age 55. Close to two-thirds of the plans (63%) allowed early retirement at age 55; 25% of them required five years' service, 27% 10 years' service, and 3% 20 years' service. [BLS National Compensation Survey: *Employee Benefits in Private Industry in the United States, 2002–2003* (January 2005), Bulletin 2573, Table 76]

Early retirement incentives have a business downside, however. In many cases, the employees who accept the offer are those who have the best prospects for getting another job. The employees who stay put may be "deadwood" who recognize that no one else would want to hire them.

Without careful planning and drafting, early retirement programs can also have a legal downside. The employer must make sure that incentives are available without unlawful discrimination. Furthermore, although it makes sense to ask early retirees to waive their claims against the employer, the waiver must be drafted with due attention to the Older Worker's Benefit Protection Act (OWBPA).

Tip: Although the OWBPA mandates a 21-day period during which employees can consider whether to take an early retirement offer, the employer can still cancel the offer—it doesn't have to remain irrevocable during that period. [*Ellison v. Premier Salons Int'l Inc.*, 164 F.3d 1111 (8th Cir. 1999)]

An early retirement program can create risks from two directions. Employees who are eligible may charge that the plan is a subterfuge for forcing them into involuntary retirement. On the other hand, employees who are not offered the incentives can charge that the unavailability of the program was the result of discrimination against them. Furthermore, if the early retirement program changes over time, employees who accepted a first offer may claim that the company should have informed them of the potential for getting a better offer by waiting longer. [This topic is discussed in more detail in Chapter 15, § 15.07, as an issue of fiduciary responsibility to make full disclosure to plan participants]

The questions of early retirement programs and retiree health benefits need to be examined in tandem, because one of the most important questions in deciding whether to retire early is the availability of health coverage. Medicare eligibility depends on age (65 or over) or disability, not employment status. Furthermore, the Medicare system does not provide spousal benefits: each spouse must qualify independently. Therefore, a potential early retiree who is younger than 65 will need retiree health coverage, COBRA coverage, or private insurance.

In order to reduce turnover and take advantage of skills and good work habits among older workers, many companies sought to recruit senior citizen workers, including those who had retired from another job. The average cost of turnover is about $2,300 for every worker that must be replaced, and workers under 30 have ten times the turnover rate of workers over 50. AARP's Web site provides links to thirteen large companies (such as Home Depot, Walgreen's, and MetLife) that are actively seeking older employees. The AARP estimates that by 2010, close to one-third of the workforce will be 50 or over. In 2004, about one-third of men and one-quarter of women aged 65 to 69 were in the labor force, whereas in 1994, 27% of men and 18% of women in that age group worked for pay. [Milt Freudenheim, *More Help Wanted: Older Workers Please Apply*, New York Times, Mar. 23, 2005, at p. A1]

The AARP's suggestions for "best practices for older workers" include retention policies (phased retirement; re-hiring workers who have retired), giving older workers more options for work schedules and locations, career counseling, assigning older workers to a mentor role, giving them more time than the FMLA requires if they are caregivers for spouses or other relatives who are sick, and recognition programs for mature workers who have long tenure with the company. The AARP concluded that many of these programs can be implemented without making a major investment. [AARP, *Staying Ahead of the Curve 2004: Employer Best Practices for Mature Workers,* August 2004 (executive summary), <http://assets.aarp.org/rgcenter/econ/multiwork_2004_1.pdf>]

§ 9.02   ADEA ISSUES OF EARLY RETIREMENT INCENTIVES

At what point does an incentive provided to motivate early retirement turn into pressure that adds up to "constructive discharge" (the equivalent of firing the employee)? The relevant statute is the Older Worker's Benefit Protection Act, which allows voluntary early retirement incentives but only if they satisfy the objectives of the ADEA: promoting employment opportunities for qualified and willing older workers.

The OWBPA allows employers to subsidize early retirement via flat dollar benefits, extra benefits, or percentage increases. Employees who retire early can be offered a more favorable benefit formula (e.g., adding a certain number of years to the number of years actually worked). It does not violate the OWBPA to impose a "window" period that is the only time that the incentive is available.

A defined benefit plan can pay a "Social Security supplement" starting at the date of early retirement, extending until the first date the retiree will be able to receive reduced Social Security benefits—or, if the employer prefers, until the retiree will be eligible for a full unreduced Social Security benefit.

Tip: The employer can amend the pension plan to raise the NRA from 65 to 67 (a change that the Social Security Administration is gradually implementing), as long as accrued early retirement benefits, including subsidies, are preserved.

A university offered early retirement incentives to both tenured professors and top-level administrators. The North Dakota district court said (and the Eighth Circuit agreed) that payments to the faculty members were not "wages" (and therefore not subject to Social Security taxes) because the payments were made in exchange for property rights in university tenure. The payments to administrators, although similar, were subject to FICA, because the administrators were at-will employees, whereas the tenured faculty could only be dismissed for grave cause. [*North Dakota State Univ. v. United States,* 85 A.F.T.R.2d ¶ 2000-332 (D. N.D. Nov. 19, 1999), *aff'd,* 255 F.3d 599 (8th Cir. 2001)] In 2000, the Federal Circuit ruled that severance payments made to retiring employees are "wages" subject to FICA because they reflect past work. In 2006, the Sixth Circuit held that early retirement incentives exchanging payments for tenure rights were subject to FICA, based on a broad definition of "compensation," and because the payments were made because of the recipients' past services for the employer, not in exchange for surrender of tenure rights. [*Appoloni v. United States/Klender v. U.S.,* Nos. 04-2068, 05-1049 (6th Cir. June 7, 2006); *Abrahamsen v. U.S.,* 228 F.3d 1360 (Fed. Cir. 2000)]

The Northern District of Illinois dismissed a complaint brought by a group of employees who were over 40 (i.e., in the ADEA-protected group) but under 50 as of March 1, 2002. Before that time, the old plan provided a premium subsidy for retiree medical coverage, based on years of active service with the employer. But on that date, a new plan was adopted, eliminating the premium subsidy except for two grandfathered-in groups. One of the groups was people who were at least 50 years old, with five or more years' service, as of February 28, 2002; the plaintiffs were excluded from this group because they were under 50. The plaintiffs filed ADEA charges with the EEOC, which did not find any violation, and brought a two-count ADEA suit. The first count charged that implementing the new plan violated the ADEA. The second count sought a declaratory judgment of the plaintiffs' standing to sue. However, the case was dismissed, because Seventh Circuit precedent does not allow a claim of age discrimination when one group of older workers is treated more favorably than another group of workers who are younger (but still are within the ADEA protected group). [*Feigl et al. v. Ecolab, Inc.*, No. 03 C 2290 (N.D. Ill. Sept. 11, 2003), <http://benefitslink.com/cases/feigl_200309.pdf>]

A school district early retirement program made cash payments to teachers retiring between the ages of 55 and 65, which resulted in a suit charging that the program violated the ADEA by denying benefits to persons over age 65. The Eighth Circuit rejected the school district's claim that it qualified for the safe harbor for voluntary early retirement plans because the plan was inconsistent with the statutory aim of eliminating arbitrary age-based distinctions. To qualify for the safe harbor, drafters should follow the statutory language about early retirement benefits in defined benefit plans or perhaps condition benefits on years of service rather than age. [*Jankovitz v. Des Moines Independent Community Sch. Dist.*, 421 F.3d 649 (8th Cir. 2005)]

§ 9.03   DISCLOSURES TO EMPLOYEES

An employee can't make a meaningful decision about whether or not to retire without understanding the choices that will be available in the near future. If the terms of the early retirement program change, people who were not eligible for the improved terms, or who elected early retirement without knowing that they could have gotten a better deal by waiting longer, may charge the employer with fraud, and may charge various parties involved with the plan with violations of fiduciary duty.

The Third Circuit announced a rule in *Fischer v. Philadelphia Electric Co.* [96 F.3d 1533 (3d Cir. 1996)] that a revised early retirement incentive has received "serious consideration," and therefore must be disclosed to potential early retirees, once senior managers discuss the proposal for purposes of implementation.

Bins v. Exxon Co. [189 F.3d 929 (9th Cir. 1999)] reached a similar conclusion. The *Bins* case was reheard in 2000. [*Bins*, 220 F.3d 1042 (9th Cir. 2000] The mandate to the fiduciary to give complete and accurate information about plan changes under "serious consideration" in response to employee queries, was affirmed. But the Ninth Circuit did not impose a duty to volunteer information employees have not asked for. Nor did the court require the employer to report changes to employees who made inquiries in the past—unless the employer volunteered to supply updated information.

Another Ninth Circuit case, *Wayne v. Pacific Bell* [189 F.3d 982 (9th Cir. 1999)], ruled that discussion of a particular early retirement proposal during collective bargaining constitutes serious consideration—even if that particular proposal is never adopted. In July, 2003, however, the Fifth Circuit refused to adopt the "serious consideration" test. Instead, the Fifth Circuit used a fact-specific test of whether the information would be relevant to a reasonable person's decision to retire, and therefore concluded that the employer did not breach its fiduciary duty by offering an early retirement plan two weeks after the plaintiffs retired. [*Martinez v. Schlumberger Ltd.*, 338 F.3d 407 (5th Cir. 2003)]

Hudson v. General Dynamics Corp. [118 F. Supp. 2d 226 (D. Conn. 2000)] found a breach of fiduciary duty with respect to two employees who asked, but were not told, that an early retirement program was under consideration. However, claims were dismissed with respect to 87 other employees who did not ask, or whose inquiries came before the company seriously considered the program.

McAuley v. IBM Corp. [165 F.3d 1038 (6th Cir. 1999)] permits retirees to sue for breach of fiduciary duty when their ex-employer adopted an early retirement plan more favorable than the one they accepted and relied on in making retirement plans.

It is a breach of fiduciary duty to inform potential early retirees that lump-sum payouts are available, without also disclosing the I.R.C. § 415 limitations on rollovers and explaining the tax consequences. [*Farr v. U.S. West Communications, Inc.,* 58 F.3d 1361 (9th Cir. 1998)] Given that the fiduciaries' common-law duty of loyalty requires them to deal fairly and honestly with plan participants, it is a violation to give them incomplete information.

To assist older employees in making decisions about Medicare Part D (the prescription drug program coming into effect in 2006), employers are required to issue a notice to all Part D-eligible employees (with disclosure to the Center for Medicare and Medicaid services as well) informing them as to whether there is prescription drug coverage under the employer's plan, and whether that coverage is creditable or non-creditable. [*See* § 9.10[B]]

§ 9.04   EEOC MANUAL ON EARLY RETIREMENT INCENTIVES

Late in 2000, the EEOC updated Section 3 of its Compliance Manual to deal with benefits. [No. 915.003, (Oct. 3, 2000) <http://www.eeoc.gov/policy/docs/benefits.html>] The agency's position is that an early retirement incentive (ERI) program is lawful as long as it's voluntary. The EEOC will not get involved if the employer chooses to:

- Set a minimum age or minimum number of years of service for employees who participate;
- Have a window (i.e., the incentive is only available for a limited time period);
- Limit the ERI to a manager, a department, a particular facility, etc.

However, ERI benefits can't be reduced or denied for older employees versus similarly situated younger employees unless the employer qualifies for one of five defenses:

- Equal cost;
- Subsidizing a portion of the early retirement benefit;
- Integrating the incentives with Social Security;
- (For a university) incentives for a tenured faculty member;
- The plan is consistent with the objectives of the ADEA.

According to the EEOC Compliance Manual (the Manual), an ERI is not voluntary if a reasonable person informed of its terms would conclude that there was no choice but to accept. Relevant factors in the analysis include, e.g., adequate time to decide; absence of coercion; lack of negative consequences for older employees who turn down the offer; and whether a particular employee had legal advice when making the decision.

The Manual provides that it is not coercion for the employer to state that layoffs will be required unless enough people accept the incentives—unless older workers are the only ones at risk of layoff. Nor is it coercion for the employer to make an offer that is "too good to refuse."

The equal cost defense probably will not be available in connection with ERIs, because the cost of early retirement benefits generally does not increase with the employee's age.

The EEOC allows the employer to limit the ERI or pay higher ERI benefits to younger employees where the benefits are used to bring early retirees up to the level of the unreduced pension they would receive at the NRA from a defined benefit pension plan. But the subsidized pension can't be greater than the pension of a similarly situated older employee who has reached NRA.

It is also permissible to offer an ERI to bridge the gap to Social Security eligibility, for a person who has not yet reached the Social Security early retirement age (currently slightly over 62). The supplement can't exceed the Social Security benefit that the employee will eventually receive as an early or normal-age retiree.

According to the EEOC, equal severance benefits are required for all similarly situated employees irrespective of their age. Employers may not deny severance on the grounds that the employee is eligible for a pension, although sometimes pension benefits can be offset against the severance pay. Denying recall rights to older workers operates as unlawful involuntary retirement. The cost of providing severance does not rise with the employees' age, so employers are not allowed to assert an equal cost defense in this context.

Retiree health benefits can legitimately be offset against severance if the retiree is eligible for an immediate pension; the retiree actually receives health benefits; and the retiree benefits are at least comparable to Medicare in type and value. If the retiree is over 65, the benefits must be at least comparable for one-fourth the value of Medicare benefits. The offset itself must be reduced by any percentage by which the pension is reduced for retirement before the NRA, and any percentage of the retiree health coverage premium that the retiree has to pay.

In the EEOC view, an ERI ignores age as a criterion (and therefore is consistent with the ADEA's objectives) as long as it gives all employees above a certain age:

- A flat dollar amount (e.g., $20,000);
- Additional service-based benefits, for instance, $1,000 for each year of service;
- A percentage of salary;
- A flat dollar increase in pension benefits, such as an extra $200 a month;

- A percentage increase (e.g., 10%) in pension benefits;
- Extra years of service and/or age used in pension computations.

§ 9.05   ERISA ISSUES

[A]   Generally

Because one of the primary purposes of ERISA is to make sure that retirement benefits will be paid in accordance with the terms of the plan, ERISA issues often arise when early retirement plans must be construed. Sometimes, ERISA welfare benefit plans will also be involved.

[B]   Preemption

It is very likely that ERISA will be held to preempt state-court cases about group health plans. In its June 2004 decision in the consolidated cases of *Aetna Health Inc. v. Davila*, and *Cigna Healthcare of Texas, Inc. v. Calad*, 542 U.S. 200 (2004), the Supreme Court found that ERISA § 502(a) completely preempts state-law claims alleging that managed care plans improperly denied care (in one case, it was claimed that the plaintiff was injured by taking a lower-cost drug rather than the safer, more expensive drug that was not covered by the plan; in the other case, alleged premature discharge from hospitalization). [*See* § 15.18] Preemption is much less likely to be found in the early retirement context. According to the Sixth Circuit, ERISA does not preempt age discrimination claims merely because the plaintiff had already retired and was collecting a pension as of the time of the suit. [*Warner v. Ford Motor Co.,* 46 F.3d 531 (6th Cir. 1995)]

The 1996 case of *Lockheed v. Spink* [517 U.S. 882 (1996)] found (among other issues) that it is not a prohibited transaction (as defined by ERISA § 406) to establish an early retirement program that is conditioned on waiving enforcement of employment claims. Under this analysis, paying benefits under any circumstances shouldn't be treated as a prohibited transaction.

In the Tenth Circuit view, ERISA does not completely preempt state-law fraud claims brought by employees who say they were induced to take an early retirement package when later retirees were offered a better deal. The Tenth Circuit stressed the difference between complete preemption under ERISA § 502(a) and conflict preemption under ERISA § 514. Conflict preemption is just a defense, and not a federal question presented on the face of the complaint. Therefore, it cannot be used as the basis for removal jurisdiction. The Tenth Circuit ruled that the district court did not have jurisdiction, because the retirees were not claiming benefits under the plan and thus could not bring an ERISA § 502(a) suit. The First, Second, Fifth, Sixth, and Eighth Circuits permit suits by former employees who claim that the employer's wrongdoing reduced the benefits they were entitled to—but the Fourth, Tenth, and Eleventh Circuits reject this approach and hold that former employees only have standing to sue under ERISA § 502(a) if they have either a colorable claim for vested benefits or a reasonable expectation of returning to employment. [*Felix v. Lucent Technologies Inc.*, 387 F.3d 1146 (10th Cir. 2004)]

[C] Fiduciary Duty

Early retirement incentives were offered as part of a downsizing plan. The information provided by corporate headquarters included a scripted presentation to be delivered at mandatory employee meetings and a letter from the company president. The letter promised that "during retirement" early retirees would be offered the benefits with the lowest deductibles and out-of-pocket caps. The letter also said they would not be affected by benefit reductions planned for active employees and those who would retire in the future. The HR manager at one plant said (both at the meetings and in private interviews) that benefits would not change and were promised for the retiree's life; the reserved right to change the plan applied only to changes of insurance carrier. A few years later, retiree health benefits were reduced and a group of retirees sued for breach of fiduciary duty. [*James v. Pirelli Armstrong Tire Co.,* 305 F.3d 439 (6th Cir. 2002)] The trial court found that, except for two plaintiffs, there was no evidence of deliberate or even accidental misstatement, and therefore dismissed the claims of the other plaintiffs. The Sixth Circuit, however, held that the test of fiduciary breach is whether materially misleading information was provided—whether there was any intent to mislead or even any negligence. The Sixth Circuit found a fiduciary breach as to all 21 plaintiffs, because they all relied on the statements in deciding to retire early. For the 10 plaintiffs who asked specific questions about the future of retiree health benefits, the inaccurate answers to the questions provide an independent basis for fiduciary breach claims.

It does not violate ERISA to deny early retirement to employees who are deemed especially valuable to the company, if the plan gives management discretion as to whether early retirement is in the company's best interests. A company's standards (as opposed to rules) are supposed to be applied flexibly and with discretion. According to the Seventh Circuit, the way this standard was implemented was not arbitrary or capricious enough to violate ERISA. [*McNab v. General Motors,* 162 F.3d 959 (7th Cir. 1998)] Another General Motors case says that the LMRA and NLRA do not preempt an early retiree's state-law claims that the employer fraudulently induced acceptance of early retirement. [*Voilas v. General Motors,* 170 F.3d 367 (3d Cir. 1999)]

A group of former employees of John Hancock prevailed at the district court level in an early retirement case. However, the First Circuit reversed, finding that a controversial plan amendment, allowing early retirement with full benefits starting at age 56 with 25 years of service, applied only to those who were actively employed at retirement, not to those whose jobs ended before retirement. The First Circuit accepted the argument made by the employer (who was also the plan administrator) that employees who left the company prior to age 50 were not eligible for a full pension until age 65, no matter how long they had worked there. The First Circuit did not believe that denial of the early retirement benefits was an abuse of discretion. The dual role as sponsor and plan administrator was not seen as a conflict of interest sufficient to impose a stricter standard of review. [*Fenton v. John Hancock Mutual Life Ins. Co.*, 400 F.3d. 83 (1st Cir. 2005)]

[D] Anticutback Rule

ERISA § 204(g) forbids cutbacks in benefits. On June 7, 2004, the Supreme Court ruled that it is a violation of the anticutback rule to amend a plan to further restrict the type of work that retirees can do without forfeiting their pensions, if the result of the amendment is that early retirement benefits that were already accrued would be suspended. [*Central Laborers' Pension Fund v. Heinz*, 541 U.S. 739 (2004)] In this case, when the plaintiffs retired, they qualified for early retirement benefits. Under their plan, they would not receive pension benefits if they undertook "disqualifying employment." At the time they retired, the plan defined disqualifying employment as being a construction worker. The plaintiffs did take post-retirement jobs, but as construction supervisors.

Then the plan was amended to expand the definition of disqualifying employment to include any work at all in the construction industry, and the plaintiffs' benefits were suspended. The Supreme Court ruled that the amendment violated the plaintiffs' legitimate expectations of benefit stability, and therefore violated the anticutback rule. *See* Rev. Proc. 2005-23, 2005-18 I.R.B. 1, adopted by the IRS to prevent plans from being disqualified because they adopted amendments of this type. The Rev. Proc. allows employers (this situation is much more common for multi-employer than single-employer plans) to return to compliance, and avoid retroactive application of the *Heinz* decision, by adopting additional remedial amendments allowing re-employment without suspension of benefits for service on or after June 7, 2004. (The plan can lawfully allow re-employment as of earlier dates as well.)

In *Bellas v. CBS* [221 F.3d 517 (3d Cir. 2000) *cert. denied*, 531 U.S. 1104 (2001)], the plaintiff was terminated for lack of work after employment between 1964 and 1997. Before 1994, the predecessor employer's pension plan offered permanent job separation benefits to employees terminated for lack of work. A 1994 amendment narrowed the definition of "permanent job separation," and the benefit was eliminated entirely for terminations occurring after September 1, 1998.

The plaintiff charged that the change in the benefit definition, and eventual elimination of the benefit, violated the anticutback rule. The Third Circuit agreed with him, finding that payment of any benefit greater than an actuarially reduced normal retirement benefit, triggered by an unpredictable contingent event such as being laid off, is a retirement-type subsidy. The benefit accrues when the benefit program is created. The Fifth and Ninth Circuits take this position, but the Sixth and Eleventh Circuits hold that job separation benefits do not accrue until the layoff actually occurs.

The practical significance of the *Bellas* decision is that, in circuit courts that follow this theory, employers can only decrease early retirement benefits prospectively. That is, once a person satisfies plan requirements, the plan cannot be amended to reduce or eliminate the early retirement benefit that has already accrued. [*See* Joseph S. Adams, *Court Rules Supplemental Benefits Must Stay in Plan*, <http://www.benefitslink.com/articles/mend001012.shtml>] The employer may have to budget a much larger amount than anticipated when the plan was amended.

A "suspension" of benefits (for exceeding the plan's limitation on employment after retirement) is not a "reduction" in benefits subject to the ERISA anticutback rule. Therefore, tougher restrictions on employment, adopted six years after the plaintiff retired, entitled the employer to suspend retirement benefits without violating ERISA. [*Spacek v. Maritime Association*, 134 F.3d 283 (5th Cir. 1998)]

In 2003, the IRS issued T.D. 9052 [2003-19 I.R.B. 879], on the requirements for notifying plan participants and beneficiaries of significant reductions in the rate of future benefit accrual—or a cutback or elimination of an early retirement benefit or retirement-type subsidiary. This Treasury Decision contains final regulations; as usual, the proposed regulations [67 Fed. Reg. 19713 (April 23, 2002)] were adopted without substantial changes. T.D. 9052 applies to defined benefit plans and to individual account plans that are subject to the § 412 funding standards. All plan provisions that could affect the benefit must be taken into account in determining whether notice is required. Whether a reduction is "significant" is calculated using reasonable expectations taking into account the relevant facts and circumstances as of the time of the amendment's adoption.

Although the basic rule is that notice must be given at least 45 days before the effective date of the amendment, small (under 100 participant) plans can comply by giving notice at least 15 days before the effective date; the 15-day notice period is also adequate for amendments relating to corporate mergers and acquisitions. If the amendment significantly reduces an early retirement benefit or subsidy, but does not significantly reduce the rate of future benefit accruals, the notice can even be given after the effective date of the amendment, as long as it is within 30 days after the effective date.

The § 204(h) notice must be written in plain English and must give enough information for participants and beneficiaries to understand the effect of the amendment (i.e., the procedures for calculating the benefit before and after the amendment takes effect). This can be done by furnishing illustrative examples; or individualized benefit statements, as long as the statements provide the approximate range of the reductions for the individual and the assumptions used to create the projections.

In general, ERISA § 204(h)'s requirements are the same as those under Code § 4980F, but there are additional penalties under § 204(h) for "egregious" failure to provide notice, over and above the excise tax imposed by § 4980F for failure to provide the required notice.

In 2004, the IRS proposed rules under which defined benefit plans could be re-designed to eliminate redundant benefit forms without violating the anti-cutback rule. The proposal also allows elimination of optional forms of benefits as long as the basic "core" payment forms are retained. In either case, the proposal requires additional protection for participants when early retirement benefits or subsidies are involved. [*See* 69 Fed. Reg. 13769 (Mar. 24, 2004)] The anti-cutback rules were further addressed by Proposed Regulations, REG-156518-04, RIN 1545-BE10, 2005-38 IRB 582. *See also* T.D. 9219, 2005-38 IRB 538. Rev. Proc. 2005-23, 2005-18 I.R.B. 991 explains how to amend a plan to remove amendments that violated § 411(d)(6) by improperly decreasing accrued benefits or adding restrictions on the right to benefits; Rev. Proc. 2005-76, 2005-50 IRB 1139 extends the time to correct the plan by amendment.

ERISA § 510 [interference with benefits] claims that the employer had a practice of forcing employees to retire early, preventing them from accruing a full pension, were unsuccessful in a 2006 case from the District Court for the District of Minnesota. The plaintiff alleged that his own pension was only 70% of what he would have received if he had worked until NRA. The District of Minnesota ruled that the practice, even if it existed, might support an ADEA charge, but not an ERISA claim. Furthermore, the plaintiff retired voluntarily, so there was no adverse employment action, and there was no proof of intent to interfere with pension vesting. [*Fischer v. Andersen Corp.,* No. 05-120 (DSD/ SRN) (D. Minn. Apr. 6, 2006)]

[E]   Other ERISA Issues

Whether a severance plan is an ERISA welfare benefit plan depends on the nature and extent of the employer's role. There is no plan without ongoing administrative responsibility for determining eligibility and calculating benefits. In *O'Connor v. Commonwealth Gas Co.* [251 F.3d 262 (1st Cir. 2001)] the employer wanted to reduce its census before a merger. The plaintiffs charge they were deceived into retiring early because the employer lied about future retirement incentives. The employer provided a one-time severance bonus calculated based on years of service. The First Circuit found that there was no ERISA "plan" because the program lasted only 15 weeks, covered only 300 workers, and involved only simple arithmetic, not discretionary judgment.

Table I-06, for valuation dates between December 31, 2005, and January 1, 2007, covering retirement occurring between 2007 and 2016 or later dates, estimates the probability (low, medium, or high) that a person will retire early, based on the retirement benefits he or she would be entitled to receive. [*See* 70 Fed. Reg.

TABLE I-06
SELECTION OF RETIREMENT RATE CATEGORY
[For plans with valuation dates after December 31, 2005,
and before January 1, 2007]

		Participant's retirement rate category is—		
Participant reaches URA in year—	Low[1] if monthly benefit at URA is less than—	Medium[2] if monthly benefit at URA is		High[3] if monthly benefit is greater than
		From	To	
2007	500	500	2,113	2,113
2008	512	512	2,164	2164
2009	524	512	2,216	2,216
2010	536	536	2,269	2,269
2011	549	549	2,324	2,324
2012	562	562	2,379	2,379
2013	576	576	2,437	2,437
2014	590	590	2,495	2,495
2015	604	604	2,555	2,555
2016 or later	618	618	2,616	2,616

[1]Table II–A.
[2]Table II–B.
[3]Table II–C.

72205 (Dec. 2, 2005) for the promulgation of this table] For 2007, for example, the "low" figure is less than $500 a month, while the "high" figure is more than $2,113. If the benefit is anywhere in between the two, early retirement probability is assessed as "medium." For 2016 and later years, the "low" figure is less than $618 a month, and the "high" is more than $2,616.

§ 9.06   PHASED RETIREMENT

In many instances, the needs of both employer and employee would be well served by the option of "phased retirement" (a gradual transition out of the work-force) rather than a bright-line test of being either fully active or retired. Employers would certainly save money if they could reduce the full-time payroll yet continue to receive part-time services from older workers, instead of offering them early retirement subsidies.

Assume that a phased retiree takes a lump sum pension payment but continues to work part-time. The one-time payment will probably be less than what the company would have to pay if the employee continued full-time work for an additional period of time, e.g., person who would have an annual pension of $36,286 by retiring at age 65 after a 40-year career with the same company, earning $50,000 a year. [Ellen E. Schultz, *"Phased Retirement" Option for Workers Is Mainly a Boon for Their Employers,* Wall Street Journal, July 27, 2000, at p. A6]

If that person takes a $263,250 lump sum at 55 and works for 10 more years, the pension will be based on only 10 years' service, not 40, so the employer will have to pay only $9,071 a year.

Current law makes it especially difficult to retire and begin taking distributions from a defined benefit or 401(k) plan prior to normal retirement age, because of limitations on "in-service distributions" that are not made on account of disability or other hardship.

Many commentators have raised the question of how to structure phased retirement equitably, e.g., by determining that a person is 50% retired, and therefore paying him or her 50% of the salary for the position, and also 50% of the retirement benefits that would be available if the person had completelyretired.

The Center for Retirement Research (Boston College), for example, suggested reducing the payroll tax obligations of over-65 phased retirees; allowing health plans to offer coverage that is secondary to Medicare for over-65 workers; and allowing proration of fringe benefits for older employees who work part-time as part of the transition to complete retirement.

Although many public-sector employers have phased retirement plans, it is unusual in the private sector, but new measures are evolving. CIGNA Corporation's Encore program, for example, provides partial benefits to supplement EGHP or Medicare benefits for retirees who work a reduced schedule of up to 80 hours per month. Pharmacia has a Retiree Resource Corporation for people who return to part-time work after six months of retirement; they are allowed to work up to 1,000 hours a year and can make 401(k) deferrals during the part-time work period.

Many pension plans (perhaps deliberately to encourage early retirement or as an unintended result of other design features) in effect grant the most rapid accrual of pension benefits when workers are in their fifties; between their mid-fifties and retirement, workers may find that pension accrual is actually negative. That is, even though they will eventually qualify for a larger pension because they work longer, they also receive the pension for one year less for each additional year worked.

IRS Proposed Regulations [REG-114726-04, 69 Fed. Reg. 61208 (Nov. 10, 2004); technical corrections at 69 Fed. Reg. 77679 (Dec. 29, 2004)] set a possible framework for permitting partial distributions from a pension plan under a bona fide phased retirement program, responding to the public comments solicited by Notice 2002-43 (July 8, 2002). The proposal permits a *pro rata* share of the employee's accrued benefit to be distributed under a *bona fide* phased retirement program, proportionate to the reduction in working hours. The IRS determined that this was the best approach to satisfy the statutory mandate that plans be maintained primarily for retirement. The IRS announced that the phased retirement rules cannot be relied on until they are finalized.

Under the proposal, phased retirement distributions can be made prior to Normal Retirement Age, but not before age 59½. A valid phased retirement program must be voluntary; employers cannot impose it on employees who wish to continue a normal employment schedule. This proposal doesn't tackle health insurance or age discrimination issues for phased retirement plans.

The proposal defines a *bona fide* phased retirement program as a written program adopted by an employer, under which employees can reduce their customary work schedule and receive phased retirement benefits. In addition to the phased retirement benefit, the employee must be allowed to participate in the plan in the same way as if he or she worked a full schedule, and must be entitled to the same benefits as a similarly situated employee who did not elect phased retirement.

Employer and employee must expect the employee's hours of work to decrease by at least 20%. All early retirement benefits, subsidies, and optional forms of benefit that would be available at full retirement must be made available upon phased retirement. However, single-sum distributions and other eligible rollover distributions are not permitted. Election of phased retirement is subject to I.R.C. § 417, including the requirement of a QJSA explanation.

In its study of the issue, the IRS concluded that it does not have authority to approve phased retirement benefits being made before age 59½; or severance from employment.

Unless there is an available exemption, the plan must test each year to see if the employee's actual working hours exceeded the expected amount by one-third or more, or if the actual hours worked were 90% or more of a normal full-time schedule. But the annual comparison ceases to be required once the employee is within three months of normal retirement age, or the compensation paid during the testing period does not exceed full-time pay times the schedule fraction. Nor is the comparison required during the first year of phased retirement, or when the employer and employee enter into an agreement calling for the employee's retirement within two years. The plan must not set its NRA so low that it constitutes a subterfuge to avoid the application of I.R.C. § 401(a). The NRA must not be below the earliest age reasonably representative of typical retirement age for the relevant workforce.

Researchers for the AARP Public Policy Institute examined a group of people who were between the ages of 51 and 61 and working full-time in 1992 to determine their retirement status in 2002: whether they were completely retired; not retired at all; partially retired (still working part-time, but for a different employer); or in phased retirement (still with the same employer, but working a reduced schedule). They found that phased retirees had greater household income and wealth than the other groups; they were more likely to be managers or have skilled white-collar jobs than members of other groups; they were better educated; tended to be white; and tended to value work for reasons other than the money they earned. Phased retirees were less likely to retire completely than people in other categories. The researchers were not surprised by their findings: phased retirement typically is available on a case-by-case basis, not as part of a program available to everyone within a company, and it tends to be available to affluent and sophisticated employees who are in a good position to cope with change. [Yung-Ping Chen and John C. Scott (AARP Public Policy Institute), *Phased Retirement: Who Opts for It and Toward What End?* <http://www.aarp.org/ppi/inb113_retire.pdf> (Jan. 2006)]

§ 9.07   RETIREE HEALTH BENEFITS: INTRODUCTION

At one time, it was very common for part of the incentive for early retirement to come in the form of health benefits to replace the employer's group health plan. Employers often promised "lifetime health benefits at no cost." However, health care costs rise significantly every year, and employees in poor health are more likely to be interested in health benefits than employees in good health. Therefore, a retiree health benefit program can become a major burden on the employer.

According to the Employee Benefits Research Institute (EBRI), the prevalence of retiree health benefits began to diminish seriously in December 1990. One of the precipitating factors was the Financial Accounting Standards Board (FASB)'s release of a standard called SFAS 106, requiring employers to record their unfunded retiree health benefit liabilities on their financial statements.

This reporting has the effect of reducing reported corporate earnings, so it is an undesirable phenomenon from the corporate accounting point of view. In response, some employers stopped providing retiree health benefits altogether; others put their plans on a defined contribution basis, added age and service requirements, or maintained the level of benefits for current retirees but reduced the benefits that would eventually be available to people retiring in the future.

Many employers adopted caps, i.e., maximum amounts that they will devote to retiree health benefits. Once the employer reaches this cap level, any additional cost increases will be 100% absorbed by plan participants. Another tactic is to impose a combination of age and service requirements for participation in the retiree health plan, e.g., limiting it to persons over 55 with 10 years' service. Or, the amount of financial contribution an employee is expected to make to the retiree health plan could be made proportional to length of service.

A survey performed for the Kaiser Family Foundation in 2005 found that respondents said that their costs went up an average of 10% between 2004 and 2005. (The amount of cost-sharing paid by retirees also went up by about 10%.) The average cost of retiree health insurance in 2005 was $4,080, of which the average employee paid $1,536 and the employer paid an average of $2,544. Employers varied widely in their cost-sharing practices: Eleven percent paid the full premium, whereas 19% paid none of the premium, allowing employees to purchase insurance out of their own pockets. Just about half of the firms capped their payment obligations; of that group, 59% said they had already hit the cap (in other words, any further cost increases would be fully borne by the retirees) and another 27% predicted that they would hit the cap within three years. About an eighth of the respondents stopped providing retiree health coverage in 2005 for anyone retiring in the future; 71% raised the premiums paid by retirees between 2004 and 2005; 34% raised copayments or coinsurance; and 24% increased deductibles imposed on retirees. [Kaiser Family Foundation, *Four in Five Large Firms to Maintain Retiree Drug Coverage [. . .]*, <http://www.kff.org/medicare/med120705nr.cfm> (Dec. 7, 2005)]

There are many ways a plan can be structured to increase cost-sharing for retirees. Traditionally, both actives and retirees were placed into a shared risk pool, but retirees can be placed into a separate pool, or premiums can be set higher for one group of retirees than another. The rationale for creating a separate risk pool is the potential for profit if retirees drop their coverage for cost reasons; accounting rules allow employers to book a gain from the reduction of liability for future health costs of retirees who leave the plan. To offset costs of covering union retirees (whose benefits cannot be reduced by the unilateral action of the employer), a company may charge salaried retirees more than the actual cost of their coverage. [Ellen E. Schultz, *Employer Actions Drive Health Costs for Retirees Higher*, Wall Street Journal, Dec. 30, 2004, at p. B1]

Some companies adopted the aggressive tactic of bringing suit against retirees (rather than the other way around) seeking a ruling that the company can reduce benefits, or that the phrase "lifetime benefits" refers to the lifetime of the CBA and not the retiree. This is a low-risk effort, because some retirees will leave the plan or die, and even if the suit is unsuccessful, the employer's reported earnings went up in the interim (because of the reduction in anticipated future obligations). The Department of Labor considers retirees ex-employees and therefore doesn't defend them, and in any event, most cases take long enough to resolve that at least some of the retiree defendants will die before the case is finished. The named retiree defendants could be chosen at random from the pool of retirees, people who complained about the retiree health plan, or union activists. [Ellen E. Schulz, *Companies Sue Union Retirees to Cut Promised Health Benefits*, Wall Street Journal, Nov. 10, 2004, at p. A1]

The TIAA-CREF Institute reported in mid-2005 that, on the average, senior citizens spend more than $9,200 a year on health care costs—not counting long-term care. About 98% of seniors are covered by Medicare, but there are many gaps in coverage. According to TIAA-CREF, retiree health benefits provide about 70% of the gap left by Medicare. [Marilyn Moon, *Trends and Issues: Retiree Health Care—Individuals Picking Up Bigger Tab*, <http://www.tiaa-crefinstitute.org/research/trends/docs/tr070105.pdf> (July 2005)]

§ 9.08   THE RIGHT TO ALTER OR TERMINATE RETIREE HEALTH BENEFITS

The general rule is that, as long as the employer drafts the plan to provide that the employer retains the right to amend, modify, or terminate the health benefits, the employer can do so unilaterally. ERISA has rules about vesting of pension benefits (i.e., the circumstances under which the right to a pension becomes non-forfeitable) but ERISA does not provide for vesting of welfare benefits such as retiree health benefits. Furthermore, ERISA preempts state law on this subject, so the states do not have the power to impose vesting requirements. [*See, e.g., General Dynamics Land Systems Inc. v.* Cline, 540 U.S. 581 (2004) (terminating retiree health benefits did not violate the ADEA) and *Int'l Union of United Auto, Aerospace & Agricultural Implement Workers v. Rockford Powertrain Inc.,* 350 F.3d 698 (7th Cir. 2003) (holding that although the company said that plans would be provided indefinitely, the right to modify or terminate the health and life insurance plans for retirees was reserved. Therefore, terminating these plans did not violate ERISA or the CBA)]

However, there are circumstances under which an employer's promise of retiree health coverage will become an enforceable contract. Under the "promissory estoppel" theory, if the employer makes an unambiguous promise of lifetime benefits, it will no longer be permitted to change the plan.

A limitation on this theory is that the plaintiff might be required to prove that he or she would have obtained comparable medical insurance at his or her own expense if the plan had not been misleading about future health benefits. Employers might also be bound by a promise of lifetime no-cost retiree health benefits if employees actually traded cash compensation or some other benefit in exchange for the employer's promise.

Another argument that employers can make to cut back or eliminate retiree health benefits is that the benefits were provided under a particular collective bargaining agreement and do not survive the expiration of that agreement unless the agreement specifically calls for their survival. Retirees are no longer employees, and therefore are not part of the bargaining unit. The bargaining agent does not have a duty to represent retirees—and there is a real potential for conflict of interest between current employees and retirees. Retiree benefits are not included among the mandatory subjects of bargaining. [*See* § 30.07[A]]

When a collective bargaining agreement determines retiree benefit rights "for the term of the agreement," it is not a violation of ERISA to terminate retiree health and life insurance benefits after a contract ends. In other words, it's a new ball game each time the CBA is renegotiated. [*Pabst Brewing Co. v. Corrao,* 161 F.3d 434 (7th Cir. 1998)]

ERISA's fiduciary duty was not breached by transferring the obligation to provide some retiree health benefits to a new company formed when a corporate division was spun off. [*Sengpiel v. B.F. Goodrich,* 156 F.3d 660 (6th Cir. 1998)] To the Sixth Circuit, the new entity's reduction of retiree health and life insurance benefits was lawful, because the power to alter benefits was retained in the plan documents. The reduction should be analyzed as a plan amendment, modification, or termination—i.e., a business decision—rather than a fiduciary decision involving discretionary issues in plan administration.

The employer's course of conduct (such as increasing health benefits for retirees when benefits for active workers increase) is probably not enough to make it unlawful for the employer to cut back on retiree benefits, especially if the benefit increases were provided gratuitously by the employer and the employees did not have to surrender anything to get them.

As a cost containment measure, in 1991 Continental Insurance offered an early retirement package including the Health Care Allowance (HCA), which was described as a "lifetime" welfare benefit. In 1995, Continental was acquired by CNA. In 1998, CNA informed the early retirees that their HCA benefit would be terminated January 1, 1999. They complained to the plan administrator but did not receive relief. They sued under ERISA and for breach of contract, estoppel, and breach of fiduciary duty.

The Seventh Circuit affirmed the district court's grant of summary judgment on all counts to the defendant. The plaintiffs admitted that, although the benefit was described as a lifetime benefit, they were not told in so many words that the benefit could not be amended or terminated. Both of the plans gave the sponsor discretion to terminate, so the "arbitrary and capricious" standard applied.

The Seventh Circuit distinguished between cases in which lifetime benefits were deemed to create a contract, but the reservation of rights clause was in a separate document. In this case, the reservation of rights clause was contained in the same document. The Seventh Circuit ruled that welfare benefits offered to retirees could be altered or amended prospectively, even after retirement, because of the reservation of rights clause. The Seventh Circuit found the state law claims to be preempted by ERISA § 502(a).

In this interpretation, to make out an ERISA estoppel claim, a plaintiff must produce a written document in which the employer makes knowing misrepresentations on which employees reasonably relied to their detriment. There is an exception for cases in which the plan documents are ambiguous or misleading, and oral representations about the meaning of the documents will be admissible. In this case, however, the Seventh Circuit concluded that the employer could have changed its policy after the acquisition. It was not reasonable for the plaintiffs to rely on the representations to mean that the lifetime benefit was vested. [*Vallone v. CNA Financial Corp.*, 375 F.3d 623 (7th Cir.), *cert. denied* 125 S. Ct. 670 (2004); *see also Hackett v. Xerox Corp,* 315 F.3d 771 (7th Cir. 2003), holding that rights do not accrue prospectively, and *Klassy v. Physicians Plus Ins. Co.,* 371 F.3d 952 (7th Cir. 2004) (ERISA preempts denial of benefits claims brought as state-law claims)]

In 2006, the Seventh Circuit permitted insurance benefits described as "lifetime" to be terminated, based on the employer's reservation of the right to alter the benefits, and under the principle that when a nonambiguous CBA expires, so does the obligation to provide any benefits that have not vested. In this reading, unless the contract provides for vesting, welfare benefits are presumed to terminate when the CBA ends, unless a party can show latent ambiguity in the contract. In the Seventh Circuit's view, contract language providing benefits for surviving spouses until their death or remarriage refers only to eligibility, not duration; the duration of the benefit is limited to the CBA term. Statements by company officials that benefits would continue for life were held not to be definitive because they could not supplant the CBA language. [*Cherry v. Auburn Gear Inc.,* 441 F.3d 476 (7th Cir. 2006). *See also UAW v. Rockford Powertrain, Inc.,* 350 F.3d 698 (7th Cir. 2003) for the proposition that benefit eligibility ends with the CBA unless the benefits are vested, and *Barnett v. Ameren Corp.,* 436 F.3d 830 (7th Cir. 2006) for the proposition that statements by company officials do not replace the contractual language]

In March 2005, the Seventh Circuit decided an unusual case, in which the plan documents did not include a reservation of the right to modify or terminate the plan provisions. Therefore, summary judgment for the defendant was reversed and the case sent back to the district court for further proceedings about benefits described as "lifetime" benefits in the summary plan description. The Seventh Circuit held that welfare benefits vest only if the employer enters into a contract with the employees. The word "vest" does not have to be used in the documents, but the intent to vest must be stated expressly. The Seventh Circuit read the plan documents to express a clear enough intention to vest to rule out the presumption against vesting. When the right to amend is not reserved, a plan's promise of "lifetime benefits" is read literally to mean benefits for life. [*Bland v. Fiatallis North America, Inc., Case New Holland, Inc. and CNH Health and Welfare Plan,* 401 F.3d 779 (7th Cir. 2005)]

An employer was denied the declaratory judgment it applied for to get court confirmation that it could unilaterally modify or terminate the CBA's retiree health benefits. The District Court for the District of Minnesota denied both the employer's application for declaratory judgment and the union's request to compel arbitration. According to the District Court, plan language must be given its common, ordinary meaning, as a reasonable person in the participant's situation would have interpreted the words. The District Court found the clauses reserving the employer's right to modify benefits to be ambiguous, because it was possible they could be interpreted to limit modifications to those required to conform to changes in the law. The CBA stated the company's commitment to continuing to pay the cost of the retiree health plan, which the District Court read as evidence that the benefits were not vested—because promising to pay for a vested benefit would be duplicative. Overall, the court found the record ambiguous as to whether the benefits were intended to be vested. The language was too confusing for the court to reach a conclusion—hence, a declaratory judgment was inappropriate. [*Rexam v. USW & IAM,* No. 03-2998 ADM/JJG, 2005 U.S. Dist. LEXIS 10055 (D. Minn. 2006)]

Although the trend is very much against plaintiffs seeking to maintain retiree benefits, a 2006 Sixth Circuit case required the restoration of lifetime health benefits for retirees—even though the corporation had reorganized in the interim and the employer retained the right to terminate or modify the benefits—because the benefits were vested under a labor contract. Management and union entered into a letter of agreement capping the employer's obligation, but stating that no covered person would have to pay any part of the excess over the cap before a stipulated date. After the merger, retirees were billed $56 a month for coverage. The employer and union set up a transition fund, but when it ran out, the premium rose to $290 and then $501 a month, leading the retirees to move for a declaratory judgment that they did not have to pay the increased premiums because of their vested right to lifetime coverage. The Sixth Circuit granted a preliminary injunction because of the risk of harm to the retirees and the likelihood that they would prevail, saying that although welfare benefit plans can expire or be changed at the end of a CBA, courts have the power to interpret ambiguous provisions that might be deemed to create vested benefit rights. (The retirees introduced substantial extrinsic evidence of intent that the benefits last for their lifetimes, including documents about lifetime coverage.) [*Yolton v. El Paso Tennessee Pipeline Co.*, 435 F.3d 571 (6th Cir. 2006)]

The Sixth Circuit ruled that, in arbitration about changes in a corporation's health plan, the union can represent retirees as well as active workers. However, although the union automatically has status to represent the actives, consent of the retirees is necessary. Although retirees are no longer part of the bargaining unit, management and union can still bargain on the subject of retiree health benefits and, once they do that, retirees can have enforceable rights to those benefits. In fact, retirees can have individual rights under LMRA § 301 that active workers do not have (because the union is their sole representative). So they must consent to being represented by the union because when the union represents them, their individual claims are waived. [*Cleveland Elec. Illuminating Co. v. Utility Workers Union of Am., Local 270*, 440 F.3d 809 (6th Cir. 2006)]

§ 9.09   TAX ISSUES FOR RETIREE HEALTH BENEFITS

Internal Revenue Code § 419A(c)(2) permits the employer to deduct the cost of retiree health benefits as part of a nondiscriminatory funded welfare plan. Key employees' retiree health benefits must be drawn from separate accounts, not the main account. Failure to maintain the separate accounts, or discrimination in furnishing retiree health benefits, is penalized by the 100% excise tax on disqualified benefits imposed by I.R.C. § 4976.

A funded welfare plan can maintain a reserve for future retiree health benefits, funded over the work lives of employees, without violating the account limit. The reserve must use a level-basis actuarial determination, making use of reasonable assumptions and current medical costs.

The Voluntary Employees' Beneficiary Association (VEBA) [I.R.C. § 501(c) (8)] is a possible funding vehicle for retiree health benefits. Caution must be exercised. The VEBA is a tax-exempt organization, so its investment income is subject to taxation. VEBAs are required to use current health costs to calculate the contributions to be made for future retirees. So if costs increase more than anticipated, or if retirees use more health care than expected, the VEBA may be exhausted.

One of the most important functions of ERISA is to make sure that pensions are properly funded in advance of the time that benefits must be paid. However, with respect to retiree health benefits, prefunding is allowed but not required. An argument can be made both for prefunding and for keeping the benefits unfunded.

Unfunded benefits are unsecured and can be changed at any time. They give rise to a large annual expense under the FASB rules. This expense generally increases over time, and can be higher than the pension expense precisely because of the mandate of prefunding pensions. There will also be a large accrued liability on the corporate books. The income received on sums that remain general assets of the corporation (because the money is not dedicated to prefunding retiree health benefits) is taxable. The employer's income tax deduction attributable to the retiree health plan is limited to the annual cost of benefits actually paid in that year.

In contrast, if the plan is funded, the money dedicated to this purpose is protected from diversion. Therefore, the plan is not very flexible. However, the corporation can accelerate its tax deduction, and there is more opportunity to manage the tax deduction. The corporation receives the investment income of a 401(h) account tax-free. Such income reduces the operating expenses of the plan and helps level out the future expenses. That makes the plan's accounting results look more favorable—and therefore the company will have less incentive to cut the benefits in the future.

Early in 2003, the Tax Court held in *Wells Fargo & Co. v. Commissioner* [120 T.C. 5 (2003)] that employers could deduct the cost of prefunding the present value of retiree medical benefit liabilities for current retirees. In this case, the employer created a trust in 1991 to fund retiree medical benefits. The plan actuary calculated the present value of the retiree medical benefits at $14 million for active employees and $27.7 million for retirees. Based on this calculation, the employer contributed the entire $27.7 million toward funding benefits for those already retired, plus $2.8 million for benefits for those who would retire in the future.

The employer deducted the entire amount under Code § 419 (c)(2) as a retiree medical benefits reserve, funded over the working lives of the covered employees, actuarially determined on a level basis using assumptions that are reasonable when taken in the aggregate. The employer's argument was that the entire present value of the projected benefit could be contributed and deducted in the first year of the fund with respect to current retirees who had already exhausted their working lives. The Tax Court treated this as a proper deduction, because if the year in which the allocation is first recognized occurs after the employee's retirement, there are no future years to which the benefit can be allocated. Therefore, there are no future normal costs, and the entire present value of the project benefit can appropriately be allocated to the first year.

§9.10   MPDIMA AND THE MEDICARE INTERFACE

[A]   In General

There are two ways a person can qualify for Medicare: either being completely and permanently disabled for a period of at least two years—or reaching age 65. Income and assets are irrelevant—and so is employment status. In other words, people who are still working can be entitled to Medicare benefits (although the employer's group health plan will usually be the primary payor) but a person under 65 who is not disabled will not qualify for Medicare merely because he or she is retired. Nor does Medicare provide benefits for the under 65 spouses of retirees (or retirees' dependent children, if the unusual case but not impossible case that they have any).

The Medicare system includes "secondary payor" rules under which retirees can elect to make Medicare the primary payor for their medical care, with the employer group health plan merely the secondary payor. However, the employer does not have this option, and is not permitted to draft the health plan to make Medicare the primary payor.

Because of its role as secondary payor, Medicare is entitled to seek reimbursement from any entity (including Medicare beneficiaries, health care providers and suppliers, and attorneys) that has received payment from a primary payor. Rules published in 2006 clarify the statutory definitions, including the legal basis for recovery when Medicare paid first although it should have been secondary. If the primary payor is an EGHP or large group health plan, all of the employers that sponsor or contribute to the plan must reimburse Medicare, whether the plan is insured or self-insured. The primary payor is relieved of its reimbursement obligation if Medicare has already recovered payment—but CMS has no duty to pursue the payee before it attempts to be reimbursed by the primary payor. [Interim Regulations, 71 Fed. Reg. 9466 (Feb. 24, 2006), effective April 25, 2006]

In a Medicare secondary payor case, Medicare incorrectly paid health care expenses for an employee who was covered by an EGHP. Medicare then sought reimbursement from the employer. The employer paid under protest and sued for a refund. The Federal Circuit ruled for the government, stating that the Medicare statute permits recoupment from any entity that is required to pay or is directly or indirectly responsible for payment. The Federal Circuit read this to mean that employers who sponsor or contribute to an EGHP are responsible. [*Telecare Corp. v. Leavitt*, 409 F.3d 1345 (Fed. Cir. 2005)]

In 2003, a federal statute known as MPDIMA (Medicare Prescription Drug, Improvement and Modernization Act of 2003 [Pub. L. No. 108-173] not only enacted the Health Savings Account form (*see* § 18.09), it called for a significant addition to the Medicare program, an optional prescription drug program. Of particular interest to the HR community is the MPDIMA program for paying subsidies to employers who offer retirees drug benefits that are at least actuarially equivalent to the Medicare provisions.

[B] MPDIMA Statute and Regulations

The Medicare Prescription Drug, Improvement and Modernization Act of 2003 (abbreviated MPDIMA) [Pub. L. No. 108-173], in addition to creating the Health Savings Account plan type discussed in § 18.09, and including provisions for the Medicare Advantage managed-care system to replace the existing Medicare+Choice plans, MPDIMA creates a program of Medicare prescription drug coverage, beginning in 2006. The prescription program is known as Medicare Part D. (In the interim, Medicare beneficiaries can get drug discount cards to reduce their prescription costs.)

MPDIMA includes provisions of especial interest to employers. Many employers will take advantage of the availability of prescription drug benefits under Medicare to terminate or cut back their own retiree health benefit programs. To limit the number of employers who will do so, Congress included a program of subsidies for employers who provide prescription drug coverage that is "actuarially equivalent" to the Medicare coverage. That phrase is in quotation marks, because there are significant accounting questions still to be resolved about what constitutes actuarial equivalence for this purpose.

According to the Society of Actuaries, a company that sponsors a pharmacy benefit plan for retirees can save more than 80% of its drug costs because of Part D. Its estimate for 2006 is that dropping the current drug plan, but paying retirees' Part D premiums, could provide an 83% saving. Companies that integrate their plans with Plan D, or have a wraparound plan, could save 31–49%. Companies that take the subsidy for maintaining their plans could save close to 30%, plus additional tax benefits. However, the Society of Actuaries predicts that savings will drop over time, except for companies that cancel their own plan and pay Part D premiums. [News Articles, *Sponsors to Reap Big Savings from Medicare Part D*, PlanSponsor.com (Jan. 10, 2006)]

Part D is voluntary: Medicare beneficiaries decide whether or not to enroll. They pay a monthly premium (estimated at $35 a month for the first year of the program's operation), then are responsible for an annual deductible of $250 before they receive any coverage under Part D. For drug costs between $250 and $2,250 a year, they are responsible for a 25% copayment. They are fully responsible for all drug costs between $2,250 and $5,100; if their drug costs are higher than that, Part D pays the full cost (except for a 5% coinsurance charge for beneficiaries whose income exceeds 150% of the poverty line). For Medicare-eligible individuals who are retired, and who enroll in Part D, Part D (and not the employer's retiree health plan) becomes the primary payor for medications.

The statute explicitly permits employers to pay Part D premiums for retirees (which could very well be cheaper than providing coverage through the plan). However, such payments will not qualify for the employer subsidy (see below). The plan can also coordinate with Part D, or "wrap around" by providing supplementary coverage—but, once again, the federal subsidy will not be payable for persons who enroll in Part D.

For 2006, the subsidy equals 28% of the retiree's prescription drug expenses that fall between $250 and $5,000 a year (minus discounts, chargebacks, and average percentage rebates). Therefore, the maximum subsidy for 2006 equals $1,300 per person: 28% of the $5,000 maximum minus the $250 deductible. CMS's Office of the Actuary estimates that the average retiree drug subsidy payment for 2006 will be $611. Because this amount is not taxable, if the corporation's marginal tax rate is 35%, the value of the average subsidy would be the same as a taxable payment of $940 per covered employee. [CMS, *Retiree Drug Coverage Under the MMA: Issues for Public Comment to Maximize*

Enhancement in Drug Coverage and Reductions in Drug Costs for Retirees,
<http://benefitslink.com/articles/retireewhitepaper.pdf>] Employers are not re-
quired to include the subsidy amounts in gross income (MPDIMA adds a new
Section 139 to the Internal Revenue Code.) In order to encourage employers to
maintain retiree health coverage, Congress gave them full flexibility with regard
to formularies and other plan design issues.

Indexed figures for 2007 were announced in April 2006. The cost threshold
(the amount of covered drug expenses that an individual must incur before the plan
sponsor can receive the subsidy; also equal to the deductible) rose from $250 to
$265; the cost limit (the maximum amount on which subsidy could be claimed)
rose from $5,000 to $5,350. The initial coverage limit (also known as the "dough-
nut hole"; the point at which the employee is responsible for 100% of the cost of
drugs) went from $2,250 to $2,400, and the out-of-pocket threshold (the maximum
amount a beneficiary can be required to pay for drugs before 95% catastrophic
coverage kicks in) went from $3,600 to $3,850. The beneficiary will be entitled to
catastrophic coverage after spending $5,100 on covered expenses in 2006,
$5,421.25 in 2007. The 2007 amounts are used to test the plan for actuarial equiv-
alence, and the subsidy is based on 28% of the claims in the range of $265 to
$5,350. Calendar year plan sponsors must submit their 2007 subsidy application by
September 30, 2006; non-calendar-year sponsors should consult their actuary
about application filing dates. [*See* Segal Capital Checkup, *CMS Announces
Indexed Medicare Part D Amounts for 2007,* <http://www.segalco.com/
publications/capitalcheckup/041106.html>, Apr. 11, 2006]

Hewitt Associates surveyed 300 large firms, covering 5.7 million retirees and
a further 16 million active workers and dependents. More than three quarters
(79%) of participants stated that they would accept the subsidy for 2006; 10%
announced an intention to supplement Part D coverage for their retirees. However,
more than a quarter (29%) of the employers taking the subsidy expected to reduce
health and prescription drug coverage for retirees who opted for Part D, and 31%
expected to reduce drug benefits for such retirees. Nine percent planned to drop
their own drug coverage for Medicare-eligible retirees. Only 56% said they would
allow retirees to reenroll in their retiree health plan if they enrolled in Part D in
2006 but were dissatisfied with it. Most respondents had no long-range plans with
respect to the subsidy; they want to see how the program progresses. [Kaiser
Family Foundation, *Four in Five Large Firms to Maintain Retiree Drug Coverage
[. . .],* <http://www.kff.org/medicare/med120705nr.cfm> (Dec. 7, 2005); Matt
Brady, *Survey: Many Employers Accept Medicare Drug Subsidies,* NU Online
News Service (Dec. 7, 2005)] A number of employers determined that it would
not be feasible to separate out the cost of offering prescription drug coverage as
distinct from the other elements of their retiree health program, and, in turn, the
viability of their retiree health coverage. These employers announced that they
would terminate all retiree health benefits for employees who elected Part D. [Milt
Freudenheim and Robert Pear, *A Drug Benefit Conundrum,* New York Times,
Oct. 4, 2005, at p. C1]

Either an ERISA welfare plan or a collectively bargained plan can operate as a qualified retiree prescription drug plan. MPDIMA uses the ERISA § 3(16)(B) definition of "plan sponsor." For plans jointly maintained by an employer and a union, the employer is the sponsor (and therefore potentially entitled to the subsidy) only if the employer provides the primary source of funding for the plan. Generally speaking, the employer will be the sponsor of a single-employer plan; the board of trustees will generally be considered the sponsor of a multi-employer plan. A qualified covered retiree is defined as one who is covered under a qualified plan; is either entitled to Medicare Part A benefits or enrolled under Part B; and has neither enrolled in a Part D plan nor in a Medicare Advantage prescription drug plan.

MPDIMA requires the plan sponsor to attest to the Department of Health and Human Services at least once a year (more often if the agency requests it) that the actuarial value of the prescription drug coverage under the plan is at least equivalent to Plan D coverage. HIPAA disclosures must be made to both the qualified covered retirees and to HHS as to the extent to which the employer's plan offers creditable coverage (*see* § 19.05).

MPDIMA and its implementing Final Regulations published in early 2005 [70 Fed. Reg. 4193 (Jan. 28, 2005)] give employers a number of choices of how to handle prescription drug benefits for retirees. It has never been mandatory for employers to offer prescription drug coverage for either active workers or former employees. MPDIMA is intended to provide incentives for employers to maintain retiree drug coverage, but doesn't require them to add coverage and doesn't forbid them to terminate existing coverage. Employers can receive a federal subsidy if they offer insured drug coverage that is at least the actuarial equivalent of the Part D drug plan. They can also create a wrap-around plan that supplements Part D (although there will be no subsidy for this option) or enter into a contract with CMS to operate a Private Drug Plan as defined by MPDIMA. (This last option will probably be taken only by very large employers.)

A wrap-around plan operates by having retirees enroll in Part D; the employer then offers coverage to the extent that Part D is less generous than the prescription drug benefits previously offered by the employer. The purpose of the wrap-around is to preserve the level of coverage previously enjoyed by the retiree, while not requiring the employer to carry the full burden of covering prescription drug costs for the retiree. To make the best decision, the employer should consult not only insurance carriers and brokers but actuaries, HR attorneys, and tax attorneys and/or accountants.

Under the Final Regulations, to receive the subsidy, an employer must:

- Provide prescription drug coverage under a program that constitutes "creditable coverage" (the concept of creditable coverage is important because it determines whether someone who delays enrolling in Part D because of being covered by another plan will be able to avoid paying the late enrollment penalty);

- Notify eligible participants whether the program qualifies as creditable coverage; notice must be given before the person first becomes eligible to enroll in
  Part D, and before the effective date of enrollment in the employer's plan. If
  coverage is not creditable, the employee or retiree must be informed of this fact
  and possible limitations and penalties on Part D enrollment;
- Cover Part D-eligible retirees and their spouses under the plan in lieu of Part D,
  but subsidies are not available for people who try to "double dip" by enrolling
  both in Part D and in the employer plan;
- Satisfy the Final Regulation's definition of actuarial equivalence;
- Submit an application to CMS by September 30 of each year, attesting to the
  actuarial equivalence of the plan and providing demographic data about the
  plan's retirees (the full name and Social Security Number of each person
  enrolled; date of birth; gender; for persons enrolled because of relationship
  to the retiree, the nature of the spousal or dependency relationship).

There are two aspects to the test for actuarial equivalence. The first is whether
the gross value of the employer's prescription drug plan is at least as valuable as the
standard Part D plan. The employer's actual claims experience, without consideration of contributions made by the retirees, is used for this test. The second prong is
a net test comparing the value of the benefit provided by the employer (gross value
minus employee contributions) to the net value of the standard Part D program.

The Final Regulation gives employers a break by determining the gross value
of the standard Part D benefit as if the sponsor's program were secondary to standard
Part D coverage, even though the rules for coordinating Medicare with Employee
Group Health Plans make the employer's plan the primary one, but only if the
employer offers a wrap-around plan to retirees who enroll in Part D. The employer
has the options of applying the actuarial equivalence test to the whole plan, or to
each benefit option within a single EGHP. Employers have complete discretion as to
how to allocate retiree contributions between prescription drug benefits and other
benefits in the same plan (e.g., medical, dental, or vision benefits).

CMS extended the deadline for applying for the subsidy from September 30,
2005, to October 31, 2005; the extension was automatic and applied to all plan
sponsors. Applications for the subsidy can be made online at <http://
www.rds.cms.hhs.gov>. The sponsor is required to file a list of retirees in
CMS' approved format. Plan administrators, PBMs, and information technology
specialists must work together to compile information for the application and then
decide who files it and who is responsible for ongoing updates. The collaborators
must also determine who will file the monthly, quarterly, or annual claims for
payment, audit claims relating to the subsidy; and work with CMS to resolve
differences between the list of participants and CMS' list of beneficiaries who
have waived Part D coverage.

Under CMS guidance, a qualifying covered retiree is a person who is eligible
for Part D but, in lieu of enrolling in it, is covered by employment-based retiree
health coverage that is actuarially equivalent to Part D. The Medicare-eligible

spouse of a retiree can qualify for Retiree Drug Subsidy (RDS) payments even if he or she is actively employed, and even if the retiree is not eligible for Medicare yet. A plan participant who is entitled to Medicare because of disability can qualify for RDS even if he or she is covered under the employer's plan as an active employee. Persons who receive Medicare because they have end-stage renal disease also qualify for RDS payments in their first 30 months of eligibility even though Medicare is only the secondary payor and the EGHP is the primary payor. [Segal's Capital Checkup, *CMS Extends Deadline for Completing Retiree Drug Subsidy Application Online and Issues Guidance on Eligibility for Subsidy Payments* (Sept. 26, 2005) (benefitslink.com)]

In February and March 2005, CMS issued additional guidance about what to do if an employer wishes to enter into a direct contract with CMS to provide retiree drug benefits, or wants to tailor the drug coverage offered to retirees by Medicare managed care plans. CMS agreed to waive some requirements that would otherwise be applicable, in the interests of making it easier for employers to set up their own full-scale Prescription Drug Plans. The technical details are beyond the scope of this book; the waivers are noted as an option your company may wish to pursue after detailed individual advice. [CMS, *Additional Part D Waiver Guidance for Employer/Union Retiree Coverage*, <http://www.cms.hhs.gov/EmpGrpWaivers/Downloads/EmployerWaiverGuidanceRev1.pdf> (Jan. 4, 2006)]

So, how should a plan sponsor handle this immensely confusing situation? Mercer HR Consulting suggests the following tactics:

- Check the plan documents to see if there are any limitations on actions affecting the plan;
- Develop an accounting strategy (see below), including the latest FASB pronouncements;
- Research the current costs the plan encounters to provide drugs that could come under Medicare Part D;
- Decide if disclosures to plan participants are required;
- Understand the available options for a drug benefit that qualifies for the subsidy versus Medicare Advantage or a wrap-around Part D plan structure;
- Review plan design options, e.g., caps, coinsurance and copayment options and Health Savings Accounts;
- Tell participants about the new laws and how the company program relates to the Medicare discount card and Part D.

[Mercer HR Consulting Employer Retiree Medical/Medicare Checklist (Jan. 9, 2004) <www.mercerhr.com>]

Research by Credit Suisse First Boston showed that large employers expect subsidies of about $4 billion over the next four years; the overall subsidy amount is projected at $14 billion over that period (including smaller private employers and public employers). Most (331) of the Fortune 500 have retiree health benefit plans, although some of these companies are financially very sound and others are in severe trouble (e.g., General Motors, which is projected to receive $1.1 billion in subsidies). CMS reported that by February 2006, plans covering 6.4 million retirees had already applied for subsidies. [Mary Williams Walsh, *U.S. to Pay Big Employers Billions Not to End Their Retiree Health Plans,* New York Times, Feb. 24, 2006, at p. C3] In mid-2005, Chicago Consulting Actuaries suggested that the employer's attitude toward the plan and its participants is an important determinant of what to do about the subsidy. Employers that take a more paternalistic view might wish to continue providing primary coverage or to become a prescription drug plan. Other companies may want to take advantage of the ability to exit the retiree health field now that Medicare drug benefits are available. [Chicago Consulting Actuaries, *Considerations in Applying for the Medicare Part D Employer Subsidy,* <http://insight. chicagoconsultingactuaries.com/Insight/Documents/MedicarePartDEmployerSubsidy. aspx> (May 26, 2005)]

To receive the subsidy, a plan must submit documentation including the Authorized Representative Verification Form, <http://www.rds.cms.hhs.gov/ news/announcements/ar_vetting_letter.htm>. The form must be submitted to CMS by mail, scanned into an e-mail, or faxed. A separate form is required for each plan sponsor ID number. The form designates the authorized representative for the plan and must be completed by someone with corporate authority to confirm that the representative has legal authority to sign the plan sponsor application and deal with CMS.

Consulting firm CCA Strategies published a checklist in 2006 reminding employers of the work to be done to qualify for the Part D subsidy:

- Compile and submit monthly updates to the beneficiary census
- Determine if any submissions have been rejected and, if so, if an appeal is warranted
- Designate an account representative and have a qualified person verify the account representative's authority
- Submit interim cost reports (either by data entry or file transfer)
- Submit payment requests
- Furnish CMS with evidence of creditable coverage for every drug benefit option (for either active workers or retirees) in which Medicare-eligible individuals can enroll; submission is due no later than 60 days after the end of the plan year or within 30 days after a plan terminates or changes its creditable coverage status
- Ninety days before the start of each plan year, submit the subsidy application, including information about the plan, designation of the authorized representative, actuary, and account manager, a census list of retirees, and the actuary's attestation that the plan is equivalent to Part D
- Send notices of creditable coverage to all Medicare-eligible plan participants (whether they are active or retired) once a year no later than November 15; before the individual's initial Part D enrollment period; before any Medicare-eligible

new participant's Medicare coverage becomes effective; when the plan's creditable coverage status changes; or when a participant asks for a notice

- Reconcile the subsidy payment files each year and submit actual drug cost data for each individual and other information required by CMS; filing is due 15 months after the end of the plan year.

[CCA Strategies Insight, *Medicare Part D Employer Subsidy Checklist*, <http://share.ccastrategies.com/Insight/Documents/PartDChecklist.aspx> (Mar. 21, 2006)]

Part D imposes notice requirements on employers: both notice to plan participants and beneficiaries, and notice to CMS, as to the status of the plan and the rights of Medicare-eligible employees and retirees.

CMS provided guidance in May 2005 on the employer's obligation, under the Medicare Prescription Drug, Improvement, and Modernization Act of 2003 (MPDIMA), to provide a Notice of Creditable Coverage, informing all Medicare Part D eligible persons covered by the plan whether the plan's prescription drug coverage is at least as good as Part D. The notice was first due November 15, 2005, unless the EGHP applied to CMS to operate a Part D prescription drug plan, or had a contract with a Part D plan to provide prescription benefits for its participants.

The guidance clarifies that a plan only needs to get attestation from a qualified actuary that its coverage is or is not creditable (i.e., Part D-equivalent or better) if the employer applies for the subsidy. A plan that does not apply for the subsidy, and that satisfies a safe harbor, is deemed creditable. The safe harbor is that the plan covers both brand name and generic drugs, offers reasonable access to retail providers; and pays an average of 60% or more of the participants' prescription drug expenses. To be creditable, a plan that does not integrate medical and drug coverage must have either drug coverage with no maximum annual benefit; an annual maximum of at least $25,000; or an actuarial expectation that it will pay at least $2,000 per Medicare-eligible person in 2005. Plans that integrate medical and drug coverage must have a deductible of $250 or less for drug coverage; no annual maximum, or a maximum of $25,000 or more; and a lifetime combined benefit maximum of at least $1 million.

The Notice of Creditable Coverage does not have to be mailed separately; it can be distributed with other information, including information about enrollment in the plan or renewing enrollment, but the Part D information must be displayed prominently. [Kaye Pestaina, *Notices of Creditable Coverage: Employer Deadline Coming Soon,* Employee Benefit News (Sept. 1, 2005)]

Disclosure is also required in another direction: from entities (e.g., health plans) that provide prescription drug coverage, informing CMS whether the coverage is creditable. Initial disclosure, in the form of posting to the CMS Web site, <http://www.cms.hhs.gov/apps/ccdisclosure/default.asp>, was due for the first time on or before March 31, 2006, and must be renewed annually thereafter within 60 days of the beginning of each plan year. A final disclosure is required within 30 days of termination of a prescription drug plan, or when its creditable coverage status changes. However, this disclosure duplicates the information submitted to receive the subsidy, so entities that have applied for subsidies are exempt. In some cases, disclosure will be required even by companies that have applied for the subsidy, with respect to eligible persons who delayed their Part D enrollment. [*See* <http://www.cms.hhs.gov/creditablecoverage> in general; January 10, 2006 update available at <http://www.cms.hhs.gov/creditablecoverage/Downloads/Disclosure2CMSGdnc.pdf>. The subsidy program's home page is <http://rds.cms.hhs.gov> (no www)] Morgan Lewis Law-Flash, *Guidance Issued on Medicare Part D Creditable Coverage Disclosure to CMS*, <http://www.morganlewis.com> (Jan. 9, 2006). For the creditable coverage guidance, and the text of the model notices to be used after May 15, 2006 (i.e., after the initial enrollment period has elapsed), *see* CMS's press release [<http://www.cms.hhs.gov/CreditableCoverage/02_CcafterMay15.asp> (Apr. 19, 2006)]

On another issue, the marketing of Medicare prescription drug plans (either standalone or as a component of a Medicare Advantage managed care plan), CMS weighed in with guidelines in mid-2005. Door-to-door sales and unsolicited e-mails to sell drug plans are forbidden. Calls to offer plan information are subject to the Do Not Call registry and consumer requests not to be called again. CMS will sanction plans that do not comply with the marketing rules, including corrective actions plans, forbidding new enrollment in the plan, civil monetary penalties, and referral to law enforcement agencies. The guidelines allow health services providers, including pharmacists, to display posters and make marketing materials for prescription drug plans available. However, they are forbidden to steer beneficiaries to a plan in which they have a financial interest. [CMS Fact Sheet, *CMS Issues Marketing Rules for All Plans Offering Medicare Drug Coverage*, <http://www.cms.hhs.gov/media/press/release.asp?Counter=1535> (Aug. 15, 2005)]

Buck Consultants summarized the status of various types of tax-favored account-based health plans for Part D purposes. When an employee participates in a health reimbursement arrangement (HRA) and its associated high deductible health plan (HDHP), a reasonable estimate of prescription drug costs should be treated as representing prescription drug claims. This amount will be credited to the HRA and will reduce the HDHP deductible. For HRAs that are not associated with HDHPs, the HRA is treated as a plan with a $0 deductible and an annual limit of the amount credited for the year, and an allocation to prescription drug expenses must be made. The employer must disclose, to all Part D–eligible participants, whether the HRA provides creditable coverage. Because of the difficulty of making actuarial calculations, CMS instructs employers to disregard FSAs when determining creditable coverage, so FSA participants need not be given notice of creditable coverage. Once a person becomes eligible for Medicare, he or she is no longer eligible to make HSA or MSA contributions; these plans are not included in the calculation of whether the employer's plan is actuarially equivalent to Part D, and notices of creditable coverage are not required with respect to HSAs and MSAs. HRAs can qualify for the subsidy; however, FSAs, HSAs, and MSAs cannot qualify because they are not creditable. [Buck Consultants LLC, *CMS Provides Information on Account Plans for Medicare Part D Purposes*, <http://www.mellon.com/hris/pdf/fyi_07_20_05.pdf> (July 20, 2005)]

[C] Accounting Issues Under MPDIMA

As soon as MPDIMA passed, companies considered the impact that future subsidies—or future reductions in the number of retirees receiving coverage under the plan (because they opted instead for the Medicare prescription plan)—would have on their projections of retiree health benefits costs. Reduction of a large cost item, in turn, would improve the company's financials.

Initially, the Financial Accounting Standards Board (FASB) issued a Staff Position, FAS 106a, that it would be premature for plan sponsors to include MPDIMA effects in their FAS 106 disclosures because of uncertainties in how MPDIMA would be implemented and enforced as well as practical considerations such as what percentage of current and future retirees would opt in to the Medicare drug plan.

This position was reversed at the FASB's January 7, 2004, meeting. The organization announced that employers who sponsor retiree health plans can take MPDIMA into account when preparing their current financial statements. They can also choose to defer accounting for MPDIMA effects until FASB issues additional guidance. FASB stated that immediate accounting could result in a material income item, resulting from the significant decrease in reported liabilities for the retiree health plan. On February 11, 2004, FASB voted to confirm that the existing rules about post-retirement benefits should continue to be used. Therefore, the projected federal subsidy should be booked as a reduction in future benefit costs—and not an income stream from continuing operations.

FASB issued Staff Position No. FAS 106-1 [*Accounting and Disclosure Requirements Related to the Medicare Prescription Drug Improvement and Modernization Act of 2003* (Jan. 12, 2004) <http://www.fasb.org/fasb_staff_positions/fsp_fas106-1.pdf>], but quickly replaced it by FAS 106-b, with the same title. [*See* <http://www.fasb.org/fasb_staff_positions/prop_fsp_fas106-b.pdf>]

FAS 106-b explains how to account for single-employer plans whose prescription drug benefits are actuarially equivalent to Medicare Part D and therefore qualify for the subsidy, which will be used to offset the employer's payments for post-retirement health benefits. This Staff Position also explains how to disclose the effects of the subsidy before the plan sponsor has determined that the plan is actuarially equivalent. However, it does not cover the situation in which the subsidy is greater than the employer's share of prescription drug costs for retirees. Plans that provide prescription drug coverage may see changes in their per capita claims costs, whether or not they receive the subsidy. FASB notes that if new plans are established, or existing ones are amended, the predicted benefit obligation will be affected by changes in benefits available to employees who have already rendered services. If a subsidy is received, it will be tax-exempt and therefore will not have to be accounted for under Statement 109.

As of FAS 106-b, until an employer is able to determine actuarial equivalence, annual or interim financial statements should disclose that MPDIMA has been passed, and that the employer's measurements do not reflect an MPDIMA subsidy because it is not yet possible to determine whether the benefits are actuarially equivalent. In interim and annual financial statements in which the subsidy is used to measure the net periodic postretirement benefit cost or the APBO, the reduction in APBO and the effect of the subsidy on measuring net periodic post-retirement benefit cost should be disclosed. So should any other information required by the 2003 revision of Statement 132 paragraph 5(r).

FASB's next pronouncement was FAS 106-2, superseding FAS 106-1 (and using the same title). [*See* <http://www.fasb.org/fasb_staff_positions/fsp_fas106-2.pdf>] The applicability of FAS 106-2 is limited to single-employer defined benefit retiree health plans that have determined that they qualify for the subsidy (because their benefits are actuarially equivalent to the Part D benefit) and expect to use the subsidy to reduce or offset the employer's share of the cost of the prescription drug coverage. This Staff Position explains how to disclose the effects of the subsidy when the employer has not yet been able to determine if the plan is actuarially equivalent or not.

[D] *Erie* Issues

The Third Circuit in *Erie County Retirees Association v. County of Erie* [220 F.3d 193 (3d Cir. 2000)] ruled that the ADEA applies to retiree benefits, including health benefits. Therefore in this reading, an employer violates the ADEA by offering Medicare-eligible retirees health benefits that are inferior to those offered to employees who are not yet eligible for Medicare, unless the employer can demonstrate that it incurred equal costs or provided equal benefits for both retiree groups. On April 16, 2001, when the case was remanded to the lower court, the Western District of Pennsylvania decided that the plan did not satisfy the equal cost/equal benefit test. [*Erie County,* 140 F. Supp. 2d 466 (W.D. Pa. 2001)]

Initially, the EEOC adopted the Third Circuit's position in Chapter 3 of its Enforcement Manual.

In July 2003, the EEOC proposed "anti-Erie" regulations that take the position that it can be legitimate (and not a violation of the ADEA; the EEOC has the power to grant exemption from ADEA requirements) for an employer to change or even eliminate retiree health benefits once the retiree becomes eligible for Medicare. The proposed ADEA exemption would also apply to health benefits for spouses and dependents of retirees. It would be permissible to alter benefits for spouses and dependents even if the benefits for the retirees themselves remain the same after they attain Medicare eligibility, and coordination of benefits would be allowed for both existing and newly created plans. [68 Federal Register 41542 (July 14, 2003), adding 29 C.F.R. § 1625.32]

The July 2003 proposal cites the trends discussed above (termination or reduction of retiree benefit programs; greater copayment responsibilities for participating retirees) and agreed with the commentators who suggested that applying the ADEA in this context would have the result of reducing health care benefits, because employers would achieve parity by reducing benefits for non-Medicare-eligible retirees rather than by increasing them for Medicare-eligible retirees.

Despite input from various constituencies, the EEOC did not believe that extending the equal benefit/equal cost test to retiree health benefits would be practical, because it would require unduly complex valuation calculations. Analyzing costs would also be complicated, because of the involvement of payroll taxes in paying for Medicare.

The EEOC proposal soon became the subject of litigation. The AARP succeeded in obtaining a 60-day delay when a federal court in Pennsylvania blocked implementation of the regulations. In March 2005, the Eastern District of Pennsylvania issued a permanent injunction against implementation of the integration regulations. Judge Anita B. Brody ruled that the EEOC rule was not entitled to deference because the agency violated the plain language and Congressional intent of the ADEA. Brody rejected the government's argument that the EEOC has the power to create ADEA exemptions as long as they are reasonable, necessary and proper, and in the public interest. Brody held that regulations are only entitled to deference if they provide rules for a topic not reached by the statute, or that clarify an ambiguous statute.

§9.11   SOP 92-6 REPORTS

The American Institute of Certified Public Accountants (AICPA) requires health and welfare benefits to prepare SOP 92-6 reports. SOP stands for "Statement of Position." Originally, the reports were supposed to start in 1996, but so many extensions were granted that many plan trustees didn't have to do their first SOP 92-6 report until 2001. Although the report is a lot of work to prepare, and involves many calculations that are not otherwise useful, at least the report establishes the plan's obligation for post-retirement benefits for the current year, and sets a benchmark for comparing the obligation to prior years' experience and trends in the plan. [*See* the online newsletter by the Segal Company, *Timing Is Everything: Anticipating and Preparing for Higher Retiree Health Expenditures,* (June 2001) <http://www.segalco.com/publications/newsletters/june01.pdf>]

The cash flow projections for the 92-6 project the amount of money needed every year to pay health costs. Although prefunding of welfare benefits is not required, it is often a good idea to create an asset pool (e.g., using a VEBA) to generate tax-free investment income that can be used for future costs.

The 92-6 report can answer questions like:

- The fund's projected trend rates for medical, drug, and dental coverage costs for future years;

- The number of active employees, retirees, spouses of retirees, and surviving spouses covered by the plan;
- Average ages of active versus retired employees;
- Average number of years of service for active employees;
- Average expected retirement age for the current crop of active employees;
- Actual retirement rate by age;
- Cost of plan benefits;
- Number of active employees eligible for full retiree health benefits;
- The postretirement benefit obligation for current retirees, dependents, and beneficiaries;
- A projection of the postretirement obligations for active workers who have not yet satisfied the requirements for full eligibility;
- Whether there have been any changes in plan design that altered the obligation for postretirement benefits;
- Total current retiree contributions;
- Expected annual rate of increase for retiree contributions;
- Percentage of total cost that comes from employee and retiree cost-sharing (deductibles and coinsurance); expected changes over the next five years.

§ 9.12   IMPLICATIONS OF THE EMPLOYER'S BANKRUPTCY

The basic rule, as created by *In re White Farm Equipment Co.* [788 F.2d 1186 (6th Cir. 1986)] is that vesting of welfare benefits is not automatic. It is a subject of bargaining, to be contracted for. In that case, the bankrupt company maintained a no-contributory, non-collectively-bargained plan that provided retiree benefits. The plaintiffs were retirees who wanted a declaratory judgment (an official statement) that their claims were both valid under ERISA and allowable as bankruptcy claims.

They also asked the court to order the employer to reinstate the plan retroactively and to resume funding it. But the court found that employee benefits regulation is strictly a federal concern. Furthermore, the employer had reserved the power to terminate the plan and could do so at that time.

Ironically, retirees of bankrupt companies may have more protection for their benefits than retirees of solvent companies. Conversely, bankruptcy may solve some of a company's problems while creating others.

Under 11 U.S.C. § 1113, a company that has filed for Chapter 11 status can ask the bankruptcy court for the right to reject an existing collective bargaining agreement, including provisions covering retiree health benefits. The company must disclose the relevant information to the union and bargain in good faith about the termination.

If the company in Chapter 11 was already paying retiree benefits, the Retiree Benefits Bankruptcy Protection Act of 1988 (RBBPA) [Pub. L. No. 100-334] requires medical and disability payments to retirees to continue, on their original terms, either until the parties agree to modify the benefits or the bankruptcy court orders a modification.

The Act includes standards for bankruptcy courts to use in deciding whether a modification is appropriate. Any modifications proposed by the bankruptcy trustee must be equitable, not just to current and former employees, but also to the company's creditors. The retirees must not have had good cause to reject the proposals. The proposed modifications must be necessary to permit the employer to reorganize in bankruptcy on fair terms.

The RBBPA also requires the employer to negotiate with retiree representatives and to disclose the best available information about the employer's financial condition. Generally speaking, the union will serve as the representative of the retirees, unless the union refuses to do so or unless the court rules that a different representative should be appointed. Any party can petition the court to appoint a committee of retirees to represent benefit recipients who are not covered by a collective bargaining agreement.

The court considering the trustee's proposal does not have the power to order benefits lower than the proposed schedule. Once the parties reach an agreement, or once the court orders changes in the benefits, the authorized representative of the retirees can petition the court for an increase, which will be granted if it appears clearly just to do so.

Tip: The RBBPA's protection does not apply to retirees, their spouses, or dependents if the retiree's gross income was $250,000 or more in the year before the employer's bankruptcy petition. The only exception is retirees who can prove they are unable to get comparable individual health care coverage. Nor does the RBBPA require bankrupt employers to maintain retiree health benefits that were provided by the union, not the employer, prior to the bankruptcy.

Congress returned to the subject of protection of retiree health benefits when the employer files for bankruptcy protection in the 2005 statute, the Bankruptcy Abuse Prevention and Consumer Protection Act (P.L. 109-8). § 1403 of this statute amends Bankruptcy Code § 1114. If the corporation, at a time it was insolvent, modified retiree benefits during the 180-day period before the bankruptcy filing, then any party in interest has the right to move for a court hearing. After the hearing, the bankruptcy court is required to order reinstatement of the provisions that were altered—unless the court finds that the balance of the equities clearly favors the modification. That is, if the modification is challenged, it is up to the employer to prove that the modification is fair; the opponents of the change don't have to prove its unfairness.

According to the Seventh Circuit, Bankruptcy Code § 1114 was not intended to be the exclusive remedy for disputes between retirees and their bankruptcy representative. Therefore, state law claims (negligence, misrepresentation, promissory estoppel) by retirees who alleged that their union failed to protect benefits that the union promised would be safe are not completely preempted by the Bankruptcy Code. Because the union's duties in bankruptcy are not identical to the duty of fair representation, the claims also are not preempted by the Labor-Management Relations Act. [*Nelson v. Stewart*, 422 F.3d 463 (7th Cir. 2005)]

A case reached the Third Circuit after a district court approved an application to modify retiree benefits under § 1114. A group of former employees appealed, taking the position that they should not be bound by the stipulation. The Third Circuit, however, upheld the district court decision and ruled that the union's agreement to the stipulation was binding on the group of retirees. The stipulation gave everyone who retired before retiree benefits were terminated a $500 administrative claim and a $5,000 unsecured claim in the bankruptcy. Persons who did not receive retirement benefits on the cut-off date did not receive any bankruptcy distributions, even if they had been eligible for benefits. The retirees who did not receive benefits were informed that the union could not represent them because it would have been a conflict of interest due to the union's support of the stipulation. Although this group of retirees obtained independent counsel, the district court, upheld by the Third Circuit, ruled that the retirees were bound by the stipulation because it was entered into in good faith by the union, which was the authorized representative of the workforce. Furthermore, there was no conflict between representing the interests of active and retired workers because all of the former employer's assets had been sold and all of the employees had been terminated. Under § 1114(b)(1), an authorized representative is designated for persons "receiving any retiree benefits covered by a CBA" so the Third Circuit said that the union was the authorized representative despite its statement that it could not represent the plaintiffs. [*Hourly Employees/Retirees of Debtor v. Erie Forges & Steel Inc.*, 418 F.3d 270 (3d Cir. 2005). *See also In re General Datacomm Indus. Inc. v. Arcara*, 407 F.3d 616 (3d Cir. 2005) (for § 1114 purposes, the term "retired employees" includes those who are forced into retirement by being terminated without cause)]

§ 9.13   401(h) PLANS

[A]   Basic Principles

The basic principle is that assets must remain within a qualified pension plan until they are distributed to participants or beneficiaries. However, the Code permits transfers of certain assets of overfunded plans to special funds known as 401(h) plans that are segregated to provide retiree health benefits.

A 401(h) plan is a pension or annuity plan that also provides incidental health benefits for retirees: benefits for sickness, accident, hospitalization, or medical expenses. The health-type benefits must be subordinate to the plan's main business of offering retirement benefits. The incidental (insurance and health) benefits must not cost more than 25% of the employer's total contributions to a defined benefit plan.

An employer that maintains a 401(h) plan must maintain separate accounts for retiree health benefits and pension benefits. The employer must make reasonable and ascertainable contributions to fund the retiree health benefits. These contributions must be distinct from the contributions to fund pension benefits.

Internal Revenue Code § 420(b)(5) permits one transfer per year to a 401(h) account for tax years beginning between January 1, 1991, and December 31, 2005. The Pension Funding Equity Act of 2004 [Pub. L. 108-218] extends the applicability of Code § 420(b) until December 31, 2013. Such transfers are not considered reversions to the employer; therefore the I.R.C. § 4980 excise tax is not imposed.

Under these Code provisions, the employer is obligated to use the transferred assets only for current retiree health liabilities. All transfers must come from excess pension assets. Excess pension assets means the fair market value minus A or B (whichever is greater) or C.

- A = 150% of the current liability under the plan;
- B = the accrued liability, including normal cost, under the plan;
- C = 125% of all liabilities under the plan to employees and their beneficiaries.

Before making a transfer to a 401(h) plan, the plan administrator must give the DOL at least 60 days' notice, and must also notify participants, beneficiaries and any union representing the participants.

The American Jobs Creation Act of 2004 (AJCA) amends I.R.C. § 420, so that, for tax years after the date of the AJCA's enactment, the determination of whether a 401(h) plan satisfies the minimum cost requirements during the five years after a transfer of pension assets permits the employer to reduce costs only as much as they would have been reduced if the employer had used the maximum amount permitted under current Regulations. In effect, overall benefit costs for all retirees can be cut by the same amount that would have been saved by reducing the number of retirees. [Ellen E. Schultz, *More Retirees May See Health Cuts*, Wall Street Journal, Oct. 14, 2004, at p. A5]

[B] Final Regulations

Effective June 19, 2001, the IRS issued Final Regulations on the I.R.C. § 420 minimum cost requirements. [T.D. 8948, R.I.N. 1545-AY43] An employer that significantly reduces its retiree health coverage during a cost maintenance period does not satisfy the I.R.C. § 420(c)(3) minimum cost requirement. This requirement institutes a five-year period during which the employer has an obligation to maintain a minimum dollar level of expenditures for covered retirees, spouses, and dependents. The period begins with the taxable year in which a qualified transfer occurs. If the requirement is satisfied, the employee doesn't have taxable income, and the employer doesn't have gross income, to the extent that funds are transferred into the 401(h) plan. The transfer is neither a prohibited transaction nor a reversion to the employer.

The Uruguay Round Agreements Act of 1994 [Pub. L. No. 103-465] shifted the focus in regulating 401(h) plans from health costs to health benefits, allowing the employer to take into account cost savings recognized in managing retiree health benefit plans, as long as the employer keeps up substantially the same level of coverage for the four years after the transfer as for the year of the transfer itself and the year before the year of the transfer.

When it was first enacted, I.R.C. § 420 was supposed to be temporary. However, the Tax Relief Extension Act [Pub. L. No. 106-170], extended it from the anticipated expiration date of December 31, 2000, to December 31, 2005. The Tax Relief Extension Act reinstated minimum cost as the appropriate test of whether the employer was handling the 401(h) plan properly. The Pension Funding Equity Act, P.L. 108-218, allows transfers until December 31, 2013. Note, however, that the AJCA, P.L. 108-357, makes it easier for employers whose qualified current retiree health liabilities are at least 5% of their gross receipts to satisfy the minimum cost requirement even if the number of covered individuals is reduced.

See also Rev. Rul. 2004-65, 2004-33 I.R.B. 300: if an employer offers to enhance pension benefits in exchange for an employee's waiver of coverage for retiree health benefits, and the employee accepts the offer, the employer has reduced the retiree health coverage as defined by § 420(c)(3)(E). The termination of coverage is an employer-initiated reduction in coverage when it must be determined whether the employer has "significantly" reduced retiree health coverage during the cost maintenance period. *See* Rev. Proc. 2006-6, 2006-1 I.R.B. 204, for the process of getting a determination letter for a 401(h) plan, covering transfers up through December 31, 2013.

Rev. Rul. 2005-60, 2005-37 I.R.B. 502, permits employers who have transferred excess pension assets to a 401(h) account to receive the retiree drug subsidy and still satisfy the minimum cost requirement under Code § 420(c)(3). The drug subsidy is not taken into account in calculating employer cost for the minimum cost requirement. CMS also permits employers who receive the subsidy to allocate the rebates across all participants in the plan, rather than making allocations based on actual usage, when the "allowable retiree costs" are calculated.

The fact pattern discussed in the Ruling is a company that made a § 420 transfer in 2005 and applied for the subsidy in 2006. The applicable employer cost was $3,600 for 2003, $3,800 for 2004, and $4,000 in 2005. In 2005, the employer received a $600 subsidy for each covered retiree in 2005. The Ruling permits the employer to disregard the subsidy and the plan to satisfy the $3,800 maintenance of cost threshold. [Deloitte's Washington Bulletin, *Additional Guidance on Retiree Drug Subsidy from IRS and CMS* (Sept. 26, 2005), <http://benefitslink.com/articles/washbul1050926.html>]

In an acquisition situation, the Final Regulations provide that the employer may (but does not have to) treat retiree coverage as not having ended if the buyer provides coverage. For the year of the sale and the rest of the cost maintenance period, the employer must apply I.R.C. § 420(c)(3) by including people receiving benefits provided by the buyer in the denominator of the applicable employer cost equation. The buyer's spending on health benefits from those individuals must be treated as qualified current retiree health liabilities.

Once the buyer starts providing the benefits, the buyer's action is attributed to the employer when determining if "employer action" terminates coverage. So if the buyer starts providing retiree health benefits but then amends the plan to stop providing the benefits, the employer has to treat the affected individuals as having lost coverage per employer action. The definition of "sale" in Final Regulation includes other transfers of business; the transferee is treated as the buyer.

The 20% cumulative test applies to transfers of excess pension assets made on or after December 18, 1999. However, coverage can be reinstated by an employer that reduced coverage by more than 20% before the first taxable year that began on or after January 1, 2002. The annual test for significant reduction applies only to taxable years beginning on or after January 1, 2002.

PART III

PENSION PLAN ADMINISTRATION

CHAPTER 10

ADOPTING AND ADMINISTERING A PLAN

§ 10.01   INTRODUCTION

The process of creating a plan and getting it approved by the IRS and Department of Labor is exacting. Many alternatives are permitted, and choosing one of them requires projections about the future of the business, the future of the workforce, trends in the economy as a whole, and the laws, court decisions, and regulations that will come into effect in the future.

Employers always have a duty to notify their employees when they adopt a plan. If the plan will be subject to ERISA Title I, the Department of Labor must be notified. It is not strictly necessary to notify the IRS of the intention to establish a qualified plan, until and unless a determination letter is sought. A determination letter is evidence of the plan's qualification, but a plan that satisfies the various requirements of the Code is entitled to tax deductions, even if there has been no determination letter.

§ 10.02   DETERMINATION LETTERS

A determination letter is the IRS' determination that a proposed plan is qualified under I.R.C. § 401(a) or 403(a)—and, if the plan is operated through a plan trust, whether the plan trust is qualified under I.R.C. § 501(a).

A plan that has a determination letter and that is amended on a timely basis to conform to changes in the law will probably be able to rebut IRS attempts at retroactive disqualification of the plan.

The application for a determination letter is made to the IRS Service Center in Covington, Kentucky (P.O. Box 192; the zip code is 41012-0192). Interested parties (current employees who will be eligible to participate if the plan is implemented) are entitled to notification that an application has been made. If the plan is collectively bargained, all employees covered by the CBA are entitled to notice. Notice to unionized employees can be given in person (e.g., printed and handed to all employees; slips placed in all pay envelopes), by mailing, or by posting in the usual place for posting employer and/or union notices. The appropriate time for giving notice to employees is 7–21 days before the IRS gets the application. If the employees are notified by mail, the notices should be mailed 10–24 days before submission of the application.

Employees must be notified because interested parties have the right to comment directly to the IRS about the application. The PBGC or a group of interested parties can also invite the Department of Labor to comment on the application. The PBGC has standing to submit its own comments directly. The comment period runs for either 45 or 60 days after the IRS receives the request for a determination letter.

In July 2002, Final Regulations were issued on the method of providing the required notice. [67 Fed. Reg. 47454 (July 19, 2002), effective for applications made on or after January 1, 2003] The Final Regulations are very similar to the proposal published at 66 Fed. Reg. 3954 (Jan. 17, 2001). Under the finalized version, notice can be provided by any method that is reasonably calculated to ensure that parties get the notice. The adequacy of a particular method is determined by considering all the facts and circumstances. In line with the IRS's program of moving toward an all-electronic system, the Final Regulation contains a safe harbor for using an electronic medium that complies with Treas. Reg. § 1.402(f)-1, Q&A 5. If the plan's employees have reasonable access to computers and are accustomed to receiving information on HR matters from the corporate Web site, the information can be placed on the site, with hard copy mailed to those who lack computer access. The notice can also be e-mailed to employees who have an e-mail address at which they can receive messages from the employer.

Mailed notices should be sent 10–24 days before the date that the application for a determination is made. Notice given other than by mailing should be given 7–21 days before the application. If the employer provides additional information that is not in the notice (for instance, the application for the determination letter, or an updated copy of the plan documents), it is permissible to use any delivery method or combination of methods reasonably calculated to transmit the necessary information.

After 60 days have elapsed, the IRS does its own investigation of the qualification of the proposed plan, including consideration of any comments that have been submitted. A reviewing agent in the relevant IRS Key District Office issues the determination letter (or denies the application). If there are questions about the application, the agent tries to resolve them by telephoning or writing to the company that applied for the determination letter.

If the IRS refuses to issue the letter, there are several levels of review within the IRS, and then the employer has the right to appeal to the Tax Court.

Determination letters are requested on official IRS forms. The IRS charges user fees, depending on the nature of the application. Furthermore, a particular plan may have to apply several times. The relevant forms are:

- Form 4461: application for a determination letter for a master or prototype defined contribution plan;
- Form 4461-A: for a defined benefit plan;
- Form 5300: application for a determination letter for an individually drafted defined benefit plan;
- Form 5302: defined contribution plan;
- Form 5309: ESOP;
- Form 5307: Prototype or master submission.

Schedule Q, demographic materials demonstrating conformity with the nondiscrimination requirements, must be attached to Forms 5300, 5303, 5307, and 5310.

The application for a determination letter must disclose:

- Information about the plan;
- Information about the employees who will be covered;

- A copy of the plan;
- Power of attorney.

[*See* Rev. Proc. 2000-8, 2000-1 C.B. 230, for user fees for these applications]

Effective February 1, 2006, the IRS implemented a new user fee schedule, based on the Office of Management and Budget's insistence that the user fees accurately represent the cost of providing the service. The fees for obtaining a ruling, previously ranging from $95 to $5,415 rose to $200 to $14,500. Effective July 1, 2006, fees under the centralized employee plan determination letter program and for opinion, advisory, and determination letters about Forms 5300, 5307, and 5310 rose from a range of $125 to $6,500 to $200 to $15,000. EPCRS fees remained unchanged. [Rev. Proc. 2006-1, 2006-1 I.R.B. 1; Rev. Proc. 2006-8, 2006-1 I.R.B. 386, discussed in Fred Schneyer, *IRS Hikes User Charges*, PlanSponsor.com (Apr. 27, 2006); Deloitte's Washington Bulletin, *Updated IRS User Fee Schedule for Employee Plans*, <http://benefitslink.com/articles/washbull051227.html>]

§ 10.03   PROTOTYPE AND MASTER PLANS

The IRS publishes master and prototype plans for the guidance of employers who want to be sure that the plan they adopt satisfies the various requirements for qualification. A prototype plan has a separate funding mechanism for each employer; a master plan has a single funding mechanism (such as a trust) that covers multiple employers.

It is frequently necessary to amend plans as the tax laws change. The IRS has launched a new six-year cycle for approval of amendments to master and prototype plans. *See* Announcement 2005-36, 2005-21 I.R.B. 1095.

§ 10.04   ROUTINE TAX COMPLIANCE

[A] Necessary Forms

Day-to-day administration of a plan involves creation of tax records and submission of many forms to the IRS and state taxing authorities, including:

- Form W-2: for each individual employee, this lists the compensation paid. The form must be submitted to the IRS and also to the employee. The normal due date for employee W-2s is January 31 following the end of the year of employment. However, employees who leave during the year have a right to demand that they get a W-2 form within 30 days of the last paycheck (or of the request, if made at a later date). The employer can use IRS Form 8809 to request additional time to file W-2s;
- Form W-3: a transmittal form filed with the Social Security Administration consolidating all the W-2 and W-2P forms for the entire company. The regular due date for any year's W-3 is February 28 of the following year;

- Form W-4P is used by employees to opt out of withholding or increase withholding on their pension and annuity payments. This form goes straight from employer to employee, no IRS filing is required;
- Forms 941/941E: these are the forms for quarterly returns of federal income tax. Form 941 is used if there are FICA taxes withheld or paid, 941E otherwise. The due date is the end of the month after the close of the calendar quarter being reported on;
- Form 945: the report on withheld taxes that are not payroll taxes (e.g., withholding on retirement plan distributions);
- Form 1041: trust income tax return, required if the plan's trust becomes disqualified (or otherwise does not operate as a tax-exempt organization) and if it also has income equal to or greater than $600. The due date is the fifteenth day of the fourth month after the end of the trust's tax year;
- Form 1099-R: 1099-series forms are used to report miscellaneous sums that might otherwise escape the attention of the taxing authorities. The 1099-R is used to report lump sums and periodic distributions. The entire group of a company's transmittal forms requires its own transmittal form, Form 1096. The filing is due by February 28 each year for the preceding year;

Tip: Within two weeks of making a distribution, the plan administrator must provide each recipient with a written explanation of the tax consequences of taking a lump sum, including how to elect lump-sum tax treatment and how to roll over the sum to another qualified plan or to an IRA.

- Form 5308: form filed in connection with a change in the tax year of a qualified plan or trust;
- Form 5330: excise tax form for failure to meet the minimum funding standard, or for receipt of an impermissible reversion of plan assets. Disqualified persons who engage in prohibited transactions are also required to file this form. There is no fixed due date: the timing depends on the nature of the transaction subject to excise tax. Form 5558 is used to request additional time to file this form;
- Form 8109: the quarterly estimated tax return when a plan trust has unrelated business taxable income (UBTI) [*see* I.R.C. § 512(a)(1)] from operation of an unrelated trade or business. UBTI is limited to business net income (after deducting the costs of generating the income). It does not include dividends, interest, annuities, loan fees, or royalties.

The IRS' project of moving all business tax form filing online is well underway. (The next important planned step is the integration of federal and state tax filings through a coordinated electronic system.) More than eight million business returns were filed electronically in 2005. (The TeleFile program, allowing telephone filing of many forms, was discontinued in mid-2005.) Business taxpayers file taxes via the Electronic Federal Tax Payment System (EFTPS), a highly secure encrypted Web site. *See* <http://www.irs.gov/efile> and IRS Publications 4132, 966, 4169, 4321, 4130, 4276, and 4048.

For tax years ending on or after December 31, 2005, corporations with assets of $50 million or more that file at least 250 returns a year, including income and employment tax and information returns, are required to file their 1120 and 1120-S forms electronically. The next year, the electronic filing requirement is extended to corporations with assets of more than $10 million who file 250 returns a year. To file electronically, large and mid-size corporations must use the IRS e-file system Modernized e-File (MeF). W-2 forms also can be submitted electronically, although those forms must be filed with the Social Security Administration rather than the IRS.

Amended returns cannot be e-filed until January 2007. No date has been announced for e-filing specialized 1120-series forms (e.g., for real estate investment trusts and life insurance companies), returns with pre-computed penalties and interests, or requests to apply a corporate tax overpayment to another account.

On the subject of routine compliance under non-routine circumstances, *see* Rev. Proc. 2005-27, 2005-20 I.R.B. 1050 for a list of 32 employee benefit issues that are affected automatically whenever the President declares a disaster. Notice 2005-73, 2005-42 IRB 723, discusses IRS relief for taxpayers affected by the 2005 hurricane season. Deadlines for time-sensitive events such as filing returns and paying taxes were deferred. "In individual assistance areas" designated by FEMA, tax relief is automatic, and taxpayers did not have to do anything to claim it. In "public assistance areas" (where FEMA deemed the damage to be more isolated) and for other taxpayers outside the affected area, they must identify themselves as hurricane victims in their IRS filings. [Janell Grenier, *Benefitsblog: Statement by Treasury Secretary John Snow on Hurricane Katrina Bill and Other Matters* (Benefitslink.com), Sept. 21, 2005.]

[B] Investment-Related Costs

The Department of Labor's Letter 2001-01A (Jan. 18, 2001) includes an advisory opinion and six hypotheticals explaining which expenses can properly be charged to a plan. Expenses to maintain tax qualification, perform nondiscrimination testing, or obtain an IRS determination letter can properly be charged to the plan, even though the employer does obtain financial benefits from the plan's tax-qualified status. [*See DOL Provides New Guidance on Payment of Expenses from Plan Assets*, <http://www.dol.gov/ebsa/regs/AOs/settlor_guidance.html>]

Rev. Rul. 86-142 says that employers are entitled to deduct (as I.R.C. § 162 ordinary and necessary business expenses) the recurring expenses of plan operation and administration directly paid by the employer. However, design studies, amendments required by corporate transitions, costs of negotiating with a union, cost studies to assess new benefits designs, and FASB 88 statement costs are not chargeable to the plan.

A Tax Court case, *Sklar, Greenstein & Scheer, PC v. Commissioner* [113 T.C. 9 (1999)], allows an employer maintaining a money purchase plan to deduct the expenses of suing the plan's investment manager. The Tax Court agreed with the company that such expenses are ordinary and necessary. The court did not agree with the IRS that only "recurring" expenses are deductible, as long as they satisfy the "ordinary and necessary" criterion.

See Mary Williams Walsh's article, "Concerns Raised Over Consultants to Pension Funds" [New York Times, Mar. 21, 2004, at p. A1] for a discussion of concerns about excessively risky investments suggested by pension consultants who are perhaps insufficiently skilled or have potential or real conflicts of interest. Although the article concentrates on public pension systems (which may have to be bailed out by taxpayers), similar issues can arise in private-sector plans.

§ 10.05   ERISA COMPLIANCE ISSUES

The Summary Plan Description (SPD) for a newly created plan must be filed with the Department of Labor within 120 days of the plan's adoption. (If this is later than the date of establishment, filing must be made within 120 days of the first time the plan covers common-law employees and therefore becomes subject to ERISA Title I.) It is wise to include a disclaimer in the SPD, to the effect that the plan instrument and not the SPD will govern in case of conflict.

ERISA § 104(a)(4)(A) gives the DOL the power to reject an incomplete SPD filing. The plan administrator has 45 days to file again to answer the DOL comments. If the second filing is not made, DOL has the power to sue for legal or equitable relief, or any other remedy authorized by ERISA Title I.

Many plans are insurance-based, so the employer will have contracts with health and liability insurers. However, insurance policies and other documents that set out the business relationship between the insured and the insurer do not always contain all of the terms and conditions mandated by ERISA for administration of a plan (including the required disclosures to plan participants). The solution is to adopt a "wrap" document that supplements the contractual language of the insurance policy with the statutory and regulatory language needed for an ERISA plan. [*See* EBIA Weekly (Feb. 7, 2002) <http://www.ebia.org>]

ERISA § 4071 allows the PBGC to impose a penalty of up to $1,100 per day for noncompliance, including failing to contact the PBGC about a reportable event, failing to report under ERISA § 4010, failure to give participants the notices required by ERISA § 4011, and failing to give notification of missing contributions when the shortfall, including interest, is greater than $1 million. PBGC policy, as expressed at 66 Fed. Reg. 2856 (Jan. 12, 2001) is that the information penalty will usually not be imposed if the premium information is filed late and the premium is also paid late, on the grounds that the late payment penalty imposes the appropriate sanction. Sometimes the PBGC rolls back a standard termination because notices were not filed or issued on time, but even in that case, the PBGC usually doesn't apply an information penalty because reversing the termination, in effect, retroactively eliminates the notice requirement. The rate for the penalty for late payment of premiums is specified by 29 C.F.R. § 4007.8, but the PBGC has discretion to determine the amount of any information penalty assessed.

The PBGC has not published a final policy statement since 1995 (60 Fed. Reg. 36837, July 18, 1995), at which time the agency set guideline penalty rates of $25 per day for the first 90 days of delinquency and $50 per day afterward, although some safety valves are in place to help smaller plans. The maximum total guideline penalty is $100 per participant. However, the policy calls for the maximum $1,100-per-day penalty to be imposed on violations of the ERISA § 4043(a) requirement of advance notice of reportable events and the ERISA § 302(f)(4) notification of missing a contribution of more than $1 million on the grounds that these two areas are so significant, and time is so much of the essence, that the full penalty is justified. A proposal, 66 Fed. Reg. 2856 (Jan. 12, 2001), has never been finalized, but in practice tends to affect the actions of PBGC staff because it provides fuller detail about when a payment failure is deemed to have occurred. [Harold J. Ashner, *Dealing with the Pension Benefit Guaranty Corporation,* <http://www.keightleyashner.com/publications/ Dealing_with[. . .]> (Jan. 6, 2006); Congressional Budget Organization, *A Guide to Understanding the Pension Benefit Guaranty Corporation,* <http:// www.cbo.gov/ftpdocs/66xx/doc6657/09-23-GuidetoPBGC.pdf> (Sept. 2005); Facts from EBRI, *Basics of the Pension Benefit Guaranty Corporation (PBGC),* <http://www.ebri.org/facts/0705fact.pdf> (July 2005)]

Starting with the 2002 plan year, some small plans (usually those having fewer than 100 participants) will be required to get a report from an independent auditor to accompany their Form 5500-series filing, even though they were excused from the audit requirement in earlier years. [65 Fed. Reg. 62957 (Oct. 19, 2000); this issue is discussed in a Reminder from BenefitsLink, *Changed 5500 Rules Will Require 2002 Independent Audit for Some Small Plans,* <http:// benefitslink.com/erisaregs/2520.104-41-final.shtml>]

Effective for plan years beginning on or after January 1, 2006, the Deficit Reduction Act of 2005, P.L. 109-171, increases the flat-rate PBGC premium to $30 for single-employer plans and $8 for multi-employer plans. The premium rates will rise each year, adjusted for increases in the national average wage index. The Required Interest Rate for the variable rate premium for the 2006 plan year is 85% of the annual yield on 30-year Treasuries for the month before the first month of the plan year. [PBGC, *What's New for Practitioners,* <http://www.pbgc. gov/practitioners/Whats-New/whatsnew/page15560.html>]

Large calendar-year plans were required to file estimated premiums using the new rates by February 28, 2006. Those who filed early using the old premiums must amend their filings to reflect the increase. There is an additional premium of $1,250 per participant for each of three years imposed on certain plans that terminate when they are underfunded. Plans with 500 or more participants have to shift all of their PBGC filings to the electronic system in 2006, a requirement that will be extended to all plans in 2007. [PBGC, *What's New for Practitioners*, <http://www.pbgc.gov/practitioners/Whats-New/whatsnew/page15560.html> (Feb. 2006); forms and instructions for the premium are at <http://www.pbgc.gov/practitioners/premium-filings/content/page1142.html> *See* 71 Fed. Reg. 31077 (June 1, 2006) for the Final Rule on efiling using My PAA]

A proposed EBSA regulation requires e-filing of Form 5500 for pension and welfare benefit plans' plan years beginning on or after January 1, 2007 (i.e., filings made in 2008). EBSA updated the EFAST system to improve security and resolve problems with electronic signatures and attachments. [R.I.N. 1210-AB04, *Electronic Filing of Annual Reports*, 70 Fed. Reg. 51541 (Aug. 30, 2005).] All Form 5500s (current, late, or amended) are filed at EBSA's EFAST office in Lawrence, Kan.] The Final Rule for EFAST filing of Form 5500 annual reports, for plan years beginning on or after January 1, 2008, was published in mid-2006, and was followed by a Proposed Rule harmonizing the changes in the Form 5500 with the annual filing requirements. [Final Rule, 71 Fed. Reg. 41359 (July 21, 2006; Proposed Rule, 71 Fed. Reg. 41392 (July 21, 2006)]

The 2005 Form 5500 no longer has a Schedule T, and Line 9 of Schedule R has been amended. The current form requires the preparer to indicate whether the ratio percentage test or the average benefit test is used to assess compliance with coverage requirements. A plan that must file a 5500 but is not a defined benefit plan (e.g., profit-sharing plans, stock bonus plans, and ESOPs) is only required to complete Schedule R if distributions were made during the year. Revised Schedule R calls for additional information about actuarial assumptions and methods (e.g., cash balance plans' assumptions for annuitizing balances). The plan's actuary must indicate if the plan is frozen or partly frozen, indicate what optional forms of benefits are available, and identify any supplemental benefits, including those available only to a subgroup of employees. [For compliance advice and help with completing the form, *see* Form5500HELP.com; *see also* Sungard Relius, *How Do You Answer the Coverage Question on the Schedule R?* <http://www.corbel.com/news/technicalupdates.asp?ID=336&T=P>]

The PBGC has updated its e-4010 Web-based application for reporting ERISA § 4010 information, including financial, actuarial, and identifying information. New options include the ability to "assign an actuary" (so someone other than the filer can access plan filings) and for plan administrators to access data already submitted instead of having to reenter it for another filing. For information years ending on or after December 31, 2005, data must be filed electronically on the e-4010 Web site <https://egov.pbgc.gov/e4010>. [Rebecca Moore, *PBGC Enhances Reporting and Disclosure Web Application,* PlanSponsor.com (Jan. 27, 2006)]

Plans in Mississippi, Louisiana, and Alabama were given until August 28, 2006, rather than February 28, 2006, to file Form 5500s that would otherwise have been due between September 23, 2005, and February 28, 2006. The deferral applies to entities within the Hurricane Katrina-affected regions and those outside the area who could not obtain necessary information from banks, insurers, or service providers affected by the hurricanes. [*See* <http://www.dol.gov/ebsa/newsroom/pr022706.html>]

In some major corporate suits (e.g., those involving Enron and WorldCom), fiduciary breach claims were made against not only the plan sponsor and its service providers, but against CEOs, CFOs, directors, plan administrators, members of plan committees, and even HR personnel. A 2006 article points out some governance strategies that corporations can use to reduce potential claims and insulate potential defendants. In many cases, individuals have been named as defendants because the plan documents failed to describe the corporation's fiduciary structure accurately or because the documents conflicted with actual practice or assigned the same function to several fiduciaries. A fiduciary structure in which the president or CEO appoints the plan investment committee and other fiduciaries is less likely to generate liability than one in which the board of directors appoints them. Members of fiduciary committees, especially the investment committee, must have enough time to devote to committee business to master all of the details. Putting the corporation's general counsel on a fiduciary committee is contraindicated because it could result in loss of attorney-client privilege. Attorneys, however, can attend committee meetings to represent the plan sponsor, but the minutes should reflect the status in which they participate.

Plan counsel should make sure that the agenda for every fiduciary committee meeting includes a report on how each investment is performing in comparison with benchmarks and peer groups; whether any of the plan's investments have dropped below their benchmark; performance evaluations of the service providers; and whether there are any liability insurance or indemnification problems. ERISA § 404(c) compliance issues should be discussed regularly: This is the provision that requires determination of whether the company stock still qualifies as "employer securities," and whether the stock is publicly traded with enough volume for prompt execution of buy-and-sell orders. The performance of company stock should be monitored just like any other investment; in fact, an increasing number of plans retain outside consultants to monitor the performance of company stock in 401(k) plans precisely because it is such an active litigation area when the company's management oversees such investments. [Stephen M. Saxon, *Attention to Details Can Make a Big Difference,* PlanSponsor.com magazine articles (Jan. 2006); *see* Jeff D. Opdyke, *Retirement Plans Get New Safeguards,* Wall Street Journal, June 21, 2005, at p. D1 for 401(k) consultants]

CHAPTER 11

COMMUNICATIONS WITH EMPLOYEES AND REGULATORS

§ 11.01   INTRODUCTION

Although ERISA does not require corporations to have employee benefit plans at all, if they choose to implement plans, there are many rules that must be followed, including procedural rules. Plan participants must be given enough information from the plan itself to understand their benefits—especially benefits available in multiple forms—so that informed choices must be made.

The Summary Plan Description (SPD) is the main document for communications between the plan and its participants, although other documents may also be required, for example when the terms of the plan are altered. If the plan is materially modified, or if there are changes in the information given in the SPD, the plan administrator has a duty to give participants a Summary of Material Modifications (SMM).

For a calendar-year plan that has undergone a material modification, the SMM must be sent to participants and beneficiaries by July 27 of the following year. Fiscal-year plans have until the 210th day after the end of the plan year.

The due date for the Form 5500 is July 31 (calendar-year plans) and the last day of the seventh month of the plan year after the plan year being reported, for plans that have a fiscal year. This is also the reporting schedule for individual statements of deferred vested benefits, to be sent to plan participants whose employment terminated during the plan year and who were entitled to deferred vested benefits at the time of termination.

For defined benefit plans only, the PBGC Form 1 is due on September 15 (calendar year plans) or eight and a half months after the close of the plan fiscal year being reported on. For all plans, the Summary Annual Report must be given to participants and beneficiaries by September 30 (or the last day of the ninth month of the plan year after the plan year in question). That is also the date that participants and beneficiaries of defined benefit plans that are less than 90% funded should be given notice of the plan's funding status and the limits on the PBGC guarantee.

At the end of 2005, the Department of Labor (DOL) announced upgrades and improvements to its compliance Web site, designed to make it easier to get information about DOL programs and employers' obligations. [<http://www.dol.gov/compliance>]

§ 11.02   SUMMARY PLAN DESCRIPTION (SPD)

[A]   Basic Requirements

ERISA § 102 imposes a duty on the plan administrator to furnish a copy of the Summary Plan Description (SPD) to each participant and to each beneficiary receiving benefits under the plan. The SPD must be furnished within 90 days of the time a person becomes a participant or first receives benefits. (For a new plan, the SPD can be furnished within 120 days of the time the plan comes under Title I of ERISA, if this is later than the 90-day period.)

ERISA § 102 requires the SPD to be written in a way that can be understood by the average plan participant. The document must be accurate and comprehensive enough to inform them of their rights and obligations. The Pension and Welfare Benefits Administration (now known as EBSA) published a Final Rule governing SPDs for pension, health, and welfare benefit plans on November 21, 2000. [*See* 65 Fed. Reg. 70226]

ERISA requires the following items to be included in the SPD:

- The formal and common names of the plan;
- The name and address of the employer (or of the organization maintaining a collectively bargained plan);
- The employer's EIN and the plan's IRS identification number;
- What kind of plan it is;
- How the plan is administered—e.g., by contract or by an insurer;
- The name and address of the agent for service of process (the person designated to receive summonses, complaints, subpoenas, and related litigation documents);
- A statement that process can be served not only on this designated agent, but also on the plan's administrator or trustee;
- The name, address, and title of each trustee;
- Disclosure of whether the plan is a collectively bargained plan, and a statement that the participant can examine the collective bargaining agreement or get a copy of the agreement from the plan administrator;
- Rules of eligibility for participation;
- The plan's normal retirement age;
- Circumstances under which plan benefits can be altered or suspended;
- How to waive the normal payment mechanism (the Qualified Joint and Survivor Annuity) and elect a different payment form, such as a lump sum;
- Procedures for QDROs and QMCSOs, either through a description in the SPD itself or disclosure that a free copy of a separate document will be provided on request;
- A description of the circumstances under which the plan can be terminated, the rights of participants and beneficiaries after termination occurs, and the circumstances under which benefits can be denied or suspended; what will happen to the plan's assets upon termination. (All amendments must be made with the necessary corporate governance steps, such as adoption of a resolution by the Board of Directors);
- If the plan benefits are insured by the PBGC; if they are not, the reason why insurance is not required; if they are, a disclosure that PBGC insurance is in place, how it works, and where to get more information (from the plan administrator or the PBGC; the PBGC's address must be given in the SPD);
- An explanation of the plan's rules for determining service to calculate vesting and breaks in service;
- Do the contributions to the plan come exclusively from the employer, or are employee contributions accepted or mandated?

- Method of calculating the contribution. (A defined benefit plan is allowed to simply say that the amount is "actuarially determined");
- The funding medium and entity for the plan. Usually this will be a trust fund, but sometimes an insurance company is involved;
- The plan's fiscal year;
- How to present a claim for plan benefits;
- If the plan will use the "cutback" rule to change the vesting or accrual rules described in the SPD, participants must be informed which provisions of the plan are subject to modification; when modified, the nature of the modification must be explained;
- Remedies that are available if a claim is denied;
- A statement of the rights of participants and beneficiaries and what protections are available for those rights. A model statement that can be used for this purpose is published at 29 C.F.R. § 2520.102-3.

After reviewing public comments, EBSA decided that the current disclosure requirements give enough information about cash balance conversions and operations, so it was not necessary to impose any special requirements.

SPDs must be given to participants and beneficiaries within 90 days after they achieve that status. For a new plan, all participants must get an SPD 12 days after the plan becomes subject to ERISA reporting and disclosure requirements. If a company offers different benefits to different groups of SPDs, the company can issue a separate SPD for each group.

> **Tip:** If a significant percentage of the participants in a plan are not literate in English, but are literate in the same non-English language, the SPD must include a notice in that language offering assistance in understanding the English SPD. In this context, a significant percentage means over 25% of the participants in a plan with fewer than 100 total participants, or the lesser of 10% of the participants or 500 people in a large plan.

The best distribution methods are handing the SPDs to the employees at the workplace, or mailing them to employees' homes. It isn't enough to put them out in the workplace, because there's no guarantee that employees will take them.

The SPD can also be distributed as an insert in an employee periodical such as one published by the company or the union. If you choose this option, be sure to put a prominent notice on the front page of the periodical, stating that this issue contains an insert that has important legal consequences, and that it should be retained for reference and not discarded.

> **Tip:** The statement of participant rights required by ERISA can be incorporated into the SPD.

If a plan is amended—and most are, sooner or later—the plan administrator must issue an updated SPD every five years (measured from the time the plan first became subject to ERISA) reflecting the changes of the past five years. Even if there are no changes at all, the administrator must provide an updated SPD to all participants every 10 years.

If there are any false statements in the SPD, ERISA disclosure regulations have been violated, and the employer could face penalties from the Department of Labor. Most plan participants never see the trust documents for the plan, so they get their information from the SPD.

Furthermore, if the SPD is ambiguous, lawsuits might be decided in favor of the employee-plaintiffs, because it is a basic legal doctrine that ambiguous documents are interpreted in the manner least favorable to the party that issued them.

In light of the general legal principle that ambiguous documents are construed against the party who drafted them (and could have been clearer!), the Ninth Circuit ruled in 2002 that the plan document itself, and not the SPD, would be applied in a case in which it conflicted with the SPD, and the plan document was more favorable to participants than the SPD. Most cases apply the SPD, on the grounds that that is the document that participants actually receive and use to make retirement decisions. [*Bergt v. Retirement Plan for Pilots,* 293 F.3d 1139 (9th Cir. 2002)]

According to the Third Circuit, the SPD determines whether benefits were fully vested when the plan was partially terminated, if the language of the cash-balance pension plan is contrary to the SPD. [*Burstein v. Retirement Account Plan for Employees of Allegheny Health Ed. & Research Foundation,* 334 F.3d 365 (3d Cir. 2003)] A Seventh Circuit case, however, rules that the documents of the plan, and not the employer's summary of benefits (which was not a formal SPD) establish the terms of the plan—including caps on pensions—for purposes of tax qualification. [*Helfrich v. Carle Clinic Ass'n,* 328 F.3d 915 (7th Cir. 2003)]

According to the Second Circuit, an employee who is denied benefits only has to prove likely prejudice from an SPD that inaccurately described the requirements for receiving benefits. In other words, the consequences of issuing an inaccurate SPD fall on the employer, not the employee. The Second Circuit refused to join other Circuits that require the employee to show that the employee actually suffered by relying on the SPD language. In this case, the employee lived with his girlfriend for eight years before they married. He died of lung cancer less than six months after the marriage. The employer's Survivor Income Benefits Plan covered both spouses and domestic partners, but domestic partners had to file a joint affidavit to be eligible for certain benefits. The employee handbook explanation of the survivor benefits did not explain the affidavit requirement.

The employee's widow (as she was then) applied for the survivor benefit, which was denied because they had been married for less than a year when the employee died. The widow appealed the denial, but missed the plan's 90-day time limit. The District Court ruled for the employer, but the Second Circuit reversed, finding that the notice was inadequate. It said that appeals "should" be filed in

90 days, but not that they "must" be filed then (the plan documents used "must" in 16 other places, implying a distinction between mandatory and optional actions). The Second Circuit also ruled that marriage should not have the effect of cutting off a person from both marital and domestic-partner benefits. [*Burke v. Kodak Retirement Income Plan*, 336 F.3d 103 (2d Cir. 2003)]

Early in 2003, the Second Circuit reminded plan administrators that it is vital to have distribution procedures for SPDs that are reasonably calculated to get the information to the intended recipients. [*Leyda v. AlliedSignal Inc.*, 322 F.3d 199 (2d Cir. 2003)] The plaintiff in this case was the widow of a person who was hired when the defendant company acquired the assets of his former employer. The acquiring company held a meeting to discuss benefits with the ex-employees of the acquired company. At this meeting, the company distributed SPDs, plan enrollment forms, and beneficiary designation forms, and left more copies around for employees who were not present. Supervisors were asked to keep track of which employees had been absent that day, but attendance was not taken at the meeting.

The decedent did not attend the meeting, and never received a copy of the SPD, so he didn't know that the new plan offered less life insurance than his former employer's plan. Assuming that the coverage provided by the employer would be the same, he purchased $40,000 in additional coverage but turned down the option to buy more. He died suddenly, and his widow received $100,000 worth of insurance, not the $160,000 she expected. She sued the defendant (in its role as plan administrator) for failure to provide the required SPD. The Second Circuit agreed that the defendant had not satisfied its responsibilities, and awarded the widow $62,250 in damages. The Second Circuit said that it was a mistake to assume that all employees who were not out sick or traveling on business would attend the meeting; and there was no procedure for finding out who did or didn't attend. The best procedure would have been to require the new hires to sign up for benefits, and have them sign a statement indicating that they received the necessary plan documents.

However, strictly speaking, it is only necessary for the court to prove that it has a reasonable method of distribution, not that the particular plaintiff actually received the SPD. Being able to document a regular business practice of mailing SPDs to the employee's last known address should be sufficient.

In a 2002 California case [*Hunter v. Lockheed Martin Corp.*, 2002 U.S. Dist. LEXIS 13797 (N.D. Cal. June 7, 2002)], a plan participant applied for disability retirement benefits more than five years after being laid off. The terms of the plan ruled out eligibility on claims filed more than two years after a layoff. When the plan administrator denied the claim as untimely, the plaintiff sued, charging that she never received an SPD or any other information about the terms of the disability plan.

Two members of the employer's HR department testified that the employer's practice was to provide copies of the SPD on an individual basis to those who, like the plaintiff, changed status from being paid on an hourly to a salaried basis, or vice versa. According to the District Court, the SPD that the plaintiff received when she was fired did not adequately disclose the time period during which disability claims had to be filed—but the SPD in effect at the time she became a salaried employee did provide adequate disclosure. Furthermore, based on testimony about the employer's practices, it was more likely than not that the plaintiff did receive the second SPD. Her disability benefit claim was denied because it was untimely under the SPD that the court ruled she had received.

A construction industry retiree brought suit under ERISA, charging that he received an unjustly small retirement benefit because some of his employers under-reported his earnings. The Second Circuit refused to impose a requirement that the pension fund audit past employers to make sure that past benefits were properly reported. Nor was it a fiduciary violation to require the claimant to produce proof (e.g., pay stubs showing covered employment) that he was not credited properly before increasing his benefit. Although pension plans do have the power to audit payroll records, they are not obligated to do so. The plaintiff did prevail on one issue: The Second Circuit held that the SPD should have disclosed the plan's requirement of submitting pay stubs as evidence of past earnings. [*Wilkins v. Mason Tenders Dist. Council Pension Fund*, 445 F.3d 572 (2d Cir. 2006)]

A married couple who worked for the same company and were covered by the same welfare plan both elected, and paid for, life insurance on dependents. Their son was later killed in an automobile accident and both of them filed claims. The wife's claim was paid, the husband's was not. The husband sued the employer, the insurer, and the welfare benefit plans. The defendants said that the case should be dismissed because the SPD ruled out duplicate coverage. The husband argued that the SPD should not control because he did not receive a copy, so the enrollment materials he did receive, which did not rule out duplicate coverage, should be treated as the SPD. The Southern District of Ohio ruled in late 2005 that the argument was strong enough to prevent his case from being dismissed. [*McKenzie v. Advance Stores Co.*, No. 04-CV-999 (S.D. Ohio Oct. 26, 2005]

[B]   Health Plan SPDs

ERISA § 104(b)(1)(B) requires that plan participants and beneficiaries be notified within 60 days of a material reduction in the services provided under an Employee Group Health Plan (EGHP). Or the plan sponsor can simply provide notices at regular intervals, not more than 90 days apart, of changes in the interim. The SPD for an EGHP must indicate if a health insurer is responsible for financing or administration (including claims payment). If an insurer is involved, the insurer's name and address must appear in the SPD.

In 1998, the Pension and Welfare Benefit Administration (now EBSA) issued a major statement on the SPD requirements for health plans [62 Fed. Reg. 48376 (Sept. 8, 1998)], including disclosures relating to COBRA, insurance portability, and the Newborns' and Mothers' Health Protection Act, and followed it up with a Final Rule. [65 Fed. Reg. 70226 (Nov. 21, 2000)] Calendar-year plans must be in compliance with the Final Rule no later than in the SPDs distributed January 1, 2003.

Group health plans SPDs must include the following:

- Participants' responsibility for cost-sharing (premiums, deductibles, coinsurance, copayments);
- Lifetime or annual caps on plan benefits; any other benefit limits;
- Procedures for Qualified Medical Child Support Orders (QMCSOs);
- Coverage of preventive services;
- Coverage (if any) of established and new drugs;
- Coverage of medical tests, devices, and procedures;
- Which health care providers are part of the network, and how the network is created;
- Circumstances under which network providers must be used; coverage, if any, for out-of-network services;
- How primary care and specialty providers must be selected;
- Conditions for getting emergency care;
- Requirements for preauthorization of treatment and utilization review;
- Information about the required length of hospital stays for childbirth, including descriptions of the federal law and any additional protection furnished by state law;
- Either a description of claims procedures or a statement that a free copy of the claims procedure is available on request. [*See* § 13.03 for a discussion of claims procedures, including another Final Rule issued on November 21, 2000];
- The role of health insurance in the plan; the EBSA says "particularly in those cases where the plan is self-funded and an insurer is serving as contract administrator or claims payor, rather than as an insurer";
- Extent to which the sponsor has the right to eliminate benefits or terminate the plan;
- Participants' rights under ERISA.

The SPD can include only a general description of the provider network, as long as the SPD explains that a separate document, available without charge, lists all the network providers.

A health plan's SPD must describe employees' and their families' COBRA rights:

- What constitutes a qualifying event;
- Premiums ex-employees must pay for continuation coverage;
- Notice procedures;
- How to make a COBRA election;
- How long coverage will last.

The SPD for an EGHP must either describe the plan's procedures for validating Qualified Medical Child Support Orders, or must inform participants that a free copy of the plan's QMCSO procedures is available on request. The description should be complete enough to assist potential alternate payees in asserting their rights.

> **Tip:** Although SPDs are often prepared by insurers, HMOs, or Third Party Administrators, the plan administrator is still legally responsible for compliance—so it makes sense to review the SPD form before it is distributed to employees, to make sure it satisfies all relevant requirements.

An EGHP is just one kind of plan that is regulated as a "welfare plan" under ERISA. EBIA Weekly points out that welfare benefit plans must issue SPDs to each participant (employees or former employees who are or may become eligible for benefits under the plan, or whose beneficiaries may be eligible). However, participants are entitled to SPDs only if they are "covered by the plan," which happens on the earliest of these dates:

- The date the plan says participation begins;
- The date the person becomes eligible to receive a benefit subject to contingencies such as incurring medical expenses;
- The date of the initial voluntary or mandatory plan contribution.

Therefore, SPDs (and SMMs) must be furnished to employees; retirees covered under the plan; the parent or guardian of a minor child who is the "alternate recipient" under a QMCSO; and spouses or other dependents of deceased participants. Although ERISA doesn't say this, some court decisions require SPDs to be furnished to guardians or other representatives of incapacitated beneficiaries.

In 2005, the Northern District of Illinois ruled that an insurer might have been required to provide an SPD to a health plan participant. After a claim was denied, a plan participant who never received an SPD brought suit against the plan, her employer, and the insurer. The insurer pointed to the ERISA provision placing the obligation to provide an SPD on the plan administrator (an amendment in 2000 removed the insurer from its role as administrator). However, in 1998, when the plaintiff's coverage commenced, the insurer was still the plan administrator. At that time, the only plan document was the insurance policy and it identified the insurer as the administrator. [*Heroux v. Humana Ins. Co.*, 2005 U.S. Dist. LEXIS 11712 (N.D. Ill. 2005)]

Plans are required under 29 C.F.R. § 2590.701-3(c) to give notice to participants, explaining the terms of any preexisting condition exclusion (PCE), before the PCE is applied to them. Plans are permitted to include this notice as part of the EGHP enrollment materials. [EBSA, *Reporting and Disclosure Guide for Employee Benefit Plans*, <http://www.dol.gov/ebsa/pdf/rdguide.pdf> (Apr. 2004)]

The Medicare Prescription Drug Improvement and Modernization Act (MPDIMA) sets up a Medicare Part D prescription drug program thus obligating health plans to notify the Centers for Medicare and Medicaid Services (CMS), the agency that administers Medicare, which plan participants and beneficiaries are eligible for Medicare and whether the plan offers prescription drug benefits that are at least actuarially equivalent to the Medicare benefit. (Employers that offer an actuarially equivalent plan may also be able to collect a federal subsidy; *see* Chapter 9.) Plans that apply for the subsidy (but not other plans) also have to get an attestation from an actuary as to whether or not the plan's coverage is creditable (i.e., comparable to Medicare).

The plan must also give everyone who is covered by the plan and who is eligible for Medicare a Notice of Creditable Coverage. (Enrollment in Medicare Part D is voluntary, but no one is allowed to enroll in Part D and also "double dip" by being covered by an employment-related pharmaceutical benefit plan.) The Notice of Creditable Coverage does not have to be mailed separately. It is permissible for the plan to distribute it with other information, including information about plan enrollment—as long as the specific Part D information is displayed prominently. [Kaye Pestaina, *Notices of Creditable Coverage: Employer Deadline Coming Soon,* Employee Benefit News (benefitslink.com) Sept. 1, 2005; the text of the notice to be used beginning May 15, 2006, is available at <http://www.cms.hhs.gov/creditablecoverage>. *See* <http://www.cms.hhs.gov/CreditableCoverage/Downloads/041206CCGuidanceUpdated-FinalOMB.pdf> for CMS guidance on providing notice]

According to *Cooperative Benefit Plan Administrators Inc. v. Whittle* [989 F. Supp. 1421 (M.D. Ala. 1997)], a manual drafted for a welfare benefit plan's administrative staff was not an SPD, even if the plaintiff relied on it—it was designed as an internal plan document, not a tool for employees to understand their benefits.

In contrast, *Feifer v. Prudential Ins. Co. of America* [306 F.3d 1202 (2d Cir. 2002)] did treat a benefits program summary distributed to employees as a plan for ERISA purposes. The summary, unlike the formal plan documents prepared several months later, did not reduce long-term disability plans by Social Security Disability Income or Workers' Compensation benefits paid to the worker; the Second Circuit required payment of the full, unreduced benefit. The Second Circuit also held that if the plan documents are silent, disability benefits vest no later than the time the employee becomes disabled. In order to use ERISA § 502(a)(1)(B) to enforce the terms of the plan, the employee does not have to prove equitable factors such as reliance or prejudice.

Because provisions stated in the SPD, but not in the plan document, are unenforceable, a group health plan could not obtain reimbursement of funds advanced from participants who received health benefits. The employer operated the plan under a wrap document covering several benefit programs. The wrap document stated that the SPD constituted part of the plan only if there was no separate formal plan document; the SPD described and was consistent with the terms of the insurance policy underpinning the plan. Therefore, the subrogation provision was not part of the plan because no insurance policy provision on that subject was introduced into evidence. In 2006, the Western District of Arkansas ruled that the employee could benefit from plan terms that are more generous than the SPD, but employees who are harmed by their reliance on the SPD are entitled to have those terms prevail in court. [*Administrative Committee of Wal-Mart Stores, Inc. Associates' Health and Welfare Plan v. Gamboa*, 2006 U.S. Dist. LEXIS 9966 (W.D. Ark. 2006); *semble Cossey v. Associates' Health and Welfare Plan*, 2005 U.S. Dist. LEXIS 4800 (E.D. Ark. 2005)]

§ 11.03   SUMMARY ANNUAL REPORT (SAR)

One of the administrator's more complex tasks is preparing the plan's annual report, usually on Form 5500. This information is then used to draft the Summary Annual Reports (SARs) that must be distributed to plan participants.

The administrator has nine months from the end of the plan year (or two years after the end of the extension, if an extension was granted for filing the underlying Form 5500). DOL regulations [29 C.F.R. § 2520.104b-10(d); *see* 68 Fed. Reg. 16400 (Apr. 3, 2003)] provide a simple "fill in the blanks" form that must be used for the SAR.

The SAR form consists of a basic financial statement about the plan and its expenses, the net value of plan assets, and whether the plan's assets appreciated or depreciated in value during the year. If the plan is subject to the minimum funding standard, the plan must disclose either that contributions were adequate to satisfy the requirement, or the amount of the deficit. Participants must also be informed of their right to receive additional information, including a copy of the full annual report, a statement of the plan's assets and liabilities, or a statement of the plan's income and expenses. Plans that have simplified reporting requirements can use alternative compliance methods to satisfy the SAR requirement.

Some plans (such as unfunded welfare plans, top-hat plans, and pension or welfare plans that are financed by employee dues) are not required to furnish SARs.

§ 11.04   INDIVIDUAL ACCOUNT PLAN DISCLOSURES

The modern trend is for plans to provide participants with a greater degree of control over the way their pension plan accounts are invested. DOL Reg. § 2550.404c-1(b), dealing with "participant directed individual account plans" (profit-sharing, stock bonus, and money purchase plans) obligates plans to offer at least three diversified categories of investments, with materially different risk and return characteristics, so that overall the participant can choose the balance between risk and return that he or she prefers. Plan fiduciaries are not liable if the participant's own investment choices result in losses, unless obeying the participant's instructions violates the terms of the plan.

Participants are entitled to receive a great deal of information in connection with individual account plans. The burden is on the plan to supply the information, not on the individual participant to request it. The mandated disclosures include:

- A description of the available investment alternatives available under the plan; the general risk and return characteristics of each, including the composition of each portfolio and how they are diversified;

- The designated investment managers for each alternative;
- When and how participants can give investment instructions; any limitations imposed on those instructions (for instance, only four changes in investment per year);
- Fees and expenses that affect the participant's account balance;
- Contact information for a fiduciary (or designee of a fiduciary) who can provide additional information about plan investments on request;
- The fact that fiduciaries are not liable if they follow the participant's investment directions, even if losses result;
- (If participants can invest in securities of the employer) Procedures to maintain confidentiality about the participant's voting and tendering shares of employer stock, and contact information for the fiduciary who monitors the confidentiality provisions.

When a participant invests in publicly traded securities and other assets subject to the Securities Act of 1933 [15 U.S.C. § 77a], the participant must be given a prospectus for the investment either before or right after making the investment. If the plan "passes through" to participants the rights to vote and/or tender the shares, the plan must provide the participant with the proxy materials and other relevant documents, and must provide instructions on how to exercise the rights.

The plan further has a duty to disclose, based on the latest information available to the plan, at least this much information (either to all participants, or on request by a participant):

- For each investment alternative, the fees and operating expenses as a percentage of the average net assets of the investment alternative;
- Whatever prospectuses, financial statements, and reports the plan has about the investment alternative;
- A description of the portfolio of each alternative;
- The value of shares in each alternative;
- The current and past performance of each alternative, net of expenses, calculated on a "reasonable and consistent basis";
- The value of the shares in the individual participant's account.

§ 11.05   NOTICES OF REDUCTION OF BENEFIT ACCRUALS

Under ERISA § 204(h), plan administrators are required to notify participants, alternate beneficiaries under QDROs, and any union representing the workers whenever a plan amendment significantly reduces future benefit accruals under any qualified plan that is subject to ERISA's minimum funding standards (e.g., defined benefit plans).

If a plan "egregiously" fails to meet the notice requirement, then the affected participants and alternate payees will be entitled to receive whatever benefits they would have received if the plan had never been amended to cut back the benefits. An "egregious" failure is intentional refusal to provide notice, or simple failure to provide most of the affected individuals with most of the information they are entitled to receive.

Regulations were proposed [*see* NPRM-Reg-136193-01 67 Fed. Reg. 19714] on April 23, 2002, covering the required disclosure when a plan is amended with respect to an early retirement benefit or subsidy, if the effect is a reduction in the rate of future benefit accruals.

The IRS issued a Final Rule in April 2003 [T.D. 9052, 2003-19 I.R.B. 879], explaining the final requirements for notifying participants and beneficiaries of significant reductions in future benefit accruals (e.g., when a plan is converted to cash balance form) or the elimination or significant reduction of an early retirement benefit or retirement-type subsidy. T.D. 9052 substantially adopts the 2002 proposals.

Tip: Plan amendments that are subject to the § 204(h)/Code § 4980F requirements may also require additional ERISA disclosures, such as issuance of the Summary of Material Modifications.

An amendment reduces the rate of future benefit accrual if it can reasonably be expected that the annual benefit commencing at NRA (or at the later actual retirement age) will decline because of the amendment. For example, if the plan provides a normal retirement benefit of 50% of the average pay for the highest five years multiplied by the number of years of participation and divided by 20, a change in either the numerator or the denominator of this fraction could produce a substantial reduction.

The required notice must be given in plain English, with enough information for participants and beneficiaries to understand the assumptions that will be used in future calculations, and the effect of the amendment on their benefit entitlement. In general, notice must be given at least 45 days before the effective date of the amendment, but advance notice can be reduced to 15 days if the plan has fewer than 100 participants, or if the amendment was made pursuant to a corporate merger or acquisition. Notice can be given after the effective date (as long as it is no more than 30 days after the effective date) if the amendment reduces or eliminates an early retirement benefit or retirement-type subsidy but does not substantially reduce the rate of future benefit accruals.

If there is an egregious failure (circumstances within the plan sponsor's control that either are intentional or lead to deprivation of information for most of those entitled to receive it), the amendment cannot be used to reduce benefits—affected individuals will continue to be entitled to receive the unreduced benefit as if there had been no amendment. *But see* Proposed Regulations [68 Fed. Reg. 40581 (July 8, 2003)] permitting amendments to defined contribution plans (e.g., 401(k)s) that reduce alternate benefit forms, without the 90-day advance notice requirement being applied, and a similar proposal for defined benefit plans at 69 Fed. Reg. 13769 (Mar. 24, 2004). *Also see* T.D. 9219, 2005-38 I.R.B. 538, for further § 411(d)(6) rules. Effective August 12, 2005, it reflects public comments on the anti-cutback rules that were submitted to the IRS and made at a June 24, 2004, public hearing. T.D. 9219 attempts to balance participants' rights against the plans' administrative convenience in being able to eliminate redundant forms of benefit that are never elected by any participants.

§ 11.06   OTHER NOTICES AND DISCLOSURES

[A]   Notice of Deferred Benefits

Frequently, an employee will leave for one reason or another ("separation from service") at a time when he or she is entitled to a deferred vested benefit, but is not yet entitled to a retirement pension. The person in that situation is entitled to a notice containing:

- The name and address of the plan administrator;
- The nature, form, and amount of the person's deferred vested benefit;
- An explanation of any benefits that are forfeitable if the employee dies before a certain date.

The notice must be given no later than the date Schedule SSA is to be filed with the IRS. [Schedule SSA is the annual report that I.R.C. § 6057 requires of pension plans and other plans that are subject to the vesting requirements of ERISA Title I, Part 3] The IRS has the power to impose a penalty of $50 per erroneous statement or willful failure to furnish a statement.

Not less than thirty, or more than ninety, days before the annuity start date of any benefit that is immediately distributable before the participant reaches 62 or normal retirement age, the participant must also be given notice of any right he or she has to defer distribution. [*See* Treas. Reg. § 1.411(a)-11(c)(2)]

[B]   Rollovers; Withholding Certificate

Not more than 90, and not less than 30, days before making a distribution, the plan administrator must notify the participant of the potential consequences of receiving a distribution that could be made the subject of a rollover. The notice should inform participants of their right to have the distribution deposited into an IRA, or to another qualified plan that will accept it.

Participants must be warned about the 20% withholding that will be imposed on all taxable distributions that are neither rolled over nor transferred—and that the sums that are received are taxable in the year of receipt. Participants must also be told that they can roll over the distribution within 60 days of its receipt to an IRA or another qualified plan. The notice must also provide information about capital gains treatment of lump sums, and the limited circumstances under which five-year averaging will be permitted. IRS Form 1099-R is used to report the taxable component of a designated distribution.

There is also a corresponding notice obligation before a plan makes a distribution that is *not* an eligible rollover distribution; the plan must send the participant IRS Form W-4P, Withholding Certificate for Pension or Annuity Payments. The W-4P informs the participant of the options he or she has with respect to withholding:

- Direct the plan not to withhold;
- Direct withholding based on marital status or the number of allowances;
- Increase withholding on periodic payments (for instance, if the participant has high outside income and might otherwise owe a large balance at the end of the tax year).

[C]   QJSA/QPSA Notice

Thirty to ninety days before receipt of benefits, a plan that permits payouts in annuity form must provide all participants with a plain English statement. [All participants—vested or otherwise—are entitled to the statement. *See* I.R.C. § 417(a)(3), Treas. Reg. §§ 1.401(a)(11), and 1.417(e)-1(b)(3)] The notice should contain:

- The terms and conditions of the joint and survivor annuity;
- The participant's right to waive the annuity, including a description of the consequences of the waiver;
- Rights of the participant's spouse;
- Description of the right to revoke the election, and consequences of the revocation.

A comparable explanation must be given about the Qualified Preretirement Survivor Annuity (QPSA), although the timing requirement is more complicated. The notice is due by the latest of:

- The period that begins on the first day of the plan year in which the participant reaches age 32, and ends at the end of the plan year before the participant reaches 35;
- A reasonable time (deemed to mean no more than a year) after a person becomes a plan participant;
- A reasonable time after the employer stops subsidizing the survivor benefit;
- A reasonable time after the I.R.C. § 401(a)(11) survivor benefit provisions become applicable to the participant. This might happen, for example, if a single or divorced person marries and acquires a spouse who could become entitled to a QPSA;

- A reasonable time after separation from service. If the employee leaves before he or she is 35, the period runs from one year before to one year after the separation.

> **Tip:** The plan can accept waivers at earlier stages (as long as the spouse consents), but the plan must give the participant a written explanation of how QPSAs work. The waiver becomes void at the beginning of the plan year in which the participant reaches age 35. If a new waiver is not signed, and the participant dies before retirement age, then the spouse gets a QPSA despite the attempt to waive this form of benefit.

The plan can omit the notice of the right to waive the QPSA/QJSA if the benefit is fully subsidized by the plan, and the participant can neither waive the QPSA/QJSA nor name a nonspouse as beneficiary. The benefit is fully subsidized if not waiving neither lowers the benefit nor results in higher costs for the participant.

An IRS Notice of Proposed Rulemaking Reg.-109481-99, R.I.N. 1545-AX34, 66 Fed. Reg. 3916 (Jan. 17, 2001)] deals with consent to non-QJSA distribution methods. The Small Business Jobs Protection Act (SBJPA) [Pub. L. No. 104-188] enacted I.R.C. § 417(a)(7), allowing the QJSA disclosure statement to be provided after the annuity starting date, as long as the period for electing to waive the QJSA is at least 30 days after the notice is rendered. The 2001 proposal (effective for plan years beginning on or after January 1, 2002) permits the explanation to be furnished either on or after the annuity starting date, and permits a retroactive starting date if the plan makes provisions for it and the participant so elects.

The proposed rules were adopted, with some modifications. [T.D. 9076, 4830–01–p, R.I.N. 1545–AX34] The Final Rule, effective July 16, 2003, applies to plan years beginning on or after January 1, 2004. A retroactive annuity starting date is allowable only if the plan provides for it and the participant specifically asks for the retroactive starting date. Benefits must be determined in a way that puts the participant in the same position as if he or she had received benefit payments starting on the retroactive annuity starting date. The participant must get a make-up amount to reflect any missed payments (and interest on those missed payments). Furthermore, although commentators requested that this provision should be extended to defined contribution plans, the Final Rule continues to limit the availability of a retroactive start date to defined benefit plans.

If the participant is married, the spouse must consent to the election of the retroactive start date if the survivor payments under the retroactive annuity are less than the QJSA with a start date after the provision of the QJSA explanation. This is true even if the actual form of the benefit elected is a QJSA. But consent is required only if the survivor annuity is less than 50% of the annuity payable during the life of the participant under a QJSA that does not commence retroactively.

As for lump sums, electing a retroactive annuity starting date cannot reduce the size of the lump sum. The distribution must not be smaller than the distribution resulting from applying the applicable interest rate and mortality table to the annuity form that was used determine the benefit amount as of the retroactive start date.

See also T.D. 9099 [68 Fed. Reg. 70141 (Dec. 17, 2003)] for guidance on how to disclose the relative value of the QJSA vis a vis optional benefit forms.

In late 2002, the IRS proposed regulations under which, for annuity starting dates on or after January 1, 2004, defined benefit plans and some defined contribution plans would have an obligation to disclose to plan participants the relative value of optional forms of benefits that they can choose to receive in lieu of a QJSA. The explanation must be hand-delivered to participants or mailed to them at their last known address. [Prop. Reg. § 1.417(a)(3)-1, REG-124667-02, RIN 1545-BA78, 67 Fed. Reg. 62417 (Oct. 7, 2002)]

Under this proposal, the value of all optional benefit forms would have to be disclosed on a consistent basis, to facilitate comparisons and provide the information needed for an informed choice. The basis for comparison can be a percentage of the QJSA, a percentage of another form of annuity, or in terms of present value. The Proposed Regulations offer guidance to the plan sponsor for selecting the interest and mortality assumptions to be used in determining relative values.

For instance, a subsidized early retirement benefit could be described as a lump sum worth a certain percentage of the value of an immediate QJSA. The QJSA must be at least as valuable as any other form offered. To avoid prohibited forfeitures, each optional form of benefit must also be at least as valuable as the plan's normal form of the normal retirement benefit.

The proposal permits the plan to disclose the financial effects and relative value of the benefit forms using generally applicable information instead of individualized information applicable to each participant—as long as participants can obtain specific information for their individual case on request.

Additional relative value requirements were published, and were initially intended to go into effect for distributions after October 1, 2004, but because of employer concerns, the effective date was deferred until February 1, 2006. [IRS Announcement 2004-58, 2004-29 I.R.B. 66; see SegalCo Bulletin, Compliance Deadline Looming, <http://www.segalco.com/nov05relativevalues.pdf> (November 2005)] In general, these are defined benefit regulations, but they also apply to 401(k) and other defined contribution plans that offer QJSAs.

To date, T.D. 9256, 71 Fed. Reg. 14798 (Mar. 24, 2006), is the IRS' final statement on disclosure of the relative value of optional forms of benefits under § 417(a)(3). In general, these rules are effective for distributions whose annuity starting dates occur on or after February 1, 2006. Compliance standards are stricter for optional forms of benefits, including lump sums, that are less valuable than the QJSA.

The Final Rules follow the proposal by allowing an optional form to be treated as actuarially equivalent to the QJSA if, using reasonable actuarial assumptions, an unmarried participant's QJSA is worth at least as much as a married participant's value. To be considered approximately equal in value to the QJSA, an optional benefit's value must fall within the range of 95–105% of the actuarial value of the QJSA. Disclosures are required for all optional forms of benefit with retroactive annuity starting dates. It is permissible for a plan to use reasonable estimates to disclose the normal form of benefit under the plan. Including participant-specific information in a disclosure (i.e., generating an individualized computerized statement) does not cause a notice to fail the requirements. If there are many substantially similar optional benefit forms, it is acceptable to make simplified presentations of their values and financial effects. [T.D. 9256 is discussed in, e.g., Deloitte Washington Bulletin, *IRS Issues Final Changes to Relative Value Disclosure Regulations,* <http://benefitslink.com/articles/washbull060403. html> (Apr. 3, 2006); Pensions & Benefits Weblog, <http://fuguerre.wordpress.com/2006/03/24/revised-regulations-for-relative-value-disclosures> (Mar. 24, 2006)]

[D] QDRO Notices

The general rule is that no one can garnish or otherwise get hold of plan benefits before they are paid. The exception to the rule is that a plan administrator not only has the right, but has the obligation, to comply with valid court orders that direct part of the benefit to the participant's separated or divorced spouse. However, not every divorce-related order must be treated as a Qualified Domestic Relations Order (QDRO).

Once a plan receives a court order, I.R.C. § 414(p) obligates the administrator to review it to see if it is qualified. The plan participant and the alternate payee (nearly always the spouse) must be notified that the plan has received an order and what the plan will do to assess its qualification. Then the administrator carries out that procedure and sends another notice to the participant and alternate payee, if the order has been determined to be qualified and therefore must be obeyed by the plan.

[E] Break-in-Service Notice

ERISA's break-in-service rules are complex and difficult for participants to understand. Participants have the right to make a written request (although only once a year) when they are separated from service, or have a one-year break in service. The notice defines their accrued benefits under the plan, and the percentage of the accrued benefits that is nonforfeitable.

[F] "Saver's Credit"

One effect of EGTRRA was to increase substantially the amount that taxpayers can contribute to IRA accounts (or defer in 401(k) or 403(b) accounts). *See* the IRS Announcement 2001-106 [2001-44 I.R.B. 416] for a description of the "saver's credit," which is an income tax credit under I.R.C. § 25B for low-income taxpayers who contribute to an IRA or pension plan. The Announcement contains a sample notice that can be given to employees explaining the credit.

[G] FASB Changes

The subject of pension accounting is highly controversial, now that so many plans have failed, are on the verge of failure, or are being frozen despite fiscal soundness. Many employers resist changes in accounting treatment of pensions because they are afraid that reductions in their bottom line will reduce the value of their stock and make it difficult to obtain operating capital. The opposing view is that current accounting practices require reform because they do not adequately disclose the true impact of future pension and benefit promises on the corporation's finances to stockholders, lenders, employees, and regulators.

In 1998, the Financial Accounting Standards Board (FASB) revised three of its standards: Statements 87, Employers' Accounting for Pensions; 88, Employers' Accounting for Settlements and Curtailments of Defined Benefit Pension Plans and for Termination Benefits; and 106, Employers' Accounting for Postretirement Benefits Other Than Pensions. The revisions were combined in a single document, Statement 132, Employers' Disclosures About Pension and Other Postretirement Benefits. FASB issued a revision, Statement 132(R), in December 2003. [*See* <http://www.fasb.org> for texts of its various documents]

On March 31, 2006, FASB released an Exposure Draft, *Employers' Accounting for Defined Benefit and Other Postretirement Plans*, No. 1025-300, amending FASB Statements Nos. 87, 88, 106, and 132(R). If the proposal is adopted, the funding status of a defined benefit pension plan would be the difference between the fair market value of the plan's assets and the projected benefit obligation. For a retiree health plan, the relevant figure would be the accumulated postretirement benefit obligation. Thus, an overfunded plan would be recorded as an asset and an underfunded plan would be recorded as a liability.

FASB announced the proposal out of a concern that current reporting mechanisms make it possible for corporations to understate the true extent of their future responsibilities for defined benefit pensions (and also for retiree health benefits). The date for calculating pension fund values would be the same as the date for calculating other corporate obligations (the employer's statement of financial position); current rules allow a gap of up to three months, which can result in better results for the pension plan if the market turns up in the interval. The proposal was immediately criticized on the grounds that it would require such large expenses to be disclosed in the balance sheet (rather than, as under current rules, in the notes to the financial statement) that many corporations would have no balance-sheet net worth for reporting purposes. However, most corporations would not experience changes in their pension and retiree health expenses on the income statement. FASB said that because the necessary information must already be collected to draft the notes in the financial statement, the cost of compliance would be minor. The proposal applies to both public and closely held corporations. [<http://www.fasb.org/draft/ed_pension&postretirement_plans.pdf>; *see, e.g.*, Aon Consulting Alert, *FASB to Change Employers' Balance Sheet for Pensions and Retiree Health Benefits in 2006,* <http://www.aon.com/alert_4_5_06.pdf> (Apr. 5, 2006); Mary

Williams Walsh, *Shocks Seen in New Math for Pensions,* New York Times, Mar. 31, 2006, at p. C1; Rebecca Moore, *FASB Issues Proposed Accounting Changes for Pensions and OPEB,* PlanSponsor.com (Mar. 31, 2006)]

FASB has also opined about stock options, in FAS 123, Transition Election Related to Accounting for Tax Effects of Share-Based Payment Awards (Nov. 10, 2005), and its revisions, including tools for defining the grant date for share-based payment awards. FAS 123(R)-4, *Contingent Cash Settlement of Stock Options* (Feb. 3, 2006), provides a safe harbor under which stock options and stock appreciation rights will not be classified as liabilities if they can be exercised only after a contingent event outside the employee's control (e.g., a corporate change in control) becomes likely to occur.

[H]   Notices About Funding Problems

If the plan is underfunded, ERISA § 4011 generally requires the administrator to notify participants and beneficiaries of the funding standards and the limitations on the PBGC's guarantee of payment of benefits. A model notice that can be used for this purpose is published at 29 C.F.R. § 2627.1-.9. The notice must be given within two months of the plan's deadline for filing its annual report for the prior plan year. (If an extension was granted, the two-month period runs from the extended deadline.) However, certain plans are not required to give this notice, even if they are underfunded: plans in their first year of PBGC coverage and plans that are exempted by ERISA § 302(d)(8) because they do not have to make deficit reduction contributions.

ERISA § 502(c)(3) imposes a penalty of up to $110 a day, or whatever relief the court deems proper, for failure to give this notice. In September 2005, the PBGC issued Technical Update 05-1 <http://www.pbgc.gov/practitioners/law-regulations-informal-guidance/content/tu15012.html> explaining how an underfunded plan can issue the necessary participant notice. This Technical Update includes a worksheet to help plan administrators decide if they are required to give this notice, and the text of a Model Notice that will satisfy the requirement.

Each year, when the PBGC republishes the ERISA 4011 Model Participant Notice, it provides an associated Technical Update containing a worksheet to determine if a participant notice is required.

The proposals seek to change the penalty structure, to $5 per participant for an initial violation, $20 per participant for repeat violations if the correction occurs pre-audit, rising to $40 and $100, respectively, for post-audit corrections. The rule in effect when the proposal was made calculated penalties primarily on the basis of number of days of violation rather than the number of participants involved: $25/day for the first 90 days of delinquency, $50/subsequent day of delinquency, subject to a cap of $100 times the number of plan participants. The proposal permits increasing or decreasing the penalty based on circumstances, such as a failure that is partial rather than complete.

The PBGC pointed out that it is expanding its enforcement of the Participant Notice requirements, with more audits to uncover and penalize noncompliance, and therefore encourages voluntary correction as an alternative. Appendix B to the Notice and Proposed Rule provides the text for a single notice that a plan can use both as the 2004 Participant Notice and as a VCP corrective notice. [PBGC Notice and Proposed Rule, *Participant Notice Voluntary Correction Program*, 29 C.F.R. Parts 4011, 4071, 69 Fed. Reg. 25792 (May 7, 2004)]

The Delinquent Filer Voluntary Compliance Program (DFVC) is DOL's program that allows plan administrators who have failed in their compliance with ERISA reporting requirements, but who have not been detected in this failure, to reduce the penalties they might eventually have to pay by voluntarily reporting and correcting the failure. The basic penalty for delinquent filings is $10 per day, capped at $750 for a small plan and $2,000 for a large (more than 100 participants) plan, for any single late annual report. There is a per plan cap of $1,500 for small plans and $4,000 for large plans that are deficient with several annual reports. [Fact Sheet, *Delinquent Filer Voluntary Compliance Program,* <http://www.dol.gov/ ebsa/newsroom/0302fact_sheet.html> (Apr. 2005). DFVC remittances are submitted to DFVC Program, EBSA, P.O. Box 530292, Atlanta, Georgia 30353-0292; the information phone number is (202) 693-8360]

[I] Notice of Termination

Between 60 and 180 days before the scheduled date of a standard or distress termination of a pension plan the administrator must give written notice to the parties affected, e.g., the amount and form of the benefit due of the proposed termination date. The notice must explain how the benefit was calculated (e.g., length of service, participant's age, interest rate and other assumptions, and other factors that the PBGC requires to be disclosed).

However, in *Thompson v. Bridgeport Hospital* [2001 Conn. Super. LEXIS 1755 (June 8, 2001)], an employee lost group health coverage when she was terminated. She sued in state court under a state law requiring employers to provide 15 days' advance notice of cancellation or discontinuation of group health coverage. She also sued under ERISA for penalties, fines, and damages for failure to provide COBRA notice. The state law claim was dismissed as preempted by ERISA § 514, on the grounds that the state law relates to the ERISA plan because it creates significant administrative duties for the employer.

§ 11.07   DISCLOSURE ON REQUEST

In addition to disclosures that must be made, and documents that must be furnished, automatically to all plan participants and beneficiaries, ERISA and the Internal Revenue Code require certain disclosures to be made only if a participant or beneficiary requests them.

Materials that can be requested include:

- A complete copy of the plan's latest Form 5500;
- The plan instrument (that is, the Collective Bargaining Agreement or trust that actually creates the plan);
- The latest updated SPD;
- A report on plan termination;
- Statement of accrued benefits (but the administrator only has to furnish this once in every 12-month period);
- Percentage of vesting; and, for participants who are not fully vested, the schedule on which full vesting will occur.

If a request is made, the information should be mailed within 30 days to the last known address of the requester. The plan is allowed to impose a reasonable charge for the information, based on the least expensive available means of reproducing the documents.

The plan documents, plan description, and latest annual report must be kept on file for participants who want to inspect them, at the plan administrator's principal office. If there is a request to make them available there, copies of the documents must also be kept at the employer's principal office and at each of the employer's locations where 50 or more employees work.

According to the Third Circuit in *Daniels v. Thomas & Betts Corp.* [263 F.3d 66 (3d Cir. 2001)], the plan administrator has a duty to provide a copy of the plan instrument to a participant or beneficiary based on a written request from the participant or beneficiary's attorney, although the Tenth Circuit says that the request has to come directly from the participant or beneficiary.

The Department of Labor can impose penalties of up to $110 a day, subject to a maximum of $1,100, for failure to furnish documents on request. The Secretary of Labor has the power to demand documents that were requested by, but not furnished to, plan participants and beneficiaries under 29 C.F.R. § 2520.104a-8 (added by 67 Fed. Reg. 784 (Jan. 7, 2002)).

The Third Circuit returned to the question of disclosure on request in 2002. A plan participant was denied benefits under a RIF plan. She hired an attorney, who made a written request for copies of the SPD and plan booklets. The plan did not respond for more than two months, by which time the plaintiff had already filed suit. She sought statutory penalties for nondisclosure. The District Court denied the penalty request, because the request was made to the company's benefits department and not to the plan administrator named in the plan documents. But the Third Circuit said this was too narrow an interpretation of ERISA § 502(c)(1). This ERISA provision does not absolutely mandate that the request go to the plan administrator, but it isn't fair to penalize the administrator for requests that the administrator never actually received. The Third Circuit said that the 30-day period for providing the documents does not begin until the request is actually received either by the plan administrator or by someone under the administrator's supervision. [*Romero v. SmithKline Beecham*, 309 F.3d 113 (3d Cir. 2002)]

Also in 2002, the Western District of New York decided a case involving a lawyer's request for a copy of the SPD covering the lawyer's client. [*Sunderlin v. First Reliance Std. Life Ins. Co.*, 235 F. Supp. 2d 222 (W.D.N.Y. 2002)] The employer did not provide the SPD, but did provide a copy of the disability insurance policy. The participant brought suit seeking disability benefits. The insurer admitted that it had lost her claim file, and agreed to settle the case. However, there still remained the question of whether the employer was liable for penalties under ERISA § 104(b)(4).

The employer's argument was that the insurance policy qualified as an SPD. The Western District of New York rejected this argument. The policy didn't contain many of the mandatory disclosure items, such as the name of the plan, its agent for service of process, the name of the plan administrator, how to contact the insurer, or the procedures for making claims and appealing denials. The policy used technical jargon and did not satisfy the ERISA imperative of understandable writing. (However, an insurance policy can be converted into a usable SPD by combining it with a "wrap document" that supplements it with the missing provisions—but if the wrap document is carelessly prepared and mentions benefits that are not provided under the policy, the employer can become liable for providing the additional benefits on a self-insured basis.)

The court also rejected the employer's argument that it did not have any other, better disclosure documents to provide, because employers have a duty to create the mandatory documents if they do not exist. The Western District imposed a substantial penalty of $17,475 ($15 a day, far less than the potential penalty of $110 a day) because of the employer's bad faith in insisting that it had provided an adequate SPD, and for failing to admit that it was the plan administrator. The employer was unsuccessful in obtaining indemnity and contribution from the insurer, because ERISA imposes the burden of providing the SPD on the plan administrator, not on insurers.

An employee sued for severance benefits and ERISA § 502(c) penalties claiming a former employer (and plan administrators) failed to provide plan documents on request. The defendant's position was that the ex-employee was not a participant, but the Third Circuit disagreed, using the test of whether the plaintiff has a colorable claim for benefits, not the likelihood that the plaintiff will prevail on that claim. The Third Circuit ruled that he did not lose participant status by seeking severance benefits after termination, because the nature of severance is that it is not limited to current employees. The court upheld the trial court's $160,000 penalty for failure to provide documents on request, finding that there had been a consistent pattern of refusal to provide mandated information, tantamount to bad faith and intentional misconduct. Although the defendant argued that certain schedules of eligible employees had not yet been compiled when the plan documents were requested, the Third Circuit negated this argument, ruling that once an employer creates a plan that requires attachment of schedules, there is a responsibility to produce timely schedules containing up-to-date information. [*Gorini v. AMP Incorporated*, 94 Fed. Appx. 913 (3d Cir. 2004)]

Two District Court cases from 2006 deal with the same issue: Should a plan administrator be penalized under ERISA § 502(c) for failing to provide documents on a timely basis and, if so, how much? In the Northern District of Illinois case, the terminated employee asked for a copy of the severance plan after his benefits were suspended; he made repeated written requests but did not receive a copy until he brought suit, 18 months after the original request. In the Southern District of Texas case, a widow made multiple written requests for copies of life insurance plan documents over a two-year period. A penalty of $20 per day for 511 days was imposed by the Northern District of Illinois and $85 per day for 656 days in the Texas case. The difference between the two stems from the Illinois court's determination that there was no reason to suspect intentional misconduct, and the delay did not really prejudice the claimant. The employee had already received an SPD containing the same information, but the court thought a modest penalty was justified because the plaintiff was inconvenienced and frustrated without good reason. The larger penalty was imposed based on the administrator's gross incompetence and neglect in the simple matter of furnishing documents. [*Reddy v. Schellhorn*, 2006 U.S. Dist. LEXIS 9329 (N.D. Ill. 2006); *Amschwand v. Spherion Corp.*, No. H-02-4836 (S.D. Tex. Mar. 6, 2006)]

In another case, a plan participant was terminated after eight years. She sought long-term disability benefits, which were denied because the plan required 10 years of service as a precondition of granting benefits for a non-work-related disability. She made several telephone calls for information, and was told each time that she was ineligible. She filed a formal benefit claim, which was denied. She sued, charging fiduciary breach and failure to satisfy the ERISA disclosure requirements. The Sixth Circuit dismissed the fiduciary breach claim because she was not deceived in any way. Even if she did not receive documents about the LTD plan until she made a request, the court ruled that plan beneficiaries are not entitled to damages based on a failure to disclose required information. Statutory penalties under ERISA § 502(c)(1)(B) were also unavailable because as soon as she made a written request, the documents were provided promptly. [*Del Rio v. Toledo Edison Co.*, 2005 U.S. App. LEXIS 7576 (6th Cir. 2005)]

An ADEA plaintiff alleged that her service with the previous employer, a company related to her subsequent employer, should have been credited toward accrual of her pension benefits. The Sixth Circuit affirmed dismissal of her ERISA § 1024 claims but reversed summary judgment on her ERISA § 1060 claim. The plaintiff's job was eliminated in a corporate restructuring; her impression was that older employees were not seen as valuable or entitled to retention. Her termination letter said that she would receive information under separate cover if she were eligible for pension benefits. She did not receive the information, and called the company to inquire. After 11 months of delay, she retained an attorney. It took 15 months after her termination to get any information, and the information provided showed that her work for the predecessor company had not been credited toward pension accrual. She claimed that failure to transfer her pension resulted in unfair devaluation of her pension benefit. The Sixth Circuit read ERISA § 1024(b)(4)

and § 1025(a) to require the administrator either to provide the requested information directly to the beneficiary, or to inform the requester's attorney that authorization is required. If the plan administrator fails to do one or the other within the
30-day time frame mandated by 29 USC § 1132(c), the district court has discretion
to impose a fine. The Sixth Circuit agreed that summary judgment should have
been granted to the defendant on the ERISA § 1060 claim, because the plaintiff
failed to prove that her former employer was a participating company under the
terms of the second employer's plan, or that the two companies were part of a
controlled group of corporations. The Sixth Circuit approved the dismissal of the
ERISA § 1024 claim because the complaint was so badly pleaded that it failed to
put the defendant on fair notice of what the plaintiff claimed it had done wrong.
[*Minadeo v. ICI Paints dba The Glidden Co.*, 398 F.3d 751 (6th Cir. 2005)]

Some 20 years after initial eligibility, an employee discovered that he had not
filled out an application and therefore was not covered by the voluntary retirement
plan. He sued for breach of fiduciary duty on the grounds that he had not been
notified that an affirmative election was required to opt into the plan. The Fourth
Circuit, however, held that adequate notice was given, even though the plan administrator could not prove that the SPD had been delivered. The employer stated that
over the 20-year period, the employee had received a number of plan-related
documents, including several SPDs, a memo informing him of his eligibility to
enroll, annual benefit statements informing him that he was not enrolled and his
balance was $0, and retirement plan newsletters.

The trial court accepted the employer's testimony that the materials had been
provided, but the Fourth Circuit ruled that the trial court erred by overlooking
testimony that the plan did not mail SPDs, but only provided them on request
(contrary to ERISA requirements). The Fourth Circuit, however, did not deem
inadequate distribution of the SPD to be a breach of fiduciary duty when other
documents provided the necessary information. The court found that the employer
had satisfied its duties by sending some documents by first-class mail and others
via an internal e-mail system that had proved to be reliable. [*Brenner v. Johns
Hopkins University*, 2004 U.S. App. LEXIS 2339 (4th Cir. 2004)]

In 2004, the Seventh Circuit imposed a penalty of $35,050 ($50 a day for 701
days) and attorneys' fees of more than $20,000 on a plan that took two years and a
court order to provide the documents requested by a surviving spouse. The plan
denied survivor benefits to the claimant, on the grounds that the plan had the
participant's and spouse's signatures to a waiver of the QJSA. However, the
spouse's signature on the document was not witnessed or notarized as required.
The plan's position was that its records were in "disarray," so it could not be
assumed that the spouse's signature was never notarized; the notarization and
witness affidavit might have been lost. The Seventh Circuit imposed half of the
penalty that was in effect for the relevant time (it has since been increased to a
possible $110 a day). Awards of attorneys' fees are not automatic in ERISA cases,
but are permitted when the opposing party took a substantially unjustified litigating
position—as the Seventh Circuit deemed to have happened where the plan tried to

take advantage of its own poor records to deny benefits. [*Lowe v. McGraw-Hill Cos.*, 361 F.3d 335 (7th Cir. 2004)]

§ 11.08   ELECTRONIC COMMUNICATIONS

The Taxpayer Relief Act of 1997 (TRA '97) [Pub. L. No. 105-34] ordered the IRS to create rules for integrating computer technology into plan administration and the disclosure process. Proposed Rules at 63 Fed. Reg. 70071 (Dec. 18, 1998) make it clear that a pension plan, including a 401(k) plan, will not lose its qualified status merely because it uses paperless electronic methods to give notice and secure consents. However, the electronic notice must:

- Be at least as comprehensible to the average plan participant as the written notice it replaces;
- Contain as much information as the paper version;
- Be written (for instance, on a Web site or as e-mail) and not oral (e.g., automated telephone system) unless it is so simple that a writing is not required;
- Advise the recipient that a paper version of the notice is available on request, at no charge. The participant must get a personal copy—posting one copy on a bulletin board is not sufficient;
- Use any technology (even if it was not available at the time the rule was proposed) that satisfies these standards.

These proposals were finalized as T.D. 8873, published as 65 Fed. Reg. 6001 (Feb. 8, 2000) and also 2000-9 I.R.B. 713, effective for years beginning on or after January 1, 2001, for using electronic media to provide notifications to plan participants (and get their consents) with respect to distributions from a qualified plan. Specifically, paperless electronic methods of communication can be used to transmit:

- I.R.C. § 411(a)(11) notice of distribution options, right to defer distribution, and the participant's consent to a distribution;
- I.R.C. § 402(f) rollover notice;
- I.R.C. § 3405(e)(10)(B) withholding notice.

Furthermore, the plan is allowed to give the notices under I.R.C. §§ 411(a)(11) and 402(f) more than 90 days before a distribution, as long as the plan offers a summary of the notices within the 90-day period before the distribution. Plans that use electronic notices must always give participants the option of getting a paper version of the notice at no charge.

Also Notice 99-1, 1999-2 I.R.B. 8 explains electronic techniques for performing administrative tasks such as enrolling participants and designating beneficiaries. Announcement 99-6, 1999-4 I.R.B. 24 allows electronic transmission of W-4P forms.

In April 2002, the Department of Labor published an additional Final Rule as a safe harbor method of communicating employee benefit information electronically. (In other words, employers will not be penalized if they follow these procedures, but they are not the only acceptable procedures.) [*See* 67 Fed. Reg. 17263 (April 9, 2002)]

To use the safe harbor, the employer must get the employee's voluntary consent to providing the information electronically. The individual must provide an address (e.g., an e-mail address) for receiving the communications. The employer must give the individual a clear and conspicuous statement, before consent is rendered, explaining the documents to which the consent applies. Employees must be informed that they can withdraw their consent to electronic notification at any time, and must be told how to update their information and/or withdraw consent. They must also be told how to obtain paper hard copies of the documents.

Tip: Under the safe harbor, employers must communicate individually with employees. Using computer kiosks in the workplace is not an acceptable method of providing the information.

The Treasury issued proposed regulations in mid-2005 covering the use of electronic media for benefit notices and the transmission of benefit elections and consents, with the limitation that the regulations cannot be relied upon until they are finalized. This proposal applies only to tax documents that the Internal Revenue Code requires to be in writing, not to ERISA communications, such as SPDs, SARs, and COBRA notices, because those documents are under the jurisdiction of DOL and PBGC. The Treasury Regulations therefore cover notices and elections for qualified plans, SEPs, SIMPLE plans, A&H plans, cafeteria plans, HSAs, and MSAs.

The Treasury Regulations provide that notices can be delivered electronically only if the consent requirement is met or if the plan qualifies for an exemption. Participants receiving an electronic notice must be informed, in a readily understandable manner, what the subject matter of the notice is and how to access it. The recipient must give explicit consent to electronic delivery and must be informed that he or she can request a paper copy at no charge and withdraw consent. Disclosure is also required about the scope of the consent, how to update contact information, and the hardware and software requirements for using the system. If the hardware/software requirements change, a new consent form is required. PINs or other security devices must be implemented to prevent unauthorized persons from accessing the system or inputting information into it. Electronic witness affidavits and notarizations are acceptable as long as a notary or plan representative physically witnesses the application of the signature.

Electronic filings of EBSA documents are now available, but will not be mandatory until 2008. [The IRS rule is at 70 Fed. Reg. 40675 (July 14, 2005);

the EBSA rule is at 70 Fed. Reg. 51542 (Aug. 30, 2005); *see, e.g.*, Tina M. Kuska and Mary K. Samsa, Proposed Treasury Regulations Regarding the Use of Electronic Media for Employee Benefit Notices, Elections and Consents, Gardner Carton & Douglas Client Memorandum 8/05 [www.gcd.com] (Aug. 2005); McKay Hochman Co. Inc., *Electronic Communications—Part One,* <http://www.mhco.com/Commentary/2005/ESIGN_Pt1_8405.htm> (Aug. 4, 2005) EBSA and the PBGC continued to publish e-filing rules and guidance: Final Rules at 71 Fed. Reg. 31077 (June 1, 2006) and 71 Fed. Reg. 41359 (July 21, 2006) and Proposed Rules to bring the changes in the structure of Form 5500 into line with the annual filing requirements: 71 Fed. Reg. 41392 (July 21, 2006)]

§ 11.09   DISCLOSURE OF DOCUMENTS TO THE DOL

ERISA required plan administrators to file all SPDs and SMMs with the Department of Labor (DOL) until it was amended by the Taxpayer Relief Act of 1997. The current version of ERISA § 104(a) requires plan administrators to respond to DOL requests by providing documents relating to an employee benefit plan—including the latest SPD, a summary of plan changes not reflected in the SPD, and the plan instrument.

However, the DOL sees its primary role in this arena as helping participants and beneficiaries get documents from the plan, so the DOL can ask for documents that participants or beneficiaries are entitled to, have requested, but have not received. But the DOL will not ask for documents that the participants and beneficiaries are not entitled to see.

If the plan administrator doesn't respond to the request within 30 days, the DOL has the power (under ERISA § 502(c)(6)) to impose civil penalties of up to $110 a day (but not more than $1,100 per request). Penalties will not be imposed if factors beyond the administrator's control prevent compliance.

The DOL's Final Rule about document disclosure and civil penalties is set out at 67 Fed. Reg. 777-789 (Jan. 7, 2002).

PBGC premium filings and payments, starting with the 2004 plan year, can be submitted electronically using the secure "My PAA" online system. Starting in 2006, mandatory online filing will be phased in, starting with plans with 500 or more participants in the previous plan year. Online filing is expected to become universal by the time filings are made for the 2007 plan year. Payments can be made through My PAA using Internet checks, credit cards, or Automated Clearing House (ACH) transfers, or outside My PAA via paper checks or Fed Wire or ACH transfer. [My PAA <https://egov.pbgc.gov/mypaa>; PBGC, *Online Premium Filing (My PAA),* <http://www.pbgc.gov/practitioners/premium-filings/content/page13265.html>; the Practitioner Call Center is available at 1-800-736-2444 or 800-400-7242 to answer questions; questions can also be e-mailed to premiums@pbgc.gov]

§ 11.10   FORM 5500

Qualified plans must report each year to the IRS, DOL, and PBGC so that these agencies can monitor plan operations and see if the plans remain qualified, are financially sound, and are operated in accordance with all applicable requirements. The basic Form 5500 covers plans with 100 or more participants; single-participant plans can use the less complex Form 5500-EZ. Only one filing is necessary—the IRS transmits the information to the DOL and PBGC. [The toll-free telephone hot line for questions about plan coverage, premiums, or terminations is (800) 736-2444]

Form 5500, like the Form 1040, consists of a basic form and various schedules that provide additional information. Form 5500 deals with four main subjects: the plan's financial statements, actuarial data, administrative data, and any benefits covered by insurance.

The annual report is due at the end of the seventh month following the end of the plan year. A plan that does not seem likely to complete the report in time should file IRS Form 5558, Application for Extension of Time to File Certain Employee Plan Returns, to get an extension of up to two and a half months. The extension will be granted automatically, until the due date for the employer's income tax return, as long as the plan year is the same as the employer's tax year, the income tax deadline has been extended to a date after the normal due date for the Form 5500, and a copy of the income tax extension is attached to the Form 5500.

The Form 5500 now consists of a basic form and the following schedules:

- A: Insurance information
- B: Actuarial information
- C: Service provider data
- D: DFE/participating plan data
- E: ESOP annual information
- G: Financial transaction schedules (there is no Schedule F)
- H: Financial information
- I: Financial information for small plans
- P: The annual return by the fiduciary of an employee benefit trust
- R: Retirement plan information
- SSA: A list of separated participants who have deferred vested benefits.

[*See* <http://www.dol.gov/ebsa/5500main.html> for documents and information about the Form 5500 for the 2005 plan year]

But, although some compliance requirements have been eased, some have become more stringent. Starting with the 2002 plan year, some small plans (usually those having fewer than 100 participants) will be required to get a report from an independent auditor to accompany their Form 5500-series filing, even though they were excused from the audit requirement in earlier years. However, audit waivers are available for plans with fewer than 100 participants, or those with participants in the 80–120 range if they filed as a small plan the year before, if at least 95% of plan assets are managed by professionals, as long as participants get additional disclosures in the summary annual report. [*See* <http://www.dol.gov/ebsa/faqs/faq_auditwaiver.html>]

A "large plan" is one with 100 or more participants as of the beginning of the plan year, and a "small plan" has fewer. If the number of participants at the beginning of a plan year was 80 to 120 and a Form 5500 was filed for the previous plan year, the plan has the right to elect to complete the Form 5500 and the schedules using the same category as the previous year.

The EFAST system is used to electronically file Forms 5500 and 5500-EZ and to download forms that will be filed as handwritten paper copies. The system, developed collaboratively by IRS, DOL, and the PBGC relies on forms in two computer-scannable formats: machine print and hand print. Hand print forms can be either downloaded from the site or ordered by calling 1-800-TAXFORM (829-3676). Consult the site for information about which proprietary forms of software and which service providers are acceptable for 5500 filings. Only approved forms can be used; non-standard or photocopies of approved forms will not be accepted.

Filing electronically requires the plan to file the Form EFAST-1 application and get a PIN identifier. Paper and electronic media (e.g., CD-ROMs and floppy disks) are mailed to EBSA's offices in Lawrence, Kan.; the address depends on whether it is paper (P.O. Box 7043) or electronic media (P.O. Box 7041) or sent via a private delivery service (3833 Greenway Drive).

Payment should not accompany the 5500 filing—instead, payment should be made directly to the appropriate government agency. [EBSA's EFAST FAQ is posted at <http://www.dol.gov/ebsa/faqs/faq_efast.html>, and the EFAST toll-free telephone information line is 1-866-453-3278. DOL's February 2, 2006 draft version of the *User's Guide for Electronic/Magnetic Media Filing of Forms 5500 and 5500-EZ* is online at <http://www.dol.gov/ebsa/pdf/efast-a.pdf>]

The DOL can assess civil penalties of up to $1,100 per day per annual report, running from the date of the failure or refusal to file and until a satisfactory report is filed, against plan administrators who fail or refuse to comply with the annual reporting requirements. A report that is rejected for failure to provide material information has not been "filed."

However, voluntary compliance is usually sought before penalties are imposed. The EBSA sends correspondence asking for additional information if data is omitted, or if the agency thinks corrections are necessary in light of the instructions or to be internally consistent with other data on the form.

The EBSA has discretion to waive all or part of the penalty based on submission of a timely statement showing reasonable cause for failure to file the complete report at the time it was due. Penalties are not assessed during the time when the DOL is considering the statement of reasonable cause.

Late in 2004, the PBGC issued a Proposed Rule on electronic annual reporting and disclosure of actuarial information. Certain identifying, financial, and actuarial information must be provided to the PBGC in a standard electronic format. Electronic reporting is also required for additional items of supporting information that are readily available to the filer. The PBGC Web site contains a standard format for ERISA § 4010 filings. The Proposed Rule calls for information about benefit liabilities to be broken down by classes (active participants, terminated vested participants, retirees and beneficiaries in pay status). If a company filed in the previous year but does not intend to file this year, it must demonstrate why filing is not required.

The proposal seeks to expand the information to be submitted on the ERISA § 4010.8(a)(3) Actuarial Valuation Report, to include the vested and nonvested current liability, computed under I.R.C. § 412, broken down according to the classes described above, the expected increase in current liability for benefits accruing during the plan year, and expected plan disbursements for the plan year. To avoid the penalty of up to $1,100 a day imposed by I.R.C. § 4071, the Proposed Rule requires filers to specify the actuarial assumptions underlying interest rates, mortality assumptions, retirement age, and administrative expenses used to calculate the ERISA § 4010.8 benefit liabilities. If plans are frozen, the PBGC seeks disclosure of the terms of the freeze (e.g., is service and/or pay frozen).

Current law requires a Power of Attorney to be provided when required information is submitted by anyone other than the filer. The PBGC proposes to eliminate this requirement as unnecessary, but figures must still be certified by an enrolled actuary, regardless of who submits the information.

Under the proposal, a forms submission made through the PBGC Web site is considered to have been transmitted when the filer performs the last act (i.e., clicking the submit button) to indicate that the form has been filed and is no longer subject to withdrawal or further editing. The PBGC says that electronic submissions made through the Web site do not require addresses; the agency takes responsibility for directing them to the proper recipient. [PBGC RIN 1212-AB01, *Electronic Filing—Annual Financial and Actuarial Information,* 69 Fed. Reg. 77679 (Dec. 28, 2004)]

CHAPTER 12

PLAN DISTRIBUTIONS

§ 12.01   INTRODUCTION

One of the major tasks of plan administration is to distribute benefits from the plan to participants and their designated beneficiaries—although sometimes determining the proper beneficiary is not as easy as it sounds. The plan administrator must communicate with participants and beneficiaries of their distribution options with respect to accrued benefits. The plan administrator has a duty to provide whatever forms are necessary to make an election.

The standard form of distribution is a single-life annuity for single participants and a Qualified Joint and Survivor Annuity (QJSA) for married participants. The plan must also provide for a Qualified Preretirement Survivor Annuity (QPSA) for married persons who die before their pension enters pay status.

But plans can permit other payment forms: lump sums and annuities offering other provisions (but not extending for a term longer than the life expectancy of the employee or the joint life expectancy of the employee and designated beneficiary). [See I.R.C. § 401(a)(9)(A)(ii)] It's up to the plan whether to offer these alternate forms, or just the standard annuities. [See §§ 12.03, 12.09]

A plan can be disqualified if it makes distributions outside the range of permitted events related to separation from service. A defined benefit or money purchase plan can only make distributions when the participant reaches Normal Retirement Age or separates from service. The rules are different for 401(k) plans: distributions can be made at retirement, death, attainment of age 59, disability, severance from employment, or hardship. Termination of service means ceasing to work for any entity that is treated as the same employer under the Code § 411 rules. However, employers are not prohibited from rehiring a former employee who has received a 401(k) distribution, although the IRS may look to whether there was a true termination or if the so-called termination was merely pretextual. The IRS might also accept distributions made to a person who is rehired for substantially different duties, and on a part-time rather than the previous full-time schedule, but there must have been an intervening period when the person was not employed by the employer.

In most cases, defined contribution plans satisfy their distribution obligations by purchasing commercial annuities with the balance in the employee's account, although the plan itself might make payments for a simple annuity for a term of years. Defined benefit plans often buy annuities, although some plans handle distribution in house to save some fees.

Tip: Choosing an annuity insurer is a fiduciary decision. DOL Interpretive Bulletin 95-1 includes a list of criteria to be used in making an appropriate choice.

The DOL added to this in Advisory Opinion 2002-14A, which clarifies that the same principles of selecting a safe annuity provider apply equally to defined benefit and defined contribution plans. A fiduciary considering the

---

availability of additional protection under a state guaranty association should consider whether the provider and the product are covered, the extent of the guaranty, and the ability of the guaranty association to meet its predictable obligations.

The normal payment method for a profit-sharing plan or stock bonus plan is a lump sum, not a periodic payment. When a participant in one of these plans dies, the entire vested balance remaining in the account must go to the beneficiary designated by the participant. The spouse's consent is required if a married participant is to designate anyone other than the spouse as beneficiary.

For plans other than pension plans, I.R.C. § 401(a)(11)(B)(iii) requires that, unless the balance in a married participant's plan is distributed before his or her death, the remainder must be paid to the surviving spouse unless the surviving spouse waives this right.

The Fourth Circuit ruled, early in 2003, that a defined benefit plan participant cannot sue to recover money allegedly lost because a distribution from the plan was not made on a specific date. The court held that such suits are not sustainable under ERISA, because they cannot be classed as seeking equitable remedies. [*Rego v. Westvaco Corp.*, 319 F.3d 140 (4th Cir. 2003)]

[A] KETRA Distributions

The Katrina Emergency Tax Relief Act of 2005 (KETRA), P.L. 109-73, contains several provisions relevant to plan distributions. This legislation remains relevant for later years in case similar provisions are enacted to respond to other natural disasters. This legislation provides that the 10% penalty on early withdrawals is not imposed on a "qualified Hurricane Katrina distribution" (QHKD) from a qualified retirement plan, 403(b) plan, or IRA. QHKDs are considered income, but they can be recognized over a three-year period, not just in the year of withdrawal. A QHKD can be returned to an eligible retirement plan within three years. Recontributed amounts are considered rollovers and therefore are not included in income.

A QHKD is defined as a distribution of up to $100,000 taken from an eligible retirement plan between August 25, 2005, and January 1, 2007, by someone whose principal residence was in the disaster area and who suffered a Katrina-related economic loss. Plans are entitled to rely on reasonable representations as to whether an employee is qualified and has suffered losses. A qualified plan is not considered to violate the Code by treating a distribution as a QHKD—as long as the aggregate amount of distributions to a particular taxpayer from the plans of the employer and its controlled group does not exceed $100,000 (even if the individual receives a total of more than $100,000 when distributions from other plans and IRAs are taken into account). A distribution taken before the hurricanes from an IRA, 401(k) plan, or 403(b) plan to buy a home in the disaster area can be recontributed to the plan if the home was not purchased or constructed because of the hurricanes.

A loan from an employer plan made after the enactment of KETRA and before January 1, 2007, to a qualified person is excluded from the borrower's income to the extent that the loan, when added to other outstanding loans from the plan, does not exceed $100,000 minus either the outstanding loan balance, or the greater of $10,000 or the participant's accrued benefit under the plan. Repayment that a qualified individual would otherwise be required to make between August 25, 2005, and December 31, 2006, is delayed for one year. This period of deferral does not count toward the requirement of repayment within five years with level amortization.

Employers have discretion to decide whether to treat distributions from their plans as Katrina distributions and are allowed to set up procedures for identifying Katrina distributions, as long as the procedures are reasonable and applied consistently. [IRS Publication 4492, *Information for Taxpayers Affected by Hurricanes Katrina, Rita and Wilma,* McKay Hochman Co. Inc., *Katrina Guidance* (Dec. 15, 2005); Janell B. Grenier, *Summary of KETRA Plan-Related Provisions* (Benefitsblog) (Sept. 23, 2005)]

Notice 2005-92, 2005-51 I.R.B. 1165, provides guidance (e.g., specifying that a taxpayer's principal place of abode is wherever he or she lives absent special circumstances), so a person who evacuated the hurricane disaster area will still be considered to have that area as a principal place of abode. Direct rollovers of Katrina distributions do not have to be offered and a § 402(f) notice is not required. A spouse's consent is still required for a non-QJSA distribution, even if it is a Katrina distribution.

[B] Roth Distributions

The enactment of Roth IRAs and Roth 401(k)s (i.e., accounts that are not tax-advantaged when deposits are made, but permit tax-free withdrawals on appropriate conditions, including retention of the sums within the account for at least five years) created a need for specialized distribution rules.

Proposed Regulations on the taxation of Roth 401(k) distributions say that the five-year holding period begins at the beginning of the tax year in which the first Roth 401(k) contribution is made and ends at the end of the fifth tax year. In a direct rollover, the holding period from the sending plan is considered under the receiving plan (this is known as "tacking"—i.e., the earlier holding period is tacked on). However, tacking is not applied if the participant makes an indirect rollover within the 60-day period. Only the taxable part of the distribution can be the subject of an indirect rollover.

Both qualified and nonqualified Roth 401(k) distributions that could otherwise be rolled over can be rolled over directly to another qualified plan that accepts Roth 401(k) contributions. Distributions to a participant can be rolled over to a Roth IRA, and the taxable part of the distribution can be rolled over to another plan that accepts Roth 401(k) funds. Even a person whose AGI is too high to make a Roth IRA contribution can roll funds over into a Roth IRA.

If one Roth plan does a plan-to-plan rollover to another Roth plan, the sending plan must inform the receiving plan that the distribution is a qualified distribution or the amount of the participant's basis and the date the five-year "clock" began to run. Participants are entitled to disclosure of the same information if they receive a distribution.

Partial distributions from a Roth plan allocate taxable income pro rata; that is, if $1,000 in a $10,000 account is income on amounts deposited into the plan, and the account owner receives a nonqualified distribution of $4,000, 10% is attributed to income and therefore is taxable income for the recipient; $3,600 is a nontaxable return of deferred amounts. Only the amount contributed to the account (not earnings) can become a hardship distribution.

In general, the proposed rules are effective January 1, 2007, but the rollover rules take effect January 1, 2006. Note that, because the Roth 401(k) is a creation of EGTRRA, it will expire in 2011 unless EGTRRA is made permanent. [71 Fed. Reg. 4320 (Jan. 26, 2006); *see* SunGard Corbel News Pension Technical Updates, *Roth Distribution Regulations,* <http://www.corbel.com/news/technicalupdates. asp?ID=332&T=P> (Jan. 26, 2006)]

The firm of McKay Hochman Co. has published a chart summarizing rollover rules for Roth 401(k) plans. The chart also explains how the five-year holding period is applied and what reporting requirements are imposed. [*Proposed Roth Distribution Regulations—Part Two,* <http://www.mhco.com/Commentary/2006/ Prop_Roth_Two_030906.htm> (Mar. 9, 2006)]

§ 12.02   CASHOUT

Although it is burdensome for a plan to make periodic payments of a very small sum, and it would be convenient to simply close the books by making a one-time payment, participants cannot be forced to "cash out" (take a lump sum instead of a stream of payments) unless their vested balance is very small—$5,000 or less. [*See* T.D. 8794, 63 Fed. Reg. 70335 (Dec. 21, 1998)] Rev. Rul. 2000-36, 2000-31 I.R.B. 140 allows a plan to make a direct rollover under I.R.C. § 401(a)(31), the default method of handling involuntary cashouts, as long as the plan participants get adequate notice that they can get the cash instead.

EGTRRA provides for automatic rollovers of cashouts from 401(k) plans in amounts between $1,000 and $5,000 to IRAs.

The calculation of the accrued benefit under I.R.C. § 411(a)(7)(B)(i) does not have to include any service with respect to which the employee has already been cashed out at a level below $3,500.

The 2002 technical corrections bill, the Job Creation and Worker Assistance Act of 2002 [Pub. L. No. 107-147] provides that employers can disregard rollovers when they determine whether or not the balance exceeds $5,000 and therefore whether or not it is subject to cashout.

The IRS provided guidance about automatic rollovers, as amended by EGTRRA, in Notice 2005-5, 2005-3 I.R.B. 337; and the Department of Labor did the same in Proposed Regulations at 69 Fed. Reg. 9900 (Mar. 2, 2004) and Final Regulations at 69 Fed. Reg. 58017 (Sept. 28, 2004).

A qualified plan can include a provision cashing out distributions under $5,000; mandatory distributions that exceed $1,000 must be rolled over to an IRA set up by the plan for the participant, unless the recipient makes an affirmative election to roll over the money elsewhere or takes it in cash. Fiduciaries are deemed to have satisfied their duties with respect to rollovers if the plan satisfies the requirements of I.R.C. § 401(a)(31)(B). These rules apply to distributions made without consent of the participant, at normal retirement age or age 62 (whichever is later). An eligible rollover distribution that is a plan loan offset is not subject to the general rules on automatic rollovers. QDROs and distributions to participants' spouses are not covered.

The DOL Proposed Rule reduces the proposal's six safe harbor conditions to five. To be cashed out, the account balance of a defined contribution plan, or the present value of the vested accrued benefit, must be under $5,000. Present value is determined as of the date of distribution, so if a balance that was over $5,000 at the time of the employee's termination drops below $5,000, cashout is permitted. The rollover must be made to an IRA. A plan that sets up IRAs for this purpose does not become a fiduciary as to future investment results. To qualify for the safe harbor, the cashed out funds must be invested in a safe product that nevertheless earns a reasonable rate of return. The investment product must be offered by a regulated financial institution such as an FDIC-insured bank, an insurance company covered by a state guarantee fund, or a registered mutual fund. Fees and expenses must be comparable to those for other IRAs. The employer must provide disclosure to the participants about the nature of the investment product, its fees and expenses, and a contact for further information. The DOL has proposed a class exemption from the prohibited transactions rule when a regulated financial institution names itself or one of its affiliates to provide such IRAs.

§ 12.03 LUMP SUMS

There is no legal requirement that plans offer lump sum distributions, although it is very common for them to do so for the convenience of retirees who either need a lump sum (to pay the entrance fee to a Continuing Care Retirement Community, for example) or who believe that they can achieve better investment results than a qualified plan, subject to fiduciary requirements, can muster.

The availability of lump sums can be involved in a "death spiral" for a troubled pension plan. In some instances, (for example, after a company sets up special fully funded retirement plans for top executives, draining off funds that could be used for rank-and-file pensions), a company's employees begin to worry about the safety of their pensions. Some of them then opt for early retirement and a lump-sum payout that they can invest. But the more money that is withdrawn from the plan, the less stable the plan becomes; the more likely the plan is to fail and be taken over by the PBGC; and the more likely the PBGC is to have to cut annuity benefits after many lump-sum payouts have been elected. [Mary Williams Walsh, *A Lump-Sum Threat to Pension Funds*, New York Times, Aug. 14, 2003, at p. C1]

A Proposed Regulation, I.R.C. § 1.402(e)-2(e)(3) says that an employee must have at least five years' participation in the plan as a prerequisite for taking a lump-sum payout.

If a plan offers both lump sums and early retirement subsidies, the plan should specify whether the subsidy can be included in the lump sum, or must be taken in annuity form.

Unless the plan provides to the contrary, the federal "mailbox rule" (evidence of timely mailing creates a presumption of timely receipt; the presumption can only be overcome with convincing evidence the document was not received) applies to an ERISA plan to determine whether a participant made a timely election of a lump-sum supplemental benefit. The plan required submission of a written election at least one year before retirement to qualify for the lump sum. In *Schikore v. Bankamerica Supplemental Retirement Plan* [269 F.3d 956 (9th Cir. 2001)], the plaintiff could prove that she mailed the election. The plan refused to pay the lump sum because it claimed it never received the election form. The Ninth Circuit said that she should get the lump sum by application of the mailbox rule.

The Fifth Circuit upheld the PBGC's determination that a lump sum distribution under a terminated plan should be calculated based on the 30-year Treasury rate in effect at the time of the distribution, accepting the PBGC's definition of "annuity start date" rather than the employer's contention that the date-of-termination rate should have been used. [*PBGC v. Wilson N. Jones Memorial Hospital*, 374 F.3d 362 (5th Cir. 2004)]

§ 12.04   ANTI-ALIENATION RULE

The underlying purpose of pension plans is to provide income to retirees and their families once the individual is no longer able to work. This purpose could not be satisfied if the pension became unavailable for some reason. Therefore, pension, annuity, stock bonus, and profit-sharing plans are subject to anti-alienation requirements under I.R.C. §§ 401(a)(13) and 404(a)(2). The benefits under such plans may not be assigned or alienated in advance. But, just as with any legal rule, there are certain exceptions to what seems to be a blanket prohibition.

Federal tax liens under I.R.C. § 6331 can be enforced; they are not considered to violate this provision. [Treas. Reg § 1.401(a)-13(b)(2)] The anti-alienation provision does not prevent the IRS from proceeding against an interest in ERISA plan benefits. [*U.S. v. McIntyre*, 222 F.3d 655 (9th Cir. 2000)]

On the grounds that pensions can be invaded to satisfy criminal fines, the Second Circuit held that it is not a violation of ERISA to invade a pension to pay a fine for traveling outside the United States to engage in sex acts with minors. [*U.S. v. Irving*, 432 F.3d 401 (2d Cir. 2005)]

Once a benefit is in pay status, a participant or beneficiary can make a voluntary revocable assignment of up to 10% of any benefit payment. However, assignments of this type cannot be used to defray the costs of plan administration.

A plan loan is not an improper alienation if:

- The plan includes a specific loan provision;
- Loans are available to all participants on a nondiscriminatory basis;
- The loan is not a prohibited transaction;
- The plan imposes a reasonable interest rate on plan loans;
- The loan is secured by the accrued nonforfeitable benefit. [*See* I.R.C. § 4975(d)(1) and § 4.18]

The Supreme Court's decision in *Patterson v. Shumate* [504 U.S. 753 (1992)] holds that ERISA's anti-alienation provisions are "applicable non-bankruptcy law" under Bankruptcy Code § 541(c)(1). Therefore, benefits from an ERISA-qualified plan can be excluded from the employee's bankruptcy estate, and will not be available to the employee's creditors.

But because of an earlier Supreme Court decision, *Mackey v. Lanier Collection Agency & Service* [486 U.S. 825 (1988)], pension benefits are protected from creditors, but welfare benefits are not. Creditors are sometimes entitled (within limits) to garnish the wages of debtors, but they cannot garnish future pension benefits. If the plan itself is terminating, creditors cannot garnish employees' interests in the plan, even if one consequence of the termination is that they will receive a lump sum instead of ongoing annuity payments. In 2005, the Supreme Court ruled, in *Rousey v. Jacoway*, 544 U.S. 320, that IRAs are entitled to the same bankruptcy protection as qualified plans. Also in 2005, Congress increased the bankruptcy protection granted to IRAs and qualified plans, via P.L. 109-8, the Bankruptcy Abuse Prevention and Consumer Protection Act (BAPCA). BAPCA also makes it harder for bankrupt employers to modify their retiree health benefits.

Once the benefits are paid, the anti-alienation provision no longer applies. [*See Robbins v. DeBuono*, 218 F.3d 197 (2d Cir. 2000)] So, unless there is a state law that offers additional protection, the funds can be attached by creditors.

ERISA's anti-alienation provisions do not prevent imposition of a constructive trust—for instance, when a family court order has been violated. [*Central States Southeast & Southwest Area Pension Fund v. Howell*, 227 F.3d 672 (6th Cir. 2000)]

Late in 2003, the District Court for the District of Kansas permitted the federal government to garnish qualified retirement benefits of a plan participant who plead guilty to wire fraud, counterfeiting, and income tax evasion. The statute governing tax levies, 18 USC § 3613, permits the government to enforce a judgment that imposes a fine "notwithstanding any other federal law"—there is no exception for ERISA. [*U.S. v. Garcia*, 72 L.W. 1311 (D. Kan. Nov. 6, 2003) 96-10049-01-JTM]

In mid-2003, the Eighth Circuit ruled that a state domestic relations order had higher priority than a prior federal tax lien. Therefore, in a case where the IRS pursued remedies against a divorced airline pilot, the QDRO in the ex-wife's favor prevailed (even though there were technical deficiencies in the order that required it to be reformed twice by the court). The Eighth Circuit read Code § 6323(a) to require the IRS to file a notice of lien to secure its priority in situations like this one, where the ex-wife had the status of a judgment lien creditor. [*U.S. v. Taylor,* 338 F.3d 947 (8th Cir. 2003)]

The First Circuit ruled that it did not violate the anti-alienation provision to require a participant to make a monthly accounting of his income to satisfy a $500,000 judgment that he owed to his daughter. Certiorari was denied. [*Hoult v. Hoult,* 373 F.3d 47 (1st Cir. 2004), *cert. denied,* 543 U.S. 1002]

§ 12.05   QJSA PAYMENTS

The normal method of paying pension plan benefits to married participants is the QJSA, payable for the lives of both the employee and his or her spouse. Once the first spouse dies, the plan can reduce the annuity payable to the survivor—although not more than 50% of the initial payment. Employers can also choose to subsidize the survivor annuity at some level between 50% and 100% of the original payment.

In addition to the QJSA/QPSA, a plan can offer term annuities and/or life annuities, and life annuities can include term certain guarantee features.

Why would a couple be willing to waive the standard form and take a payment other than a QJSA? For one thing, the payments might be larger in the short run. The participant might be the first spouse to retire, with additional funds expected in the future from the other spouse's pension. If the spouse who is expected to survive will have ample funds (e.g., from personal assets and insurance on the life of the other spouse), then a reduced or absent survivor annuity may not create problems.

I.R.C. § 417(d) provides that QJSAs are required only if the participant was married for one year or more before plan payments begin, with an exception for participants who marry in the year before payments begin and remain married for one year. To avoid tracking problems, most plans simply offer QJSAs to all married participants whatever the duration of the marriage.

Because of a 1984 federal law, the Retirement Equity Act, the employee spouse cannot waive the QJSA without the written consent of the other spouse. There is a 60-day window for making the waiver, starting 90 days before the annuity start date (the first day of the employee spouse's first benefit period under the plan), ending 30 days before the annuity start date. However, the Small Business Job Protection Act [Pub. L. No. 104-188] amended the Internal Revenue Code to allow QJSA disclosures to be given even after the annuity starting date.

The final regulations, promulgated at T.D. 8796, 63 Fed. Reg. 70009 (Dec. 18, 1998), loosen up the notice requirements somewhat. Distributions from the plan can be made less than 30 days after the notice is given, but participants and beneficiaries still must be given at least seven days notice. QJSA disclosure can be deferred until after the annuity starting date. However, the participant can revoke the election until the annuity starting date or seven days after notice is given—whichever comes later. [*See also* Treas. Reg. 109481-99 R.I.N. 1545-ZX34, effective for plan years beginning on or after January 1, 2002, the QJSA explanation can be furnished on or after the annuity starting date]

A waiver of the right to receive the pension in QJSA form must be in writing, and must either be notarized or witnessed by a representative of the pension plan. [*See* Treas. Reg. § 1.417(e)-1(b)(3)] Furthermore, the waiver must be expressed in a document specifically related to the plan; a prenuptial agreement between the employee and his or her spouse won't work for this purpose. [Treas. Reg. § 1.401(a)-20, Q&A 28] The waiver binds only the spouse who signs it; if the employee and spouse divorce, any subsequent spouse is still entitled to a QJSA unless he or she waives it. [I.R.C. § 417(a)(4)]

In this context, ERISA preempts community property law [*Boggs v. Boggs*, 520 U.S. 833 (1997)], so a spouse who waives the right to a QJSA can't later assert community property rights in those benefits.

The Eleventh Circuit ruled that survivor benefits under a top hat plan's joint and survivor annuity were not payable to the employee's second spouse when the employee was married to his first spouse when the benefit payments started. When the former employer was acquired by another corporation, the acquiring corporation decided to accelerate payments under the plan by offering lump sums based on a single-life expectancy for the life of the retiree (without consideration of the current spouse). The Eleventh Circuit said that distributing lump sums was legitimate because the plan reserved the right to accelerate benefits, and the lump sum was the full equivalent of the value of the future benefits. The Eleventh Circuit ruled that *Boggs v. Boggs* is inapplicable, because top hat plans are not subject to the ERISA participation and vesting rules. Even if there had been a QJSA requirement, a survivor annuity is available only to the person who was married to the employee at the time when benefits commenced, not to spouses married subsequently. In addition, because top hat plans are exempt from ERISA's fiduciary rules, there could not have been a fiduciary violation. [*Holloman v. Mail-Well Corp.*, 443 F.3d 832 (11th Cir. 2006)]

Internal Revenue Code § 417(a)(1)(A)(ii) allows the plan participant to revoke the waiver of QJSA payment at any time before payments begin. The spouse's consent is not required for the revocation, because it has the effect of increasing, not decreasing, the spouse's rights.

A Sixth Circuit case tackled some issues for QJSA waivers. The plan participant retired at 62, opting for a single life annuity. His wife, the plaintiff in the eventual litigation, waived the QJSA. The plan approved payment of benefits (monthly annuity checks) retroactive to his retirement date. He died after receiving only six checks. The plaintiff raised the issue that her signature had been forged on the waiver. The plan denied her benefit claim based on its determination that the waiver was valid. The Sixth Circuit ruled that the plan acted appropriately; the determination that the waiver was valid was not arbitrary or capricious. Under ERISA § 1055(c)(2)(A), the "applicable election period" for QJSA waivers is the

90-day period ending on the annuity starting date—the first date of the first period in which an annuity payment is due. The participant was an early retiree, so the choice of when to receive benefits rested entirely with him, not with the plan. He did not designate a specific start date, so the plan was justified in concluding that payments should be made as soon as possible. Therefore, the waiver was not untimely and should be given effect. [*Shields v. Reader's Digest Ass'n Inc. Retirement Plan*, 331 F.3d 536 (6th Cir. 2003)]

Regulations were proposed, under Reg. § 1.417(a)(3)-1 on October 7, 2002 [*see* 67 Fed. Reg. 62417], to revise and consolidate the required content of the information about the QJSA that must be given to participants to allow them to make a valid choice among alternate forms of benefit. The value of the other benefit forms can be disclosed as a percentage of the QJSA, a percentage of another form of annuity that is the normal distribution form under the plan, or in terms of present value. The relative value comparisons can be expressed in chart form.

This issue is most significant for defined benefit plans, because 401(k) plans usually don't provide QJSAs. However, if a defined contribution plan does offer a QJSA, it must disclose which optional forms of benefit are available, conditions of eligibility to receive each, and the financial effect of taking each one as compared to the QJSA.

For defined contribution plans, participants must be informed that purchasing contracts from an insurance company will provide annuity benefits. The descriptions of financial effects can be based on reasonable estimates of the yield of the annuity contracts that will be purchased, as long as participants are told they can request a detailed calculation of their individual benefits. Before the regulation was issued, only one request for a detailed calculation could be made; this limitation is removed by the proposal.

These Proposals were finalized, with some changes, in T.D. 9099. [4830-01-p RIN 1545-BA78, 68 Fed. Reg. 70141 (Dec. 17, 2003)] Under the Final Regulations, the description of the relative values of the QJSA and the optional benefit form must provide the participant with a meaningful comparison of their relative economic values; the participant must not be required to make calculations using interest or mortality assumptions to compare them. The plan must convert the benefit options under the alternative payment forms to a uniform format, taking into account life expectancies and the time value of money. Although employers are not required to disclose the plan's actuarial assumptions in this notice, participants must be given information about these assumptions on request. The description of the financial effects of an annuity form can be based on the plan's reasonable estimates of the amount that will be payable—but where estimates are used the notice must say that the figure is an estimate and that an exact calculation is available on request.

The Final Regulations permit a plan to use a uniform basis for comparison for both married and unmarried participants, as long as the benefit options are the same for both. To avoid excessive complexity, certain disclosures can be simplified. If the actuarial present value of all the forms is at least 95% of the actuarial present value of the QJSA, all the forms can be treated as approximately equal.

Delivery is adequate if the participant receives hand delivery, or if the notice is sent by first class mail to the participant's last known address. Posting the notice on a physical bulletin board is not adequate notice. The Final Regulation doesn't address electronic methods of giving notice, but further guidance is anticipated.

The IRS returned to the subject of relative value disclosure in 71 Fed. Reg. 14798 (Mar. 24, 2006). In general, the IRS will not penalize plans that make good faith efforts to disclose the relative value of benefits, but for lump sums and some other alternate forms of benefit, plans are required to be in compliance with the 2003 Final Regulations for annuity starting dates on or after October 1, 2004. [*See* Deloitte's Washington Bulletin, *IRS Issues Final Changes to Relative Value Disclosure Regulations,* <http://benefitslink.com/articles/washbull060403.html> (Apr. 3, 2006)]

[A] 2005 Proposed Regulations

In May of 2005, the IRS published Proposed Regulations systematizing the rules for several distribution issues that arise under I.R.C. §§ 415 and 417. [70 Fed. Reg. 31214 (May 31, 2005).] Generally speaking, the proposals apply to limitation years that begin on or after January 1, 2007. Employers are permitted to rely immediately on some of the new rules if they prefer not to defer implementation.

The IRS's last set of regulations on these topics was issued in 1981, so many statutory modifications must be taken into account.

The 2005 Proposed Regulations make it clear that the entire accrued benefit, vested or not, and including benefits under an annuity contract distributed to the participant, is counted toward the I.R.C. § 415(b) limit. The maximum permissible annual benefit under a defined benefit plan is the average of the participant's three highest years of compensation, and is also limited to $160,000 a year. Only compensation earned as an active participant in the plan is included, and compensation is not included if it is higher than the I.R.C. § 401(a)(17) limitation. Actuarial adjustments must be made to bring early (pre-age 62) or late (post-age 65) benefit commencements into line.

The 2005 proposal explains the methodology to be used when a participant has more than one annuity starting date under the plan (e.g., because the participant's account received transfers from another defined benefit plan). The procedure is necessary to make sure that a single amount is not counted twice against the plan limitations.

The proposal also simplifies the calculation that is performed to ensure that a benefit that is not paid as a straight life annuity is actuarially equivalent to a straight life annuity and makes it clear that if a benefit is partially paid as a QJSA and partially in another form (e.g., a lump sum) the survivor annuity paid to the surviving spouse under the QJSA is not subject to the I.R.C. § 415 limitations.

§ 12.06   POST-DEATH PAYMENTS

The terms of the plan, and the fact situation, determine whether payments must continue after the death of the plan participant. For instance, if the employee was unmarried and received a life annuity, or if the employee was married and the employee and spouse validly waived the QJSA in favor of a life annuity, the plan will have no post-death obligations. Usually, however, the plan will be required to make a single or ongoing distributions to a beneficiary designated by the employee, or named as beneficiary under the terms of the plan.

Internal Revenue Code § 401(a)(9)(B) provides that if an employee dies when an annuity or installment pension with a survivorship feature is in pay status, the plan continues distributions in the same manner, but to the beneficiary rather than the retiree. The general rule is that the plan has five years from the death of the employee to complete distribution of the decedent's entire interest.

The five-year rule does not apply if the decedent's interest is payable to a designated beneficiary in life annuity form, or in installments that do not extend past the beneficiary's life expectancy. In this situation, the plan must begin the distributions no later than December 31 of the year following the date of the employee's death.

Qualified plans are required to provide Qualified Preretirement Survivor Annuities (QPSAs) if a vested plan participant dies before benefits begin. [I.R.C. § 401(a)(11)] The QPSA for a defined benefit plan participant who was eligible to retire at the time of death must be at least as great as what the spouse would have received if the employee had retired with the QJSA on the day before the actual date of death.

In the case of a person who was not yet retirement-eligible on the date of death, the defined benefit plan must calculate the survivor annuity that would have been available if the employee had separated from service on the date he or she died, and survived until the plan's earliest retirement date. The QPSA must be at least equivalent to the QJSA that would have been payable if the employee spouse had died the day after retiring with a QJSA on the plan's earliest retirement date.

In a defined contribution plan, the QPSA must be actuarially equivalent to at least 50% of the nonforfeitable account balance as of the time of death.

The designated beneficiary can also be an irrevocable trust that is valid under state law and has identifiable beneficiaries. It's the responsibility of the employee who wants to take this option to provide the plan with a copy of the trust.

According to I.R.C. § 401(a)(9)(B), if an employee dies once payment of an annuity or installment pension has begun, the plan simply continues the distributions in the same manner—unless, of course, they are supposed to stop at the employee's death.

Plans are allowed to reduce pension benefits to fund the QPSA. Therefore, participants (with the consent of the spouse of a married participant) have the right to waive the QPSA in order to prevent this reduction in the pension amount.

The plan must notify participants of the right to waive the QPSA. The notice must be given in the period that starts on the first day of the plan year in which the participant reaches age 32 and ends with the close of the plan year before the plan year in which the participant reaches age 35. [I.R.C. § 417(a)(3)(B)]

The notice must disclose:

* The terms and conditions of the QPSA;
* The effect of waiving it;
* The spouse's right to invalidate the waiver by withholding consent;
* The participant's right to revoke the waiver and reinstate the QPSA.

The D.C. Circuit ruled, in mid-2003, that trustees for a union retirement fund correctly refused to pay the pension to the estate of a beneficiary who had disappeared more than 15 years earlier and was presumed dead. In 1982, a beneficiary receiving benefits as a surviving spouse disappeared. The trustees suspended the payments, stating that payments would resume if the beneficiary returned. Eventually a state court declared her dead. The administrator of her estate filed a claim for benefits, which was denied by the trustees on the grounds that there was no evidence that she was alive, and thus entitled to continued benefit accruals, after disappearing. The D.C. Circuit treated the date of death as a fact question, to be resolved by submission of evidence to the trustees; but there was no evidence one way or the other, to be submitted. It was proper for the trustees, designated by the plan as sole judges of the standard of proof for benefit claims, to deny the claim. [*Fuller v. AFL/CIO*, 328 F.3d 672 (D.C. Cir. 2003)]

According to the Eastern District of Michigan, posthumous QDROs are acceptable. The case arose when a Ford employee who left the company in 1989 became eligible to receive early retirement benefits starting in 2003. He was in default on his child support payments, and the state filed a $51,000 lien against his plan interest as a result. A QDRO was entered in 2001, entitling the ex-wife to 100% of his plan benefits. An amended QDRO was filed early in 2002—at which point the plan and the ex-wife became aware of the ex-employee's death several months earlier. The Ford plan took the position that the ex-employee's death terminated the ex-wife's benefit eligibility, but the Eastern District ruled in the ex-wife's favor, treating the state lien as a QDRO and also noting that the ex-wife had submitted a proposed QDRO in 1998, well before the ex-employee's death. [*Galenski v. Ford Motor Co. Pension Plan*, 421 F. Supp. 2d 1015 (E.D. Mich. 2006)]

The Ninth Circuit ruled that entering the code "ES" on a life insurance beneficiary designation to indicate the estate was not a valid designation because it did not specify a particular beneficiary. The decedent wrote "as indicated in my will" as the name of the beneficiary. The will named his first wife as beneficiary, but they divorced the next year. The beneficiary designation was signed soon after the divorce. At the time of his death, he was remarried, but had not changed either his will or the beneficiary designation form. The divorce revoked his will, so he died intestate. Initially, the benefits were awarded to his second wife, but when it was discovered that he had an out-of-wedlock son, the case was remanded to apportion the funds between the second wife and son. [*Metropolitan Life Ins. Co. v. Parker*, 436 F.3d 1109 (9th Cir. 2006)]

In another case, a plan participant named his wife as the beneficiary of the death benefit of his pension and of his employment-related life insurance. The couple later divorced. The wife waived her rights to these benefits, but the participant died with the previous beneficiary designation still intact. The benefits were paid to the ex-wife, and the decedent's estate sued to recover the benefits, citing the wife's waiver of benefit eligibility. The Michigan Court of Appeals upheld the waiver on the grounds that the divorce decree effectively waived the wife's rights in the plan. [*Moore v. Moore*, 266 Mich. App. 96, 700 N.W.2d 414 (Mich. App. 2005)] Likewise, the Eastern District of Kentucky awarded 401(k) benefits to a deceased participant's parents, because his beneficiary designation of his then-wife was revoked by their subsequent divorce. He did not have a new spouse or surviving children, so his estate, of which his parents were the beneficiaries, was the appropriate recipient. [*Dudley v. NiSource Corp. Servs. Co.*, No. 5:05-217-JMH, 2006 U.S. Dist. LEXIS 26395 (E.D. Ky. Apr. 18, 2006), discussed in Fred Schneyer, *Participant's Parents to Get 401(k) Proceeds*, PlanSponsor.com (Apr. 28, 2006)]

Late in 2005, the District Court for the District of Massachusetts awarded $208,000 in group life insurance to the parents of an employee who committed suicide. The employee was separated from his wife, although not legally divorced, and the employee had not designated a beneficiary. The plan called for payment to one or more of the surviving spouse, child, parent, or sibling of the employee. The decedent's wife alleged that this was a hierarchy, but the District Court interpreted the plan to permit benefits to any of those, with no required order. [*Forcier v. Forcier*, 406 F. Supp. 2d 132 (D. Mass. 2005)]

The Northern District of California ruled that a deceased participant's beneficiary designation form was invalid, even though the spouse signed a consent to make the children beneficiaries of the account. The form required married plan participants to obtain the signature of their spouses to name a beneficiary other than the spouse, but failed to satisfy ERISA's requirement that the spouse acknowledge the effect of the consent. The form was also invalid because it failed to explain the rights surrendered. Another problem was that the signature was neither witnessed by a plan representative nor notarized. [*Sun Microsystems Inc. v. Lema*, No. C 04-04968 JF, 2006 U.S. Dist. LEXIS 4176 (N.D. Cal. Feb. 2, 2006)]

§ 12.07 THE REQUIRED BEGINNING DATE

[A] Theory and Application

Congress' initial reasons for passing ERISA, and for allowing Individual Retirement Accounts (IRAs) revolved around providing current income for workers for the time period between retirement and their death. Not only was estate planning with qualified retirement benefits not considered important, it was not even considered a worthwhile objective—the benefits were supposed to be used up during the individual's lifetime. Therefore, distributions from qualified plans and IRAs were required to start no later than a Required Beginning Date (RBD). The RBD was defined as April 1 of the year after the year in which the individual reached age 70½. An excise tax penalty was imposed on the failure to make at least the Minimum Required Distribution (MRD) each year.

Over the years, theories in Congress and at the IRS have changed. Estate planning for benefits is now treated as a legitimate objective. Furthermore, although the RBD/MRD requirements remain in effect for IRAs, and for qualified plan participants who are corporate officers or directors, or who own 5% or more of the stock in the employer corporation, they have been abolished for rank-and-file employees. If plan participants choose to defer retirement and remain at work past age 70½, they will no longer suffer a tax penalty for doing so.

For plan years beginning on or after January 1, 1997, I.R.C. § 401(a)(9)(C) sets the RBD for a rank-and-file employee at the later of April 1 following the year in which the individual reached age 70½ or that person's actual retirement date. The plan must make actuarial adjustments to the pensions of persons who continue to work after age 70½.

The eventual pension must be at least the actuarial equivalent of the benefits payable as of the date the actuarial increase must begin, plus the actuarial equivalent of any additional benefits that accrue after the starting date, reduced by the actuarial equivalent of whatever retirement benefits are actually distributed after the annuity start date. Employees who stay at work after age 70½ can be given the option of suspending distributions from the plan until they actually retire.

[B] Excise Taxes

The basic tax rule is that amounts received by a plan participant from a plan are taxable income for that year. (Any after-tax contributions made by participants were not deductible when they were made, and will not be taxed again when they are withdrawn. Participants who made after-tax contributions are therefore allowed to calculate an exclusion ratio, so part of each distribution is tax-free to the extent that it can be traced back to past after-tax contributions.)

A 10% excise tax (over and above the normal income tax) is imposed on "premature" distributions. The general rule is that a distribution made before age 59½ is premature. Distributions under a QDRO are not subject to this excise tax. Nor is a distribution considered premature if it is made to a person who has reached age 55 and separated from service. Distributions are not subject to the 10% penalty if they are made after the participant's death, or to employees who are so totally disabled as to be unable to engage in any substantial gainful activity.

The premature distribution excise tax is imposed on lump sums, but not on distributions made over the life, lives, or joint life expectancies of the participant or the participant and one or more beneficiaries. Defined benefit plans are subject to additional rules on this topic. Finally, if a plan participant's unreimbursed medical expenses are high enough to be tax-deductible (over 7.5% of adjusted gross income), plan distributions are not considered premature, even if the participant does not actually use the distributions to pay the medical bills.

See also Coleman-Stephens v. Commissioner [T.C. Summ. Op. 2003-91 (2003)], holding that a plan participant who suffered from ongoing depression and was hospitalized twice in three years was "disabled" and therefore the premature distribution penalty did not apply to her withdrawals from the plan. (However, this opinion was issued under Code § 7463(b), which means that it cannot be reviewed by any other court, and cannot be cited as precedent, although it does give an indication of Tax Court thinking.)

Before 1996, plan participants could find themselves between a rock and a hard place. Not only was an excise tax penalty placed on premature withdrawals; a different penalty was imposed on excess lifetime withdrawals from a pension plan but also on excess accumulations of pension benefits within the estate. The SBJPA suspended the tax on excessive distributions for the period 1996–1999, but retained the tax on excessive accumulation in the estate. The Taxpayer Relief Act of 1997 permanently repealed both excise taxes, greatly increasing the financial and estate planning flexibility available to plan participants.

[C] 2001–2002 Rules

An IRS Proposed Regulation [66 Fed. Reg. 3928-3954 (Jan. 17, 2001)] covers required minimum distributions from qualified plans, IRAs, and I.R.C. § 403(b) and § 457 (government and nonprofit-organization) plans. The Proposal substantially simplifies earlier Proposed Regulations issued in 1987 under I.R.C. § 401(a)(9). The 2001 Proposal is effective for distributions for 2002 and subsequent calendar years. [*See* Announcement 2001-18, 2001-10 I.R.B. 791, for more guidance on timing issues]

The 1987 rules did not allow a participant who had designated a beneficiary before the Required Beginning Date (RBD) to change the designation after the RBD, even if there were sound planning reasons to make a change. Under the 1987 rules, unless the designated beneficiary was the employee's spouse, the balance remaining as of the employee's death would have to be distributed relatively quickly. Yet many financial plans favor "stretching out" the distribution, to provide income over a longer time while also reducing the amount of taxable income received in each year.

The 2001 proposal enacts a single Minimum Distribution Incidental Benefit (MDIB) table, in Treas. Reg. § 1.401(a)(9)-2, to be used to calculate the RMD. The table provides for distributions during the employee's life, ranging from 25.2 years (at age 70) to 1.8 years (at ages 115 and older!). The same table can be used whether the beneficiary is a natural person (the employee's spouse or otherwise), or an entity such as a spouse or charity. Under prior law, the balance would have to be distributed faster after death if the beneficiary was an entity, because entities do not have a life expectancy over which the balance can be distributed.

The MDIB table uses the same assumption in all cases: that the beneficiary is 10 years younger than the employee (no matter what their actual ages are). Distributions are made over the predicted life expectancy of a person 10 years younger than the employee. Even greater "stretch-out" is allowed if the beneficiary is the employee's spouse, and is actually more than 10 years younger than the employee, because in that case the calculation of the RMD can be based on the spouse's actual life expectancy. If the employee fails to designate a beneficiary, the RMD is calculated based on the employee's own life expectancy, reduced by one year every year.

With respect to post-death distributions, the 2001 Proposed Regulations allow a beneficiary to be designated even after the RBD, up to the end of the year following the year of the employee's death, in case the employee's executor wants to do post-mortem estate planning. Beneficiaries now have the right to cash out small account balances. If receiving the benefits is financially not advantageous to them, they can disclaim their status as beneficiaries.

The general rule for post-death distributions is that the benefits remaining when the employee dies must be distributed over the life expectancy of the designated beneficiary. The calculation is made in the year the employee dies. If more than one beneficiary is designated (for instance, two or more of the employee's children), then the beneficiary with the shortest life expectancy is treated as the designated beneficiary—whether the employee dies before or after the RBD. If the employee dies without designating a beneficiary, then distribution must be made to his or her intestate distributees, over a period of five years.

In May 2002, the proposals were finalized in substantially the proposed form. However, the final rule, Notice 2002-27, 2002-18 I.R.B. 814, makes it easier to distribute benefits to separate accounts with different beneficiaries, slightly simplifies the RMD calculation by eliminating some of the mathematical factors used in the calculation, and requiring the beneficiary of a decedent's account to be named by September 30 (rather than December 30) of the year of death. This last change was made to make it clear that distribution to the beneficiaries must start in the year of death.

[D] 2004 Final Rule

Guidance duly arrived in mid-2004, in T.D. 9130, RIN 1545-BA60, Final Regulations published at 69 Fed. Reg. 33288 (June 15, 2004) (*See also* 68 Fed. Reg. 68077 (Nov. 23, 2004) for technical corrections to T.D. 9130.). T.D. 9130 applies to the required minimum distributions from defined benefit plans, and also to annuity contracts distributed in satisfaction of defined contribution plan accounts. The IRS responded to public comments to make some modifications in the 2002 rules.

Under the 2002 rules, benefits could increase because of, e.g., cost of living increases and plan amendments. T.D. 9130 also allows the purchase of variable annuities for plan participants, and for regular increases in plan benefits under specified circumstances.

The Final Rule includes a table for determining whether a joint and survivor annuity with a person other than the participant's spouse satisfies the "incidental benefit" rule. Such an annuity fails the test if the percentage of payments to the non-spouse beneficiary is higher than the percentage given in the table (ranging from 100% for age differences under 10 years to 52% if the age difference is greater than 44 years).

To prevent abusive estate planning devices (e.g., payments extending over decades because a grandchild is chosen as a joint annuitant), the Final Rule forbids a joint and survivor annuity with a 100% survivor benefit if the beneficiary is more than 10 years younger than the employee. Additional adjustments are required if the employee starts to receive benefits before age 70 (because the earlier start means that more payments will be made).

The Final Rule allows changes in the form of distribution. For annuities with no life contingency, the recipient can change the form that future distributions will take at any time. When a person retires, or when the plan terminates, the form of distribution can be changed prospectively. An employee who marries can change the annuity to a joint and survivor annuity.

Code § 401(a)(9)(F) permits certain payments of an employee's accrued benefit to the employee's child to receive the same favorable treatment as payments to the employee's spouse. Under the Final Rule, such treatment is permitted for payments made until the child reaches majority (or dies, if he or she dies while still a minor)—as long as the payments are payable to the employee's surviving spouse when the child reaches majority or dies. The same rule applies to students under age 26 and disabled children of any age.

§ 12.08   DIVORCE-RELATED ORDERS

[A]   QDROs and QMCSOs

For many couples, one spouse's interest in a retirement plan is a major marital financial asset. In fact, it may be the only significant marital financial asset. Given our society's high divorce rate, plan administrators are often confronted with court orders incident to an employee's separation or divorce—or are faced with conflicting claims after the death of an employee who divorced, remarried, and eventually died without having changed the beneficiary designation from the first to the second spouse.

Although the general rule is that plan benefits cannot be anticipated or alienated, there is an important exception for family law orders that fit the definitions of Qualified Domestic Relations Orders (QDROs) or Qualified Medical Child Support Orders (QMCSOs). [On QMCSOs, *see* the HHS/DOL Final Rule on National Medical Child Support Notice, 65 Fed. Reg. 82128 (DOL) and 65 Fed. Reg. 72154 (HHS), and the Compliance Guide for Qualified Medical Child Support Orders (Aug. 13, 2003) <http://www.dol.gov/ebsa/publications/qmcso.html>], as discussed at § 18.16]

Technically speaking, welfare benefit plans are not required to have QDRO procedures, because the QDRO requirements appear in ERISA Title I, Part 2, which does not apply to welfare benefit plans. However, five of the Circuits (the Second, Fourth, Sixth, Seventh, and Tenth) have concluded (in cases about life insurance) that QDRO procedures are required because ERISA doesn't specially say that welfare benefit plans do not have to have QDRO procedures. (The issue for health plans is covered by the QMCSO procedure.)

Once the administrator determines that a court order has the status of a QDRO, payments can legitimately be made to the alternate payee: i.e., the separated or divorced ex-spouse of an employee.

A QDRO is a court order based on a state domestic relations law (including community property law) dealing with child support, alimony, or marital property rights. No court is allowed to use a QDRO to order a plan to make payments in any type or form not allowed by the plan documents. A QDRO cannot force a plan to pay benefits that have already been assigned to someone else under an earlier QDRO, or to increase the actuarial value of benefits to be paid. The Department of Labor's introduction to the subject of plan administration of QDROs can be found at <http://www.dol.gov/ebsa/faqs/faq_qdro.html>.

To be entitled to recognition by the plan, a QDRO must contain at least this much information:

- The recipient's right to plan benefits;
- The names and addresses of the parties;
- The amount or percentage of the plan benefit to be paid to the alternate payee named in the order;
- The time period or number of payments covered by the order;
- The plan(s) it applies to (the same employee might be covered by more than one plan).

Generally, the alternate payee does not receive distributions under the QDRO before the date the employee would be entitled to them. However, distributions can be made from any plan on the earliest date the participant could get the distribution after separation from service, or when the participant reaches age 50—whichever is later. If the plan is drafted to allow it, QDROs can require immediate distribution, or at a time that is not related to the age of the employee spouse.

For QDROs issued when the employee spouse is still working and has not retired, the payments are calculated based on the present value of the normal retirement benefits already accrued as of that time. Early retirement subsidies are not taken into account. The QDRO can provide for recalculation at the time of retirement, in case an early retirement subsidy is actually paid.

The question of who should get benefits under an ERISA welfare benefit plan is a question of federal law. Therefore, the Sixth Circuit says that ERISA preempts state-law claims that undue influence was exercised to get an employee to change his beneficiary designation. [*Tinsley v. General Motors*, 227 F.3d 700 (6th Cir. 2000)]

A marital dissolution order requiring the plan participant to name his children as beneficiaries of the plan was held by the Ninth Circuit not to be a QDRO. The court's rationale was that the dissolution agreement was not specific enough to be a QDRO: It did not require the plan to take action; did not assign the death benefits to the children; did not specify when payments were to begin or the amount, calculation or form of payment; and did not explain what would happen to the QPSA. The Retirement Equity Act permits termination of a QPSA only if the spouse consents to the designation of another beneficiary, and a QDRO can override the QPSA only by naming a former spouse as a beneficiary. [*Hamilton v. Washington State Plumbing & Pipefitting Industry Pension Plan*, 433 F.3d 1091 (9th Cir. 2006)]

An unpublished 2005 decision of the District of New Jersey says that a QDRO naming the employee's ex-wife as alternate payee was invalid. The divorce agreement, which satisfied the QDRO requirements, ordered payments of $232 a month once the husband started to receive monthly pension benefits. However, he continued working past NRA and died before retiring and before the pension was in pay status. The surviving spouse applied for benefits. The plan administrator denied the wife's benefit claim. She sued in state court, and was granted an amended QDRO naming her as surviving spouse for the QPSA and alternate payee. The plan still wouldn't pay her claim, so she sued in federal court, where summary judgment was granted for the plan on the grounds that the court order that purported to be a QDRO could not give the ex-wife rights in survivor benefits that did not exist at the time of the participant's death. The order in effect required the plan to increase the actuarial value of benefits, because it would have required the creation of a pre-retirement survivor annuity that was not in existence at the time of his death. The District of New Jersey distinguished the *Files* case, where language granting the ex-wife half of the pension created a separate interest in the pension to the ex-wife who could have enforced that right to a benefit before her ex-husband died, so the post-death order did not increase the actuarial value of the benefit. The District Court held that a plan administrator's review of a purported QDRO has to include not only the way the pension is divided during life, but what happens if the participant dies before receiving distributions and whether the alternate payee can affect the forms of distribution that the participant can elect. [*Sanzo v. NYSA-ILA Pension Trust Fund*, No. 04-300(WGB), 2005 U.S. Dist. LEXIS 37572 (D.N.J. Dec. 29, 2005) (unpublished); *Files v. Exxon Mobil Pension Plan*, 428 F.3d 478 (3d Cir. 2005)]

Under the January 2001 proposals, as implemented in 2002, the ex-spouse who is entitled to some or all of the benefits will be considered a spouse for distribution purposes, even if the QDRO does not make explicit reference to I.R.C. §§ 401(a)(11) and 417—and even if the employee has more than one ex-spouse. Distributions to the alternate payee named by the QDRO must begin no later than the employee's Required Beginning Date. However, the calculation will be based on the employee's life expectancy. If the ex-spouse is more than

10 years younger than the employee, the actual joint life expectancies of the employee and ex-spouse will be used in the calculations.

Although ERISA explicitly covers only QDROs dealing with pension plans, courts sometimes use a similar rationale to divide welfare benefits such as life insurance. [*See, e.g., Deaton v. Cross*, 184 F. Supp. 2d 441 (D. Md. 2002); *Seaman v. Johnson*, 184 F. Supp. 2d 642 (E.D. Mich. 2002)] In both these cases, the court held that the divorce-related court order should prevail over the beneficiary designation filed with the plan.

[B] QDRO Methodology

Under the "separate interest" method of distribution under a defined benefit plan, the alternate payee gets future payments based on his or her life expectancy, not that of the plan participant. [*See, e.g., In re Marriage of Shelstead*, 66 Cal. App. 4th 893 (1998)] The nonemployee wife was awarded a 50% community property interest in the employee husband's pension plan. The order said that, if the wife died before the husband, she would be able to designate a successor in interest to receive her community-property share. But the California Court of Appeals decided that, although this was a divorce-related order, it was not a QDRO because it did not settle the rights of an alternate payee, and she could leave her share to anyone, not just another acceptable alternate payee.

Under the "shared payment" method, the alternate payee gets a portion of each pension payment made to the plan participant, so both the participant and the alternate payee use the same timing schedule and form of annuity. The alternate payee gets to take advantage of any early retirement incentives elected by the participant. The enhanced benefit under an early retirement plan is actuarially reduced if the alternate payee is younger than the participant (this is often the case, especially if the participant is male and his ex-wife is younger than he is), but is not increased if the alternate payee is older than the participant.

In a defined contribution plan, the beneficiary is always named, usually at the time of plan enrollment, and remains the same until and unless the participant changes it. Defined contribution plans always use the separate interest method. A plan participant can make his or her subsequent spouse a named beneficiary, but an alternate payee who remarries does not have the right to choose a joint-and-survivor payment option with respect to the participant ex-spouse's pension. [*See* Darren J. Goodman, *Transferring the Alternate Payee's Retirement Benefits at Death: A Look at* Shelstead, Family Law News (Winter 1998), <http://library.findlaw.com/1999/Jul/1/126422.html>]

Under a defined benefit plan, unless the QDRO stipulates a preretirement death benefit for the ex-spouse, the ex-spouse will receive nothing if the participant spouse dies before the benefit starts. On the other hand, the effect of the death of the nonparticipant spouse before benefits begin is that the participant spouse will be entitled to 100% of the benefit.

See Kazel v. Kazel [No. 163, N.Y. Nov. 18, 2004]: a QDRO that amends an interest in the husband's pension plan does not automatically include the plan's pre-retirement death benefit. Provisions for the death benefit must be stated explicitly and separately. New York's Court of Appeals ruled that a divorce court's failure to consider the QPSA did not automatically entitle the participant's former wife to receive it.

According to the District Court for the District of Vermont, a valid QDRO can be entered retrospectively after the participant's death. (The plan participant died after a divorce decree awarded part of his 401(k) account to his ex-wife, and after a proposed QDRO was submitted to the plan, but before either court approval of the proposed order or a plan decision on its validity.) [*IBM Savings Plan v. Price*, No. 2:04-CV-187 (D. Vt. 2004), <http://nysd.uscourts.gov/courtweb/pdf/D02VTXC/04-08579>]

A valid QDRO gives the alternate payee the status of an ERISA "beneficiary." Sometimes the alternate payee gets even more protection, as a "participant." If the QDRO is issued when the employee spouse's pension is already in pay status, the shared payment method will be used. If the nonemployee spouse dies first, his or her share of the QJSA reverts to the surviving employee spouse. The alternate payee is just a beneficiary, and can only dispose of his or her interest in the plan by naming another alternate beneficiary as contingent alternate beneficiary in the QDRO.

But where the separate interest method is available (in defined contribution and 401(k) plans, or if the divorce occurs before benefits are in pay status), the alternate payee's status is more like that of a plan participant, because he or she can choose the form of pension payment. Some forms of payment (e.g., an annuity for a term certain) allow the payee to designate someone to receive unpaid benefits at the payee's death.

[C] The Administrator's Response

When a plan administrator receives a court order, the first step is to determine whether the order is entitled to QDRO status. However, once ERISA compliance is determined, the administrator must comply with the QDRO, without inquiring as to its acceptability under state law. An employee who opposes the terms of the QDRO has to litigate with the ex-spouse in state court; the plan administrator is not liable for complying with the QDRO. [*Blue v. UAL Corp.*, 160 F.3d 383 (7th Cir. 1998)]

If the administrator believes that a document described as a QDRO is a sham, or at least questionable, PWBA Advisory Opinion #99-13A [(Sept. 29, 1999) <http://www.dol.gov/ebsa/regs/AOs/ao1999-13a.html>] provides guidance. The administrator who requested the opinion received a series of 16 purported QDROs, many of them from the same lawyer. The documents gave the same address for the plan participant and the alternate payee, although they were supposed to be separated or divorced. The administrator was aware of a publication suggesting sham divorces as a means of accessing ESOP benefits during employment.

The advisory opinion says that administrators are "not free to ignore" information casting doubt on the validity of an order. If the administrator finds that evidence credible, the administrator must make a case-by-case determination of the validity of each order, "without inappropriately spending plan assets or inappropriately involving the plan in the state domestic relations proceeding."

The PWBA Advisory Opinion says that appropriate action could include informing the court of the potential invalidity of the order; intervening in a domestic relations proceeding; or even bringing suit. However, an administrator who can't get a response within a reasonable time from the agency that issued the order "may not independently determine that the order is not valid under state law." [PWBA Advisory Opinion #99-13A (Sept. 29, 1999) <http://www.dol.gov/pwba/programs/ori/advisory99/99-13a.htm> ERISA Opinion Letter 94-32A says that it is improper to charge either the participant or the alternate payee a fee for processing a QDRO.

This determination must be made within a reasonable time. The employee and the proposed alternate payee must be notified promptly that the order was received. The administrator must explain to them how the plan will determine the validity of the alleged QDRO. The funds in question must be segregated, and separately accounted for, until the determination has been made. There is an 18-month limit on keeping the funds in the segregated account. [See EBSA Advisory Opinion 2000-09A, (July 12, 2000) <http://www.dol.gov/ebsa/regs/AOs/ao2000-09a.html>] for a discussion of what to do when an alternate payee is named under a plan that limits beneficiary designations to spouses, minor children, and parents—but not former spouses]

EBSA's Advisory Opinion 2004-02A, dating from February 17, 2004, explains what to do when an administrator receives a DRO that changes the previous assignment of benefits, reducing the amount assigned to the alternate payee. EBSA's position is that a court can modify its previous order, with the modified order serving as a QDRO as long as it names the payee and the amount or percentage to be paid, and does not require the plan to make distributions in a form that the plan does not provide for. However, modified orders operate as QDROs only prospectively. EBSA says that there are no grounds for the plan to seek repayment from the alternate payee of amounts that were paid under the earlier QDRO that would not be payable under the modified order. [EBSA Advisory Opinion 2004-02A (Feb. 17, 2004) <http://www.dol.gov/ebsa/regs/aos/ao2004-02a.html>]

According to the Western District of Kentucky, a plan participant's ex-wife who was designated as the surviving spouse in a domestic relations order lost surviving-spouse status by failing to provide the plan with a signed copy of the order before the participant retired. The court did not accept the ex-wife's argument that the plan had constructive knowledge of the order. Without the signed DRO in the plan's files, the "surviving spouse" was the woman he was married to at the time of his death. [Singleton v. Singleton, 2003 WL 22658184 (W.D. Ky. 2003)]

The District Court for the District of Maine held that the decedent's agreement to name his children as beneficiaries of his qualified plan was not a QDRO. Therefore, it violated the anti-alienation rule and was not enforceable. The benefits went to his second wife, who had been designated as the sole beneficiary under the plan. [*McKay v. Estate of Harris*, 2004 U.S. Dist. LEXIS 2849 (D. Me. 2004)]

[D]   QDRO Case Law: *Egelhoff* and After

According to an EBSA Advisory Opinion 2001-06A [(June 1, 2001) <http://www.dol.gov/ebsa/regs/AOs/ao2001-06a.html>] an income-withholding notice issued by a welfare department or county child support agency can be treated as a "judgment, decree, or order" dealing with state family or domestic relations law. In the PWBA's view, ERISA does not absolutely insist that valid QDROs be issued by a court, as long as they relate to child support, enforce an order, and are issued by an agency with jurisdiction over child support matters.

The Supreme Court decided, in *Egelhoff v. Egelhoff* [532 U.S. 131 (2001)] that ERISA preempts a Washington State law that made all beneficiary designations (in life insurance as well as qualified plans) invalid when the employee or insured person divorced. The Supreme Court decided that the state law "relates to" ERISA plans, and therefore is preempted, because qualified plans can be regulated only by federal, and not state, law.

Other courts soon applied the *Egelhoff* decision. An ex-spouse tried to use California community property law to collect benefits under an employee benefit plan providing life insurance. The Ninth Circuit held, in *Metropolitan Life Insurance v. Buechler* [19 Fed. Appx. 678 (9th Cir. 2001)] that the disposition of insurance proceeds is a core ERISA concern, where community property laws are preempted. Therefore, the postdivorce designation of a new beneficiary governed.

The Texas Supreme Court refused to award pension benefits to an ex-wife who was still named as beneficiary in the plan's records, because she waived the benefits in the divorce settlement. In this reading, ERISA does not prevent plan administrators from looking beyond the plan documents. The Texas court considered the purpose of ERISA to be creating nationwide uniformity, and therefore applied a common-law rule under which waivers will be given legal effect as long as they are knowing, voluntary, and specific. [*Keen v. Weaver*, 2003 Tex. LEXIS 82 (Texas June 19, 2003)]

A divorcing couple expressly waived rights to each other's life insurance, including insurance under ERISA plans. The husband cited *Egelhoff* for the principle that ERISA preempts any such wavier, because the policy is part of a welfare benefit plan. However, the Michigan state court treated it as a waiver case, and not a preemption case, holding that ERISA does not preempt a knowing, voluntary, good-faith waiver of ERISA benefits made by a non-participant. [*Estate of Rowley v. MacInnes*, 260 Mich. App. 280 (Mich. App. 2004)]

The Western District of Wisconsin decided in mid-2002 that an employer-sponsored life insurance policy was an ERISA welfare benefit plan, and an order governing the distribution of policy proceeds after the employee's death was a valid QDRO; therefore, ERISA did not preempt state laws about distribution of insurance proceeds. The Western District required a trial to decide whether the court order or the decedent's beneficiary designation should govern. [*Principal Life Insurance Co. v. Fields*, 2002 U.S. Dist. LEXIS 22730 (W.D. Wis. July 29, 2002). *See also Barrs v. Lockheed Martin Corp.*, 287 F.3d 202 (1st Cir. 2002)]

Delaware had a slightly different law: one that said that property (here, a 401(k) account) could not be transferred before a divorce-related property settlement became final. The plan participant tried to remove his ex-spouse as beneficiary of his 401(k) plan and make his children the beneficiaries. The Family Court said that ERISA preempts the state law. But to remove incentives to violate state law, the court decided that the 401(k) account should be considered marital property for division as part of the divorce. [*Jones v. Jones*, 789 A.2d 598 (Del. Fam. Ct. 2001)]

ERISA doesn't rule out payments made on the basis of a QDRO approved after the plan participant's death, because the purpose of the statute is to protect ex-spouses and children (even if sometimes this will defeat the plan participant's preferred estate plan). [*Trustees of the Directors Guild of America-Producer Pension Benefit Plans v. Tise*, 234 F.3d 415 (9th Cir. 2000)].

In 2002, the Seventh Circuit interpreted *Egelhoff* to mean that state laws cannot be used to displace the designation of beneficiaries made under ERISA, because ERISA preempts the state law completely. [*Metropolitan Life Ins. Co. v. Johnson*, 297 F.3d 558 (7th Cir. 2002)] In light of this decision, the Seventh Circuit refused to allow the state-law remedy of imposing a constructive trust to be used to pay the benefits of a deceased, divorced employee's life insurance plan to his 14-year-old daughter (as required by the terms of his divorce agreement) rather than to his ex-wife (who was still named as the beneficiary in the plan documents). Although the divorce agreement included boilerplate waivers of interest in the other spouse's financial assets, the Seventh Circuit did not believe this was specific or explicit enough to disclaim the ex-wife's interest in the ex-husband's benefit plans. [*Melton v. Melton*, 324 F.3d 941 (7th Cir. 2003)]

The Tenth Circuit permitted the designation of an ex-spouse as beneficiary to be revoked by a state law that was enacted after the beneficiary designation, and after the annuitant had divorced and remarried. At the time of the divorce, state law said that an ex-spouse's rights as insurance beneficiary ended on divorce only if the divorce instruments specified that result. Later, state law was changed to create a presumption that divorce revokes property dispositions—unless the divorce instrument maintains the disposition. The Tenth Circuit applied the new law, on the theory that failure to change the beneficiary usually just reflects inertia, not a desire to make financial provision for the former spouse. [*Stillman v. TIAA-CREF*, 343 F.3d 1311 (10th Cir. 2003)]

A September 2002 Eighth Circuit case obligates the employer to pay plan benefits to a surviving spouse. In this case, the deceased ex-husband had been a participant in the defendant company's pension plan. The couple's divorce decree awarded the wife half of the "present retirement funds," to be set out in a QDRO, but no order dividing the retirement benefit was issued. Less than a year after the divorce, the ex-husband died, at age 48, and not remarried. The Chancery Court entered an order naming the ex-wife as alternate payee with respect to the benefits. The company said that the ex-wife was not entitled to benefits as a surviving spouse, because a QDRO cannot be entered posthumously. The Eighth Circuit disagreed, and did not review the plan's decision deferentially to see if there was an abuse of discretion, because the administrator interpreted the divorce decree rather than the terms of the plan. The Eighth Circuit ruled that, as long as the order issues within 18 months of the divorce decree, it could be valid even if the employee spouse has died in the interim. [*Hogan v. Raytheon Co.*, 302 F.3d 854 (8th Cir. 2002)]

An order was treated as an enforceable QDRO even though the surviving spouse submitted it long after the divorce in a 2003 case from the District of New Jersey. The decedent had been a participant in a defined benefit plan. Two years after his employment terminated, he divorced. He died eight years after the divorce. The surviving ex-spouse gave the plan administrator a copy of the divorce decree and a property settlement from the time of the divorce, assigning her 50% of the employee spouse's pension.

The plan administrator refused to pay, on the grounds that the order was not a valid QDRO. The administrator argued that not only was it untimely, but it failed to include vital information such as the type of benefit involved, the amount or percentage of the benefit to be paid, how to determine the benefit, and the time period for making the payment. The District Court for the District of New Jersey did not accept these arguments, holding that the order was a valid and enforceable QDRO despite the irregularities. [*Smith v. Estate of Smith*, 248 F. Supp. 2d 348 (D.N.J. 2003)]

In yet another case involving post-death distribution of benefits, the parties to a divorce agreed that their settlement would include four payments. Two of the payments were secured by the employee spouse's 401(k) plan interest. There was no QDRO. Before the due date of the first secured payment, the plan participant remarried, named the new spouse as beneficiary of the 401(k) plan, and died. A month after his death, the entire 401(k) balance was distributed to his second wife. Two months after the participant's death, the ex-wife's divorce lawyer submitted the divorce decree to the plan as security. The plan denied the ex-wife's claim for payment on the grounds that the participant's interest in the 401(k) plan did not operate effectively as security for the payment.

The decedent's ex-wife sued the plan, the plan administrator, and the plan sponsor to have the decree enforced as a QDRO, and also for breach of fiduciary duty. These claims were denied. The Third Circuit ruled that the so-called security interest was not a benefit under the plan that could be assigned by a QDRO. Nor did the plan have notice of the divorce decree before the participant's death. Submitting the decree did not create a fiduciary duty, because by the time it was submitted, the plan had already distributed the benefits (to the second wife) in accordance with the information it possessed at that time. [*Winters v. Kutrip*, 47 Fed. App. 143 (3d Cir. 2002)]

A defined benefit plan began making payments of survivor benefits to the plan participant's third wife, who he was married to at the time of his death. His first wife, who was legally separated but never divorced from the participant, claimed entitlement to the benefit (although she had remarried). The participant died in Texas; under Texas law, the third wife was entitled to be treated as his spouse because although her marriage was invalid, she entered into it in good faith. The first wife accepted the benefits of a divorce decree (by remarrying) and therefore was not allowed to challenge the validity of her "divorce." [*Central States Pension Fund v. Gray*, 2003 U.S. Dist. LEXIS 18282 (N.D. Ill. Oct. 8, 2003)]

When a couple divorced, a QDRO was issued relating to the husband's pension plan. However, at that time the parties did not realize that he was covered by two pension plans rather than one. He died before retirement age, without remarrying. A lump-sum payment was made to the ex-wife on the basis of the QDRO. She inquired because it was smaller than she expected, and discovered the existence of the second pension plan. Even though the two pension plans had merged into a single plan, the plan administrator refused to make any distribution from the second plan to the employee's ex-wife. The ex-wife went back to state court and got a retroactive order, dating back to before the ex-husband's death, giving her a share in the second pension plan. The plan administrator refused to treat this order as a QDRO, on the grounds that QDROs must be given to the plan before the participant's death. The Tenth Circuit, however, did not find that the language of ERISA imposes any such requirement. The Tenth Circuit also held that the order was valid because it did not require the plan to pay additional benefits, or benefits in forms that would otherwise be unavailable. [*Patton v. Denver Post Corp.*, 326 F.3d 1148 (10th Cir. 2003)] However, the Third Circuit did say in 1999 that a beneficiary's entitlement is established on the day the plan participant dies, which rules out retroactive orders, even if they are backdated. [*Samaroo v. Samaroo*, 193 F.3d 185 (3d Cir. 1999)]

During the era of "New Economy" prosperity, divorcing couples often fought over stock options and how to divide the future appreciation in the couple's stock portfolio. Under current conditions, disposal of unwanted underwater stock options and apportionment of stock losses are the significant issues—especially if the QDRO relates to a plan in which the participants can direct investments, and the market drops after the QDRO is issued.

The message of the Supreme Court's 1997 ruling in *Boggs v. Boggs*, 520 U.S. 833 (1997) is that, although QDROs are saved from ERISA preemption, other domestic relations orders issued by state courts are preempted. If a plan complies with an order that is not a QDRO, it is guilty of improper alienation of plan benefits, and may lose its status as a qualified plan. The decision about whether a QDRO is valid is made by the plan administrator; courts defer to the decision as long as it is reasonable, even if the judge might have reached a different conclusion based on the same facts. [*Fox v. Fox*, 167 F.3d 880 (4th Cir. 1999); *Feder v. Paul Revere Life*

Ins. Co., 228 F.3d 518 (4th Cir. 2000)] An early 2003 case holds that each spouse has an equal share of risk of loss in the value of retirement plan assets when a QDRO is awarded. In this case most of the couple's assets consisted of stock. The valuation took into account the two-month period from the date the employer segregated the plan assets for the wife to the date she was permitted to withdraw the assets. The court required the valuation of the falling stock to be adjusted, so the wife would not shoulder the entire loss herself, under the court's authority to interpret a document to carry out the intention of the parties. [*Duran v. Duran*, 2003 S.D. 15, 657 N.W.2d 692 (2003)]

ERISA preempts state "slayer statutes" (denying financial benefit to anyone who killed the plan participant, insured, etc.). Therefore, federal and not state law determines the proper beneficiary of a life insurance policyholder who was murdered by her husband. The policy was part of an employee benefit plan, so the Ohio Court of Appeals ruled that the slayer statute, like the law struck down by *Egelhoff*, interfered with ERISA's goal of uniform nationwide rules. [*Ahmed v. Ahmed*, 73 LW 1240 (Oh. App. Sept. 24, 2004)]

A bankruptcy debtor's undistributed interest in the former spouse's qualified retirement plan, obtained under a QDRO, is exempt in the debtor's bankruptcy proceedings and does not become part of his bankruptcy estate. (In other words, the QDRO entitled the husband to a lump sum from his ex-wife's retirement plan, but he filed for bankruptcy protection before the lump sum was distributed to him.) At the commencement of his bankruptcy case, the funds had not been received, so the money qualified for the bankruptcy exclusion of interests in plans or trusts that have enforceable restrictions under applicable non-bankruptcy law: in this case, ERISA's anti-alienation provisions. [*In re Nelson*, 322 F.3d 541 (8th Cir. 2003)]

Matters were simpler in a 2004 Eleventh Circuit case, holding that the will of a life insurance plan participant could be used to change the beneficiary designation, even though the participant failed to file a change of benefit form with the employer. ERISA preemption was not an issue because no state law was invoked that might have been preempted by the federal statute. In this interpretation, plans can allow multiple methods of changing the designated beneficiary. [*Liberty Life Assurance Co. of Boston v. Kennedy*, 358 F.3d 1295 (11th Cir. 2004)]

The statute of limitations for breach of fiduciary duty claims is the earlier of six years from the last action constituting the breach, or three years of actual knowledge of the breach. Therefore, a participant's 2005 suit was time barred. He knew in 1990 that a QDRO awarded part of his pension to his ex-wife, and that payments began in 1991, so it was too late to charge that the payments breached fiduciary duty. [*Angell v. John Hancock Life Ins. Co.*, 421 F. Supp. 2d 1168 (E.D. Mo. 2006)]

§ 12.09   REDUCTION OF BENEFIT FORMS

Qualified plans must always offer payments in the form of QJSAs and QPSAs. What if a plan originally adopts additional, optional forms of benefit payments, then later finds that some of them are unpopular or hard to administer? For years beginning after December 31, 2001, as a result of EGTRRA, I.R.C. § 411(d)(6) and ERISA § 204(g) have been amended to make it easier for defined contribution plans to cut back on the number of benefit options that they offer, especially in connection with plan mergers and other transitions.

A defined contribution plan will not be penalized for reducing participants' accrued benefits if the plan adopts amendments that reduce the number of benefit options—provided that the participant is always entitled to get a single-sum distribution that is based on at least as high a proportion of his or her account as the form of benefit that is being eliminated under the plan amendment. EGTRRA obligates the IRS to issue new regulations no later than December 31, 2003, to this effect, applying to plan years beginning after December 31, 2003 (or earlier, if the IRS so specifies).

On a related issue—Final Regulations issued in April 2003 to implement the Code § 4970F/ERISA § 204(h) rules about significant reduction in the rate of future benefit accrual and reduction in early retirement benefits and subsidies— see T.D. 9052, RIN 1545-BA08, 2003-19 I.R.B. 879.

Similar relief was proposed for defined benefit plans in 69 Fed. Reg. 13769 (Mar. 24, 2004). Redundant optional forms of benefit can be eliminated, as long as another form in the same "family" remains available (the proposal defines six families of optional benefit forms), and as long as the "core" options remain available. A plan amendment changing the availability of benefit forms cannot be effective for any distribution with an annuity start date within 90 days after adoption of the amendment.

The core options that must be preserved are the straight life annuity, the 75% joint and survivor annuity, life and 10-year certain annuity, and the most valuable option the plan provides for participants with a short life expectancy. As a general rule, lump sum payouts cannot be eliminated by making use of this proposal, and plan amendments eliminating non-core options do not apply to start dates within four years after adoption of the amendment. The proposal imposes additional requirements to protect participants when early retirement benefits and subsidies are altered.

T.D. 9176, 4830-01-p, RIN 1545-BC35, 2005-10 I.R.B. 661, is a Final Regulation on elimination of forms of distribution from defined contribution plans. It finalizes, with some revisions, the proposals published at 68 Fed. Reg. 40581 (July 8, 2003). It is no longer necessary for plans to give 90-days notice of plan amendments that are otherwise acceptable under I.R.C. § 411(d)(6)(E) as enacted by EGTRRA. However, the plan amendment can apply only to distributions whose annuity starting date is later than the adoption of the amendment, not to distributions already commenced.

Regulations were proposed in 2005 under § 411(d)(6), covering the way that the anti-cutback rules work with the nonforfeitability requirements under § 411(a), addressing questions such as how to apply the utilization test and how the rules on permitted forfeitures interact. The proposal reflects the *Central Laborers Pension Fund v. Heinz* decision, 541 U.S. 739 (2004), and sets out a new utilization test that can be used to reduce or eliminate certain benefit forms. *Heinz* holds that

ERISA § 204(g) forbids a plan to increase the categories of postretirement employ-ment that require the suspension of payment of early retirement benefits that have already accrued. [Prop. Regs., REG-156518-04, R.I.N. 1545-BE10, 2005-38 I.R.B. 582; *see also* T.D. 9219, 2005-38 I.R.B. 538]

The IRS announced in Rev. Proc. 2005-23, 2005-18 I.R.B. 991, that it will not retroactively disqualify a plan solely because of a plan amendment before June 7, 2004, that expanded the criteria for suspending benefits—as long as the plan adopts a reforming amendment. The Proposed Regulations state that a plan amendment that decreases accrued benefits or imposes greater restrictions on the right to benefits violates § 411(d)(6), even if the restriction or condition is otherwise acceptable under the § 411(a) vesting rules. But a plan amendment is permitted to the extent that it applies to benefits that accrue after the date of the amendment. Rev. Proc. 2005-76, 2005-50 I.R.B. 1139, provides extensions for time periods to take corrective action to satisfy *Heinz.*

The Second Circuit ruled that Xerox's method of offsetting a rehired em-ployee's pension benefits by prior plan distributions violated the anti-cutback rule. The "phantom account" offset (the rehired employee's pension was reduced by the plan distribution amount he had already received) was not added to the plan until a 1998 amendment, and participants were not properly notified at that point. The court ruled that a plan amendment does not occur until there has been proper notice; merely changing the operation of the plan is not enough. [*Frommert v. Conkright*, 433 F.3d 254 (2d Cir. 2006)]

§ 12.10   ROLLOVERS

Because of termination of employment, or termination of a plan itself, a person of working age may become entitled to a plan distribution. If he or she does not need the funds immediately, and would encounter an unwelcome income tax liability, one solution is to "roll over" the funds by placing them into another qualified plan or an IRA within 60 days.

The funds that are rolled over are not available to be spent by the plan participant, and therefore the participant is not taxed.

Tip: Although employees have a right to roll over these funds, the qualified plan that is the intended recipient does not have an obligation to accept rollovers. So it makes sense for the distributing plan to require employees to submit a statement that the potential recipient is not only qualified to take rollover contributions, but is willing to do so. The recipient plan is allowed to impose conditions, such as the form in which it will accept rollovers and the minimum amount it will accept as a rollover. The recipient plan is also entitled to set its own distribution rules and does not have to follow the rules of the original plan.

A direct rollover is considered a distribution, not a transfer of assets. [Treas. Reg. § 1.401(a)(31)-1] Therefore, the participant and spouse may have to sign a waiver because plan benefits are not being paid in QJSA form.

Rollovers can be carried out either by the plan administrator of the first plan sending a check or wire transfer to the trustee or custodian of the transferee plan, or by giving the participant a check payable to the IRA, plan trustee, or custodian.

A distribution to a spouse, or a QDRO distribution to an ex-spouse, can also be rolled over, but only to an IRA, not to a qualified plan.

EGTRRA increased the number of circumstances in which funds can be rolled over between plans. One result is that the notice given to employees about their rollover rights became obsolete. The IRS therefore drafted a new version of the Safe Harbor Explanation. [Notice 2002-3, 2002-2 I.R.B. 289] It is permissible to adapt the safe harbor notice by leaving out portions that do not apply to the plan.

The Notice advises, "even if a plan accepts rollovers, it might not accept rollovers of certain types of distributions, such as after-tax amounts. If this is the case, and your distribution includes after-tax amounts, you may wish instead to roll your distribution over to a traditional IRA or split your rollover amount between the employer plan in which you will participate and a traditional IRA."

The notice must explain:

- The rules for transferring a distribution to another qualified plan;
- The requirement for withholding income tax on amounts that are eligible for rollover but are not rolled over;
- The obligation to make a rollover within 60 days of receiving the funds;
- Any applicable information about early withdrawal penalties, hardship withdrawals, withdrawals to buy a house or pay medical or education expenses, and distributions of the employer's own securities.

Rev. Rul. 2004-12 [2004-7 I.R.B. 478] provides that eligible retirement plans that separately account for amounts attributable to rollover contributions can permit distribution of amounts attributable to a rollover whenever the participant requests. (If the plan requires spousal consent for distributions, it will be required in this situation too.) When funds are transferred from one of an employer's plans to another plan maintained by the same employer but of a different type (e.g., from a money-purchase plan to a profit-sharing plan), the assets remain subject to the rules for the transferor plan, unless there is separate accounting for the transferred assets and their income.

If a plan provides for cash out of benefits that do not exceed $5,000 (remember, it is illegal to impose a mandatory cash out if the plan balance is greater than $5,000), EGTRRA requires the plan to make a direct rollover the default distribution method for cash outs that fall between $1,000 and $5,000. [*See* I.R.C. § 401(a)(31)(B) and Prop. Regs. at 69 Fed. Reg. 9900 (Mar. 2, 2004)]

Also see I.R.C. § 411(a)(11)(D), which was added by EGTRRA, providing that when determining whether someone's balance is low enough to be subject to involuntary cash out, rollover contributions and interest on rollover contributions don't have to be included in the calculation. The Job Creation and Worker Assistance Act of 2002 [H.R. 3090, Pub. L. No. 107-147] made technical corrections to make it easier for the employer to disregard rollovers in cash out calculations. *See* Notice 2005-5, 2005-3 I.R.B. 337, and 69 Fed. Reg. 58017 (Sept. 28, 2004), as discussed at § 12.02.

§ 12.11   WITHHOLDING

A designated distribution is any amount of $200 or more that the participant could roll over, but chooses not to. Under I.R.C. §§ 401(a)(3) and 3405(c), plan administrators have to withhold a mandatory 20% of any designated distribution.

All or part of an employee's balance in a qualified plan is eligible for rollover, except:

- A series of substantially equal periodic payments, made at the rate of at least one payment a year, over the life of the employee or the joint lives of the employee and designated beneficiary;
- Payments made for a term of at least ten years [*See* I.R.C. § 402(c)(4)];
- The RMDs under I.R.C. § 401(a)(8) for officers, directors, and 5% stockholders.

In the case of a partial rollover, withholding applies only to the part that the employee withdraws from the plan, not the part that is rolled over.

For amounts that are neither annuities nor eligible rollover distributions, optional withholding can be done at a rate of 10%. The employee can direct the plan not to withhold. During the six months immediately preceding the first payment, and at least once a year once benefits are in pay status, the plan must notify participants of their right to make, renew, or revoke a withholding election. The employer can either include the withheld amounts in each quarterly Form 941 filing, or use Form 941E to report withholding.

The plan administrator is responsible for withholding unless the administrator directs that the insurer or other payer of benefits perform this task. [Treas. Reg. § 31.3405(c)-1]

Whenever designated distributions (i.e., those eligible for withholding) are made, the employer and plan administrator become responsible for making returns and reports to the IRS, participants, and beneficiaries.

A penalty of $25 per day is imposed by I.R.C. § 6047(d), up to a maximum of $15,000, for failure to meet this requirement, although the penalty can be waived if the plan has a good excuse for noncompliance. [*See* I.R.C. § 6047(b) for the required records; under § 6704(b), record-keeping violations can be penalized by up to $50 per failure per year, up to a maximum of $50,000 per year]

§12.12   PLAN LOANS AS DEEMED DISTRIBUTIONS

Code § 72(p) sets out the rules under which plan loans that fail to conform to the requirements will be treated as taxable distributions from the plan, rather than as tax-neutral loans. Regulations on this issue were proposed in 2000 and finalized at the end of 2002. [67 Fed. Reg. 71821 (Dec. 3, 2002)] The Final Regulations apply to loans, assignments, and pledges made on or after January 1, 2004 (although plans can adopt the rules earlier). An exemption is available for loans made under an insurance contract that was in effect on December 31, 2003, that is obligated to offer loans to unsecured contract holders.

A loan will not be treated as a deemed distribution if the plan suspends loan repayment when the borrower is on leave of absence for active military service, even if the leave lasts more than a year, as long as repayments resume when the borrower returns from military service, and repayment is complete by the normal term plus the term of military service. Before these regulations were finalized, the Proposed Regulation imposed a limit of only two loans per plan participant; additional loans would be treated as deemed distributions. The Final Regulations remove the two-loan limit, and allow credit card loans to be secured by amounts in a participant's account.

In a 2004 Tax Court case, a plan participant received a plan loan in June, 2000. In that month, he was transferred to another division within the employer company. Payments were not deducted from his paychecks. At the end of the year, the loan was declared in default (because there hadn't been any payments). A Form 1099-R was issued, treating the entire loan as a table distribution (Code § 72(p)). The plan participant did not include the loan balance in taxable income, so the IRS issued a Notice of Deficiency and imposed the 10% early-distribution penalty under § 72(t). The participant claimed that he never received any notices (and offered evidence that the plan sent at least one of them to an incorrect address). However, the Tax Court ruled against the taxpayer, holding that he must have been aware that he was not making loan payments. Therefore, a deemed distribution occurred, and there was no reason to remit the penalty. Furthermore, under § 7453(b), no other court could review the decision. Nor can the decision be cited as a precedent; it's discussed here for an indication of Tax Court thinking. [*Leonard v. Commissioner*, T.C. Summary Opinion 2004-11 (2004)]

Tip: If a plan loan is made to a party in interest, *see* Rev. Rul. 2002-43, 2002-28 I.R.B. 85, for an explanation of the calculation of the prohibited transaction excise tax, including situations in which the loan is outstanding for more than one year so multiple prohibited transactions occur. Also note that § 402 of the Sarbanes-Oxley Act [Pub. L. No. 107-204] forbids publicly traded corporations to make loans to their officers and directors. Because this modifies the existing ERISA rule that plans must make loans available to all participants on equal terms, some fiduciaries were worried that they might be charged with violating this provision if they refused plan loans to directors and officers. [*See* DOL Field Assistance Bulletin 2003-1 (Apr. 15, 2003) <http//www.dol.gov/ebsa/regs/fab_2003_1.html> for an explanation that denying a loan that violates Sarbanes-Oxley is not a violation of ERISA § 408(b)(1)'s requirement of loan availability to all participants]

CHAPTER **13**

PROCESSING AND REVIEWING CLAIMS AND APPEALS

§ 13.01   INTRODUCTION

All pension and welfare benefit plans that are subject to ERISA Title I are required to maintain a "reasonable claims procedure." An appropriate claims procedure is one that is described in the SPD: does not place undue restrictions or inhibitions on the processing of claims, and satisfies the relevant regulations about filing claims, reviewing submitted claims, and informing participants when a claim is denied. [DOL Reg. § 2560.503]

At the very least, the procedure must give claimants (or their authorized representatives) the right to apply to the plan for review, *see* the pertinent documents, and submit written comments and issues for resolution.

The plan must give a specific reason if it denies a claim. Claimants must be referred to the relevant plan provision. They must be given information about how to appeal the denial. [*See* § 13.03, below, for further discussion of the EBSA Final Rule adopted in November 2000]

Research by Towers Perrin shows that claims administration is failing to meet quality goals. The industry standard for paying out claims in error is supposed to be limited to 1% or less, whereas in both 2002 and 2003, erroneous payments were more than three times as high as the goal. The quality benchmark is that 3% or fewer of claims should have errors, but in 2002, 6.3% of claims had financial errors and 2.5% had non-financial errors. In 2003, the percentages were 6.6% and 1.9%, respectively. One reason for financial errors is that health plans are frequently amended. Claims administrators look for more efficient ways to process claims; however, sometimes the constant pace of change means that things "fall between the cracks." The more standardized the system, the more items get kicked out by the system to be hand processed—which leads to errors and omissions. [Vanessa Fuhrmans, *Oops!* Wall Street Journal, Jan. 24, 2005, at p. R4]

§ 13.02   THIRD-PARTY ADMINISTRATORS (TPAs)

[A]   Use and Benefits of TPAs

About two-thirds of covered workers in the United States get their benefits from plans that use some degree of third-party administration instead of handling all plan administration in house.

A TPA is an outsourcing firm that handles administrative tasks. It could be a consulting firm or a broad-based benefits administration firm. There are no federal licensing rules for TPAs, although some states impose their own requirements.

If the plan has unexpectedly high claims, TPAs usually provide stop-loss protection with back-up insurance that benefits the plan itself (rather than the employees with high expenses). Having a stop-loss plan doesn't turn a self-insured plan into an insured plan for ERISA purposes.

[B] TPA Case Law

A plan sued its TPA for making an improper payment. Benefits were paid to a plan participant who was badly hurt in an automobile accident while he was driving under the influence of alcohol (however, no criminal charges were brought against him). The plan excluded coverage of injuries occurring in the course of illegal acts, including DWI. The plan had stop-loss coverage, but the stop-loss insurer refused to pay because the injured person's blood alcohol level had been three times the legal limit. The plan sued the TPA for breach of contract and breach of fiduciary duty (for making the improper payments), and also sued to make the stop-loss carrier pay if the TPA did not.

The TPA said that the illegal-acts provision was ambiguous, because it was not clear whether a conviction was required. The Eastern District of Arkansas disagreed. [*SGI/Argis Employee Benefit Trust Plan v. The Canada Life Assurance Co.,* 151 F. Supp. 2d 1044 (E.D. Ark. 2001)] DWI is illegal whether or not there is a conviction. The court held that the stop-loss insurer was not required to reimburse the plan for the payment made by the TPA, but allowed the case to continue to determine whether the payment was in fact improper.

A TPA can be considered an ERISA fiduciary as long as it satisfies the statutory requirement of holding "any authority or control," even if it does not have discretionary control over the assets of the health plan it administers. The Sixth Circuit held that a TPA's authority to write checks on the plan's account (which continued to be exercised to pay the TPA's fees even after the contract with the plan sponsor ended) provided the necessary degree of authority or control to impose liability after the sponsor company went bankrupt and many employees had unpaid medical bills. [*Briscoe v. Fine*, 444 F.3d 478 (6th Cir. 2006)]

The Southern District of New York ruled that TPAs and fiduciaries are entitled under ERISA to apply for attorneys' fees and costs after a settlement. ERISA § 410(a) (ban on indemnification of fiduciaries) prevents a fiduciary who has been found guilty of breach from recouping expenses from the plan, but indemnification is acceptable if the fiduciary wins the case and is vindicated. The Southern District held that barring indemnification from the plan after a settlement provides excessive relief for the plaintiff. [*Martinez v. Barasch*, 2006 U.S. Dist. LEXIS 6914 (S.D.N.Y. 2006)]

§ 13.03 HEALTH PLAN CLAIMS

The Department of Labor's Pension and Welfare Benefits Agency (PWBA; later renamed EBSA) published a wide-ranging Final Rule on claims procedures for health and disability plans, amending 29 C.F.R. § 2560.503-1. [*See* 65 Fed. Reg. 70246-70271 (Nov. 21, 2000); 66 Fed. Reg. 35887 (July 9, 2001)]

The Final Rule applies to ERISA health and disability plans, dental and vision plans, and health Flexible Spending Accounts, but not to plans offering long-term care benefits. The Final Rule requires plans to speed up decision making and appeals, especially in situations where an employee files a claim for urgent care.

The Final Rule draws a distinction between preservice claims (advance approval of health care services) and postservice claims (where medical care has already been provided). The distinction is made because postservice claims are much less urgent. The employee has already been treated, so the question becomes who will pay the bill, not whether potentially necessary care will be available or not.

Under the Final Rule, a plan must make a decision within 15 days on ordinary preservice claims, and within 72 hours for urgent care claims. (The plan is bound by the treating physician's characterization of a claim as urgent.) Decisions on postservice claims can wait for 30 days. For adjudicating pre- or postservice claims (but not urgent claims), the plan can get one extension of time of up to 15 days. If a defective claim is filed (for instance, some of the information fields have been left blank), the plan must notify the claimant and can't reject the claim because of procedural defects.

In comparison, before the Final Rule, the plan gave employees 60 days to appeal; the Final Rule not only gives them 180 days to appeal, but expands their right to sue based on claims denials.

For "concurrent care decisions" about continued reimbursement for treatment that has already started, the plan participant must be given a right to request review before the plan terminates or even reduces the benefits. Employees must be given enough advance notice to use the appeal rights under the plan. If the employee's treating physician considers the request to extend benefits to be urgent, then the plan must resolve the dispute within 24 hours.

The Final Rule also increases the amount of disclosure the employer must provide. Employees are now entitled to a detailed explanation of the plan's claims procedures and why a claim has been denied. Internal protocols used to make decisions must be disclosed. Plans must also have a mechanism for making sure that claims are decided uniformly by the different decision makers.

Plans are not allowed to impose any fees or costs for appealing a denial. The reviewer cannot be either the person who made the initial denial or someone who works for that person. Whenever there is an issue of medical judgment, such as when treatment is necessary, the plan must consult appropriate health care professionals. The reviewer must examine the claim de novo (from the beginning), not just to see if the initial decision involved an abuse of discretion. The employee is allowed to introduce new facts that they did not provide earlier—even if these facts would not be admissible as evidence in a suit.

Plans are entitled to two options. They can have either a single level of review of denied claims, or two sequential levels of review (like a trial court and an appeals court). But plans that impose a second level of review don't get any additional time. Both levels of review must be completed within the normal time frame.

Health plans are allowed to include an arbitration requirement as part of the process. Employees are entitled to full disclosure of how the arbitrators are chosen and how the procedure works. The claimant must agree to arbitration, and can't be compelled to arbitrate unwillingly. Arbitration can only be used as an intermediate step after the plan's own internal appeals procedure has been completed.

The Employee Benefits Security Administration has summed up the various queries it has received about the claims standards in a Frequently Asked Questions page at <http://www.dol.gov/ebsa/faqs/main.html>.

The FAQ clarifies that the regulation only applies to coverage determinations that are part of a claim for benefits; a question about eligibility that does not also apply for benefits accordingly is not covered. However, if a plan requires "pre-service" claims (e.g., requests for preauthorization) to be submitted, then it "is not entirely free" to ignore inquiries (especially from an attending physician, and especially if specific medical conditions and specific treatments are mentioned) that might involve preservice claims, even if the procedure is not fully followed.

The claims standards apply to dental benefits and prescription drug benefit programs, whether they are a stand-alone plan or part of an EGHP. However, contract disputes between health care providers and insurers or managed care organizations are not covered by the requirements unless the dispute affects claimants' rights to benefits.

The regulation sets up time frames for making claims decisions—but does not govern the timing for actual payment of benefits. However, failure to make payments within a reasonable time may trigger ERISA fiduciary liability issues.

If a claimant authorizes someone else to act as a representative, then the plan should provide information and notifications directly to the authorized representative—although the plan can legitimately communicate with both the claimant and the authorized representative.

The FAQ says that the time for making an initial claims determination starts when the claim is filed under the plan's reasonable filing procedures—even if it is not a "clean claim" (one that contains all the necessary information). The plan may have to make a decision even before certain information (such as "coordination of benefit" information) has been submitted. However, for a nonurgent claim, the plan administrator can unilaterally decide that an additional 15-day period is needed for reasons beyond the control of the plan, such as the claimant's failure to supply required information.

The direct supervisor of the person who makes initial claim determinations can serve as the fiduciary who reviews claims on appeal—the regulation merely bans the person who made the initial determination, or his or her subordinates, from performing the review.

A sales representative, 25% of whose work time involved driving (800 to 1,000 miles per week), had a stroke that permanently impaired the vision in one eye. The plaintiff's doctor said that it would be dangerous for him to drive, but also described him as having "no restrictions." Disability benefits were initially awarded and later terminated on the grounds that the plaintiff's condition was improving. The plaintiff submitted evidence that he was permanently impaired. The insurer relied on an unidentified vocational consultant who said that driving was not a material duty of working as a sales representative. The Fifth Circuit agreed with the plaintiff that the insurer failed to satisfy the requirements of the claims regulation, holding that ERISA requires review of the specific ground for denying the application as well as disclosure of the identity of the vocational expert. According to the Fifth Circuit, these are not trivial technical points, but issues that go deeply to the plaintiff's ability to receive meaningful review of the termination of benefits. [*Robinson v. Aetna*, 443 F.3d 389 (5th Cir. 2006)]

§ 13.04   HIPAA EDI STANDARDS

One reason for high medical costs is that a lot of time and effort is devoted to processing, transmitting, and analyzing information. A number of different standards evolved for storing and displaying health information. To streamline this process, HIPAA requires a uniform set of EDI standards to be placed into effect for health and welfare funds.

Standard code sets, such as the HCFA Common Procedure System and the CPT-4 [Physicians' Current Procedural Terminology, 4th ed. (Celeste G. Kirschner et al., American Medical Ass'n Annual)] must be applied uniformly. The standards cover both the format and the content of electronic files used to submit health care claims, transmit payment information, coordinate benefits among plans, enroll and disenroll plan beneficiaries, and related tasks.

HIPAA's EDI standards apply to insured and self-insured EGHPs, health insurers and HMOs, but not to small, self-administered health plans with fewer than 50 participants. Employers are covered only if they administer their own health plans.

Failure to comply can be penalized by up to $100 per plan per violation, up to a maximum penalty of $25,000 per calendar year for each transaction standard to which a plan is subject.

Tip: Even plan sponsors that are not directly subject to the rule will probably have to make changes in their computer systems to exchange information with their health insurers and managed care organizations.

---

§ 13.05   CASE LAW ON CLAIMS

[A]   Generally

Many cases have been litigated over questions of the proper way to handle and process claims within a plan—and especially over the standard of review that courts should apply when reviewing the decisions of plan administrators.

[B]   Experimental Treatment

EGHPs typically refuse to cover experimental treatment, and new forms of treatment are very often more expensive than the ones they replace. There is a long line of cases attempting to distinguish between experimental treatments and those that are novel but are accepted as scientifically valid by the medical community.

A Tenth Circuit case says that if a plan's definition of experimental treatment is treatment not generally accepted by the medical community, then the plan is entitled to exercise its discretion as to which treatments are in this category. [*Healthcare America Plans Inc. v. Bossemeyer*, 166 F.3d 347 (10th Cir. 1998)] When the decision is reviewed, the court should not examine the evidence de novo; it should merely determine whether the plan's decision was arbitrary and capricious.

In *Zervos v. Verizon New York, Inc.*, [277 F.3d 635 (2d Cir. 2002)] the insurer refused to pre-authorize a new kind of high-dose chemotherapy and blood cell transplant, based on an independent medical expert's opinion that this procedure was only as effective as conventional chemotherapy. The Second Circuit said that the insurer had improperly imposed a requirement that experimental treatments be superior to more accepted treatments—treatment should be covered as long as there is scientific evidence of their validity.

The sponsor of a self-insured benefit plan sued its stop-loss insurer for reimbursement of benefits the plan paid for an autologous peripheral blood stem cell transplant. The company, in its role as plan administrator, preauthorized the treatment. The insurer objected on the grounds that the treatment was experimental and not medically necessary. However, the District Court for the District of Iowa ruled in late 2002 that the stop-loss policy incorporated the terms of the plan document, including the plan administrator's discretionary powers. To avoid ERISA coverage, the insurer intentionally separated claims review from decision-making. Therefore, the insurer ironically found itself in the position usually occupied by plan beneficiaries seeking coverage: It had to prove abuse of discretion by the plan administrator. The court held that the plan administrator acted reasonably, by relying on the medical opinion of the patient's doctors and on the independent utilization review system approved by the insurer. [*Computer Aided Design Sys., Inc. v. SAFECO Life Ins. Co.*, 235 F. Supp. 2d 1052 (D. Iowa 2002)]

[C]   Other Exclusions

A plaintiff's treating physician sent her to a rehabilitation facility after she suffered severe head injuries. The program provided daily structured retraining in basic physical and cognitive skills. The health plan administrator denied the claim as a custodial service that was not covered under the plan. The district court affirmed the denial of benefits, holding that the plan had not abused its discretion. However, the Ninth Circuit reversed. [*Castillo v. CIGNA Healthcare*, 11 Fed. Appx. 945 (9th Cir. 2001)]

When a plan's cosmetic-surgery exclusion specifically mentioned gastric bypass and other procedures used primarily to treat obesity, it was reasonable to deny coverage of a gastric bypass that was medically rather than cosmetically indicated (although the procedure on the 470-pound claimant would probably have been covered if the exclusion had not specifically listed gastric bypass). [*Manny v. Central States Pension and Health and Welfare Funds*, 388 F.3d 241 (7th Cir. 2004)]

All of the doctors treating the plaintiff agreed that the services were needed to gain functional improvement and independence, so the care was not custodial in nature. The services also met the plan's definition of rehabilitation therapy likely to result in clear and reasonable improvement in normal, necessary physical movement, within a three-month time frame.

In the case of *Mitchell v. Dialysis Clinic, Inc.* [18 Fed. Appx. 349 (6th Cir. 2001)], the plaintiff and her husband were covered by the employer's self-funded medical plan. The plaintiff submitted a claim when her self-employed husband was injured while working. The plan denied benefits under its exclusion for on-the-job injuries or illnesses. The plaintiff said that the exclusion was inapplicable because her husband did not have Worker's Compensation insurance. The Sixth Circuit upheld the benefits denial. It is true that the plan excluded work-related injuries "for which the covered person is entitled to benefits under any Worker's Compensation law," a category that did not include the plaintiff's husband. However, coverage was also limited to nonoccupational injuries (injury that "does not arise out of (or in the course of) any work for pay or profit"), with no mention of Worker's Compensation. Therefore, the plan did not act arbitrarily or capriciously in denying the claim.

According to the Second Circuit, it was not arbitrary and capricious to apply the plan's "illegal acts" exclusion to deny coverage of injuries sustained in an accident for which the participant was cited for traffic infractions. The court deferred to the administrator's discretion, even though traffic infractions are not considered crimes in New York; the court nevertheless found this interpretation to be reasonable. [*Celardo v. GNY Automobile Dealers Health & Welfare Trust*, 318 F.3d 142 (2d Cir. 2003)]

The Western District of Missouri held that it was not unreasonable for a health plan's administrative committee to exclude treatment of hand injuries caused by a fist fight under the plan's "violent behavior" exclusion. The exclusion still applied even if the employee was telling the truth about acting in self-defense to stop a fight. [*Jennings v. Administrative Committee of Wal-Mart Stores Inc. Assocs. Health and Welfare Plan*, (W.D. Mo. 2005); Rebecca Moore, *Fist Fight Falls Under Health Plan's Violent Behavior Exclusion* (PlanSponsor.com) Jan. 11, 2006]

The exclusion for benefits in excess of a stated lifetime maximum was the issue in *Combe v. La Madeleine, Inc.* [2002 U.S. Dist. LEXIS 21602 (E.D. La. Nov. 6, 2002)] The employee received pre-approval for jaw surgery, but was notified that actual benefits would be determined after the claim was processed, and the amount payable would be based on the applicable eligibility provisions, including maximum benefit limitations. The plan paid only $8,000 of the $120,000 cost of the treatment. The employee received an Explanation of Benefits saying that the lifetime maximum for the service had been reached although no formal denial letter was issued for about a year, when the plaintiff sued. A few weeks before the plaintiff filed suit, the plan notified the employee that treatment for TMJ was subject to a lifetime maximum of $1,000, and the plan wanted the plaintiff to return $7,000.

Once suit was filed, the employer took the position that she failed to follow the plan's claims procedures, which require an appeal to be filed within 60 days of the date of the original Explanation of Benefits. The court rejected this argument, not only because there was no evidence that the employer was prejudiced by the plaintiff's actions—it could and did review the plaintiff's case file—but because there was evidence that the plaintiff did send a hand-written note requesting review within the 60-day period). The court also found that the denial was an abuse of discretion because there was no evidence that her treatment was related to TMJ, and the surgery as performed did not resemble the TMJ exclusion set out in the plan documents.

An uninsured patient's doctor diagnosed probable irritable bowel syndrome and recommended that she have a colonoscopy to determine if she had inflammatory bowel disease. Shortly after this consultation, she married and became covered by her husband's EGHP. She was hospitalized, had the colonoscopy, was diagnosed with irritable bowel syndrome, and was treated. The health plan refused to pay on the grounds that preexisting conditions were not covered for a year after enrollment. The District Court for the Middle District of Pennsylvania decided in 2006 that the recommendation of the colonoscopy triggered the exclusion because the plan terms referred not only to conditions that were treated, but those for which treatment was recommended or suggested but not received. [*Hoagland v. Amerihealth Administrators*, 2006 U.S. Dist. LEXIS 1570 (M.D. Pa. 2006)]

[D] Timing

One of the most significant questions in tort law is when a potential plaintiff can be expected to be aware that an injury has occurred—and therefore when the clock starts for determining whether a claim is timely. A 2004 case from the Eighth Circuit began when a plaintiff broke his arm and leg in a fall. He applied for benefits from an ERISA-covered self-funded health plan. The claim was denied, and he sued the plan and its administrator in state court.

The defendants removed the case to federal court and moved to dismiss, saying that the suit was time-barred. The terms of the plan required suits to be brought within three years of the expiration of the time when proof of claim was required. He was injured August 4, 1994, the claim was denied February 8, 1995, and he sued in February of 2002. The plaintiff, of course, argued that the claim was timely in light of the plan provision allowing suit within "such longer period as required by applicable state law." He pointed to a Missouri law imposing a 10-year statute of limitations for suits to enforce a defendant's written promise to pay money. The Eighth Circuit ruled that ERISA plans can contractually incorporate a state statute of limitations—and this plan chose to do so. In this reading, the parties intended plan participants to have at least three years to bring suit, even if state law provided for a shorter time. But plan participants would also be entitled to any longer period allotted by state law. The Eighth Circuit drew an analogy between self-insured plans and ordinary contracts, finding the claim to be more like an ordinary contract claim than an action to enforce an insurance policy. [*Harris v. The Epoch Group*, 357 F.3d 822 (8th Cir. 2004)]

The plaintiff in *Watts v. Bellsouth Telcoms Inc.* [316 F.3d 1203 (11th Cir. 2003)] applied for short-term disability (STD) benefits; the claim was denied. Instead of filing a plan appeal within the 60-day time frame, she consulted an attorney about filing suit, and then filed a plan appeal that was rejected by the plan as untimely. However, she won in court: the Eleventh Circuit ruled that the SPD said that claimants "may" use the plan's procedure to appeal denials, and also said "you may file suit in a state or federal court" if a claim is denied. According to the Eleventh Circuit, this language could reasonably be interpreted to mean that the plan's appeals procedure is optional, not mandatory.

When long-term disability benefits were discontinued on the ground that the participant no longer fit the definition of disability, the participant appealed. Sixty-seven days after the appeal, the insurer replied that it was reviewing the appeal. About 30 days later, the insurer asked the participant's attorney for additional medical records. Three months later, the insurer wrote again to say it was still considering the appeal but waiting for an independent medical examination scheduled in 10 days. In the interim, the participant filed suit. The plaintiff said she had standing to sue because the appeal had not been decided within the time frame prevailing at that time (60 days, or 120 days with special circumstances). The Southern District of New York, however, dismissed the case because the insurer made a good-faith effort to investigate the claim, and the process should be given a reasonable time for completion as long as there is no bad faith. The court ordered the insurer to decide the appeal within 30 days of receiving the results of the independent examination, although the plaintiff could re-file the suit if the claim was denied or the insurer failed to decide within the 30-day period. [*Nichols v. Prudential Ins. Co. of America*, 2004 U.S. Dist. LEXIS 3041 (S.D.N.Y. 2004)]

A nuclear engineer continued to work for about a year after a diagnosis of chronic abdominal pain and irritable bowel syndrome. Then his doctor gave him a week off work, a period that was extended by the doctor for more than six months, during which time he also saw a gastroenterologist and a psychologist. He was cleared to return to work, but when this did not work out, he was placed on medical leave of absence. The employer filed an LTD application with the insurer, saying that his last date worked was December 1, 1999, but he returned to work June 19, 2000. The insurer asked the plaintiff for more documentation, which he provided.

He claimed that his disability began December 2, 1999, and his last work date was August 1, 2000. The insurer denied his claim, finding that there was no medical documentation of the irritable bowel syndrome diagnosis and no evidence of inability to perform the job. The plaintiff hired a lawyer, who furnished additional documentation to the insurer, including the Social Security Administration's determination of disability. The Fourth Circuit ruled that the time starts for determining disability (including elimination periods) based on proof of total disability; it is an abuse of discretion to make a determination based on a particular date where proof is submitted relating to a different date. [*Evans v. Metropolitan Life Ins Co.,* 358 F.3d 307 (4th Cir. 2004)]

In a Nebraska case, the plaintiff's doctor requested preauthorization for surgery to improve the plaintiff's fertility. A doctor employed by the defendant health plan denied the request on the grounds that infertility services were not covered by the plan. The plaintiff's attorney made a written demand for payment of surgical expenses. The defendant informed the attorney that this would be treated as a written appeal of an initial denial of coverage, which would be resolved within 45 days—but the defendant did not resolve the appeal. The plaintiff sued, seeking a declaratory judgment that the services were covered; the defendant moved to dismiss the case for failure to exhaust administrative remedies within the plan. However, the District Court ruled that the defendant's failure to act operated as the denial of an administrative appeal, so exhaustion of remedies would have been futile and the plaintiff was not obligated to continue pursuing remedies within the plan. [*Theil v. United Healthcare of the Midlands, Inc.,* 2001 U.S. Dist. LEXIS 935 (D. Neb. Jan. 23, 2001)]

After her disability benefits were terminated, a claimant filed an appeal. After 197 days, the insurer had not made a decision so the participant sued under ERISA. (The rules in effect at the relevant time required a decision within 60 days or within 120 days if there were grounds for an extension of time.) The District Court dismissed the case on the grounds that, because the insurer had not resolved the case, the plaintiff had failed to exhaust her administrative remedies. The Second Circuit, however, ruled that an insurer cannot be deemed to be in substantial compliance with ERISA if the deadline is allowed to pass without a decision being rendered. Although the insurer's position was that a decision had been delayed by the plaintiff's failure to provide medical evidence, DOL guidance implies that insurers cannot impose indefinite delays because of missing evidence. [*Nichols v. Prudential,* 406 F.3d 98 (2d Cir. 2005)]

In an Eighth Circuit case, disability benefits were terminated on the basis of medical improvement. The recipient brought an appeal under the plan. He lost on appeal and, instead of bringing the second-level appeal mandated by the plan, he brought a federal suit. The Eighth Circuit upheld the dismissal of his case. The plaintiff argued that the plan violated ERISA by imposing a 60-day time period on second-level appeals. However, although 29 C.F.R. § 2560.503-1(h)(1) requires plans to provide full and fair review of adverse benefit determinations, defined to require that claimants be given at least 180 days to appeal after an adverse benefit determination, it is permissible for the plan to have a second level of internal appeals before claimants can sue (*see* 29 C.F.R. § 2560.503-1(c)). The Eighth Circuit held that the second-level appeal cannot be considered an "adverse benefit determination." The statute does not set a time limit for second-level internal appeals, but the Eighth Circuit, reasoning by analogy from 29 C.F.R. § 1560.503-1(h)(2), a general ERISA provision not specific to disability plans, decided that 60 days is a reasonable time limit for second-level appeals. The plaintiff argued that that was not long enough to produce the necessary evidence but, because it was the second level of reconsideration, the plaintiff had already had a six-month period to adduce evidence. [*Price v. Xerox Corp.*, 445 F.3d 1054 (8th Cir. 2006)]

ERISA's guarantee of the right to appeal benefit denials includes the right to review pertinent documents. The plan participant who sued in *Simpson v. Ameritech Corp. Inc.* [2000 U.S. Dist. LEXIS 14607 (E.D. Mich. Aug. 30, 2000)] said she was denied access to documents relevant to her claim for LTD benefits. The District Court denied relief, because she didn't even ask for the documents until the appeals procedure was complete. *But see* an earlier case, *Ellis v. Metropolitan Life Insurance Co.* [126 F.3d 228 (4th Cir. 1997)], holding that the DOL regulations imply a requirement that the plan administrator or fiduciary inform participants of their right to review documents.

The notice requirement of § 2560.503(f)(1)-(2) is satisfied if the denial letter cites a specific plan provision, and the physician's report buttresses the denial. [*Regula v. Delta Family-Care Disability Survivorship Plan*, 266 F.3d 1130 (9th Cir. 2001)] It says that benefit plans need not permit claimants to review every document in their administrative files—only the ones that influenced the plan's decision. *See also DiGregorio v. Hartford Comprehensive Employee Benefit Service Co.*, 423 F.3d 6 (1st Cir. 2005), holding that, in order to get her claim for benefits remanded, the First Circuit required a long-term disability plan participant to show that she was prejudiced by the administrator's failure to provide her with the entire claim file. Prejudice would occur if, without a complete copy of the claim file, she did not understand what evidence would be required to rebut the administrator's conclusion that she was not disabled.

[E] Other Issues

Health plan fiduciaries have a duty to consider all pertinent available information and to make a decision based on substantial evidence. The District of Connecticut ruled [*Crocco v. Xerox Corp.* [969 F. Supp. 129 (D. Conn. 1997)] that the employer failed to provide the required "full and fair review" when it relied on its Utilization Review firm and therefore approved payment for only 30 days of a four-month psychiatric hospitalization. The plan administrator had a duty to review the medical records and make an independent determination of the correctness of the Utilization Review firm's decision. It wasn't good enough to permit an appeal after denial of the claim.

The Eighth Circuit reversed the lower court's grant of summary judgment to the employer, because the plaintiff should have been permitted to respond to the independent medical examiner's report to offer evidence that her obesity, alone or in conjunction with post-polio syndrome, rendered her totally disabled. The plaintiff applied for long-term disability benefits and submitted medical documentation of her progressive loss of strength, although her doctor said that losing weight and exercise would be beneficial. The LTD plan's examining nurse concluded that the record did not contain sufficient medical evidence to support a claim of permanent and total disability. The independent medical examiner deemed the plaintiff to be capable of sedentary or light-duty work, considering obesity and depression more significant than post-polio syndrome in explaining the plaintiff's condition. The plaintiff submitted a functional capacity evaluation, showing a decline in her ability to work, and a letter from the former employer explaining that her job was 40 rather than 20 hours a week—an important matter when her capacity for sustained work was at issue. The appeals deadline lapsed without a decision being rendered, or notice of extension given, by the plan committee. The medical reviewer denied the claim about a month after the deadline on the ground that if the plaintiff could work six hours a day, she could work full-time. The District Court affirmed the denial, finding no abuse of discretion. The Eighth Circuit reversed and remanded, requiring the plan to consider the effects of obesity on the plaintiff's ability to work, and giving her a chance to respond to the adverse medical evidence.

The Eighth Circuit interprets the requirement of full and fair review imposed by 29 USC § 1133/29, C.F.R § 2560.5031(h), to provide the right to review all information relevant to the claim and an appeal process that considers all the information submitted by the claimant. Because the plaintiff didn't have access to the second medical report, she could not participate meaningfully in the appeals process without understanding why the plan considered her claim to be inconsistent. Because morbid obesity is at least potentially a disabling condition, it should have been considered. When the plan's own medical examiner specifically identifies a potentially disabling condition, the plan is not permitted to ignore such evidence. [*Abram v. Cargill Inc.*, 395 F.3d 882 (8th Cir. 2005)]

An employee received 24 months of LTD benefits for mental illness. When those benefits ended, she sued, claiming physical disability benefits for other health problems, and providing documentation from her primary care physician and specialists. The insurer denied the claim on the ground of insufficient medical information, stating that the claimant's doctor failed to submit "office notes or test results." The plaintiff provided additional data, but again was denied because the rheumatologist's findings were not supported by "test results." The Eastern District of Pennsylvania refused to grant summary judgment for either side, criticizing the insurer for failure to give a comprehensible explanation of what the plaintiff could do to qualify. [*Scott v. Hartford Life & Accident Ins. Co.*, 2004 U.S. Dist. LEXIS 8702 (E.D. Pa. 2004)]

The Tenth Circuit held that it was arbitrary and capricious for the administrator to deny benefits without properly investigating the participant's claim that he was unable to work because of his use of prescription painkillers. The court obligated fiduciaries to access any readily available evidence supporting the claimant's position—particularly when the fiduciaries do not have any independent information about the matter. [*Gaither v. Aetna Life Ins. Co.*, 394 F.3d 792 (10th Cir. 2004)]

A Seventh Circuit case highlights the problems of integrating coverage under EGHPs with different or inconsistent terms. The plaintiff was covered by two EGHPs: one through her own employer, the other through her husband's job. Her plan said that employees covered by another EGHP are automatically covered under a sub-plan with a limit of $1,000 per person per calendar year and a "no-loss" provision. The no-loss provision stated that the plan would pay the difference if the participant received lower benefits when this plan was combined with his or her other plan than if he or she were covered by major medical insurance. The wife's plan's coordination of benefits (COB) provision said that not more than 100% of covered charges could be paid or reimbursed (i.e., employees could not get a windfall by having both individual and spousal coverage). The other plan's position was that it was primary coverage for its own plan participants, secondary coverage for dependents of its participants. The second plan's coordination of benefits provision said that if the other plan does not have a COB provision, that plan would be primary and its plan would be secondary. If part of the other plan coordinated benefits and the other did not, the second plan treated the first plan as two separate plans.

The plaintiff submitted $160,000 in medical bills to both plans. The first plan said that its exposure was limited to $1,000, because she was in the sub-plan, and her husband's plan was responsible for the rest. The husband's plan brought suit, taking the position that the wife's plan was responsible for the entire bill. The Seventh Circuit adopted the position of the wife's plan: The wife was entitled to $1,000 coverage under the sub-plan, and the husband's plan was liable for the rest. In this reading, ERISA does not mandate the type or amount of employee benefits and does not cover coordination of benefit issues. If the provisions of two EGHPs are clear and can be applied together, the court will apply them as written. The sub-plan arrangement under the wife's plan was a benefit design, not a COB rule, so it did not fall within the husband's plan's provision ruling out coordination with a plan that does not use the normal coordination rules. [*Trustees of Southern Ill. Carpenters Welfare Fund v. RFMS*, 401 F.3d 847 (7th Cir. 2005)]

Prevailing plan participants who succeed in challenging a benefit denial are entitled to attorneys' fees in any case unless there are special circumstances that rule out a fee award. [*Martin v. Arkansas Blue Cross/Blue Shield*, 270 F.3d 673 (8th Cir. 2001)]

The Second Circuit permitted interest to be awarded on benefits based on an unreasonable delay in reinstating them (disability benefits were suspended for a year while the administrator considered whether evidence of disability was sufficient). [*Dobson v. Hartford Financial Services Group Inc.*, 389 F.3d 386 (2d Cir. 2004)]

A chiropractor approached the DOL for clarification after several claims had been denied by a self-insured plan. The chiropractor's question was whether health care professionals consulted by fiduciaries (to see if the claim is medically justified) have to be licensed in the state where the services are provided or in the state where the claimant lives. The DOL stated that fiduciaries can properly consult anyone who is licensed and accredited in the relevant medical field, even if the license was issued by another state. (Because the query involved a self-insured plan, the DOL did not address the question of state external review laws that require insurance companies to have a review panel of medical experts; it is possible that state law will require an in-state license for the experts.) [DOL Advisory Opinion 2005-16A, <http://www.dol.gov/ebsa/regs/aos/a02005-16a.html> (June 10, 2005)]

[F] Ambiguity

Especially in a situation in which one party has more resources and more power and is able to draft a document which the other party is not in a position to negotiate, courts will often be faced with allegations that a document is ambiguous, and should be construed in favor of the less-powerful party: here, the plan participant rather than the plan, plan administrator, or insurer.

The general rule is that the reviewing court will look only at the documents themselves. However, if a document is ambiguous, "extrinsic" (outside) evidence can be used to aid in its interpretation. In *Tumbleston v. A.O. Smith Corp.* [28 Fed. Appx. 231 (4th Cir. 2002)], however, a person disabled by clinical depression sought coverage under a disability policy both for depression and for lumbosacral disc disease with sciatica. Benefits were terminated after 24 months, the maximum duration of plan benefits for mental and nervous disorders. The plaintiff alleged that the plan language was ambiguous as to people suffering both physical and mental ailments, but the Fourth Circuit disagreed, ruling that the plan language was not ambiguous and was interpreted in a reasonable manner. [*Johnson v. General Am. Life Ins. Co.*, 178 F. Supp. 2d 644 (W.D. Vir. 2001) reaches a similar conclusion on a similar fact pattern]

In a 2001 Eighth Circuit case [*Walke v. Group LTD Ins.*, 256 F.3d 835 (8th Cir. 2001)], another case involving termination of mental health disability benefits after 24 months on the grounds that the claimant was no longer totally disabled, the court found that the plan language was ambiguous. (The provision required "satisfactory proof of Total Disability to us.") The court construed the ambiguity in favor of the claimant, reviewed the claim de novo, and found in favor of the plaintiff.

Although the question of ambiguity often arises in the context of disability policies, it is not limited to them. In *Bablitz v. E.I. DuPont de Nemours & Co.* [171 F. Supp. 2d 906 (S.D. Iowa 2001)] a class of employees sought severance benefits under a change-in-control provision that offered benefits to employees who resigned or retired for "stated good reasons." The severance committee was given explicit power to review the reasons asserted by employees and then determine their eligibility. The court refused to admit extrinsic evidence, because the plan was not ambiguous.

Similarly, the Northern District of California decided in a 2001 case that a severance plan that defined "job elimination termination" as a termination solely because the employer has ended the employee's position and has not offered the employee another job anywhere else was not ambiguous, and the provision was reasonably applied by the plan administrators. [*Thomas v. Silgan Containers Corp.*, 2001 U.S. Dist. LEXIS 7088 (N.D. Cal. May 24, 2001)]

However, the Southern District of New York examined extrinsic evidence in *Keiser v. CDC Inv. Mgt. Corp.* [160 F. Supp. 2d 512 (S.D.N.Y. 2001)], a claim about denial of long-term disability benefits for a plaintiff disabled by a car accident at a time she was receiving severance benefits. The court accepted the plaintiff's argument that the plan term *active employment* was ambiguous.

[G] Estoppel

Estoppel is another legal doctrine, one which holds that in certain circumstances, a party will be "estopped" (prevented) from asserting a right that would otherwise apply—e.g., an employer that prevents an employee from filing a timely claim will not be allowed to reject claims on the grounds that they are untimely.

In *Devlin v. Empire Blue Cross & Blue Shield* [274 F.3d 76 (2d Cir. 2001)], employees who retired between 1989 and 1993 challenged the employer's 1998 decision to reduce life insurance coverage for retirees. The plaintiffs claimed estoppel on the grounds that, before 1987, the plan's SPD did not reserve the right to amend the plan. Furthermore, the SPD and other communications to employees referred to lifetime benefits. The retirees charged that reduction of benefits was an extraordinary circumstance that would justify granting an estoppel claim under ERISA. The Second Circuit ruled that mere unfairness does not constitute an extraordinary circumstance. However, the court also held that a reasonable trier of fact could have concluded that the workers were promised lifetime benefits.

In contrast, a First Circuit case involved a plaintiff who was vested in a pension plan. When the plaintiff was first employed, the plan calculated benefits on the basis of career average salary; then it was amended to use final average salary in the calculations. The plaintiff said that he went back to work for the employer in 1988 (after quitting in 1980) and that he turned down better jobs elsewhere because he believed that the amended plan terms would be applied to his earlier period of employment. [*Mauser v. Raytheon Co. Pension Plan*, 239 F.3d 51 (1st Cir. 2001)] His estoppel claim was dismissed; the court found it unfair to grant the estoppel claim, because it was almost identical to a claim that the SPD did not provide adequate disclosure, and the plaintiff failed to prove that he experienced ill effects because of reliance on the amended document. *Also see Aguilar v. Ford Motor Co.* [2001 U.S. Dist. LEXIS 8984 (E.D. Mich. May 23, 2001)], in which the employer got summary judgment because the plaintiff's estoppel claim, based on detrimental reliance on the language of the SPD, was vague, and the plaintiff failed to show inconsistencies between the language of the plan and the language of the SPD.

The doctrines of ambiguity and estoppel are often raised in cases involving plan amendments limiting benefits for those who have already retired. *See* Chapter 9 for retiree health benefits in general, and Chapter 14 for a discussion of the implications of amending a plan.

§ 13.06   THE STANDARD OF REVIEW

If and when a plan participant sues in connection with plan benefits, one of the most important questions is the "standard of review" the court will use to assess the plan administrator's decision. The two possibilities are "de novo" review, under which the court considers the question as if it were a new case, or review to see if the administrator abused his or her discretion. Many more plan decisions will be reversed—and many more claimants will win their cases—if the court can look at all the factors underlying the matter, and not just to see if there was an abuse of discretion.

The basic rule, as set by the seminal case of *Bruch v. Firestone Tire & Rubber* [489 U.S. 101 (1989)], is that plan administrators' decisions will be reviewed on a de novo basis, unless the plan itself is drafted to give the fiduciaries discretion over the way the plan operates. If the plan sponsor reserved this discretion, the court's only role is to see whether the administrators abused their discretion.

However, if the fiduciary that made the decision had a conflict of interest, then de novo review might be imposed, or the conflict might be treated as a factor in determining whether discretion was abused. [*Torres v. Pittston Co.,* 346 F.3d 1324 (11th Cir. 2003)]

The Eighth Circuit applied the heightened standard of judicial review when an employer had a conflict of interest because it retained control over claims decisions, and disability benefits were paid directly out of operating expenses and therefore affected the employer's profits. The employer claimed that, because it had delegated claims processing to a TPA, the proper standard of review would be "arbitrary and capricious," but the employer had the power to give the TPA specific, binding instructions about specific claims. Nevertheless, even when applying the heightened standard, the Eighth Circuit did not deem the plaintiff to be entitled to benefits. [*Williams v. BellSouth Telecomms, Inc.,* 373 F.3d 1132 (11th Cir. 2004)]

In 2001, the Seventh Circuit held in *O'Reilly v. Hartford Life & Accident Ins. Co.* [272 F.3d 955 (7th Cir. 2001)] that conflict of interest is merely one factor to be considered in determining the standard of review, but the Eighth Circuit uses a "sliding scale" to select the standard, depending on the severity of the conflict. [*Clapp v. Citibank, NA Disability Plan,* 262 F.3d 820 (8th Cir. 2001). *Also see Lain v. UNUM* [279 F.3d 337 (5th Cir. 2002) (insurer's financial incentives created a significant conflict of interest, so the denial would not stand up under either standard of review)]

The Tenth Circuit uses a two-tiered approach. If there is a conflict of interest, but only the standard one (the claimant does not establish a serious conflict), then the plan's dual role is a factor in determining whether it acted arbitrarily. But if the conflict is inherent (e.g., the insurer serves as plan administrator), then the decision-maker must provide substantial evidence of the validity of the decision. [*Fought v. UNUM Life Ins. Co. of America*, 379 F.3d 997 (10th Cir. 2004)]

According to the Ninth Circuit, a disability plan that required "satisfactory written proof" of disability, but did not say in so many words that the administrator had discretionary authority, was subject to de novo review. [*Kearney v. Standard Ins. Co.*, 175 F.3d 1084 (9th Cir. 1998)]

In contrast, the Seventh Circuit case of *McNab v. GM* [162 F.3d 959 (7th Cir. 1998)] involved an early retirement plan giving management discretion to reject early retirement applications from employees who were deemed so valuable that their early retirement was contrary to the employer's best interests. The Seventh Circuit interpreted this as a standard rather than a rule—standards can be applied flexibly and with discretion. Denying early retirement to the plaintiffs was not sufficiently arbitrary or capricious to violate ERISA.

A later Seventh Circuit case says that, for a sponsor to reserve discretion, the plan documents must demand more than claimants prove or give satisfactory proof of entitlement to benefits. The rationale of *Herzberger v. Standard Insurance Co.* [205 F.3d 327, 331 (7th Cir. 2000)] is that an ERISA plan is a contract, to be interpreted by the courts and not by the party who drafted the language. But the court approved this language as enough to trigger the arbitrary and capricious standard: "Benefits under this plan will be paid only if the plan administrator decides in his discretion that the applicant is entitled to them."

According to the Eighth Circuit, a termination of disability benefits should have been reviewed de novo. The plan in the insurer's claim file affidavit did not grant discretion to the insurer, whereas the brief for the insurer included a different copy of the plan, with no affidavit of authenticity. This version did grant discretionary authority. The Eighth Circuit ruled that the District Court should not have used the second version without resolving the explanation for the disparity. [*Barham v. Reliance Standard Life Ins. Co.*, 441 F.3d 581 (8th Cir. 2006)]

The Eastern District of Wisconsin found that it was arbitrary and capricious for a plan to deny coverage of a medically necessary feeding tube, for a patient who was unable to swallow, using the theory that meals were available in the hospital: "An administrator is not free to give ordinary words bizarre or obscure interpretations." [*See Schneider v. Wisconsin UFCW Unions*, 985 F. Supp. 848, 850 (E.D. Wis. 1997)]

Other recent cases on this issue include:

- *Gritzer v. CBS Inc.* [275 F.3d 291 (3d Cir. 2002)]: The de novo standard applies when plaintiffs sue after a claim (in this case, for early retirement rather than health benefits) is denied and the plan ignores the plaintiff's claim letter. However, even under this standard, the defendant won: The Third Circuit read plan language saying that the pension committee "may" treat service with a successor employer as its own service to provide discretion to grant or deny any benefit, including the early retirement benefit in contention.

- *Jebian v. Hewlett-Packard Co.* [310 F.3d 1173 (9th Cir. 2002)]: The de novo standard is proper when the case involves a claim that, under the plan language, was automatically deemed denied if the administrator did not respond within six days. When the administrator does not exercise discretion, a court cannot determine whether or not discretion was abused. However, in 2003, the Ninth Circuit withdrew that opinion and issued a substitute opinion, affirming that the de novo standard is appropriate where benefits are "deemed denied" through the passage of time alone—but withdrawing the instruction that the appellant's claims be considered in light of the "treating physician rule" (which has been invalidated by the Supreme Court). [*Jebian v. Hewlett-Packard,* 349 F.3d 1098 (9th Cir 2003); earlier opinion withdrawn on Oct. 25, 2003)] *Gilbertson v. Allied Signal Inc.* [328 F.3d 625 (10th Cir. 2003)] also holds that failure to render a decision within the plan's time frame constitutes a failure to exercise discretion such that de novo review is applied. *See also Linder v. BYK-Chemie USA Inc.,* 313 F. Supp. 2d 88 (D. Conn. 2004) (*semble,* for a claim that stock option compensation should have been included in pension calculations).

The Fifth Circuit permitted an administrator to terminate benefits shortly after granting them without proof of substantial change in the participant's condition; the court refused to impose a heightened standard of proof when the administrator says that it made a mistake and tries to correct it. [*Ellis v. Liberty Life Assurance Co. of Boston,* 394 F.3d 262 (5th Cir. 2004, revised Jan. 13, 2005)]

§ 13.07   CASE LAW ON CLAIMS PROCEDURAL ISSUES

A fiduciary, including a life insurance company, has a right under ERISA § 502(a) to seek appropriate equitable relief from the courts in order to enforce plan provisions. Therefore, the fiduciary can bring an interpleader action (a suit asking for court guidance on how to dispose of funds whose ownership is disputed) if there are conflicting claims to insurance proceeds—for instance, based on a beneficiary designation and community property law. [*Aetna Life Ins. Co. v. Bayona,* 223 F.3d 1030 (9th Cir. 2000)]

It is a reasonable exercise of discretion for an insurer to deny life insurance benefits that violate state law. An employee who quit his job was offered the right to convert his life insurance under an employee welfare plan to a group policy, contingent upon whether he lived in a state that approved such a continuation. The application to convert was denied by the plan's insurer because at that time, the state where he lived (Michigan) did not permit portable term insurance coverage.

Three years later, the applicant died, and over a year after that his widow submitted a claim for the death benefits that would have been payable if the conversion application had been accepted. The surviving spouse sued for the life insurance benefits, plus statutory penalties for failure to provide plan documents. The Sixth Circuit ruled that the insurer, as fiduciary, had discretion to interpret the plan, making the standard of review whether the determination had been arbitrary and capricious. Insofar as converting the policy would have been unlawful at the time of the application, the insurer was not guilty of any wrongdoing. Furthermore, the claim for benefits accrued at the time of the original denial of the application, so the surviving spouse's claim also had exceeded the three-year statute of limitations. [*Morrison v. Marsh & McLennan*, 439 F.3d 295 (6th Cir. 2006)]

A beneficiary of a self-funded health plan sued his spouse's employer (the plan administrator and fiduciary) under the plan's claims procedure. The District Court for the District of Massachusetts denied summary judgment for the employer because the employer's consideration of the appeal failed to provide a full and fair review. The employer improperly deferred to the claims administrator's initial determination because it asked the administrator only for information supporting its decision, not the full file. In deciding the internal appeal, the employer used the claims administrator's guidelines, but did not include the guidelines in the denial notice or inform the claimant how to obtain them. Nor did the employer disclose the scientific or clinical judgments used in the determination. The District Court remanded the claim to the employer for reconsideration, ordering that all relevant information be given to the beneficiary, and that the employer consider additional information. [*Krodel v. Bayer Corp.*, 345 F. Supp. 2d 110 (D. Mass. 2004) on remand 2005 U.S. Dist. LEXIS 26833 (D. Mass. 2005)]

[A] HMO and TPA Involvement in Claims

Yet another facet in the complex picture comes from the involvement of HMOs and TPAs in the claims process. The legal questions become much more complex than a simple relationship between employee/plan participant and employer/plan sponsor.

In a Fifth Circuit case from 2002, a diabetic plan participant suffered a foot amputation after he had to wait a week to have his infected toes treated. He sued his HMO in state court, alleging that the HMO caused the delay by refusing to recognize his treating physician as a primary care physician who could refer patients for hospital treatment. The Fifth Circuit ruled [*Haynes v. Prudential Health Care,* 313 F.3d 330 (5th Cir. 2002)] that the HMO's determination about the doctor's status as a primary care physician was an administrative rather than a treatment decision. Therefore, it was preempted by ERISA. (However, if the case had arisen after the regulations discussed at § 13.03 were in effect, it would have been an urgent care claim on which a decision would have been required within 72 hours.)

In the wake of the Supreme Court's consolidated decision in *Aetna Health Inc. v. Davila*, and *Cigna Healthcare of Texas, Inc. v. Calad*, 542 U.S. 200 (2004), note that plan participants who claim that they were improperly denied necessary health care by a Managed Care Organization will have to bring the cases in federal court. The Supreme Court ruled that ERISA § 502(a) completely preempts state laws purporting to regulate managed care decisions about whether or not to provide treatment.

A former employee who had elected COBRA continuation coverage applied for benefits when he was injured lifting a heavy object in the course of a home business. The health plan paid the claim, but the employer contacted the third-party administrator, stating that it was afraid that the injuries were caused by the ex-employee's martial arts activities and were therefore excluded under the policy's hazardous-sports provisions. Without reviewing the medical records, the TPA concluded that the injury was excluded and tried to recoup the payments it had made to health care providers. The injured person denied that the injury was sports-related; the TPA finally reviewed the records and concluded that the injury was excluded because it was in the scope of employment. When the injured person brought suit against the health plan, the District Court for the District of Oregon ruled that the plan's inconsistent positions, denial of the claim without having all the facts, and the plan's partially self-funded status all pointed to a conflict of interest requiring heightened scrutiny. The court ordered payment of benefits, because the exclusion for employment-related injuries was not relevant to the plaintiff's home-based business outside regular working hours. [*Olcott v. Vision Plastics Inc. Health Care Plan*, 2004 U.S. Dist. LEXIS 14010 (D.Ore. 2004)]

[B] Exhaustion of Remedies

Exhaustion of remedies is a traditional legal doctrine under which parties will not be permitted to litigate a claim until they have satisfied the applicable administrative requirements—whether that means filing a claim with a state or federal antidiscrimination agency or using the appeals procedures provided by a health or welfare benefit plan. This is an important doctrine for employers, who can eliminate many suits at their earliest stages if the employees had an obligation to access plan remedies but failed or refused to do so.

Cases on this issue include:

- *Harrow v. Prudential Ins. Co.* [279 F.3d 244 (3d Cir. 2002)]: The plaintiff wanted the plan to provide Viagra for his diabetes-related impotence. His ERISA § 502(a)(1)(B) claim was dismissed for failure to exhaust administrative remedies. His only action in seeking coverage prior to filing suit was making a single phone call.
- *Davenport v. Abrams, Inc.* [249 F.3d 130 (2d Cir. 2001)]: The plaintiff argued that she had no obligation to exhaust administrative remedies, and the court abused its discretion by failing to hold that exhaustion of remedies would have

been futile. But the Second Circuit held that there was no clear and positive showing of futility, and requiring exhaustion of remedies promotes ERISA's statutory objective of letting plan administrators manage the plans in accordance with ERISA.

- *Guerrero v. Lumbermen's Mutual Casualty Co.* [174 F. Supp. 2d 1218 (D. Kan 2001)]: A disability plan had two levels of administrative review. The plan forbade bringing suit unless the participant had timely sought review. An employee went through the first level of review but did not explicitly make a timely request for the second level of review. The District Court rejected her argument that the plan failed to provide adequate notice of the consequences of bypassing the second level of review. Nor did the court accept the plaintiff's argument that going to the second level would have been futile, because the original reviewers did not do the second review.

A number of plaintiffs, including a group of participants in several self-insured medical plans, brought suit against several TPAs. The plans paid for out-of-network services on the basis of usual, customary, and reasonable amounts (UCR). If the actual out-of-network charge was higher than the plan's UCR, the participant had to pay the difference. The TPAs set the charges based on typical charges in the same or a similar area, whereas the plaintiffs alleged that the plan language required the UCR to be supported by appropriate data.

The Southern District of New York dismissed the suit, treating it as a claim for benefits due and fiduciary breach claim [*AMA v. United Healthcare Corp.*, 2001 U.S. Dist. LEXIS 10818 (S.D.N.Y. July 30, 2001)] The claim for benefits due was inappropriate, because such claims can only be made against a plan or a plan administrator, not a TPA. In the Southern District view, the cause of action for fiduciary breach exists to protect plan assets, not to benefit individuals. Even if the allegations are correct, in effect the plan paid less than it should have, so plan assets would be preserved, not dissipated. The plaintiffs also said that their denial notices were not specific enough, but the Southern District ruled that this is not the TPA's responsibility: The plan itself has to provide such information, including information about UCRs.

CHAPTER 14

AMENDING A PLAN

§ 14.01   INTRODUCTION

It is very likely that, no matter how carefully a plan was drafted, amendments will be required over the course of time. The company's line of business or work-force may change. The business may suffer reverses. And it's more than likely that ERISA and the tax code will change in ways that require corresponding amendments to the plan. Each new tax bill that requires amendments includes a schedule for when plans are required to make their conforming amendments.

Plan amendments can be adopted either prospectively or retroactively. Retroactive amendments can be made until the last day (including extensions) for filing the income tax return for the year the plan was adopted.

The Department of Labor must be notified whenever a plan is materially modified or the information called for by ERISA § 102(b) changes. The DOL must receive an updated SPD when the participants and beneficiaries do. The DOL can reject an incomplete submission, giving the plan administrator 45 days for corrections. The 5500-series form filed with the IRS also requires reporting of the plan amendments and changes in the plan description that occurred during the year.

In most cases, the Internal Revenue Code does not require that employees be notified in advance that the plan will be amended. So they don't have a right to comment on the proposed amendment (although they do have a right to comment on the plan's initial application for a determination letter). The exception is that advance notice is required if the amendment changes the vesting schedules of participants who have three years or more of plan participation, because they have the right to choose between the new and the old schedules. However, ERISA does impose a notice requirement. Once a plan is amended, ERISA §§ 102(a)(1) and 104(b)(1) require participants to get a Summary of Material Modifications (SMM) within 210 days of the end of the plan year in which the change is adopted.

§ 14.02   FLEXIBILITY THROUGH AMENDMENT

To preserve flexibility, it's a good idea for the sponsor to draft the plan reserving the right to amend the plan in the future. Plans can be amended to change or eliminate:

- Ancillary life insurance provided in connection with a pension plan;
- Accident or health insurance that is incidental to a pension plan;
- Some Social Security supplements;
- Availability of plan loans;
- Employees' ability to direct investment of their plan accounts or balances;
- The actual investment options available under the plan;
- Employees' ability to make after-tax contributions to the plan, or to make elective salary deferrals to a plan that is not a 401(k) plan;

- Administrative procedures for the plan (although even after the amendments, participants must have a right to fair redress of their grievances);
- Dates used to allocate contributions, forfeitures, earnings, and account balances.

But any amendment must take into account I.R.C. § 411(d)(6), which forbids amendments that reduce accrued benefits, including early retirement benefits and retirement-related subsidies—even if the employees affected by the change consent to it. Furthermore, the general rule is that protected benefits cannot be reduced or eliminated when a plan is merged or its benefits are transferred to another plan.

A current, but not a former, employee can go to court to get a declaratory judgment that a plan has lost its qualification after an amendment. [*Flynn v. C.I.R.*, 269 F.3d 1064 (D.C. Cir. 2001)] The D.C. Circuit considers ex-employees "interested parties" only with respect to termination of a plan.

However, a plan that is subject to the I.R.C. § 412 minimum funding standard can be amended retroactively to reduce accrued benefits—as long as the plan sponsor can prove to the DOL that the sponsor is undergoing substantial business hardship that mandates a cutback in benefits. The amendments must be adopted within 2½ months of the end of the plan year. They must not reduce anyone's accrued benefit for plan years before the beginning of the first plan year that the amendment applies to. IRS approval is required for amendments of this type, and the DOL may have to be notified.

A plan can be amended to change its vesting schedule as long as no participant loses any nonforfeitable accrued benefits.

Even if an amendment is allowed, participants who have at least three years of service with the plan must be given a chance to choose between the new and the old schedules. [I.R.C. § 411(a)(10)(B)] The plan can provide that, once employees make this election, it is irrevocable. The period for making the election must start by the date the amendment is adopted. It cannot end before 60 days after the date the amendment is adopted, the date it becomes effective, or the date the participant gets written notice of the amendment—whichever comes last. *See* the Proposed Regulations published by the IRS on April 23, 2002, at 67 Fed. Reg. 19713, explaining how to give notice of reduction in early retirement subsidies or other benefits.

A defined benefit plan can lose its qualified status if it adopts an amendment that increases plan liabilities, if the result is that the funded current liability falls below 60% for the plan year. The employer can preserve the plan's qualification by posting "adequate" security. Either the corporation must place cash and securities in escrow, or it must obtain a bond from a corporate security company that is acceptable under ERISA § 412. [*See* I.R.C. § 401(a)(29) and ERISA § 307]

Plan amendments also are required when the law changes to permit novel forms of benefit plans and new types of plans (e.g., the introduction of Roth IRAs and Roth 401(k) plans). Notice 2006-44, 2006-20 I.R.B. __, provides sample language to be used in amending 401(k) plans to reflect a participant's ability to make Roth contributions. However, the sample amendment does not address the issue of the extent to which participants can designate that distributions be made from the Roth account rather than their other accounts, so the plan language will have to be drafted to specify. (Because it is a sample amendment, plans do not have to adopt it verbatim to get favorable tax treatment.) Allowing designated Roth contributions requires a discretionary amendment, so Notice 2005-95, 2005-51 I.R.B. 1172, must be followed.

Notice 2005-95 explains the interaction of various timing requirements when plan amendments are needed to maintain compliance as rules change. Notice 2005-95 refers to Rev. Proc. 2005-66, which sets different deadlines for discretionary amendments than for amendments dealing with disqualifying provisions (i.e., provisions that could result in the plan's failure to satisfy the requirements of the Code). Discretionary amendments must be adopted by the end of the plan year in which the amendment is effective.

Amendments to allow a plan to have designated Roth contributions are discretionary amendments. That makes the deadline the end of the plan year in which the amendments are effective. Plan amendments to allow "qualified Katrina distributions" to persons affected by the 2005 hurricane season can be made up until the last day of the first plan year beginning on or after January 1, 2007. [*See* P.L. 109-73] If the plan does not provide for loans or hardship distributions, but wishes to permit "qualified Katrina distributions," it must have been amended for this purpose no later than the end of the first plan year beginning after December 31, 2005. *See* § 12.01[A] for further discussion of qualified Katrina distributions.

In a late 2004 decision, the Third Circuit held that the doctrine of ratification cannot be used to apply a pension plan change retroactively if that would have the effect of reducing accrued benefits. When the plaintiff was hired in 1983, the defendant had a defined benefit plan. Amendments were proposed in 1997 under which younger, short-term employees were transferred to a cash balance plan, and longer-term employees were grandfathered in the defined benefit plan. The plan amendments included a "rehire rule" under which long-term employees who left the company but were subsequently rehired would be enrolled in the cash balance plan rather than the old plan. But, because plan amendments must be made in writing, the formal adoption of the plan did not occur until December 31, 1998 (the date the CEO signed the document adopting the amendments). The plaintiff left the company the day after the changes were supposed to take effect and was rehired 22 days before the amendment was signed. Although the District Court accepted the defendant's argument that the plan changes had already been announced and the CEO's signature retroactively ratified a plan that was already in force, the Third Circuit held that amendments could not be ratified later if they retroactively reduce the rights of plan participants or other third parties. [*Depenbrock v. CIGNA Corp.*, 389 F.3d 78 (3d Cir. 2004)]

§ 14.03   CHANGE IN PLAN YEAR

IRS Determination letters are not limited to initial qualification of a plan: They can also be obtained for plan amendments. The current employees who are eligible for plan participation are "interested parties" and must be notified of the application for a determination letter. If the proposed amendment changes eligibility for participation, then all employees at the same workplace as the original interested parties must be notified.

The request for change in a retirement plan's plan year is made on Form 5308. IRS approval is automatic as long as:

- No plan year is longer than 12 months. In other words, a year can be broken up into two short years, but two short years can't be consolidated into a long one;
- The change does not have the effect of deferring the time at which the plan becomes subject to changes in the law;
- The plan trust (if any) remains tax-exempt and does not have any Unrelated Business Taxable Income in the short year;
- Legal approval for the change is granted before the end of the short year;
- (Defined benefit plans) The deduction taken for the short year is the appropriate prorated share of the costs for the full year.

§ 14.04   REDUCTION IN FORMS OF DISTRIBUTION

Although it is not permitted to amend a qualified plan in any way that reduces any participant's accrued benefit, it is permissible to amend a plan to eliminate optional forms of benefits (such as periodic payments other than the required QJSA/QPSA). EGTRRA provides that, for plan years beginning after December 31, 2001, defined contribution plans can eliminate certain forms of benefit payout. *See* § 12.09 for details.

In particular, if funds are transferred from one qualified plan to another (e.g., in connection with a merger or acquisition), the transferee plan will not be required to provide all the payment options that the transferor plan provided. [*See* I.R.C. § 411(d)(6)(D) and ERISA § 204(g)(4)] However, if payout forms are eliminated, the plan participants must be allowed to take their distributions in lump-sum form.

In 2004, the Supreme Court ruled [*Central Laborer's Pension Fund v. Heinz*, 541 U.S. 739 (2004)] that a plan amendment increasing the varieties of postretirement employment that would cause a suspension of benefit payments violated the anti-cutback rule. However, in Rev. Proc. 2005-23, 2005-18 I.R.B. 991, the IRS ruled that *Heinz* will not be applied retroactively to disqualify plans that suspended benefits in this way—as long as they adopt a timely corrective amendment. Rev. Proc. 2005-76, 2005-50 I.R.B. 1139, extends the time to adopt the amendment (and the time during which participants can elect retroactive benefits) from January 1, 2006, to January 1, 2007.

Regulations were proposed at 69 Fed. Reg. 13769 (Mar. 24, 2004) reflecting the requirements of *Heinz*. Under the proposal, a plan amendment that reduces accrued benefits, or imposes greater restrictions on the right to benefits, is permissible only if it does not impair the rights of any plan participant to an extent that is more than minimal.

The regulations were finalized in T.D. 9219, 2005-38 I.R.B. 538. A plan amendment that decreases accrued benefits or places greater restrictions on the right to receive a benefit protected under I.R.C. § 411(d)(6) is in violation of § 411(d)(6) even if the restriction or condition is acceptable under the § 411(a) vesting rules. However, plans can be amended to restrict the availability of benefits accruing after the date of the amendment.

The Second Circuit has ruled that a plan amendment does not occur when the plan administrator changes the way the plan operates; it occurs when the employees are properly notified of the change. In one case, Xerox amended its plan to implement a "phantom account offset" (i.e., employees who left the company and were later rehired had a pension calculated after a deduction of the lump sum they received the first time they left), but the notice was not given until 1998. The court ruled the amendment could not be applied to anyone rehired before 1998, as it would violate the anti-cutback rule. [*Frommert v. Conkright*, 433 F.3d 254 (2d Cir. 2006)]

§ 14.05   EGTRRA CONFORMING AMENDMENTS

It is common for plans to require amendments to conform to changes in tax and labor law (or to take advantage of additional options that have opened up for employers). The Economic Growth and Tax Relief Reconciliation Act of 2001 (EGTRRA) [Pub. L. No. 107-16] made many sweeping changes in pension administration and taxation. Areas in which plan amendments may be required, or may be desirable, include:

- Higher limits on amount of employer contributions to both defined benefit and defined contribution plans;
- Higher elective deferrals in 401(k) plans;
- Extra catch-up contributions made by employees age 50 and over;
- Faster vesting for employer's matching contributions to a qualified plan;
- Changes in the way 401(k) plans are tested to make sure they do not discriminate in favor of highly compensated employees;
- Higher deductions for employers on account of their contributions to qualified plans;
- Changes in the minimum funding rules that apply to defined benefit plans;
- Greater mobility between plans because rollovers between plans have been liberalized.

Because EGTRRA increased the limit on compensation that can be used in certain benefit calculations from $170,000 a year to $200,000 a year (it has since been raised to $220,000 a year), the IRS has ruled that a plan design that takes pre-2002 compensation into account with respect to accruals or allocations can use the $200,000 ceiling when calculating post-2001 accruals or allocations on pre-2002 compensation—for instance, when calculating a five-year average of compensation. [*See* Notice 2001-56, 2001-38 I.R.B. 277]

It does not violate this "anti-cutback" rule to terminate a COLA that was added to the pension plan after the plaintiffs retired, as in *Board of Trustees of Sheet Metal Workers Nat'l Pension Fund v. CIR* [318 F.3d 599 (4th Cir. 2003)] However, an employer that amends its plan to correct an alleged violation of the anti-cutback rule can still be sued with respect to the alleged violation, because the plan could be amended again to terminate the benefits once again. [*Adams v. Bowater Inc.,* 313 F.3d 611 (1st Cir. 2002)]

§ 14.06   ERISA 204(h) NOTICE

The plan administrator has a duty to notify employees when a defined benefit plan (or any other plan that is subject to the minimum funding requirement) is amended in a way that significantly reduces the rate at which future benefits will accrue. In effect, this is an early warning system that signals to employees that their eventual pensions may be smaller than anticipated.

EGTRRA supplements the rules found at ERISA § 204(h) with a comparable Internal Revenue Code provision, I.R.C. § 4980F, which also imposes an excise tax on failure to make the required notification. *See* 67 Fed. Reg. 19714 for additional Proposed Regulations on this topic.

Final Regulations on this topic were published on April 9, 2003, applicable to plan amendments with an effective date on or after September 2, 2003 (or January 1, 2004 in some situations). [T.D. 9052, 2003-19 I.R.B. 879] The Final Regulations contain examples of required disclosures in many situations, including the complex situation in which a cash balance conversion occurs and the rate of benefit accrual is altered. Converting a money purchase plan into a profit-sharing plan will be considered a significant reduction in the rate of future benefit accrual, so notice will be required. In general, notice must be given 45 days in advance of the effective date of the amendment, although exceptions are allowed for some small plans and some actions in connection with corporate transitions. If necessary, the notice can be given before the adoption date of the amendment.

The notice must be understandable to the average plan participant, and must give enough information for him or her to understand approximately how much his or her benefit entitlement will be reduced by the amendment.

In some instances, providing the required "204(h) notice" (by delivery to each participant's last known address, when the address records have been kept reasonably up to date) will also be treated as furnishing the required Summary of Material Modifications (SMM).

In mid-2003, however, the IRS backed away from this position, proposing regulations [68 Fed. Reg. 40581, July 8, 2003] under which defined contribution, including 401(k) plans, could be amended to reduce alternate benefit forms without a 90-day advance notice requirement. Plans would, however, still have to issue a timely Summary of Material Modifications or revised SPD describing the change. The proposal would become effective only upon adoption of Final Regulations, so plan amendments in the interim must still comply with the advance notice requirement.

A counterpart for defined benefit plans was proposed in March 2004 [69 Fed. Reg. 13769 (Mar. 24, 2004)] for eliminating redundant optional forms of benefit within a "family" of benefit options, and for cutting back the number of options offered provided that the "core" benefits such as the straight life annuity and 75% joint and survivor annuity are preserved.

§ 14.07   AMENDMENTS TO A BANKRUPT SPONSOR'S PLAN

The general rule is that plan benefits may not be increased while the plan sponsor is a bankruptcy debtor. [*See* I.R.C. § 401(a)(33)] Amendments are forbidden if the plan's liabilities rise because of the benefit increase, or because of a change in the rate of accrual or nonforfeitability of benefits. However, amendments that take effect after the effective date of the plan of reorganization are allowed. So are amendments to plans, whose funded current liability percentage is 100% or more, or amendments approved by the IRS, or amendments required to maintain compliance with tax law changes.

The Bankruptcy Abuse Prevention and Consumer Protection Act (BAPCPA), P.L. 109-8, the bankruptcy reform legislation adopted in 2005, alters the treatment of retirement plans in bankruptcy. Bankruptcy Code § 1114, as amended, prevents a Chapter 11 debtor from terminating or modifying retiree welfare benefits without negotiating with retiree representatives. Benefits must be maintained unless the bankruptcy court approves a change. In addition, the court can set aside amendments to a retiree benefit plan made within 180 days before a bankruptcy filing unless the court finds that it is clearly equitable to modify the plan.

The Third Circuit ruled that a plan amendment, adopted just before a Chapter 11 filing, that doubled or even quintupled the pension benefits payable to a group, including many corporate insiders, was void because it was a fraudulent transfer. One factor in the court's decision was the fact that the amendment was described to the board of directors as an "administrative formality," when in fact it was a significant modification to the plan. [*Pension Transfer Corp. v. Beneficiaries Under the Third Amendment to the Fruehauf Trailer Corp. Retirement Plan,* 444 F.3d 203 (3d Cir. 2006)]

§ 14.08   ISSUES HIGHLIGHTED BY THE IRS

IRS' Employee Plans division listed more than a dozen issues that frequently require plan amendments. These issues often prevent the IRS from closing a case until the issues are resolved to the agency's satisfaction:

- Defined benefit plans that do not apply I.R.C. §§ 415(b)(2)(E) and 417(e) properly;
- Defined contribution plans that do not reflect changes in the calculation of the maximum contributions;

- Plans that use the wrong procedure to waive the QJSA;
- Plans that don't meet the effective date requirements of amendments to the Code;
- Plans that can't prove that they complied with earlier tax and pension laws;
- Plans that have not been amended to forbid rollovers of 401(k) plan hardship distributions;
- Plans that do not define "highly-compensated employee" properly;
- Top-heavy plans that have not been updated in view of current laws.

[*See Recurring Plan Issues in Determination Case Review*, <http://www.irs.gov/pub/irs-tege/sum01.pdf#page=15>]

CHAPTER 15

ENFORCEMENT AND COMPLIANCE ISSUES FOR QUALIFIED PLANS

§ 15.01 INTRODUCTION

The underlying purpose of ERISA, and of various later pieces of legislation, is to make sure that plan participants and their beneficiaries receive the promised benefits. Therefore, the focus of enforcement is to make sure that plans remain sound, and that participants and beneficiaries do not fall victim to outright fraud, mistake, negligence, poor administration, or declines in the sponsoring company's financial fortunes. Certain types of transactions are prohibited—although "prohibited transaction exemptions" can be obtained in cases where payment of benefits is not placed at real risk. [*See* § 15.15[C]]

In addition to private suits by participants and beneficiaries, the Department of Labor (DOL) and the IRS carry out administrative enforcement efforts and become involved in litigation about plan compliance and participant and beneficiary rights.

A pension plan is a legal entity that can sue or be sued under ERISA Title I. [*See* ERISA § 502(d)] Unless somebody is found liable in an individual capacity, the plan is responsible for paying all money judgments.

Because the management of plan assets for the sole benefit of participants and beneficiaries is so central to plan operation, the identification, duties, and liabilities of fiduciaries are central to plan enforcement.

ERISA § 402(a)(1) requires all plans either to have a named fiduciary, or to explain in the plan document how fiduciaries will be selected. Under ERISA § 411, a convicted felon is not permitted to serve as plan administrator, fiduciary, officer, trustee, custodian, counsel, agent, consultant, or employee with decision-making authority for 13 years after his or her conviction or the end of his or her prison term, whichever comes later.

§ 15.02 WHO IS A FIDUCIARY?

In general legal terms, a fiduciary is anyone responsible for another party's money or property. Fiduciaries have a legal duty to behave honestly and conscientiously, and to avoid promoting their own self-interest at the expense of the owner of the assets.

Many types of people who deal with pension and benefit plans are considered fiduciaries under ERISA—including some people who do not think of themselves in that way or do not understand their responsibilities and potential liabilities.

Fiduciary liability extends far beyond embezzlement and other criminal acts. It is even possible for one fiduciary's mistake or wrongdoing to get a group of other fiduciaries into trouble.

An individual, business, or institution that deals with a plan becomes a fiduciary whenever, and to the extent that, he or she:

- Exercises any discretionary authority (i.e., is able to make decisions) or control over the management of the plan;

- Exercises any authority (even if it isn't discretionary) over the management and disposition of plan assets. The distinction is made because the greatest potential for abuse exists when money is at stake;
- Receives direct or indirect compensation for giving the plan investment advice about its assets;
- Has any discretionary authority or responsibility for day-to-day plan administration (as distinct from plan management).

In other words, if a plan hires attorneys, accountants, or actuaries to provide advice, those professionals will usually not become fiduciaries of the plan, because they do not control the direction that the plan takes. They merely provide technical information that the administrator and other fiduciaries use to make decisions.

Just having custody of plan assets doesn't make the custodian a fiduciary, so a law firm did not become a fiduciary by acting as an escrow agent for funds belonging to one of its clients. (The issue arose when a partner in the law firm embezzled some of the money.) [*Burtch v. Ganz* (*In re Mushroom Transport Co. Inc.*), 382 F.3d 325 (3d Cir. 2004)]

However, in *L.I. Head Start Child Development Services v. Frank* [165 F. Supp. 2d 367 (E.D.N.Y. 2001)], the court held that attorneys can be liable for breaches of fiduciary duty committed by an insolvent health fund, if the lawyers knew that their legal fees were paid from funds improperly accumulated by the fund and not used for the exclusive benefit of participants and beneficiaries. In effect, nonfiduciary professionals can become liable through knowing participation in a fiduciary's breach of duty. A financial consulting firm that appraised the employer's stock is not a fiduciary, and is not liable for an Employee Stock Ownership Plan's losses. [*Keach v. U.S. Trust Co.*, 234 F. Supp. 2d 872 (C.D. Ill. 2002)]

Tip: If the professional adviser is not a fiduciary, ERISA probably will not preempt state-law malpractice suits brought by the plan.

Similarly, a stockbroker who simply executes the fiduciaries' orders to adjust the plan's investment portfolio is not a fiduciary—but an investment manager who has a role in setting the plan's investment policy is very definitely a fiduciary.

The Ninth Circuit held that being a fiduciary for ERISA purposes does not necessarily entail being a fiduciary as defined by Bankruptcy Code § 523(a)(4), the Bankruptcy Code provision that prevents bankruptcy discharge of debts for fiduciary fraud. [*Hunter v. Philpott*, 373 F.3d 873 (9th Cir. 2004)]

Two pilots were told, when their employer was acquired by another airline, that the balances in their pension accounts would be transferred to a comparable 401(k) plan. The notice was sent by the benefits consulting firm hired to administer the 401(k) plan. The actual account transfers occurred weeks or months after the time given in the notice. The plaintiffs sued the acquiror company and the consulting firm, charging that they violated ERISA § 502(a)(2) by misrepresenting how and when the balances would be transferred, and that their accounts had lost value by remaining in the ex-employer's failing plan longer than necessary. The Fifth Circuit ruled that TPAs are not fiduciaries when they merely perform administrative duties. The question is whether they acted as fiduciaries with respect to the specific acts or omissions that are charged as ERISA violations. Even if the plaintiffs' allegations are accepted as true, the plaintiffs did not allege that the TPA exercised any control or discretion over the content of the notices, the transfer of funds, the length of the blackout period, or investments in the account. The court rejected the plaintiffs' theory that their claim inured to the benefit of the plan as a whole, ruling that they merely sought individualized relief for particularized harm. The court reached this conclusion because the plaintiffs sought to have damages allocated among individual accounts in proportion to losses. Nonmembers of the class would not receive anything from a plaintiff victory, because no funds would be added to their accounts. The Supreme Court has restricted the ERISA § 502(a)(2) cause of action to cases that benefit the whole plan, based on factors such as whether all plan participants benefit directly (via an increase in all account balances), whether the alleged fiduciary breach targeted the plan as a whole, and whether all the participants or only a subset bring suit. The Fifth Circuit ruled that in this case, only a few participants sued, and only for their own accounts, so they lacked standing under ERISA § 502(a)(3) because they acted on behalf of their own subclass only. [*Milofsky v. American Airlines Inc.,* 404 F.3d 338 (5th Cir. 2005). The Fifth Circuit has agreed to rehear *Milofsky,* and several other circuits (the Third, Sixth, and Eighth) have permitted a group of participants in a 401(k) or other individual account plan to seek money damages for losses resulting from alleged breach of fiduciary duty (retention of employer stock in the plan after its value had declined), even if the breach affected only a portion of the participants, not all of them. [*In re Schering-Plough Corp. ERISA Litigation,* 420 F.3d 231 (3d Cir. 2005)]

A TPA can be considered an ERISA fiduciary even if it does not have discretionary control over the assets of the health plan it administered; the statutory language is "any authority or control." The Sixth Circuit held that a TPA's authority to write checks on the plan's account (which continued to be exercised to pay the TPA's fees even after the contract with the plan sponsor ended) provided the necessary degree of authority or control to impose liability after the sponsor company went bankrupt and many employees had unpaid medical bills. [*Briscoe v. Fine,* 444 F.3d 478 (6th Cir. 2006)]

Similarly, the Tenth Circuit found the power to receive plan contributions, deposit them into its business account, and write checks to the plan's investment adviser on its behalf was sufficient to make the TPA a fiduciary. [*David P. Coldesina D.D.S. P.C. Employee Profit Sharing Plan v. Estate of Simper,* 407 F.3d 1126 (10th Cir. 2005)]

An insurance broker who was accused of keeping the money remitted to him to pay insurance premiums was a fiduciary, despite his lack of discretionary control, because of the allegation that he exercised practical control over plan assets by seizing them. [*Chao v. Day,* 436 F.3d 234 (D.C. Cir. 2006)]

According to the Southern District of New York, when the PBGC calculated the benefits due under a terminated plan to former employees of an airline, the agency acted as a statutory trustee and not a government guarantor. Therefore, it can be sued for breach of fiduciary duty if the calculations were incorrect. [*Pineiro v. PBGC,* 318 F. Supp. 2d 67 (S.D.N.Y. 2003)]

The contract between a plan sponsor and a plan administrator permitted the administrator to keep funds resulting from discounts given by health care providers. The Sixth Circuit ruled that the administrator was not acting as a fiduciary when, in accordance with the contract, it retained these sums—so there couldn't have been a fiduciary breach. Adhering to a contract that does not call for exercise of discretion does not make a party a fiduciary. [*Seaway Food Town Inc. v. Medical Mutual of Ohio,* 347 F.3d 610 (6th Cir. 2003)]

In October 2001, a Tennessee district court ruled that an insurer acting under an Administrative Services Only (ASO) contract could be sued for breach of fiduciary duty, even though it was not named in the plan documents as a fiduciary, because of the discretion it exercised in managing the plan's assets and keeping its records. [*Guardsmark Inc. v. Blue Cross and Blue Shield of Tennessee,* 169 F. Supp. 2d 794 (W.D. Tenn. 2001)]

The court treated the insurer as a "functional fiduciary" subject to claims that it wrongfully approved some claims and lost documentation for other claims, and that it overcharged the plan for its services and failed to provide proper documentation. The District Court also ruled that state-law claims were not preempted by ERISA, to the extent that some of the plan's claims against Blue Cross were not covered by ERISA.

The owner of a grocery store was held personally liable, to the tune of more than $5 million, for wrongfully terminating a voucher program that provided groceries to retirees. The program was treated as an ERISA pension plan. The store owner was not liable as an administrator, but he was liable as a fiduciary, for failure to fund the plan and for terminating it without making provision for rights already funded under the plan. [*Musmeci v. Schwegmann Giant Super Markets,* 332 F.3d 339 (5th Cir. 2003)]

Harold Ives Trucking Co. v. Spradley & Coker Inc. [178 F.3d 523 (8th Cir. 1999)] holds that, even though its service contract had language to the contrary, a Third-Party Administrator (TPA) became a fiduciary by making an independent determination that a rehab facility was covered under an Employee Group Health Plan.

Fiduciary conduct is examined on two levels. Fiduciaries must satisfy their affirmative obligations (to choose proper investments for the plan; to diversity investments unless diversification itself is imprudent; to maintain proper liquidity; to obtain a reasonable yield on plan investments; and to make proper administrative decisions). They are also forbidden to engage in prohibited transactions.

The Pension and Welfare Benefit Administration (now EBSA) published a Final Rule on January 5, 2000 [65 Fed. Reg. 615], creating a safe harbor for insurance companies that manage pension funds as part of their general accounts. Insurance policies do become plan assets, but for policies issued on or before December 31, 1998, the insurance company will not be an ERISA fiduciary as to the plan, if the insurer provides adequate annual disclosure to plan participants. Furthermore, if the insurer unilaterally modifies the policy in a way that has a material adverse effect on the policyholder, 60 days' advance notice is required.

§ 15.03   FIDUCIARY DUTIES

[A]   ERISA Requirements

ERISA imposes four major duties on fiduciaries:

- Loyalty;
- Prudence;
- Acting in accordance with the plan documents;
- Monitoring the performance of anyone to whom fiduciary responsibility has been delegated.

The source of the duty of loyalty is the ERISA mandate that plan assets be held for the exclusive benefit of participants and beneficiaries. Once assets have been placed into the plan trust, or used to buy insurance, they can no longer be used for the benefit of the employer.

The duty of prudence requires fiduciaries to behave with the level of care, skill, prudence, and diligence that a hypothetical prudent person would use to handle the same tasks. This hypothetical prudent person is familiar with the plan and its situation—not the "man on the street" who lacks specialized knowledge.

Although trust law requires every asset within a trust to satisfy the prudent person test, DOL Reg. § 2550.404a-1(c)(2) allows the fiduciary to select assets by considering the relevant facts and circumstances, including the role of the individual investment within the portfolio. Relying on expert advice is encouraged, but it does not guarantee that an investment choice will be considered prudent.

In 2002, the Sixth Circuit examined the scope of fiduciary duty, in a case brought by pension plan trustees, a participant, and the plan itself, alleging that the defendants breached their fiduciary duties as plan trustees by failing to make required contributions, collect repayment of plan loans, and file the necessary annual reports. The Sixth Circuit's ruling in *Best v. Cyrus* [310 F.3d 932 (6th Cir. 2002)] is that ERISA incorporates the concepts of fiduciary duty created by trust law. Therefore, trustees are subject to additional duties even if the duties are not spelled out in the plan documents. In other words, the plan document can't limit the general fiduciary duties owed by trustees. However, in this case the trustee was not responsible for filing the Form 5500 annual report, because that obligation falls on the plan administrator.

[B]   Diversification

The general rule is that ERISA requires fiduciaries to diversify unless diversification is imprudent (the fiduciary has to prove this). The fiduciary is supposed to select a balanced portfolio that is responsive to current conditions. The portfolio's liquidity and current return must be considered in light of anticipated needs for cash flow. Fiduciaries are not restricted to a "legal list" of investments, and are permitted to take a certain amount of risk, as long as the risk is reasonable in the context of the entire portfolio.

In early 2002, the failure of Enron Corporation highlighted the entire question of investment in employer securities. The basic ERISA rule is that plans can invest in employer securities only if they are "qualifying employer securities" such as stock and eligible debt instruments. Defined benefit plans are subject to additional limitations on holdings of employer securities. [*See* § 6.09[C] for additional discussion of this issue in the context of 401(k) plans]

A Fifth Circuit case held that a pension administrator did not breach fiduciary duty by investing 65% of the plan's assets in undeveloped land. [*Metzler v. Graham,* 112 F.3d 207 (5th Cir. 1997)] The court decided that there was no real risk of a large loss, so the investment was prudent at the time it was made. Most of the plan participants were young, so there was enough time to make up for losses if they did occur, and there was plenty of time for appreciation in the land's value. The fiduciary was familiar with the local real estate market and thus able to select good investments. Historically, real estate has played an important portfolio role as an investment hedge.

In the view of the Central District of Illinois, it was not a violation of fiduciary duty for ESOP trustees, after a merger, to continue to invest two-thirds of the assets of the terminated profit-sharing plan in the sponsoring employer's stock. When the case was appealed, the Seventh Circuit affirmed this finding and ruled that it was not a fiduciary breach for the terminated plan to take 18 months to distribute plan assets to the employees. Because there was no fiduciary breach, the fiduciaries were not liable for losses the plan incurred during that 18-month period. [*Steinman v. Hicks,* 252 F. Supp. 2d 746 (C.D. Ill. 2003), *aff'd,* 352 F.3d 1101 (7th Cir. 2003)]

[C]   Investments

The question of how to invest plan assets becomes even more salient in a down market, when many plans face losses, than during a roaring bull market. Additional problems arose in 2003 and 2004, in connection with SEC and state investigations of securities-law violations allegedly committed by mutual funds. In 2004, the DOL offered guidance for fiduciaries worried about their potential for being dragged into liability because of the mutual funds they invested in. The DOL announced that it would investigate ERISA issues about fund advisers and mutual fund investments.

DOL acknowledged that fiduciaries could not have predicted that mutual funds would be accused of late-trading and market-timing abuses, but now fiduciaries are on notice and must review their investments to consider the impact of these abuses. Fiduciaries must consider the appropriateness of continuing to invest in a fund that has faced charges or has settled a case. The decision depends on factors such as the nature of the allegations; the potential effect of abuses on the plan's investment; what the mutual fund has done to prevent future losses; and remedial actions taken to make investors whole. DOL cautions fiduciaries that the mere fact that a particular mutual fund has not faced charges does not mean it is free from abuses. Fiduciaries should consider asking fund managers how they identify and police improper trading practices.

The problem is that fiduciaries are required to provide full disclosure of information plan participants need to make informed choices—but securities law forbids the release of certain nonpublic information. If there has been clear fraud, the fiduciary probably has to disclose nonpublic information, but perhaps disclosure would not be required in other situations. Plaintiffs have seldom been so successful with claims that it was not prudent for a fiduciary to continue to invest in the employer's stock. [(no by-line) *Retirement Plan Litigation Expected to Wend Its Way to Appeals Courts*, 72 LW 2539 (Mar. 16, 2004)]

Two recent district court decisions state that it is not "discrimination" under ERISA § 510 for a plan to forbid round-trip trades over $75,000, or to require high-volume traders to make their trading requests in writing [*Straus v. Prudential Employee Savings Plan,* 253 F. Supp. 438 (E.D.N.Y. 2003)], and held that trading restrictions on a 401(k) separate account were justified by plan language reserving the right to defer or stop participants' ability to direct contributions and transfers to a separate account within the 401(k) plan. [*See Borneman v. Principal Life Ins Co.,* 291 F. Supp. 935 (S.D. Iowa 2003)]

The Ninth Circuit not only found a fiduciary breach, but also held a plan manager personally liable for the plan's losses when he used plan assets to buy complex derivative securities that were illiquid and very risky. This was held to be imprudent because fiduciaries must investigate their purchases in advance. Relying on a trusted broker isn't good enough. [*Gilbert v. EMG Advisors Inc.,* 1999 U.S. App. LEXIS 4719 (9th Cir. Mar. 17, 1999)]

But fiduciaries are not liable merely because adverse consequences happened on their watch. An employer's purchase of Guaranteed Investment Certificates (GICs), for individual pension accounts, from a company that was eventually seized by regulators, was not a breach of fiduciary duty. [*In re Unisys Savs. Plan Litig.,* 173 F.3d 145 (3d Cir. 1999)] The employer acted with adequate prudence by delegating investment responsibility to appropriate parties, who made an adequate investigation before recommending the purchase. [*Bussian v. RJR Nabisco Inc.,* 21 F. Supp. 2d 680 (S.D. Tex. 1998), reaches a similar conclusion for annuities purchased from an insurer that later became bankrupt]

In a merger situation, plan participants wanted to sell some of their holdings of the employer's stock to take advantage of the post-merger increase in value.

The fiduciaries of a stock bonus plan refused to permit this. The Ninth Circuit found that the refusal did not breach the fiduciaries' ERISA § 404 duty of prudence, because it would have been an ERISA violation to permit them to sell off more stock than the terms of the plan allowed. The Ninth Circuit pointed out that the duty to act in accordance with the plan sometimes prevents fiduciaries from deciding issues the way that participants want. [*Wright v. Oregon Metallurgical Corp.*, 360 F.3d 1090 (9th Cir. 2004)]

Plan participants who charged that Sears caused them to invest their 401(k) plans in employer stock without telling them that the company was aware of mistakes in its 2001 SEC filings were permitted to maintain a class action against the company, its board of directors, top executives, and investment committee members for breach of fiduciary duty. The Northern District of Illinois refused to dismiss their case even though the information in question was nonpublic. [*In re Sears, Roebuck & Co. ERISA Litigation*, 2004 WL 407007 (N.D. Ill. Mar. 2, 2004)]

Conseco agreed to pay $10 million to settle an employee class action charging ERISA violations in connection with stock losses when the company went bankrupt in 2002. The suit, brought in the District Court for the District of Indiana, charged Conseco and current and former officers with breach of fiduciary duty because they allowed 401(k) plan participants to remain invested in employer stock without disclosing the company's true financial state. [Rupal Parekh, *Conseco Settles Employees' ERISA Class Action*, Business Insurance, Mar. 17, 2005 (law.com)]

The First Circuit ruled that ESOP participant plaintiffs could survive a motion to dismiss by charging that fiduciaries knowingly allowed them to invest in the employer's stock when the fiduciaries knew the price of the stock was artificially inflated. The First Circuit conceded that it would be difficult to actually win the case, but the claim gave the employer fair notice that it had inflated the stock price by concealing its financial problems. The First Circuit refused to accept the district court's hard and fast rule that it is presumptively reasonable to invest in employer stock, so ESOP fiduciaries cannot be in breach of their fiduciary duty until the company is on the brink of collapse. [*Lalonde v. Textron Inc.*, 369 F.3d 1 (1st Cir. 2004)]

Because fiduciaries are obligated to act in the best interests of plan participants and beneficiaries, self-dealing (engaging in transactions for the fiduciary's own benefit) is always at least suspect, and is often a breach of duty, although it can be excusable if no detriment to the plan or its participants occurs.

The Eighth Circuit held in 2002 that ERISA § 408(c)(2) provides a separate exemption for self-dealing by fiduciaries if the compensation paid was reasonable [*Harley v. Minnesota Mining & Mfg. Co.*, 284 F.3d 901 (8th Cir. 2002)], even though the relevant DOL regulations [29 C.F.R. § 2550.4086-2(e)] do not allow an exemption when the fiduciary gets paid for providing services to the plan. In this case, the Eighth Circuit believed that the fiduciaries made a mistake by investing in collateralized mortgage securities without fully understanding this type of investment, but any loss in the value of assets in an overfunded plan essentially harms the plan sponsor (which may have to make up the difference) and not the plan's participants and beneficiaries. Self-dealing came into the picture because the fee for the plan's investment advisor was tied to the value of the mortgage securities.

In 2002, the Eastern District of Pennsylvania approved a settlement of ERISA claims on behalf of 401(k) plan participants. The claims arose because the participants were required to allocate their employer matching contributions to the employer's stock. The settlement requires the plan to be amended to eliminate this requirement. Participants with two or more years of service will be allowed to invest the matching contributions in any investment option offered under the plan.

An independent advisor will be retained to review the educational materials given to participants to teach them about investment choices. A second independent advisor will review and report to the fiduciaries about the comparative performance of employer stock versus the other investment options. The settlement does not provide any monetary relief for plan participants, because the court believed that the plan amendment would eventually make the plan more valuable; a large cash award would depress the value of the employer's stock, perhaps harming participants in the long run; and many of the plaintiffs were also involved in a class action that resulted in a settlement of securities fraud claims against the employer. [*In re IKON Office Solutions Inc. Securities Litigation* (*Whetman v. IKON*) 209 F.R.D. 94 (E.D. Pa. 2002)]

The fiduciaries of a plan delayed more than a year making a requested distribution from the plan (because they were directors of the sponsor company, and also relatives of the plan participant who stood to inherit if the plan balance went into the participant's estate instead of being distributed to the designated beneficiary, as the court ruled should have been done). Complicating the serious problem of fiduciary breach was the decline in value of the account, which lost 40% of its value, falling from $1.5 million to about $900,000. (The fiduciaries failed to diversify, leaving 55% of the fund invested in just one stock.)

The Northern District of Ohio granted summary judgment for the employer, finding that the retiree did not show that the plan's method of making distributions *pro rata* from all of a defined contribution plan participant's investment funds, rather than from just one fund selected by the participant, violated ERISA. The plaintiff filed an administrative appeal from the denial and sought financial data and documentation for one of the funds. He sued when the appeal was denied. The Northern District found that the proper standard of review for the denial was arbitrary and capricious, because the plan granted the committee full discretionary power. [*Hickey v. Pennywitt*, 2004 U.S. Dist. LEXIS 10734 (N.D. Oh. 2004)]

A question that continues to arise is the extent of liability when a corporation's stock value plunges and participants who remained invested in the stock experience losses.

The District Court for the District of Kansas permitted participants to maintain a suit for breach of fiduciary duty in keeping employer stock in the plan because the defendants were fiduciaries. The CEO could not escape liability by claiming that he was not obligated to monitor the investment committee's performance, because that would render his duty to appoint and remove committee members meaningless. Nor would the court extend the presumption that investing in employer stock is prudent to a plan that was not an ESOP. [*In re Westar Energy Inc. ERISA Litigation*, 74 L.W. 1240 (D. Kan. Sept. 29, 2005). *See In re McKesson HBOC Inc. ERISA Litigation*, 74 L.W. 1192 (N.D. Cal. Sept. 9, 2005) (the special mission of an ESOP is to invest in employer stock, so ERISA permits an ESOP to retain employer stock even if it would be prudent to disinvest)]

Of course, the terms of the individual plan will affect the outcome of a challenge to the plan's administration. The Eastern District of Michigan and the Southern District of Illinois, however, permitted participants to maintain breach of fiduciary suits for continued investment in the employers' stock. [*Sherrill v. Federal-Mogul Corp. Retirement Programs Committee*, No. 04-72949 (E.D. Mich. Feb. 9, 2006); *Lively v. Dynegy Inc.*, No. 05-cv-0063-MJR (S.D. Ill. Feb. 15, 2006), both 74 L.W. 1528] In contrast, the Southern District of Texas held that keeping the employer's stock in the defined contribution plan was not a breach of fiduciary duty because the plan clearly stated that employer stock must be an investment option at all times. Thus, the employer and the administrative committee did not have the authorty to remove the stock. Alleged misrepresentations made to the SEC were not breaches of fiduciary duty because filing forms with the SEC was an issuer action, not a fiduciary action. [*In re Reliant Energy ERISA Litigation*, 74 L.W. 1496 (S.D. Tex. Jan. 18, 2006)]

[D] Fiduciary Duties in Health Plans

According to the Supreme Court, an HMO is not acting as a fiduciary when, acting through its doctors, it makes a "mixed" decision about medical treatment and health plan eligibility. [*Pegram v. Herdrich*, 530 U.S. 211 (2000)] Therefore, even if plan participants are right that the plan refused them necessary treatments in order to increase its profits, they have not stated a cause of action for breach of fiduciary duty.

The Supreme Court returned to the question of review of HMO coverage decisions in mid-2004: *Aetna Health Inc. v. Davila* and *Cigna Healthcare of Texas, Inc. v. Calad*, 542 U.S. 200 (2004). One of the plaintiffs alleged harm caused by denial of coverage of an expensive arthritis drug; the other claimed that she was prematurely discharged from the hospital, leading to complications of surgery. They sued under a Texas state law dealing with HMO negligence. The Supreme Court held that ERISA completely preempts the state law, because ERISA covers all cases where someone claims that coverage was denied under a plan that is a welfare benefit plan for ERISA purposes. However, in this case, the Supreme Court clarified its earlier *Pegram v. Herdrich* decision. In that case, HMOs were held not to be fiduciaries to the extent that they act through their physicians to make mixed eligibility and treatment decisions. The 2004 decision says that HMOs are fiduciaries when they make pure eligibility decisions. The consequence is that if patients sue in state court, claiming that they were wrongfully denied health benefits, the case is completely preempted by ERISA and can be removed to federal court.

In September 2004, the Third Circuit ruled that ERISA preempts Pennsylvania's statute that awards remedies for bad-faith failure to pay insurance claims. (The case involved a long-term disability plan that terminated the plaintiff's benefits after determining that he was no longer disabled.) The Third Circuit found conflict preemption because the state statute awards punitive damages, which are not part of Congress's ERISA enforcement scheme. After *Calad/Davila*, the Third Circuit no longer believed that the statute could qualify for the savings clause for statutes that regulate insurance, because it did not substantially affect the transfer of risk between insured and insurer, in that bad-faith breach of the insurance contract is not a risk of loss the insurer agrees to bear for its insured as part of the contract. ERISA preempts state laws that duplicate, supplement, or seek to replace the ERISA enforcement system. [*Barber v. UNUM Life Ins. Co. of America*, 383 F.3d 134 (3d Cir. 2004)]

A health plan participant was not informed that, after losing an internal appeal of a denied claim, his only further redress was to file for arbitration within 60 days. However, he would have known this if he had consulted the SPD. The Ninth Circuit ruled that failure to disclose the arbitration requirement violated ERISA § 404(a), which obligates fiduciaries to act solely in the interests of plan participants and beneficiaries. [*Chappel v. Laboratory Corp. of Am.*, 232 F.3d 719 (9th Cir. 2000)] The fiduciary must provide written notice of the steps that must be taken to invoke arbitration.

An insurer denied claims under an EGHP because the policy had lapsed as a result of the employer's failure to pay the premiums. The plan participants were not informed of the lapse. A plan participant's estate sued the insurer, charging it with breach of fiduciary duty by denying the claim and failing to inform her that her coverage had been canceled. The District Court for the District of Nebraska held, in early 2004, that the insurer was not the plan administrator, that the policy made the employer responsible for providing notification, and that the insurer's denial was not a fiduciary action because there was no coverage available so there was no discretion involved in denying the claim. [*Nakazawa v. Principal Financial Group*, No. 8:01CV624 (D. Neb. Feb. 26, 2004)]

A self-funded group health plan sued its Third-Party Administrator (TPA) claiming that the TPA was a fiduciary that breached its duties by mismanaging claims administration and retaining the interest earned on the plan's checking account. The district court agreed that the TPA was a fiduciary, because the plan was not detailed enough to render the TPA's role purely ministerial. The TPA decided the vast majority of the claims. All of the TPA's requests for more money to write checks were approved, so in effect the TPA had access to all the plan funds. But, although the Western District of Tennessee decided that the TPA was a fiduciary with respect to writing checks and claims administration, retaining the interest was not a breach of fiduciary duty, because it was a negotiated item of compensation under the TPA's contract with the plan. [*Guardsmark, Inc. v. Blue Cross & Blue Shield of Tenn*, Civ. No. 01-2117 (W.D. Tenn. 2004)].

An employee's spouse, covered by an EGHP, received physical therapy for a stroke for about three months. At that point, she was informed that the plan limited physical therapy coverage to 60 visits a year, so no more could be covered. She sued the employer and insurer, alleging that the SPD permitted an unlimited number of therapy visits. However, what she referred to as the SPD was actually the enrollment guide for the plan (although she was also furnished with an SPD). According to the Western District of Louisiana, the terms of the SPD (which limited PT visits to 60 a year) would have to govern in case of conflict with other plan documents. [*Bailey v. CIGNA Ins. Co.*, No. 01-1115 (W.D. La. Sept. 5, 2002), *aff'd* 87 Fed. Appx. 347 (5th Cir. 2004)]

§ 15.04   DUTIES OF THE TRUSTEE

Usually, pension and welfare benefit plans will be organized in trust form. Every trust must have at least one trustee. ERISA § 403(a) provides that the trustee can be named in the instrument itself, appointed under a procedure set out in the plan, or appointed by a named fiduciary.

The trustee has exclusive authority and discretion to manage and control the plan's assets. If there are multiple trustees, they must jointly manage and control, although ERISA § 403(a) permits them to delegate some duties. Certain fiduciary duties can be delegated—it depends on whether trustee responsibility or other duties are involved.

A plan can be drafted to make its trustee subject to a named fiduciary who is not a trustee—for example, to make the trustee report to an administrative committee. If this is done, the trustee must comply with "proper" directions given by the named fiduciary, if they are in accordance with the plan's procedures and not contrary to law.

If there has been a proper appointment of an investment manager, the trustee does not have to manage or invest the assets placed under the investment manager's control. Crucially, the trustee will not be liable for the acts or omissions of the investment manager. The trustee has a duty to make sure that the manager charges reasonable fees; performance-based fees, rather than flat fees determined in advance, are allowed.

A DOL Field Assistance Bulletin issued late in 2004 provides guidance when a plan uses directed trustees to carry out transactions on the basis of instructions from a named fiduciary. Even though some trustees' authority or discretion is limited, a plan trustee is always a fiduciary. The Bulletin cites *In re Enron Corp Securities Litigation*, 284 F. Supp. 2d 511 (S.D. Tex. 2003), which holds that a directed trustee has at least some fiduciary status and duties. A directed trustee's knowledge of a fiduciary breach can render him or her liable as a co-fiduciary unless the directed trustee takes reasonable steps to remedy the breach. However, the directed trustee's duties under ERISA § 403(a)(1) are narrower than those assigned to a discretionary trustee under common-law trust principles.

A directed trustee is subject to "proper" directions of a named fiduciary; a proper direction is one that does not violate ERISA and conforms to the terms of the plan. A directed trustee is not permitted to follow a direction that he or she knows or should know is inconsistent with the plan terms, and therefore there is a duty to review the relevant plan documents to learn about appropriate directions.

The named fiduciary carries the primary responsibility for determining whether a particular transaction is prudent, and the directed trustee's responsibility is limited; the DOL does not require the directed trustee to second-guess the named fiduciaries or make an independent assessment of the prudence of every transaction. This is particularly true when the direction is to purchase publicly traded securities at the market price. The DOL noted that stock prices habitually fluctuate, so even a sharp drop would not necessarily make it imprudent to retain the stock within the plan's portfolio.

A directed trustee's obligation to question transactions in publicly traded stock on the ground of prudence is very limited. When there are clear and compelling public indicators, such as a bankruptcy filing or data on a Form 8-K, the directed trustee might be placed on notice that the company is not viable as a going concern. Additional inquiry may be required if a directed trustee gets a direction to buy or hold the stock of the company that employs the fiduciary after the company or its officers or directors have been charged with financial irregularities. [DOL Field Assistance Bulletin No. 2004-03 (Dec. 17, 2004), <http://www.dol.gov/ebsa/pdf/fab-2004-3.pdf>]

The Eastern District of Virginia ruled in September 2005 that a directed trustee of a retirement plan does not have a fiduciary duty to question the named investment fiduciary's retention of employer stock in the plan, where there was no available public information that would inform the directed trustee of the worthlessness of the stock. The term "directed trustee" does not appear in the text of ERISA, but it is widely understood to mean a trustee subject to the direction of a named fiduciary who is not a trustee. However, in October 2005, the same court denied summary judgment for the airline, this time holding that there was a triable issue of fact as to the prudence of maintaining company stock as an investment for the 401(k) plan. The Eastern District granted summary judgment for the airline on the issue of whether it breached its fiduciary duty by failing to provide adequate investment information. [DiFelice v. US Airways Inc., 74 L.W. 1202 (E.D. Va. Sep. 27, 2005) and 74 L.W. 1263 (E.D. Va. Oct. 18, 2005)]

A directed trustee of an ESOP is not liable for breach of fiduciary duty for holding the company's stock despite its significant drop in value. A directed trustee is liable only for failing to act on reliable and trustworthy information and has no duty to advise the ESOP committee on investing or to investigate the correctness of its investment choices. [Summers v. UAL Corp. ESOP Comm., 74 L.W. 1256 (N.D. Ill. Oct. 12, 2005)]

Early in 2005, the Southern District of New York ruled that Merrill Lynch was a directed trustee for ERISA purposes (with a limited fiduciary role), and it was not guilty of breach of fiduciary duty when it did not prevent the holders of 401(k) accounts from investing in WorldCom stock. The Southern District ruled that Merrill merely followed WorldCom's instructions, and did not have any material non-public information that would require Merrill to inquire. In this reading, a directed trustee does not have a duty of inquiry merely because it is aware that the company has financial difficulties, or even that an SEC investigation is under way, although the result might be different where actual suits or criminal charges have been filed. [*In re WorldCom Inc. ERISA Litigation*, 2004 W.L. 2338151 (S.D.N.Y. Oct. 18, 2004), discussed in Michael Bobelian, *Merrill Lynch Wins Workers' Suit Over WorldCom 401(k) Choices*, New York Law Journal, Feb. 2, 2005 (law.com)]

A father and son, the owners of a business that shut down, were both found liable for failing to deposit nearly $43,000 in amounts deferred by employees into the 401(k) plan. (After the company went out of business, the DOL brought suit for breach of fiduciary duty.) Both of them were trustees who exercised control over the contributions. Although the father claimed to be retired, the Northern District of New York pointed out that he continued to draw a paycheck and went to the office on most days. Furthermore, his abdication of responsibility facilitated his son's ability to misappropriate funds from the plan. [*Chao v. James C. Docster Inc.*, N.D.N.Y., No. 3:01-CV-827, 3/31/06; *see* Rebecca Moore, *Father and Son Held Liable for Not Forwarding Employee Contributions*, PlanSponsor.com (Apr. 6, 2006)]

§ 15.05 THE EMPLOYER'S ROLE

Although it might be predicted that the heaviest liability for plan misconduct would fall on the company that sponsors the plan, this is not always the case. The corporation might not be a fiduciary, or might not be acting in a fiduciary capacity in a particular case.

To prevent conflicts of interest, ERISA §§ 403, 4042, and 4044 allow fiduciaries to perform certain actions without violating the duty to maintain the plan for the sole benefit of participants and beneficiaries. Employer contributions can be returned if:

- The contributions were made based on a mistake of fact;
- The plan is not qualified under I.R.C. §§ 401(a) or 403(a);
- The income tax deduction for part or all of the contribution is disallowed;
- The contribution could be treated as an excess contribution under I.R.C. § 4975.

Nor is there a conflict of interest if the fiduciary follows PBGC requirements for a distribution incident to a plan termination.

§ 15.06   INVESTMENT MANAGERS

[A]   Qualified Managers under ERISA

If the plan so permits, ERISA allows fiduciaries to delegate their investment duties to a qualified investment manager.

There are four categories of qualified investment managers:

- Investment advisers who are registered under the federal Investment Company Act—whether they are independent consultants or in-house employees of the plan;
- Trust companies;
- Banks;
- Qualified insurance companies.

ERISA requires the manager to acknowledge in writing that he, she, or it has become a fiduciary with respect to the plan.

DOL Reg. § 2510.3-21(c) explains who will be deemed qualified to render investment advice:

- Those who give advice about the value of securities or recommend investing, buying, or selling securities (or other property, such as real estate);
- Those who are given discretion to buy or sell securities for the plan;
- Those who give advice, on a regular basis, under an oral or written agreement, if the advice is intended to serve as a primary basis for investing plan funds.

As long as the fiduciaries were prudent when they chose the manager (and continued to review the manager's performance), the fiduciaries will not be liable for acts and omissions committed by the manager.

A broker-dealer, bank, or reporting dealer does not become a fiduciary if its only role is to take and execute buy and sell orders for the plan. [DOL Reg. § 2510.3-21(d)(1)] The investment manager is a fiduciary only as to whatever percentage of the overall investment he or she can influence (except in situations where ERISA § 405(a) makes the investment manager responsible for breaches by co-fiduciaries).

In mid-2005, DOL and the SEC released suggestions for fiduciaries to help them choose and monitor investment consultants (complementing earlier DOL guidance about doing the same for employee benefit plan service providers such as recordkeepers). The SEC's concern is that investment consultants can experience conflicts of interest, especially in "pay to play" arrangements whereby the consultants are compensated by brokers or money managers for offering access to the consultant's plan clients.

The two federal agencies released a list of issues that a fiduciary must consider:

- Is the consultant registered as an investment adviser? If so, the fiduciary should review the disclosures on Part II of SEC's Form ADV.
- Get written acknowledgment that the consultant is a fiduciary and will comply with fiduciary obligations.
- Find out if the consultant or a related company has relationships with the money managers recommended and whether the consultant receives payments or trades by the money managers that the consultant recommends.
- Ask about the consultant's policy on conflicts of interest.

DOL suggests including questions on these topics in any request for proposals for a new consultant—and perhaps even seeking written answers from existing consultants. The RFP also can be used to obtain representations and warranties of compliance, collect information about the consultant's insurance coverage and willingness to indemnify the client. Plans should determine when the contract can be terminated either for cause or for the convenience of the parties; the plan's right to continue using materials developed by the service provider for the plan; liquidated damages for failure to satisfy contractual standards; and any pending litigation or complaints outstanding against the service provider. [McDermott Newsletters, *Recent Guidance on Selecting and Monitoring Service Providers* (benefitslink.com) (June 27, 2005)]

[B]   The Role of the Insurer

The Supreme Court's decision in *John Hancock Mutual Life Insurance v. Harris Trust* [510 U.S. 86 (1993)] holds that assets held in an insurer's general account and not guaranteed by the insurer are plan assets subject to ERISA's fiduciary requirements.

DOL issued interim regulations covering insurance contracts sold before December 31, 1998; later contracts are all covered by ERISA fiduciary rules. DOL's Interpretive Bulletin 95-1 says that a fiduciary who chooses annuities to distribute plan benefits has a fiduciary duty to choose the safest available contract, based on factors such as the insurer's size and reputation, the insurer's other lines of business, and the size and provisions of the proposed contracts.

§ 15.07   DUTY TO DISCLOSE

Employees have a right to information about their benefit options, and fiduciaries have a corresponding duty to make complete, accurate disclosure. Furthermore, they need information about the way the plan is expected to evolve, so they can make future plans.

The classic test, stemming from *Fischer v. Philadelphia Electric Co.* [96 F.3d 1533 (3d Cir. 1996)] is that plan participants who inquire must not only be informed about the current structure of the plan—they must be informed of proposals that are under "serious consideration" by management. [Some cases say that, although information must be provided to those who ask for it, it need not be volunteered if there is no request, e.g., *Bins v. Exxon Co.*, 220 F.3d 1042 (9th Cir. 2000); *Hudson v. General Dynamics Corp.*, 118 F. Supp. 2d 226 (D. Conn. 2000). But other cases say that there is a fiduciary duty to give information whenever silence could be harmful to beneficiaries' financial interests. *See Krohn v. Huron Mem. Hosp.*, 173 F.3d 542 (6th Cir. 1999).] The Fifth Circuit refused to adopt the "serious consideration" test: *Martinez v. Schlumberger Ltd.*, 338 F.3d 407 (5th Cir. 2003), even though seven Courts of Appeals use this test. The Fifth Circuit assesses whether the information that was not given would have been material to a reasonable person's decision to retire.

The Seventh Circuit held, in mid-2004, that an employer is an ERISA fiduciary only in connection with benefits under an existing plan or amendments to existing plans. Therefore, it could not have been a breach of fiduciary duty to misinform an employee about the possibility of adoption of a separate plan that did not occur until after the plaintiff's retirement. (The employee asked if his department would be offered a voluntary separation package, and was told it would not.) In the Seventh Circuit's reading, fiduciary duties are plan-specific, and the employer is not a fiduciary when it decides whether or not to establish a plan, or what benefits should go into the plan. [*Beach v. Commonwealth Edison Co.*, 388 F.3d 1133 (7th Cir. 2004)]

The fiduciary must provide complete and accurate information about the tax consequences of options under a plan. [*Farr v. U.S. West Communications Inc.*, 58 F.3d 1361 (9th Cir. 1998)] But it is not a fiduciary breach to distribute benefits in accordance with the participant's own instructions, even if the fiduciary allegedly gave inaccurate tax advice. [*Glencoe v. TIAA*, 69 F. Supp. 2d 849 (S.D.W.V. 1999)]

Failure to provide this information on request is a breach of fiduciary duty. [*McAuley v. IBM Corp.*, 165 F.3d 1038 (6th Cir. 1999)] The fiduciaries' common-law duty of loyalty requires honest, fair dealings with plan participants. The Second Circuit position is that even long-range contingency plans must be disclosed. In *Caputo v. Pfizer* [267 F.3d 181 (2d Cir. 2001)], the court held that the fiduciary breached his duty by saying "a golden handshake (early retirement incentive) will never appear in your lifetime" when the fiduciary knew that the company was considering additional downsizing, and early retirement incentives are common in downsizing companies.

In the Ninth Circuit view, the employer did not actively misrepresent the availability of an enhanced severance program when it posted a message on its Web site saying that it did not intend to offer that program at a specific facility: the program was not under serious consideration at that time. However, once management decided to implement the program for workers in the HR department, it was a breach of fiduciary duty not to tell the other workers at the refinery about severance benefits that would be available in connection with a RIF. [*Mathews v. Chevron Corp.*, 362 F.3d 1172 (9th Cir. 2004)]

Although many cases have arisen in the context of early retirement programs, fiduciary disclosure issues can come up in other contexts as well. There is a clear fiduciary duty to provide employees with copies of certain plan documents. According to the Second Circuit, ERISA § 104(b)(4) requires the plan administrator to provide copies of "plan documents" on request. However, actuarial evaluation reports do not fall into this category, and need not be disclosed. The Sixth Circuit reached the opposite conclusion. [*Compare Board of Trustees of CWA/ITU Negotiated Pension Plan v. Weinstein*, 107 F.3d 139 (2d Cir. 1997), *with Bartling v. Fruehauf Corp.*, 29 F.3d 1062 (6th Cir. 1994)]

In 2002, the Sixth Circuit held that affirmatively misleading employees about the continuation of health benefits, inducing them to retire early, is a fiduciary breach, even though not all the plaintiffs asked specific questions about future benefits. The appropriate test is whether the information is materially misleading, whether or not the employer intended to mislead or was negligent in providing the misleading information. There were 21 plaintiffs; the court ruled that all of them relied on the statements in deciding when to retire. The employer provided the information on its own initiative, so *Sprague* did not apply. The 10 plaintiffs who did ask specific questions about health benefits had a separate and independent claim for fiduciary breach. [*James v. Pirelli Armstrong Tire Co.*, 305 F.3d 439 (6th Cir. 2002)]

Plan language that employees would "keep" or "continue" their benefits after retirement did not cause vesting at retirement. Therefore, the insurer's termination of life insurance benefits was not a breach of contract. However, the Eleventh Circuit reinstated claims that the employer breached fiduciary duty by engaging in a systematic pattern of misrepresentation encouraging employees to believe that insurance benefits would not be changed after they retired. [*Jones v. American General Life Ins. Co.*, 370 F.3d 1065 (11th Cir. 2004)]

An employee was initially hired as a part-time worker who was not eligible for participation in the employer's long-term disability plan. Later he was shifted to a full-time schedule and became eligible. He alleges that he was not informed about the LTD plan and did not receive an SPD. The First Circuit ruled that, although fiduciaries have a duty to answer questions accurately, there is no general duty to provide information about benefits unless there is some reason for the fiduciary to know that failure to inform could be harmful. [*Watson v. Deaconess Waltham Hosp.*, 298 F.3d 102 (1st Cir. 2002)]

§ 15.08   PENALTIES FOR FIDUCIARY BREACH

A fiduciary that breaches the required duties can be sued by plan participants, plan beneficiaries, and/or the Department of Labor. Penalty taxes can be imposed for improper transactions involving the plan. Generally speaking, ERISA § 509 grants relief to the plan itself; participants and beneficiaries find their remedies under ERISA § 502(a)(3).

A large, overlapping, and potentially confusing variety of Civil Monetary Penalties (CMPs) can be imposed under various provisions of ERISA. The same action often violates several different sections, with penalties at least potentially assessed for each, such as:

- § 209(b) failure to furnish or maintain records
- § 502(c)(1)(A) failure to notify participants of their rights to COBRA benefits
- § 502(c)(1)(B) failure to provide required information on a timely basis
- § 502(c)(2) failure or refusal to file an annual report
- § 502(c)(3) failure to notify participants and beneficiaries when the plan fails to satisfy the minimum funding requirements; failure to give notice when excess pension assets are transferred to a 401(h) retiree health benefits account
- § 503(c)(5) failure or refusal to file information required under ERISA § 101(g)
- § 503(c)(6) failure or refusal to comply with a participant's or beneficiary's request for information subject to disclosure under ERISA § 104(a)(6).

Most penalties are defined as a maximum amount per day—usually $110 or $1100. Courts hearing such cases have the discretion to reduce or even abate the penalty, based on factors such as the employer's inability to pay, its basic good faith, or extenuating factors such as destruction of records in circumstances beyond the employer's control.

These odd amounts are dictated by inflation adjustments. [Pub. L. No. 104-134, the Debt Collection Improvement Act of 1996, requires inflation adjustments to the level of CMPs at least once every four years] The inflation-adjusted penalties are rounded up to multiples of $10 (for penalties up to $100), in multiples of $100 for penalties $100–$1,000, multiples of $1,000 in the $1,000–$10,000 range, multiples of $5,000 in the $10,000–$100,000 range, $10,000 in the $100,000–$200,000 range, and multiples of $25,000 for penalties greater than $200,000.

Early in 2003, the Department of Labor and the Pension and Welfare Benefit Administration (now known as EBSA) published the latest round of adjustments at 68 Fed. Reg. 2875 (Jan. 22, 2003), effective for violations occurring after March 24, 2003; *See also* 68 Fed. Reg. 3734 (Jan. 24, 2003). Because inflation was fairly low, only two penalties were affected. The § 502(c)(5) penalty went from $1,000 to $1,100 a day, and the § 502(c)(6) penalty rose from $100 a day (up to a limit of $1,000 per request) to $110 a day (limited to $1,100 per request).

It should be noted, though, that the penalties as imposed are seldom collected. In January 28, 2004, testimony before Congress, Assistant Secretary of Labor Patrick Pizzella said that EBSA undertook 11,882 enforcement actions in its 2003 fiscal year. About half of these (5,283) were taken against small entities (with 100 or fewer plan participants). When a small entity was involved, the penalty was reduced or even waived entirely in nearly every case (5,223 out of the total of 5,283). Penalties were lowered in 5,342 of all civil penalty cases—i.e., about half of them. The total amount of penalties actually collected in FY 2003 was about $9.3 million lower than the amount initially assessed. [*See* 72 L.W. 2447]

A fiduciary who is guilty of a breach of duty is personally liable to the plan and must compensate it for any loss in asset value caused by the violation. The fiduciary must also "disgorge" (surrender) any personal financial advantage improperly obtained: *see* ERISA § 409. However, there is liability only if there is a causal connection between a breach and the loss or the improper profits. Fiduciaries are not expected to guarantee that the plan will never lose money.

A plan can get a court order removing a faithless fiduciary from office. The removed fiduciary can be ordered to pay the plan's attorneys' fees plus interest on the sum involved. But plan participants cannot get an award of punitive damages, no matter how outrageous the fiduciary's conduct (although some courts will order punitive damages payable to the plan itself). In the most serious cases, a fiduciary can be subject to criminal charges instead of, or in addition to, civil penalties.

Plans can have "bad boy" clauses. For example, under ERISA § 206(d) and I.R.C. § 401(a)(13)(C) fiduciaries who are also plan participants can have their pensions reduced if they breach fiduciary duty, if they are convicted of crimes against the plan, or if they lose or settle a civil suit or enter into a settlement with the Department of Labor or PBGC.

Unless the crime involved an ERISA pension plan, and restitution to the plan is ordered, a federal court sentencing a person convicted of a crime does not have the power to order that undistributed funds from the convicted person's pension plan be used to pay restitution. [*United States v. Jackson*, 229 F.3d 1223 (9th Cir. 2000).

§ 15.09   ERISA § 502

[A]   Generally

ERISA § 502 gives participants and beneficiaries, the DOL, and fiduciaries many remedies against abuses and risks to the plan. In fact, an important part of litigation planning is deciding which subsection of ERISA § 502 to invoke—defendants can get a case dismissed if the wrong subsection is charged or if the plaintiff asks for remedies that are unavailable under that subsection.

Under ERISA § 502, "participant" means an employee or ex-employee who is or may become eligible to receive any benefit under the plan. "Beneficiary" either means someone eligible or potentially eligible to receive benefits under the plan terms, or as designated by a participant.

Participants and beneficiaries (but not the DOL, the employer, or the plan itself) can use ERISA § 502(a)(1)(B) to sue for benefits due under the terms of the plan, to enforce rights under the terms of the plan, or to clarify rights to future benefits under the terms of a plan.

Civil actions under ERISA § 502(a)(2) can be brought by participants, beneficiaries, or the DOL when a breach of fiduciary duty is alleged.

The DOL, participants, beneficiaries, or fiduciaries can sue under ERISA §§ 502(a)(3) and (a)(5) to enjoin violations of ERISA Title I, to get equitable relief under Title I, or to impose penalties on PIIs for engaging in prohibited transactions. The remedies under ERISA § 502(a)(3) can include ordering return of misappropriated plan assets, plus the profits improperly earned on them—but this remedy is not available in situations where the defendant did not hold or profit from plan assets.

The Second Circuit did not permit a health plan participant to seek equitable relief for alleged deceptive practices by the plan's insurer. An injunction was held to be unavailable because any harm could be compensated by money damages. The proper cause of action would have been under ERISA § 502(a)(1)(B) for the value of benefits wrongfully denied. [*Nechis v. Oxford Health Plans*, 421 F.3d 96 (2d Cir. 2005)]

An ERISA § 502(a)(3) suit for individual equitable relief can be maintained against a company that deceived its employees about benefit safety if they were transferred to a new division that was spun off by the company. The Supreme Court ruled that the corporation was acting as a fiduciary when it lied about benefit security. [*Varity Corp. v. Howe*, 514 U.S. 1082 (1996)]

The Southern District of Ohio permitted a suit to go on when an employee charged ERISA violations in an employer's termination of its pension plan when the way it was terminated permitted the savings on benefits to revert to the employer. The employer's defense was that the suit was improper because it sought money damages, but the Southern District ruled that the plaintiff was not seeking money damages in the sense of additional benefits—only equitable relief in the form of reversal of the reversion. [*Clevenger v. Dillards Inc.*, 74 L.W. 1512 (S.D. Ohio Jan. 31, 2006)]

A party in interest to a prohibited transaction with a plan can be liable under ERISA § 502(a)(3), even if the defendant is not a fiduciary [*Harris Trust v. Salomon Brothers*, 530 U.S. 238 (2000)]

According to the Fifth Circuit, there is no gap in statutory remedies under I.R.C. § 502(a)(3) that has to be filled in by consulting federal common law. Therefore, if a person totally disabled by non-work-related injuries violates the contract and refuses to reimburse the health plan out of a lump sum received from Social Security disability income, the plan's fiduciary cannot argue that federal common law entitles the fiduciary to recoupment to prevent unjust enrichment. [*Cooperative Benefit Adm'r Inc. v. Ogden*, 367 F.3d 323 (5th Cir. 2004)]

The domestic partner of a deceased plan participant was not entitled to recover the $500,000 value of benefits that the partner would have received if the plan had not delayed 16 months in telling him he was the beneficiary, because ERISA § 502(a)(3) equitable relief does not include compensation for the beneficiary's losses sustained as a result of fiduciary breach. [*Goeres v. Charles Schwab & Co.*, 2004 U.S. Dist. LEXIS 20358 (N.D. Cal. 2004)]

Beneficiaries who are wrongfully deprived of coverage can be reinstated in the plan—but they can get only the benefits that would have been payable if they

had been covered all along. They are not entitled to "disgorgement" of the money
the employer saved by failing to provide the benefits at the appropriate time.
[*LaRocca v. Borden, Inc.*, 276 F.3d 22 (1st Cir. 2002)]

The Sixth Circuit did not permit a plan participant to use I.R.C. § 502(a)(3) to
impose a constructive trust to recover benefits that the plaintiff said should have been
paid under his cash balance plan. The plaintiff elected a lump sum payout after the
employer company was sold and he lost his job. Initially, the plan administrator
calculated the plaintiff's balance at $48,732; the plaintiff protested; the adminis-
trator re-calculated and came up with a figure of $52,013. The plaintiff then brought
suit, claiming that he was entitled to $57,262 because the plan's assumptions were
contrary to ERISA. He did not sue under ERISA § 502(a)(1)(B) (recovery of benefits
under the terms of the plan) because he alleged that the terms of the plan provided
less than ERISA mandated. He lost because the Sixth Circuit ruled that payment
of money constitutes money damages and not equitable relief; and there were no
ill-gotten gains to be disgorged and placed in the constructive trust sought by the
plaintiff. [*Crosby v. Bowater Inc. Ret. Plan*, 382 F.3d 587 (6th Cir. 2004)]

An employee (in this case, an early retiree) who is misled about the tax
consequences of taking a lump sum payout is entitled to rescission as other equitable relief under ERISA § 502(a)(3), but the Fourth Circuit allowed only partial
rescission when the employee's unreasonable delay in seeking a remedy was
prejudicial to the employer. [*Griggs v. DuPont*, 385 F.3d 440 (4th Cir. 2004)]

Usually, an employer is not acting as a fiduciary when it amends a plan, but if
benefits were vested, reducing them violates the plans and breaches fiduciary duty.
[*Devlin v. Empire Blue Cross/Blue Shield*, 274 F.3d 76 (2d Cir. 2001)]

In the Seventh Circuit view, the employees of a bankrupt company raised a
sufficient claim by alleging that the company's executives breached their fiduciary
duty by failing to provide ongoing funding for a health plan that was terminated as
part of the bankruptcy process. The executives were fiduciaries because they had
control over the committee that invested the plan's assets. However, the Seventh
Circuit dismissed the claims of breach of fiduciary duty by not giving notice of the
likelihood of plan termination, because there is no duty to disclose likely future
termination unless plan participants are deliberately misled. [*Baker v. Kingsley*,
387 F.3d 649 (7th Cir. 2004)]

The Third Circuit says that a grant of interest on benefits wrongfully withheld
is proper, because it is "other appropriate equitable relief." A 1999 Eighth Circuit
case disagreed with this position [*see Kerr v. Charles V. Vaterott & Co.*, 184 F.3d
939 (8th Cir. 1999)], but in 2004, the Eighth Circuit held that, when a beneficiary
wins a breach of fiduciary duty case against an insurer, prejudgment interest on the
profits that the insurer wrongfully obtained by withholding benefits can be awarded
to the plaintiff as ERISA § 502(a)(3) appropriate equitable relief, because not
awarding the interest could lead to unjust enrichment. The plaintiff in this case
was a diabetic who could not work because of complications of her condition.
Initially, she was denied LTD benefits; then the benefits were granted; then they
were suspended for failure to show that her disability was permanent.

The employee charged that suspension of benefits was a breach of fiduciary duty. The insurer said that it reinstated benefits voluntarily, so there was no judgment relative to which pre-judgment interest could be granted. The Eighth Circuit allowed an award of interest when the award is equitable and prevents unjust enrichment. [*Parke v. First Reliance Standard Life Ins. Co.*, 368 F.3d 999 (8th Cir. 2004)] [*Fotta v. Trustees of UMW Health Retirement Fund*, 165 F.3d 209 (3d Cir. 1998).] However, if benefits are denied under a long-term disability plan, the plaintiff cannot recover the expenses of medical treatment, because this is the kind of extracontractual, compensatory damages that the *Mertens* case rules out. [*Rogers v. Hartford Life & Accident Ins. Co.*, 167 F.3d 933 (5th Cir. 1999)]

A late-2002 Third Circuit case was brought by a plaintiff claiming that she was terminated to interfere with her benefit rights, as well as wrongful denial of benefits. She also sought civil penalties because the plan administrator missed the statutory deadline for providing the documents. She lost her benefit claims (because it was not an abuse of discretion to determine that she was ineligible for enhanced retirement benefits). The § 510 claim also failed, for lack of evidence that her discharge was motivated by an intention to avoid paying benefits. However, the Third Circuit held that § 502(c)(1) should be interpreted to impose personal liability on the plan administrator even if the request for information was not addressed to the current plan administrator. However, the administrator will be liable only if the request remains unfilled 30 days after it is actually received by the plan administrator or someone supervised by the administrator. [*Romero v. Smithkline Beecham*, 309 F.3d 113 (3d Cir. 2002)]

If the ERISA § 105 requirement of providing benefit statements is violated, the DOL, participants, or beneficiaries can sue under ERISA § 502(a)(4). Only participants or beneficiaries can sue, under ERISA § 502(a)(1)(A), to collect a penalty of $110 a day when a plan fails to supply the information required by Title I. The DOL can sue under ERISA § 502(a)(5) for equitable relief for employees who were misclassified as project, supplementary, or temporary rather than permanent workers, even though the employees can use ERISA administrative proceedings to obtain benefits themselves. [*Herman v. Time Warner*, 56 F. Supp. 2d 411 (S.D.N.Y. 1999)]

Section 502(a)(6) authorizes civil actions by the DOL to collect the excise tax on prohibited transactions or the penalty tax on fiduciary violations. State governments (but NOT the DOL) can sue under § 502(a)(7) to enforce compliance with a Qualified Medical Child Support Order (QMCSO). The states have a role to play here because they have traditionally been empowered to deal with family law issues such as child support.

Funds from an insurance contract or annuity purchased in connection with termination of participant status can be secured by a suit under § 502(a)(9). Suit can be brought by the DOL, fiduciaries, or persons who were participants or beneficiaries at the time of the violation—but suit can only be brought if the purchase of the policy or annuity violated the terms of the plan or violated fiduciary obligations.

ERISA § 502(c) allows the Department of Labor to impose a penalty of $110 per day (dating from the date of failure or refusal to furnish the documents) against a plan administrator who doesn't comply with a participant's or beneficiary's request for plan documents within 30 days. Administrators can be penalized even if the failure is not deliberate—but not if it is due to matters beyond their reasonable control.

Both the federal and the state courts have jurisdiction under § 502(e) when participants or beneficiaries bring suit to recover benefits, clarify their rights to future benefits, or enforce rights under any plan that falls under ERISA Title I. Although ERISA does not rule out binding arbitration of claims, any other Title I claim can only be heard in a federal, not a state, court.

In late 2004, SmithKline Beecham Corporation agreed to pay $5.2 million in an ERISA class action brought by workers who claimed that they were denied pension benefits because they were improperly classified as "temporary." The plaintiffs survived summary judgment on fiduciary breach claims against Smith-Kline based on the company's initial and continuing failure to make them eligible and give them vesting credits; by requiring them to prove eligibility; and by failing to notify them of their appeal rights under the plan. [Shannon P. Duffy, *SmithKline to Pay $5.2 Million to Settle ERISA Suit,* Legal Intelligencer, Oct. 15, 2004 (law.com)]

ERISA § 502(i) requires the DOL to impose a civil penalty on fiduciaries who violate the fiduciary responsibility provisions of Title I. A nonfiduciary who knowingly participates in a fiduciary violation can also be penalized under this section. The base penalty is 20% of the penalty that the court orders under ERISA § 502(a)(2) or (a)(5). If the fiduciary or person who assisted the fiduciary in the breach settled with the DOL to avoid being taken to court, the base penalty is 20% of the amount of the settlement. The penalty can be reduced or even waived if the person acted reasonably and in good faith. Because the main objective of this section is to safeguard the plan, a reduction or waiver can also be obtained if the fiduciary or helper would not be able to reimburse the plan without severe financial hardship if the full penalty were assessed.

Section 502(k) permits plan administrators, fiduciaries, participants, and beneficiaries to sue the Department of Labor itself in district court in order to compel the agency to undertake an action required by ERISA Title I, to prevent the Department from acting contrary to Title I, or to review a final order of the Secretary of Labor.

Section 502 also permits fiduciaries to ask the court to remove another fiduciary from office, or to issue an injunction against anyone who has violated ERISA Title I or the plan's own terms.

It is mandatory for the DOL to impose civil penalties, under § 502(l), against a fiduciary who knowingly violates the Title I provisions on fiduciary responsibility, and also against anyone who knowingly participates in a violation. The basic penalty is 20% of the court order under §§ 502(a)(2) or (a)(5), or the settlement with DOL in such a case. However, any penalty imposed under § 502(i), or any prohibited transaction excise tax, can be used to offset the § 502(l) penalty. The Secretary of Labor has discretion to reduce or waive the penalty in two circumstances: if the fiduciary acted reasonably and in good faith—or if waiver permits the fiduciary to reimburse the plan for its losses.

[B]   Issues under *Knudson, Sereboff,* and *McVeigh*

In 2002, the Supreme Court decided *Great-West Life & Annuity Ins. Co. v. Knudson* [534 U.S. 204 (2002)]. The Supreme Court ruled that a health plan and its administrator cannot sue under ERISA § 502(a)(3) when they claim that beneficiaries violate the terms of the plan by refusing to reimburse the plan for amounts the plan spent on the beneficiaries' medical care. The Supreme Court reached this conclusion because § 502(a)(3) refers to cases that traditionally came under the heading of "equity." Contract suits traditionally were considered suits at "law," not "equity."

After *Knudson*, plans faced three hurdles in bringing claims for restitution. First, the defendant (in many such cases, the plan participant, because the plan itself is the plaintiff) must have been unjustly enriched. In some cases, the defendant will have to have possession of specific property that really belongs to the plaintiff—and equitable relief must be appropriate.

In mid-2006, the Supreme Court revisited ERISA subrogation issues twice. In *Sereboff v. Mid Atlantic Medical Services Inc.* [No. 05-260, <http://laws.findlaw .com/us/000/05-260.html> (May 15, 2006)] the petitioners were covered by an ERISA plan that included a subrogation provision. The petitioners settled tort claims related to an automobile accident. Their insurer sued under ERISA § 502(a)(3) to recoup medical expenses paid on their behalf. The petitioners set aside part of the tort recovery, corresponding to the insurer's claim. The Supreme Court ruled that the insurer was entitled to recover the amount expended on the petitioners' medical care. The insurer acted as a fiduciary seeking "appropriate equitable relief" to enforce plan terms, as permitted by ERISA § 502(a)(3). Unlike *Knudson*, the disputed funds in this case were in the petitioners' possession and set aside in a separate account. The Supreme Court treated the insurer's claim as equitable not because it was a claim for subrogation, but because it was the equivalent of an action to enforce an equitable lien created by agreement.

A month later, in *Empire Healthchoice Assurance, Inc. v. McVeigh* [No. 05-200, <http://laws.findlaw.com/us/000/05-200.html> (June 15, 2006)] ruled that an insurer's attempt to recover health care costs paid on behalf of an injured federal employee had to be litigated in state court rather than federal court: there was no jurisdiction under 28 U.S.C. § 1331. Although the worker was covered under the Federal Employees Health Benefits Act, a statute that includes a provision that the terms of the federal plan's insurance contracts will preempt state or local law about health benefit plans, the Supreme Court held that the case for reimbursement does not "arise under federal law" and therefore there is no federal jurisdiction.

§ 15.10   ERISA § 510

ERISA § 510 makes it unlawful to interfere with ERISA rights, or to discharge or discriminate against a participant for exercising ERISA rights. The typical examples are firing an employee to prevent benefit accrual, or firing someone in retaliation for making a claim for plan benefits. ERISA preempts state-law wrongful termination claims in these circumstances. [*Ingersoll-Rand v. McClendon*, 498 U.S. 133 (1990)] Section 510 applies to welfare benefit plans as well as pension plans. [*Inter-Modal Rail Employees v. Atchison, Topeka & Santa Fe Railroad*, 520 U.S. 510 (1997)]

However, refusal to rehire laid off workers who have credited service, as part of a policy of reducing pension obligations, does not violate § 510 because the people who seek to be rehired have not yet been hired or promised benefits. [*Becker v. Mack Trucks Inc.*, 281 F.3d 372 (3d Cir. 2002)]

After their jobs were outsourced, a group of former Honeywell employees sued under ERISA § 510, charging that their employment was terminated with intent to interfere with their pension benefits. They also brought Title VII and ADEA claims. The district court dismissed all the claims, and the Eighth Circuit affirmed. The plaintiffs worked at a plant that Honeywell managed on behalf of the Department of Energy. A consultant concluded that outsourcing certain functions would improve efficiency; the plaintiffs applied for the remaining jobs but were not chosen. However, they were offered and accepted employment with the outsourcing company. They continued to earn at least as much after the transfer as before, and gained access to potential bonuses that were not available when they worked for Honeywell. Their suit alleged that they were not offered a portable pension plan, even though other business units had a portable plan. While they worked for Honeywell, they participated in its defined benefit plan. That ceased when they were re-employed, but the new unit set up two defined contribution plans for the outsourced employees. Honeywell valued the defined contribution plans as worth 90 to 95% of the value of the terminated plans, or 105% if bonuses were considered. The Eighth Circuit found that, although the plaintiffs made out a *prima facie* case, the defendant had a legitimate, non-pretextual business reason (pleasing the Department of Energy; improving the efficiency of the sub-par facilities and utilities engineering management department) for outsourcing, and the benefit package was improved when the outsourcing company determined that it was worth less than the original defined benefit plan. [*Register v. Honeywell Federal Mfg.*, 397 F.3d 1130 (8th Cir. 2005). The Eighth Circuit applies *McDonnell Douglas* in § 510 cases: *Griffith v. City of Des Moines*, 387 F.3d 733 (8th Cir. 2004)]

At the end of 2003, employees raised an interesting but unsuccessful argument in a case before the Fifth Circuit. They claimed that the employer interfered with their right to enhanced retirement benefits by *not* discharging them during a RIF. The court pointed out that § 510 does not forbid retaining employees, from whatever motivation. [*Bodine v. Employers Casualty Co.*, 352 F.3d 245 (5th Cir. 2003)]

In 2001, the Northern District of Oklahoma ruled that the McDonnell Douglas Corporation violated ERISA § 510 when it closed down a plant. Despite the company's argument that it had a valid business reason for the shutdown, the District Court ruled that the closing was motivated by a desire to avoid paying benefits under two pension plans and a retiree health plan. However, in May 2004, the Tenth Circuit reversed, finding that employees were not entitled to back pay after the plan closing, because back pay is not "equitable relief" of the type provided by ERISA § 502(a)(3). [*Millsap v. McDonnell Douglas Corp.*, 162 F. Supp. 2d 1262 (N.D. Okla. 2001), *rev'd* 368 F.3d 1246 (10th Cir. 2004)]

She sued under ERISA § 510 for damages (including her medical expenses related to cancer treatment), claiming that she was fired to relieve her employer of the obligation to pay her medical bills. However, she lost her case, because § 510 requires proof of the employer's specific intent to interfere with an ERISA right. Although the court found the employer's policy to be harsh and unreasonable, it was not illegal, and it was uniformly applied to all employees.

A § 510 claim arose when corporate assets were sold. The contract of sale provided that all of the selling corporation's employees who were actively at work on the day of the sale, or who were on vacation or non-extended leave on that day, would automatically be employed by the buyer corporation and covered by the buyer's health plan without interruption of coverage. Employees who were on medical, disability, Worker's Compensation, or other extended leave on the day of the sale were eligible for transfer to the buyer company only if they returned to active employment. Six employees were not transferred, including the plaintiff, who had been on Worker's Compensation leave for more than two years. She sued the seller and buyer corporations under state law and the Americans with Disabilities Act. The District Court converted the state law claims into ERISA § 510 claims.

The Ninth Circuit ruled that it violates § 510 to choose employees on medical or disability leave for termination and denial of benefits. The Ninth Circuit read the sales contract to presume that such individuals were discharged until they returned to work. The contract itself was direct proof of discriminatory intent. It would have been permissible to transfer all of the employees to the buyer corporation subject to a reduction in benefits for all of them, but a selected group could not be excluded for health reasons. The case was remanded for the District Court to allocate liability between the buyer and seller corporations. [*Lessard v. Applied Risk Mgmt.*, 307 F.3d 1020 (9th Cir. 2002)]

§ 15.11   OTHER ENFORCEMENT ISSUES

[A]   Generally

Criminal penalties can be imposed under ERISA § 511, making it a crime, punishable by up to one year's imprisonment and/or a fine of $10,000, to use or threaten force, fraud, or violence to restrain, coerce, or intimidate a participant or beneficiary, in order to interfere with or prevent exercise of any right under the terms of the plan or under Title I.

Rev. Rul. 2002-45, 2002-29 I.R.B. 116 sets out circumstances under which amounts placed in a defined contribution plan's trust will be treated as contributions in various situations involving fiduciary breach.

The first scenario described a plan whose employer has invested an unreasonably large portion of the plan's assets in a high-risk investment that becomes worthless. The plan participants bring suit for breach of fiduciary duty. The employer settles the suit without admitting a breach of duty but makes a payment to the plan equivalent to the plan's losses due to the improper investment; the payment is allocated to the individual accounts within the plan.

The second scenario uses the same facts, but without a lawsuit. Knowing that the participants are contemplating legal action, the employer determines that there is a reasonable likelihood of suit and reimburses the plan for its losses.

The IRS ruled that payments made under either scenario are "restorative payments." Restorative payments are not treated as plan contributions, with two implications. First, the limitations on allowable contributions do not apply—but the payments are not deductible. A restorative payment is a payment made to make up for plan losses resulting from a fiduciary action or failure to act that created a reasonable risk of liability for breach of fiduciary duty. However, payments made to a plan to "top it up" after investment losses are generally treated as plan contributions.

Payments made to a plan under a DOL order or court-approved settlement are generally treated as being made on account of a reasonable risk of liability. But payments required by the plan, or by the Code, are not restorative payments even if the required payment was delayed or not made because of a fiduciary breach. Therefore, a payment of delinquent elective deferrals or employee contributions as part of a voluntary correction, or an EPCRS payment to correct a qualification failure, is not a restorative payment even if the payment was delayed or omitted because of a fiduciary breach, but an adjustment required under EPCRS to reflect lost earnings is a restorative payment.

ERISA § 409(a) makes a breaching fiduciary personally liable to the plan to make up for losses caused by the breach (such as the difference between what the plan would have earned given appropriate investments, minus its actual earnings). The breaching fiduciary is also liable for any other legal and equitable remedies the plan chooses to impose.

However, in *Peacock v. Thomas* [516 U.S. 349 (1996)], the plaintiff won an ERISA case against his employer, but could not collect the judgment, allegedly because a corporate officer who was not a fiduciary misappropriated the funds that could have been used to satisfy the judgment. The plaintiff could not "pierce the corporate veil" and make the corporate officer personally liable, for various technical legal reasons. For one thing, the case was not closely enough related to ERISA for the federal courts to get involved. Anyway, a federal court cannot enforce a judgment against someone who was not liable for it in the first place.

The Department of Labor has authority under ERISA § 504(a)(2) to investigate whether a Title I violation has occurred so the employer might be ordered to submit books, papers, and records for DOL examination. This can be done only once per 12-month period unless the DOL has reasonable cause to believe that Title I was violated. The DOL also has subpoena power over books, records, and witnesses under § 504(c), but the subpoena can be enforced only if the agency shows that the investigation has a legitimate purpose, the inquiry is relevant to that purpose, and the government does not already have the information.

ERISA § 515 permits a civil action against an employer for delinquency in making contributions. This section does not have a statute of limitations, so most courts that have considered the issue use a six-year statute of limitations (typical for contract cases). The statute of limitations is clear under a similar provision, ERISA § 4003(e)(1) (which correlates with I.R.C. § 412(n)). If an employer fails to make a required contribution to the plan, at a time when the plan's funded current liability percentage is lower than 100% and the employer owes the plan more than $1 million (including interest), then all of the employer's real and personal property becomes subject to a lien in favor of the plan.

The plan that was supposed to, but didn't, make the payment has an obligation to notify the PBGC within 10 days of the payment due date. The PBGC has six years from the date of the missed payment, or three years from the time it knew or should have known about the missed payment, to sue in federal District Court to enforce the lien. Fraud or concealment by the employer extends the statute of limitations to six years from the PBGC's discovery of the true state of affairs.

Although confidential communications with an attorney, for the purpose of getting legal advice, generally are privileged, there is a "fiduciary exception" to this rule. Under the fiduciary exception, fiduciaries are supposed to act on behalf of the plan's participants and beneficiaries, so an attorney advising a fiduciary about plan administration is really working for the participants and beneficiaries. [See *Coffman v. Metropolitan Life Ins. Co.*, 24 F.R.D. 296 (S.D.W.V. 2001)]

ERISA gives the federal courts subject-matter jurisdiction to hear interpleader actions (a case in which the holder of disputed property asks the court for guidance about what to do with the property) when an insurance company needs to determine the proper beneficiary under a benefit plan. The insurance company is acting as a fiduciary, and interpleader is one of the types of equitable relief that can be granted to a fiduciary in order to enforce the terms of the plan. [*Aetna Life Ins. v. Bayona*, 227 F.3d 1070 (9th Cir. 2000)]

In general, standing to sue under ERISA, as a participant or beneficiary, is determined as of the time the suit is filed. However, in *McBride v. PLM Int'l Inc.* [179 F.3d 737 (9th Cir. 1999)], a whistleblower employee objected to the termination of an ESOP plan and to using the value of common rather than preferred stock in making termination distributions from the ESOP. According to the Ninth Circuit, the plaintiff was a plan participant, despite being fired and despite the termination of the plan. Therefore, he was a whistleblower, as defined by ERISA

§ 1140, with standing to sue. As the Ninth Circuit pointed out, a contrary result would actually encourage employers to fire dissident employees and terminate plans—not exactly the results ERISA was supposed to achieve!

[B]   Sarbanes-Oxley Act Changes

The penalty for willful violation of reporting or disclosure rules [29 U.S.C. § 1311] was increased dramatically by the Sarbanes-Oxley Act [Pub. L. No. 107-204]. The maximum penalty under this provision (whether or not the violator is a publicly traded corporation) is $100,000 rather than $5,000 for an individual; ten years rather than one year of imprisonment; and $500,000 rather than $100,000 if the violator is a corporation.

See the DOL Final Rule [68 Fed. Reg. 3729 (Jan. 24, 2003)] for the effects of the Sarbanes-Oxley Act on penalties. Although the main focus of this Rule is on the penalties (up to a maximum of $100 per affected participant per day) imposed pursuant to ERISA § 502(c)(7) for failure to provide proper notice of a blackout period, the Sarbanes-Oxley Act made several changes in penalty levels that apply to all ERISA violations, not just those involving corporate governance. The maximum penalty under ERISA § 502(c)(2) is $1,000 per day; starting on the date the plan administrator failed or refused to file the annual report. The maximum penalty under ERISA § 502(c)(5) is $1,000 per day (for violations occurring after March 24, 2003, the penalty can be up to $1,100 a day. [*See* 68 Fed. Reg. 2875 (Jan. 22, 2003)] Failure to furnish documents on request of plan participants, beneficiaries, or their designates can be penalized by up to $100 a day, subject to a maximum of $1,000 per request.

In all these cases, the plan administrator is entitled to notice and hearing before imposition of the penalty, and the administrator will be permitted to introduce evidence of why it would not be equitable to impose a penalty (e.g., the administrator acted in good faith and the non-compliance was due to factors beyond his or her control).

Sarbanes-Oxley also limits the availability of plan loans to the officers and directors of the sponsor corporation. EBSA issued a Field Assistance Bulletin that such limitations do not violate ERISA. [EBSA Advisory Opinion 2003-04A <http://www.dol.gov/ebsa/regs/aos/ao2003-04a.html>]

§ 15.12   LIABILITY OF CO-FIDUCIARIES

If a plan's assets are held by more than one trustee, the general rule is that all the trustees are jointly responsible for management, unless the plan's trust instrument either makes a specific allocation of responsibility, or sets up a procedure for allocating responsibility.

Every trustee has a legal duty to use reasonable care to make sure the other fiduciaries do not breach their duties. Any fiduciary's misconduct implicates all the others. Fiduciaries are liable for the acts and omissions of their fellow fiduciaries if:

- They knowingly participate in, or knowingly conceal, a breach on another party's act;
- They facilitate someone else's breach by failing to perform their own fiduciary duties as stated by § 404(a)(2);
- They know about a breach by another fiduciary, but fail to take reasonable steps to remedy it.

Under a 1993 Supreme Court case, the plan can also get equitable remedies (but not damages) from a nonfiduciary who cooperated with a fiduciary who breached fiduciary duty. [*Mertens v. Hewitt Assocs.*, 508 U.S. 248 (1993)] An attorney who knowingly participates in a fiduciary breach may have to make restitution to the plan, or have a constructive trust imposed on his or her legal fees received as a result of the fiduciary's breach—even if the attorney is not a fiduciary him- or herself. [*Long Island Head Start Child Dev. Servs. v. Frank*, 165 F. Supp. 2d 367 (E.D.N.Y. 2001)]

Some courts have applied *Mertens* to prevent any claims by plans against nonfiduciaries. This only puts more pressure on the fiduciaries, because then they are the only possible defendants if something goes wrong. But fiduciaries cannot be liable for other fiduciaries' conduct occurring before they themselves became fiduciaries. Nor do they have a duty to remedy breaches that occurred before their tenure or after they cease to be fiduciaries.

But see a 2004 case in which the Middle District of Illinois allowed trust fiduciaries who were found to have breached their fiduciary duty to seek contribution and indemnification from non-fiduciaries who marketed a severance plan. In effect, the non-fiduciary was treated as a co-fiduciary because of its role in the breach. However, the non-fiduciaries were not liable under RICO. [*Daniels v. Bursey*, 73 LW 1112 (M.D. Ill. Aug. 5, 2004)]

The Fourth Circuit reversed dismissal of a complaint charging 401(k) plan fiduciaries with breach of the duty of prudence when they liquidated two of the plan's investment funds at a loss. The district court dismissed the complaint because it said that the plan's sponsors had amended the plan to eliminate those two funds, and that the amendment was a "settlor act" that did not trigger fiduciary duty analysis. The Fourth Circuit allowed the plaintiffs to pursue their claim because the amendment did not remove the fiduciaries' discretion to maintain the funds, so the decision to liquidate them could be imprudent. [*Tatum v. RJ Reynolds Tobacco Co.*, 392 F.3d 636 (4th Cir. 2004)]

ERISA § 405(c)(1) allows a plan to make an explicit allocation of fiduciary responsibility (other than the responsibility of trustees) among the named fiduciaries. The plan can also have procedures for fiduciaries to designate a party other than a named fiduciary to carry out fiduciary responsibilities under the plan. In general, a fiduciary who designates someone else will not be responsible for the acts or omissions of the designee. The two major exceptions occur when making or continuing the designation violates the designor's duties under ERISA § 404(a)(1), or when ERISA § 405(a) makes the designor responsible for the co-fiduciary's breach.

§ 15.13   BONDING

The basic rule set down by ERISA § 412(a) is that all fiduciaries, and plan officials who are not fiduciaries but who handle plan assets, must be bonded. Generally, the employer will maintain a single bond covering all of its plans that are subject to ERISA Title I. Recovery on behalf of one plan must not be allowed to reduce the amount available to the other plans below the minimum requirement.

The exceptions are some banks and insurance companies with assets over $1 million, and administrators, officers, and employees who deal with unfunded plans. (An unfunded plan is one whose assets come from the general funds of the employer or a union, even if the funds derive in part from employee contributions.) A bond is not required for amounts characterized as general assets of the employer until they are transferred to the insurers that pay the actual benefits.

Various forms of bonds are acceptable:

- Blanket bond (covering all the fiduciaries and everyone who handles the plan's money);
- Individual bond;
- Name schedule bond (covering a group of named individuals);
- Position schedule bond (covering whoever fills certain jobs or stands in certain relationships to the plan).

The bond must be issued by a corporate surety that holds a Department of Treasury Certificate of Authority. To be acceptable, the bond must not have a deductible, and must cover claims discovered after termination or cancellation of the bond. The amount of the bond must be large enough to cover the plan's potential losses caused by plan officials' dishonesty or fraud. In general, the bond must be 10% of the funds handled, but not less than $1,000 or more than $500,000.

Tip: A company in sound financial condition can save the cost of the bond by applying to the DOL for an opinion that payments are not at risk, and therefore the administrators of funded plans need not be bonded.

---

§ 15.14   INDEMNIFICATION

ERISA § 410 says that language in a plan, or in a side agreement with a fiduciary, is void as against public policy if it limits the fiduciary's liability for breach of fiduciary duty. However, the employer (as distinct from the plan) can permissibly indemnify the fiduciary or buy insurance covering the fiduciary. The fiduciary can also buy his or her own insurance coverage. [*See* § 43.08 for more discussion of fiduciary liability insurance] The sponsor corporation can also agree to use corporate assets to indemnify the fiduciary. This is allowed by the Department of Labor, and it is not considered a prohibited transaction.

The Southern District of New York ruled in 2006 that ERISA empowers fiduciaries and TPAs to apply for attorneys' fees and costs after a settlement. ERISA § 410(a) forbids provisions that indemnify fiduciaries, so a fiduciary who has been found guilty of a breach cannot recoup expenses from the plan. However, that does not prevent a fiduciary who has been found not guilty from being indemnified. The Southern District of New York held that ERISA permits a contract provision calling for indemnification to be enforced after a settlement because preventing plans from providing indemnification would grant excessive relief to plaintiffs. [*Martinez v. Barasch,* 2006 U.S. Dist. LEXIS 6914 (S.D.N.Y. 2006); *see* Rebecca Moore, *Plan Fiduciaries and TPAs May Recover Fees After Settlement,* PlanSponsor.com, Mar. 3, 2006]

§ 15.15   PROHIBITED TRANSACTIONS

[A]   Generally

Objectivity is one of the most important fiduciary characteristics. ERISA bans certain types of transactions between a plan and parties who might lose objectivity because of those transactions. "Parties in interest" and "disqualified persons" are blocked from certain categories of transactions, even if a particular transaction is fair.

Title I of ERISA makes any one of these a prohibited transaction if it occurs between the plan and a party in interest:

- Sale, exchange, or lease of property, including the plan's assumption of a mortgage, or a mortgage placed on the property by a party in interest during the 10 years before the transfer of the property to the plan;
- Extensions of credit;
- Furnishing goods or services;
- Transfers or uses of plan assets for the benefit of a party in interest;
- Acquisition or holding of employer securities that are not qualified, or in excess of the normal limit (usually 10% of the fair market value of the plan assets);
- Use of plan income or assets by a fiduciary in her or her personal interest or for his or her own account;
- Payments to a fiduciary for his or her own account, made by anyone who deals with the plan;

- Conflict of interest: the fiduciary acts on behalf of a party, or representing a party, in any transaction representing the plan—if the interests of the party the fiduciary represents are adverse to the interests of the plan or of its participants and beneficiaries.

ESOP trustees engaged in a prohibited transaction when they approved the purchase of convertible preferred stock from the employer without adequate research. The Northern District of New York required the trustee to reimburse plan participants for the difference between what they paid for the stock and what they would have paid if the trustee had performed an adequate investigation and discovered the true fair market value of the stock. [*Henry v. Champlain Enterprises, Inc.*, No. 01-CV-1681, 73 LW 1176 (N.D.N.Y. Sept. 3, 2004)] In 2006, the Second Circuit vacated and remanded the lower court's decision on the grounds that the issue is the prudence of the fiduciary's decision, not the scope of the documentation of the investigative process. The case was remanded to determine the adequacy of the actual investigation. [No. 05-0606 (2d Cir. Apr. 26, 2006)]

A group health plan was sued by an outpatient surgery center in a dispute over the amount of payment to the center. The plan raised an interesting argument by counterclaiming that the surgery center was an ERISA party in interest, and tried to engage in a prohibited transaction by trying to collect amounts in excess of reasonable compensation for services. This counterclaim was dismissed: A party in interest has to render services directly to the plan itself, not its participants, and the services provided by the surgery center did not contribute to the establishment or administration of the plan. [*Surgicore, Inc. v. Midwest Operating Engineers Health and Welfare Fund*, 2002 U.S. Dist. LEXIS 24152 (N.D. Ill. Dec. 6, 2002)]

[B] Parties in Interest

ERISA § 3(14) defines "party in interest" (PII) very broadly:

- Any fiduciary or relative of a fiduciary;
- Plan employees or persons who provide counsel to the plan—or their relatives;
- The plan's service providers and their relatives;
- Any employer or employee organization (e.g., union) whose members are covered by the plan;
- Anyone who owns 50% or more of the employer corporation, whether ownership is direct or indirect; relatives of the 50% owner;
- A corporation, partnership, trust, or estate that is 50% or more controlled by anyone in one of the categories above (unless they are involved only as relatives of a person involved with the plan);
- Employees, officers, and directors of organizations in the list (or anyone with similar powers and responsibilities without the formal title);
- Employees, officers, and directors (or those with similar rights and duties) of organizations in the list;

- Employees, officers, and directors of the plan;
- Anyone who has a direct or indirect 10% share ownership in the plan or an organization closely related to the plan;
- Anyone with a direct or indirect 10% interest in the capital or profits of a partnership or joint venture with anyone on the list.

Any participant, beneficiary, or plan fiduciary can bring suit for "appropriate equitable relief" under ERISA § 406 when an individual or business that is a "party in interest" (e.g., the employees and service providers of the plan) enters into a prohibited transaction—even if this individual or business is not an ERISA fiduciary. [*Harris Trust & Savings Bank v. Salomon Smith Barney*, 530 U.S. 238 (2000)] Therefore, the party in interest can be enjoined by a court, or required to make restitution to the plan, if the prohibited transaction results in financial losses to the plan.

A disqualified person who engages in a prohibited transaction can be required to pay an excise tax, even if he or she didn't know the transaction was prohibited. The excise tax is 15% of the amount involved per year. An additional tax of 100% of the amount involved is imposed when the IRS notifies the disqualified person that the transaction is prohibited, but the transaction is not rescinded within 90 days of receipt of the notice. The excise tax is payable to the IRS. In addition, the Department of Labor can impose a civil penalty that is more or less equivalent to the excise tax if a plan that is not qualified under Title I engages in a prohibited transaction.

The rules for welfare benefit plans are slightly different: The excise tax, under ERISA § 502(i) and I.R.C. § 4975(f)(5), is 5% of the amount of the prohibited transaction, and this amount is cumulated if the prohibited transaction continues over several years. There is a 100% excise tax for failure to correct a prohibited transaction after receipt of notice from the IRS.

[C]   Prohibited Transaction Exemptions

Because the prohibited transaction rules are so broad, the DOL has the power to grant "Prohibited Transaction Exemptions" for technically improper transactions that in fact are advantageous to the plan and benefit the plan's participants.

Exemptions fall into two main categories: the specific exemptions set out in ERISA § 408, and those granted by DOL and the Treasury after conferring. Before granting an exemption, the federal agency must decide that the proposed exemption is administratively feasible; serves the best interests of participants and beneficiaries; and protects the rights of participants and beneficiaries.

To get an individual exemption, a plan must apply to the relevant agency or agencies, and also give notice to affected parties and publish a notice in the Federal Register. Affected parties can place their comments (positive or negative) on the record. In some cases, a hearing will be required before the exemption is granted (e.g., when a fiduciary seeks permission to deal with the plan for his own account or to represent an adverse party).

ERISA includes statutory exemptions for loans to PIIs who are also plan participants or beneficiaries, as long as the loans are made on fair terms; for payment of reasonable compensation to PIIs for services they provide to the plan, rental of real estate to the plan at reasonable rates, and other deals that are the equivalent of arm's length transactions. There is also a statutory exemption for investing more than 10% of the plan's assets in qualifying employer securities and real property, as long as the plan purchases these items at a reasonable price and does not have to pay a commission to acquire them from the employer. Depending on the type of security, the plan will not be permitted to hold more than 25% to 50% of the entire issue.

"Class exemptions" have also been adopted for frequent transactions that are not harmful to the plan or its participants. Class exemptions have been granted, for instances, in connection with interest-free loans; mortgage loans to PIIs; and hiring PIIs to provide investment advice to the plan.

In February 2003, the DOL and EBSA proposed a class exemption for transactions in connection with settlement of litigation against a plan. [68 Fed. Reg. 6953 (Feb. 11, 2003)] For example, sometimes the best way to resolve an improper purchase of property from a party in interest is to re-sell the property to another party in interest. DOL received many inquiries about settlements of securities fraud class actions that overlap with ERISA cases. The Department has determined that it would be appropriate to provide an exemption for parties in interest in order to facilitate the settlement of litigation with plans. DOL proposes a retroactive (to 1975) and prospective exemption from restrictions in connection with release by the plan of legal or equitable claims against a party in interest in exchange for consideration in settlement of litigation; and extension of credit by the plan to the party in interest in connection with settlement, when the party in interest makes installment repayment of amounts owed to the plan.

A class exemption was granted in November 2002 to expedite voluntary correction [Prohibited Transaction Exemption 2002-51, 67 Fed. Reg. 70623 (Nov. 25, 2002)] in connection with four types of transactions: failure to make timely contributions; plan loans to parties in interest; sale or leaseback of real estate; and purchase or sale of other assets. The exemption will not apply if the amount of assets involved in the transaction is more than 10% of the total FMV of plan assets at the time of the transaction, and any transaction that uses the exemption must be fair (e.g., loans to parties in interest must be made at a fair market interest rate) and property transactions must be made on terms at least as favorable to the plan as arm's length transactions would be.

If a plan has failed to transmit contributions to the pension plan within the time frame required by 29 C.F.R. § 2510.3-102, or loan repayments have not been placed into the plan within a reasonable time of being withheld or received by the employer, the failure can be corrected by depositing the sums into the plan within 180 calendar days of receipt by the employer.

In general, relief will be denied if similar relief was granted within the previous three years under the VFC program. To obtain an exemption, the applicant must meet all the requirements of the VFC program and obtain a no-action letter from the EBSA—but merely getting the no-action letter doesn't prove that all the conditions have been satisfied.

Within 60 calendar days of submitting the application to the DOL, the plan must give notice to interested persons (e.g., plan participants and beneficiaries)—and plan assets can't be used to pay for the notice.

Early in 2006, EBSA issued two class exemption amendments, facilitating transactions with a wide range of insurers and financial institutions. The amendment to PTE 75-1 permits transactions with broker-dealers, reporting dealers and banks that are fiduciaries of the plan, as long as the institutions or their affiliates do not have investment authority over the plan assets and do not provide investment advice. Similarly, PTE 84-24 has been amended to permit insurance agents and brokers, pension consultants, and mutual fund underwriters to sell insurance and receive commissions. In EBSA's view, the changes reflect consolidation in the financial services industry, which has increased the number of affiliations among entities. However, to qualify for exemption, transactions must be as favorable to the plan as if they were negotiated at arm's length. [Fred Schneyer, *EBSA Changes Prohibited Class Transaction Rules,* PlanSponsor.com (Feb. 2, 2006)]

§15.16   PAYMENT OF PLAN EXPENSES

One of the EBSA's top enforcement priorities is to make plan sponsors reimburse plans for expenses that were paid out of plan assets but should have been paid by the sponsors themselves. The DOL said that its regional offices would be conducting more plan expense audits than before. If a violation is found, not only must the employer reimburse the plan, but anyone involved in the transaction is subject to a 20% penalty. The Department of Labor can refer the case to the IRS for collection of the excise tax on prohibited transactions.

"Settlor functions" (decisions about establishing a plan or about plan design) are discretionary and not subject to the ERISA fiduciary requirements. Therefore, the expenses of performing settlor functions are not expenses of plan administration, and it is improper to use plan assets to pay them.

DOL Advisory Opinion 97-03A says that plan assets can be used to pay the expenses of terminating the plan itself, if the plan was silent about paying expenses, or if the plan permitted the payment of necessary administrative expenses. Plans that required the sponsor to pay such expenses can be amended to make the plan responsible for the expenses—but only expenses incurred after the amendment.

The DOL provided additional guidance in Advisory Opinion 2001-01A and a separate group of fact patterns. Under this Opinion, formation of a plan is a settlor activity, and the plan should not pay for it. Maintaining qualified status could involve fiduciary activities that the plan can pay for. Depending on whether they are incurred before or after a plan amendment, and whether they are reasonable and necessary for plan administration, these expenses could be legitimate plan expenses:

- Minimum funding valuations;
- Requests for determination;
- Processing fees;
- Preparation and submission of reports required by government agencies;
- Sending copies of such reports to participants;
- Making disclosure to, and communicating with, plan participants;
- Gathering information to make investment decisions for the plan;
- Amending the plan when complying with the law requires an amendment;
- Asset valuations in connection with a plan merger or spinoff (as long as the valuation is done after the plan is amended to cope with the transition);
- Winding up a terminated plan (including preparing valuations for the PBGC and distributing the plan's assets);
- Paying PBGC premiums;
- Preparing and auditing the plan's financial statements;
- Paying investment expenses.

Advisory Opinion 2001-01A says that the following are not allowable expenses that can be charged against the plan:

- Comparing benefit structures;
- Studies for outsourcing services that were previously performed by the sponsor at no cost to the plan;
- Preparing plan amendments that are not required for the sake of compliance;
- Preparing the financial disclosures that the sponsor is required to make under accounting standards;
- Getting valuations as part of deciding whether a merger or spinoff is worthwhile;
- Penalties imposed on the plan administrator;
- Analyses of whether to adopt early retirement incentives;
- Analyses of whether to terminate the plan.

In May 2003, EBSA ruled that it was permissible for a plan to pass along operating costs on a per-participant basis. However, the costs of creating a plan are entirely the financial responsibility of the employer. Cost allocation to individual participants is allowed for calculation of benefits, hardship withdrawals, and QDRO processing. This last is a reversal of a long-standing policy: in 1994 PBGC said that it was not permitted to impose a charge for processing a QDRO. [Kathy Chu, *Employees May Pay More on Retirement Plans*, Wall Street Journal, June 24, 2003, at p. D3]

§15.17   SERVICE PROVIDERS

Part of the fiduciary's duty of prudence is intelligent and informed selection of service providers for the plan, followed by monitoring of the job that the service providers do. Although it is understandable that fiduciaries will think first of their friends, colleagues, or relatives in selecting a service provider, the baseline is that they must deal only with people who have at least the minimum qualifications and experience to do the tasks they are hired for. A thorough reference check should be performed.

Compensation must be at least reasonably comparable to market rates for the same work. Selection by competitive bidding is helpful. Before retaining a service provider, it is vital to determine whether the fee that is quoted covers all the necessary services, or whether it is possible or likely that additional fees will be incurred, based on the predicted activities of the plan. The fiduciary doesn't always have to select the low bidder, but must be able to justify the selection as providing the best value on balance.

The job of the plan committee, or the responsible officers, is to choose investment options that, individually and in the aggregate, are suitable and prudent for the plan and its participants. Many of the financial service companies that market 401(k) plans provide investment advice at either the plan or the participant level. A plan that uses advisory services must have a prudent process for choosing the advisor and reviewing its activities. ERISA's investment rules are based on Modern Portfolio Theory so this should be the default choice for the plan's investors to use, unless it is prudent to select a different methodology. The advisor should give the committee a written explanation of its methodology, representing that it adheres to generally accepted theories and follows practices prevailing within the investment industry. The advisory firm must have employees with proper credentials or should have contracts with persons who have such credentials. Disclosure to the committee should include the software that the advisor uses to choose stocks and the advisors' criteria for rating stocks. The advisor should provide the committee with performance reports and benchmarks that can be used to assess how well the advisor is doing. For advice rendered at the plan rather than the individual level, the advisor should report to the committee in writing at least annually about the results achieved. The investment committee should check with other clients to see what they think of the advisor's performance and on a periodic basis (perhaps once every three years) the committee should verify that the advisor renders services that are, at least, of market standard as to effectiveness, quality, and fees. [Fred Reish, *Prudence in Advice Selection*, Magazine Articles, PlanSponsor.com (Mar. 2006)]

On August 20, 2002, the DOL issued Advisory Opinion 2002-08A, <http://www.dol.gov/ebsa/regs/AOs/ao2002-08a.html>, which permits fiduciaries to cause plans to enter into contracts with actuarial firms and other service providers that contain limitation of liability and indemnification provisions. When service providers are chosen, the fiduciary has an obligation to engage in an objective process to get the information needed to assess the provider's qualifications, the quality of the services offered, and the reasonableness of the fees charged for the services. Soliciting bids is an acceptable way to get this information, including the service provider's policies about indemnification and limitation of liability.

In the DOL view, such indemnification or limitation of liability is not necessarily per se imprudent under ERISA § 404(a)(1)(B) or unreasonable under § 408(b)(2), but it must be construed in connection with the reasonableness of the entire agreement and by considering whether participants and beneficiaries are placed at risk.

Fiduciaries must assess the potential risk of loss, and the cost to the plan, if the service provider causes loss to the plan and is indemnified. Furthermore, indemnification or waiver of liability that relates to willful misconduct or fraud is void as against public policy, and it is neither prudent nor reasonable for fiduciaries to agree to such provisions.

DOL's Advisory Opinion 2005-23A (December 2005) applies ERISA's requirements of prudence, avoidance of prohibited transactions, and operation of the plan for the exclusive benefit of participants to many of the recommendations that financial planners and investment advisors give about the assets in qualified individual account plans. Paid investment professionals can be fiduciaries even though they work for the individual plan participants rather than the plan itself—especially if they have discretionary authority to manage the participants' investments. They can be fiduciaries even without discretionary authority if they give regular, individualized investment advice in return for a fee, with the expectation that the participant will act on the advice. Therefore, they can be liable under ERISA if their investment recommendations are not prudent, but ERISA preempts any contractual or state law limitations on their liability. These planners and advisors are subject to the prohibited transaction rules, so they are forbidden to engage in self-dealing (e.g., advising a client to take a distribution from a qualified plan in order to invest it in an IRA managed by the advisor). The plan's other fiduciaries do not have a duty to advise the participant about the advice given by the participant's own advisor, nor are the other fiduciaries liable for decisions made by a participant's advisor. [Gregory L. Ash, *The Fiduciary Corner: Individual Financial Planners May Be ERISA Fiduciaries,* <http://www.spencerfane.com/article.asp> (Feb. 2006); Rebecca Moore, *Participant-Chosen Financial Advisor Is a Plan Fiduciary* (Jan. 20, 2006)]

§ 15.18   ERISA LITIGATION

[A]   Generally

The provisions of ERISA are enforced both by the federal government and by private litigation. EBSA announced that in its 2005 fiscal year, it achieved $1.7 billion in enforcement recoveries (although 2004 recoveries were higher).

The 2005 total included $709 million in assets restored to plans plus benefits to individual workers. The agency fielded 160,000 inquiries and recovered $88.4 million in benefits for workers and their families through the informal resolution of individual complaints (vs. $76 million in 2004). In FY 2005, EBSA closed 3,782 civil investigations, about three quarters of which resulted in corrective actions, including monetary recoveries for the plans. EBSA closed 196 criminal investigations; the number of criminal cases closed via conviction or guilty plea was up 13% from the previous year. In addition, 106 people were indicted for offenses related to employee benefit plans. Nearly 1,000 applications for the Voluntary Fiduciary Correction Program were filed (up 108% since 2004), and $7.4 million worth of assets were returned to plans under this program. [DOL Fact Sheet, <http://www.dol.gov/ebsa/newsroom/fs2005enforcementresults.html> (Feb. 2006); *see* Rebecca Moore, *BSA Achieves $1.7 Billion in Enforcement Actions Results*, PlanSponsor.com (Jan. 30, 2006)]

In ERISA litigation, as in many other types of cases involving plans, the basic questions include who can be sued, the proper court for the case, when the suit must be filed to be timely, and what remedies can be ordered if the case is proved.

In 2002, the Seventh Circuit ruled that pilots could not bring suit in the Southern District of Illinois against a plan administrator located in Atlanta. The presence of two plan participants (out of a total of 2,740) in the district does not provide sufficient contacts to justify bringing suit in that district. [*Waeltz v. Delta Pilots Retirement Plan*, 301 F.3d 804 (7th Cir. 2002)]

In 1997, the district court for the District of Colorado ruled that plan participants' ERISA claims to recover benefits under a severance plan are legal, not equitable. Therefore, a jury trial would be available. But this was very much a minority view—nine Circuits had already ruled that jury trials are not available in such cases. In 1998, the Tenth Circuit joined the others. [*Adams v. Cyprus Amax Mineral Co.*, 149 F.3d 1156 (D. Colo. 1997)]

Jury trials are usually unavailable in ERISA § 502(a)(1)(B) and (a)(3) cases. Another possibility is that a jury will be empanelled in these cases, but it will only determine the part of the case relating to breach of contract. The judge in the case will decide claims of breach of fiduciary duty.

By and large, ERISA cases are treated like contract cases. Therefore, the damages available to a winning plaintiff basically put the plaintiff in the position he or she would have been in if the contract had been complied with. "Extracontractual" damages (like damages for negligent or intentional infliction of emotional distress) will probably not be available. In most ERISA cases, punitive damages are also ruled out.

In any ERISA action brought by participants, beneficiaries, or fiduciaries, the winning side (whether plaintiff or defendant) can be awarded reasonable costs and attorneys' fees if the court thinks this is appropriate. Usually the attorneys' fee award starts out with the "lodestar" figure. This is the number of hours the winning lawyer spent on the case, multiplied by an hourly rate the court considers reasonable. In rare cases, the lodestar is reduced: if the court thinks the lawyer wasted time, for instance. Sometimes the fee award is greater than the lodestar amount, if the case was especially difficult, the lawyer broke new ground with innovative legal theories, or took on an unpopular case.

Although ERISA § 502(a)(3) is limited to equitable relief, the Sixth Circuit ruled in early 2006 that District Courts had subject matter jurisdiction to award attorneys' fees in a suit to enforce the reimbursement provisions of an EGHP after the defendant-plan participant received an automobile accident settlement. The Sixth Circuit drew analogies from non-ERISA Supreme Court decisions. [*Primax Recoveries Inc. v. Gunter*, 433 F.3d 515 (6th Cir. 2006)]

As Chapter 40 shows, arbitration assumes an increasingly large role in the resolution of disputes within the U.S. legal system. In some compliance cases, the question is whether the proper forum is litigation or arbitration. The Ninth Circuit ruled that the arbitration clause in an investment management agreement between an employer and its investment advisor did not obligate a plan participant to arbitrate fiduciary breach claims. (The participant charged that the advisor imprudently invested in Internet stocks that declined in value.) The Ninth Circuit rejected the employer's argument that the plan participant was a third-party beneficiary who was bound by the arbitration agreement because there was no proof that the participant knowingly exploited the agreement that included the arbitration clause. There was no evidence that the agreement, which was not signed by the plan participants, was intended to affect their rights to sue. [*Comer v. Micor Inc.*, 436 F.3d 1098 (9th Cir. 2006)]

[B]   Preemption

In many instances, cases involving benefits will have to be brought in federal rather than state courts, because of ERISA preemption. It should be noted that ERISA preempts state law in connection with voluntary benefit programs, with the result, for example, that an employee who charges irregularities in connection with a voluntary disability insurance plan will have to sue in federal court and will not be able to receive punitive damages. According to the Tenth Circuit, ERISA does not preempt claims about promises of job security, but it does preempt claims about promises involving employee benefits. [*Wilcott v. Matlack Inc.*, 64 F.3d 1458 (10th Cir. 1995)]

According to the Seventh Circuit [*Metropolitan Life Ins. Co. v. Johnson*, 297 F.3d 558 (7th Cir. 2002)], the federal doctrine of "substantial compliance" preempts state law for suits involving alleged changes in the beneficiaries of a plan. In this case, life insurance benefits went to the children of a deceased beneficiary who failed to fully comply with the plan's provisions for beneficiary designation, because the court ruled that the decedent gave proof of his intent and took steps to carry out a change of beneficiary.

In its *Aetna Health Inc. v. Davila*, and *Cigna Healthcare of Texas, Inc. v. Calad*, 542 U.S. 200 (2004), decision, the Supreme Court ruled that ERISA completely preempts HMO participants' claims that they were improperly denied health care.

ERISA doesn't preempt state common-law fraud claims by a plan against a participant who concealed his divorce in order to maintain plan coverage for his ex-wife. ERISA doesn't have a mechanism for plan administrators or fiduciaries to recoup benefits obtained by fraud, so state tort claims can still be maintained for this purpose. [*Trustees of the AFTRA Health Fund v. Biondi*, 300 F.3d 765 (7th Cir. 2002)]

In general, ERISA will preempt state laws in cases requiring interpretation of plan documents. There is an exception to preemption for "the business of insurance"—so a number of cases deal with the question of whether federal or state courts should handle certain cases in which health or other insurance is involved in a benefit plan.

The preemption issue is very significant in these emotive cases, because if the case can be heard in state court, punitive damages could be available—and a sympathetic jury could impose heavy punitive damages.

More recently, courts ruled that ERISA preempted state-law causes of action in these situations:

- A claim that the employer was negligent and breached its fiduciary duty by failing to enroll the employee's husband in its accident insurance plan; the court did not accept the employee's argument that it was a negligence claim. [*Page-Walters v. Discovery Financial Services Inc.*, 71 L.W. 1680 (Ohio App. Apr. 15, 2003)]
- State bad-faith laws that give insured persons additional remedies (such as punitive and consequential damages) have been held by the Tenth Circuit to be preempted by ERISA, because the additional damages are inconsistent with ERISA's regulatory scheme. [*Kidneigh v. UNUM Life Ins. Co. of America*, 345 F.3d 1182 (10th Cir. 2003) (Colorado state law); *Conover v. Aetna U.S. Health Care Inc.*, 320 F.3d 1076 (10th Cir. 2003) (Oklahoma state law). *See also Hollaway v. UNUM Life Ins. Co. of America*, 2003 OK. 90 (Okla. 2003)]

But preemption was held not to occur in these instances:

- A plan brought state claims (e.g., malpractice, breach of contract, promissory estoppel) against its actuary, claiming that the actuary's wrongdoing resulted in the plan being underfunded. However, the actuary was not a fiduciary and the Second Circuit held that ERISA does not preempt state-law negligence claims against non-fiduciaries. But the court also ruled that the remedies under ERISA are the only remedies available—the plan could not get consequential damages against the actuary. [*Gerosa v. Savasta & Co.*, 329 F.3d 317 (2d Cir. 2003)]
- Claims of malpractice, negligent misrepresentation, and breach of contract were brought by ESOP participants against an investment firm they allege

undervalued that plan's stock during the process of terminating the plan. (When the company was sold after the plan was terminated, the per-share price was much higher than the price plan participants received for their ESOP shares.) Resolving the charges against the investment firm did not require interpretation of the plan, so the case could be remanded to state court. ERISA's civil enforcement provisions were not triggered because the plaintiffs did not charge fiduciary breach, nor did they seek to recover plan benefits. [*Clark v. Ameritas Investment Corp.*, D. Neb., No. 4:05CV3251 (Dec. 27, 2005)]

• Action by a group of employees under state mechanic's lien law, to recover contributions that the employer failed to make to the benefits trust fund; the mechanic's lien law is not preempted because it is a law of general applicability that does not relate to the benefit plan. [*Betancourt v. Storke Housing Investors*, 31 Cal. 4th 1157 (Cal. 2003)]

Another question is removal—whether a state case can be removed to the federal court system. In the view of the Eleventh Circuit, the employer cannot get the case removed to federal court, even for the limited purpose of deciding the preemption issue, if the plaintiff's state claims relate to benefits that are not covered by ERISA, even though they are bundled with an ERISA plan. [*Kemp v. IBM*, 109 F.3d 708 (11th Cir. 1997)]

When an employer ceased contributions to its plan and some employees were no longer entitled to plan benefits, a group of employees brought claims under state law. The employer had the case removed to federal court on the grounds of ERISA preemption. The Western District of New York, however, ruled that the employees were no longer entitled to plan benefits so they were not entitled to ERISA civil enforcement remedies, and the case should therefore be remanded to state court. [*Bialy v. Honeywell Int'l Inc.*, W.D.N.Y., No. 04-CV-0980E(Sc), (Jan. 24, 2006)]

The SPD for a disability plan stated that actions to recover benefits could be filed in either state or federal court. Where the benefit claimant chose to file in state court, the Seventh Circuit ruled that the clause did not prevent the plan administrator from removing the case to federal court. The provision was not a forum selection clause, merely a quotation of the relevant provision of ERISA. [*Cruthis v. Metropolitan Life Ins Co.*, 356 F.3d 816 (7th Cir. 2004)] *See* § 15.09[B] for discussion of 2006 developments in treatment of subrogation and removal of cases to federal court. Also note that, for cases filed after the February 18, 2005, effective date of the Class Action Fairness Act (P.L. 109-2), the federal system may be the only appropriate venue for certain class actions brought by health plan participants.

According to the Eleventh Circuit, an employer's payments under a sickness and accident plan came from the employer's general assets, not from a welfare benefit plan. This was a "payroll practice" exempted from ERISA. Because it was not subject to ERISA, it was also not preempted by ERISA, so the defendant could not remove an employee's state breach of contract case (when payments were stopped). [*Stern v. IBM*, 326 F.3d 1367 (11th Cir. 2003)]

An employee sued in state court for negligence and breach of fiduciary duty, alleging that his employer failed to disclose an impending merger that would have affected the employee's decision about taking an ESOP distribution. The Eleventh Circuit would not permit removal of the claims. The plaintiff sought remedies outside the scope of ERISA § 502(a), so ERISA did not preempt the claims. He wasn't seeking clarification of his rights under the plan, or even seeking to enforce his rights under the plan—he asserted pure state-law claims of fiduciary breach. [*Ervast v. Flexible Products Co.*, 346 F.3d 1007 (11th Cir. 2003)]

A group of ex-employees sued in state court, seeking compensatory damages for the decline in value of company stock held in their retirement plan. The Sixth Circuit ruled that the claims involved only state-law issues of business judgment, so even though the ESOP in question was an ERISA plan, the case could not be removed. [*Husvar v. Rapaport*, 337 F.3d 603 (6th Cir. 2003)]

[C] Exhaustion of Remedies

The court system is supposed to handle major conflicts, not minor everyday disputes that can and should be addressed in less complex and less socially expensive ways. Therefore, plaintiffs often have a legal duty of "exhaustion of remedies." That is, they will not be permitted to bring court cases until they have pursued all the administrative remedies within the system they are challenging. ERISA requires every plan to have a system for pursuing claims and appealing claims denials. So the general rule is that would-be plaintiffs must go through these steps before filing suit. This is not stated in so many words in ERISA itself, but judges have looked to ERISA's legislative history and other labor laws to determine when this requirement should be implied.

Plaintiffs clearly have to exhaust their remedies within the plan when their case involves benefits. Courts are split as to whether ERISA § 510 plaintiffs (interference with protected rights; see above) are required to exhaust their remedies. Exhaustion of remedies will not be required if:

- Going through channels would be futile;
- It was impossible to pursue plan remedies because the defendant wrongfully denied the plaintiff access to the plan's claims procedures;
- Irreparable harm would ensue if exhaustion of remedies was required;
- Participants and beneficiaries did not know how to enforce their rights, because they were deprived of information about claims procedures.

The Third Circuit required exhaustion of remedies in a case in which the plaintiffs charged the plan administrator with fiduciary breach for failure to provide full vesting of benefits after partial termination of a plan, on the grounds that this is essentially a claim for plan benefits. [*D'Amico v. CBS Corp.*, 297 F.3d 287 (3d Cir. 2002)]

The estate and surviving child of a mentally ill person who committed several murders and then committed suicide brought suit against the utilization review company that performed services for the decedent's health plan. The plaintiffs alleged that the decedent was discharged too soon from a mental institution, and should have been monitored more closely. The Fourth Circuit ruled that, because the utilization review company was not involved in health care decisions, the state-law claim related exclusively to plan administration. Therefore, it was preempted by ERISA. That left the only possible cause of action a claim for fiduciary breach. The court ruled that the complaint focused on decisions made by health care providers and did not demonstrate fiduciary breach by the utilization review firm. [*Marks v. Watters*, 322 F.3d 316 (4th Cir. 2003)]

[D]   Statute of Limitations

ERISA § 525 permits a civil action against an employer for delinquency in making contributions. This section does not contain an express statute of limitations; most courts use a six-year statute of limitations, treating the case as the equivalent of an action to enforce a written contract.

The statute of limitations for an ERISA § 409 case (breach of fiduciary duty) derives from ERISA § 413. The suit must be brought within three years of the time the plaintiff discovered the alleged wrongdoing, or six years from the date of the last breach or the last date on which the omission could have been cured—whichever is earlier.

The Third Circuit found that ERISA's six-year statute of limitations for fiduciary breaches barred claims about misrepresentations of pension benefits. The statute began to run when the allegedly misleading statements were made, not when the participants relied on the representations to their detriment. [*Ranke v. Sanofi-Synthelabo Inc.*, 436 F.3d 197 (3d Cir. 2006)]

ERISA has an explicit statute of limitations for claims of breach of fiduciary duty, but not for participants' claims for plan benefits. According to *Wetzel v. Lou Ehlers Cadillac Group Long Term Disability Insurance Program* [222 F.3d 643 (9th Cir. 1999)], the crucial issue is whether the plaintiff provided proof of continuing disability for each month. The general federal rule is that a claim accrues as soon as a claimant knows or had reason to know that his claim had been denied. This rule would apply in any month in which adequate proof of loss was provided. But a separate three-year statute of limitations would be applied to determine whether claims were timely or time-barred for each month in which adequate proof of loss was not submitted.

The District Court dismissed as untimely a claim that the fiduciary violated the plaintiff's ERISA rights by failing to deposit and invest funds in accordance with his instructions. He made many unsuccessful attempts to get a complete accounting. To the District Court, the applicable statute of limitations was three years [29 U.S.C. § 1113(2)], and the cause of action accrued in December 1995 and therefore the case had to be filed by December 1998. However, the Third

Circuit reversed this decision. [*Roush v. New England Mutual Life Ins. Co.*, 311 F.3d 581 (3d Cir. 2002)] The Third Circuit ruled that the statute of limitations is triggered by the plaintiff's actual knowledge of the breach or violation—and actual knowledge means knowledge of all relevant facts supporting the argument that fiduciary duty was breached. In this case, the plaintiff knew in 1995 that his instructions had not been followed, but he did not have a complete, accurate accounting and did not know that the defendant's actions had caused harm or would have harmful consequences.

Similarly, the Sixth Circuit ruled that a suit was untimely where trustees began to worry about their financial advisor some six to seven years before bringing suit. They consulted three independent financial consultants, who concluded that the plan had been harmed by improper advice. At that point, the trustees terminated the relationship with the adviser, but they didn't hire a lawyer for more than a year, and did not file suit for more than three years. The Sixth Circuit's test is knowledge of the conduct that forms the basis for the suit; otherwise, plaintiffs could extend the statute of limitations indefinitely merely by failing to get legal advice. [*Wright v. Heyne*, 349 F.3d 321 (6th Cir. 2003)] The Third and Fifth Circuits start the statute of limitations running with knowledge that the facts constitute a breach of fiduciary duty; the Sixth, Seventh, Ninth, and Eleventh Circuits use the knowledge of the underlying facts; and the Second Circuit uses a hybrid test—knowledge of all the facts necessary to constitute a claim, including expert opinions and understanding of harmful consequences.

Because § 510 does not include an explicit statute of limitations, the First Circuit held that the *state* statute of limitation for the most similar type of case should be applied in § 510 cases. Furthermore, the First Circuit used the state's three-year statute of limitations for personal injury cases, not the six-year statute of limitations for contract cases—so the plaintiff's suit was dismissed as time-barred. [*Muldoon v. C.J. Muldoon & Sons Inc.*, 278 F.3d 31 (1st Cir. 2002)]

According to the First, Third, Seventh, Eighth, Ninth, and District of Columbia Circuits, the six-year statute of limitations under ERISA § 413 "in case of fraud or concealment," can be applied only when both fraud and concealment are charged. The Second Circuit disagrees, allowing the six-year statute of limitations for claims of either fraud or concealment. [*Caputo v. Pfizer Inc.*, 267 F.3d 181 (2d Cir. 2001)]

If the source of the suit is a fiduciary's omission rather than a wrongful action, the time limit is six years from the last date the fiduciary could have cured the problem.

§ 15.19   CORRECTION PROGRAMS

[A]   Plan Deficiency Aids

One of the central tenets of tax and ERISA enforcement for plans is that, wherever possible, plans should be encouraged to determine where they fall short of compliance, and to correct the problems before regulators detect them. The IRS publishes Alert Guidelines, Explanations, & Plan Deficiency Paragraphs [<http://www.irs.gov/retirement/article/0,,id=97188,00.html>] so businesses can see the standards that IRS reviewers use when they review retirement plans for compliance. Each worksheet comes with explanatory text. The IRS Checksheets, also known as Plan Deficiency Paragraphs, are standardized text that plans can use to draft provisions that will satisfy IRS requirements.

[B] Voluntary Correction

The IRS has engaged in ongoing efforts to allow plans to correct failures without losing qualification. The Department of Labor encourages voluntary return to compliance by plan administrators. Over time, these programs have evolved. The IRS consolidated a number of programs into the EPCRS program. Self-correction actions can be undertaken without a formal filing with the IRS, and no fees are involved. The IRS policy is that a plan will not be disqualified because of any error that was self-corrected.

For the latest information about IRS' Voluntary Correction Program (VCP), *see* Rev. Proc. 2006-27, 2006-22 I.R.B. 945, which modifies and supersedes Rev. Proc. 2003-44, 2003-1 C.B. 1051, the previous comprehensive statement of the Employee Plans Compliance Resolution System (EPCRS) rules. EPCRS provides three levels of corrections of inadvertent errors that do not involve deliberate engagement in abusive tax strategies (e.g., inappropriate tax shelters):

- The Self-Correction Program (SCP) allows the least complex types of plans (403(b), SEPs, and SIMPLE IRAs) to correct minor operational failures. These corrections are performed purely in house, do not generate penalties, and need not involve or even be disclosed to the IRS.
- The Voluntary Correction Program (VCP) permits a plan sponsor who detects mistakes before an audit to correct those mistakes and pay a fee that is smaller than the penalties that would be imposed on deficiencies uncovered in an audit.
- The Correction on Audit Program (Audit CAP) permits correction in response to an audit, with sanctions reflecting the extent and seriousness of the deficiency.

Rev. Proc. 2006-27 changes the rules for applying for a determination letter after certain failures have been corrected via plan amendment and allows terminating "orphan plans" (whose sponsor is no longer in existence) to use VCP and Audit CAP. In appropriate cases, if the failure constitutes a lack of satisfaction of the § 401(a)(9) minimum distribution requirements, the § 4974 excise tax will be waived.

DOL updated the Voluntary Fiduciary Correction (VFC) program in April 2006, effective May 19, 2006. The VFC now applies to 19 transactions that could involve fiduciary breach or prohibited transactions. The 2006 changes are based on the 2005 revision, including a model application form, lower paperwork burdens for applicants, easier calculations of sums to be returned to the plan, and relief from

ERISA § 502(i) civil penalties for some health plan transactions). More plans can qualify for participation because the definition of "under investigation" has been clarified. VFC can now be used by plans that have paid certain expenses that were properly the responsibility of the employer; by plans that made loans to participants that violated the requirement of level amortization (as long as correction is also made under IRS' EPCRS program); and by plan that sold illiquid assets to parties in interest. If, on the other hand, the plan has purchased an asset from a party in interest, the plan would be permitted to keep the asset, rather than selling it to correct the transaction. The VFC program does not apply to IRAs that are exempt from ERISA. [71 Fed. Reg. 20261 (Apr. 19, 2006); 71 Fed. Reg. 20135, of the same date, updates PTE 2002-51, the prohibited transaction class exemption that remits the I.R.C. § 4975 excise tax, to accommodate the changes in the VFC program. DOL's April 18, 2006 press release was posted to <http://benefitslink.com/pr/detail.php?id=39677>]

DOL announced a new mailing address for the Directed Fiduciary Voluntary Correction (DFVC) program in March 2006: Items sent by mail go to DFVC Program-DOL, P.O. Box 70933, Charlotte NC 28272-0933. Those sent via private delivery service go to DFVC Program-DOL QLP Wholesale Lockbox NC 0810 Lockbox #70933, 1525 West WT Harris Blvd., Charlotte, NC 28262.

Voluntary correction is also permitted if the deficiencies exist in a health benefit rather than a pension plan. EBSA has stepped up enforcement efforts such as auditing for compliance with HIPAA's requirements of nondiscrimination and health insurance portability; mental health parity; and the Women's Health and Cancer Rights Act. Over 1,200 welfare benefit plans have been audited for compliance with 42 requirements, including notice requirements. Violations—usually notice deficiencies—were reported in 60% of the audited multi-employer plans.

In February 2003, EBSA announced H-CAP, the HIPAA Compliance Assistance Program, including distribution of materials, live training sessions, and compliance aids. [*See* <http://www.dol.gov/ebsa/compliance_assistance.html#section2>]

[C] Removing Assets

Although Rev. Proc. 2001-17, 2001-7 I.R.B. 589 describes limited circumstances under which assets can be removed from the plan to effect correction of a qualification failure, the better strategy is to prevent excess assets from entering the plan in the first place. Section 6.02(2)(c) of the Procedure permits removal of the assets only if the Code, Regulations, or other generally applicable guidance allows correction by way of distributing assets or participants or beneficiaries, or returning assets to the employer or plan sponsor. This section also says that if an excess allocation is made for a plan participant (other than a 401(k) participant), and the allocation does not exceed the I.R.C. § 415 limit, then the excess allocation should be corrected by reallocating it to other participants or reducing the sponsoring employer's future contributions. [*Removing Assets from a Plan to Effect Correction*, BenefitsLink Correcting Plan Defects Q&A, (Dec. 3, 2001) <http://benefitslink.com/cgi-bin/qa.cgi?database_id=164&mode=read&database=qa_plan_defects>] The funds should not be returned to the sponsor. If the funds are excess because the plan fails the ADP antidiscrimination test, funds may be returned to participants. The funds must be returned to participants if a deferral is greater than the I.R.C. § 402(g) maximum (which is $13,000 for 2004, $14,000 for 2005, and $15,000 for 2006 and thereafter) and the required minimum distribution is not made under I.R.C. § 401(a)(9).

CHAPTER 16

EFFECT OF CORPORATE TRANSITIONS ON PENSION AND BENEFIT PLANS

§16.01 INTRODUCTION

A qualified plan can change its form for several reasons: by amendment, by termination, or as a response to a change in form in the corporation that sponsors the plan. The sponsoring corporation can merge with or be acquired by another company, and some or all of the first plan's employees can become employees of the new or surviving corporation. The transition may be primarily motivated by corporate needs or primarily to change the form or operation of the plan (e.g., combining several existing plans for ease of administration or to cut costs).

Basic fiduciary principles continue to apply during a transition, and plans must still be maintained for the sole benefit of participants and beneficiaries. Therefore, the Supreme Court decided that plan participants and beneficiaries can sue under ERISA §502(a)(3) to get equitable relief for themselves, when a company spun off its money-losing divisions to a new, financially unstable corporation and then lied to employees about the safety of their benefits if they transferred to the new corporation. [*Varity Corp. v. Howe,* 516 U.S. 489 (1996)]

However, because pension benefits vest but welfare benefits (including retiree health and insurance benefits) do not, ERISA fiduciary duty is not violated by transferring the obligation to pay nonpension retiree benefits to a new company spun off from the former employer. Nor will the courts hear an ERISA contract claim.

Part of the due diligence that must be undertaken prior to purchasing another business, or selling a business, is the effect of the change on each corporation's employee benefit plans. For example, if it is discovered that the seller's plan is underfunded, the sales documents might be redrafted to obligate the seller to correct the underfunding—or the sales price might simply be reduced accordingly. Sometimes, the deciding factor in structuring the deal will be the way the deal partners intend to treat their benefit plans.

A change in corporate structure can have unintended effects on plans, such as violation of nondiscrimination, minimum participation, and anticutback rules. The buyer must be particularly careful to find out if defined contribution plans are unfunded, or defined benefit plans are underfunded.

The presence or absence of golden parachutes, retiree health benefit obligations, and COBRA obligations must be determined. Worker Adjustment and Restraining Notification Act (WARN) [29 U.S.C. §2101 *et seq.*] notification may also be required if there is a significant reduction in the workforce after the corporate transition. [*See* §30.10] Plan discrimination testing must also be repeated after a change of corporate organization. [*See* §4.22]

Changes in ownership or the form of ownership of a corporation sponsoring a plan will frequently be "reportable events" of which the PBGC must be notified (in case the plan is unable to meet its payment obligations and the PBGC has to take over).

The reorganization of a plan's contributing sponsor makes the successor corporation responsible for certain plan liabilities such as the plan's accumulated funding deficiencies, including those previously waived by the IRS. [*See* ERISA §§ 4062(f) and 4069(b)] A party that engages in a transaction within five years before a plan termination, if the transaction was intended to evade liability in connection with the plan, becomes a contributing sponsor who is liable for those amounts. In other words, the effect of the transaction is precisely the opposite of what was intended.

When operations are terminated at a facility and 20% or more of the participants separate from service, the employer must either fund the plan's guaranteed benefits immediately or make provisions for the funding. There is also likely to be a WARN Act event. [*See* § 30.10]

The test of whether two companies are alter egos (and therefore one must make up for the other's delinquent contributions to a pension plan) comes from basic corporate law. Does one company control the other so closely that the second corporation has no independent existence? Is the second corporation only a sham used for fraudulent purposes?

Although the "golden parachute" (large payments due to top executives who lose their jobs because of a corporate transition) gained the lion's share of attention, sometimes "tin parachutes" (payments to rank-and-file workers) are also possible. In late 2004, the tin parachute regained some of its popularity as a takeover defense. This strategy peaked in the early 1990s, then declined as a result of situations in which the payments to rank-and-file employees didn't cost enough to discourage unsolicited takeover bids. [David Enrich, *"Tin Parachute" Payouts Make Return*, Wall Street Journal, Dec. 15, 2004, at p. B3D]

There are also tax, labor law, and unemployment insurance consequences of corporate transitions.

In mid-2003, the Eighth Circuit ruled that a predecessor employer's alleged promise to pay severance benefits if employees were fired by the successor employer was not based on an ERISA plan and did not amend any existing plan. It was simply a one-time promise. Because there was no ERISA plan involved, employees who did get fired and did not receive severance were permitted to pursue state-law claims in state court. [*Eide v. Grey Fox Technical Servs. Corp.*, 329 F.3d 600 (8th Cir. 2003)]

IRS Form 5310-A, Notice of Plan Merger or Consolidation, Spinoff, or Transfer of Plan Assets or Liabilities, was revised in April 2006. The form must be filed to give notice of the combination of two or more plans into a single plan, splitting a plan into two or more spinoff plans, or a transfer of assets or liabilities to another plan. However, Form 5310-A is not filed in certain cases, such as when defined contribution plans are merged, but the sum of the account balances in each plan equals the fair market value of the plan assets; or two defined benefit plans are merged when the total liabilities of the smaller plan are less than 3% of the assets of the larger plan. The form must be filed at least 30 days before the transition; all forms must be filed with the IRS office located at P.O. Box 192, Covington, Kentucky, 41012-0192.

§ 16.02   CHOICE OF FORM

[A]   Generally

Although there are almost infinite variations, there are several basic ways to structure a transaction. Two companies could merge, either creating a new successor company or with one company merged into the other. One company could buy all of the other's assets, or one company could buy all of the other company's stock. The consequences of stock and asset purchases are different.

In either a merger or a stock purchase, the buyer acquires the seller's liabilities as an automatic part of the deal. The buyer will become the sponsor of the seller's employee plan benefits unless:

- Action is taken to terminate or freeze the plan. Both corporate action (resolution of the Board of Directors; perhaps affirmation by the stockholders) and pension plan action (plan amendment) will be required;
- The plan is transferred away from the acquired entity (e.g., to a parent corporation that is selling one of its subsidiaries);
- The transaction is set up so the seller retains plan sponsorship.

In this situation, if the plan is not assumed, employees might end up forfeiting benefits that had not vested as of the time of the sale. But if the transaction has the legal effect of a partial termination of the plan, vesting will be required.

In contrast, in an asset sale, the buyer is traditionally deemed to assume only the specific liabilities it agrees to assume. Thus, the buyer becomes a successor plan sponsor only if it takes action to become one, such as adopting the existing plan or a plan that is a spinoff of the existing plan. A spinoff divides one plan into two or more, for instance by assigning a spun-off plan to each of several divisions. There are many reasons why an asset buyer might prefer to avoid adopting the seller's plan—because of underfunding or other liability triggers, or a bad match with the buyer's existing deferred compensation plans.

But asset purchases have their own risks. Some recent court cases make the purchaser liable for pension liabilities such as the asset seller's unpaid pension contributions and termination liability. This could occur even if the asset buyer did not expressly assume the obligations, and even if it is not a successor under the general principles governing corporate transitions, as long as there is continuity of operations and the seller bought the assets knowing that the liabilities existed.

Two former Honeywell employees instituted a class action, claiming that the shareholder vote approving a merger with General Electric triggered their rights to accelerated benefits under the Honeywell Stock Plan. The Eighth Circuit dismissed the case, finding that the language of the stock plan was not ambiguous. Government regulators prevented the merger from occurring. Honeywell's approval of the merger did not constitute an acceleration event, which would have required a consummated merger that ended Honeywell's existence as an independent publicly owned corporation. [*Bohan v. Honeywell Int'l Inc.*, 366 F.3d 606 (8th Cir. 2004)]

[B] T.D. 8928

[1] Generally

T.D. 8928, 66 Fed. Reg. 1843 (Jan. 10, 2001), provides that, when a corporation makes an asset sale (of substantially all the assets of a trade or business, or an asset as substantial as a factory or a corporate division), it is treated as the successor employer if the seller entirely ceases to provide group health plans, and the buyer maintains business operations using the assets. A transfer (e.g., in bankruptcy) is considered an asset sale if it has the same effect as a sale would have.

The plans that the seller maintained before the transaction could be retained, frozen, or terminated. A buyer who adopts an existing plan could agree to assume liability only going forward, with the seller retaining liability for violations of the plan rules that occurred before the sale. As for plans maintained by the buyer before the transaction, the buyer's and seller's plans could merge. [*See* below for the anticutback rules and the requirement of crediting prior service to the new plan]

Like all rules, this has exceptions. If the transaction is in effect a merger rather than an asset sale, liabilities will be characterized as they would be in a merger. If the buying corporation is a mere continuation of the selling corporation, or if the transaction is a fraud intended to escape liability, the transaction will be disregarded.

If only plan assets, and not the operating terms of the two plans, are merged, then the transaction is not considered a plan amendment that has the effect of reducing plan accruals. However, if the plans merge and one adopts the other's formulas and definitions, the original plan is deemed to have been amended. If benefits are reduced, notice must be given under ERISA § 204.

[2] ERISA Issues

In most instances, duplicative plans are merged, or some of them are eliminated. The seller's plan generally transfers assets (and related liabilities) either to the buyer's existing plans or to a newly created plan. ERISA does not require employees to be represented in the negotiations; but once the deal is consummated, the surviving and new plans must be operated subject to fiduciary standards, and mandatory communications must be made to employees.

A corporation's decision to terminate or amend a plan, or to spin off part of a plan, is a discretionary "settlor" function, and the plan sponsor does not act as a fiduciary. The amount of assets to be assigned to a spun-off plan, or the decision to transfer employer securities to a new plan created as part of a spin-off, is not a fiduciary decision. However, the fiduciaries of the plan making the transfers must comply with the plan merger and asset transfer standards set out in ERISA § 208.

Many transactions are structured so that the buyer assumes the seller's responsibility for providing unfunded benefits, such as retiree health coverage. The seller's decision to transfer the liability, and the buyer's commitment to accept it, are also settlor functions and therefore cannot give rise to a claim for breach of fiduciary duty. However, ERISA § 208 does require that each participant receive at least as good a benefit package if the plan were terminated just after the transaction as he or she would have received if the plan had terminated just before the transaction. It should also be remembered that plan assets must not be used for purposes other than paying benefits.

When the seller's defined contribution plan is merged into the buyer's, or assets and liabilities are transferred from seller to buyer, the investment options available to participants in the seller's plan usually replace those available under the buyer's plan. Fiduciary breach claims made by employees of the buyer will probably be rejected. There's one possible exception: if the assets of a diversified seller's plan are liquidated and concentrated too much in the buyer company's stock. The seller's employees are likely to be subject to a blackout period (a time when they cannot take plan loans or change the investment of their accounts). There are problems if both plans offered self-directed investments. Many of the plan participants will fail to return the forms for investment instructions, with the result that the blackout period will be extended.

An administratively simpler option is "mapping": comparing each of the investment options under the old plan to those available under the new plan, with automatic transfers to the comparable option. The downside is that ERISA § 404(c)'s relief for fiduciaries will probably be lost, because that exemption applies only if the participant has exercised actual control over the investment of the account. If the "mapping" notice is given in plenty of time before the blackout period begins, perhaps the argument will succeed that mapping constitutes an implied direction by employees who do not make other choices that they consent to have their account balances "mapped."

On another ERISA issue, the Ninth Circuit ruled in late 2002 that two companies violated ERISA § 510 (the ban on taking adverse employment action against a person to prevent access to plan benefits) when, under an asset purchase agreement, the seller's active employees were hired and given health coverage, but employees who were on extended leave of absence were denied coverage until they returned to work. [*Lessard v. Applied Risk Management*, 307 F.3d 1020 (9th Cir. 2002)] The Ninth Circuit ruled that it violates § 510 to select for presumptive termination and benefit loss on the basis of being on medical or disability leave. The seller would not have been able to terminate the benefits of employees because they took leave, so the buyer could not either. It was improper to structure the program so that the employees with the worst disabilities received the worst deal. The Ninth Circuit remanded the case to apportion liability between the buyer and seller companies.

In the view of the District Court for the Central District of Illinois, it was not a violation of fiduciary duty for an ESOP's trustees, after a merger, to continue to invest two-thirds of the assets of a terminated profit-sharing plan in the stock of the sponsoring employer. Nor was it a fiduciary breach for the plan to take 18 months to distribute its assets to the employees; because there was no breach, the trustees were not liable for losses the plan incurred during that 18-month period. Trustees are not insurers of the financial results of their plan. [*Steinman v. Hicks,* 252 F. Supp. 2d 746 (C.D. Ill. 2003), *aff'd,* 352 F.3d 1101 (7th Cir. 2003)]

An employee sued in state court, alleging negligence and breach of fiduciary duty because the employer did not notify him of an impending merger that would have affected his decision about taking an ESOP distribution. The Eleventh Circuit ruled that such claims cannot be removed to federal court. They are not preempted by ERISA, because the remedies that the plaintiff seeks are not within the scope of ERISA § 502(a). The plaintiff was not seeking clarification of his rights under the plan, or even seeking to enforce the terms of the ESOP. [*Ervast v. Flexible Products Co.,* 346 F.3d 1007 (11th Cir. 2003)]

Plaintiffs in an Eighth Circuit case were paid a guaranteed base salary plus commissions for loans that they closed. They were also eligible for benefits under a Change in Control Severance Pay Program, which provided for benefits if they resigned for "good reason" within 24 months of a change in control. Good reason was defined to mean a reduction of 10% or more in base compensation unless base compensation was replaced by other guaranteed compensation. Their employer merged with another company, resulting in a partial change of control for severance purposes. Several months later, the plaintiffs resigned and filed claims for severance benefits. When the claims were denied, they brought ERISA and state-law breach of contract claims as well as claims for statutory penalties for late payment of earned commissions. Six weeks before their resignation, they received an addendum to the new plan that gave them guaranteed non-recoverable draws equal to their previous guaranteed base salary. Therefore, the severance committee ruled that there had not been an "occurrence" under the severance program because their compensation level could not decline.

The Eighth Circuit held that the state law claims were properly dismissed, because ERISA civil enforcement provisions are the exclusive remedies for benefits under an ERISA plan. The court of appeals agreed with the severance committee that the plaintiffs did not have good cause to resign, because they were not at risk of loss of compensation. When the plaintiffs quit, they were given a final commission payment minus the guaranteed draws that had been paid under the post-merger plan. When they protested, the deductions were reversed. They asserted a violation of the state law mandating payment of commissions within 24 hours of resignation. The Eighth Circuit ruled that the commissions were never earned because their employment contracts before the merger required the CEO's approval before commissions could be paid to an employee who quit. The CEO did not approve the payments. Because the plaintiffs alleged that they never accepted the post-merger compensation plan, their entitlement to commission depended on the pre-merger plan. [*Johnson v. U.S. Bancorp,* 387 F.3d 939 (8th Cir. 2004)]

After their employer merged with another company, a group of participants in a stock bonus plan wanted to sell some of their holdings of employer stock to take advantage of the post-merger increase in value. The fiduciaries of the plan refused. When the participants sued, the Ninth Circuit held that it was not a breach of the ERISA § 404 fiduciary duty of prudence. In fact, it would have violated ERISA to permit them to sell off any more shares than the plan permitted. Fiduciaries do not have a duty to resolve every issue of interpretation as the plan participant wishes. [*Wright v. Oregon Metallurgical Corp.*, 360 F.3d 1090 (9th Cir. 2004)]

The Fifth Circuit reinstated an arbitrator's award of about $1.5 million to employees who were denied severance benefits as a result of a last-minute amendment to a welfare benefit plan, imposed the night before the merger. The Fifth Circuit agreed that the arbitrator correctly decided that it was a violation of fiduciary duty to deny severance claims. [*Kergosien v. Ocean Energy Inc.*, 390 F.3d 346 (5th Cir. 2004)]

The Sixth Circuit held that a group of former employees of SKF USA Inc. immediately became employees of Tyson when SKF was sold to Tyson. The employees were never laid off and therefore there was no triggering of immediate vested benefits under the SKF pension plan. [*Morgan v. SKF USA Inc.*, 385 F.3d 989 (6th Cir. 2004)]

[C] Labor Law Implications of Choice of Form

Labor law follows the basic rule that a merger or sale of stock obligates the acquiring company to assume the liabilities of the acquired or selling company. This includes the Collective Bargaining Agreement (CBA). But in an asset sale, the CBA is not assumed unless the purchaser voluntarily takes it on, or unless there is another reason to view the buyer as a successor or surrogate of the seller.

Yet even if the company is not fully bound by its predecessor's CBA, it could still have a duty to bargain in good faith with the existing union, based on continuity linking the old and new enterprises. If a transaction lacks real substance, the successor could be forced to assume the predecessor's labor-law obligations. The main test is whether there has been a significant practical change or whether operations continue despite a nominal change in ownership.

In addition to situations in which one entity replaces another, two or more enterprises can be treated as a "single employer" for labor-law purposes. One might be treated as an alter ego (surrogate) of the other. If a parent company and its subsidiary engage in the same line of business, the NLRB will probably treat them as a single enterprise, not two. Furthermore, "joint employers" that are separate entities but share decision making about labor issues may be treated together by the NLRB.

Either a purchaser must be prepared to take on the predecessor's union contracts and other labor-law obligations, or must structure the transaction to be free of such obligations. Also note that a change in corporate ownership (even if corporate structure remains the same) can lead the state to revoke the privilege to self-insure against Worker's Compensation claims.

A new company that adopts an existing operation can unilaterally change the wage scale, unless it's "perfectly clear" that the new owner will hire all of the old employees. In a "perfectly clear" case where the new owner does not consult with the union and there is no evidence of what would have emerged if there had been negotiations, the employees are given the benefit of the doubt. It is assumed that the former wage rate would have continued and would not have been diminished. So new ownership in a "perfectly clear" case cannot lead to wage cuts unless the union agrees.

In its 1999 decision in *St. Elizabeth's Manor* [329 N.L.R.B. 341 (1999)], the NLRB created a "successor bar" rule under which an incumbent union would be given a reasonable amount of time, after a corporate takeover, to bargain with the successor employer without challenges to the union's majority status. However, the NLRB overruled this decision in mid-2002. Under the new rule, in a successorship situation the incumbent union is entitled to rebuttable presumption of continuing majority status—but if there is evidence to rebut the presumption, an otherwise valid challenge to majority status will be allowed to proceed. [*MV Transportation,* 337 N.L.R.B. 129 (2002)]

[D] Transitions and Unemployment Insurance

Although it is a comparatively minor cost, the acquiror of a business may wish to take advantage of the amount of FUTA tax already paid by the transferor of the business for the part of the year before the transition. The successor employer can rely on wages paid (and therefore on FUTA payments made) by the predecessor if either one of two circumstances exists. The first is that the transferee acquires substantially all the property used in the transferor's entire trade or business (or in a separate unit of the trade or business). The other is that, whether or not the property was acquired, at least one employee from the old business remains employed immediately after the transfer.

Tip: A multistate operation will usually be permitted to combine wages paid in the various states for FUTA purposes.

The IRS' view, for FICA and tax withholding as well as FUTA purposes, is that, in a statutory merger or consolidation, the surviving corporation is the same taxpayer and the same corporation as the predecessor corporation(s). Of course, that means that the successor will have to pay any taxes due but unpaid by the predecessor—unless the successor gives the local administrative agency adequate written notice.

However, most state unemployment laws provide that companies remain subject to unemployment insurance laws for at least two years once they have acquired an experience rating—with the result that the transferor may remain liable in a year after it ceases operations, unless it applies to the local administrative agency for a determination that it is no longer an employer.

If the predecessor has acquired a good experience rating, the successor will probably be able to take over the experience rating with the rest of the operation, as long as operations remain more or less the same, at the original business location, and the workforce remains stable. Altering these important factors in effect creates a new enterprise, which will have to acquire its own experience rating.

[E]   COBRA Issues

Depending on the structure of the transaction, it is likely that some of the employees of one or both of the companies involved in a transition will lose their jobs. Perhaps as a result of the deal, some individuals will remain employed but will cease to be covered by an Employer Group Health Plan (EGHP). If a COBRA event occurs, unless the organization is too small to be covered, it will be necessary to provide COBRA notice. In the context of a corporate transition, that raises the question of who is responsible for providing the notice.

The crucial question is whether there has been a qualifying event. If there has, the structure of the transaction (stock sale versus asset sale) will determine the allocation of the notice burden. COBRA provides that an M&A qualified beneficiary may have a qualifying event if he or she was last employed by the acquired corporation (in a stock sale) or was last employed in connection with the assets being sold in an asset sale. However, a stock sale is not a COBRA qualifying event if the employee continues to be employed by the acquired organization after the transactions, even if the employee is no longer covered by an EGHP.

An asset sale results in a qualifying event for those whose employment is associated with the purchased assets, unless the buying corporation is a successor employer and the employee is employed by the buying corporation immediately after the sale. There is no COBRA event after an asset sale for people who retain their coverage under the selling corporation's EGHP. A successor employer is either a mere continuation of the former employer company; an entity that results from the merger or consolidation of the employer corporation; or a continuation of the business operations associated with the purchased assets.

If a COBRA event does result, and the selling corporation continues to maintain an EGHP, it is responsible for providing continuation coverage (and COBRA notice) to the M&A qualified beneficiaries. If the selling corporation does not continue to maintain an EGHP, in a stock sale the EGHP of the buying corporation has the COBRA duties. In an asset sale, the EGHP of the buyer corporation is responsible for COBRA only if the buyer corporation continues the business operations associated with the assets without interruption and without substantial change. The buyer and seller corporations can re-allocate the burden by contract—but if the party who agrees to undertake the COBRA obligations fails to do so, the originally responsible party still retains its legal liability.

[Kenneth W. Ruthenberg Jr., *Don't Pick up COBRA as Part of Your Next Deal—Negotiating COBRA Liability in Business Transactions* (Sept. 10, 2002) <http://www.seethebenefits.com/CRLframeset.asp . . . >]

For stock sales and assets sales effective on or after July 7, 2003, Rev. Rul. 2003-70, [2003-27 I.R.B. 3], provides guidance on how to determine the number of employees in the appropriate entity (and therefore whether the COBRA threshold of 20 employees has been reached). In a stock sale, where two employers are now treated as a single employer, the EGHP maintained by the combined entity is subject to COBRA as of the date of the stock transfer, if the combined entity has 20 or more employees. If there is an acquisition of assets, and the buyer and seller do not become a single employer, the successor is exempt until it reaches the 20-employee level. Q&A 8(c) of Reg. § 54.4980B-9 says that a buyer of substantial assets becomes a successor employer of the seller only if it continues the business operations without substantial change, and the seller ceases to provide EGHP coverage. But if the buyer does become a successor employer, it has to provide COBRA coverage to any M&A qualified beneficiaries at the seller company—even if the buyer company would otherwise be exempt under COBRA.

[F] Bankruptcy as a Transition

In a weak economy, many businesses will go through the involuntary transitions provided by the bankruptcy system. DOL's document about bankruptcy and benefits provides some useful factors to consider. [DOL Fact Sheet, *Your Employer's Bankruptcy: How Will It Affect Your Employee Benefits?*, <http://www.dol.gov/ebsa/Newsroom/fsbankruptcy.html>] When the company operates as a Debtor in Possession under Chapter 11, the benefit plans will usually remain in operation during the reorganization process, but a Chapter 7 liquidating bankruptcy will probably lead to termination of the plans.

The PBGC does not get involved in a standard termination because the plan has adequate assets to satisfy its obligations. If a distress termination occurs, the PBGC is required to pay the guaranteed benefits. The PBGC allows distress terminations in Chapter 11 bankruptcy cases if the bankruptcy court makes a determination, under ERISA § 1341(c), that the employer will not be able to pay all of its debts under a reorganization plan and will not be able to stay in business unless the pension plan is terminated.

The court has to decide whether there is any feasible reorganization plan that would preserve the pension plan; it is not restricted to considering the plan proposed by the debtor. An important question is whether financing could be obtained to continue the business—and if the parties that might provide the financing insist on termination of the pension plan. The company must explore alternatives, such as eliminating only some pension plans and maintaining others; exploring funding waivers; freezing future benefit accruals, but not terminating the plan; and looking for non-pension means of saving money.

The PBGC is entitled to press two types of claims against the bankrupt sponsor of the plan: a plan asset insufficiency claim and a claim for unpaid funding contributions accruing after the petition. A plan insufficiency claim is a general unsecured claim to the extent that it involves plan benefits employees earned before the petition. The unpaid funding contributions get priority as administrative expenses. [Daniel J. Morse, *Distress Termination of Pension Plans in Ch. 11*, American Bankruptcy Institute Journal, <http://www.gcd.com/files/Publication/48d1bf73[. . .] (Mar. 2006). *See, e.g., In re Aloha Airgroup*, 2005 WL 3487724 (Bank. D. Haw. 2005) for a case in which the only option for financing was contingent on plan termination; but *In re Philip Services Corp.*, 310 B.R. 802 (Bank. S.D. Tex. 2004) refused to permit termination, finding that termination was only desirable and not essential to reorganization)]

A corporation contemplating bankruptcy will have to determine the future of its plans, including who will serve as administrator and trustee before and after bankruptcy and how benefits will be distributed from a terminated plan.

Severance benefits usually come from the employer's assets, and may have the status of a priority claim in bankruptcy. The Bankruptcy Abuse Prevention and Consumer Protection Act (BAPCA; P.L. 109-8), 2005's bankruptcy reform legislation, affects the treatment of pensions and employee benefits in several ways.

When an employer files for bankruptcy protection, wage and benefit claims for 180 days (rather than prior law's 90 days) are priority claims, and $10,000 per employee in wages and benefits (raised from the previous level of $4,000) counts as a third-priority claim. The bankruptcy trustee can avoid transfers made to or for the benefit of corporate insiders during two years (rather than one) prior to the filing. Transfers made under an employment contract can be avoided by the trustee—whether or not the transfers caused the employer to become insolvent—if they occurred outside the ordinary course of business. BAPCA also places limits on retention bonuses and severance benefits that can be paid to corporate insiders.

The employer's creditors are not permitted to reach amounts contributed by employees, or withheld from their wages for contribution, to a plan when the amounts are in the employer's hands because they have not yet been placed into the plan.

If the employer modified retiree welfare benefits (e.g., retiree health plans) within the 180 days before filing of the bankruptcy petition, any party of interest can apply for a court order. The modification will be enjoined unless the court rules that the balance of equities clearly supports the modification.

Usually conflicts arise when bankruptcy results in a reduction of benefits. The Third Circuit ruled that plan amendments adopted just before a Chapter 11 filing, which resulted in the doubling or even quintupling of pension benefits for certain participants (including corporate insiders), was invalid as a fraudulent conveyance. The court also criticized the introduction of the amendment to the board of directors as an "administrative formality" as evidence of bad faith and the use of a surplus in the union side of the pension accounts to fund the new benefits.

[*Pension Transfer Corp. v. Beneficiaries Under Third Amendment to Fruehauf Corp. Retirement Plan*, 444 F.3d 203 (3d Cir. 2006)]

See Chapter 19 for a discussion of the obligation to provide continuation coverage under COBRA. Even if a health plan is terminated, outstanding claims will have to be satisfied. Under HIPAA (also discussed in Chapter 19) employees are entitled to certificates of creditable coverage showing their date of enrollment in the plan, so they can establish their entitlement to purchase individual coverage.

Your benefits plan may also be affected by the bankruptcies of others, because plans are required to offer special enrollment to those otherwise eligible (even outside the normal enrollment season) if they had other coverage that was lost not more than 30 days earlier as a result of the employer's bankruptcy.

§ 16.03   THE ANTICUTBACK RULE

Internal Revenue Code § 411(d)(6) forbids amendments that reduce accrued benefits, including early retirement benefits and the availability of additional forms of payment over and above the required QJSA and QPSA. But according to *Board of Trustees of the Sheet Metal Workers Nat'l Pension Fund v. C.I.R.* [117 T.C. 220 (2001)], only employees, not retirees, can "accrue" benefits. Therefore, eliminating post-retirement Cost of Living Increases doesn't violate the anticutback rule, because the benefits weren't "accrued."

In 2004, the Supreme Court ruled [*Central Laborer's Pension Fund v. Heinz*, 541 U.S. 739 (2004)] that an amendment increasing the varieties of postretirement employment that would cause the suspension of benefit payments violated the anticutback rule. However, in Rev. Proc. 2005-23, 2005-18 I.R.B. 991, the IRS ruled that *Heinz* will not be applied retroactively to disqualify plans that suspended benefits in this way—as long as they adopt a timely corrective amendment. Rev. Proc. 2005-76, 2005-50 I.R.B. 1139, extends the time to adopt the amendment (and the time during which participants can elect retroactive benefits) from January 1, 2006, to January 1, 2007.

Regulations were proposed at 69 Fed. Reg. 13769 (Mar. 24, 2004) reflecting the requirements of *Heinz*. Under the proposal, a plan amendment that reduces accrued benefits, or imposes greater restrictions on the right to benefits, is permissible only if it does not impair the rights of any plan participant to an extent that is more than minimal.

The regulations were finalized in T.D. 9219, 2005-38 I.R.B. 538. A plan amendment that decreases accrued benefits or places greater restrictions on the right to receive a benefit protected under I.R.C. § 411(d)(6) is in violation even if the restriction or condition is acceptable under the § 411(a) vesting rules. However, plans can be amended to restrict the availability of benefits accruing after the date of the amendment.

Former highly compensated employees who were transferred to the new employer after the sale of the subsidiary at which they worked were not entitled to receive lump-sum deferred compensation benefits after the transfer. Because the plan was an exempt top-hat plan, eliminating the deferred compensation plan did not violate the anticutback rule. [*Cogan v. Phoenix Life Ins. Co.,* 310 F.3d 238 (1st Cir. 2002)]

In contrast, *Michael v. Riverside Cement Co. Pension Plan* [266 F.3d 1023 (9th Cir. 2001)] says that the employer violated the anticutback rule by eliminating a provision that gave re-employed employees full benefits (without reduction for benefits paid at their first retirement) when they finally retired for a second time.

If a plan is spun off, the spin-off plan is required to maintain the old plan's payment options as to benefits accrued before the spinoff.

In a merger, employees are permitted to retain their premerger pay-out options. In practice, this means that if a merged plan wants to have a single pay-out structure, it must improve the less-favorable plan to equal the options under the more-favorable plan.

Section 411(a)(10)(B) requires that individuals who had three years of service before the corporate transition will be entitled to keep the old vesting schedule, if it is more favorable to them than the newly adopted one. Employers have an obligation to inform employees of this option.

According to I.R.C. § 414(l), if plans (even plans maintained by the same employer) merge or consolidate, or if a plan's assets and liabilities are transferred to another plan, each participant's benefit immediately after the transition, calculated on a termination basis, must be at least as great as his or her benefit would have been if the plan had terminated immediately before the transition.

The regulations for this section say that a transfer of assets and liabilities from one plan to another will be treated as a spinoff followed by a merger. This usually means that Form 5310-A has to be filed at least 30 days before the merger, spinoff, or asset transfer.

Section 414(l) requires a plan's actuaries to make reasonable assumptions about expected retirement age, mortality, and interest rates before and after the asset transfer. The termination assumptions that the PBGC uses offer a safe harbor because using them is always deemed reasonable, but their use is not mandatory.

According to *Systems Council EM-3 v. AT&T Corp.* [159 F.3d 1376 (D.C. Cir. 1999)], a plan sponsor can spin off part of a plan to another corporation in the same controlled group, and keep some or even all of the assets of the original plan. The participants in the spun-off plan are not entitled to a share of the surplus assets, even though they would have been distributed in a termination.

The Secretary of the Treasury has the power to enforce ERISA § 208, which is very similar to I.R.C. § 414(l). The Department of Labor has indirect enforcement powers under ERISA § 208, because of its enforcement powers over fiduciary conduct.

Adams v. Bowater Inc. [313 F.3d 611 (1st Cir. 2002)] ruled that a lawsuit challenging a plan amendment that cut back an early retirement benefit was not necessarily moot even though the defendant company repealed the plan amendment and reinstated the benefit. The First Circuit reached this decision because the company could always reinstate the challenged practice by amending the plan again, so the plaintiffs were entitled to a courtroom determination of whether the amendment did or didn't violate the anticutback rule.

The Second Circuit ruled that a plan amendment occurs once the participants are properly notified, not when the operation of the plan changes. Therefore, a change in the method of handling pension benefits for employees who left the company and were later rehired violated the anti-cutback rule because the change in the calculation was not written down until a 1998 plan amendment—and was not properly communicated even then. [*Frommert v. Conkright*, 433 F.3d 254 (2d Cir. 2006)]

Internal Revenue Code § 414 has separate rules for merging two defined contribution plans; two defined benefit plans; and one plan of each type to make sure that participants' entitlement to benefits is not reduced as a result of the transaction. There are further requirements to be observed if one of the plans is fully funded but the other is underfunded. For defined benefit plans, this section serves two policy purposes. It avoids manipulation of funding by means of moving plan assets between the plans of a controlled group of corporations, and it prevents the dilution of benefits within the ERISA § 4044 priority order for categories of assets during a termination.

The priority order is as follows:

- Assets are allocated to benefits coming from participant contributions;
- Benefits going to individuals who were already getting benefits during the three years before the termination;
- Benefits to persons who could have been getting benefits during that three-year period;
- PBGC-guaranteed benefits;
- Other nonforfeitable benefits;
- Everything else.

§ 16.04   NOTICE OF REDUCTION OF BENEFITS

ERISA § 204(h) requires notices of reductions in future benefits. This provision was amended by EGTRRA. Now, notice must be given before the effective date of any amendment that eliminates or reduces an early retirement benefit or early retirement subsidy. An excise tax is imposed on failure to provide proper notice.

Notice is due a reasonable time before the effective date of the plan amendment. The notice can be given before the formal adoption of the amendment, as long as there is no material change before the amendment is finally adopted. If there is an "egregious" failure to provide notice, then the amendment cannot take effect, and individuals affected by the change get the larger of the pre- or post-amendment form of the benefit.

The Pension and Welfare Benefits Administration (PWBA; renamed EBSA) has its own provision for informing employees of the effect of a transition on their benefits. [The agency has published a 32-page booklet, *Pension and Health Care Coverage: Questions and Answers for Dislocated Workers* at <http://www.dol. gov/ebsa/publications/dislocated_workers_brochure.html>]

In April 2003, the IRS published Final Regulations on the notice requirements of ERISA § 204(h). [T.D. 9052, RIN 1545-BA08, http://benefitslink.com/ taxregs/204h-final-2003.shtml] Under the final rule, notice must generally be given 45 days in advance of the event (even if this is earlier than the adoption date of the plan amendment that institutes the cutback). A small plan (one with fewer than 100 participants) is allowed to give less notice: 15 days. The 15-day rule also applies when a § 204(h) amendment is adopted in connection with a corporate acquisition or disposition.

Furthermore, if the amendment is adopted to deal with transfers of liabilities from one plan to another in connection with a transfer, merger, or consolidation of assets or liabilities under Code § 414(l), and the amendment cuts back on early retirement benefits or subsidies but does not significantly reduce the rate of future benefit accrual, the notice can be given after the amendment takes effect—but not more than 30 days afterward. The Final Regulations are in Q&A form, and provide model text that can be used to provide notice.

The IRS modified its position in July 2003, allowing defined contribution plans (including 401(k)s) to reduce alternate benefit forms without 90 days' advance notice—as long as the change was reflected in a timely revised SPD or Summary of Material Modifications. [68 Fed. Reg. 40581 (July 8, 2003)] Similar relief was proposed for defined benefit plans. [69 Fed. Reg. 13769 (Mar. 24, 2004)]

Proposed Regulations [70 Fed. Reg. 47155 (Aug. 12, 2005)] cover the interaction of the anti-cutback rules with the § 411(a) nonforfeitability requirements. There are two ways to reduce or eliminate a benefit: (1) if the benefit is redundant, that is, duplicates another benefit in the same family, 90 days' notice is required; or (2) if the benefit is a core option, such as the straight life annuity and the 10-year certain/life annuity, four years' notice is required. Benefits also can be eliminated when they have been available for a meaningful length of time but no one ever elected them.

§ 16.05   THE MINIMUM PARTICIPATION RULE

Initially, minimum participation rules were applied to both defined contribution and defined benefit plans. However, the Small Business Job Protection Act of 1996 [Pub. L. No. 104-188] eliminated this rule for defined contribution plans— now only defined benefit plans are required to have a minimum number or percentage of participants. This is significant in the context of corporate transitions because asset buyers often decline to adopt the seller's plan. If the plan is not adopted, there is a risk that the new plan will fail to cover the mandated number or percentage of employees.

Some relief is available under I.R.C. § 410(b)(6)(C), which allows one year after an acquisition or the disposition of a corporation to satisfy the minimum participation requirement. But after that, the plan is likely to become disqualified—unless it has been terminated in the interim.

A possible strategy is to freeze the plan. However, if too many participants choose to cash out, that creates difficulties. Two or more plans can be merged into a larger plan, offering a benefit structure at least as favorable as the most favorable of the merged plans, no later than the fifteenth day of the tenth month after the end of the plan year.

Rev. Rul. 2004-11, 2004-7 I.R.B. 480, permits a qualified plan to hold off on compliance testing during a transition period that runs from the date of an acquisition or disposition until the last day of the plan year after the year of the corporate transition. The transition relief is unavailable, however, if the plan's terms or coverage are substantially altered during the transition period other than as a result of the transition itself—so it is probably unwise to amend the plan during the transition unless it is certain that the amended plan passes the relevant discrimination tests.

On a related issue, *see* T.D. 9072, 2003-37 I.R.B. 527, Final Regulations, under § 414(v) for catch-up contributions by persons over 50, in plans such as 401(k)s, SEPs, and SIMPLE IRAs. The T.D. is effective July 8, 2003, and is applicable to contributions in taxable years beginning on or after January 1, 2004. If a plan satisfied the "universal availability" requirement (i.e., the right to make catch-up contributions was uniformly applied) before an acquisition or disposition described in Reg. § 1.410(b)-2(f), it will be deemed to satisfy the universal availability requirement up through the end of the period described in I.R.C. § 410(b)(6)(C). In other words, the employer gets until the end of the plan year after the plan year of the transaction to bring the plan into compliance with the universal availability requirement with respect to the restructured workforce.

§ 16.06   IN-SERVICE DISTRIBUTIONS AND REHIRING

The underlying purpose of pension plans is to provide postretirement financial security. Therefore, "in-service distributions" (distributions from the plan while the individual is still working) are severely discouraged by the Code. There is some interest in modifying this requirement in order to make it easier for workers to make a transition out of the workforce by taking "phased retirement" rather than terminating workforce participation entirely.

There are some special rules governing taxation of in-service distributions during a transition. Treasury Regulation § 1.401-1(b)(1)(i) provides that defined benefit plans cannot make in-service distributions before the employee's retirement or termination of employment—unless the plan itself is terminated. But a defined contribution plan that is not a 401(k) plan can use the two-year/five-year rule. That is, contributions can be withdrawn from the plan after the contributions have been in the plan for two years, or the participant has five years of plan participation.

> **Tip:** EGTRRA eliminates the "same desk" rule for 401(k) plans. In other words, when there is a merger consolidation, or liquidation, participants in a 401(k) plan will be entitled to take a distribution from the plan even if the successor company hires them and they have not separated from service. Congress intended to increase the portability of pensions in this situation.

Because of the abolition of the same desk rule, distributions can be made from the seller's plan in either an asset or a stock sale, to employees who go to work for the buyer or stay at the subsidiary that has been sold, as long as that subsidiary drops participation in the plan by the time of the sale. Distributions are not allowed if the subsidiary that is the subject of the sale retains the plan, the buyer takes over as plan sponsor, or assets are transferred to a plan maintained by the buyer corporation. In most cases, a plan amendment will be required. It probably makes sense to permit distributions to any participant who is transferred out of the seller's controlled group as a result of a stock sale, sale of assets, or other corporate transaction. Note that, because this is an EGTRRA provision, it is subject to the January 1, 2011, sunset date of the entire statute.

Similarly, employees who took substantially similar jobs with the buyer corporation were not "released" from employment and therefore were not entitled to severance pay. [*Cassidy v. Akzo Nobel Salt Inc.,* 308 F.3d 613 (6th Cir. 2002)] The termination plan defined release as permanent separation initiated by the employer for reasons such as lack of work, RIF, or unsatisfactory performance by the employee.

§ 16.07   TAX ISSUES

[A]   Attributes of Successor Plans

If, after a merger, liquidation, or reorganization, the surviving company maintains the predecessor corporation's qualified plan, I.R.C. § 381 generally provides that the original plans' tax attributes are passed on to the successor plan. If two qualified plans consolidate, the deductions taken by each employer before the consolidation will not be retroactively disqualified by the consolidation.

The acquiring corporation can keep up the plan for the benefit of those covered by it under the old ownership—with no obligation to cover the workers who were its own employees before the acquisition.

Revenue Procedure 99-50, 1999-52 I.R.B. 757 sets forth the basic and a separate elective procedure for preparing tax forms (e.g., Form 1099; Form 5498) when a successor business acquires substantially all of the assets used in a trade or business. The standard procedure is that both predecessor and successor companies have to file the relevant forms for the year of the acquisition. But, to relieve burdens, the alternate procedure allows the predecessor and successor companies to agree that the successor company will take over the entire reporting burden for the year of the acquisition.

[B] Golden Parachutes

The risk of acquisition or merger makes corporate recruitment more difficult, because top candidates have a realistic fear that they will lose their jobs during a shake-up. Employment agreements with prominent candidates often include "golden parachutes" (providing generous compensation if the job is lost because of a corporate transition) and "golden handcuffs" (retention bonuses that are forfeited if the individual quits shortly after being hired).

Most of these programs have a double rather than a single trigger. That is, they do not take effect when the employees quit voluntarily, only if they have involuntary job loss. A modified double trigger plan contains a window period, during which payments will be made even if the employee quits voluntarily. The window is often placed in the thirteenth month of the agreement, when the 20% excise tax on excess parachute payments can be minimized. In fact, if a company is particularly insistent on hiring a particular top executive, it may even agree to "gross up" the payment—that is, to take over payment of the excise tax on the excess parachute payment.

Parachute payments deal with the risk that current top management will be ousted if there is a change in control. The acquirer may face the opposite problem: Managers whose skills are needed for success may quit because of the transition. A "stay bonus" for remaining with the new owner is a fixed benefit (and therefore a fixed incremental cost for the business buyer). The bonus is paid after the employee has remained for a certain period of time. It could also be combined with a golden parachute. For instance, the executive could be offered two months' salary as a bonus for staying a year, or given a severance package of three months' salary and outplacement assistance if terminated without good cause within 18 months of the transition.

Internal Revenue Code § 280G does not allow corporations to deduct "excess parachute payments." Any "disqualified person" who receives an excess parachute payment is subject to a 20% excise tax, under I.R.C. § 4999. A parachute payment is a payment of compensation, contingent on a change in ownership, and equal to three times or more of the base amount (roughly speaking, the base amount is the individual's normal compensation).

In August 2003, the IRS issued Final Regulations on golden parachutes. A corporation that qualifies as a Subchapter S corporation but has not made a Sub S election can be treated as a small business corporation exempt from the excess parachute rules—but a foreign corporation cannot be treated as a small business corporation.

Only one change in ownership or control will be deemed to have occurred with respect to any one transaction. Accelerating the vesting of a stock option creates value that counts in determining whether a parachute payment has been made.

The excise tax on excess parachute payments can be prepaid in the year of the change in control or any later year—but prepayment cannot be made with respect to a cash payment if the present value of the payment could not be reasonably ascertained under the I.R.C. § 3121(v) rules on FICA taxation of nonqualified deferred compensation. In other words, the amount, form, and commencement date of the payments must be known. Employers are not allowed to prepay the excise tax on any part of the excess parachute payment that results from continuing to provide health benefits to the recipient of the payment.

A correction published in October 2003 rewords Reg. § 1.280 and clarifies that the Regulations apply to payments contingent on change in ownership or control occurring on or after January 1, 2004. Taxpayers can rely on the Regulations after August 4, 2003, for the treatment of any parachute payment. [68 Fed. Reg. 45745 (Aug. 4, 2003), corrected 68 Fed. Reg. 59114 (Oct. 14, 2003). *See also* Rev. Proc. 2003-68, 2003-34 I.R.B. 398, issued in conjunction with the Final Rule, explaining how to reflect changes in the term of an option or the volatility of the underlying stock in the valuation of the parachute payment; the IRS revoked its earlier proposals on taxation of golden parachutes, found in Rev. Proc. 2002-13, 2002-8 I.R.B. 549]

Rev. Rul. 2004-87 discusses several scenarios as to whether there has been a change in ownership or control as defined by I.R.C. § 280G and I.R.C. § 4999, and whether contingent payments have been approved by shareholders and therefore are exempt under I.R.C. § 280G(b)(5)(A)(ii). In the first situation, the corporation files a voluntary Chapter 11 petition. The bankruptcy court approves a plan of reorganization after negotiations with the unsecured creditors' committee and the equity committee. The plan calls for cancellation of all shares of common stock and issue of new shares, with the unsecured creditors receiving 75% of the stock, and no single unsecured creditor gets 20% or more of the shares. The second situation has the same fact pattern, but the largest creditor receives 25% of the outstanding shares. The third situation refers to a public corporation in Chapter 11 whose stock is delisted; the fourth has the same facts but after delisting, the shares still trade over the counter. The bankruptcy court approves a sale of more than one-third of the fair market value of the corporation's assets. An executive who is entitled to a golden parachute payment because of the sale petitions the bankruptcy court to treat the parachute payments as administrative expenses of the bankruptcy estate. The court agrees; the payment is made and the assets are acquired.

The IRS position is that the purpose of I.R.C. § 280G is to discourage excessive payments in connection with an acquisition that absorb too much of the money that should go to shareholders. The exception under I.R.C. § 280G(b)(5)(A)(ii) is available only for payments approved by at least 75% of the shareholders, in corporations that did not have readily tradeable stock. In the first situation, the creditors were not acting as a group to acquire the stock, so there was no change in control based on group action. In the second scenario, a change in control is presumed because one creditor acquired more than 20% of the stock in a 12-month period. The presumption can be rebutted by a showing that the major creditor would not in fact act to control management and policies. There would be a change in ownership in the third situation because more than one-third of the FMV of assets was acquired, but if the disclosure and shareholder approval requirements are met, the payments are not parachute payments. In the fourth case, there has been a change of ownership, and the payments are exempt if the disclosure and voting requirements are satisfied, because a corporation's bankruptcy impairs the trading of its shares on the OTC market. When the stock is not readily tradeable, the payments are not parachute payments.

The Tax Court ruled that lump sum payments to corporate executives, under agreements entered into after a change in control, were excess parachute payments and were not deductible to the extent that they exceeded reasonable compensation for the executive. Under Prop. Reg. § 1.280G-1, Q&A 22, 23 (later finalized essentially intact), an agreement that is executed after a change in control but pursuant to a legally enforceable agreement made before the change in control, will be treated as if it had been made before the change in control. In this case, in order to retain a group of executives at the acquired company, the acquirer negotiated incentive agreements to replace the prior golden parachute agreement. Eleven executives received close to $15 million in retention payments and supplemental retirement benefits, as well as significant pay increases (for some, their current compensation quadrupled). The acquirer deducted $10.4 million of this amount, but the IRS disallowed $7.6 million as constituting excess parachute payments.

The Tax Court agreed with the IRS: a new agreement was negotiated as a replacement for an earlier agreement whose payments were contingent on a change in control. In the Tax Court view, reasonable compensation would be the 90th percentile of compensation for comparable executives at comparable companies. Therefore, although the executives were not parties to the suit, this result made it likely that the 20% excise tax on excess parachute payments, under Code § 4999, would apply to them. [*Square D Co.*, 121 T.C. No. 11 (2003)]

§ 16.08   THE PBGC EARLY WARNING PROGRAM

PBGC's Early Warning Program is supposed to reduce the agency's risk of loss in the context of corporate transitions. PBGC's Technical Update 00-3 (July 24, 2000) explains that the program focuses on below-investment-rated companies that have plans with current liability over $25 million, or plans with over $5 million in unfunded current liability. The PBGC gets to review the transactions of these companies to see if a transaction weakens the plan's financial support to the extent that the PBGC might become liable to take over benefit payments.

The early warning program is designed to identify transactions that significantly increase the PBGC's risk of loss. Although the agency has never published standards for what it considers a significant increase in risk, certain types of transactions have been identified as potential problem areas: the breakup of a controlled group; a leveraged buyout; major divestiture by a company that retains significantly underfunded pension liabilities; or transfer of significantly under- funded pension liabilities in connection with sale of a business. [This program is discussed in Harold J. Ashner, *Dealing with the Pension Benefit Guaranty Corporation*, Tax Management Compensation Planning Journal, <http://www. keightleyashner.com/publications/Dealing_with[. . .]> (Jan. 2006)]

§16.09 STOCK OPTIONS

During the late lamented Internet boom, stock options were greatly cherished by employees because of the possibility of purchasing stock for a few dollars and being able to resell it at a much higher price—especially if the company was a start- up with the potential for a high-flying Initial Public Offering. Under current depressed stock market conditions, far fewer employees hold options that can be exercised profitably. However, in the hope that conditions will turn around again, the topic is worth discussing.

The Financial Accounting Standards Board's (FASB's) Opinion 25 and Opinion 16, "Business Combinations," tackled the treatment of stock options after an acquisition. Before 2004, the question was whether APB Opinion 16 would apply, or whether, instead, Opinion 25, the general pronouncement on most stock option issues, would be relevant. In 2004, FASB replaced Opinion 25 with a proposal, *Share-Based Payment—An Amendment of Statements No. 123 and 95.* Under the proposal, equity instruments and options on equity instru- ments must be accounted for on the basis of fair value as of the grant date. FASB continued to develop pronouncements on share-based compensation, issuing a revised statement, No. 123(R), also called *Share-Based Payment*, on December 16, 2004. The statement carries forward the theme that the most appropriate meth- od of valuing transactions involving share-based payments is on the basis of the fair value of the equity or liability instruments that the corporation issues to compen- sate its employees. FASB concluded that this approach gives investors the most complete and objective view of the true cost of share-based compensation. [FASB News Release, *FASB Issues Final Statement on Accounting for Share-Based Payment,* <http://www.fasb.org/news/nr121604_ebc.shtml> (Dec. 16, 2004). This process is ongoing: *see, e.g.,* FAS 123(R)-3, *Transition Election Related to Accounting for Tax Effects of Share-Based Payments* (Nov. 10, 2005) and FAS 123(R)-4, *Contingent Cash Settlement of Stock Options* (Feb. 3, 2006)]

Mergers raise many questions about stock options, including:

- Do employees of the acquired company forfeit their outstanding options?
- Are their options bought out?
- Do they receive options in the acquiror company in exchange?

Incentive stock options must be granted under a plan that is approved by the grantor corporation's stockholders within 12 months either before or after the date the plan is adopted. However, the Final Regulations on ISOs published in August 2004 include an illustration of what happens when two companies (one of which has an ISO plan and one of which doesn't) merge. The new combined entity will make ISO grants in the future. Because there is a new plan, the shareholder approval requirement is triggered—but if the merger agreement describes the plan and states that it will survive the consolidation, the shareholder approval requirement is deemed satisfied, and the plan is deemed to have been approved on the date the consolidation agreement itself is approved. [T.D. 9144, 69 Fed. Reg. 46401 (Aug. 3, 2004)]

When a parent company divests itself of a business, or a parent company buys back a minority interest in a company that was earlier sold to the public, there are accounting problems in valuing the exchange of options in the subsidiary's stock for options in the parent company's stock. Sometimes the value is adjusted; sometimes options in the parent's stock are substituted for those in the subsidiary's stock; and sometimes "founder's grants" are offered in a spinoff or IPO situation. The availability of severance benefits after a corporate transition was also at issue in *Winterrowd v. American General Annuity Ins. Co.* [321 F.3d 933 (9th Cir. 2003)] The Ninth Circuit ruled that the benefits in question were not offered under either an amendment to the existing ERISA plan nor under a new ERISA plan. Therefore, ERISA did not preempt state-law breach of contract claims. The case was brought by a group of commissioned salespersons who worked for Independent Advantage Financial and Insurance Services (IAF). American General Corporation (AG) acquired IAF and decided to shut it down and terminate its workforce. At that time, IAF salaried employees were eligible for a Job Security Plan that provided severance and other termination benefits.

Although they worked on commission only and were not eligible under this plan, the plaintiffs were offered a severance package in return for staying at work during an interim transition period. They were offered a lump-sum deal (ranging between $99,000 and $200,000 for the individual plaintiffs) based on a 10-month rolling average of sales commissions. After they accepted the offer, they were told that the lump sums had been recalculated on the basis of a six-month average, reducing the benefits to a range of $48,000 to $117,000. At first, they sued for breach of contract, but lost, because the District Court adopted the defendants' theory that it had amended its ERISA plan to include the plaintiffs. The plaintiffs then filed an amended complaint raising ERISA claims.

The Ninth Circuit held that the defendant could not use the argument that the plan had been retroactively amended to include the plaintiffs, because an amendment that denies rather than expands plan benefits cannot be retroactive. The defendant could not argue that a new plan was created covering the plaintiffs, because a plan has to have an ongoing administrative structure, and it must be possible to ascertain who is entitled to benefits, how large the benefits will be, and how to apply for benefits. The letters sent to the plaintiffs offering the benefit package were not a "plan," because they did not include these necessary elements.

One of the factors fueling the economic boom of the late 1990s and early 2000s was the incentive to mergers and acquisitions offered by "pooling of interest" accounting. When pooling of interest was available, it allowed two companies to exchange equity securities and pool their bookkeeping and accounting thereafter. The net result was that the company's reported earnings would be higher, because there was no need to amortize goodwill as an expense. In contrast, if the transaction had to be accounted for under the purchase method, the acquirer would be deemed to purchase the acquired company, and the financial statements of the combined entity must reflect the fair value of the company's assets and liabilities. However, for most transactions initiated after June 30, 2001, pooling of interest accounting is unavailable—the purchase method must be used instead.

In a transaction accounted as a purchase, if the acquiring company does not take any steps with regard to the acquired company's outstanding options, then the terms of the plan under which the options were granted governs their treatment. In most plans, this will mean that all outstanding stock options vest upon a change in control, with a limited period (e.g., 30–60 days) to exercise vested options. The acquiring company can also buy out the outstanding options, or exchange options on its own stock for options on the acquired company's stock—allowing employees of the acquired company to get some value for their unvested options, and giving them upside potential, without the acquirer having to spend any cash to deal with options. [*See* § 22.02 for further discussion of stock options]

§16.10 CORPORATE CULTURE AND HR'S ROLE IN TRANSITION PLANNING

In economic boom times, there tend to be a lot of corporate transitions, because corporations with high-valued stock can take on aggressive acquisition programs. In bad times, there tend to be a lot of transitions, because that is often the only way a weakened company can survive! In 1998, there were almost 11,500 merger or acquisition transitions, with an aggregate value of more than $1.6 trillion, and in 2000, the aggregate value of mergers was about $1.8 trillion (12.9% higher than the corresponding figure for 1999).

Some business combinations fail for lack of business logic, but in many cases, the problem is irreconcilability of the corporate cultures. Getting both HR departments involved earlier, and giving them a larger role, could have smoothed the transition. In some cases, analysis by HR can point to potential problems that rule out a transaction.

The corporation's board of directors has a duty of due diligence: Transactions that can affect the corporation's continued existence or that can change its form must be studied thoroughly. A transaction can be recommended only if it is in the best interests of stockholders. It may be legally necessary to consider other constituencies as well, such as employees, retirees, and the community as a whole.

Therefore, it is important to determine if a potential merger partner has committed discrimination, labor-law violations, or wage and hour violations. Even if the potential partner has behaved lawfully in every respect, it may have a more generous pension or benefit structure that will have to be maintained for current employees. If the partner's investment performance is poor, or its actuarial assumptions are defective, then additional funds may be required to prop up its pension plans.

CHAPTER 17

PLAN TERMINATION

§ 17.01   INTRODUCTION

When companies start a pension plan, they usually do so in good faith, and with the intention of keeping the plan in operation as long as it is necessary to provide benefits. However, ERISA and the Internal Revenue Code recognize that sometimes it will be necessary to terminate a pension plan—usually because the sponsoring corporation is ceasing operations, being absorbed by another company, or has financial difficulties so severe that it cannot continue to meet its obligations. There are even some rare circumstances under which the plan is *over* funded, and the employer is able to terminate the plan, distribute its assets, and retain the plan surplus for its own benefit.

Plan termination is usually voluntary, premised on the employer's decision to shut down the plan. However, courts, based on a determination that the economic security of plan participants is at risk, can order involuntary terminations. The legal system provides structures for winding up pension plans in an orderly way. Usually, the plan's assets are applied to purchase annuities that will pay participants' pensions as they become entitled to receive them.

Under the relevant legal and tax rules, a plan termination can be either complete or partial. When a termination occurs, all accrued benefits vest immediately—including benefits that would not vest until later under the plan's normal vesting schedule. This requirement is imposed to reduce the temptation to terminate expensive and inconvenient plans!

Terminating a plan involves both the IRS and the Department of Labor (DOL). Both ERISA and the IRC must be consulted. There are forms to be filed, consents to be secured, and disclosure obligations to the participants and beneficiaries of the plan. Then, the plan's assets are distributed within an "administratively reasonable time" (generally defined as one year or less). But if the process continues for too long, the plan may be treated as if it had not terminated, and reports under I.R.C. §§ 6057–6059 will still be required. Section 6059 applies only to defined benefit plans.

> **Tip:** Under some circumstances, a Reduction in Force (RIF) is deemed to cause a partial termination (for which vesting will be required). Therefore, before implementing an RIF, the company should determine the pension implications of the program.

A federal agency called the Pension Benefit Guaranty Corporation (PBGC) plays an important role in the termination of defined benefit plans. When a plan termination is contemplated, the plan notifies the PBGC, which has 60 days (or longer, if the plan consents to an extension) to review the proposed termination for any improprieties.

The PBGC also has the power to ask the federal court system to close down a pension plan (even if the employer has not sought to terminate the plan) and supervise the orderly distribution of its assets. The PBGC is not involved in the termination of defined contribution plans, because each participant in such a plan has an individual account that can be distributed to him or her.

There are certain exceptions to these general rules. Benefits are not guaranteed if they become nonforfeitable only because of the termination; nor does the agency guarantee benefits in full if the plan was in effect for less than 60 months before it terminated. If a benefit was scheduled to increase under a plan amendment that was either made or took effect within 60 months prior to the termination, the PBGC will not guarantee the increase. The benefits of "substantial owners" (those owning 10% or more of the company's stock) are not guaranteed. In April 2002, the PGBC liberalized its rules, giving participants in terminated plans more alternatives for receiving benefits. [*See* 67 Fed. Reg. 16949 (April 8, 2002). *See* § 17.03[B]]

Although in most cases, termination will be performed by the plan sponsor, an "abandoned" or "orphan" plan is one which no longer has a plan sponsor, or whose sponsor has ceased to conduct business. In March 2005, the DOL issued guidance for winding up of orphan plans by Qualified Termination Administrators (QTAs) who have the power to distribute the benefits from individual account plans when they deem the plan to be abandoned (e.g., there have been no contributions to, or distributions from, the plan over a 12-month period; the sponsor corporation has been liquidated in a Chapter 11 bankruptcy proceeding). A QTA must be a person or entity who could serve as an IRA trustee, such as a bank, insurer, or mutual fund.

The QTA must give notice of the intended termination to the sponsor at its last known address; if the sponsor does not acknowledge this communication, the QTA must take further steps, such as asking other entities known to have provided services to the plan how to locate the sponsor. The sponsor has 30 days to object to the proposed termination.

The QTA must also notify the DOL that the plan is abandoned, that it intends to serve as QTA, the estimated value of the plan assets, and similar items; the DOL proposal contains a Model Notice that can be used for this purpose. The QTA's duty is to wind up the plan by calculating the benefits and distributing them to the appropriate persons. There is a safe harbor for the QTA if it rolls over balances to IRAs. The abandoned plan is then deemed terminated 90 days after the QTA gives notice to the DOL; a termination report must also be rendered to the IRS, and the DOL must be informed that termination has been carried out. [70 Fed. Reg. 12045 (Mar. 10, 2005). *See also* 71 Fed. Reg. 20820 (Apr. 21, 2006), DOL's rules for orphan 401(k) plans, comprising procedures under which financial institutions can distribute benefits to plan participants; a safe harbor for fiduciaries who distribute such benefits even though no election was filed stipulating a distribution procedure; and a template for a simple terminal report for an orphan 401(k) plan]

§ 17.02   TERMINATION TYPES

[A]   Generally

There are two types of voluntary termination: standard and distress. *See* 29 C.F.R. Part 4041 for Regulations. A standard termination, governed by ERISA § 4041, is used by plans that have at least enough assets to pay the benefits guaranteed by the PBGC. All terminations are handled as standard terminations unless the PBGC permits a "distress termination," which imposes lower obligations on the plan.

Under ERISA § 4044, there are six priority categories of accrued benefits. When the plan's assets are distributed, all Category-1 claims must be paid, then all Category-2 claims, and so on, until the assets are exhausted. Therefore, in many instances some of the classes will go unpaid. The categories, in descending order of priority, are:

- Voluntary employee contributions made to the plan. (NOTE: These amounts are NOT guaranteed by the PBGC, because they fall outside the definition of "basic benefits";
- Mandatory contributions that employees made to the plan, plus 5% interest;
- Annuity benefits that derive from employer contributions, if the annuity was or could have been in pay status three years or more before termination of the plan. ("Could have been" refers to the situation in which employees continue to work despite their eligibility for early retirement);
- All other PBGC-guaranteed benefits;
- All other nonforfeitable benefits;
- All benefits that are accrued but forfeitable.

Before a plan administrator can actually make any distributions, there is a legal obligation to determine the plan's ability to pay benefits at the level deemed appropriate by the PBGC. The plan administrator must notify the PBGC if the plan is unable to pay the guaranteed benefits. The PBGC makes its own determination and issues notices. If, on the other hand, the administrator determines that the PBGC-guaranteed benefits, but not all the guaranteed liabilities, can be paid, then the plan should distribute the assets but notify the PBGC.

If the PBGC affirms the administrator's characterization, it will issue a Notice of Liability resolving the issue of the plan's sufficiency. The plan administrator is obligated to provide a new valuation of the plan's liabilities and guaranteed benefits. An enrolled actuary must certify the valuation.

Hughes Aircraft Co. v. Jacobson [525 U.S. 432 (1999)], which involved several other pension issues, also affects plan termination. This case involves a plan partially funded by mandatory employee contributions. The employer suspended its own contributions at a time when the plan had a surplus. The employer created a new, noncontributory plan for new plan participants. Participants in the existing plan charged the employer with ERISA violations in connection with the amendment.

The Supreme Court's ruling is that the changes in the plan structure did not constitute a voluntary termination under ERISA § 4041(a)(1), and the employees were not entitled to an order terminating the plan voluntarily. The employees asserted a "wasting trust" theory (that the original plan had been wound up because it satisfied all of its objectives), but the Supreme Court refused to accept this theory, deeming it inconsistent with ERISA's detailed provisions for terminating a plan. [*Id.*]

The Supreme Court ruled that neither a standard nor a distress termination is appropriate as long as a plan continues to provide benefits to participants and to accumulate funds to make payments in the future. [*Id.*]

An employer in Chapter 11 sought to terminate its pension plan, but the PBGC objected. The employer purchased annuities to effect a standard termination and refused to consider the union's suggestion of merging the plan into the union's multi-employer pension fund. The Bankruptcy Court and the District Court agreed with the union: It was a breach of fiduciary duty not to at least give the union's suggestion serious consideration. The employer's litigating position was that the board of directors did not have a duty to consider the suggestion because it made a non-reviewable business decision. However, the Ninth Circuit held that ERISA § 4041 provides for several methods of terminating a plan other than annuity purchase. The Ninth Circuit concluded that the employer chose the annuity option because of the possibility of reversion—a possibility that would not exist if the plan had merged into the multi-employer plan. Hence, there was a breach of fiduciary duty because the interests of participants were not placed first. [*Beck v. PACE Int'l Union*, 427 F.3d 668 (9th Cir. 2005)]

A qualified plan must provide protection for its beneficiaries whenever the plan is merged or consolidated with another plan, or when its liabilities are transferred to another plan. [*See* I.R.C. §§ 401(a)(13), 404(a)(2), and 414(l), and ERISA § 206(d)] Each participant must receive a benefit immediately after a hypothetical merger, consolidation, or transfer of the plan at least as great as the participant would have received if the plan had terminated before the transaction occurred.

[B] Standard Termination

The appropriate PBGC form for carrying out a standard termination is Form 500 (Standard Termination Notice).

Within 120 days after the proposed termination date, the plan administrator must submit a Schedule EA-5 of the Form 500, a certificate prepared by a PBGC-enrolled actuary to the PBGC. The certificate estimates the value of the plan assets and the present value of plan liabilities, so that the actuary can certify that assets are adequate to satisfy the liabilities. The administrator must also furnish any other information the PBGC requests. The plan administrator must certify under penalty of perjury that the actuary's certificate is correct, and that the information given to the PBGC has been accurate and complete.

Once all the assets are distributed, the administrator must file PBGC Form 501 within 30 days of the final distribution, to prove that the assets were distributed. The penalty for a late form can be up to $1,100 a day. [*See* 29 C.F.R. § 4010.13] Late filing can also have the effect of creating a last, short plan year for the plan—thereby reducing the refund of the PBGC premium that the employer would otherwise be entitled to receive.

The ERISA § 204(h) notice of the amendment (including disclosure of its effective date) must be given. Question 16 in the Q&A for the Final Rule explains that an amendment providing for the end of benefit accruals on a specific date is subject to ERISA § 204(h). A plan terminated in accordance with Title IV is deemed to have satisfied ERISA § 204(h) no later than its termination date, so no additional benefits have to accrue after the date of the termination. But if the amendment reducing future accruals is effective earlier than the termination date, then ERISA § 204(h) does apply. [*See* § 5.07 for further discussion of this issue.]

[C] Notification

At least 60 days but not more than 90 days before the proposed date of a voluntary termination, the plan administrator must provide notice of the intended termination. [ERISA § 4041(a)(2)] Notice must be given to plan participants; their beneficiaries; alternate payees under domestic relations orders; and the employees' collective bargaining representative (if the workplace is unionized). The notice must give the date of the termination and must explain that the PBGC guarantee ends as soon as the benefits are distributed. The notice must also disclose the name and address of the insurance company chosen to provide annuities to participants. (If the choice has not yet been made, the names and addresses of possible choices must be disclosed.)

Tip: Selection of the insurer is a fiduciary decision, subject to the normal rules of fiduciary duty. The notice must also identify a contact person who will answer questions about the termination process.

Items to be disclosed include:

- The name of the plan and of its sponsor;
- The plan's tax number;
- The sponsor's Employer Identification Number;
- A statement that service credit and benefits will continue to accrue until the termination, or that benefit accruals have been frozen or will be frozen on a specified date—whichever is applicable;
- A promise to provide written notification of the benefits each affected party will receive under the termination;

- A promise to each retiree that retirement benefits in annuity form will not be affected by the termination;
- Disclosure that standard termination is available if and only if the plan has adequate assets to cover its liabilities to all participants and all beneficiaries of deceased participants;
- A statement that further notice will be given if the termination does not occur as contemplated.

When a distress termination rather than a standard termination is intended, the disclosure requirements [ERISA § 4041(c)] are fundamentally similar. However, parties must be informed whether the plan's assets are sufficient to pay all guaranteed benefits or all benefit liabilities. Notice is also required of the extent to which the PBGC guarantees payment of benefits, and an explanation of any benefit reductions that may be imposed, based on the PBGC's maximum guarantee.

The plan's filing of PBGC Form 500 (Standard Termination Notice) triggers the obligation to issue another notice to participants and beneficiaries, in a comprehensible, nontechnical form. This Notice of Plan Benefits [PBGC Reg. § 4041.23, .24] explains the factors determining benefit entitlement (e.g., age, length of service, wages, interest assumptions), and how payments will be made. It is also necessary to disclose that benefits might be either higher or lower than the estimate.

For benefits already in pay status, disclosure is required of the amount and form of benefits that will be payable. For individuals who have named a retirement date and elected a form for the payout, but whose benefits are not yet in pay status, the projected benefit start date must be announced, with disclosure of the form and amount of benefits payable as of that date, and the date for any scheduled increase or reduction in benefits. If the benefit start date is not known for benefits not in pay status, disclosure is required of the benefits available at normal retirement age or after the death of a participant, with special attention to any benefits that can be paid as lump sums.

Another notice is required when underfunding is very significant: e.g., $50 million or more in the plan year before the year of the notice. Notice is also required if a lien could be imposed on plan assets, or the IRS granted a minimum funding waiver covering more than $1 million. The notice informs plan participants about the financial status of the plan, its sponsor, and the sponsor's controlled group of corporations. [See PBGC Reg. § 4010] The information must be provided within 105 days of the end of the corporation's information year.

ERISA § 4011 calls for notification of funding status when plans fail to meet their full funding limitation, and their PBGC premium is increased to compensate for the underfunding. The PBGC Regulations include a model notice. Participants and beneficiaries must be warned of the underfunding and of the limitations on the PBGC's obligation to insure benefits. This notice is due two months after the deadline for filing the annual report for the year in which the plan was underfunded.

Information about plan termination must also be provided in the Summary Plan Description (SPD) furnished to plan participants. EBSA's Final Rule about SPDs [65 Fed. Reg. 70226-70244 (Nov. 21, 2000)] requires disclosure of:

- A summary of the plan's provisions authorizing the sponsor, or other party, to terminate the plan or eliminate some or all of its benefits;
- Circumstances that might trigger termination or elimination of some benefits;
- The benefits, rights, and obligations of plan participants and beneficiaries if and when the plan is terminated. In pension plan SPDs, the accrual and vesting consequences of plan termination must be disclosed. (This is not an issue in welfare plan SPDs, because such benefits do not vest);
- How the plan assets will be disposed of on termination.

In December 2004, the PBGC adopted a Final Rule (effective January 1, 2005) covering the interest rate assumptions to be used for valuing and paying benefits under a terminating single-employer plan. The interest rate assumptions are those in Part 4044, Appendix B (valuing benefits for allocation purposes under I.R.C. § 4044); those in Part 4022, Appendix B (used by the PBGC to decide if a benefit is payable as a lump sum and, if so, the size of the payment); and Part 4022, Appendix C rates for pension practitioners to use based on the PBGC's historical methodology. [PBGC, *Benefits Payable in Terminated Single-Employer Plans; Allocation of Assets in Single-Employer Plans; Interest Assumptions for Valuing and Paying Benefits*, FR Doc. 04-27443, 69 Fed. Reg. 74973 (Dec. 15, 2004), supplemented most recently by F.R. Doc. 06-3572, 71 Fed. Reg. 19429 (Apr. 14, 2006)]

[D] Distress Termination

A plan that does not have enough assets to pay all the benefit liabilities can apply to the PBGC for a "distress" termination, which is available only if the plan's sponsors (and the other corporations that are part of a controlled group of corporations with the sponsor) can prove financial hardship, e.g., involvement in voluntary or involuntary bankruptcy or insolvency proceedings. *See* 29 C.F.R § 4041.41–4041.50. If a company makes a Chapter 11 filing, seeking bankruptcy reorganization, a distress termination will be permitted only if the bankruptcy court decides that terminating the plan is necessary, or that the company cannot remain in business and pay its debts if it maintains the plan. [*See* Daniel J. Morse, *Distress Termination of Pension Plans in Ch. 11*, <http://www.gcd.com/files/Publication/48d1bf73/[...]> (Mar. 2006)] The PBGC's *Distress Termination Filing Instructions* are available online at <http://www.pbgc.gov/docs/600_instructions.pdf>.

Distress termination might also be permitted if the sponsor proves to the PBGC that terminating the plan is essential to paying its debts and remaining in operation. A distress termination might also be available if pension costs have become intolerable only because of the decline in the covered workforce—loss of stock market value of the plans' assets would not be considered an acceptable rationale.

To request a distress termination, the plan must file PBGC Form 600 and 601 to notify the PBGC and the plan's participants, respectively. Affected participants must get at least 60 days' notice but not more than 90 days' notice. Form 601 must be filed on or before the 120th day after the proposed termination date. The duty to notify participants is more or less the same for standard and distress terminations. A distress termination calls for actuarial certification, using Schedule EA-D of the Form 601.

If the plan has enough assets to pay the guaranteed benefits, the PBGC issues a "distribution notice." Within 15 days of receiving this notice, the plan administrator must give each participant and beneficiary a notice of impending distribution. Unless an extension has been granted, the distribution must begin within 60 days and be completed within 240 days. Then PBGC Form 602 (Post-Distribution Certification) must be filed within 30 days of the completion of distribution of the assets.

As soon as possible after receiving an application for a distress termination, the PBGC is supposed to rule on the application. If the agency turns down the application and the plan has enough assets to satisfy its liabilities, a standard termination is carried out. But if the assets are inadequate and the PBGC is not cooperative, the plan cannot go through a voluntary termination at all.

Mortality rates for 2006 valuation dates (effective January 1, 2006), under ERISA § 4044, have been published for determining the present value of annuities when a single employer plan goes through an involuntary or distress termination. The PBGC revises its tables when private-sector insurers do, so it has replaced the 1983 Group Annuity Mortality tables with their 1994 counterpart. [R.I.N. 1212-AA-55, <http://www.pbgc.gov/practitioners/Mortality-Table/content/page1511.html> and 70 Fed. Reg. 72205 (Dec. 2, 2005), adopting Regulations proposed at 70 Fed. Reg. 12429 (Mar. 14, 2005)>]

[E] Partial Termination

Full vesting is required when a plan is terminated or partially terminated, but there is no simple definition of "partial termination." The IRS says that partial termination occurs when there is a substantial reduction in the number or percentage of plan participants. Partial termination is presumed not to occur at 20%, presumed to exist at 50% reduction. In between, the facts and circumstances of the case are determinative.

The problem is that RIFs usually target higher-paid, long-tenure employees, so the question of whom to count is very important.

Rev. Rul. 2002-42, 2002-28 I.R.B. 76, provides that converting a money purchase plan to a profit-sharing plan is not a partial termination, if all the covered employees remain covered by the new plan and vest under the same schedule, and if the transferred assets and liabilities retain the same characteristics. However, it is required that the notice of significant reduction of benefit accruals be given to the participants of the money purchase plan.

The Seventh Circuit rule is that events from more than one plan year can be used to determine if a partial termination has occurred, when an employee alleges that his balances should vest fully because of the termination. [*Matz v. Household Int'l Tax Reduction Investment Plan,* 227 F.3d 971 (7th Cir. 2000). *See also Sea Ray v. Robinson,* 164 F.3d 981 (6th Cir. 1999)] The Sixth Circuit's rationale in this situation is that, if review was limited to a single year, employers would be able to escape liability by firing some employees in December, some in January. [*Sea Ray,* 164 F.3d 981]

On a related issue, the *Matz* court required counting of both vested and nonvested participants to determine whether a partial termination occurred. However, the Supreme Court ordered the court to reconsider its opinion because of *United States v. Mead Corp.* [53 U.S. 218 (2001)], a Supreme Court case about the extent to which courts have to abide by the rules of administrative agencies. This time, the Seventh Circuit decided that only nonvested participants should be counted in deciding if there has been a partial termination. [*Matz v. Household Int'l Tax Reduction Investment Plan,* 265 F.3d 572 (7th Cir. 2001)] This ruling makes it less likely that a partial termination will be found, especially in close cases where the percentage of terminated participants is close to the 20% threshold.

In late 2004, the *Matz* case returned, and more than three years after rejecting the IRS's formula for identifying a vertical partial termination, the court accepted the IRS's formula, because an at-will employee can be fired at any time and doesn't have any reasonable expectation of receiving benefits before he becomes vested. The Seventh Circuit excluded vested participants from both the numerator and the denominator of the equation, and set 20% as the dividing line. When the reduction in plan participation was less than the 20% figure, there would be a rebuttable presumption that there had not been a partial termination; over that level, there would be a rebuttable presumption of partial termination. The Seventh Circuit suggested that there would be a conclusive presumption that no partial termination had occurred below the 10% level, and a conclusive presumption that it had occurred when plan participation was reduced by 40% or more. [*Matz v. Household Int'l Tax Reduction Investment Plan,* 388 F.3d 570 (7th Cir. 2004)] At the end of 2005, the Northern District of Illinois certified a class of participants charging that their plan was partially terminated by the constructive termination of much of the workforce. The plan opposed class certification on the grounds that only the named plaintiff could show exhaustion of administrative remedies. The Northern District found that argument unpersuasive and did not believe that individual determinations would have to be made as to who had quit voluntarily and who had been constructively terminated. In March 2006, the Seventh Circuit held that as long as the named plaintiff had exhausted administrative remedies, the other class members with similar claims did not have to. The court reasoned that the defendant was already on notice of the claims against it and requiring individual class members to pursue and exhaust administrative remedies would cause more litigation for no reason. [74 L.W. 1448 (N.D. Ill. Dec. 19, 2005), *aff'd* 441 F.3d 500 (7th Cir. 2006)]

§ 17.03   THE PBGC'S ROLE

[A]   PBGC Guarantee

Defined benefit plans pay premiums to the PBGC annually, providing funds for the federal agency to supervise plan terminations and, if necessary, assume payment of a terminating or terminated plan's obligations to its participants. The Deficit Reduction Act of 2005, P.L. 109-171, increased the PBGC premium for single-employer plans from its long-held $19 per employee per year to $30. DRA '05 also institutes inflation-indexing of the premium. For the years 2006-2010, terminations of single-employer plans under ERISA §§ 4041(c)(2)(B) or 4042 are subject to a special premium of $1,250 per participant. If, however, the termination occurs in conjunction with a bankruptcy case filed on or after October 18, 2005, the special premium is suspended and does not have to be paid until the bankruptcy case is dismissed or the plan sponsor is discharged in bankruptcy.

The PBGC guarantee is intended to protect the employees of the plan, not the sponsor corporation. If the assets of a terminating plan are not large enough to pay the benefits, the PBGC makes the payments and then seeks recoupment from the corporation. However, an employer's liability to the PBGC is capped at 70% of its net worth, or 75% of the unfunded guaranteed benefits.

In the case of a single-employer plan, the PBGC guarantees payment of all nonforfeitable benefits. However, the PBGC guarantee is subject to a maximum limitation, with the result that some participants will not receive the full benefit they would have received had the plan not terminated.

In the Sixth Circuit view, the PBGC's announcement that it was terminating a plan extinguished participants' expectation in continued benefit accruals. Therefore, the agency is not liable for $95 million worth of collectively bargained but unvested shutdown benefits from the bankrupt company's assets, because the participants should have known that the PBGC was terminating the plan. [*PBGC v. Republic Technologies Int'l*, 386 F.3d 659 (6th Cir. 2004)]

In 2006, the PBGC faced a plethora of challenges. The PBGC was responsible for guaranteeing 30,300 private-sector pension plans covering 44 million workers and retirees. At the end of FY 2005, the PBGC's single-employer insurance program was $22.8 billion in deficit (assets of $56.5 billion, but liabilities of $79.2 billion). The PBGC paid out $3.7 billion in benefits in 2005. [Figures come from AARP Public Policy Institute, *The Pension Benefit Guaranty Corporation 2005 Fiscal Year Report*, <http://assets.aarp.org/rgcenter/econ/fs125_pension.pdf> (no www) (Mar. 2006)]

The PBGC guarantees "basic benefits." (The PBGC has legal authority to set up a separate trust fund to guarantee nonbasic benefits, but it has chosen not to do so.) The basic benefit guaranteed by the PBGC is a monthly life annuity that lasts for the participant's life. (This is in contrast to the joint and survivor annuity that is the normal payment form for a married participant to receive under an ongoing plan.) The annuity begins at age 65. For 2005, the PBGC's maximum guarantee for a single life annuity at age 65 is $3,801.14 per month ($45,614 per year); for 2006, the maximum is $47,659 per year on the same terms. [AARP Public Policy Institute, *The Pension Benefit Guaranty Corporation 2005 Fiscal Year Report,* <http://assets.aarp.org/rgcenter/econ/fs125_pension.pdf> (no www), (Mar. 2006); Employee Benefit Research Institute, *Basics of the Pension Benefit Guaranty Corporation (PBGC),* <http://www.ebri.org/facts/0705.fact.pdf>]

When a plan is to be terminated, the PBGC:

- Determines if the benefit is nonforfeitable and payable in periodic installments; if so, it is a guaranteed basic benefit;
- Performs actuarial calculations to convert benefits in other forms to straight life annuities commencing at age 65.

The PBGC has the power to assess penalties if an employer was late in paying its PBGC premiums, or if the employer failed to provide the required notices to employees.

Late in 2003, an Eastern District of Virginia bankruptcy judge ruled that US Airways was required to use the existing regulations, rather than a more favorable newer method, in calculating pensions for its pilots. Terminating plans are required to use the interest rate assumptions that apply to group annuities issued by insurers. US Airways wanted permission to use rate assumptions similar to the projections of the return a prudent investor would obtain. In effect, Judge Stephen Mitchell applied ERISA rather than bankruptcy rules to the situation. The result was that the pilots would recapture some of the benefits lost when the pension plan failed in March 2003 and was taken over by the PBGC. The decision meant that unsecured creditors—including, ironically, the PBGC—would get less because the pilots would get more. The judge intended to frustrate the tactic of using Chapter 11 bankruptcy to isolate assets from pension obligations (in effect, looking for a federal subsidy in the form of a PBGC takeover). The PBGC's view was that some companies deliberately understated their pension obligations to workers, cutting the amount of employer contributions, and placing the benefits at risk. Employers, however, argued that they were at the mercy of investment forces rather than deliberate underfunding, and requiring larger contributions will be harmful to business soundness.

PBGC Executive Director Steven A. Kandarian praised the decision as a victory for the financial integrity of the PBGC guarantee program, preventing companies from using the PBGC as a cheap way out of their financial problems. [Statement of PBGC exec director Steven A. Kandarian on US Airways decision (Dec. 30, 2003), <http://www.pbgc.gov/news/press_releases/2003/pr04_17.htm>]

[B]   Proposal on Payment Forms

PBGC No. 02-14 (Dec. 22, 2000) [65 Fed. Reg. 81456 (Dec. 26, 2000)] announces proposed regulatory changes for payments to participants when the

PBGC takes over a plan. Under the proposal, participants would be allowed to select alternative annuity benefit forms. (The spouses of married participants would have to consent.) Nonspouse beneficiaries could be named. The proposal distinguishes between separation from service and retirement, and determines who will inherit benefits that are payable to a deceased participant. The proposal also simplifies the application of the maximum guaranteed benefit rules if the same individual is entitled to benefits both as a plan participant and as a survivor of another participant (e.g., a deceased spouse who was a co-worker).

Under the proposal, the PBGC would make benefits available as straight life annuities and annuities for five, ten, or fifteen years certain and continuous. The proposal also includes joint and 50, 75 or 100% survivor annuities and joint and 50% survivor "pop-up" annuities. (in a pop-up annuity, the participant's benefit increases to the unreduced level if the beneficiary dies before the participant). Joint life annuities would only be available to two natural persons—not a person plus a trust or a charity.

The PBGC's intention is to make all of these payment forms available on termination of a plan, even if the plan did not offer all of them while it was in operation. The proposal gives the PBGC the power to promulgate further regulations that add additional forms of benefit payment, although it does not plan to do so for particular plans, only overall.

The proposal defines the Earliest PBGC Retirement Date (EPRD)—a concept that is needed because some plans allow participants to receive a lump sum well before normal retirement age. The EPRD is the earliest retirement date allowed by ERISA Title IV—i.e., the earliest date to receive an immediate annuity, or to receive a lump sum if the plan permits this. The EPRD is either the earliest annuity date or, for dates before age 55, either 55 or the time when the participant could retire, given consideration of all facts and circumstances.

The proposal calls for the PBGC to adjust the survivor's benefit under a joint and survivor annuity if the agency determines that there was an underpayment or overpayment as of the time of the first spouse's death.

Under current law, the PBGC sets an aggregate limit on the amount of benefits it will guarantee in three situations:

- Benefits payable to the same person under multiple plans;
- Benefits payable to the same person relative to two or more participants;
- Benefits with respect to a participant who has more than one beneficiary.

Under the proposal, the PBGC will waive the limit with respect to a person who is dually entitled to benefits as both worker and survivor, but aggregation will continue for multiple beneficiaries, who will have to divide the benefit.

The PBGC finalized these proposals more or less intact in April 2002: 67 Fed. Reg. 16949 (April 18, 2002). Some changes were made in the definition of "earliest PBGC Retirement Date." The Final Rule defines this as the earliest date the plan participant could retire for the purposes of ERISA Title IV. Usually, this will mean either age 55 or the first date the participant could retire and collect an immediate annuity, whichever is later.

[C] Penalties and PBGC Enforcement

Revenue Procedure 2000-17, 2000-11 I.R.B. 766 explains how a plan can get a waiver of the I.R.C. § 4971(b) 100% tax that is imposed when accumulated funding deficiencies under I.R.C. § 412 remain even after the 10% tax has been imposed. The Secretary of the Treasury can waive the 100% tax for certain terminated single-employer plans, even if the accumulated funding deficiency has not been reduced to zero.

In general, the PBGC debt collection rules found at 29 C.F.R. Part 4903 allow the agency to collect penalties by diverting tax refunds or other amounts the federal government would otherwise owe the employer. But under the proposal, this collection technique will not be applied if there is a safe harbor or other law or regulation that allows a waiver; if the employer had a reasonable cause for not making the payment or for making only a partial payment; if the employer's failure to pay was based on an incorrect interpretation of the law; or if collection would violate the purposes of ERISA.

Section 32 of the proposal defines reasonable cause as circumstances beyond the employer's control, which the employer could not have avoided by exercising ordinary care and prudence. Section 34 goes into more detail: Reasonable cause includes the absence of the person who was supposed to make the payment; fire or other casualty; or reasonable reliance on incorrect evidence given by the PBGC (either orally or in writing).

But the larger the size of the organization and its staff, the higher the standard of care it will be expected to satisfy. Of course, the larger the amount of premium that the government seeks to collect, the greater the enforcement effort that will be expended.

[D] QDROs in Plans Under PBGC Control

Qualified Domestic Relations Orders (QDROs) are discussed in detail at § 12.08 If the PBGC takes over a plan some of whose benefits must be paid to alternate payees (ex-spouses and separated spouses of participants), it issues two standard QDRO forms (Model Separate Interest; Model Shared Payment) for use by domestic relations courts. PBGC QDROs either specify or give the alternate payee discretion to control the time at which benefits begin, how the benefits are paid, the percentage of the pension payment going to the alternate payee, and how long the alternate payments begin.

QDROs cannot require the PBGC to provide any benefit type or option that would not otherwise be available under the plan or that would not otherwise be offered by the PBGC. Nor can the court order increase the amount that the PBGC would have to pay relative to the employee spouse's pension account.

The PBGC's Model Separate Interest form can be used only if the order is entered before the employee's pension is in pay status. It is appropriate when the alternate payee's benefits are fixed and do not depend on when the participant starts to get benefits or the form in which the participant receives them. The effect of this form is to divide the pension account under the PBGC's control into two parts: one for the participant, one for the non-employee alternate beneficiary. The Shared Payment form, in contrast, operates at the level of each individual payment. As each payment comes due, it is divided between the employee and the alternate beneficiary. The alternate beneficiary will not receive benefits after the employee's death unless the order specifically provides for survivor benefits.

§ 17.04   INVOLUNTARY TERMINATION

[A]   Basic Procedure

ERISA § 4042 governs involuntary termination proceedings brought when the plan assets are less than the total of guaranteed benefits. The PBGC asks the appropriate federal district court to oust the plan administrator and appoint a trustee to wind up the plan. ERISA § 4062(b)(1) makes the employer liable to the PBGC for the total amount of unfounded plan liabilities on the termination date, plus interest starting on the termination date.

The PBGC is empowered to ask for involuntary termination if:

- The plan has failed to meet its minimum funding standards;
- The plan cannot pay benefits when due;
- The plan has been required to report one or more distributions to a "substantial owner" (10% shareholder);
- The fund's liabilities will increase unreasonably if the plan is not terminated.

In those situations, it is a judgment call: The PBGC decides whether or not to seek involuntary termination. If the situation is even worse (the plan does not even have enough assets to pay its current benefits, much less to keep paying benefits as they come due; the plan has applied for a distress termination but lacks money to fund the guaranteed benefits), the PBGC has an obligation to seek involuntary termination.

Many of the PBGC's financial challenges stem from problems within the airline industry. The District Court for the District of Columbia ruled that it was not arbitrary for the PBGC to involuntarily terminate an airline's defined benefit plan for its flight attendants. The court ruled that the PBGC's motivation of preserving its settlement agreement with the airline was not legitimate, because the agency cannot preserve its bottom line at the expense of its duty to encourage maintenance of pension plans. Nevertheless, the termination was still permissible because the agency also had other, acceptable rationales, so the decision to terminate was not fatally tainted by the PBGC's self-protection. [*Association of Flight Attendants v. PBGC*, 74 L.W. 1464 (D.D.C. Jan. 13, 2006) 05-1036]

The Seventh Circuit held that the agreement between United Airlines and the PBGC that required the PBGC to consider involuntary termination of the pension plan was lawful. The union said that the agreement improperly sidestepped the collective bargaining process, but the Seventh Circuit held that the statute permits involuntary termination no matter what a CBA says. [*In re UAL Corp.*, 428 F.3d 677 (7th Cir. 2005)]

The Eastern District of Virginia rejected United Airlines' union's contention that the termination date of the plan should be set at March 14 or later (which would have meant $88 million more in benefits for union members). The termination date was ruled to be March 11, 2005, the date that United Airlines' ground workers received notice that the PBGC was involuntarily terminating the plan. The court ruled that notice was adequate because it was published in seven major newspapers. [*PBGC v. UAL Inc.*, 74 LW 1336 (E.D. Va. Nov. 10, 2005) 05-0269]

[B] The Role of the Trustee

If the district court appoints a trustee, the plan must be terminated. The PBGC can also force termination of a plan even without such an appointment. If a trustee is appointed, his or her duty is to keep the plan administrator, participants, beneficiaries, unions, and employers with potential ERISA liability informed about the progress of the termination. The trustee has the power to demand turnover of some or all of the plan's records and assets. The trustee has a choice of either continuing the pattern of benefit payments in place before the trustee's appointment, or limiting payment of benefits to the basic benefits.

Under ERISA § 4062(d), the employer is liable for the unpaid contributions to the trustee plan. The employer must provide the trustee with cash, or securities acceptable to the trustee, in an amount equal to:

- The accumulated funding deficiencies under I.R.C. § 412(a);
- Any funding deficiencies that the IRS waived under I.R.C. § 412(c) before the termination date;
- All decreases in the minimum funding standard permitted by I.R.C. § 412(e) before the termination date, plus interest running from the termination date.

Under certain circumstances outlined in ERISA § 4069(b), a successor corporation can become liable for such amounts, if the sponsor reorganizes; the purpose of the reorganization was to evade liability; and reorganization occurred within the five years before a plan termination that would have caused liability. In this context, reorganization means a merger, consolidation, or becoming a division of another company; changing identity, form, or place or organization; or the liquidation of a subsidiary into its parent.

Also note that ERISA § 4062(b) provides that when an employer ceases operations at a facility, leading to separation from service of 20% or more of the total number of plan participants, the employer either has to fund the guaranteed benefits immediately, or make provision for their funding.

[C] Calculations for Involuntary or Distress Terminations

Under 29 C.F.R. Part 4044 (Appendix D, Table I-06), benefits under a plan going through an involuntary or distress termination are calculated based on a determination of the likelihood (low/medium/high) that the participant will retire early in various years. Then, once early retirement benefits are computed, the total value of benefits under the plan can be computed. The process uses the Unreduced Retirement Age, which is either the normal retirement age or the earliest age at which a pension can be paid without actuarial reduction—whichever is earlier.

Valuation of early retirement benefits based on the annuity starting date (if a date for retirement has been elected) or the expected retirement age (if it has not) is required by 29 C.F.R. § 4044.51(b). Appendix D to Part 4044 provides tables for determining whether the probability of a participant retiring early is high, medium, or low; it depends on the year he or she would reach the age at which an unreduced retirement benefit would be available, and the monthly benefits that would be available at that point.

In this table, "year" means the year in which the unreduced benefit becomes payable. The "low" and "high" benefits are dollar amounts; the "medium" benefits are a range between the two figures. The current table is Table I-06, to be used for valuation dates falling between December 31, 2005 and January 1, 2007.

Year	Low	Medium	High
2007	500	500–2,113	2,113
2008	512	512–2,164	2,164
2009	524	524–2,216	2,216
2010	536	536–2,269	2,269
2011	549	549–2,324	2,324
2012	562	562–2,379	2,379
2013	576	576–2,437	2,437
2014	590	590–2,495	2,495
2015	604	604–2,555	2,555
2016 and later	618	618–2,616	2,616

§ 17.05 PLAN REVERSIONS

Before ERISA, it was legal for an employer to simply wind up a plan and take back its assets. But under current law, a plan provision that calls for reversion (or increased reversion) cannot become effective until the end of the fifth calendar year following the year of adoption. In other words, employers have to wait at least five years to take advantage of a reversion opportunity. Furthermore, if the plan called for mandatory contributions, once the benefits are paid off, assets must be allocated to mandatory contributions before the reversion occurs.

An employer that is entitled to a reversion must pay 50% of the reversion amount as an excise tax. However, if the employer establishes a qualified replacement plan or amends the terminating plan to increase benefits, the excise tax is reduced to 20%. IRS Form 5330 is used to pay the excise tax. It is due the last day of the month after the month in which the reversion occurred.

§ 17.06   EFFECT ON BENEFITS

[A]   Forfeit of Benefits

Benefits become nonforfeitable when a plan terminates or partially terminates. A defined contribution plan's benefits become nonforfeitable if and when the employer completely ceases its contributions to the plan. If a defined benefit plan terminates within 10 years of its creation, I.R.C. § 411(d)(2) imposes limits on the benefits that can be paid to the 25 highest-compensated individuals covered by the plan. This rule prevails even if it results in the loss of some accrued benefits.

In the Seventh Circuit view, the employees of a bankrupt company raised a sufficient claim of breach of fiduciary duty by alleging that the company's executives failed to provide ongoing funding for a health plan that was terminated as part of the bankruptcy process. The executives were fiduciaries because of their control over the committee that invested the plan's assets. However, the Seventh Circuit dismissed claims of breach of fiduciary duty by not giving notice of the likelihood of plan termination, on the ground that there is no duty to disclose likely future termination unless plan participants are deliberately misled. [*Baker v. Kingsley*, 387 F.3d 655 (7th Cir. 2004)]

[B]   The Anticutback Rule

Whether deliberately or inadvertently, employers sometimes make cutbacks in a plan, or scale it down. The effect can be inadvertent if the employer lacks the money to make a required deposit, or simply is ignorant of what the legal requirements are. The consequences are not always those intended by the employer. The worst-case scenario is that the plan will be treated as partially terminated, and then retroactively disqualified, obligating the employer to pay back taxes for prior plan years. Retroactive disqualification also harms employees, who are likely to owe back taxes. Furthermore, distributions from a disqualified plan cannot be rolled over to a qualified plan.

A plan is frozen if it is amended to keep the plan trust in existence, but without further contributions or accrual of benefits. A frozen plan is still subject to the top-heavy plan rules, and still has to provide QJSAs and QPSAs on the same terms as if it had not been frozen.

Most plans are subject to I.R.C. § 412, so whenever a plan is partially terminated as defined by I.R.C. § 411(d)(3)(A), immediate 100% vesting is required. Full vesting for employees makes it more likely that the plan will discriminate in favor of HCEs or will yield reversions to the employer. That's because employees in a frozen plan are often given the choice of withdrawing their accrued benefits immediately, or keeping them within the plan until the normal time for distribution. But if too many rank-and-file employees choose withdrawal, the unintended result could be that the plan becomes discriminatory because too high a proportion of HCEs keep their benefits within the plan.

A plan is usually deemed partially terminated if more than 20% of the plan's participants lose their jobs. A "vertical partial termination" occurs when a group of employees lose coverage under the plan. A "horizontal partial termination" occurs when the potential for reversion of plan assets to the employer increases unduly.

If it is uncertain whether there has been a partial termination, Form 5300 can be filed to request an IRS determination letter. If the IRS rules that there has been a partial termination, the event must be reported to the PBGC (as must a 20% cut in the workforce, or a plan amendment that reduces the accrual of benefits by 50% or more for 50% or more of the workforce).

§ 17.07   REPORTING AND COMPLIANCE

When a plan is terminated, IRS Form 5310 is used to request an IRS determination letter stating that the associated plan trust did not become disqualified or lose its exempt status. Form 6088 must be filed in conjunction with this form, listing up to 25 owners or 5% shareholders of the employer corporation who received any distribution from the plan during the preceding five years.

The general rule is that Form 5310-A must be filed 30 days or more before a transfer of plan assets to another qualified retirement plan because of a merger, consolidation, or change in ownership of assets or liabilities. When two defined contribution plans merge or a defined contribution plan is spun off, or a defined benefit plan engages in a merger or spinoff that has only minimal effects, the Form 5310-A filing is not required.

In the somewhat unlikely case that the trust of a terminating plan has more assets than are needed to pay all the plan benefits, and therefore the employer recovers those excess assets, Form 5319 must be filed by the last day of the month after the month in which the employer recouped the assets. This is also the form the employer uses to pay the excise tax on the recouped funds.

The Form 5500-series annual report must be filed for the year of the merger, consolidation, division, or termination. If a trust is frozen (the plan maintains its assets, although benefit accruals have stopped), the 5500-series filing is required in every year until all the assets have been distributed.

§ 17.08   PAYMENT OF EXPENSES

It is appropriate for fiduciaries to use plan assets to pay the expenses of an ongoing plan. However, the decision to terminate a plan is a business decision made by the plan's settlor, and not a fiduciary decision. That means that some of the termination expenses relate to settlor functions—and it violates ERISA to use plan assets to pay settlor expenses. Therefore, allocation is necessary. DOL's ERISA Opinion Letter No. 97-032A (February 1997) recommends that the allocation be made by an independent fiduciary.

These expenses are considered fiduciary expenses that can properly be paid out of plan assets:

- Getting an audit;
- Preparing and filing the final annual report;
- Amending the plan to carry out the termination;
- Calculating benefits;
- Preparing benefit statements;
- Notifying participants and beneficiaries about their rights incident to termination.

However, the cost of maintaining the plan's tax-qualified status—including the cost of getting determination letters—is a settlor expense.

PART IV

BENEFIT PLANS

CHAPTER 18

EMPLOYEE GROUP HEALTH PLANS (EGHPs)

§ 18.01   INTRODUCTION

What started out as a modest Depression-era plan to make sure that doctors got paid for their services (and not in chickens or home-made preserves, either) has had immense implications for the American workplace and the economy as a whole.

The first health insurance plan was originated at the behest of doctors. During World War II, workers were very hard to find (because of military and defense-plant needs), and the federal government froze wages but not benefits. Therefore, offering health insurance was one of the few ways in which employers could compete to offer incentives to recruit workers. After the war ended, unions had a powerful role in an industrialized economy, and negotiations for health plans were an important part of negotiations for each new Collective Bargaining Agreement.

For many years, health care costs, and therefore insurance costs, rose much faster than inflation, until employers faced a heavy burden. In the 1970s and 1980s, there was a vast shift from indemnity insurance [*see* § 18.12] to some form of managed care. The promise of managed care was that eliminating waste and keeping employees healthier would reduce costs.

However, by the end of the twentieth century, managed care was a problem in and of itself. Insurers began to charge the kind of double-digit annual premium increases that caused so much pain in the 1970s. Many patients were dissatisfied with managed care, charging that they were often denied access to necessary care. Doctors were dissatisfied, with the restrictions on their freedom to prescribe, with the amount of paperwork they had to do, and with both the size and speed of their reimbursement from managed care organizations (MCOs).

Just as there has been a transition from defined-benefit to defined-contribution or employee-funded retirement plans, health plans have shifted from the once-predominant indemnity plan to a heavy dominance of some form of managed care. Some employers have always chosen to self-insure rather than purchase insurance; others have switched to self-insurance to cut costs. A new form that is emerging is the so-called defined contribution or consumer-oriented health care plan.

One of the most important differences between ERISA's pension plan provisions and its welfare benefit plan provisions is that, by and large, welfare benefits do not vest, and can be altered or terminated if the plan document retains the sponsor's discretion to do so. However, in some situations, the employer will be deemed to have a contractual obligation to maintain the plan. In a unionized company, the CBA will impose further limitations on the employer's ability to alter the health plans it maintains. [For the requirements for Summary Plan Descriptions (SPDs) for health plans, *see* § 11.02[B]]

§ 18.02   THE HEALTH CARE LANDSCAPE

Although initially the employer group health plan market was divided only between self-insured and indemnity insurance plans, today managed care is dominant. There are many types of managed care plans. At one time the Health

Management Organization (HMO) was the dominant managed care form, but today its predominance is yielding to plans that provide somewhat more flexibility and provider choice for patients.

Although questions of how states and the federal government can regulate managed care are very important in our legal system, these fast-moving issues are by and large outside the scope of this book.

Tip: Two Web sites that contain excellent current information about state regulation of managed care plans are Families U.S.A. <http://www.familiesusa.org> and the Kaiser Family Foundation <http://www.kff.org>. Many states require managed care organizations to maintain review processes so neutral outsiders who do not have a financial interest in restricting the plan's costs can review claims denials. State laws also deal with issues such as access to emergency care, access to specialists, and limits on financial incentives given to doctors to induce them to reduce the number of treatments.

In March 2005, BLS data showed that nearly 70% of workers in private industry had access to work-related health insurance, with the employer paying part or all of the cost. However, about three quarters of private industry workers didn't have a choice of plans: 30% were not offered a plan and 44% had only one available plan. Another 12% of workers were offered two plans, and only 3% could choose among five or more plans. [Carl Barsky, *Medical Plan Choices in Private Industry, 2005*, DOL, Bureau of Labor Statistics, Compensation and Working Conditions Online <http://www.bls.gov> (Aug. 31, 2005)]

"Association plans"—health insurance sold by an association of persons having a common interest (e.g., people who belong to an organization such as the Rotary Club; members of a profession)—have been hailed as a valuable tool in slowing down the pace of health care inflation. However, a report by consumer advocates Families USA, released in March 2004, warned that association plans are too vulnerable to control by the insurers of the health policies. Families USA also criticized association policies for offering artificially low "teaser" rates, followed by high premium increases—or even misrepresentation of policy benefits to close the sale, leaving insured persons with high medical bills for non-covered procedures. Association plans are also marketed to individuals who have lost group coverage (e.g., they are retired or unemployed and have not elected or have exhausted COBRA coverage). These people, who tend to be economically vulnerable, are sometimes deceived as to whether they are receiving true group coverage or merely dressed-up individual policies. [Chad Terhune, *Report Raps Association Insurance,* Wall Street Journal, Mar. 11, 2004, at p. D3. *See also* The Families USA report, *The Illusion of Group Health Insurance: Discretionary Associations* is available online at http://www.familiesusa.org/assets/pdfs/Disc_brief_summary 350f.pdf]

The traditional role of workplace clinics was to cope with on-the-job injuries and, perhaps, to perform drug testing. Now, some employers are looking to these clinics as a way to cut health care costs and make it easier for employees to get treatment and follow-up care and return to work promptly. Workplace clinics also can interface with wellness programs to keep employees healthier. Usually, in-house clinics hire third-party providers to manage the facility, so employees can be assured that privacy will be protected. In 2003, the Washington Business Group on Health commissioned a study of a small group of large employers with in-house clinics; 68% said the facilities were effective in improving the health of employees, 59% said that costs were managed effectively, 56% said employees were more satisfied, and 54% said the facilities improved productivity. [Angela Maas, *On-Site Medical Clinics: New Take on Old Model*, Employee Benefit News, <http://www.benefitnews.com/pfv.cfm?id=7379> (Apr. 15, 2005)]

§18.03 BENEFITS MANDATES

[A] Generally

Although as a general rule, employers have complete discretion to determine which benefits will be included in the plan, and the ratio between benefits, there are certain legislative mandates that temper this discretion.

The regulations call for penalties of up to $100 per day per person affected by noncompliance if states fail to enact, or enact but fail to enforce, consumer health statutes such as the ones discussed in this section. [*See* 45 C.F.R. Part 150, Interim Final Regulations issued by the agency then known as HCFA (now it is called CMS, for The Centers for Medicare and Medicaid Services) on August 20, 1999; 64 Fed. Reg. 45786] For a database about state laws on mandated health benefits, sorted by state and type of benefit, *see* <http://www.insure.com/health/lawtool.cfm>.

According to the Council for Affordable Health Insurance's March 2006 paper, a total of 1,818 state health insurance mandates had been enacted, with 295 new mandates added in 2004 alone. Mandates can refer to the type of provider entitled to reimbursement (e.g., chiropractors or Certified Social Workers providing behavioral health care), benefits (e.g., breast reconstruction after mastectomy), or covered populations (e.g., newborns or children adopted by plan beneficiaries). Many of the states mandate as many as 40 to 50 types of coverage. All the states mandate coverage of mammograms, 45 require coverage of alcoholism treatment, 47 require coverage of diabetic supplies, and 46 require coverage of emergency services. All of the states require coverage of infants born to plan participants, and 42 mandate coverage of children adopted by participants. In the Council for Affordable Health Insurance's view, mandates raise the cost of health insurance by 20 to 50% (depending on the number and type of mandates in a given state). They attribute one-fourth of the uninsured to the effect of mandates. [Victoria Craig Bunce and J.P. Wieske (Council for Affordable Health

Insurance), *Health Insurance Mandates in the States 2006* (Mar. 2006), <http://www.cahi.org/cahi_contents/resources/pdf/MandatePub2006.pdf>]

On February 26, 2003, the Employee Benefits Security Administration (the DOL department formerly known as the Pension and Welfare Benefits Administration) announced a new compliance assistance program to help EGHPs satisfy the portability and nondiscrimination requirements of HIPAA as well as the mental health parity requirement and the requirements dealing with women's health issues such as mastectomy and childbirth. The EBSA site (<http://www.ebsa.gov>) has a health sector that gives information about the agency's compliance workshops, held at various locations nationwide. The site includes a self-assessment tool with 40 questions that plans can use to check compliance, a chart setting out the various health-related required notices, and a checklist of compliance tips.

Some useful pointers from the site:

- Plans should be reviewed for "hidden" pre-existing condition limitations, such as conditioning coverage of treatment for accidental injuries to circumstances in which the person was covered under the plan when the accident occurred. Such provisions must be removed from the plan unless they can be administered in conformity with the pre-existing condition rules.
- Any waiting period for coverage should run concurrently with the pre-existing condition exclusion—the pre-existing condition limitation period cannot be timed to start after the waiting period ends. In addition to general notice to all plan participants, employees should be given individual notice if they present evidence of creditable coverage but are still subject to a pre-existing condition limitation.
- Make sure certificates of creditable coverage that you issue are complete (i.e., reflect information about dependents and waiting periods).
- Plans must not have provisions that deny eligibility based on a health factor, even if the provision applies only to late enrollees.

[B] Maternity Stays

The Newborns' and Mothers' Health Protection Act of 1996 (NMHPA) [Pub. L. No. 104-204] and the Taxpayer Relief Act of 1997 [Pub. L. No. 105-35] combine ERISA and tax code provisions to mandate that group health plans (both insured and self-insured, whatever the number of participants) provide at least a minimum hospital stay for childbirth. The minimum is 48 hours after a vaginal delivery, 96 hours after a Caesarian section.

Mother and child can be discharged earlier if, after consulting the mother, the mother's attending physician allows it. However, the plan is not allowed to offer financial incentives to the physician or the mother to shorten the stay. If the plan does not provide hospitalization benefits for childbirth, it is not required to add those benefits because of this legislation. The NMHPA does not preempt state laws that require an even longer maternity stay.

Rules to implement the NMHPA were jointly issued by the IRS, Pension and Welfare Benefit Administration, and Health Care Financing Administration (now renamed Centers for Medicare and Medicaid Services). [29 C.F.R. § 2590.711]

Under these rules, when a baby is delivered in the hospital, the stay begins at the time of the delivery (or the last delivery, in a multiple birth). If the mother is admitted to the hospital after giving birth elsewhere, the stay begins at the time of admission. These rules forbid health plans to penalize health care providers for complying with the NMHPA. It is permissible to offer post-discharge follow-up after an early discharge, as long as the services offered do not exceed those that would be provided during the 48- or 96-hour stay required by the NMHPA.

Violation of the NMHPA is subject to the I.R.C. § 4980D penalty of $100 per participant per day, starting when the failure occurs and running until it is corrected. No penalty will be imposed if the failure to provide an adequate postpartum stay was unintentional, and is corrected within 30 days. If the failure is unintentional but is not corrected, the maximum penalty is $500,000 a year, or 10% of the EGHP's expenses for the year before the failure—whichever is less.

[C] Women's Health and Cancer Rights Act (WHCRA)

The Women's Health and Cancer Rights Act (WHCRA) [Pub. L. No. 105-277], became law on October 21, 1998, effective for plan years beginning on or after that date. The Act provides that if an EGHP covers mastectomies, it must also cover reconstructive breast surgery if the patient wants it and her attending physician prescribes it. This includes reconstruction of the mastectomized breast; surgery on the other breast to balance the patient's appearance; prostheses; and treatment of physical complications of mastectomy. Deductibles and co-insurance for reconstructive surgery must be comparable to those imposed on other procedures.

EGHPs (and the insurers and HMOs that provide the medical and surgical benefits) have an ongoing obligation to notify new plan participants of their WHCRA rights, and to renew the notice annually. (It is not necessary for both the EGHP and insurer or HMO to furnish the notice, as long as one of them does.) The notice must satisfy the DOL requirements for Summary Plan Descriptions. [*See* 29 C.F.R. § 2520.104b-1] The annual notice doesn't have to be given in the first year of enrollment, because it would only duplicate the initial enrollment notice.

Annual notices must be delivered by a method that is reasonably likely to get the information to the plan participant: e.g., first-class mail or e-mail. The notice can be included with an SPD, Summary of Material Modification, or Summary Annual Report; with a benefits newsletter or union newsletter; open enrollment information for the plan; or other written plan communication.

The DOL has furnished this model notice that will satisfy the compliance burden: "Did you know that your plan, as required by the WHCRA, provides benefits for mastectomy-related services including reconstruction and surgery to achieve symmetry between the breasts, prostheses, and complications of mastectomy (including lymphedema)? Call your Plan Administrator [insert phone number] for more information." [<http://www.dol.gov/pwba/pubs>]

After a double mastectomy, the plaintiff had problems with the implants and tissue expanders used in reconstructive surgery. Her insurer approved a new implant at a university hospital, but refused a request to have the surgery performed at a hospital closer to her home. She brought suit under the WHCRA and also asserted state-law claims. The state-law claims were dismissed (as preempted by ERISA). The WHCRA claim was dismissed because she brought suit directly under this suit; the court held that the WHCRA does not have any separate enforcement mechanisms apart from ordinary ERISA enforcement. [*Howard v. Coventry Health Care of Iowa, Inc.,* 158 F. Supp. 2d 937 (S.D. Iowa 2001)]

The plaintiff in a 2004 case from the same court was equally unsuccessful. The plaintiff had a mastectomy and reconstruction many years before becoming a participant in her current health plan. While she was covered by this plan, one of her breast implants ruptured. The plan refused to cover any additional reconstructive surgery, not only because it was a preexisting condition. The plan's position was that the WHCRA was not applicable, because the initial surgery was performed to treat fibrocystic breast disease, not cancer. For several reasons, including untimely filing, the court dismissed the plaintiff's claim. The court accepted the plan's argument that it was not obligated to provide benefits for follow-up surgery that was not provided under the plan. [*Davidson v. Wal-Mart Assocs. Health and Welfare Plan,* 2004 U.S. Dist. LEXIS 2598 (S.D. Iowa 2004)]

[D] Contraceptives

A December 14, 2000, EEOC decision [available at <http://www.eeoc.gov/docs/decision-contraception.html>] agrees with the charging parties, a group of female employees, that it violates Title VII for a plan to fail to cover prescription contraceptive drugs and devices when it covers other types of preventive medical care, and when it covers vasectomy and tubal ligation (permanent surgical methods of contraception). The EEOC treats the distinction as discrimination on the basis of sex (in that only women use birth control pills, diaphragms, and IUDs) and pregnancy.

The EEOC's rationale is that the Pregnancy Discrimination Amendment (PDA) [42 U.S.C. § 2000e(k). *See* § 34.06] forbids discrimination on the basis of potential as well as actual pregnancy. Employers can lawfully exclude coverage of abortion, but not of contraception. In this case, the employer said that contraception was not covered because only abnormal health conditions were covered— but the plan covered sterilization of healthy persons based on their desire not to procreate in the future.

The EEOC also noted that plans frequently cover vaccination and preventive examinations, which, like contraception, prevent healthy employees from developing unwanted health conditions. The EEOC required the plan to cover the full range of available prescription contraceptives, because a woman employee's needs might change in the course of employment.

Employers spent an average of $43.36 per year per employee for contraceptives, 5.1% of all pharmaceutical costs. Most of this was for oral contraceptives (an average of $29.52). SHRM found that 70% of employers covered contraceptives in 2002 and 82% covered them in 2005. The federal government requires its health plans to cover contraceptives, and at least 21 states mandate this for fully insured health plans. [*Contraceptive Coverage Grows*, BenefitNews Connect, Aug. 30, 2005 (benefitslink.com)]

State law is also a factor. According to the National Conference of State Legislatures, the states of Arizona, California, Connecticut, Delaware, Georgia, Hawaii, Illinois, Iowa, Maine, Maryland, Massachusetts, Missouri, Nevada, New Hampshire, New Mexico, North Carolina, Rhode Island, Texas, Vermont, Virginia, Washington, and West Virginia mandate inclusion of contraceptive coverage in EGHPs. However, 13 of the states allow employers with a religious objection to providing contraceptives to assert a conscience clause. According to the District Court for the District of Nebraska, the Pregnancy Discrimination Act's definition of "women affected by pregnancy" is broader than "pregnant women," so the risk of pregnancy must be treated at least as favorably as other similar health risks. The court was not persuaded by the employer's argument that contraceptives for men were also excluded from the plan because all contraceptives actually affect the potentially pregnant female body. [*In re Union Pacific R.R. Employment Practices Litigation*, 378 F. Supp. 2d 1139 (D. Neb. July 22, 2005)]

In June 2001, the Western District of Washington granted summary judgment for the plaintiff in the first federal case after the EEOC ruling. In other words, the employer had an obligation to cover contraceptives under the EGHP. [*Erickson v. Bartell Drug*, 141 F. Supp. 2d 1266 (W.D. Wash. June 12, 2001).

After the District Court ruling, the defendant appealed to the Ninth Circuit. The case was settled in 2003. Bartell included prescription drugs and devices and related contraceptive clinical services in its plan in mid-2001. Under the settlement, the defendant agreed to continue doing this. All class members still employed by Bartell receive contraceptive services without copayment obligations until 2006. Class members who are no longer employed received $100 each.

A mid-2003 Washington State case holds that state law does not require health plans to cover all forms of prescription contraceptives that have been approved by the FDA—only the services offered by the health plan. [*Glaubach v. Regence Blue Shield*, 74 P.3d 115 (Wash. 2003)]

A class action of female Wal-Mart employees protesting the exclusion of female contraceptives from the health plan was certified in the Northern District of Georgia in August of 2002. The judge rejected as plaintiffs wives of male employees and female employees who did not use birth control pills, and also dismissed the named plaintiff's claims for compensatory and punitive damages. (The suit continued with respect to claims for back pay of about $300 per plaintiff per year to cover the cost of excluded contraceptives.) Wal-Mart's position was that it excluded contraceptive coverage on a gender-neutral basis, for the valid business reason of saving money.

A class action suit was filed against AT&T (*Stocking v. AT&T*) alleging that the health care and contraceptive reimbursement available to female AT&T employees was not equal to that available to male employees, in that Viagra and vasectomies were covered but oral contraceptives, jellies, foams, implants, and contraceptive injections were excluded. In July of 2003, the AT&T plan began to cover oral contraceptives, but only by mail-order prescription. The suit continued with respect to the other forms of contraception.

The District Court for the District of Arizona granted final approval of settlement of a nationwide class action against Albertson Grocery and Pharmacy on February 9, 2004. Six employees complained to the EEOC on behalf of 200,000 female employees nationwide. Albertson's agreed to cover all FDA-approved prescription contraceptives and related medical services on a parity with other preventive drugs and devices. Employees who incurred out-of-pocket expenses for birth control pills at a time when they had been plan participants for at least 90 days received vouchers of $50 to $150 (depending on tenure).

A class action, *Mewborn v. CVS Pharmacy,* was filed in January of 2002. In June of that year, the defendant reviewed its benefits package and added contraceptive coverage. In February 2004, the district court rejected an additional filing by the plaintiff on the grounds that, because she was no longer a CVS employee, she no longer had standing. Furthermore, the court ruled that the addition of contraceptive coverage had mooted her request.

The Northern District of Texas ruled on December 13, 2001, that the benefits sought by the flight attendant plaintiff in *Alexander v. American Airlines,* 2002 U.S. Dist. LEXIS 7089 (Pap smears, contraceptives, and infertility treatment), were not required by federal law and, because she had never filed a plan claim for contraceptives, she lacked standing to sue.

The California Supreme Court required Catholic Charities of Sacramento, Inc., to cover prescription contraceptives under its health and disability insurance plans. This employer brought suit, challenging the validity of the state statute because it required Catholic Charities to reimburse for contraceptives despite its moral opposition to contraception. The statute offers an exemption for religious employers, but the state Supreme Court rejected that characterization of Catholic Charities, which was not organized to inculcate religious tenets, was not a nonprofit organization, and did not primarily serve and primarily employ members of a particular religion. Therefore, it was subject to the general mandate to reimburse the cost of prescription contraceptives. [*Catholic Charities of Sacramento, Inc. v. Superior Court of Sacramento County,* 72 LW 1529 (Cal. 2004), *cert. denied* No. 03-1618 (Oct. 2004)]

The Women's Health and Wellness Act, a New York state statute, requires contraceptive coverage in all plans that cover prescription drugs. The statute has a religious exemption, but it is a narrow one (covering only organizations dedicated to religious worship and excluding those that provide, e.g., social services under faith-based control). The New York Court of Appeals upheld the validity of the statute. The language of the religious exception, which limits coverage to employers whose main purpose is promotion of theological values and who primarily employ and serve members of their own faith, is drawn from a California law that also has survived challenge. [*Catholic Charities of the Diocese of Albany v. Serio*, 96621 (N.Y. 2006); *see* John Caher, *N.Y. Court Rejects Employers' Challenge to Contraception Law*, N.Y.L.J., Jan. 13, 2006 (law.com)]

Early in 2006, New Jersey enacted a statute requiring health insurance providers that cover outpatient prescription drugs to cover prescription contraceptives (birth control pills, diaphragms, other FDA-approved devices) for women. The statute applies to individual and group health plans, HMOs, and the state's Health Benefits Program. An exemption is available however if compliance would conflict with the bona fide beliefs and practices of a religious employer. [Fred Schneyer, *New Jersey Adds Contraceptives Coverage Mandate*, PlanSponsor.com (Jan. 10, 2006)]

[E] Mental Health Parity

A very controversial 1996 federal statute, the Veterans' Affairs, Housing and Urban Development and Independent Agencies Appropriations Act [Pub. L. No. 104-204] imposed a requirement of parity in EGHPs with more than 50 participants. Under the parity provision, plans that did not impose lifetime or annual limits on medical and surgical benefits could not do so on mental health benefits. Most plans do impose limits—so the limits would have to be the same for mental and physical ailments. In 1996, this requirement was made part of ERISA.

The Mental Health Parity Act was permitted to expire in 2001. Subsequently, it received many temporary leases on life, although legislation to make it permanent never achieved passage. *See* the 2002 Appropriations Act, Pub. L. No. 107-116; the Job Creation and Worker Assistance Act of 2002, Pub. L. No. 107-147; Mental Health Parity Reauthorization Acts of 2002, Pub. L. No. 107-313, and 2003, Pub. L. No. 108-197, with an implementing Final Rule at 69 Fed. Reg. 2004 (Jan. 26, 2004); and Working Families Tax Relief Act, Pub. L. No. 108-311; see 69 Fed. Reg. 75798 (Dec. 17, 2004). The federal requirement was extended to December 31, 2006, by the Mental Health Parity Act Extension, P.L. 109-151 (Jan. 3, 2006). [*See also* 71 Fed. Reg. 13937 (Mar. 20, 2006) and <http://www.dol.gov/elaws/ebsa/health>]

A December 2004 issue brief by the American Academy of Actuaries [American Academy of Actuaries, *Mental Health Parity: Often Separate, Usually Unequal* (Issue Brief, Dec. 2004), <http://www.actuary.org/pdf/health/parity_1204.pdf>] points out that despite the nominal requirement of parity, plans can provide a lower level of benefits for behavioral health without violating the law. They can impose "inside limits" such as restricting the number of behavioral health office visits permitted per year, or the number of days of hospital care. They can also impose higher cost-sharing for mental health than for other forms of health care.

Thirty-five states have mental health parity laws that are broader than the federal requirement. Some of the states use a broad definition of mental health, but others require parity only in the case of specified biologically based mental illnesses. State insurance regulation may also require insurers to make additional mental health benefits available through an extra-cost rider to the policy. In 2005, South Carolina became the 35th state to have its own state parity mandate. Effective July 1, 2006, the mandate covers nine severe mental illnesses, including depression and anxiety. [Jonathan Maze, *Mental Health Bill Now Law,* Charleston Post and Courier (May 26, 2005) (benefitslink.com)] State laws requiring mental health parity in insured plans are preempted by ERISA with respect to self-funded plans. [*Daley v. Marriott Int'l Inc.,* 415 F.3d 889 (8th Cir. 2005)]

Before the original Mental Health Parity Act of 1996 (MHPA), almost all EGHPs covered mental health disorders, but benefits were generally more restricted than for physical illnesses (shorter duration of coverage, lower annual and lifetime benefit maximums). According to the National Compensation Survey, the MHPA has greatly reduced the percentage of employees whose health plans imposed more restrictive limits on behavioral health than on physical health. In 1997, 55% of plans had lower limits for outpatient mental health care and 41% had lower inpatient limits, whereas both percentages dropped to 7% in 2002. However in 1997, 61% of employees were entitled to fewer inpatient days for mental health—a percentage that rose to 77% in 2002. The MHPA does not cover the treatment of substance abuse, although attempts have been made to amend the statute to do so, in part because of the immense economic cost of drug abuse. [John D. Morton and Patricia Aleman, *Trends in Employer-Provided Mental Health and Substance Abuse Benefits,* Monthly Labor Review, <http://www.bls.gov/opub/mlr/2005/04/art3full.pdf> (Apr. 2005)]

Fears about the cost of health care parity may be exaggerated. In 2001, the Federal Employees Health Benefit Program (FEHBP) began a pilot project to see what would happen if mental health and substance abuse services were covered to the same extent as treatments for physical illnesses. Some managed care techniques (such as only reimbursing treatment from network providers and requiring approval from the plan) were applied. Results were published in the New England Journal of Medicine in 2006. The proportion of federal employees using mental health services went up 1.35 to 2.75% over a two-year period, which was no faster than the increase in a comparable large private-sector plan that did not offer mental health parity. Employees covered by FEHBP had lower out-of-pocket spending on mental health services. [Vanessa Fuhrmans, *Findings Support Coverage of Costs for Mental Health*, Wall Street Journal, March 30, 2006, at p. D3] Because of managed behavioral health care, in part, the cost of mental health parity was not as high as predicted. In the states with mental health parity requirements, the cost of maintaining a health plan increased less than 2% because of the requirement; the implementation of behavioral care management sometimes resulted in a cost decrease. In Minnesota, the parity requirement (enacted in 1995) was estimated to have raised costs by only 1–2% for state employees. Rhode Island, whose parity requirement is limited to severe mental illnesses only, has seen a cost increase of 0.33% since 1994. [Steve Melek, *The Costs of Mental Health Parity*, Health Section News, Mar. 2005 (benefitslink.com)]

For employers seeking to improve their plans' treatment and management of behavioral health issues, guidelines from the National Business Group on Health suggest:

- Screening employees who have chronic health conditions for depression;
- Having disease management vendors perform the screening;
- Improving the coordination among general medical care, behavioral health care, and disease management;
- Providing reimbursement under the EGHP for primary care doctors and specialists other than psychiatrists for screening, assessing, diagnosing, and treating mental illness and substance abuse; and
- Involving the employee assistance program, if established, to help employees using psychiatric disability benefits get back to work.

[BenefitNews Connect, *Guide Helps Firms Improve Mental Health Benefits*, benefitslink.com (Dec. 15, 2005)]

[F] Other Inclusion Issues

The Supreme Court affirmed, without opinion, the Seventh Circuit's decision in *Doe v. Mutual of Omaha*. [179 F.3d 557 (7th Cir. 1999)] The Seventh Circuit ruled that it is not a violation of Title II of the Americans With Disabilities Act for either an insured or a self-insured health plan to impose a lower lifetime cap on AIDS-related conditions than on other conditions (e.g., $25,000 versus $1 million). The rationale is that Mutual of Omaha didn't refuse to sell policies to people with AIDS, although the policy was worth far less to a person with AIDS or an AIDS-related condition than someone with other health problems.

EGHPs are forbidden to discriminate against employees or their dependents who suffer from end-stage renal disease (ESRD). Internal Revenue Code § 5000 imposes a heavy penalty: 25% of the employer's health care expenses (not just the amount that would have been paid for ESRD coverage in the absence of discrimination). Also note that ERISA § 609(d) requires plans to maintain their coverage of pediatric vaccines at least at the May 1, 1993, level.

Twelve states have a mandate for coverage of infertility treatment: Arkansas, Connecticut, Hawaii, Illinois, Maryland, Massachusetts, Montana, New Jersey, New York, Ohio, Rhode Island, and West Virginia. California and Texas do not have a mandate, but require insurers to offer infertility coverage as an option. Approximately 25% of employers offer some coverage, but it is usually very limited (e.g., diagnosis of conditions causing infertility). [Jill Elswick, *Employers Are Wary As Demand Swells for Infertility Treatment*, Employee Benefit News, <http://www.benefitnews.com/pfv.cfm?id=8329> (Dec. 2005)]

In January 2003, the Second Circuit ruled that it is not a violation of Title VII for a plan to exclude coverage of surgical procedures to correct infertility that are performed only on women, because infertility affects male and female participants equally. The District Court hearing this case applied the "equal access" standard often used in ADA cases, asking whether all employees have equal access to plan benefits. However, the Second Circuit held that this is not an appropriate standard in a Title VII case, in which the relevant standard is whether sex-specific conditions exist. If they do, the next inquiry is whether excluding coverage of those conditions results in a plan that has inferior coverage for one sex. The Second Circuit said that the Pregnancy Discrimination Act's ban on discrimination on the basis of pregnancy or related conditions does not extend to discrimination on the basis of infertility, because both men and women have reproductive capacity and can be infertile. [*Saks v. Franklin Covey Co.*, 316 F.3d 337 (2d Cir. 2003)]

Late in 2002, the Second Circuit upheld a plan administrator's decision that gender reassignment surgery was not medically necessary. When the plan administrator provides sufficient evidence that a desired treatment is not medically necessary as a general rule, the patient and doctor must offer evidence that the patient is different and the treatment is necessary in his or her specific case. [*Mario v. P&C Food Markets Inc.*, 313 F.3d 758 (2d Cir. 2002)]

A 2002 Seventh Circuit case ruled that a former employee was not entitled to recover the medical expenses resulting from a heart attack, because he never properly enrolled in the ex-employer's health plan. The plaintiff was hired in March 1998. He claims that he was promised health insurance coverage. He signed a letter of commitment accepting the proffered compensation package; the letter did not mention health insurance. He was faxed a health insurance enrollment form. He never completed the form, claiming that some of the questions violated his privacy. He says that he was not told that failure to complete the form would prevent the issuance of coverage. He finished his assignment with the employer, quit his job, and suffered a heart attack shortly thereafter.

The Seventh Circuit did not accept the plaintiff's argument that he would have completed the application if the employer had not misled him. The Seventh Circuit ruled that the employer did not knowingly misrepresent the terms of the plan. A promise to provide insurance is not the equivalent of a promise to provide coverage even for people who fail to enroll in the relevant plan, and the plan' fiduciaries behaved appropriately and issued the appropriate communications. [*Kamler v. H/N Telecommunications Servs., Inc.*, 305 F.3d 672 (7th Cir. 2002)]

Traditionally, plans covered dependent children of employees only until the child reached age 18, or age 22 or 23 if he or she was a full-time student. However, several states have legislation requiring a long coverage period.

New Jersey P.L. 2005 ch. 375, effective for insurance contracts issued or renewed on or after May 12, 2006, provides that insured plans must either extend dependent coverage to age 30 or have a COBRA-like provision for dependents who lose coverage before age 30 to elect to continue it up to age 30. For this purpose, dependents must be unmarried, New Jersey residents or full-time students in New Jersey, and must not have other group health coverage. Continuation can be elected within 30 days before aging-out, and the continuation coverage must be identical to the previous coverage. Like COBRA, the provision permits the insurer to charge a premium of up to 102% of the difference between family and single coverage for continuation coverage. Parents of dependents who can make the election are entitled to notice in the insurance certificate for the group plan and also from the employer when an election to continue coverage becomes available. [Morgan Lewis Law-Flash, *New Jersey Extends Dependent Medical Coverage to Age 30*, <http://www.morganlewis.com/Eb_NewJerseyAge30_LF_23jan06.pdf> (Jan. 23, 2006)]

Colorado has a law (applying both to group and individual policies) requiring the coverage of dependents until they turn 25, and legislation has been introduced there to permit grandparents to elect coverage for their dependents' dependents. According to the National Conference of State Legislatures, Massachusetts, Utah, and New Mexico have also passed laws covering adult dependents. [M.P. McQueen, *Health Insurer Must Cover Adult Children*, Wall Street Journal, Apr. 11, 2006, at p. D1]

[G] 2003 California Legislation

Shortly before being recalled, then-Governor Gray Davis of California signed the state's Health Insurance Act. This statute created a "pay or play" requirement under which employers of 560 or more employees would have to either provide health insurance in compliance with state standards or pay into the state's existing risk pool. The statute exempted companies with under 20 employees entirely, had a delayed effective date for companies with 20 to 50 workers, and required companies with at least 200 workers to offer dependent coverage as well. However, in late 2004, 50.9% of the state's voters voted against Proposition 72, a measure to allow the Health Insurance Act of 2003 to take effect. Therefore, the statute was not implemented. [*See, e.g.*, Judy Greenwald, *Californians Vote to Repeal Health Insurance Mandate*, Business Insurance (Nov. 3, 2004); Milt Freudenheim, *Many California Employers Face Health Care Mandate*, New York Times, Sept. 17, 2003, at p. A14]

[H] "Wal-Mart" Bills

The traditional principle has been that employers are free to decide whether or not to offer health insurance coverage and to design their plans. That principle may be eroding. Early in 2006, Maryland passed the first bill mandating a minimum level of health care spending by large employers. The law requires companies with more than 10,000 employees to either devote at least 8% of payroll to health benefits or make up the difference in taxes. The governor vetoed this "Wal-Mart law" (so-called because Wal-Mart was the only employer subject to it; the other equally large companies already had health plans), but the state legislature overrode the veto. Similar legislation was introduced in about 30 other states. [Tresa Baldas, *Novel Health Benefit Bill Sparks Debate*, Nat'l Law Journal, Jan. 24, 2006 (law.com); Matt Brady, *Union Wins Big Employer Health Bill Victory*, NU Online News Service, Jan. 13, 2006)] The AFL-CIO's position on this requirement is that Americans pay $113 billion each year to cover uninsured workers (in the form of higher premiums for the insured and Medicaid benefits). Twenty states disclosed information about employed Medicaid beneficiaries, and in each of these states, Wal-Mart employees led in the total. [Judy Ward, *Total Benefits: Picking up the Tab* [PlanSponsor.com articles, Mar. 2006] In July 2006, the District Court for the District of Maryland ruled that the state's law was invalid and unenforceable because it was contrary to the ERISA statutory objective of permitting multi-state companies to maintain plans that are uniform rather than subject to a variety of state requirements. The state announced its intention to appeal this determination. [*Retail Industry Leaders Ass'n v. Fielder*, No. 1:06-cv-00316-JFM (D. Md. July 19, 2006); *see, e.g.*, Reed Abelson and Michael Barbaro, *Judge Gives Wal-Mart Reprieve on Benefits*, N.Y. Times July 20, 2006, at C1; Kris Hudson, *U.S. Judge Grants Wal-Mart a Win on Health Outlays*, Wall St. J. July 20, 2006 at B2]

In response to criticisms, Wal-Mart announced that it would make its lowest-cost EGHP more accessible and reduce the period of employment required to enroll from 24 months. The company announced that its nine in-store pilot clinics would be joined by more than 50 other clinics where employees could receive their health care in the workplace. [News Articles, *Wal-Mart Unveils Employee Health Coverage Improvements*, PlanSponsor.com (Feb. 23, 2005)]

Massachusetts took another approach to increasing coverage with its April 2006 enactment of a law that imposes tax penalties on individuals who had access to affordable health care coverage, but did not elect it. The bill also provides subsidies and sliding-scale premiums so low-income persons can purchase health care coverage. [Steve LeBlanc (AP), *Mass. Governor Oks Landmark Health Bill*, Verizon.net (Apr. 12, 2006)]

§ 18.04   DENTAL PLANS

Many medium-sized and large companies offer some form of dental coverage. As with most health-related benefits, the prevalence of the benefit increases directly with the size of the company.

Most dental plans offer fee for service coverage, although some plans use HMOs or PPOs. An emerging new form, endorsed by the American Dental Association in 1996, is the direct reimbursement plan: a fee-for-service plan where employees choose their own dentists. The plan sets a limit; up to the limit, the employee is entitled to payment of a percentage of dental expenses, e.g., full coverage of the first $100 in expenses, 50% reimbursement of the next $1,800, phasing out at a plan limit of $1,000 in benefits. [*Id.*]

Dental plans are subject to COBRA's continuation coverage requirement.

The basic structure of a dental plan is a schedule of covered procedures and payments for each (which might be defined as dollar amounts or percentages). The dentist who renders the care is paid for each service to covered employees (in a fee-for-service plan) or receives capitated or other prearranged compensation under an HMO or PPO plan. There is an increasing trend to require advance approval of large non-emergency claims.

The general rule is that the percentage of coverage is inversely related to the expected cost of the service. Low-cost procedures like X-rays and examinations get a higher percentage of reimbursement (often, 100%, but limitations to two exams and cleanings per year are also common) than fillings, root canals, and dental surgery (typically reimbursed at an 80% level). Prosthetics and orthodontia are typically reimbursed at a 50% level. Dental plans typically exclude cosmetic dentistry, hospitalization for inpatient dental procedures, and amounts that would be covered by other insurance (including Worker's Compensation). Usually, dental plans impose an annual maximum. BLS's survey of 2002–2003 benefits and compensation, released January 2005, shows that 72% of dental plans had a deductible; 71% imposed only a yearly deductible (in 47% of the cases, a $50 deductible)(Table 59); 86% of plans specified a maximum dental benefit that could be provided in a year. In 34% of the plans, the maximum was $1,000 a year; in 27% it was $1,500 a year; only 15% had a maximum greater than $1,500 a year, so the average maximum benefit limitation was $1,356 a year.

§ 18.05 PRESCRIPTION DRUG COVERAGE

Many companies' EGHPs provide at least some coverage of prescription drugs, as a complement to medical treatment. Some employers offer separate prescription drug plans with the objective of saving money by ordering in bulk. Some prescription drug plans also cover employees' dependents—often, with some degree of financial responsibility on the employee's part. *See* Chapter 9 for a discussion of the effect of Medicare Part D (prescription drug coverage) on EGHP and retiree health plan operations.

The typical prescription drug plan covers only outpatient drugs; drugs taken by hospital patients come under the hospital care benefit. The usual plan imposes a copayment on each prescription (e.g., $5–$25). Overall dollar limitations on reimbursement per plan year are common. However, many plans are bedeviled by high increases, such as 15–20% a year, in prescription drug costs.

In an effort to keep costs down, or at least to tamp down the speed of the rate of increase, plan sponsors are altering prescription drug plan design, incorporating features such as imposing higher copayments; imposing a coinsurance percentage instead of a flat amount; requiring doctors to get prior authorization for expensive drugs; requiring a trial of a less expensive drug before a more expensive one is prescribed ("step therapy"); and having two or even three tiers with a $100 copayment in the highest tier and lower copayments for generics and less expensive branded drugs. According to Hewitt Associates, less than 10% of plans had copayments of more than $30 in 2001, but nearly 40% of plans imposed copayments at that level in 2005. However, to prevent employees with chronic conditions from going off medication (and increasing the risk of expensive hospitalization), some plans waive copayments on maintenance drugs (e.g., insulin). "Reference pricing" in effect adopts a usual and customary cost schedule for drugs; plan participants pay a percentage (e.g., 25%) of the reference price, plus any difference between the actual cost and the reference price. [Barbara Martinez, *Drug Co-Pays Hit $100*, Wall Street Journal, June 28, 2005, at p. D1]

Some plans allow repeat prescriptions to be dispensed by mail, allowing savings due to centralized cost processing. However, a mail order plan is not well suited to short-term, acute medications. A mail order plan can be combined with a nationwide panel plan, where a network of pharmacies agrees to sell prescription drugs at the panel's schedule prices. Participating pharmacies accept membership cards from enrolled employees; the pharmacies submit their claims for payment directly to the plan.

The majority of retail drug prescriptions are handled by Pharmacy Benefit Management (PBM) companies that permit economies of scale. Plans often try to reduce costs by encouraging the use of generic rather than brand-name drugs (e.g., by imposing higher copayments on brand-name drugs; limiting reimbursement to drugs appearing on a formulary set in advance; refusing reimbursement for drugs that are not deemed safe and effective or cost-effective; and requiring prior approval of prescriptions so doctors will test the less expensive drug before prescribing the more expensive alternative.

Maine became the first state to pass a law, effective September 2003, regulating PBM operations. Under the law, PBMs were mandated to disclose the terms of their arrangements with drug manufacturers to the employers hiring the PBM. In some cases, disclosure would also be required to consumers. An association of major PBMs sued the State of Maine to enjoin the law from taking effect. Their contention was that drug companies would restrict the availability of discounts if the discounts had to be disclosed, and therefore the law would lead to higher prescription-drug prices. In March 2004, a preliminary injunction was issued in federal court, suspending the law's effective date. [Barbara Martinez, *Drug-Benefit Managers Win Round,* Wall Street Journal, Mar. 11, 2004, at p. D6] But the First Circuit upheld the law, finding it to be constitutional. The First Circuit held that the statute does not relate to ERISA plans and therefore is not preempted by ERISA. The law also does not impair ERISA's ultimate objective of creating nationwide uniformity in the administration of benefit plans. [*Pharmaceutical Care Management Ass'n v. Rowe*, 429 F.3d 294 (1st Cir. 2005); the statute is 22 Maine Rev. Stat. Ann. § 2699]

In response to major increases in prescription drug costs, some plans are moving toward two- or three-tier copayment systems, where participants pay the lowest percentage for generic drugs, the highest percentage for proprietary drugs that are not included in the plan's formulary, and an intermediate amount for proprietary drugs on the formulary. The "therapeutic focus" approach requires an especially high copayment for prescription drugs for which one or more OTC counterparts are on the market. Some plans require preauthorization for especially expensive drugs or drugs at high risk of abuse. Another option is excluding coverage of drugs prescribed for off-label uses (i.e., prescribing a drug for a condition other than the one the FDA has approved).

A 2003 First Circuit ERISA case was brought by a group of plaintiffs suing plan sponsors and a related nonprofit entity that provides prescription drug benefits. The plans impose fixed copayments, such as $5 per prescription. In some instances, the copayment is higher than the actual cost of the drug, although usually it's much less. The plaintiffs claimed that any excess of the copayment over the plan's cost for the medicine is wrongly taken from the plan's beneficiaries, contrary to the plan's terms and to fiduciary duty. However, the District Court and the First Circuit concurred: The plan provision was perfectly reasonable, and was fairly communicated to plan participants, so there was no violation of fiduciary duty. [*Alves v. Harvard Pilgrim Health Care Inc.*, 316 F.3d 290 (1st Cir. 2003)] See § 9.10 for discussion of the employer's role in providing prescription coverage for employees and retirees who are Medicare-eligible, after the Medicare Part D prescription drug program takes effect in 2006.

§ 18.06   DOMESTIC PARTNER BENEFITS, CIVIL UNIONS, AND SAME-SEX MARRIAGE

[A]   Current Trends

Not all employees fit neatly into the categories of "married" or "single." Some employees live with a domestic partner, whether in a nonmarital cohabitation relationship or with a same-sex partner. An increasing number of companies are offering health or other benefits to the unmarried domestic partners of employees.

The general rule is that the employer has discretion to offer—or refuse to offer—domestic partner benefits. The advantage is that the plan can be a powerful motivator; the disadvantages are cost, administrative complexity, and possible offense to employees and recruitment candidates who are offended by nonmarital relationships.

The federal Defense of Marriage Act means that self-insured plans are not required to recognize same-sex marriages. However, in a state that does not have a DOMA, a fully insured plan will be subject to state insurance regulation and may have to recognize same-sex marriages. Of those offering domestic partner coverage, over half (60%) had adopted the policy within the previous five years. Companies that do offer these benefits find that they are seldom used, for many reasons: for instance, domestic partners are usually employed and have benefits through their own employment, and employees are often wary of tax consequences if they do use domestic partner benefits. Two-thirds of employees who did use domestic partner benefits did so for a same-sex partner. Eighty-eight percent of the companies offering the benefit required proof of the nature of the relationship before granting benefits, and 73% would only grant benefits for a relationship that had lasted for at least a minimum duration. [Jessica Wohl, (Reuters) *More Firms Offer Partner Benefits-Survey*, Feb. 2, 2005 (Yahoo! News; law.com)]

As an additional difficulty, domestic partner benefits that are subject to federal tax are probably subject to state tax in a DOMA state, but probably would not be taxable in a non-DOMA state—especially one that recognizes same-sex marriage or domestic partnership. This disparity could create problems of reporting and for payroll accounting. Claims could also be raised by same-sex couples if the plan provides benefits for "spouses" but does not define the term, so it is probably a good idea to include a definition reflecting your company's policy—but only after consultation with your legal department and your insurer. If corporate policy to date has been to cover unmarried domestic partners because marriage is not an option for same-sex couples, you might wish to revise the policy either to require marriage as a condition of benefit eligibility or to clarify the status of cohabiting couples (same-sex or two-sex). Consideration must also be given to all the state laws in which a multi-state corporation operates.

It is possible that, in states and localities that forbid employment discrimination on the basis of sexual orientation, cases will be litigated claiming that domestic partners should receive the same benefits as married couples. It is likely that ERISA will preempt such claims. However, if the plan does not define "spouse," or does not limit it to male/female couples, or if domestic partners are explicitly included, then the employer may be required to cover the same-sex life partners of employees.

Plans that cover domestic partners use criteria such as:

- The partners are adults
- They are competent to enter into a contract.
- They are not married or in another domestic partnership.
- They intend their relationship to be long-term.
- They live together and/or combine their finances (e.g., through jointly owned property and joint accounts).

Such plans often require the employee-partner to submit affidavits of domestic partner status, and typically require that the relationship have lasted for a period of time, such as six months or a year, rather than permitting the immediate enrollment of a domestic partner.

A same-sex partner is not a "spouse" whose consent must be obtained before someone else can be named as beneficiary of a defined contribution or 401(k) plan, although the employer could add this requirement to the plan as an optional feature.

So far, there is no legal guidance as to whether giving effect to a "QDRO" covering a same-sex spouse would violate the anti-alienation rule.

The Social Security Act (SSA) uses a gender-based definition of "husband" and "wife." Although the SSA also says that the legality of a marriage is determined under state law (*see* 42 USC § 416(h)), the federal DOMA prevents same-sex spouses from receiving Social Security spousal benefits. DOMA probably also prevents the use of HSA funds on a pre-tax basis to pay medical costs for the employee's domestic partner, unless the domestic partner is also the employee's dependent. Domestic partners probably do not qualify for the HIPAA special enrollment period that applies when an employee marries. Especially in states that have laws recognizing domestic partnership or same-sex marriage, there may be laws requiring insurers to offer domestic partner coverage, or to make it available as an option on request. In contrast, Virginia insurance laws forbid domestic partner coverage. However, ERISA does not preclude an employer that wishes to cover same-sex spouses from amending its plan to do so.

Another coverage issue is whether plans that cover domestic partners should have provisions for determining when a domestic partnership has been terminated. California, Hawaii, and New Jersey law provide standards for this that can be adopted or adapted. Because of the DOMA, becoming a domestic partner or terminating a domestic partnership is not a change in status event permitting a change in cafeteria plan elections, nor is a court order governing distribution of same-sex partners' property a QDRO. [Laura Haltzel and Patrick Purcell, CRS Report for Congress, *The Effect of State-Legalized Same-Sex Marriage on Social Security Benefits and Pensions*, <http://benefitslink.com/articles/4s21897.pdf>; David N. Levine and Robert A. Imes, *Same-Sex Domestic Partner Benefits—Current Legal and Plan Drafting Issues*, <http://www.groom.com/files/articles/79.pdf>]

A state university's denial of health insurance benefits to the same-sex domestic partners of faculty members has been held to violate the Oregon state Constitution. *Tanner v. Oregon Health Sciences Univ.* [971 P.2d 435 (Ore. App. 1998)] holds that unmarried same-sex couples constitute a true class. They are not permitted to marry, and therefore discrimination against them represents unconstitutional discrimination on the basis of sexual orientation and not, as the university claimed, a distinction on the basis of marital status.

Montana ruled in late 2004 that it violates the state constitution's equal protection clause to provide health insurance to opposite-sex common-law spouses while denying benefits to same-sex domestic partners. The court found that it was discriminatory to draw the line based on an illusory difference in marital status, because common-law marriage depends on third parties' recognition that the relationship constitutes a "marriage," which could also be true of a same-sex relationship. [*Snetsinger v. Montana University System*, 325 Mont. 148, 104 P.3d 445 (Mont. 2004); a similar rationale was applied in *Alaska Civil Liberties Union v. State*, 122 P.3d 781 (Alaska 2005)]

According to the Southern District of New York, neither Title VII nor the Equal Pay Act is violated when a company grants domestic partner benefits to same-sex couples but denies them to unmarried heterosexual couples. [*Foray v. Bell Atlantic,* 56 F. Supp. 2d 327 (S.D.N.Y. 1999)] The court's rationale is that male-female couples who want access to family benefits have the option of getting married to secure them, whereas same-sex couples do not have this choice.

According to *Irizarry v. Chicago Board of Educ.* [251 F.3d 604 (7th Cir. 2001)], the practice of limiting domestic partner benefits to same-sex furthers the legitimate government interest of recruiting and retaining qualified employees who have same-sex life partners.

As of January 2006, Massachusetts was still the only state authorizing gay marriage (marriages could be solemnized only for state residents, not for those coming from other states to marry). There were domestic partnership or civil union statutes in California, Connecticut, Hawaii, Maine, New Jersey, and Vermont. Forty-one states had statutes defining marriage as a relationship between a man and a woman (Alaska, Arkansas, Arizona, California, Colorado, Delaware, Florida, Georgia, Hawaii, Idaho, Illinois, Indiana, Iowa, Kansas, Kentucky, Louisiana, Maine, Maryland, Michigan, Minnesota, Mississippi, Missouri, Montana, Nebraska, Nevada, New Hampshire, North Carolina, North Dakota, Ohio, Oklahoma, Pennsylvania, South Carolina, South Dakota, Tennessee, Utah, Vermont, Virginia, Washington, West Virginia, and Wyoming). (In January 2006, a judge found the Maryland statute unconstitutional, but it continued to be enforced.) In addition to family law statutes defining marriage, 19 states had language in their constitutions defining marriage as a relationship of one man and one woman (Alaska, Arkansas, Georgia, Hawaii, Kansas, Kentucky, Louisiana, Michigan, Mississippi, Missouri, Montana, Nebraska, Nevada, North Dakota, Ohio, Oklahoma, Oregon, Utah, Texas). The statutes or constitutions of a number of those states explicitly provide that same-sex marriage is a violation of public policy and/or deny recognition to same-sex marriages solemnized elsewhere.

The states of Connecticut, Massachusetts, New Jersey, New Mexico, New York, Rhode Island, and Wisconsin have neither a constitutional nor a statutory ban on same-sex marriage.

In states that recognize civil unions or domestic partnerships, insurers will probably be obligated to cover domestic partners as spouses. The laws of Maryland and Virginia permit, but do not require, spousal coverage for domestic partners. At one time, Virginia had a statute forbidding domestic partner insurance coverage, but it was amended, effective March 28, 2005, by 2005 Virginia Acts Chapter 871.

EBRI's March 2004 paper reports that ERISA preempts state laws that relate to employee benefits (other than state laws that regulate insurance). Therefore, ERISA preempts any requirement that Vermont civil unions would have to be treated as marriages for benefit purposes. However, state family leave benefits and Worker's Compensation are not under the jurisdiction of ERISA, so civil union partners must be treated as spouses for this purpose. Starting January 1, 2001, Vermont insurers were required to offer coverage to civil union participants if they offer coverage to married couples—but employers are not required to provide "spousal" coverage to civil union participants.

Under California Assembly Bill 25, when a couple files a Declaration of Domestic Partnership with the Secretary of State, the partners are treated as spouses, and domestic partner benefits are not subject to state tax.

New York City passed an Equal Benefits Law, mandating that contractors providing services to the city provide domestic partner benefits for their employees on par with benefits for spouses. The law was vetoed by New York City Mayor Bloomberg, who believed the bill would increase the cost of municipal contracts; the veto was overturned. San Francisco, Seattle, and Los Angeles already had similar statutes. The New York Supreme Court ordered the administration of New York City to enforce the Equal Benefits Law (the law mandating city contractors to provide domestic partner benefits). [Fred Schneyer, *NY Justice to Mayor: Enforce Domestic Partner Benefits Law,* PlanSponsor.com (Nov. 12, 2005)] Then, in February 2006, the state's highest court, the Court of Appeals, struck down the statute on the grounds that it impermissibly prescribed terms for ERISA plans. Although the U.S. Supreme Court recognizes a marketplace participant exception, it is limited to situations in which the state is not attempting to set policy. The statute is also preempted by the state's competitive bidding law because it has the effect of eliminating possible bid winners. [*Council of the City of N. Y. v. Bloomberg,* 2006 N.Y. LEXIS 149 (N.Y. Feb. 14, 2006) <http://www.courts.state.ny.us/ctapps/decisions/feb06/6opn06.pdf>]

In the view of the District Court for the District of Maine, ERISA preempts a local ordinance requiring an employer that receives certain types of housing and community development funds to provide coverage for employees' domestic partners. Plans maintained by Catholic Charities would normally be exempt, but the organization filed a form with the IRS opting into ERISA. [*Catholic Charities of Maine Inc. v. Portland, Maine,* 304 F. Supp. 2d 77 (D. Maine 2004)]

[B] Taxation of Domestic Partner Benefits

Under Treas. Reg. § 1.106-1, employees are not taxed on coverage provided to their spouse or dependents. However, there is no regulatory language about domestic partners. Therefore, unless the relationship is recognized by the state as spousal, or unless the domestic partner qualifies as a dependent under I.R.C. § 152(a)(8) (i.e., the employee domestic partner provides at least half the support for the other domestic partner), the employee will have taxable income equal to the value of the dependent coverage. However, if the cohabitation relationship is illegal under local law, I.R.C. § 152(b)(5) forbids treatment of the non-employee domestic partner as a dependent of the employee domestic partner.

If the non-employee domestic partner can be claimed as a dependent of the employee domestic partner, then the cost of domestic partner benefits is exempt from FICA and FUTA. But if the cost is taxable to the employee, both FICA and FUTA will apply in addition to income tax. Under Treas. Reg. § 1.61-21(b)(1), the gross income for the employee is the fair market value of the taxable fringe benefit, minus any amount the employee paid for it. Because the employee was taxed at the time the coverage was provided, neither the employee nor the domestic partner will be taxed if, for instance, health insurance or other reimbursement is provided later on.

In 2001, the IRS issued a Private Letter Ruling (PLR 20018010) stating that health plan coverage of a domestic partner who is the employee's dependent is not taxable to the employee, and is not subject to employment taxes. But if (as is usually the case) the domestic partner is not the employee's dependent, then the value of employer-provided domestic partner coverage is treated as wage income for the employee. Furthermore, I.R.C. § 152 now provides that a dependent must earn less than $3,100 (I.RC. § 151(d) exemption amount). So employers who choose to provide domestic partner coverage and receive certification that the partner is the employee's dependent must revise their forms to reflect the income test. [Carol V. Calhoun, *Working Families Tax Relief Act Affects Domestic Partner Benefits*, Employee Benefits Legal Resource Site, Oct. 29, 2004, <http://benefit sattorney.com/modules.php?name=News_file=article&sid . . . >]

Massachusetts published a Technical Information Release in mid-2004 explaining tax issues for same-sex couples. They can file either joint or separate state returns, but will still be single filers for federal tax purposes. A same-sex spouse who qualifies for federal head of household status will not so qualify for Massachusetts purposes, because that status requires being unmarried. If one same-sex spouse does not claim a personal exemption from his or her own employer, the other spouse can submit the M-4 (state withholding exemption certificate) to claim spousal exemption for state withholding purposes. The Adjusted Gross Income of both same-sex spouses is used to determine the eligibility for the state medical/dental expense deduction (which, like the federal, is limited to expenses in excess of 7.5% of AGI). All employee benefits that would be tax-exempt for state purposes when provided to a conventional spouse or children will also be tax-exempt if provided to a same-sex spouse. [*MA Tax Issues Associated With Same-Sex Marriage*, Massachusetts Technical Information Release 04-17 (July 8, 2004), <Commissioner@dor-domo.dor.state.ma.us>]

§ 18.07   TAX ISSUES IN EGHPS

For both the employer and the employee, the major EGHP tax issues fall under I.R.C. §§ 104–106. It is often in the best interests of both employer and employee for benefits to be provided under a plan of accident and health insurance (A&H). This result is desirable because the employer can deduct its costs of offering such a plan, and the employee does not have taxable income because the plan exists.

Section 104 provides that an employee does not have gross income when he or she receives A&H insurance benefits that the employee paid for, or that derive from employer contributions that have already been taxed to the employee. For years after 1996, amounts paid under other arrangements having the effect of A&H plans will be taxed as if they did, in fact, come from an A&H plan.

Section 105 provides that amounts an employee receives from an A&H plan are taxable if they are paid by the employer or stem from employer contributions not already taxed to the employee. If the employer reimburses medical expenses incurred by the employee for him- or herself and family, if the expenses would be deductible under I.R.C. § 213 (medical diagnosis and treatment, rather than cosmetic or experimental procedures), and if they have not already been deducted by the employee, then the employee has no gross income as a result of the medical expense reimbursement.

The employee can rely on I.R.C. § 105 to exclude amounts that were not received from an insurance policy, as long as they were received under a "plan." For this purpose, a plan is a structured arrangement—although it need not be legally enforceable or even written. The purpose of the plan must be to provide benefits to common-law employees (not independent contractors or self-employed persons) in the event of personal injury or sickness. If the plan is not legally enforceable, Treas. Reg. § 1.105-5 imposes the additional requirement that it be communicated to employees before they encounter any covered health expenses.

The third section of the trilogy, I.R.C. § 106, provides that employees do not have gross income if their employers provide them with A&H insurance.

Notice 2004-79, 2004-49 I.R.B. 898, provides guidance on WFTRA's effect on the I.R.C. § 106 exclusion of coverage under an accident and health insurance plan from the recipient's taxable income. Under I.R.C. § 152(c), as amended by WFTRA, a "qualifying child" is a person who satisfies relationship, residency, and age tests, and does not provide more than half of his or her own support. The age requirement is under 19, or under 24 and a full-time student, or permanently and totally disabled. I.R.C. § 152(d)(1) provides that a qualifying relative is a person who is not a qualifying child; has income below the exemption amount; and receives at least 50% of his or her support from the taxpayer. The value of coverage provided by the employer is taxable income if it benefits a person who is not a qualifying child and does not meet the income definition for a qualifying relative. Dependent status under I.R.C. § 105(b) is determined without reference to the amended I.R.C.§ 152(b) and § 152 (d), so the previous definition of "dependent" remains in effect.

Rev. Rul. 2002-3, I.R.B. 2002-316 (Dec. 12. 2001), disapproves a widely marketed tax avoidance scheme. Promoters of the scheme claim that the employer can reimburse employees for health insurance premiums they pay via pre-tax salary reduction, without creating taxable income for the employee, so that after-tax pay is the same as it would be if there had been no salary reduction and no reimbursement payments. For example, if an employee earns $800, and gets free health insurance, and if the employee's rate of income tax and FICA is 20%, then the employee's take-home pay would be $640 (80% of $800). The tax shelter scheme calls for imposing a $200 salary reduction on the employee's salary, so that his or her take-home pay becomes $480 (80% of $800 minus the $200 salary reduction), and then reimbursing the employee $160 for health insurance premiums. The employee then has the same amount of cash as the original after-tax amount, but the employer has saved $40 and paid a smaller FICA amount—which constitutes the motive for tax avoidance and the reason why the IRS disapproves of the plan.

The Revenue Ruling says that the salary reductions are actually insurance premiums paid by the employer, and therefore are excluded from gross income under I.R.C. § 106, and excluded form withholding under I.R.C. § 3401. However, the reimbursements are not excluded from income, because the employee has not actually paid a premium that the employer can reimburse. Nor are the amounts excluded under I.R.C. § 105, because they do not reimburse the employees for medical expenses. They are also subject to FICA and FUTA tax.

Rev. Rul. 2002-58, 2002-38 I.R.B. 451 covers a fact pattern in which an employer set up a self-insured medical expense reimbursement plan on December 1, effective retroactively as of January 1 of that year. Participating employees are eligible for reimbursement of expenses incurred by themselves, their spouses, and their dependents during the plan's calendar year. The employee in question became a participant as soon as the plan was established. Before the plan was established, the employee had incurred qualified medical expenses, and submitted claims in December, receiving reimbursement for pre-establishment expenses. The Revenue Ruling, citing cases such as *Wollenberg v. U.S.* [75 F. Supp. 2d 1032 (D. Neb. 1999)] holds that reimbursements for expenses incurred prior to the establishment of a plan are not excludible from gross income, because they cannot be paid or received under a plan before the plan was created.

Rev. Rul. 2003-62, 2003-25 I.R.B. 1034, provides that amounts that are distributed from a qualified retirement plan and used by the recipient to pay health insurance premiums under a cafeteria plan must be included in the recipient's gross income. This is also true of amounts distributed by a qualified retirement plan for direct reimbursement of medical expenses. This result follows from the principle that all distributions from retirement plans are taxable other than rollovers and net unrealized appreciation in the employer's own securities.

Regulations were proposed under § 4980G, the excise tax on employers who do not make "comparable" contributions to employees' HSAs. Although employers who have an HSA program do not have to make any contributions, if they contribute to any employee's HSAs, comparable contributions must be made for all "comparable participating employees." That is, HSAs cannot be "top hat" plans for executives only. The proposals makes it clear that HSA contributions made by independent contractors, sole proprietors, and partners are not taken into account for comparability rule purposes. The comparability rules are applied separately to three groups of employees: current full-time employees, current part-time employees, and ex-employees (other than those who retain coverage under the employer's HDHP because they have made a COBRA election). Thus, the comparability rules apply within a category only if the employer contributes to the HSA of any employee within the category. But the employer is not permitted to place unionized employees covered by a collective bargaining agreement in separate groups for comparability testing. Comparability is tested separately for HSAs and Archer MSAs, but if an employee has both types of account, the employer can contribute to only one, not both. If the employer makes HSA contributions through a cafeteria plan, the comparability rules do not apply—but the § 125 nondiscrimination rules, which serve a similar purpose, do apply. [70 Fed. Reg. 50233 (Aug. 26, 2005)]

§ 18.08   HEALTH-BASED DISCRIMINATION

On January 5, 2001, HHS, the PWBA, and the IRS jointly issued an interim final regulation on discrimination based on health factors. For questions and answers about the rule, *see* <http://www.dol.gov/ebsa/faqs/faq_hipaa_ND.html>. Note that whether a plan provision complies with HIPAA doesn't determine whether or not it violates the Americans with Disabilities Act (ADA).

The interim final rule implements I.R.C. § 9802/ERISA § 702 (added by HIPAA), which prohibits discrimination in health coverage. Group health plans and insurers are not allowed to discriminate against—or charge a higher premium to—individual participants or beneficiaries on the basis of any individual "health factor":

- Health status;
- Mental or physical condition;
- Claims experience;
- Past health care;
- Medical history;
- Genetic information;
- Disability;
- Insurability.

Group and self-insured plans must make coverage uniformly available to all similarly situated individuals, whether or not they have health factors. Restrictions on benefits must apply uniformly to all similarly situated individuals. Benefits can legitimately be limited or excluded in relation to a specific disease or condition, for certain types of drugs or treatments, or based on a determination that a procedure is experimental or is not medically necessary—just as long as all similarly situated individuals, not just those with health factors, are affected by the limitation.

The interim final rule says that modifying a plan to restrict benefits for the treatment of a condition for which an individual has already filed a claim violates HIPAA if the plan amendment takes effect before the beginning of the next plan year—unless there are other facts on record to show that the plan was changed for reasons independent of the claim.

"List billing" (using separate individual rates that vary by health factors in connection with a group health plan) is forbidden by the interim final rule, even if the employer absorbs the higher cost and does not pass them along to employees who have health factors. Underwriting can still be used to set group premiums, but the insurer must use claims experience as part of rate-setting for the group as a whole.

Employees can be placed in valid employment-based classifications consistent with the employer's usual business practices: e.g., full-time versus part-time employees, unionized and non-unionized, participants and beneficiaries, beneficiaries of full-time or part-time employees, and employees in different occupational classes or work locations. In fact, health benefits can differ by occupation or geographic location, even if this is based on health factors of the entire group. What is forbidden is taking individual health factors into account.

The general rule is that plans may not deny enrollment or increase premiums or copayments because a person is unable to engage in normal life activities. Permissible distinctions can be drawn between employees on the basis of the services that they render to the company.

Tip: It would not violate the interim final rule to offer benefit packages to current employees that are not available to COBRA "qualified beneficiaries," but it would violate COBRA. Both COBRA and the antidiscrimination rules allow the plan to impose a higher premium for COBRA coverage during the disability extension than during other COBRA election periods.

"Nonconfinement clauses" (provisions that deny eligibility to a participant or beneficiary who is hospitalized on the date coverage would otherwise become effective) are forbidden under the interim final rule. "Actively at work" clauses that deny coverage or raise copayments for people out sick on the day coverage would otherwise begin are also improper. However, the plan or insurer can legitimately require the individual to begin work before coverage actually becomes effective.

The interim final rule permits employers to provide more favorable treatment to people who have above-average health care needs. It is acceptable to extend the period of coverage for disabled former employees, or to cover a disabled dependent child who has reached an age at which dependent coverage would ordinarily terminate.

Certain plans are exempt from the interim final rule, such as benefits that are not covered by HIPAA (e.g., long-term care insurance); single-participant plans; and self-funded plans that elect under 45 C.F.R. § 146.180 to opt out of the non-discrimination requirements.

Employers are permitted to offer bona fide "wellness programs" (*see* 66 Fed. Reg. 1420 (Jan. 8, 2001) to encourage healthful behaviors. It is not considered discriminatory to offer incentives, such as discounts on premiums, and lower copayments to employees who, for example, quit smoking or take up exercise programs.

However, the Eighth Circuit ruled that it was not an abuse of discretion for an insurer to rescind a health insurance policy because when the applicant completed the EGHP enrollment form, he answered "No" to questions about past ailments. A few months later, after several doctor visits for respiratory problems, he was diagnosed with Chronic Obstructive Pulmonary Disease and cancer. The insurance was rescinded retroactive to its effective date for failure to fully disclose colds, a sinus infection, and bronchitis, which were deemed to be related to the COPD eventually diagnosed. [*Shipley v. Arkansas Blue Cross and Blue Shield,* 333 F.3d 898 (8th Cir. 2003)]

§ 18.09   HEALTH SAVINGS ACCOUNTS (HSAs) AND ARCHER MSAs

[A]   MSAs

In addition to imposing health insurance portability requirements, HIPAA enacted I.R.C. § 220, which adds a new type of health plan for taxable years that begin after December 31, 1996. The "Medical Savings Account" (MSA), started out as a small-scale pilot project for the years 1997–2000, designed to terminate once 750,000 accounts had been created. A limited number of individuals were permitted to open accounts that combine an IRA-like savings account (contributions are tax-deductible, within limits) with a high-deductible health insurance policy but no other health insurance coverage.

The MSA account is tax exempt as long as it remains an MSA. Account owners do not get a tax deduction when they withdraw funds from the account to pay medical expenses, because the contributions have already received favorable tax treatment. Funds taken from the account for any other purpose are not only taxable income but subject to a 15% excise tax.

IRS Announcement 99-95, 1999-42 I.R.B. 520, extended the MSA project. The Community Renewal Tax Relief Bill of 2000 (H.R. 5652), passed on December 15, 2000, renamed the account the Archer MSA (after Representative Bill Archer, Republican of Texas) and extended its lifetime for a further two years. Then the Job Creation and Worker Assistance Act of 2002 [Pub. L. No. 107-147], extended the availability of Archer MSAs until December 31, 2003.

	2003	2004	2005	2006
Individual Deductible	1,700–2,500	1,700–2,600	1,750–2,650	1,800–2,700
Family Deductible	3,350–5,050	3,450–5,150	3,500–5,250	3,650–5,450
Individual OOP Cap	3,350	3,450	3,500	3,650
Family OOP Cap	6,150	6,300	6,450	6,650

The version of IRS Publication 969 (Health Savings Accounts and Other Tax-Favored Plans) released for 2005 returns, <http://www.irs.gov/pub/irs-pdf/p969.pdf>, includes a discussion of the qualifications for participation, contribution limits, and participation rules for HSAs, health FSAs, and HRAs. Earlier editions dealt only with MSAs.

[B] HSAs Under MPDIMA

Division B of the Medicare Prescription Drug Improvement and Modernization Act of 2003 (MPDIMA; P.L. 108-173) is called the Health Savings
and Affordability Act of 2003. MPDIMA provides for two new kinds of accounts:
the Health Savings Security Account (HSSA) and the Health Savings Account
(HSA). *See* § 9.10 for a discussion of the effect of MPDIMA's Medicare
prescription drug plan on retiree health benefits and corporate accounting.

HSSAs are designed for uninsured persons or those who are covered only under
a high deductible plan. This discussion focuses on the employment-related HSA plan
structure, which is much easier to understand in the context of Archer MSAs and
other plans than when viewed in isolation. Starting January 1, 2004, individuals
under age 65 who have a qualified health plan can contribute to HSAs, with the
maximum contribution limited to the HDHP's deductible. The limit is increased for
persons aged 55-65, who are allowed to make catch-up contributions ($500 a year in
2004; increasing until it reaches $1,000 a year in 2009). If both spouses are 55 or
over, a married couple is allowed to make two catch-up contributions.

MPDIMA § 224 provides that for an eligible individual, there is a tax deduction
equal to the aggregate amount of cash paid to the HSA, subject to a monthly limitation. The monthly limitation is $1/12$ of the annual deductible of coverage under the
high deductible health plan (HDHP). Amounts paid to Archer MSAs, HSSAs, and
amounts paid for family members' HSAs are aggregated and subjected to the same
limits. Employees can deduct contributions they make to their HSAs even if they
take the standard deduction rather than itemizing deductions. [Treasury Dept Office
of Public Affairs JS-1045 *Treasury Secretary Snow Statement on Health Savings
Accounts* (Dec. 8, 2003) <http://treas.gov/press/releases/js1045.htm (no www) >]

An eligible individual is a person who is covered under an HDHP and is not
covered under any other health insurance plan that is not an HDHP and that
duplicates benefits offered by the HDHP. Coverage (through insurance or
otherwise) for accidents, disability, dental or vision care, or long-term care
constitutes "permitted insurance" that is disregarded in this context. In plans
with large deductibles (e.g., $1,000), some insurers make an exception and will
cover preventive care even before the deductible has been met so insured persons
won't skimp on necessary screenings. For HSAs, immunization, weight-loss programs, smoking cessation, routine prenatal and well-child care, periodic health
evaluations, and screening can be covered before the deductible has been met
without plan ceasing to be an HDHP. However, there is no insurance industry
standard for what is preventive. Doctors may fail to identify services as such,
and some of the services in a given visit may be included and some excluded
from the definition of "preventive services." [Sarah Rubenstein, *Care Quandary:
What's 'Preventive'?* Wall Street Journal, Aug. 24, 2005, at p. D4]

The HSA itself is a trust created exclusively for the purpose of paying the
qualified medical expenses of an eligible person. The term "qualified medical
expenses" has the same definition as in Code § 220(d)(2).

The trust must be drafted so that contributions (other than rollovers from another HSA or from an MSA or HSSA) can only be made in cash. All contributions must come either from the beneficiary or the beneficiary's employer, and contributions must not exceed the maximum set by MPDIMA. The statute forbids investing HSA trust assets in insurance contracts, and trust assets cannot be commingled with other property (except in a common trust fund or common investment fund). The HSA trustee must either be a bank or an insurance company or an individual who demonstrates that the trust will be administered in accordance with the MPDIMA requirements. As long as the trust continues to satisfy the HSA requirements, it is not a taxable entity.

For 2005, HDHP minimum deductibles for HSAs are unchanged; the maximum out-of-pocket amount (deductibles, copayments, and other amounts—but not premiums) rises to $5,100 for an individual, $10,200 for a family.

For 2006, the minimum deductible is $1,050 for an individual and $2,100 for family coverage; the out-of-pocket maximum is $5,250 for an individual and $10,500 for a family.

One reason HSAs are attractive is that they reduce the premiums that employers pay. According to the Kaiser Family Foundation, the average annual premium that an employer would pay for single coverage would be $3,413 per employee. However, an HDHP would cost the employer only $2,270 a year. For family coverage, the average for all plans is $8,167 a year and $6,245 a year for HDHPs.

HSAs also reduce payroll taxes for companies that adopt them, because employees' HSA contributions are typically exempt from FICA and FUTA. In a 1,000-employee company whose employees put $1.5 million into their HSAs in a year, the payroll tax reduction could reach $150,000—enough to cover the plan's administrative costs. Employers also get a tax deduction for the HSA contributions they make. In effect, the HSA could do the same thing for (or to) EGHPs that 401(k)s did for pensions. Instead of the employer having the responsibility and risk, much of the burden is transferred to employees. America's Health Insurance Plans reported that in early 2006 about three million people had HDHPs, and about a million of those had HSAs. [Theo Francis and Ellen E. Schultz, *Health Accounts Have Benefits for Employers,* Wall Street Journal, Feb. 3, 2006, at p. B1]

In mid-2004, the IRS released Model HSA trust and custodial account forms, 5305-B (trust account) and 5350-C (custodial account): <http://www.irs.gov/pub/irs-pdf/f5305b.pdf> and <http://www.irs.gov/pub/irs-pdf/f5305c.pdf>. [*See* Treasury Press Release JS-1748 (6/25/04), <http://www.treas.gov/press/releases/js1748.htm> (June 25, 2004)] IRS's Revised Notice 2004-50, 2004-33 I.R.B. 196 (July 23, 2004, revised August 9, 2004), provides that any insurance company or bank can serve as an HSA trustee or custodian; it doesn't have to satisfy the Internal Revenue Code definition of "life insurance company" or "bank."

If funds are paid or distributed out of an HSA, and are used to pay the account beneficiary's qualified medical expenses, they do not constitute taxable income for the beneficiary. However, amounts that are distributed but are used for other purposes not only constitute gross income for the employee, but are subject to a

15% excise tax penalty. The excise tax is waived if the distribution is made after the beneficiary's death; after the beneficiary becomes totally disabled; or after the beneficiary becomes eligible for Medicare.

On the compliance front, MPDIMA adds a new Code § 106(e) that states that an employer's contributions to an HSA are considered to be contributions under an Accident & Health plan. The employer's contributions are not subject to FICA or FUTA—but they must be shown on the employee's Form 1099. Failure to provide the mandated reports is penalized under Code § 6693(a). An employer that commits to making HSA contributions for employees, but fails to do so, is penalized under Code § 4980G.

MPDIMA specifies that a plan does not cease to be an HDHP merely because it does not impose the deductible on preventive care services. Nor does a PPO plan cease to be an HDHP if the annual deductible for out-of-network services is higher than the maximum that would otherwise be permitted, or if participants can encounter a higher out of pocket expense for out of network services than would be permitted otherwise.

In April 2004, the Department of Labor's Field Assistance Bulletin 2004-1 stated that HSAs are not subject to ERISA if participation in the plan is voluntary and the employer's role is limited. In that case, the DOL will treat the HSA as a personal savings arrangement controlled by the employee, and not as a group insurance arrangement. The presence of employer contributions does not always make the plan an ERISA welfare benefit plan, but excessive involvement by the employer (e.g., limiting the employee's ability to transfer funds between HSAs, imposing conditions on the use of HSA funds, accepting compensation in connection with the HSA, defining the HSA as a welfare benefit plan) can trigger ERISA coverage. On the other hand, an HDHP, which might be offered in connection with an HSA, will be treated as a welfare benefit plan unless it qualifies for an exemption (e.g., as a government or church plan). It should be noted that exemption from ERISA is not necessarily helpful to the employer, because it opens up the possibility that state-law claims will be asserted. [DOL Field Assistance Bulletin 2004-1 (4/7/04), <http://www.dol.gov/ebsa/regs/fab_2004—1.html> (Apr. 7, 2004)]

The problem, from the employees' point of view, is that HDHPs can have very negative financial effects. The Commonwealth Fund concluded that close to a quarter of low-income workers had to spend 5% or more of their income on out-of-pocket health expenses, and 40% of low-paid workers reported doing without a prescription, doing without a recommended medical test, or not seeing a doctor at all when they were sick. This was twice the percentage of higher-income workers who refrained from getting medical care for reasons of cost. The organization's research also showed that about half of adults insured by an HDHP experienced problems paying medical bills, or went into debt to do so—whereas only 31% of those with lower-deductible plans did so. HDHP owners were also more likely to have access problems in getting the care they need (38% in the HDHP group versus 27% of those with other insurance) and more likely to do without necessary treatment for reasons of cost. [Commonwealth Fund press release, *Half of Insured Adults With High-Deductible Health Plans Experience Medical Bill or Debt Problems* (Jan. 27, 2005), <http://www.cmwf.org/newsroom/ newsroom_show.htm?doc_id=257751>; Vanessa Fuhrmans, *Health-Care Cost Surge Set to Ease*, Wall Street Journal, Oct. 6, 2004, at p. A2]

Another issue is the role of states, because states are the primary regulators of health insurance and decide which insurers will be permitted to issue HDHPs. The IRS announced transition relief until 2006, when treatment incidental or ancillary to preventive care or medication to prevent disease will be permitted under an HDHP before the deductible is satisfied. After the transition period ends, an HDHP that covers prescription drugs with low or no deductible will not be eligible for use in conjunction with an HSA.

In some states, HSAs are limited or unavailable because of state-law problems. For example, in New York, HMOs are the only form available to individual purchasers. HSA HDHPs have to have a deductible of at least $1,000, but New York law won't allow HMOs to impose deductibles on services of in-network providers. Six other states have benefit mandates that interfere with the HSA minimum deductible, and five states (e.g., Illinois, Ohio, Missouri) have copayment requirements that conflict with HSA rules. Even if there's no legal problem, would-be HSA owners may not have easy access to a financial institution to serve as HSA custodian. [Sarah Lueck, *Legal Conflict*, Wall Street Journal, June 20, 2005, at p. R4]

The state-tax treatment of HSAs is still evolving. Areas still being considered include the relation of HSAs to state benefit mandates, high-risk pools, and whether MSA funds can be rolled over to an HSA.

In five states, HSA contributions are exempt from state income tax, all as a result of bills passed in 2005: Arkansas (H.B. 1064), Mississippi (S.D. 2633 and H.B. 1213), Nevada (S.B. 240), Oklahoma (H.B. 1848), and Pennsylvania (S.D. 300 and H.B. 107). Legislation was introduced in 2005 but failed to pass in a number of states (e.g., California, Illinois, Kentucky, Maine, Massachusetts, Michigan, Minnesota, Mississipi, New Jersey, Ohio, and Wisconsin). Alaska, Florida, South Dakota, Texas, Washington, and Wyoming don't have a state income tax.

Eleven states, including California, New Jersey, Pennsylvania, Kentucky, and Minnesota, explicitly make employees taxable on HSA contributions, but even at the maximum state tax rate and the maximum contribution, only a few hundred dollars would be involved. Therefore, a high-income account holder would still probably achieve federal tax savings that would make an HSA a more tax-favored investment than a 401(k). [Tom Anderson, *Eleven States Tax Health Savings Accounts*, Employee Benefit News, <http://www.benefitnews.com/ pfv.cfm?id=7378> (Apr. 15, 2005)]

Federal law about MSAs has a list of preventive care measures that are not subject to the deductible. However, some states require health plans to offer "first-dollar" coverage without a deductible for certain types of care, which can prevent high-deductible health plans getting licensed in those states. The federal HSA legislation included transition relief, so that state mandates in place on January 1, 2004, would not disqualify a plan as an HDHP until January 1, 2006. Several states (e.g., Arizona, California, Colorado, Indiana) adopted or introduced legislation to eliminate mandates so that HDHPs could be approved. However, North Dakota and Rhode Island added new "first-dollar" mandates in 2005 (mental health and substance abuse coverage for North Dakota; early intervention for developmentally disabled children for Rhode Island).

Some of the states that have high-risk pools for the medically uninsurable use HSAs to administer the plans; this is true of Alabama, Arkansas, Colorado, Idaho, Kentucky, Louisiana, Maryland, Minnesota, Missouri, Nebraska, and South Dakota. Several states (e.g., Florida, Iowa, Missouri, and South Carolina) have submitted proposals to the federal government to use HSAs as part of their Medicaid programs. [CAHI (Council for Affordable Health Insurance) HSA State Implementation Report, <http:.www.cahi.org>]

[C] IRS Guidance on MSAs and HSAs

Shortly after MPDIMA was passed, the IRS provided guidance in Notice 2004-2, 2004-2 I.R.B. 269.

Notice 2004-2 parallels the initial guidance about Archer MSAs. The Notice covers five issues: what an HSA is and who is eligible to have one; how to establish an MSA; making contributions; distributions from the HSA; and other issues. Although MPDIMA doesn't mention this point, the Notice says that HSAs can be either self-insured by the employer or insured by a commercial health insurer. It also says that HSAs are not subject to COBRA.

A person or entity that has already been approved as an IRA trustee, or the trustee for an Archer MSA, can serve as an HSA trustee without additional approval from the IRS. Any other would-be trustee (other than a bank) must apply under Reg. § 1.408-2(e). IRS Announcement 2003-54, 2003-40 I.R.B. 761 lists all non-bank trustees that had secured approval as of the date of the announcement.

The Notice provides that, for an individual who has family coverage, it is forbidden to make any distributions from the HSA (other than for preventive care) until the entire family deductible has been satisfied. Contributions to an HSA can be made either monthly or as a lump sum at any time before the tax return is due. But if part of the contribution is attributable to months when the individual was not eligible for the HSA, that part of the contribution can be subject to the excise tax penalty unless the plan returns those funds to the individual.

Q-4 of the Questions and Answers in the Notice says that a plan that would otherwise qualify as an HDHP can set the out-of-pocket expense limit for out-of-network services higher than the limit permitted for an HDHP; the same is true for the plan's deductible for out-of-network services. In other words, the limits are determined on the basis of the plan's coverage of in-network care.

Q-6 fleshes out the definition of "permitted insurance" that can be used to supplement the HDHP without the insured person losing HSA eligibility: insurance substantially all of whose coverage relates to worker's compensation, certain specified types of disease or illness insurance, coverage for tort claims, automobile insurance or other coverage relating to ownership or use of property, and insurance that pays a fixed amount per day or other period of hospitalization.

Neither the trustee nor the contributing employer is responsible for making sure that distributions from HSAs are used only for qualifying medical expenses. Because there are no substantiation rules for HSAs, the special substantiation rules of Notice 2003-43, 2003-28 I.R.B. 50, do not apply, although electronic payments cards can be used in conjunction with an HSA.

A family member who is an eligible individual can make contributions on behalf of another family member who is also an eligible individual. The eligible individual on whose behalf the contributions were made—and not the donor—gets the deduction. Although HSAs resemble Archer MSAs in many ways, contributions can be made on behalf of an eligible individual even if the contribution exceeds that person's compensation (or if he or she has no compensation). Anyone who can be claimed as a dependent on another taxpayer's return cannot be an eligible individual. [*See* Q-11, Q-12, and Q-18] Q-15 tackles the problem of coordination when both spouses have family coverage. For married persons, both are considered to have family coverage if either one does. If each has family coverage under a separate plan, both of them are considered to be covered under the plan with the lower deductible. The contribution limit for spouses is the lowest deductible amount, equally divided between the two unless they agree on a different division.

Q-17 clarifies that if an employee deducts an HSA contribution, he or she cannot also deduct the same amount as a Code § 213 medical expense.

Contributions for a tax year can be made in one or more payments at any time until the deadline for the eligible person's tax return for the year (the original deadline, without extensions)—usually that makes the last date to contribute April 15 of the following year. But contributions for a tax year can't be made before the beginning of the tax year.

Q-22 states that contributions made by the employer on behalf of an employee are included in the employee's gross income to the extent that they exceed the limits, or are made on behalf of someone who is not an eligible individual. Excess contributions made by either employers or employee are subject to an excise tax of 6% per year, unless they are removed by the due date for the tax return.

Even after the Notice, certain important questions remain unresolved. It's unclear how HRAs and Health FSAs can be integrated with HSAs. Some state laws require certain benefits other than preventive care to be covered without a deductible, creating possible qualification problems for HSAs in these states. Nor is it clear how to apply the nondiscrimination rules under Code § 125 to HSAs, although Q-32 says that an employer that makes HSA contributions must make comparable contributions on behalf of all comparable participating employees (eligible employees with comparable coverage). Contributions are comparable if they are made either in the same dollar amount or the same percentage of the HDHP deductible. Comparability is not required of amounts rolled over from an MSA or another HSA, or to contributions made through a cafeteria plan.

Comparability testing is done separately for part-time workers—defined as those who are customarily employed for under 30 hours a week.

Speaking of rollovers, Q-23 provides that although the general rule is that HSA contributions must be made in cash, rollover contributions can be in other forms (e.g., stock) if they come from an Archer MSA or another HSA. Nor does the contribution limit apply to these rollovers. However, rollovers from an IRA, HRA, or FSA to an HSA are not allowed. [The News release is at <http://www.ustreas.gov/press/releases/js1061.htm>]

In March 2004, the IRS issued four further pronouncements on HSAs:

- Rev. Rul. 2004-38, 2004-15 I.R.B. 717 clarifies the interaction of HSAs with other health plans. A person is not an "eligible individual" who can have an HSA if the person is covered by both an HDHP and any other insurance plan, unless the second plan fits the definition of "permitted insurance" or "permitted coverage." More specifically, this ruling says that a person who has an HDHP that does not cover prescription drug benefits, and also has a separate prescription drug plan or rider, that person will not be an "eligible individual"—unless the separate prescription coverage is itself in the form of an HDHP.
- But see Rev. Proc. 2004-22, 2004-15 I.R.B. 727, permitting transition relief (only for the months prior to January 1, 2006) for an individual who has both an HDHP and a separate prescription drug plan or rider that offers drug benefits until the HDHP's minimum annual deductible has been satisfied. Such an individual will be an eligible individual for this brief period. The IRS adopted this position because plans do not have much time to coordinate their provisions with the MPDIMA requirements for HSAs.
- Notice 2004-23, 2004-15 I.R.B. 727 offers guidance for implementation of the Code § 223(c)(2)(C) safe harbor, under which HDHPs can offer preventive care benefits without imposing the normal high deductible—even if no deductible is imposed on preventive care at all. This is a permissive rather than a mandatory provision. There is no federal requirement that plans provide preventive care benefits at all, although there may be state mandates that apply to the plan. In this context, preventive care means, e.g., periodic health evaluations; screening; immunizations; programs for quitting smoking; weight loss programs; and routine prenatal and well-child care. However, services or benefits for the treatment of an existing illness, injury or condition do not constitute preventive care.
- Notice 2004-2 stated that expenses would be qualified only if they were incurred after the HSA was established, not those already owed before the HSA was set up. Notice 2004-2 permitted an employee to continue to use HSA funds for qualified expenses after he or she ceased to be qualified to make additional contributions to the account.

Further transition relief was provided under Notice 2004-43, 2004-27 I.R.B. 10, permitting HSA contributions for months prior to January 1, 2006, even if the HDHP associated with the HSA provided benefits before the taxpayer satisfied the annual deductibles—if those benefits were provided as a result of a state mandate.

The lengthy (88 Q&As!) Notice 2004-50, 2004-33 I.R.B. 196, provides guidance on additional issues. Q-1 says that an employee offered a choice between a low-deductible plan and an HDHP is eligible for an HSA if he or she elects coverage only under the HDHP, because the test is actual coverage rather than coverage potentially available.

A person who is eligible for Medicare but not yet enrolled is eligible to maintain an HSA, but can no longer make HSA contributions once he or she actually enrolls; prior to enrollment, a Medicare-eligible person can make catch-up contributions under I.R.C. § 223(c)(1)(Q-2,3). Someone who is covered under TRICARE, the military health plan, is not eligible to have an HSA (Q-6). The general rule is that benefits for "permitted insurance" under I.R.C. § 223(c)(3) must be provided under insurance contracts rather than self-insurance. Q-8 makes an exception for benefits such as Worker's Compensation that are mandated by statute and provide secondary or incidental medical care benefits; such benefits are considered to be permitted insurance even if they are self-insured.

Q-9 of Notice 2004-50 says that discount cards for products or services do not rule out HSA participation if the cardholder is required to pay the (reduced) costs of the products or services until the HDHP deductible is satisfied. Employee Assistance Programs, disease management programs, and wellness programs do not preclude HSA participation (Q-10). Even a state high-risk insurance pool can qualify as an HDHP if its benefits are not triggered below the minimum annual deductible for HDHPs (Q-13). HDHPs can impose lifetime limits on benefits under the plan, as long as the limit is reasonable. Payments made by a person who has exhausted the lifetime limit are not treated as out-of-pocket expenses with respect to the annual out-of-pocket maximum, but Q-14 says that a lifetime limit is not reasonable if it is designed to circumvent I.R.C. § 223(c)(2)(A)'s maximum annual out-of-pocket amount.

It is reasonable to limit benefits to the usual, customary, and reasonable charge for those services (Q-16), and therefore amounts that a patient must pay over and above the usual, customary, and reasonable charge are not included toward the maximum out-of-pocket amount. Q-19 tackles a question that is also affected by Notice 2004-2, 2004-2 I.R.B. 269, stating that if the plan imposes 10% coinsurance on medical bills after the deductible has been satisfied, but 20% coinsurance if the patient failed to obtain pre-certification for consulting a specific provider (or consults an out-of-network provider), the extra 10% does not count toward the out-of-pocket maximum.

Treatment of a related condition during preventive care or screening (e.g., removing polyps during a diagnostic colonoscopy) still falls within the preventive-services safe harbor (Q-26). Drugs also fall under the preventive care safe harbor if they are prescribed to prevent disease based on risk factors, but not if they treat disease that has already manifested itself (Q-27).

Q-28 clarifies that any person, including an employer and a family member, can make HSA contributions on behalf of an eligible person; there is no requirement that the account owner contribute all the funds to the account. HSA contributions (except for catch-up contributions) on behalf of a married person are divided equally between the spouses unless they agree on a different division (Q-32)—but they can allocate the contributions however they want, including all to one spouse. Q-36 provides that if an account beneficiary's spouse or dependents are covered under an insurance policy that is not an HDHP, distributions from the HSA for their qualified medical expenses do not constitute gross income for the account beneficiary.

Although the general rule is that long-term care insurance premiums cannot be paid out of a cafeteria plan, Q-40 says that the account beneficiary can use HSA distributions to pay LTCI premiums even if the HSA is funded by cafeteria plan salary reductions, because the HSA rather than the LTCI is "offered" under the cafeteria plan. Note, however, that Q-41 provides that I.R.C. § 213(d)(1) limits on deductibility of LTCI premiums restrict the size of the distribution that can be excluded from income as an HSA-qualified medical expense. Q-42 says that distributions from an HSA used to purchase long-term care services are qualified medical expenses and thus are excluded from the taxpayer's gross income. However, payments for long-term care made from an FSA are included in gross income.

A retiree who is 65 or older can receive tax-free distributions from an HSA to pay his or her contribution toward self-insured retiree health coverage (Q-43). A Medicare-eligible retiree's use of HSA funds to reimburse Medicare premiums that were deducted from his or her Social Security benefit is a qualified medical expense (Q-45).

Only one rollover contribution to an HSA can be made during any one-year period, and the funds must be paid over to the HSA within 60 days of receipt. But, as with IRAs, trustee-to-trustee transfers don't count, and can be made as often as the account holder directs (Q-55, Q-56).

Although an eligible individual can have multiple HSAs and contribute to more than one (subject to the maximum contribution limit), a married couple cannot have a joint HSA. Each spouse must have a separate HSA, which can have only one account beneficiary (Q-63, Q-64).

The permissible investments for an HSA are the same as for an IRA, so bullion and coins are permissible investments, but life insurance contracts and collectables are not. The trust document or custodial agreement is permitted to restrict investments, for example, to certain designated investment funds (Q-65). Reasonable investment restrictions can also be imposed, such as the minimum size and maximum frequency of contributions that will be accepted (say, only $X per month, or requiring a contribution of at least $50) (Q-80).

Q-81 explains that the employer's only responsibilities are to determine:

- If the employee is eligible to maintain an HSA
- His or her maximum contribution

- Whether or not the employee is covered by an HDHP and, if so, the amount of the deductible
- The employee's age (to see if he or she is entitled to make catch-up contributions, employers are legally entitled to rely on birthdates as provided by employees)

If a bank or insurer contributes cash credits as an incentive to open an HSA account, that does not constitute a prohibited transaction for ERISA or tax purposes. EBSA's advisory opinion on the topic covers two scenarios. In the first, an insurer offered both HSAs and HDHPs to individuals. In the second, the insurer provides group HDHPs and also has a contract with a bank that provides HSAs to persons covered by the HDHPs. The incentive contribution was $100 credit in the HSA; there was no way for the individual to divert the contribution before it was placed into the HSA. EBSA ruled that (unless the HSA in the second scenario is an ERISA Title I plan) there is no prohibited transaction because the cash contribution is not a prohibited sale or exchange of property, a transfer of assets for the benefit of a disqualified person, or self-dealing by the bank or insurer. [EBSA Advisory Opinion 2004-09A, <http://www.dol.gov/ebsa/regs/aos/ao2004-09a.html>, Dec. 22, 2004]

IRS Regulations were proposed in August 2005 that cover comparability rules for employer contributions to HSAs, with exceptions when the employer contributions are made through a cafeteria plan. [Prop. Treas. Reg. §§ 54.4980G-1 through 54.4980G-5 (Aug. 26, 2005) <http://www.irs.gov/pub/irs-regs/13864704.pdf>]

[D] Plan Comparisons

Given the variety of plan options under the Internal Revenue Code and ERISA, it's understandable that confusion often reigns when it comes to deciding which plans should be offered to employees and how to administer them in compliance with all the relevant rules. (*See* § 18.10 below for Medical Expense Reimbursement Plans, § 18.11 for Flexible Spending Accounts (FSAs), and § 18.18 for Health Reimbursement Arrangement (HRA) plans.

The broad distinction between an HRA and an HSA is that HRAs are solely funded by employer contributions and can be used for qualified medical expenses and premiums designated by the employer. Funds also can carry over from year to year. HSAs are tax-exempt trusts or custodial accounts. Contributions are deductible and are not taxable income for the employee if they are made by the employer or made by the employee in the form of pre-tax salary reduction contributions. Any employer can sponsor either type of plan. However, self-employed persons, including partners and owners of more than 2% of the shares in a Sub S corporation, cannot participate on a tax-favored basis in these plans.

Under Notice 2004-50, HSA-permitted insurance benefits have to be provided through contracts and not self-insured; however, self-insurance is permissible for secondary benefits (e.g., Worker's Compensation) that are incidental to other benefits. Rev. Rul. 2004-23, 2004-11 I.R.B. 585, says that a prescription drug program is not considered permitted insurance.

HRAs are welfare benefit plans, so ERISA requirements for written plan documents and fiduciary conduct must be followed. SPDs also are required, and Form 5500 must be filed unless there is a small plan or other exemption available. DOL Field Assistance Bulletin, No. 2004-1, says that HSAs are not generally welfare benefit plans if the employer's involvement is limited (the employee pays the full premium; participation is voluntary).

Notice 2002-45, 2002-28 I.R.B. 93, allows an employee to participate in both an HRA and a health FSA in the same year. If both can cover a particular expense, the HRA has to pay it first unless the HRA plan makes the FSA responsible. It should be noted that Rev. Rul. 2004-45 does not allow participation in a health FSA, HRA, and HSA at the same time unless the FSA and/or HRA are allowed only to reimburse dental, vision, and preventive care costs.

HSA contributions must be made in cash (Notice 2004-2, 2004-2 I.R.B. 269) and can be made by the employee, employer, a family member, or other third party. [Notice 2004-50, 2004-33 I.R.B. 196] Notice 2004-2 also provides that HSAs can be invested in any vehicle that would be permitted for an IRA (i.e., life insurance and collectables are not allowable investments). Notice 2004-50 also provides that administrative and account maintenance fees paid, directly to the trustee or custodian of the account, by the account holder or employer are not counted toward the maximum contribution. However, contributions (even catch-up contributions) cannot be made in or after the month in which the account holder enrolls in Medicare.

HRA contributions are subject to forfeiture, but HSA contributions are not. Therefore, HSA balances can be rolled over tax-free to another HSA. MSA funds can also be rolled over into an HSA. However, IRA, HRA, and Health FSA amounts cannot be rolled over to an HSA. Notice 2004-2 says that HSA owners can take distributions at any time, and the trust or custodial agreement cannot restrict distributions to medical expenses. The owner can take the distribution for any reason, although distributions that are not used for medical care are included in gross income and are subject to a 10% penalty unless the distribution was taken after disability, death, or attainment of Medicare eligibility.

The employer determines what an HRA can reimburse and when. The claims procedure, to which the participant is bound, must be set out in the SPD and satisfy ERISA § 503. A withdrawal to reimburse qualified medical expenses is not considered gross income (*see* §§ 105–106), but if any amount can be taken from an HRA in cash or other taxable or nontaxable benefits, Notice 2002-45 makes all HRA benefits taxable. Furthermore, if an HRA is cashed out upon the participant's death, the HRA program is disqualified and all its participants are subject to tax.

The employer has the power to design the program in an HRA and therefore has the right to place restrictions on withdrawals. The employer cannot restrict HSA withdrawals, but Notice 2004-50, 2004-33 I.R.B. 196, allows a trustee or custodian to impose reasonable restrictions, such as a certain number of distributions per month. However, the trust or custodial agreement cannot restrict the account owner's ability to roll over or transfer amounts from the HSA. The owner of the account (not the trustee or custodian) has the burden of maintaining records to prove that distributions were taken for qualified medical expenses.

If the employer designs the program to reimburse for qualified medical expenses, HRA owners can receive reimbursement from the account after termination of employment even if the employee does not make a COBRA election. The employer can set requirements (e.g., age and service) for reimbursement after termination. HSAs are inherently portable and non-forfeitable.

COBRA and HIPAA apply to HRAs because they are considered EGHPs. COBRA does not apply to HSAs. [*See* Notice 2004-2, Q&A 35] HIPAA applies to HSAs if, and only if, they are ERISA welfare plans.

After the participant dies, survivors can withdraw the balance if the HRA is designed that way, and HRA coverage can be continued if the survivor is a COBRA-qualified beneficiary. For HSAs, if the survivor is the named beneficiary, the HSA becomes the survivor's HSA and the balance qualifies for the marital deduction. Notice 2004-2 Q&A 31 provides that the surviving spouse does not have gross income in this situation. But if the HSA passes to a named beneficiary other than the spouse, § 223(f)(8) provides that the account ceases to be an HSA as of the date of death. The beneficiary has gross income equal to the FMV of the HSA's assets as of the date of death, minus any amount used in the year after the death to pay qualified medical expenses incurred by the decedent. If no beneficiary has been designated, the account ceases to be an HSA as of the date of death, and the FMV of assets is included in the decedent's gross income in the year of the death—even if, in fact, the account passes to the surviving spouse as distributee.

HRAs are subject to the nondiscrimination requirements under § 105(h) and therefore must benefit at least 70% of all employees or 80% of eligible employees. HCEs also cannot receive greater benefits. HSAs that contain only employee contributions are not subject to nondiscrimination requirements. However, if the HSA is funded by pre-tax salary reductions under a cafeteria plan, Notice 2004-50, Q&A 47 applies the § 125 nondiscrimination rules. If the employer contributes to employees' HSAs, § 2980G mandates that the contributions be comparable.

An HRA cannot be transferred to another person while the owner is alive, but § 223(f)(7) permits HSAs to be transferred pursuant to a divorce or separation agreement, with the ex-spouse becoming the new owner. The distribution is not taxable to either spouse and is not subject to the 10% penalty on premature withdrawals. [Chicago Consulting Actuaries, *HRAs or HSAs, How Does an Employer Decide?* (Nov. 9, 2005) (benefitslink.com); originally published in the Journal of Deferred Compensation (Aspen), Winter 2005)]

In mid-2005, CMS published guidance about which of the "account-based group health plans" (FSAs, HRAs, Archer MSAs, and HSAs) count as "creditable coverage" for which employers can claim the prescription drug plan subsidy. (*See* Chapter 9 for more discussion.) According to CMS, FSAs are nearly always not creditable coverage because their actuarial value is so hard to determine (because it is unpredictable how much employees will contribute and how much of that will be spent on drugs). HRAs are creditable under certain circumstances, and employers can count their HRA contributions in the calculation of actuarial equivalence. However, contributions by retirees to HRAs (through COBRA, for example) must be deducted when the employer calculates actuarial equivalence. People who are eligible for Medicare are not allowed to contribute to Archer MSAs or HSAs; these plans are therefore not creditable coverage for MPDIMA purposes. As a result, FSAs, Archer MSAs, and HSAs are not required to send notices of creditable coverage (because their coverage is not creditable under any circumstances); however, HRAs must provide the notice to inform participants if their coverage is creditable or not. [CMS, *Treatment of Account-Based Health Arrangements Under the Medicare Modernization Act*, <http://www.cms.hhs.gov/medicareform/pdbma/employer.asp>, discussed in Segal Bulletin, *Treatment of Account-Based Health Arrangements Under the MMA: CMS Guidance*, <http://www.segalco.com/publications/bulletins/july05<Usguidance.pdf> (July 2005). Segal has also summarized the guidance on its own site, <http://www.segalco.com/publications/presentations/accounts.pdf>]

Rev. Rul. 2004-45, 2004-28 I.R.B. 33, provides guidance as to the interaction of various plan forms by explaining when someone who is covered by an HDHP and also by a health FSA or HRA can make an HSA contribution. The ruling covers five scenarios.

In the first, the taxpayer has an HDHP imposing 20% coinsurance after the deductible has been satisfied and also has a health FSA under a cafeteria plan and an HSA that complies with Notice 2002-45, 2002-28 I.R.B. 93. The FSA and HRA pay or reimburse whatever I.R.C.§ 213(d) medical expenses the taxpayer encounters that are not covered by the HDHP; benefits are coordinated as required by Notice 2002-45. The second scenario has the same facts, except that the FSA and HRA are limited-purpose for vision and dental care, and also provide preventive care benefits as described by Notice 2004-23, 2004-15 I.R.B. 725.

The third scenario is the same as the second, but there is no FSA and under the HRA, the taxpayer elects to forgo payment or reimbursement of medical expenses other than "excepted medical expenses" as defined by I.R.C. § 223(c)(1)(B). The fourth has the same fact pattern as the first, but the FSA and HRA only pay or reimburse medical expenses after the HDHP's minimum annual deductible has been satisfied. In the fifth and final scenario, the fact pattern is the same as in the first but there is no FSA and the HRA only reimburses medical expenses incurred after retirement.

I.R.C. § 223(c)(1)(B) allows certain coverage to be disregarded when calculating whether the HDHP deductible has been satisfied: "permitted insurance" and "permitted coverage." The term "permitted insurance" refers to Worker's Compensation, tort liability, property insurance, and policies that are limited to a specific disease or illness (e.g., cancer) or pay a fixed amount per day of hospitalization. "Permitted coverage" (which can but doesn't have to be provided by insurance) means accident disability, dental care, vision care, or long-term care.

Notice 2002-45 defines a tax-favored HRA as one that is solely paid for by the employer; is not furnished under a cafeteria plan; and provides reimbursement for medical care expenses up to a maximum dollar amount, with unused surpluses carrying over to the following year. Health FSAs and HRAs are considered "other coverage" under I.R.C. § 223(c)(1)(A)(ii), with the result that a person with an FSA or HRA generally will not be an eligible individual for HSA purposes. A spouse's coverage (e.g., under an FSA that covers family members) can also prevent the other spouse from being HSA-eligible.

Furthermore, Rev. Rul. 2004-38, 2004-15 I.R.B. 717, says that a person who has a high-deductible health plan without prescription drug coverage, plus a separate prescription drug plan or rider that provides benefits before the deductible has been satisfied, is not an HSA-eligible individual. The deductible for the HRA or FSA need not be the same as the deductible for the HDHP, as long as the employee cannot receive any coverage until he or she has paid the HDHP deductible out of pocket. If the deductibles are different, contributions to the HSA are limited to the lower deductible. A limited-purpose Health FSA or HRA does not rule out HSA eligibility, nor does a suspended HRA—until the suspension ends.

If an HSA is funded by cafeteria plan salary reductions, the salary reduction election must indicate that the reduction goes only to the HSA offered in conjunction with the HRA, and not to the HRA itself.

Employees are not entitled to have the same expense reimbursed by more than one plan but, subject to the ordering rules in Notice 2002-45, an FSA or HRA can pay or reimburse an expense as long as the individual certifies to the employer that the expense has not yet been reimbursed and the employee will not seek reimbursement under any other plan.

§18.10 MEDICAL EXPENSE REIMBURSEMENT PLANS

Maintaining a medical expense reimbursement plan is yet another option employers have to coping with employees' health care needs. The plan must cover employees, although it is not a legal requirement that it cover all employees. The plan can be informal. There is no legal requirement that the plan be in writing, unless it is an "welfare benefit plan" for ERISA purposes. In any case, employees must be given reasonable notice of the plan's existence and of how it operates.

Medical expense reimbursement plans usually reimburse employees directly for their medical expenses. Payment comes from the employer's resources, not from an insurance policy. Usually, the plan sets a maximum: e.g., only claims of $X per year will be covered. The plan can also be coordinated with insurance, so that the employer pays up to a certain amount, with insurance covering the rest.

For tax purposes, the most important question is whether the plan shifts risk to a third party (other than the employer and employee). A plan that uses a third- party administrator (TPA) to handle administrative or bookkeeping services does not shift risk to the TPA. The employer's costs of maintaining a self-insured plan will probably be deductible, as ordinary and necessary business expenses.

Internal Revenue Code § 105(h) governs self-insured medical expense reimbursement plans—those whose benefits are not payable exclusively from insurance. Plans of this type must satisfy coverage and nondiscrimination tests to qualify:

- The IRS issues a determination letter stating that the plan is nondiscriminatory;
- The plan covers at least 70% of all employees;
- At least 70% of all employees are eligible for the plan, and 80% or more of the eligible employees are actually covered.

However, the plan need not count employees who are younger than 25 years old, those who have been working for the company for less than three years' service, part-time or seasonal employees, or employees covered by a collective bargaining agreement that made accident and health benefits the subject of good-faith bargaining.

The plan is not discriminatory if the benefits provided for highly compensated employees (HCEs) and their dependents are also provided for other employees. The plan can impose a dollar maximum on the benefits paid on behalf of any individual, but cannot set the maximum at a percentage of compensation, because that would improperly favor HCEs.

If a self-insured medical reimbursement plan is discriminatory, then the HCEs (but not the rank-and-file employees) will have taxable income equal to the employer's plan contributions on their behalf. If taxable income does result from a self-insured medical expense reimbursement plan, the income will be subject to income tax withholding, but not to FICA or FUTA. [*See* I.R.C. § 3121(a)(2)(B)]

§ 18.11   FLEXIBLE SPENDING ACCOUNTS (FSAs)

[A]   Generally

An FSA is an arrangement under which an employer diverts some cash compensation into a separate account, which must be identified for specific use: either for dependent care expenses, or for medical expenses that are not reimbursed by insurance or directly by the employer.

The amount that can be placed into a dependent care FSA is limited by the Internal Revenue Code's limits on deductible dependent care expenses. Funds targeted for medical care cannot be used for dependent care, and vice versa. A medical expense FSA must last at least twelve months, although a short first year, when the plan is initially adopted, is allowed. Premiums for other health coverage cannot be reimbursed by the FSA.

An FSA can either be part of a cafeteria plan or a separate plan. Stand-alone FSAs are subject to the same nondiscrimination rules as cafeteria plans.

IRS regulations define an FSA as a benefit program that reimburses an employee for specified, incurred expenses. The maximum amount of reimbursement that can be made "reasonably available" to a participant during a period of coverage is limited to 500% of the total premium for the coverage. FSA reimbursement must be made available at least monthly, or when the level of expenses reaches a reasonable minimum amount such as $50.

To receive reimbursement, the FSA participant must submit a written statement from an independent third party (such as the doctor or medical office administrator) to confirm that a medical expense of $X has been incurred, and that this expense was neither reimbursed by nor eligible for reimbursement under any other plan.

Pre-2005 law required all FSA plans (stand-alone or in cafeteria plans) to operate on a "use it or lose it" basis. In other words, if an employee puts $3,000 into a medical expense FSA, but has only $1,000 in unreimbursed medical expenses, the other $2,000 is forfeited. Forfeitures can be refunded to the participants as a whole, based on a reasonable and uniform method of allocation, based on the amount of contributions to the plan, but not based on reimbursement from the plan. Unofficial IRS statements hint that forfeitures can be used to pay the plan's administrative expenses, or can be returned to participants pro rata. Some relief was provided by IRS Notice 2005-42, 2005-23 I.R.B. 1204. Employers now have the option of amending their plan no later than the end of a plan year, to provide that employees have 2½ months after the end of that plan year to seek payments or reimbursement from the FSA for expenses incurred during the plan year. The general "use it or lose it" rule remains in the Tax Code, but there is a grace period. Cafeteria plans are not permitted to cash out unused benefits during the grace period, nor may they convert them to any other type of benefit (whether or not the benefit is taxable).

Notice 2005-85, 2005-46 I.R.B. 961, explains who is eligible to make HSA contributions during the type of cafeteria plan grace period described in Notice 2005-42, 2005-23 I.R.B. 1204. A health FSA participant who is covered by the grace period is generally barred from making an HSA contribution until the first day of the first month after the end of the grace period. (Limited-purpose FSAs, which are limited to preventive, dental and vision care, and post-deductible FSAs, which provide reimbursement only after the HDHP deductible has been satisfied, are exempt from this ban.) However, cafeteria plans can be amended to make an FSA limited purpose or post-deductible during each grace period, so that health FSA participants will also be HSA-eligible during the grace period. Note that, even if the FSA has reached its limit, an employee covered under an FSA grace period cannot contribute to an HSA for the same time period. [Notice 2005-86, 2005-49 I.R.B.]

An FSA (or an HRA or other employer-provided health plan) is permitted by Rev. Rul. 2003-102, 2003-38 I.R.B. 559, to reimburse employees for over-the-counter drugs. Such reimbursement will not have to be included in the employee's gross income for tax purposes as long as the OTC medication is used to treat or alleviate sickness or injuries of the employee or employee's dependents. The ruling uses the examples of antacids, allergy medications, and pain relievers. However, vitamins and dietary supplements that are merely beneficial to promoting general health don't qualify for this treatment.

A taxpayer wrote to the IRS asking the agency to change its policy, so that the rental cost of an electric breast pump could be reimbursed by a health FSA, given the importance of breastfeeding to infant health. A Treasury official responded that health FSA funds can be used only for medical care. Breast pumps are beneficial to general health, but are not used for medical treatment, so FSA funds cannot be used. [Treasury Tax Correspondence, 2004 TNT 118-51 (June 8, 2004) and 2004 TNT 103-23 (Nov. 12, 2003)]

Under Rev. Rul. 2003-43, 2003-21 I.R.B. 935, a plan that is a combined FSA and Health Reimbursement Account will be permitted to make electronic reimbursements of medical expenses (for instance, by issuing credit or debit cards that can be used to pay for health care). As long as the plan includes safeguards to make sure that only permitted medical expenses are reimbursed, the plan will not result in taxable income for participants.

[B] HIPAA Exemption for FSAs

In 1997, the IRS, the Department of Labor's Pension and Welfare Benefits Administration (renamed EBSA), and the Department of Health and Human Services joined to publish a "clarification of regulations" that appears at 62 Fed. Reg. 67688 (Dec. 29, 1997).

Under this document, health insurance portability is not required for certain health FSAs, because they rank as "excepted benefits" under ERISA §§ 732 and 733(c) and I.R.C. §§ 9831 and 9832(c).

According to this document, a health FSA is a "benefit program that provides employees with coverage under which specified, incurred expenses may be reimbursed (subject to reimbursement maximums and any other reasonable conditions) and under which the maximum amount of reimbursement that is reasonably available to a participant for a period of coverage is not substantially in excess of the total premium (including both employee-paid and employer-paid portions of the premium) for the participant's coverage." FSAs usually cover medical expenses excluded by the primary EGHP.

An FSA is not "creditable coverage" subject to the HIPAA portability requirements if the employee's maximum FSA benefit for the year is not greater than twice the employee's salary reduction election under the FSA for the year, as long as the employee has other EGHP coverage, and as long as the FSA provides at least some benefits that are not "excepted benefits."

§ 18.12   EGHP STRUCTURES

Originally, indemnity plans were the standard; now, that role is held by managed care plans of various types. Within the managed care category, HMOs were once dominant, but now must share the spotlight with other plan forms that offer greater choice of health care providers. Recently, attention has been given to defined contribution and voucher plans.

Indemnity plans were the original model for EGHP coverage. In response to uncontrolled increases in health care costs, most plans switched to some form of managed care (see below). However, now that managed care costs are rising out of control, there may be renewed interest in indemnity plans.

Usually, indemnity plans are divided into "basic" and "major medical" models. Basic coverage encompasses surgery, hospitalization, and care provided by physicians during a hospital stay. A major medical plan pays when other coverage is exhausted. A comprehensive major medical plan combines basic and major medical features, whereas a supplemental plan offers pure excess insurance.

The standard model for indemnity insurance calls for the patient to be responsible for paying a deductible each year (e.g., $X, or $X per family member) before the plan has any responsibility for payments. Most plans also impose a co-insurance responsibility: In an 80/20 plan, for example, once the deductible is satisfied, the patient is responsible for 20% of the bill—or 20% of the "schedule amount" that the plan pays for the service, plus the full difference between the actual charge and the schedule amount. It is also typical for indemnity plans to include a "stop-loss" provision that represents the maximum out-of-pocket spending an individual or family will incur under the plan. But the plan, in turn, usually limits its exposure by imposing overall limits on each employee's coverage, whether per year or over a lifetime.

Reimbursement to providers under indemnity plans is generally made on the basis of the table of "usual, customary and reasonable charges" promulgated by the insurer. These are either historical figures or a schedule of charges for various items.

§18.13 MANAGED CARE

[A] Concepts and Models

Managed care was a response to the climate of the 1970s and 1980s, when employers were faced with explosive increases in insurance premiums. The general concept of managed care includes many kinds of entities and relationships among patients, employers, and health care providers. The theory is that adding management skills to the health care equation will save money by increasing cost-consciousness and reducing employees' tendency to extravagant health care consumption. However, the analogy between health care and other forms of consumption is rather strained, because the doctor or other health care provider, and not the patient, determines the services that the patient will attempt to claim from the health plan. Furthermore, it is hard to imagine anyone jeopardizing his own health—much less the health of his children—merely to save money for an insurance plan.

A common feature of managed care plans is utilization review. Patients may be required to consult a "gatekeeper" primary care physician before they can be referred to a specialist. Nonemergency procedures may have to be approved in advance by a claims reviewer. Patients' operations and hospital stays will be assessed for medical necessity.

In some managed care models, the employee is required to get all care within a closed network of providers; otherwise, reimbursement will not be available for out-of-network care (except in emergencies or when necessary care is not available within the network). But the trade-off is that the employee either gets care within the network at no additional charge, or pays only a small amount per visit, per prescription, or per service.

Managed care plans typically have their own payment schedules, which may be significantly lower than actual health care costs encountered in the community. The managed care plan's reimbursement to the patient may be defined in terms of this schedule, with the result that the patient has very significant copayment responsibilities. If a patient has satisfied the deductible and is charged $1,000 for a procedure and the health plan's schedule amount is $800; it pays 80% of the schedule amount, or $640, making the patient responsible for the remaining $360.

Generally, employees will be given one open enrollment period a year. During this time, employees who have just become eligible will be able to select one of the options available under the plan. Employees who have already selected a plan option will be able to change their selection. Once made, a decision is usually irrevocable until the next open enrollment period. Most open enrollment periods occur in the autumn, but this is by custom; it is not a legal requirement.

Although a full discussion is beyond the scope of this book, two recent Supreme Court HMO cases should be mentioned briefly. The Supreme Court upheld state "any willing provider" laws (statutes requiring MCOs to accept all licensed health care providers who apply; about half the states have such laws). The MCOs' argument was that closed networks control costs by imposing lower fees, but the Supreme Court said that extending the freedom of health care providers to offer care, and making more options available to patients, should be accorded higher priority. [*Kentucky Ass'n of Health Plans v. Miller,* 538 U.S. 329 (2003)]

The Eighth Circuit decided in 2005 that Arkansas' "any willing provider" law (requiring managed care organizations to permit any qualified health provider to join the network) regulates insurance. Therefore, it is not preempted by ERISA, except with respect to self-funded ERISA plans (which are not treated as insurers). [*Prudential Ins. Co. of Am. v. National Park Med. Ctr., Inc.,* 413 F.3d 897 (8th Cir. 2005)]

The April 7, 2003, case of *Pacificare Health Sys., Inc. v. Book* [538 U.S. 401 (2003)] holds that RICO claims (that MCOs engaged in a pattern of offenses by failing to reimburse doctors for services provided to MCO plan participants) can be subject to a mandatory arbitration clause in the contract between the doctors and the MCOs. The doctors argued (unsuccessfully) that arbitration could not be compelled because the RICO statute allows awards of treble damages to prevailing plaintiffs, whereas the arbitration agreement specified that punitive damages could not be awarded. The Supreme Court ruled that the RICO treble-damage provision is remedial and not punitive. As for other questions, the Supreme Court left those up to the arbitrator to decide.

[B] Health Maintenance Organizations

The Health Maintenance Organization, or HMO, is both a network of providers and a mechanism for financing health care. The theory is that participating providers are paid on a "capitated" basis. That is, they receive a fee "per head" covering all medical services under the plan for a particular employee or dependent of an employee. The theory is that, because providers do not receive more if their patients get additional health services, they will not be motivated to order unnecessary services for purely financial reasons.

In a "staff model" HMO the health professionals are salaried employees of the HMO. In the more prevalent Individual Practice Association (IPA) model HMO, the health professionals enter into contracts with the IPA, and the IPA negotiates with the HMO to set a reimbursement schedule for each service on the schedule.

Under the "group model," the HMO enters into contracts with independent group practices that are responsible for administrative tasks and are usually paid on a capitated basis. The "network model" HMO's doctors practice primarily in fee-for-service mode, However, they also agree to provide certain services to HMO patients, once again generally in exchange for a capitation fee.

Employees who want HMO coverage can sign up with the HMO during a stated open enrollment period each year. There are also rules for switching from one HMO to another if several are available in the relevant geographic area, and rules for disenrolling from the HMO and returning to an indemnity plan (if the employer still offers one).

A federal law, the Health Maintenance Organization Act of 1973, imposes some degree of uniformity and federal regulation (by the Department of Health and Human Services) on HMOs that wish to call themselves "federally qualified." (It is legal for a state-licensed HMO to do business even if it is not federally qualified.)

Federally qualified HMOs must provide an obligatory package of services including both primary and specialty physician services; hospital inpatient and outpatient care; emergency medical treatment; short-term outpatient mental health treatment; referrals and treatment of substance abuse; home health care; and preventive health care. Federally qualified HMOs can also provide additional, optional services such as long-term care, longer-term mental health treatment, dental and vision care; physical therapy; and prescription drugs. Optional services do not have to be provided on a capitated basis, and the HMO can impose fees on such services.

[C] Preferred Provider Organizations (PPOs)

A PPO is an administrative structure under which health care providers become "preferred" by affiliating with the structure. Employers negotiate with the PPO to set the rate scale for specified health services.

There is no set enrollment period for employees to join a PPO. Nor is there a single centralized entity that has complete financial responsibility for the enrollees' care. Sponsorship of PPOs is quite diverse: They might be created by a hospital or other health care provider, a health insurer, entrepreneur, or group of doctors.

In 2005, the PPO was the most common type of EGHP plan. Average PPO premiums for employees rose 76% between 2000 and 2005 (from $342 to $603) and the average deductible for single coverage went from $186 in 1999 to $323 in 2005. According to the Center for Studying Health System Change, 20 million families had trouble paying their health bills in 2003—and two thirds of those families were insured, not uninsured. [John Leland, *When Even Health Insurance Is No Safeguard,* New York Times, Oct. 23, 2005, at p. A1]

[D] Point of Service (POS) Plans

A point of service plan is a hybrid of indemnity and HMO concepts. Participants can select their providers from a network, but they are not obligated to get their care within the network. If they do, their only copayment responsibility is a small amount per visit. Indemnity concepts such as an annual deductible and a co-insurance percentage apply when they choose out-of-network care. POS plans usually impose a high coinsurance percentage, such as 40%, on out-of-network care.

[E] Managed Care Cost Reduction Techniques

Utilization review (UR) is a cornerstone of managed care cost-cutting. In traditional fee-for-service medicine, the health care provider determines which treatments will be used, and the payor reimburses for part or all of the care ordered by the provider.

Managed care adds "gatekeepers"—reviewers who determine whether a claim satisfies the requirements of the plan. In many instances, the plan will require prior approval of claims, and will deny or reduce claims for non-emergency services that did not receive this approval in advance. UR also includes concurrent review (e.g., reviewing the need for continued hospitalization while the patient is still in the hospital) and retrospective review (after treatment is completed).

Procedural controls are common. Most plans will pay for a second opinion prior to surgery, but will not pay for surgery unless the second opinion confirms the recommendation for surgery. Cost-cutting techniques also include adopting a fixed payment schedule, and favoring outpatient and home care over hospitalization.

A carve-out is a discount mechanism under which particular forms of medical expense, or high-cost conditions, are managed separately from the rest of the health plan.

It should be noted that HMO limitations on hospital stays for childbirth led to the passage of federal law. [*See* the discussion of the Newborns' and Mothers' Health Protection Act, Pub. L. No. 104-204]

Tip: It is fairly common for audits of health plans to discover that 10–15% of employees have listed an ineligible person as a dependent, although in most cases this is probably an honest mistake rather than an attempt to cheat the company. For this reason, companies often provide an amnesty period for correcting the records, or for submitting proof in questionable cases. Another cost-saving measure is auditing high-cost claims to make sure that they were properly filed and in the correct amount. According to Towers Perrin, the number of audit requests rose 50% in 2003. These audits don't raise privacy flags, because they examine personnel records (e.g., to see if a dependent "child" is really 32) rather than personal health information. [Vanessa Fuhrmans, *To Stem Abuses, Employers Audit Workers' Health Claims*, Wall Street Journal, Mar. 31, 2004, at p. B1]

[F] Cost Trends

Managed care became popular because of undesirable increases in the cost of indemnity health plans. However, managed care has not lived up to its promise of reducing health care costs. Furthermore, participants in indemnity plans decide how much health care they want to receive. Managed care participants often feel (whether accurately or not) that they are denied access to medically necessary care so that the plans can increase their profits.

A complicating factor in the equation was the ongoing development of more and more sophisticated drugs. This is good, to the extent that it saves lives, reduces suffering, and allows people to be treated at home instead of in a hospital—but it is bad, to the extent that the new drugs are even more expensive than the older ones they replace. Therefore, for many plans, increases in prescription drug costs drove health care cost inflation.

Since 2000, "employers confront explosive health cost increases" has been about the least surprising of news items (though one of the most upsetting for HR professionals).

The growth rate for both public and private health spending in 2004 was 7.9%—the smallest increase since the 6.3% increase in 2000, but it's still much faster than gross domestic product (GDP) growth. Prescription drug spending in 2004 increased 8.2%, the first time in a decade below 10%. Hospital spending rose 8.6%, a slight increase over past years. [Sarah Lueck, *Health-Care Spending Growth Slows*, Wall Street Journal, Jan. 10, 2006, at p. A2]

The most common employer response has been to shift an ever-increasing portion of the cost to employees, by raising the premiums they must pay, increasing deductibles and coinsurance, imposing a formulary for prescription drugs, using a "tiered" system under which reimbursement is higher for generic than for brand-name drugs, or restricting or eliminating family benefits.

Health care costs for employers rose an average of 6.1% in 2005 (with a predicted 6.7% increase in 2006), but Mercer Health & Benefits said this was achieved more as a result of cost-shifting to employees than because costs grew more slowly. The average per employee cost of EGHPs was $6,679 in 2004 and $7,089 in 2005. Mercer's survey found that 22% of the largest companies offer a CDHP, but only 2% of business with less than 500 workers offered one—even though CDHPs were designed in part to alleviate small businesses' health planning problems. [Vanessa Fuhrmans, *Growth in Medical Costs Slows As Firms Shift Tab to Workers*, Wall Street Journal, Nov. 21, 2005, at p. B9]

The bulk of cost increases are due to family coverage, so many employers are raising the family premium; refusing to cover spouses who have access to coverage through their own employment; adding larger payments for larger families; or imposing monthly surcharges for family coverage.

Other, more drastic, measures include firing employees who have high health costs, requiring employees to get maintenance medications for chronic illnesses from mail order pharmacies (which presumably would offer better prices than local pharmacies), increasing premiums for employees who have risk factors such as smoking or obesity.

Some common medications (e.g., for heartburn and allergy) have recently been sold over the counter instead of as prescription drugs—good news for employers that do not cover OTC drugs, that require advance authorization for coverage of over-the-counter drugs, or that have to pay less for the OTC pills than their prescription counterparts; but bad news for employees who have to pay more for these medications. This trend is expected to accelerate, as more prescription medications are in the pipeline for FDA approval for over-the-counter sales. [Barbara Martinez, *Forcing Employees to Buy Drugs Via Mail,* Wall Street Journal, Feb. 18, 2004, at p. D1]

In 2004 and 2005, employers became more proactive in cutting costs, not just shifting them to employees: for example, by opening in-house clinics, although only companies with many employees at a particular location can do this (e.g., Perdue Farms, Pitney-Bowes, Sprint, Quad/Graphics). Quad/Graphics, a printing company in Wisconsin, found that its medical costs were 30% less than the state average, and workers had below-average hospitalization rates and above-average medical compliance once most primary care was shifted in-house. However, unionized companies and those with a bad labor relations history might find it impossible to implement in-house medical care.

A group of 50 major employers, working with the Human Resources Policy Association, set up a buyer's association. The association plans to negotiate directly with drug manufacturers to gain lower drug prices for 50 common drugs on behalf of some 5 million active and retired employees and family beneficiaries. They adopted this as an alternative to using pharmacy benefit managers (PBMs) to provide discounted rates, because of the difficulty in getting accurate cost information from PBMs. The collaborative approach was also used to extend coverage to part-timers and other uninsured workers, although past collective efforts have failed because of disagreements over priorities. [Vanessa Fuhrmans, *One Cure for High Health Costs: In-House Clinics at Companies*, Wall Street Journal, Feb. 11, 2005, at p. A1; Milt Freudenheim, *Big Employers Join Forces in Effort to Negotiate Lower Drug Prices*, New York Times, June 12, 2004, at p. C1; Milt Freudenheim, *Companies Band Together as a Way to Offer Health Care to Part-Time Employees*, New York Times, May 13, 2004, at p. C3]

Early in 2005, a group of 60 major corporations, including General Electric and IBM, announced plans to promote medical discount cards and low-cost insurance to help reduce the numbers of their employees who were uninsured. However, a year later, the program was mired in difficulties. Only 10 of the initial 60 employers signed up for the National Health Access program when it became available. Only about 6,000 employees signed up (out of 900,000 or so who were eligible, and 133,000 who were eligible and uninsured), and nearly all of them came from a single company. Most of the plan's offerings were fairly modest (discount on doctor visits), and the major medical insurance failed to attract low-income workers. [Vanessa Fuhrmans, *Few Uninsured Workers Opt for Employers' New Health Plans*, Wall Street Journal, Feb. 8, 2006, p. B1 and *Low-Cost Plans for Health Care Are to Be Offered*, Wall Street Journal, Jan. 28, 2005, at p. B3]

[G] Choosing a Managed Care Plan

Most employers can choose among several or many managed care plan vendors (although they won't be able to take advantage of this to bargain for low prices!). When an employer chooses a plan, cost considerations are important, but they don't tell the whole story.

Employees may initially be glad to sign up with an HMO that imposes low copayments, but they will be dissatisfied if they have to travel too far to find a network provider, or wait too long for appointments. Other possible sources of discontent are difficulties in getting referrals to specialists, and denial of access to prescriptions, tests, and treatments that the patients and/or doctors think are likely to be beneficial.

When an HMO account representative approaches you, collect as much information as you can about the plan, its history, and its results (including references from other subscribers). A telephone or face-to-face appointment with the HMO's medical director is useful to research staff quality. The medical director can let you know how the HMO chooses its affiliated physicians and how much input physicians have on HMO policies. Also find out if the plan is good at keeping its physicians, or whether it has a problem of high turnover. An important issue to explore is how doctors in the network resolve problems among themselves—and with the HMO—about preferred treatment methods.

Your state insurance department will probably have information about the HMO's operations, loss ratios (percentage of premiums used to pay claims rather than profits or administrative expenses) and how complaints have been resolved in the past.

There are various objective measures of HMO quality. The National Commission on Quality Assurance accredits HMOs. The standard survey instrument for managed care plans is HEDIS (Health Plan Employer Data and Information Set); plans should provide their HEDIS results on request.

Factors to consider are:

- Number of health care providers in the network or participating in the plan;
- Qualifications of health care providers (board certification or eligibility; hospital affiliations; any past complaints or suits);
- How the provider pattern fits your employee census (are there too many obstetricians and not enough cardiologists, or vice versa?);
- Quality of hospitals and other facilities involved with the plan;
- Utilization review and other cost-control measures;
- Availability of primary care physicians at off hours (to cut down on the number of emergency room visits);
- Use of claims management to coordinate treatment of serious illness and injury to promote rehabilitation;
- How premiums compare to those of other MCOs—however, a low premium may simply mean that you will face exceptionally large increases in the future;
- Measures the plan takes to promote consumer satisfaction (telephone help lines, clear explanations of claims procedures, swift resolution of claims disputes, periodic surveys to assess consumers' reactions to the plan.

A good HMO should have plenty of staff to respond to patients' questions (whether to go to the doctor; how to handle minor ailments or accidents; claim and benefit questions).

Early in 2004, a GAO study highlighted the growing problem of "health insurance" plans that are unauthorized or simply fraudulent, and that collect premiums but do not provide coverage when claims are filed. In effect, these entities operate like Ponzi schemes: they attract business by mimicking the names of legitimate insurers, offer below-market rates, and initially use some of the premiums collected to pay other claims, but eventually stop paying claims covered by the terms of the fraudulent policies. Fraudulent insurers also often market their products through licensed agents, so purchasers cannot protect themselves merely by maintaining a relationship with an insurance agent.

For the period 2000–2002, the GAO found that 144 companies sold about 200,000 invalid policies, resulting in over $250 million in unpaid claims.

The Department of Labor shut down some of the abusive companies, and 30 states issued a total of 108 cease-and-desist orders. Every state had at least five bogus insurers; Texas had the most, with 31 of them operating in the state. Over one-fourth of the fraudulent plans were offered through associations of employers or individuals, compromising the image of association health plans that have been touted as a valuable means of reducing health costs. Another 26% were identified as employee leasing firms providing administrative services. [GAO, *Private Health Insurance: Unauthorized Or Bogus Entities Have Exploited Employers and Individuals Seeking Affordable Coverage,* GAO-04-512T, (March 3, 2004), <http://www.gao.gov/new.items/d04512t.pdf>; the Senate Finance Committee held a hearing on this topic on March 3, 2004: "Health Insurance Challenges: Buyer Beware." A transcript can be found at <http://www.kaisernetwork.org/health_cast.uploaded_files/030304_Senate_Finance_transcript.pdf>]

[H] Self-Insured Plans

As insurance premiums increase, more and more employers adopt, or at least consider adopting, self-insured plans. However, a self-insured plan has a heavy administrative and disclosure burden. Reinsurance is vital, because even a young and healthy group of employees can incur catastrophically high claims if even one employee is in a serious accident or has a child with major health care needs. Furthermore, health care providers tend to shift costs onto self-payors.

One coping mechanism is to use a Blue Cross or other entity as a Third-Party Administrator (TPA), which could give your plan access to the insurer's discount structure.

Late in 2003, the Fourth Circuit held that it was proper to certify a class action charging that negligent administration by the plan's TPA caused the collapse of the plan. The defendant opposed certification, claiming that the employer and the employees covered by the plan had opposing interests—but the Fourth Circuit said that few claims would be brought against defendants if employers and employees were not permitted to litigate together. However, the court rejected the certification of "subclass actions" against the insurance agents who marketed the health plan. [*Gunnels v. Health Plan Services Inc.,* 348 F.3d 417 (4th Cir. 2003)]

In a specific stop-loss plan, the insurer agrees to reimburse the employer or other plan sponsor for any claim that exceeds a specified amount (the "retention"). An aggregate stop-loss plan covers all claims above the retention in a particular year. In effect, a stop-loss plan works like an insurance policy with a very high deductible. But from the insurer's viewpoint, a specified stop-loss plan is more favorable, because although the insurer collects premiums in either case, it has no direct liability to the employees covered by a stop-loss plan, and cannot be sued by them for allegedly improper denials of claims or refusals to pre-approve treatment. A stop-loss plan ends on a particular date, and the insurer is not responsible for claims that accrued by that date but have not yet been filed. In contrast, an insured plan is responsible for these "tail" or IBNR (Incurred But Not Reported) claims.

§ 18.14   EMPLOYER LIABILITY FOR HMO ACTIONS

[A]   Generally

The managed care relationship has three parts: the HMO or other managed care organization (MCO) that provides care; the employer that enters into a contract with the MCO; and the employee or dependent that receives health care. When there is a bad result (whether or not malpractice occurred), the employee might want to sue the employer as well as the MCO.

One of the most controversial topics in our legal system is precisely how much control the legal system should have over medical practice, and the extent to which physicians, HMOs, and employers can be held liable for the results of HMO coverage decisions. Initially, employers usually avoided liability because the HMO provided the actual treatment (or claims denial). In many cases, HMOs escaped liability as well, because ERISA preempts state law but says virtually nothing about HMOs' obligations. This state of affairs led to many demands for increased regulation (especially state regulation) of HMO operations in the interests of protecting health care consumers. Many of these explosive issues are beyond the scope of this book, because they involve the employer and the EGHP only indirectly.

The Supreme Court has tackled some of these issues. *Humana Inc. v. Forsyth* [525 U.S. 299 (1999)] permitted EGHP members to bring a RICO suit for insurance fraud when they alleged that they were overbilled as part of a conspiracy to force them to make excessive copayments. The significance of a RICO suit is that treble damages can be ordered. The defendant claimed that the McCarran-Ferguson Act [15 U.S.C. §§ 1011–1015] (which exempts "the business of insurance" from antitrust regulation) preempts the RICO suit. However, the Supreme Court held that RICO does not invalidate or supersede state insurance laws, so the McCarran-Ferguson Act does not bar the RICO suit.

The Supreme Court returned to EGHP ERISA issues in April 1999, finding in *UNUM Life Ins. Co. of America v. Ward* [526 U.S. 358 (1999)] that ERISA does not preempt state "notice-prejudice" laws. These laws prevent insurers from denying claims because they were filed late, unless the delay actually prejudiced the insurer's interests. This decision does not harm employers who administer EGHPs, because it says that although the employer is the insurer's "agent," the employer's role "relates to" an ERISA plan and therefore ERISA preempts suits against the employer with respect to this role.

In mid-2000, the Supreme Court decided, in *Pegram v. Herdrich* [530 U.S. 211 (2000)], that when an HMO, acting through its doctors, makes a mixed decision about medical treatment and health plan eligibility (rather than a purely medical decision about what kind of operation is proper for a particular diagnosis, or a purely financial decision), then the HMO is not acting as a fiduciary. Therefore, even if patients are correct that the HMO refused them necessary and medically valid treatment because the HMO wanted to increase its profits by cutting the amount of care available to subscribers, this would not state a cause of action for breach of fiduciary duty.

When an insurance policy is converted from an EGHP to an individual policy, state law claims about that policy no longer "relate to" a benefit plan, and therefore are not preempted by ERISA. [*Waks v. Empire Blue Cross/Blue Shield,* 263 F.3d 872 (9th Cir. 2001)]

In mid-2004, the Supreme Court ruled that ERISA completely preempts HMO participants' claims of improper denial of health benefits. Therefore, any such suits that are filed in state court can be removed to federal court. Only the ERISA remedies, and not state tort remedies such as punitive damages, will be available. In the Supreme Court's view, ERISA contains a complete set of remedies, which Congress intended to be exclusive. However, ERISA stands for "Employee Retirement Income Security Act," and although the statute contains lengthy provisions about pension plans and their administration, it has far less to say about welfare benefit plans such as health plans—and nothing at all to say about the activities of health insurers—who are third parties in the employer/employee relationship anyway. [*Aetna Health Inc. v. Davila, Cigna Healthcare of Texas, Inc. v. Calad,* 542 U.S. 200 (2004)]

To reduce its liability exposure, the employer should negotiate and draft its contracts with MCOs accordingly:

- Have doctors and other individual health care providers acknowledge that they are independent contractors, not employees of the corporation sponsoring the plan, and that they are fully responsible for their own professional actions;
- Make sure that patients can use an alternative dispute resolution procedure to handle their complaints;
- Set up a feedback mechanism so providers can protest UR-related denials of services the providers deem necessary;
- Require providers to maintain at least a specified minimum level of malpractice coverage, because the less coverage the provider has, the more likely a dissatisfied patient is to feel that additional defendants need to be brought into a dispute;
- Make sure that medical specialists are consulted about all decisions involving specialty referrals;
- Maintain adequate documentation of the disposal of each claim.

[*See* Chapter 13 for federal requirements about health care claims. To learn more about legal issues affecting MCOs, *see, e.g.,* the Kaiser Family Foundation Web site, <http://www.kff.org>, for ongoing coverage of HMO legal issues]

[B] ERISA Preemption Issues

One of the themes of this book is that the balance between state and federal law is critical to the entire subject of employment law. In many cases, plaintiffs who are seeking faster resolution or a greater breadth of remedies will file cases in state court. Often, the employer will then claim that the case can be heard (if at all) in the federal courts, because ERISA preempts the state-law cause of action.

Many older cases became irrelevant in light of the *Davila/Calad* decision, the Supreme Court's ruling that ERISA completely preempts HMO participants' claims of improper denial of health benefits. This ruling rendered invalid the managed care patients' rights laws of ten states (Arizona, California, Georgia, Maine, New Jersey, North Carolina, Oklahoma, Oregon, Texas, Washington, and West Virginia), and required ERISA plan participants to litigate their claims in federal court (where certain state tort remedies, including punitive damages, are not available). The Supreme Court gave little discussion to ERISA § 514(b)(2)(A), the provision in the statute that exempts from preemption state laws that "regulate insurance." In the Supreme Court view, where there is an overpowering federal policy, even statutes that regulate insurance are preempted. However, to date Congress has had little to say in ERISA about appropriate coverage decisions in managed care plans, or remedies for plan participants who believe they have been wrongfully deprived of health care services. [*Aetna Health Inc. v. Davila*, and *Cigna Healthcare of Texas, Inc. v. Calad*, 542 U.S. 200 (2004)]

In July 2004, the Fifth Circuit, citing *Davila*, found that ERISA preempts state-claim claims by an employee and her doctor against a health plan administrator who rejected the proposed treatment as "experimental." The Fifth Circuit refused to extend the principle that mixed treatment/eligibility decisions are not preempted to a traditional indemnity insurer. [*Mayeaux v. Louisiana Health Svce and Indemnity Co.*, 376 F.3d 420 (5th Cir. 2004)]

In September 2004, the Third Circuit ruled that ERISA preempts the Pennsylvania statute providing remedies for bad-faith failure to pay insurance claims. (The case arose when LTD benefits were terminated on the basis of a determination that the claimant was no longer totally disabled.) The Third Circuit found conflict preemption because the state statute awards punitive damages, which are not part of Congress's ERISA enforcement scheme, and ERISA preempts state laws that supplement, duplicate, or attempt to replace ERISA enforcement. After *Calad/Davila*, the Third Circuit no longer believed that the statute could qualify for the savings clause for statutes that regulate insurance. In this reading, the statute did not substantially affect the transfer of risk between insured and insurer, because bad-faith breach of the insurance contract is not a risk of loss that the insurer agrees to bear for its insured as part of the contract. [*Barber v. UNUM Life Ins. Co. of America*, 383 F.3d 134 (3d Cir. 2004)]

However, the Supreme Court ruled in mid-2006 that certain claims must be litigated in state, not federal, court. [*Empire Healthchoice Assurance, Inc. v. McVeigh*, No. 05-200, <http://laws.findlaw.com/us/000/05-200.html> (June 15, 2006)] The injured employee was covered by a plan subject to the Federal Employees Health Benefits Act (FEHBA). FEHBA says that the terms of insurance contracts insuring federal employees preempt state or local law about health benefit plans. Nevertheless, when an insurer sought reimbursement of amounts it spent on the care of a federal employee who received an automobile injury settlement, the Supreme Court required the case to be heard in state court. The Supreme Court ruled that there was no federal jurisdiction under 28 U.S.C. § 1331, because the claim for reimbursement did not arise under federal law, so federal jurisdiction could not be triggered.

See § 18.06[A] for ERISA preemption issues in connection with same-sex spouse and domestic partner benefits.

§ 18.15 LABOR LAW ISSUES IN THE EGHP

A 1996 NLRB ruling holds that an employer's reservation of the right to "amend or modify" the health plan did not give the employer the power to replace the existing fee-for-service plan with a managed care plan. Such a change is so sweeping that the employer cannot implement it unilaterally without bargaining. [*Loral Defense Systems-Akron,* 320 NLRB No. 54 (Jan. 31, 1996), *aff'd,* 200 F.3d 436 (6th Cir. 1999)]

When negotiations reach an impasse, the employer cannot replace the union-sponsored health (and retirement) plans with employer-proposed plans that did not form part of the pre-impasse negotiations. [*Grondorf, Field Black & Co. v. NLRB,* 107 F.3d 882 (D.C. Cir. 1997)]

A unionized company that wants its employees to pay 30% of the premium thereby has an obligation to release information to the union about the health care claims of non-union employees and their dependents. The information is not confidential, because the employer has opened up the issue of health care costs and cost containment. [*Carr v. Gates Health Care Plan,* 195 F.3d 292 (7th Cir. 1999)]

§ 18.16 QUALIFIED MEDICAL CHILD SUPPORT ORDERS (QMCSOs)

Divorce courts often issue orders explaining how to divide an employee spouse's retirement benefits with the divorcing non-employee spouse. These orders are called Qualified Domestic Relations Orders, or QDROs. [*See* § 12.08] The counterpart for the EGHP is the QMCSO, which supplements COBRA continuation coverage as an additional means of protecting children against loss of health care coverage as a result of their parents' divorce. [*See* § 12.08[A]] A QMCSO is a court order that requires a parent covered by an EGHP to take whatever steps are necessary to enroll the child ("the alternate recipient") in the health plan—whether that includes notifying the plan or paying insurance premiums.

A valid QMCSO must identify:

- Every plan it applies to;
- The period of time covered by the order;
- The type of coverage the plan must give each alternate recipient (or a method of determining the coverage);
- The name and last known mailing address of the employee parent and each alternate recipient.

When a health plan receives a document described as a QMCSO, the plan has an obligation to review it to see if it is a valid order. Every health plan must have a written document setting out its procedure for reviewing QMCSOs. Courts do not have the power to order benefits that are not provided under the plan—so, for instance, if a plan does not offer dependent coverage, a QMCSO cannot create this coverage.

The plan administrator must notify the participant and the alternate recipients that the order has been received, and how the plan will analyze the order's validity. If, as usually happens, the plan approves the order as valid, then the participant and alternate recipients must be notified. Because the alternate recipients are children, they can designate a parent, stepparent, or attorney to receive copies of the notice on their behalf.

State governments (but NOT the DOL) can sue under I.R.C. § 502(a)(7) to enforce compliance with a Qualified Medical Child Support Order (QMCSO). The states have a role to play here because they have traditionally been empowered to deal with family law issues such as child support.

A 1998 law, the Child Support Performance and Incentives Act [Pub. L. No. 105-200], requires state child-support enforcement agencies to protect children's rights to medical coverage. The DOL and HHS published a Final Rule giving the text for the National Medical Child Support Notice. [*See* 65 Fed. Reg. 82128 and 82154 (Dec. 27, 2000)] State agencies have been required to use the form to enforce child support orders since October 1, 2001.

The Notice includes Parts A and B. Part A, the Employer Withholding Notice, informs the employer of the facts of the medical child support order. The employer must either:

- Inform the child-support enforcement agency that forwarded the order that the employer doesn't provide health care coverage to the employee who is the subject of the order;
- Inform the agency that the person named in the order is no longer an employee (the agency must also be notified if the employee is subsequently terminated); or
- Forward Part B of the form to the plan administrator within 20 business days, if health care coverage for a child is applicable.

The next step is for the plan administrator to decide whether the child(ren) covered by the order is or are enrolled in the health plan. If so, any appropriate withholding amount is taken from the employee's wages to provide medical coverage for the children. These deductions cannot exceed the amount of medical support specified by the order. They are also subject to federal and state limitations on wage assignments.

Employers can be sanctioned under ERISA and state law if they fail to carry out the wage deductions—or, on the other hand, if they fire or discipline employees because they have medical child support obligations.

It is the plan administrator's responsibility to send Part B to the child support enforcement agency. The form indicates whether the administrator deems the notice to be a valid QMCSO and, if so, what coverage options are available and which options the child(ren) has or have been enrolled in. The administrator has 40 business days to assess the validity of an alleged QMCSO.

In August 2003, EBSA issued a 26-page compliance guide, available online. The guide clarifies that if a National Medical Support Notice (NMSN) is issued to a plan by a state child support enforcement agency, the administrator must treat it as a QMCSO.

An employee who is eligible for enrollment but is not enrolled in the plans is considered a participant, so an order naming such an employee can be a QMCSO. If the order is in proper form, the plan must cover the child. If the plan requires an employee to be enrolled as a condition of covering his or her dependents, the guide says that the plan has to enroll both.

An order can also be a QMCSO even if the employee has not yet satisfied the plan's waiting period; the administrator should arrange for the child to be covered as soon as the parent's waiting period is up.

The IRS (which has jurisdiction over COBRA eligibility questions) has ruled that a child enrolled in an EGHP under a QMCSO who loses coverage as a result of a qualifying event (for instance, the parent is no longer employed; the child marries, ceases to be a full-time student, or reaches age 23) is a qualified beneficiary who is entitled to make a COBRA election.

HIPAA applies to children covered by QMCSOs—so if there is a generally applicable pre-existing condition limitation under the plan, the child will be subject to it. But when the plan gets a QMCSO, any time it takes to determine the validity of the order will not count toward the 63-day period for determining if creditable coverage is still present or if there has been a break in coverage. [Compliance Guide for Qualified Medical Child Support Orders, (Aug. 13, 2003), <http://www.dol.gov/ebsa/publications/qmcso.html>]

§18.17   THE EMPLOYER'S RIGHT OF SUBROGATION

In the typical subrogation case, a plan participant is injured, and the plan provides funds for treatment of his or her injuries. Then the injured person settles a case, or wins a judgment, against the person responsible for the injuries. In practical terms, that usually means a liability insurance company gets involved. The EGHP then attempts to recover the benefits from the injured person's tort recovery.

If, as is often the case, the injuries occurred in an automobile accident, automobile insurers often get involved. [*See Community Insurance Co. v. Morgan,* 54 Fed. Appx. 828 (6th Cir. 2002); *Lasky v. State Farm Mutual Auto Ins. Co.,* 2001 U.S. Dist. LEXIS 13636 (W.D. Mich. Aug. 31, 2001)]

Subrogation is a legal concept under which a party that advances expenses can recover them when the person who received the funds is reimbursed for those expenses. More specifically, if an EGHP covers the medical treatment of an injured employee, or dependent of an employee, the EGHP will have a legal right to part of the verdict or settlement that the employee receives from suing whoever caused the accident or manufactured the dangerous product.

For the plan to have a right of subrogation, the plan language, or the insurance covering the plan, must provide this right explicitly. State law must also be consulted to see if limitations are imposed on subrogation.

California, for example, has a state antisubrogation statute that says that a health insurer is not entitled to reimbursement out of a victim's medical malpractice recovery. The statute has been upheld as enforceable and not preempted by ERISA (which has an exception for laws under which states regulate the business of insurance). [*Medical Mutual of Ohio v. deSoto*, 234 F.3d 298 (6th Cir. 2000)]

The question becomes whether the antisubrogation law is a state law that is preempted by ERISA. *Bauhaus USA, Inc. v. Bill Benson and Bancorp South* [2003 U.S. Dist. LEXIS 1966 (N.D. Miss. Feb. 6, 2003)] finds that the state law is preempted.

Arana v. Ochsner Health Plan Inc. [338 F.3d 433 (5th Cir. 2003)] reaches a similar conclusion: the state law preventing subrogation is completely preempted by ERISA. According to the Fourth Circuit, a claim that an HMO violated a state antisubrogation law is not preempted by ERISA, because of the exemption for state regulation of insurance. However, because the plaintiff in this case wanted relief under ERISA § 502(a), the defendant had the right to remove the case to federal court. [*Singh v. Prudential Health Care Plan Inc.*, 335 F.3d 278 (4th Cir. 2003)]

See also Levine v. United Healthcare Corp. [3d Cir. 2005], holding that New Jersey's anti-subrogation statute conflicts with ERISA. Therefore, health insurers are entitled to seek reimbursement of medical expenses from insured persons who get a personal injury settlement or judgment from a third party. When the plaintiffs were injured, New Jersey had a law permitting subrogation, so they reimbursed their health plans for care received. Then New Jersey's highest court struck down the statute, and it was repealed. The plaintiffs sued to recover the funds they had turned over to the plans, but they lost on ERISA preemption grounds. The Third Circuit refused to apply the saving clause for laws that regulate insurance because the statute in question governed all recoveries in civil actions. Although it usually was applied to health insurance policies, that was not the sole purpose of the law. [*Levine v. United Healthcare Corporation*, 402 F.3d 156 (3d Cir. 2005)]

The Ninth Circuit held that ERISA does not preempt a plan administrator's state-law claim seeking reimbursement out of a personal injury settlement. The court treated this as a pure contract claim not requiring plan interpretation. [*Providence Health Plan v. McDowell*, 385 F.3d 1168 (9th Cir. 2004)]

By contrast, some state laws facilitate subrogation: for instance, by requiring the participant to agree to subrogation as a condition of receiving benefits under the plan.

The Supreme Court decided a subrogation case. [*Great-West Life & Annuity Ins. Co. v. Knudson*, 534 U.S. 204 (2002)] In this case, the plan called for recovery from plan beneficiaries if they recovered any payments from third parties. The plan paid most of the $411,157.11 in medical expenses when a car crash rendered an employee quadriplegic. She settled her tort case; the settlement allocated only $13,828.70 to past medical expenses. The Supreme Court refused to allow the plan to sue under ERISA § 503(a)(3) (civil action to enjoin an act or practice violating the terms of the plan), or to obtain equitable relief to collect more of the funds it had advanced. The Supreme Court refused to permit the plan to bring such a suit, ruling that compelling payment of money due under a contract is not an "equitable" remedy.

Shortly after this decision, the Northern District of Illinois ruled that ERISA does not preempt a suit brought by a health plan against a plan participant who still has continuing control over the money that the health plan wants to recover. [*Administrative Committee of Wal-Mart Stores Health and Welfare Plan v. Varco,* 2002 U.S. Dist. LEXIS 530 (N.D. Ill. Jan. 13, 2002)] Therefore, the concept of "constructive trust" (segregating funds that legitimately belong to someone else) can be applied. This does not conflict with *Great-West,* because in that case the funds had already been placed into a trust to be used for future medical care, and had been used to pay attorneys' fees; the funds did not remain in the injured person's hands. The Seventh Circuit affirmed the District Court on this issue (although it also ruled that the District Court was wrong about the way it applied the common fund doctrine to the award of attorneys' fees): *see* 338 F.3d 680.

The Fourth Circuit ruled that a PPO plan was entitled to recover the $75,000 it had advanced from the personal injury settlement received by two injured plan participants. The plan contained a subrogation provision, subject to a deduction for attorneys' fees for obtaining third-party payments. The injured participants were asked several times to execute subrogation agreements, but did not do so, and they refused to reimburse the PPO after the settlement was made. The plan sued the participants under ERISA § 502(a)(3), seeking equitable relief to enforce the provisions of a plan. The Fourth Circuit ruled that, pursuant to *Knudson,* a lien would constitute equitable restitution because there were identifiable funds that, in equity, belonged to the plan and were in the custody of the plan participants. The court also cited the plan's right to reimbursement as clear under the plan documents. Certiorari was granted in late 2005. [*Mid Atlantic Med. Servs., LLC v. Sereboff,* 407 F.3d 212 (4th Cir. 2005). *Aff'd* No. 05-260, <http://caselaw.lp.findlaw.com/us/000/05-260.html> (May 15, 2006). The Supreme Court treated the insurer's civil action as "appropriate equitable relief" as defined by ERISA § 502(a)(3)(B) because, unlike the fact pattern in *Knudson,* the injured plan participants agreed to set aside part of their tort recovery (in an amount equal to the reimbursement sought by the insurer), so they became trustees with respect to the funds specifically set aside in case it was determined that the insurer should be reimbursed]

The Tenth Circuit granted equitable relief from the terms of a subrogation clause, finding that the plan acted arbitrarily and capriciously by imposing a new condition on the injured person that was not in the plan or the SPD. (In order to receive vested medical benefits, the plaintiff was required to file a third-party action against the other driver in the accident. He was required to file suit within a year of the accident and to pay his own legal bills, but was ordered not to settle the case without consent of the plan.) The Tenth Circuit ruled that it was unfair to impose these requirements; however, because of the subrogation provision in the plan, the health plan had the legal right to sue the driver itself to protect its rights to reimbursement. [*Gorman v. Carpenters' & Millwrights' Health Benefit Trust Fund*, 410 F.3d 1194 (10th Cir. 2005)]

The "make-whole" doctrine also has to be considered in cases where the injured person has received a recovery, but less than an amount necessary to compensate for all injuries received. This doctrine absolves the injured person of having to reimburse the plan until he or she has been "made whole." Yet another factor is the "common fund" doctrine: whether the EGHP's right of recovery is reduced to account for attorneys' fees paid to the injured person's attorney. The rationale for this doctrine is that without the attorney, there would have been no "common fund" for the injured person and the plan to share, and therefore both of them should contribute toward the fees. *See Palmerton v. Associates' Health and Welfare Plan* [2003 Wis. 2d 41, 659 N.W.2d 183 (Wis. App. 2003)], which holds that the plan document for the EGHP was properly drafted to make both these doctrines inapplicable. Therefore, the EGHP's right of reimbursement was not limited by the attorney's fee.

According to the Eighth Circuit, a health plan can recover the "reasonable" value of the services it provided to injured employees. This is defined as the fee-for-service fee schedule. The employer's right of subrogation is not limited to the actual amount that the health plan paid to the health care provider (health plans typically pay providers less than the schedule amount). [*Ince v. Aetna Health Management Inc.*, 173 F.3d 672 (8th Cir. 1999)]

In another case involving discounted rates, the district court for the District of Rhode Island awarded more than $4 million in damages, plus interest, to plan participants who challenged an HMO's practice of imposing copayments based on billing rates, even though the HMO actually had negotiated a lower, discounted rate that it paid to health care providers. [*Corsini v. United HealthCare Servs. Inc.*, 145 F. Supp. 2d 184 (D.R.I. 2001)]

In a Sixth Circuit case, the employee received about $18,000 in medical expense reimbursement after a car accident. [*Smith v. Wal-Mart Assocs. Group Health Plan*, 2000 U.S. App. LEXIS 33993 (6th Cir. Dec. 27, 2000)] She got a tort judgment of $25,000 against the other driver. One-third went to her lawyer as a contingent fee. The plan's subrogation clause allowed the plan to recover benefits already paid, to the extent of "any payment resulting from a judgment or settlement." However, the Sixth Circuit said that the attorney's one-third share of the judgment should have the effect of reducing the amount the plan could receive: The employee had received only two-thirds of the $25,000. The plan would have to sue the lawyer to recover the rest.

> **Tip:** The problem in the case mentioned above can be avoided by drafting the subrogation clause to clarify that the plan can recover against the full, unreduced amount of any settlement or judgment.

§18.18   DEFINED CONTRIBUTION, CDHP, AND HRA PLANS

[A]   Generally

Some employers prefer to avoid the difficulties, expenses, and controversy involved in EGHP management, and prefer to give employees health care vouchers so they can purchase their own coverage. The employer agrees to give the employee a fixed amount that can be applied to a menu of health care choices. The employer's exposure is limited and is not subject to health care price increases. In effect the voucher works like a defined contribution or 401(k) plan, shifting control to the employees—but also putting them at risk of bad or simply unlucky decisions.

A defined contribution health plan, also known as a "consumer-driven" plan, is another way of limiting the employer's exposure to cost increases.

In 2005, consumer-driven health plans, including HSAs and HRAs, represented 2% of the market, covering 2.7 million people and $16 million in premium volume. Employers wishing to add an HSA option to their plans can choose among many options offered by banks, insurers, technology companies, and even debit card vendors. There are three main types of HSA vendors: custodians (e.g., banks) who hold the funds in interest-bearing accounts, issue debit cards, process transactions, and offer investment services; administrators; and stand-alone debit card vendors. Some debit card vendors are integrating with PBMs so that consumers can present their debit cards at pharmacies to have their drug purchases subtracted from their HSAs. [Tom Anderson. *Vendors Offer Employers a Dizzying Array of HSA Options,* Employee Benefit News, <http://www.benefitnews.com/pfv.cfm?id=7452> (May 2005)]

Mercer Health & Benefits Consulting found that three years after CDHPs were introduced, they remained largely the domain of very large employers. Looking at all employers with 10 or more employees, only 2% had a CDHP in 2005, and only 1% of eligible employees were enrolled. But in 2005, 10% of the employers with 5,000–9,999 employees and 19% of employers with 10,000–19,000 employees had CDHPs. Among large employers who had CDHPs, 52% of the large companies had an HRA. In 2005, the average cost per employee of CDHP coverage (including the employer's contribution to the account) was $5,480, 18% lower than the average cost of a PPO ($6,480) and 13% below the average HMO cost ($6,210). [Fred Schneyer, *CDHP Adoption Rate Still Slow, Halting,* PlanSponsor.com (Feb. 1, 2006)]

Watson Wyatt Worldwide's survey performed for the National Business Group on Health found that in 2006, 29% of all employers offered a consumer-directed health plan (HSA or HRA), more than double the 13% level of 2005. Median enrollment was 7% of employees. Eighty percent of employers found CDHPs at least somewhat effective in getting employees more involved in health care decisions, but only 59% found it somewhat effective in slowing down health care cost increases. [Rebecca Moore, *CDHPs a Growing Health Care Offering from Employers,* PlanSponsor.com (Mar. 16, 2006)]

In a fixed-dollar contribution plan, the employer offers a choice of health plans and gives each worker a certain amount of compensation to buy insurance. Employees who want a more expensive policy must use their own pretax dollars to pay the difference. In a fixed-percentage contribution plan, the employer's contribution is defined as a percentage of the premium, with the rest paid by the employee.

Employers could also combine a high deductible health plan with a funded or unfunded account for medical expenses. The employer might set up an account in which funds are accumulated on behalf of active employees, to be used for their eventual retiree health expenses.

Defined contribution plans are touted as means of improving employees' consumerism and health care shopping behavior, although that was also an argument used in favor of managed care, which is now failing to control costs.

If the arrangement constitutes a Flexible Spending Account, then Internal Revenue Code requirements will have to be satisfied. If the arrangement is trust-funded, it may become an ERISA welfare benefit plan, with additional requirements to meet. Very possibly, the IRS will treat the arrangement as a self-insured medical plan, in which case there may be nondiscrimination, COBRA, and HIPAA compliance obligations. Questions of dependent coverage will have to be worked out.

CDH plans can be combined with HRAs (see below), and the plan can be set up so that the employee is required to satisfy a deductible before accessing HRA funds. Another option is for the employer to cover up to 100% of preventive care services, or require employees to use HRA amounts for this purpose. The employer can also impose a cap, such as $3,000 a year, on the amount that can be rolled over from year to year within an HRA.

An integrated pharmacy benefit works by giving participants an electronic card that the pharmacist can check to see if funds are available under the HRA. If not, the participant pays for the drugs out of pocket until the deductible is met, and then a PPO or POS plan takes over. CDH plans showed good ability to control costs for employers in 2002—but it is possible that the results of the small sample of available plans are not representative of what will happen if these plans become more popular. There is also the risk of "bait and switch"—employers who adopt CDH plans might later be hit with very heavy cost increases. Furthermore, employees paid as much or more than they would have under non-CDH plans.

One interpretation is that CDH plans save money for the employer because participants become more active, better-informed consumers. But of course the major challenge for any health plan is not offering services to young, healthy people, but to a mixed population that includes older people and perhaps some suffering from chronic illnesses. It should also be remembered that the reason for offering EGHPs in the first place is to motivate employees, an objective that will not be achieved if they resent the increased burden placed on them. For example, data allowing price comparisons between health care providers is not easy to find. It should also be kept in mind that many of the same advantages were touted for MSAs, yet these plans have never achieved popular acceptance. [Vanessa Fuhrmans, *Insurer Reveals What Doctors Really Charge,* Wall Street Journal, Aug. 18, 2005, at p. D1 and *Patients Give New Insurance Mixed Reviews,* Wall Street Journal, June 14, 2005, at p. D1; Allison Bell, *Study: Health Plans Still Skimp on Cost Information,* NU Online News Service, Nov. 10, 2005]

A study by Rand Health, published in the Journal of the American Medical Association in 2004, found that when copayments doubled, the average use of prescriptions declined 31% among people with allergies, 27% among people with arthritis, and 23% among diabetics. Even modest increases in copayments can cause health setbacks because patients not merely shift away from higher-priced to less-expensive drugs but stop taking their medicine altogether, with a result that many very expensive complications occur. For example, the study showed a 17% increase in emergency room visits and a 10% increase in hospital stays for people with diabetes, asthma, and gastric acid disorders. Between 2000 and 2003, the average copayment for a preferred prescription rose 46% (to $19) and increased 71% (to $29) for a nonpreferred prescription. [Vanessa Fuhrmans, *Higher Co-Pays May Take Toll on Health,* Wall Street Journal, May 19, 2004, at p. D1]

While CDHPs are being promoted, the opposite tack is also being marketed, in the form of "mini-medical" or "limited-benefit" plans that are inexpensive for employers and employees. The catch is that they have low annual caps (e.g., $10,000 a year) and have very little coverage for emergency services and hospitalization. These plans can cost as little as $40 a month (about a quarter of the cost of a major medical plan, and less than an eighth of the cost of a typical EGHP); however, coverage of doctor visits is usually limited to four and 10 per year, and some laboratory tests and prescription drugs, so even a person without a health crisis can easily run through the coverage. These plans were initially offered for part-time and temporary employees, so they have become more popular as the use of part-time and contract workers increases. Limited benefit plans have also been adopted by some employers for full-time workers. In effect, these plans "zig" where CDHPs "zag"; sometimes combining a limited benefit plan with a CDHP can provide full coverage at lower cost than conventional insurance. [Vanessa Fuhrmans, *More Employers Try Limited Health Plans,* Wall Street Journal, Jan. 16, 2006, at p. D1]

[B]   2002 IRS Guidance

In 2002, the IRS issued two documents to inform employers about Health-Related Arrangements (HRAs) and their differences from FSAs and MSAs. [Rev. Rul. 2002-41, 2002-28 I.R.B. 75, and Notice 2002-45, 2002-28 I.R.B. 93] Some—but not all—defined contribution health plans will qualify as HRAs. Treasury Secretary Paul O'Neill announced that the publication of these rulings clears the way for employers to offer employees plans featuring patient-directed features, offering more choice and greater participant control over their coverage. An FSA (as defined by Code § 106(c)(2) and Prop. Reg. § 1.125-2, Q&A-7(c)) is a benefit program for the reimbursement of specified, incurred expenses qualifying under Code § 213, subject to reasonable conditions such as maximum reimbursement amounts. The maximum reimbursement for a period of coverage must not exceed 500% of the value of the coverage. A health FSA is subject to the Proposed Regulations governing cafeteria plans, and unused benefits cannot be carried over from year to year. For COBRA and HIPAA purposes, a health FSA is a group plan. It is also an ERISA welfare benefit plan, and is subject to Code § 105(h)'s nondiscrimination rules for self-insured medical expense reimbursement plans.

An MSA, as defined by Code § 220 (now known as an Archer MSA), is a trust or custodial account that accumulates funds on a tax-preferred basis that may eventually be used for medical payments. Contributions made by the employer to the MSA are excludible from the employee's gross income pursuant to § 106(b). Contributions made by an employee are AGI deductions, within limits. Amounts distributed from the MSA for medical expenses are excluded from gross income. Amounts distributed from an MSA but not used for medical expenses are not only included in income, but are subject to a 15% penalty (unless the distribution is made at or after age 65 or in the event of death or disability); relief is available for rollovers and distributions made in connection with divorce. There is a 6% tax on excess contributions. Under Code § 105(b)(5), MSAs are not subject to COBRA or the prohibited transactions excise tax under Code § 4975. It is not absolutely clear, but MSAs are probably welfare benefit plans subject to ERISA rules.

Before Notice 2002-45 and Rev. Rul. 2002-41 were issued, the IRS refused to issue rulings as to whether employer-provided coverage used for § 213 medical expenses can be excluded from income if unused amounts can be carried over from year to year. The IRS has finally agreed that carryovers are permissible.

An HRA is a plan that is 100% funded by employer contributions and provides reimbursement for medical expenses incurred during the 12-month plan year (but not before). In fact, carryover of unused amounts is not only permitted, it is mandatory. The balance in the HRA may be used to provide coverage of medical expenses; and the balance must be used for this purpose if a COBRA event occurs. Distributions for any purpose other than paying medical expenses jeopardizes the exclusion from income of all distributed amounts. Notice 2002-45 says that any expense that qualifies under § 213(d) can be reimbursed from the HRA, including insurance premiums, with one major exception. Because of § 106(c), no amount that constitutes a "qualified long-term care service" under § 7702B(c) can be reimbursed because health FSAs are not allowed to cover long-term care.

HRA distributions can be made to employees, former employees, COBRA qualified beneficiaries, and spouses or dependents of employees. However, if the HRA makes distributions as bonuses, severance pay, or payments to the estate of a deceased participant, all distributions from that account in that tax year become taxable, even if they were used to pay medical expenses. This result comes from Reg. § 1.105-2, which says that amounts cannot be excluded from income if the taxpayer would be entitled to receive them whether or not he or she had medical expenses.

An HRA can be offered in conjunction with a cafeteria plan. The HRA account is offered with a major medical plan whose premiums are paid via salary reduction. If the pre-tax salary reduction amounts can be contributed directly to the HRA, the arrangement loses its status as an HRA and becomes subject to the cafeteria plan rules. This is a problem, because HRAs generally are not drafted to satisfy the cafeteria plan requirements, and failure to do so will probably make amounts distributed from the HRA includible in the recipient's gross income for tax purposes.

HRAs are subject to the Code § 105(h) nondiscrimination rules, so if the employer's contribution level differs for different employees, it's important to make sure that the differences are not discriminatory. The Notice does not address the limitations on contributions to an HRA. If the HRA is funded through a VEBA, the limitations of Code §§ 419 and 419A apply. One question that remains to be resolved is whether employees who could have participated in the HRA, but declined to do so, will be counted when discrimination testing is performed.

Unfunded HRAs come under Code § 404. The IRS hasn't ruled specifically, but tax experts suggest that the employer will not be entitled to take a deduction for an unfunded HRA until funds are paid out for medical expenses. HRAs are subject to COBRA, and the premium charged when a qualifying event occurs does not have to vary with the balance of the HRA account. The premium can be calculated as a reasonable actuarial estimate of the cost of providing coverage for similarly situated beneficiaries.

The 2002 guidance from the IRS fails to address whether the HIPAA ban on charging different premiums on account of health status applies to HRAs. Nor do these two documents tackle the ERISA welfare benefit issues—perhaps the DOL, rather than the IRS, will be the federal agency that rules on issues such as whether the HRA must be held and administered in trust form, and if so whether there must be a trust document and a set established policy.

It should also be noted that, as the employees' entitlement under the HRA grows, the employer's unfunded liability would also increase. Because this liability presumably would have to be reflected on the corporate balance sheet, with corresponding depressing effect on the bottom line, some employers will prefer to use a VEBA to fund the HRA rather than maintaining it as an unfunded plan.

Rev. Rul. 2005-24, 2005-16 I.R.B. 892, permits employers to contribute accumulated vacation and sick days to retirees' HRAs. However, the ruling clarifies that HRAs will lose their tax benefits if they provide anything except reimbursement of qualified medical expenses. Three of the four fact patterns considered in Rev. Rul. 2005-24 result in disqualification. The only qualifying situation is one in which the employer has an obligation to contribute the value of all or part of the unused days off to the HRA, and the employee has no ability to "cash out" the unused days—which could create problems in states that have laws requiring employers to cash out unused leave days. [Watson Wyatt Insider, *IRS Issues New Guidance on HRA Contributions and Distributions*, <http://www.watsonwyatt.com/us/pubs/insider/ printable.asp?ArticleID=14572[. . .]> (June 2005)]

In Rev. Rul. 2005-25, 2005-18 I.R.B. 971, the IRS ruled that amounts paid under a reimbursement plan are not exempt from the employee's gross income if the plan pays the employee unused reimbursement amounts in cash or other benefits. The fact situation in this ruling is an employer plan that reimburses current and former employees and their spouses and dependents (including survivors of deceased employees) for substantiated "medical care expenses" as defined by I.R.C. § 213, subject to an annual maximum dollar amount. The plan is fully employer funded and does not involve employee contributions or a cafeteria plan. In one scenario, most of the reimbursement account is forfeited if a balance remains unused at the end of the year (or when the employee dies), but some of it is carried forward to future plan years. The second scenario allows some or all of the unused balance to be paid to the employee in cash at the end of the plan year or when the employee's employment terminates. The third scenario pays unused reimbursement amounts to the designated beneficiary or estate of a deceased employee. The fourth plan gives employees the option to transfer part of the reimbursement amount that would otherwise be forfeited to a retirement plan, or to receive part of it in cash.

The Revenue Ruling says that if an employee is entitled to receive a payment whether or not medical expenses have been incurred, none of the payment can be excluded from gross income under I.R.C. § 105(b)—whether or not the employee actually has medical expenses that are reimbursed by the plan. Therefore, the only type of HRA that qualifies for tax-favored treatment under I.R.C.§ 105(b) and I.R.C. § 106 is one in which employees and their families can receive only reimbursement for medical expenses, and cannot receive cash or other benefits equivalent to their unused plan balances. The Revenue Ruling specifies that this principle applies to plans that cover only retirees as well as plans covering active employees only or both actives and retirees.

CHAPTER 19

HEALTH INSURANCE CONTINUATION AND PORTABILITY (COBRA AND HIPAA)

§ 19.01   INTRODUCTION

The two dominant mechanisms for providing health insurance coverage in our society are employee group health plans (EGHPs) and the Medicare system for senior citizens and the disabled. However, there are many instances in which a person has lost coverage under one EGHP and is not (or is not yet) covered by another one, and is not eligible for Medicare. Individual health coverage is expensive—and furthermore, the ex-employee or a member of his or her family might have a medical condition that makes insurance harder to obtain or raises its cost even higher.

Two federal statutes, the Comprehensive Omnibus Budget Reconciliation Act (COBRA) and the Health Insurance Portability and Accessibility Act (HIPAA) work together to make the transition between EGHPs, or from EGHP coverage to individual health coverage, at least somewhat smoother. Both statutes impose responsibilities on the employer, so the health plan administrator must be aware of these duties.

§ 19.02   COBRA CONTINUATION COVERAGE

Continuation coverage is the right of a "qualified beneficiary" (i.e., a former employee or his or her spouse and dependents) to maintain coverage under the employer's group health plan after a "COBRA event."

[A]   Qualifying Events

A COBRA event is either personal or work-related and poses a threat to coverage under the ordinary circumstances:

- The employee is terminated or has hours reduced (unless termination is for gross misconduct);
- The employee divorces or becomes legally separated;
- The employee's dependent child ceases to be covered by the plan (usually because of "aging out");
- The employee's employer files for bankruptcy protection;
- The employee becomes Medicare-eligible (which entitles the employee's spouse to COBRA coverage);
- The employee dies (obviously, this is only a COBRA event for the survivors).

It should be noted that a protective order issued during a divorce proceeding is not a "legal separation" that triggers the right to COBRA notice. There must be a final court decree that adjudicates legal rights, but maintains marital status. [*Simpson v. T.D. Williamson Inc.*, 414 F.3d 1203 (10th Cir. 2005)]

The Trade Act of 2002 [Pub. L. No. 107-210 (signed Aug. 6, 2002)] enacts a tax credit under Code § 35, equal to 65% of the premiums paid for COBRA coverage and extended COBRA coverage to certain displaced workers (displaced by factors such as overseas business or imports). The credit can also be used for other programs, such as state-law continuation coverage that is broader than the federal COBRA requirement, or state risk-sharing pools for insuring high-risk individuals.

The credit is refundable (i.e., a person whose tax liability is less than $0 can receive a tax refund). The credit amount can be forwarded to the health plan, so qualifying individuals only have to pay 35% of the COBRA premium out of pocket.

The credit applies only to people who are not covered by other government or private insurance programs. Qualifying individuals are:

- Aged 55–64 and receiving monthly guarantee payments from the PBGC, or
- Unemployed and eligible for Trade Adjustment Assistance benefits under the Trade Act. The Department of Labor and state labor agencies certify that jobs were lost for this reason, and the effective date of job loss.

Workers who qualify for TAA benefits get an additional 60-day COBRA election period, if they are found to be TAA-eligible within six months of their loss of group insurance coverage. If they make an election, COBRA coverage begins on the first day of the special election period. Furthermore, the period from the initial loss of EGHP coverage to the beginning of the special election period is not counted in determining whether there has been a 63-day interruption of coverage for HIPAA purposes.

The IRS published guidance for administrators of Trade Act-Related Health Coverage Tax Credit Plans. [*See* <http://www.irs.gov/individuals/article/0,ii=109977,00.html> and <http://www.irs.gov/pub/irs-utl/hctc_health-plan-adminstrator_guide.pdf>]

Trade-displaced individuals, or persons receiving pension benefits from the PBGC contact IRS' HCTC Customer Contact Center to apply. If they are found to be qualified, they send 35% of the premium each month to a payment center designated by the IRS. The payment center adds the remaining 65% of the premium and forwards the funds to the health plan. Since August 2003, eligible individuals have been able to claim the credit in advance, to help them pay the premiums.

To receive payment from the HCTC, the administrator of an eligible health plan must register online as a vendor and submit instructions for electronic funds transfer. (If the administrator doesn't register the plan, eligible individuals can still claim the credit on their tax returns, but will not be able to participate in the advance payment program.) However, the IRS guidance does not explain what happens if an EGHP is justified in terminating an individual's coverage if the HCTC Transaction Center is tardy in sending the payments.

The employer's and administrator's only reporting obligation is to respond to HCTC requests to verify a particular person's participation in the plan or payment history. The plan is also required to give eligible individuals a health plan invoice that allocates between the cost of basic coverage and excepted benefits (e.g., dental or vision coverage; health FSA coverage; coverage for family members who are not qualified) that are outside the scope of HCTC.

The Summary Plan Description (SPD) for an EGHP must include COBRA information: *see* DOL Regulation § 2520.102-3(o). The required statement of ERISA rights (ERISA § 102-3(t)) requires COBRA disclosures. Proposed regulations say that SPDs for health plans should disclose the potential availability of a special second election period under the Trade Act. Many plans provide the same information in COBRA notices and in the SPD, so changing one requires changing the other—which, in turn, may require a plan amendment and possibly a Summary of Material Modifications. DOL considers it acceptable to use the SPD to meet the initial COBRA notice requirement, but that will probably require amending the SPD to include all the mandatory provisions. *See* § 1.18 for a discussion of the health care continuation rights of the family of reservists called to active duty. [EBIA Weekly Questions of the Week *How Do the DOL's Proposed COBRA Regs Affect Our Group Health Plan's SPD Disclosures?* (July 23, 2003), <http://www.ebia.com/weekly/questions/2003/COBRAS030723.jsp>]

Although COBRA does not define "gross misconduct," the standard is probably the same as "willful misconduct"—substantial and willful disregard of the employer's best interests. [*Chatterjee v. School Dist. of Philadelphia*, 170 F. Supp. 2d 509 (E.D. Pa. 2001). *But see Lloynd v. Hanover Foods Corp.*, 72 F. Supp. 2d 469 (D. Del. 1999) (a factory worker fired for ruining a batch of product was merely negligent, and therefore was entitled to COBRA notice; the plan had to pay $3,000 of her medical expenses, plus a $25,250 civil penalty ($50 a day) for failure to give notice]

A truck driver was fired for attending to personal business instead of making a scheduled delivery. At the time of termination, he was informed orally about his COBRA rights and received a written notice with his last paycheck. The District Court for the District of Minnesota ruled that although oral COBRA notice is sometimes adequate, it was not clear in this case whether the plaintiff received enough information to make an informed decision. The plaintiff also claimed that he telephoned the employer several times to get information, which could be considered evidence that the employer had not provided proper written notice. The employer also charged that the employee was not entitled to make a COBRA election because his gross misconduct made him ineligible, but the District Court refused to grant summary judgment and required the case to be tried. [*Rengo v. Lakehead Oil Co., Inc.*, 2005 U.S. Dist. LEXIS 8422 (D. Minn. 2005), <http://www.nysd.uscourts.gov/courtweb/pdf/Do8MNXC/05-02891.PDF>]

Whenever a "qualifying event" occurs, anyone who performs services for the employer and is covered by the EGHP must be given COBRA rights—including partners, self-employed people who are allowed to participate in the plan, and eligible independent contractors.

Even persons who are not covered by the EGHP may have some legal rights; Reg. § 54.4980B-3 says that workers are considered to have coverage that was denied or not offered because of a violation of applicable law. The Southern District of New York refused to dismiss COBRA and ERISA claims in a case brought by a worker who had a contract with the defendant giving strong indications that she was an independent contractor and not a common-law employee, on the grounds that the contract was not dispositive of her status, and she had a right to prove that she was a common-law employee and that she was entitled to COBRA coverage. [*Baraschi v. Silverwear, Inc.*, 2002 U.S. Dist. LEXIS 24515 (S.D.N.Y. Dec. 18, 2002)]

> **Tip:** Continuation coverage is also available if the ex-employee's child is no longer a dependent because he or she has reached age 19 and is not a full-time student.

Long-term disability (LTD) coverage was denied for a work-related injury on the ground that the injured person was a temporary employee who was not eligible for the plan. He sued for wrongful denial of benefits, claiming that his transition from permanent to temporary status should have triggered a COBRA notice. However, the Eastern District of Louisiana ruled that LTD benefits provide income replacement, not health coverage, so they are exempt from COBRA. Ancillary medical benefits under an LTD plan, however, are subject to COBRA. [*Goldman v. Hartford Life & Accident Ins. Co.*, 2004 U.S. Dist. LEXIS 18266 (E.D. La. 2004)]

An employer's cessation of contributions to a plan is not a COBRA event, even if it results in a loss of coverage. Termination of employment is a qualifying event, however, and the plaintiffs lost their jobs about a year after the employer stopped making contributions to its multiemployer plan. The District Court for the District of New Jersey held that the trustees breached their fiduciary duty by failing to tell the employees in time about the effects of the employer's delinquency. Therefore, the court required the plan to provide benefit coverage up to the date the employees were notified of the termination of coverage. [*Martinez v. District 1199J Nat'l Union*, 2003 U.S. Dist. LEXIS 15605 (D.N.J. Sept. 9, 2003)]

A terminated employee sued his ex-employer for a variety of employment-related causes of action, including failure to offer COBRA coverage. The COBRA claim was dismissed because the plaintiff did not make a credible claim of having vested benefits. Therefore, he was not a plan participant, and failed to state a claim for benefits or damages from failure to receive benefits. However, he was given 14 days to amend the complaint if he could show his participant status. [*Lakin v. Skaletsky*, 2003 U.S. Dist. LEXIS 15449 (N.D. Ill. Sept. 4, 2003)]

An employee applied for health insurance, but the insurer never received the application. Months later, the employee was terminated. Post-termination, the employee was hospitalized, accruing medical bills of over $100,000. The District Court for the Middle District of Florida dismissed the COBRA claim (because the employee never achieved coverage under the EGHP in the first place), but suit was allowed to proceed on ERISA claims of breach of fiduciary duty and negligence claims based on state agency law. [*Kobold v. Aetna US Healthcare*, 258 F. Supp. 2d 1317 (M.D. Fla. 2003)]

If a cafeteria plan includes health benefits, COBRA applies only to benefits actually elected by a plan participant, not those that he or she declines. COBRA does not apply to Flexible Spending Accounts, Medical Savings Accounts, or to plans that are substantially limited to qualified long-term care services, because these are not deemed to be conventional health plans.

When a person makes a COBRA election, health insurance coverage continues under the EGHP—but the employee, not the employer, pays the premium. (The employer can also agree to subsidize the COBRA premium, e.g., as an early retirement incentive.) The employer can impose an administrative charge of up to 2% of the premium, but no other fees or charges. The COBRA premium is set once a year, in advance.

[B] Covered Businesses

Businesses are subject to COBRA if they have 20 or more employees on a typical workday, and if they maintain a group health plan (either insured or self-insured). Most of the states (all except Alabama, Arizona, Delaware, Hawaii, Idaho, Indiana, Michigan, Montana, Pennsylvania, Virginia, and Washington) have COBRA expansion statutes that require companies with fewer than 20 employees to provide the equivalent of the federal COBRA notice and continuation coverage rights.

The District Court for the District of Puerto Rico ruled in 2002 that an employer who had 27 workers employed at two stores was subject to COBRA, even though two of those were owners of the business and seven were relatives of the owners, and only 10 people were covered under the plan. In this analysis, family relationship is irrelevant, and COBRA exempts small employers but not small health plans. [*Jiminez v. Mueblerias Delgado Inc.*, 196 F. Supp. 2d 125 (D.P.R. 2002)]

Unpaid part-time officials of a not-for-profit organization were not "employees" for purposes of determining whether there were 20 employees, so the general manager (a paid employee) was unable to bring a COBRA suit. [*Giddens v. University Yacht Club Inc.*, 2006 U.S. Dist. LEXIS 10631 (N.D. Ga. 2006)]

The length of the continuation coverage period can be anywhere from 30 days (in Oklahoma) to 24 months (Connecticut); the most common duration is 18 months, required in California, Colorado, Florida, Kentucky, Maryland, Massachusetts, Minnesota, Nevada, New Hampshire, New York, North Carolina, Rhode Island, South Dakota, West Virginia, and Wisconsin. [This information comes from State Health Facts Online: State Continuation Coverage for Small Firm Employees (COBRA Expansions) on the Kaiser Family Foundation Web site, <http://statehealthfacts.org/cgi-bin/healthfacts.cgi?action=compare . . . >]

See Rev. Rul. 2003-70, 2003-27 I.R.B. 3 (effective for stock sales and asset sales on or after July 7, 2003) for guidance on COBRA compliance when an employer only reaches the 20-employee level as a result of a stock or asset acquisition. If a transfer of stock means that two previously separate employers are now treated as a single employer, then the employees of both during the previous year are aggregated. If the total is 20 or greater, the combined entity is subject to COBRA as of the date of the stock transfer. However, if it is an asset acquisition, and the buyer and seller do not become a single employer, then the successor is exempt from COBRA until it has 20 employees.

Under Reg. § 54.4980B-9 Q&A 8(c), the buyer of substantial assets (e.g., substantially all of the assets of a trade or business, or at least of a division or a plant) becomes the seller's successor employer only if it continues the business operations without substantial change—and if the seller stops providing group health plans to all employees in connection with the sale. However, if the buyer company does become a successor employer, its group health plan must make COBRA coverage available to any M&A qualified beneficiaries of the seller corporation—even if the buyer corporation would otherwise be exempt from COBRA.

In 2002, the District Court for the District of Columbia ruled that a successor employer was subject to COBRA because there had been a sale or transfer of substantial assets of the selling corporation (for instance, databases and intellectual property). The acquirer continued to use the seller's business location and equipment, and most of the seller's employees were re-hired at the same salary. The plaintiff was awarded attorney's fees, although not in the amount requested. The court ruled that the award of fees was justified because this was the first case to interpret COBRA's regulations on successor liability, and the plaintiff's position was substantially justified by the regulations. On rehearing, the court affirmed the fee award. [*Risteen v. Youth for Understanding Inc.*, 245 F. Supp. 2d 1 (D.D.C. 2003)]

Note, however, that employees probably will not be able to sue in state court if they allege that COBRA claims were denied in bad faith, because this is an area in which ERISA preempts state enforcement. [*Estate of Coggins v. Wagner Hopkins Inc.*, 183 F. Supp. 2d 1126 (W.D. Wis. 2001); *Harrelson v. Blue Cross/Blue Shield of Alabama*, 150 F. Supp. 2d 1290 (M.D. Ala. 2001). The *Coggins* case also says that the ex-employee cannot sue the employer, insurer, or plan administrator to recover medical expenses that she had to pay out-of-pocket when her COBRA coverage was improperly terminated]

Self-insured plans are subject to COBRA, too. The "premium" for them is a reasonable estimate, using reasonable actuarial assumptions, of the cost of providing health coverage for employees similarly situated to the qualified beneficiary.

Continuation coverage must be the same as active employees receive, although continuation coverage can change as the underlying plan changes. If the employer terminates or reduces coverage in an EGHP, qualified beneficiaries must be allowed to elect coverage under whatever plan the employer continues to maintain for similarly situated active employees. The employer cannot condition continuation coverage on submission of evidence of insurability. [*See* I.R.C. § 4980B(f)(2)(D)]

This discussion has centered around the employer, but what about the insurer, another important party when coverage rights are at stake? The Eastern District of Louisiana permitted an insurer that prematurely terminated COBRA coverage (because of an administrative error) to be sued in state court for money damages. In the court's view, the action dealt with the business of insurance, and not administration of a qualified plan. In this case, the plaintiff was denied benefits because of inefficient handling of paperwork, not on the basis of an exercise of discretion in interpretation of plan terms. However, ERISA did preempt the claims charging the insurer with breach of contract and bad faith. [*Duchesne-Baker v. Extendicare Health Services, Inc.*, 2003 WL 22327192 (E.D. La. Oct. 9, 2003)]

[C] Family Rights

The employee's spouse and children may also have independent rights to maintain coverage: for instance, after a divorce, when the former employee dies, or when the former employee becomes eligible for Medicare. (In this situation, the former employee no longer has COBRA rights—but, because Medicare does not cover spouses or dependents, these family members have COBRA rights.)

Continuation coverage is available if the ex-employee's child is no longer a dependent (e.g., reaches age 19 and is not a full-time student).

The one-time employee can exercise the COBRA election on behalf of his or her spouse and children, and the spouse can exercise the election on behalf of the children. However, only plan participants, not their beneficiaries, are entitled to receive penalties if the plan administrator fails to provide COBRA notice. [*Wright v. Hanna Steel Corp.*, 270 F.3d 1336 (11th Cir. 2001)]

Rev. Rul. 2002-88, 2002-52 I.R.B. 995 tackles the issue of when COBRA coverage has to be made available to an ex-spouse based on the employee ex-spouse's termination of EGHP coverage. The plan referred to in the Ruling allows the employee spouse to terminate spousal coverage, removing the non-employee spouse from the EGHP at the end of the month of the notice. The plan terms also say that eligibility is lost as of the date of divorce from an employee spouse. If the employee, anticipating a divorce, removes the non-employee spouse from coverage, the plan must make continuation coverage available to the non-employee spouse as of the date of the divorce. COBRA does not require, or even make provision for, extending continuation coverage before a qualifying event has occurred. Also note that, under Reg. § 54.4980B-6, the qualified beneficiary does not have to be offered the right to elect continuation coverage unless the plan administrator receives notice of the divorce or legal separation within 60 days of the date of the divorce or legal separation or the date the qualified beneficiary would lose coverage—whichever is later.

While a divorce case was pending, the court issued an order requiring the husband to maintain health insurance during the divorce action. The administrator of the husband's plan learned about the court order and notified the wife that there had been a COBRA event (legal separation); her coverage was terminated; and she was entitled to make a COBRA election. Although she made the election, neither spouse paid the premiums, and eventually her coverage was canceled for nonpayment. When the final divorce decree was granted, the wife made a second COBRA election. The plan administrator did not respond, and she brought suit. The state in question (Oklahoma) does not have a statutory definition of "legal separation," and there was no state precedent. On public policy grounds, the Northern District of Oklahoma ruled that living apart under a temporary court order does not constitute a legal separation and, therefore, is not a COBRA qualifying event. The court ordered the administrator to give COBRA notice and pay damages for out-of-pocket medical expenses as well as penalties for notice failure. [*Simpson v. T.D. Williamson Inc.*, 2003 U.S. Dist. LEXIS 25498 (N.D. Ok. 2003) and 2004 U.S. Dist. LEXIS 11531 (N.D. Ok. 2004)]

In light of Massachusetts' same-sex marriages and civil unions and domestic partnerships in several other states (*see* § 18.06), employers may wonder whether their ex-employees' same-sex partners are entitled to spousal coverage under COBRA. Because COBRA is a federal law, the existence of a federal Defense of Marriage Act means that in general a same-sex partner will not be treated as a spouse under, e.g., I.R.C. § 105, § 106, and § 125, unless the same-sex partner is the employee's dependent.

There is another limited exception in the case of a plan that has chosen to cover same-sex partners, because COBRA gives all qualified beneficiaries the same open enrollment rights as a similarly situated active employee who has not had a COBRA qualifying event. If an employee covered by a plan that covers same-sex partners loses coverage, the partner could therefore be added to the plan during the annual enrollment period.

It is also possible that a state "mini-COBRA" law will require domestic partner coverage; this is true in Massachusetts and Vermont. In Massachusetts, employers that are not subject to COBRA but have between two and twenty employees must offer continuation coverage, although self-insured plans are not required to do so. Group health policies and some HMOs must offer continuation coverage triggered on termination of membership in an insured group, an insured employee's death or layoff, plan closing, divorce, or legal separation.

Vermont provides civil union partners covered by EGHPs rights that do not exist under COBRA. The EGHP must permit continuation of coverage for up to six months after the employee dies or is terminated; there is a divorce or legal separation (including dissolution of a civil union); or a dependent child ceases to be a dependent under the policy.

If the employer has voluntarily chosen to extend domestic partner benefits, it might also want to amend the plan to create a COBRA-type right; if this coverage is offered voluntarily, the employer will not be required to cover all COBRA events or to extend coverage for the statutory COBRA periods. In this situation, the employer should make sure that the plan and SPD clearly identify the events triggering continuation coverage for domestic partners, and spouses and domestic partners covered under the plan should receive appropriately tailored notices. [Todd A. Solomon, Joseph S. Adams, Elizabeth A. Savard, *What COBRA Rights Exist for "Same-Gender Relationships"?* Thompson Publishing Group, Mandated Health Benefits-The COBRA Guide, <http://www.thompson.com/libraries/benefits/heal/samplenews/heal0408.html> (August 2004)]

[D] Duration of Coverage

COBRA specifies minimum obligations that employers must meet; they always have discretion to provide additional coverage.

The basic duration of COBRA continuation coverage for ex-employees is 18 months, starting with the qualifying event. However, if the ex-employee satisfies the Social Security Administration definition of total disability (basically, is incapable of substantial gainful activity), the employee and family members are entitled to 29 months of continuation coverage not 18. But for the 11 months after the end of the normal 18-month term, the employer can lawfully charge the employee 150% of the premium, not just the normal 102%.

Qualified beneficiaries can get 29 months of continuation coverage with respect to the same qualifying event if they are qualified with respect to a termination of employment or a reduction in hours; they became disabled within the first 60 days of COBRA continuation coverage; and they give the plan administrator a copy of the determination of disability within 60 days of the date it was issued and also within the initial 18-month COBRA period.

The ABA Joint Committee on Employee Benefits has an annual meeting with DOL officials at which the officials provide informal guidance on benefit matters. Under COBRA, plans can require notification that the individual continues to be disabled as a condition of extending coverage from 18 to 29 months. The DOL representatives were asked if a plan can refuse the extension on the grounds that the beneficiary did not provide the certification if the plan did not disclose the obligation. The DOL said that notice must be given before enforcing the requirement. But if the plan has given notice, it can enforce the requirement even if the beneficiary gets less than 60 days to provide notice. The coverage period is extended to 36 months when there is a second qualifying event (e.g., a divorce). The plan can require notice of the second qualifying event, but the minimum period for notice is 60 days from the date of the event, the date when the coverage would be lost due to the event, and the date on which the beneficiary is informed of the obligation to provide notice and how to do it—whichever is latest. [<http://www.abanet.org/jceb/2005/qa05dol.pdf>; *see* EBIA Weekly, *DOL Officials Offer Informal Views on Disability and Second Qualifying Event Notices from Qualified Beneficiaries* (benefitslink.com), Oct. 27, 2005]

If the qualifying event is the ex-employee's becoming eligible for Medicare, his or her qualified beneficiaries are entitled to 36 months of continuation coverage. *See* Rev. Rul. 2004-22, 2004-10 I.R.B. 553, providing that Medicare entitlement is not a second qualifying event for a beneficiary who would not have lost coverage under the plan as a result of Medicare entitlement. If the plan does not terminate coverage for the employee's spouse, the spouse is entitled to only 18 months of continuation coverage because there has not been a second qualifying event.

However, COBRA entitlement ends if:

- The employer terminates and does not replace the EGHP for active employees (in effect, there is no longer any plan whose coverage can be continued);
- The qualified beneficiary fails to pay the COBRA premium;
- The employee becomes eligible for Medicare (although family members still have COBRA rights);
- The qualified beneficiary gains coverage under another EGHP.

When there is a second qualifying event (here, a dependent beneficiary reached age 25) and the plan becomes aware of it (the plan was notified by the insurer and also by the dependent's father, who was also a qualified beneficiary), the qualified beneficiary under the second qualifying event is entitled to COBRA notice. When the son did not receive notice, he sued the employer in its role as plan administrator, seeking statutory penalties. The employer's position was that the young man's mother (who worked for the employer) had the obligation to inform the plan. The Western District of West Virginia held that notice from the father—another qualified beneficiary—was acceptable, so the case was remanded for trial as to whether the father gave proper notice. [*Birkhead v. St. Anne's-Belfield, Inc.*, 2005 U.S. Dist. LEXIS 18836 (W.D. Va. 2005)]

The Supreme Court ruled, in *Geissal v. Moore Medical Group* [524 U.S. 74 (1998)], that the employer can terminate COBRA coverage if the employee gains access to other coverage AFTER making a COBRA election, but cannot terminate COBRA eligibility on the basis of coverage (for instance, coverage under a spouse's plan) that the employee had access to before the COBRA election.

By the time the case was remanded to the district court, the plaintiff had died, and his estate maintained the litigation. The estate contended that the plan was unjustly enriched by refusing to provide benefits, so ERISA § 502(a)(3) entitled it to equitable relief. The district court disagreed saying that the estate sought money damages, which are not considered "equitable relief" for this purpose. [*Geissal v. Moore Med. Group*, 158 F. Supp. 2d 957 (E.D. Mo. 2001)] Years later, the case was still in the court system. The Eighth Circuit required Moore to pay the Geissal estate $217,369 in attorneys' fees and court costs, and certiorari was denied—so the effect was that the estate was not entitled to recover the expenses that were paid by the surviving spouse's EGHP, even though those expenses should have been paid by the decedent's EGHP. [*Geissal v. Moore Medical*, 338 F.3d 926 (8th Cir. 2003)].

A terminally ill employee lost eligibility under a welfare benefit plan as a result of her reduced work schedule. The employer permitted her to elect to continue EGHP benefits for 18 months. The COBRA notice outlined the benefits she could maintain, including medical, dental, vision, and life insurance. She elected continuation coverage, but the coverage was terminated for failure to pay premiums. When she died, her surviving spouse sued over denial of life insurance benefits. Summary judgment for the employer was denied, because there were factual disputes that would have to be resolved by a trial. The court found the notice unclear and might have led the employee to believe her life insurance coverage would continue for 18 months after her last day of work, not 18 months after her initial illness-related reduction in hours. The District Court for the District of Minnesota applied a COBRA analysis to continuation of life insurance benefits, even though COBRA is a health coverage statute. [*Murphy v. Board of Social Ministry*, 2004 U.S. Dist. LEXIS 12593 (D. Minn. 2004)]

[E] COBRA Regulations

The IRS published important Proposed Regulations at 63 Fed. Reg. 708 (Jan. 7, 1998), adopted as 26 C.F.R. § 54.4980B-1 to conform COBRA to HIPAA (see below), the Small Business Job Protection Act [Pub. L. No. 104-188], and various other statutes. As a result of these changes, qualified beneficiaries can get 29 months (rather than the basic 18 months) of COBRA coverage with respect to the same qualifying event if:

- They are all qualified with respect to a termination of employment or a reduction in hours;
- They became disabled (as defined by the Social Security Administration) within the first 60 days of COBRA continuation coverage;
- They gave the plan administrator a copy of the determination of disability within the initial 18-month COBRA period and also within 60 days of the date the determination was issued.

During the 11-month extension, the employer can charge a premium that is 150% of the applicable premium, whereas the employer is limited to charging 102% of the premium during the 18-month basic COBRA period. Charging 150% is not considered premium discrimination on the basis of health status, so I.R.C. § 9802(b) is not violated. If there is a second qualifying event during a disability extension, then COBRA coverage can last for 36 months, with the 150% premium charged until the end of the 36-month period.

HIPAA entitles children born to, or adopted by, covered employees during a period of COBRA coverage to be covered by COBRA. The child's maximum coverage period runs from the date of the employee's qualifying event, and not from the child's birth or adoption. The effect is that the child's COBRA coverage ends at the same time as the coverage of other family members.

Under the January 7, 1998 rule, Medical Savings Accounts and plans substantially all of whose coverage is for qualified long-term care services (as defined by I.R.C. § 7702B) are not subject to the COBRA continuation coverage obligation.

The IRS' next move was to finalize regulations first proposed in 1987. The Final Rule at 64 Fed. Reg. 5160 (Feb. 3, 1999) includes rules for coping with EGHPs during corporate transitions. [*See* § 16.01] It is effective for qualifying events that occur in plan years beginning on or after January 1, 2000. If the EGHP provides both core health coverage and noncore coverage (e.g., vision and dental), it is no longer necessary to allow qualified employees to elect only the core coverage.

Treasury Decision 8928, 66 Fed. Reg. 1843 (Jan. 10, 2001) supplements the February 1999 Final Rule. Treasury Decision 8928's effective date is January 10, 2001, and it applies to qualifying events that occur on or after January 1, 2002. Under this Treasury Decision, all benefits offered by a business are treated as a single plan, unless the governing instruments make it clear that the benefits come from separate plans.

If a plan claims exemption from COBRA on the grounds that it has fewer than 20 employees, part-time employees will be reflected in the calculation on the basis of Full-Time Equivalents (i.e., 80 persons working 10 hours a week = 20 FTEs), no matter how they are scheduled. This provision was included to deter employers from manipulating scheduling.

Treasury Decision 8928 also finalizes rules about COBRA requirements in business reorganizations. The purchaser of a substantial asset such as a plant or corporate division or of substantially all the assets of a trade or business will be treated as a successor employer if the seller entirely ceases to provide group health plans, and the buyer continues business operations involving the assets. A transfer that has the same effect (including a bankruptcy-related transaction) can be treated as an asset "sale" even if it takes some other form for official purposes. Under the T.D., in an asset sale, employees have a qualifying event if they terminate employment and do not receive continuation coverage from the successor—even if they are then rehired in the same job.

[F] HRAs

A Health Reimbursement Account (HRA) is a plan that offers specified dollar amounts to reimburse employees for health expenses they have paid. The IRS provided guidance under Notice 2002-45, 2002-28 I.R.B. 93 and Rev. Rul. 2002-41, 2002-28 I.R.B. 75. HRAs are considered group health plans, and therefore are subject to COBRA. If the HRA satisfies the safe harbor allowed under the IRS's 2002 guidance, balances can be rolled over from year to year, tax-free. The COBRA premium must be set in advance for each 12-month period, calculated based on the cost of covering similarly situated beneficiaries who did not experience a COBRA event. Self-funded plans must either determine the premium actuarially or calculate it on the basis of past costs. (Therefore, a new HRA that does not have claims experience will probably have to make actuarial calculations.) The premium must be set at the same level for each category of HRA qualified beneficiaries—the individual account balances must not affect the calculation. To cover administrative costs, the premium can be set at 102% of the employer's cost, or 150% during the COBRA disability extension.

The HRA must increase its maximum reimbursement amount at the same time, and by the same increment (and reduce it for reimbursed claims) on the same basis. Although there is no formal IRS guidance as to how to allocate the balance for a participant who has a spouse and/or children, the IRS's informal position is that account balances should be allocated based on the history of claim use within the family.

§ 19.03   COBRA AND THE FMLA

Taking FMLA leave [*see* Chapter 38] is not in and of itself a COBRA-qualifying event. But if an employee who was covered by the EGHP before or during the FMLA leave fails to return to work after the FMLA leave, there is a qualifying event for this person (and any dependent at risk of losing health coverage) as of the last day of the FMLA leave. The employer is not allowed to make the ex-employee reimburse the employer for health premiums paid during the leave.

However, there is no qualifying event if, while the employee is on leave, the employer eliminates EGHP coverage for the entire group of workers the person on leave belonged to. The rationale is that the worker would have lost health coverage even if he or she had not taken leave.

The qualifying event for an employee who does not return to work occurs on the last day of the FMLA leave, and the regular COBRA notice must be given. The qualifying event occurs even if the employee had an obligation to pay health insurance premiums during the leave but failed to do so. State laws that require a longer leave than the 12-week FMLA period are disregarded in determining whether a qualifying event has occurred.

§ 19.04   COBRA NOTICE

[A]   Generally

One of the most important tasks in COBRA administration is timely issuance of the proper notices, as provided by I.R.C. § 4980B(f)(6)(A) and ERISA § 606. There are two types of COBRA notice: one given to employees as soon as they become eligible for participation in the health plan (informing them of COBRA rights they might have in the future), and the other given to a qualified beneficiary in connection with a COBRA event. The employer has an obligation to notify the plan administrator when employment-related qualifying events occur, such as when an employee is terminated or laid off, or when the company files in Chapter 11 for bankruptcy protection. The responsibility for reporting personal qualifying events, such as divorce or separation, rests on the qualified beneficiary.

There are three timing requirements. The employee must give notice to the plan that a qualifying event has occurred within 60 days of the event. At that point, the employer has 30 days to notify the plan administrator that there has been a qualifying event for which COBRA notice must be provided; and the plan administrator has a further 14 days to actually issue the notice.

In May, 2003, the Department of Labor published Proposed Rules to clarify the requirements for giving COBRA notice (including notice for people qualified for Trade Adjustment Assistance benefits). *See* 68 Fed. Reg. 38132 (May 28, 2003). The proposal includes updated model notices.

The notice should explain:

- Who can be a qualified beneficiary;
- What events trigger the right to continuation coverage;
- How and when to elect coverage;
- The right to reject the coverage (e.g., for financial reasons);
- Rights of the other qualified beneficiaries if one qualified beneficiary waives the election;
- Obligation to pay the premiums on time;
- How long the coverage will last;
- Events that will allow the employer to terminate continuation coverage.

Finalization occurred about a year after the proposals, via Final Rules published at 69 Fed. Reg. 30083 (May 26, 2004). The Final Rules retain the same structure as the proposals, but make some changes to reflect comments from the public. The May 2004 document also contains updated texts for the model notices to be used by single-employer plans. The new rules must be obeyed for notice obligations arising on or after the first day of the first plan year that starts on or after six months after the May 26, 2004, publication date. Therefore, for calendar-year plans, compliance is required as of January 1, 2005.

The Final Rules require notice to be furnished to covered employees and covered spouses on the earlier of two dates: 90 days from the first date of coverage (or the date on which the plan first becomes subject to COBRA, if that happens later), or the date on which the plan administrator has to provide a COBRA election notice.

Based on comments, DOL eliminated the proposal's requirement that the initial notice describe the obligation of beneficiaries receiving continuation coverage to provide notice of a second qualifying event. This information is potentially confusing at the initial stage, and the information is provided in the SPD and also in COBRA election notices, which will be given closer to the actual event.

The DOL decided to retain the provision in the proposal that the initial notice can be combined with the SPD. Also carried over are the provisions for employers to give notice to the plan administrator of events such as the employee's termination of employment or death, and the requirement that plans set up reasonable procedures for plan beneficiaries to use when they are required to report events (e.g., divorce or disability).

The Final Rules clear up the 44-day question by stating the this rule only applies to cases in which the employer has an obligation to give notice of an event to the plan administrator. The election notice must be furnished within 44 days of the qualifying event—or the date the qualified beneficiary ceases to be covered under the plan, if the plan's terms date the start of COBRA coverage from the loss of plan coverage.

The Final Rules liberalize the requirements for the 11-month disability extension. To get the extension, the qualified beneficiary has 60 days to submit notice of a Social Security Administration (SSA) determination of total disability. The 60-day period runs from the date of the official disability determination; the date of the qualifying event; the date on which the qualified beneficiary would lose COBRA coverage without the extension; or the date on which the qualified beneficiary is notified of the obligation to provide proof of the SSA determination—whichever is latest. This assists beneficiaries who, for technical reasons, might not be able to get the extension under the strict terms of the COBRA statute.

Unlike the proposal, the Final Rules say that the COBRA election notice does not have to inform qualified beneficiaries about alternative coverage available to them instead of COBRA. Nor must they be informed of options to convert their coverage after COBRA eligibility ends. Nevertheless, if the plan allows conversion to individual coverage, conversion must be made available for 180 days after qualified beneficiaries exhaust their COBRA eligibility.

The Final Rules require plan administrators to provide notice of termination of COBRA coverage, and notice when coverage is unavailable. There are no model notices for this purpose; plans have to draft their own. The notice of unavailability must be given within 14 days of receiving notice of a qualifying event when the plan denies coverage—whether or not the notice was given in proper form. Termination notices must be given as soon as practicable after the plan administrator determines that continuation coverage is ending.

Although the COBRA notice must be written, an oral waiver of the election has been held to be valid and enforceable. [*Hummer v. Sears, Roebuck & Co.*, 1994 U.S. Dist. LEXIS 3659 (E.D. Pa. March 21, 1994)] However, in 2002 the Eighth Circuit ruled that while the initial COBRA notice (given when a person becomes eligible for health plan participation) must be in writing, the notice about the availability of the COBRA election can be given orally to a terminating employee. [*Chesnut v. Montgomery*, 307 F.3d 698 (8th Cir. 2002)] The court found that adequate oral notice was provided (even though the beneficiary was not told information such as how to make an election or when to make the first premium payment). Failure to provide an election notice to the employee's spouse was treated as a technical violation. No penalties were ordered, because the employer acted in good faith and the plaintiff was not harmed by the notice failure. In a case arising before the 2003 Proposed Regulations, the Eastern District of Pennsylvania held that notice of the right to elect COBRA coverage was validly provided orally, during a telephone conversation between an employee's spouse and a representative of the employer. [*Heebner v. Nationwide Mutual Ins. Co.*, 2003 U.S. Dist. LEXIS 19569 (E.D. Pa. Sept. 30, 2003)]

Tip: Under Department of Labor Final Rules published on April 9, 2002, COBRA notices can be given electronically (for instance by e-mailing employees who consent to receive notice in electronic form), [*See* 67 Fed. Reg. 17263].

Although some cases have found that the employer's business records, showing that the COBRA notice was mailed, are adequate to prove that notice was given, even if the employer cannot produce a copy of the letter that was actually mailed [*Ramos v. SEIU Local 74 Welfare Fund*, 2002 U.S. Dist. LEXIS 5849 (S.D.N.Y. Apr. 5, 2002); *Roberts v. National Health Corp.*, 133 F.3d 916 (4th Cir. 1998)], the First Circuit reversed summary judgment for the employer that was granted on the basis of a sworn declaration of compliance by the employer's custodian of records, stating that the notice was sent by certified mail, return receipt requested—but the employer did not receive the receipt. The First Circuit reversed, holding that there was insufficient evidence of mailing, in that the sworn declaration was really just a note stating that the notice had been sent. The First Circuit remanded for trial on the fact issue of adequacy of notice. [*Claudio-Gotay v. Becton Dickinson Caribe, Ltd.*, 375 F.3d 99 (1st Cir. 2004)]

The Eastern District of New York ruled in favor of an employee who said he never received the COBRA notice that his employer claimed had been mailed. The court found that the employer, who was also the plan sponsor and administrator, failed to establish a presumption that the notice was mailed. There was no formal written policy; testimony of the person who allegedly mailed the notice was not introduced; there was no indication that the election notice had been mailed; and another terminated employee testified that he did not receive notice—all of which implied the absence of an effective procedure. [*Tufano v. Riegel Transp., Inc.*, No. 03-CV-0977 (E.D.N.Y. Feb. 11, 2006)]

According to the Fifth Circuit, the employer satisfies its duty by sending the notice by certified mail to the employee's last known address—even if the employer learns that the employee did not actually receive the notice [*Degruise v. Sprint Corp.*, 279 F.3d 333 (5th Cir. 2002)] The Southern District of Ohio reached a similar conclusion where the letter was returned to the plan administrator, marked "unclaimed"; the administrator is not required to prove actual receipt, only that a reasonable method was used to transmit the information. [*Holmes v. Scarlet Oaks Retirement Community*, 2003 U.S. Dist. LEXIS 14250 (S.D. Ohio July 24, 2003). The Northern District of California ruled similarly, that COBRA doesn't require that the employee actually receive the notice, only that the employer make a reasonable good faith effort to provide it. The evidence was undisputed that the employer prepared and mailed the notice in the ordinary course of business, relieving it of liability. [*Maya v. Inspro Corporation*, 2004 U.S. Dist. LEXIS 22880 (N.D. Cal. 2004); *see also Farrell v. AstraZeneca Pharm's LP*, 2005 U.S. Dist. LEXIS 18866 (D. Del. 2005)]

The Fourth Circuit found that it was not a breach of fiduciary duty for an HR manager not to discuss COBRA when the mother of a hospitalized ex-employee (who had quit his job the week before) called to ask about his medical coverage. A timely COBRA notice was sent to the employee's address, but nobody opened it during the brief time between his hospitalization and his death, and he did not make a COBRA election. The estate sued on grounds that it was a breach of duty not to provide the information, but the Fourth Circuit ruled that the employer satisfied its duty by sending the notice. The manager who spoke to the former employee's mother probably should have done more, but his duties were purely ministerial and he was not an ERISA fiduciary. [*Estate of Weeks v. Advance Stores Co. Inc.*, 2004 U.S. App. LEXIS 10637, No. 03-1926 (4th Cir. June 1, 2004)]

If the ex-employee clearly fails to make a timely election, this will excuse the plan administrator's mistake in putting an incorrect return date on the notice. [*Deering v. O.K. Indus.*, 9 Fed. Appx. 569 (8th Cir. 2001)]

In a failure-to-provide-notice case, the employer admitted that it did not provide COBRA notice, but that there was no bad faith because it believed that a letter sent by its health care provider several months after the termination complied with the statute. When the suit was filed, the employer offered COBRA coverage. The plaintiff declined. He had only one post-termination medical bill, for $285. To take up the coverage, he would have had to catch up on the back premiums, which would have cost much more than $285. The Southern District of New York granted summary judgment for the defendant, on the theory that the plaintiff had suffered no real damages. The court declined to exercise its discretion to impose statutory penalties, probably because it did not believe that the employer had committed any meaningful misconduct. [*Soliman v. Shark Inc.*, 2004 U.S. Dist. LEXIS 14254 (S.D.N.Y. 2004)]

Department of Labor Advisory Opinion 99-14A allows the health plan to satisfy the notice requirement by sending a single notice to multiple beneficiaries living at the same address: e.g., one first-class letter covering the employee, spouse, and dependent children. But there must either be a separate election notice in the mailing for each qualified beneficiary, or an explanation of their independent rights to elect coverage. [*See* <http://www.dol.gov/ebsa/regs/AOs/ao1999-14a.html>] In light of this Advisory Opinion, *McDermott v. Case Windham Pub. Schools* [225 F. Supp. 2d 180 (D. Conn. 2002)] dismissed a COBRA claim brought by a teacher who claimed that, although she received adequate COBRA notice from the school district that fired her, the minor children living with her were entitled to separate COBRA notices.

In another 2004 case, the plaintiff charged that after he was terminated, his minor daughter did not receive adequate notice of her COBRA rights. A notice, referring to "you and/or your covered dependents," was mailed to the employee's last known address. The plaintiff said that neither he nor his daughter ever received a notice, so he did not make a COBRA election. His daughter required surgery, generating a large medical bill. The District Court for the District of Minnesota rejected the plaintiff's contention that the daughter was entitled to separate COBRA notice. Although the employer's records about notice mailing were not perfect, the court held that the employer had met its burden of proving that notice was mailed, and it is presumed that properly sent notices will be received. [*Starr v. Metro Systems Inc.*, 2004 U.S. Dist. LEXIS 15744 (D. Minn. 2004)]

However, because of common-sense factors about the behavior of divorcing couples, it does not fulfill the notice obligation for a plan administrator, notified by an employee of the employee's divorce, to give the employee the COBRA notice to deliver to his or her ex-spouse! [*Phillips v. Saratoga Harness Racing Inc.*, 233 F. Supp. 2d 361 (N.D.N.Y. 2002)]

Qualified beneficiaries must be given a period of at least 60 days to either accept or waive continuation coverage. The election period must begin no later than the time EGHP coverage would end if there were no election. In other words, notice must be given early enough to prevent any gap in coverage. The Eleventh Circuit has ruled that if the COBRA notice fails to specify the 60-day period, then the right to make the election extends indefinitely. [*Branch v. G. Bernd Co.*, 955 F.2d 1574 (11th Cir. 1992)] The Fifth Circuit ruled that an employer can have a COBRA election period of any length, as long as the period is at least 60 days. Participants in a plan that failed to set an election deadline could therefore make a COBRA election at any time during the 18 months following the qualifying event. [*Lifecare Hosps. Inc. v. Health Plus of Louisiana Inc.*, 418 F.3d 436 (5th Cir. 2005)]

If an ex-employee needs only a certain number of months of COBRA coverage (usually the waiting period for eligibility in a new plan), COBRA does not permit the ex-employer's plan to require the ex-employee to pay for a full 18 months of retroactive coverage. [*Popovits v. Circuit City Stores Inc.*, 185 F.3d 276 (7th Cir. 1999)]

The first premium payment is not due until 45 days after the election. Qualified beneficiaries get an automatic grace period of at least 30 days, during which coverage cannot be terminated for nonpayment of premiums—even if the underlying EGHP has a shorter grace period. But if the plan provides a longer grace period, the employee must be permitted to take advantage of it.

Several months after being laid off, an employee asked about COBRA. He was allowed to make the election but was required to catch up on seven months' of premiums since he had been laid off. He made that back payment but did not pay the premium for the next month. After the grace period elapsed, his coverage was terminated. He sued the employer and its TPA for failure to provide a timely election notice, and for wrongful termination of COBRA coverage. The Northern District of California dismissed the claims against the TPA but awarded a $2,300 penalty against the employer for failure to provide notice. (A notice was mailed, but to the employee's former address which was not the last known address in the employer's payroll records.) Summary judgment was granted for the employer on the claim of wrongful termination of coverage, because the employee had no right to insist that his back payments be applied prospectively, and because coverage would not have been terminated if the employee had continued to make timely payments. [*Chaganti v. Sun Microsystems*, 2004 U.S. Dist. LEXIS 24243 (N.D. Cal. 2004)]

A plan that permits retirees to continue coverage at their own expense for an indefinite time (after the COBRA requirement ends) nevertheless must issue COBRA notices at retirement, because retirement is a COBRA event. [*Mansfield v. Chicago Park Dist. Group Plan*, 997 F. Supp. 1053 (N.D. Ill. 1998)]

In *Fallo v. Piccadilly Cafeterias Inc.* [141 F.3d 580 (5th Cir. 1998)], an employee was entitled to an 11-month COBRA extension, after the normal 18-month period, because his wife became disabled during the 18-month period. The terms of the plan echoed the COBRA statute, requiring that notice of the Social Security Administration's determination of disability be given before the initial 18-month period expired. But the SPD merely required that notice be given to the plan within 60 days of the SSA disability determination and did not rule out extensions for disabilities beginning late in the 18-month period. The SPD was the document given to employees, and therefore the document that the Fifth Circuit chose to enforce. In late 2002, the Supreme Court denied certiorari [123 S. Ct. 487 (2002)], thus leaving the Fifth Circuit decision in place.

An employer that mistakenly extended continuation coverage longer than the collectively bargained date could lawfully terminate the coverage as soon as it discovered the mistake, even though the former employee's wife had encountered $45,000 in hospital bills in the meantime. The case of *Coker v. TWA* [165 F.3d 579 (7th Cir. 1999)] holds that it was not reasonable of the plaintiff to rely on the employer's mistake, because the plaintiff received an accurate written explanation of the benefits when he was laid off.

An independent contractor who was covered by an EGHP as part of his contract became eligible for COBRA upon the contract's termination. However, a COBRA notice was issued 10 months later. The notice erroneously stated that his plan eligibility terminated that month. After one year of paying premiums (rather than the 18 months he expected), he was told that his entitlement expired and his coverage would end in one month. He sued the employer and asked for a temporary injunction to maintain the coverage. The Eastern District of Wisconsin refused to grant an injunction, holding that the late notice did not extend the COBRA coverage period. He did not show a critical need for health care, only that out-of-pocket payment could be expensive. However, the court warned the employer that the lateness of the notice might entitle the plaintiff to statutory penalties and to other relief under ERISA § 502 if the lateness of the notice prevented the plaintiff and his wife from obtaining replacement coverage without preexisting-condition exclusions. [*Koopman v. Forest County Potawatomi Member Benefit Plan*, No. 06-C-0163 (E.D. Wis. Feb. 15, 2006)]

The Eighth Circuit affirmed an award of $8,030 in statutory penalties for COBRA notice failure plus $11,550 in ERISA statutory penalties for failure to supply an SPD on written request. The employer was also ordered to provide a certificate of life insurance for $38,000 minus the premiums the plaintiff would have paid to exercise the right to convert the policy to individual insurance.

The plaintiff was placed on disability leave, and was terminated when she was unable to return to work after leave expired. The termination letter, sent November 15, 2000, described the effective date of her termination as October 29, 2000, and also said she would receive further information about benefit eligibility. An important benefit was the ability to continue life insurance coverage without proof of insurability, because the plaintiff's health condition made it hard for her to buy insurance.

The SPD, which was printed in the employee handbook, explained the various benefit issues, but the plaintiff left her copy in her locker, and it was thrown out when she was on disability leave. The plaintiff made at least two telephone calls to get information and was told the information would be provided. Then she hired a lawyer, who sent two written requests for benefit information. COBRA and insurance conversion forms were finally provided in late February 2001. The plaintiff tried to exercise the life insurance conversion option, but it was denied as untimely (past the 31-day deadline). The standard for awarding penalties is whether the plan abused its discretion and, if so, to what extent. The Eighth Circuit ruled that it is unfair to deny a request as untimely if the plan said information would be forthcoming and repeatedly failed to provide the information. The court also accepted restoration of life insurance coverage as a valid equitable remedy, because it placed the plaintiff in the position she would have been in if the defendant had not acted improperly. [*Brown v. Aventis Pharmaceuticals Inc.*, 341 F.3d 822 (8th Cir. 2003)]

Similar issues arose in a case in which, some two months after termination, a former employee received a document described as a COBRA enrollment application, plus a cursory cover letter from the employer. The employee never responded. The employer nevertheless continued coverage for about five months after employment ended. At that point, the employer terminated coverage. After a letter from the ex-employee's lawyer, coverage was reinstated, but in a way that left a coverage gap of a month and a half. The ex-employee sued the ex-employer under ERISA § 502(c), seeking damages purely for the failure to provide adequate COBRA notice. (The employee did not incur any medical expenses that were not reimbursed because of the lack of notice.) The Third Circuit upheld the imposition of a penalty of $2 a day (a small penalty, because despite the employer's failure to meet its duty, there were no real consequences) for 521 days (starting 44 days after the end of employment, ending at the end of the 18-month COBRA notice period). The court also awarded $5 a day for 243 days for failure to provide a copy of the plan's SPD on request. [*Veneziano v. Long Island Pipe Fabrication & Supply*, 79 Fed. Appx. 506 (3d Cir. 2003)]

An employee who had COBRA coverage under a former employer's plan got a new job. The new employer reimbursed the employee's out-of-pocket expenses for that coverage. The employee was never covered by the second employer's health plan. When the second job ended, the employee did not receive COBRA notice and brought suit. He claimed—unsuccessfully—that reimbursement of his COBRA premiums created a new EGHP, separate from the regular plan, entitling him to COBRA notice under this separate plan when he was terminated. The Southern District of Ohio disagreed and entered summary judgment for the employer because the notice obligation would only have existed if the plaintiff had been covered by the second employer's EGHP on the day before employment ended; reimbursement for the COBRA premiums was an item of compensation, not a benefit plan. [*Cox v. Transit Group Transp.*, 2005 U.S. Dist. LEXIS 21698 (S.D. Ohio 2005)]

Similar issues were raised when a Mississippi plaintiff got a new job. He claimed that his new employer agreed to transmit the COBRA election form to the ex-employer and to pick up the premiums for 60 days, until the plaintiff would be eligible for participation in its health plan. The new employer did not do this. The plaintiff went back to work for his ex-employer, who had continued coverage for the plaintiff and had paid large medical bills for his wife. The first employer tried to recoup these amounts from the health care providers. The providers tried to get the plaintiff to pay them directly, and the employee sued the administrator of the ex-employer's plan. The Northern District of Mississippi dismissed the case. All the first employer was required to do was provide COBRA notice, which it did; the first employer was not responsible for any failures on the part of the second employer. [*Lloyd v. Harrington Benefit Servs., Inc.*, 2006 U.S. Dist. LEXIS 13287 (N.D. Miss. 2006)]

The inadequacy of termination and COBRA notices led to reinstatement of a plan beneficiary's claims for medical and severance benefits for his deceased wife. A company shut down operations at one location, transferring some employees to another location and terminating all those who were not transferred. The decedent had tuberculosis and was HIV positive and was frequently out sick. She elected to participate in a special severance program for employees who worked until the scheduled plant closure. About two weeks before the plant closed, the decedent was hospitalized, and died a few months later. Nine days before she entered the hospital, she received a letter saying she had been retroactively "separated." This was her only notice of termination or COBRA eligibility. She did not return the COBRA election form, so her coverage was terminated. Because she was ill at the time of the closing, she did not receive the severance payment.

The District Court granted summary judgment for the employer, but the Third Circuit permitted suit to proceed. The Third Circuit found the termination letter inadequate because it did not explain the term "qualifying event"; lay people cannot be presumed to be familiar with this term. The inadequacy of the notice made the employer liable for the decedent's health care costs. A full trial was required to determine the decedent's eligibility for severance benefits; evidence was required as to whether she was terminated or placed on medical leave of absence. Even if she was terminated, it was possible that she had a medical "early release" that qualified her for the severance benefit. [*Emilien v. Stull*

Technologies Corp., No. 02-1422, 2003 U.S. App. LEXIS 14515 (3d Cir. July 8, 2003)]

A plaintiff brought suit (two years minus two days after being fired), alleging failure to pay wages within 72 hours as required by federal law, and also alleging failure to satisfy the COBRA notice requirement. He sought the court's permission to amend his complaint to assert a claim of breach of fiduciary duty, and to seek damages under 29 U.S.C. § 1132(c)(1) for failure to comply with a request for plan information. The employer opposed the motion, stating that it had in fact provided COBRA notice, but that the COBRA claims were time-barred. COBRA itself does not include a statute of limitations, so a statute of limitations has to be "borrowed." The Southern District of West Virginia refused to use the statute of limitations for breach of contract cases, preferring to use the one for unfair insurance-related practices. That was only one year, so the COBRA notice claims were time-barred. [*Harvey v. Mingo Logal Coal Co.*, Civ. No. 2:02-1177 (S.D.W.V. Aug. 5, 2003)]

The Fifth Circuit held that a suit filed more than four years after the employer's alleged failure to give COBRA notice was time-barred. The court applied the state's statute of limitations for unfair insurance practices (two years). The case also involved an ERISA § 510 claim, which was also time-barred because it was also subject to a two-year statute of limitations. The Fifth Circuit noted that in other COBRA cases, a one-year statute of limitations has been applied (under a different insurance bad faith law), as has a six-year period as a claim for economic damages. [*Lopez v. Premium Auto Acceptance Corp.*, 389 F.3d 504 (5th Cir. 2004); the Southern District of New York also applied the unfair insurance practices statute of limitations (although in New York, it is a three-year period); the court rejected the employer's suggestion that the one-year-plus-30-day statute of limitations for negligence applied: *Treanor v. Metropolitan Transp. Auth.*, 2005 U.S. Dist. LEXIS 35861 (S.D.N.Y. 2005)]

The day after his EGHP coverage ended, a terminated employee had surgery. He had not been given a chance to make a COBRA election. He sued the plan to get it to pay for the surgery and for statutory penalties. A two-year statute of limitations applied; the question was when the two-year period began to run. In the employer's view, two letters from health care providers indicating the plaintiff's uninsured status triggered the running of the statute of limitations. The plaintiff denied receiving the letters. The Fifth Circuit held that summary judgment was inappropriate because it could not be presumed that the plaintiff received the letters; it was a factual issue to be resolved at trial. The second letter was sent by certified mail, but there was no delivery receipt—and it was sent to the wrong address. [*Burton v. Banta Global Turnkey Ltd.*, 2006 U.S. App. LEXIS 7271 (5th Cir. 2006), <http://www.ca5.uscourts.gov/opinions/unpub/04/04-20721.0.wpd.pdf>]

COBRA-qualified beneficiaries have been treated as unsecured creditors of the employer, if the employer sells its assets and then goes bankrupt. [*In re ABC Fabrics of Tampa, Inc.*, 259 B.R. 759 (M.D. Fla. 2001)]

In a Southern District of New York case, an employee signed a separation agreement releasing all employment-related claims in exchange for the employer's agreement to pay premiums for the first six months of COBRA coverage. Despite the release, she filed ADA charges with the EEOC and eventually brought suit. In 2003, the Southern District dismissed the suit, finding the release to be valid and enforceable. The promise to pay the COBRA premiums was valid consideration and adequate for the release. At that stage, the Southern District did not accept the plaintiff's argument that the release was fraudulently obtained in that she had not received a COBRA notice. The court said that she signed before the end of the 44-day notice period, at a point when the employer's obligation to provide the notice had not matured.

In 2004, however, the Southern District affirmed its basic decision to dismiss most of the claims but reinstated one of the claims: the allegation that the employer violated COBRA by not providing the election notice. At this stage, the Southern District ruled that the release did not vitiate the duty to provide notice because it was not clear whether the employee fully comprehended her rights when she signed the release. The release itself could not be considered an adequate COBRA notice because it did not contain all the mandated items, and it was not timely under the COBRA calendar. [*Knoll v. Equinox Fitness Clubs*, 2003 U.S. Dist. LEXIS 23086 (S.D.N.Y. Dec. 11, 2003), *modified* 2004 U.S. Dist. LEXIS 3690 (S.D.N.Y. Mar. 9, 2004)]

In another case involving releases, an employee scheduled for RIF was given 45 days to decide whether to accept a severance package, including payment of COBRA premiums. The severance package was conditioned on signing a release of all employment-related claims. Before she signed the release, she received a COBRA information packet from the employer and other COBRA materials from the employer's TPA. The employee accepted most of the severance payments, then sued the employer, alleging employment discrimination. The plaintiff charged that the release was invalid because it was obtained under duress; she said she was threatened with loss of COBRA benefits if she did not release her claims. The Washington Court of Appeals was not persuaded because there was insufficient evidence that she had been misled about COBRA rights, and she had been given correctly phrased COBRA materials before she signed the release. The court accordingly dismissed her discrimination claims. [*Goh v. American President Lines, Ltd.*, 2005 Wash. App. LEXIS 922 (Wash. App. 2005)]

[B] Penalties for Notice Failure

The Internal Revenue Code and ERISA § 502(g) impose a penalty of $110 per day per beneficiary for noncompliance, subject to a maximum of $220 per family per day. There is also a limit of the smaller of $500,000 or 10% of the amount the employer paid (or incurred obligations for) its EGHPs in the preceding year. Furthermore, a health plan that does not conform to COBRA does not generate I.R.C. § 162 "ordinary and necessary business expenses." Therefore, the employer is denied a deduction for health plan costs.

The penalty is imposed on the employer. It can also be imposed on the individuals responsible for administering the plan or providing benefits under it, if those individuals have contractual responsibility for running the plan. A third-party administrator (TPA) would fall into this category unless factors beyond the administrator's control prevented the notice from being given.

In *Hall v. CWR Construction, Inc.* [42 Fed. Appx. 593 (E.D. Ark. 2002)], a terminated employee who did not receive COBRA notice sued both the employer and the insurance agency serving as its TPA for notice failure. The employer and TPA each claimed that the other was the plan administrator responsible for giving notice. The Eastern District of Arkansas dismissed COBRA claims as against the TPA but not against the employer. Because the plan failed to designate a plan administrator, the employer was responsible for this role. The employer was permitted to sue the TPA for breach of contract in failing to issue the notice.

There is a cap of $2 million for all plans administered, for an administrator who fails to satisfy all the COBRA requirements, but who is not guilty of willful neglect and who did have reasonable support for his or her decisions.

The penalty can be reduced or waived if no one had reason to know that the appropriate notices were not given, or if the failure to notify was corrected within 30 days after a responsible person became aware of the failure.

Statutory penalties are not available in a suit for denial of benefits, only for refusal or failure to provide the necessary notice. [*Moreno v. St. Francis Hosp. & Health Ctr.*, 2001 U.S. Dist. LEXIS 17206 (N.D. Ill. Oct. 17, 2001)]

The Southern District of Ohio imposed $1,020 in statutory penalties on a plan that failed to send a COBRA notice. The court rejected the employer's argument that the ex-employee could not afford the premiums and therefore was not damaged by the notice failure. [*Chenoweth v. Wal-Mart Stores Inc.*, 159 F. Supp. 2d 1032 (S.D. Ohio 2001)]

In addition to the statutory penalties, any person or organization can be sued under ERISA Title I by someone who lost coverage because of the defendant's actions or inaction.

For instance, *Wright v. Hanna Steel Corp.* [270 F.3d 1336 (11th Cir. 2001)] affirms the District Court's award of $75/day penalties to the participant when the employer failed to provide COBRA notice. However, the Eleventh Circuit reversed the District Court's award to the participant's spouse and children.

In this case, the plaintiff quit his job at the end of 1996, and did not receive a COBRA notice. He started a new job right away and applied to transfer his family's coverage to the new employer's plan. The transfer application was denied because the insurer's records showed that he was still covered by the former employer's plan. A couple of months later, the plaintiff told the former employer about the situation and asked it to check its records, but he got no reply. Several months after that, the plaintiff's wife was diagnosed with cancer. The insurer treated her illness as a non-covered preexisting condition. Eventually, the insurer agreed to cover the wife's cancer treatment. The plaintiff sued the employer for statutory penalties for failure to provide notice, for failure to provide the notice, and for attorneys' fees. The District Court awarded a total of $93,000: $75/day to the employee and his wife, $10/day to the children for a period of 18 months, plus $24,000 in attorneys' fees.

The Western District of Michigan imposed a penalty of $55 a day (i.e., half the possible penalty), for a total of $27,610, when the employer failed to provide proper notice after the qualifying event. More than a year later—and after suit had been filed—the employer offered COBRA coverage. The employee refused, because the employer demanded a lump-sum payment of premiums, and the plaintiff was at risk of denial of retroactive claims.

The District Court ordered the employer to renew and clarify the COBRA offer, requiring a new 60-day election with monthly (not lump-sum) premiums, but did not order the employer to pay medical expenses the plaintiff had incurred in the interim. The District Court also ordered the employer to pay $23,730 in attorneys' fees to the plaintiff, in part because of the employer's bad faith, calculated at the $150/hour market rate for the locality, but without a "multiplier." [*Holford v. Exhibit Design Consultants,* 218 F. Supp. 2d 901 (W.D. Mich. 2001). A $55/day penalty was also assessed in *Burris v. Five River Carpenter District Council Health and Welfare Fund,* No. 3:01-cv-30091 (S.D. Iowa Jan. 15, 2004); only half the maximum was assessed based on a finding that the plan eventually offered full retroactive COBRA coverage, and had not acted maliciously.]

An unusually high $100/day penalty for 215 days (a level of $5–$20 a day is more common) was awarded in *DiGiovanni v. The Guardian Life Ins. Co. of America* [2002 U.S. Dist. LEXIS 12380 (D. Mass. June 28, 2002)] The plaintiff received long-term disability benefits for more than three years. The employer, who was also the insurer, terminated the disability benefits and her medical coverage. Seven and a half months after termination of the disability benefits, the employer sent the plaintiff a letter saying that her separation date was the date of termination of disability benefits, and she could elect COBRA coverage, retroactive to the first day after the separation date, by paying $3,300 as a premium for the first eight months of COBRA coverage. She did not accept this offer, and sued the employer for statutory penalties for failure to provide notice, plus her medical expenses from the date of separation to the date of COBRA notice.

The employer argued that its COBRA obligation had expired, because the qualifying event occurred more than three years earlier, when the plaintiff stopped working and began to receive disability benefits. However, the court held the employer to the separation date given in the letter—and therefore the notice was 215 days late, resulting in prejudice to the plaintiff by forcing her to pay a large sum for retroactive coverage, whereas paying $400 a month for current coverage might have been more affordable. But, because the plaintiff had not paid any premiums, the court held that the employer was not required to reimburse her medical expenses.

When the trial court granted $80/day penalties for 505 days, the plan administrator (the plaintiff's former employer) moved to reduce the penalty and limit its application to a shorter period—either when the suit was filed or when the administrator filed its response. The District Court for the District of Puerto Rico ruled that the penalty period started on the 45th day after the termination of the plaintiff's employment (because the administrator has 44 days to issue the notice). Because notice was not given, the penalty period did not end until the last day of potential COBRA coverage—18 months after termination. Although the District Court found the $80/day penalty level reasonable, it reduced it to $65 because the plaintiff did not object. [*Rodriguez v. International College of Business and Technology Inc.*, 2005 U.S. Dist. LEXIS 2351 (D. P.R. 2005)]

However, penalties were not granted in *Kerkhof v. MCI Worldcom, Inc.* [282 F.3d 44 (1st Cir. 2002)] because the failure to provide notice was not in bad faith, and the plaintiff was not harmed because she was given the full 60 days to make the election and declined coverage anyway.

A plan administrator failed to carry out its standard procedure for mailing COBRA notices. There was no record of mailing and no one could recall sending the notice. The District of Minnesota accordingly required the plan to pay $113,000 medical expenses, minus premiums and copayments had the election been made, incurred by an ex-employee's minor daughter who, the ex-employee claimed, was deprived of the opportunity to make a COBRA election. However, the court refused to award statutory penalties, for lack of proof that the failure reflected a disregard of obligations under COBRA. [*Starr v. Metro Sys. Inc.*, 2005 U.S. Dist. LEXIS 20443 (D. Minn. 2005)]

Not only were statutory penalties not awarded in *Moreno v. St. Francis Hospital & Health Ctr.* [2002 U.S. Dist. LEXIS 1672 (N.D. Ill. Jan. 31, 2002)], but the plaintiff's lawyer (not the plaintiff) was ordered to pay part of the defendant's attorneys' fees. The court ruled that it was unreasonable to continue to maintain an ERISA claim even after getting payment of COBRA benefits under the dental plan. The court blamed the attorney rather than the plaintiff, thus explaining the award. [For a detailed discussion of the case law, *see* Greta E. Cowart, *Recent COBRA Cases* (May 2002) <http://www.abanet.org/tax/groups/benefits/cobra>]

When a plan administrator is aware that a COBRA notice was not delivered, the good-faith requirement is not satisfied if the administrator fails to send another notice. [*Wooderson v. American Airlines, Inc.*, 2001 U.S. Dist. LEXIS 3721 (N.D. Tex. March 23, 2001)]

The same court held that it is not necessary to exhaust administrative remedies within the plan before suing for failure to provide COBRA notice (although it is required before an ERISA claim). An employer cannot get a failure-to-notify case dismissed because it acted in good faith. Statutory damages can be awarded whether or not the plaintiff has actual damages, and whether or not the employer acted in good faith, although these factors can affect the amount of damages. [*Thompson v. Origin Technology in Business*, 2001 U.S. Dist. LEXIS 12609 (N.D. Tex. Aug. 20, 2001)]

In a case that might have seemed a slam-dunk for the plaintiff, the former employer nevertheless prevailed. A terminated employee sent a letter and check to his former employer electing COBRA and paying the initial premium even though he had not received a COBRA notice. He hand-delivered two more premium checks, which the ex-employer did not submit to the insurer, which in turn resulted in coverage loss). The Northern District of Illinois ruled that the suit was improper because the employee was subject to an arbitration agreement requiring arbitration of "any differences, claims or matters in dispute" arising out of or connected with the employment agreement. The court rejected the plaintiff's argument that the claim arose post-termination and therefore was not subject to the arbitration clause. Because it was employment-related, arbitration was required. [*Maroney v. Triple "R" Steel, Inc.,* No. 05 C 1249 (N.D. Ill. Aug. 11, 2005)]

§ 19.05   HEALTH INSURANCE PORTABILITY

[A]   Coverage

The Health Insurance Portability and Accountability Act of 1996 (HIPAA) [I.R.C. Chapter 100, §§ 9801-9806], also known as the Kennedy-Kassebaum Act, copes with the situation in which a person leaves employment with one employer, gets another job, and experiences health care bills before he or she is covered by the new employer's plan, or where the new plan might exclude coverage of the ailment as a pre-existing condition.

For plan years beginning after June 30, 1997, the HIPAA "creditable coverage" requirement in effect allows coverage to carry over from one plan to the other, as long as employees use COBRA (or other means) to make sure that there is never a gap of 63 days or more in coverage.

Although plans can control costs by imposing pre-existing condition limitations, the scope of the limitation is restricted. Under HIPAA, the most stringent definition of "pre-existing condition" that a plan can apply is a mental or physical condition for which medical advice, diagnosis, care, or treatment was sought during the six-month period before the enrollment date. In general, the maximum duration for a pre-existing condition limitation is 12 months from the enrollment date for the current health plan. The enrollment date is the earlier of the first day of the waiting period for enrollment or the date of actual enrollment. Late enrollees (who fail to enroll in the plan during the open enrollment period, or the first period of eligibility) can be subject to an 18-month rather than a 12-month pre-existing condition limitation.

The fact that someone underwent genetic testing is not a "pre-existing condition" (even if susceptibility to a disease or condition is revealed), as long as there is no actual diagnosis of an existing illness. Pre-existing condition limitations cannot be imposed on pregnancy. There are very few situations in which newly born or adopted children can be deemed to have a pre-existing condition. Plans that include dependent coverage must offer a "dependent special enrollment period" lasting at least 30 days during which a new dependent acquired by marriage, birth or adoption can be added to the plan. HIPAA's PCE rules do not apply to disability benefit plans. [*Schleicher v. Ascension Health,* 2006 U.S. Dist. LEXIS 14485 (M.D. Tenn. 2006)]

"Creditable coverage" means coverage from another EGHP, from individual health insurance, from Medicare Part A or B, or from Medicaid. Health plan coverage ceases to be creditable, and therefore is not portable to a new plan, if there is a break of 63 days or more during which the employee is completely without health insurance. The so-called affiliation period (the waiting period after a new employee enrolls in a new health plan) is not considered a period of being uninsured.

Tip: HIPAA obligates EGHPs to provide a certification of the dates creditable coverage began and ended, whenever a former participant gains or loses entitlement to COBRA continuation coverage. The ex-participant can also request the certification at any time within 24 months of the COBRA event, so he or she can submit it to a new plan to prove the existence of creditable coverage. Insured (rather than self-insured) plans are exempt from the certification requirement if they have a procedure for having the insurer issue the certificates.

The mental health parity requirement applies to HIPAA. [*See* EBSA rules at 62 Fed. Reg. 66957 (Dec. 22, 1997)]

At the end of 2004, the DOL, HHS, and the Treasury joined to publish additional final and proposed rules on HIPAA portability. The new rules are similar to those promulgated in 1997. They take effect for plan years starting on or after July 1, 2005 (i.e., January 1, 2006, for calendar year plans). The document includes new sample forms, e.g., for certificates of creditable coverage under an EGHP or Medicaid, explaining the interaction with the FMLA.

EGHPs and insurers must not impose excessively strict preexisting condition exclusions (PCEs) for employees who change jobs or are fired. The plan must have written procedures for obtaining a certificate of creditable coverage. Plans provided by foreign governments must be treated as creditable coverage. The certificate of creditable coverage must include an educational statement of beneficiary rights. The initial notice of rights with regard to preexisting conditions must be given with whatever written application materials the plan distributes.

PCEs cannot be applied in regard to pregnancy, and a plan provision that denies pregnancy coverage during the first year the employee is covered by the plan is an unlawful subterfuge that violates HIPAA because it excludes benefits for preexisting pregnancies. It is forbidden to impose a new PCE when there is a switch in benefit options (for example, from PPO to HMO) or when the plan's insurer changes.

The rule forbids "hidden preexisting condition exclusions": exclusions that seem to be neutral on their face, but have the effect of penalizing preexisting conditions, e.g., by counting benefits received under a different health plan toward the plan's lifetime limit, or a requirement that coverage for accidental injuries be used only for injuries that occur while the person is covered.

There is no statutory definition of "dependent," so the Rule adds one: someone who is entitled to coverage under the plan because of a relationship to a plan participant. The rule also adds coverage under a State Children's Health Insurance Program as a form of creditable coverage for HIPAA purposes.

As long as an HSA is not subject to ERISA, it is exempt from the HIPAA portability requirements. Employer-sponsored HDHPs associated with HSAs, however, are subject to the portability rules if they are group health plans. Some health FSAs are exempt from the portability requirements: limited-scope dental or vision coverage that is provided under a separate insurance arrangement and is not an integral part of the health plan.

The proposals include extending the time to exercise HIPAA rights by a person who was not promptly notified of loss of coverage, and HIPAA coverage during FMLA leave. For HIPAA purposes, FMLA leave for which the person has not elected continuation coverage does not count toward the 63-day limit on time without creditable coverage. A HIPAA certificate of creditable coverage must be issued automatically when FMLA leave begins, although the agencies acknowledge that most such certificates will not be needed, because the person on leave will return to work. But if the employee does not return to work after leave, he or she—and his or her dependents—is entitled to a special enrollment period that begins when leave ends. If the certificate of creditable coverage is delayed, the special enrollment period is extended correspondingly.

Retirees and other former employees are protected by HIPAA, if they are covered by a group health plan that also includes at least two active employees. Presumably, then, a plan that covers only retirees is exempt from HIPAA. [The rules, affecting 26 C.F.R. Parts 54 and 602, 29 C.F.R. Part 2590, and 45 C.F.R. Parts 144 and 146, were published at 69 Fed. Reg. 78719 (Dec. 30, 2004); the agency's explanatory Press Release was posted to <http://www.dol.gov/ebsa/pdf/pr123004.pdf>]

[B] Nondiscrimination Requirements

HIPAA forbids discrimination in benefits in health plans. (In this context, discrimination is closer to the Title VII sense than the pension plan sense of not favoring highly compensated employees.) Under HIPAA, it is unlawful for a plan to base its rules for eligibility or continued eligibility, or its definition of the waiting period, on an employee's or dependent's:

• Health status;
• Physical or mental health condition;
• Claims experience;
• Past receipt of health care;
• Medical history;
• Genetic information;

- Evidence of insurability;
- Disability.

None of these factors can be used to increase the premium or other contribution that an individual plan participant has to pay, when compared to other
similarly situated participants. HIPAA does not limit the premiums or copayments
that employers can require participants to pay. It is also legitimate to offer employees discounts, rebates, or reductions in their copayment obligations based on
their participation in health promotion and disease prevention programs (such as
smoking cessation or weight loss programs).

[C]   Insurers' Obligations

One of Congress's rationales in passing HIPAA was that employers, especially small companies, often had difficulty getting insurance—and once they had
insurance, they often faced cancellation of coverage or at least excessively high
rate increases.

HIPAA imposes obligations on insurers with respect to group health policies.
The rules are different for "small employer" coverage (2–50 employees) and
"large employer coverage" (groups of more than 50 employees). HIPAA's general
requirement is that insurers who sell small employer coverage within a state must
sell to all small employers who want to purchase the coverage, although there is no
corresponding obligation to sell to would-be large-group buyers.

In either the small or the large-group market, the insurer has an obligation to
renew coverage or continue it in force as long as the purchase chooses, unless the
purchaser:

- Stops paying the premiums;
- Commits fraud related to the policy;
- The insurer withdraws from the relevant market within the state;
- Plan enrollees move outside the service area for a network plan;
- (In a plan based on association membership) enrollees cease to be members of
  the association;
- The purchaser violates the rules on participation or contributions to the plan.

If an insurer discontinues one kind of group coverage but maintains others, all
affected plan sponsors, participants, and beneficiaries are entitled to 90 days'
notice of the discontinuance. The plan sponsor must be given the option to
purchase the other coverage that the insurer offers in that market.

The insurer must act uniformly, without considering the existing or potential
health problems of plan participants and beneficiaries, or the claims experience of
the plan sponsor. An insurer that chooses to discontinue all of its coverage in the
small- or large-group market must give state insurance regulators 180 days notice
of intent to discontinue. An insurer that withdraws will be barred from re-entering

the market for five years. This requirement is imposed to prevent insurers from leaving and re-entering the market purely based on their own needs.

A health plan participant incurred over $265,000 in hospital bills. The plan applied to renew its stop-loss coverage and submitted the claim to the stop-loss insurer. The stop-loss insurer rejected the claim (the plan said that it did not give a reason) and refused to renew the policy. The hospital brought an ERISA claim against the health plan seeking payment. The hospital's claim was dismissed on the grounds that the plan was a government plan not subject to ERISA. Then the plan sued the stop-loss insurer and its agent, claiming that the refusal to renew violated HIPAA's requirement of guaranteed renewability, restrictions on preexisting condition limitations, and the ban on discrimination on the basis of participants' health status. The Northern District of Illinois ruled in 2004 that there is no private cause of action to enforce these provisions; enforcement power belongs only to HHS and state authorities. Furthermore, stop-loss policies generally are not group health coverage (although a policy with a low attachment point might be group health coverage) and thus are not subject to HIPAA in any event. [*Northwestern Memorial Hospital v. Village of South Chicago Heights Health and Welfare Fund*, 2004 U.S. Dist. LEXIS 14411 (N.D. Ill. 2004)]

[D]   Exceptions to the Portability Rule

Plans of certain types are not subject to the portability rules, because they are not deemed to be health benefit plans:

- Plans that offer accident and/or disability insurance;
- Liability insurance plans;
- Insured plans that provide medical benefits that are secondary or incidental to other benefits;
- Limited scope plans providing, e.g., dental, vision, or long-term care benefits;
- Coverage that is limited to a specified disease or illness;
- Fixed-indemnity plans (e.g., hospitalization insurance);
- Medicare Supplementary (Medigap) insurance.

Plans that cover only a single current employee are not subject to portability requirements.

Flexible Spending Accounts (FSAs) are "excepted benefits" under ERISA §§ 732 and 733(c) and I.R.C. §§ 9831 and 9832(c). Therefore, health insurance portability is not required for these plans. [*See* the "clarification of regulations" jointly issued by the IRS, the Pension and Welfare Benefit Administration, and the Department of Health and Human Services at 62 Fed. Reg. 67688 (Dec. 29, 1997)] The FSA is excepted from HIPAA if the employee's maximum FSA benefit for the year does not exceed twice the employee's salary reduction election for the year, as long as the employee has other EGHP coverage and as long as the FSA provides at least some benefits that are not "excepted benefits."

Another IRS/DOL/HCFA joint clarification, published at 62 Fed. Reg. 67689 (Dec. 29, 1997) does not allow plans to establish rules for initial or continued eligibility on the basis of health status (including medical condition, claims experience, receipt of health care, medical history, genetic testing, insurability, or disability. Employees and their dependents (even late enrollees) cannot be required to pass a physical examination in order to enroll in the health plan.

HCFA's Program Memorandum 00-04 says that HIPAA forbids the use of "actively at work" provisions (i.e., limiting coverage under a new plan to people who were working on the day on which a plan changes its carrier) to discriminate on the basis of disability or other health factors.

[E] Penalties and Enforcement

Health plans are subject to a penalty tax, under I.R.C. Chapter 100, for failure to comply with the HIPAA portability rules. The basic penalty rate is $110 per person per day of noncompliance. The maximum liability that a single-employer plan can incur is the smaller of $500,000 or 10% of the amount paid or incurred by the EGHP for the preceding year.

Liability can be waived or reduced if the person responsible for the error or omission did not know, and could not have known, of the defect; if the cause of the failure was reasonable; and no willful neglect was involved. Penalties can also be avoided if the failure is corrected within 30 days of the first date it could have been detected. If the source of the problem is the insurer's error or misconduct, plans with 2–50 employees will not be subjected to the penalty tax.

However, a minimum tax that cannot be waived is imposed if the HIPAA compliance failure is found after the plan has received notice of income tax examination. In that case, the tax is the lesser of $2,500 or the tax that would otherwise be imposed.

Although the interim final rule about CMPs for violation of HIPAA's administrative simplification rules, dealing with issues such as privacy, security, unique health identifiers, transaction and code sets, was supposed to expire September 16, 2004, it was extended for a further year: see 69 Fed. Reg. 55515 (Sept. 15, 2004). The CMP level is $100 per violation, up to a maximum of $25,000 per calendar year for multiple violations of the same requirement. Administration of the penalties has been delegated to the Office for Civil Rights for the privacy component and to the Centers for Medicare and Medicaid Services for transaction and code sets, security, and unique health identifiers. Informal comments from HHS showed that no CMPs had been imposed before the extension of the interim final rule.

[F] Data Privacy and Security

As discussed in I.P.C. § 26.07, HIPAA also penalizes misuse of Protected Health Information (PHI). "Covered entities"—typically, an insurer or self-insured plan—are not permitted to use or disclose PHI without the consent of the subject of the information. [*See* 45 C.F.R. Parts 160 and 164 and HHS's FAQ at http://www.hhs.gov/ocr/hipaa/privacy.html] The privacy rules are limited to health plans, not other welfare benefit plans (including disability plans), and PHI can lawfully be used for payment, treatment, or health care operations. In an insured EGHP, the insurer rather than the plan is the covered entity. The covered entity must provide privacy notices to plan members explaining their rights to data confidentiality.

A final enforcement rule was published, at 71 Fed. Reg. 8390 (Feb. 16, 2006), effective March 16, 2006, covering the HIPAA privacy, security, and EDI rules and the rules about unique identifiers. The final rule follows the ongoing themes of HIPAA enforcement: investigating reported violations and offering conciliation and technical assistance to resolve violations, with money penalties imposed only as a last resort. When HHS determines that penalties are appropriate, it must issue a notice of proposed determination describing the violation and the penalty sought (a maximum of $100 per day of violation, capped at $25,000 per year for the same violation). The party from whom the penalty is sought is entitled to a formal hearing before an ALJ, and the ALJ's decision can be appealed to HHS' Departmental Appeals Board (DAB). Going to the DAB completes the process of exhausting administrative remedies, so court review can be sought at that point.

The HIPAA notice of privacy practices took effect April 14, 2003, so large plans had to issue reminder notices by April 14, 2006. For small plans, which got an extra year to comply, the first reminder is due April 14, 2007. An HHS Frequently Asked Questions listing says that the reminder can be provided by resending the original notice or issuing a new version; mailing covered individuals a reminder that the notice is available and explaining how to get it; or posting a reminder in a plan publication. [Epstein, Becker & Green Client Alerts, *Reminder: HIPAA Privacy Notice of Privacy Practices*, <http://ebglaw.com> (Mar. 2006)]

A standard Interpretation Letter added to OSHA's Web site on August 18, 2004, clarifies that there is no general requirement that employers edit the OSHA 300 log of injuries and illnesses to remove names before disclosing the log to someone authorized to request it (e.g., a union). [*See* 73 LW 2103]

The Third Circuit upheld the constitutionality and validity of HIPAA's "routine use" exception to the medical records privacy rules brought by nine individuals and 10 patients' rights organizations. Although due process claims can be raised for violation of the right to privacy in medical records, only disclosures by government action, not by private providers, can support the claim. [*Citizens for Health v. Leavitt*, 428 F.3d 167 (3d Cir. 2005)]

Tip: However, a health FSA is considered a self-insured plan, so employers that maintain FSAs must comply with the privacy rule and security rules. Furthermore, if the health care FSA and the insured EGHP are administered as a single plan, the combined entity is subject to many HIPAA rules. However, FSAs with fewer than 50 participants are exempt from certain

HIPAA requirements, but FSAs (no matter what the number of participants) must comply with the administrative requirements if they use a TPA. [*See* Chicago Consulting Actuaries Health & Welfare Insight, *HIPAA Privacy Requirements and Health Care Flexible Spending Accounts: Have Smaller Employers Forgotten Something?* (Mar. 21, 2005), <http://share.ccastrategies. com/Insight/Documents/HIPAAPrivacyRequirements.aspx>]

Data confidentiality protects the patient against improper disclosure of PHI by health care providers and insurers. The related subject of "data security" is tackled by a final rule appearing at 68 Fed. Reg. 8333 (Feb. 20, 2003). Covered entities are required to carry out technical, physical, and business procedures to protect PHI from unauthorized access (e.g., by hackers), and to have compliance programs so their employees carry out the program.

After his termination, a Fire Department paramedic sued the Fire Department, seeking discovery of the employer's records (medical records, return-to-work evaluations, information about fitness for duty) of leave taken by other paramedics for psychological or substance abuse treatment. The employer claimed that HIPAA's Privacy Rule, as well as federal and state rules making substance abuse records confidential, prevented the disclosure. The Northern District of Illinois, however, held that the employer was not a "covered entity" as defined by HIPAA. The employer held the records in its capacity as an employer rather than for health care purposes, so the HIPAA Privacy Rule didn't apply. Furthermore, even covered entities can release protected health information in connection with a court case if appropriate conditions are met, as they were here. Because the plaintiff's suit involved only federal claims, the Northern District didn't consider the state statute relevant. However, the court found that some of the records were subject to psychologist-patient privilege. It ordered the employer to review all the records to find those that were privileged on this basis, and required the parties to negotiate a protective order limiting the use and distribution of the records that were not privileged. The Employee Benefits Institute of America's comment on this case was that it was good news for employers that the court clarified that an employer does not become a HIPAA-covered entity by hiring a professional to perform a fitness for duty evaluation unless the professional also treats the employee. [*Beard v. City of Chicago*, 2005 U.S. Dist. LEXIS 374 (N.D. Ill. 2005)]

A health care provider informed a patient's employer that the patient apparently had altered a narcotic prescription for a work-related injury to allow refills. The employer fired the employee, who sued the provider for violating the HIPAA privacy rule. The HIPAA claim was dismissed on the grounds that not only did the disclosure not violate the privacy rule, but in any case there is no private right of action under the privacy rule: the statute only calls for enforcement by HHS. [*Rigaud v. Garofalo*, 2005 U.S. Dist. LEXIS 7791 (E.D. Pa. 2005), <http:// www.paed.uscourts.gov/documents/opinions/05D0552P.pdf>]

An FBI agent sued the agency, charging that information about his medical history, taken from his fitness-for-duty evaluations, had been disclosed to his supervisors and others in the chain of command. The District Court for the District of Columbia dismissed the case, also on the grounds that there is no private cause of action under the HIPAA privacy rules. However, it should be noted that federal employees can file privacy complaints with the HHS Office for Civil Rights. State court actions as well as criminal complaints with the Department of Justice may be possible. HIPAA's nondiscrimination provision, unlike the privacy provision, does permit private suits, but those provisions are part of ERISA. [*Runkle v. Gonzales*, 2005 U.S. Dist. LEXIS 22219 (D.D.C. 2005)]

The EEOC brought a disability discrimination suit against an employer. The employer applied for a court order granting permission to contact psychologists who had interviewed the plaintiff, without EEOC or plaintiff's attorneys being present. The Eastern District of New York decided that the HIPAA privacy rule, rather than state law about psychologist-patient privilege, determined whether the psychologist could release information about the plaintiff. HIPAA has no provisions about "ex parte" communications (the party's lawyer is not present). The Eastern District decided that the proper balance was to allow the employer to contact the psychologists only via a court order that spelled out what information could be released, or when there was a subpoena or discovery request that conformed to the HIPAA privacy rule. [*EEOC v. Boston Market Corp.*, 2004 U.S. Dist. LEXIS 27338 (E.D.N.Y. 2004)]

A nurse was fired for misuse of narcotics when caring for a patient. In connection with the hospital's administrative disciplinary process, she subpoenaed the patient's medical records. The hospital, citing HIPAA's criminal penalties, refused to produce the records. The New York Supreme Court held that the HIPAA privacy rule permits disclosure pursuant to a subpoena, although in this case the subpoena was procedurally defective. The court ordered the hospital to produce the records, but only after removing certain identifying information, and on condition that the nurse return or destroy the information when the court case was over, and could not use it in any way outside the case. [*Chapman v. Health and Hospitals Corps.*, 2005 N.Y. Misc. LEXIS 518 (N.Y. Sup. Ct. 2005)]

CHAPTER **20**

DISABILITY PLANS

§ 20.01   INTRODUCTION

Because of an acute illness, a chronic illness, or an injury (work-related or otherwise), many working-age individuals will go through brief, extended, or permanent periods during which they are unable to perform their normal jobs.

The DOL's latest figures, from 2003, show 1.3 million workers suffered illnesses or injuries requiring time off from work. About one third of the employers surveyed by Marsh and Mercer Human Resource Counseling said that the incidence of short-term disability (STD) increased between 2004 and 2005; more than a quarter said that was true of long-term disability (LTD) incidence. However, the number of employers offering disability plans fell: in 2005, 88% of employers offered LTD and 77% offered STD. According to MetLife, however, only 60% of employees had access to disability coverage. [Kelley M. Butler, *Rising Claims, Restricted Coverage Creates Disability Disconnect*, Employee Benefit News, <http://www.benefitnews.com/pfv.cfm?id=8060> (Sep. 15, 2005)]

According to UnumProvident, a major disability insurer, the most common long-term disabilities for persons in the 40–60 age bracket are musculoskeletal disorders such as back problems (25% of cases), cancer (17%), cardiovascular and circulatory disorders (8%), and mental/behavioral illness (7%). Buck Consultants said that 1.66 out of every 1,000 workers under 40 were disabled for more than 180 days; the rate was 3.49/1,000 for those aged 40–49 and 9.6/1,000 for those over 50. Workers 55 or over average 12 days of absence per year. [Steve Davolt, *Words to the Wise—Engaging and Empowering Baby Boomers to Prevent and Treat Disabilities,* Employee Benefit News (Apr. 1, 2006)]

In 2005, combined premiums for group disability (including both short- and long-term) insurance was $11.2 billion, about 6% higher than the 2004 level, although the increase was much greater for long-term (7%) than for short-term (4%) policies. Sales of both kinds of insurance rose 3%, generating more than $1.9 billion of new annualized premiums. The disability insurance market is quite concentrated: Twenty-nine carriers share more than 95% of the group market, and the top 10 carriers wrote 76% of new short-term business in 2005 and more than 82% of new long-term business. [*Disability Premiums Up 6% Last Year: JHA*, NU Online News Service (Apr. 26, 2006)]

Late in 2005, UnumProvident Corp. settled with California about rules for long-term disability (there had been a multistate settlement, requiring $15 million in fines and the reopening of 215,000 claims denied or terminated between January 2000 and November 2004, but California and Montana opted out). California settled for an $8 million fine and a set-aside of $75 million to cover the cost of reexamining and, if necessary, paying, 26,000 old claims. An independent, but non-binding, review procedure was set up for claimants whose claims continued to be denied or terminated on review. California regulators sought to apply changes in definitions not just to UnumProvident policies, but to all California disability policies. During the own-occupation period, the new definition is that total disability means a disability that renders the person unable to perform with reasonable continuity the substantial and material acts necessary to pursue the usual occupation in its usual and customary way. During the any-occupation period, total disability is disability that renders the insured incapable of performing with reasonable continuity another occupation which he or she could reasonably be expected to perform satisfactorily in light of age, education, training, experience, station in life, physical capacity, and mental capacity. UnumProvident agreed not to include any policy provisions giving the company discretionary authority over contracts issued after the settlement. Post-settlement contracts also will not mandate participation in rehab programs. [Settlement documents posted to <http://www.sec.gov/Archives/edgar/data/5513/000119312505195355/dex101.htm>; *see* Arthur D. Postal, *California Forces Changes in LTD Definitions*, NU Online News Service (Oct. 3, 2005)]

There are both public (Social Security Disability Income; Worker's Compensation) and private systems for dealing with disability. The Supreme Court ruled that the Commissioner of Social Security reasonably construed the definition of disability to deny benefits to a claimant who was healthy enough to do her former job (elevator operator) even though that job no longer exists in significant numbers within the national economy. [*Barnhart v. Thomas*, 540 U.S. 20 (2003)] Some states require employers to provide disability benefits; in other states, employers often do this as an employee benefit.

§ 20.02   EMPLOYMENT-BASED PLANS

Usually, a short-term disability (STD) is defined either as one that lasts less than six months, or one that lasts less than a year. Long-term disability benefits typically terminate after a period of years (e.g., five years) or at age 65, when the employee would presumably be retiring anyway.

A typical arrangement is for the employer to self-insure for short-term disability, but to buy LTD insurance (possibly with the covered employees contributing part of the cost). It is also typical for STD and LTD plans to use different definitions of disability. The long-term plan has more restrictive definitions, because the employer's possible exposure is greater.

Using an "own occupation" definition (the person is disabled when unable to carry out the duties of the predisability occupation) makes it easier to qualify for benefits than using an "any occupation" definition (benefits stop as soon as the person is able to return to any work, or any work suitable to his or her education and training). Another frequent plan design is for the definition to start out as "own-occ" but switch after two years to inability to perform any occupation suitable to the individual's education and training.

LTD plans usually replace 60–70% of predisability income; 60% is the most common level. The plan may also limit income replacement from all sources, including Worker's Compensation and Social Security, to a percentage such as 75% of predisability income. Many plans offset (reduce) disability benefits to account for government benefits and damages received from tort suits or settlements (e.g., if the employee was injured in an accident or by a defective product).

Another cost-saving measure is to have benefits start after a waiting period, so that the plan covers situations in which work ability is impaired for a long time, but not ordinary illnesses and minor injuries (which are probably covered by sick leave anyway).

Mercer HR Consulting found that 24% of respondents dismiss workers on long-term disability after a set number of months; 27% do this as soon as LTD benefits begin; 15% terminate the disabled person at normal retirement age; 18% do not have a policy; and 16% use other criteria for termination. This is a new finding: five or even three years ago, most survey respondents paid LTD until retirement age. When employees are terminated, they continue to receive LTD checks, but lose health and life insurance. Some companies have a policy of paying COBRA premiums for persons in this situation, but most do not. (However, the impact is tempered somewhat by Medicare eligibility once a person has been totally disabled for two years.) [Joseph Pereira, *To Save on Health-Care Costs, Firms Fire Disabled Workers,* Wall Street Journal, July 14, 2003, at p. A1]

A Taft-Hartley plan is a temporary disability plan jointly run by employers and a union. The plan's goal is to assist employees who are in financial need because of a disability, while also helping them return to work as soon as possible (if they can be rehabilitated adequately).

Highly compensated employees, who often experience crushing income loss after disability (because disability benefits are capped at a level far below their pre-disability income) can be good subjects for corporate disability buy-up policies— supplemental group disability plans providing additional income replacement.

The buy-up plan could be either employer paid, in which case the employer can deduct the premiums and the employee does not have taxable income because of the premium payments, but benefits will be taxable when received; or the employer sponsors the plan, allowing insurers to sign up employees who pay for their own coverage but can then receive benefits tax-free. The second approach is more popular. A disability buy-up can also be included in a cafeteria plan, so that premiums are paid with pre-tax dollars but benefits are taxable. In this case, the coverage will be portable, and employees can take it with them when they change jobs. In a hybrid plan, the employer pays the premiums for a select group of employees; other employees can participate by paying premiums.

Buy-up plans are structured with two tiers. The first tier is a guaranteed issue policy issued at standard rates without underwriting. The second tier has limited underwriting, which may lead to higher premiums or some coverage restrictions.

Insurers want to do business in this select market, so discounts may be available. For example, an executive earning $300,000 a year might be covered by a group plan whose coverage is limited to $10,000 a month. Most carriers would discount the coverage by approximately 25% as a marketing tool—the executive would be treated as having a monthly benefit of only $7,500 rather than $10,000. The insurer then issues a first-tier benefit of $2,500 a month and a further $2,500 second-tier benefit. The end result is that, if disabled, the executive would receive a potential benefit of $15,000 a month, or 60% rather than 40% income replacement. [Stanley B. Siegel, *Corporate Disability Buy-Ups,* <http://www.aicpa.org/pubs/jofa/dec2002/siegel.htm>]

As an incentive for rehabilitation, the plan may continue benefits at a low level while the individual engages in a trial period of re-employment, or undertakes part-time or lower-level work in an attempt to re-enter the workforce. [*See* Chapter 37 for a discussion of Age Discrimination in Employment Act (ADEA) [29 U.S.C. § 621 *et seq.*] implications of disability plans]

The role that psychological factors play in long-term disability is attracting increasing attention. Between 1990 and 1998, the incidence of mental-nervous claims almost tripled. There is growing recognition that early intervention helps to prevent injured workers from feeling hopeless and that they can never recover.

Many companies have succeeded in controlling costs through integrated disability management (whether or not the disability is occupational in origin). Using a single source to manage rehabilitation of injured workers and administer disability and Worker's Compensation benefits can be an effective tactic. [*See, e.g.,* Dianne Dyck, *Disability Management Best Practices*, <http://www.wsib.on.ca/wsib/wsibsite.nsf . . . >]

In a December 2003 article, Barry J. Goldberg and William M. Mon provide guidance about the factors involved in choosing between self-insured and insured disability programs. The main factors are the exposure risk (the ultimate responsibility for payments to disabled workers); administration (who decides how the plan will be run) and funding (how the benefits are paid). The plan might encounter a higher number of claims than anticipated, and disabled workers might be slower to return to work than predicted. A self-insured plan will be affected directly by its investment success; an insured plan will be indirectly affected, as premiums rise to make up for lacunae in the insurer's portfolio.

An insured plan offers a certain predictability of costs—but self-insurance can save at least 10–20%, because it is not necessary to pay for the insurer's taxes, risks, profit charges, and the time value of money. Many administrative burdens are removed by purchasing insurance for the plan (although it's also possible to self-insure and hire a TPA).

Tip: Although self-insured plans are not subject to the same kind of minimum funding requirements as certain pension plans, FAS 112 does require recognizing unfunded obligations on the corporate books. FAS 112 requires insured plans to recognize their insurance premiums. A company that switches from self-insurance to an insured plan and transfers liability for current claimants to the insurer will be required to recognize the additional premiums.

On the other hand, a company that moves from an insured plan to self-insurance can either adopt a pay-as-you-go strategy or use a VEBA to fund

---

the benefits. [Barry J. Goldberg and William M. Mon *Long-Term Disability Program—Self-Insured vs. Fully Insured*, Journal of Compensation and Benefits (November/December 2003) <http://www.buckconsultants.com/pdf/long-term_disability . . . >]

§ 20.03   STATE MANDATES

In five states (California, Hawaii, New York, New Jersey, Rhode Island), employers are required to provide TDI (Temporary Disability Insurance) coverage for between 26 and 52 weeks of non-occupational temporary disability for industrial and commercial workers. Either the state administers a fund from which employer contributions are distributed to disabled employees, or the state maintains a fund but gives employers the choice of self-insuring, buying insurance, or paying into a union-sponsored disability plan.

TDI benefits are offset (that is, reduced) by Worker's Compensation and unemployment benefits.

§ 20.04   COMPLIANCE ISSUES

[A]   ERISA Compliance

For ERISA purposes, most disability arrangements are welfare benefit plans, and therefore subject to disclosure, filing, and fiduciary requirements. Some disability plans, however, are top-hat plans that only cover executives, so the employer's disclosure obligations are more limited. If a plan is maintained only to comply with Worker's Compensation or state mandates, then ERISA § 4(b)(3) exempts the plan from ERISA compliance obligations. ERISA compliance is also excused in situations where an employer makes payments out of its general assets to an employee who is out of work for medical reasons. [*See* 29 C.F.R. § 2510.3-1(b)(2)]

The plaintiff in *Turnoy v. Liberty Life Assurance Co.*, [2003 U.S. Dist. LEXIS 1311 (N.D. Ill. Jan. 30, 2003)] was an insurance agent who described himself as an independent contractor. The District Court held that ERISA applied to his disability plan, because the company he worked for was the sponsor of the policy, and eligibility for participation in the disability plan depended on meeting production standards set by the plan sponsor. The insurance agent was an ERISA beneficiary because ERISA covers any individual entitled to benefits under the terms of a plan, even though he was not a common-law employee.

According to the Fifth Circuit, a doctor who was an employer-shareholder in a group medical practice was a working participant in an ERISA plan. Therefore, the ordinary criteria applicable to ERISA plans applied, and the long-term disability insurer was justified in rescinding a policy issued to the doctor, because he lied about never having been treated for substance abuse or mental illness. [*Provident Life & Accident Ins. Co. v. Sharpless*, 364 F.3d 634 (5th Cir. Apr. 9, 2004)]

Claims were made under an LTD policy offered by the employer but for which the employee had paid the premiums. After denial of a claim, the employee sued in state court for breach of contract. The insurer removed the case to the federal courts and asserted ERISA preemption. The trial court agreed, holding that the LTD coverage did not conform to the ERISA safe harbor for voluntary employee-pay-all coverage; it was an ERISA plan. The Eleventh Circuit upheld the District Court, because the plan was established and maintained by the employer, which selected the policy, set up a fund to pay benefits, made representations about the plan, was involved in benefit payment, and determined eligibility. The plan documents described the plan as an ERISA plan and named the employer as plan administrator. [*Anderson v. UNUM Provident Corp.*, 369 F.3d 1257 (11th Cir. 2004)]

After a corporate acquisition, employees were given a "program summary" explaining their benefits. The summary did not require LTD benefits to be reduced by Social Security Disability Income or Worker's Compensation benefits received by a disabled employee. The actual plan documents had not been prepared at the time of the transaction, and in fact were not prepared until several months later. The Second Circuit ruled that the program summary was a "plan" for ERISA purposes, and therefore the plaintiffs were entitled to receive LTD benefits without SSDI or Worker's Compensation offset. Unless a plan document provides to the contrary, disability benefits vest no later than the time of disability, and the employer cannot take away vested rights through the terms of a later document. [*Feifer v. Prudential Ins. Co. of Am.*, 306 F.3d 1202 (2d Cir. 2002)]

If the employee pays all the premiums for LTD insurance, and the employer's only role is to administer the payments (without giving its approval of the policy), then ERISA does not preempt a suit by the employee against the insurer claiming bad faith termination of benefits. There are three tests for deciding whether ERISA preempts litigation about a disability policy:

- Was there a "plan, fund or program"? In this case, a plan was clearly present—but it was not an ERISA plan;
- Does the arrangement qualify for the ERISA safe harbor? The safe harbor is available if the employer does not make any contributions to the plan; the plan is completely voluntary; the employer does not profit from the plan (although it can legitimately receive a reasonable administrative fee); and the employer allows one or more insurers to publicize the availability of the program, but does not endorse or recommend it;
- Is the employer's sole function under the plan collecting premiums, or does it have deeper involvement? [*Bagden v. Equitable Life Assurance Society of the United States*, 1999 U.S. Dist. LEXIS 7066 (E.D. Pa. May 11, 1999)]

ERISA does not preempt state "notice-prejudice" laws. Such laws prevent insurers from denying a claim on the basis that the insured person did not give timely notice of the covered event, unless the delay really causes harm to the insurer. [*Daug v. UNUM Life Ins. Co.*, 1999 WL 238236 (10th Cir. 1999); *Cisneros v. UNUM*, 134 F.3d 939 (9th Cir. 1999)]

According to the Seventh Circuit, the plaintiff in *Feldman v. American Memorial Life Insurance Co.*, [196 F.3d 783 (7th Cir. 1999)] was not totally disabled throughout the 90-day elimination period in her disability insurance policy. Therefore, her ERISA § 510 claim, that the employer fired her to prevent her from collecting benefits, had to fail. She never became eligible for the benefits, and therefore the employer could not have been motivated to terminate her to prevent payment of benefits she had earned.

The Northern District of Georgia would not allow a Long Term Disability insurer to recover three years of overpayments made to a partially disabled person who gave the insurer proper notice that he was working part-time (which would have justified termination of payments). But ERISA does allow termination of the payments on a prospective basis.

A plan participant who was denied benefits under a LTD plan sued under ERISA § 502(a)(3). The participant got a default judgment covering disability expenses, medical benefits, prejudgment interest, and attorneys' fees. [*Rogers v. Hartford Life & Accident Ins. Co.*, 167 F.3d 933 (5th Cir. 1999)] The plan got the court to reopen the case. The Fifth Circuit reduced the damages, on the grounds that the cost of medical treatment lay outside the disability plan's terms. The *Mertens* case [508 U.S. 248 (1993)] says that the I.R.C. § 502(a)(3) remedies are all equitable, so therefore compensatory damages are not available.

The plaintiff was hired as a part-time employee, ineligible for disability coverage. Later, he became an eligible full-time employee and was enrolled in the LTD plan. After several years, he began to experience heart problems; a year later, he reduced his hours to cope with his medical needs. He asked an HR staffer about the effect of return to part-time work on his medical and dental benefits, but did not ask about the effect on the LTD plan. Eventually he became unable to work, and applied for LTD benefits, which were denied, both because of his pre-existing condition and because he was a part-time worker.

He sued, but lost, because the First Circuit ruled that, unless there is a promise or a misrepresentation, a plan administrator has no duty to volunteer information about plan coverage. Fiduciaries are obligated to answer questions honestly, but do not have a duty to inform unless they have reason to know that failure to inform could be harmful. [*Watson v. Deaconess Waltham Hosp.*, 298 F.3d 102 (1st Cir. 2002)]

A plaintiff was usually classified as an independent contractor and paid directly by the company for whom she performed graphic design services for many years. However, sometimes she was a temporary worker providing services through a third-party company. She became ill and asked for benefit information, but was told that she was not eligible for benefits because she was not an employee. She sued and applied for disability benefits. The benefit claims were rejected because of her non-employee status. She did not appeal the denial under the plan's claim procedure. The defendant employer won, not only because she did not exhaust her administrative remedies, but also because she was a non-employee and not eligible for plan coverage (which was limited to those who were paid W-2 wages). [*Jaeger v. Matrix Essentials*, 236 F. Supp. 2d 815 (N.D. Ohio 2002)]

An independent contractor commodities trader was affiliated with a trading firm that provided disability benefits to affiliates. In 1999, as a result of chronic headaches, he applied for benefits under a plan that provided benefits when trading income fell below 80% of the person's average monthly income. The insurer denied the claim for lack of evidence of a disabling condition. The trader sued in federal court, raising state insurance and tort law claims.The District Court ruled for the insurer, finding that ERISA preempted state law and the insurer's decision was not arbitrary and capricious. While the appeal was pending, the Seventh Circuit ruled that independent contractors can be beneficiaries of ERISA plans. The plaintiff's argument that the disability coverage was not a welfare benefit plan as defined by ERISA was invalid because the clearing firm paid part of the premiums. The Seventh Circuit refused to apply a heightened standard of review on the grounds of conflict of interest, stating that exposure under a single claim does not affect the company's decision making. Furthermore, despite the plaintiff's contention that he was bedridden and totally disabled, a private investigator hired by the insurer observed the plaintiff carrying out a full range of activities. He also earned net profits of $600,000 from floor trading at the time he claimed total disability. His health clearly reduced his income potential, but the only medical report he supplied exaggerated the extent of his limitations. [*Shyman v. Unum Life Ins. Co.*, 427 F.3d 452 (7th Cir. 2005); the principle that independent contractors can be beneficiaries of ERISA plans comes from *Ruttenberg v. United States Life Ins. Co.*, 413 F.3d 652 (7th Cir. 2005), coincidentally also involving a floor trader. For the proposition that a large company does not have a meaningful conflict of interest because the status of a single claim cannot affect the company much, *see Hess v. Reg-Ellen Machine Tool Corp.*, 425 F.3d 653 (7th Cir. 2005); *Leipzig v. AIG Life Ins. Co.*, 362 F.3d 406 (7th Cir. 2004)]

A mortgage loan officer disabled by back injury was required to apply for SSDI as a condition of her LTD benefits continuing. She applied for and was granted SSDI. She was then required to repay part of the LTD benefit because of receipt of benefits from an alternative source for the same disability. Later, she was required to have a functional-capacity evaluation, which determined that despite her limitations in ability to sit, there were some jobs that she could handle, and that were available in the local economy. Her benefits were then terminated. She appealed the denial and provided letters from her doctor and supporting evidence as to her permanent total disability. The plan retained a neurosurgeon to review the records; he concluded that the claimant had always been able to perform her own occupation, had no work limitations, and had no objective evidence of disability. Her administrative appeal was denied, and she sued under ERISA. The Sixth Circuit ruled that an SSA determination was, at the very least, support for the plaintiff's contention that she was totally disabled, although it is just one factor—it does not conclusively prove that denial of benefits was arbitrary and capricious. In this case, however, the Sixth Circuit found that the file review was not thorough and failed to rebut or even mention important evidence like the SSA determination, X-rays, and CAT scans, and the functional capacity evaluation. [*Calvert v. Firstar Fin., Inc.,* 409 F.3d 286 (6th Cir. 2005)]

[B] Tax Issues

Whether an employer can get a tax deduction for the cost of its disability plan depends on satisfying I.R.C. § 162 (ordinary and necessary business expenses). The employer's contributions must also satisfy I.R.C. § 104.

From the employee's viewpoint, the key section is I.R.C. § 106, which excludes employer coverage under an accident and health insurance (A&H) plan from the employee's gross income. This section is usually interpreted to include the premiums that the employer pays to maintain an insured disability plan, as well as the value of coverage under a self-insured disability plan. After a disability occurs, the benefits received by the employee under A&H or disability insurance must be included in income to the extent that they are attributable to previously excluded employer contributions. Amounts paid directly by the employer to the employee are also includible in gross income.

However, benefits paid for permanent loss (or loss of use) of a body part or its function, or for disfigurement, are not included in the employee's income, as long as the benefit is computed without regard to absence from work.

The I.R.C. § 22 tax credit, often referred to as the Credit for the Elderly, also applies to individuals who retired at a time when they were permanently and totally disabled.

In *Thomas v. Commissioner,* [2001 T.N.T. 173-7 (2001)] the employer sponsored an insured disability plan. It was a "premium conversion plan" (this type is also known as a premium-only or premium-payment plan). Participants could pay with pretax dollars, but the plaintiff elected to pay with after-tax dollars. He suffered several months of disability and collected about $5,000 in disability benefits, which he did not report as taxable income. However, because he used after-tax dollars, the benefits were tax-free under I.R.C. § 104(a)(3).

Rev. Rul. 2004-55, 2004-26 I.R.B. 1081, permits employees participating in an employer-sponsored disability plan to make an election at the start of any plan year to change the employer contributions from pre- to post-tax dollars (if the plan permits this). Employees who choose the after-tax option can exclude benefit payments from their income; older employees or those who expect to collect extensive health benefits might wish to exercise this option. However, both the employer's and employee's share of after-tax payments are subject to employment taxes. When the benefits are received, those attributable solely to after-tax employee contributions are excluded; those attributable solely to pre-tax employer contributions are included in the employee's gross income. The election must be made before the beginning of the plan year in which the election takes effect, and is irrevocable, but a new election can be made for each plan year, or the plan can permit carryover until the employee affirmatively makes a change in tax treatment. The ruling was requested for a long-term disability plan, but the IRS says that the result would be the same for short-term disability. However, it does not address the tax treatment of disability benefits paid with pre-tax employee contributions under a cafeteria plan. A later Private Letter Ruling, Pvt. Ltr. Rul. 200527012 (Apr. 1, 2005), reached a similar conclusion: *see* <http://www.irs.treas.gov/pub/irs-wd/0527012.pdf>.

Tip: Enrollment materials for the plan should explain the consequences of paying with pretax versus after-tax dollars.

[C] ADA Compliance

It should also be noted that a disability plan that imposes lower limits for mental health care than for care of physical ailments may violate the Americans with Disabilities Act (ADA). The Mental Health Parity Act [42 U.S.C. § 300gg] makes it unlawful for employee group health plans to set lower limits for mental health care than for treatment of physical illnesses. This statute, however, is not applicable to disability plans.

Early in 2000, the Supreme Court affirmed (without opinion) [528 U.S. 1106 (2000)] the Seventh Circuit's decision in *Doe v. Mutual of Ohio.* [179 F.3d 557 (7th Cir. 2000)] It does not violate the ADA's public accommodations title for an insured or self-insured health plan to impose a lower cap on benefits for AIDS-related illnesses or conditions than for other ailments. The Supreme Court would not grant privileged status to diseases that cause ADA disability over other diseases that do not.

ADA Title IV immunizes insurer and benefit plan decisions based on underwriting, classifying, or administering risk, as long as the decisions are not a subterfuge to escape ADA compliance. Decisions that have actuarial support are likely to qualify for this safe harbor.

According to *Weyer v. Twentieth Century Fox Film Corp.,* [198 F.3d 1104 (9th Cir. 2000)] ADA Title I was not violated by imposing different caps for mental and physical ailments. In this case, the plaintiff was totally disabled and could not perform essential functions of the job even with accommodation. Title III was not violated because there was no public accommodation involved, and insurance underwriting decisions are protected by the Title IV safe harbor.

Disability insurers seldom litigate mental disability cases until the second year. They may take a more proactive stance if they face the potential of claims with the same limits as physical disability claims, or without any limits at all.

The victim of a work-related brain injury received disability benefits under SSDI and the employer's ERISA plan on the basis of total and permanent disability. Later, he applied for reinstatement. The Seventh Circuit ruled that the representations made to obtain those benefits were inconsistent with a later ADA claim because the benefits were dependent upon a showing that the claimant could not perform his former occupation even with reasonable accommodation. [*Opsteen v. Keller Structures, Inc.*, 408 F.3d 390 (7th Cir. 2005). Under *Pals v. Schepel Buick*, 220 F.3d 497 (7th Cir. 2000) accommodation to a short-term disability may be required, but a permanently and totally disabled person is not "qualified" for ADA purposes]

[D]   EEOC Compliance Manual

EEOC directives do not have the force of law. Even Regulations promulgated by this agency have often been invalidated by court decisions. However, you should consult Section 3 of the EEOC's Compliance Manual, issued October 3, 2000 [<http://www.eeoc.gov/policy/docs/benefits.html>] for EEOC policy on what constitutes discrimination on the basis of age or handicap, and what "equal" benefits mean in the context of disability benefits.

The revised Compliance Manual permits employers to reduce long-term disability benefits to account for Social Security Disability Income, Worker's Compensation, and other non-age-based government benefits. LTD benefits paid to older workers can also be reduced by pension benefits that come from employer contributions, under two conditions. Either the employee voluntarily opts to receive the pension (at any age) or has reached age 62 of the plan's normal retirement age (whichever is later) and is eligible for a full, unreduced pension. In plans partially funded by employee contributions, the employer is only permitted to reduce benefits that can be traced back to its own contributions, not employee contributions.

The Eighth Circuit also allowed a plan sponsor to offset disability benefits (under the pension plan and Disability Income Plan) by the amount of the Worker's Compensation award—but not by the amount of attorneys' fees the claimant paid to litigate the issue. The Eighth Circuit reached this result because the terms of the plan explicitly permitted offsets of benefits that are of the same general character as plan benefits, and the plan administrator had discretion to decide whether Worker's Compensation fell into this category. The Eighth Circuit ruled that attorneys' fees are not of the same general character as plan benefits. [*Leonard v. Southwestern Bell Corp. Disability Income Plan*, 341 F.3d 696 (8th Cir. 2003)]

The EEOC position is that disability retirement benefits are not equal if they are calculated on the basis of the number of years the employee would have worked until NRA, because that approach favors younger employees. But disability benefits under government programs can legitimately be used to reduce disability benefits paid by the employer.

[E]   Other Compliance Issues

Disability benefits are not considered "medical care," so when an employee is terminated, the right to COBRA continuation coverage [*see* Chapter 19] extends to the employee group health plan but not to the long-term disability plan.

See, e.g., Goldman v. Hartford Life & Accident Ins. Co. [2004 U.S. Dist. LEXIS 18266 (E.D. La. 2004)], a suit for wrongful denial of LTD benefits brought by a person whose claim was denied on the ground that he was a temporary employee and hence ineligible. The employee alleged that COBRA notice was due when he changed from permanent to temporary employee status and lost eligibility for LTD coverage, but the Eastern District of Louisiana ruled against him, on the ground that LTD provides income replacement rather than health coverage and therefore is not subject to COBRA. Disability plans are specifically exempt from HIPAA's portability requirements, including the rules about preexisting conditions, so it was not a violation of HIPAA for an LTD plan to deny a claim on the basis that the illness existed during the plan's three-month look-back period. [*Schleicher v. Ascension Health,* 2006 U.S. Dist. LEXIS 14485 (M.D. Tenn. 2006)]

The Family and Medical Leave Act [P.L. 103-3. *See* Chapter 38] may entitle the employee to claim unpaid leave for personal medical needs, or the need to care for a sick family member. UnumProvident commissioned a Lost-Time Progression Study in 2005 to determine the relationship between FMLA leave and disability leave as aspects of time lost from work. From 2002 to 2004, 11% of almost 150,000 employees studied had a lost-time event, an average of 4.5 claims per 1,000 employees. More than half (58%) were FMLA claims, 36% short-term disability, 2% Worker's Compensation claims, and only 1% long-term disability claims. However, 65% of those with a lost-time event combined FMLA leave and a disability claim within a six-month period. Of the FMLA claims, 66% were to treat the employee's own serious health condition, 20% for parenting leave, and 17% to care for a sick family member. Only 2% of the employees surveyed used intermittent FMLA leave, but that time off represented about one fifth of all FMLA leave used. One quarter of the intermittent leaves progressed to other types of time-off benefits. Companies that integrated leave management had a lower claim cost (by almost $12,000 per 100 disability claimants) than companies that tried to manage their disability plans but did not coordinate those plans with FMLA time off. [Kenneth Mitchell and Carol Davis, *Reducing Lost Time: The Correlation Between Family-Medical Leave and Short-Term Disability,* Employee Benefit News, <http://www.benefitnews.com/pfv.cfm?id=8968> (May 2006)]

In the view of the Ninth Circuit, the ADEA may be violated by calculating disability retirement benefits using the age at the time of hiring. The plan at issue calculated the benefit on the basis of years of service lost as a result of disability, based on the length of service between age 55 (presumed retirement date) and the date the claimant became a public employee. Under *Hazen,* [*see* § 42.11[D]] calculations based on actual years of service are acceptable, because a younger person might have more years of service, and vice versa. But this is a slightly different question, because the age at hire had a strong effect on the potential disability benefit. The Ninth Circuit remanded the case to the District Court for disposition. [*Arnett v. California Public Employees Retirement Sys.,* 179 F.3d 690 (9th Cir. 1999)] Later, perhaps reflecting a different judicial environment, the Sixth

Circuit ruled that it was not a violation of the ADEA to compute disability retirement benefits on the basis of the number of years someone would have worked if he or she had not become disabled. Under this plan, a person who became disabled after becoming eligible for retirement therefore received only normal retirement benefits. Although this method put older workers at a disadvantage, the court held that the plan was valid because it was adopted to compensate the younger workers for the greater number of years of income they would lose, not to discriminate against older workers. [*EEOC v. Jefferson County Sheriff's Dep't*, 414 F.3d 467 (6th Cir. 2005)]

At least according to the First Circuit, a Social Security Disability Insurance (SSDI) determination is relevant to the question of whether a person receiving LTD benefits continues to be disabled. But the SSDI determination is not controlling, because ERISA-regulated disability plans and SSDI have different standards. [*Pari-Fasano v. ITT Hartford Life and Accident Ins. Co.*, 230 F.3d 415 (1st Cir. 2000)]

Also with respect to SSDI, an Eighth Circuit case involved a worker who experienced pulmonary symptoms. A lung specialist imposed permanent work restrictions on dust, fumes, chemicals, and smoke. He kept trying to get a job at the plant that he could do safely, but there were no such jobs available. He filed charges of age and disability discrimination and retaliation, which were settled for a package of cash and outplacement assistance. The settlement called for distribution of his thrift and pension accounts in accordance with the normal plan rules. The plan also allowed for disability retirement for workers of at least 10 years' tenure, who are certified by a physician as permanently disabled, when disability existed for at least 26 weeks.

He applied for and received SSDI, based on the Social Security Administration's conclusion that he was totally disabled, as well as veterans' benefits based on post-traumatic syndrome from events in the military. As a result of a permanent diminution in lung function, he received Worker's Compensation at a 60% permanent partial disability level.

The plaintiff applied for disability retirement under the former employer's plan, citing evidence from the SSA, VA, and Worker's Compensation determination. The defendant in this case, the plan administrator, denied disability retirement benefits on two grounds. First, that he had not separated from service because of disability, but had resigned pursuant to the settlement agreement; second, that he was not totally and permanently disabled. He filed an internal appeal. Although the plan set a deadline of 60 days if there is no appeal hearing, 120 days if there is one, more than 18 months passed with no decision by the review panel.

The Eighth Circuit reviewed the release that the plaintiff signed to make sure that it was obtained without violations of fiduciary duty. The court concluded that the plaintiff did not surrender his retirement benefits by settling discrimination charges; state law requires contracts to be interpreted to avoid unduly harsh results.

The rule in the Eighth Circuit is that a review panel's failure to act on an appeal increases the standard of scrutiny from abuse of discretion to de novo review only if the failure raises serious doubts about the conclusion reached by the plan administrator. [*Seman v. FMC Corporation Retirement Plan for Hourly Employees*, 334 F.3d 728 (8th Cir. 2003); the rule about de novo review comes from *McGarrah v. Hartford Life Ins. Co.*, 234 F.3d 1026 (8th Cir. 2000)]

The question of ERISA preemption (whether the federal law and courts, not their state counterparts, will govern) often arises in the pension and benefits context. [*See* § 18.17, *infra.*]

According to the Tenth Circuit, ERISA preempts claims that disability benefits were denied in bad faith. [*Kidneigh v. UNUM Life Ins. Co. of America*, 345 F.3d 1182 (10th Cir. 2003); *Conover v. Aetna U.S. Health Care Inc.*, 320 F.3d 1076 (10th Cir. 2003)] The court reached its decision by noting that state laws that provide additional remedies (such as punitive and consequential damages) are preempted because they conflict with ERISA's enforcement scheme. Although there is an exception from preemption for state laws that regulate insurance, this applies only to laws that are integral to the process of pooling risk.

§ 20.05   CASE LAW ON "TOTAL DISABILITY"

In many instances, the question is not how to interpret the plan—the question is whether or not the claimant satisfies the plan's definition of "total disability." It may be inability to perform the applicant's own occupation, or any occupation for which his or her education and training qualifies him or her—or the definition may shift depending on the length of the period of disability.

Even if the question is ability to engage in "any gainful occupation," most courts will require consideration of the individual's earnings history and the availability of jobs in the relevant geographic area. [*See, e.g., Mossa v. Provident Life & Casualty Ins. Co.*, 36 F. Supp. 2d 524 (E.D.N.Y. 1999)]

It was permissible for the insurer to terminate LTD benefits, based on its conclusion that an actuary/business executive with hearing loss in both ears was able to do a variety of jobs appropriate for his experience and physical limitations. He submitted a report that there was no job available to him paying more than $45,000 a year, but the insurer reasonably relied on the Chicago Society of Actuaries' conclusion that there were many jobs, some of them paying six figures, that a hearing-impaired person could perform. [*O'Reilly v. Hartford Life & Accident Ins. Co.*, 272 F.3d 955 (7th Cir. 2001)]

The employee in *Whatley v. C.N.A. Insurance*, [189 F.3d 1310 (11th Cir. 1999)] lost his job on September 29. Later, he applied for disability benefits, claiming that he became totally disabled on October 3. The benefits were denied, on the theory that he could not have been disabled on September 29 (because he worked on that day), so any disability must have arisen after employment was terminated. According to the Eleventh Circuit, however, he might have been totally disabled at the end of September. Summary judgment should not have been granted—fact questions remained to be settled, including medical evidence about the actual onset of total disability.

Summary judgment was granted at the District Court level for the insurer, on the grounds that it did not abuse its discretion in denying disability benefits. The Fourth Circuit, however, reversed the District Court. The plaintiff, a nuclear engineer, kept working for about a year despite a diagnosis of chronic abdominal pain and Irritable Bowel Syndrome (IBS). Then his doctor ordered a week off work, which was extended for more than six months. He was cleared to return to work but this was not successful; he was placed on medical leave of absence. He filed for LTD benefits, claiming that disability began at the end of 1999 and his last work date was the unsuccessful attempt to return in mid-2000. The insurer denied his claim on the basis that there was no medical documentation that he had IBS and no evidence of inability to work (the plaintiff submitted a great deal of documentation, including an SSA disability determination).

According to the insurer, the proper date for determining disability was the initial time off plus a six-month elimination period, whereas the plaintiff said the determination should have been made as of the unsuccessful attempt to resume work. The Fourth Circuit held that disability should be determined based on sufficient proof of total disability. The insurer abused its discretion by basing its determination on a particular date when evidence was submitted relating to a different date. [*Evans v. Metropolitan Life Ins Co.*, 358 F.3d 307 (4th Cir. 2004)]

Riedl v. General American Life, [248 F.3d 753 (8th Cir. 2001)] holds that the plaintiff should not have been granted summary judgment against the insurer: there was no clear evidence that he was totally disabled. The plan imposed a six-month waiting period. After that, an applicant would be deemed totally disabled if, for 24 months after the injury or illness, the applicant would be unable to work at his or her regular job or another reasonable job available within the employer company. After that 24-month period, the applicant would be considered totally disabled if unable to work at any occupation.

The plaintiff (a shift supervisor) went on medical leave in April 1995 and had surgery in August 1995. In September 1995, his cardiologist cleared him to return to work without restrictions. Soon thereafter, he accepted an early retirement severance package. In November 1995, he applied for LTD benefits. In December 1995, his attending physician and his cardiologist said he was totally disabled for his own job, but could do other work. The Eighth Circuit said that summary judgment was inappropriate, because the finder of fact would have to hear all the facts to decide the question of disability.

An orthopedic surgeon supplemented his disability insurance (which covered total disability—the inability to perform the material and substantial duties of his occupation) with a rider making disability from his own occupation total disability. He also purchased a "residual" (partial) disability rider covering the inability to perform one or more daily duties of his occupation or the inability to maintain his usual pre-disability work schedule. Injuries from a piloting accident prevented him from standing at an operating table and thus precluded him from continuing to practice as an orthopedic surgeon, although he could and did perform other medical tasks on a part-time basis (although his income was only one eighth of its pre-accident level). The Eighth Circuit upheld the trial court's grant of summary judgment for the insured doctor, agreeing that his inability to carry out the most important part of his previous occupation rendered him totally disabled under the terms of the policy and riders. [*Dowdle v. National Life Ins. Co.*, 407 F.3d 967 (8th Cir. 2005)]

The Eighth Circuit, finding substantial reason for the denial, upheld a termination of LTD benefits when the insurer determined that a person who had to leave her nursing job because of a latex allergy was nevertheless capable of other occupations. [*Smith v. UNUM*, 305 F.3d 789 (8th Cir. 2002)] The court followed *Ferrari v. TIAA*, [278 F.3d 801 (8th Cir. 2002)], which holds that when the standard is abuse of discretion, a decision must be affirmed if a reasonable person could have made that decision, not that a reasonable person necessarily would have made the same decision. When there are conflicting medical opinions, it is not an abuse of discretion to accept a reasonable opinion that the person is not disabled. A treating physician's opinion is entitled to more deference than the opinion of a reviewer who just reviews the records, but not more deference than the opinion of a doctor who performs an independent examination. [*Delta Family-Care Disability & Survivorship Plan v. Marshall*, 258 F.3d 834 (8th Cir. 2001)] Relying on the opinion of the independent examiner is not proof that the fiduciaries lacked reasonableness or prudence. [*Coker v. Metro Life Ins. Co.*, 281 F.3d 793 (8th Cir. 2002)] Similarly, the First Circuit upheld a grant of summary judgment for the employer: it was not arbitrary and capricious for the plan to conclude that the plaintiff was not unable to work at any occupation she was qualified for. The plan acted on the basis of expert opinions, including a Functional Capacity Evaluation indicating that the plaintiff could perform sedentary work. The medical reports submitted by the plaintiff said that she couldn't work full time, but did not indicate what she would be capable of doing. [*Matias-Correa v. Pfizer Inc.*, 345 F.3d 7 (1st Cir. 2003)]

A bank loan officer with fibromyalgia filed for short-term disability benefits. The claim was approved. When the short-term disability period ended, her claim was automatically converted to a long-term disability claim. She was told that she was eligible but would have to submit periodic updated medical information to justify continued benefits. Six months later, benefits were terminated. She appealed within the plan, then sued in Texas state court. The defendant moved the case to the federal system. Although the district court awarded benefits to the plaintiff, the Fifth Circuit reversed, finding that the district court misinterpreted the policy provision "unable to perform all duties" of her own occupation as "not able to perform any one of the duties." Because the plaintiff could not prove she was unable to perform all of the material and substantial duties of her occupation, the Fifth Circuit deemed that she was not entitled to long-term disability benefits. [*Ellis v. Liberty Life Assurance Co. of Boston*, 394 F.3d 262 (5th Cir. 2004), revised Jan. 13, 2005]

Another fibromyalgia case holds that it was not arbitrary for a plan to give credence to its reviewing physicians rather than the plaintiff's treating physicians. The plaintiff failed to provide medical support for her claim that she was unable to work in her own, sedentary occupation of secretary. [*Jordan v. Northrop Grumman Corp. Welfare Benefit Plan*, 370 F.3d 869 (9th Cir. 2004)]

Of course, even a decision that is reviewed de novo might survive the review. For instance, an editor with back problems quit his job and applied for LTD benefits. The benefits were denied on the grounds that he was not totally disabled. At about the same time, he qualified for SSDI. He appealed the denial, but the insurer upheld the denial because he could perform at least some of the duties of his regular occupation. The Fourth Circuit reviewed the matter de novo, because the plan document did not clearly grant discretionary authority. However, the Fourth Circuit found that the insurer used an objectively reasonable description to define the claimant's job and evaluated his medical condition against those duties, reaching a reasonable (although not inevitable) conclusion that he was not totally disabled. The court did not accept the plaintiff's contention that substantial weight had to be given to the SSDI finding, because there was no evidence that the Social Security Administration used the same definition of disability as the plan did. [*Gallagher v. Reliance Standard Life Ins. Co.*, 305 F.3d 264 (4th Cir. 2002)]

§ 20.06   EFFECT OF PLAN AMENDMENTS

In late 1999, the Eighth Circuit offered yet another lesson in the importance of careful drafting of plan documents. Ceridian Corporation used to pay insurance premiums for disabled individuals as part of its long-term disability plan. When it discontinued this practice, a group of disabled ex-employees sued. The SPD reserved the right to amend the plan, but did not specify whether it could be amended with respect to people who were already disabled at the time of the change. [*Barker v. Ceridian Corp.*, 193 F.3d 976 (8th Cir. 1999)] The Eighth Circuit held that the SPD provision was ambiguous. That opened the way for testimony about the company's intentions. The Eighth Circuit ordered Ceridian to continue paying for insurance for the group of ex-employees already disabled at the time of the change in the plan.

According to a 2006 Second Circuit decision, the standard for judicial review of an administrator's benefit determination is the SPD that was in effect when the plaintiff became disabled—and not the amended SPD in effect when the application was denied. (The later SPD granted discretion to the plan administrator; the earlier one did not.) The right to benefits vested when the plaintiff became disabled, so the second SPD could not apply. [*Gibbs v. Cigna*, 440 F.3d 571 (2d Cir. 2006)]

§ 20.07   CLAIMS PROCEDURES AND THE STANDARD
           OF REVIEW

[A]   Generally

See Chapter 13 for a discussion of claims procedures. The Department of Labor's final rule on claims procedures [65 Fed. Reg. 70246 (Nov. 21, 2000)] sets the time frame for resolving disability claims. At the initial level, claims must be resolved within 45 days of the time the plan receives the claim. But, as long as the claimant receives a notice explaining the reason for the delay, resolution can be deferred for 30 days due to factors beyond the control of the plan. A second 30-day extension is possible. If the decision is adverse to the claimant, the appeal usually has to be decided within 45 days. If the plan is unable to complete review within the original time period, a 45-day extension is possible.

An EBSA advisory opinion letter [No. 2005-06A, <http://www.dol.gov/ebsa/pdf/ao2005-06a.pdf> (Apr. 11, 2005)] says that an ERISA plan providing accidental death and dismemberment (AD&D) benefits in a lump sum, based on a schedule of covered losses (e.g., for blindness or loss of a body part) is not a disability plan and therefore is not subject to the special claims requirements set for disability plans by 29 C.F.R. § 2560.503-1. Although the insurer retained the right to demand medical examinations or autopsies, EBSA opined that an award of benefits did not depend on an assessment of the claimant's ability to engage in gainful activity, so it was not a disability plan.

Under the current version of the claims regulations (*see* Chapter 13), whenever there is an adverse benefit determination (e.g., reduction or termination of benefits), the plan administrator has a legal obligation to consult an independent medical expert—an appropriately trained health care professional who has relevant experience. Disability benefits were terminated after 24 months based on a determination that the claimant was not disabled using an "any-occupation" standard. As part of the appeal, the claimant had to submit to examination by a psychologist hired by the company doctor. The Southern District of Ohio agreed with the plaintiff's contention that the psychologist was not an independent medical expert because he was hired by the doctor who made the initial adverse determination. Furthermore, the role of the consultant is to review the existing record, not to add more data to it. [*Neiheisel v. AK Steel Corp.,* 2005 U.S. Dist. LEXIS 4639 (S.D. Ohio 2005)]

In order to get her claim for benefits remanded, the First Circuit required a LTD plan participant to show that she was prejudiced by the administrator's failure to provide her with the entire claim file. Prejudice would occur if, without a complete copy of the claim file, she did not understand what evidence would be required to rebut the administrator's conclusion that she was not disabled. [*DiGregorio v. Hartford Comprehensive Employee Benefit Serv. Co.*, 423 F.3d 6 (1st Cir. 2005)]

An investment banker, who was covered under an LTD policy, had a stroke a few months after he was hired. He went back to work despite slurred speech and hand and leg weakness and worked for more than a year. In 1999, he was diagnosed with permanent partial disability and his return to unrestricted professional employment was considered unlikely. He was later terminated the same year. He received STD for part of the 1996–1998 period. In 2000, his claim for total disability benefits was denied for reasons including late submission of claim, lack of cooperation, and prejudice to the insurer because of the delay. The state law extends the statute of limitations to three years from the date proof of loss is required. For a continuing-loss claim such as LTD, proof of loss is due 90 days after the end of the period of disability. For a discrete loss date claim, proof of loss is due 90 days from the discrete loss. By that standard, the suit would be timely because it would have to be filed within three years and 90 days from the time the insured ceased to be totally disabled, and the claimant continued to be disabled. The Eighth Circuit did not accept the insurer's contention that proof of loss was due at the time of the stroke, because the claimant went back to work and worked for two years afterward. [*Weyrauch v. Cigna Life Ins.*, 416 F.3d 717 (8th Cir. 2005)]

[B] De Novo or Abuse of Discretion?

An LTD plan directed the administrator to pay benefits if the participant submits "satisfactory proof of total disability." According to the Eighth Circuit, courts must review these determinations using a de novo standard of review. [*Walke v. Group Long Term Disability Ins.*, 256 F.3d 835 (8th Cir. 2001)] The Ninth Circuit made a similar ruling in *Kearney v. Standard Insurance Co.* [175 F.3d 1084 (9th Cir. 1998)] The Eighth Circuit view was that this was ambiguous language, normally found in non-ERISA contexts; if the insurer chose to include this language, it must deal with consequences of the administrator not being awarded discretion.

To the Fourth Circuit, the arbitrary and capricious standard of review applies only if the plan gives the administrator discretion. De novo review is required for all other plans. The long-term disability plan construed in *Feder v. Paul Revere Life Insurance Co.* [228 F.3d 518 (4th Cir. 2000)] said that a physician was eligible if he or she was totally disabled and unable to perform professional duties. Total disability meant injury or sickness that completely precluded work and made the doctor unable to perform the central duties of the medical specialty.

The plaintiff, a surgeon, was terminated in 1993, and submitted a LTD claim for disabling mental illness. Benefits were paid as of February 1994. In June 1996, the insurer gave notice that benefits were being terminated because the doctor no longer qualified. The Fourth Circuit reversed the grant of summary judgment for the plan, because its insurer did not reserve discretion—it merely required submission of written claims, which is an inevitable part of all insurance claims processes.

According to the Seventh Circuit, for a sponsor to reserve discretion, the plan documents must say more than that claimants must prove or give satisfactory proof of entitlement to benefits. The rationale of *Herzberger v. Standard Insurance Co.*, [205 F.3d 327 (7th Cir. 2000)] is that an ERISA plan is a contract, which is interpreted by courts and not the party who drafted the language. However, the court approved this language as adequate to secure deferential review: "Benefits under this plan will be paid only if the plan administrator decides in his discretion that the applicant is entitled to them."

The Seventh Circuit ruled that a denial had to be reviewed *de novo* because the LTD plan did not have appropriate language to reserve discretion: Requiring "proof satisfactory to us" for benefits does not put the participant on notice of the administrator's power to interpret the plan. [*Diaz v. Prudential Ins. Inc.*, 424 F.3d 635 (7th Cir. 2005)]

According to the Eighth Circuit, a termination of disability benefits should have been reviewed *de novo*. The plan in the insurer's claim file affidavit did not grant discretion to the insurer, whereas the brief for the insurer included a different copy of the plan, with no affidavit of authenticity. This version did grant discretionary authority. The Eighth Circuit ruled that the District Court should not have applied the second version without resolving the discrepancy. [*Barham v. Reliance Standard Life Ins. Co.*, 441 F.3d 581 (8th Cir. 2006)]

Although insurers generally prevail in suits over LTD and other health claims, the Eighth Circuit reversed a grant of summary judgment for an insurer, finding that the insurer had abused its discretion by denying an application. The plaintiff, a surgical technician, was discharged after his heart medication caused dizziness, and his doctor said that he could work but could not be on call. After his medication was adjusted, he was reassigned to a lower-salaried job with fewer responsibilities. He resigned, claiming that he planned to seek other job opportunities. He claimed LTD benefits because of his heart condition and hearing impairment, listing two audiologists and a cardiologist in support of his claim. The insurer decided that he wasn't disabled and could perform other health care jobs. The Eighth Circuit said that one of the medical reviewers erred seriously by making unsupported conclusions (e.g., inappropriate conclusions about the plaintiff's conflicts with employers and alcohol abuse) and misstating the facts of the case (saying that the plaintiff was fired for poor performance rather than resigning after a demotion). The Eighth Circuit did not accept the plaintiff's argument that a higher standard of review was required because of the insurer's conflict of interest, but did agree with the plaintiff that the medical evidence in the record showed he was unable to perform his own occupation safely and therefore the insurer had abused its discretion. [*Torres v. Unum Life Ins. Co. of Am.*, 405 F.3d 670 (8th Cir. 2005)]

Usually, a court that reviews a plan decision de novo will restrict its review to the administrative record. For example, in a 2005 First Circuit case, a medical technician received LTD benefits on account of drug dependency and depression. The policy limit was five years of benefits. After three years, the claimant filed a second claim based on back problems. The insurer denied this claim. The claimant sued and the District Court granted summary judgment for the insurer. The First Circuit affirmed in 2005, holding that the medical record did not show total disability due to back pain. The plaintiff argued that evidence outside the administrative record should have been admitted on the issue of disability, but the First Circuit ruled that this would have been improper—what is reviewed in the federal courts is the final ERISA administrative decision, and adding more documents later offends the interest in finality and the requirement of exhaustion of administrative remedies. [*Orndorf v. Paul Revere Life Ins. Co.,* 404 F.3d 510 (1st Cir. 2005)]

However, according to the Tenth Circuit [*Hall v. UNUM Life Ins. Co.*, 300 F.3d 1197 (10th Cir. 2002)], the court can supplement the record with other evidence if the circumstances clearly establish the need for the material to perform an adequate review. The party seeking to supplement the record has the burden of showing that evidence is needed that could not have been submitted during the claims review process, and that the evidence does not duplicate evidence already in the record. Factors that could justify admitting additional evidence include the complexity of the medical issues involved; possible doubt about the credibility of medical experts; need for evidence to interpret plan terms; and possible conflict of interest on the part of the plan administrator. The Tenth Circuit expects that the test will be met only in unusual circumstances; in most cases, de novo review will still be restricted to the administrative record.

The Second Circuit permits evidence outside the administrative record to be examined if there is good cause to do so; but the administrator's conflict of interest, viewed in isolation, is not enough to go outside the record. Outside evidence can be examined if the plan administrator lacks adequate procedures to process claims fairly. [*Ocher v. UNUM Life Ins. Co. of America*, 389 F.3d 288 (2d Cir. 2004)]

A case reviewed de novo (because the plan terms did not give the plan administrator interpretive discretion) granted summary judgment for the defendant insurer, because there was ample medical evidence, including statements from the claimant's own doctors releasing him for work, that the claimant was not totally disabled. Plans have the option—but not the obligation—to obtain independent medical review of claims. Once a participant's own treating physicians indicate he can return to work, the plan has no obligation to look any further. [*Wallace v. Reliance Standard Life Ins. Co.*, 318 F.3d 723 (7th Cir. 2003)]

An insurer's denial of disability benefits is not entitled to deference from the courts if the denial is based on a selective rather than a comprehensive reading of the medical evidence, and if the plan's own experts called for additional tests but the plan did not carry them out. (The question was whether a corporate manager's sleep disorder was totally disabling.) In this case, the insurer both funded and administered the plan, so this potential conflict of interest required a heightened standard of review. [*Ferguson v. Hartford Life and Accident Ins. Co.*, 268 F. Supp. 2d 463 (E.D. Pa. 2003)]

The Eighth Circuit looked at the problem of conflict of interest in *Farfalla v. Mutual of Omaha Ins. Co.*, 324 F.3d 971 (8th Cir. 2002), concluding that although the defendant was both the insurer and the plan administrator, it was not necessary to apply de novo review to the defendant's decision to terminate the plaintiff's disability benefits. There was substantial evidence that the plaintiff, despite significant health problems, was still able to perform certain types of work and thus was not totally disabled. In this reading, conflict of interest triggers de novo review only if the conflict is palpable or there is a serious procedural irregularity that causes a serious breach of fiduciary duty—a standard that comes from *Woo v. Deluxe Corp.* [144 F.3d 1157 (8th Cir. 1998)]

The *Farfalla* decision also rules that a plan administrator is not bound by the Social Security Administration's determination that a person qualifies for Social Security Disability Income benefits—especially where, as here, the SSDI benefits reflect an onset date later than the ERISA plan's claims determination. The Seventh Circuit held in 2006 that it was not necessarily arbitrary and capricious for an in-house doctor employed by the administrator of a disability plan to rule, after a records review, that the claimant was not disabled. The doctor was just as capable of rendering an objective opinion as a non-employee doctor retained by the administrator. There was no inherent conflict of interest, and the plan administrator did not have to retain an outside doctor to verify the in-house doctor's conclusions. Nor was it necessary for the in-house doctor to examine the claimant or speak to his attending; file review was adequate. [*Davis v. Unum*, 444 F.3d 569 (7th Cir. 2006)]

In contrast, the Eleventh Circuit ruled in late 2003 that whenever a benefits determination is made by a party that will be required to make payments if coverage is granted, the fiduciary has a conflict of interest. Therefore, a heightened standard of review should operate—even in a factual situation rather than a case involving interpretation of the terms of the plan. [*Torres v. Pittston Company*, 346 F.3d 1324 (11th Cir. 2003)]

The First Circuit position is that the mere possibility that the insurer-cum-administrator will have to pay claims out of its own assets does not create a conflict of interest. [*Wright v. R.R. Donnelley & Sons Group Benefit Plan*, 402 F.3d 67 (1st Cir. 2005); *Glista v. Unum Life Ins. Co. of America*, 378 F.3d 113 (1st Cir. 2004)]

The Seventh Circuit was dismissive of a plaintiff's argument that the decision of his disability insurer to deny benefits should not be granted deference because of the potential for conflict of interest. (The insurer ruled that the plaintiff's coronary artery disease, hypertension, and gout did not prevent him from being able to hold down a job as a commodities dealer.) The District Court, affirmed by the Seventh Circuit, ruled that such a decision was not arbitrary or capricious, because individuals with cardiac problems have often proved capable of holding stressful jobs. Furthermore, the Seventh Circuit found that the conflict of interest argument was weak, because insurers are diversified enough to escape financial risk from any individual case. [*Leipzig v. AIG Life Ins. Co.*, 362 F.3d 406 (7th Cir. 2004)]

Periodic review (based at least in part on an irrelevant report) led to disqualification for long-term disability benefits. The recipient appealed the disqualification. The employer requested an independent medical examination by a doctor it designated. The plan administrator relied on this examination to uphold the termination of benefits, despite other information in the file (including an SSA disability determination and reports from the employee's two doctors) indicating ongoing disability. The recipient went to federal court, suing for wrongful denial of benefits. The trial court upheld a benefits termination. It ruled that it was not arbitrary and capricious to terminate benefits, although the employee's two doctors stated that the employee was disabled, and there was an SSA disability determination in the file. The Third Circuit reversed the district court, finding that an overly deferential standard of review was applied. The Third Circuit required a sliding scale to be used to account for financial conflict of interest and procedural bias (i.e., the employer got involved by demanding an independent examination when there was already ample evidence of disability). The case was remanded for the trial court to reexamine the case using a heightened standard of review. [*Kosiba v. Merck & Co.*, 384 F.3d 58 (3d Cir. 2004)]

A plan's "deemed denial" provision caused failure to issue a decision within 120 days of receipt of a claim for review to be treated as a denial. The denial would constitute exhaustion of administrative remedies, thus permitting the claimant to bring suit to contest the denial of benefits. The plaintiff received short-term disability but was denied long-term disability, and appealed the long-term disability denial. She received an extension of time to file additional medical reports. Her attorney sent a letter enclosing a medical report and stating that a second report would follow. The attorney and the plan administrator agreed that review of the appeal would continue until the plaintiff submitted a report from an evaluator of her choice. But at that point, communications broke down for about two years. The plaintiff claimed that the report was submitted, the defendant that no report was received. Finally, the appeal was resolved and denial of long-term disability benefits was affirmed because the administrator concluded from review of the records that the plaintiff did not suffer from disabling conditions covered by the policy. About three months after this denial, the plaintiff sued, claiming that she was entitled to benefits because she satisfied the policy's definition of total disability.

The plan argued that because the SPD and plan require suit to be filed within four years of the "occurrence of the loss for which the claim is made," that is, when the disability occurred, a timely suit must be filed within four years of the last date that the plaintiff was able to work. However, the Ninth Circuit ruled that the plan's delays stopped them from asserting a statute of limitations defense, because the plaintiff reasonably refrained from filing a lawsuit while the plan induced her to believe that her claim was under review. There were several contacts between the plaintiff and defendant in which the defendant could have asserted that the claim was untimely, but it did not do so. However, on the substantive issues of the case, the Ninth Circuit held that after the *Nord* case, the opinions of treating physicians should not be given more deference than those of reviewing physicians. [*See* § 20.07(C)] The proper standard for reviewing the denial decision should be the more generous "abuse of discretion" rather than subjecting the decision to *de novo* review, because the plan exercised its discretion to grant an extension of time to the plaintiff. The Ninth Circuit did not want to punish the plan for allowing the plaintiff additional time. [*LaMantia v. Voluntary Plan Administrators, Inc.*, 401 F.3d 1114 (9th Cir. 2005)]

[C] The Treating Physician Rule

When the Social Security Administration decides whether an applicant is entitled to receive SSDI benefits, it uses the "treating physician" rule. In other words, the opinion of a physician who actually treats the claimant is given more weight than the opinion of a physician-reviewer who looks at the patient's medical file but doesn't actually examine the patient. There was a Circuit split as to whether this rule should be applied in the context of an ERISA plan. For example, the Sixth Circuit adopted the treating physician rule [*Darland v. Fortis Benefits Ins. Co.*, 317 F.3d 516 (6th Cir. 2003)] but the Second Circuit refused to apply the rule when plan administrator's decisions were being reviewed on a de novo basis. [*Connors v. Connecticut General Life Insurance Co.*, 272 F.3d 127 (2d Cir. 2001)]

The Supreme Court resolved the Circuit split through its May 2003 decision in *Black & Decker Disability Plan v. Nord.* [538 U.S. 822 (2003)] The Supreme Court ruled that the Social Security rule does not have to be followed in cases involving private ERISA plans rather than public benefits. According to the Supreme Court, neither the ERISA statute nor the Department of Labor's regulations demand any special deference for the opinion of the treating physician. Furthermore, in January 2005, the Sixth Circuit ruled that not only is the treating physician rule not mandatory, but an ERISA plan administrator is not bound by the Social Security Administration's determination that a person is totally and completely disabled to the extent that payment of SSDI benefits is justified. The court ruled that it was not arbitrary and capricious for the plan to base its conclusion that the plaintiff was not disabled on the opinions of an independent neurologist and psychiatrist who reviewed the plaintiff's medical records. [*Whitaker v. Hartford Life and Accident Ins. Co.*, 404 F.3d 947 (6th Cir. 2005)]

The Eighth Circuit held that it was reasonable for an insurer to reject the opinion of a claimant's treating physician. The plan booklet gave the sponsor discretionary authority. The sponsor delegated authority to the insurer, so the standard of review was abuse of discretion. The insurer obtained an independent physician's report, which stated that the plaintiff was capable of sedentary or light work. Reports by the treating doctor were contradictory—some saying he was capable of sedentary work, others denying it. Given the contradictions in the treating doctor's opinions, it was reasonable to accept the reviewing doctor's opinion. [*Groves v. Metropolitan Life Ins. Co.*, 438 F.3d 872 (8th Cir. 2006)]

The Sixth Circuit ruled that it was arbitrary and capricious to terminate LTD benefits (for a former office worker who qualified for Social Security disability because of uncontrolled severe hypertension and thumb pain) because the reviewer disregarded her treating physician's repeated statements that the claimant's hypertension was not treatable and that she was not able to work. That is, the problem was not merely that the treating physician's conclusion was not accepted—it was that the reviewer failed to give proper weight to the evidence. [*Moon v. Unum Provident Corp.*, 405 F.3d 373 (6th Cir. 2005)]

§ 20.08 APPEALS OF CLAIM DENIALS

A plan participant sued an insurer, Hartford Life and Accident Insurance Company, for benefits allegedly due under a long-term disability policy issued to the Hartford Multi-Employer Trust. The insurer raised the defense that it was not the plan, and therefore was not a proper defendant. However, the SPD for the plan failed to identify a proper agent for service of process, so the court permitted the case to go forward against the insurer because it was impossible to name the plan as a defendant. [*Penrose v. Hartford Life and Accident Ins. Co.*, 2003 U.S. Dist. LEXIS 13497 (N.D. Aug. 4, 2003)]

The insurer (which also administered the plan) denied plaintiff's initial LTD benefit claim. The initial denial letter stated that the participant was not "totally disabled" under the plan's definition, and advised her to submit additional information. She appealed the denial, providing more medical data. The administrator denied the claim once again, in a more detailed letter. [*Olive v. American Express LTD Benefit Plan*, 183 F. Supp. 2d 1191 (C.D. Cal. 2002)] The Central District ruled that the initial denial letter was inadequate because it was ambiguous and failed to inform the claimant whether her claim was substantively defective (her medical condition wasn't really totally disabling), procedurally defective (she didn't submit all the necessary records), or both.

The Seventh Circuit upheld the district court's determination that it was not arbitrary and capricious to deny disability benefits to a plaintiff who asserted that he was totally disabled and unable to walk, stand, or sit. It was a post-*Davila* case, so the Seventh Circuit treated the insurer as a fiduciary when it denied benefits. The terms of the plan gave the insurer discretion to interpret the plan and make determinations. The Seventh Circuit treated an insurer's decision as entitled to great deference, and can be overturned only if it was clearly unreasonable. In this case, the plaintiff failed to produce specific evidence that the fiduciary had a conflict of interest. The reports from the plaintiff's doctors, stating that he could not work at all, were founded in the plaintiff's subjective complaints of pain and were not supported by objective evidence. In fact, one of the plaintiff's doctors said he could perform at least some standing, sitting, and walking, so the rejection of his claim was not irrational. [*Ruiz v. Continental Casualty Co.*, 400 F.3d 986 (7th Cir. 2005)]

The Seventh Circuit ruled that, although the insurer was a fiduciary because of its discretionary authority, a denial of benefits was not adversely affected by the conflict of interest alleged by the plaintiff. The Seventh Circuit did not find any contract of interest other than conflicts inherent to any contract. [*Rud v. Liberty Life Assurance Co. of Boston*, 438 F.3d 772 (7th Cir. 2006)]

A 2006 Eighth Circuit case arose when long-term disability benefits were terminated on the grounds of medical ineligibility. The recipient was notified that he had 180 days to file an appeal, but he asked for and was granted a 90-day extension. His internal appeal was denied. He was notified that he had 60 days to file for the plan's second-level internal appeal. However, instead of pursuing the internal appeal, he brought suit against the plan and plan sponsor. His litigating theory was that the plan violated ERISA by imposing the 60-day time limit on second-level appeals. The Eighth Circuit dismissed his case for failure to exhaust administrative remedies. The ERISA regulations require claimants to be given at least 180 days to appeal an adverse decision. The regulations permit, but do not require, plans to have a second level of internal appeal before claimants are allowed to go to court. Furthermore, the regulations do not specify a time frame for second-level appeals and thus do not mandate a second 180-day period. The Eighth Circuit, reasoning by analogy with ERISA plans in general, accepted 60 days as a reasonable time limit for second-level appeals. A shorter time frame was acceptable because the claimant has already had the first-level appeal period to gather evidence. [*Price v. Xerox Corp.*, 445 F.3d 1054 (8th Cir. 2006)]

In 2006, the Eastern District of New York ruled that the administrator of a disability plan acted reasonably in terminating benefits on the basis of the job description provided by the employer—a description that the employee did not object to until late in the appeal process. The claimant, a collection specialist, claimed that she regularly had to lift packages weighing more than 20 pounds; the employer described the job as sedentary. [*Greenberg v. Unum Life Ins. Co. of Am.*, E.D.N.Y., No. CV-03-1396 (CPS), (E.D.N.Y. Mar. 27, 2006)]

When it reviews a case, the trial court should only look at the administrative record that was available to the insurer when it denied the claim. Evidence submitted after the expiration of the appeals period should not be considered. [*Alford v. DCH Found. Group LTD Plan*, 311 F.3d 955 (9th Cir. 2002)]

The Eighth Circuit ruled that a plan abused its discretion by concluding without substantial evidence that a claimant could perform sedentary work. A fact-based disability determination is reasonable if it is supported by substantial evidence, considering only the evidence that was available to the administrator at the time of claim denial. In this case, there was no new medical evidence of improvement to support this conclusion, so the benefits were improperly terminated. [*Norris v. Citibank, N.A. Disability Plan and Aetna Life Ins. Co.*, 308 F.3d 880 (8th Cir. 2002)]

A sales representative, 25% of whose work time involved driving (800–1,000 miles per week) had a stroke that permanently impaired the vision in one eye. The plaintiff's doctor said that it would be dangerous for him to drive, but also described him as having "no restrictions." Disability benefits were initially awarded and later terminated on the grounds that the plaintiff's condition was improving. The plaintiff submitted evidence that he was permanently impaired. The insurer relied on an unidentified vocational consultant who said that driving was not a material duty of working as a sales representative. The Fifth Circuit agreed with the plaintiff that the insurer failed to satisfy the requirements of the claims regulation, holding that ERISA requires review of the specific ground for denying the application and also requires disclosure of the identity of the vocational expert. According to the Fifth Circuit, these are not trivial technical points, but issues that go deeply to the plaintiff's ability to receive meaningful review of termination of benefits. [*Robinson v. Aetna*, 443 F.3d 389 (5th Cir. 2006)]

ERISA does not authorize suits by beneficiaries to get interest when long-term disability benefits are reinstated after an appeal. The Eleventh Circuit ruled that ERISA was written with a limited range of remedies, and does not specifically provide for interest. One Circuit did admit the possibility of an interest award (but only if the plan documents specifically provide for it). The Eleventh Circuit interpreted ERISA § 502(a)(3)(B) to limit the successful plaintiff to equitable remedies; interest on overdue contract payments is a classic legal, rather than equitable, remedy. [*Flint v. ABB, Inc.*, 337 F.3d 1326 (11th Cir. 2003)]

CHAPTER **21**

INSURANCE FRINGE BENEFITS

§ 21.01   INTRODUCTION

In addition to plans in which insurance operates behind the scenes (health plans; pension plans funded by insurance contracts), some fringe benefit plans exist to provide insurance coverage to employees. This chapter covers life insurance and long-term care insurance (LTCI) fringe benefits.

§ 21.02   LIFE INSURANCE FRINGE BENEFITS

[A]   Favorable Tax Treatment

Life insurance plays a valuable part in employees' financial planning through their entire planning cycle. For young employees who have not accumulated many assets, insurance is valuable as the source of a potential "instant estate." Older employees with greater accumulation of assets nevertheless value the benefits that life insurance can provide for survivors. Traditionally, life insurance was given favorable treatment for estate tax purposes, although as a result of EGTRRA, a larger number of estates will be exempt from estate taxation, making this a less important consideration.

The Internal Revenue Code authorizes several mechanisms under which employers can provide life insurance to employees at little or no income tax cost to the employees. (These mechanisms are distinct from the "key-person" insurance coverage that pays benefits to the corporation itself when it becomes necessary to replace a top executive or creative person.) The basic rule is that, if the employer pays the premiums and the insurance proceeds go to the beneficiary designated by the employee, the employee will have taxable income and the employer will be able to deduct the cost of providing the insurance. (The employer gets a deduction only for "ordinary and necessary business expenses.") However, the Code also provides certain relief measures that limit or eliminate the tax cost of these fringe benefits.

In mid-2005, the IRS issued T.D. 9223 to forbid abusive transactions involving "springing value" life insurance policies transferred to employees. The transactions are abusive because the purpose is to have an employee who has received a policy from a § 412(i) plan taxed at the cash surrender value of the policy, which is low. T.D. 9223 makes the employee taxable on the full fair market value (FMV) of the transferred life insurance contract. [*Final Regulations: Value of Life Insurance Contracts When Distributed from a Qualified Retirement Plan*, 2005-39 I.R.B. 591 (Aug. 26, 2005); 2004 Proposed Regulations were published at 69 Fed. Reg. 7384; *see also* Rev. Proc. 2004-16, 2004-10 I.R.B. 559, and Rev. Rul. 2004-20, 2004-10 I.R.B. 546]

An individual insurance contract plan is exempt from the minimum funding requirement of I.R.C. § 412 if it satisfies six requirements:

1. It is funded exclusively by the purchase of individual annuity and/or insurance contracts from a licensed life insurance company, although

        purchases can be made either directly by the employer or through a trust
        or custodial account.

2. The contract provides for level premium payments, either annual or more
frequent.

3. The benefits under the plan equal benefits provided under each contract
at the plan's Normal Retirement Age, guaranteed by the carrier to the
extent premiums have been paid.

4. The premiums payable for the current and all previous plan years were
paid before lapse (or the contract is reinstated).

5. There has never been a security interest at any time during the plan year
affecting rights under the contract (although a security interest created
after the distribution of the contract to the participant is permissible).

6. There are no policy loans outstanding at any time during the plan year
prior to distribution of the policy.

The employer can deduct contributions used to pay premiums on the insurance
contract if the plan holds the contract until the employee's death or until the
contract is distributed or sold to the employee (e.g., at retirement).

The IRS targets plans involving specially designed life insurance policies
whose cash surrender value is temporarily set far lower than the premiums paid.
Such policies are distributed or sold to employees at the artificial cash surrender
value; the "springing" feature then returns the value of the policy to something
more commercially realistic. The Final Regulations carry over the principle from
the 2004 proposal that a property distribution is included in the recipient's income
at FMV, including the value of all rights under the agreement, including
supplemental agreements (whether or not they are guaranteed). A transfer of property to a plan participant for less than FMV is considered a distribution by the plan
to the extent of the difference.

The Regulations under Code §§ 79 and 83 have also been modified to make
FMV controlling with respect to life insurance contracts under those sections as
well. Rev. Proc. 2005-25, 2005-17 I.R.B. 962, gives safe harbors for determining
the FMV of a life insurance contract; taxpayers can rely on it for all periods. Relief
under Notice 2002-8, 2002-1 C.B. 398, is still available for pre-January 28, 2002,
split-dollar life insurance arrangements and for transfers of life insurance contracts
under a split-dollar arrangement entered into before September 17, 2003, and not
materially modified since then.

Announcement 2005-80, 2005-46 I.R.B. 967, lists § 412(i) defined benefit
plans and 20 other tax-saving devices; certain users of these devices must surrender
improperly obtained tax benefits to the IRS, and in some cases will be subject to
penalties. Section 412(i) plans tend to use life insurance policies with a guaranteed
return to fund defined benefit plans because reporting is simplified by having a
guaranteed return. The § 412(i) programs targeted by the IRS include plans in
which the life insurance death benefits are greater than the benefits specified in
the plan documents, or those in which the rights of plan participants to buy life

insurance contracts under the plan are extremely unequal. [<http://www.irs.gov/pub/irs-drop/a-05-80.pdf>; discussed in Allison Bell, *Settlement Offer Could Affect Small DB Pension Plans,* NU Online News Service (Oct. 28, 2005)]

[B] Employee-Owned, Employer-Paid Insurance

It is common for employers to pay the premiums for life insurance owned by the employees covered by the plan. Treas. Reg. § 1.1035-1 gives the employer an income tax deduction for the cost of the plan, provided that the employer is not the beneficiary, and also limited by the I.R.C. § 162 "ordinary and necessary" rule.

The premiums that the employer pays are taxable income for the employee, but the insurance proceeds are not taxable income for the beneficiary who receives them. [*See* I.R.C. § 101)] If the employee borrows against the policy, interest on the loan (unlike most forms of personal interest) is deductible.

> **Tip:** Employer-pay life insurance plans are not subject to nondiscrimination requirements, so it is perfectly legitimate for the employer to furnish insurance to the employees the employer particularly wants to motivate, without making the plan available to the whole workforce.

[C] Company-Owned Life Insurance (COLI)

Under this variation, the policies are owned by the company itself, and can be used to finance death benefits paid under the employer's benefit plans. Cash-value insurance can be used to finance retirement benefits. The beneficiary of the plan, or the estate of the deceased employee, does have income under I.R.C. § 101(a), because the death benefits are deemed to be paid directly by the employer and not by an insurer.

When the employer owns the COLI policy and uses it only to fund the death benefit, the employee does not have taxable income during his or her life from either the policy's cash surrender value or the premium payments that the employer makes—as long as the employee's beneficiary is only an unsecured creditor with respect to the proceeds of the policy.

Usually, the corporation is not entitled to a deduction for the premiums it pays for COLI, because of the employer's interest as a beneficiary. However, there is an exception to this rule for premiums paid for certain annuity contracts used in connection with COLI plans.

In 2002 and 2003, a series of articles in the *Wall Street Journal* severely criticized COLI (calling it "janitor insurance" or "dead peasant insurance"), because in some instances, a corporation collects significant insurance benefits on the lives of low-paid workers who had little or no personal or company-provided insurance and whose families therefore were left poorly provided for. Insurance benefiting the company when nonkey employees die was criticized as unfair, because the insurance is sometimes maintained on retirees and other ex-employees, so companies benefit by the death of persons who are no longer employees at all, much less key employees. (Initially, corporations were only deemed to have an insurable interest in the lives of key employees, but this rule was changed in the 1980s.)

This type of insurance can also be used by corporations for financial manipulation. Corporations can deduct the insurance premiums they pay for this purpose; and, because they are insurance policies, the buildup of cash value is not taxed, and increase in cash value can be used to improve the financial results on the company's books. The insurance proceeds are not taxable income, so the company can get a windfall if someone dies after a short period of employment. The insurance can also be used as collateral for loans, or policy loans can be taken against the insurance.

According to Ellen E. Schultz and Theo Francis, the Wall Street Journal reporters who raised interest in this issue, corporate sales now make up 25–30% of all insurance sales. They charge that corporations derive tax breaks of close to $2 billion a year from insurance on employees' lives—a larger amount than the tax relief given to encourage business in economic empowerment zones.

Schultz and Francis trace a number of steps in the evolution of COLI. Key-man insurance has been used to cover top executives and business owners since the 1980s. However, in 1986 Congress imposed a $50,000 limit on the interest deduction for a loan to purchase a single policy. Many employers responded by purchasing many smaller policies on rank-and-file employees. In 1996, the interest deduction for policy loans was phased out. Starting in 1996, the trend was to use "manager's insurance" with the objective of paying for retiree medical benefits and executive deferred compensation. However, when an insured person dies, the policy benefits become part of general corporate assets, and their use is not restricted to these purposes. [Theo Francis, *Workers' Lives: Best Tax Break?*, Wall Street Journal, Feb. 19, 2003, at p. C1; Ellen E. Schultz and Theo Francis, *Death Benefit: How Corporations Built Finance Tool Out of Life Insurance,* Wall Street Journal, Dec. 30, 2002, at p. A1; Theo Francis and Ellen E. Schultz, *Tax Advantages of Life Insurance Help Lift Income,* Wall Street Journal, Dec. 30, 2002, at p. A8]

Also in 2002, there was trouble brewing between a number of large employers and the insurers (e.g., American International Group, Pacific Mutual, CIGNA, Metropolitan Life) that sold "Super-COLI" products. After Wal-Mart settled with the IRS as to the tax treatment of COLI, the retailer sued American International Group, seeking damages of $235 million, alleging that the insurer had failed to disclose the tax risks inherent to the plan. (At about the same time, about 20 other companies also settled IRS claims on this issue.) A Texas District Court ruled that Wal-Mart could not collect on a COLI policy because it did not have an insurable interest in the life of the insured person; Wal-Mart was not permitted to maintain a suit for breach of fiduciary duty and fraud against the insurers and insurance brokers that sold COLI to Wal-Mart. Wal-Mart charged that it was denied the financial advantages that were the purpose of the plan, but the Delaware Chancery Court said that the claims were time-barred because the claim accrued many years earlier, when the insurance was purchased. Equitable tolling was not available because Wal-Mart was aware of the risks of the plan. [*Wal-Mart Stores v. AIG Life Ins. Co.*, 72 LW 1600 (Del. Ch. Mar. 2, 2004)]

In *Dow Chemical Co.*, [2003-1 U.S.T.C. ¶ 50,346 (D. Mich. Mar. 31, 2003)] the court ruled that a pre-HIPAA arrangement involving complex loan transactions did have economic substance, and the corporation did have a legitimate economic interest in the policies, so the transaction was not a sham. In early 2006, the Sixth Circuit ruled that Dow could not deduct the interest on loans taken to purchase COLI because the plans were economic shams. The Sixth Circuit held that the District Court's cash flow analysis incorrectly included the positive cash flows predicted by Dow for the later years of the plan. These cash flows were highly contingent; if they were not included, the cash flows obviously would have been negative, indicating a sham transaction. The Sixth Circuit said that future profits contingent on a taxpayer's future actions can be considered by a court only if they are consistent with the taxpayer's past conduct. Dow had never infused cash into the plan before, so it was unrealistic to conclude that they would do so, especially when there was no legal obligation. The current rules limit deductibility of interest for borrowing to provide coverage of more than $50,000 on the lives of key persons, so this ruling is of greatest significance to companies that have pre-1996 COLI plans and have not settled with the IRS. [*Dow Chemical Co. v. United States*, 435 F.3d 594 (6th Cir. 2006)]

The Sixth Circuit agreed with the IRS that American Electric Power Company was not justified in claiming federal income tax deductions for interest due on loans using COLI policies as collateral. In effect, the Sixth Circuit found that the plan, covering 20,000 employees, was a sham because it was elaborately set up to generate tax deductions rather than to provide genuine insurance benefits. [*American Electric Power Co. v. U.S.*, 328 F.3d 737 (6th Cir. 2003)] *Winn-Dixie Stores, Inc. v. Commissioner*, 254 F.3d 1317 (11th Cir. 2001), also treats a COLI arrangement as a sham.

In August 2002, the Third Circuit ruled that company-owned life insurance policies funded by "loading dividends" were shams, and the whole transaction lacked economic substance. Therefore, IRS penalties against the corporation for inaccuracies in stating income were upheld. [*In re CM Holdings, Inc., IRS v. CM Holdings*, 301 F.3d 96 (3d Cir. 2002)]

The company bought COLI policies for 1,430 employees, naming itself as beneficiary of the policies. It paid a large premium in policy years 1–3, and then took a policy loan equal to most of the premiums paid. For the next four years, the company paid the annual premium for the policies plus accrued interest on the loan. The insurer treated nearly the entire premium as an expense charge, and then it returned nearly all of the expense charge to the company, describing it as a loading dividend. The company took interest deductions based on the highest of several available interest rates. When the interest deduction for COLI loans was phased out, the company stopped paying premiums and instructed the insurer to let the policies revert to a smaller amount of paid-up insurance. That was also the year of the company's bankruptcy filing. A year later, the IRS filed proof of claim in the bankruptcy case for $4.4 million in taxes, $1.8 million in prepetition interest, and $1.35 million in accuracy-related penalties (charged for misstatement of corporate tax items).

Courts look at two related aspects of a transaction to see if it has economic substance and therefore is entitled to be respected for tax purposes: objective results and subjective business motivation. This COLI plan fails both tests, because it obviously had no purpose and made no sense except as a means of generating tax deductions. It also looks bad for borrowers to choose a high interest rate, because it implies that they are tax-motivated and not interested in saving money.

Tip: Texas does not permit companies to get insurance on non-key employees. [*Mayo v. Hartford Life Ins. Co.,* 354 F.3d 400 (5th Cir. 2004); California, Illinois, Michigan, Minnesota, New York and Ohio require the consent of the employee whose life is insured.

An employer purchased life insurance on the lives of all its employees, but concealed this fact. The company collected $340,000 when one of its rank-and-file employees died. The personal representative of the decedent's estate sued under a state statute permitting the insured or a representative of the insured to bring suit whenever a party without an insurable interest purchases life insurance. The Tenth Circuit ruled for the representative of the estate, finding that the mere fact that a company encounters recruitment and training costs to replace a deceased employee does not create an insurable interest unless the employee is a key employee or somehow special to the corporation. However, the Tenth Circuit dismissed the unjust enrichment claim because this was an equitable cause of action and the plaintiff had adequate legal remedies under the statute. [*Tillman v. Camelot Music Inc.,* 408 F.3d 1300 (10th Cir. 2005)]

Despite the spate of unfavorable decisions, business life insurance continues to be valuable in some circumstances. It can be a good funding vehicle for deferred compensation liabilities (although probably not optimal for companies that have no tax liability and therefore don't need deductions or for companies subject to alternative minimum tax). Companies that have taxable income and have strong cash flows into their plans may want to use COLI as a funding vehicle to supplement mutual funds. It should be noted that funding deferred compensation with life insurance policies requires a good deal of administration, including monitoring the deferrals going to policies; allocating premiums appropriately; and adjusting investment options within a variable, universal, or variable-universal policy. COLI is not very liquid, so it is not a good choice for plans whose distributions exceed their contributions. Making a § 1035 policy exchange also calls for caution because the plan sponsor has to pay acquisition costs again for the new policy. [John N. Smith III, *The Bottom Line: Insurance Policies,* PlanSponsor.com magazine articles (Feb. 2006)]

COLI is still quite popular in the Fortune 1000 as a funding mechanism for nonqualified deferred compensation plans. In 2004, 63% of those large companies used COLI for this purpose—a percentage that rose to 70% in 2005. In 2004, 64% used COLI to fund supplemental executive retirement plans (SERPs), and 74% did so in 2005. Furthermore, 83% of health care companies and 100% of the largest utility companies in the Fortune 1000 had SERPs. [*Survey: COLI Use Rises,* NU Online News Service (Nov. 8, 2005)]

[D]   Section 79 (Group-Term Life)

Internal Revenue Code § 79 allows an employer to establish a written, non-discriminatory plan to provide term life insurance policies to a group of employees. (Term life insurance is pure insurance, with no cash value.) Employees can receive up to $50,000 worth of coverage under the plan with no tax consequences to them. But if the employer provides coverage over $50,000, the employee does have taxable income. The calculation is based on an official IRS table. The excess coverage is subject to FICA tax but not FUTA tax or income tax withholding. [I.R.C. § 3121(a)(2)]

The table was revised effective July 1, 1999. [*See* 64 Fed. Reg. 29788 (June 3, 1999)] The new rates are much lower than the old ones—especially for older employees:

Employee's Age	Prior Law	Revised Rates
Up to 25	.08	.05
25–29	.08	.06
30–34	.09	.08
35–39	.11	.09
40–44	.17	.10
45–49	.29	.15
50–54	.48	.23
55–59	.75	.43
60–64	1.17	.66
65–70	2.10	1.27
>70	3.76	2.06

A Section 79 plan must either be available to all employees, or to groups of employees defined in a way that does not allow selection of employees based on individual characteristics. So the plan can condition eligibility on factors related to age or employment, but not on the amount of the corporation's stock that the person owns. Nor can the amount of coverage be based on individual factors (although it can be proportionate to compensation). As a general rule, Section 79 plans must cover at least ten employees.

To satisfy the nondiscrimination test, the plan must benefit at least 70% of the sponsoring company's employees, and not more than 15% of the participants may be key employees. If the group-term life insurance plan is part of a cafeteria plan, it must also satisfy the I.R.C. § 125 rules. If the plan fails the nondiscrimination test, then highly compensated employees will have to include the full cost of coverage (not just the coverage over and above $50,000) in income.

[E] Split Dollar

Until 2001, split dollar plans were a regulatory backwater where nothing ever happened. A split dollar plan is a benefit arrangement that divides ownership, and possibly premium payments, between an employer and an employee. Each year the employer makes a contribution equal to the policy's increase in cash value for the year. Under the "endorsement method," the employer owns the policy. The policy is endorsed to allocate cash value and death benefit between employer and employee. Under the "collateral assignment" method, either the employee or a third party owns the policy and then assigns it to the employer. At the employee's death, the employer receives either the cash value of the policy or an amount representing the premiums paid; the rest of the benefits go to the employee's designated beneficiary. If the plan is an "equity split dollar plan," the employer is entitled to repayment of the premiums it paid, while the rest of the proceeds go to the designated beneficiary.

Split dollar plans became popular as a way to enhance the compensation of top executives without angering the shareholders by disclosing the full value of the compensation package. Executives liked the plans because they can be more secure than a corporate pension as they are backed by the insurer's resources. If the employer corporation goes bankrupt, its creditors can reach the pension funds, but not insurance policies. [For historical perspective on split dollar, *see, e.g.,* Theo Francis and Ellen E. Schultz, *Insurers Move to Protect Executive Policy,* Wall Street Journal, Dec. 30, 2002 at p. C1]

However, beginning in 2001, the IRS launched an attack on split dollar as a compensation mechanism. Another factor was the Sarbanes-Oxley Act's ban on personal loans to the directors and officers of public corporations, a provision that brought new sales of corporate split dollar policies to a halt because of uncertainties as to whether split dollar arrangements would be treated as interest-free loans to executives.

The IRS's first rulings on the taxation of split dollar arrangements, Rev. Rul. 64-328 and Rev. Rul. 66-110, covered only the endorsement and collateral assignments types of split dollar. They did not tackle the equity form. In 2001, the IRS took its first steps to remedy this by issuing Notice 2001-10 [2001-5 I.R.B 1], applying Code §§ 83 and 7872 in the split dollar context. In this Notice, the IRS published a new table, Table 2001, to be used both in valuation of split dollar arrangements and in calculations for qualified retirement plans.

In 2002, however, the IRS reversed itself, withdrawing Notice 2001-10 and replacing it with Notice 2002-8. [2002-4 I.R.B. 398] Notice 2002-8 gives a simple scheme for characterizing split dollar arrangements as either "transfers" or "loans." The most important factor for tax purposes is ownership of the policy. If the employer owns the policy (endorsement method) the transfer rules apply; if the employee owns it (collateral assignment method), then loan rules apply. Notice 2002-8 allows either Table 2001 or the one-year term rates published by the insurance company to be used to value the policies used in the split dollar program.

In July 2002, the IRS issued Proposed Regulations RIN 1545-BA44 [67 Fed. Reg. 45414] calling for taxation under either an economic benefit theory or a loan theory. The Proposed Regulations give rules for determining who is the owner. If only one party is named in the policy, that party is the owner; if two or more are designated, the first one named is generally treated as the owner.

Next, the IRS issued Notice 2002-59 [2002-36 I.R.B. 481] targeting "reverse split dollar" (a plan under which the employee owns the policy and its cash value; when the employee dies, the employer receives the basic death benefit; the employer often reimburses the employee for the annual term cost of the death benefit). The agency stated that in some arrangements, the party with the right to current life insurance protection uses manipulative techniques (e.g., inappropriately high term insurance rates) to achieve financial benefits other than insurance coverage.

Notice 2002-59 does not allow a party who has a right to any current life insurance protection to use Table 2001 or lower published rates. If the employer is the party with the right to current insurance protection, the employer's payment of the premium can create a taxable benefit for the employee, and neither Table 2001 nor the insurer's lower published rates can be used to value the taxable benefit. Also *see* REG-165754-01 RIN 1545-BA44 [68 Fed. Reg. 24898 (May 5, 2003)], a Notice of Proposed Rulemaking intended to clarify the valuation of split dollar arrangements for tax purposes.

In September, the IRS issued T.D. 9092 [2003-46 I.R.B. 1055], Final Regulations designed for appropriate taxation of split-dollar arrangements. The IRS press release announcing the regulations says that companies can no longer use split-dollar life insurance as a tax-free compensation mechanism.

Where the executive owns the policy, payments of premiums made by the employer are treated as loans to the executive. Unless the loan provides for market-rate interest, the executive recipient will be taxed on the difference between the market rate and actual rate of interest. Nominal interest is disregarded if it is called for but is in effect paid by the lender or a related person.

However, where the employer owns the policy, the employer's payments of premiums are taxable economic benefits to the executive. The Final Regulations do not address the Sarbanes-Oxley implications of making loans to executives of public companies, because those matters are under SEC, rather than IRS, jurisdiction.

Also note that Rev. Rul. 2003-105 says that because T.D. 9092 is comprehensive, it makes Rev. Ruls. 64-328, 66-110, 78-420, and 79-50 obsolete. However, taxpayers can continue to rely on these rulings with respect to arrangements that were entered into on or before September 17, 2003, as long as the arrangements are not materially modified afterwards. [Press release from IRS Office of

Public Affairs JS-726, *Treasury and IRS Issue Final Regulations for Split-Dollar Life Insurance Arrangements* (Sept. 11, 2003) <http://treas.gov/press/releases/js726.htm]

In the fall of 2005, the IRS sought comments on the treatment of older split dollar insurance plans in light of the I.R.C. § 409A rules about nonqualified deferred compensation. The IRS plan was to have most of the § 409A proposals take effect January 7, 2007, but certain provisions could be applicable in 2006 to taxpayers who appeared to be acting in bad faith. Although most commenters to the IRS said that split dollar plans should be excluded from the § 409A rules, the IRS claims that sometimes split dollar operates as deferred compensation. The IRS position is that § 409A should not apply to arrangements that merely provide death benefits, or where the employer makes a loan to pay for the split dollar plan. However, the endorsement method could be deferred compensation, as could the employer's irrevocable promise to pay future premiums. [Allison Bell, *Feds Propose Regs for Nonqualified Deferred Compensation Plans*, NU Online News Service (Sept. 29, 2005)]

[F] Case Law on Life Insurance Fringe Benefits

Cehrs v. Northeast Ohio Alzheimer's Research Center [155 F.3d 755 (6th Cir. 1998)] involves an employer that had a life insurance plan. A disabled employee was told that he did not fit the plan's definition of disability, so the employer would not maintain his life insurance coverage. However, the employer did not give any reason for the determination or explain how to appeal it. After the ex-employee's death, his family brought suit under ERISA § 503. The employer's litigating position was that the family failed to mitigate (reduce) his damages by investigating and discovering that the employer's position was incorrect. The Sixth Circuit rejected this argument, taking the position that when a plan fails to provide the notices required by law, employees are not able to mitigate their damages. Requiring mitigation would actually reward the plan for failing to provide the mandatory notices.

The estate of a wrongfully terminated employee was entitled to recover the face value of employer-provided insurance that was lost as a result of the discharge, minus the proceeds of the insurance policy that the deceased ex-employee bought as a replacement. [*Sposato v. Electronic Data Sys. Corp.*, 188 F.3d 1146 (9th Cir. 1999)] The Ninth Circuit used the amount of insurance, not just the premiums that the employer would have paid, as the standard of measurement.

When Kenneth Howell died in 1966, he had a life insurance policy under a welfare benefit plan. In 1994, his second wife (he already had three children from a prior marriage) sued for divorce. In 1995, a family court ordered both spouses to refrain from transferring or otherwise disposing of marital assets during the divorce proceedings. Proceedings were still pending when he died. However, contrary to the court order, he had changed the beneficiary designation from his second wife to his children. The pension fund brought an interpleader action under ERISA. [*Central States, Southeast & Southwest Areas Pension Fund v. Howell*, 227 F.3d 672 (6th Cir. 2000)] The court order did not qualify as a QDRO, because it did not have mandatory information such as the number of payments and how the participant's benefits were to be allocated. Because there was no QDRO, ERISA preempted state-law allocation principles. The beneficiary card filed with the plan, directing payment to the children, governed. However, the case was remanded to the District Court to see if a constructive trust should be imposed, i.e., whether the benefits should be treated as if a trust had been established with provisions reflecting equity and justice.

Initially, a plan participant named his mother as the beneficiary for his basic and supplemental coverage under the life insurance plan. When he married, he used the plan's form to name his wife as beneficiary of the basic coverage. The form did not refer to the supplemental coverage. When the participant died, the mother and the surviving spouse disputed the disposition of the supplemental benefits. The surviving spouse produced a letter allegedly sent by the participant to the employer several years before his death complaining about lack of response to his notifications that he wanted his wife to be his sole beneficiary. (The employer did not have a copy of this letter.) The wife's position was that this letter substantially complied with the plan's requirements, thus entitling her to the supplemental benefit, but the Third Circuit disagreed. Even if the letter was authentic, it was not sufficient because under New Jersey state law, the plan participant has an obligation to make every reasonable effort to make sure that a desired beneficiary change is carried out. [*Metropolitan Life Ins. Co. v. Kubichek*, 83 Fed. Appx. 425 (3d Cir. 2003)]

The Ninth Circuit held that entering an "ES" code on a life insurance beneficiary designation to indicate that benefits should be paid to his estate did not make a proper designation. The case was remanded to the District Court to determine the proper recipient of the benefits. To the Ninth Circuit, relationship codes such as "ES" do not specify a particular beneficiary—they identify categories of persons or entities that might be beneficiaries. The decedent wrote "as indicated in my will" as the name of the beneficiary, and the Ninth Circuit found this insufficient. In 1990, the decedent made a will naming his first wife as beneficiary. They divorced the next year. Shortly after the divorce, he signed the life insurance beneficiary designation form, which called for five pieces of information (beneficiary name; relationship to insured; relationship code; percentage of benefits allocated; and Social Security number). The beneficiary designation form was incomplete, specifying only "ES" under relationship code and 100% to pass according to his will. Nine years after filling out the form, the employee remarried, then died without having made a new will or changed the beneficiary designation. He lived in a state where divorce revokes previous wills, so he died intestate. Initially, all the benefits were paid to his second wife, until it was discovered that he had an out-of-wedlock son. The case was remanded to determine which plan applied at the time of his death, and who was the proper recipient of the benefits. [*Metropolitan Life Ins. Co. v. Parker,* 436 F.3d 1109 (9th Cir. 2006)]

In a 2004 case, the widow of a plan participant charged the employer with breach of fiduciary duty for telling the insurer to pay death benefits to the participant's children rather than his surviving spouse. The participant had named the children as beneficiaries, but tried to change the designation shortly before his death. The designation forms gave complete instructions for making a valid change of beneficiary. The employer's HR department rejected the form for noncompliance. The Northern District of Illinois ruled that the employer didn't know that there was a dispute about the coverage, and had no duty to determine the participant's intentions or learn about the conflict between the surviving spouse and the children. The court found that it was not arbitrary or capricious to impose formal requirements for change of beneficiary or to reject a defective form. [*Gassner v. IBM*, 2004 U.S. Dist. LEXIS 10869 (N.D. Ill. 2004)]

A married couple, both of whom worked for the same employer and were covered by the same welfare plan, both elected and paid for dependent life insurance. Each of them filed a claim when their son was killed in an automobile accident. The wife's claim was paid, while the husband's was denied. The husband sued the employer, insurer, and several of the welfare plans. The defendants sought dismissal of the case because the SPD ruled out duplicate coverage. The plaintiff-husband said that he did not receive a copy of the SPD, and the enrollment materials he did receive did not exclude the potential for duplicate coverage. The Southern District of Ohio refused to dismiss the case because a proper SPD had not been provided. [*McKenzie v. Advance Stores Co.,* No. 04-CV-999 (S.D. Ohio Oct. 26, 2005)]

The Sixth Circuit held that an insurer is not obligated to provide life insurance benefits that are contrary to state law, so the District Court was correct to dismiss a surviving spouse's claim. When the decedent resigned from his job, he was given the right to convert the life insurance under an employee welfare plan to a group policy—contingent upon whether he lived in a state that approved such a continuation. He lived in Michigan, which at that time forbade portable term insurance coverage, so the conversion application was denied. Three years later, the ex-employee died. More than one year later, his widow submitted a request for the death benefits that would have been payable if the conversion application had not been rejected. When the claim was denied, she sued for the life insurance benefits and statutory penalties for failure to provide plan documents. The Sixth Circuit held that the insurer, as fiduciary, had the right to interpret the plan, so its decision must be reviewed under the "arbitrary and capricious" standard. Because converting the policy at that time would have been illegal, the plan administrator didn't do anything wrong. Furthermore, the benefit claim accrued at the time of the original denial of conversion, not the date when the surviving spouse attempted to access plan benefits, so the claim was untimely under the applicable three-year statute of limitations. [*Morrison v. Marsh & McLennan,* 439 F.3d 295 (6th Cir. 2006)]

§ 21.03 LONG-TERM CARE INSURANCE PLANS

Although many employers are aware of long-term care issues and want to help employees cope, very few employees are knowledgeable about or interested in these issues. According to James Barrett, President of American Worksite Insurance Marketing, slightly over 4% of employees have work-related long-term care insurance (LTCI). The 2004 MetLife survey found that close to two-thirds of the mature workers they surveyed (aged 40 to 70) are not aware of the facts about LTCI. Forty percent believed they were entitled to basic LTC coverage under Medicare; 63% were unable to estimate the cost of LTCI if purchase was deferred to an advanced age.

According to America's Health Insurance Plans (a trade association), more than 900,000 LTCI policies were sold in 2002, the largest number to that time. Almost a third of those were purchased through employment, although many of those were part of the federal LTCI program rather than in the private sector.

In contrast, Eastbridge Consulting Group reached a different conclusion in its 2004 study of worksite sales of insurance. According to Eastbridge, LTCI accounted for only 1.8% of the market (a large drop from 6.3% in 2003); life insurance and disability insurance dominate the employment market, together accounting for about half of workplace-related insurance sales.

Worksite programs tend to achieve enrollment rates of only about 7 to 10%, because there are so many other demands on employees' paychecks. Workplace marketing of life insurance riders is more successful—typically, 30 to 35% of workers enroll—probably because employees are more familiar with life insurance as a product. These riders increase the cost of life insurance by about 3%; they pay out a part of the death benefit (e.g., 2% per year for home care, 4% for nursing home care). However, because the average life insurance benefit is only $100,000, a percentage of that sum provides only a small fraction of the actual cost of long-term care.

The National Association for the Self-Employed found that owners of very small businesses had much greater interest in LTCI than their employees did. The survey included 618 owners of businesses with 1–10 employees. One quarter of respondents said that LTCI is one of the three most important benefits for themselves (outranking life insurance or paid sick leave, and almost as popular as dental insurance) but only 6% of respondents considered LTCI one of the top three benefits to offer employees. [Allison Bell, *Mom and Pop Worry About Nursing Home Bills*, NU Online News Service (Oct. 5, 2005)]

Long-term care insurance (LTCI) is private insurance, sold by life and health insurers, that covers the cost of home and institutional care for the frail elderly and disabled. There is an increasing trend for employers to offer group long-term care insurance plans as an employee benefit—and to permit employees not only to purchase coverage for themselves and their spouses, but for their parents. Individual coverage for senior citizens can be difficult to find, and is often expensive when it is available.

Unlike most types of employee benefit, however, the typical LTCI plan is completely paid for by the employee. The employer's role is purely to administer the plan, and make it easier for employees to get insurance (frequently without proof of insurability) and at lower, group rates than if they purchased policies individually. Workplace LTCI sales can either take the form of a master policy with certificates issued under it, or a group discount of perhaps 5–10% for purchase of individual policies.

Although full discussion is beyond the scope of this book, it should be noted that the federal government's LTCI program for its employees and their relatives did a great deal to raise the profile of workplace LTCI sales when it was launched in 2002.

But see Johanna Bennett, *Corporate Care,* Wall Street Journal, Dec. 10, 2002, at p. R6, warning that group policies may lack features such as hospice or respite care coverage, may offer inadequate home care and inflation protection benefits, and may actually be more expensive than individual policies that the employees could buy outside the workplace.

CHAPTER 22

OTHER FRINGE BENEFITS

§ 22.01 INTRODUCTION

This book has already dealt with issues of setting and administering current compensation (pay planning), deferred compensation (pension planning), and the provision of several of the major types of fringe benefits: health plans, disability coverage, and life insurance plans.

It is common, however, for employers to provide other forms of benefits as compensation and as incentives. This chapter traces their tax, ERISA, and state-law consequences.

For tax purposes, the most relevant sections include I.R.C. § 162 (allowing a deduction for all of the employer's ordinary and necessary business expenses, including the employer's contributions to unfunded welfare benefit plans) and I.R.C. §§ 419 and 419A, which set limits on the deductions.

In general, employers will be able to deduct direct payments of benefits or expenses. Employers can make contributions that bear a reasonable actuarial relationship to the amounts that will be needed to pay benefits in the future. In some circumstances, a statutory safe harbor allows deductible contributions.

If a funded welfare plan earns income (e.g., from investments), that income will probably be taxed to the employer that maintains the plan. Unrelated business taxable income (UBTI) earned by the plan will almost certainly be taxed to the employer. [*See* Chapter 1, §§ 1.08, 1.12 for a discussion of some of the issues of determining who is an "employee" who is or might be eligible for plan participation]

As of March 2005, 70% of workers in private industry had access to health plans and 53% participated in the plans (reasons for non-participation could include access to coverage elsewhere, or inability to afford financial obligations under the plan). Sixty percent of private-industry employees had access to retirement plans and 50% participated in one or more plans. Defined contributions plans were by far the most common—53% had access and 42% participated. More than three quarters of private-sector employees (77%) were entitled to paid holidays and vacations, and 69% were entitled to leave for jury duty and 48% could be paid while on military leave. Over half of private-sector workers had access to workplace-related life insurance benefits (52% access; 49% participation). Participation was almost universal among the 40% of workers with access to short-term disability benefits and the 30% with access to long-term disability benefits. [Bureau of Labor Statistics (DOL) *National Compensation Survey: Employee Benefits in Private Industry in the United States, March 2005 (Summary 05-1)*, <http://www.dol.gov/ebsm0003.pdf> (Aug. 2005)]

§ 22.02 STOCK OPTIONS

[A] Generally

Both the corporation and its employees benefit when the price of the company's stock increases. This common-sense observation inspired widespread creation of plans under which employees are awarded stock options, with the intention that employees would be able to purchase stock in the employer corporation at below-market rates, and would have a personal incentive to work hard so the value of the stock would continue to climb. Depending on the company's circumstances, and the incentives it wants to provide, stock options could be granted widely, or restricted to top executives.

Giving stock options to employees, or allowing them to participate in a stock purchase plan, is also a way to create incentives, give additional compensation, and qualify for a tax deduction, without actually spending cash from the corporate coffers. Stock option plans were also very popular among startup companies that had little cash but high hopes.

For practical and tax reasons, the employer will probably want to impose some limitations on the options. A typical restriction is the employee's obligation to put (resell) the stock back to the corporation on termination of employment. An arrangement like this includes a method of calculating the put price (e.g., book value or a set P/E ratio).

A stock bonus plan is very similar to a profit-sharing plan from both the labor law and tax perspectives. However, distributions are generally made in the employer's common stock rather than in cash. Employees must be given put options obligating the employer to repurchase shares of stock that are not readily tradeable on an established market.

An Employee Stock Ownership Plan (ESOP) is a stock bonus plan or a plan combining stock bonus and money-purchase features. ESOPs invest primarily in the employer's common stock. The Internal Revenue Code contains additional rules for leveraged ESOPs that borrow the funds used to purchase the stock. ESOPs are often adopted as a defense against hostile takeovers of the issuing corporation. [*See* Prop. Reg. § 31.3121(a)-1(k) and 31.3306(b)-1(e)]

Stock appreciation rights (SARs) are really a form of cash compensation. The grantee of SARs gets money from the corporation, based on the price of the company stock. If, for instance, a corporate Vice President has SARs for 1,000 shares, the corporation will pay him or her the difference between the FMV of those shares at the time of exercise and the FMV at the time of grant. SARs are not usually issued by themselves. Generally they accompany qualified or nonqualified stock options. Often, they can be exercised with the stock options, giving the employee some of the cash needed to pay for the optioned shares.

IRS Notice 2005-1, 2005-2 I.R.B. 274, which primarily deals with nonqualified deferred compensation (*see* Chapter 8), also has some implications for options plans. As long as stock options are issued "at the money" rather than at a discount, they are not subject to the new I.R.C. § 409A.

Nor does I.R.C. § 409A apply to stock appreciation rights (SARs) that are issued by a public company if the rights are settled in employer stock; they are not discounted, and therefore do not have the effect of deferring compensation.

IRS Notice 2006-4, 2006-3 I.R.B. 307, provides interim guidance on applying § 409A (*see* Chapter 8) to stock options and SARs granted before January 1,

2005 (before the enactment of § 409A as part of the American Jobs Creation Act of 2004, P.L. 108-357, and therefore before nonqualified plans were aware of the requirements of that legislation). Notice 2006-4 permits application of the principles of Reg. § 1.422-2(e)(2): When the issuer made a good-faith attempt to set the exercise price of a stock option or SAR granted before January 1, 2005, to equal or exceed the FMV of the stock, the exercise price will qualify for exclusion from the recipient's gross income. For stock options granted between January 1, 2005, and the effective date of Final Regulations under § 409A, if the exercise price was intended to equal or exceed the FMV on the date of grant, and a reasonable valuation method was used, the valuation will be acceptable for tax purposes whether or not it satisfies Reg. § 1.409A-1(B)(5)(i)(B) in the October 4, 2005 Proposed Regulations published at 70 Fed. Reg. 57930.

A junior stock plan is another motivational device. Executives are given the right to buy junior stock (stock in the employer corporation with reduced dividend rights and voting powers). Owners of junior stock can convert it to ordinary common stock by achieving specified performance goals.

A late-2002 Texas case holds that the measure of damages when an employer fails to deliver stock options as promised is the value of the stock on the date that the promise was breached, and not the subsequent appreciated value of the stock once it became publicly traded [*Miga v. Jensen,* 96 S.W.3d 207, 46 Tex. Sup. J. 89 (2002)], because the Texas rule is that contract damages are measured as of the time of the breach, not the market value of the goods by the time the case gets to trial.

The case of *Lucente v. IBM* [310 F.3d 243 (2d Cir. 2002)] raises many of the complicated issues caused by stock options in a declining market. The plaintiff participated in IBM's Variable Compensation and Long-Term Performance Plan, both of which called for forfeiture of his unexercised stock options and restricted stock grants if he went to work for a competitor after leaving employment with IBM. The forfeiture provision did not place any limitations on the time, place, or scope of the noncompete clause. At retirement, the plaintiff was awarded about 125,000 stock options; he did not exercise any options before retirement. The plaintiff retired early, before 60, and went to work for another company; IBM let him keep the stock options because it did not view the plaintiff's new employer as a competitor.

Then the plaintiff accepted another job and asked IBM if that company was considered a competitor; IBM said that it was. The plaintiff went to work for this company nonetheless. IBM canceled his stock options (which were underwater at that point, but regained profitability later). The plaintiff sued IBM for breach of contract by canceling the stock options and for refusing to accept the check he tendered to try to exercise the options. IBM countered by saying that he violated his noncompete agreement. Although the plaintiff won at the District Court level (after a lot of procedural maneuvering), the Second Circuit held that Lucente voluntarily quit his job with IBM, refusing to accept his argument that he was forced out. As for the noncompete clause, the contract was supposed to be interpreted under

New York law, and New York law is opposed to restrictive employment covenants and will only enforce them to the extent they are necessary to protect a valid business interest. However, New York also follows the "employee choice doctrine": a covenant will be enforced if the employee exercises an informed choice between not competing with the ex-employer, and retaining benefits, or competing but losing the benefits. Furthermore, Lucente acted as if he believed his stock options had been canceled, so he could not ask the court to enforce his right to exercise those options.

In *Cochran v. Quest Software Inc.*, [328 F.3d 1 (1st Cir. 2003); the Massachusetts unjust enrichment rule comes from *Harrison v. NetCentric Corp.*, 744 N.E.2d 622 (Mass. 2001)] stock option questions mingled with wrongful termination claims in a First Circuit case. The plaintiff sued his former employer, alleging that he lost valuable unvested stock options as a result of wrongful termination, that some options were unlawfully rescinded prior to his termination, and that he was cheated in the valuation of options that vested before termination. However, the employer prevailed on all the claims. The plaintiff signed a vesting schedule explaining the rate at which options became vested; all vesting was contingent on his continued employment. In January 2000, he was told that his work was inadequate and some of his options might be recalled, and a few months later, before any options had become vested, he was notified that 27,500 unvested options had been canceled. At that point, he still had further unvested options on 62,500 shares. Days later, the stock split two-for-one, and a day later he reached his first vesting milestone, for about 25,000 shares. He was fired about four months later. Subsequently, he bought 25,000 shares at $1.19 and sold them at $55; the rest of the options lapsed when he was fired.

Although the plaintiff alleged that the vesting schedule turned him into an employee for a term of years, the First Circuit ruled that he was an at-will employee who could be terminated at any time. (The letter offering him a job stated that he would be working at-will, and the option agreement and employee handbook stated that he had no fixed term of employment.)

The employer corporation had the right to cancel the unvested options, and the rescission of the 27,500 options was also lawful, as a mutually agreed-upon modification of the employment agreement. The plaintiff's continuing to work provided consideration for the modification, and he signed a memorandum setting out the terms. It's true that Massachusetts makes an exception to the at-will employment rule for termination that unjustly enriches the employer by depriving the employee of compensation for work already performed. However, unvested options are not compensation for past services, because they are contingent on continued employment.

The Fourth Circuit denied damages under state wage and hour law in a case in which the plaintiff alleged that his employer refused to let him exercise stock options. There was no unconditional promise of options as part of his compensation package as a salaried employee, so the options were not recoverable as remuneration for work. [*Varghese v. Honeywell Int'l*, 424 F.3d 411 (4th Cir. 2005)]

[B] Incentive Stock Options (ISOs)

Internal Revenue Code § 422 creates a specially tax-favored category of Incentive Stock Options (ISOs). An ISO plan is permitted to discriminate in favor of highly compensated employees. However, favorable tax consequences are available to the employee only if he or she retains the shares for at least one year from the exercise of the option or two years from the grant of the option.

ISOs must be granted pursuant to a plan that states the aggregate number of shares that can be issued under option, and indicates which employees can receive them. The corporation's shareholders must approve the plan, during the time period running from 12 months before to 12 months after the adoption of the plan. Options can only be granted during the 10-year period after the adoption of the plan, but the corporation can simply adopt further ISO plans after the initial 10-year period expires.

The option price must be at least equal to the fair market value of the stock at the time the option is granted. In other words, ISOs cannot be issued at a bargain price, although NQSOs can be. The employees must wait for the stock's value to appreciate to benefit from the options.

Employees themselves can only exercise ISOs, during their lifetimes. Employees are only allowed to transfer ISOs by will or intestacy. If, at the time of the grant, the grantee owns 10% or more of the corporation's stock, the option price must be set higher, and only five years can be given to exercise the option, not ten.

Furthermore, the aggregate fair market value of each employee's stock cannot exceed $100,000 (measured as of the date of the grant of the option) in the first calendar year for which the options are exercisable. The $100,000 limit does not have to be written into the ISO plan document. It is applied automatically, and amounts over $100,000 simply are not characterized as ISOs.

Section 251 of the American Jobs Creation Act of 2004 (P.L. 108-357) amends I.R.C. § 3121(a), § 421(b), and § 423(c) to provide that FICA and FUTA "wages" do not include remuneration derived from exercising an Incentive Stock Option or an option to buy stock under an ESOP. (Nor does this remuneration count toward the person's future Social Security benefits.) The spread (the difference between the stock's FMV and the option price) is not income at the time of the exercise. However, if the statutory holding period is satisfied, it does constitute capital gain once the stock is disposed of. This treatment is effective for stock acquired through options exercised after the enactment of the AJCA. Because of the ACJA, a Notice of Proposed Rulemaking, published at 66 Fed. Reg. 57023 (Nov. 14, 2001), which would have imposed FICA and FUTA withholding on ISOs, became obsolete and was withdrawn.

In mid-2003, the IRS consolidated and systematized the rules about taxation of stock options, making it clear that warrants are considered options, and giving more details about the situations in which stockholder approval of option plans is required. [68 Fed. Reg. 34344 (June 9, 2003)] For a plan to qualify as an ISO plan, the maximum number of shares for all types of options and other stock-based awards must be specified. However, as long as the maximum number of authorized shares is disclosed, it is permissible for the plan to provide for the number of authorized shares to increase over the life of the plan.

Generally speaking, an ISO can be exercised only by the employee, his estate or his heir—but the 2003 rules permit an option to remain an ISO after it has been transferred to a trust, as long as the employee is the sole beneficial owner of the option after the transfer (under both the Internal Revenue Code and state law). Transferring an option to an ex-spouse in connection with a divorce terminates ISO characterization, but transferring the actual stock acquired under an ISO in connection with a divorce does not result in a disqualifying disposition.

ISOs are limited to stock with a Fair Market Value (measured at the time of the option grant) of not more than $100,000 exercisable in any taxable year. Under the latest IRS proposal, if the ability to exercise an option is accelerated by events such as a change in control, options exercised before the event, but in the year of the event, are still treated as ISOs, even if the effect of acceleration is to make over $100,000 in options exercisable in the year of the acceleration.

Code § 425 provides that an ISO loses its entitlement to favorable tax treatment if it is modified, unless the modified option meets the ISO requirements as of the date of the modification. But some changes in terms are not considered modifications if they are made in connection with corporate transactions. The proposal expands the definition of "corporate transaction"—and no longer requires that a significant number of employees be discharged or transferred to a new employer for the exception to apply. The proposal also clarifies that as long as the option itself provides for employer discretion (e.g., to pay a bonus or make a loan when an option is exercised), the exercise of discretion is not a modification of the option.

Although it took 20 years, the IRS eventually released Final Regulations for Incentive Stock Options: T.D. 9144, 69 Fed. Reg. 46401 (Aug. 3, 2004). Generally, these rules took effect August 3, 2004, albeit with transition rules for ISOs already issued and those to be granted before 2006. After December 31, 2005, all ISOs are subject to the Final Regulation.

The hallmark of an ISO (Code I.R.C. §§ 421-422) is that an employee can receive shares of the employer stock without taxable income when the option is granted or exercised, and gains on subsequent sale of the stock are taxed as capital gains rather than ordinary income if the holding period is satisfied. There is a $100,000 limit on the market value of options issued to any employee and first exercisable in any calendar year. The $100,000 figure does not include any part of a grant it turns into NQSOs because of cancellation, modification, or transfer before the year in which they would be exercisable. However, options over and above the permissible $100,000 limit become NQSOs and do not get favorable tax treatment. Separate stock certificates can be issued when options are exercised, designating only some of the stock as ISOs.

Under the Final Regulations, a plan that grants ISOs must disclose the aggregate number of ISO shares that can be issued. If the plan also covers NQSOs and other kinds of equity-based compensation, it must specify the number of ISO shares that can be issued, but it need not specify the number of other shares. Therefore, a plan amendment will be required if the plan does not already call for disclosing the number of ISO shares.

When ISO shares are subject to a substantial risk of forfeiture after exercise, an effective I.R.C. § 83(b) election can be made for the Alternative Minimum Tax that would otherwise be applicable. A timely I.R.C. § 83(b) election can avoid AMT on vesting, if an optionee receives nonvested shares (for example, as restricted stock) if the ISO provides for immediate exercise at the time of the grant—at which point the exercise price is, by definition, equal to the fair market value.

The Final Regulations clarify that a person remains an employee while he or she is on leave but is entitled to reemployment under the Family and Medical Leave Act (FMLA) or the Uniformed Services Employment and Reemployment Rights Act (USERRA).

Under the Final Regulations, a change that shortens the exercise period of an option is not a "modification," although the grant of a new option is a modification, as is a change that extends the period of exercise, adds new benefits, or makes the payment terms on exercise more favorable. If a plan is inadvertently modified so that ISO treatment is lost, the modification can be canceled before the earlier of the end of the calendar year of the modification or the exercise of the ISO, without imperiling the plan's ISO status. When one company acquires another, the Final Regulations do not require the acquiror's shareholders to approve the grant of substitute ISOs in the acquiror company to the target's shareholders. But if the acquiror's plan does not allow ISOs or did not get shareholder approval, then shareholders must approve any future grants of ISOs. [Haynes Boone, *Final Incentive Stock Option Regulations*, <http://www.haynesboone.com/knowledge/ knowledge_detail.asp? . . .>]

[C] Nonqualified Stock Options (NQSOs)

Nonqualified stock options (NQSOs) are stock options that do not satisfy the I.R.C. § 422 rules. Sometimes NQSOs are issued "in the money": that is, the price at which the option can be exercised is lower than the current value of the stock, not just the anticipated future value of the stock at the time the option can be exercised.

There is no tax effect at the time of the grant of an NQSO, as long as the option itself does not have a readily ascertainable market value (i.e., the options are not traded actively). When the option is exercised, the employee has taxable income, equal to the FMV of the stock minus the consideration paid for the option. However, if the stock received by exercising the option is not transferable, and is subject to a substantial risk of forfeiture, then income is not taxed until the condition lapses. At that time, the amount of gain is determined, using the then-current FMV of the stock.

The FMV of the stock at the time of the exercise of the option, minus the price of the option, is a preference item for Alternative Minimum Tax purposes.

The American Jobs Creation Act of 2004, P.L. 108-357, changed the tax effectiveness of discount stock options (non-qualified stock options with an exercise price lower than the stock's fair market value on the grant date). Under prior law, the question was whether the discount was so deep that the grant should be treated as direct issuance of the stock. For example, if options were granted to buy $10/share stock for a penny a share, that would be treated as a direct grant; but if the exercise price for the same stock were $8, the option feature would be recognized, and there would be a taxable event only at exercise of the option.

The AJCA subjects discount stock options to the I.R.C. § 409A deferred compensation rules (*see* Chapter 8). Deferred compensation can be paid only on the occurrence of specified events: death, separation from service, disability, change in control, unforeseen financial hardship, or the arrival of the date specified in the plan. If a discount stock option can be exercised at the grantee's discretion, then the grantee will have taxable income when the option vests. The taxable income equals the option spread (the exercise price minus the current FMV of the stock). The spread is also subject to a 20% excise tax penalty. For example, if an option is immediately exercisable when granted, and the option price is $8 for a stock worth $10, on the grant date the employee has $2 ordinary income per share and owes 40 cents in penalty tax. If vesting is delayed for a year after the grant, and the stock is worth $15 when it vests (versus $10 when granted with an $8 exercise price), then on the vesting date the employee has $7 ordinary income and $1.40 in penalty tax per share—whether or not the option is exercised. (Warrants that are issued as part of an investment unit and are not stock options granted as compensation are not subject to I.R.C. § 409A.)

Rev. Rul. 2004-60, 2004-24 I.R.B. 1051, provides that a transfer of interests in nonstatutory stock options from an employee to a non-employee spouse pursuant to a divorce does not constitute "wages" for FICA/FUTA purposes. However, the employment taxes come into play when the options are exercised, as if the employee spouse had received them. Therefore, NQSOs are subject to FICA/FUTA when the recipient non-employee spouse exercises them. These payments constitute FICA wages for the employee spouse because they relate to the employee spouse's employment. The non-employee spouse's income is subject to withholding, deducted from the payments made to the non-employee spouse. W-2 reporting is not required because the recipient is not an employee. Instead, the employer issues a 1099-MISC to the non-employee spouse and reports the withholding on its Form 945.

[D]   Option Taxation Under I.R.C. § 83

Internal Revenue Code § 83 governs all transfers of property in exchange for performance of services, so it is important to stock option taxation but also has broader applicability. Under I.R.C. § 83, the person who performs the services has taxable income, at ordinary income (not capital gains) rates at the time that the rights in the property become transferable or are no longer subject to a substantial risk of forfeiture.

The amount of ordinary income to be recognized equals the fair market value (FMV) of the property minus any amount the employee paid for it. The options can be made forfeitable if the employee leaves before a certain number of years of employment. That motivates the employee to stay longer by offering tax incentives: There is no taxable income until the restriction lapses.

The point at which an option becomes subject to I.R.C. § 83 depends on whether it has an ascertainable market value (for instance, if it is traded on an established market). If so, and if the option is vested, it is taxed as soon as it is granted—not at the later point when it is exercised. Options that have no ascertainable FMV do not become subject to I.R.C. § 83 until they are exercised, on the theory that an option with an FMV can be sold as a separate asset.

Therefore, the employee faces taxation at two stages. The first is when the option can be exercised and the stock purchased; the second is when the stock is sold. (Gains from the sale of stock are capital gains; they do not generate ordinary income.)

Stock options are vested when the stock is transferable and there is no longer a substantial risk of forfeiture. (Sometimes stock awarded to employees is endorsed on its face to prevent transfer.) Section 83 holds that property is subject to a substantial risk of forfeiture if the right to receive the property is conditioned on future performance of substantial services ("earn-out restriction").

There's no bright-line test for when services are substantial; it depends on factors such as the regularity with which services are supposed to be performed and the amount of time needed to perform them. A retiree whose consulting agreement allows him or her to keep the stock while failing to perform the services is not performing substantial services.

Under I.R.C. § 83, refraining from performing services (e.g., under a non-compete clause) can also give rise to a substantial risk of forfeiture.

If the employer company's stock is publicly traded and it is a "reporting" company under the Exchange Act of 1934 [15 U.S.C. §§ 77b-e, etc.], major executives who are corporate officers, directors, or 10% shareholders will probably be subject to the Exchange Act's ban on "short-swing" profits earned by corporate insiders who trade in the company's stock. Internal Revenue Code § 83(c)(3) provides that rights are not vested at any time that the person receiving stock options cannot sell the stock without violating the short-swing profit rules. That means that the insider who gets a stock option has no income either for six months or until the first day that the stock can be sold.

In the usual stock option situation, until the option vests, the corporation is still considered the owner of the stock. The dividends on the stock are considered additional compensation for the employee. On the other hand, the corporation can deduct these dividends (as employee compensation) even though under ordinary circumstances a corporation cannot deduct the dividends that it pays.

The employee has the right to elect immediate taxation in the year of the transfer of the property, even if I.R.C. § 83 would not otherwise impose tax. This is a reasonable choice where otherwise the appreciation on the stock would be taxed as compensation.

> **Tip:** If the employee pays the tax right away and later has to forfeit the options (e.g., by quitting his or her job), the tax already paid is not refundable.

The employer can deduct the compensation that the employee includes in income under I.R.C. § 83 (as long as the compensation is reasonable). The deduction is taken in the employer's tax year that includes the year in which the employee includes the sum in his or her income. Nearly all employees pay taxes on a calendar-year basis, whereas most corporations operate on a fiscal year. The employer gets an immediate deduction if the property is vested as soon as it is transferred, or if the employee exercises the election to be taxed immediately.

To sum up the ISO/NQSO distinction, when an individual is granted NQSOs:

- (At time of grant) If there is no readily ascertainable FMV, there is no tax effect;
- (At time of grant) If there is an ascertainable FMV, § 83 governs taxation;
- (At time of exercise) The employee has taxable income equal to the FMV of the stock minus consideration paid for the option. However, if the stock received on exercise of the option is nontransferrable and subject to a substantial risk of forfeiture, taxable income is not a factor until the condition lapses. At that point, gain is determined based on the FMV at the time of the lapse. If the employee actually sells the stock purchased under the option, then he or she will have capital gain or loss on the sale;
- The employer gets a deduction equal to the individual's gain.

If the employee gets ISOs instead of NQSOs:

- (At time of grant) The employee has no taxable income;
- (At time of exercise) The employee has no income;
- (At time of disposition of stock) The employee has capital gain or loss, with consequences depending on the length of the holding period;
- The employer does not get a deduction. [I.R.C. § 421(a)(2)]

If an employee disposes of shares obtained under an ISO within two years of the grant of the option or one year of exercising the option, any gain is ordinary income, and the employer is entitled to a tax deduction equal to this amount.

The value of a publicly traded stock at a particular time can easily be determined by consulting published price quotations. However, options are (or at least used to be) often issued by nonpublic companies, especially startups. In 2002, the IRS issued two documents about valuations of stock options. Rev. Proc. 2002-13,

2002-8 I.R.B. 549, creates a "safe harbor" method for valuing stock options that generates acceptable values by considering the volatility of the stock; the exercise price of the option; the value of the stock at the time of valuation, and the term of the option as of the valuation date. Rev. Proc. 2002-13 applies to the tax on "excess golden parachutes" [see § 3.03[D]] and therefore must be taken into account when a company is acquired and its golden parachutes are triggered.

Later in 2002, the IRS modified Rev. Proc. 2002-13 in Rev. Proc. 2002-45, 2002-27 I.R.B. 40, but revoked those pronouncements in 2003 when further guidance on valuation of stock options under § 280G was issued. [Rev. Proc. 2003-68, 2003-34 IRB 398] For § 280G purposes, options must be valued when a payment in the nature of compensation includes the grant or vesting of a stock option in connection with a change in corporate ownership or control. Rev. Proc. 2003-68 does not apply to valuation of payments in cash or property where the size of the payment is determined by reference to the cancellation of a stock option.

Options on either publicly or non-publicly traded stock can be valued by any method that is consistent with GAAP (e.g., FAS 123) and that takes into account the factors set out in Reg. § 1.280G-1 Q&A 13. The valuation of a stock option depends on factors such as the spread between the value of the stock at the time of the change in control and the option's exercise price; the volatility of the underlying stock; and the term of the option. The Revenue Procedure allows a safe harbor for Black-Scholes-based valuation using four factors: the volatility of the underlying stock; the exercise price of the option; the spot price of the stock at the time of the valuation; and the term of the option on the valuation date. The Revenue Procedure includes a table of calculations for this safe harbor. The taxpayer must characterize the volatility of the stock (as low, annual standard deviation 30% or less; medium, 30% to 70%; or high—over 70%). For stocks that are not publicly traded, the spot price must be reasonable and consistent with the price determined for the stock in other parts of the same transaction.

If the value of an option is recalculated because the term of the option changed (because of termination of employment or greater or lesser volatility of the stock), parachute payments and excess parachute payments must be recalculated using the new valuation. The employer's deduction under § 83(h), for transfers of property other than money as compensation, is equal to the amount included in the employee's gross income because of the transfer. The question facing the Federal Circuit in mid-2003 was whether the deduction is the amount includible as a matter of law, or merely the amount actually included. The Court of Federal Claims had ruled that the deduction was limited to the amount that was actually included, either on the employee's tax return or after the IRS issued a final determination that became binding on the employee. However, the Federal Circuit reversed this ruling.

The taxpayers were the sole shareholders of a group of related S Corporations. The group entered into an employment agreement with its Chief Operating Officer, giving him a 10% ownership interest, vesting gradually with partial forfeiture if he terminated his employment early. He paid $2 million for the stock. The stock came under § 83(a) because it was part of his salary and was conveyed subject to restrictions on his ownership rights. For property conveyed subject to such restrictions, the employee has income equal to the bargain element in the year that the employee's rights in the property are no longer subject to a substantial risk of forfeiture. The employee has a right under § 83(b) to elect (within 30 days of the transfer) to recognize the income in the year of receipt. The employee immediately becomes taxable on the amount of the compensation, but any appreciation in value between the time of the transfer and the lapse of the restrictions can be treated as capital gains. The employer's deduction is the amount included in the employee's gross income for the taxable year of the person providing the services.

In 1995, the COO made a § 83(b) election but did not report any income because he said that the $2 million he paid for the stock was its fair market value, so there was no bargain element. The stockholder-taxpayers, on the other hand, say that the stock was worth $28.8 million, not $2 million. Three years later, the COO was terminated, and the corporate group bought back the part of COO's stock that had vested. The group paid $13.2 million, based on a total value for the company of $165 million. On finding out about the § 83(b) election, the group issued corrected W-2s for 1995 reflecting that valuation, increasing the ex-COO's wage income by more than $20 million, The corporate group paid the employer's share of employer taxes, based on that valuation. The stockholders filed an administrative claim with the IRS for a refund. The IRS denied their application, and they sued in the Court of Federal Claims and lost.

The Federal Circuit reversed, cross-referencing § 61 to conclude that "included" means included in the recipient's gross income as a matter of law. The IRS said that the taxpayer's position puts the agency at a risk of being caught by employer-employee conflicts about the value of the stock, especially if both litigate and achieve inconsistent results. However, the Federal Circuit ruled that at least the IRS can participate in both tax cases, whereas the employer is not a party to the employee's tax case if the employee is audited on § 83 issues. [*Robinson v. U.S.*, 335 F.3d 1365 (Fed. Cir. 2003)]

[E] Securities Law Issues for Stock Option Plans

Federal securities laws and state Blue Sky Laws must be consulted before offering stock options (or any other form of securities-based compensation). Public companies have an established obligation to disclose option transactions to their shareholders, and to reflect them in SEC filings and on proxy statements. The Exchange Act also forbids insiders to take short-swing profits.

For fiscal years ending on or after March 15, 2002, and for proxies for shareholder meetings or shareholder actions on or after June 15, 2002, the SEC has imposed additional disclosure requirements on reporting companies that offer stock compensation plans. Disclosure is now required of plans offering equity compensation, whether or not approved by security holders.

For each category, the reporting company must put a table in the Form 10-K (the annual report) and in the proxy statement whenever shareholders are asked to approve a compensation plan that includes securities. The table should have three columns:

- Number of securities to be issued on exercise of outstanding options, rights, and warrants;
- The weighted average exercise price for the outstanding options, rights, and warrants;
- Securities not reflected in the first column, still available to be issued in the future under equity compensation plans. [*See New Disclosure Rules for Stock Plans,* Watson Wyatt Insider, <http://www.watsonwyatt.com/us/pubs/insider/showarticle.asp?ArticleID=9588&Component=The+Insider>]

In mid-2003, the SEC released a document approving the amended listing requirements of the NYSE and NASDAQ. Under the modified listing rules, companies require shareholder approval for most of their equity compensation plans, including stock option plans and material revisions of plans. The NYSE version defines equity compensation plans as plans that deliver newly issued equity securities or treasury shares of the company to any service provider (including an employee or director) as compensation for services. The definition extends to compensatory grants of equity securities (including options) that are not made under a plan. However, the rule does not extend to deferred compensation plans under which employees pay the full market value of the shares they receive, inducement awards when a new employee is recruited, and dividend reinvestment plans and other plans available to all shareholders generally. [SEC Release No. 34-48108, Self-Regulatory Organizations (June 20, 2003) <http://www.sec.gov/rules/sro/34-48108.htm>]

The SEC's 2006 Final Rule on disclosure of executive compensation requires public corporations to discuss stock options in the Compensation Discussion and Analysis disclosed to stockholders. Effective for fiscal years beginning on or after December 15, 2006, annual reports, proxy statements, and registration statements will have to give far more detail about option grants to and exercises by top management. A Summary Compensation Table is required, giving dollar amounts for stock awards and stock option awards (measured as of the grant date, using FAS 123R; see below). If the closing market price on the grant date is higher than the exercise price, the closing price must be disclosed. To prevent abusive back-dating of options, the date that the decision to make the grant of options must be disclosed, if it is different than the stated grant date. If the exercise price of an option is different from the closing market price on the grant date, the methodology for calculating the price must be disclosed. [SEC Press Release, *SEC Votes to Adopt Changes to Disclosure Requirements Concerning Executive Compensation and Related Matters,* <http://www.sec.gov/news/press/2006/2006-123.htm> (July 26, 2006)]

[F] Accounting Issues

Traditionally, the Financial Accounting Standards Board (FASB) did not require corporations to expense their stock options; the cost merely had to be reflected in the footnotes to the financial statement. Expensing means that the cost of the options is deducted in the year the option is offered. Although taxpayers usually want to increase their deductions to cut their tax bills, there is a counter-vailing pressure on corporations to report high earnings, so anything that depresses their earnings is unattractive.

The rules began to change when FASB amended FAS 123, *Accounting for Stock-Based Compensation,* in FAS 148, *Accounting for Stock-Based Compensation—Transition and Disclosure.* FASB initially planned to announce option-expensing rules in 2003, but postponed rulemaking until 2004 to give corporations more time to prepare—and to permit FASB to harmonize its rules with the International Account Standard Board's rules. In December 2004, FASB issued a revised Statement 123, designated as FASB 123(R), *Share-Based Payment.* Legislation (H.R. 3574) was introduced in Congress to prevent FASB from requiring that stock options be expensed, and while it attracted many votes, it ultimately did not pass.

Effective July 1, 2005, FASB adopted rules requiring expensing of stock options, although non-public companies have until January 1, 2006, to comply. In October 2004, FASB deferred the effective date of the option-expensing rule for six months, so that it would begin in the third calendar of 2005 for calendar-year public companies. Ironically, this relief was made available at a time when the popularity of options had declined for other reasons, such as uncertainty about future stock prices.

Statement 123(R) requires "share-based compensation" (stock options) to be expensed in financial statements. Several kinds of grants are covered: not just actual shares of stock, but options (the right to purchase shares in the future at a set price) and Stock Appreciation Rights (SARs; the employee is awarded the increase in the value of the employer's stock). Statement 123(R) does not affect the accounting treatment of shares issued to non-employees, nor does it change the rules for Employee Stock Ownership Plans (ESOPs).

The employer must calculate the fair value of the grant at the date of issuance, then recognize this amount as a compensation cost over the period that begins with the issue date and ends on the vesting date. If the option itself is traded on a market, then the fair market value of the option is its market price. If it is not traded, then the company must use a standard option pricing model (such as Black-Scholes-Merton) for valuation, although FASB stepped back from mandating the use of any single pricing model.

The Chicago Consulting Actuaries firm points out that under the new rules, employers can put conditions on their stock options without adverse consequences. So it may be worthwhile to use indexed options (the exercise price moves with economic or industry indices, so if the particular company outperforms the market, employees will derive even more benefit) or to require employees to hit performance marks to qualify for option vesting. [Chicago Consulting Actuaries, *FAS 123(R): Expensing Stock Options* (Mar. 21, 2005), http://insight. chicagoconsultingactuaries.com/Insight/Documents/StockOptions3.aspx (no www); Mary Rivlin, *Regulators Adopt Tighter Rules on Accounting for Stock Options*, New York Times, Dec. 17, 2004, at p. C5.

In 2005, the FASB offered an alternate computation method for compliance, available to companies that lack the information about net excess tax benefits required by Statement 123. Proposed FASB Staff Position FAS 123(R)-b offered guidance on the definition of "grant date" for share-based payment awards. One of the factors is whether the employer and employee have reached a mutual understanding on the key terms and conditions of the award. In practice, the grant date is generally the date that the corporation's governance structure approves the grant, as long as the employee is informed within a reasonable time. The FASB staff position is that the date of board or other corporate approval will be deemed the date of mutual understanding as long as the recipient does not have the power to negotiate terms, and the key terms are communicated as expeditiously as can be done under the company's usual HR practices. [FAS 123(R)-3, (*Transition Election Related to Accounting for Tax Effects of Share-Based Payment Awards*)]

FAS 123 was amended again on February 3, 2006 (FAS 123(R)-4). FASB described the Statement, *Contingent Cash Settlement of Stock Options,* as a practical accommodation to protect against employee stock options and SARs being reclassified as liability awards merely because the plan included a feature permitting contingent cash settlement. If the cash settlement feature can be exercised only when a contingent event outside the employee's control occurs (e.g., the corporation has an initial public offering; there is a change in control), liability classification does not occur until it becomes probable that the event will actually happen. Once the occurrence of the event becomes likely, the reclassification is treated as turning an equity award to a liability award. Before the issuance of 123(R)-4, stock options and SARs had to be classified as liabilities if there was any contingency, no matter how implausible, under which the company might be required to settle the award in cash or property. In mid-2005, Deloitte Consulting reported that 75% of survey respondents had reacted to FASB Statement 123's requirement of expensing stock options by reducing, or planning to reduce, the number of options granted. However, 91% of respondents said that they had not reduced option grants to their senior management, whereas 45% of the companies who reduced option grants did so at levels below management. As Deloitte's Mike Kesner said, options are returning to their historical use as part of the top-management compensation package. Nearly everyone surveyed (83%) did not expect FASB's rule change to affect the price of their stock very much. [Ellen Sheng, *Stock-Option Cuts to Hit Employees in Lower Ranks,* Wall Street Journal, July 13, 2005, at p. D3]

The SEC offered guidance in Staff Accounting Bulletin (SAB) No. 107 (March 29, 2005), stating that public companies can use any valid option-pricing model. Once they adopt a pricing model, they are not stuck with it—they can change occasionally, and can use multiple models. Once a company makes assumptions and estimates value, the SEC will not subsequently challenge good-faith estimates even if they do not play out in the real world. Estimates can be made in-house; it is not necessary to retain a third-party expert. The SEC will permit acceleration of vesting of stock options (so they will not become subject to the new rules) as long as the company makes adequate disclosure that this is being done. *See* SAB 107 for additional disclosures about equity compensation that should be made in the Management Disclosure and Analysis (MD & A) portion of the financial statement. [Frederick W. Cook & Co., *SEC Staff Releases Guidance on Option Valuation Under Statement 123(R)*, Apr. 4, 2005, <http://www.fwcook.com/alert_letters/4-4-05 . . . > (benefitslink.com)]

The compensation consulting firm of Pearl Meyer & Partners made some suggestions for expensing stock option grants:

- Set up a team to make decisions about fair value accounting.
- *See* if FAS expenses can be managed better by restructuring options and/or accelerating vesting of options; check past Form 4s, 8-Ks, and proxy statements for trends in your long-term incentive programs.
- Analyze your history of grants and exercises to *see* how long the expected life of the options is (for use in valuation); *see* how your company would have fared using various valuation methods, and compare historical volatility to predicted future volatility.
- Analyze the competitiveness of your long-term incentive plan.
- Value estimated current and future grants to *see* effect on earnings over the vesting period; use grant guidelines to determine annual and total potential dilution and compare them to industry norms.
- If necessary, amend plan to include the appropriate long-term incentives; compare the effectiveness of the various alternatives for incentives, and if they are appropriate for your company based on the impact they can be expected to have.
- *See* if the mix of incentives fits your business objectives, reward strategy, and has acceptable financial impact; consider adding nonqualified deferred compensation or a SERP.
- Check out proxy voting guidelines for institutional investors; *see* if your metrics are reliable predictors and whether the options are discounted.
  *If the instruments aren't going to deliver value to you, consider restructuring the program and finding alternatives to reduce the earnings charge.
- Update the plan documents for the proxy statement; *see* if any changes require a plan amendment or shareholder approval. After plan changes are approved, file a Form 8-K and outline changes to compensation plans in the proxy statement Compensation Committee report. [SmartPros, *10 Critical Steps to SFAS 123(R)* (Mar. 29, 2005), http://accounting.smartpros.com/x47572.xml (via benefitslink.com)]

[G] Coping with Underwater Options

An option is said to be "underwater" if the value of the stock on the open market declines below the exercise price given in the option. In that case, of course, the employee will not have any advantage from exercising the option. Workforce. com has published a very useful chart of strategies that can be used in this unfortunate (though quite common) situation, listing eight possible strategies, when each is appropriate, and the pros and cons of each. For example, the issuer corporation can refrain from taking any action (although this is likely to anger employees). The next scheduled grant of options could be speeded up, especially if the corporation expects that its price has bottomed out and is due to recover. If the company is very interested in keeping employees happy, and can afford to do so, it can buy back underwater options from employees, based on the economic value of the options, and then grant more options at FMV at least six months and a day after the repurchase.

A number of companies shifted from options to grants of restricted stock, in part because of the potential for misconduct or excess risk on the part of optionees willing to go too far to increase the value of their options. Restricted stock is particularly useful for mature, dividend-paying companies, less effective for start-ups in high-growth industries. There are trade-offs. Risk-averse employees probably prefer restricted stock, for its lower risk and the fact that the stock is unlikely to become absolutely worthless even though its value may decrease. But stock options offer at least the possibility of becoming rich through an IPO or increase in the value of the stock. For tax purposes, the employee has taxable income when the restricted stock vests (an event under the control of the corporation, not the employee) whereas the employee can control when options are exercised and can engage in tax planning. [Elayne Robertson Demby, *The Rise of Restricted-Stock Grants,* Workforce Management (January 2004), <http://www.workforce. com/archive/feature/23/58/99/235901.php>]

[H] Change of Control Issues

One of the numerous issues that has to be resolved in a merger or acquisition (*see* Chapter 16 for a general discussion) is what will happen to stock options in the transition. The problem is especially acute when only part of a company (for instance, a division or subsidiary) is sold, and there are arguments pro and con as to whether the plan's "change in control" threshold (which would lead to immediate vesting of options) has been reached. A further twist is added when the options are profitable on some dates, but underwater on others, because people who were unable to exercise options at a profit may bring suit over the factors that prevented them from doing so. Qualcomm, for example, settled a class action over the sale of a division, in which the class of employees alleged they were pressured into surrendering their rights to sue over lost options, by distributing $11 million to over 800 employees.

A common provision says that unvested options are forfeited when a person terminates employment other than in a change-of-control situation, and employees of the merged or acquired company are given a limited time (such as three months) to exercise their stock options; under the original option plan, they might have had as much as ten years to exercise the options. In 2001, the Fourth Circuit ruled that a company's CEO did not have a fiduciary duty to disclose to an employee that the employee's options vested fully and became exercisable when part of the company was sold: *Black v. Hoffman,* 2001 WL 369673 (4th Cir. 2001).

§ 22.03   CAFETERIA PLANS

[A]   Plan Characteristics

A cafeteria plan, as defined by I.R.C. § 125, is a written plan under which the employer offers a "menu" of benefits, permitting employees to choose between cash and a group of benefits. The plan must offer at least one taxable and one nontaxable benefit. Other than a 401(k) plan, the cafeteria plan may not offer any pension or deferred compensation benefits.

The I.R.C. § 125 requirements for a valid cafeteria plan are

- All plan participants are employees (although the Proposed Regulations allow ex-employees to be included in the plan, as long as it is not predominantly for their benefits. Spouses and children of employees can receive benefits under the plan, but cannot actively participate (e.g., by choosing the benefits);
- The participant chooses between cash and one or more benefits, although the amount of cash does not have to be as great as the entire cost of the nontaxable benefit [Prop. Reg. § 1.125-1];
- The plan does not discriminate in favor of highly compensated employees (HCEs);
- The benefits provided to HCEs do not exceed 25% of the total benefits for the year;
- The election to take benefits rather than cash must be made before the beginning of the plan year;
- Changes in the election must conform to the Regulations.

The allowable benefits include:

- Accident and health plans;
- Group-term life insurance;
- Disability coverage, including accidental death and dismemberment (ADD) plans;
- Dependent care assistance;
- Benefits that fail nondiscrimination tests and therefore are not part of a qualified plan;

- Vacation days;
- Group automobile insurance or other taxable benefit purchased by the employee with after-tax dollars.

Cafeteria plans are not permitted to include long-term care insurance. Neither can Flexible Spending Accounts [*see* § 18.11] because FSAs are not allowed to be used to pay insurance premiums.

The nontaxable benefits that can be included in a cafeteria plan are group-term life insurance, medical expense reimbursement, and accident and disability benefits as defined by I.R.C. § 106, dependent care assistance, and paid vacation days.

In a pretax premium plan, a "mini cafeteria" salary reduction plan is used to provide after-tax dollars for the employees to pay insurance premiums. The most common application is health insurance coverage for dependents, in plans where the employer covers employees but dependent coverage is on an "employee pay all" basis. The employer adopts a plan that allows the employee, before the start of the plan year, to elect a reduction in compensation sufficient to pay the employee's share of the premium. These salary reductions are not subject to the employer share of FICA.

A cafeteria plan must be designed as a "use it or lose it" plan: Unused benefits cannot be carried over to subsequent years. Participants can be given a chance to use their vacation days, sell them back to the employer for cash, or buy extra vacation days—as long as the plan is not used to defer the receipt of compensation to a later plan year. [*See* Prop. Reg. § 1.125-1, Q&A 7]

If a cafeteria plan fails nondiscrimination testing, then the HCEs will have taxable income. The test for discrimination in benefits is whether contributions are made for each participant in a uniform relationship to compensation. If contributions for each participant are equal to the cost of coverage that the plan incurs for HCEs, or if contributions for each participant are at least equal to 75% of the cost for the similarly situated plan participant who has the highest cost of benefits, the plan satisfies the nondiscrimination tests.

Nontaxable cafeteria plan benefits are not subject to employer or employee FICA taxes. However, amounts placed into a 401(k) plan are subject to both employer and employee shares of FICA and FUTA.

Generally, participants will be given a 30-day period at the end of every year to make the election for the following year. The period might close a few days, or even a month, before the end of the year to give the plan administrators time to process the election request.

Rev. Rul. 2002-27, 2002-20 I.R.B. 925 provides that it is permissible to set up a cafeteria plan to provide automatic enrollment of employees for group health insurance. Elective employee contributions used to purchase health insurance are not included in the purchasing employee's gross income. However, an automatic-enrollment plan must notify the employees of the provision and give them the option to take cash instead of health insurance coverage.

ERISA § 403 does not require cafeteria plans to be managed by a trust (although the terms of the plan itself can require trust management). However, if the plan allows after-tax contributions for the purchase of benefits, such contributions must be placed into trust unless they are used to buy insurance policies.

[B] Cafeteria Plans After HIPAA

Proposed and Temporary Regulations for bringing cafeteria plans into conformity with HIPAA were published at 62 Fed. Reg. 60165 and 60196 (Nov. 7, 1997). Then, in March 2000, the IRS replaced the 1997 Temporary Regulations with T.D. 8878, 65 Fed. Reg. 15548, 2000-15 I.R.B. 857 (March 23, 2000). These Regulations, which were supposed to be final, clarified the circumstances under which employees participating in cafeteria plans can change their elections in connection with accident, health, or group-term life insurance coverage. For example, a change might be needed when a Qualified Medical Child Support Order (QMCSO) is granted, or when the person gains or loses eligibility for Medicare or Medicaid.

At the beginning of 2001, the IRS revised this Treasury Decision. [*See* T.D. 8921, 66 Fed. Reg. 1837 (Jan. 10, 2001)] T.D. 8921 modifies the T.D. 8878 Final Regulations by allowing cafeteria plan participants to increase or decrease their coverage whenever they have a change-of-status event.

Changes were always allowed on the basis of marriage or divorce. Thanks to T.D. 8921, changes are also permitted when a dependent is born or adopted. An employee who decreases or cancels coverage under the cafeteria plan because of coverage under a spouse or dependent's plan has to certify that he or she is getting other coverage.

The cafeteria plan election can be changed to conform to a domestic relations order, but only if the spouse or former spouse actually provides coverage for the child; T.D. 8921 also allows elections to be changed when the employee's responsibility for payments under the plan increases or decreases significantly. The plan's payment for dependent care cannot be greater than what the employee earns.

§ 22.04 EDUCATION ASSISTANCE

Employers offer education assistance both because anything that employees consider a valuable benefit is a good motivator, and because a better-educated workforce promotes efficiency and productivity. However, the tax status of this benefit has fluctuated over the past decades.

There were no Code provisions allowing employees to receive educational assistance tax-free before I.R.C. § 127 was enacted in 1978, as a five-year pilot project. Under I.R.C. § 127, employees did not have taxable income because of qualified employer educational assistance. The employer was entitled to a deduction for maintaining a qualifying educational assistance plan. Even without a plan, educational assistance spending might be deductible as a working condition fringe benefit under I.R.C. § 132 Internal Revenue Code § 127 contains a dollar limitation ($5,250 a year). [*See* IRS Publication 508, *Tax Benefits for Work-Related Education*]

Since 1983, the provision has been saved from expiration several times. The Small Business Job Protection Act of 1996 [Pub. L. No. 104-188] allowed employees to exclude qualified educational assistance received during the period January 1, 1995–May 31, 1997. The income exclusion was extended again, for courses beginning before June 1, 2000, by the Tax Relief Act of 1997. [Pub. L. No. 105-34] The Ticket to Work Act [Pub. L. No. 106-170] extended the exclusion for undergraduate (but not graduate-level) education assistance until the end of 2001.

EGTRRA not only made the exclusion permanent, it repealed the earlier limitation of assistance to undergraduate-level education. Congress intended to resolve employers' insecurities about establishing a plan that could be eliminated by later tax legislation.

Although employers are increasing their offerings of education assistance, this is not a widely used benefit—perhaps because of poor communication of information about the benefits. Hewitt Associates found that more than three quarters of their survey respondents offered education assistance benefits, and the average tuition reimbursement was $5,000 per participating employee per year. In 2004, the Society for Human Resource Management reported that 71% of employers provided education assistance for undergraduate studies, and 67% for graduate work. But only 5–10% of employees used these programs. Traditionally, this benefit came with strings attached, such as a commitment to remain with the company or restricting reimbursement to work-related curricula (or reimbursing more tuition for work-related studies). As for employees concerned about paying their children's tuition, many companies try to reduce the number of 401(k) plan loans taken for this purpose by making it easier (e.g., by payroll deduction) for employees to invest in tax-favored I.R.C. § 529 plans. [Susanna Duff Barnett, *College Conundrum: More Companies Are Offering Education Benefits, But Workers Do Not Take Advantage,* Employee Benefit News, <http://www.benefitnews.com/pfv.cfm?id=7427 (May 2005)]

§ 22.05   EMPLOYEE ASSISTANCE PROGRAMS (EAPs)

The purpose of the Employee Assistance Program (EAP) is to help employees cope with stress and other problems. The theory is that sympathetic listening, and referrals for whatever professional services are needed, will ease employees' anxieties and make them more productive. EAPs can offer any combination of one-on-one counseling, information and referral, hotlines and crisis intervention, and informational seminars.

EAPs typically deal with problems such as substance abuse, dependent care, and problems with spouses and children. Many companies have found that early intervention makes it possible to shorten the damage and amount of time that would otherwise be involved, for instance, when the employee "hits bottom" with a drug or alcohol problem, or when an untreated mental illness requires inpatient hospitalization in a crisis. Each dollar invested in EAP services is estimated to return anywhere from two to eight dollars in health and productivity savings.

EAPs also take a role in coordinating an employee's return to work after recuperating from an accident or illness (which may include a shortened or flexible schedule, intermittent FMLA leave, or other accommodations).

The services can be provided in house by the HR department, or contracted out to outside vendors. The second course is more expensive, but it may make the EAP more credible to employees, or may reassure employees that their confidentiality will be protected.

§ 22.06   MISCELLANEOUS FRINGES

Employees do not have taxable income if they receive certain minor fringe benefits provided by the employer on a nondiscriminatory basis to all employees. Under I.R.C. § 132, the benefits are not taxed to the employees. FICA, FUTA, and federal income tax withholding are not required, and the employer share of these taxes does not have to be paid. Generally, the employer will be able to deduct the cost of the program (which is supposed to be nominal, in any case) as long as it fits the definition of an ordinary and necessary business expense.

The categories of miscellaneous fringe benefits authorized under I.R.C. § 132 are:

- No-additional-cost services of the employer company (e.g., air travel for an airline employee; a simple will prepared by a law firm for a non-attorney staffer). The employee must gain access to services normally sold to customers, but the employer must not incur any substantial cost. In effect, the employees are given access to the business's excess capacity;
- Employee discounts; the discount must not exceed the gross profit percentage for goods, or 20% of the cost of services;
- De minimis fringe benefits, such as free beverages at work or small Christmas presents—anything too trivial to account for separately;
- An on-premises eating facility such as a low-cost cafeteria that prepares meals on premises for the convenience of the employer (because employees can take shorter meal breaks because the subsidized dining facility is available). The facility must be owned or operated by the employer, must generate revenue at least equal to its operating costs, and must provide meals during the workday or right before or right after it. It must also be in or near the workplace, and must be operated by the employer (possibly through a contract with a third-party management company);

- Working condition fringe benefits—goods or services the employee could deduct if he or she paid for them personally. Typical examples are business travel and the use of company cars;
- An on-premises gym for the exclusive use of employees and their families;
- Reimbursement of employment-related moving expenses that would be deductible if the employee paid them directly (but have not in fact been deducted by the employee);
- Up to $205 (2006 level) for parking, and up to $105 (2006) a month for transit passes or highway vehicle transport (i.e., van pooling).

In Rev. Rul. 2004-98, 2004-42 I.R.B. 664, the IRS noted that an attempt to gross up qualified transportation fringes, when the employer reimburses employees for parking expenses with the result that net after-tax pay is the same as if there had been no reduction in compensation, does not satisfy Reg. § 1.132-9(b). (In this example, an employee's $1,500 gross income was $1,301.45 after withholding: the employer set up an arrangement under which the employee's pay was reduced by $100 to pay for parking; the employer withheld $105 FICA and $73 income tax, then paid the employee an additional $79.75 to reimburse for the parking deduction, yielding the same net monthly pay of $1,301.45, albeit with smaller FICA and income tax payments.) The IRS ruled that parking expenses can be excluded from gross income only if they are actually incurred out of pocket. The IRS rejected the employer's claim that the reductions can be given effect and yet the reimbursement payments can be excluded from employees' gross income and not subject to FICA or FUTA. The IRS held that the employees did not really incur parking expenses and therefore could not receive tax-free "reimbursement" of amounts not actually incurred. It doesn't matter whether the reduction is mandatory or elective, or whether the employer initially offered free parking and then entered into a payroll arrangement to balance a purported charge.

Another Code section, I.R.C. § 119, governs meals and lodging furnished on premises for the convenience of the employer, e.g., a room for a hotel manager who must be around to handle problems as they arise. Such benefits are not taxable income for the employee.

Financially pressed companies are always on the lookout for low-cost benefits that can improve employee satisfaction (e.g., flextime, child and elder care referral services, weight-loss programs, smoking cessation help, and medical FSAs). Voluntary insurance benefits also are popular with both employers (who pay only small administrative costs) and employees (who can get much better premium rates as part of a group than as individuals). Another benefit gaining popularity is giving employees the chance to buy health insurance—for their pets; veterinary health insurance has increased from being offered in 1% of companies in 2000 to 5% in 2005 (and 10% of large employers). Typical monthly premiums for dog owners range from $15 to $30. Other benefits are theoretically more expensive, but don't cost the company much because only a small percentage of the workforce ever use them (e.g., domestic partner benefits for same-sex partners and adoption assistance). [Kris Maher, *Popular . . . But Cheap*, Wall Street Journal, Jan. 24, 2006, at p. R4; Kerry Hannon, *More Employers Are Offering Pet-Insurance Benefits*, Wall Street Journal, Nov. 12–13, 2005, at p. B3]

During the dot-com boom, tech companies strove to offer the most generous perks available. This crashed to a halt with the dot-com bust, but by 2005, the trend returned, with companies making services such as grocery shopping, car detailing, massages and haircuts available at the worksite. This time, however, the new twist was that employees were expected to pay much or all of the cost of the services, which were now considered a productivity tool rather than a way to recruit scarce workers by pampering them. For example, Google runs a shuttle bus between San Francisco and its headquarters, 33 miles away—equipped with wireless Internet so the commuters can spend the trip working! [Pui-Wing Tam and Mylene Mangalindan, *Parking-Lot Perks: Haircuts, Car Washes for Busy Tech Workers*, Wall Street Journal, Nov. 9, 2005, at p. A1]

§ 22.07   VOLUNTARY EMPLOYEE BENEFIT ASSOCIATIONS (VEBAs)

A Voluntary Employee Benefit Association (VEBA), as defined by I.R.C. § 501(c)(9), is a trust that is funded by employer contributions (with or without employee contributions) and is used to pay benefits to employees who voluntarily exercise the option to participate in the association. VEBAs provide life, sickness, accident, or similar benefits to employee members and their dependents and designated beneficiaries. Benefits that can be offered by a VEBA safeguard or improve health or protect against a contingency that threatens the employee's earning power. But VEBAs are not allowed to offer reimbursement of commuting expenses, profit sharing, or stock bonuses.

The trust itself is not a taxable entity, but VEBA benefits constitute taxable income to the employee unless they are specifically exempted.

The VEBA must be controlled by its employee membership, by a bank or other independent trustee, or by fiduciaries chosen by or on behalf of the membership. A VEBA is considered a welfare plan under ERISA, and therefore is subject to ERISA Parts 1 (notice and reporting), 4 (trust and fiduciary responsibility), and 5 (enforcement).

The Sixth Circuit ruled that the portion of the VEBA contribution used to fund long-term disability benefits was deductible, but the portion used to fund post-retirement benefits and medical benefits for union members was not deductible, because the employer failed to satisfy the I.R.C. § 419A(c)(2) requirements for accumulating assets to prefund the benefits. [*Parker-Hannifin Corp. v. Commissioner*, 139 F.3d 1090 (6th Cir. 1998)]

§ 22.08 FRINGE BENEFIT PLANS: TAX COMPLIANCE

[A] Reporting Requirements

The reporting requirements for a fringe benefit plan are set out in I.R.C. § 6039D. The plan must report:

- Number of employees at the employer company;
- Number of employees eligible to participate in the plan;
- Number actually participating;
- Number of highly compensated employees in each of the above categories;
- The plan's total cost during the year;
- The employer's name, address, and Employer Identification Number;
- The nature of its business.

If any fringe benefits are taxable, the employer can either add them to the regular wages for a payroll period, or withhold federal income tax at the rate for supplemental wages. [The relevant IRS publication is 15-B, Employer's Tax Guide to Fringe Benefits.]

IRS Notice 2002-24, 2002-16 I.R.B. 785 sets out the requirements for cafeteria plans, education assistance plans, and adoption assistance plans to file Form 5500 as annual disclosure forms. These plans are not required to file the Schedule F information return.

[B] The Employer's Tax Deduction

When it comes to pensions, the tax rules are devised to make sure that the employer contributes enough to fund the plan. In contrast, when it comes to welfare benefits, the tax focus is preventing excessive prefunding of benefit plans. So the relevant Code sections (I.R.C. §§ 419 and 419A) specify a maximum funding level for welfare benefit trusts. If this level is exceeded, the trust is no longer tax-exempt.

Although the employer receives a tax deduction for maintaining a welfare benefit trust, the deduction is limited to the "qualified cost" of the benefit plans for the year. That means the direct cost of funding benefits, plus whatever amount I.R.C. § 419A permits to be added to the account for the year as a safety cushion.

Reference should also be made to I.R.C. § 4976, which imposes a 100% excise tax on disqualified benefit distributions made from funded welfare benefit plans. For instance, retiree health and life insurance benefits for highly compensated employees are supposed to be kept in a separate account from comparable contributions for rank-and-file employees.

Therefore, benefits paid to HCEs from the general account would be disqualified. VEBA benefits to HCEs that violate nondiscrimination requirements are also disqualified, as are amounts that revert to the employer. (An erroneous contribution which is withdrawn by the employer after a determination that it is not deductible is not considered a reversion.)

§ 22.09   ERISA REGULATION OF WELFARE BENEFIT PLANS

[A]   Creation and Administration

Although most of the attention goes to ERISA's regulation of pension plans, ERISA also covers welfare benefit plans—a category roughly equivalent to fringe benefit plans. An ERISA welfare benefit plan is created (generally by a corporate resolution passed by the Board of Directors and managed by the relevant corporate officials) and administered to provide one or more of these benefits to plan participants and their beneficiaries:

- Medical benefits;
- Health care;
- Accident insurance;
- Disability benefits;
- Death benefits;
- Supplemental unemployment benefits;
- Vacation benefits;
- Training (e.g., apprenticeship);
- Day care centers (but not dependent care spending reimbursement accounts);
- Scholarships;
- Prepaid legal services;
- Any benefit described in the Labor-Management Relations Act § 302(c) [29 U.S.C. §§ 141–144, etc.] other than death benefits, pensions, or insurance coverage for pensions or death benefits.

The people receiving the benefits must be common-law employees and not independent contractors. For this purpose, employee status depends on agency principles such as who controls and supervises the person, and whether the person can recognize profit or loss from the work relationship. It does not depend on the "reasonable expectations" of the parties. [*Mutual Insurance Co. v. Darden*, 503 U.S. 318 (1992)]

Welfare benefit plans are subject to ERISA Title I. The Eleventh Circuit has ruled that a Title I plan exists if circumstances lead a reasonable person to ascertain the intended benefits, intended beneficiaries, financing sources, and procedure for receiving benefits under the plan. [*Donovan v. Dillingham*, 688 F.2d 1367 (11th Cir. 1982)] A plan can be deemed to exist even if the ERISA rules are not observed, and in fact, even if there is no written instrument.

Severance pay plans are sometimes treated as pension plans, but are more likely to be characterized as welfare benefit plans. DOL Advisory Opinion 84-12A says that a severance pay plan is not a pension plan if:

- Its benefits are not contingent on the employee's retirement;
- Total payments do not exceed twice the employee's compensation for the year before the termination;
- Payments are completed within 24 months after termination of service for the employer.

Under a similar analysis, bonus programs are not treated as pension plans for ERISA Title I purposes unless the payments are systematically deferred at least until termination of employment. DOL Reg. § 2510.3 says that an employer plan that supplements retirement benefits (e.g., until early retirees can qualify for Social Security benefits) can be either a pension or a welfare benefit plan, depending on its terms and how it is administered.

ERISA Title I does not apply to certain payroll practices:

- Extra pay for nonstandard working hours (overtime, shift premiums, holiday premiums);
- Compensation paid when the employee is on sick leave, taking a sick day, or otherwise medically unable to work;
- Compensation paid for other absences, such as vacation days, sabbaticals, and military leave.

In mid-2004, EBSA issued an advisory opinion as to whether a vacation pay plan was a "welfare benefit plan" as defined by ERISA § 3(1). The plan provided paid vacation to eligible employees, based on average hours worked, length of service, and level of employment. Hourly employees could accrue a maximum of 6.67 vacation hours per month; salaried employees could accrue up to 13.3 hours per month. Some hours could be carried over from year to year, and salaried employees with six months of service or hourly employees with a year of service could be paid accumulated but unused vacation balances on termination. The EBSA opined that 29 CFR § 2510.3-1 draws a distinction between a welfare benefit plan and a payroll practice, such as paying vacation benefits out of the employer's general assets. The factors in the determination of a welfare benefit include whether the employee's right is contingent on a future occurrence or whether the employee undertakes some risk other than ordinary employment risk. If there is a VEBA or trust involved, ERISA coverage depends on whether the trust is a bona fide separate fund; whether it has a direct legal obligation to pay plan benefits; if the employer's obligation to make contributions is legally enforceable; and whether the contributions are actuarially determined or established via collective bargaining. EBSA ruled that although the plan had a trust that was legally obligated to pay benefits, the benefits were not related to the plan's accruing liability, nor had the administrator exercised its power to set up a rate of per-person contribution based on actuarial factors. EBSA concluded that the trust was just a pass-through vehicle for the distribution of ordinary vacation pay. [EBSA Advisory Opinion 2004-08A, 7/2/04, <http://www.dol.gov/ebsa/regs/aos/a02004-08a.html>]

[B] ERISA Case Law on Welfare Benefits

A brokerage firm created an association of small firms (under 225 employees) so the members could maintain a self-funded health benefit plan. The Third Circuit ruled that the members lacked the requisite commonality of interest, and therefore the plan was not an "employee welfare benefit plan" as defined by ERISA. [*Gruber v. Hubbard Bert Karle Weber Inc.,* 159 F.3d 780 (3d Cir. 1998)]

Where failure to make complete disclosure could be harmful to benefit participants, a benefit plan administrator had a fiduciary duty to give complete and accurate information about the plan. If it is clear that a participant is unaware of important features of the plan, it is not enough simply to answer questions. [*Krohn v. Huron Mem. Hosp.,* 173 F.3d 542 (6th Cir. 1999)]

Vega v. National Life Insurance Services Inc. [188 F.3d 287 (5th Cir. 1999)] involved a plan sponsored by a married couple that owned a business. The plan administrator (which was a subsidiary of the insurer that wrote the plan's policies) denied a health claim for the wife. The administrator relied on information from the wife's doctor that the claim was for surgery planned before the policy was obtained.

The Fifth Circuit decided that even if a plan administrator has a conflict of interest when it denies a claim (which, in this case, would have been paid by the administrator's parent company) ERISA does not impose an additional duty of reasonable investigation before denying the claim. Even an administrator who has a conflict of interest can reach a valid decision, but when a court reviews the transaction for abuse of discretion, the conflict of interest is evidence.

PART V

THE HR FUNCTION

CHAPTER **23**

HIRING AND RECRUITMENT

§ 23.01   INTRODUCTION

Efficient hiring practices benefit the company at all levels. Prompt, economical selection of the best person to do the job (whether from inside the company or brought in from outside) will keep operations running smoothly and encourage innovation that will keep the business competitive.

On the downside, bad hiring practices create many kinds of risks.

The most obvious risks are employment discrimination charges brought by ex-employees or job applicants. The employer might be held liable for negligence in hiring or retaining a person who commits a crime in the workplace, or who sexually harasses other workers.

Subtler risks come from poorly chosen employees who absorb too much training time, drag down the efficiency of an entire department, make costly mistakes— or who must be discharged and replaced, setting the whole cycle in motion again.

A majority of survey respondents (81%) told the National Association of Manufacturers that they expect moderate or even severe shortages of skilled production workers over the next three years, and over half of them said that they have 10% or more of their job openings unfilled because they can't find a qualified candidate. About a third (35%) anticipated shortages of scientists and engineers within three years, as did 25% for unskilled production workers, but only 8% for consumer service employees. However, in 2001, a similar survey showed the same percentage of companies expected trouble in filling skilled jobs.

Additional problems will be caused as the Baby Boom generation starts retiring. Many Boomers will continue to work past age 65, for financial and/or personal reasons, but the National Association of Manufacturers warns that there could be a shortfall of five million skilled workers between 2010 and 2012. However, if a job category is no longer needed, the impending retirement of many of the people trained for the job is not necessarily cause for concern. [Timothy Aeppel, *Firms' New Grail: Skilled Workers*, Wall Street Journal, Nov. 22, 2005, at p. A2; Kelly Greene, *Bye-Bye Boomers?* Wall Street Journal, Sep. 20, 2005, at p. B1]

According to a 2004 survey by the Society for Human Rights Management, about 60% of respondents contract out some of their HR functions. The most common is partial outsourcing of the administration of health care benefits, pensions, and payroll. Fifty-six percent of respondents said they outsourced to cut operating costs; 41% did so to reduce staff and staff-related expenses. Although about half of the respondents said that outsourcing decreased job opportunities for HR professionals, another quarter said that it increased opportunities. [Kris Maher, *The Jungle*, Wall Street Journal, July 20, 2004, at p. B4]

§ 23.02   PRODUCTIVE HIRING

Unless the plan is specifically to hire someone for a short-term or temporary assignment, an important objective is to find someone who will develop loyalty and will want to stay with the company for a long time. Training is both expensive and inconvenient, and it takes time for a new hire to get used to the job, so turnover is very harmful to productivity.

The best candidate is not necessarily the one with the most impressive resume. In fact, someone with great credentials might be constantly "head-hunted" and inclined to jump ship when a better offer comes along. The company is probably better off hiring someone who is suited to the job as it exists now and as it will develop in the future.

Current employees can be a great starting point for recruitment (and many companies offer bonuses if a current employee recruits someone who is hired and completes a minimum period satisfactorily), but they should not be the only source of recruitment—especially if you want a diverse workforce.

College and graduate school recruitment should not be restricted to those nearby, or only to a small class of Ivy League schools. If nationwide recruitment is a cost problem, the Internet allows nationwide recruiting and low cost. However, resumes posted on the Internet are no more or less truthful than those delivered by traditional means, so reference checks are still required.

"Temp to perm" or "temp to hire" arrangements provide a means for employers to size up employees on a more substantive basis than a job interview and for employees to get a feeling if they want the job on a permanent basis. Employment Line, a staffing service in New York City, found that in 2005 more than 75% of the new hires they placed started out as temps—versus about 25% five years ago. Even professional jobs are sometimes filled in this way. Generally, the contract between employer and staffing agency does not require the payment of an additional fee when a temp is converted to a permanent employee. [Tanya Mohn, *A Way to Try a Job on for Size Before Making a Commitment*, New York Times, Mar. 12, 2006, at § 10 p. 1]

§ 23.03 ANALYZING JOB REQUIREMENTS

In many cases, poor hiring decisions are made because of lack of insight into the real demands of the job. A candidate is chosen who matches the formal, written job description, but there's a mismatch, because the real job isn't very much like the job description. Often, people are hired on the basis of technical skills, but those skills are seldom used on a day-to-day basis.

The job should be analyzed to see how much time is actually spent on tasks such as:

- Meeting and conferring with others;
- Using specific computer hardware and software;
- Selling the company's products;
- Working with machinery;
- Supervising other people's work;
- Writing and analyzing reports;

- Creating policy for the organization;
- Carrying out policy set by others;
- Heavy lifting or repetitive stress;
- Driving;
- Business travel.

It is important to understand the physical demands of the job, to see who can meet them without accommodation, and what accommodations can reasonably be made to the needs of individuals with disabilities. [*See* § 36.05 for a discussion of reasonable accommodation.]

The job's role within the organization should also be analyzed. Maybe the whole operation could become more productive if the responsibilities assigned to the job were changed, or if the job were moved higher or lower on the grading system or organization chart. Maybe there have been problems because the job reports to one person, when it would make more sense to report to someone else.

The job must be identified as exempt or nonexempt for wage and hour purposes. Sometimes it makes economic sense to restructure job duties so that the job becomes exempt from overtime requirements. However, the change must be real, not just a meaningless title.

Reasons for job turnover should also be analyzed and steps taken to improve retention. In the late 2000s, companies faced a serious seller's market, and had to compete heavily to attract and retain good workers. The current economic downturn makes it more of a buyer's market, but it is still a good idea to remain competitive with the working conditions, salary, and benefits available elsewhere.

The job interview, and especially follow-up interviews with various people in the corporate hierarchy, should be used to give the potential employee strong insight into the resources available and what will be expected if he or she is offered, and accepts, the job.

There should be a written job description indicating:

- Job title;
- When it has to be filled;
- Why the organization needs someone for that position at all (perhaps the duties could be delegated to existing employees, outsourced, or assigned to temporary or part-time employees);
- Required educational qualifications;
- Necessary skills;
- Standards for defining inadequate, satisfactory, good, and excellent performance; the educational qualifications, skills, and experience that are really needed to perform the job; and standards (as objective as possible) for defining inadequate, satisfactory, good, and excellent performance.

The job description should indicate reporting relationships (whom the jobholder reports to; who reports to him or her). It should explain the promotion potential for the job, including conditions (such as getting an MBA or meeting performance goals). If your company has a grading system, the job grade should be indicated. The job description should also include the salary range.

§ 23.04   RECRUITMENT

[A]   Generally

It is probably worthwhile to consider promoting existing employees to fill important positions, although sometimes it is necessary to look outside—or desirable to get new skills and viewpoints. Even a policy of promoting from within requires recruiting, to fill entry- and mid-levels that have been vacated by the promoted employees. According to the DirectEmployers Association (which runs Jobcentral.com), in 2005 51% of all new hires came from the Internet, making it the largest hiring source. Employers' own Web sites were the best source of leads. Companies spent 27% of their recruitment ad budget on general job board ads; however, those ads generated only 15% of new hires. [Rebecca Moore, *Internet Now Primary Source of New Hires*, PlanSponsor.com (Feb. 10, 2006)]

Blogs—Weblogs—are taking on a role in recruitment and hiring. A corporate blog can provide insight into the daily life of the corporation, using personal, even quirky, material about the company. Third-party blogs about a particular industry can integrate company information, industry news, and job postings; some of these blogs include paid advertisements. And, of course, if a job applicant has a blog, the recruiter can learn a lot about the applicant by reading it. [Kris Maher, *Blogs Catch On as Online Tool for Job Seekers and Recruiters*, Wall Street Journal, Sept. 28, 2004, at p. B10]

[B]   Recruitment from Within

Many companies create incentives for employees to do well by stressing internal transfers and promotions. These workers do not have to leave (or threaten to leave) to advance or earn more money if they are given access to job postings and given a real chance to compete for jobs. Internal recruitment also saves money that would otherwise go to advertisements and search firm fees. The company can get a detailed view of the employee's past performance by consulting their own records. Internal promotion also means that the person selected will be familiar with the corporate culture. However, sometimes supervisors deliberately torpedo the promotion chances of their best employees, because they don't want to lose them!

In most companies, job postings literally are posted on a bulletin board, leaving the notice up for five to ten days. More and more companies are using the corporate Intranet for this purpose. The posting should explain the nature of the job (although another advantage of recruiting from within is that the applicants will be fairly familiar with it already); the qualifications required; and whether there are any limitations. For instance, seniority is a very significant factor in promotions in a unionized workplace. Some companies have a policy that employees are not allowed to apply for internal vacancies unless they have held their current job for at least six months with satisfactory or better performance appraisals. The usual policy is to keep the application confidential from the applicant's immediate supervisor, until there is the possibility that the promotion will be offered.

[C] Competitive Recruiting

If at least some outside applications are solicited, the question becomes how to stay competitive in the job market. Attractive features can include:

- High cash compensation;
- High overall compensation package, taking health and other benefits into account;
- High job security;
- Prestige within the industry;
- Ability to work on cutting-edge projects;
- Availability of stock options;
- Pleasant working environment;
- Easy commute;
- Family-friendly policies (although these are neutral or even a disadvantage for unmarried employees).

Companies that send letters to rejected candidates often include the polite phrase, "We will keep your resume on file," but few of them actually review the filed resumes when they have another job to fill—although this can be a simple and inexpensive source of candidates.

The state employment service can be a good resource for low-level jobs, and even some higher-level technical jobs. Unemployment benefits are not available to workers who have voluntarily quit, or who were fired for wrongdoing, so workers receiving benefits are probably not unstable or a bad risk merely on account of being unemployed. Also, people who are employed but want a new job sometimes register with the state employment office because it has contacts with a wide range of employers and because it does not charge jobseekers a fee. To fill higher-level positions, if a local company has had a major downsizing recently, check with the company that handles their executive outplacement.

[D] Avoiding Improprieties

If you hire someone who held a senior position at one of your competitors, it is possible that the individual had an employment contract with the company that contained a covenant not to compete. Another possibility is that, when his or her severance package was negotiated, a covenant not to compete was signed at that time. Therefore, it is important to find out if a job applicant is subject to such an agreement, and whether taking the job that is offered would violate it.

Even without a covenant not to compete, a competitor could charge that you hired its ex-employee to misappropriate the competitor's customer lists and trade secrets. If you recruited the ex-employee, you might be charged with interference with contractual relationships. So make it part of the interview process to make a record about the circumstances of the contact.

In mid-2003, two office supplies companies agreed to a $5.8 million settlement where one allegedly raided the other by hiring away its employees and gaining access to confidential information, after the plaintiff company sought a strategic buyer—a deal that had to be renegotiated, unfavorably, allegedly as a result of the raid. The defendant began to recruit away sales representatives (some of whom had non-compete agreements) by offering them guaranteed salaries and exceptionally high bonuses. Recruitment also extended to truck drivers, warehouse workers, and operations managers. The defendant company and its CEO were held responsible for $4.85 million of the settlement, paid by insurance. Another insurer paid $750,000 on behalf of the defendant company, and the first insurer also paid $100,000 on behalf of an investment banker involved in the situation. [*USOP Liquidating v. Allied Offices Supplies Inc.*, 2001 Bankr. LEXIS 825 (D. Del. 2001), discussed in Danielle N. Rodier, *Corporate Raiding Case Settles for $5.8M,* The Legal Intelligencer, Aug. 11, 2003 <http://www.law.com>]

In early 2005, the Eighth Circuit ruled that there is no Minnesota cause of action for corporate raiding (in the sense of hiring away another company's employee), so claims such as interference with contract relations, inducing breach of contract, and breach of fiduciary duty failed for lack of proof of damages when a start-up company (which was later acquired by Cisco) hired 27 Storage Technology engineers. [*Storage Tech. Corp. v. Cisco Sys. Inc.*, 395 F.3d 921 (8th Cir. 2005)]

A 2003 Seventh Circuit case [*International Union of Operating Engineers, Local 150 v. NLRB,* 325 F.3d 818 (7th Cir 2003)] raises some interesting questions about recruitment practices. For 40 years, a highway contractor has maintained the same hiring policy. Applications from current or former employees, or people they refer, get priority over applications from unknown or walk-in candidates. However, under a conciliation agreement with the DOL, to avoid perpetuating past patterns of discrimination, the company also gives preferential consideration to candidates referred by equal employment opportunity service providers. The case arose when a union local, knowing that the company had a big new job and presumably would need to hire many workers, sent a number of applicants wearing union insignia.

The Seventh Circuit rule is that it's improper to refuse to hire someone merely because of their union sentiments, membership, or activities [*Bloedorn v. Francisco Foods Inc.,* 276 F.3d 270 (7th Cir. 2001)], or even because they're union "salts" (people "salted" into the workforce to spread pro-union ideas).

[*Hartman Bros. Heating & Air Conditioning Inc. v. NLRB,* 280 F.3d 1110 (7th Cir. 2002)] However, the Seventh Circuit found that the company's hiring procedure was not tantamount to a refusal to hire or consider pro-union applicants. As long as an employer is not motivated by anti-union animus, for labor law purposes it can freely exercise its business judgment when deciding whom to hire. [*NLRB v. Louis A. Weiss Mem. Hosp.,* 172 F.3d 432 (7th Cir. 1999)] Even the NLRB itself takes the position that preferring current employees, ex-employees, and people referred by management cannot be interpreted as anti-union discrimination. [*Custom Topsoil, Inc.,* 328 N.L.R.B. 446 (1999). *See* Chapter 30 for more about labor law concepts]

[E] Rehiring

Sometimes downsizing goes too deep, and employees can be recalled at a later time. Employees leave because of differences of opinion, personality conflicts, or because they have been offered another job. Rehiring a former employee has both advantages and disadvantages. The ex-employee needs less training than an outsider, because he or she is already familiar with procedures and the corporate culture. However, there is a risk of morale problems, both arising out of the original termination and on the part of other employees who feel that they were insufficiently rewarded for loyally sticking to the company all along.

§ 23.05 SEARCH FIRMS

For a rank-and-file job, putting out the word to employees, or within the neighborhood could be enough to fill the vacancy. For an entry-level job, recruiting from high schools, colleges, and vocational training programs often works well. Newspaper classified ads, ads in specialty journals, and to an increasing extent, Internet job search sites, can result in a good match between needs and job candidates.

However, the stakes are higher when a top executive or prominent professional has to be replaced. The successful candidate will set the company's policy and/or creative agenda. A good choice strengthens the company's long-term competitive position; the wrong choice could lead to long-term damage. The person hired might have excellent credentials and work hard, but might have a vision for the company that is incompatible with the rest of management.

For those and other reasons, businesses often look to search firms when a major job needs to be filled. This is a costly option. Search firm fees can be the equivalent of a year's salary—or more!—for a highly compensated executive. But it pays off in productivity if the right candidate is selected and gets to work quickly.

There are two main types of firms in the search professional. Contingency firms are usually used to find candidates for jobs paying $40,000–$80,000 a year;

an executive search firm usually gets involved only with jobs paying $75,000 a year or more. A search firm works directly for the company seeking to hire an executive. Usually, its contracts require the company to pay for its services whether or not a candidate is hired. In contrast, a contingency firm's clients include both job seekers and companies looking to hire someone, and the company pays a fee if and only if hiring results.

A search firm's fee can be anywhere from 25% to 100% of the first year salary. Contingency firms usually charge less, perhaps 20% to 33% of the first year's salary. Only cash compensation, not bonuses or stock options, is included in the calculation. Both kinds of firms often give refunds if the new hire leaves or has to be discharged during a probationary period such as 90 days.

Many companies are not familiar with search firms, so they do not know what to expect or how to assess the quality of the firm's performance. John Marra, president of the recruitment firm Marra Peters & Partners, has some suggestions:

- Be clear on the criteria you use to judge the firm's performance;
- Get references from past clients and follow them up;
- Tell the search firm what you expect the successful candidate to accomplish the first six months and the first year after hiring, and how you will assess the new hire's performance;
- Ask the search firm to send only candidates who are a good match with your requirements;
- Get the search firm's promise to keep working with you until the vacancy is satisfactorily filled (if necessary, after someone has been hired, terminated after a probationary period, and a new search performed).

Some of the provisions to look for in a recruitment contract are:

- Clarification that the firm does not have the authority to hire someone on behalf of your company, or to promise terms and conditions of employment—only your company's authorized agent can do that;
- A statement that your company is committed to equal employment opportunity principles;
- The firm's agreement that it will be responsible if it commits discrimination in referring candidates to you—and that it will indemnify your company for any liability resulting from its discriminatory referrals;
- A clear statement of the firm's responsibilities, including screening candidates and checking their references;
- Recruiting expenses that your company agrees to pay;
- Whether you have to pay if you hire a candidate obtained through another channel, or only if the recruiter sends the successful candidate to you;
- The recruiter's promise not to contact or solicit your new hire for a period of at least two years.

§ 23.06   JOB APPLICATIONS

Frequently, the first real contact between the corporation and the potential employee occurs when the applicant submits a formal job application. The application is a legal document that can have serious consequences: both as a source of promises that the employer can be held to, and as a source of information whose correctness the applicant can be held responsible for. For example, false statements on an application can constitute "after-acquired evidence" of wrongdoing that can limit the damages available to a successful employee plaintiff. [See § 42.10[C]]

It often makes sense to have a candidate fill out a job application even if he or she has submitted a resume. The resume only includes the information the candidate wants to disclose. The application form is standard, and resumes are very variable, so it is easier to compare applicants if you have the same information about each. The application might ask for:

- Positions held with the last three or four employers;
- Dates of employment;
- Job title;
- Salary;
- Name of immediate supervisor;
- Why the candidate left that job (unless he or she is still employed);
- Permission to contact the supervisor for a reference.

Tip: In several states (e.g., California, Delaware, Minnesota, Wisconsin), if you require applicants to sign their applications, the state privacy law also requires you to give them a copy of the completed application, or lets employees copy personnel files including job applications.

The application should make it clear that the form is a legal document that can have serious ramifications. It is important to require the applicant to state that all the information given on the application is complete and accurate—and that it will be grounds for discipline or dismissal if the applicant is hired and the employer later finds out that false information was given on the application.

There should be a separate signature line if the employer wants to get a credit report to indicate release of this information. Applicants should be informed when reference checks will be done. The form should clarify that application is being made for at-will employment. If the job offer is conditional on the applicant's passing a physical examination and/or drug and alcohol testing, this should be indicated on the application.

Check state law about which questions are permissible, and which are ruled out by antidiscrimination laws.

> **Tip:** It could make sense to indicate that applications will be rejected if the applicant includes extraneous information that was not requested on the application. Some applicants use this material tactically: for instance, if they volunteer information about union activism, they might claim that they were discriminated against by the employer. [*See* Timothy S. Bland and Sue S. Stalcup, *Build a Legal Employment Application*, HR Magazine, March 1999, at p. 129]

Late in 2003, West Virginia ruled that it is not an invasion of privacy to require a job applicant to take a drug test, even though state law forbids mandatory drug testing of persons who are already employees, because employees have a higher expectation of workplace privacy than applicants. [*Baughman v. Wal-Mart Stores Inc.*, 215 W. Va. 45 (W. Va. 2003)]

See 70 Fed. Reg. 58,947 (Oct. 7, 2005) for DOL's Office of Federal Contract Compliance Programs' Final Rule covering federal contractors' records maintenance obligations with respect to Internet-based job applications. If possible, contractors should collect data on the gender, race, and ethnicity of applicants (including those who apply online). Contractors are required to maintain records of Internet-based expressions of interest that resulted in the contractor considering an applicant for a particular job. Records retention is not required if an applicant merely asked generally about job opportunities at the company, or submitted queries that did not satisfy the company's requirements for job applications. Federal contractors reacted with displeasure, many of them believing that the records would not only be unduly burdensome to create and maintain, but also create a new paper trail that could spur a wave of new discrimination lawsuits. [Tresa Baldas, *New Web Hiring Rules Cause Corporate Consternation*, National Law Journal, Dec. 7, 2005 (law.com)]

§ 23.07   ESTABLISHING TERMS AND CONDITIONS

The interview should stress the at-will nature of employment if your company wants the flexibility to terminate employees without a formal structure. Train interviewers to avoid statements such as "If you do a good job, you'll be set for life here" or "We never lay anybody off, no matter how tough the economy gets." Interviewers should also avoid statements about corporate procedure ("We go through all the channels before anybody gets fired") unless they accurately reflect corporate policy and practice.

Interviewers are agents of the company, and even if the employee handbook says that the company is only obligated if there are written contracts, in fact the company is likely to be held accountable for promises made by the interviewer (for instance, about vacation terms, the availability of leave, and education benefits).

Many companies set a salary range rather than an explicit pay rate for a particular job. Interviewers should understand whether or not they can negotiate a salary with a promising candidate, or if that matter will have to be referred to a higher-up. Interviewees should always be told clearly who else is involved in the interview process, what the powers are of each person, and who has the power to actually make a job offer.

§ 23.08   REFERENCE CHECKS

Not every statement made on an application or in an interview is strictly accurate! At the worst, criminals may seek a job where they can plunder the corporate funds, so it is often worthwhile to have an arrangement with a third-party provider that checks criminal record databases. In the case of an especially unusual or sensitive job, it can make sense to do a detailed investigation, or even hire a private investigator, before extending a job offer.

On a less dramatic scale, basically honest people often exaggerate their credentials, turn attendance at a program into a degree, or claim more credit for results than they are entitled to. Companies that are sensitive to the risk of defamation may limit the amount of information that they provide about former employees, but they should at least be able to confirm the dates of employment and the positions held.

Reference checks on employees (rather than applicants) can also be useful. A lack of candor can be a valid reason for denying a raise or promotion, and "after-acquired evidence" discovered as late as the preparation for a discrimination suit can be used to reduce the recovery a plaintiff can obtain.

Nearly all (96%) of SHRM members surveyed said that their company always checks applicants' credentials and/or references. ResumeDoctor.com checked out more than 1,000 resumes that had been posted to its site (verifying educational background, dates of employment, and job titles or duties) and found that 42.7% included at least one inaccurate item, and 12.6% had two or more errors of fact. [Cheryl Soltis, *Eagle-Eyed Employers Scour Resumes for Little White Lies*, Wall Street Journal, Mar. 21, 2006, at p. B7]

Assessing truthfulness during a face-to-face interview is very difficult. An interviewee who fidgets and looks shady could be truthful, and merely nervous about the interview. On the other hand, an experienced liar is also likely to be a good actor. Tips for spotting lies include comparing spoken statements with the data given on the resume and application, and asking pointed questions focusing on the details of the disparity. Follow up inconsistencies and contradictions during the interview, and ask for contact names to verify the information.

Tip: Be aware that sometimes failure to pay traffic fines is reported by a state database as a "violation of probation," so follow up the nature of the "violation."

Usually, a criminal-record check starts with a trace on the applicant's Social Security number, which generates a list of previous addresses. (Of course, this implies that the applicant was operating "on the books" and using his or her own name!) A complete search looks for outstanding wants and warrants (misdemeanors as well as felonies), motor vehicle reports, credit reports, academic qualifications, and verification of past employment.

Firms that perform checks charge an average of $35 to $50 for a basic search for a low-level candidate, and perhaps $150 to $200 for a more senior employee; it could cost about $300 for a three- to five-day turnaround on a search.

Tip: Make sure that the outsourcing firm fully understands the Fair Credit Reporting Act limitations on use of investigative credit reports—and make sure they have plenty of liability insurance if they could be required to indemnify your company!

A good criminal record check goes back at least seven years. Because many court systems have automated records going back only one to six years, it is often necessary for the research firm to do a manual search (which often costs extra). It is also common for misdemeanor and felony records to be kept in different places, which could also lead to higher fees for separate searches. [Merry Mayer, *Background Checks in Focus,* HR Magazine, Jan. 2002, at p. 59]

A comparatively new problem, affecting companies with defense contracts, is the question of security clearance. So many applications have been filed that the federal background-checking staff had a 12-month backlog of 423,000 applications as of February 2004. Depending on the level of clearance required for a task, the background check could be anything from a superficial review of references to an in-depth investigation, complete with interviews with contacts and a polygraph examination of the person being cleared. There is no general mechanism for a worker to obtain a security clearance on a prospective basis; clearances are performed only when someone already has a job requiring a clearance. Some employers cope with this potential catch-22 by hiring applicants with a military service background, who have already been cleared—or even by acquiring companies with workers who have clearances. The National Security Scholarship program encourages college juniors and seniors to get clearances before graduating, so offering internships to participants can also speed the clearance process. [Gary Fields, *Security Vetting of Employees Is Highly Prized,* Wall Street Journal, Feb. 24, 2004, at p. B1]

Forty-six million Americans have been convicted of some kind of criminal offense, so employers will often discover criminal records when they do background checks—even checks for the kind of entry-level jobs that parolees and people who have served their sentences are encouraged to apply for. It's a delicate situation—everyone wants ex-convicts to support themselves honestly instead of returning to a life of crime, but employers are understandably reticent about hiring them. Prisoner advocates say that instead of using background checks to enforce a zero-tolerance policy, employers should consider whether the conviction was relevant to the job. The Fair Credit Reporting Act requires employers to provide a copy of the credit report if they reject an applicant for having a conviction, but it's easy for employers to say that the application was rejected for a different reason. The FCRA does not apply to searches that the employer does itself (for example, by searching Internet databases). [Ann Zimmerman and Kortney Stringer, *As Background Checks Proliferate, Ex-Cons Face Jobs Lock*, Wall Street Journal, Aug. 26, 2004, at p. B1]

§ 23.09 NONDISCRIMINATORY HIRING

Federal law bans discrimination in employment, which definitely includes hiring. Discrimination on account of age, sex, race, disability, religion, and/or national origin is banned. However, even a company that strives to avoid deliberate prejudice can find it hard to eradicate "disparate impact"—apparently neutral practices that actually disadvantage members of one group more than others. For instance, a minimum height requirement screens out more women and certain ethnic groups than white males. That does not mean that employers cannot impose height requirements, as long as it really is necessary to be taller than a certain height to do the job properly.

Other potential sources of disparate impact include:

- Educational standards;
- Preemployment testing;
- Requirements of military service;
- Referrals from your current workforce (who tend to know people of their own ethnic group);
- Rules about facial hair (which could disadvantage religious applicants, or black men who have ingrown hairs that make shaving painful);
- Refusing to hire anyone who has ever been arrested, filed for bankruptcy, or had a child out of wedlock.

Your attorney should review hiring practices to make sure that they are not discriminatory and that all requirements can be justified in terms of the practical needs of the business and skills that will actually be used on the job. For each position, you should also determine the physical capacities that are central to the job, those that are sometimes used but are peripheral, and those that are never invoked by the job.

If employees request flextime (for parenting needs, as an accommodation to disability, as a religious accommodation, or simply for convenience), you should either be able to grant the request or demonstrate a legitimate business reason why conventional business hours or standard shifts must be observed.

There are two important criteria for assessing interview questions:

- Do the questions relate to legitimate workplace issues, rather than just satisfying curiosity?
- Are they asked uniformly, rather than only to a group of people chosen on the basis of preconceived notions? For instance, it is discriminatory to ask a woman if her husband "lets" her travel on business, but not discriminatory to discuss the amount of travel required with all applicants, including the number of overnight or prolonged stays required, and to ask all candidates if they are able to travel that much.

Equal employment opportunity law assumes that many candidates will be interviewed for each opening, and there are many reasons why the successful candidate will be selected. There is no reason to collect a great deal of information about candidates who have no real chance of selection. Therefore, some questions are acceptable when a conditional job offer is made that would not be allowed at a first-stage interview.

For instance, marital status and having children are very relevant to participation in an employee group health plan, but irrelevant if the person is not going to get a job offer. So this information should either be requested only after hiring, or collected on a separate sheet of paper and not consulted until after hiring. [See § 36.09 for a discussion of acceptable and unacceptable pre-employment inquiries and tests in the disability context]

It is not acceptable to ask an interviewee about his or her history of receiving Worker's Compensation benefits, but anyone who gets a conditional job offer can be asked about past injuries that may require accommodation.

There are also circumstances under which the company's commitment to equal employment opportunity must be put into writing: if the company is a federal contractor, for instance.

The majority of the states have laws protecting employment and other rights of smokers and persons who engage in other lawful pursuits. However, in the states that do not, some companies are refusing to hire smokers (even if they only smoke away from the workplace). They could do pre-employment nicotine testing, or test employees. The rationale is cutting health benefit costs and maintaining a healthier workforce. [Tresa Baldas, *Heat Rises Over "No Smokers Hired" Policy*, Nat'l Law Journal, Jan. 25, 2005 (law.com); the case of *Grusendorf v. City of Oklahoma City*, 816 F.2d 539 (10th Cir. 1989), allows an employer, for health and safety reasons, to forbid employees to smoke even off-premises]

§ 23.10   PRE-EMPLOYMENT TESTING

[A] Permissible Testing

It is legitimate for an employer to test job applicants to see if they have relevant skills. Title VII permits the use of professionally developed ability tests that are not designed or administered with a discriminatory motive. A valid test is one that is neither explicitly nor implicitly discriminatory against protected groups; one that tests skills that are actually used in the job; and one that has been validated by psychologists or other experts so that it really offers insight into the issues needed for effective hiring.

A Supreme Court case, *Albemarle Paper Co. v. Moody* [422 U.S. 407 (1975)] holds that if a test has a disproportionate negative effect on a minority group, the test is permissible only if professionally accepted methods verify the test's ability to predict important elements of work behavior. As *Griggs v. Duke Power Co.* [401 U.S. 424 (1971)] says, the point of pre-employment testing is to measure the applicant's performance in the context of a specific job, not in the abstract. Even if the company's pre-employment test is valid, it is discriminatory to give the test only to minority-group members.

[B] Validating a Test

If your company adopts a pre-employment test and monitors the results, discovering that the test has an adverse impact on women and/or members of minority groups, then you should either get rid of the test, change it to remove the adverse impact, or do a validity study that confirms both that the test is a business necessity and that it accurately predicts the skills needed for successful job performance. The Civil Rights Act of 1991 [Pub. L. No. 102-166] says that it is not acceptable to grade minority applicants' tests on a "curve," or to have a lower passing grade for minorities.

Publications about psychological testing are good for finding out which tests have already been validated. Three types of validation are accepted:

- Criterion-related (the test is an accurate predictor of work behavior or other criteria of employee adequacy);
- Content-related (the test accurately duplicates the tasks that will actually be called for in the workplace);
- Construct-related (the test identifies general mental and psychological traits needed to do the job, such as the ability to remain cool under pressure and respond courteously to angry customers).

§ 23.11   IMMIGRATION ISSUES

[A] Employment Requirement

Although it is hard to specify exactly how many illegal immigrants are working in the United States, the Pew Hispanic Center estimates that there are 7.2 million undocumented workers. This is 5% of the whole workforce, but some industries have a much larger percentage of illegals—perhaps 20% of cooks, 22% of maids and cleaners, 27% of meat processing workers, and 29% of agricultural workers.

The Department of Homeland Security is testing a project, Basic Pilot, to verify names and Social Security numbers submitted by employers against government databases. Basic Pilot is designed to identify Social Security numbers that do not match up with names, but the system is not sophisticated enough to detect better organized forms of identity theft. Under current law, employers have an obligation to get copies of documents from new hires, but are not required to verify the accuracy of the documents. [June Kronholz, *Business Groups Fault U.S. Plan to Identify Illegal Workers*, Wall Street Journal, Mar. 16, 2006, at p. B1]

Most estimates indicate that the volume of illegal immigration has increased in most years since 1992, but administrative actions against businesses for employing illegal aliens, once fairly common, have been almost discontinued since 2000. In 1999, the agency then known as the INS assigned 9% of its personnel to workplace enforcement; the current Bureau of Immigration and Customs Enforcement assigns only 4% of its staff to that task. Fines for employing illegal immigrants sometimes are as low as $275 per worker, and the Bureau of Immigration is receptive to downward negotiations. [Eduardo Porter, *The Search for Illegal Immigrants Stops at the Workplace*, New York Times, Mar. 5, 2006, at Business at p. 3]

Before the September 11 attack, the focus was on making sure that employers hired only noncitizens who were permitted to work in this country. Since then, the focus has shifted more in the direction of security, and there has been a crackdown on people who overstay their visas.

If an alien wishes to enter this country on the basis of employment, he or she must not only have a definite job offer from a U.S. employer, but the employer must have "labor certification." [<http://workforcesecurity.doleta.gov/foreign/hiring.asp>] That is, the Department of Labor must certify that the job is "open" because the company cannot recruit a qualified U.S. worker at the prevailing wages. First, the employer must use the State Employment Service and post and advertise the job opportunity. The employer must interview any applicants who come through that route, and must file a recruitment report with the DOL explaining why none of those applicants was suitable for the position.

However, certain occupations are considered "shortage" occupations because of a documented difficulty in filling the jobs: nursing, physical therapy, and people of demonstrated exceptional ability in business, science, or the arts. Multinational executives, outstanding university-level teachers, researchers, and people whose jobs are in the national interest do not displace American workers, so labor certification will not be required for such jobs.

[B]   Immigration Categories

Employment-based immigration is regulated under the Immigration Act of 1990. [Pub. L. No. 101-649] There are various categories of employable immigrants, e.g.:

- Priority workers individuals of extraordinary ability and/or vocational responsibility;

- Professionals with advanced degrees and/or exceptional ability;
- Other workers (skilled workers, professionals without advanced degrees; unskilled workers who have DOL certification that there is a shortage of U.S. workers with similar skills);
- Special immigrants (e.g., religious workers sent to the U.S. by a religious hierarchy);
- Immigrants who have the financial capacity to invest at least $1 million within the United States, employing at least 10 U.S. workers;
- H-1B "specialty occupation" workers who reside temporarily within the United States, and work here, but do not become citizens;
- H-2 temporary non-agricultural workers.

The Save Our Small and Seasonal Businesses Act of 2005 is Title IV of P.L. 109-13. It changes the calculation of the number of H-2B visas that will be allowed, restricts the entrance of H-2B visa holders to only half the number during the first half of the fiscal year, and raises the penalties for misconduct by employers. Under Proposed Regulations, the original two-step application process has been reduced to a single form that employers e-mail to the Department of Homeland Security to certify compliance with the requirements. [Proposed Regulations: 70 Fed. Reg. 3983 (Jan. 27, 2005)] Another provision of P.L. 109-13 allows up to 10,500 Australians to receive non-immigrant E visas based on employers' attestations that they are needed for specialty occupations.

[C] Employer Responsibilities

U.S. labor and immigration law places a burden on the employer (or on an agency that gets a fee for recruitment or making referrals) to determine whether job applicants are legally permitted to work in this country. No later than three business days after hiring, the employer must ascertain if the new hire is a U.S. citizen or a legal immigrant who is not only permitted to reside in this country but to work here.

The employer responsibilities stem from the Immigration Reform and Control Act of 1986 (IRCA). [7 U.S.C. § 1324a] The employer is responsible for checking documents presented by potential new employees to demonstrate their identity and authorization to work within the United States. (There are people who are lawfully permitted to enter and reside in this country, but not to work here, so there is more to the matter than distinguishing illegal aliens from lawful immigrants.)

The information must be obtained in a way that is not discriminatory against dark-skinned people, or people whose first language is not English.

Both the U.S. Citizenship and Immigration Services (USCIS) and the DOL are entitled to inspect a company's immigration-related forms, but to enter a workplace they must either have a warrant or give 72 hours' notice.

Employment of immigrants requires the employer to work with both the DOL's Employment and Training Administration and the USCIS, which is part of the Department of Homeland Security. Employers can obtain permission to hire foreign workers on either a temporary (e.g., nurses; seasonal agricultural workers; specialized professional workers) or a permanent basis, depending on the facts of the case and the conditions within the U.S. labor market. The overarching policy is that employment of a foreign worker depends on proof that there is a shortage preventing the hiring of U.S. workers for the job. Furthermore, the law requires lawful immigrant workers to receive at least the prevailing wage for their jobs, so immigrant workers cannot be used to depress wages.

Labor certification is the process of petitioning DOL's Employment and Training Administration; the ETA certifies to the USCIS that permitting the person the employer wishes to hire is appropriate because no U.S. worker is available to fill the job. The application is ETA Form 9089, Alien Employment Certification, describing the job duties, qualifications, and experience required. The employer must obtain a prevailing wage determination from the state work-force agency.

After labor certification is obtained, the employer files USCIS Form I-140, Immigrant Petition for an Alien Worker, on behalf of the alien worker. [The DOL's explanation of the process can be found at *Hiring Foreign Workers*, <http://www.workforcesecurity.doleta.gov/foreign/hiring.asp> and *Permanent Labor Certification*, USCIS has published *The Form I-9 Process in a Nutshell*, <http://uscis.gov/graphics/servicds/employerinfo/EIB102.pdf> (Oct. 7, 2005) as a guide to the process]

It is illegal to knowingly hire an ineligible person. Knowledge includes constructive knowledge (reasonable inferences from facts and circumstances, to the degree that a person acting with reasonable care would have to be aware). According to USCIS regulations [*see* 8 C.F.R. § 274a], these circumstances create an inference of constructive knowledge:

- The employer actually has some information that the person is not eligible for U.S. employment;
- The applicant refuses to complete the I-9 form, or does it improperly;
- The employer acts with "reckless and wanton disregard" of the consequences of hiring ineligible persons.

However, accent and appearance are not acceptable sources of constructive knowledge. Once the employer knows that the hiree is (or has become, because of a change of status) ineligible to work in the United States, continuing employment is unlawful. [*See* 8 U.S.C. § 1324a]

Presidential Executive Order 12989 [61 Fed. Reg. 6091 (Feb. 13, 1996)] debars federal contractors from getting further federal contracts after they have been caught knowingly hiring illegal aliens.

The Seventh Circuit tackled an unusual immigration-related issue in mid-2003. An HR administrator was fired after three years' tenure. She brought suit under Title VII, charging racial and national origin discrimination and also charged that state law was violated by retaliating against her for complying with immigration law. Her argument was that Illinois state law forbids firing someone who tries to keep undocumented workers off the payroll. The plaintiff claimed that the Social Security Administration notified the employer that some of the W-2 forms it submitted did not have valid Social Security numbers. The plaintiff investigated, and attributed the problem to employees who furnished falsified numbers. The plaintiff's boss told her to send letters to the employees in question. The plaintiff said that she refused to do this because it was illegal, and subsequently suffered retaliatory discharge.

The District Court said that a federal statute [8 U.S.C. § 1324b(a)(5)] provided a complete remedy, and therefore the state-law retaliatory discharge claim was preempted. But the Seventh Circuit held that the District Court was wrong about this. That federal law forbids retaliation for complaining about national origin or citizenship discrimination. The plaintiff, however, claimed that she was trying to prevent the company from employing illegal aliens—a different situation altogether. However, the Seventh Circuit did not find that she had a valid claim under state law, because the plaintiff did not have the power to enforce her personal interpretation of immigration law; and her employer merely followed directions from the Social Security Administration. Furthermore, immigration law is an inherent area of federal power, with no role for state law. [*Arres v. IMI Cornelius Remcor, Inc.,* 333 F.3d 812 (7th Cir. 2003)]

[D] Employment Verification Documents

Hired individuals prove their eligibility to work within the United States either by showing that they are U.S. citizens (e.g., showing a U.S. passport or birth certificate evidencing birth within the United States) or by showing that they have a so-called green card. (The document, Form I-551, is no longer actually green.)

Since 1997, the Immigration and Naturalization Service has issued Form I-766, a tamper-resistant card issued to aliens whose immigration status permits work within the United States. The I-766 is a List A Employment Authorization Document (EAD): that is, it establishes both the job applicant's identity and his or her entitlement to work.

There are three categories of documents. List A documents can be used to prove both identity and employability; List B documents prove identity only; List C documents prove employability only.

A DOL Proposed Rule establishes a 45-day window during which employers must file an application with the Department of Homeland Security after labor certification has been granted for a particular non-citizen worker. However, the application is not transferable, and a new labor certification application must be filed if the person for whom the certification was applied for is unavailable to take the job. Previous practice accommodated the long period for getting approval by allowing substitutions. [71 Fed. Reg. 7655 (Feb. 13, 2006); *see DOL Proposes Barring Name Substitutions by Employers on Green Card Applications*, 74 L.W. 2492 (Feb. 21, 2006)]

[E] H-1B Visas

The H-1B visa is a non-immigrant visa for temporary workers in "specialty occupations." This means jobs that apply a highly specialized body of knowledge in both a theoretical and a practical way. Most H-1B visa holders work in high-tech businesses, such as software development. The initial duration of the visa is three years, although it can be extended for three more years. The worker must have at least a bachelor's degree in his or her specialty field, or must have equivalent qualifications and expertise. If the job requires a state license, the visa holder must have the license.

H-1B workers must be paid either the salary the employer would otherwise pay for the job, or the prevailing wage in the area. This requirement is designed to prevent employers from hiring foreign workers simply to lower wage costs. Willful violation of this requirement or the layoff requirement can be penalized by a $35,000 fine and three years' debarment from federal contracts.

Employers usually recruit workers from foreign students in the United States on student visas and about to graduate from a program that gives them the necessary specialized skills. Immigration law requires the employer to wait until the student graduates before making a job offer. You can get around this problem by having the student get permission from the Immigration and Naturalization Services to add a year of PGPT (post-graduate practical training) to his or her student visa, so you can apply for the H-1B visa during this extra year. The holders of student visas are required to leave the United States by July of the year in which they graduate, unless they have PGPT authorization.

The American Competitiveness and Workforce Improvement Act of 1998 (ACWIA) [Pub. L. No. 105-277] modifies the H-1B visa process. [*See* DOL Interim Final Regulations, 65 Fed. Reg. 80109 (Dec. 20, 2000)]

H-1B visa holders may not be hired until the employer has first attempted to recruit qualified U.S. workers, although a more qualified H-1B applicant can legitimately be preferred to a less-qualified U.S. citizen. Employers are also forbidden to terminate U.S. workers for the purpose of replacing them with H-1B workers. Temporary agencies and other suppliers of contingent workers are forbidden to make any placements of H-1B workers with any company that has displaced U.S. workers.

The DOL regulation not only protects U.S. jobs, it protects the H-1B workers from exploitation. They must be given benefits on the same basis as their U.S. counterparts. Whenever their employer places them in a nonproductive category (e.g., there is a temporary lull in work), they must be kept at full salary. It is unlawful for employers to require H-1B workers to reimburse them for the cost of filing the employment petition, or to penalize workers for terminating their work assignment prematurely.

To encourage reporting of misconduct, protection is extended to applicants, employees, and ex-employees who assist the Departments of Labor and Justice in their investigations. In fact, H-1B whistleblowers can be permitted to remain in the United States for up to six years.

Also see the H-1B Visa Reform Act of 2004, enacted as part of P.L. 108-447, the appropriations act. Up to 20,000 H-1B visas can be granted exempt from the cap of 65,000 per year that would otherwise apply. Visa holders under the exemption must have a Master's or higher degree from a U.S. educational institution. There is a filing fee of $2,300 or $3,000 per application (the higher fee is imposed on companies with more than 25 employees), and the application can be expedited and processed within 15 days if the $1,000 premium processing fee is paid. Interim Final Rules were published in mid-2005. [70 Fed. Reg. 23775 (May 5, 2005), discussed at 73 L.W. 2636, 2666. *See also* <http://www.foreignlaborcert.doleta/gov/foreign/h01b.asp>]

[F]   Case Law on Immigration Issues in Employment

Undocumented aliens are employees entitled to vote in representation elections, even if their status has been challenged under the IRCA. [*NLRB v. Kolkka,* 170 F.3d 937 (9th Cir. 1999)] But an illegal alien is not an "employee" for Worker's Compensation purposes, and therefore cannot receive Comp benefits for an on-the-job injury. [*Granados v. Windson Development Corp.,* 257 Va. 103, 509 S.E.2d 290 (1999)], or back pay in a suit alleging unlawful layoff. [*Hoffman Plastic Products Inc. v. NLRB,* 535 U.S. 137 (2002)]

The New York Supreme Court (in New York, that is an intermediate rather than the state's highest court) ruled in 2004 that undocumented aliens can bring suit in state court for wages lost as a result of work-related injuries. This case treated immigration status as merely a factor to be considered with respect to future lost wages. The *Hoffman* case was not applied, because that was a federal case dealing with back pay; this was a state court case involving future wages. [*Celi v. 42nd St. Develop. Project, Inc.,* No. 37491/01 (N.Y.Sup. 2004), discussed in Mark Faas, *Illegal Immigrant Ruled Able to Sue for Lost Earnings from On-the-Job Injuries,* New York Law Journal, Nov. 19, 2004 (law.com); *Majlinger v. Cassino Contracting Corp.,* 802 N.Y.S.2d 56 (N.Y.A.D. 2005) also allows an injured illegal worker to recover back wages in a tort suit on the grounds that federal immigration law was not intended to cover tort suits, nor should employers be protected from liability for one form of wrongdoing (having an unsafe workplace) because they committed another form of wrongdoing (hiring illegal workers)] Two slightly later New York cases require the awards of lost wages to be based on home-country, not U.S., wages. The Appellate Division reached this conclusion from a policy determination that undocumented workers should be encouraged to pursue any valid claims they have against their employers—but they should not be given a windfall. [*Sanango v. 200 East 16th St. Housing Corp.* (N.Y.A.D. Dec. 28, 2004), *Balbuena v. IDR Realty LLC* (N.Y.A.D. Dec. 28, 2004), both 73 LW 1396; *Cano v. Mallory Management*, 195 Misc. 2d 666 (N.Y. Sup. 2003) (denies a motion to dismiss a negligence action brought by an illegal immigrant worker)]

It was an unfair labor practice to contact the INS right after the union won an election, telling eleven employees that they could not work until they straightened out their immigration status. This was a departure from the employer's normal practice. The NLRB said that, although IRCA compliance is important, it must not be used as a smokescreen for anti-union animus. [*Nortech Waste,* 336 N.L.R.B. 79 (2001)] In 2004, the Seventh Circuit ruled that employees cannot state a RICO claim by alleging that the employer deliberately hired illegal aliens to keep wages down. In such a situation, the defendant company is the "enterprise," so there is no one for it to conspire with for RICO purposes. [*Baker v. IBP Inc.,* 357 F.3d 685 (7th Cir. 2004)] The Eleventh Circuit, however, disagreed, ruling that both RICO and state law claims were raised by allegations that the employer conspired with temporary agencies to hire illegal workers and use false documentation, with the objective of lowering wages and escaping Worker's Compensation responsibilities. The Supreme Court granted certiorari in December of 2005, but dismissed certiorari as improvidently granted in June 2006 and sent the case back to the 11th Circuit to resolve some minor issues. [*Williams v. Mohawk Industries Inc.,* 411 F.3d 1252 (11th Cir. 2005), *cert. granted but dismissed as improvidently granted,* No. 05-465 (June 5, 2006)]

[G]   EEOC/DOJ Memorandum of Understanding

Under the Memorandum of Understanding (MOU) between the EEOC and the Department of Justice's Office of Special Counsel for Immigration Related Unfair Employment Practices [*see* 63 Fed. Reg. 5518 (Feb. 3, 1998)] each agency can act as the other's agents to receive complaints about immigration-related discrimination charges. The two agencies will coordinate to limit duplication of efforts. Document abuse, intimidation, and retaliation will be treated as immigration-related unfair labor practices. The EEOC has agreed not to ask if the charging party is a U.S. citizen, national, or work-authorized alien as a condition for referring charges to the DOJ.

However, according to the Fourth Circuit, only a citizen or an alien with a valid work visa is a "qualified" employee who can make out a Title VII prima facie case. [*Egbuna v. Time-Life Libraries Inc.,* 153 F.3d 184 (4th Cir. 1998)]

On October 26, 1999, the EEOC issued "Enforcement Guidance on Remedies for Undocumented Workers Under Laws Prohibiting Employment Discrimination," No. 915.002. At that time, the EEOC took the position that undocumented workers would be entitled to hiring, reinstatement, and back pay if they were victims of discrimination as defined by the ADEA, ADA, or EPA, to the extent the remedies could be provided consistently with IRCA and other immigration laws. At that time, the EEOC view was that antidiscrimination laws protect all workers, and employers should not be given encouragement to violate such laws, compounding their wrongdoing in hiring undocumented workers at all.

However, after the Supreme Court rendered its *Hoffman Plastics* decision, the EEOC rescinded the Enforcement Guidance. [*See* <http://www.eeoc.gov/docs/undoc-rescind.html>] But also see a General Counsel memo from NLRB General Counsel Arthur F. Rosenfeld, in which he informs regional office personnel that undocumented aliens are nonetheless employees, so an employer is still liable for unfair labor practices against them. Undocumented workers can vote in elections under NLRB supervision. If an employer knowingly hired an undocumented worker and then fired that person, the NLRB can order the worker's reinstatement, if the worker can satisfy the IRCA requirements. However, a back pay award is ruled out by *Hoffman Plastics*. [<http://www.nlrb.gov/gcmemo/gc02-06.html>]

§ 23.12   ADA COMPLIANCE IN HIRING

The ADA protects qualified individuals with a disability. The employer must determine whether to extend a job offer to a candidate with a disability, a question that includes consideration of accommodations that may be needed in the course of employment. Some pre-employment inquiries are simply unacceptable; others are permissible only after a conditional job offer has been made.

The EEOC's Technical Assistance Manual for implementation of the ADA defines these pre-hire questions as improper:

- Have you ever been treated for these diseases?
- Have you ever been hospitalized? Why?
- Are there any health factors that prevent you from doing the job you applied for? (However, if the inquiry is restricted to specific job functions, it is permissible to ask about ability to perform those particular functions, and about potential accommodations.)
- How much sick leave did you take last year?
- Are you taking any prescribed medications?
- Have you ever been treated for substance abuse?

When it comes to pre-employment testing, it is discriminatory to give a test in a form or manner that requires the use of an impaired sensory, speaking, or manual skill, unless the point of the test is the degree to which that skill is present. So an assembly-line job may legitimately require manual dexterity. But if the point is to test keyboarding speed, a hearing-impaired person may have to be given a test that includes nonverbal commands as to when to start and stop. It may be necessary to have a test read aloud to a blind or dyslexic person, or to have a sign language interpreter. Every effort should be made to administer the test in a room that is wheelchair-accessible.

> **Tip:** Tell applicants if there will be a test as part of the interview process. Then it is up to them to explain the nature of any accommodation they need to take the test.

Pre-employment medical examinations are allowed only if the candidate has already met the other criteria, and a conditional job offer has been extended. The examination must be required of everyone in that job category who gets a conditional offer. Once the offer has been made, it is acceptable to ask about past injuries and Worker's Compensation claims.

An unresolved legal issue is the extent to which employers can use hiring screening to eliminate persons who are not currently disabled, but are at risk of disability—for example, overweight workers or those who smoke. A Wal-Mart internal memo suggests adoption of a policy of altering job duties so that all jobs require physical exertion in order to discourage applicants who are restricted to sedentary work. [Ann Zimmerman, Robert Guy Matthews, and Kris Hudson, *Can Employers Alter Hiring Policies to Cut Health Costs?* Wall Street Journal, Oct. 27, 2005, at p. B1]

The Ninth Circuit reversed dismissal of privacy, ADA, and California Fair Employment and Housing Act (FEHA) claims brought by three HIV positive applicants for jobs as flight attendants. The applicants passed the initial selection process and were given conditional offers of employment, contingent on background checks and medical examinations, which included filling out medical histories and providing blood samples. When the applicants asked why the blood sample was taken, the nurse said that it was being checked for anemia. The applicants did not disclose their HIV positive status or the medications they took, although they completed forms that stated that failure to disclose medications or medical history, or false or fraudulent information, would be grounds for termination. Once the blood samples were taken, the job offers were rescinded.

The three brought suit on privacy and ADA and California FEHA grounds and the district court granted summary judgment for the airline, but the Ninth Circuit allowed the suit to proceed (except with respect to one plaintiff's claim of intentional infliction of emotional distress). The plaintiffs alleged that they were not told what the medical examination would entail. They were notified about, and only gave their consent to, urine testing. In the Ninth Circuit view, for a job offer to satisfy the requirements of the ADA and California law, the employer either must have completed all non-medical parts of the application process or be able to prove that it could reasonably have done so before making the offer. The ADA requires medical examinations (if given at all) to be a separate, second step of the selection process occurring only after all other selection issues have been resolved. The Ninth Circuit held that job applicants can keep their medical condition private until the last stage of the hiring process; at that point, they can decide whether or not to disclose the condition. Therefore, the Ninth Circuit held that the so-called conditional job offers were not real, because the applicants were required to undergo an immediate medical examination prematurely, while both medical and non-medical conditions on hiring remained. Although the airline testified that it had to streamline the application process to remain competitive with other airlines for applicants, the Ninth Circuit held that the airline failed to prove that there were no reasonable alternatives that would put the medical examination in its proper place—at the end of the selection process.

The California Constitution's right of privacy is broader than the federal one, because it imposes obligations on private parties as well as state actors. The appellants charged that the airline violated their privacy rights by performing blood tests without notice or consent. The court found that the blood tests implicated a protected privacy interest. Whether an expectation of privacy is reasonable is a fact question that can't be determined without a full trial, so summary judgment was inappropriate. Although the applicants consented to blood testing, they did not consent to any and all use that might be made of their blood samples, or to blood tests outside the ordinary and accepted range of pre-employment testing. However, claims of intentional infliction of emotional distress were dismissed, because there was no proof that the blood tests, even if illegal, were extreme or outrageous enough to violate norms of decency. [*Leonel v. American Airlines, Inc.,* 400 F.3d 702 (9th Cir. 2005)]

Post-offer medical examinations are considered nondiscriminatory, and therefore it is not necessary to provide proof of business necessity. But if the applicant with a disability is in fact qualified for the job, and the offer is withdrawn subsequent to the examination, the employer must show job-related business necessity for canceling the offer, and must also prove that reasonable accommodation to the disability could not be made without undue hardship.

In two late-2002 Advisory Letters, the EEOC warned against asking disability-related questions before extending at least a conditional job offer, giving as examples whether a person is diabetic, takes prescription drugs, or has used illegal drugs or been in drug rehabilitation in the past. After an offer has been made, the employer can conduct a test of physical ability. Physical ability and fitness tests are not considered medical if they do not include medical factors such as measuring heart rate and blood pressure. However, if the test is used to screen for disability, the test must be job-related and justified by business necessity. [*See* 71 L.W. 2536 (2002)]

In late 2005, the EEOC issued an Advisory Letter stating that there is an exception to the ADA's ban on disability-related inquiries before making a job offer if the employer has an affirmative action program for people with disabilities. To qualify, the employer's program must include an interview that gives the person with a disability a real opportunity to compete for a job; the information sought must not be greater than what is needed to determine eligibility for the interview; and the applicant must voluntarily provide the information. [EEOC Advisory Letter, <http://www.eeoc.gov/policy/docs/preemp.html> (Nov. 8, 2005)]

For active employees, medical examinations and inquiries about the nature and severity of disability can be required only if they are job-related and consistent with business necessity: For instance, someone has been ill or injured, and the question is fitness to return to work.

The ADA also requires disability-related information to be kept confidential. In fact, it should be collected and maintained on separate forms, and even stored in files separate from general personnel information, although there are certain exceptions to the general rule of confidentiality:

- Supervisors and managers can be informed about work restrictions or accommodations that are needed;
- If emergency treatment might be required for a disabled employee (e.g., an epileptic might have a seizure; a diabetic might go into insulin shock or coma), first aid and safety personnel can be informed, so they will be prepared;
- A special post-September 11 rule allows collection of information about special needs for evacuation in an emergency;
- Government officials investigating ADA compliance are entitled to information about the number of employees with disabilities, and the nature of the disabilities.

EARN is the Department of Labor's Employee Assistant Referral Network [<http://www.earnworks.com>], a resource for putting employers in touch with qualified individuals with disabilities. DOL also maintains a Job Accommodation Network for information about how to make workplace accommodations affordable. [<http://www.jan.wvu.edu] The DOL points out that even in the boom times of the 1990s, only about 48% of persons with disabilities were employed. But one in five Americans has a disability, and the BLS projects that there will be only 20 million workers available to fill 55 million new jobs by 2008, so employers will have to become more flexible about finding talent in unconventional places.

The tax code provides various employer incentives, such as the § 44 disabled access credit, available for small businesses that make their premises accessible; and the § 190 barrier removal deduction for removing physical, structural, and transportation barriers on business premises. The § 190 deduction can be taken by any size business, but is not available for construction of new premises, only retrofitting; it is limited to $15,000 a year, but larger amounts can be depreciated.

§ 23.13   CREDIT REPORTING IN THE HIRING PROCESS

A federal law, the Fair Credit Reporting Act (FCRA) [15 U.S.C. § 1681a *et seq.*], as amended by the Consumer Credit Reporting Reform Act of 1996

(CCRRA) [Pub. L. No. 104-208], governs the use of credit reports and investigative credit reports not only for making loans and approving credit card applications, but in the employment context as well.

The FCRA provides that a consumer report is a written or oral communication from a consumer reporting agency, dealing with a consumer's entitlement to credit, "character, general reputation, personal characteristics, or mode of living."

An investigative credit report is different in that it involves personal interviews with people who have personal knowledge of the individual. The CCRRA requires employers to give job applicants a written disclosure statement, and to get their consent in writing, before requesting either a consumer report or an investigative consumer report. Furthermore, if the employer wants an investigative report, it must explain to the applicant (via a written disclosure mailed no later than three days after the report is requested) that this type of report covers matters like character and conduct.

The FCRA [see 15 U.S.C. § 1681b(3)(B)] says that "employment purposes" are legitimate reasons for requesting a credit report or investigative credit report. "Employment purposes" means "evaluating a consumer for employment, promotion, reassignment or retention as an employee." Because the FCRA specifically authorizes the use of credit reporting information in the hiring process, doing so is not employment discrimination.

An "adverse action" includes "denial of employment or any other decision for employment purposes that adversely affects any current or prospective employee." When the credit report is negative, leading to adverse action, the employer must provide oral, written, or electronic (for instance, fax or e-mail) notice of the adverse action. It must also explain how to review the credit report file, correct errors (the negative report might refer to someone else with a similar name, or someone who has appropriated the job applicant's identity) and contest items that the consumer believes to be untrue. Notice must be given after the employer makes the decision, but before the adverse action is implemented.

The CCRRA also imposes an obligation on the employer. Before it gets any reports from a reporting agency, it must give the agency a statement that the employer complies with the various consumer protection requirements of credit reporting law.

As a result of a later statute, the FACTA (Fair and Accurate Credit Transactions Act of 2003; Pub. L. N. 108-159), 15 U.S.C. § 1681a has been amended to add a new subsection (x). Under the new law, a communication is not treated as a consumer report—and therefore is not subject to the FCRA requirements—if the purpose of the communication is job-related and not related to the person's creditworthiness.

To qualify for the FACTA exemption, the communication must be made to an employer as part of an investigation of suspected employment-related misconduct, or in compliance with laws or regulations (including the rules of a self-regulatory organization such as a stock exchange), or under the employer's pre-existing written policies. Reports of this type must not be disclosed to anyone except the employer or its agents, government officials, or self-regulatory organizations, unless disclosure is mandated by law. Furthermore, once the employer gets the information, if the information is the basis of any adverse action against the person, the employer must provide the person with a summary of the communication—but does not have to disclose the sources furnishing the information.

CHAPTER 24

RECORDKEEPING

§ 24.01   INTRODUCTION

[A]   Employer Responsibility in General

Employee records are important in setting compensation, assuring that it is paid appropriately, and administering benefit plans. Proper records are necessary to handle insurance matters, comply with court orders, fill out tax returns and other government documents, and demonstrate EEO and immigration compliance.

In addition to determining its internal needs for gathering, processing, and deleting information, the company must be aware of legal requirements for record retention, and limitations on document destruction. Destroying documents that are subject to discovery in a court case is at least a civil offense, and may constitute contempt of court or even a criminal offense, depending on circumstances.

In a 2003 Ninth Circuit case, a participant in an ERISA pension plan sought information about fees that the plan paid to its service providers. The participant sued under ERISA § 104(b)(4), covering documents that the plan must provide on written request. The court dismissed that claim, holding that the ERISA provision applies only to the instruments under which the plan is established or operated. However, the court found that the fiduciaries violated § 107 (the statutory provision governing recordkeeping) and general fiduciary principles. Because the plaintiff was only asking for equitable relief, not monetary damages, it was not necessary to prove monetary losses suffered by the plan as a result of the alleged violation. [*Shaver v. Operating Eng. Local 428 Pension Trust Fund,* 332 F.3d 1198 (9th Cir. 2003)]

All documents in personnel files should be date-stamped when they are received, because it may be necessary to determine what was in the file at a particular time.

> **Tip:** If it is legal and practical to destroy a document, make sure that all paper copies have been destroyed, as well as all computer files (including back-ups, copies on disks, and data uploaded to an Internet site for safekeeping). Just because someone has deleted a file does not mean that it has even been removed from that computer, much less from the entire network.

Many of the states have laws that guarantee employees access to their own employment records. If your state has such a law, check to see if ex-employees are entitled to access, or if only current employees do.

Whether the records are on paper or electronic, the goal of the corporate record retention policy should be to store and manage information on- and off-site in a systematic and cost effective manner. When necessary, the system must be able to handle litigation-related requests for documents, and managing risk. The policy must satisfy the statutory and regulatory requirements for record retention, applicable statutes of limitations, and best practices for business. Publicly traded companies are subject to additional requirements imposed by the Sarbanes-Oxley

Act (for example, communications with the company's audit firm must be retained). The Public Company Accounting Oversight Board (PCAOB) requires accountants to retain audit work papers for at least seven years. Early in 2003, the SEC covered record retention issues in Exchange Act Release No. 47241.

A Sarbanes-Oxley provision enacted at 18 U.S.C. § 1519 calls for imprisonment of up to 20 years for knowing alteration, destruction, mutilation, falsification, or cover-up of records or documents with the intent to obstruct investigation of any matter under the jurisdiction of a federal department or agency. Even document destruction that occurred before a proceeding commenced can be prosecuted.

Courts have imposed major—even multi-million-dollar—sanctions on companies that destroyed key evidence in violation of court orders. Litigation parties that destroy evidence have also been precluded from introducing their own evidence as a penalty. It is increasingly clear that once litigation begins, a "litigation hold" should be placed on destruction of paper and electronic documents. Once the company becomes aware of impending litigation, employees should be informed of the possibility. They should receive copies of the relevant court orders, and be informed of the penalties for destruction of evidence.

However, if a company has a reasonable policy for when documents should be retained and when they should be destroyed, and the policy is consistently applied, then courts will probably find that it is unreasonable to expect the company to produce documents destroyed pursuant to the policy. If records are destroyed when the policy did not call for their destruction, then questions arise as to whether the documents were destroyed to prevent unfavorable revelations. [Robert L. Levy *"Is It OK to Throw Away These Papers?"—Legal and Ethical Considerations Regarding Record Retention Programs,* <http://www.haynesboone.com>]

Early in 2006, EBSA sought public comments on the reporting process, asking for information about whether the summary annual report requirements should be modified. [71 Fed. Reg. 9839 (Feb. 27, 2006)]

[B] 2002 DOL Final Rule

The Department of Labor published Final Rules Relating to Use of Electronic Communication and Recordkeeping Technologies by Employee Pension and Welfare Benefit Plans, updating 29 C.F.R. Part 2520, at 67 Fed. Reg. 17264 (Apr. 9, 2002). This document provides final rules under ERISA Title I for using electronic media to disclose benefit plan information to participants (a topic discussed in Chapter 27) and enacts a safe harbor for using electronic methods of disclosing and maintaining records. The Final Rule is effective October 9, 2002.

Under the Final Rule, electronic media can be used for maintenance and retention of records, if:

• The system has reasonable controls to ensure integrity, accuracy, authenticity, and reliability of the records.

- The records are maintained in reasonable order, in a safe and accessible place, so they can reasonably be inspected.
- The records can readily be converted into legible and readable hard copy from electronic form.
- The electronic data is labeled, securely stored, and backed up so it can be recovered if the main data repository is destroyed or corrupted.
- The employer retains paper copies of any data that cannot be seamlessly transferred to the electronic system.

The Final Rule permits destruction of paper records that have been transferred without error to the electronic system, unless there is a requirement (under the terms of the plan or an applicable law) that duplicate or substitute records be maintained in paper form.

On the practical side, it should also be noted that properly archived paper records are very durable and are immediately accessible—which is not the case with records stored on obsolete electronic storage media such as IBM Mag Cards, 8¼″ floppy disks, or eight-track tapes, especially if they also use obsolete software programs or very early software versions that are no longer supported by their vendors.

On July 14, 2005, the Department of the Treasury proposed regulations covering the use of electronic media in employee benefit notices, elections, and consent forms for qualified plans, accident and health plans, and plans such as health savings accounts and medical savings accounts. A notice can be given electronically rather than by paper hard copy if the employee consents, or if the situation fits one of the statutory exemptions. Notice to obtain employee consent must disclose the subject matter of the communication, what the extent of the consent is, how to update contact information, how to withdraw consent, and how to request a paper copy of the document. There is an exemption when the recipient is able to access the electronic medium and has been informed that a paper hard copy is available without charge. This proposal supplements the ERISA rules and does not apply to ERISA communications (e.g., SPDs and COBRA notices), which are under the jurisdiction of the DOL or PBGC. The Treasury announced that the proposal cannot be relied upon until it is finalized. [Tina M. Kuska and Mary K. Samsa, *Proposed Treasury Regulations Regarding the Use of Electronic Media for Employee Benefit Notices, Elections and Consents*, Gardner Carton & Douglas Client Memorandum (Aug. 2005), <http://www.gcd.com . . . >]

§ 24.02 OSHA RECORDS

[A] Injury and Illness Recordkeeping

Complying with the Occupational Safety and Health Act [*see* Chapter 31] requires constant accumulation of data on a day-by-day basis, followed by compilation of annual records.

Effective January 1, 2002, OSHA changed the reporting requirements found in 29 C.F.R. Part 1904 ("Recording and Reporting Occupational Injuries and Illnesses"). The new requirements are simplified, streamlined, and work better with computer technology than the old requirements. The new forms can be downloaded from <http://www.osha.gov> or ordered by telephone from the OSHA publication office at (202) 693-1888. The Final Rule appears at 66 Fed. Reg. 5916 (Jan. 19. 2001). Although most of the changes went into effect as scheduled, the effective date of the rules about hearing loss and reporting of musculoskeletal disorders were delayed until January 1, 2003. [*See* 66 Fed. Reg. 35113 (July 3, 2001)]

Under the prior rules, employers were required to make incident reports on Form 101, Supplementary Record of Occupational Injury and Illnesses. The replacement form is Form 301, the Injury and Illness Incident Report.

The prior rules called for the employer to collate all the 101 forms to create the annual Form 200, Log and Summary of Occupational Injuries and Illnesses. The new forms are 300, Log of Work-Related Injuries and Illnesses, and 300A, Summary of Work-Related Injuries and Illnesses. [*See* 29 C.F.R. § 1904.4]

The forms are used to report new cases of work-related illness or injury. The OSHA 301 Incident Report must be completed within seven calendar days of receiving information about the incident. The OSHA 300 log requires a short description of each incident. The OSHA 300-A summary is compiled at the end of the year, using this log.

All businesses have to make a report of OSHA if an incident in the workplace results in a death, or if three or more workers are hospitalized. However, it is not necessary for companies in low-hazard businesses such as retail, service, finance, real estate, or insurance to maintain OSHA illness and industry records unless OSHA specifically requests such records. [*See* <http://www.osha-slc.gov/OshStd_data/1904_New/1094_0002.html> for information about the exemption]

OSHA issued compliance manual CPL 2-0.131 in late 2001, which has been somewhat amended as CPL 02-00-135. [*Recordkeeping Policies & Procedures Manual* (Dec. 30, 2004), <http://www.osha.gov/pls/oshaweb/owadisp.show_ document [. . .], more easily reached by selecting "Recordkeeping" in the A-Z listing at the OSHA home page]

Tip: In a "privacy concern case" (e.g., one involving mental illness, sexual assault, HIV status, or other sensitive issues), the employee's name should not be entered on the OSHA 300 Log. Effective January 1, 2004, other illnesses can also be treated as privacy concern cases, and the employee's name omitted at the request of the employee. [68 Fed. Reg. 38607 (June 30, 2003)]

According to a standard interpretation letter posted on August 18, 2004, on the OSHA Web site, HIPAA does not require the employer to edit the

---

> OSHA 300 injury and illness log to remove employees' names before granting access to the data (for example, in response to a union request). [*See* 73 LW 2103]

[B] Asbestos, Lead, and Noise Monitoring Records

If the workplace noise level is high, the employer not only must monitor exposure, but must maintain records for two years. Records of employees' hearing tests must be retained at least as long as they work for the employer. Exposure monitoring records and asbestos and lead medical surveillance records should be retained for at least 30 years after termination of employment of the individual monitored.

Asbestos monitoring records should indicate:

- Each monitored employee's name, Social Security number, extent of exposure;
- If a respirator was worn; if so, what kind;
- Date the asbestos level was monitored;
- The workplace operation or process that was monitored;
- How the samples were taken and evaluated;
- Evidence supporting the scientific validity of the sampling methodology;
- How long the sampling process lasted; number of samples taken; sampling results.

For each employee subject to medical surveillance, the record should give his or her name and Social Security number, the employee reports of asbestos-related medical conditions; and a written report from the doctor who performs the surveillance, indicating whether the employee actually is suffering effects of asbestos exposure.

For testing of lead rather than asbestos, the employer must maintain written records of tests determining whether the ambient lead level exceeds the Permissible Exposure Limit (PEL). The test record should indicate:

- Name and Social Security number of each monitored employee;
- Date of the test;
- Area that was monitored;
- Previous airborne lead readings taken at the same place;
- Employee complaints that might be related to lead exposure;
- Any other evidence suggestive of lead exposure.

[C] OSHA Postings

Employers must post a notice of OSHA rights, as mandated by 29 C.F.R. § 1903.2(a). Failure to post is subject to a civil penalty of up to $7,000 per violation, but normally the penalty will be $1,000.

An employer who receives an OSHA citation must post a copy of the citation near each place where a violation occurred. The copy must be left in place for three working days or until the violation is corrected—whichever comes first. Posting is also required if the employer contests a citation or files a petition for modification of abatement. Failure to make these postings can result in a $1,000 fine.

§ 24.03   TITLE VII RECORDKEEPING AND NOTICE REQUIREMENTS

The Equal Employment Opportunity Commission (EEOC) requires companies with 100 or more employees to file an annual report. The Employer Information Report (EEO-1) is a simple two-page form that tracks the composition of the workforce. The due date is September 30 of each year. A copy of the most recent report must be kept on file at every company required to file (either at the "reporting unit" or the company's or division's headquarters). The EEOC also has the right to require other reports about employment practices if the agency thinks additional reports are necessary to carry out Title VII or the Americans With Disabilities Act.

Records of application forms, requests for accommodation, and other employment-related data must be preserved for one year. The one-year period starts either when the data is collected or the personnel action is taken, whichever is later. Personnel records of fired employees must also be kept for one year after employment ends. [Press Release, *Recordkeeping Guidance Clarifies Definition of "Job Applicant" for Internet and Related Technologies,* Mar. 3, 2004 <http://www.eeoc.gov/press-3-3-04.html>; a notice appeared in the March 4, 2004, Federal Register]

Late in 2005, a Final Rule was issued [70 Fed. Reg. 58,945 (Oct. 7, 2005)], with few differences from the proposal. Under the Final Rule, a person is considered an "Internet applicant" if the federal contractor accepts expressions of interest in a job through the Internet, e-mail, the employer's Web site, or a resume databank. The applicant must have used the Internet or related means to submit an expression of interest in the job; the contractor must have considered the person for a particular position; the expression of interest must have demonstrated that the applicant had at least the basic qualifications for the job; and the person must have never removed him- or herself from consideration for the job before receiving a job offer. Contractors are not required to maintain records of electronic expressions of interest unless the contractor actually considered the person for a particular job. Federal contractors are permitted to have rules under which they reject general expressions of interest in working for their company that are not submitted for a particular position. It also is lawful to reject expressions of interest that do not meet the contractor's requirements.

The EEOC proposed revisions to the EEO-1 form in mid-2003 [68 Fed. Reg. 34,965 (June 11, 2003)] and finalized them in late 2005 [70 Fed. Reg. 72,194 (Nov. 28, 2005)]. Except in cases in which the employer cannot get Internet access, filing must be done electronically; *see* the instructions at <http://www.eeoc.gov/ eeo1survey/howtofile.html>. The version of the report to be filed on or before September 30, 2006, is available at <https://apps.eeoc.gov.eeo1/eeo1.jsp>; the report format to be filed by September 30, 2007, can be found at <http://www.eeoc.gov/ eeo1/index.html>. *See* <http://www.eeoc.gov/eeo1/qanda.html> for guidance.

The revised EEO-1 form increases the five racial/ethnic categories to seven: There is a new "two or more races" category, and the "Asian or Pacific Islander" category has been divided into "Asian" and "Native Hawaiian or other Pacific Islander." The category "Black" has been changed to "Black or African American," "Hispanic" is now "Hispanic or Latino," and the job category of "Officials and Managers" has been divided into an Executive/Senior Level category and a First/Mid-Level Officials and Managers group. Business and financial occupations are now to be disclosed as Professionals rather than as Officials and Managers. The EEOC wants racial and ethnic categories to be determined by employees' self-identification, not visual identifications made by the employer.

If a discrimination charge is made, all records relating to the employment action involved in the charge must be retained until there has been a final disposition of the charge. According to 29 C.F.R. § 1602.14, this means that either the case is over, or the employee's time to sue has elapsed.

Users of pre-employment tests must maintain records about the validation of the test, including statistical studies to determine if the test has adverse impact on protected classes of applicants and employees.

Employers also have to make records that are relevant to charges of unlawful employment practices and maintain those records. [*See* 42 U.S.C. § 2000e-8(c)]

One of the many notices that must be posted in the workplace is the official EEOC notice about equal employment opportunity and how to file a charge. [42 U.S.C. § 2000e-10] If the employer willfully violates this requirement, a fine of up to $100 can be imposed for each separate offense.

§ 24.04   FMLA RECORDS

Federal law does not impose any specific form for keeping FMLA records, so any paper or electronic method can be used to record the necessary information:

- Basic payroll data for each employee, such as hours worked; pay rate; supplemental wages or wage deductions; total compensation paid;
- Dates on which FMLA leave was taken;
- Hours of leave (if less than a day was taken);
- Copies of the employee's notice to the employer of impending leave;
- Copies of the employer's disclosure materials about FMLA rights;
- Documentation of the employer's leave policy;
- Records of payment of premiums for employee benefit plans;
- Records of any dispute about when employees are entitled to leave or reinstatement after a leave.

> **Tip:** Because employee medical records, including certification of serious medical condition and fitness to return to work, are confidential, they should be kept physically separate from the employee's other records, to prevent unauthorized access to the data. [*See* § 26.07 about privacy requirements]

§ 24.05   IMMIGRATION RECORDS

The information collected to verify identity and eligibility to work in the United States [*see* § 23.11[D]] must be retained for three years after the date of hiring. Records should be retained for three years from the date of recruiting or referral with respect to applicants who were not hired or who did not accept a job offer. Certifications of employment eligibility furnished by state employment services must also be retained for three years. For former employees, the record-retention period is the later of three years after hiring, or one year after termination.

§ 24.06   EMPLOYMENT TAX RECORDS

Newly hired employees should be asked to provide a W-4 (withholding exemptions) form, so the appropriate number of exemptions can be used to withhold income taxes. An employee about to retire should be asked for Form W-4P to determine whether pension withholding should be done, and if so, in what amount.

IRS Publication 15, Employer's Tax Guide, requires at least the following information to be collected by the employer and made available for IRS review on request:

- Dates and amounts of all payments of wages and pensions;
- Fair market value of any wages paid other than in cash (e.g., in merchandise or services);
- Each employee's name, address, Social Security number, and job title;
- Dates each employee started and terminated employment;
- Dates and amounts of any payments made by the employer, or by an insurer or other third party, to employees who were out sick or injured;
- Copies of W-4 and W-4P forms;
- W-2 forms sent to employees but returned as undeliverable;
- Copies of all tax returns;
- Records of dates and amounts of tax deposits.

§ 24.07   UNEMPLOYMENT INSURANCE RECORDS

FUTA records must show the total amount of remuneration to employees in the calendar year, the amount of wages subject to tax, and the contributions made to the state unemployment insurance funds of each state in which the company does business. The records must be kept open to inspection by the IRS and state unemployment tax officials.

Records must be organized by pay period (dates the period starts and ends; total remuneration including commissions paid in the period) and by employee. The records to be kept for each worker include:

- Name;
- Social Security number;
- Date of hiring (or rehiring) and termination;
- Place of work;
- Wages for each payroll period;
- Wage rate;
- Date wages were paid;
- Amount of expense reimbursement granted;
- Time lost when worker was unavailable for work.

Although unemployment insurance information can be released to government agencies other than the employment security agency (child support enforcement agencies, for example), in general the information is confidential and should not be disclosed to unauthorized parties.

§ 24.08   RECORD-RETENTION REQUIREMENTS

Various state and federal laws require retention of records (about individual employees and summaries reflecting the entire corporate experience). The enterprise should draft its record-retention policies to comply with statutory requirements:

- Title VII: Personnel and employment records as well as EEO-1 reports must be kept for six months. Records relating to a discrimination charge must be retained until the charge is disposed of;
- Equal Pay Act: Records of a pay differential imposed on the basis of sex must be kept for two years;
- FMLA: Records must be retained for three years;
- FICA/FUTA: Records of withholding and paying these taxes must be retained for four years;
- ERISA: The record-retention period is six years;
- Federal contractors: Information about the employer's contractor status must be retained for three years;
- OSHA: The record-retention requirement for employee exposure to toxic substances is very long: 30 years;
- Tax records: The minimum retention period is four years;

- ADEA: 29 C.F.R. § 1627.3(b)(2) requires a benefit plan that is subject to the ADEA to be kept on file while the plan is in operation, and for at least one year after its termination.

Just as the IRS is developing methods of making the transition from a paper-based tax filing system to an electronic one, other government agencies are creating transition rules. The Department of Labor published final rules at 67 Fed. Reg. 17264 (Apr. 9, 2002), enacted as 29 C.F.R. § 2520.104b-1, creating a safe harbor for plans to store records and communicate with participants and beneficiaries in electronic form.

The PBGC followed up the general safe harbor by proposing rules on digital filings and record retention. [PBGC Proposed Rule, RIN 1212-AA89, 68 Fed. Reg. 7544 (Feb. 14, 2003)] The PBGC's announced intention is to implement the Government Paperwork Elimination Act by removing unnecessary obstacles that stand in the way of electronic filing of government documents and other electronic communications. The proposed rules, which amend 29 C.F.R. Part 4000, are divided into five parts; Part E contains the recordkeeping requirements, which track the 2002 safe harbor rules very closely. *See* <http://www.pbgc.gov/mypaa> for coverage of the MyPlan Administrative Account System available for plan years after 2004. [*See, e.g.,* <http://www.pbgc.gov/media/news-archive/2004/pr04-67.html> for discussion]

> **Tip:** The administrator of a plan that uses a service provider to create, maintain, or take custody of records is responsible for making sure that the service provider complies with the federal requirements.

CHAPTER **25**

CORPORATE COMMUNICATIONS

§ 25.01 INTRODUCTION

Communications within the corporation, and from the corporation to outsiders, have tremendous practical and legal consequences. To avoid trouble, everyone in a position to speak for the corporation should be aware of these potential ramifications and should be very careful about what is communicated (because not only are there things that should not be said, but items that must be accurately disclosed in various contexts) and in what form.

§ 25.02 EMPLOYMENT CONTRACTS

[A] Basic Considerations

Labor law aspects of Collective Bargaining Agreements between an employer and a union are discussed in Chapter 30. For employees who are not union members, there are both advantages and disadvantages to entering into a written employment contract. The written contract reduces uncertainty, and that is good—but it also limits flexibility, and that can create problems. If an employee has a written employment contract, disputes with the employer must be handled as contract cases; a suit for wrongful termination will not be available. [*Claggett v. Wake Forest Univ.*, 486 S.E.2d 443 (N.C. App. 1997)]

An individual written employment contract should cover issues such as:

- Duration of employment;
- Renewal provisions (including the amount of notice to be given);
- The duties the employee will perform;
- Promotion possibilities;
- Compensation and benefits, including contingent compensation—contingent on results and/or bonuses and stock options;
- Rights in inventions and other intellectual property developed by the employee during the contract term; treatment of intellectual property developed while the contract is in force but not during working hours, or not of the type the employee was hired to produce;
- Covenant not to compete with the employer, and agreement not to solicit its employees and customers, even after termination of employment. To be enforceable, these agreements must be reasonable in both duration and geographic scope, and must not be so severe that they prevent the individual from earning a living;
- Severability: If any contract provision is invalid, that provision will be removed from the contract, and the rest of the contract will remain valid and enforceable;
- Alternative Dispute Resolution: Whether disputes about the contract will be resolved by an arbitrator, mediator, or other decision maker other than a court.

[B] Employment Contract Case Law

A California case from mid-2000 allows a company to alter its established employment policies, as long as:

- Vested benefits are preserved;
- Employees get reasonable notice of the change;
- There is a reasonable phase-in period for the new rules.

According to *Asmus v. Pacific Bell,* [23 Cal. 4th 1, 999 P.2d 71 (Cal. 2000)] the employer does not have to provide additional consideration to employees to support the change. [*See* Kevin Livingston, *Employers Win Right to Rescind Job Promises,* The Recorder (June 5, 2000) (law.com)]

The case arose when Pacific Bell established a policy in 1986 giving job security to managers who satisfied the company's business expectations. The company said it would maintain the policy as long as "there is no change that will materially alter Pacific Bell's business plan achievement." The job security policy was canceled in 1992 in a memo saying the company needed greater flexibility in order to stay competitive in its economic environment. Sixty ex-managers sued for an injunction against implementation of the changes. They also sought ERISA damages and damages for breach of contract, breach of fiduciary duty, and fraud. The California Supreme Court held that the company had a right to change its policies, and the managers accepted the changed policy by continuing to work.

In contrast, another California case, *Guz v. Bechtel National Inc.*, [100 Cal. Rptr. 2d 352 (Cal. 2000)] finds that there was an implied contract, creating triable issues at to whether the employee still worked at will, because of contradictory statements in the employer's personnel policies. The policies said that the employee worked at will—but also said they could be terminated only for cause, which is a contractual concept.

The Statute of Frauds is another fundamental contract rule, one that says that a contract that lasts a year or more can only be enforced if it is in writing. In a Washington State case, the employee had an oral five-year contract, allowing either party to end the contract on six months' notice. The employee was fired after spending about eleven months with the company.

When he sued for breach of contract, his argument was that the Statute of Frauds should not apply because the contract could have been wrapped up in less than a year, and that is what happened. He lost his case—the court said that the Statute of Frauds applies only to employment contracts with an indefinite duration, not those with a specific term such as five years. With no written agreement, he also did not have a case against the employer. [*French v. Sabey Corp.,* 134 Wash. 2d 547, 951 P.2d 260 (1998)]

Oral promises that an employee who relocated would be fired only for good cause did not add up to a contract. Therefore, as an at-will employee, she could be fired even without cause. Here, the problem for the employee wasn't the Statute of

Frauds, but the failure to form an enforceable contract at all. [*Montgomery County Hosp. Dist. v. Brown,* 965 S.W.2d 501, 41 Tex. Sup. Ct. J. 537 (Tex. 1998)]

An employee was orally promised a bonus of a percentage of the employer's profits. The bonus could not be figured out until after the year ended. The employer said that the Statute of Frauds prevented enforcement of the contract, because the calculation required a period of more than a year. The employee's argument (which prevailed in a New York court which allowed enforcement of the oral contract) was that he worked at will and certainly could be fired in less than one year. [*Cron v. Hargo Fabrics, Inc.,* 91 N.Y.2d 362 (N.Y. 1998)]

In an Eighth Circuit case from early 2003, the plaintiff had a contract under which a telecommunications firm agreed to pay him 25% of gross margin on all guaranteed revenue from the outsourcing contracts the plaintiff negotiated for the defendant. The plaintiff charged breach of contract (failure to pay full commission on two contracts). The defendant counterclaimed, however, and charged the plaintiff with fraud and fraudulent concealment.

One of the disputed contracts had a term of six years, but could be terminated. The defendant therefore said that guaranteed revenue under the contract lasted for only two years. Later, the client agreed to eliminate the termination clause; still later, it was replaced after another contract modification. The Eighth Circuit said that only the first modification should affect the plaintiff's entitlement to commissions, because the second one occurred more than 90 days after the execution of the contract, which is the time period given for calculating commissions. Full commissions were also ordered under another disputed contract, because even though the defendant canceled long-distance service under the contract, the cancellation occurred more than 90 days after the date of the contract, so commissions were due on the initial amount of the contract including long-distance service. Minnesota law requires [Minn. Stats. § 181.14(1)(a)] that commissions earned but unpaid as of the time of an employee's resignation must be paid in full no later than the first scheduled payday after the employee's last day at work. The statute also provides that the court "shall" (not just "may") order the employer to pay the employee's court costs and attorneys' fees. [*Cousineau v. Norstan, Inc.,* 322 F.3d 493 (8th Cir. 2003)]

The perils of raiding employees were graphically illustrated in a Third Circuit case. The trial ended in November 2002 with a verdict of close to $685,000 in compensatory and $1.3 million in punitive damages. An occupational therapy firm had charged a nursing home management company with tortious interference with the OT firm's contracts by inducing two nursing homes to stop doing business with the OT firm and by hiring five therapists who were covered by a "non-raiding clause." The nursing homes that got their OT services through the plaintiff promised not to hire any of its independent contractor therapists for one year after terminating their contracts with the plaintiff.

The jury found the defendant had committed tortious interference both by inducing termination of therapy contracts with nursing homes that the defendant managed, and by recruiting away the therapists. On appeal in February 2004, the

Third Circuit found that only the second claim was valid, reduced compensatory damages to $109,000, and ordered a new trial on punitive damages. The second jury awarded $30 million in punitive damages. This heavy punitive damage award was granted because it took the plaintiff's business six months to recover from the raid, and $30 million represented six months' profit for the defendant. Because the defendant was a management company, it was the agent of the nursing homes, so the Third Circuit ruled it had a qualified privilege to recommend termination of the therapy contracts. Under Pennsylvania law, it is not necessarily tortious to hire another company's at-will employees, but it is tortious to systematically hire away workers for the purpose of destroying a business organization rather than to recruit quality employees. In mid-2005, the Eastern District of Pennsylvania reduced the damages yet again, with the $30 million punitive damage award falling to $2 million because the judge found it plainly excessive when compared to the $190,000 compensatory damages: still a 19:1 ratio, but far lower than 275:1. [*CGB Occupational Therapy Inc. v. RHA/Pennsylvania Nursing Homes Inc.,* 354 F.3d 375 (3d Cir. 2004) and *"Excessive" Damages Slashed by $28M,* The Legal Intelligencer, Jul. 14, 2005 (law.com)]

[C] Noncompete Case Law

In a buyer's market, employers can impose—and enforce—noncompete agreements. Even if the economy strengthens, companies that want to retain their top executives may continue to enforce the clauses. A company that wants to hire someone who is subject to a noncompete agreement can ask the former employer to release the employee, but this concession is unlikely to be granted—opening the way for a lawsuit on the issue of whether the two employers are really competitors. [Ellen L. Rosen, *More Employers Tighten Ties That Bind Workers to Them,* New York Times, Oct. 24, 2004, § 10 at p. 1]

Contract terms also become significant after termination of the employment relationship, in the context of covenants not to compete.

An accounting firm's employment contract, requiring ex-employees to compensate the firm if they worked for any of the firm's clients during the 18 months following termination of employment, was too broad, and therefore unenforceable. [*BDO Seidman v. Hirshberg,* 93 N.Y.2d 382 (N.Y. App. 1999)] The court considered it inappropriate to forbid ex-employees to work for clients they had not had contact with during their employment tenure, or to forbid them to work for personal clients they had brought to the ex-employer firm.

In a fast-moving business such as information technology, for instance, a one-year term (that might be acceptable in a conventional retail environment) could be deemed unreasonable and unenforceable. [*See, e.g., EarthWeb v. Schlack,* 71 F. Supp. 2d 299 (S.D.N.Y. 1999), *remanded without opinion* 205 F.3d 1322 (2d Cir. 2002)]

California law actually forbids noncompete agreements, although, in the right case, California might agree with the 20 states that accept the "inevitable disclosure" doctrine—i.e., that an ex-employee can be enjoined from going to work for a competitor of the former employer, if the inevitable result would be disclosure of the ex-employer's trade secrets, even if the ex-employee does not intend to do so.

Also note that even though California law bars covenants not to compete, a California court does not have the power to issue an injunction forbidding the parties in a California suit from bringing suit in a different state to enforce the covenant not to compete. [*Advanced Bionics Corp. v. Medtronic Inc.*, 29 Cal. 4th 697, 59 P.3d 231, 128 Cal. Rptr. 2d 172 (2002)] The theory is that judges should respect the powers of other judges, especially those in other states.

In Florida, as in most states, reasonable covenants not to compete are enforceable. In April 2003, the Florida Supreme Court decided a case about the applicability of noncompete agreements signed by employees with one employer when a successor employer wants to enforce the agreements after a corporate acquisition. [*Corporate Express Office Prods., Inc. v. Phillips*, 2003 Fla. LEXIS 521 (2003)] There were three employees involved: two of them had worked for a company whose stock was acquired by the plaintiff company, one had worked for another company whose assets were acquired by the plaintiff. The noncompete agreements lasted for one year and covered seven counties in Florida. The ex-employees' position was that not only did they not sign any noncompete agreements with Corporate Express, but the agreements that they did sign with their former employers were not assigned to Corporate Express, and didn't even include provisions for assignment. The Florida Supreme Court concluded that when there is a stock sale, the corporation whose stock is sold continues in existence and the purchaser of the stock can continue to enforce the sold corporation's contracts. This is also true when two corporations merge. In an asset sale, however, the covenant not to compete is enforceable only if the employee consents to the assignment.

The general rule is that employees who are not bound by employment agreements or termination agreements containing noncompete clauses are free to compete with the employer after they leave. A top executive may be considered a fiduciary as to the employer. A principle of corporate law called the "corporate opportunity doctrine" imposes a duty on a current employee to disclose to the employer whenever a business opportunity arises that is appropriate for the corporation.

It is improper for an executive to take advantage of the opportunity personally. [*See Hanover Ins. Co. v. Sutton*, 46 Mass. App. 153, 705 N.E.2d 279 (1999)] In this analysis, the opportunity is an asset of the corporation, and the executive is no more permitted to take advantage of it without the corporation's knowledge than he could help himself to one of the office computers.

It can be considered improper to contact the employer's customers while still employed—especially if the employee worked in a position of special confidence that provided contact with the customers and access to information about them. [*Dalton v. Camp*, 519 S.E.2d 82 (N.C. App. 1999)]

You might guess that an employee with a good memory would not be allowed to memorize the employer's customer list and use it after leaving employment if an employee with a bad memory would not be allowed to write down or photocopy the information. However, a Washington State trial court refused to treat a memorized list as a protectable trade secret. But then the state's Supreme Court granted protection to the information itself. [*Ed Nowogroski Ins. Inc. v. Rucker,* 137 Wash. 2d 427, 971 P.2d 736 (1999)]

In a Minnesota case [*Kallok v. Medtronic, Inc.,* 573 N.W.2d 356 (Minn. 1998)], a company that hired a person away from a direct competitor was found liable for tortious interference with the covenant not to compete. It was ordered to reimburse the first employer for the $90,000 in attorneys' fees it encountered when suing the employee to enforce the covenant. When the recruited employee got the job offer, he informed the recruiting company about the covenant, which barred employment in a field in which he had worked or had access to confidential information in the preceding year. The term of the agreement was two years. The recruiting company asked its outside attorney if hiring the competitor's employee would create legal problems. The lawyer said that it would be acceptable because the employee worked in a different field and did not have confidential information.

Once the employee changed companies, the first employer got a court order forbidding the employee to work for the new company. The competitor was also penalized for interfering with the employment contract. Proving a case of tortious interference requires proof of five elements:

- Existence of a contract that could be breached;
- The defendant's knowledge that the contract existed;
- Intentional action breaching or promoting breach of the contract;
- Lack of justification for the action;
- The injured contracting party suffers damages.

The Minnesota court decided that the competitor did not investigate enough. Simple inquiries would have uncovered the real provisions of the noncompete agreement. Therefore, the hiring company was not justified in its actions. Its actions forced the first employer to sue its ex-employee, so the hiring company was rightly ordered to reimburse the first employer for legal fees directly resulting from this wrongdoing.

The Wisconsin Supreme Court decided in late 2002 that a "no-hire" provision in a contract between a nursing home operator and an employment agency that provided physical therapists was invalid. Under the contract, the nursing home agreed not to offer permanent jobs to any of the agency's therapists without the agency's consent. A penalty of 50% of the therapist's salary was agreed on for violations. Despite the contract, the nursing home hired some physical therapists. The agency sued. The agency won at the trial-court level, but the appeals courts ruled that the provision was invalid because it was an unlawful restraint of trade in violation of public policy. Under Wisconsin law, a covenant not to compete is valid and enforceable if its restrictions are reasonably necessary to protect a business, but unreasonable restraints are void. Because the agency had similar contracts with other nursing homes, the effect was to substantially limit employment options for physical therapists, so the provision could be construed as an illegal territorial restriction. Furthermore, therapists were not even informed of these contract provisions (much less consenting to them), so the provisions were harsh, oppressive, and contrary to public policy. [*Heyde Cos. v. Dove Healthcare LLC,* 258 Wis. 2d 28, 654 N.W.2d 830 (2002)]

The Sixth Circuit ruled, early in 2004, that a former employer could not sue an ex-employee for breach of the covenant not to compete. The company claimed that the ex-employee sold equipment and solicited the former employer's customers in the forbidden geographic area. The court read the employment contract to forbid starting a business physically located within the target area. The defendant, however, started his new business physically outside the target area, although it's true that about one-third of his customers were within the area named in the covenant not to compete. In the Sixth Circuit view, operating a business means locating the business premises there, not doing business with customers who can be found there. [*United Rentals (North America) Inc. v. Keizer,* 355 F.3d 399 (6th Cir. 2004)]

After the company he worked for was acquired, an employee was asked to sign a one-year covenant not to compete, forbidding him to solicit the acquired company's customers or potential customers whom he had dealt with while working for the acquired company. He refused, and was fired. He sued for wrongful termination in violation of public policy, asserting that he had been fired for refusing to sign a covenant not to compete that was unenforceable under California law. The trial court agreed with the acquiring company that the covenant not to compete was lawful and enforceable, because it was narrowly tailored and protected a legitimate interest in customer information. The California Court of Appeals reversed, ruling in favor of the ex-employee. Although the clause was less restrictive and had a less drastic anticompetitive effect than a broad traditional covenant not to compete, it nevertheless had an anticompetitive effect. In California, covenants not to compete are void unless they protect trade secrets or confidential or proprietary information—matters that were not involved in this case. [*Thompson v. Impaxx, Inc.,* 113 Cal. App. 4th 1425, 7 Cal. Rptr. 3d 427 (Cal. Ct. App. 2003)]

The Eleventh Circuit ruled that a non-compete agreement (NCA) was unenforceable under Georgia law—but ruled that the District Court abused its discretion by issuing an injunction forbidding the company from seeking to enforce the NCA against its ex-employee in any court anywhere.

Although the NCA called for application of Ohio law, the District Court applied Georgia law instead. The case was sent to the Supreme Court of Georgia, which ruled that Georgia law would apply as long as the transaction involved significant contacts with Georgia and application of another state's law would violate Georgia public policy. The Eleventh Circuit held that Georgia law could properly be applied because the ex-employee lived and worked in Georgia, so that was where the effects would be felt. Therefore, the public policy of the state of Georgia was involved.

The NCA was considered overbroad, and hence unenforceable, because it forbade working for any competitor of the ex-employer. Because the corporation was a multinational, in effect that covered the entire world. Another problem with the way the agreement was drafted was that the geographic reach could not be determined until the date of termination, violating Georgia law, which holds that territorial restrictions that change in the course of the agreement are invalid. The NCA's ban on solicitation of customers was also unenforceable because it was too broad, did not have valid geographic limitations, and imposed a blanket restriction against solicitation, even of parties with a prior business relationship with the employee. However, the Eleventh Circuit refused to extend the injunction against enforcement of the agreement to cover any state except Georgia. [*Keener v. Convergys Corp.*, 342 F.3d 1264 (11th Cir. 2003)]

In 2005, the Eleventh Circuit followed up on *Keener.* An insurance executive entered into two non-compete agreements, one when a company of which he was a one-third owner was sold, the second in connection with exercise of a stock options package. The district court found both the agreements unenforceable under Georgia law, and granted an injunction against their enforcement within Georgia. The Eleventh Circuit ruled that a full trial was required to determine whether the first agreement should be analyzed as related to the sale of a business or as an employment-related agreement.

Under Georgia law, sale-related agreements get a low level of scrutiny, and a court can re-form the agreement to bring it into line with local law. But employ-ment-related covenants are enforceable only if they are strictly limited in time and place, and are otherwise reasonable. The second agreement was clearly employ-ment-related, and Georgia courts will not enforce employment-related agreements that prevent the employee from accepting unsolicited business from former clients. The second agreement included a provision of this type. Therefore, the whole agreement was invalid and unenforceable in Georgia. Although the defendant said that it waived enforcement of the invalid provisions, the Eleventh Circuit, as a matter of policy, would not allow an employer to revise its own invalid agreement. The Eleventh Circuit also ruled that, based on *Keener*, the scope of injunctive relief was properly limited to Georgia—but a final declaratory judgment in a case involving a non-compete agreement prevents the issue from being re-litigated in any other state. [*Meathe v. Marsh & McLennan Cos. Inc.*, No. 03-16248 (11th Cir. Apr. 1, 2005). The case about unsolicited business is *Waldeck v. Curtis 1000 Inc.,* 583 S.E.2d 266 (Ga. App. 2003); the precedent about declaratory judgments is *Hostetler v. Answerthink*, 599 S.E.2d 271, 275 (Ga. Ct. App. 2004)]

Choice of law questions also came into play in a 2006 Eighth Circuit case. The Eighth Circuit upheld a grant of summary judgment on behalf of three former employees who worked as managers in Nebraska for a Delaware corporation whose principal place of business was Ohio. The managers' non-compete agreement barred them from engaging in contract cleaning services within a 100-mile radius of their place of employment for one year after termination of their employment for any reason. The contract's choice of law provision called for interpretation under Ohio law. However, Nebraska law was applied because Nebraska had a much greater interest in the contract, and applying Ohio law would have violated Nebraska public policy. In a diversity case, federal courts apply the law of the state in which they sit, and all of the meaningful contacts with the case occurred in Nebraska. An Ohio court will reform a non-compete agreement to make it conform to law, whereas Nebraska will not. Hence, the Eighth Circuit decided that enforcing the unduly broad 100-mile limitation would violate Nebraska public policy because it was unduly harsh and oppressive to the employees and extended further than necessary to protect the employer's legitimate interests. The Eighth Circuit defined an acceptable agreement as one that restricted working for, or soliciting, clients that the person actually worked for during the previous employment. [*DCS Sanitation Management Inc. v. Castillo*, 435 F.3d 892 (8th Cir. 2006); the rule against reforming non-compete agreements comes from *H&R Block Tax Servs. Inc. v. Circle A Enterprises*, 693 N.W.2d 548 (Neb. 2005), and the Nebraska public policy is stated in *Professional Bus. Servs. Co. v. Rosno*, 680 N.W.2d 176, 184 (Neb. 2004)]

Cameco Inc. v. Gedicke [157 N.J. 504, 724 A.2d 783 (N.J. Sup. 1999)] holds that an employee can be liable for breach of the duty of loyalty for assisting the employer's competitors, even if there is no direct competition. It depends on the nature of the employer/employee relationship. It also depends on the level of assistance the employee provided to competitors. Under this analysis, an employee has a duty to inform the employer of his or her plans before establishing a moonlighting business that could conflict with the employer's business. Appropriate damages for the breach of the employee's duty of loyalty could include the injury to the employer's business plus the profits the employee earned from inappropriately competitive moonlighting.

The Seventh Circuit upheld a preliminary injunction forbidding two defendants from providing any services to a company they formed with a former customer of their ex-employer. The plaintiff is a beef importer; the defendants were senior sales representatives of one of the plaintiff's largest customers. The customer proposed a deal to the plaintiff, but negotiations broke down, and the customer withdrew most of its business. The defendants approached the customer about creating a new importing company. They incorporated a business, quit their jobs with the plaintiff, and became a division of the customer's company. The ex-employer applied for an injunction based on breach of fiduciary duty and improper appropriation of corporate opportunity. The Seventh Circuit found that breach of duty had occurred (even though the defendants were not corporate officers; they were highly paid, were paid on the basis of results, and had significant autonomy and discretion) and that secret negotiations with a potential competitor are necessarily improper. An injunction was the proper remedy (rather than damages) because the value of a business relationship is difficult to calculate; the defendants had no significant personal assets; and the new company was a startup with little money with which to pay damages. [*Foodcomm Int'l v. Barry*, 328 F.3d 300 (7th Cir. 2003)]

Although a recent Ninth Circuit case began as an FLSA case, eventually it was resolved by analysis of duty of loyalty issues. The District Court ruled that Hawaii law imposes a duty of loyalty on employees, obligating them to avoid competition with their former employers. The defendants worked for a sewer pipe company; they formed a partnership, competed against their employer for a public contract, won the contract, were fired, and sued for unpaid overtime under the FLSA. The employers counterclaimed, charging them with breach of the duty of loyalty.

The Ninth Circuit affirmed the District Court, quoting Restatement (Second) of Agency § 393 to impose a duty of loyalty: an agent, including an employee, has a duty not to compete with the principal with respect to the subject matter of the agency. Merely preparing to compete with the employer is not a breach of the duty, but placing a competing bid is equivalent to soliciting the employer's customers, which is expressly forbidden by the Restatement. The ex-employees claimed that they were not subject to the duty because they were merely rank-and-file employees, not executives, but the Ninth Circuit ruled that ordinary employees are not exempt. The Ninth Circuit also ruled that the proper statute of limitations in this case was six years (for contracts) rather than two years (for torts) because the breach of loyalty claim is a hybrid that includes elements of recovery of a debt founded on a contract, obligation or liability. [*Eckard Brandes, Inc. v. Riley*, 338 F.3d 1082 (9th Cir. 2003)]

§ 25.03   EMPLOYEE HANDBOOKS

[A]   Generally

Employee handbooks are traditional in large corporations, as a means of creating a uniform culture and distributing information to what can be a large, diverse, and widely disseminated group of employees. Handbooks are useful in training new hires about the employer's expectations. They provide a ready reference about work rules—and employee discipline often revolves around claimed infractions of these rules, so employees must be informed of the rules.

Not all handbooks are printed; more and more companies are using the Web or an intranet to provide information.

Employee handbooks can be extremely useful, but unless they are drafted carefully and kept up to date, they can create at least as many problems as they solve. Sometimes, statements made in a handbook will be deemed to create a binding contract—although this is not necessarily what the employer wished to do.

Furthermore, once the employer is deemed to have created a contract, some courts will say that the employer can no longer amend that contract whenever it wants to, without providing additional consideration to the employees in return for the change. Although some courts say that the fact that the employee continues to work for the employer provides consideration, others require the employees to get some additional benefit if the employer wants to alter the contract.

> **Tip:** Many federal and state statutes limit the policies that employers can adopt. For example, a policy against leaves of less than one day could violate the Family and Medical Leave Act, or might be a refusal to make a reasonable accommodation required by the Americans With Disabilities Act.

Typical subjects for coverage in the handbook include:

- Training;
- Benefits (health plan, dental plan, disability, etc.);
- Access to profit-sharing plans;
- Defined benefit, defined contribution, 401(k), and other pension plans;
- Stock options;
- Vacations, leave (including sick leave, pregnancy, and military leave), holidays, and time off;
- Explanation of employees' rights under the Family and Medical Leave Act (FMLA) (the Department of Labor's Wage and Hour Division publishes a standard FMLA Fact Sheet, if you don't want to have to draft your own explanation);
- Employer's policy of checking all references provided;
- Policy of employing only U.S. citizens and noncitizens who can lawfully work within the United States;
- Drug-free workplace policy, including circumstances under which drug testing will be required;
- Policies about e-mail and Internet use in the workplace;
- Policies about employment of both spouses in a couple, or more than one family member;
- Antiharassment policy; commitment to investigate charges; alternative reporting procedures if the supervisor is the alleged harasser;
- Policies about conflict of interests and acceptance of gifts from suppliers;
- Confidentiality of the employer's intellectual property;
- Employees' patent rights (if any) in inventions they develop while they are working for the employer;
- What will be considered a disciplinary offense;
- Discipline procedure (e.g., oral reprimand, followed by a written warning; suspension after two written warnings for the same offense; retention of warnings in the personnel record for at least a year; and termination; immediate termination will be permitted in the case of a serious, dangerous, or criminal act);

[B] At-Will Employment

For employees who are not unionized, and who do not have individual employment contracts, it is often a good idea to put a disclaimer in the handbook:

- Employees are hired at will;
- They can be fired when the employer sees fit; it is not necessary for the employer to demonstrate good cause for the discharge;
- The information in the handbook is for guidance only, and does not bind the employer to a contract.

To be legally effective, a disclaimer must be clear and conspicuous. It cannot be buried in small print somewhere in the back of the book. In fact, the first page is an excellent location. When a disclaimer is issued, it does not apply to people who were already employees and working under the old policy.

The mere fact that the employer has a system of progressive discipline, spelled out in the handbook, does not mean that the employee is no longer an at-will employee. However, it makes sense to include a disclaimer explaining the function of the disciplinary system.

The more specific a provision is, the more likely that courts are to construe it as creating a formal contract. However, in order to win when they charge breach of this implied contract, employees may have to show detrimental reliance (i.e., that they relied on the provision, and this reliance was harmful for them). At the very least, employees will have to prove that they read the handbook, because it is hard to claim reliance on an unread provision.

[C] Orientation Checklists

It is a good idea to provide orientation to train new hires. It is even better to standardize the orientation process, with standard documents for welcoming and instructing new employees. Both the employee and the supervisor handling the orientation should sign the document, so that later on the employee will not be able to claim that lifetime employment was promised if the document clearly states that employment is at will.

The orientation checklist should cover subjects such as:

- The company's equal employment opportunity policies;
- The company's position on unionization and union activity (get legal advice before promulgating a policy!);
- Which unions (if any) that are already recognized as bargaining agents for the employees;
- The terms of the formal probation process (if there is one);
- What a new hire has to do to become a permanent employee, but make sure that no promises are made of indefinite tenure or lifetime employment;

- The new employee's job title, duties, and promotion path;
- The compensation and benefit package for the job (including vacation days, vacation banking, disability benefits, sick leave, options under the group health plan, and severance pay);
- Work rules;
- Circumstances under which the employee can be terminated.

Even if the manual indicates the employees will be on probation for a certain length of time after being hired, they will still be entitled to good faith and fair dealing from the employer. In fact, some courts will allow probationary employees to sue for wrongful termination, if the employer did not offer them long-term employment after the end of the probation period.

[D] Legal Consequences of Handbooks

When a union challenges one provision in a handbook, then it can open the door to a challenge from NLRB that involves the handbook as a whole. In the case of *Lafayette Park Hotel,* [326 N.L.R.B. 69 (1998)] the handbook included a ban on false, vicious, profane, or malicious statements about the hotel or its employees. The NLRB struck down this rule, on the grounds that the employees were not given adequate notice of what constituted improper conduct. The NLRB also invalidated another rule that required employees to leave the premises as soon as they finished their shift. This rule was unacceptable because it restricted access to nonwork areas such as the parking lot.

In earlier NLRB cases, the agency allowed employees to reveal wage and benefit information to the union during contract negotiations, despite a work rule prohibiting disclosure of confidential information. A work rule against "derogatory" statements could not be enforced to prevent the union from making truthful statements that questioned the quality of care provided by the employer (a hospital). [*See* A. Michael Weber, *Unions Challenge Employee Handbook Language,* National Law Journal, Feb. 8, 1999, at p. S7]

Early in 2004, the NLRB ruled that it violates federal labor law to promulgate a handbook provision that restricts employee communications with other employees and the press about the terms and conditions of employment (such as wages and grievances). The employer could not forbid discussion of company issues in public areas other than the casino floor. Discussions on the casino floor, however, could be banned by analogy with the retail sales area of a store. It was improper for the handbook to forbid communicating any information about the company to the media without management approval; even a rule that is never enforced can have a chilling effect. [*Double Eagle Hotel & Casino*, 341 NLRB No. 17 (Jan. 30, 2004)]

Two Indiana workers were fired when a supervisor found them on the roof of the plant. They said, probably truthfully, that they had been ordered up to the roof to clean the gutters. However, the supervisor smelled marijuana in the attic through which the roof was reached. After their discharge, the workers sued the employer because the grievance procedures given in the handbook were not followed before their discharge. Not only did the employer win, but the case was dismissed without a full trial. In Indiana, handbook provisions create a contract only if the employee provided some consideration over and above merely taking the job. Anyway, the handbook didn't promise that the procedures would be followed in every case. In fact, it said that immediate dismissals could occur when necessary. [*Orr v. Westminster Village N.,* 689 N.E.2d 712 (Ind. 1997)]

In May 1999, an Arizona court decided that handbook provisions requiring good cause for termination implied that the employees had a contract. Therefore, even though the handbook contained a provision stating that it was not an employment contract, and even though the employer reserved the right to amend the handbook, the employer lost the power to make unilateral amendments. Employees had to be notified, and give their individual consent, for the changes to become operative. [*Demasse v. ITT Corp.,* 194 Ariz. 500, 984 P.2d 1138 (Ariz. 1999)]

§ 25.04   WORK RULES

Some organizations are small enough, informal enough, or simple enough in operation that they do not need written work rules. But in the larger organization, or even a small operation where the work rules could become an issue, a written list of rules (in the handbook or set out separately) can be very useful.

The work rules document should make it clear that the employer is the only one to make work rules and that the employer has the right to modify them at any time. The rules themselves are not a contract with the employees that has to be negotiated, or that has to be maintained in its original form.

Work rules deal with issues such as:

- Workplace safety and security (not letting in unauthorized persons; wearing protective equipment in construction areas or where hazardous chemicals are present);
- Emergency procedures in case of fires, chemical spills, etc.;
- Where (if anyplace!) smoking is allowed in the workplace; if smoking is banned inside the workplace, limitations on going outside for smoking breaks;
- Requirement of on-time arrival and staying until the end of the work day or shift;
- Dress and grooming rules—are uniforms required for any job titles? Which days are "casual" days, and what is acceptable business casual clothing? Are there any limitations or bans on facial hair, hairstyles, makeup, or jewelry? (Make sure that these rules do not violate employees' rights to reasonable accommodation of their religious practices);
- Availability of paid and unpaid leave; how to request leave. Some companies maintain a no-fault absence policy, under which employees get a certain number of days off no matter what the reason is, but discipline can be imposed for excessive absence. A paid leave bank is similar, but allows unused days to

be carried over or cashed out. Get legal advice about harmonizing your leave policy with legal requirements for disability and unpaid family leave;

- Bans on horseplay, substance abuse, possession of alcohol in the workplace, and removing products or materials (even waste or spoiled items) without permission;
- Bans on harassment, fighting, and weapons;
- Control of solicitation within the workplace. A "no-solicitation" rule can be very helpful, not only in restricting union activity, but in improving efficiency and avoiding conflict among employees. It can get pretty expensive to come to work each day if you are asked to contribute to everyone's favorite charity and chip in for presents for people who are getting married, leaving the company, having a baby, in the hospital, etc. An effective no-solicitation rule must be appropriately communicated to employees, it must be nondiscriminatory, and it must be applied uniformly. So if one employee is given permission to sell raffle tickets for the Catholic Church, while another is denied permission to raise money for the NAACP (or vice versa), it will appear that the employer is guilty of discrimination;
- The extent to which employees are permitted to inspect their own personal records or show them to an attorney, union representative, etc. Check your state law: It probably requires employees to have access to their records, and also protects privacy rights by limiting disclosure of personal information to anyone except the employee without the employee's consent. [*See* § 26.07 for rules on privacy of health records];
- Ethical standards imposed on employees: for example, when they are allowed to accept gifts from a potential supplier; use of inside information; lobbying, political activities, and donations;
- How to find additional work-related information and answers to questions: for instance, through the HR department, the Employee Assistance Program, or the corporate intranet.

Tip: Even though the work rules are not contractual in nature, it is a good idea to have employees sign a notice stating that they received a copy of the work rules and had a chance to read and become familiar with them. The notice may come in handy later if the employee claims that he or she never saw the rules or didn't understand them.

---

§ 25.05 SYSTEMS OF PROGRESSIVE DISCIPLINE

One approach to at-will employment is for the employer to take and maintain a consistent position that only the employer determines the quality of the employee's work performance. Employees can therefore be disciplined or fired based on the employer's sole determination that their work is unsatisfactory. In a unionized workplace, it is almost certain that the collective bargaining agreement will require a system of progressive discipline, where all the steps, from a verbal warning through levels of reprimands, must be followed before the employee can be fired.

There are various reasons why even a nonunion workplace might have a progressive discipline system. It could improve efficiency. Sometimes, employees really do not know that their work is below par, so it is better to show them how to improve instead of firing them. Also, if the employer voluntarily adopts a progressive discipline system, this could make employees less interested in unionizing.

The downside is that having specific rules to follow limits the employer's flexibility. Even in a nonunion setting, the disciplinary system may be treated by courts as a contractual obligation, so that once the system is set up, it has to be maintained in the future.

Usually, a system of progressive discipline begins with an oral warning explaining why the supervisor is dissatisfied with the employee's performance. The next step is a written warning. If performance is still unsatisfactory, discipline proceeds to a probationary period or suspension (usually unpaid, lasting three–five days), then demotion or termination.

All the steps, including oral warnings, should be documented in the employee's personnel record. The written warning should include a place for the employee's signature, indicating that the document has been read. The employee should be given a copy for reference. It is often helpful to let the employee include a brief written statement giving his or her side of the story.

Tip: It has always been permitted for unionized workers to bring a representative to interviews that could result in disciplinary action; the NLRB's position is that even nonunionized workers have the same right.

It is important to monitor the reasons for an employee's lateness or absence. Discipline or discharge could constitute a violation of a statute if the employee has been injured (and qualified for Worker's Compensation), is disabled as defined by the ADA, or is taking care of a sick family member and therefore is entitled to FMLA leave.

All investigations should be documented, to show that the employer is acting on the basis of facts and not discrimination against members of a protected group.

An objective party should review all termination decisions. The best time is after tempers have had a chance to cool, but promptly enough to demonstrate the employer's efficiency and involvement. Before a termination, review the process to see that the employee received the appropriate warnings; the investigation gave enough weight to the employee's explanation; and the employee was treated fairly, objectively, and on a par with other similarly situated employees.

In general, employees who are discharged for cause are not entitled to severance pay [*see* Chapter 3] However, the employee handbook may have been written in such general terms that it constitutes a contract to pay severance benefits, even in connection with a discharge for cause. Severance policies that are written and communicated to workers may become welfare benefit plans subject to ERISA. If there is no formal plan, and the employer has not entered into an express or implied contract, then it is completely at the employer's discretion to grant or withhold severance benefits.

§ 25.06 EMPLOYEE EVALUATIONS

Regular evaluations of employee performance can be critical in making sure that the organization meets its goals. Employees who are not performing up to par can be identified and given the training, encouragement, or whatever they need to improve. When it's time to award merit raises and bonuses, the performance appraisal should identify the stars.

A well-done performance appraisal identifies real problems in employee performance and gives insights into solutions. Some of the basic issues for performance reviews include:

- Whether the quantity of work performed by the employee has been satisfactory;
- Quality of the work;
- The employee's knowledge of the job;
- His or her dependability, initiative, and adaptability;
- The extent to which the employee has learned new skills, and seems likely to be able to acquire the skills that will be needed in the future;
- The extent of the employee's cooperation, attendance, and punctuality;
- Areas in which the employee needs to improve.

However, performance appraisals must be carefully done. If they're mishandled, the result is often to subject the employer to liability for wrongful termination or employment discrimination. There are many reasons why the appraisal process itself doesn't work well:

- Managers do not have time to do a thoughtful job of appraising performance, so they decide to err on the side of generosity;
- The appraisals do not seem to actually be used for anything, so managers put down whatever seems uncontroversial—or simply update the previous year's forms without much thought;
- In a large work group, managers may not know very much about what individual employees are doing;
- Managers want to be liked by the employees who report to them; they're afraid that a tough-minded appraisal could create hostility and reduce motivation;
- Ambitious managers want to give themselves an indirect pat on the back, hoping that they will be seen as outstanding leaders if all their subordinates are doing a great job;

- A bad appraisal could be attacked as the product of racism, sexism, sexual harassment, or retaliation. However, the answer is **not** to give everyone good marks because it looks very suspicious if the employer claims that someone who got a long line of excellent appraisals was fired for poor performance.

At a minimum, the employee should be shown a written performance appraisal, be given an opportunity to discuss it, and should be asked to sign a statement that he or she has read the document. Some states make it a legal requirement that the employee must be allowed to add comments; it is a good idea anyway.

The modern form of appraisal is the "360-degree review," which has input from more than one person, including co-workers and customers. However, it can be hard to gather all the necessary information, and not everyone will be candid. An alternative might be to have more frequent but informal reviews: for instance, at the end of every project, or every quarter or twice a year.

§ 25.07   MANDATORY PREDISPUTE ARBITRATION PROVISIONS

Employers, faced with the delay, high costs, and significant risks of employment litigation, often seek to require in advance that employees will raise any discrimination claims using the arbitration process rather than litigation. *See* Chapter 40.

However, it takes skillful drafting to use the employee handbook for this purpose. Cases like *Paladino v. Avnet Computer Technologies Inc.*, [134 F.3d 1054 (11th Cir. 1998)] *Phox v. Allied Capital Advisers*, [74 Fair Empl. Prac. Cas. (BNA) 809 (D.D.C. 1997)] and *Trumbull v. Century Marketing Corp.* [12 F. Supp. 2d 683 (N.D. Oh. 1998)] have refused to enforce these provisions, because they did not give the employees enough notice of their rights.

To have a chance of enforcement, a handbook provision must make it clear which statutes are covered, and clearly and explicitly indicate that arbitration is the sole remedy. It makes sense to have the employee sign a document when he or she receives the handbook—not only stating that the handbook has been received, but that the employee has read its contents and understands them.

In recent years, most cases have come down on the side of arbitration, even if it is compelled by a mandatory predispute arbitration clause (i.e., if employees had to agree to arbitrate their claims as a condition of being hired)—a proposition that was approved by the Supreme Court in *Circuit City v. Adams*. [532 U.S. 105 (2002)] There are some exceptions to this rule: New York's Court of Appeals ruled early in 2003 that the only way an employee can validly waive statutory employment rights is through an explicit, affirmative agreement unmistakably showing intent to waive. Merely continuing to work after receiving an employee handbook that contains a waiver clause is not sufficient. [*Leodori v. CIGNA Corp.*, 814 A.2d 1098 (N.J. 2003)]

The California Court of Appeals ruled early in 2006 that an arbitration clause that forbids class action arbitration is acceptable and is not an unlawful contract of adhesion because it gives employees the opportunity to opt out of the arbitration program and adequate time to make the decision whether to do so. [*Gentry v. Superior Court of Los Angeles*, 135 Cal. App. 4th 944 (Cal. App. 2006)]

However, an employer seeking to enforce an arbitration agreement must be careful to abide by the agreement itself. In late 2005, for example, the Ninth Circuit ruled that an employer that unilaterally imposed an arbitration policy had to arbitrate an employee's claims of wrongful termination (the employer said that she was fired for falsifying a time sheet). The employee sued in state court; the employer removed the case to federal court and sought to compel arbitration, but the federal courts refused to compel arbitration because the employer had failed to cooperate with the requirements of AAA arbitration required by the arbitration policy. [*Brown v. Dillard's Inc.*, 430 F.3d 1004 (9th Cir. 2005)]

The Ninth Circuit initially ruled that employees can't be fired for refusing to accept predispute arbitration [*Duffield v. Robertson Stephens*, 144 F.3d 1182 (9th Cir. 1998)] but then, in 2002, the Ninth Circuit decided another case overturning the *Duffield* decision. [*EEOC v. Luce, Forward, Hamilton & Scripps,* 303 F.3d 994 (9th Cir. 2002)] The 2002 ruling was upheld on appeal in 2003, affirming the validity of mandatory predispute arbitration clauses. [345 F.3d 742 (9th Cir. 2003)] [For history of this case, see two articles by Jason Hoppin (both available from law.com): Jason Hoppin, *9th Circuit Grapples with Duffield,* The Recorder, Mar. 28, 2003 (law.com); Jason Hoppin, *Employer Can Insist on Arbitration Agreement,* The Recorder, Sept. 4, 2002 (law.com)] An important focus in recent cases that accept the basic validity of predispute arbitration agreements is whether a particular agreement contains unfair terms that place too great a burden on employees who might seek to arbitrate grievances. The important California case of *Armendariz v. Foundation Health Psychcare Services, Inc.* [24 Cal. 4th 83 (2000)] imposes fairness requirements (the arbitrator's award must be appealable, and employees must not be required to pay unaffordable sums to arbitrate a claim). However, it has been held that *Armendariz* only applies to arbitration of claims of employment discrimination barred by federal or state statutes, and not to claims that someone was wrongfully terminated in violation of public policy. [*Little v. Auto Stiegler, Inc.*, 29 Cal. 4th 1064, 63 P.3d 979, 130 Cal. Rptr. 2d 892 (2003)]

The employer's failure to give the employee a copy of the arbitration rules was not a "special circumstance" that would invalidate the mandatory predispute arbitration agreement, even though the U-4 form that the employee signed said that she was familiar with the rules. The Second Circuit held that it was up to the employee to resolve any questions she had before signing the agreement; after signing, it was conclusively presumed that she was aware of the contents of the agreement. [*Gold v. Deutsche Aktiengesellschaft*, 365 F.3d 144 (2d Cir. 2004)]

In a case involving claims about pension entitlement rather than about allegations of violations of antidiscrimination statutes, the Eighth Circuit held late in 2002 that a pension plan's mandatory arbitration clause, requiring the employee to pay half the arbitration costs of a benefit determination dispute, is invalid because it prevents full and fair review of denied claims. That, in turn, violates the ERISA § 503 requirement of reasonable opportunity for full and fair review. [*Bond v. Twin Cities Carpenters Pension Fund,* 307 F.3d 704 (8th Cir. 2002)]

The Sixth, Tenth, and D.C. Circuits have ruled that a provision requiring employees to pay arbitration costs is automatically unfair. The Sixth Circuit says that the court must determine whether employees get an opportunity, before mandatory arbitration is imposed, to prove that the potential costs are high enough to discourage themselves and other people in similar situations from seeking arbitration to enforce their rights. [*Morrison v. Circuit City Stores Inc.,* 317 F.3d 646 (6th Cir. 2003)] The Fourth Circuit uses a similar analysis, but looks at the situation of the individual claimant, not the individual and others in similar situations. [*Bradford v. Rockwell Semiconductor Systems Inc.,* 238 F.3d 549 (4th Cir. 2001)] In the *Morrison* case, the Sixth Circuit did find that fees ranging from $1,125 to $3,000 were unfair and did improperly discourage employees from going to arbitration.

Even if part of an arbitration clause is ruled to be unfair, that doesn't necessarily mean that the employer loses everything. A number of cases allow the invalid part of the clause to be severed, and the rest of the clause to be enforced. [*See,* for instance, the *Little* case mentioned above, and *Spinetti v. Service Corp. Int'l,* 324 F.3d 212 (3d Cir. 2003)]

At the end of 2003, the Ninth Circuit ruled that an employer that failed to pay for arbitration to settle employee claims (the employee charged the employer with breach of the employment contract by failure to make the agreed-upon payments and stock option grants) was in default under § 3 of the Federal Arbitration Act. Therefore, despite the arbitration clause in the plaintiff's employment contract, the employer could not compel a stay of litigation or enforce the arbitration clause as to those claims. [*Sink v. Aden Enters., Inc.,* 352 F.3d 1197 (9th Cir. 2003)]

§ 25.08   DEFAMATION

A hostile or unflattering statement that a company or one of its agents makes about a job applicant, employee, or former employee could become the focus of charges, or even a lawsuit. However, there are several circumstances under which negative statements are legally protected. For one thing, the statement might have been demonstrably true. They might have been made without malice, or in a privileged context.

Slander is defined as communicating a defamatory statement orally or otherwise informally. Libel means communicating a defamatory statement more broadly ("publishing" it). A defamatory statement is one that attributes serious misconduct to someone else. The victim of slander or libel can sue and obtain tort damages, unless the statement was privileged in some way.

The basic rule is that a plaintiff not only has to prove that defamation occurred, but also that some actual damages were suffered because of the defamation. But there are some statements so negative that they are automatically presumed to damage the reputation of the person about whom they are made. A plaintiff who proves such "defamation per se" can win without proving actual damages (concrete injury attributable to the defamation).

To support a suit, the alleged slander or libel must be a statement of fact, not a mere opinion or a general, imprecise statement ("Marcia is hard to work with"; "Steve seems to be working through some problems in his life."). A pure opinion cannot be defamatory, because it is not a statement of fact, but a statement of fact backing up that opinion can be defamatory. A corporation is liable for the statements of its employees and agents, as long as they were acting within the scope of their employment.

Truth is always a defense to a defamation charge: For instance, it is not defamatory to say that an employee was fired for stealing office supplies if this is what actually happened. If the employer believes a statement is true, and the statement is communicated without malice, then the employer is entitled to a defense. The jury, not the judge, decides whether or not a statement was communicated with malice.

A statement has not been "published" to the extent that a libel charge can be made if it is communicated only to the plaintiff, or to someone who is acting on behalf of the plaintiff (including a friend or an investigator who calls to find out what the employer is saying about the employee). Courts take different positions about communications that stay within the employer corporation. Some courts say that this is so narrow that no publication has occurred, whereas others accept the plaintiff's argument that dissemination was broad enough to constitute libel.

The idea that communication within the corporation cannot be defamatory, because the corporation is "talking to itself," has been adopted in Alabama, Georgia, Louisiana, Missouri, Oklahoma, Tennessee, Washington, and Wisconsin.

A mid-level manager was assigned to work on a corporate project. His direct supervisor, infuriated by his employee's "wasting time" on the project, engaged in an angry, profane tirade in the presence of two non-management employees. The mid-level manager sued in state court, claiming that the verbal abuse constituted defamation per se under Kentucky law, because it accused him of inability or unfitness for his duties. The case was removed to federal court as a diversity case, and then dismissed for failure to state a claim. The Sixth Circuit's conclusion was that, although the supervisor did so in highly unparliamentary language, he merely said that the plaintiff was spending time on the project (which was true) and did not call him unfit or incompetent. [*Gahafer v. Ford Motor Co.*, 328 F.3d 859 (6th Cir. 2003)]

On the other hand, the Restatement of Torts (2d) § 577 says that expression within a corporation clearly constitutes publication, and this is the position taken by the states of California, Connecticut, Florida, Illinois, Indiana, Kansas, Massachusetts, Michigan, Minnesota, New York, Nevada, and Oregon. These states view the purpose of defamation law as protecting reputation within the business community, and an intraoffice communication could certainly endanger reputation.

A school bus driver was randomly chosen for drug testing, under federal rules requiring a urine specimen of at least 45 milliliters. According to the plaintiff, his specimen was adequate; the testimony of the tester is that the sample was insufficient. No controlled substances were found in the sample. The plaintiff was suspended for violating regulations that do not permit anyone to drive a commercial vehicle who has refused to submit to a required test. An inadequate sample is treated as a refusal to submit to testing. The plaintiff was ordered to get an assessment by a substance abuse professional and submit another sample. He did not submit the sample, and sued the school district, charging it with defaming him by making untrue statements (that he had failed or refused to take the test) to a third party.

The District Court dismissed the defamation claim, but allowed the jury to rule on a claim under the state law forbidding unlawful disclosure of government data. The jury awarded $108,000 for pain and suffering and loss of reputation, $10,000 for lost earnings, $2,000 for future medical expenses, and a nominal $100 punitive damages.

The Eighth Circuit agreed that the defamation claims should have been dismissed, because the plaintiff failed to meet his burden on essential elements of the defamation cause of action. If there was damage to his reputation, it was caused by his publication of the letter from the superintendent requiring the additional sample. The disclosure was made at the plaintiff's own instance; he was not compelled to make embarrassing disclosures about himself. The statement that he had refused to take the test was accurate, given the language of the federal regulation. The Eighth Circuit also dismissed the claims relating to government data, because he failed to prove a connection between the statements and loss of reputation or financial damage. He should not have received an award for lost earnings, because he was paid for the days he was suspended. The school district offered to reinstate him, but he refused. Nor was there any proof of ongoing treatment, so there should not have been an award for future medical expenses. [*Anderson v. Independent Sch. Dist.,* 357 F.3d 806 (8th Cir. 2003); on compelled self-publication, *see Kuechle v. Life's Companion PCA Inc.,* 653 N.W.2d 214 (Minn. App. 2002)]

§ 25.09   PRIVILEGED STATEMENTS

[A]   Generally

Some kinds of communication are essential to the operation of businesses and the legal system, so they are afforded special treatment. They are referred to as "privileged," and by definition cannot be defamatory.

For instance, a case from California holds that a supervisor's statements made in an employee's performance review generally cannot be considered defamatory unless the supervisor falsely accuses an employee of criminal conduct, lack of integrity, incompetence, or reprehensible behavior. In other words, to lose the privilege, the supervisor must actually lie, not just be wrong about the employee. Even unjustified or bad-faith statements might be treated as privileged if they are opinions held by the supervisor. [*Jensen v. Hewlett-Packard Co.,* 14 Cal. App. 4th 958 (1993)]

Restatement of Torts (2d) § 596 permits a privilege when the publisher and the recipient of the information share a common interest, such as making sure that honest, qualified individuals are hired and retain their jobs.

Information about a teacher's dismissal for sexually harassing students, and his subsequent reinstatement after arbitration, was newsworthy and of public interest. Therefore, comments by school district officials to the local newspaper were privileged and were not defamatory. [*Corbally v. Kennewick Sch. Dist.,* 973 P.2d 1074 (Wash. App. 1999)]

In addition to absolute privilege, "qualified" privilege exists in some circumstances. A qualified privilege is one that can be taken away under some circumstances, whereas an absolute privilege survives all kinds of challenges. If the employer asserts a qualified privilege, it has the burden of proving that it is entitled to the privilege.

The District of Columbia Court of Appeals ruled in 1998 that employee evaluations are not absolutely privileged. The employer is entitled to a qualified privilege when communications remain within the firm. However, the privilege can be forfeited if information is disclosed outside the firm, if too much information is communicated, or there is a malicious motivation for the communication. [*Wallace v. Skadden, Arps, Slate, Meagher & Flom,* 715 A.2d 873 (D.C. App. 1998)]

The California Court of Appeals says that there is a qualified privilege for reports of workplace harassment (as § 35.02 shows, the employer has a duty to investigate harassment charges), and dissemination of these reports is defamatory only if the person communicating the report acts with malice. [*Bierbower v. FHP, Inc.,* 70 Cal. App. 4th 1, 82 Cal. Rptr. 2d 393 (1999)]

If a corporation has an audit committee, discussion of possible embezzlement or securities violations are probably entitled to qualified privilege as long as they remain within the committee, and are not disclosed (other than to law enforcement officials, which is the subject of another privilege). If there has been an investigation about workplace matters, disclosing the results of the investigation to the employees at large would probably also be privileged.

Even though they are not law enforcement officials, the EEOC and unemployment officials are close enough so that communications to them are privileged. There is at least a qualified privilege to make statements in the course of processing a union grievance or issuing dismissal letters required under a collective bargaining agreement. In fact, in some states (Michigan, New Mexico, Louisiana, Missouri) the privilege is absolute, not qualified.

California [Cal. Civ. Code § 47(c)] gives employers a qualified privilege for statements made without malice and on the basis of credible evidence. Alaska presumes [Alaska Stats. § 09.65.160] that employers act in good faith when they discuss their employees with other prospective employers. However, if the employer acts recklessly, maliciously, or contrary to the employee's civil rights, the privilege is no longer available.

In any state, employers are probably entitled to a qualified privilege when they make good-faith comments on employee performance to someone who has a legitimate right to the information. However, some degree of caution must be exercised. Not all co-workers necessarily have a legitimate interest in performance appraisals.

There is a qualified privilege to protect the safety of employees who might hurt themselves, or might be hurt by others. (Communications that are privileged in the context of a defamation suit are probably also privileged if the employee sues for violation of privacy instead of, or in addition to, defamation.)

However, even if a privilege initially exists, it can be sacrificed—most typically, by failure to act in good faith, or by making statements without proof and with reckless disregard as to whether or not they are true.

[B]   Attorney-Client Privilege

To do a good job, lawyers must learn all the facts of the situation, not just the facts that put their clients in a favorable light. Certain information is privileged if a client communicates it to a lawyer. The lawyer cannot be required to disclose this information—in fact, in most instances, it is unethical for the lawyer to disclose the information without the client's consent.

The factors that determine the availability of attorney-client privilege include:

- Whether the client approached the lawyer specifically to seek legal advice (as distinct from a casual chat, or when the lawyer played another role, such as giving business advice or serving as a director of a company);
- Whether the lawyer is acting as a lawyer, not a director or business advisor;
- Whether the communication relates to the lawyer-client relationship;
- Whether the client intends the information to be confidential;
- Whether the client did anything (deliberately or inadvertently) to remove the privilege; for instance, material distributed by the corporation will not be privileged.

It can be hard to determine the status of corporate documents.

A report might be confidential only if it were drafted specifically as a confidential document for transmission to the attorney.

The EEOC was not allowed to introduce a report prepared by the employer's attorneys about their investigation of a sexual harassment charge.

If the primary purpose of a communication is to get legal advice, a secondary business motive will not take away the privilege. But the privilege will be waived (that is, surrendered) if the corporation voluntarily distributes the document to non-attorneys, or discloses or allows the disclosure of a significant part of the document. For instance, if a corporation issues a press release about a development, or sends an employee to read a technical paper at an industry conference, it will not be able to argue that the press release or the technical paper is confidential.

However, a statement made by an employee who is not acting as an agent of the employer, but is simply an independent witness to an event probably will not be confidential, no matter why the statement was made.

In addition to the attorney-client privilege, the law of evidence contains a separate "work product" privilege. Work product is material prepared by attorneys and their employees as part of representing a client. Work product is also confidential and cannot become part of the discovery process before litigation.

[C] Self-Critical Analysis

Companies that want to improve diversity and eliminate discrimination often make studies of their employment and HR practices. Can discrimination plaintiffs require the company to disclose those documents, and use them to prove that the company used discriminatory employment practices?

Several federal courts have recognized a "self-critical analysis privilege": in other words, that these reports are internal documents that should not have to be revealed to plaintiffs, because companies should be encouraged to be candid about their discrimination problems instead of suppressing what they know to avoid embarrassing disclosures in lawsuits. [*See* Eric J. Wallach, Leslie Reider and Anthony C. Ginetto, *Employment Law,* National Law Journal, June 26, 1997, at p. B9; Michael Delikat and Ruth Raisfeld, *Litigation Over Corporate Diversity Programs,* New York Law Journal, July 14, 1997, at p. S5]

The opposite view is that the documents were prepared as part of the company's Title VII compliance program, would eventually be reported to the EEOC, and therefore could not reasonably be described as privileged. Even under this argument, a distinction might be drawn between a self-critical analysis that a company originated voluntarily and one that is mandated by the EEOC or by federal contract regulators. Or the court might require the company to produce hard information like statistics about workplace diversity, but permit the analytical part of the report to remain confidential.

It also helps to control dissemination of sensitive documents. The fewer people who have access to the document, and the more they agree that the company needs to analyze its performance in order to improve, the less likely they are to disclose the document in a way that is harmful or embarrassing to the corporation.

§ 25.10 DUTY TO COMMUNICATE

Not only are there situations in which an employer becomes liable for defamation or other disclosures; sometimes the employer can get into trouble for failing to communicate. There might be a duty to disclose dangerousness, so that other employers will not hire someone who puts their other employees or customers at risk. A subsequent employer may sue if the first employer fails to reveal relevant information, such as a job applicant's dismissal for stealing or workplace drug dealing.

Employers have a legal duty to protect customers and co-workers. That makes them negligent if they know that someone is dangerous, but they still retain him or her as an employee. This is true even if the risk is of conduct outside the scope of employment. An employer who knows that an employee has violent tendencies can be liable because of workplace assaults committed by that person, even if the assaults are not only not part of the job, but are contrary to the employer's policy and work rules. However, if the injured person is a fellow employee, it is very likely that the employee's only remedy will be through the Worker's Compensation system. [*See* § 33.03 for the concept of WC exclusivity]

Employers can be sued for negligent hiring or negligent entrustment if they hire someone for a safety-critical job but fail to check that person's references. In some contexts (such as hiring workers for a nursing home or day care center) there may be a duty to consult a special database maintained by the state or by a licensing organization to list individuals who are ineligible for employment because they have been convicted of a crime.

An employer will probably be exempt from liability for negligent hiring if a thorough investigation is performed before hiring; but if an employer fails to discover information that would have been disclosed by an ordinary background check, liability is a possibility.

Discrimination plaintiffs sometimes add a negligent hiring claim to their complaints. Their theory is that the employer was negligent in hiring and/or retaining a supervisor who was racist, sexist, or otherwise prone to engage in discriminatory conduct. The advantage to the plaintiff is that, although the discrimination claim is subject to the Civil Rights Act of 1991 (CRA '91) cap on damages [*see* § 42.12[B]], the negligent hiring claim is not. Also, it is hard to introduce evidence into a discrimination case about acts of discrimination or harassment carried out against employees other than the plaintiff, but this is relevant evidence in a negligent hiring case.

The employer might also be liable for negligent supervision, if the court or jury accepts the argument that the supervisor would not have been able to carry out the act of discrimination or harassment if the employer had managed the facility better.

§ 25.11   RESPONSES TO REFERENCE CHECKS

The employer has to steer between two hazards: neither committing defamation, nor failing to disclose information that must be divulged. One approach that often works is just to confirm the start and end dates of a former employee's employment, and then say that it is against company policy to discuss ex-employees. Another possibility is to disclose only information that is fully documented by HR files.

> **Tip:** If your state gives employees the right to review their files and make their own comments, make sure that any response to an inquiry includes the employee's comments. For instance, "Ms. Jones was dismissed for excessive lateness and poor performance. However, she said that other people were late just as often, and we should have been more sympathetic about her performance because her mother had just died." That way, the questioner gets both sides of the story.

According to employment lawyer Wendy Bliss, it is perfectly legitimate for a former employer to provide information about the candidate's performance as a member of a work team, and the adequacy of his or her work habits. But information should be disseminated only if it is truthful, work-related, and can be supported by documentation. Bliss suggests that employers should have a written policy about what kind of information will be given in references—and who will be allowed to provide this information. Information should not be released without a signed consent and release form (including a liability waiver) from the employee.

A new business sector is emerging: consultants who inform job applicants what their former employers are saying about them; in late 2003, a Google search found at least 10 companies performing these reference checks for $50–$90 fees. [Marci Alboher Nusbaum, *When a Reference is a Tool for Snooping,* New York Times, Oct. 19, 2003, at Business p. 12]

If an employee's resignation or termination is being negotiated, one area of negotiation is what will be said in response to reference checks.

It may be easier to get reference check information by asking about a job candidate's strengths and accomplishments as an employee, rather than stating or implying that you want negative information. No one is going to sue for defamation for being described as "hard working," "effective," or "creative"!

The growing trend toward outsourcing functions opens new risks if background checks are omitted, but the law is not clear as to whether the employer or the staffing agency is responsible for performing the checks. Hence, employers who are concerned about liability risks should either perform or make sure that the staffing agency performs background checks on:

- Anyone working in a customer's home
- Anyone working with children or vulnerable adults (e.g., the elderly or disabled)
- Anyone with access to bank accounts, Social Security numbers, trade secrets, or other confidential information

The employer's contract with the agency should include a warranty that the agency has performed background checks on all agency workers and certification that the check did not show anything precluding placement of the worker. The agency should warrant that background checks were performed in accordance with the FCRA and state laws. Employers should make sure that the agency maintains adequate liability insurance and should seek indemnification from the agency. [Tresa Baldas, *Outsourced Employees Triggering More Suits*, National Law Journal, Feb. 22, 2006 (law.com)]

A negligence suit brought by an employer against a staffing service was dismissed. The staffing service referred a bookkeeper who turned out to be a convicted embezzler, and who stole again from the employer. The staffing agency won the case because the employer did not specifically request a criminal background check, so the staffing service relied on testimonials from two other ex-employers who said the bookkeeper was honest. [*See* Joann S. Lublin, *Who Must Check a Prospect's Work History?* Wall Street Journal, July 31, 2001, at p. B1]

San Benito Bank & Trust Co. v. Landair Travels [31 S.W.3d 312 (Tex. App. 2000)] says that under Texas law, an employer does not have a duty to report embezzlement to law enforcement authorities or warn the new employer, because the first employer no longer controlled the employee's actions. There was no duty to prevent future crimes (she also embezzled funds from the subsequent employer). In fact, even a current employer does not have a duty to prevent off-duty wrong doing by employees.

§ 25.12   NEGOTIATED RESIGNATIONS

In some cases, an employee has been guilty of misconduct so serious (securities fraud or embezzlement, for example) that immediate removal is needed to reduce the risk to the corporation. In other cases, it will be less clear that employment must be ended—situations that fall under the Hollywood euphemism "creative differences." In such a situation, both parties benefit if they negotiate a resignation. The employee will leave on a stipulated date, and will release the company from all claims of employment-related discrimination. [*See* Chapter 37, § 37.07[A] for the specific problems of drafting a release that will satisfy the provisions of the Older Workers Benefit Protection Act (OWBPA). Pub. L. No. 101-433]

A resignation agreement is a contract and therefore is subject to the ordinary rules of contract law. For instance, if the employer deliberately misleads an employee, or subjects him or her to undue influence, the resignation agreement will be void and the employer will not be able to enforce it against the employee. The implications of the agreement are serious enough that first-line supervisors should not be allowed to negotiate. Either a trained HR staffer or an attorney should take on this role.

The agreement covers issues such as:

- The employee represents that he or she has not already filed any charges, or instituted litigation against the employer. If legal action is already in the works, settlement discussions or conciliation from the antidiscrimination agency is in order, but it is too late to negotiate a simple resignation agreement;
- The employee waives all claims against the employer. Drafting the proper, enforceable language is an intricate legal task;
- The employee agrees to treat the resignation as voluntary, and therefore not to apply for unemployment compensation;
- The employer should state that it does not admit liability of any kind, but is only using the agreement to clarify the issues;
- The employer should specify the kind of reference it will give the employee, and how it will handle reference checks from potential future employers;
- The employee should waive any merit-based bonuses that would otherwise be payable in the year of the resignation;
- The employee should agree to return all materials in his or her possession containing trade secrets or other proprietary materials of the employer, and should agree to refrain from using the employer's proprietary/trade secret information in any later employment;
- The employee should agree to keep the terms of the agreement confidential.

§ 25.13   RELEASES

An employee who has already filed discrimination charges may be willing to settle those charges, receiving some consideration in exchange for releasing the employer from further threat of suit by that employee. (However, a suit brought by another employee, or by the EEOC, continues to be a risk.) During the negotiations before a resignation, the employer and employee could agree on a severance package that winds up their relationship, making it clear that the soon-to-be-ex-employee will not bring any discrimination charges.

> **Tip:** If the terminating employee is a senior executive or creative person, and the risk of lawsuit, unfair competition, or solicitation of your employees or customers is a significant one, it could make sense to offer a consulting agreement after termination of employment. That way, at least he or she will be on your side instead of becoming an opponent.

A release is a contract, a legal agreement for surrendering claims that already exist. A release can be quite general, simply referring to "all claims" or quite specific, spelling out a whole laundry list of claims. A release of liability could be combined with reasonable covenants not to compete and provisions about the employer's intellectual property.

Courts might refuse to enforce a release that is too general, on the grounds that it is not specific enough to inform employees of their rights. But a release that is too detailed can put ideas into the heads of employees who had no real intention of bringing suit—or who didn't know the vast and exotic variety of ways in which they can make trouble for the employer!

Before payments of pensions and benefits begin, the plan might require the potential participant or beneficiary to sign a release stating that the plan has computed the amounts of benefits correctly, or that the participant or beneficiary waives all claims against the plan except the right to receive benefits as specified by the plan.

Courts are split as to whether such mandatory releases are enforceable. If all plan participants and beneficiaries have to sign, the release becomes part of ordinary plan administration, and there is no additional consideration for it. The employer gets something (freedom from suits and other claims) but doesn't give up anything in return (the benefits would be available under the plan anyway).

All contracts require consideration to be enforceable. Each party must receive something under the contract. In a typical release situation, the employer provides additional benefits (e.g., extra severance pay; outplacement assistance; early retirement incentives) over and above normal severance. The employee offers the employer a release of all claims, thus sparing the employer the risk of having to defend against charges. If each party gets something of value, the court probably won't worry about exact equivalence, as long as the parties knew their rights and understood all the implications of the release.

A general release covers all claims in existence at the time of the release; a limited release covers only the types of claims named in the release itself.

Tip: A release covering an injured worker who is entitled to Worker's Compensation is valid only if it is approved by a Worker's Compensation judge. Special care is required in drafting the release. If the worker releases claims relating to compensable physical injury, he or she will still have the right to bring suit on other grounds, such as claims that the employer acted in bad faith or intentionally inflicted emotional distress on the employee.

States take varying approaches about what can be covered by a general release. Some states say that they can cover all claims, known or unknown, but other states say that a general release is not effective for claims that the employee did not know about or suspect at the time the release was signed. Under this theory, people can only give up claims that they know about and decide are worth less than the benefits under the release.

In exchange for her employer's agreement to pay the premiums for the first six months of COBRA coverage, an employee signed a separation agreement releasing all employment-related claims, including ADA claims. Nevertheless, she filed EEOC charges and sued the former employer. The Southern District of

New York granted the former employer's motion to dismiss, finding the release to be valid and enforceable. The promise to pay the COBRA premiums constituted adequate consideration. Even though the coverage was mistakenly terminated, the release was still valid, because coverage was quickly reinstated. The court rejected the plaintiff's argument that the release was fraudulently obtained because she did not receive a COBRA notice; the employer's obligation to provide notice had not yet matured, because the release was signed prior to the end of the 44-day period during which notice must be given.

Later, the Southern District of New York reaffirmed its earlier decision to dismiss but reinstated one of the dismissed claims: the allegation that the employer violated COBRA by failing to provide a notice of election. The release did not relieve the employer of the duty to give notice because it was not clear whether the employee fully understood her rights when she signed the release. The duty to provide notice is triggered by termination and loss of EGHP coverage. The release could not be considered an adequate notice in and of itself because it did not satisfy the COBRA timing requirement, and because it did not include all of the mandated items that must be included in a notice. [*Knoll v. Equinox Fitness Clubs,* 2004 U.S. Dist. LEXIS 3690 (S.D.N.Y. 2004); 2003 U.S. Dist. LEXIS 23086 (S.D.N.Y. 2003)]

§ 25.14   SARBANES-OXLEY NOTICES

The Sarbanes-Oxley Act of 2002 [Pub. L. No. 107-204] became law in July 2002. It is a wide-ranging piece of legislation; many of the issues it covers are outside the scope of this book because they involve corporate governance and accuracy in accounting. However, the Sarbanes-Oxley Act also deals with "blackout periods" in individual account plans such as 401(k) plans. If a blackout period does occur, the corporation is required, by Sarbanes-Oxley Act § 306(b), to provide advance notice to plan participants that their ability to control their plan accounts will be limited during the blackout period, and a plain English explanation of the effect on their rights. [*See* 68 Fed. Reg. 3715 (Jan. 24, 2003) for DOL's Final Rule on this subject]

The general rule is that the notice must be given at least 30 days, but not more than 60 days, before the start of the blackout period, although exceptions are recognized if circumstances make it unfeasible to give the notice at the regular time. The notice must disclose the start and end dates of the blackout period and explain the extent to which participants' ability to change their plan investments or get distributions or loans from the plan will be affected. The notice must be written, rather than verbal, but it can be distributed electronically.

Civil money penalties of up to $100 per participant per day can be imposed on the plan administrators as individuals if the required notice is not given (although DOL also has discretion to suspend penalties if the imposition of penalties would be unjust). The Final Rules for Sarbanes-Oxley civil penalties were published by the DOL at 68 Fed. Reg. 3729 (Jan. 24, 2003).

The notice must be in writing—so a speech to the workforce wouldn't count—but it can be handed to participants, mailed, or distributed electronically. [*See* 68 Fed. Reg. 3729 (Jan. 24, 2003) for the text of a model notice that can be used to comply with the disclosure requirement] The model notice ("Important Notice Concerning Your Rights Under the [Plan Title] Plan") includes:

- The reason why a blackout period is imposed
- The extent of the restrictions, including the statement "whether or not you are planning retirement in the near future, we encourage you to carefully consider how this blackout period may affect your retirement planning as well as your overall financial plan"
- The expected beginning and ending dates of the period; a toll-free telephone number or URL the participants can access to check to see if the blackout period is still in effect
- A warning of the need to check and perhaps re-balance the participant's overall investment strategy because of the effect of the trading restrictions
- (If the full 30-day notice is impossible) The reason why the regular notice could not be given
- Name, address, and telephone number of a contact person who can answer questions about the blackout period and its effects.

CHAPTER 26

PRIVACY ISSUES

§ 26.01   INTRODUCTION

For the employee, a significant part of each working day is spent in the workplace. The employer takes on some of the roles of the government. Do employees have the same civil rights with respect to their employers as citizens have with respect to their governments? In some ways, the answer is "Yes," but in other ways, the legal system balances the employer's need for honesty, sobriety, and efficiency in the workplace against the employees' desire for privacy. Many (if not most) constitutional rights are limitations on government power, not the power of private entities such as employers.

Many of the topics in this book are either completely regulated by federal laws, or federal laws are dominant, but in the privacy arena, state laws are very significant. Most states have laws on access and copying of personnel files, so that employees can view and copy their own files, but access by outsiders is restricted.

Most states also protect privacy of medical records, especially those involving genetic testing or reports of substance abuse treatment. States often impose limitations on the extent to which employers can collect and record information about employees' lawful off-premises activities. For instance, many states make it illegal to investigate the religious, political, and social organizations that employees belong to.

Three HIV positive persons applied for flight attendant positions with American Airlines. They were given conditional offers of employment, contingent on passing medical exams and background checks. At this point, they were required to fill out medical histories and provide blood samples. None of them disclosed their HIV positive status or the medications they took, although the job application stated that false or fraudulent information, or failure to disclose medical conditions or medication use, would be ground for termination. When the blood samples were processed, the airline rescinded the job offers on the basis of failure to disclose their HIV status.

The three brought suit on privacy, ADA, and California FEHA grounds. The district court granted summary judgment for the airline, but the Ninth Circuit allowed the suit to proceed (except with respect to one plaintiff's claim of intentional infliction of emotional distress). The plaintiffs alleged that they were not told what the medical examination would entail. They were only notified about, and gave their consent to, urine testing. The plaintiffs asked for an explanation of why blood samples were taken, and were told that they were being checked for anemia. In the Ninth Circuit view, for a job offer to satisfy the requirements of the ADA and California law, the employer either must have completed all non-medical parts of the application process or be able to prove that it could reasonably have done so before making the offer. The ADA requires medical examinations (if given at all) to be a separate, second step of the selection process occurring only after all other selection issues have been resolved. The Ninth Circuit held that job applicants can keep their medical condition private until the last stage of the hiring process; at that point, they can decide whether or not to disclose the condition. Therefore, the Ninth Circuit held that the so-called conditional job offers were not real, because the applicants were required to undergo an immediate medical examination prematurely, while both medical and non-medical conditions on hiring remained. Although the airline testified that it had to streamline the application process to remain competitive for applicants with other airlines, the Ninth Circuit held that the airline failed to prove that there were no reasonable alternatives that would put the medical examination in its proper place—at the end of the selection process.

The California Constitution's right of privacy is broader than the federal one, because it imposes obligations on private parties as well as state actors. The appellants charged that the airline violated their privacy rights by performing blood tests without notice or consent. The court found that the blood tests implicated a protected privacy interest. Whether an expectation of privacy is reasonable is a fact question that can't be determined without a full trial, so summary judgment was inappropriate. Although the applicants consented to blood testing, they did not consent to any and all use that might be made of their blood samples, or to blood tests outside the ordinary and accepted range of pre-employment testing. However, claims of intentional infliction of emotional distress were dismissed, because there was no proof that the blood tests, even if illegal, were extreme or outrageous enough to violate norms of decency. [*Leonel v. American Airlines, Inc.*, 400 F.3d 702 (9th Cir. 2005)]

§ 26.02   POLYGRAPH TESTING

There are many problems with using polygraphy ("lie detector tests") in the workplace setting. These tests are expensive and not very reliable. The real test is whether the employee is nervous, and a practiced liar may be far less nervous than a timid but honest employee.

There are outright bans on polygraph testing in the workplace in Massachusetts, Michigan, Minnesota, and Oregon. Alaska, Connecticut, Delaware, Hawaii, Maine, Nebraska, New Jersey, New York, Rhode Island, West Virginia, and Wisconsin forbid employers to require, request, or even suggest testing. In one of these states, it violates public policy to fire someone for refusing to take a polygraph test, because the test cannot be demanded as a condition of employment. In Illinois, Maine, Michigan, Nevada, New Mexico, and Virginia, testing is not forbidden, but polygraph operators have to be licensed.

The Federal Employee Polygraph Protection Act of 1988 [Pub. L. No. 100-347, 29 U.S.C. § 2001] forbids most private employers from using polygraph tests for pre-employment screening. In the workplace itself, it is permissible to polygraph employees but only the course of an ongoing investigation about economic loss or injury to the employer's business. (In this context, drug tests and written or oral "honesty tests" are not considered polygraph examinations.)

Under the federal law, an employee can be asked to submit to polygraph testing only if:

- He or she has access to the property involved in the inquiry;
- The employer has a reasonable suspicion about the employee's involvement;
- Before the examination, the employer provides the employee with a specific written statement about the nature of the investigation and the basis for the employer's suspicion of the employee.

The employer is required to keep these statements on file for three years after they are issued.

The employer must advise the employee of his or her rights:

- To refuse the test or stop it after it has begun;
- To seek representation by a lawyer or other person (such as a union representative);
- To review the questions before the test;
- To review the results before the employer uses them as a premise for adverse employment action.

The employee must be notified that test results may be turned over to prosecutors.

In the view of the Seventh Circuit, an employer may have violated the Employee Polygraph Protection Act by asking for a taped voice sample from an employee for analysis to see if he had left a threatening voice mail for another employee. Because the sample was used to analyze truthfulness, and not just for a simple comparison between the employee's voice and the threatening message, it fell under the statutory definition of "lie detector." [*See Veazey v. Communications & Cable of Chicago, Inc.,* 194 F.3d 850 (7th Cir. 1999)]

The situation is different when the employee actually seeks the test. In 2006, the Eleventh Circuit ruled that a company did not violate the Employee Polygraph Protection Act by accepting the union's proposal that miners who were fired for theft be allowed to take a polygraph test so they could clear their names and be rehired. The company was not liable because the proposal was for the employee's own good, and there was no evidence that the company exerted pressure on the union to propose the testing. Nor was the union liable, because it acted on behalf of its members. [*Watson v. Drummond Co.,* 436 F.3d 1310 (11th Cir. 2006)]

§ 26.03   DRUG USE IN THE WORKPLACE

[A]   A Pervasive Problem

Workplace drug use is a serious problem for many reasons. Some drug users are able to restrict their substance abuse to off-work hours and off-premises locations. Some of them are able to pay for drugs by legitimate means. Even in this "best-case" scenario, drug residues are likely to affect their performance during working hours. That's why many states either deny Worker's Compensation to anyone who was drunk or drug-impaired at the time of an accident, or presume that substance abuse was the cause of any accident unless the injured person can prove otherwise. Quest Diagnostics, which provides workplace drug tests, says that the number of positive tests for amphetamines rose 17% between 2001 and 2002 alone. The problem of addiction to painkillers such as Oxycontin and Vicodin is also increasing. [Melinda Ligos, *Dealing With Addiction and What Comes After,* New York Times, July 20, 2003, at Business p. 8]

According to InfoLink Screening Service, in 2005, the type of workplace with the most drug test failures was the education system (12.7% of applicants), nearly twice as high as the 6.5% rate in the next highest category, the automobile industry. [PlanSponsor.com News Articles, *New Report Reveals Results of Background Checks* (Jan. 27, 2006)]

Many, if not most, drug users are unable to be so moderate in their drug consumption, and are likely to be impaired during working hours. They may use or even deal drugs in the workplace. If they can't afford to pay for their drugs, they are very likely to steal, embezzle, or commit industrial espionage to get drug money. Employees who are already breaking the law by illegal drug use may lose their inhibitions against committing other crimes as well.

Early in 2004, the Wall Street Journal reported on a new screening mechanism: a "drug wipe," a plastic tool that looks like the wand for a home pregnancy test, can be applied to surfaces to detect drug residues left by skin contact. This is less invasive than an individual test; does not raise privacy issues (workers do not have an enforceable interest in not having the office furniture screened!); and is less expensive than a conventional drug test. A general assessment of the office environment for five drugs costs about $10 per employee, versus about $35 for a single urine test. However, the problem becomes what to do if drug residues are found (one testing company says that residues are found on about half of premises), because it's hard to track who has touched particular objects. [Kris Maher, *Armchair Drug Detection,* Wall Street Journal, Jan. 20, 2004, at p. B1]

Two caveats should be noted. First, there is a tremendous "anti-drug-test" industry marketing substances (often effective) to be used to mask the presence of drug metabolites. The development of these products relies on the same research used to test for drug use; there's a kind of "arms race" between the two, and testing for the chemical adulterants that mask drug use is becoming more common. Be aware, therefore, that a person who tests negative may be a well-prepared drug user rather than a "clean and sober" individual. [Daniel Nasaw and Jennifer Saranow, *Don't Say No: Foiling Drug Tests Is Cottage Industry,* Wall Street Journal, Dec. 12, 2002, at p. D6]

Second, the fairly widespread condition of "paruresis" (shy bladder syndrome) renders some people incapable of producing urine for random drug testing. Of course, this doesn't mean that they use illegal drugs or are not effective workers.

Department of Transportation regulations allow a person with this condition who has documentation from a physician to be tested with alternative evaluation methods, and it makes sense to have alternatives available if you perform drug testing. [Sana Siwolop, *For Some, Drug Tests Are Almost Impossible,* New York Times, Apr. 14, 2002, at Business p.1] Note that at the end of 2002, Ohio struck down a state law [Rev. Code. Ann. § 4123/54(A)(2)] requiring drug and alcohol testing of all injured workers (even without suspicion) and imposing a rebuttable presumption that anyone who refuses testing is impaired. The court found this statute to violate the Fourth Amendment by authorizing unreasonable searches—unless the worker is employed by an industry that is especially safety-sensitive, or unless the injured person had a demonstrated history of substance abuse. [*State ex rel. Ohio AFL-CIO v. Ohio Bureau of Worker's Compensation,* 97 Ohio St. 3d 504, 780 N.E.2d 981, 2002 Ohio 6717 (2002)]

The abuse of legal substances, such as alcohol and prescription drugs, also creates problems for employers. Although the problems are reduced, because laws are not violated, they are problems nonetheless, and the Employee Assistance Program should make help available for those who need a substance abuse program or support group.

Under the Federal Drug-Free Workplace Act, [41 U.S.C. § 701] companies with federal procurement contracts over $25,000 (and many companies are federal contractors) must certify to the contracting agency that they will provide a drug-free workplace. The contract will not be awarded if they do not make the certification.

The contractor-employer's obligations are to:

- Notify employees that using, possessing, and selling drugs is prohibited, and what the penalties will be if these rules are violated;
- Set up a drug-free awareness program;
- Order employees to abide by the program and notify the employer if they are convicted of a drug offense (even one occurring off-premises);
- Notify the contracting agency within ten days of receiving such a report from an employee;
- Impose penalties on all employees convicted of drug violations that are related to the workplace;
- Continue to make a good-faith effort to keep drugs out of the workplace.

If the employer is a defense contractor, it must do regular drug tests on employees in "sensitive positions," in other words, those with access to classified information.

A Connecticut statute [Conn. Gen. Stat. § 31-51x] prohibits urine testing for drugs unless the employer has a reasonable suspicion that the employee is using drugs or alcohol in a way that does or could adversely affect job performance. However, this statute does not apply to tests on consent of the employee (here, because an employee accused of theft agreed to take a test to reduce the disciplinary consequences of the theft). [*Poulos v. Pfizer,* 711 A.2d 688 (Conn. 1998)]

[B] Case Law on Drug Testing

Department of Transportation rules have been held to protect the public, not transportation workers. Therefore, it is legitimate for employers to delegate the administration of the testing program to an outside company. If the outside company mixes up the urine specimens, it is liable for the mistakes, and the employer that hired it is not. [*Carroll v. Federal Express Corp.,* 113 F.3d 163 (9th Cir. 1997)]

Pre-employment drug testing is more likely to be upheld by the courts than testing of current employees, on the theory that employees have a legitimate right of privacy. (For example, in late 2003 West Virginia ruled that because of the lower expectation of privacy, it is permissible to require job applicants to take a drug test even though state law bars mandatory testing of employees. [*Baughman v. Wal-Mart Stores Inc.,* 215 W. Va. 45 (W. Va. 2003)]) In 1997, the California Supreme Court took the position that urine testing for drugs can be required of persons who have received conditional job offers, but not employees who are under consideration for promotions. The rationale is that the Fourth Amendment allows drug testing that is not connected to specific suspicion, but only if there is a special need and the employee's privacy is impaired only minimally, as compared to the special interests of public employers. [*Loder v. Glendale, California,* 14 Cal. 4th 846, 927 P.2d 1200 (1997)]

In another California case, a job offer was extended conditioned on the applicant's passing a drug test. The applicant had to move to take up the new job, and logistics kept him from actually taking (and failing) the drug test until he was already on the payroll. The employer fired him, and he claimed that he was already an employee so a suspicionless drug test was improper. The California Court of Appeals did not accept that argument. [*Pilkington Barnes Hind v. Superior Court,* 66 Cal. App. 4th 28, 77 Cal. Rptr. 2d 596 (1998)] The distinction between job applicants and employees exists because employers have a chance to observe their active employees, and in appropriate cases detect signs of drug abuse that give rise to reasonable suspicion. The employer had not yet had a chance to observe the plaintiff.

Cases in Arizona and California say that it does not violate public policy to discharge a worker based on his or her refusal to take a drug test. [*AFL-CIO v. California Unemployment Ins. Appeals Bd.,* 23 Cal. App. 4th 51, 28 Cal. Rptr. 2d 210 (1994); *Hart v. Seven Resorts Inc.,* 191 Ariz. 297 (Ariz. App. 1997)] In a Fourth Circuit case, two employees charged that, although they were nominally fired for refusing to take a drug test, the real reason was that they were union activists. The court held that neither imposing the drug testing requirement nor firing the two workers violated the National Labor Relations Act.

Even though the testing program was implemented only one week after a strike, it was applied uniformly to all employees so could not be cited as an example of anti-union animus. Furthermore, since six out of 20 employees tested positive, the employer had a valid concern about drug use in the workforce.

Eldeco Inc. v. NLRB [132 F.3d 1007 (4th Cir. 1997)] says that drug testing policies are valid as long as they are not disparately enforced (e.g., on the basis of racial stereotyping or union membership).

In *Smith v. Zero Defects Inc.*, [132 Idaho 881 (1999)] the employer's policy called for termination of any employee testing with a detectable level of alcohol or illegal drugs. The plaintiff tested positive for amphetamines during a random test; he was not impaired at that particular time. However, Idaho (like Nebraska, Nevada, Oklahoma, and Utah—but unlike Arizona, Kansas, Oregon, and Washington) considers violation of an employer's zero-tolerance policy to be misconduct that is serious enough to prevent the employee from getting unemployment insurance benefits, even if he or she was not impaired at the time of the test. In other words, off-duty drug use can be serious enough to block unemployment benefit eligibility.

It was legitimate for a school board to fire a teacher who refused to take a drug test that was ordered after a local law-enforcement sweep found marijuana in her car parked in the school parking lot. The demand did not violate the teachers' contract requirement for either consent or a search warrant for search of teachers' personal property in the school building. The demand for testing was appropriate in light of the violation of the school's drug and alcohol policy. [*Hearn v. Board of Pub. Educ.,* 191 F.3d 1329 (11th Cir. 1999)]

According to the California Court of Appeals, it is legitimate to fire an employee who tests positive for marijuana, even if he claims that he used the drug pursuant to the state's Compassionate Use Act because it relieved his back pain. Employers have no duty to accommodate drug use that violates federal law. [*Ross v. Ragingwire Telecommunications Inc.,* 132 Cal. App. 4th 590 (Cal. App. 2005)]

An arbitrator's award, requiring reinstatement of an employee who was fired after failing a drug test, could not be enforced, because it violated the well-established public policy against allowing drug users to keep safety-sensitive jobs. [*Exxon Corp. v. Esso Worker's Union,* 118 F.3d 841 (1st Cir. 1997)] However, two years later, the Tenth Circuit upheld an award reinstating a truck driver who admitted to smoking marijuana two days before an accident. The arbitrator read the CBA's requirement of discharge only for "just cause" to require proof of on-the-job drug use, drug dealing, or impairment, not just off-hours drug use. [*Kennecott Utah Copper Corp. v. Becker,* 195 F.3d 1201 (10th Cir. 1999)]

A later case on arbitration and drug testing arose when an oil refining company imposed a nationwide zero-tolerance drug policy at all its facilities. The union filed two grievances, charging that the policy was improperly implemented, without bargaining. One arbitrator upheld the policy in all respects. The second arbitrator generally upheld the reasonableness and validity of the policy, except for the provision that called for immediate termination of employees with a positive drug test, with no potential for rehabilitation or a last chance agreement. The employer brought suit in district court to challenge the arbitration award. The district court confirmed the arbitration award, but the Third Circuit reversed, finding that this was one of the rare cases in which an arbitration award could be disturbed. In this case, the arbitrator exceeded his discretion by ruling against the zero-tolerance policy, which was clearly within management's powers to adopt. The arbitrator's award substituted the arbitrator's own judgment for management's. Therefore, the award did not draw its essence from the CBA, and so it could be invalidated by the Court of Appeals. [*Citgo Asphalt Refining Co. v. Paper, Allied-Industrial Chemical, and Energy Workers Int'l Union Local No. 2-991*, 385 F.3d 809 (3d Cir. 2004)]

Decisions in several states (Illinois, Louisiana, New York, Wyoming) allow a person fired because of a false-positive drug test to sue the testing firm for failing to meet its duty of due care in collecting, handling, and processing the specimens, but in the views of the Fifth Circuit, and courts in Texas and Pennsylvania, testing firms do not have an enforceable duty to the employee, because the employer is the one that hires the testing company. [*Duncan v. Afton*, 991 P.2d 739 (Wyo. 1999); *Ney v. Axelrod*, 723 A.2d 719 (Pa. Sup. 1999)]

In the view of the Texas Supreme Court, an employer does not owe a duty to an at-will employee to use reasonable care in carrying out mandatory drug testing. It was permissible for a trucking company to use its own employees rather than an independent laboratory to collect urine samples, despite the importance of the task. (Employees could be fired for testing positive.) The plaintiff, a former truck driver, tested positive for marijuana, although he denied that he had used marijuana. Later on, he passed an independent lab's hair-follicle test, but it was so much later (84 days) that it didn't really resolve the question of drug use at the relevant time. In the safety-regulated trucking industry, employers are required to review two years' back tests performed by other employers, so the plaintiff was unable to secure another trucking job. At the trial court level, the jury found the defendant negligent and held that it acted with malice, thus awarding more than $900,000, including $100,000 in punitive damages, to the plaintiff—an award that was reversed by the Texas Supreme Court. [*Mission Petroleum Carriers Inc. v. Solomon*, 106 S.W.3d 705 (Tex. 2003)]

Federal Railroad Administration rules about drug testing of transportation workers do not preempt state common-law claims (negligence, breach of contract, defamation, invasion of privacy, intentional infliction of emotional distress) against a lab that allegedly reported that two employees' urine samples were "not consistent with human urine," resulting in their being fired. Code of Federal Regulations Title 49 § 219.11(d), says that employees cannot be required to waive liability for negligent handling of drug-test specimens. The Ninth Circuit has interpreted the federal regulations to permit common-law negligence claims in state court. The Fifth Circuit held that the DOT drug testing regulations preempt common-law claims, but that case involved claims against the employer, not the allegedly negligent laboratory. [*Chapman v. Lab One*, 390 F.3d 620 (8th Cir. 2004); *Ishikawa v. Delta Airlines Inc.*, 343 F.3d 1129 (9th Cir. 2003); *Frank v. Delta Airlines*, 314 F.3d 195 (5th Cir. 2002)]

It is probably inappropriate to impose a drug testing requirement that covers lawful prescription and over-the-counter medications. The Tenth Circuit granted an injunction against an employer's drug policy that required its employees to notify, and get permission from, their supervisors if they took prescription medications. The court treated this as a violation of the Americans with Disabilities Act, as a forbidden inquiry about disability. [*Roe v. Cheyenne Mountain Conference Resort Inc.,* 124 F.3d 1221 (10th Cir. 1997)]

Tip: However, the ADA's protection is limited to "qualified individuals with a disability," so if side effects of a prescription medication (such as falling asleep or losing coordination) make it unsafe for a person to perform a particular job, then that person is not qualified for ADA purposes.

Furthermore, current substance abuse is not a disability for ADA purposes (although it is unlawful to discriminate against someone who is now clean and sober because of a past history of substance abuse). "Current" drug use means use that is recent enough for the employer to conclude that drug abuse is an ongoing problem. [*Zenor v. El Paso Healthcare System, Limited,* 176 F.3d 847 (5th Cir. 1999)] Drug use several weeks prior to termination can fit this definition. [*See, e.g., Shafer v. Preston Mem. Hosp.,* 107 F.3d 274 (4th Cir. 1997); *Collings v. Longview Fibre Co.,* 63 F.3d 828 (9th Cir. 1975)]

The ADA has a safe harbor [42 U.S.C. § 12114(b)] for people who have completed a rehab program. Just entering a program isn't enough; the safe harbor is for people with a history of staying clean.

§ 26.04   CRIMINAL RECORD AND CREDIT CHECKS

A federal law, the Fair Credit Reporting Act (FCRA), [15 U.S.C. § 1681] as amended by the Consumer Credit Reporting Reform Act of 1996, [Pub. L. No. 104-208] governs the access of businesses to credit reports. Although credit reports are most commonly used in the context of loans or merchandise sales, it is also fairly common for potential employers to run a credit check before making a job offer.

Under the FCRA, employers must notify applicants before they seek credit information as part of the application process. A civil penalty is imposed for ordering a credit check without the mandatory notification. The employer must also notify applicants and employees before any negative employment-related action is taken on the basis of an investigative credit report.

The FCRA allows credit reporting agencies to disclose the information they have gathered to companies that use the information for "employment purposes," i.e., evaluating the subject of the credit report for employment, promotion, retention as an employee, or reassignment. The reporting agency is allowed to furnish a report discussing the job applicant's or employee's creditworthiness, standing, character, and reputation.

In addition to federal regulation of the use of credit reports, some states (Arizona, California, Connecticut, Florida, Kansas, Kentucky, Maine, Maryland, Massachusetts, Montana, New Hampshire, New Mexico, New York, Oklahoma, and Texas) impose additional requirements on employer use of credit reports.

If a third party performs a drug test, it might be treated as a "credit report" or "investigative credit report" under the federal Fair Credit Reporting Act. However, if the employer performs the test itself, the FCRA is not involved, because the statute does not apply to transactions between a consumer and the entity that makes the report. Therefore, an employee fired after a urine test that was positive for marijuana cannot use the FCRA to sue the employer that performed the test. [*Chube v. Exxon Chem. Ams.,* 760 F. Supp. 557 (M.D. La. 1991)]

2003 legislation, the Fair and Accurate Credit Transactions Act (FACTA; P.L. 108-159) amends 15 USC § 1681a, enacting a new subsection (x) under which a communication will not be treated as a consumer report (and therefore will not be subject to FCRA requirements) if it is a job-related communication not related to the creditworthiness of the individual. The communication must be made to the employer as part of an investigation of suspected workplace misconduct, or under the employer's pre-existing policies or under any law or regulation. To qualify for the exemption, the information must be disclosed only to the employer or to government officials or self-regulatory officials—unless broader disclosure is mandated by law. If the employer uses the information as the basis of any adverse action against the subject of the investigation, the subject must be furnished a summary of the information. The employer, however, is not obligated to disclose the sources of the information.

Under the Intelligence Reform and Terrorism Prevention Act of 2004, P.L. 108-458 (Dec. 17, 2004), private employers can access the FBI criminal records database to obtain information about employees or applicants for private security jobs. The statute applies to full-time or part-time, uniformed or non-uniformed, armed or unarmed personnel, but not to persons hired to monitor electronic security systems. Section 6403 of the statute provides that, on the written consent of the employee or applicant, the employer can submit fingerprints or other means of identification to the state's investigative agency for a background check. (States can opt out of the background check system by passing a law, or if the state governor issues an order to this effect.) The United States Attorney General has the power to respond to a request from the state agency to view the FBI data. Then the state investigative agency notifies the employer whether, in the previous 10 years, the employee or applicant has been convicted of a felony, an offense involving dishonesty, or a false statement. Employers must be notified of offenses involving physical force against another person in the previous 10 years, as well as any unresolved felony charges within the previous 365 days. The employer has an obligation to disclose the information to the employee. [*See also* § 23.08]

There was steady growth in the number of FBI fingerprint checks performed for private employers between 1992 (when about 3.5 million such checks were done) and 2004 (when the number was more than nine million). By 2005, half of the FBI fingerprint checks were vocationally related rather than for criminal cases. States accept fingerprint records, compare them to state criminal records, and then forward them to the FBI, who maintains the only federal fingerprint database, the Integrated Automated Fingerprint Identification System, which contains 44 million sets of prints. The use of fingerprint checks has not only expanded to cover far more occupations, but is often applied by nonprofit organizations to volunteers. [Gary Fields, *Ten-Digit Truth Checks,* Wall Street Journal, June 7, 2005, at p. B1]

The increasing prevalence of outsourcing to cut labor costs raises questions about whether the employer or the staffing agency is responsible for background checks. Clearly, both are at risk of being sued in connection with any harm caused by an outsourced worker. It is prudent for employers to get background checks at least on anyone who works in clients' homes; has access to trade secrets, bank accounts, or Social Security numbers; or works with children or the elderly. Employers that work through agencies should get the staffing agency to agree to indemnify the worksite employer, carry adequate insurance, and name the worksite employer as an additional insured. [Tresa Baldas, *Outsourced Employees Triggering More Suits,* National Law Journal, Feb. 22, 2006 (law.com)]

§ 26.05   GENETIC TESTING

There are already more than 500 genetic tests available, although they are too expensive for widespread use. More than half the states make it unlawful to impose a requirement of genetic testing (e.g., for sickle cell trait or susceptibility to cancer) as a condition of employment, as a condition of insurance, or as a factor in raising insurance premiums.

The state laws focus on different areas. Some of them make the results of genetic testing confidential, while others limit the extent to which insurers can deny coverage or raise premiums on that account. Another group of statutes focuses on hiring.

On February 8, 2000, then-President Clinton issued an Executive Order that prevents mandatory genetic testing, or use of genetic information in employment-related decisions, in federal workplaces.

In mid-2002, the Burlington Northern and Santa Fe Railroad agreed to pay $2.2 million to settle an EEOC suit involving claims brought by 36 employees about the employer's attempt to conceal improper genetic testing of workers who filed Worker's Compensation claims. (The purpose of the testing was to argue that the injured people had a genetic susceptibility to carpal tunnel syndrome.) The railroad agreed not to use genetic testing in required medical examinations, and to provide additional training in ADA issues to its medical and claims staff. This was the first federal case to be resolved. [Leigh Strope (Associated Press), *Railroad Agrees to Pay $2.2 Million to Workers It Genetically Tested* (May 9, 2002) (law.com)]

According to the National Conference of State Legislatures, the majority of the states (33 of them) forbid employment discrimination based on genetic information. Of the state laws, 16 prohibit the use of genetic tests by employers; 18 forbid employers to ask applicants or employees for genetic information; and 25 forbid employers to mandate that employees be tested.

Federal legislation is also in the works. In 2005, the Senate passed a bill forbidding genetic discrimination in employment, and parallel legislation was introduced in the House. IBM claimed that it was the first major corporation to take a stance against genetic testing in employment when, in late 2005, it adopted a policy forbidding the use of genetic test data in hiring or benefits decisions. The company's intention was to use its size and status to start a trend. Aetna pledged not to drop coverage or raise rates because of genetic test results.

The advocacy group The Genetic Alliance reports receiving an average of two discrimination complaints per week, and in 2005, the Genetics in Medicine Journal reported survey results that 40% of those queried were afraid of losing jobs or health care coverage as a result of genetic test results. Comparatively few lawsuits have been brought, perhaps because of difficulties of proof or the lack of consensus as to whether there is a private cause of action for violation of statutes governing genetic testing. [Tresa Baldas, *Tension Grows Over Genetic Testing of Employees,* National Law Journal, Nov. 3, 2005 (law.com); Charles Forelle, *IBM Policy Bars Use of Gene Data in Employment,* Wall Street Journal, Oct. 11, 2005, at p. B2; Steve Lohr, *I.B.M. to Put Genetic Data of Workers Off Limits,* New York Times, Oct. 10, 2005, at p. C1]

§ 26.06   SEARCHES AND SURVEILLANCE

[A]   Constitutional Limits on Employees

Although the Constitution puts limits on unreasonable searches and seizures, the focus is on the activities of public agencies such as the police and the military. Therefore, it is very unlikely that the actions of a private employer would have a constitutional dimension, or that the employee would be able to invoke the Fourth Amendment as protection against searches and seizures.

However, an employer's surveillance activities might constitute an invasion of privacy, which could furnish grounds for a suit by an employee.

An employer can legitimately order a workplace search if there is a good reason in the first place (such as getting evidence of embezzlement, theft of products, or other work-related misconduct) and the scope of the search is appropriate to satisfying that purpose. But, because the employer controls the workplace but employees control their own personal possessions such as coats and handbags, get legal advice about how to handle a search.

There is no general state or federal ban on video surveillance of nonprivate areas within the workplace (areas that are open to the public or that are open to inspection of other employees).

Surveillance programs are most likely to survive legal challenge if:

- They are created in response to a real problem (e.g., inventory shrinkage) or a real threat (e.g., potential employer liability);
- Employees are accurately informed of the purposes and content of the program;
- Surveillance is restricted to the least intrusive method that is still effective.

The Third Circuit ruled that Labor Management Relations Act (LMRA) § 301 does not preempt state laws about wiretaps and privacy, so state tort claims about workplace surveillance are not ruled out. Suit was brought to protest audio and video surveillance of the time clock area that was imposed without notice to the employees. The court held that it is not necessary to interpret the CBA to determine whether surveillance violated employee rights; merely looking at the CBA to see if it has a surveillance clause is not a contract interpretation. Tort claims are pre-empted by LMRA § 301 only if they involve a duty of care imposed by a CBA. [*Kline v. Security Guards Inc.*, 386 F.3d 246 (3d Cir. 2004)]

The First Circuit says that it does not violate the Fourth Amendment for a public employer to use silent video cameras for surveillance of the work area. In this case, the work environment was an open space with no assigned offices, cubicles, workstations, or desks, so the court concluded that it would not be reasonable to assume that privacy would be available in such an environment. [*Vega-Rodriguez v. Puerto Rico Telephone Co.*, 110 F.3d 174 (1st Cir. 1997)]

However, in a unionized company, it might be an unfair labor practice to install surveillance devices, at least without the consent of the union. In 1997, the NLRB decided. [*Colgate-Palmolive Co.*, 323 N.L.R.B. 82 (1997)] that installation of hidden surveillance cameras is a mandatory bargaining subject, not a management decision. To the NLRB, only subjects like product lines and capital investments are management prerogatives.

The Seventh Circuit obligated a unionized employer to engage in collective bargaining about the use of hidden surveillance cameras. The employer also had to disclose the location of the cameras to the union. The court required bargaining because it compared the use of surveillance cameras to drug, alcohol, and polygraph tests—all of which are mandatory bargaining subjects. Furthermore, the employer was not forbidden to exercise its management prerogative to install security cameras—only ordered to bargain collectively on the subject. [*National Steel Corp. v. NLRB*, 324 F.3d 928 (7th Cir. 2003)]

Early in 2002, the Supreme Court permitted unionized employees to sue in state court for invasion of privacy because of video surveillance of company bathrooms. The employer, a trucking company, said that the cameras were installed to frustrate drug dealing and drug use, and were not aimed at urinals or bathroom stalls. The issue in *Consolidated Freightways v. Cramer* [534 U.S. 1078 (2002)] was whether LMRA § 301 preempts the state law forbidding undisclosed videotaping of employees. The Supreme Court held that it does not, so state-law suits can go forward—even though the case might be interpreted as involving interpretation of a collective bargaining agreement (the usual test for LMRA § 301 preemption).

The NLRB ruled that it was a violation of federal labor law to install hidden surveillance cameras in the workplace without bargaining. (The employer suspected that a room was being used by employees to use and sell illegal drugs; 16 workers out of 18 observed by the cameras were disciplined for leaving their work areas and using drugs.) The NLRB ordered the company to bargain on the issue. [*Anheuser-Busch Inc.*, 324 NLRB No. 49 (July 22, 2004)] In 2005, the D.C. Circuit ruled that surveillance, as a subject plainly germane to the work environment, is a mandatory bargaining subject because it is not within the core of entrepreneurial control. However, the court ruled that while the employer must bargain over the use of cameras and the general reason why surveillance is necessary, the employer is not obligated to inform the union of the location of the cameras or when they will be in use. The D.C. Circuit remanded the case to determine whether the employees observed on the videotape would be entitled to individualized relief if the employer discovered their misconduct unlawfully. [*Brewers and Maltsters v. NLRB*, 414 F.3d 36 (D.C. Cir. 2005); *National Steel Corp. v. NLRB*, 324 F.3d 928 (7th Cir. 2003) (also treats surveillance cameras as a mandatory bargaining subject)]

The railroad Metro-North found out the hard way that surveillance outside the workplace is often a bad idea. An employee sued under the Federal Employee Liability Act (which covers all railroad employees) for job-related back injuries. The railroad hired a private investigator to videotape her daily activities, hoping to prove that her claim was faked. Instead, the footage showed a severely debilitated person trying to cope with degenerative arthritis that resulted when she suffered a herniated disc. Naturally, the company didn't plan to introduce the video at trial, but when the plaintiff's attorney found out about the tape (as part of the discovery process), the plaintiff introduced the tape to impeach the testimony of a witness for the defense. The New York court ruled that the plaintiff could introduce the tape. Video surveillance is fairly common in employment injury cases, so plaintiff's lawyers usually ask if tapes have been produced; about a quarter of the tapes turn out to be beneficial to the plaintiff rather than the defense. [Mark Fass, *Video of Hurt Worker Shows How Surveillance Can Backfire*, New York Law Journal (Dec. 9, 2004) (law.com)]

A Department of Corrections research analyst was told, after holding a job for two years, that she would have to take a psychological examination to keep it. (The record does not explain why this was required.) She took the test, then brought suit under 42 U.S.C. § 1983 against the Department of Corrections and two officials (her immediate supervisor and the official who imposed the testing requirement) in their individual capacity. The plaintiff alleged that the inquiries into her personal life constituted an unreasonable search and seizure. To obtain supplemental jurisdiction, she alleged that even if the test was not a search, making it a job requirement invaded her privacy and deliberately inflicted emotional distress (an Indiana common-law tort). She sought damages and an injunction expunging the test results. The District Court dismissed the case on the grounds that the individual defendants were immune because there was no clearly established right at the time the plaintiff sued; it dismissed as against the Department of Corrections, finding that it was not a person that could be sued under 42 U.S.C. § 1983. Because there were no remaining federal claims, the district court dismissed the state claim. The Seventh Circuit ruled that the official immunity defense applies only to liability for damages, but U.S.C. § 1983 injunctive relief is not available against state officials sued as individuals. Because there was no physical contact, the Seventh Circuit did not deem the required test to be a search, although the opinion implied that it was unreasonable to require a researcher who did not carry a gun or have access to prisoners to undergo psychological testing.

The Seventh Circuit dismissed, noting that although there appeared to be valid state claims, they should be pursued in state court. [*Greenawalt v. Indiana Dep't of Corrections*, 397 F.3d 587 (7th Cir. 2005)]

[B] Wiretapping

Wiretapping, and other forms of interception of wire, oral, and electronic communications, including e-mail (or electronic or mechanical interception of conversations) are covered by the federal Omnibus Crime Control and Safe Streets Act of 1968 [18 U.S.C. § 2511 *et seq.*] Interceptions by the employer are regulated. Interceptions are prohibited only if the employee had a reasonable expectation that the communication would not be subject to interception.

For instance, if a telephone salesperson has known from the beginning of the job that contact with customers is subject to monitoring, there would be no reasonable expectation of privacy. But even if interception of calls is legitimate, the employer must cease the interception if it is clear that a particular call is personal and not business-related. One of the parties to a communication has a right to intercept it; so does anyone with explicit or implicit consent to intercept.

The federal statute imposes penalties for improper interception that can be as high as $10,000. Punitive damages can be imposed on an employer that acted wantonly, recklessly, or maliciously.

To investigate charges of misuse of the police paging system, the city of Reno monitored pagers. The district court for the District of Nevada held [*Bohach v. City of Reno*, 932 F. Supp. 1232 (D. Nev. 1997)] that there was no search, and federal wiretap statutes were not violated, because the pager technology required centralized storage of the messages, defeating any reasonable expectation of privacy.

[C] Internet and E-Mail Monitoring

Apart from the fact that employees are not supposed to use the company computer system for personal purposes, employee e-mails can subject the employer to liability (in the context of sexual or racial harassment, for example, or concealment of improprieties).

When the American Management Association surveyed 840 companies in 2004, it found that 60% of them use software to monitor the e-mails their employees send and receive. In 2001, only 47% did this. In all the states other than Connecticut and Delaware, employers are not restricted in the scope of their surveillance of traffic on company computers or using company e-mail accounts. Although internal communications (between employees of the same company) carry high risks of getting the company into trouble, in 2004 only 27% of companies monitored internal e-mail communications. Originally, surveillance software looked only for obscenities and sexual content; now more sophisticated monitoring programs look for references that might hint at industrial espionage, malicious hacking, or insider trading in securities—or simply long periods of time when the employee is apparently not working! There is an increasing trend to monitor Instant Messaging and employees' blogs (Weblogs) to make sure that trade secrets and competitive information are not being released. [Pui-Wing Tam, Erin White, Nick Wingfield, and Kris Maher, *Snooping E-Mail by Software Is Now a Workplace Norm,* Wall Street Journal, Mar. 9, 2005, at p. B1]

Tip: Attorney Clifford R. Atlas points out that surveillance of employee e-mail usage during a union organizing campaign could lead to ULP charges. [Riva Richmond, *Do You Know Where Your Workers Are?* Wall Street Journal, Jan. 12, 2004, at p. R1; Lothar Determann, *When No Really Means No: Consent Requirements for Workplace Monitoring,* 72 L.W. 2243 (Nov. 4, 2003); Marci Alboher Nusbaum, *New Kind of Snooping Arrives at the Office,* New York Times, July 13, 2003, at Business p. 12]

The collaboration software technology used to facilitate telecommuting can also be used to monitor employees' computer and Internet use at the workplace, e.g., by detecting and/or blocking attempts to access non-business sites. Not all types of work are equally amenable to such monitoring: it's one thing to determine how many calls a call-center worker completes, or how many forms a claims processor processes, another thing to decide if a programmer who writes more lines of code is more productive or just sloppier than a co-worker.

Tip: Employers should be aware that peer-to-peer software (e.g., Morpheus, Kazaa) can create significant problems for office networks. Not only are these applications typically used by employees for non-work purposes (e.g., downloading songs and movies), they can slow down a corporate network, spread viruses, and give outsiders access to the network. Many employers have adopted or strengthened policies against file-sharing at work, or even installed programs to detect and block access to unauthorized peer-to-peer sites (although it's a constant struggle between providers of up-to-date security software and ambitious hackers). [Anna Wilde Mathews, *Companies Deplore File Sharers,* Wall Street Journal, June 26, 2003, at p. B1]

It has long been traditional for blue-collar workers to punch a time clock. Some enterprises are shifting from a paper-based to an electronic time-logging system (e.g., swiping an electronic badge instead of writing down hours on a time card). More sophisticated electronic measures are now being adopted in the white-collar, salaried context, to track employees' presence at their workstations and what they're doing. For example, a large law firm requires its paralegals and clerical workers to indicate their presence with a touchpad sensor. Mitsubishi Motors workers log their hours on a Web-based desktop system, and the accounting manager's system is set up to permit checking on any subordinate's computer system. However, if employees feel that they are being infantilized by being subjected to excessive suspicion and surveillance, the increase in insubordination could outweigh any productivity gains. [Kris Maher, *Big Employer is Watching*, Wall Street Journal, Nov. 4, 2003, at p. B1]

State and federal wiretap statutes typically include a "provider exception," under which the provider of communications is allowed to intercept messages on the system. An employer is clearly a provider when it owns the equipment on which the employees communicate.

In *Smyth v. Pillsbury Co.*, [914 F. Supp. 97 (E.D. Pa. 1996)] an employer was held not to have invaded the privacy of an employee who was fired after sending hostile e-mail messages to a supervisor. The court applied the provider rule because the employer company owned the communications equipment, even though the employees were told that their e-mails were confidential and would not give rise to employee discipline. Therefore, this exception might not be available if an Internet service provider actually handles the e-mail service.

According to the Iowa District Court, discharge for violation of the corporate e-mail policy constitutes disqualifying misconduct that will prevent the receipt of unemployment insurance benefits (and therefore will not result in deterioration of the employer's experience rating). [*Mercer*, Unempl. Ins. Rep. (CCH) ¶ 9042 (Iowa Dist. Ct. 2002) (the discharged employees continued sending sexually explicit e-mails after receiving a warning—also e-mailed—from their supervisor; they had signed the employer's procedures for Internet, e-mail, and telephone usage at work, so they were familiar with the rules)]

In the Third Circuit view, an employer's decision to review an employee's stored e-mails does not violate the Electronic Communications Privacy Act, because that legislation only forbids interception at the time of transmission, not afterwards when the data is in storage. The owner of the e-mail system is exempt from claims of illegal seizure of stored messages. [*Fraser v. Nationwide Mut. Ins. Co.*, 352 F.3d 107 (3rd Cir. 2003)]

The employer's right to monitor computer use may depend on whether the employee-computer user had a reasonable expectation of privacy. The Second Circuit held in 2001, for example, that a public employee had such an expectation because he had a private office with a door and had exclusive use of the computer and other office equipment. However, in a Connecticut case involving a state employee who was convicted on state and federal charges after child pornography was found on his office computer, the defense attorney argued that the defendant was the registered owner of the computer and did not have to take any extra steps to protect his privacy. The Connecticut Superior Court ruled in 2002 that the defendant did not have a reasonable expectation of privacy, because he did not block his files from being accessed by other network users. [*Leventhal v. Knapek,* 266 F.3d 64 (2d Cir. 2001); *State v. Lasana,* 2002 Conn. Super. LEXIS 25 (Conn. Super. Ct. 2003)]

[D] Identification Numbers

It is convenient, but not always good policy, to use Social Security numbers as employee IDs. Business is becoming more and more internationalized, so overseas personnel will not have Social Security numbers. The European Union's privacy requirements are quite stringent, and must be obeyed when doing business outside the United States. [*See* Susan J. Wells, *You've Got Their Numbers—And They Want Them Back,* HR Magazine, Dec. 1998, at p. 3] Wells suggests choosing an identification system that does not rely on Social Security numbers or nine-digit numbers that could be confused with Social Security numbers. For most companies, a six-digit number (which allows 999,999 options!) will be satisfactory. It's better to assign numbers at random, not sequentially. If the numbers are assigned based on hiring dates, a hacker who knows when some people were hired could guess other employees' numbers. Your payroll and database programs impose standards: You may have to start each ID number with a number not a zero, blank space, or character such as an asterisk or ampersand.

[E] How-Tos for Employers

Attorney Jonathan A. Segal [Jonathan A. Segal, *Security vs. Privacy,* HR Magazine, Feb. 2002, at p. 93; *Searching for Answers,* HR Magazine, March 2000, at p. 59] provides some useful guidance for employers:

* Notify employees that working areas in the workplace are not private, and employees and their belongings are subject to search there, to rebut later charges that employees felt their reasonable expectation of privacy was violated or that private information about them was made public;
* Inform employees that their cars can be searched when they are parked on company property;
* Make it clear that the employer has the right to search employees' lockers, even if they are locked (providing the locks can reinforce this message as well as making it easier to open them when needed);
* Reserve the right to search all employees, not just individuals on the basis of reasonable suspicion. However, given the potential for hostility, in practice searches should only be done in emergencies, or on a reasonable-suspicion basis;

- Impose a work rule that refusal to be searched will be considered serious misconduct that justifies termination;
- Tell workers that they do not have an expectation of privacy in their e-mails, voice mails, computer hard drives, network access, and Web usage histories on company computers, even if they have been issued, or have chosen, a password;
- Put a message on the voice mail system indicating that messages can be recorded and reviewed. This puts outsiders as well as employees on notice that there is potential for monitoring;
- Ask employees for their written consent to monitoring of telephone conversations and voice mail;
- Inform employees that mail that they have addressed to them at the workplace can be opened by the employer—even if it is marked Personal or Confidential. (Federal law makes it illegal to obstruct mail delivery—but the Post Office's position is that once mail is delivered to the workplace, it has been delivered, so the employer does not obstruct mail delivery by opening mail before the employee gets it.)

Segal points out the need to balance reserving legal rights against employees' (and perhaps customers') reactions to a full-surveillance program. He stresses the absolute need for documentation: why a search was ordered, and what it found, for instance; or the nature of an emergency that required broad-based searches without individual suspicion.

He counsels employers to rely on observed or alleged behavior, and not profiling characteristics such as race, religion, or union advocacy. Wherever possible, searches of female employees should be performed by women, and searches of male employees by males. There should be a witness to all searches, and the shop steward should be allowed access if he or she wishes to be present.

To avoid later claims of harassment or battery, don't touch employees who refuse to be searched, and don't detain employees (which could constitute false imprisonment) except in security emergencies where it is necessary to detain the employee until the police arrive.

It is common for companies that do drug testing to appoint an independent Medical Review Officer (MRO). In fact, an MRO has to be used for all drug tests required by federal law, and some state laws also impose this requirement. Samples are sent to the testing lab, and the lab reports all the results. The MRO then contacts all employees who tested positive to see if there is a legitimate explanation—such as use of a prescription drug. If there is a legitimate explanation, then the MRO reports the result to the employer as a negative.

Even if the employer has the right to monitor conversations, or to open mail, the best policy is to terminate observation once it is clear that the communication is personal. Under the federal Electronic Communications Privacy Act [P.L. No. 99-508], messages are considered intercepted only if they are acquired in the course of transmission. It is not clear when an e-mail or voice mail is considered transmitted; it could be either when the sender completes the process of sending it, or when the receiver receives the message. *Fraser v. Nationwide Mutual Ins. Co.* [135 F. Supp. 2d 623 (E.D. Pa. 2001)] says that a message is intercepted only if it is viewed before the intended recipient accesses it.

More than half of the states (30) have "smoker's rights" laws, either limited to tobacco or making it unlawful for employers to ban any form of legal activity engaged in away from the workplace (e.g., drinking alcohol). Michigan does not have such a law, and in early 2005 the New York Times profiled a Michigan company whose policy calls for random testing of employees for tobacco use; evidence of smoking (even away from the premises and outside working hours) is ground for termination. Some other companies refuse to hire smokers and perform nicotine testing of employees. The rationale for smoking bans is that, according to the Centers for Disease Control, smokers cost their employers an average of $3,391 a year in extra health care costs and lost productivity. [Jeremy W. Peters, *Company's Smoking Ban Means Off-Hours, Too,* New York Times, Feb. 8, 2005, at p. C5]

Some employers are providing incentives to encourage employees to stop smoking (e.g., paying for smoking cessation classes or offering a bonus); others are imposing penalties on those who smoke (e.g., higher insurance premiums), even outside the workplace. Scotts Miracle-Gro Inc. announced that after a period of time allotted to allow employees to quit smoking, employees who smoke would be terminated. Four employees of a small medical benefits administration firm were fired because they refused to take a "breathalyzer"-type test that checked for tobacco use. [Ilan Brat, *A Company's Threat: Quit Smoking or Leave,* Wall Street Journal, Dec. 20, 2005, at p. D1]

In 2006, the Sixth Circuit ruled [*Spero Electric Corp. v. International Brotherhood of Electrical Workers, AFL-CIO, Local Union No. 1377,* 439 F.3d 324 (6th Cir. 2006)] that an employer had the right to unilaterally modify its work rules to ban smoking anywhere in the workplace. (The employer previously permitted smoking in designated areas, and imposed progressive discipline for smoking outside those areas.) Although the District Court had ruled that an employee could not be fired for a first-offense violation of the No Smoking rule, the Sixth Circuit upheld the employer's right to implement a zero-tolerance policy.

§ 26.07   HIPAA PRIVACY RULES

Congress passed the Health Insurance Portability and Accessibility Act (HIPAA) [Pub. L. No. 104-191], covering many issues related to health insurance and health care. The statute ordered Congress to issue federal health care privacy standards by August 21, 1999. However, Congress failed to meet this deadline, which gave the Department of Health and Human Services the right to draft regulations.

The HIPAA Regulations published on December 28, 2000 [65 Fed. Reg. 82511, amending 45 C.F.R. Parts 160 and 164] initially required most entities to comply by April 14, 2003, with an extra year for small health plans to get up to speed. Final modifications to the 2000 rules were published at 67 Fed. Reg. 53182 (Aug. 14, 2002), but the modifications leave the essential structure unchanged.

An Interim Final Rule was published, setting civil monetary penalties for violating the privacy and security rules. Although it was supposed to expire September 16, 2004, 69 Fed. Reg. 55515 (Sept. 15, 2004) extends it for an additional year. The penalty is $100 per violation, subject to a maximum of $25,000 per year for violations of the same requirement. The Office for Civil Rights administers the privacy component of the rule, although as of September 2004 they had not in fact imposed any civil penalties.

HHS published a Final Rule on HIPAA enforcement in February 2006. [71 Fed. Reg. 8390 (Feb. 16, 2006), discussed in Segal Capital Checkup, *Final HIPAA Enforcement Rule,* <http://www.segalco.com/publications/capitalcheckup/031509no2.html> (Mar. 15, 2006)] The rule takes the position that HIPAA enforcement relies largely on complaints of violations, which can then be investigated by HHS, leading to efforts to secure voluntary compliance by conciliation. Civil monetary penalties are imposed only if conciliation fails. HHS also carries out compliance reviews independent of complaints.

Changes to the privacy rule (e.g., the elimination of patient consent requirements for routine use and disclosure of PHI) were challenged by a citizen group, but the Third Circuit upheld the validity of the changes, finding that HHS did not abuse its discretion. [*Citizens for Health v. Leavitt,* 428 F.3d 167 (3d Cir. 2005)] The Fourth Circuit upheld the validity of the privacy rule, finding that it was not an impermissible delegation of legislative authority to the executive branch, and that HHS had adequate guidance and properly understood and carried out the congressional purpose. [*South Carolina Medical Ass'n v. Thompson,* 327 F.3d 346 (4th Cir. 2003); *Association of Am. Physicians & Surgeons, Inc. v. U.S. Dep't of HHS,* 224 F. Supp. 2d 1115 (S.D. Tex. 2002), reached the same conclusion]

There is no private right of action for violation of the HIPAA privacy rules (i.e., employees cannot sue if they claim their PHI was improperly disclosed or used). [*Runkle v. Gonzales,* 2005 U.S. Dist. LEXIS 22219 (D.D.C. 2005) (disclosure of medical information to co-workers); *Rigaud v. Garofalo,* 2005 U.S. Dist. LEXIS 7791 (E.D. Pa. 2005) (disclosure of information required to comply with a Worker's Compensation law)]

The HHS Office of Civil Rights can do compliance reviews and investigate complaints. HIPAA does not require amended SPDs to reflect the privacy rules, but plans that wish to issue an amendment may do so.

If the EGHP is funded by insurance and the employer-plan sponsor has no access to PHI, the insurer has full responsibility for privacy compliance. A plan sponsor that does have access to PHI has an obligation to amend the plan document to institute privacy procedures under which participants can inspect (and, if necessary, correct) their PHI and control disclosure of the PHI to others. The plan sponsor must give the plan a certificate of complying amendments and safeguards. The plan must have a privacy officer, and it must modify contracts with business associates to make sure that PHI is protected.

A self-insured or self-administered plan doesn't have an insurer in the picture to handle privacy concerns, so the plan document must be amended to control dissemination of PHI; privacy safeguards and certification are required; a privacy officer must be appointed; and business associates' access to PHI must be controlled.

Tip: The privacy rules apply only to health plans, not to other types of welfare benefit plans (for instance, short-term and long-term disability plans, Worker's Compensation, and sick pay) even though administering these plans requires insight into the health status of employees.

With one important exception (self-insured plans) EGHPs are not directly affected by the privacy rules. The theme of the HIPAA privacy rules is that the individual must give specific authorization before a covered entity can use protected health information for any reason other than payment, treatment, or health care operations. State health care laws are not preempted if they furnish even greater protection of patient confidentiality.

A covered entity is a health plan, health care clearinghouse, or health care provider that ever transmits health information electronically. PHI means all individually identifiable information that is transmitted or maintained in any form by a covered entity. A group health plan is permitted to disclose PHI to a plan sponsor only if the sponsor certifies to the plan that it will comply with the privacy rules about use and disclosure of the information.

The plan sponsor has a duty to amend the plan document governing the health plan to describe its use of PHI. Once this has been done, the sponsor has a duty to certify to the group health plan that the required amendments have been made. The plan sponsor can only use PHI for plan administration activities that constitute payment or health care operations.

The plan does not need individual employees' consent to provide summary (rather than individual) health information to the sponsor for administrative activities such as getting bids from other insurers or for amending or terminating the plan. A covered entity can "de-identify" individual data by stripping out all of the 19 identifying factors (for instance, birth date, photograph, phone number, Social Security number) laid out in the regulation.

A group health plan that provides its benefits entirely through an insurer or an HMO, and that does not create, maintain, or receive PHI other than summary health information and enrollment information is not required to designate a private official/contact person or satisfy the other administrative requirements of 45 C.F.R. § 164.530.

A fully insured group health plan is not required to issue the Notice of Privacy Practices to its plan participants. The HMO or issuer of the plan has this responsibility. However, a self-insured plan does have to provide the Notice. For people already in the group, notice is required as of the plan's compliance date (and within 60 days after a material revision). New participants get the notice at enrollment.

To comply with the regulation, the notice must:

- Be written in plain English or otherwise effectively communicated (for instance, a video could be used to convey the information);
- Prominently display this header: "This notice describes how medical information about you may be used and disclosed and how you can get access to this information. Please review it carefully";
- Describe when the covered entity can or must use PHI without authorization from the individual;
- Describe the entity's procedures for disclosing information to the plan sponsor;
- Explain when authorization is required for disclosure of information;
- Disclose the individual's right to revoke authorization; restrict uses and disclosures; get confidential communications; inspect, copy, and amend PHI; find out what disclosures were made; and get a paper copy (if the original notice was electronic);
- Disclose the entity's duty to maintain privacy;
- Reserve the right to change the privacy policy and apply the new policy retroactively;
- Explain how to file complaints about privacy right violations;
- Give contact information for a plan representative who can handle questions about, and resolve problems with, the policy;
- Contain the effective date for notice.

Enforcing this Regulation is the responsibility of the Department of Health and Human Services' Office of Civil Rights, which handles a spectrum of tasks from providing technical guidance and doing compliance reviews to complaint investigations, assessing civil penalties, and making referrals for criminal prosecution.

A covered entity that violates the rules can be subjected to civil penalties of up to $100 per incident, up to a maximum of $25,000 per person per year for each standard violated. [See 68 Fed. Reg. 18895 (Apr. 17, 2003)] Criminal penalties can be imposed for improper access or disclosure of information, obtaining personal health information under false pretenses, or making malicious use of confidential information, especially if there was a profit motive.

Although employers and plan sponsors of insured plans are not directly subject to these rules, they do have to restrict the way in which they collect and use personal information. When employers and sponsors receive PHI from a covered entity such as an insurer or HMO, the plan sponsor must agree to control re-use of the information. Employers are not permitted to use PHI for employment-related functions or functions for other benefit plans.

The rule requires certain information to be included in the plan document:

- A description of how PHI can be used and disclosed;
- The sponsor's access to PHI if it has provided certification as to the necessary plan amendment and conditions on the use of PHI;
- Description of security measures such as firewalls, restriction of access to authorized persons, and mechanisms for resolving charges of noncompliance with the privacy rules.

The mandatory certification is the employer's commitment not to use or disclose PHI except as permitted by HIPAA or required by law—a ban that includes not using PHI for employment-related actions. The employer must agree to make PHI accessible to the individuals involved and to let them correct mistakes. The employer must account for its disclosures, and must provide the Department of HHS with compliance information about its information practices. Any subcontractors or agents who get access to PHI must agree to abide by the same limitations. The employer must use firewalls to preserve data security. To the extent feasible PHI must be returned to the supplier of the information—or be destroyed—when the data is no longer needed.

One of the few major changes between the 2001 and 2002 Final Rules is that, under the 2002 version, covered entities are no longer required to get written consent from participants before using PHI for payment, treatment, or health care operations. But a covered entity must get advance written consent from plan participants to use PHI for marketing purposes, other than face-to-face encounters or communications involving a promotional gift of nominal value. [*See* HHS Fact Sheet, *Modifications to the Standards for Privacy of Individually Identifiable Health Information—Final Rule* (Aug. 9, 2002) <http://www.hhs.gov/news/press/2002pres/20020809.html>]

In addition to the basic privacy rules, a related Final Rule on data security was published at 68 Fed. Reg. 8333 (Feb. 20, 2003). Most covered entities must comply with the security rule by April 21, 2005, but small health plans get until April 21, 2006. Covered entities are required to create the appropriate administrative, technical, and physical safeguards to keep PHI data (whether in paper or electronic form) from inappropriate access or other forms of harm (intentional corruption by hackers, for example). The approach that these rules take is to provide general principles and implementation processes, rather than detailed mandates or specifications of required technologies.

Businesses that are covered entities under the general privacy rule are also covered entities under the security rule. Provisions are organized into four areas:

- Ensuring the confidentiality, integrity, and availability of electronic PHI created, received, maintained, or transmitted by the covered entity
- Protecting against predictable hazards to the security or integrity of the data

- Protecting against reasonably foreseeable improper use or disclosure of the data
- Ensuring compliance by workers who have access to the data.

Employees can request that employers omit their names from the OSHA 300 log in privacy-concern cases [for example, HIV status or sexual assault; *see* 68 Fed. Reg. 38607 (June 30, 2003)]. But, according to a standard interpretation letter posted on August 18, 2004, on the OSHA Web site, there is no general HIPAA requirement that employers edit the OSHA 300 log to remove the names before granting access to the log (for example, in response to a union request). [*See* 73 LW 2103]

After his termination, a Fire Department paramedic sued the Fire Department, seeking discovery of the employer's records (medical records, return-to-work evaluations, information about fitness for duty) of leave taken by other paramedics for psychological or substance abuse treatment. The employer claimed that HIPAA's Privacy Rule, as well as federal and state rules making substance abuse records confidential, prevented the disclosure. The Northern District of Illinois, however, held that the employer was not a "covered entity" as defined by HIPAA (*see* § 19.05[F]). The employer held the records in its capacity as an employer rather than for health care purposes, so the HIPAA Privacy Rule didn't apply. Furthermore, even covered entities can release protected health information in connection with a court case if appropriate conditions are met, as they were here. Because the plaintiff's suit involved only federal claims, the Northern District didn't consider the state statute relevant. However, the court found that some of the records were subject to psychologist-patient privilege. It ordered the employer to review all the records to find those that were privileged on this basis, and required the parties to negotiate a protective order limiting the use and distribution of the records that were not privileged. The Employee Benefits Institute of America's comment on this case was that it was good news for employers that the court clarified that an employer does not become a HIPAA-covered entity by hiring a professional to perform a fitness for duty evaluation unless the professional also treats the employee. [*Beard v. City of Chicago*, 2005 WL 66074 (N.D. Ill. Jan. 10, 2005), <http://www.ilnd.uscourts.gov/recent opinions/casenumber3527>]

CHAPTER 27

THE ROLE OF THE COMPUTER IN HR

§ 27.01   INTRODUCTION

Corporate human resource functions have always been number-intensive, from calculating a payroll to preparing reports on the nature of the workforce. Therefore, the HR department was an "early adopter" of all kinds of technology, going as far back as tabulating machines, through mainframe computers using punched cards, to the desktop PC, to today's networked systems. (Ironically, computer networks have something in common with the old-style mainframe with "dumb terminals" linked to it.)

Not only are computers used within the business, and not only are functions such as payroll preparation and tax reporting compliance often outsourced by electronic means, computerized communications continue to gain in importance. The Internet provides vast information and calculation resources for the HR department.

A corporate intranet (private computer network) can be developed to transmit information to, and receive information from, employees. Instead of printing a lengthy employee manual, then reprinting it to respond to changes in laws and corporate policy, the material can be input in a form that a computer can use and displayed on the intranet, with access limited to authorized persons.

An intranet can be set up with various levels of security, possibly password-protected, so that all employees have access to basic information like the employee handbook and work rules, but only those who need to know have access to salary information and employee performance ratings. Intranets can also be used for training, for job postings within the organization, and to advise employees how to save for retirement and manage their benefits.

The "wiki"—an easy-to-use Web page that anyone with authorized access can easily edit—is another means of assisting collaboration within an organization, or between an organization and its customers. Wikis are much less expensive and have a shorter learning curve than traditional collaboration software. Getting a number of people to collaborate on a wiki page can be more productive than exchanging e-mails on the same subject. [Michael Totty, *Togetherness, Wiki Style*, Wall Street Journal, Jan. 12, 2004, at p. R4]

According to the computer security company Websense, 93% of workers spent at least some time using the Web during working hours in 2005—7% higher than a year earlier. The average Web time used during the workweek was 10.5 hours, 18% more than in 2004. For employees who access the Internet during working hours, 51% spend 1–5 hours per week at nonwork sites; 5% spend 6–10 hours, and 2% spend 11 hours or more; the average is 3.4 hours per week per employee. Websense did find, however, that 73% of Internet usage in the workplace is work-related. Forty-two percent of employees never go to a nonwork-related site while they are at work, but 62% of men and 54% of women engage in personal-use Internet access at work. [Richard Breeden, *More Employees Are Using the Web at Work*, Wall Street Journal, May 10, 2005, at p. B4]

In addition to time spent at the office for personal matters, employees' Web use can create other problems for the employer—including the introduction of viruses and worms into the company's computer system, and liability for copyright infringement relating to the illegal downloads of music and movies. Use of instant messaging or Internet telephony can also create problems because these communications are not logged, and some companies (e.g., in the financial services industry) require a record to be made of all electronic communications. [Shawn Young, *Security Fears Prod Many Firms to Limit Staff Use of Web Services*, Wall Street Journal, Mar. 30, 2006, at p. A1]

§ 27.02 INTERNET RESEARCH

Many Web sites specialize in providing information about the HR function. The Society for Human Resources Management (SHRM) has a secure commerce server for online book orders, so credit card orders are safe. [*See* <http://shrmstore. shrm.org> (no www)] HR Magazine's site has a "conference room" for online chat with other HR professionals. The articles archive for HR Magazine appears at <http://www.shrm.org/hrmagazine/articles> (members only).

Law firm Web sites are also an excellent source of up-to-date information about court cases, new tax rulings, and compliance matters.

If you need information about outplacement, or need to find an experienced professional in your area, *see* the Association of Career Firm's site, <http:// www.aocfi.org>. The International Foundation of Benefit Plans can be found at <http://www.ifebp.org>.

The best government sites, such as <http://www.irs.ustreas.gov> are full of useful forms, explanations, and news summaries, as well as offering the full text of new regulations. It is worth scheduling time to regularly review the Pension and Welfare Benefit Administration and Occupational Safety and Health Administration sites to monitor ongoing developments; to see if you want to post an official comment on a proposal or testify at a hearing; or if there are new forms and publications available.

The Department of Labor has an immense bank of information online. Their main site is <http://www.dol.gov>. The Bureau of Labor Statistics reports the relative strengths of various employment sectors and employment cost trends. [*See* <http://www.bls.gov>] It also disseminates statistics on occupational safety and health. [*See* <http://www.bls.gov/bls/safety.htm>. OSHA's home page is http://www.osha.gov>] Federal contracting compliance information is available from the Employment Standards Administration. [*See* <http://www.dol.gov/esa/ ofcp_org.htm>]

In August 2004, the DOL announced a new e-mail subscription service, allowing subscribers to receive information and links to information on the HR subjects of interest to them: for example, the first test of the system was a fact sheet about the agency's Fair Pay Initiative. *See* <http://www.govdocs.com>. [DOL Press Release, *U.S. Department of Labor Unveils E-Mail Subscription Service Website* (Aug. 10, 2004), <http://benefitslink.com/pr/detail.php?id=38219>]

The Employee Benefits Security Administration, a subagency of DOL, has its site at <http://www.dol.gov/ebsa>. For Worker's Compensation information, *see* <http://www.dol.gov/esa/owcp_org.htm>. The Wage and Hour Division's Web presence is <http://www.dol.gov/esa/whd>. *See* <http://www.doleta.gov> for the DOL's Corporate Citizenship Resource center, with profiles of companies that have implemented exceptional work-family programs. *See* <http://www.pbgc.gov> for coverage of the expansion of PBGC information technology.

There are so many HR resources available that it could be too time-consuming to use an ordinary search engine to find them all. Therefore, "meta-indexes" have been developed: Web home pages that offer links to information-rich sites. *See,* for instance,

- Labor lawyer David Rhett Baker's Web "bibliography," <http://www.benefitslink.com/articles/usingweb.html>;
- HR Professional's Gateway to the Internet, <http://www.hrprosgateway.com/www/index2.html>;
- Nottingham Trent University (Britain) Human Resources Management Resources on the Internet, <http://www.nbs.ntu.ac.uk>;
- Employment Law Links, <http://www.contilaw.com/links.html>.

These are some private sites that may be helpful:

- Work & Family Connection, <http://www.workfamily.com>;
- Wageweb (survey data on typical compensation level for various jobs—designed for use in pay planning), <http://www.wageweb.com>;
- Benefitslink Benefits Buzz shows news clips for events of the previous 48 hours, with links to the full text of articles. There is also an archive of past issues that can be searched by topic, <http://www.benefitslink.com/buzz/>. Benefitslink also has two daily online newsletters, one dealing with pensions and one with benefit issues;
- Sites by consulting firms, such as Aon Consulting, <http://www.aon.com>;
- For technical information about plan design, see the Enrolled Actuaries Report, <http://www.actuary.org>;
- The National Underwriter online Life and Health edition, although written from the insurance industry perspective, has a good deal of useful benefit information, <http://cms.nationalunderwriter.com/cms/NULH/website/eNewsletters>;
- PlanSponsor.com's free daily newsletter NewsDash, <http://www.plansponsor.com>;
- The Employee Benefits Research Institute has a very comprehensive site at <http://www.ebri.org>, although some of the best material is members-only;
- Wall Street Journal Career Journal, <http://www.careerjournal.com>.

Helpful employment blogs include, e.g., two blogs by Ross Runkel: Employment Law Blog, <http://www.lawmemo.com/blog/>, and Arbitration Blog,

<http://www.lawmemo.com/arbitrationblog/>, and two by B. Janell Grenier: ERISAblog, <http://www.benefitscounsel.com/erisablog/>, and Benefitsblog, <http://www.benefitscounsel.com/benefitsblog/>.

§ 27.03   RECRUITING VIA THE INTERNET

By 2005, 51% of all new hires came via the Internet, making it the primary recruiting source. Newspaper ads produced only 5% of hires. Recruiting usually took place through the employer's own site (21% of hires), general job boards (6%), social network Web sites (5%), and commercial resume databases (4%). Companies devoted 27% of their recruiting ad budget to general job boards—the largest category of spending—but only 15% of new hires came from this source. (This information comes from DirectEmployers Association, which operates the Jobcentral.com site.) [Rebecca Moore, *Internet Now Primary Source of New Hires*, PlanSponsor.com, Feb. 10, 2006]

If your corporation has a Web site, it's easy and inexpensive to add an area for posting job opportunities. You can include an electronic form so even candidates who do not have an electronic resume can submit their qualifications. The form can be used for initial screening of applicants.

To an ever increasing extent, performing a Web search on candidates' names is becoming a normal part of recruitment and hiring—for example, to see if inconsistent resumes have been posted to help-wanted sites, or to check out the candidate's blog (which might, for instance, include indiscreet material about the candidate's current employer, or negative comments about a competitor or an industry as a whole). According to the Committee to Protect Bloggers, about a dozen people were fired in 2004 for blog-related reasons; for example, a Delta Airlines flight attendant says she was fired for including a picture of herself in uniform in her blog—but, she says, there was no official ban on doing this. Litigation is ongoing between Apple Computer and bloggers who allegedly included confidential information about the company in their blogs. [Jason Boog, *Employers Wrestle With Blogosphere*, National Law Journal, Apr. 5, 2005 (law.com); Erin White, *The Jungle,* Wall Street Journal, Oct. 12, 2004, at p. B8. The Apple Computer case is *O'Grady v. Apple Computer,* No. H028579, pending before the California Court of Appeal]

Many corporations set up their own blogs as a recruiting tool, so that job seekers can gain an insight into the corporation's daily life and culture. Another option is for a company to become a sponsor of a third-party blog (for example, one that covers the news of a particular industry) and pay to be highlighted on the site or to post job openings. [Kris Maher, *Blogs Catch On as Online Tool for Job Seekers and Recruiters,* Wall Street Journal, Sept. 28, 2004, at p. B10] A small but increasing number of corporations (in 2005, it was estimated that only 4% of major corporations had publicly accessible blogs) used corporate blogs to increase the corporation's profile by making content about the firm widely available. Some corporations even assigned employees to create blogs, much as they had corporate Webmasters to manage Internet sites. [Sarah E. Needleman, *Blogging Becomes a Corporate Job; Digital "Handshake"?* Wall Street Journal, May 31, 2005, at p. B1] A 2006 Wall Street Journal article puts the matter in a nutshell by saying "Employee blogs can put a human face on companies. But that's not always a good thing." Small companies can get extremely valuable publicity at low cost. However, corporate image specialists warn that having a lot of employee blogs can create conflicting messages about what the company is like, and lawyers warn about liability potential and security problems about new products, trade secrets, and proprietary formulas. Companies need to have policies about when employees can post to their blogs at work—and what they can say when they're posting from home. Even anonymous blogs can be tracked back, so many company policies require employees to use their real names on work-related blogs. [William M. Bulkeley, *The Inside View*, Wall Street Journal, Apr. 3, 2006, at p. R7]

Federal contractors who accept Internet-based job applications are subject to DOL's Office of Federal Contract Compliance Programs' Final Rule on record-keeping. The Final Rule covers jobs for which the contractor accepts expressions of interest via the Internet, e-mail, employer Web sites, or resume databanks. Federal contractors are required, wherever possible, to obtain data on the sex, race, and ethnicity of their employees and job applicants—including those who apply over the Internet. An Internet applicant is one who uses the Internet or related technology to submit an expression of interest and who demonstrates at least basic qualifications for the position, who the federal contractor has considered for a particular position, and who never took him- or herself out of consideration for the job before an offer was made. The rule requires federal contractors to maintain records of Internet-based expressions of interest that resulted in the contractor considering the applicant for a particular job (the OFCCP decided it would be too burdensome to make them retain records of non-specific applications). It is acceptable for federal contractors to discard expressions of interest that do not relate to a particular position or that do not meet the contractor's standards for submitting applications. [70 Fed. Reg. 58,945 (Oct. 7, 2005)]

§27.04 BENEFITS MANAGEMENT ONLINE

There are many reasons to limit the corporate content that is publicly available on the Internet: Premature disclosure of confidential information could result in loss of privacy, premature release of corporate plans, exposure of trade secrets, securities law violations, or the like. Corporations also generate a tremendous amount of information that is not security-sensitive, but is not of interest outside the organization.

The cost of implementing an intranet depends on the scope of the project, and whether the project requires full-scale programming or can be implemented wholly or partially with off-the-shelf commercial software packages. Another important question is whether the in-house information technology staff can handle the job, or whether a consultant will be needed.

In recent years, employers have been strongly interested in finding low-cost benefits that they can add (because benefits are an important employee motivator, in any economic environment). A new option is allowing employees to pay their bills online via deductions from their paychecks; the system can also be set up to allow employees to buy online from retailers that accept credit cards or agree to debit the account (subject to a maximum balance, such as 2.5% of annual pay). Payments for such purchases can be deducted automatically from several paychecks, without interest, with a six-month interest-free period allowed for big-ticket items. The employee gets a monthly statement of purchases and returned items. To protect employee privacy, the employer gets reports about account balances but not individual purchases. [Marianne Kolbasuk McGee, InformationWeek (Mar. 3, 2002) <http://www.informationweek.com/shared/printableArticle?doc_id=IWK20030228S0019>]

Spencer Benefits Reports showed very positive results of HR technology, in that Web-based self-service modes not only reduced the HR department's workload but improved the accuracy and timeliness of data that could be harvested from the system. Sixty percent of employers reported a decrease in workload. About half (47%) found that self-service reduces the administrative burden on the HR department. The Web is replacing other service delivery systems, such as paper-based and voice response systems. In fact, half of the respondents said that in 2004 a Web site would be the sole means of enrollment for the plan, and 90% expected to make their HR policies viewable online. In 2003, two-thirds allowed online changes of personal data; 89% expected to do so in 2004. In 2003, 86% granted self-service access to job postings, 83% to HR policies, and 71% allowed online applications for posted jobs. However, it was rare for companies to provide online access to compensation and benefit statements. Intranet access is convenient for salaried employees (93% of whom can access the intranet at the office) but is more difficult for hourly employees, especially in manufacturing, who tend not to use computers in their work. To extend access to such groups, companies are experimenting with kiosks and shared PCs at work sites. [Spencer Benefits Reports, *Web-Based HR Technology Increases Productivity, Towers Perrin Survey* Finds, Nov. 24, 2003) <http://www.benefitslink.com/links/20031124 . . . >]

§ 27.05   LEGAL IMPLICATIONS OF E-MAIL

The benefits of e-mail in providing a simple method of communications are obvious. However, unencrypted e-mail is not secure. It is much more like a post-card that can be read by anybody than it is like a sealed letter—much less a coded message. Merely clicking a "delete" icon does not remove a message completely and permanently from the entire computer system, network, or service provider that offers e-mail service. So a message that is embarrassing or worse (e.g., one involving racial epithets, sexual harassment, or evidence of corporate wrongdoing) can be found by hostile parties—including plaintiffs' lawyers.

If a company provides e-mail access at work, it should inform employees of the company's policies with respect to e-mail. A reasonable e-mail policy might involve

- Disclosure that the company has the right to monitor employee e-mail. [*See* § 26.06[C] for a discussion of privacy issues] It would be illegal to fire, or otherwise take action against, an employee who uses e-mail to engage in protected concerted activity such as complaining about safety risks. Threatening or inflammatory messages are not protected under labor law, but a direct protest to management certainly would be. Employee-to-employee communications are probably protected unless they actually threaten the harmonious and efficient operation of the business enterprise;
- Restriction of e-mail to business use. Inexpensive software is available to uninstall or disable games on office computers or networks, and to track usage (e.g., to see if gambling or pornographic sites are being accessed). However, although such measures may increase productivity, they must be balanced against the resentment employees may experience;
- No forwarding of copyrighted materials (for example, newspaper stories or cartoons);
- No use of obscene or suggestive language or slurs against any group;
- No discussion of matters that might have legal consequences (e.g., price fixing or industrial espionage);
- Asking employees to think before they send a message if there is anything in the message that they would not want publicized, or that could put the employer in a bad light.

In 2005, a New Jersey court found a business negligent and therefore liable for failing to contact law enforcement authorities when an employee was found transmitting child pornography from a work computer; the plaintiff was the child's mother—and the employee was the child's stepfather. The defendant company had investigated and found the pornography, but reacted only by telling the employee to stop accessing pornographic Web sites at work. The implication is that if a company is going to engage in monitoring at all, it must react when the monitoring provides evidence of illegal activity. Employers that wish to monitor employee Internet use should disclose that they plan to do so; should follow through by monitoring and keeping records; and take reasonable care to respond to detected illegal activities. [*Doe v. XYC Corp.*, 74 L.W. 1432 (N.J. Super. 2005), discussed in Lyda Phillips, *After Employer Found Liable for Worker's Child Porn, Policies May Need to Be Revisited,* 74 L.W. 2563 (Mar. 28, 2006)]

§ 27.06   FEDERAL RULES ON DIGITAL COMMUNICATIONS

Many of the rules affecting HR functions were drafted before the heyday of the personal computer, when plan administration generated mounds and mounds of paper (but nothing but paper). Two trends coalesced in the 1980s: personal computing and the drive to make government more efficient and reduce unnecessary paperwork. Obviously, the often-proclaimed Paperless Office never arrived, but to an increasing extent, documents are not only being created on computers but also distributed and retained electronically.

Department of Labor regulations [29 C.F.R. § 2560.104b-1] create a safe harbor (added by 67 Fed. Reg. 17274 (Apr. 9, 2002)) for using electronic methods of satisfying the obligation to give various notices to government agencies, plan participants, and beneficiaries under the plan. The overriding objective is finding a method that is reasonably calculated to make sure that the information actually gets into the hands of those who are entitled to it.

Materials that are subject to disclosure (either mandatory or on request by a participant or representative) can be disclosed through electronic media, as long as the delivery system is reasonably calculated to result in actual receipt of the information (for instance, by using a system that "bounces" undelivered e-mail messages). The electronic communication must use content, format, and style consistent with the requirements for paper documents. When documents are furnished electronically, participants and beneficiaries must also receive a notice (whether hard-copy or electronic) explaining the significance of the document if it is not immediately apparent. Recipients must also be advised that they have the right to request a paper copy of the document. Furthermore, electronic distribution is permitted only for plan participants who have effective computer access at work, and for participants and beneficiaries who have expressly consented (whether electronically or on a paper document) to receiving digital documents. Documents can properly be furnished online only to people who have provided an e-mail address, given affirmative consent, or confirmed consent electronically, in a manner that shows they can effectively access the means the plan will use to communicate the information.

A valid consent requires advance provision of a clear and conspicuous statement (digital or hard-copy) of the kind of documents covered by the consent; that consent can be withdrawn at any time without financial penalty; how to withdraw consent; how to get hard copies of electronic documents; and the hardware and software requirements for accessing digital documents.

The following year, the PBGC proposed a rule on electronic filing, notice issuance, calculation of time periods, and record retention [RIN 1212-AA89, 68 Fed. Reg. 7544 (Feb. 14, 2003)] building on the rules in the 2002 document. The PBGC Proposed Rule appears at 29 C.F.R. Part 4000. It provides that any document that must be submitted to the PBGC can be submitted by hand, mail, or commercial delivery service. It can also be delivered to a fax number or e-mail address listed on the <http://www.pbgc.gov> Web site, or obtained from a PBGC customer service center: (800) 736-2444 for professionals, (800) 400-7242 for plan participants.

The 2003 Proposed Rule is divided into five subparts:

- Methods for filing documents with the PBGC
- Methods for issuing notices to parties other than the PBGC

- Determination of date on which notices were submitted
- Calculation of time periods
- Record-keeping requirements.

As long as the sender complies with the PBGC's requirements, most documents are deemed filed on the date they were sent. However, certain items (applications for benefits, advance notice of reportable events, notice of failure to make contributions) are deemed filed when they are received, no matter what method was used to transmit them. A submission received on a weekend or federal holiday, or after 5 P.M. on a business day, is deemed filed on the next business day.

Most documents can be submitted to the PBGC by e-mail attachment, or on a floppy disk or CD-ROM. However, the PBGC must be given a contact telephone number of someone who can be reached if the PBGC is unable to access the digital data.

The PBGC moved closer to complete digital compliance management by publishing rules in late 2003 for the Web-based MYPAA (My Plan Administration Account Authentication Records) secure system that became operational February 3, 2004. Once established, the account can be used for filings, premium payments, disclosure of the intent to terminate the plan, asking the PBGC questions, and making reports of events that are reportable under 29 USC § 1343. When the system made its debut, Forms 1, 1-ES and 1-EZ, and Form 1 Schedule A could be filed (and signed) electronically, with plans for phasing in additional e-filing.

The account is created by an authorized "filing coordinator" (plan sponsor, administrator, or practitioner such as an enrolled actuary) registering with the PBGC. The coordinator must submit his or her name, employer, contact information (including e-mail address, pension plan name, and the EIN and plan number for the plan). The PBGC verifies the submitter's authorization to speak for the plan by having the submitter state the number of participants reported to the PBGC in the most recent premium filing and the PBGC premium paid for the year.

If the information checks out, the PBGC issues a temporary user ID and password for the system; even if it doesn't, conditional status is granted until the PBGC can re-check the records or contact the applicant for confirmation. [PBGC Press release, *Federal Pension Insurer Takes First Step to Automate Premium Filing Process,* Feb. 18, 2004 <http://benefitslink.com/pr/detail/php?id=37753>; 68 Fed. Reg. 74655 (Dec. 24, 2003); *see* "Online Premium Filing" link at <http://www.pbgc.gov>]

At the end of 2004, the PBGC issued a proposal for electronic filing of a broad range of data relating to ERISA plans. The proposal explains how to submit standardized electronic reports under ERISA § 4010 (identifying financial and actuarial information about the plan). Reporting instructions are found on the PBGC Web site. The proposal states that a data submission made to the PBGC site is considered transmitted when the plan performs the last act indicating that the submission has been filed and can no longer be edited or rescinded. Electronic submissions do not have to be addressed to specific PBGC departments or personnel; the PBGC will direct them to the proper place. [PBGC RIN 1212-AB01, *Electronic Filing—Annual Financial and Actuarial Information*, correction to Notice of Proposed Rulemaking, 69 Fed. Reg. 77679 (Dec. 28, 2004)]

In mid-2005, the Treasury weighed in with its own proposal for using electronic media to give plan participants and beneficiaries notices and secure benefit elections or consents. These proposals apply only to documents that the Internal Revenue Code requires to be in writing—and that are not covered by ERISA, or under DOL or PBGC jurisdiction. (Thus, the rule does not apply to SPDs, COBRA notices, or the like, but does apply to various documents under retirement and welfare plans). Notices can be delivered electronically only if the recipient has consented, or an exception applies and consent is not required. The exemption from the consent requirement applies if the recipient has the ability to access the electronic medium and has been informed that a paper copy is available free of charge. The plan participant or beneficiary must be informed what the communication is about and how to access the notice. Benefit elections and consents can be obtained electronically (instead of by signatures on paper) as long as the person can access the electronic method of delivery; the system is reasonably designed to preserve security (e.g., PIN numbers are required); the employee has the chance to review or modify his or her consents before they become final; consent is confirmed (either electronically or by generating a paper copy); and communications are at least as understandable in electronic form as in printed form. Because the proposals are designed to conform to eSign, the federal law permitting electronic "signatures," consents that have to be witnessed or notarized are valid as long as the notary or plan representative physically witnesses the participant or beneficiary "signing" the document electronically. [REG-138362-04, 2005-33 I.R.B. 299; *see* Tina M. Kuska and Mary K. Samsa, *Proposed Treasury Regulations Regarding the Use of Electronic Media for Employee Benefit Notices, Elections and Consents* (Aug. 2005), www.gcd.com. For the EBSA counterpart on filing annual reports electronically, *see* Proposed Rule, 70 Fed. Reg. 51,541 (Aug. 30, 2005)]

Final standards for data security under the HIPAA privacy rule (*see* Chapter 26) appear at 68 Fed. Reg. 8333 (Feb. 20, 2003). The data security standards take effect in 2005 (with a one-year extension granted to small plans). The security rules apply only to Personal Health Information (PHI) that exists in digital form, not to all health information. Nor do the security rules apply to employment records maintained by a plan sponsor, even if they incidentally include PHI. However, plan sponsors who have access to PHI in electronic form have an obligation to amend the plan to certify that the sponsor will comply with the data security rules.

Also note that Rev. Rul. 2003-106, 2003-44 I.R.B. 936, provides that a reimbursement plan for deductible travel and entertainment expenses is entitled to favorable treatment as an accountable plan if it uses electronic receipts and expense reports. The ruling gives the example of a business credit card whose users are personally liable for the bills, but where the credit card company gives the employer daily itemized electronic reports and allocates between business and personal expenses. An electronic receipt satisfies the requirements of Code

§ 274 if it provides information such as date, place, and amount to characterize the payment.

On a related issue, the Seventh Circuit permitted the application of the federal Computer Fraud and Abuse Act, and civil penalties, in the case of an ex-employee who maliciously erased files from the ex-employer's computer system when he left to set up his own business. The statute, intended to penalize computer hacking, applies to transmission of computer code with the intention of damaging a computer system. [*International Airports Centers v. Citrin*, 440 F.3d 418 (7th Cir. 2006); *see* Pamela A. MacLean, *Erasing Computer Files Might Create Employee Liability*, National Law Journal, Mar. 29, 2006 (law.com). An earlier Seventh Circuit ruling on the Computer Fraud and Abuse Act, *U.S. v. Mitra*, 405 F.3d 492 (2005) defined "computers" very broadly, so that wireless networking stations and cell phones might also be included in the statute's reach]

WORK-FAMILY ISSUES

§ 28.01   INTRODUCTION

Work-family issues didn't arise when most people were subsistence farmers and the whole family worked together to raise crops for survival. The problems were muted when most family units consisted of a male breadwinner and a house-wife. Since World War II (when many women had to do factory and other work to replace men away at war), however, many employees have had trouble reconciling their family obligations with the needs of paid jobs.

Over 70% of women of working age are in the workforce. Pregnant women are working until closer to their due dates and returning sooner than in the 1970s. Between 1996 and 2000, 56.6% of women worked full time up to the ninth month of their first pregnancy. In the 1996–1999 period, two thirds of first-time mothers returned to paid work within a year, and one seventh were back at work within a month of delivery. The Forte Foundation (a nonprofit promoting business leader-ship opportunities for women) found that half of women feel that taking time away from work to raise children impairs their employment opportunities; 83% took another job at the same level or accepted a demotion, and 61% changed industries. Even women who can rebut the assumption that they are not interested in senior positions once they have children have to cope with the assumption that child-rearing means that they lose current skills. [Kelley M. Butler, *Today's Working Women Seek Mentors, Motherhood Transition,* Employee Benefit News, Apr. 1, 2006 (benefitslink.com)]

Trends in the employment of mothers are hard to interpret. In 2000, almost 76% of married women who had a child aged 6–13 also held paid jobs. This percentage fell to 74% in 2005. However, the Center for Economic Policy Research pointed out that the percentage of women with no children holding jobs also fell, suggesting involvement of economic factors in job availability.

Recessions in the 1980s and 1990s did not slow down the growth of female labor force participation, but the 2001 recession did. Traditionally, women worked in "pink collar" jobs (like nursing and secretarial work) that were fairly recession-proof, but now that the occupational range is wider, women are also more vulner-able to the effects of recession. In 2004, among women aged 25–54, the workforce participation rate of mothers was 8.2% lower than the rate for childless women; in 2000, the gap was 9.9%, and in 1993 it was 14.4%. [Eduardo Porter, *Stretched to Limit, Women Stall March to Work,* New York Times, Mar. 2, 2006, at p. A1; Eduardo Porter, *Mothers' Flight from Job Force Questioned,* New York Times, Dec. 2, 2005, at p. C2]

The Department of Labor's 2004 figures show that the average working woman spends about twice as much time doing housework and child care as the average working man. For full-time employees aged 25 to 54 who are parents, men spend 8.87 hours a day at paid work, women 7.74 hours. However, men averaged 0.83 hours a day caring for family members and 0.73 hours on housework—versus 1.55 hours for family care and 1.44 hours for housework for women. Eighty-five percent of men, and 78% of women, were employed. On an average day, two-thirds of women did housework and prepared meals. Nineteen percent of men did housework and 34% helped with cooking or meal clean-up. [Edmund L. Andrews, *Survey Confirms It: Women Outjuggle Men*, New York Times, Sept. 15, 2004, at p. A23]

Concerns have been raised that there are many "off-ramps" for mothers to leave the workforce, but fewer "on-ramps" to return. Employers wishing to keep one-time employees connected to the firm after they leave to take care of children often offer training and mentoring so they can keep their skills current; invite them to meetings and office parties so they won't lose touch with the workforce; use internal recruiting to find suitable jobs for them when they're ready to return; and allow them to work at home on temporary projects. Companies such as Lehman Brothers and Merrill Lynch use these programs to prevent the loss of highly trained employees who would be hard to replace. [Sue Shellenbarger, *Employers Step Up Efforts to Lure Stay-at-Home Mothers Back to Work*, Wall Street Journal, Feb. 9, 2006, at p. C1]

An approach that is being tested, especially in the financial services industry, is to offer a formal leave of absence covering several years. The person on leave doesn't receive benefits, but still maintains a connection with the firm. The company docs not guarantee re-hiring when the person on leave is ready to return, but does make an effort to find a job. Sometimes the company allows workers on leave to use the company's e-mail and intranet, and may offer continuing professional education and coaching for licensing exams. Once workers return from leave, they may be offered special classes or mentoring to get them back up to speed. [Lisa Belkin, *Goodbye Doesn't Need to Mean Forever*, New York Times, Mar. 11, 2005, at § 10 p. 1; Teri Cettina, *Leaving, But Not Left Behind*, Human Resource Executive, <http://www.workindex.com/hrexecutive/feature2.asp>]

But a new trend is emerging: for both parents to work while the children are very young, then for mothers to quit paid jobs and stay at home with middle- and high-school students, who are seen as having greater needs for active parenting. [Jeffrey Zaslow, *Should You Quit Work to Stay Home with the Baby? No, Wait till He's 11*, Wall Street Journal, Aug. 29, 2002, at p. D1]

The Wall Street Journal's Sue Shellenbarger predicts that in the future, mothers and fathers will alternate paid work and staying at home with the children, and which parent works will often depend on factors such as the availability of health insurance and other benefits. [Sue Shellenbarger, *Bob's Mobile Office and Day-Care Center, and Other Innovative Balancing Acts*, Wall Street Journal, Dec. 26, 2002, at p. D1; in a later column, Shellenbarger noted that employment rates for married women whose youngest child is 14–17 have stayed stable (at about 80%) between 2000 and 2005, but parents of teenagers are now far more likely to work at home so they can supervise their teenagers. Among corporate employees who telecommute, 17.5% have teenagers at home. And almost 20% of employees who work at home on a part-time basis are parents of teenagers. Sue Shellenbarger, *Work & Family Mailbox*, Wall Street Journal, Mar. 2, 2006, at p. D4]

There are new kinds of families developing (single parents, blended families, grandparents raising grandchildren). Greater involvement of fathers in hands-on child care also increases the demand for FMLA leave or flexible hours for fathers. [*See* Chapter 38] for the FMLA; however, paternity leave has never really caught on.

A late-2005 survey by the Families and Work Institute showed that in 1998, 28% of survey respondents offered maternity leave at full pay, which dropped to 19% in 2001 and 17% in 2005. Much of the decline was a product of rising health care costs putting pressure on benefits. About two thirds of the respondents said they provided partial pay for maternity leave, but 19% said that the amount of compensation depended on the situation; only 13% said this in 1998. Most large employers have private short-term disability leave plans, under which it is often possible to claim temporary disability resulting from childbirth. [Sue Shellenbarger, *Employers Cut Back on Full Pay for Maternity Leave,* Wall Street Journal, Oct. 13, 2005, at p. D2]

According to the National Bureau of Economic Research (NBER), a long maternity leave (at least three months) helps prevent postpartum depression. New mothers who take at least three months of leave show 15% fewer depression symptoms after their return than those who took six weeks or less. Leaves of eight weeks or more cut symptoms by 11%. The NBER estimate is that 50 to 70% of new mothers have postpartum "blues," which escalates to full-blown depression for 10 to 20% of them. [Sue Shellenbarger, *Baby Blues: The Dangers of the Trend Toward Shorter Maternity Leaves,* Wall Street Journal, May 20, 2004, at p. D2. Resources for postpartum depression include <http://www.workoptions. com>'s 19-page guide to maternity leave, including sample language for leave requests; <http://www.psych.org> (a fact sheet for new mothers by the American Psychiatric Association); <http://www.postpartum.net>; and <http://www. yourmedicalsource.com/library/depressionpregnancy.DPR_how.html>]

Additional issues arise when an employee has a special needs child. The Center for Child and Adolescent Health Policy (MassGeneral Hospital for Children) and the MetLife Division of Estate Planning for Special Kids offer suggestions for ways employers can support employees in this situation.

The Families and Work Institute says that 20% of families have a child with some significant physical or mental health problem. Data from the Archives of Pediatric and Adolescent Medicine shows the incidence of disabling conditions affecting children and teenagers rose from 2% in 1960 to 7% today. MassGeneral's estimate is that a 2,000-worker company would probably have close to 175 special-needs children in the families of its workforce.

Most companies are unaware that there is even a need for services for this employee group, but a few have useful programs such as onsite support programs for special-needs parents and seminars explaining topics like public benefits and educational rights of special-needs children. Offering these services can be crucial to employee retention: The federal Maternal and Child Health Bureau says that 30% of parents have to quit their jobs or cut back on working hours if they have a child with a disability.

MetLife found that 29% of parents in this group have made no financial plans for their child's future, less than half have designated a guardian for their child to serve after their own deaths, and close to two thirds experience barriers in getting information they need. Employers can furnish valuable information about, e.g., Medicaid planning, creating trusts to manage the assets of persons incapable of self-care, and tax issues. However, parents in this situation may be afraid to raise the issue, in case they suffer discrimination based on prejudice against persons with disabilities or because of a perception that the company's health plan will become too costly to be afforded. [Kelley M. Butler, *It Takes a Village: Employers Have Key Role in Supporting Employees With Special-Needs Children*, Employee Benefit News, Jan. 2006, <http://www.benefitnews.com/pfv.cfm?id=8461>; Sue Shellenbarger, *Employers Begin to Provide Assistance for Parents of Children With Disabilities,* Wall Street Journal, Oct. 13, 2005, at p. D1; MassGeneral has a manual about workplace benefits, online at <http://www.massgeneral.org/ebs>]

Nor is child care the only issue. People in mid-life are sometimes called the "sandwich generation" because they have responsibilities for aging parents as well as growing children. The Department of Labor Women's Bureau is a good resource for work-family issues. [*See* <http://www.dol.gov/wb/childcare/b2bintro.htm>] So is the National Partnership for Women and Families. [*See* <http://www.nationalpartnership.org>]

Work-life programs have gained prominence since 2001, as hard-pressed companies looked for ways to motivate employees without burdening themselves with very high capital obligations. There are several broad categories of work-life programs:

- Family-friendly benefits such as day care, information and referral services (I&R), offering leave in excess of FMLA requirements, lactation rooms, adoption assistance, and domestic partner benefits
- Alternative work arrangements and time off (flextime; telecommuting; temporary or project-based work; paid time off for volunteer activities; sabbaticals)
- Health and wellness benefits
- On-site amenities (an ATM or bank branch; concierge service)
- Financial assistance (tuition reimbursement; personal use of frequent flyer miles earned at work; prepaid legal services)

[The categories come from Tara Pickering, *Work/Life Programs: Not Just Another Employee Benefit,* The CEO Refresher, <http://www.refresher.com/ !tpworklife. html>]

The theoretical availability of work-life benefits doesn't solve all of employees' problems in this area. A number of surveys show that management and HR departments have more faith in employees' willingness to use these programs than employees have that they can take a leave or use other work-family benefits without harming their careers. SHRM says that women workers, and all employees under 35, name work-life balance as the most important component in job satisfaction—whereas men over 35 rate it only fourth. A survey by Work & Family Connection showed that a third of respondents said their company's culture did not support work-life programs, and 38% said that championship of the programs by management would improve the situation—especially if top management figures used the program themselves.

The usefulness of work-life programs can be improved by:

- Surveying workers to find out what they need and want
- Communicating this information to managers
- Keeping workloads under control
- Associating work-life benefits and business objectives
- Keeping track of the return on investment of work-life programs
- Basing assessments of employee performance on the results they achieve, not how late they stay or how many hours they work
- Creating guidelines for negotiating flexible work arrangements and making the guidelines available to all employees
- Letting employees know that they will not be penalized for accessing work-life benefits

[Kelly Pate Dwyer, *Still Searching for Equilibrium in the Work-Life Balancing Act*, New York Times, Dec. 4, 2005, at § 10 p. 1; Leah Carlson, *Work-Life Benefits Do Not Guarantee Work-Life Balance*, Employee Benefit News, Aug. 2005 (benefitnews.com)]

Since, and perhaps as a result of, the September 11 attack, employers are more sensitive to the need for workplace response to the deaths of co-workers. ResponseWorks, an organization that deals with traumatic events of all kinds, reports that the U.S. workforce loses 15,000 people a year to suicide, 6,000 to accidental workplace deaths, and more than half a million to illness. In 2002, 12% of companies had grief recovery programs, a number that rose to 14% in 2003.

All of a company's departments, including the Employee Assistance Program, can help grieving employees communicate with co-workers (who often don't know how to express their sympathy effectively), and working through productivity issues. The HR department is responsible for setting up and administering bereavement policies, including arranging for insurance benefits, time off, emergency loans, perhaps donations of time off from the leave bank. [Kathryn Tyler, *Helping Employees Cope With Grief*, HR Magazine, Sept. 2003 <http://www.shrm.org/hrmagazine/articles/0903/0903tyler.asp>; Jeffrey Zaslow, *Grieving at Work: The Struggle to Cope With the Sudden Death of a Colleague*, Wall Street Journal, Aug. 28, 2003, at D1; The Grief Recovery Institute's site includes brochures such as "When a Co-Worker Dies" and "A Manager's Guide to Grief in the Workplace": <http://www.grief.net>]

In addition to changing demographics, some employers find themselves confronted by changes in attitude. A slowing economy may result in a lessening of ambition and competitive feelings among employees, some of whom will turn against corporate cultures that insist on extended hours, preferring to spend more time with their families even if they have to accept lower pay and smaller benefits to do so. Employers that want to retain their employees or recruit good new workers may have to respect these priorities.

From the employer's point of view, there's another potential downside to the new attitudes: increased litigation. The Families that Work research center (located at American University) reports that there is a small but growing number of suits filed charging employers of discrimination against, or harassment of, working parents. The first such case dates all the way back to 1979, but about three-quarters of the total has been filed since 1990. In 1999, for example, there was a $3 million verdict in Pennsylvania awarded to a chemical engineer who was denied promotion for being a working mother. [Associated Press, *More Working Parents Suing Employers* (Aug. 28, 2002) <http://news.findlaw.com/ap/f/1310/8-28-2002/20020828151503_33.html>]

The "sex-plus" cause of action charges that women with family responsibilities (as mothers, or as caregivers for the elderly) are denied raises, promotions, and/or access to leave because of assumptions about their family responsibilities. There were 15 cases of this type resolved in the 1980s, and more than 74 since 1999. [Dee McAree, *"Sex-Plus" Gender Bias Lawsuits Are on the Rise*, National Law Journal, Mar. 14, 2005 (law.com); *see, e.g.*, the suit filed in the Southern District of New York by 12 woman employees alleging a pattern of disparate pay and promotions and denial of access to the management development program after they took FMLA leave for childbirth: *Velez v. Novartis*, No. 04 Civ 09194 (GEL)]

Also note that, as discussed in more detail in Chapter 38, in 2002 California passed S.B. 1661, a pioneering law calling for payment of temporary disability benefits to individuals who are not disabled themselves, but who take time off to care for a newly born or adopted child, or a sick family member. In other words, unlike the Family and Medical Leave Act, this is paid rather than unpaid leave. (This leave must be taken concurrently with FMLA leave; the California statute doesn't create an entitlement to leave over and above the 12-week FMLA annual limit.) The California program is funded by mandatory employee contributions (so it doesn't cost the employer anything), with contributions starting January 1, 2004. There is a seven-day waiting period before coverage begins, and only six weeks of benefits (ranging between $50 and $728 a week) can be paid in any twelve-month period.

California's State Employment Development Department reported that in the first year of the program, about 1.1% of eligible workers took paid family leave (approximately 138,000 out of 13 million employees), collecting about $300 million in benefits. Nearly 88% of the claims were for the care of a new baby, and 70% of those who took leave to care for a family member were female. [Judy Greenwald, *Calif. [sic] Paid Leave Program Draws 1% of Workers*, Business Insurance, July 5, 2005 (benefitslink.com)]

The Families & Work Institute's 2005 National Study of Employers [James T. Bond, Ellen Galinsky, Stacy S. Kim, and Erin Brownfield, <http://www. whenworkworks.org>] found that employers offered 17 types of flexibility in work scheduling. Companies with 50 or more employees nearly always allowed a gradual return to work after a childbirth or adoption leave (86% of respondents did this); 83% allowed time off for job skill training; 78% gave employees at least some discretion in setting their break times; 77% allowed paid time off for family and personal needs; and 73% allowed lengthy breaks to respond to family needs. However, most employers limited these flexible options to only some workers, not the entire workforce. Although most benefits and perquisites are found more frequently the larger the size of the employer, small employers were much more likely to offer flexible scheduling than large ones—perhaps because small companies do not have large bureaucracies, or because to stay competitive for good employees, they have to provide greater flexibility because they cannot necessarily compete on the basis of compensation.

When it comes to maternity leave, the study found that 22% provided less than 12 weeks of leave; 50% offered 12 weeks' leave, and 29% more than 12 weeks. Only 19% offered over 12 weeks of paternity leave, with 52% offering 12 weeks and 29% offering less. Adoptive and foster parents were granted more than 12 week's leave by 19% of respondents, 12 weeks by 58%, and less than 12 weeks by 22%. Only 19% offered more than 12 week's leave for care of a seriously ill child; 59% offered 12 weeks, and 21% offered less in this situation. (Not all survey respondents were subject to the FMLA, so they did not necessarily meet FMLA standards.) Despite changes in the economy, the survey found little difference between leave availability between 1998 and 2005.

No-cost and low-cost child care options were the most common, with 45% of respondents offering dependent care assistance plans and 34% offering information and referrals about child care, but only 7% of employers of 50 or more offering child care at or near the workplace.

An AFL-CIO study done in 2004 showed that 93% of working women considered paid sick leave important—but 31% of them were not entitled to paid sick leave; the Institute for Women's Policy Research says that there are 24 million low-wage workers who do not get paid time off for illness, much less for their needs as caregivers for sick relatives. [Leah Carlson, *Flexible Benefits: Swinging Away from 9 to 5*, Employee Benefit News, <http://www.benefitnews.com/ pfv.cfm?id=7384> (Apr. 15, 2005). For a perspective on men's attempts to balance work and family, *see* Hilary Stout, *The Daddy Diaries: Fathers Juggle Work, Kids and Stress, Too*, Wall Street Journal, May 5, 2005, at p. D4]

§ 28.02   EMPLOYER-PROVIDED DAY CARE

One option, perhaps the most appreciated by employees, is for the employer to maintain an on-site day care center. Calculating the costs and benefits of running a day care center can be difficult. Initial expenses can be high, but this perk is valuable in recruiting good employees and retaining employees who need quality care for their children.

On-site care is only feasible for large companies—and probably is more workable outside big cities because metropolitan rents are often prohibitive. An employer-sponsored day care center has to be licensed. It will be subject to ongoing inspections. The employer company could become liable if, for example, a child were injured on the premises, or several children developed a contagious illness. The standard Worker's Compensation insurance policy also excludes injuries that occur in an employer-operated day care center.

It can be convenient for the employer to contract out daily operations to an experienced provider of high-quality child care, although this adds further expenses. The employer can also co-sponsor a nearby child care center that offers care to employees of several companies.

However, it is much more common for employers to reimburse employees for some of their child care expenses. [See § 28.07 for a discussion of child care fringe benefits and their tax implications. A smaller-scale program gives employees "I&R" (information and referral) to child care resources, but does not actually furnish services or funds]

Consulting firm Circadian Technologies Inc. concluded, in mid-2003, that companies that offer on-site child care for extended hours (outside the 7 a.m.–7 p.m. time frame) had a potential Return on Investment (ROI) of 100% over a five-year horizon. Circadian found that less than 1% of employers provided child care for the 24 million extended-hours employees who work mid- or night shifts, even though 31% of the extended-hours workers have minor children. About 28% of American women regularly work nights, evenings, or weekends, which means that 3.5 million extended-hours workers are the mothers of children under 18. The result is absenteeism, high turnover, and excess overtime costs for workers who cover for employees with child care problems. Circadian reported that companies that made extended-hours child care available saw a $300 annual reduction in absenteeism costs, and had an average 20% reduction in absenteeism. Turnover rates dropped from 9.3% to 7.7%—highly beneficial because recruiting and training a new extended-hours employee costs an average of $25,000. Overtime also decreased from 12% to 8% when child care was available. [SmartPros Editorial Staff, *The ROI of On-Site Child Care Centers,* Aug. 13, 2003 <http://hr.smartpros.com/x40012.xml (no www)>]

Hewitt Associates reports that large companies take a more active child care role (just as they typically offer more generous benefit packages than smaller companies). Twelve percent of large firms offer day care on or near the premises, 10% negotiate for discounts when employees send their children to neighborhood day care centers, and 43% provide information and referral. These percentages increased about 2% between 1995 and 2001.

Although the federal government and half the states have adopted tax credits to motivate employers to offer child care, and in some situations the credit can provide as much as $100,000 in tax relief, the credits are seldom used and therefore have not motivated many employees to change their policy. The National Women's Law Center studied credit utilization in 20 states. In 5 states, no company applied for the credit, and in 11 states there were fewer than 5 applications. State credits are a problematic way to motivate employers anyway, because 93% of state corporate filers don't have enough tax liability to take full advantage of the credits, and 57% don't owe any state taxes at all, even without credits. [Kelley M. Blassingame, *Tax Breaks Fail to Facilitate Childcare Benefits,* Employee Benefit News (March 2003) <http://www.benefitnews.com/pfv.cfm?id=4131>. The states with tax incentives for employers are Arkansas, California, Colorado, Connecticut, Florida, Georgia, Illinois, Kansas, Maine, Maryland, Mississippi, Montana, Nebraska, New Jersey, New Mexico, Nevada, Ohio, Oklahoma, Oregon, Pennsylvania, Rhode Island, South Carolina, Tennessee, Texas, and Virginia]

§ 28.03   BREAST FEEDING IN THE WORKPLACE

Breast feeding for at least the first six months of life, and preferably a year, is the medical recommendation for newborn babies. So either new mothers must choose bottle feeding; delay their return to work until they are ready to stop breast feeding; or participate in a workplace lactation program that either allows them to feed their babies at the workplace or gives them an appropriate private place to pump and store breast milk. [*See* Kathryn Tyler, *Got Milk?* HR Magazine, March 1999, at p. 69]

Workplace lactation programs are a good value for employers, because they aid employee retention. Furthermore, breast-fed babies are often healthier than formula-fed babies, so their parents need less time off to deal with babies' illnesses. The Los Angeles Department of Water and Power found that every dollar invested in the lactation program provided a return of $3.50–$5.00. The program cut absenteeism by 27% and reduced health care costs by 35%.

The demands of a lactation program are modest. Participating employees need a private, reasonably quiet and pleasant place to express breast milk and a refrigerator or cooler to keep it cool, plus a sink to wash up. Typically, employees will need two 30-minute, or three 20-minute, breaks to express milk.

According to *Breast-Feeding In the Workplace: What Should an Employer Do?* [WestGroup Employment Alert, March 16, 2000, at p. 1] the PDA and the ADA do not cover breast feeding. In general, courts hearing cases on this issue have not required the employer to provide personal leave, modified schedules, or changes in job routine for employees who breast feed after returning from maternity leave. In this analysis, lactation is a natural function, and is neither a pregnancy-related medical condition nor a disability.

However, there are some relevant state statutes. Hawaii has enacted a law making it unlawful discrimination to refuse to hire, or to discharge or discriminate against a woman who breast feeds or expresses milk in the workplace.

States such as California, Florida, and New York have general statutes allowing mothers to breast feed in public places where they are not trespassing, but these laws do not specifically cover workplace issues. Hawaii, Georgia, Minnesota, Oregon, and Tennessee have statutes that require or at least allow employers to provide unpaid break time so lactating employees can express breast milk. The employer also has to make reasonable efforts to provide a more suitable place than a toilet stall to do this. A Texas law grants businesses a "mother-friendly" designation if they offer flexible work schedules, private spaces for breast feeding and expressing milk, and hygienic storage for expressed breast milk.

In 2005, the Wall Street Journal's Sue Shellenbarger reported that new legislation about workplace lactation has lost momentum. Between 1998 and 2001, six new statutes were passed, and employers offered more support. The number of employers offering support for lactation tripled between 1998 and 2002, but still reached only a level of 19%. No new laws have been passed since 2001, and employers are reducing lactation support programs as part of an overall quest to trim benefits budgets. [Sue Shellenbarger, *Employer, State Support Stalls for Mothers Who Nurse at Work*, Wall Street Journal, Nov. 22, 2005, at p. D4]

A Treasury official turned down a taxpayer's suggestion that the IRS should make the cost of renting an electric breast pump reimbursable from a health FSA because breastfeeding is so important to infant health. According to the official, breast pumps are beneficial to general health but do not treat a specific medical condition, so FSA reimbursement is inappropriate. [Treasury Tax Correspondence, 2004 TNT 118-51 (June 8, 2004) and 2004 TNT 103-23 (Nov. 12, 2003)]

§ 28.04   ADOPTION ASSISTANCE

Under I.R.C. § 137, as amended by EGTRRA, employers can establish a written adoption assistance program, providing benefits for employees who adopt children. This is not a very common benefit. According to the Society for Human Resources Management's 2005 survey, only 20% of employers offer adoption assistance—still a much higher percentage than the 16% who did so in 2001. [Charley Hannigan, *Adopting a New Benefit,* The Post-Standard, Feb. 5, 2006 (benefitslink.com)] Employees who receive such assistance may be able to exclude as much as $10,000 in employer assistance from income (and they may also qualify for an income tax credit of up to $10,000 when they adopt a child). [*See* I.R.C. § 23] Under pre-EGTRRA law, a larger amount could be excluded if the adoptee had special needs, but current law harmonizes the two.

As adjusted for inflation, the 2006 amount is a maximum credit of $10,960 per child. The credit phases down for taxpayers whose adjusted gross income exceeds $164,410 and is eliminated when AGI reaches $204,410.

The 2002 tax bill, the Job Creation and Worker Assistance Act of 2002 (JCWAA) [Pub. L. No. 107–147] makes it clear that if an employee receives adoption assistance for a special-needs child, the full credit can be taken even if the actual adoption expenses are less than the maximum credit amount. However, expenses incurred for pre-2002 tax years are subject to the limit prevailing in the year of the adoption. If a special-needs child is adopted in a tax year beginning after 2002, then the JCWAA provides that the credit is reduced by any qualified adoption expenses for the same child in earlier years.

Adoption assistance can be offered under a cafeteria plan—a structure that provides tax benefits for employees with no direct cash outlay by the employer. Adoption assistance programs provided to members of the armed forces are automatically treated as qualified, even if they would not otherwise satisfy the § 137 rules. But illegal adoptions, adoptions involving surrogate mothers, adoption of a stepchild, or adoption of an adult do not qualify under § 137. [See the adoption assistance FAQs at <http://benefitsguides.com/portals/benefits_guides/adoption/adoption_assistance_faqs.html>]

IRS Notice 2003–15, 2003–9 I.R.B. 540 provides safe harbors (depending on the type of immigration visa the adopted child uses to enter this country) for determining when the adoption of a foreign-born child is final for Code § 137 purposes. [See Deloitte & Touche Washington Bulletin (Mar. 3, 2003) <http://benefitslink.com/print.php> (no www)]

Hewitt Associates says that, among employers who provide adoption assistance, the average benefit is $3,700. Less than half of 1 percent of the workforce uses this benefit each year, but it creates a lot of good will.

The employer's rationale is often that since it covers childbirth costs via the health plan, coverage of adoption costs is only equitable. Furthermore, adoption costs a lot more than having a baby (about $12,000 versus $4,000), so employees who adopt have a heavier financial burden to start with. [Garry Kranz, *Adoption Programs Gaining Ground,* Workforce Management, April 2004 <www.workforce.com>]

§ 28.05   CORPORATE ELDER CARE ACTIVITIES

Everybody knows that the U.S. senior citizen population is growing, and soon the huge Baby Boom generation will reach retirement age. The vast majority of care provided to assist elderly people with their illnesses and limitations imposed by aging is unpaid, informal care from family members and friends.

Caring for the disabled elderly has an immense impact on the caregivers' family life—and on their productivity as employees. A 1995 study by AARP and the National Alliance for Caregiving estimates that U.S. industry loses at least $11.4 billion a year in productivity because employee caregivers have to take emergency time off, leave early, or are interrupted at work. The same organizations' 1996 survey estimates that there are about 14.4 million employee caregivers in the United States.

Caregivers spend an estimated average of 15 hours a week taking care of their aging relatives. Some of these tasks have to be performed during normal working hours. In some instances, caregivers have to switch from full-time to part-time work, or quit their paying jobs entirely. Stress can greatly reduce the productivity of caregiver employees when they're in the office.

"Who Cares," a 1999 study by the National Alliance for Caregiving and AARP, reports that about one-quarter of caregivers take care of a person with Alzheimer's Disease or other dementia-causing illness, and that there may be anywhere from 1.9 million to 4 million cases of Alzheimer's in the United States. That adds up to at least 2%, and maybe as much as 12%, of the senior citizen population. Caring for a person with Alzheimer's is very time-consuming and stressful. If the employer can offer supportive services for employees who have relatives with dementia, this is likely to pay off in terms of more employees retaining their jobs, and fewer quitting to become full-time caregivers—as well as greater productivity while they are still employed. [GAO/HEHS-98–16, *Alzheimer's Disease: Estimates of Prevalence in the United States,* (January 1998)]

The MetLife Mature Market Group and the National Alliance for Caregiving released a report. [*Family Caregiving in the U.S.: Findings From A National Survey,* (1997)] The survey showed that almost one-fourth of all U.S. households included one or more persons with caregiving responsibilities. Almost two-thirds of those caregivers were employed; more than 50% worked full-time. That meant 14.4 million Americans combining caregiving and employment responsibilities.

MetLife's conclusion was that lost productivity and extra supervisory time for resolving caregiving problems cost American business $11.4 billion a year (to replace employees, cope with absenteeism and partial absenteeism, and deal with interruptions during the work day). The estimated average cost to business, per caregiver employee, was $1,142 a year: $69 traced to absenteeism, $85 to partial absenteeism, $657 for workday interruptions, $189 for employees leaving work to deal with crises, and $141 for supervisory involvement. In addition, replacing employees who quit to become full-time caregivers was estimated to cost almost $5 billion a year more. Furthermore, because caregiving is so stressful, caregivers are unusually heavy consumers of health and counseling services, increasing the employer's plan costs.

The majority of caregivers are women, taking care not only of their own parents but of their in-laws. A small but useful study [*The MetLife Juggling Act Study: Balancing Caregiving With Work and the Costs Involved,* MMI_MetLifemetlife. com (1990)] identifies key themes in the caregiving experience:

- Caregivers often underestimate how hard it is to be a caregiver, or how much effort will be required over how long a time;
- Not only do they make informal adjustments to their work schedules, 84% of survey respondents made formal adjustments, such as leaving their jobs, taking early retirement, or using sick and vacation days;
- Caregivers lost access to promotions, training, transfers, and other avenues toward improved career status;

- Close to two-thirds of caregivers lost some income, and therefore forfeited abilities to save and build wealth. The estimated median loss over the total period of caregiving was $243,761; the estimated mean loss was $566,443;
- Caregivers' own retirement becomes precarious. If they work less, earn less, and save less, they will also be entitled to smaller pensions from their employers and smaller Social Security benefits;
- Most caregivers also provide financial assistance as well as practical help to their relatives or friends. On the average, financial help was provided over a period of two to six years, at an average figure of almost $20,000. These gifts reduced caregivers' ability to invest in home improvements, make consumer expenditures, and pay for their children's education;
- Many caregivers found that their own health deteriorated: 20% reported serious health problems related to caregiving;
- One-quarter of respondents found that their productivity at work declined because of caregiving; 10% felt it declined significantly for this reason.

§ 28.06   THE CORPORATE ELDER CARE ROLE

In 2005, 79% of companies reported offering unpaid time off for elder care; 29% provided information and referrals, but only 6% directly paid for elder care programs. Half of large companies, but only 25% of small ones, offered elder care Information & Referral (I&R), but the percentage of companies offering time off and financial support were very similar. [Bond et al., *The Families & Work Institute 2005 National Study of Employers*, <http://www.whenworkworks.org>]

One problem with corporate elder care efforts is that they often use a child-care template that is not very effective—child care doesn't require tangling with the Medicare Part D labyrinth, for example! Another problem is that, in a time of soaring benefit costs, corporations are far more willing to provide low-cost I&R than more costly benefits such as paying for geriatric care management or offering paid leave to employees with elder care problems. The I&R system could be limited in scope and could be poorly edited, so that obsolete listings remain, or poor-quality providers are not eliminated. Even if the I&R system is excellent, employees still face a lot of hard work in creating and managing the elder care plan.

Figures from the National Alliance for Caregiving show that as the number of weekly hours of care provided by an employee increases, so does the effect on the employee's work performance—with full-time caregivers far more likely to retire early, refuse promotions, take a leave of absence, or move to part-time work. In fact, 80% of those who provided 87 hours of care per week or more were late to work, left early, or spent work hours on elder care tasks—twice as many as caregivers who provided only four hours of care a week. [Jane Gross, *As Parents Age, Baby Boomers and Business Struggle to Cope*, New York Times, Mar. 25, 2006, at p. A1]

Tip: In 2004, AARP released five state surveys about working caregivers in Delaware, Kentucky, Maine, Ohio, and Vermont, focusing on the support workers receive from their employers under existing programs, with suggestions for new programs. The home page for the study is <http://research.aarp.org/econ/caregiving_work.html>

Tip: When the federal Older Americans Act [Pub. L. No. 38–73] was re-authorized at the end of 2000, a new National Family Caregiver Support program was created and funded with $125 million nationwide. Helping employees access benefits they are entitled to under government programs is clearly a win-win for employer and employee. Be sure to work with your local Area Agency on Aging to put caregiver employees in touch with these programs.

Under an I&R (information and referral) plan, the HR department, Employee Assistance Program, or other relevant department maintains listings of nursing homes, home health agencies, government agencies for the aging, and other resources.

Other elder care resources that employers can provide include:

- Seminars about relevant topics such as Medicare and Medicaid;
- Support groups for caregivers;
- Hotlines giving elder care information;
- Subsidized phone consultations with resource or elder care experts (including those in other geographic areas, where employees' relatives live);
- Directories and other publications;
- Caregiver fairs, providing exhibits from public agencies as well as voluntary organizations and for-profit service vendors;
- Counseling from a psychologist or clinical social worker;
- Subsidies for adult day care for the parent;
- Respite care;
- Emergency care (including care in the home of the elderly person);
- Paratransit, such as wheelchair-accessible vans, to provide transportation to medical appointments and other trips that would otherwise require the employee's services as driver;
- Subsidizing the cost of pagers that the parent can use to contact the employee in an emergency;
- Case management—services of social workers or geriatric care managers (GCMs), who advise the employee about creating and managing a complete elder care plan (The employer could pay care managers to provide in-home assessments of the care needs of employees' elderly relatives; the care manager

produces a written report and research recommendations, saving employees a lot of research time. Ceridian Lifeworks estimates that employers can save three dollars for every dollar spent on a program like this.);

- "Elder-proofing" services to make a senior citizen's home safer;
- Monthly or other regularly scheduled seminars for caregiver employees;
- Special outreach efforts during May (Older Americans Month) and October (National Caregivers Month);
- Discounts on eldercare-related products such as incontinence supplies and nutritional supplements;
- An in-house elder care coordinator (especially if the company has a large workforce, or a workforce with a preponderance of middle-aged and older people who can be expected to have elder care needs);
- Adding elderly dependent parents to the coverage of dependent care accounts.

For the unionized workplace, *see* the AFL-CIO's worksheet, "Bargaining for Eldercare," available at <http://www.aflcio.com>.

According to the Shea article cited above, Bon Secours Richmond Health System pays half the cost of home care for up to ten days a year for elderly relatives of the system's health care professionals. Sometimes short-term placements can be arranged in Bon Secours' Assisted Living Facilities to provide respite for caregivers.

LifeCare and the National Association of Professional Geriatric Care Managements teamed up to offer Web, intranet, phone, and print service to provide employees with personalized information, resources, and referrals, including in-home assessments and care planning. [*LifeCare Teams With National Geriatric Association to Offer Elderly Care,* BenefitNews Advisor, Jan. 7, 2004 <http://www.benefitnews.com/pfv.cfm?id=5489>; LifeCare: <http://www.lifecare.com>; National Association of Professional Geriatric Care Managers: <http://www.caremanager.org>]

Some companies have found that their elder care benefits are underutilized and have not succeeded in improving productivity. Utilization of services is typically in the range of 3% of the workforce. The main reason for these disappointing results is that communications with employees and employee education are at fault. The New York Business Group on Health's focus groups with users and non-users of corporate elder care plans revealed that:

- Employees have different definitions of elder care, so the employer must clarify the benefits available;
- Caregivers may be in denial about their needs or may feel that they have to do everything themselves, without help;
- Some parts of an organization may be better at communicating the availability of elder care benefits than others;
- The immediate manager the person reports to is crucial in encouraging use of elder care benefits;
- Users of elder care perceive the employer as being more receptive to employees' use of these benefits than non-users do.

[Richard Federico, *Elder Care Benefits Cry Out for Better Employer Communications,* Employee Benefit News, Jan. 2004 <http://www.benefitnews.com/pfv.cfm?id=5471>]

The Health Insurance Portability and Accountability Act (HIPAA) of 1996 [Pub. L. No. 104–191] cleared up some previously murky tax questions. It enacted Code § 7702B, which provides for tax deductions for some LTCI purchasers. In effect, HIPAA places "qualified" long-term care insurance plans on the same footing as Accident & Health (A&H) plans, so the employer will be entitled to a tax deduction (if it does contribute to the premiums) and employees will not have taxable income on account of employer contributions. But HIPAA also makes it clear that LTCI cannot be provided through either a cafeteria plan or a flexible spending account.

§ 28.07   DEPENDENT CARE ASSISTANCE PLANS

The Internal Revenue Code recognizes, and gives favorable tax treatment to, plans under which the employer makes direct payments to provide dependent care to employees, or the employer reimburses employees for certain dependent care expenses. [I.R.C. § 129] The employer is not obligated to pre-fund the plan. It can pay benefits as they arise, out of current income, with no need to maintain a separate account. However, the employer is required to provide reasonable notice to eligible employees that the program is in existence and how it operates.

Employees do not have taxable income because of participation in an I.R.C. § 129 plan. However, the plan cannot pay more for dependent care than the employee earns. (In other words, the plan can't be set up as a perk for employees who are, in essence, on parenthood leave and earn very little.) Furthermore, in effect the plan only assists employees who are single parents, or who are part of a two-career couple, because the employee will have taxable income if the I.R.C. § 129 benefits exceed the income of the employee's spouse, unless that spouse is a full-time student or disabled.

In addition to these limitations, the maximum employer contribution to an I.R.C. § 129 plan that can be excluded from income is $5,000 per employee. This is further reduced to $2,500 in the case of married employees who file separate returns.

For this purpose, dependent care expenses are household services and other expenses that are incurred to permit the employee to hold a job outside the home. In the I.R.C. § 129 context, "dependents" means dependent children under age 15, or a spouse or other dependent (e.g., an aging parent) who is physically or mentally incapable of self-care.

The Code defines a qualified dependent care assistance plan as a written plan for the exclusive benefit of employees, subject to a classification created by the employer but approved as nondiscriminatory by the IRS. To be considered non-discriminatory, not more than 25% of the contributions to the plan or benefits received from the plan may relate to shareholders, 5% owners, or their families. The average benefits provided under the plan to employees who are not highly compensated must be 55% or more of those provided to highly compensated employees.

If the plan fails to be qualified for this reason, then HCEs (but not other employees) will have taxable income as a result of plan participation. Every year, by January 31, employees must be given a written report of the amounts paid or expenses incurred by the plan for that employee's dependent care in the previous year. An employer-provided day care center is deemed to be a welfare benefit plan, but a dependent care plan that involves reimbursement of employees' dependent care expenses is not.

Dependent-care plans are linked to the Code provisions for a dependent care credit that taxpayers can take. As amended by the JCWAA, the I.R.C. § 21 credit is up to 35% of qualifying expenses. The credit is a sliding-scale percentage (a higher percentage for lower-income people) of qualifying dependent care expenses up to a maximum.

DIVERSITY IN THE WORKPLACE

§ 29.01   INTRODUCTION

At one time, most workforces were quite homogeneous, with a workforce drawn from the surrounding area. Sons would follow their fathers into the "mill" or the office, joined by their brothers and cousins, eventually retiring at 65 with a gold watch. Women worked as clerical or sales workers, or teachers or nurses—not engineers or executives. They quit their jobs when they got married, or when they had children. Handicapped people were kept out of sight. There might be a few people in the workforce who were considered too masculine (if they were women) or not masculine enough (for men). They might even be suspected of homosexuality—if so, they'd be at pains to deny it; they certainly wouldn't show up at the company picnic with a same-sex life partner.

Although the workers might be immigrants or the children of immigrants, it was a pretty safe bet that the managers would be college-educated, Anglo-Saxon white males. Whatever the problems and tensions within the operation, relatively few of them would be caused by racial, religious, nationalistic, or cultural friction—simply because different groups seldom came in contact.

Today, the picture has changed significantly! Although the majority of the U.S. workforce is male, there is a high proportion of female workers—not all of whom hold traditionally feminine jobs. There are many first- and second-generation immigrants in the work force, but now they are more likely to come from Asia and the Pacific, or from Latin America, than from the European countries that dominated earlier waves of immigration. [For 2005 statistics on the workforce in general, managers, and professionals by ethnic group in 1985, 1998, and 2003, *see* Joi Preciphs, *Moving Ahead . . . But Slowly*, Wall Street Journal, Nov. 14, 2005, at p. R3]

The expansion of diversity in the workplace has not been achieved without a struggle. Nor do all the problems come from the proverbial "angry white males." Anyone can be prejudiced, hostile, blinded by stereotypes, ignorant of other peoples' traditions, or just plain hard to work with. Furthermore, a company can be doing its best to offer equal opportunity—while women and minorities believe that they have little access to mobility within the organization, and white males simultaneously believe that they are at a disadvantage.

The National Urban League surveyed 5,500 workers in 2004, concluding that workers are not averse to diversity in the work setting—but they don't think top management has done a good job in promoting the case for diversity. Only one-third of respondents believed their employer company had an effective diversity program. Close to two-thirds of respondents (63%) considered marketing to be the most important area for diversity initiatives, so that companies can communicate their messages to a customer base that embraces potential purchasers in the U.S. and internationally. [William J. Holstein, *Diversity as Policy, Not as Window Dressing*, New York Times, Sept. 12, 2004, at Business p. 10]

The HR department's mission is to promote efficiency and cooperation—not to eliminate differences or even prejudices. A company's workforce doesn't have to worship together, enjoy the same sporting events, celebrate the same holidays, or even like each other. They do have to understand the factors shaping other peoples' behavior, strive to avoid offending others, be tolerant of unintended offensive remarks and actions, and work together harmoniously and productively. For some tested techniques of diversity management, *see* Career Magazine's Diversity Initiative Program Web site, <http://www.careermag.com>.

There are pros and cons for employers that already have employee resource groups for female and minority employees to adopt similar programs for gay employees. The Human Rights Campaign reported that in 2005, about two thirds of the large companies they surveyed had affinity groups for gay employees—a significant increase from the 41% figure in 2002. Some industries (e.g., financial services; technology) are more amenable to having these groups, and they tend to be a Blue State phenomenon. Having such groups can stress the company's commitment to diversity and can help in recruiting; however, they also can create controversy by offending other workers. In addition, not all gay employees are willing to identify themselves as such at work. [Kathryn Kranhold, *Groups for Gay Employees Are Gaining Traction*, Wall Street Journal, Apr. 3, 2006, at p. B3]

§ 29.02   THE GLASS CEILING

Unfortunately, some people are actively and consciously hostile to those different from themselves. They engage in whatever discriminatory actions they think they can get away with. However, overt hatred and resentment are not the only factors that block full advancement for qualified women and members of minority groups. There are other, subtler forces at work, sometimes affecting people who on a conscious level are objective and tolerant.

The prejudices of the past cast a long shadow. If law and business schools used to discriminate against minorities and women, then the supply of members of these groups with professional degrees, and with decades of business experience, will be limited. If a company hardly ever recruits women or members of minority groups for its training program, and if its policy is to promote from within, then it will look to its (overwhelmingly white male) middle managers when it's time to fill senior posts.

These subtler barriers to advancement are sometimes called the "glass ceiling": Advancement up to a point is reasonably easy, but there are invisible barriers to achieving the really top jobs. *See* the reports of a federal commission convened under the Glass Ceiling Act, a provision of the Civil Rights Act of 1999. [Pub. L. No. 102-166]

According to the main report, "Many judgments on hiring and promotion are made on the basis of a look, the shape of a body, or the color of skin." [*A Solid Investment: Making Full Use of the Nation's Human Capital*, <http://www.ilr.cornell.edu/library/catherwood/collections . . . >]

Although the Glass Ceiling report acknowledges that some factors (such as educational systems and social attitudes) are beyond corporate control, the report identifies some factors that business can control:

- Whether recruitment is narrow or broad-based;
- Extent of outreach efforts;
- Degree to which new hires are assigned to marginal areas or staff jobs that have less promotion potential than more central, line jobs;
- Presence or absence of mentors;
- Whether good performance is rewarded with access to training and prime assignments;
- Access to social events and informal networks (e.g., social and sporting events);
- Help and support from colleagues, versus hostility and demeaning treatment;
- Whether evaluations are objective or merely reflect prejudices.

Certain characteristics are shared by successful diversity programs:

- The CEO actively supports the program;
- The program is comprehensive and inclusive;
- The program has a genuine goal of advancing the most talented people, whatever their background;
- Results are reviewed, and managers are accountable for results;
- The company has long-range relationships with community organizations, not a single effort that is quickly abandoned;
- Recruitment is genuinely diverse;
- Recruiters consult sources such as www.diversityee.com, www.newsjobs.com, www.diversity-services.com, and www.HireDiversity.com to obtain resumes from people from a wide variety of backgrounds;
- The program makes out a business case for diversity and communicates it to employees.

There are about 10,000 Board of Director seats on the Fortune 1000 companies' boards; in 2003, about 80% of those companies had at least one woman board member, 75% one ethnic minority person—but only 15% of directors are female, 5% black, and 1.9% Hispanic. Observers believed that one effect of Sarbanes-Oxley would be broader recruiting of board members for major corporations, in addition to the traditional method of top executives nominating their friends and acquaintances. Organizations that promote diversity, and organizations representing various groups, can be good sources of candidates with significant top-level business experience. Some of the advocacy organizations also provide specialized training for women and minority-group leaders tapped as board members. [Julie Bennett, *For Women and Minorities, Reaching the Boardroom Remains a Rough Ride*, Wall Street Journal, Oct. 12, 2004 (special advertising section at p. B11)]

§ 29.03   DIVERSITY TRAINING

Corporations frequently attempt to defuse hostilities within the workplace by offering (or requiring) diversity training. Usually, it is provided by outside contractors. The training could be a voluntary initiative by management, part of a negotiated settlement with the EEOC or a state antidiscrimination agency, or part of the settlement of a court case. The mission of the training is to make employees examine their assumptions and to relate to other employees in a more professional manner.

The goals of diversity training include:

- Finding areas in which the organization is defective;
- Setting goals for improvement;
- Identifying specific steps for reaching the goals;
- Training employees to carry out those steps.

The focus of diversity training has changed over time. In the 1970s, the prime topics were race relations and collaboration between male and female employees. The 1980s focused on disabilities and language issues, and sexual orientation became an issue examined by some companies. In the 1990s, sexual orientation, generational differences, and cross-cultural communications were highlighted. Twenty-first century diversity issues tend to involve operating in a global marketplace; balancing work and life; religious issues and spirituality; and intergenerational issues. [Laura Egodigwe, *Back to Class*, Wall Street Journal, Nov. 14, 2005, at p. R4]

However, diversity training is not without risks and disadvantages. The program can wind up furnishing evidence for a Title VII or other discrimination suit. A well-intentioned program to promote understanding and harmony can worsen the anger and resentment already simmering below the surface. Employees can feel that discussion of other religions or lifestyles is an insult to their own deeply held beliefs. [This point is raised by Simon J. Nadel, *Religion and Sexual Orientation at Work May Produce Combustible Combination*, 68 L.W. 2163 (Sept. 28, 1999)] A 2004 case illustrates this risk. AT&T Broadband maintained a diversity policy requiring all employees to "recognize, respect, and value differences." A fundamentalist Christian employee refused to sign the certificate, because his religion teaches that some differences are sinful and do not deserve to be valued. The District of Colorado found that he put the employer on notice of his religious objection to the policy, requiring the employer to start the interactive process of accommodation; not doing so violated the employee's right to religious accommodation. [*Buonanno v. AT&T Broadband LLC*, 2004 WL 782648 (D. Colo. Apr. 2, 2004)] An attempt to reach out to traditionally disfavored groups could be construed as reverse discrimination. And, in any event, a diversity training program (which could be viewed as purely cosmetic) is no substitute for effective hiring or for making sure that no one is subjected to a hostile environment in the workplace.

§ 29.04   DIVERSITY AUDITS

The prospect of performing a diversity audit raises a similar mix of questions. A company that has central-office commitment to diversity might have very different conditions at the shop-floor level. Furthermore, a multi-unit company can find it difficult to maintain uniform policies throughout.

A well-designed audit can pinpoint the problems and lead to their resolution. However, a badly designed survey does not generate any useful information, but it does generate data that could be damning if a plaintiff discovers it. Doing a diversity audit shows that management cares about the issue. However, that could backfire, if employees expect real change that doesn't come.

> **Tip:** If a lawyer performs or supervises the audit, there is at least a possibility that potentially embarrassing material can be protected by attorney-client confidentiality. But don't forget that confidentiality is sacrificed if the information is publicized.

Labor lawyers Christine Amalfe and Heather Akawie Adelman give some suggestions for an effective diversity audit:

- The first step is advice from a qualified employment lawyer;
- Concentrate on facts, not subjective comments, when collecting information;
- Destroy the individual survey responses and interview notes once statistical data has been compiled;
- Mark the finished report "privileged and confidential";
- Keep the reports separate from other HR information;
- Control distribution, and do not disclose the results to anyone who does not have a legitimate need to know.

Cummins Incorporated, a manufacturer of diesel engines and power generator products, uses an audit team to make sure that all locations stay on the same page. (The company is careful to make sure that the composition of the team is diverse in and of itself.) The team goes out to each site and interviews about 10% of the employees over a period of three to four days. The team reviews the demographics of each operation, goes over its personnel policies, and does a walkthrough to see if there are any hostile environment issues (e.g., pin-ups that could make some workers uncomfortable). The team makes suggestions there and reports back to the central office. [Lin Grensing-Pophal, *A Balancing Act on Diversity Audits*, HR Magazine, November 2001, at p. 87]

§ 29.05   ENGLISH-ONLY RULES

In many (if not most) workplace situations, the ability to speak and understand English fluently is a valid job qualification. However, a person can be fluent in English even though it is not his or her first language. He or she may be more comfortable speaking other languages. According to the 2000 U.S. Census, 18% of the residents of the United States (47 million people) spoke a language other than English when they were at home. However, this has not frequently been raised as a legal issue: In 1996, the EEOC received a mere 32 complaints about English-only policies, up to only 155 in 2004. [Miriam Jordan, *Employers Requiring "English Only" at Work May Face Bias Suits* and *Employers Provide Language Aid*, Wall Street Journal, Nov. 8, 2005, at pp. B1, B13]

If the employer bans languages other than English in the workplace, it is easy for national-origin minority groups to show disparate impact.

As of early 1999, almost half the states (most of them in the South or Northwest) had passed statutes declaring English to be the official language of the state: Alabama, Alaska, Arkansas, California, Colorado, Florida, Georgia, Hawaii, Illinois, Indiana, Kentucky, Louisiana, Massachusetts, Mississippi, Missouri, Montana, Nebraska, New Hampshire, North Carolina, South Carolina, North Dakota, South Dakota, Tennessee, Virginia, and Wyoming. Most of these statutes include certain exceptions (e.g., the criminal trial of a person who does not speak English; when health and safety requires communication in another language). About 40 cities also had similar laws of their own.

According to the Federal Reserve Bank of Atlanta, in states with English-only laws, men who were not fluent in English earned an average of 9.3% less than fluent English speakers. However, the wages of women who were not fluent in English did not differ significantly in the two groups of states. [This information comes from Alejandro Bodipo-Memba, *Wage Gap Widens in "English-Only" States*, Wall Street Journal, Feb. 25, 1999, at p. A2]

An employer who imposes such a rule must be able to demonstrate job-relatedness and business necessity: for instance, that there is no other way to meet customer needs or communicate in an emergency. But it would be hard to establish business necessity for forbidding employees to converse in other languages during meals or breaks, or when they are in the restroom or a locker room.

The EEOC's National Origins Guidelines say that merely implementing an English-only rule has a disparate impact. However, the Ninth Circuit rejected these guidelines, requiring proof that the rule creates a hostile work environment for persons whose first language is not English, or proof that the rule is imposed on employees who experience difficulty in speaking English. [*Garcia v. Spun Steak Co.*, 998 F.2d 1480 (9th Cir. 1993); the EEOC guidelines are at 29 C.F.R. § 1606.7. The Northern District of Texas upheld the rule, saying that it was within the EEOC's jurisdiction to adopt it. *See EEOC v. Premier Operator Services, Inc.*, 75 F. Supp. 2d 550 (N.D. Tex. 1999)]

> **Tip:** A workplace English class, centering around work-related vocabulary and concepts, can be an excellent idea, especially if employees speak many languages, so that English becomes a central means of communication.

Where a high percentage of employees or customers speak languages other than English, or where the company does a good deal of business in non-English-speaking countries, bilingual employees (whether native speakers or those who have learned the language) can be invaluable. The question then becomes whether the pay rate should be higher for bilingual employees.

According to *Roman v. Cornell University*, [53 F. Supp. 2d 223 (N.D.N.Y. 1999] it is permissible for an employer to require bilingual employees to speak English on the basis of complaints that non-Spanish-speaking employees felt excluded from conversations. The rules must be rational; they must be communicated clearly; and must cover all languages other than English instead of singling out one in particular. Furthermore, it could be hostile environment discrimination to apply a rule in a way that shows hostility toward a particular nationality. [*Velasquez v. Goldwater Mem. Hosp.*, 88 F. Supp. 2d 257 (S.D.N.Y. 2000); *Gotfryd v. Book Covers Inc.*, 1999 U.S. Dist. LEXIS 235 (N.D. Ill. Jan. 5, 1999)]

In September, 2000, the EEOC arranged a settlement of close to $200,000 with an Illinois company that agreed to provide back pay for seven Hispanic workers who quit or were fired under the company's English-only rule, plus punitive damages. [No by-line, "Employer's English-Only Policy Brings a Settlement of $192,500," *New York Times*, September 2, 2000, at p. A12]

§ 29.06 PROMOTING DIVERSITY

Steps to take to promote equality in the workplace—or simply to avoid getting sued—include:

- Broaden your recruitment efforts. Don't recruit only at the nearest colleges, or only at the Ivy League. Low-cost public colleges attract some excellent students who can't afford private institutions, so don't rule them out as sources of recruitment;
- Reward managers who increase the diversity of their workforces (with raises, bonuses, and promotions);
- Compare your diversity efforts to those of competitors;
- Provide newly hired female and minority candidates with the training, access to information, mentoring, and networking that they need to succeed;
- Remind employees to avoid ethnic slurs and statements that could create a hostile environment in all written documents, e-mail, and voice mail messages—and also remind them that supposedly deleted materials can often be restored!

The April 2003 issue of the journal Workforce has some interesting words of caution about naive acceptance of the proposition that setting up a diversity program (whether or not high-priced seminars and products are purchased, the diversity training industry earns an estimated $8 billion a year) will necessarily create harmony in the workplace—much less improve the company's bottom-line results. [*See* Fay Hansen, *Diversity's Business Case Doesn't Add Up* (Apr. 2003) <http://www.workforce.com/section/11/feature/23/42/49/index.html>]

Hansen cites MIT professor Thomas A. Kochan for the proposition that gender and racial diversity have no significant effects (either positive or negative) on business performance. Kochan performed a five-year study of whether large companies derive financial benefits from effective maintenance of a diverse workforce. He found that valid published information was hard to find—none of the 20 corporations in his study actually had company-wide measurements of the impact of diversity. Professor Kochan says that to change long-term behavior, managers must be trained to deal with group process issues, not just to "value diversity." Furthermore, anyone can set up in business as a diversity consultant and book high fees; the question is what these people actually have to offer their clients.

However, another article by Hansen in the same issue does give some cautious grounds for optimism. [*Tracking the Value of Diversity Programs* (Apr. 2003) <http://www.workforce.com/archive/feature/23/42/49/234251.php>] Ryder System, Inc. measures the return on its diversity program by checking to see if women and minority-group members have access to key jobs and promotions— and whether litigation costs go down. The company finds that the program has been very effective in reducing litigation costs. Each business unit has a hiring and promotion scorecard. Accounting giant PriceWaterhouseCoopers reports that clients value diversity when they engage an accounting firm, so diversity can be considered part of marketing. The firm has ROI metrics for assessing recruitment, retention of top-performing employees, and employee satisfaction. Real estate services company Cendant measures its return on its diversity program investment by checking the population of new hires, the volume of services provided by minority suppliers, the number of its minority franchisees, and the amount of business generated by multicultural marketing initiatives.

PART VI

EMPLOYEE RELATIONS

CHAPTER **30**

LABOR LAW

§ 30.01   INTRODUCTION

In the broadest sense, labor law covers the entire relationship between employers and employees. However, the term is usually used in a much narrower sense: to mean the body of law dealing with whether a union will be allowed to organize a workplace; union elections, challenges to elections, and decertification of a union that is guilty of misconduct or that no longer represents employee interests; negotiating a Collective Bargaining Agreement (CBA); interpretation of the CBA; and strikes. Labor law sets rules for conduct by both management and unions.

In most cases, labor law is a matter of federal law. Congress has preempted this issue, in the interest of creating a single, uniform body of law that prevails throughout the country.

In 2005, 7.8% of private-sector workers belonged to a union—about the same percentage as in 2004, but only one third as great as the peak figure in the early 1970s, when about one quarter of private-sector workers were union members. (The rate of union membership among government employees has always been much greater than for private-sector workers.) In 2005, unionized workers made about 23% more per week than nonunionized workers. Depending on perspective, that means that unions either have done an excellent job for their members—or have priced themselves and their members out of the market. The union movement also experienced a volcanic change when the Teamsters Union and the Service Employees International Union, two of the nation's largest unions, left the AFL-CIO and created a new organization, the Change to Win Coalition. [Eduardo Porter, *Unions Pay Dearly for Success,* New York Times, Jan. 29, 2006, at Business p. 4; Kris Maher, *Share of the U.S. Work Force in Unions Held Steady in 2005*, Wall Street Journal, Jan. 21–22, 2006, at p. A4; Gary Fields, Kris Maher, and Ann Zimmerman, *Two Unions Quit AFL-CIO, Casting Cloud on Labor*, Wall Street Journal, July 26, 2005, at p. A1]

The easiest kind of operation for a union to organize is a large factory with many well-paid blue collar workers who believe they can improve their job security and enhance their pay and benefits by unionizing. The workers must be secure enough to be able to make a credible threat of going out on strike. They have to believe that they will be able to survive economically during a strike, that they will be rehired afterwards, and that the employer needs to end the strike quickly for its own economic benefit.

But there are many instances in which these conditions are not met, and either workers are afraid to unionize, or believe that they have nothing to gain (and in fact may lose by becoming the pawns of a corrupt union, or may undergo job loss if the employer goes out of business or relocates in another state or a foreign country). Recently, unions have been concentrating on organizing service workers, whose jobs can't be relocated easily, and putting pressure on employers to recognize unions by consent, rather than having a representation election. (There are still about 3,000 representation elections each year, and the results are pretty evenly divided between union and employer victories.)

§ 30.02   SOURCES OF LABOR LAW

[A]   Generally

The NLRA was supplemented in 1947 by the Labor-Management Relations Act (LMRA) [29 U.S.C. §§ 141–144, etc.], popularly known as the Taft-Hartley Act. The LMRA extends the powers of the NLRB. It outlaws certain kinds of strikes, including jurisdictional strikes, strikes to enforce unfair labor practices (rather than strikes to protest them), and secondary boycotts. A secondary boycott is an attempt to pressure a neutral company to keep it from dealing with a company that the union has a dispute with. For example, union activities, including a mock funeral procession, used to force a hospital to stop dealing with a nonunion contractor and its labor recruiter, constituted a secondary boycott forbidden by the LMRA. The Eleventh Circuit upheld an interim injunction, which was proper to prevent further harm. [*Kentov v. Sheet Metal Workers' Int'l Ass'n Local 15*, 418 F.3d 822 (11th Cir. 2005)] Where there was evidence that employees of neutral contractors were discouraged from working on construction projects, a contractor-employer could get a new trial on the issue of whether an unlawful secondary boycott occurred at the neutral gate between two construction sites. [*Ruzicka Electric v. IBEW*, 427 F.3d 511 (8th Cir. 2005)]

The Landrum-Griffin Act, known as the Labor-Management Reporting and Disclosure Act of 1959 [Pub. L. No. 86-257], forbids hot-cargo agreements (agreements not to carry the merchandise of a company involved in a labor dispute). It allows prehire agreements in the building and construction industries, and makes it an unfair labor practice to picket in order to force an employer to recognize or bargain with a union.

The Labor-Management Reporting and Disclosure Act (LMRDA) requires employers to make an annual filing, using the LM-10 form, to disclose payments made to unions and union officials. Payments under $250 a year are excluded. The DOL published new guidelines in Q&A form on March 7, 2006. The guidelines respond to concerns that DOL guidelines proposed in 2005 imposed reporting obligations too broadly. The LM-10 form is due 90 days after the end of the employer's fiscal year. [DOL, *Form LM-10-Employer Reports—Frequently Asked Questions*, <http://www.dol.gov/esa/regs/compliance/olms/LM10_FAQ.htm>, discussed in Dechert On Point, *Department of Labor Issues New LM-10 Guidelines*, <http://www.dechert.com/library/Labor_and_EB_03-06.pdf> (Mar. 2006)]

The Norris-LaGuardia Act severely limits the situations in which an employer can secure an injunction against a union. However, injunctions are still available in certain circumstances. In *Burlington Northern Railway v. IBT Local 174* [170 F.3d 897 (9th Cir. 1999)], for instance, an injunction was upheld to prevent a union from picketing a site where nonunionized contractors loaded goods onto trains. Because no collective bargaining agreement or organizing effort was at stake, there was no "labor dispute" as defined by the Norris-LaGuardia Act.

Although federal law usually preempts state law in the labor arena, the states do have a limited role in protecting their own legitimate interests. They can pass certain labor laws that will not be federally preempted: For instance, there is a legitimate state interest in preventing violence, so states can regulate how and when picketing can be done. States can legislate in areas such as minimum wages, child labor, and employment discrimination.

States can also cope with issues that are only peripheral to the main purposes of the LMRA. This category includes defamation suits brought by employers against unions, suits dealing with continuation of welfare benefits during strikes, and internal union affairs. States are also allowed to legislate in the area of union security, for instance by passing right-to-work laws forbidding union shops and agency shops. [*See* § 30.06]

The National Labor Relations Board's (NLRB) jurisdiction is limited to work performed in the United States; the agency has no jurisdiction over temporary work assignments in Canada. [*Asplundh Tree Expert Co. v. NLRB*, 365 F.3d 168 (3d Cir. 2004)]

[B] NLRA Section 7

The National Labor Relations Act of 1935 (NLRA), also known as the Wagner Act, is one of the bedrock federal labor statutes. The NLRA establishes the National Labor Relations Board (NLRB) as a kind of referee between management and unionized labor.

Section 7 of the NLRA says that employees have the right to engage in "protected concerted activities." In other words, they can act together to form a union, join a union, present grievances, bargain collectively, go on strike, and picket peacefully.

> **Tip:** Once a union is certified, the employer is justified in doing away with its entire benefit package and negotiating "from scratch" with the union, even if the result is a less generous benefit package that the union agreed to in exchange for concessions in other areas. The employer can legitimately explain this phenomenon to workers considering whether or not to vote for the union.

Wearing buttons opposing forced overtime was a protected collective activity by hospital nurses (they did not, for instance, engage in a work stoppage), and therefore the hospital violated the NLRA by forbidding and confiscating the buttons. [*Mt. Clemens Gen. Hosp. v. NLRB*, 328 F.3d 837 (6th Cir. 2003)]

It was also protected concerted activity for two employees to complain to one of the employer's customers about the employer's policies. (The customer paid a bonus to the employer based on the number of injury-free hours worked; presumably the bonus was supposed to be distributed ot the employees, but the employer distributed only half and used the rest to pay for the company Christmas party; the employees complained.) Therefore, firing the employees in question violated the NLRA. [*Bowling Transp., Inc. v. NLRB*, 352 F.3d 274 (6th Cir. 2003)]

An investment counseling firm violated federal labor law by firing a financial consultant for protesting the compensation terms and practices involving himself and other financial consultants. The company failed to apply progressive discipline. Others who made complaints were not fired, so characterizing the plaintiff as a "troublemaker" and "not a team player" did not prove that he would have been fired even if he had not engaged in protected concerted activity. [*Citizens Investment Servs. v. NLRB*, 430 F.3d 1195 (D.C. Cir. 2005]

The NLRB ruled in mid-2003 that it is a violation of federal labor law to fire a worker for trying to take family leave when his pregnant wife was hospitalized. (He wasn't eligible for FMLA leave because he had been employed there for less than a year.) Talking to a co-worker and a manager about the federal and state family leave laws (see Chapter 38) constituted protected concerted activity, because it embraces the public policy of granting such benefits to eligible workers. The employer charged the worker with three very minor incidents during training, six months earlier, as grounds for termination, but these incidents were not made the subject of progressive discipline at the time. The NLRB concluded that there was no legitimate reason to terminate the employee, and therefore ordered his reinstatement with back pay. [*Phillips Petroleum Co.*, 339 NLRB No. 111 (July 31, 2003)]

An employee was fired for lying during a coercive interrogation resulting from her distribution of flyers criticizing layoffs. The employer said that although the distribution was concerted activity, it was not protected because it violated company policy against distribution of any unofficial materials. The D.C. Circuit found that the concerted activity was protected, and the employer's ban was presumptively invalid because it covered all working hours, not just the employee's work time, and extended to the whole building, including the break room and cafeteria. Furthermore, the employee didn't really lie; she merely replied evasively to avoid retaliation for engaging in protected activity. [*United Services Automobile Ass'n v. NLRB*, 387 F.3d 908 (D.C. Cir. 2004)]

The NLRB permitted the termination of an employee for soliciting a co-worker to serve as a witness on behalf of her sexual harassment claim. In the NLRB view, although this was concerted activity, it was not protected by NLRA § 7 because the employee was interested only in her own case, not the situation of other employees. [*Holling Press Inc.*, 343 N.L.R.B. 45 (Oct. 15, 2004)]

[C] Unfair Labor Practices

Either a union or an employer can be guilty of an "unfair labor practice" (ULP) as defined by the NLRA and the LMRA. The NLRB has the power to issue a "cease and desist" order if it deems that an unfair practice has occurred.

The NLRB also has powers to order positive actions, such as ordering an employer to bargain with a union.

NLRA § 8 defines unfair labor practices to include:

- Refusal to engage in collective bargaining—whether the recalcitrant party is management or union;
- Employer domination of a union;
- Retaliation against employees for filing charges with the NLRB or testifying before the agency;
- Discrimination against employees based on either union activities or refusal to join a union. In this context, discrimination includes firing, refusal to hire, refusal to reinstate, demotion, discrimination in compensation, discrimination in work assignments. etc. However, if a union security clause is in place, employees can be required to pay union dues or the equivalent of dues, but they cannot be required to actually join the union;
- Deliberately inefficient work practices that require the employment of excessive numbers of workers ("featherbedding");
- Certain practices occurring during strikes or picketing.

The LMRA penalizes unfair labor practices by unions, including:

- Restraining or coercing employees when they exercise their right to bargain collectively, choose a representative, or vote against unionization;
- Causing an employer to discriminate against any employee;
- Refusing to participate in collective bargaining, once the union becomes the authorized bargaining representative for the employees;
- Engaging in strikes or concerted activity for the purpose of boycotting one employer, forcing another employer to recognize an uncertified union, forcing any employer to recognize a particular union when a different union is actually the authorized bargaining representative, or when a determination of jurisdiction still has to be made;
- Requiring union members in a union shop to pay excessive initiation fees or excessive dues;
- Featherbedding.

It is not an unfair labor practice for an employer to put work rules in the employee handbook against abusive and threatening language and limiting solicitations and distributions within the workplace; pro-union employees can make their point of view known without threatening their opponents, so the rules do not interfere with protected collective activity. [*Adtranz ABB Daimler-Benz Transp. v. NLRB*, 253 F.3d 19 (D.C. Cir. 2001)]

The Seventh Circuit held that a company violated the NLRA by threatening to fire employees who joined a union, and by telling employees to report if they were solicited to sign union authorization cards. The employer said that employees were told to report threats or harassment by union proponents, but apparently there were no threats. The Seventh Circuit would not presume that current employees who testify against their employers are necessarily truthful, but did state that the testimony is likely to be reliable because it's adverse to their pecuniary interests. The court found that the employer targeted union supporters, so the NLRB was not unreasonable to conclude that the NLRA was violated. [*Bloomington-Normal Seating Co. v. NLRB*, 357 F.3d 692 (7th Cir. 2004)]

The First Circuit upheld the NLRB's determination that it was an unfair labor practice to terminate an employee who was known to be pro-union. The employer's contention—that she was a probationary employee who had a poor attendance record—was an obvious pretext, where the employee followed the procedure for reporting before her shift that she had to take her son to the hospital Emergency Room. Nor was the employer's situation improved by discharging an employee who served as an anti-union spy at the same time as the pro-union worker was fired. [*E.C. Waste Inc. v. NLRB*, 359 F.3d 36 (1st Cir. 2004)]

The NLRB overruled the ALJ and held that it was lawful to fire seven employees (most of whom were pro-union) for failure to disclose their criminal records on job applications. (The ALJ had concluded that six of them were fired for union activism and the seventh to obscure the employer's anti-union animus.) The undisclosed convictions included serious felonies, and the NLRB found that the company had a zero-tolerance policy for application fraud, and applied it in an even-handed manner. [*Overnite Transportation Co.*, 343 NLRB 134 (Dec. 16, 2004)]

The NLRB ruled, early in 2004, that management violated federal labor law by threatening, suspending, and eventually firing a pressman who called his supervisor a "bastard redneck son of a bitch" during a discussion of perceived racism in the distribution of work within the organization. The angry comments were part of the protected activity of protest about working conditions. [*Media General Operations Inc. dba Winston-Salem Journal*, 341 NLRB No. 18 (Jan. 30, 2004)]

The NLRB affirmed an ALJ's decision that it was a violation of labor law to refuse to promote an employee to supervisor because of his union activity. But the NLRB refused to adopt the ALJ's suggested remedy of imposing the promotion, because that would infringe on management's hiring prerogative. Instead, the Board ordered the employer to reconsider the promotion—and to provide back pay making up the difference between rank-and-file and supervisory pay until the employee is actually promoted. [*Georgia Power Co.*, 341 NLRB 77 (Apr. 7, 2004)]

[D]   LMRA Preemption

Many cases turn on whether § 301 of the Labor-Management Relations Act (LMRA) should be applied. This section gives federal District Courts jurisdiction over suits for violations of a collective bargaining agreement, as well as suits by one union against another. This section is often applied to bring labor questions into the federal courts—and keep them out of state courts when issues such as wrongful termination and unfair employee discipline are raised.

The most important issue in deciding whether LMRA preemption exists is the relationship between the controversy and the collective bargaining agreement. State laws are preempted whenever it is necessary to interpret the CBA. However, the Supreme Court decided in 1994 that a mere need to refer to the CBA is not enough to justify preemption. The underlying dispute must really involve searching out the meaning of the terms of the contract. [*Lividas v. Bradshaw*, 512 U.S. 107 (1994)]

If the CBA includes a contractual grievance or arbitration provision (and most do), then potential plaintiffs have to exhaust their remedies (complete the entire process) before bringing suit under §301. Plaintiffs are entitled to demand jury trials in LMRA §301 cases. [*Nicely v. USX*, 709 F. Supp. 646 (W.D. Pa. 1989)]

In 1996, two Circuits found that state laws that penalize employers for late payment of wages are preempted by LMRA §301. In one case, this conclusion was reached because the CBA had to be interpreted, in the other because the state law was treated as an "end run" around the limitations imposed by the LMRA. [*Antol v. Esposito*, 100 F.3d 1111 (3d Cir. 1996); *Atchely v. Heritage Cable Vision Ass'n*, 101 F.3d 495 (7th Cir. 1996)]

Other cases in which preemption was found include:

- Failure to rehire, negligent and intentional infliction of emotional distress (because deciding the case required interpretation of the CBA's seniority provisions);
- A claim that a worker was denied reinstatement after a period of disability in retaliation for filing a Worker's Compensation claim, because the issue here was the management's exclusive right to hire and fire under the CBA "management rights" clause;
- Alleged failure to promote because of racial discrimination and union activity, because the CBA covers promotion, seniority, and training. [*Weisbart v. Hawaiian Tug & Barge Corp.*, 1994 U.S. App. LEXIS 13061 (9th Cir. May 31, 1994); *Martin v. Shaw's Supermarkets, Inc.*, 105 F.3d 40 (1st Cir. 1997); *Reece v. Houston Lighting and Power Co.*, 79 F.3d 485 (5th Cir. 1996)]
- A claim that the employer engaged in fraud, negligent misrepresentation, and conversion by depriving the employee of benefits he was entitled to under the CBA, and failing to deposit money in the relevant benefit funds. The claims were directly based in the CBA, and therefore §301 was controlling. [*Williams v. George P. Reintjes Co. Inc.*, 361 F.3d 1073 (8th Cir. 2004)] A similar result was reached with respect to charges that a bankrupt employer violated state law by failing to make supplemental payments to laid-off workers as mandated by a CBA extension negotiated in anticipation of a plant shutdown, because the CBA had to be interpreted to determine who was entitled to such payments. [*Baker v. Kingsley*, 387 F.3d 649 (7th Cir. 2004)]

However, preemption was not found in these situations, on the grounds that the court did not have to interpret the CBA to decide the case:

- Retaliatory discharge;
- Discharge of an employee for reasons violating public policy;
- False imprisonment (unreasonable detention of an employee by a security guard);
- Claims about oral contracts other than the CBA (for instance, a verbal promise of lifetime employment) or implied contracts;
- Claims under state antidiscrimination laws on issues that are not normally bargained away during contract negotiations.
- Plaintiffs alleged that a management negotiator knowingly lied to them by making individual promises and personal guarantees that the plant where they worked would stay open for six years and that their jobs would be safe. They charge that they relied on these representations and ratified a CBA that did not ensure re-employment. The Sixth Circuit held that their state-law fraud claims were not preempted by LMRA § 301; if they did not charge breach of contract, the federal law would not preempt claims that they were induced to sign the contract by fraud. [*Alongi v. Ford Motor Co.*, 386 F.3d 716 (6th Cir. 2004)]

State wrongful-termination law is preempted in deregulated industries where not only the CBA but the deregulation law must be consulted. In this case involving a utility company, the plaintiffs' position was that the deregulated plan prohibited layoffs or demotions for 30 months after a transfer of ownership, and the employer company was merged. The Seventh Circuit said that the deregulation agreement did not provide rights independent of the CBA, so preemption occurred. [*Tifft v. Commonwealth Edison Co.*, 366 F.3d 513 (7th Cir. 2004)]

A union-management settlement terminated and superseded the CBA, so former employees of a shut-down plant cannot litigate in federal court about the contract, benefit claims under the EGHP, or the supplemental unemployment benefits plan. Once the CBA was terminated, the district court no longer had jurisdiction over a hybrid LMRA § 301 suit covering breach of contract and breach of the union's duty of fair representation. [*Bauer v. RBX Industries Inc.*, 368 F.3d 569 (6th Cir. 2004)]

LMRA § 301 does not preempt a state-law claim involving the employer's obligation to make reasonable accommodations to an employee's disability. [*Humble v. Boeing Co.*, 305 F.3d 1004 (9th Cir. 2002)] The plaintiff argued that she was entitled to a light-duty assignment to prevent her shoulder injury from getting worse. The defendant said that the availability of light-duty assignments is governed by the CBA, but the Ninth Circuit ruled that it was not necessary to interpret the CBA to determine if the employer had met its duties under state disability discrimination law.

Although LMRA §301 says that labor unions can "sue and be sued" in federal courts, that provision does not automatically provide federal jurisdiction whenever a union wants to sue in federal court. The union must abide by the normal rules of civil procedure, so there must be diversity jurisdiction (the parties are citizens of different states and the alleged damages exceed a required minimum amount) or a federal question must be involved. [*K.V. Mart Co. v. United Food & Commercial Workers*, 173 F.3d 1221 (9th Cir. 1999)]

LMRA §301 precludes union members from bringing malpractice suits against attorneys hired by the union to represent them in labor disputes. [*Carino v. Stefan*, 376 F.3d 156 (3d Cir. 2004)]

As to what constitutes a federal question, *Textron v. UAAIW* [523 U.S. 653 (1998)] holds that an allegation of a CBA violation by an employer presents a federal question. However, a charge that the employer fraudulently induced the union to enter into a contract, and got a no-strike pledge, by promising not to subcontract out work did not come under LMRA §301, and did not present a federal question.

A federal court can compel arbitration of claims that an employer's conduct during an organizing campaign violated an agreement with the union. The Ninth Circuit held that the dispute comes under LMRA §301 because contract issues outweigh representational issues. The agreement can be interpreted without going into the question of whom the union represents. [*Service Employees' Int'l Union v. St. Vincent Med. Ctr.*, 344 F.3d 977 (9th Cir. 2003)]

The LMRA itself can be preempted by other statutes. In a Sixth Circuit case, employees and a union sued under LMRA §301 to recover nonguaranteed pension benefits. The court ruled that ERISA, not the LMRA, prevailed, because of 1987 amendments to ERISA that make the employer liable to the PBGC for benefits that are unfunded at the time a plan terminates. [*United Steelworkers of Am. v. United Eng'g Inc.*, 52 F.3d 1386 (6th Cir. 1995)]

§30.03 EMPLOYEE STATUS

[A] Definition of Employee

The NLRA defines the rights of "employees," so an important basic question is who fits into this category. Independent contractors are not employees, but common-law employees under the employer's control in terms of hiring, firing, work methods and results, provision of tools and materials, and employee discipline, are also employees for NLRA purposes.

Employee status is maintained during a temporary layoff, if the worker reasonably expects to be recalled in the future. A sick or injured worker continues to be an employee either until he or she takes another permanent full-time job, or is permanently unable to return to work for physical reasons.

In some contexts, retirees will not be considered employees once they are off the company's active payroll and have no right to be rehired or any reasonable expectation of being rehired.

[B]   Part-Time and Temporary Workers

Temporary or casual workers will probably not be considered employees. Part-time workers are considered employees, although sometimes it is inappropriate to put them in a bargaining unit with full-timers, if their interests are adverse. In August 2000, the NLRB ruled that temporary workers can be included in the same collective bargaining unit as permanent employees, as long as the characteristics of the job are similar. [*M.B. Sturgis Inc.*, 331 N.L.R.B. 173 (Aug. 25, 2000)]

This reverses earlier NLRB decisions saying that temporary workers could be organized in a bargaining unit with permanent workers only if neither the "supplier employer" (the temp agency or other company that supplied the workers) nor the "user employer" (the place where the work was actually performed) objected. As you can imagine, one or both usually did object!

The NLRB ruled that the union has the right to show that the two companies are really joint employers of the workers, because they both determine the terms and conditions of employment. However, the user employer can rebut the union's contention by showing that the supplier employer maintains the real control over the workers.

The *M.B. Sturgis* decision, rendered in 2000, was overturned in November 2004. The NLRB returned to its original policy: that separate employing entities can only be required to negotiate as a multi-employer entity if they consent to do so. However, in the 2004 decision, the NLRB said that a bargaining unit consisting only of emloyees of two joint employers, without any individuals employed by only one of them, can be an appropriate bargaining unit even if the joint employers do not consent as long as they jointly co-determine the terms and conditions of employment for the employees. This decision is limited to the context of representation elections and does not apply to joint-employer Unfair Labor Practices cases. Temporary agency workers who want to unionize must name the contracting joint employer in the petition; each joint employer would have to consent to organization of employees assigned to multiple companies. It is not clear if bargaining units organized under *Sturgis* have lost their validity, and whether or not petitions for decertification can be filed on the basis of *H.S. Care*. [*H.S. Care LLC,* 343 NLRB 76 (Nov. 19, 2004); *see* John Lambremont and Andrew Marks, *Bush Board Overrules M.B. Sturgis Rule Regarding Bargaining Units That Include Leased Employees*, ASAP (Littler, Mendelson newsletter), Dec. 3, 2004 (law.com)]

Late in 2001, the NLRB ruled that temporary warehouse workers supplied by staffing firms and jointly employed by the staffing company and Tree of Life fit the definition of "drivers and warehousemen," so it was an unfair labor practice for the company not to apply the CBA's terms on working conditions to the temporary workers. [*Tree of Life Inc.*, 336 N.L.R.B. 77 (Oct. 1, 2001)]

Tip: The law firm Nixon Peabody LLP suggests that user employers avoid giving referred employees the same uniforms, badges, or ID cards as their

---

permanent work force. They should not be given copies of the policy manual or handbook. The supplier employer rather than the user employer should be responsible for disciplining the referred employees. [Nixon Peabody LLP, Employment Law Alert Issue 71 (January 2001)]

The Seventh Circuit held that seasonal employees at a factory were eligible for inclusion in the bargaining unit with permanent employees, based on shared interests and the seasonal workers' reasonable expectation of future employment. The seasonal workers constituted a large part of the workforce; they came from a definable, static group of workers (the local Hispanic population), and all new permanent hires came from the pool of seasonal workers. The Seventh Circuit reached this conclusion although the seasonal employees did not receive the same benefits as the permanent employees; and the employer did not try to recruit former seasonal workers when new workers had to be hired. [*Winkie Mfg. Co. v. NLRB*, 348 F.3d 254 (7th Cir. 2003)]

[C] Supervisors

The text of the NLRA [29 U.S.C. § 152] says that "supervisors" such as foremen and forewomen are not "employees," for the common-sense reason that supervisors promote management interests and therefore do not fit in well with rank-and-file workers, who have different and often opposing interests.

A supervisor is someone who has a formal job title indicating supervisory status, has been held out as a supervisor by management, or is perceived as a supervisor by rank-and-file workers. A supervisor makes independent, individual judgments, can reward or discipline employees (up to and including firing them) and has authority to adjust employee grievances.

To be a supervisor, someone must have supervisory authority on a consistent basis (whether or not it is exercised). Sporadic or limited authority, such as power to take over in an emergency, doesn't make a rank-and-file worker into a supervisor. Courts have expanded the statutory definition, so that managers are not considered employees either, because of their discretion and ability to set corporate policy.

In mid-2001, the Supreme Court resolved a conflict about the status of Registered Nurses in nursing homes. Because the RNs direct the activities of non-RN staff, they are supervisors and cannot be organized in the same unit as the other staffers. [*NLRB v. Kentucky River Community Care Inc.*, 532 U.S. 706 (2001)]

In May 1997, the First Circuit held that a TV station's technical directors were not supervisors, and therefore should have been included in the bargaining unit. [*Telemundo de Puerto Rico v. NLRB*, 113 F.3d 270 (1st Cir. 1997)] But in late 2001, the Eighth Circuit ruled that TV producers and assignment editors are not supervisors. Although they assign work to other journalists, they do not use independent judgment, either because the assignment involves mechanical application of routine or because decisions are made collectively. [*Multimedia KSDK Inc. v. NLRB*, 285 F.3d 759 (8th Cir. 2001)] But then, in 2002, the Eighth Circuit decided that the NLRB used the wrong standard: The court said that *Kentucky River* invalidated the determination that the producers did not exercise independent judgment and therefore were not supervisors—judgment based on professional or technical skill or experience should be treated as independent judgment. [*Multimedia KDSK Inc. v. NLRB*, 303 F.3d 896 (8th Cir. 2002)]

In the case of *Dreyer's Grand Ice Cream, Inc. v. NLRB*, [140 F.3d 684 (7th Cir. 1998)] two pro-union workers held the post of "super-coordinator." They were in charge of several work teams, including interviewing job applicants, recommending hiring and pay raises, and disciplining team members. The super-coordinator job was eliminated after a year, and the two employees kept their increased salaries but were not promoted to the newly created post of "facilitator."

There was an unsuccessful attempt to unionize the workplace, and the two former super-coordinators were fired. The NLRB ordered reinstatement. Dreyer's sought review on the grounds that even after the super-coordinator positions were eliminated, the two workers were supervisors who did not belong in the bargaining unit. However, the Seventh Circuit agreed with the NLRB, because the two did not continue to exercise authority after they had been demoted.

The NLRB said that "shift supervisors" in a college security department were not really supervisors, but the Second Circuit disagreed. There was evidence that the shift supervisors assigned work to their co-workers and directed and disciplined them. [*NLRB v. Quinnipiac College*, 256 F.3d 68 (2d Cir. 2001)]

[D] Union Organizers

A paid union organizer can qualify as a protected "employee" under the NLRA. The fact that he or she is paid a salary by the union does not deprive him or her of the protection of federal labor law. This concept has been extended to treat a volunteer union organizer who is not paid by the union as an employee. [*NLRB v. Town & Country Electric Inc.*, 516 U.S. 85 (1995); *NLRB v. Fluor Daniel*, 102 F.3d 818 (6th Cir. 1996)]

In general, the LMRA prevents employers from making payments to any union representative, but this rule is not violated by continuing to provide full pay and benefits to a long-tenure employee who served as shop steward and worked full-time representing employees who had grievances. The Ninth Circuit held that it was in the employer's best interests to have grievances handled expeditiously. The shop steward was an employee of the company and not the union because the company controlled his work week; he reported to the company's HR director; and his workplace was the shop floor, not the union hall. [*International Ass'n of Machinists v. B.F. Goodrich*, 387 F.3d 1046 (9th Cir. 2004)]

An employer is allowed to maintain a policy against moonlighting (refusal to employ anyone who holds another job)—as long as the policy is nondiscriminatory and is applied uniformly. If the employer has a policy of this type, it is not unlawful discrimination to refuse to hire someone who also works as a paid union organizer. However, the union can win in this situation by showing that the policy really was not neutral, and that the company refused to hire union organizers but tolerated other forms of moonlighting. [*Architectural Glass and Metal Co. v. NLRB*, 107 F.3d 426 (6th Cir. 1997); *H.B. Zachry Co. v. NLRB*, 886 F.2d 70 (4th Cir. 1989)]

If the NLRB charges that employees were fired for pro-union activity, and not for a legitimate reason (such as poor work performance or the employer's financial need to reduce the payroll) the NLRB has the duty of proving the anti-union motivation. It is not up to the employer to prove legitimate reasons for the discharge. [*Schaeff Inc. v. NLRB*, 113 F.3d 264 (D.C. Cir. 1997)]

The basic rules about what happens when a company refuses to hire union organizers come from *FES v. NLRB* [301 F.3d 83 (3d Cir. 2002)]. The prima facie case against an employer shows that the company was hiring, or had concrete plans to hire, at the time of the alleged unlawful conduct. The union organizer-applicants either had the relevant experience or training for the job, or the employer didn't adhere to its own stated hiring requirements or the requirements were pretextual; and anti-union animus at least contributed to the decision not to hire the organizers. If a prima facie case is made, the employer can defend itself by showing that it would not have hired those applicants even if they had not been affiliated with the union. Furthermore, some courts require proof that there were enough job openings to accommodate all of the rejected applicants. [*Starcon, Inc. v. NLRB*, 176 F.3d 948 (7th Cir. 1999)]

On another status issue, the NLRB ruled in January 2000 that a full-time paid union organizer who was denied employment as an electrician because of his admitted intention to organize the workplace was entitled to back pay for the period of time he was unable to work at that job. Furthermore, his union salary should not be subtracted from the back pay award because the NLRB treated it as "secondary employment," not interim earnings that would offset the award. [*Ferguson Elec. Co.*, 330 N.L.R.B. 75 (Jan. 19. 2000)]

A construction company was ordered to reinstate a terminated employee and to offer a welding test to another person; the company had taken action against the two because of their status as union organizers. The test of whether an employer has committed a ULP is whether the NLRB can show by a preponderance of the evidence that the action was motivated by antiunion animus. If the NLRB is able to do this, the employer has the right to assert an affirmative defense that it would have taken the same action even if protected labor activity had not been going on. Here, the hiring process was supposed to be based on skill tests; it violates the NLRA to deny union members equal opportunities to compete for the positions. [*Kamtech, Inc. v. NLRB*, 46 Fed. Appx. 265 (6th Cir. 2002)]

In appropriate cases, the employer can assert the defense that the union "salts" who applied for jobs were not entitled to be hired because they had a disabling conflict with the employer's interests. However, according to the D.C. Circuit, the disabling conflict defense can only be asserted if a union organizer seeks work while engaged in an economic strike against the employer, or if what is described as protected union organizing activity is actually a cloak for unlawful conduct aimed at sabotage or driving the employer out of business. [*Casino Ready Mix v. NLRB*, 321 F.3d 1190 (D.C. Cir. 2003)] In this case, the union salts responded to an advertisement, and were clearly qualified for the job, so refusal to assign work to them was unlawful discrimination. However, in 2003 the Seventh Circuit held that a construction company's hiring system, which gave preference to former employees and referrals from trusted sources did not violate the LMRA. The union "salts" were not hired—but that was not because of their union affiliation, but because they were walk-ins, the lowest-priority category in the employer's classification. [*International Union of Operating Eng'rs, Local 150 v. NLRB*, 325 F.3d 818 (7th Cir. 2003)]

§ 30.04   ELECTIONS, CERTIFICATION, AND RECOGNITION

[A]   Generally

To gain "certification," and thereby become the bargaining agent for the employees (whom the employer must deal with), a union has to win an election supervised by the NLRB. There is a one-year period after the certification election during which no rival union is allowed to seek certification.

A union organizing campaign begins with a petition for certification. Typically, the petition is filed by the union or by an individual employee who is a union supporter. Most organizing work is done by pro-union employees, because employers can and usually do bar non-employees from soliciting on business premises during working hours. [*But see* § 30.04[H] for exceptions to this rule] If there are two or more unions trying to organize the same workplace, the employer is allowed to express a preference for one over the other.

A certification petition is valid only if at least 30% of the employees in the bargaining unit indicate their interest. Acceptable indications of interest are:

- Authorization cards;
- Union membership cards;
- Applications for membership;
- Records of union dues;
- Employee signatures on certification petitions.

It is a serious unfair labor practice for employers to retaliate against workers because of their union activism, so it is important to document good business reasons for any disciplinary action taken against less-than-optimal workers who also happen to be union activists.

The employer has the right to request a representation election when a majority of the employees have submitted signed authorization cards designating a particular union as their bargaining agent. However, an employer that engages in serious ULPs forfeits the right to call for an election, and can be compelled to bargain with the union, because an employer loses the right to call for an election if it engages in conduct that is likely to disrupt the election. [*NLRB v. Orland Park Motor Cars*, 309 F.3d 452 (7th Cir. 2002)]

The Seventh Circuit upheld the NLRB, requiring reinstatement of workers (nearly all of them pro-union) who were laid off during an organizing drive; the company owner and supervisors showed anti-union animus in many statements (including threats of violence), threatened to close down the company if the union won the election, and actually hired as permanent workers a group of temporary workers at the same time as the Reduction in Force. [*Huck Store Fixture Co. v. NLRB*, 327 F.3d 528 (7th Cir. 2003)]

The Seventh Circuit upheld the NLRB's determination that an employer never voluntarily recognized the union, and therefore withdrawing recognition and refusing to bargain with the union (after management's unilateral change in workers' starting times) was not a violation of NLRA § 8. The court noted that a company can voluntarily recognize a union without an election, and voluntary recognition can be explicit or implicit (i.e., the employer's conduct shows a commitment to enter into negotiations with the union). Merely reviewing authorization cards is not the equivalent of recognizing a union. The two sides disagreed about whether bargaining had taken place; the NLRB concluded that the discussion was closer to an informational session than the kind of give-and-take that characterizes bargaining. In the Seventh Circuit view, court review of NLRB orders is narrow: the NLRB must be upheld as long as the agency's factual findings were supported by substantial evidence and have a reasonable basis in the law. [*International Union of Operating Eng'rs, Local 150 v. NLRB*, 361 F.3d 395 (7th Cir. 2004); the principle that review of cards is not recognition comes from *Jefferson Smurfit Corp.*, 331 NLRB 809 (2000)]

[B] Consent Elections

The NLRB is responsible for determining the validity of the representation petition. If the employer does not oppose holding the election, the election is a consent election. The employer and union sign a contract permitting an election. The NLRB will probably have to accept the consent agreement's definition of the appropriate bargaining unit, unless it violates the law (for instance, by including guards in a mixed bargaining unit).

Within seven days of the time that the appropriate NLRB Regional Director approves a consent agreement, the employer has a duty to submit the "Excelsior List" to the Regional Director. This is a list of the names and addresses of every worker eligible to vote in the consent election. The Regional Director distributes the list to all interested parties. [The name comes from the NLRB case of *Excelsior Underwear Inc.*, 156 N.L.R.B. 271 (1986)]

> **Tip:** It is an unfair labor practice for an employer to recognize a union that does not represent the majority of workers. So the employer has a duty to at least examine the authorization cards before agreeing to a consent election. But if an NLRB hearing is anticipated, it is better not to examine the cards. Disciplinary actions will be less vulnerable to challenge if the employer did not know which employees expressed pro-union sentiments, and therefore could not have retaliated against them on this basis.

Also see *Consolidated Diesel v. NLRB*, [263 F.3d 345 (4th Cir. 2001)] holding that it was improper for an employer to investigate charges that anti-union workers felt harassed by pro-union workers "talking up" the union. The Fourth Circuit's interpretation is that the employer interfered with the right to organize, because it is impossible to maintain an organization campaign without saying anything that could be potentially offensive to anyone.

[C] NLRB Hearings

If the employer objects, but the NLRB finds that there is reasonable cause to believe that the union might be an appropriate representative for the employees, the NLRB holds a nonadversary hearing to determine if there is a question of representation. (Employers who are dissatisfied with the Regional Director's decision can appeal to the central NLRB for review.) This type of hearing cannot be used to raise claims of unfair labor practices by either side.

In most instances, the hearing will result in setting a date for a secret ballot election under NLRB supervision. The NLRB will then certify the result: whether or not the union has secured a majority vote.

A union will be certified as bargaining representative for the unit if it wins the votes of a majority of the voters (not a majority of those eligible to vote). But the election will not be valid unless a "representative number" of eligible employees actually voted. There is no bright-line test for whether the number of voters was representative. Many factors, such as the voter turnout, adequacy of the employees' notice of the election and opportunity to vote, and the presence or absence of unfair practices by the employer, are considered to see if there was a high enough turnout.

[D] Election Procedure

Usually, the election will be held at the workplace, because that is accessible to all employees. However, if there is good cause shown for holding an election somewhere else, or for allowing voting by mail, the NLRB will supervise the out-of-plant election. Elections are held by secret ballot. The voters enter the voting location, have their employee status checked, and then mark their ballots in a closed booth where their selections are not visible. The ballots are collected for later tallying.

According to *San Diego Gas & Electric*, [325 NLRB 218 (1998)] voting by mail should be allowed not only in the tense situation of an election during a strike or picketing, but also whenever potential voters would have to travel a significant distance to the polls and are so scattered that simply relocating the polling place would not be effective. Another indicator for mail balloting is a workforce with varying schedules, so that they cannot be assembled in one place at a particular time.

Before a certification or deauthorization election, the employer must post an election notice in a conspicious place in the workplace. The notice must be up for at least three full working days before 12:01 A.M. of the day scheduled for the election. Failure to post the notice can result in the election results being set aside. The notice must give the date, time, and place of the election, and must show a sample ballot so employees will know how to mark it to indicate their choice.

If there are objections to the eligibility of certain voters, or to the mechanics of the election, either the employer or union can file an objection with the NLRB within seven days of the ballot tally. There is no absolute right to get a hearing on the validity of the election: The NLRB Regional Director decides when one is needed.

The NLRB held that a worker who put an X in the "Yes" box but also wrote in a question mark nevertheless expressed a preference for the union—with the result that the UAW won the election by one vote. [*Daimler-Chrysler Corp.*, 338 NLRB No. 148 (Apr. 18, 2003)]

If an employer relies on the results of an invalid election to change policies within the workplace, the Ninth Circuit said that the appropriate remedy is to hold a new election. [*Gardner Mechanical Servs. v. NLRB*, 89 F.3d 586 (9th Cir. 1996)] A bargaining order is improper unless there is proof that it would be impossible to hold a valid election.

[E] Voter Eligibility

The simple answer is that all "employees" in the "bargaining unit" are entitled to vote in a representation election. However, it can be hard to determine the appropriate bargaining unit, and there are some questions about who retains employee status.

A worker who has taken a voluntary leave of absence is entitled to vote unless the relationship with the employer has been severed. If the employee on leave retains seniority and is still in the employer's pension and benefit plans, he or she is probably an eligible voter. Employees on sick leave or maternity leave are entitled to vote, unless they have been formally or constructively terminated from employment.

For laid-off workers, the question is whether they have a reasonable expectation of recall (determined as of the date of the election, not the date of the NLRB pre-election hearing). Laid-off workers with no such reasonable expectation cannot vote in an election about whether the union from the old plant can continue to represent workers after the employer's move to a smaller, more automated plant. [*Hughes Christensen Inc. v. NLRB*, 101 F.3d 28 (5th Cir. 1996)]

A person who was lawfully fired before the date of the election is not eligible to vote, but someone who is unlawfully discharged for union activity retains employee status, and therefore is entitled to vote.

Economic strikers [*see* § 30.09[B] for characterization of strikes] who have not been replaced as to the date of the election are entitled to vote. During the 12 months after the beginning of an economic strike, economic strikers are still entitled to vote if they have been replaced—even if they are not entitled to immediate reinstatement after the strike ends. Employees who are on the preferential reinstatement list are also entitled to vote. But if the election is held more than 12 months after the beginning of a strike, replaced economic strikers are not entitled to vote, even if they still have a reasonable expectation of recall.

Replacement workers hired during an economic strike are entitled to vote in the election, but only if they were employed before the eligibility cutoff date for the election. Unlike economic strikers, unfair labor practice strikers are always eligible to vote in representation elections, but their replacements are never entitled to vote.

Undocumented aliens are employees entitled to vote in representation elections, even if their status has been challenged under the IRCA, [*NLRB v. Kolkka*, 170 F.3d 937 (9th Cir. 1999)] but they cannot be awarded back pay when they are laid off, even unlawfully. [*Hoffman Plastics Compounds, Inc. v. NLRB*, 535 U.S. 137 (2002)]

[F] Electioneering and Communications

During a certification campaign, both employer and union are entitled to communicate their viewpoints to employees. The employer is considered a "person" entitled to exercise free speech rights, subject to limitations of accuracy and fairness. If the employer overreaches, the election results will be set aside, and the employer will have to go through the whole process again, perhaps with more employee sympathy for the union. In egregious cases, the employer might have to answer charges of an unfair labor practice.

The "critical period" is the time between the filing of a representation petition and the election itself. (For a runoff or rerun election, the critical period begins at the first election, and even conduct occurring before the certification petition was filed might be considered relevant as to the fairness of the election.) The NLRB will observe the conduct of both sides, and has the power to invalidate elections, even if the misconduct is not serious enough to constitute an unfair labor practice. The employer is held responsible for the conduct of its agents, including its lawyers and labor relations consultants.

> **Tip:** An employer can avoid liability for an inappropriate statement by an agent if it repudiates the statement promptly, admitting that it was out of line, restating it in proper form, and giving at least as much publicity to the retraction as to the original communication.

Certification elections are supposed to provide "laboratory conditions" (i.e., pure and untainted) for workplace democracy. Employers are not allowed to conduct pre-election polls, or even ask employees their opinions about unionization, if the inquiry is too close to the time of the election. However, it is accepted labor law that employers can call a meeting of workers on company time for management to assert its arguments against unionization. If the union is permitted to solicit employees during meals and other breaks, the employer can call a mass meeting without giving the union equal time to reply.

During the 24-hour period just before the election, neither management nor union is allowed to make speeches to massed employees on company time. If the employer does this, it is not an unfair labor practice, but it could lead to invalidation of the election. The employer is allowed to distribute printed materials to workers during this time. The employer can also conduct antiunion meetings away from the workplace during the 24-hour period, as long as attendance is voluntary and employees choose to come in on their own time.

These are examples that have been found to constitute unfair labor practices by the employer:

- Announcing benefits on election day;
- Explicitly promising benefits if the union loses;
- Threatening to withhold benefits if the union wins;
- Using a supervisor (even a low-level one) as an election observer [*Family Serv. Agency, San Francisco*, 331 N.L.R.B. 103 (July 24, 2000)];
- Announcing new benefits during the critical period to show that the employer offers a better deal than the union—unless the benefits were decided before the representation petition was filed, or there is economic justification for providing them at that time. The employer can increase the amount of information available about benefits [*Beverly Enters. Inc. v. NLRB*, 139 F.3d 135 (2d Cir. 1998)], even though actually increasing benefits before the election would be unacceptable;
- Delivering paychecks at the voting site for a decertification election, rather than at the workplace. [*United Cerebral Palsy Ass'n of Niagara County*, 327 N.L.R.B. 14 (1998)] The NLRB requires a legitimate business reason for changing the procedure for delivering paychecks within 24 hours of an election. Usually, a higher voter turnout is good—but in a decertification election, increased turnout benefits the employer rather than the union;

- Telling employees that their yearly merit raises would end if the company unionized. [*LaSalle Ambulance, Inc.*, 327 N.L.R.B. 18 (1998). *See also More Truck Lines v. NLRB*, 324 F.3d 735 (D.C. Cir. 2003)] It would have been acceptable to state that the yearly raises were a term of condition of employment that could not be altered without bargaining, not a new issue that could not be implemented without bargaining. A new election was ordered after a 6-6 vote, based on a manager's statement that the company's profit-sharing program might not be available if the union won. This was a threat to terminate benefits. The NLRB did not accept the argument that the current year's bonus had already vested and future bonuses would be subject to negotiation. [*Cooper Tire & Rubber Co.*, 340 N.L.R.B. No. 108 (Oct. 28, 2003)];
- Telling employees that unless they returned to work the next day without a union contract, the business would be closed down, and its equipment would be leased, was a threat (an unfair labor practice) and not just a permissible prediction of future events. It was a threat because it referred to events wholly within the employer's control [*NLRB v. Gerig's Dump Trucking Inc.*, 137 F.3d 936 (7th Cir. 1998)];
- A company-wide increase in employer contributions to the 401(k) plan was announced three days before an election to the employees participating in the election; the good news was not given to employees in the company's other units until later [*Waste Management of Palm Beach*, 329 N.L.R.B. 20 (2000)];
- Moving a security camera to videotape employees handing out union literature during the period before a representation election. [*Robert Orr-Sysco Food Servs.*, 334 N.L.R.B. 122 (2001); *National Steel & Shipbuilding Co. v. NLRB*, 156 F.3d 1268 (D.C. Cir. 1998) holds that the employer's videotaping union rallies outside the plant interferes with protected activities, unless the employer can provide objective justification for the surveillance. However, *Metropolitan Regional Council, United Brotherhood of Carpenters & Joiners*, 335 N.L.R.B. 67 (Aug. 21, 2001) says that it is also an unfair labor practice for a union to photograph and videotape employees of a nonunion contractor as they crossed a picket line.]
- The Seventh Circuit ruled that it was a violation of federal labor law to threaten stricter enforcement of rules and possible plant closure if the union won the election—but it was legitimate to forbid posting union literature on a bulletin board where personal notices were allowed but there was a consistently applied ban on materials from any group or organization. [*Fleming Cos v. NLRB*, 349 F.3d 968 (7th Cir. 2003)]

It has been deemed to be an unfair labor practice by the union promising to throw "the biggest party in Texas" if the union won. [*Trencor, Inc. v. NLRB*, 110 F.3d 268 (5th Cir. 1997)] In the case of *Overnite Transportation Co. v. NLRB* [140 F.3d 259 (D.C. Cir. 1998)], pro-union employees photographed and videotaped other employees. The court refused to overturn the union's election victory because the employees were not acting as union agents, and they did not create an atmosphere of fear and reprisal that would prevent a fair election.

The Eleventh Circuit invalidated a pro-union result in a representation election because of violence committed by a pro-union worker against an antiunion worker (the pro-union worker speeded up the production line to dump hot rubber near the co-worker) three days before the election. The court concluded that other workers were likely to fear further acts of retaliation if they voted against the union. [*Associated Rubber Co. v. NLRB*, 296 F.3d 1055 (11th Cir. 2002)] The NLRB decided that threats by two pro-union employees to another employee during the critical period did not create an atmosphere of fear and reprisal sufficient to invalidate the election results (the union won). Here, the threats did not directly involve violence (it was implied that in a unionized workplace, male employees would be at risk of being fired based on fabricated sexual harassment charges). The NLRB used five factors to analyze a situation of threats: the nature of the threat; whether the entire unit was affected; whether all the employees were aware of the threat; whether the person uttering the threat was capable of carrying it out; and whether the threat was repeated close to the time of the election. [*Accubuilt Inc.*, 340 NLRB No. 161 (Jan. 6, 2004)]. Employees were permitted to proceed with their claim that it was a violation of privacy for unions to use their license plate numbers to get their home addresses to visit them during an organizing campaign, although the Eastern District of Pennsylvania noted that a litigation exception could apply if the information was gathered for use in, or even anticipation of, NLRB proceedings. [*Pichler v. UNITE,* 339 F. Supp. 2d 665 (E.D. Pa. 2004)]

The NLRB ordered King Electric to bargain with the IBEW; King challenged the certification of the union because of union conduct around the time of the election. The D.C. Circuit agreed with the employer that giving employees a benefit during an election campaign that they would not otherwise be entitled to (in this case, employment referrals to a Joint Apprenticeship Training Committee) is objectionable, even if the benefit was not conditioned on how the employees vote in the election. Nor could the action of half the employees who quit after the election be ignored. However, the union did not engage in improper electioneering because during the voting, the union representatives were 40–50 feet away from the polling booth and not on the employer's property. Although they did talk to voters, they did not violate NLRB instructions. [*King Electric v. NLRB*, 440 F.3d 471 (D.C. Cir. 2006)]

However, these have been held not to be improper practices by the employer:

- Delaying pay raises until after the election, as long as timing is the only issue—raises will be paid no matter who wins the election;
- Distributing fact-based (not coercive or threatening) handbills during an organizing drive, saying that unionization would lead to long, bitter negotiations and possibly an ugly strike [*General Elec. Co.*, 323 N.L.R.B. 91 (2000)];
- Announcing two new floating holidays the day before the election. The election was nevertheless valid because the holidays affected thousands of employees

throughout the employer's parent company. The timing of the announcement was logical within the company's fiscal year; it was just a coincidence that it was right before the election. [*Network Ambulance Servs. Inc.*, 329 N.L.R.B. 13 (1999)]

The NLRB reversed its own decision of four years earlier and ruled in November 2004 that an employer's threat to close down a facility if the workers vote for the union will not be presumed to be disseminated throughout the bargaining unit. The NLRB pointed out that the burden of proof for an issue usually rests with the objecting party, given the difficulties of proving a negative. The changed rule applies prospectively only. [*Crown Bolt Inc.*, 343 NLRB 86 (Nov. 29, 2004)]

The NLRB imposes a five-part test, all of which must be met, to determine when it is legitimate for an employer to ask employees to appear in an anti-union video. Direct solicitation is considered improper, but it is permissible to make a general announcement seeking volunteers, with a guarantee that employees who do not wish to participate will not be penalized. The Third Circuit approved the NLRB test, finding it to be a rational balance between the employer's right of free expression and employees' right to be free of coercion. Employees must not be pressured into making a decision while a supervisor is present. The employer must not have engaged in other forms of coercion or unfair labor practices during the union campaign, and the process of seeking employees to appear in the video must not be used to spy on the union. [*Allegheny Ludlum Corp. v. NLRB*, 301 F.3d 167 (3d Cir. 2002)]

The NLRB did not abuse its discretion by extending the certification year for an additional six months, and by ordering the employer to reinstate its bargaining proposals, where the employer withdrew all its proposals just before the certification year ended. [*NLRB v. Beverly Health & Rehab Servs. Inc.*, 187 F.3d 769 (8th Cir. 1999)]

In *Waldinger Corp. v. NLRB* [262 F.3d 1213 (11th Cir. 2001)], a supervisor advocated the union at a meeting at which many authorization cards were signed. The Eleventh Circuit held that the supervisor's actions did not taint the cards, and therefore the employer was not justified in withdrawing recognition of the union. Although there is a legal concept of "supervisory taint," it is present only if the supervisor gives a false impression that the employer favors the union, or that employees are at risk of coercion or retaliation.

In late 2002, the Sixth Circuit upheld the NLRB, which overturned an election (in which the employer won by a narrow margin) but certified the second election, which resulted in a broad union victory. The employer interfered with the first election by banning pro-union posts on bulletin boards, and by soliciting employee grievances to redress (to create the idea that the union is not necessary to resolve grievances). The second election was valid because there was no proof that the union did anything to limit the employees' free choice. [*NLRB v. V&S Schuler Eng'g Inc.*, 309 F.3d 362 (6th Cir. 2002)]

The Third Circuit ruled that it was an abuse of discretion for the NLRB to refuse to hold an evidentiary hearing when an employer objected to an election that the union won. The employer alleged that former employees who talked to current employees were union agents. If this was true, the election must be set aside, because no matter what they were talking about, prolonged conversations in the polling place between voters and union agents make an election invalid. [*Trimm Assocs. v. NLRB*, 351 F.3d 99 (3d Cir. 2003)]

[G]   Buttons and Insignia

The right to free speech extends to employees in the workplace to the extent that workers must be allowed to wear union buttons. They must be allowed to wear union buttons to the poll, even though blatant electioneering like this would not be allowed in a general election.

Wearing union insignia is protected by NLRA § 7, and interfering with this right violates § 8(a)(1), unless the union materials cause a real safety hazard, or there is a real risk of violence between union supporters and opponents. The mere possibility of violence is not enough.

There is a partial exception. Employees who work with the public, and who are required to wear a uniform, can be forbidden to wear all kinds of jewelry, including union buttons. They can be required to wear the standard uniform, not a union T-shirt. But the employer must be careful to communicate the uniform policy, and to enforce it across the board, not just against union insignia.

An employer can permissibly forbid employees to display any decals not issued by the employer on their hard hats. According to the Fourth Circuit, the ban served a legitimate function. [*Eastern Omni Constructors Inc. v. NLRB*, 170 F.3d 418 (4th Cir. 1999)] The employer-issued decals promoted workplace safety by identifying workers certified to use particular pieces of equipment. The employees' free expression was not stifled because they could display union insignia on other articles of clothing.

Although Wal-Mart Stores' no-solicitation rule was lawful, it was not a violation of the rule for a pro-union employee to wear a t-shirt with a union message, or to invite three co-workers to a union meeting. These actions were not solicitation because of the lack of demand for an immediate response, and because the employee did not interrupt the work of others. The NLRB found that pro-union t-shirts fall within the accepted right to wear union insignia on corporate premises. [*Wal-Mart Stores Inc.*, 340 NLRB No. 76 (Sep. 30, 2003)]

The other side of the coin can also be legally recognized. Employees who were ordered to wear both employer and union insignia at work filed an NLRB complaint against the employer and union, charging violations of their First Amendment rights and their right to refrain from concerted activity. The plaintiffs were not union members; the uniform policy applied to both union and nonunion workers. The NLRB dismissed the claim on the ground that special circumstances applied: the collectively bargained logo policy advanced the employer's business objective of maintaining a favorable public image. The Fourth Circuit vacated the NLRB's decision, holding that the CBA provision violated 29 USC § 157, so there was no need to consider the First Amendment question.

The court ruled that employees have a presumptive right to wear union insignia as part of the NLRA § 7 right to engage in concerted organizing and collective bargaining activities. But § 7 also protects employees who choose to refrain from union activities, so there must be a reciprocal right to refuse to wear the union logo. The Fourth Circuit says that an employer can lawfully ban a display of union insignia that unreasonably interferes with the employer's business plan and public image. The converse is true—employers cannot mandate the display merely for customer exposure. In this case, there was no evidence that the union logo carried the intended message of a trouble-free work environment; in fact, the public might associate the union logo with service disruptions. Customers would also reasonably conclude that the person wearing the insignia was a union member and supporter, which was not true of the petitioners. [*Lee v. NLRB*, 393 F.3d 491 (4th Cir. 2005)]

[H] Access by Non-Employees

In most instances, a workplace is private property, not a public space. Therefore, union organizers do not automatically have a right to leaflet or distribute literature if this is contrary to the wishes of the employer or other owner of the property.

An exception might occur in a "company town" situation, where in effect all property is owned by the employer, so there is no public space where the union can distribute literature. [*See, e.g., Lechmere v. NLRB*, 502 U.S. 527 (1991)] Another exception might be a place that is so remote geographically that the union has no reasonable means of communicating with employees outside the workplace.

The Ninth Circuit held that it was an unfair labor practice for a store to have union representatives arrested for picketing and handbilling in the store's private parking lot. [*NLRB v. Calkins*, 187 F.3d 1080 (9th Cir. 1999)] The court refused to apply *Lechmere* on the grounds that the case was decided under Connecticut law, which allows union organizers to be excluded from private property as trespassers. California law offers broader free-speech protection and allows union representatives to picket and distribute literature on private property. The Ninth Circuit ruled that the California Constitution requires private shopping centers to respect free speech rights, so a rule against distribution of literature naming a mall tenant, owner, or manager was invalid and could not be used to ban distribution of handbills criticizing Disney and Capitol Cities/ABC. [*Glendale Assocs. Ltd. v. NLRB*, 347 F.3d 1145 (9th Cir. 2003)] A later case, in contrast, holds that it is not a violation of California law for a stand-alone grocery store on private property to bar union organizers from distributing literature. [*Waremart Foods v. NLRB*, 354 F.3d 870 (D.C. Cir. 2004)]

The Sixth Circuit found that it was an Unfair Labor Practice for a non-union nursing home to require employees distributing union literature to leave non-working areas of the premises. The court found that the rights of employees who worked at other sites to receive the information outweighed the employer's property rights. There was no proof that nursing home residents would be any more distressed by the presence of union organizers than any other stranger. [*First Healthcare Corp. v. NLRB*, 344 F.3d 523 (6th Cir. 2003)]

The Tenth Circuit said it was legitimate for the City of Denver to bar the musicians' union from picketing and leafleting on the pedestrian walkway of the city-owned art center. The walkway was not a public forum and had no history of being used for public expressive activities. [*Hawkins v. Denver*, 170 F.3d 1281 (10th Cir. 1999)]

The Second Circuit used a very similar analysis in late 2002 to decide that Lincoln Center, the arts complex in Manhattan, can legitimately forbid a food service worker's union from holding a rally or leafleting in Lincoln Center's plaza, where expression has always been limited to artistic or performance-related, rather than political, events. [*Hotel Employees & Restaurant Employees Union v. City of N.Y.*, 311 F.3d 534 (2d Cir. 2002)]

However, in 2001 the Ninth Circuit said that a sidewalk built on private property, to replace the public sidewalk that was demolished when the street was widened, is still a public forum for First Amendment purposes, giving the union the right to picket there. [*Venetian Casino Resort LLC v. Local Joint Executive Bd. of Las Vegas*, 257 F.3d 937 (9th Cir. 2001)]

The Third Circuit has found that the NLRA is not violated when an employer denies access to its property to union representatives who want to distribute handbills accusing the employer of using underpaid nonunion labor. In this context, the employer's property rights clearly prevail over the union's free speech right— especially because general information aimed at the public, not an actual certification election, was involved. [*Metropolitan Dist. Council of Phila. v. NLRB*, 68 F.3d 71 (3rd Cir. 1995)] In contrast, where employee interests outweighed the employer's security and property rights concerns, the D.C. Circuit ruled that off-site employees must be allowed to distribute pro-union handbills in the plant parking lot. [*ITT Indus. v. NLRB*, 413 F.3d 64 (D.C. Cir. 2005)]

The employer also has a right to control the use of plant bulletin boards and to forbid the posting of union materials on those boards. [*Guardian Indus. Corp. v. NLRB*, 49 F.3d 317 (7th Cir. 1995)] Following the principle that there is no special exception requiring access in support of union organizing activity [*Sandusky Mall Co. v. NLRB*, 242 F.3d 682 (6th Cir. 2001)], the Sixth Circuit ruled in 2002 that it is not an Unfair Labor Practice for a store chain to let some charitable organizations solicit on their premises (despite a policy forbidding all types of solicitation) while denying access to non-employee union representatives. [*Albertson's Inc. v. NLRB*, 301 F.3d 441 (6th Cir. 2002)]

Can a business located in a shopping mall forbid the distribution of union literature in that mall? The Eighth Circuit says that a business that is just a tenant (and therefore does not have exclusive rights to the corridor outside its business location) cannot forbid union handbilling. But the Sixth Circuit says that a mall owner can ban solicitation by union representatives who are not employed at the mall, even if other kinds of solicitation (e.g., for charity) are allowed. [*O'Neil's Markets v. United Food & Commercial Workers*, 95 F.3d 733 (8th Cir. 1996); *Cleveland Real Estate Partners v. NLRB*, 95 F.3d 457 (6th Cir. 1996); *Riesbeck Food Markets Inc. v. NLRB*, 91 F.3d 132 (4th Cir. 1996)]

The NLRB says that a mall can demand that it be given advance notice of the names of people who propose to give out union handbills, but once this is done, the mall cannot forbid handbillers to refer to mall tenants by name. That strikes a balance between permitting free speech but allowing malls to exclude people who had behaved improperly in the past. [*Glendale Assocs.*, 335 NLRB 8 (Aug. 23, 2001)]

The Fourth Circuit, reversing the NLRB, held that it was not a violation of labor law for a resort to call the police to deal with union representatives picketing on a busy public road near the entrance to the hotel. The Fourth Circuit viewed the picketing as a cause of potential danger that justified law enforcement involvement. [*CSX Hotels Inc. v. NLRB*, 377 F.3d 394 (4th Cir. 2004)]

Picketing is a particularly confrontational practice and has the potential to create conflict and danger, especially when persons who wish to enter the premises are told not to cross the line. The District Court for the District of Maryland ruled that it was permissible for a union to display a large banner outside the offices of a law firm that hired a nonunion subcontractor, treating the banner as purely informational—the equivalent of leafletting—not a confrontational barrier. [*Gold v. MidAtlantic Regional Council of Carpenters*, 74 L.W. 1432 (D. Md. Dec. 22, 2005)] The Ninth Circuit ruled that the NLRB was not entitled to a preliminary injunction to prevent a union from putting "Labor Dispute" banners outside stores that hire nonunion contractors because banners do not threaten, coerce, or restrain employees or potential customers. [*Overstreet v. United Bhd. of Carpenters & Joiners of Am.*, 409 F.3d 1199 (9th Cir. 2005)]

§ 30.05 THE APPROPRIATE BARGAINING UNIT

Even after winning an election, a union cannot be certified unless it is organized as the appropriate bargaining unit for the enterprise. NLRA § 9(b) gives the NLRB power to determine the appropriate bargaining unit. The basic standard is whether there is a community of interest among the unit members, not just employees in general (who can be expected to want higher wages and better benefits). Neither employer nor union can tell in advance what will be considered the appropriate unit, or how large the unit will be.

The appropriateness of a bargaining unit depends on the duties, skills, and working conditions of the employees who are supposed to have common interests. If there are competing proposed bargaining units for the same company, their relative popularity with employees is highly significant.

A union can be organized by employer, craft, or plan, or a subdivision of one of these categories. A union decision to organize as a craft unit is legally protected. The NLRB does not have the power to decide that a different unit would be more appropriate.

Employees and supervisors cannot be in the same bargaining unit. In fact, in many instances, supervisors cannot unionize at all, because they are considered a part of management. As a general rule, professionals and nonprofessionals cannot be included in a unit, but this rule can be waived if a majority of the professional employees vote to be included. (The nonprofessionals do not get veto power over inclusion of professionals.)

Determination of professional status does not depend entirely on job title. The factual determination is whether the work is predominantly intellectual, is not routine, requires discretion and independent judgment, mandates specialized knowledge, and cannot be standardized as to time. Professionals can still be unionized, but they must consent to inclusion in a nonprofessional bargaining unit instead of having their own.

If plant guards are unionized, they must have their own bargaining unit. They cannot be organized with other employees, because the employer would not feel very secure during a strike if several guards were union activists—much less if one of them was the shop steward!

The NLRB required registered nurses for a comprehensive regional medical system to be included in the same bargaining unit whether they work at the main campus or in outlying facilities, because they do similar work, attend the same meetings, and sometimes workers are assigned to different units within the system. [*Stormont-Vail Healthcare, Inc.*, 340 NLRB No. 143 (Dec. 3, 2003)]

In mid-2002, the Fourth Circuit ruled that the NLRB was wrong to order Sara Lee to recognize the union at three newly acquired, nonunionized plants. The NLRB treated the workers at the new locations as "accreted" (absorbed by) the two existing bargaining units. However, the Fourth Circuit held that each facility should be presumed to be a separate bargaining unit. When a group of non-union employees joins a unionized company (e.g., as a result of a corporate acquisition), accretion is only proper if the circumstances show that it is certain that the self-determination of employees would not be frustrated by including them in the union. [*Sara Lee Bakery Group Inc. v. NLRB*, 296 F.3d 292 (4th Cir. 2002)]

The Seventh Circuit agreed with the NLRB that it was appropriate to order a representation election for eleven employees as a substantial and representative complement of a 300-employee workforce, when the employer planned to expand and merge subsidiaries with a new plant acquired a mile and a half away. The employer failed to demonstrate that a majority of the employees would decline employment at the new location. [*NLRB v. Deutsche Post Global Mail Ltd.*, 315 F.3d 813 (7th Cir. 2003)]

§ 30.06   UNION SECURITY

[A]   NLRA Prohibitions

Closed shops (where only union members can be hired) are illegal. The NLRA also forbids "preferential hiring" situations under which the employer is obligated to hire only union members unless the union is unable to fill all vacancies with qualified workers.

However, the LMRA authorizes "union shops," where all current employees must be union members, and new hires can be required to join the union after hiring (within seven days in the construction industry, within 30 days in other industries), and "agency shops," where payment of initiation fees and union dues is mandatory, but actual membership is optional. "Union security" measures are available to a union that is the bona fide bargaining representative of the employees in the bargaining unit and there has not been a deauthorization election certified in the year preceding the effective date of the union security agreement.

It is not a breach of a union's duty of fair representation for it to enter into a CBA that contains a union security clause that echoes the wording of NLRA § 8(3)(a). [*Marquez v. Screen Actors Guild*, 525 U.S. 33 (1998)] The plaintiff claimed that she should have been notified of her right not to join the union and to pay the union only for its representational activities.

The NLRB ordered a hospital to comply with the CBA's union security provision by firing nurses who had not paid their union dues. The Eighth Circuit upheld the NLRB's order because failing to abide by a CBA provision constitutes a refusal to bargain collectively. [*St. John's Mercy Health Sys. v. NLRB*, 436 F.3d 843 (8th Cir. 2006)]

If the union wants "automatic dues checkoff" (deduction of dues from the paycheck, so the union doesn't have to bill the member), it must have its members provide a written assignment lasting until the contract expires, or for one year, whichever comes first. The NLRB ruled that it was permissible for casinos to unilaterally stop making payroll deductions for union dues after the union contract expired—but the Ninth Circuit said the agency was wrong. In the Ninth Circuit view, the obligation to collect dues stops when the CBA ends if, but only if, the CBA has a union security clause, because union membership can only be made a condition of employment under a CBA. [*Local Joint Executive Board of Las Vegas v. NLRB*, 309 F.3d 578 (9th Cir. 2002)]

Under the NLRA [29 U.S.C. § 169], employees who have a religious objection to unionization cannot be forced to join or support a union—even if the workplace is subject to a union security measure. However, to prevent financial windfalls, the employee can be required to contribute the equivalent of the initiation fee to a nonreligious charity of the employee's choice.

Tip: It's OK for the union to require independent corroboration from a reliable third party (e.g., the employee's pastor) when an employee asserts a religious objection to paying the dues; it doesn't violate the union's duty of reasonable accommodation of religious needs. [*Bashouse v. Local Union 2209*, 70 L.W. 1236 (N.D. Ind. Oct. 2, 2001)]

Communications Workers of America v. Beck [487 U.S. 735 (1988)] says that employees who do not want to join a union, but who are subject to a union security clause in the CBA, can be charged fees that can be traced back to collective bargaining, contract administration, and pursuing grievances. But they can prevent the union from using their money for political or other "nonrepresentational purposes."

It was a ULP for a union to fail to inform members of their legal rights under *Beck* if they resigned from the union; by not honoring resignations made during a strike; and by improperly assessing a second initiation fee when ex-members rejoined the union. [*International Bhd. of Teamsters Local 492*, 346 N.L.R.B. 37 (Jan. 31, 2006), <http://www.nlrb.gov/nlrb/shared_files/decisions/slip346.asp>]

A union can include organizing expenses as an element in the agency fees charged to nonmembers. The NLRB allows this [*see United Food & Commercial Workers*, 329 N.L.R.B. 69 (Sept. 30, 1999)] because of the positive effect of unionization on a company's wage scales, benefiting workers who do not join.

A "Hudson notice" (the name comes from *Chicago Teachers Union v. Hudson* [475 U.S. 292 (1986)]) informs non-members of a union of the "fair share" fees that they are charged to cover their fair share of the union's cost of negotiating and enforcing the CBA. Courts disagree about what constitutes an adequate Hudson notice. According to the Ninth Circuit, it's not good enough to say that the figures explaining the calculation of the fair share come from an audited statement. The Ninth Circuit view is that although a formal audit is not always required, the union must provide independent verification that the expenses really were incurred. The notice must provide at least certification from the auditor that the figures have been audited and are correct. [*Cummings v. Connell*, 316 F.3d 886 (9th Cir. 2003); *Wessel v. City of Albuquerque*, 299 F.3d 1186 (10th Cir. 2002); *Harik v. California Teachers Ass'n*, 298 F.3d 863 (9th Cir. 2002)] However, according to the Third Circuit (at least for public employees), the union must get an independent auditor to verify the charges, no matter how small the union local is. But the case did allow calculation of fair-share costs including litigation costs pooled with costs of other unions, because the industry as a whole at least arguably benefited by sharing the costs. [*Otto v. Pennsylvania State Educ. Ass'n*, 326 F.3d 142 (3d Cir. 2003)]

Executive Order 13202, mandating that federal agencies awarding contracts can neither require nor prohibit the contractors from entering into or adhering to agreements with unions, has been upheld by the D.C. Circuit. The court found this to be proprietary action, not regulation, and therefore to be a constitutional exercise of presidential power that is not preempted by the NLRA. [*Building & Constr. Trades Dep't v. Allbaugh*, 295 F.3d 28 (D.C. Cir. 2002)]

President Bush's Executive Order 13201 [66 Fed. Reg. 11,219 (Feb. 22, 2001)] requires federal contractors to post a "Beck notice" informing employees of their right to avoid joining a union, and their right to object to use of funds for nonrepresentational purposes—and that they can seek a refund of funds used in this way over their objections.

The *Beck* notice rules were finalized, in much the same form as the proposal, at 69 Fed. Reg. 16375 (Mar. 29, 2004).

In 2002, the District Court for the District of Columbia held that Executive Order 13201 was invalid because it was preempted by the NLRA. However, in 2003, the District of Columbia Circuit overruled the District Court, finding that the NLRA does not preempt, and therefore upholding the validity of the order. [*UAW-Labor Employment and Training Corp. v. Chao*, 325 F.3d 360 (D.C. Cir. 2003)]

The NLRA preempts a California law that forbids employers who receive more than $10,000 a year in state funds to use those funds to either assist or deter unionizing efforts. The Ninth Circuit found that the state law is preempted because it chills employers' free speech. [*Chamber of Commerce of the U.S. v. Lockyer*, 422 F.3d 973 (9th Cir. 2005)]

The converse of union security is a state "right to work" law that says that unwilling employees cannot be compelled to join unions or pay dues. Alabama, Arizona, Arkansas, Georgia, Louisiana, Mississippi, Nebraska, Nevada, North Dakota, South Carolina, Texas, Utah, and Virginia have adopted such laws.

The "project labor agreement" (*see* NLRA § 8(f)) is an arrangement under which a construction employer can deal with a union even if its majority status has not been certified. An exception to the usual labor law rules is available because of the high turnover in the construction industry and other obstacles to union organization. General Motors entered into a project labor agreement under which it agreed to deal only with contractors who pay wages equal to the union scale. An arbitration panel awarded a union local damages of $1.6 million against a contractor that violated the agreement. Although the District Court vacated the arbitration award on the grounds that it violated public policy by extending the benefits of a CBA to employees who had chosen not to unionize, the Sixth Circuit reinstated the award. As Chapter 40 shows, it's always difficult to overturn an arbitration award; and in this case, the Sixth Circuit ruled that the effect of the arbitration award was merely to enforce a lawful project labor agreement. [*Eisenmann Corp. v. Sheet Metal Workers Int'l Ass'n Local No. 24*, 323 F.3d 375 (6th Cir. 2003)]

[B] Hiring Halls

Under a union security option, the employer decides who to hire, but the union may be able to get hirees to join or pay dues. A hiring hall works differently. It is a mechanism under which the union selects workers and sends them to the employer, based on the employer's requisition (for six plasterers and two electricians, for example). The union decides which union or nonunion workers will be referred for the job.

It was an unfair labor practice for a union to refuse to refer a worker for a construction job covered by a CBA because he was behind on his union dues. The agreement with the contractor did not have a union security clause, nor did it incorporate the master agreement's union security clause by reference, so the union could not make the argument that it was enforcing a union security provision. [*NLRB v. IBEW Local 16*, 425 F.3d 1035 (7th Cir. 2005)]

An exclusive hiring hall is a relationship under which the employer gets all its workers through union referrals. This is not considered a union security arrangement, so it is legal in the right-to-work states. A nonexclusive hiring hall makes union referral only one of the ways in which the employer can find new workers.

The NLRA provides that it is unlawful for a union to give preference to union members over equally qualified nonmembers in the operation of a nonexclusive hiring hall. The operation and structure of a hiring hall is a mandatory bargaining subject.

§ 30.07   THE COLLECTIVE BARGAINING PROCESS

[A]   Basic Issues

Under the NLRA, the purpose of certifying a union is to provide an ongoing process of collective bargaining between employer and union on important work-related issues, leading to the adoption of a union contract, or Collective Bargaining Agreement (CBA). Even after a CBA is in place, it is still necessary to bargain on "mandatory" issues, and allowable to bargain on "permissive" issues. [*See* 29 U.S.C. § 158(a)(5)] There are some subjects on which it is illegal to bargain. For instance, it is illegal to implement a closed shop, even if both employer and union are willing.

Mandatory bargaining subjects include:

- Drug testing;
- Dues checkoff (the employer's practice of deducting union dues from paychecks, then forwarding these amounts to the union);
- Work rules;
- Bans on moonlighting by employees;
- Transfers of work out of the bargaining unit;
- Contracting out work done by employees in the bargaining unit (contracting out work done by nonunionized employees is not a mandatory subject of bargaining);
- Bonuses;
- Medical insurance;
- Clauses that forbid strikes and lockouts.

Mandatory bargaining subjects are those that materially or significantly affect the terms or conditions of employment. Issues that have a remote or incidental effect on the work environment are permissible subjects of bargaining.

Where bargaining is required, the employer has a duty to meet with the union at reasonable times to confer over the terms and conditions of employment (such as wages and hours). Insisting that bargaining sessions be held during regular business hours and making negotiating committee members use paid leave to attend the sessions was a management ULP because it interfered with the right to bargain collectively. [*Ceridian Corp. v. NLRB*, 435 F.3d 352 (D.C. Cir. 2006)]

Refusal to bargain is an unfair labor practice. On the other hand, certain issues are established as managerial prerogatives that can be decided unilaterally, without bargaining:

- Complete termination of operations;
- Sale of an entire business;
- A partial closing that has business motivations, and is not the result of anti-union animus;
- Relocation of bargaining-unit work that is motivated by a basic change in the nature of the employer's operations, where the work at the new location is significantly different from the work at the old one.

The basic rule is that bargaining is required if a decision is undertaken to save labor costs, but not if the employer takes on a program of modernization or environmental compliance that costs more than the potential savings on labor costs. Even if the employer has the right to make a decision without union involvement, it has an obligation to engage in "effects bargaining": that is, it must notify the union that the decision has been made, and must bargain about the effects the change will have on union members.

Changing the methods of production is considered a managerial prerogative, although employees who believe that they are adversely affected by the change can file a grievance or seek effects bargaining about the change.

Unilateral elimination of a long-standing practice of letting employees donate blood during working hours (with paid time of up to four hours twice a year for this purpose) was an Unfair Labor Practice. The D.C. Circuit held that this was a mandatory bargaining subject because of its clear effect on wages and other terms and conditions of employment. [*Verizon N.Y. Inc. v. NLRB*, 360 F.3d 206 (D.C. Cir. 2004)]

A Gissel bargaining order (stemming from *NLRB v. Gissel Packing Co.* [395 U.S. 575 (1969)] is an order compelling management to bargain in good faith with a union. Early in 2003, the D.C. Circuit upheld an NLRB order requiring a movie theater chain to bargain with union locals before making the theaters "manager-operated" and firing the union projectionists. Although technological improvements have greatly reduced the amount (and skill level) of the work done by projectionists, eliminating a job classification does not come under the heading of "new or improved work methods" that can be introduced without bargaining. Transfer of work always requires bargaining if it results in loss of bargaining unit jobs. [*Regal Cinemas Inc. v. NLRB*, 317 F.3d 300 (D.C. Cir. 2003)]

The D.C. Circuit ruled that a hospital did not violate its CBA by imposing a mandatory on-call policy or by coaching some nurses in an effort to improve morale. The hospital was not obligated to negotiate the policy before adopting it, and there was no refusal to bargain on mandatory issues. The morale-building initiative also did not interfere with protected concerted activity. [*Enloe Med. Ctr. v. NLRB*, 433 F.3d 834 (D.C. Cir. 2005)]

The Seventh Circuit says that CBA management rights clauses allow the employer to unilaterally impose a policy controlling employees' use of drugs and alcohol both on and off the job. Although in general drug testing is a mandatory bargaining subject, the Fifth Circuit allows the employer to impose its policy unilaterally after a bargaining impasse. [*Chicago Tribune Co. v. NLRB*, 974 F.2d 933 (7th Cir. 1992); *Steelworkers v. ASARCO, Inc.*, 970 F.2d 1448 (5th Cir. 1992)]

Bargaining must be done in good faith. Neither side is obligated to make concessions or give in where it thinks surrender would be imprudent. If the bargaining process comes to an impasse—i.e., neither side is introducing new proposals or yielding on proposals already on the table—then the employer can lawfully cease negotiating and simply put its own proposals into place.

Early in 2003, the Tenth Circuit agreed with the NLRB that a company had failed to bargain in good faith, and therefore could not be permitted to unilaterally implement increased managerial powers that it claimed were necessary to keep the company competitive in a deregulated environment. The determination of whether bargaining was done in good faith depends on the totality of the circumstances, including the terms of the management proposals. To issue a valid bargaining order, the NLRB does not have to assert the illegality of any particular proposal, if it can show that the company acted in bad faith by demanding acceptance of proposals that would undermine the union's ability to represent the workers. If there has been no reasonable attempt at good-faith bargaining, an impasse cannot occur, and therefore it will not be possible for the employer to implement its proposals unilaterally. [*Public Serv. Co. of Oklahoma v. NLRB*, 318 F.3d 1173 (10th Cir. 2003)]

A non-profit corporation employing disabled individuals was required to bargain with the union. Although the corporation was formed to assist the disabled, it purchased the worksite (a factory) as a for-profit subsidiary after its former owner declared bankruptcy. The workforce remained essentially the same after the purchase, and employees' working conditions also remained the same. [*Shares Inc v. NLRB*, 433 F.3d 939 (7th Cir. 2006)]

"Regressive bargaining"—withdrawing an offer if the union is unable to meet the employer's time frame—has been upheld by the NLRB in *White Cap, Inc.* [325 N.L.R.B. 220 (1998)], unless it is done specifically for the purpose of avoiding a contract. Where the employer has a legitimate business reason for wanting to resolve the issue quickly, regressive bargaining is permissible.

TruServ Corp. v. NLRB [254 F.3d 1105 (D.C. Cir. 2001)] holds that the NLRB was wrong: The parties had reached a bargaining impasse, and the employer was entitled to act unilaterally. Hard bargaining had gone on for eight days; the employer submitted its last, best, and final offer, but the union refused to submit this offer for a member vote; and the parties were far apart on critical issues such as wages, holidays, and health care. To establish that an impasse had occurred, the D.C. Circuit used factors such as bargaining history, good faith, length of negotiations, importance of the unresolved issues, and what the parties believed about the progress of negotiations.

After the breakdown of negotiations, a nursing home declared an impasse and imposed its final offer. Management stopped collecting union initiation fees, although the CBA required fees to be remitted to the Union. This resulted in a pay increase (because there was a serious labor shortage in the health care sector). The union called a strike and filed Unfair Labor Practice charges. The Sixth Circuit ruled that failing to collect the initiation fees was a ULP, even though the union had failed to enforce this provision in the past. It was also a ULP unilaterally to increase wages during wage negotiations. It's unlikely that the union would have objected to a wage increase!—but the union certainly did not waive its right to negotiate on this issue. However, the Sixth Circuit did not find a ULP with respect to the employer's proposal for a buy-back of pension and holiday benefits. The employer's refusal to change its position was not necessarily a failure to bargain in good faith, and the court found that impasse truly had been reached on this issue, so unilateral action was legitimate. After the strike, three-quarters of the unionized employees voted to withdraw, so the employer was justified in withdrawing recognition of a union that no longer represented a majority of the work force. [*Pleasantview Nursing Home, Inc. v. NLRB*, 351 F.3d 747 (6th Cir. 2003)]

After a collective bargaining agreement expires, there is nothing left to be enforced under contract law. But labor law [NLRA § 8(a)(5)] obligates the employer to maintain the status quo, at least until an impasse is reached and the employer can start implementing its own proposals unilaterally. The employer cannot take advantage of a bargaining impasse to unilaterally impose new provisions, or any provisions more favorable to its own cause than the provisions that were on the table during negotiations.

In 2002, the NLRB held that a union's failure to act with due diligence can relieve an employer of the duty to bargain. [*AT&T Corp.*, 337 N.L.R.B. 105 (May 24, 2002)] In this case, AT&T announced closure of a facility because technical improvements reduced the number of operators required. The employer gave notice of intent to close the facility. The CBA allowed the employer to unilaterally declare future layoffs on 60 days' notice; the union then has 45 days to propose an alternative plan. According to the NLRB, the union's failure to request bargaining when the notice was given relieved the employer of the obligation of collective bargaining about the closing.

However, in the spring of 2003, the Seventh Circuit ruled (in a case involving a union's request for information about hidden surveillance cameras in the workplace) that the right to bargain about a mandatory bargaining subject can only be waived by a clear and unmistakeable expression of an intention to waive. [*National Steel Corp. v. NLRB*, 324 F.3d 928 (7th Cir. 2003)] The cameras are mandatory bargaining subjects because, like drug and alcohol tests, they involve the terms and conditions of employment. Furthermore, the employer was merely ordered to bargain and provide the union with information about the cameras; it was not forbidden to use security cameras or ordered to make public disclosure of the location of the cameras. The deployment of hidden surveillance cameras was also treated as a mandatory bargaining subject by *Brewers & Maltsters v. NLRB*, 414 F.3d 36 (D.C. Cir. 2005), because subjects plainly germane to the work environment are mandatory bargaining subjects, unless they are at the core of entrepreneurial control of the workplace.

[B]   Typical CBA Clauses

Although the actual contract that emerges from bargaining will reflect the individual needs of the business, and the comparative strengths of management and union, the following are issues that are often addressed in Collective Bargaining Agreements:

- Description of the bargaining unit;
- Management rights;
- Workday and workweek;
- Overtime;
- Classification of jobs for wage purposes;
- Compensation, bonuses, health, and other benefits;
- Paid time off (who is eligible, scheduling time off, who must be notified, which paid holidays are provided);
- Sick leave (number of days available; waiting period; doctors' notes; discipline for misusing sick leave);
- Seniority (what counts as a break in continuous service; effect of corporate transitions on seniority);
- Subcontracting;
- Plant closing and successorship;
- Severance pay;
- Hiring halls;
- Union security;
- Access to premises by non-employee union staff;
- Progressive discipline (the steps such as reprimands, conferences, and written warnings that will be provided before an employee is discharged);
- Drug testing;
- Grievance procedures (scope of disputes covered; how employees can present grievances; whether binding arbitration is required).

[C]   Bargaining on Modification, Termination

The employer has an obligation to notify the union whenever it intends to modify or terminate a CBA. The employer must also notify the Federal

Mediation and Conciliation Service of the intended action. Sixty days before the contract is scheduled to expire (or 60 days before the intended modification or termination), the employer must notify the union, inviting it to negotiate a new or amended contract. Notice to the FMCS is due 30 days after the notice to the union. Failure to give the required notice is an unfair labor practice. [29 U.S.C. § 158(d)]

The 60-day notice period is referred to as the cooling-off period. The contract remains in effect during this period, and neither strikes nor lockouts are permitted.

Employers need not volunteer information, but they have a duty to provide the union with whatever information the union requests in order to represent the employees adequately. Information relating to wage rates and job descriptions is presumed relevant. However, employers do not have to disclose confidential or privileged information, or anything not relevant to the bargaining process. The union has to show a specific need for access to the employer's nonpublic financial information. The union can see financial data if the employer claims that it cannot afford a wage increase. In case of dispute, the NLRB determines what has to be disclosed and what is privileged. For example, in late 2003 the D.C. Circuit ruled that sending a letter to employees during CBA negotiations, explaining that the employer's bargaining position was intended to restore profitability, did not trigger an obligation to disclose financial information to the union. Management did not state that its bargaining position was based on inability to pay more, so there was no need to open the books to prove it. Management's statement that sales and revenues were declining was a claim of short-term losses, not inability to pay. [*Lakeland Bus Lines Inc. v. NLRB*, 347 F.3d 955 (D.C. Cir. 2003)]

A CBA's "evergreen" clause said the CBA remained in effect after the original expiration date unless either party gave 60 days' written notice to terminate it. On May 1, 2003, the union notified management of its intent to reopen negotiations for the agreement expiring July 5, 2003. A new agreement was ratified on May 4, 2004. In March 2004, one employee was terminated and another was disciplined, which resulted in union grievances under the terms of the expired agreement. The grievances were not resolved, and the union sought arbitration. Management opposed arbitration, taking the position that arbitration was unavailable because the agreement had expired. The District Court ruled for the employer, holding that the letter from the union constituted notice of termination of the agreement. The Seventh Circuit reversed, finding that "reopening" an agreement is different from "terminating" it. Furthermore, the employer continued to carry out check-off of union dues, suggesting that the employer believed the contract continued in force. The basic rule is that obligations end when the CBA term ends, except for terms and conditions within the unilateral power of the employer (because those provisions do not require the consent of the employees, whereas other CBA provisions do). [*Office & Prof'l Employees Int'l Union Local 95 v. Wood County Telephone Co.*, 408 F.3d 314 (7th Cir. 2005)]

§ 30.08   ELECTIONS AFTER CERTIFICATION

Representation elections are not the only kind that can be ordered and supervised by the NLRB. Federal labor law allows a rerun or runoff election to be held to redress an improper election. Once a union is in place, employees can ask that it be deauthorized or decertified. The employer also has the right to challenge a union's majority status.

A rerun election is held if there were election improprieties, or if two unions competed for representation; the ballot included a "no union" choice, and "no union" got as many votes as the other alternatives. (If there is only one union on the ballot, a tie vote means that the union loses, because it failed to attract a majority of the voters.)

A runoff election is held if no choice gets a majority. Only one runoff election can be held, although there could be both a rerun and a runoff election in the same organizing campaign.

A company that had been operating under a CBA with one union since 1998 had a representation election in April 1999 with three choices: the incumbent union, another union, and no union. None of the three options gained a majority of the votes. A runoff election between the two unions was scheduled for May 1999. The company announced that, if the challenger union was elected, it would cease to follow the established pattern of annual wage increases, because those increases were provided under the CBA with the incumbent union, which would be terminated as a result of the election. The challengers filed a ULP charge against the employer. The incumbent union won the runoff election. The NLRB, upheld by the D.C. Circuit, ordered a second runoff election and ordered the employer to stop making threats to end the annual raises. The raises had become incorporated into the terms and conditions of employment, and would be required to continue even if the challenger union won the runoff election. [*More Truck Lines Inc. v. NLRB*, 324 F.3d 735 (D.C. Cir. 2003)]

A deauthorization petition is filed by a group of employees who want to remove the union's authority to enter into a union shop contract. Therefore, there are no deauthorization petitions in right-to-work states, because there aren't any union shops either. When a majority of the bargaining unit (not just a majority of the voters) vote for deauthorization, the union remains the authorized bargaining representative for the employees, but the employees no longer have to pay union dues.

The purpose of a decertification petition is to remove the union's bargaining authority. The petition can be filed by an employee, a group of employees, or someone acting on behalf of the employees. The employer does not have the right to file a decertification petition, but it does have a free-speech right to inform employees of their right to remove a union that they feel has not represented them adequately.

A decertification petition requires a showing of interest by 30% of the employees in the bargaining unit. Most petitions that are filed get the necessary vote (a majority of actual voters, not eligible voters) and therefore result in decertification of the union.

Decertification petitions cannot be filed at certain times: one year after certification of a union; a reasonable time after an employer's voluntary recognition of a union; or within 12 months of another decertification petition.

The ballots of 27 strikers had to be counted in a decertification election, because the employer did not prove that their jobs had been permanently eliminated. [*Omahaline Hydraulics Co.*, 340 NLRB 104 (Oct. 15, 2003)]

The employer has the right to petition the NLRB to determine that the union has lost its majority status. The employer must offer objective evidence of the change, such as employee turnover so heavy that few of the original pro-union workers remain; the union's failure to process employee grievances; or a strike that yielded no benefits for employees. If an employer has information that leads it to doubt the union's majority status, it is an unfair labor practice to enter into a contract with this union and then try to disavow the contract based on those doubts. The appropriate action is to refuse the contract. [*Auciello Iron Works Inc. v. NLRB*, 517 U.S. 781 (1996)]

In 2001, the NLRB issued a decision, *Levitz Furniture Co. of the Pacific*, [333 NLRB 105 (2001)] eliminating the good faith reasonable doubt standard in withdrawal-of-recognition cases. Under *Levitz* (which only applies prospectively, not retroactively), the employer will have to show that the union has actually lost majority status to justify unilateral withdrawal of recognition from an incumbent union. Nor can the employer cite employee discontent with the union arising after an unlawful refusal to bargain as evidence of reasonable uncertainty about majority status, because the refusal to bargain itself taints the employer's relations with the union, which can only be repaired through good-faith bargaining. [*Marion Hosp. Corp. v. NLRB*, 321 F.3d 1178 (D.C. Cir. 2003); *Prime Servs. Inc. v. NLRB*, 266 F.3d 1233 (D.C. Cir. 2001)] The Eighth Circuit ruled that an employer committed ULPs, and could be ordered to bargain with the incumbent union, after the employer notified the union that it could not reach a CBA unless the union could show that a majority of unit members currently supported the union. The company sent a letter to all the employees asking for an election; the letter said it was a "sad occasion" because the union was preventing the employees from getting a wage increase. Further letters said that the company would reduce the health insurance contributions employees had to make. Then a number of employees signed a petition to decertify the union. The employer informed the union that it would not bargain with the union any more. The company announced additional improvements in employee benefits. The Eighth Circuit upheld the NLRB: In this case, the employer committed ULPs by undermining the union and communicating directly with employees. [*NLRB v. Miller Waste Mills*, 315 F.3d 951 (8th Cir. 2003)]

The Eighth Circuit upheld the NLRB's determination that an employer failed to bargain in good faith, and engaged in improper "surface bargaining" as part of a plan to get the union decertified as soon as the certification year ended. The evidence of intent to seek decertification was that, after several months of productive bargaining, the employer made several regressive proposals, and statements by supervisors showed the intent to get the union removed. [*NLRB v. Hardesty Co.*, 308 F.3d 859 (8th Cir. 2002)]

The general rule, known as the CBA bar, is that no union election can be held while a collective bargaining agreement is in force. However, if there has been a substantial increase in personnel since the contract was signed, a new election may be proper if the union no longer represents a majority of the current workforce.

There used to be another "bar" in effect, the "successor bar" rule of *St. Elizabeth's Manor*, [329 NLRB 341 (1999)] under which an incumbent union would be given a reasonable amount of time after a corporate takeover to bargain with the successor employer without challenges to its majority status. However, in 2002, the NLRB overruled that decision [*MV Transportation*, 337 N.L.R.B. 129 (July 19, 2002)] and now takes the position that the incumbent union gets a rebuttable presumption of continuing majority status, but that will not bar an otherwise valid challenge to majority status. It violates federal labor law for an employer to withdraw recognition of a union prematurely, without engaging in bargaining for a reasonable period of time. (However, pursuing reasonable bargaining will remove the taint of an earlier refusal to bargain.) In this case, there were only five bargaining sessions, and apparently the parties were close to reaching agreement when recognition was withdrawn, so the D.C. Circuit upheld the NLRB's ruling against the employer. [*Lee Lumber & Building Materials Corp. v. NLRB*, 310 F.3d 209 (D.C. Cir. 2002)]

§ 30.09 STRIKES

[A] Right to Strike

The NLRA gives employees the right to engage in "protected concerted activities"—joining together to organize, protest, and otherwise assert their interests in a lawful manner. This includes going on strike if a new contract cannot be negotiated, or based on a union's claim that working conditions are bad enough to justify a strike.

A striking union's gamble is that the employer will need to maintain continuous operations and therefore will grant significant concessions before the employees lose too much income by stopping work. But at other times employers actually benefit from strikes, if they can save payroll for a while, shut down an unproductive location, relocate to a lower-cost area (in another state or even another country) or bringing in "striker replacements."

Violence, sabotage, and threats are not protected activity. If a threatened strike would imperil the national health or safety, the President of the United States can order the U.S. Attorney General to petition the appropriate federal court for an 80-day cooling-off period, during which the strike is enjoined.

Secondary strikes and secondary boycotts—actions taken against one employer to put pressure on another employer that does business with the first employer—are banned by NLRA § 8(b)(4). A company that is the victim of a secondary strike or boycott can sue for damages under LMRA § 303.

According to the Seventh Circuit, employees who went out on strike in sympathy when a popular supervisor was fired were overreacting to the firing, so the strike was not protected concerted activity. [*Bob Evans Farms Inc. v. NLRB*, 163 F.3d 1012 (7th Cir. 1998)]

In 2002, the Eighth Circuit upheld a jury verdict of $81,000 in damages awarded to an employer and against a union that engaged in picketing that was, in effect, a work stoppage and an improper substitute for grievance arbitration. The employer and union belonged to the National Master Automobile Transports Agreement, which imposes a requirement of mandatory arbitration before any work stoppage or strike, and 72 hours' written notice before a strike. The union called a strike without giving the notice, ended the strike without negotiating about the problems that led to the strike, and picketed for three days, making the backup in work that occurred during the strike even worse. [*Allied Sys. Ltd. v. Teamsters Local 604*, 304 F.3d 785 (8th Cir. 2002)]

[B] Types of Strike

Employees can lawfully engage in a work stoppage in three situations:

- An economic dispute with the employer;
- A claim that the employer has committed unfair labor practices;
- A claim that workplace conditions are so unreasonably dangerous that they should not be required to continue work.

An "unfair labor practices" strike is caused in whole or part by unfair labor practices. There must be a causal connection between the strike and the employer practices. If the practices are simply cost-related (such as shift changes), then the strike should be characterized as an economic strike. But a strike that begins as an economic strike can be converted to an unfair labor practices strike if the employer acts unfairly or refuses to accept legitimate offers for return to work.

The main difference between an economic strike and an unfair labor practices strike is the extent of employees' reinstatement rights after the strike ends and they want to go back to work. Some issues are areas of managerial prerogative, so employees cannot lawfully strike to challenge management's decisions in these areas.

29 U.S.C. § 143 makes it a protected concerted activity for employees to refuse to work if there is measurable, objective evidence of undue hazards (not just a subjective feeling that something is wrong). The employees must also articulate goals that the employer can respond to: replace a defective machine or install guard rails, for instance, not just "make the workplace safer." [*See* Chapter 31 for information about occupational safety and health]

According to a mid-2002 Sixth Circuit decision, the right to engage in a good-faith work stoppage due to abnormally dangerous conditions applies whether or not the employees have a no-strike clause in their CBA, and the employer does not have the right to hire permanent replacements in such a situation. However, in this particular case, the Sixth Circuit found that the workers' belief that conditions were abnormally dangerous was not objectively supported. It's true that NIOSH found that the workers had high uranium levels, but the levels were within limits permitted by the state and by the Nuclear Regulatory Commission. [*TNS Inc. v. NLRB*, 296 F.3d 384 (6th Cir. 2002)]

The Sixth Circuit refused to enforce an NLRB order that five physical therapists were unlawfully discharged for engaging in protected activities. In response to an announcement of wage reductions, the therapists drafted a letter stating their wage and working condition demands. They met with management and, without using terms such as "strike" or "work stoppage," they said they would stay on the premises and do paperwork but would not treat their patients. One of the five went home early, and the other four were sent home. They considered picketing but decided against it. The next day, they faxed letters to top management asking for a grievance meeting. They were fired that day and brought ULP charges. In the Sixth Circuit view, the refusal to see patients was a partial strike that was not protected concerted activity because the employees sought to retain the benefits of working without performing their assigned tasks. In this view, the only protected activity for striking workers is to stop working completely. [*Vencare Ancillary Servs., Inc. v. NLRB*, 352 F.3d 318 (6th Cir. 2003)]

If the underlying strike is lawful, then a sympathy strike (workers outside the striking bargaining unit refuse to cross the picket line) is probably protected concerted activity as defined by the NLRA. A 2003 decision of the Ninth Circuit says that a no-strike provision in a CBA does not bar a sympathy strike for another bargaining unit within the same local union, because the CBA clause did not clearly and unmistakeably waive the right to call a strike in support of fellow union members. [*Standard Concrete Prods. Inc. v. General Truck Drivers Office, Food & Warehouse Union*, 353 F.3d 668 (9th Cir. 2003)]

In contrast to those protected activities, a sitdown strike (an illegal takeover of the employer's premises) is unlawful. A wildcat strike, called by the rank and file without authorization from the union, is not protected activity if the workers want to usurp the union's role as sole bargaining representative for the workers.

A collective bargaining agreement can lawfully be drafted to include a no-strike clause. It is not protected concerted activity to call an economic strike in violation of a no-strike clause. Therefore, the employer can legitimately fire the strikers and deny them reinstatement after the strike ends.

Because of the special risks involved, NLRA § 8(g) requires unions at health care facilities to give at least 10 days' notice before a strike, picket, or concerted refusal to work. The employer must be notified of the date and time the action will commence. The NLRB ruled that starting the strike four hours later than the time stated in the notice violates the notice requirement. Unions are not permitted to make unilateral extensions of strike notices. Therefore, it was not an unfair labor practice to fire nurses involved in the strike. [*Alexandria Clinic PA*, 339 NLRB No. 162 (Aug. 21, 2003)]

[C] Lockouts and Other Employer Activity

The lockout is the employer's counterpart to the union's strike. In a strike, the employees refuse to come to work. In a lockout, the employer refuses to let them in. An employer that undertakes a lockout for business reasons can hire replacement workers. It can enter into a temporary subcontract for the duration of the lockout. However, the employer is not allowed to use the lockout to permanently contract out work formerly performed by employees. Lockouts are lawful if and only if they have a business motivation, not if they are used to prevent the workers from organizing a union, or to avoid bargaining with an incumbent union. However, a lockout is a justified response to a strike that violates a CBA no-strike clause.

It is an unfair labor practice for an employer to institute a lockout that is inherently destructive of the rights of employees. It is also an unfair labor practice to institute a lockout without having legitimate economic business justification (not just the employer's convenience). The mere possibility of a strike if contract negotiations break down is not a sufficient justification for a lockout during collective bargaining; and it might be treated as an unlawful refusal to bargain. Lockouts are analyzed even more stringently outside the strike context, because the union's power is weaker and there is less need for the employer to counterbalance it.

Employers are allowed to close a business, or shut it down temporarily, with economic motivations. But doing it to harm the union is an unfair labor practice. A "runaway shop" (transferring work between existing locations or opening a new location) is an unfair labor practice if it is based on antiunion motivation rather than a desire to enhance profitability.

During a strike, the employer is not permitted to alter the terms and conditions of employment that affect strikers. However, once a CBA expires, the employer is allowed to change those terms as they affect striker replacements.

After impasse, a company locked out all of its production and maintenance workers other than those who were still in their 90-day probation period. The NLRB deemed this to be a legitimate means of applying bargaining pressure to the employees with the greatest stake in the negotiations. In general, it is not an Unfair Labor Practice to lock out permanent employees and work with temporaries after an impasse. The NLRB held that it was permissible to distinguish between union members and probationary employees, because the distinction between the two groups was a rational one. [*Bunting Bearings Corp.*, 343 NLRB 64 (Oct. 29, 2004)]

The NLRB ruled that it was illegal for a group of hospitals to refuse to give temporary employment to nurses who were on strike against two other hospitals in the area. The agency found that there was no legitimate justification for refusal to hire the nurses, because the defendant hospitals were not involved in the strike. [*Allina Health Systems*, 343 NLRB 67 (Oct. 29, 2004)]

An employer committed a ULP by imposing a partial lockout (locking out those employees who were on strike at the time the union unconditionally offered to return to work, but not those who agreed to go back to work before the strike ended). The employer failed to produce substantial evidence of the operational necessity of the partial lockout or that the lockout was needed to exert economic pressure on the holdouts to bring the strike to an end. (During the strike, the company was able to stay open with managers and temporary workers.) Where an employer's refusal to reinstate strikers has more than a temporary effect on the collective bargaining process and is inherently destructive of important employee rights, the union does not have to prove anti-union motivation. Inherently destructive activities are lawful only if there is a business justification that outweighs the damage to employee rights. However, activities for which there is a business justification are lawful if the harm to collective bargaining is comparatively slight. [*IBEW Local 15 v. NLRB*, 429 F.3d 651 (7th Cir. 2005)]

[D]   Striker Replacements

During a strike, employers are entitled to keep their operations open by hiring replacements. Employers can always hire replacements for jobs that are described as temporary stopgaps until the strike ends. The question is whether the employer can hire permanent replacements, outsource functions formerly performed by employees, or keep the replacements and deny reinstatement to the strikers post-strike.

It is not an unfair labor practice to discharge strikers who have lost their employee status, and therefore their protection under the NLRA. The NLRA protects only lawful strikes that are conducted in a lawful manner, are called for a protected purpose, and are authorized by the bargaining unit representative (if there is one).

A strike is lawful if it occurs after the expiration of a CBA, if it is either an economic or an unfair labor practices strike, or if it demands concessions from the employer. Wildcat strikes, sitdown strikes, and strikes contrary to a CBA no-strike clause are not protected. Excessive violence removes employee status, although a minor instance of violence would not prevent the perpetrator from being considered an employee.

In an economic strike, the employer can permanently replace the strikers and keep the replacement workers after the end of the strike. However, strikers are entitled to reinstatement after the strike if they have not been replaced. Delay in reinstating them counts as an unfair labor practice. Even after being replaced, an economic striker is still considered an employee. If the former economic striker makes an unconditional application for reinstatement, the employer must reinstate him if the replacement worker quits or is terminated. If no jobs are available at the

§ 30.09[E]   HUMAN RESOURCES AND THE LAW

time of the application, the employer must reinstate the ex-striker when a job becomes available.

However, the former striker does not have to be reinstated if:

- He or she gets regular and substantial employment somewhere else;
- The employer has a legitimate business reason (violence or sabotage during the strike, for instance) for denying reinstatement;
- The job itself has been eliminated (e.g., due to new technology).

The NLRB's position, which has been upheld by the Seventh Circuit, is that the main issue is whether the replacement workers have a reasonable expectation of recall after being laid off. Strikers are entitled to reinstatement if the replacements did not have a reasonable expectation of recall—unless the employer can prove that the job is vacant or there is good cause not to rehire the striker. A "Laidlaw vacancy," otherwise known as a "genuine job vacancy," occurs if the replacement worker cannot reasonably expect recall after layoff.

Unless there is a legitimate and substantial business reason to depart from the rule, a reinstated economic striker must be treated equally with nonstrikers and permanent replacements, with the same benefits, including paid vacations and accrual of seniority. Normally, reinstatement should return the worker to status quo, but he or she can be demoted for a legitimate business reason such as a risk of sabotage.

A health care union sent some notices, but not notices that were adequate under NLRA § 8(g), to disclose the intention to strike or picket a health care institution. Therefore, the employer was correct that the strike was illegal, and the employer had no obligation to reinstate 450 former strikers. The D.C. Circuit overturned the NLRB finding that the nursing home chain violated the NLRA by failing to reinstate 450 employees after a three-day strike. [*Beverly Health & Rehab. Servs. v. NLRB*, 317 F.3d 316 (D.C. Cir. 2003)] The D.C. Circuit disagreed with the NLRB as to whether it was an Unfair Labor Practice to videotape the picketers. It would be illegal to videotape employees engaged in lawful picketing, but here the employer presented evidence that it believed that trespass, not lawful picketing, occurred.

[E] Subcontracting

When a strike is imminent, employers who have a pressing business reason, and who are not acting out of antiunion animus, can legitimately subcontract out work that was performed by the bargaining unit, even though employees are displaced. NLRA § 8(a)(3), which penalizes employer actions that are intended to discourage union membership, can be invoked even if there is no direct proof of the employer's motivation—if the employer's action is inherently destructive of important rights of the employees. Subcontracting is a mandatory bargaining subject, so the employer can act unilaterally if a bargaining impasse has been reached.

30-46

Contracting out in-house security functions (and therefore firing all the newly unionized employees) violates the NLRA. [*Reno Hilton Resorts v. NLRB*, 196 F.3d 1275 (D.C. Cir. 1999)] The D.C. Circuit reached this conclusion because the employer did not provide enough evidence of the connection between outsourcing and declining revenues (the reason given for the move).

The NLRB held that the employer violated NLRA §§ 5 and 8(a)(1) by denying the Union information about its use of outside contractors for bargaining work. The Fourth Circuit affirmed the agency determination and ordered disclosure of certain information, but remanded on the issue of producing contractor cost data. The Fourth Circuit says that whether a union is entitled to information depends on the relevance of the material and whether it is useful to the union in carrying out its statutory role. If relevance is obvious on the face of the request, the union does not have to inform the company of why the information is relevant. But if the requested information relates to the employer's financial condition (e.g., profit data), the union must demonstrate its specific need for the material. A company that claims it cannot afford to meet union demands opens up the question of financial condition. The Fourth Circuit pointed out that an employer cannot complain about the burdensomeness of repeated requests—if the union had to keep requesting information that the company failed to provide. [*West Penn Power Co. v. NLRB*, 394 F.3d 233 (4th Cir. 2005)]

§ 30.10 THE WARN ACT

The Worker Adjustment Retraining and Notice Act ("WARN Act") [29 U.S.C. § 2101] requires employers of 100 or more full-time employees (or a combination of full- and part-timers adding up to at least 100 people and 4000 work hours a week) to provide notice of a plant closing or mass layoff. At least 60 days' notice must be given to employees, unions, and the federal government. The Act defines a plant closing as employment loss (termination, prolonged layoff, serious cutback in work hours) affecting 50 or more workers during a 30-day period.

A mass layoff has a lesser effect on the individual workers (e.g., potential for recall) and affects 500 people or one-third of the workforce. Anyone rehired within six months, or anyone who elected early retirement, should not be counted in determining if a mass layoff has occurred.

WARN Act notice must be given to laid-off employees who have a legitimate expectation of recall. *Kildea v. Electro-Wire Products Inc.* [144 F.3d 400 (6th Cir. 1998)] says that these people are "affected employees" because of the likelihood that plant closing will lead to job loss. Although the WARN Act refers to a "group" of laid-off employees, employers cannot avoid the application of the act by performing layoffs one at a time. All economically motivated layoffs within a 90-day period are aggregated toward the 50-employee figure. [*Hallowell v. Orleans Regional Hospital*, 217 F.3d 379 (5th Cir. 2000)]

If the employer fails to give the required notice, each affected employee is entitled to up to 60 days' back pay (work days, not calendar days) and benefits.

A federal civil penalty of up to $500 can also be imposed for every day that the failure to give notice continued. A union can sue for damages on behalf of its members.

The Northern District of California allowed a suit by employees of an acquired law firm to proceed, because it was possible that the acquisition of the firm by another law firm was a "sale" of the first firm's business, triggering WARN Act obligations. The defendant said that it avoided structuring the transaction as a merger, but the Northern District noted that, although the second firm was not the alter ego of the first firm as defined by California law, there were still enough signs of continuity to justify continuation of the suit. [*McCaffrey v. Brobeck, Phleger & Harrison*, 2004 WL 3452 31 (N.D. Cal. Feb. 17, 2004)]

The Eighth Circuit ruled that the seller of a business was protected by the WARN Act's sale-of-business exclusion. The buyer promised to hire a substantial number of the seller's employees (and in fact did so), so the seller believed that fewer than 50 employees would lose their jobs. A seller is responsible for providing WARN Act notice up to and including the sale date, but at that point, the purchaser becomes responsible for giving notice of a plant closing. In the Eighth Circuit view, only the party actually causing employment loss must give notice. When a business is sold as a going concern, the sale-of-business exception creates a presumption that the buyer is the employer if the seller continues to employ its employees on the day of the sale. [*Wilson v. Airtherm Products Inc.*, 436 F.3d 906 (8th Cir. 2006). *See also Smullin v. Mity Enters. Inc.*, 420 F.3d 838 (8th Cir. 2005): where a sale closed on Friday, 44 of the 68 employees were employed by the buyer, and operations resumed on Monday, there was no plant closing and hence notice was not required]

A company that provided payroll management services for other companies was not a WARN Act "employer" and could not be held liable for failure to provide notice, because it did not order the closing. Even though the employees in question received Workers' Compensation and health benefits under the management service company's plans, the workers did not perform any services for the management service company, which was not a joint employer with the company they actually worked for. [*Administaff Cos., Inc. v. New York Joint Board, Shirt & Leisurewear Div.*, 337 F.3d 454 (5th Cir. 2003)]

The 2003 Northern District of Oklahoma decision in *Millsap v. McDonnell Douglas Corp.* was unusual because it was one of only three cases holding that a plant closing violated ERISA § 510 (the provision that makes it unlawful to interfere with the attainment of benefits under an ERISA plan). The parties settled the case after trial, and the settlement included $36 million in damages for lost pension and health benefits (as well as attorneys' fees and costs of close to $10 million). However, in 2004, the Tenth Circuit reversed, holding that the District Court was wrong to make a back pay award, because back pay (or other damages stemming from back pay) is not the kind of "equitable relief" that ERISA § 502(a)(3) provides for plan participants. [162 F. Supp. 2d 12 (N.D. Ok. 2003), rev'd 368 F.3d 1246 (10th Cir. 2004)]

A West Virginia state court took the position that back pay and damages awarded under the WARN Act are not covered by a state law mandating timely payment of "wages"—even though the statute describes the damages as back pay. [*Conrad v. Charles Town Races Inc.*, 206 W. Va. 45, 521 S.E.2d 537 (W.Va. 1998)]

WARN Act responsibilities continue after a bankruptcy filing. However, if a company ceases to operate as a going concern and winds up its affairs, it is no longer an "employer" and therefore cannot be held liable if it fails to give WARN Act notice. [*Official Committee of Unsecured Creditors v. United Healthcare Sys. Inc.*, 200 F.3d 170 (3d Cir. 1999)]

The Ninth Circuit ruled that two corporations under common control (one with 88 employees, the other with 18 employees, with at least 1,000 hours of employment during the relevant period) were a single employer for WARN Act purposes. The companies claimed exemption for having fewer than 100 employees or, in the alternative, defenses of good faith, financial difficulties, and unforeseen business difficulties. The Sixth Circuit disagreed, and ordered $60,000 in damages (60 days' wages) and attorneys' fees of $123,000. Although the companies got around the legal requirements for common ownership, they shared directors and officers; one company de facto controlled the other; and their operations were mutually dependent. The employer failed to prove good faith (which is an affirmative defense—i.e., it's up to the party asserting it to prove it). The court did not accept the argument that the bank's refusal to continue a line of credit was a sudden and unforeseeable act leading to the plant shutdown; there were many reasons for the closure, most of them developing over a period of time. The "faltering company" WARN Act exemption is narrowly construed and applies only to plant closings, not mass layoffs. It can be used only where the employer had a reasonable belief that giving WARN Act notice would have impaired raising the capital needed to continue the business. [*Childress v. Darby Lumber Inc.*, 357 F.3d 1000 (9th Cir. 2004)]

The Sixth Circuit accepted the company's argument that, when it posted a notice of immediate and permanent closing of a facility, it did not violate the WARN Act, because unforeseen business circumstances precluded giving 60 days' advance notice. The employer discovered that its prime customer was going to shift to another supplier, and then was told that the customer was not going to pay for a large order—circumstances that the Sixth Circuit agreed qualified for the notice exception for sudden, dramatic circumstances outside the employer's control. The plaintiffs argued that there were many other signs that the business was in trouble, but the court ruled that the question is whether, in the business' commercially reasonable business judgment, the need to shut down could have been predicted 60 days in advance—and in this case it was not. [*Watson v. Michigan Indus. Holdings Inc.*, 311 F.3d 760 (6th Cir. 2002)]

The Seventh Circuit reversed the District Court and permitted the plaintiffs to pursue a WARN Act case in which the issue was whether the plant shutdown was reasonably foreseeable and therefore notice could have been given. The employer, a meat packing plant, was subject to inspection by the U.S. Department of

Agriculture. The on-site inspectors issued citations called NRs (Noncompliance Records) when unsanitary conditions were detected. In the year before the plant shutdown, over 30 NRs were issued, and on several occasions production was stopped temporarily to clean up. The USDA eventually forbade the company to ship any products, and ordered unsanitary products to be destroyed. The company decided to terminate operations, and the next day employees were notified. The employer's argument was that the USDA's actions constituted business circumstances that were not reasonably foreseeable 60 days in advance. The Seventh Circuit found that there were triable issues as to whether the USDA action could have been predicted, and even if it could not, whether WARN Act notice should have been issued, although on a shorter-than-normal schedule. [*Pena v. American Meat Packing Corp.*, 362 F.3d 418 (7th Cir. 2004)]

§ 30.11 LABOR LAW ISSUES OF SHARED LIABILITY

[A] Possible Scenarios

There are many situations in which more than one company may be deemed to be a particular person's "employer." Sometimes, both companies will be liable, or the actions of one will be attributed to the other, with respect to unfair labor practices, defining the appropriate bargaining unit, or enforcing a collective bargaining agreement.

Vested benefits under a collective bargaining agreement are transferable when the employer transfers employees to another one of its locations, which is covered by another CBA with another union. [*Anderson v. AT&T Corp.*, 147 F.3d 467 (6th Cir. 1998)]

When one company merges with or takes over another, it is common for many or all of the first company's employees to be retained. Whether the acquiror is now the employer, and whether it is bound by the former employer's CBA and other promises to its workers is a factual question, depending on whether or not real operational changes were made.

In connection with CBAs, a "successor company" is one that continues the same business and hires at least half of the old employees. A successor employer is not bound by the predecessor's contracts, but does have an obligation to recognize and consult with the union. The Supreme Court has ruled that a new company becomes a successor if it is clear that all the former employees will be retained. [*NLRB v. Burns Int'l Security Servs. Inc.*, 406 U.S. 272 (1972)] *Canteen Corp. v. NLRB* [103 F.3d 1355 (7th Cir. 1997)] holds that a company can also be treated as a successor employer if it fails to give employees enough information about the new wages and working conditions to make a meaningful choice about accepting a job offer from the new employer.

After a merger or the purchase of a business, a successor has a duty to bargain collectively and can be liable for unfair labor practices committed by the predecessor if there is "continuity of identity" with the ex-employer, such as using the same facility to produce identical products and services, using the same or substantially the same labor force, without changes in job description, working conditions, supervision, equipment, or production methods.

An alternate test is whether there is a new corporate entity to replace the predecessor, whether there is a hiatus in the enterprise's operations, and whether the employment relationship with the prior workforce was terminated. If it is perfectly clear under the *Burns International* standard that the new owner will hire the entire existing workforce, then the incoming employer has a duty to consult with the union about wage scales. It cannot unilaterally impose cuts. If there is no such consultation, it is presumed that the negotiations would have continued the prior wage scale.

However, in *Monterey Newspapers Inc.* [334 NLRB 128 (Aug. 9, 2001)], a publishing company that acquired a newspaper was allowed to set up a separate "pay band" system for persons hired after the acquisition. The pay band system was adopted unilaterally, without bargaining with the newspaper union. The acquiror recognized the union four days after an acquisition in which most of the existing workforce was rehired. The NLRB interpreted the acquiror's rights under *Burns International* to include setting new initial terms and conditions of employment. But once the new hires joined the work force, any later changes in their compensation would become a mandatory bargaining subject.

The Sixth Circuit treated the purchaser of a hotel and the management company running the hotel as joint employers, and also as successor employers to a company that had recognized and bargained with the union. The predecessor's voluntary recognition of the union created a presumption of majority status after the transition. Therefore, it was a violation of labor law to refuse to recognize and bargain with the housekeeping workers' union. [*3750 Orange Place LP v. NLRB*, 333 F.3d 646 (6th Cir. 2003)]

Another possibility is that two or more enterprises might be deemed to be "alter egos" (substitutes) for one another, even if they are not formally under common control. Alter egos may be held liable for each other's unfair labor practices. The test is whether transferring business from one alter ego operation to another benefits the transferor by eliminating labor relations obligations. The alter ego theory became part of labor law to prevent "double-breasting": the practice of pairing commonly owned firms, one with a union and one nonunionized. If the double-breasted firms are actually alter egos, a federal district court can require the nonunion firm to abide by the union firm's labor agreements, even if there has been no NLRB determination of a single bargaining unit.

Two or more entities organized as legally separate entities might be treated as a "single employer" if there is an integrated enterprise. The factors that determine integration include common ownership, common management, integrated business operations, and centralized control of labor relations.

These tests are similar to the tests to see if companies are alter egos. The difference is that the two alter ego companies are not considered a single enterprise, so all their employees are not necessarily in the same bargaining unit.

A parent company and its subsidiary would probably be treated as a single employer if they were fundamentally in the same industry or business enterprise. This would be manifested by sharing supervisory, technical, and professional personnel; sharing workforce and equipment; having common officers and directors; and operating under the same labor relations policies.

The NLRB might group separate entities together as "joint employers" if they "codetermine" (i.e., make decisions jointly) about essential terms and conditions of employment. Under this theory, the crucial factor is not whether the companies have overlapping ownership, but whether they make joint decisions about hiring and firing, working conditions, compensation, and supervision of employees.

These principles came into play in *Aldworth Co.* [338 N.L.R.B. 22 (Sept. 30, 2002)] Dunkin' Donuts Mid-Atlantic Distribution Center and its labor supplier were deemed to be joint employers, both liable for the many ULPs committed during an organizing campaign, because Dunkin' Donuts was involved in most employment decisions and in day-to-day direction of leased drivers' helpers and warehouse workers. However, only the labor supplier could be made subject to a Gissel bargaining order. The union demanded recognition only from the labor supplier, and thereby waived bargaining rights as against Dunkin' Donuts. In 2004, the D.C. Circuit ruled that Dunkin Donuts was a joint employer of the leased employees, and furthermore the bargaining order was justified because multiple ULPs had been committed. [*Dunkin Donuts Mid-Atlantic Distrib. Ctr. v. NLRB*, 363 F.3d 437 (D.C. Cir., 2004)]

[B] Agents of the Employer

An employer company will be liable for the actions of any "agent" of the company acting in the employer's interest. For example, a labor consultant is considered the employer's agent, but a Chapter 7 bankruptcy trustee is not. The determination uses factors similar to those used in deciding if someone is a common-law employee. The employer's degree of control is crucial: the right to hire and fire the agent; furnishing tools and materials; prescribing what the agent will do and how to do it.

Someone can become an agent of the company either by actual agency (explicitly granted) or apparent agency (where a principal says that the agent can speak for it, or knowingly lets the agent exercise authority). An employer is responsible for the actions performed by a supervisor in the course of actual or apparent authority. Even if a supervisor acts without authority, the employer can become liable by ratifying the supervisor's action (i.e., offering support for it after the fact). In general, however, the employer will not be responsible for actions for someone who is not an employee, or perhaps not a supervisory employee, unless the employer initiates, promotes, or ratifies the conduct. If the agent's improper conduct was an isolated, unpremeditated act, or if the employer repudiates the conduct, it is possible that the employer will be relieved of liability.

In general, the NLRB will blame the employer for an unfair labor practice only if it was committed directly by the employer, or by the employer's agent. But in a representation proceeding, a finding of agency is not required to set aside an election if the election was unfair enough to prevent employees from exercising a rational, unforced choice.

Tip: Unions are also liable for actions taken by their agents, including rank-and-file union members advancing union goals. Unless the union takes preventive or corrective action to stem inappropriate picket-line behavior, the union is likely to be held liable for unfair labor practices. But when several unions engage in joint picketing during an organization drive, *Washington v. HCA Health Services of Texas Inc.* [152 F.3d 464 (5th Cir. 1998)] says that one union is not responsible for the actions of the others just because they share the objective of organizing the workplace.

---

§30.12 EMPLOYER DOMINATION

In Europe, "codetermination," where union representatives collaborate closely with management, and where joint management-labor committees play an important decision-making role, is well accepted. However, under U.S. law, employer domination of a labor organization is an unfair labor practice. [*See* NLRA §8(a)(2)] Although this provision was originally enacted to bar "sweetheart unions" (formed or taken over by the employer), it has been applied more broadly.

A Sixth Circuit case concerned a plant council that was created just after the employer won a certification election. [*NLRB v. Webcor Packaging Inc.*, 118 F.3d 1115 (6th Cir. 1997)] The plant council met during working hours to discuss work rules, wages, and benefits. The council, made up of five employees and three management representatives, reviewed ideas from the Suggestion Box and made proposals to management, some of which were accepted.

The DOL challenged the council as an employer-dominated labor organization. The NLRB and the Sixth Circuit agreed, because it fit into the statutory definition. It represented employees, dealt with the employer, and was concerned with conditions of employment. Employer domination was present because management created the committee and could disband it; it met during working hours; and management representatives were always present.

In 1992, the NLRB ruled that an "action committee" created by the employer in response to employee dissatisfaction was improperly employer-dominated. [*Electromation, Inc.*, 309 NLRB 163 (1992)] The NLRB considered it a labor organization, not a way to improve communications, because its purpose was to solve employee grievances and because the employee members acted in a representative capacity. The agency's decision was upheld by the Seventh Circuit in 1994. [35 F.3d 1148 (7th Cir. 1994)]

In 1993, the NLRB found that six joint labor-management safety committees, and a joint committee on fitness, were also labor organizations, because their purpose was to deal with the employer, and because they dealt with important issues such as safety, incentive awards, and exercise facilities for employees. [E.I. DuPont de Nemours, 311 NLRB 88 (1993)]

It was a violation of the NLRA for an employer to unilaterally implement a workplace ethics program (WEP) (after consulting with the employees, but not bargaining with the union). Under the WEP, employees could invoke either the WEP process or the grievance procedure to review management decisions about discharge, discipline, or demotion, although the WEP yielded when arbitration was invoked. Grievance procedures are a mandatory bargaining subject, and the CBA already contained a grievance procedure. The Eleventh Circuit held that the employer would have been required to bargain to eliminate the existing grievance procedure, so they could not use the workplace ethics program to perform an end-run around the CBA's grievance procedure. [*Georgia Power Co. v. NLRB*, 427 F.3d 1354 (11th Cir. 2005)]

To avoid NLRB characterization of a work team or quality circle as an unduly dominated "labor organization," the employer should consider these steps:

- Look for a neutral meeting place away from the workplace, such as a local library, Rotary club, or City Hall;
- Rotate membership of the team, to involve as many people as possible and get new viewpoints;
- Focus the team on productivity and workplace issues, not compensation;
- Don't use the team to avoid contract negotiations;
- Employee representatives, not management, should draft the bylaws under which the team operates. [*Polaroid Corp. & Scivally*, 329 NLRB 47 (1999); *EFCO Corp.*, 327 NLRB (1998); *NLRB v. Webcor Packaging Inc.*, 118 F.3d 1115 (6th Cir. 1997); *Electromation, Inc.*, 309 NLRB 163 (1992)]

§ 30.13   NLRB JURISDICTION

The National Labor Relations Board has the power to get involved in a situation if:

- It is a labor dispute—i.e., there is any controversy about conditions of employment or representation of workers. Strikes, walkouts, picketing, and employer refusals to bargain are labor disputes;
- It affects interstate commerce. The threshold is so low that virtually any business will be deemed to affect interstate commerce;
- Employers and employees, rather than independent contractors and their clients, are involved;
- The dispute involves working conditions.

When it has issued a complaint or filed an unfair labor practices charge, the NLRB can ask a federal District Court to issue a temporary injunction. In fact, the agency has an obligation to seek an injunction if it charges unlawful secondary activity (such as striking one employer to put pressure on another), some forms of improper activity, or certain boycotts. However, permanent injunctions are very rare, because of the Norris-LaGuardia Anti-Injunction Act.

Theoretically, the NLRB has jurisdiction over all unfair labor practice claims that require interpretation of a CBA that is still in effect. In practice, the NLRB often declines to exercise its jurisdiction, allowing the parties to use the contract's grievance arbitration machinery, to proceed with ongoing arbitration, or to enforce an arbitration award. However, it is up to the NLRB to intervene or stay out. The employer and union cannot deprive the NLRB of jurisdiction by agreeing to arbitrate.

Wal-Mart published employee benefits booklets denying profit-sharing participation, health coverage, and 401(k) plan participation to unionized employees. (That language has since been removed from the booklets on orders from the NLRB.) Employees brought suit against Wal-Mart, raising ERISA claims that the "union exclusion" clause was used to undermine employees' right to unionize. The District Court dismissed the case, holding that it did not have jurisdiction over claims involving unionization—the NLRB had sole jurisdiction. The Eighth Circuit reinstated the suit early in 2006, finding that the ERISA claims were not inextricably entwined with the NLRA claims and could be decided separately. [*Lupiani v. Wal-Mart Stores Inc.*, 435 F.3d 842 (8th Cir. 2006)]

The NLRB did not abuse its discretion in extending the certification year by six months, and ordering the employer to reinstate its bargaining proposals, in a case where the employer withdrew all its proposals just before the certification year ended. [*NLRB v. Beverly Health & Rehab Servs.*, 187 F.3d 769 (8th Cir. 1999)]

In 1997, the Court of Appeals for the District of Columbia Circuit overturned a long-held belief that the NLRB has the power to order an employer to reimburse the union for negotiating and litigation effects if the employer has been found to have committed unfair labor practices during collective bargaining. But the D.C. Circuit decided that the National Labor Relations Act is not specific enough on this point to justify a departure from the normal American rule that litigants have to pay their own litigation costs. [*Unbelievable Inc. v. NLRB*, 118 F.3d 795 (D.C. Cir. 1997)]

The Seventh Circuit upheld the NLRB's imposition of a corporate-wide remedial order against a corporation that operates about 900 separate nursing homes. Remedies at the corporate level were proper because violations were found in a number of facilities, not just one, and the company is centrally administered. [*Beverly California Corp. v. NLRB*, 227 F.3d 817 (7th Cir. 2000)]

A group of employees traditionally worked 7½-hour days with an unpaid half-hour lunch break. Their employer set up a new production schedule, with overlapping shifts. A few months later, after voluntary furloughs, the employer reinstated the 7½-hour day, then went back to 8-hour shifts when business improved. About six months later, the department was unionized. Four months after the union was recognized, the employer once again went back to 7½-hour shifts. Not only was there no bargaining, the union wasn't even notified of the latest change. The NLRB ruled that unilateral reduction of working hours of bargaining unit members violated NLRA §§ 8(a)(1) and (a)(5). The NLRB applied for judicial enforcement of its order, and the employer challenged the move on the grounds that the NLRB's chosen remedy (return to the 8-hour shift; back pay for workers whose hours were cut) was invalid. The First Circuit ruled that it lacked jurisdiction over the defendant's challenge. Except in extraordinary circumstances, courts do not have jurisdiction over any issues that were not raised before the NLRB [*NLRB v. Saint-Gobain Abrasives, Inc.*, 426 F.3d 455 (1st Cir. 2005)]

The Tenth Circuit applied the NLRB's standard formula for back pay, even though it resulted in a windfall to delivery service drivers who were wrongfully terminated for union activity (they received higher wages because of truck expenses, but those expenses were not deducted from the back pay award). [*NLRB v. Velocity Express Inc.*, 434 F.3d 1198 (10th Cir. 2006)]

Documents such as briefs, motions, and requests for permission to appeal in representation cases can be filed electronically at the NLRB e-filing home page, <http://gpea.nlrb.gov; no www>, by filling out a form, attaching the document to the form, and e-mailing it to the NLRB's Office of the Executive Secretary. The agency prefers files in .pdf format, but .doc and .txt files are also acceptable.

§ 30.14   LABOR LAW IMPLICATIONS OF BANKRUPTCY FILINGS

The general rule is that the "automatic stay" on litigation as soon as a bankruptcy petition is filed will protect the company that files from being sued. However, because the NLRB is considered a unit of the federal government exercising its regulatory powers, NLRB unfair labor practices hearings are exempt from the automatic stay. However, the bankruptcy court has the power to enjoin the NLRB from doing anything that would prevent the reorganization of the bankrupt company.

Part of the bankruptcy process is a decision about which executory contracts (i.e., contracts to be performed in the future) will be carried out by the reorganized company and which can and should be rejected. The company seeking bankruptcy protection can petition the court to allow it to assume or reject a CBA. The court's standard for granting a rejection request is whether it would be fair to reject the contract, or whether the union unreasonably refused to accept contract modifications proposed by the employer. The employer does not have to prove that the proposed plan of reorganization will fail unless the contract can be rejected.

However, if the collective bargaining agreement expires while bankruptcy proceedings are pending, the whole issue becomes moot, because there is nothing for the employer to either accept or reject.

The circuit courts are approaching bankruptcy labor law issues differently. For example, United Airlines made a deal with the PBGC to terminate all four of its pension plans. In exchange for the airline paying $1.5 billion to the PBGC, the agency took over as trustee, which resulted in major pension cuts for many employees and saved the airline about $4.5 billion in future pension obligations between 2005 and 2010. The Seventh Circuit upheld the agreement. [*Association of Flight Attendants v. United Airlines Inc.*, 33 B.R. 436 (N.D. Ill. 2005), aff'd *In re UAL Corp.*, 428 F.3d 677 (7th Cir. 2005)] In 2003, the D.C. Circuit upheld a negotiated settlement with the PBGC covering pension issues. [*Allied Pilots Ass'n v. PBGC*, 334 F.3d 93 (2003)] The Third Circuit allows § 1113 to be triggered only if it is required to prevent liquidation in the short run, not as a long-term planning device. [*Wheeling Pittsburgh Steel v. United Steelworkers*, 791 F.2d 1074 (3d Cir. 1986)] In the Second Circuit, the test for rejecting a labor contract is whether rejection is needed to make a successful reorganization more likely. [*Truck Drivers Local 807 v. Carey*, 816 F.2d 82 (2d Cir. 1987); Pamela A. MacLean, *A Savvy Way to Trim Pensions*, National Law Journal, Nov. 16, 2005 (law.com)]

The Bankruptcy Abuse Prevention and Consumer Protection Act of 2005, P.L. 109-8 (BAPCPA), includes various provisions not only extending the exemption of individual debtor's retirement accounts from the bankruptcy estate, but altering the treatment of retirement plans in corporate bankruptcy. The employer's bankruptcy estate does not include funds that the employer withheld or funds received by the employer from employee wages to be paid to ERISA plans, such as defined contribution plans or benefit plans. [*See* BAPCPA § 323]

Bankruptcy Code § 1114, as amended by BAPCPA § 1403, permits the bankruptcy court to set aside modifications of retiree health plans that the employer made within the 180 days before filing, unless the court finds that the balance of equities clearly supports the changes. (Section 1114 is the provision that requires Chapter 11 debtors to negotiate with retiree representatives rather than unilaterally modifying or terminating retiree welfare benefits. After a bankruptcy filing, the benefits must be maintained unless the bankruptcy court orders or permits modification.)

BAPCPA raises the amount of wages and benefits earned by an employee before the employer's bankruptcy filing, but not paid before the filing, that can be treated as a priority claim. The amount is now $10,000, rather than $4,925 in unpaid wages and benefits per employee, earned within 180 days before the filing (rather than only 90 days pre-filing under prior law). BAPCPA also limits the amount of severance or retention bonuses that can be paid to insiders of a bankrupt company.

Chapter 31

OCCUPATIONAL SAFETY AND HEALTH

§ 31.01   INTRODUCTION

The federal Occupational Safety and Health Act and the agency that administers it, the Occupational Safety and Health Administration (both abbreviated OSHA) have as their mission protecting employees against unreasonably hazardous workplaces. All employers must satisfy the "general duty standard" of maintaining a workplace that is reasonably free of recognized dangers. Additional standards are imposed in some circumstances, particularly in the construction industry.

Employers are not held to an impossible standard of a hazard-free workplace, but they must be prepared to deal with known hazards (including disease and chemical toxicity as well as accident). They must use the reasonably available methods and technology to keep the dangers within bounds.

In 2004, there were 5,703 fatal at-work injuries, the third lowest amount in 12 years. According to Forbes.com, the rate of fatal injuries at work fell from 5.3 per 100,000 (1994) to 4.1 per 100,000 (2004). Workplace deaths fell 17% between 1992 and 2004, at a time when non-workplace fatalities rose 14%. The highest rate of fatalities occurred in agriculture, followed by mining. Construction ranked fourth. About a quarter of workplace deaths were automobile related; falls were the next most common cause of fatalities. In 2004, about 6.8 million workers suffered serious injuries that were not work-related, about twice the number of work-related serious injuries. The National Safety Council estimates that off-the-job injuries caused 165 million lost days of production time, compared to 80 million workdays lost to workplace injuries. [Data from the National Safety Council, <http://www.nsc.org>. *See Safety Council: Out-of-Work Injuries an Increasing Workplace Issue,* Plan Sponsor.com (Feb. 7, 2006) and *Workplace Deaths Higher in 2004 but Still Comparatively Low*, PlanSponsor.com (Jan. 9, 2006)]

In 1997, a Texas trial court combined 20 plaintiffs' "toxic soup" claims of occupational exposure to multiple substances. In 2004, the Texas Supreme Court reversed the consolidation, finding that the plaintiffs' claims were too varied, and the jury would be confused by consolidated argument about different work sites, occupations, durations of exposure, and damages. [*In re Van Waters & Rogers Inc.*, 145 S.W.3d 203 (Tex. 2004)]

Wood v. Chao [275 F.3d 107 (D.C. Cir. 2001)] involves a discharged worker who alleges that his discharge occurred in retaliation for reporting unsafe conditions at a facility for disposal of military chemical weapons. The employer says he was discharged for insubordination (he refused to work in a toxic area because the employer had not provided him with corrective lenses for his protective mask; he had already received a final reprimand for refusal to work in the past). The Department of Labor refused to file suit on his behalf, on the grounds that the right to refuse to work is very narrow. The DOL's position was that he did not satisfy the necessary criteria, so discharging him did not violate OSHA. The D.C. Circuit said that it is up to OSHA to decide what investigations and lawsuits are appropriate, and employees cannot sue the Department of Labor to force it to bring suits on their behalf.

Also note that in late 2002, the Sixth Circuit ruled that ERISA does not require employers to pay overtime for the time newly hired workers spend completing company-sponsored training (OSHA's ten-hour general construction safety course). In the Sixth Circuit's view, employees were better off being allowed to take the course in four sessions after regular working hours (even without overtime pay) than they would be if hiring were deferred until after they completed the course. [*Chao v. Tradesmen Int'l Inc.*, 301 F.3d 904 (6th Cir. 2002)]

§ 31.02   OSHA POWERS

Under the OSH Act, OSHA has the authority to inspect workplaces, order correction of violations, and impose penalties if correction does not occur as mandated. It has been held that it is not a violation of the OSH Act, or the Fourth Amendment's ban on unreasonable searches and seizures, for an OSHA compliance officer to videotape a construction site from across the street before going to the site and presenting his credentials. The theory is that looking at a site (to determine if fall protection techniques were adequate) is not a "search," so no warrant is required. [*L.R. Willson & Sons Inc. v. OSHRC*, 134 F.3d 1235 (4th Cir. 1998)]

The OSH Act also requires employers to keep records of workplace injuries and to use this information to generate annual reports (which must be disclosed to the workforce as well as being submitted to OSHA).

All employers whose operations affect commerce among the states are subject to OSHA. There is no minimum number of employees. However, small-scale or low-risk enterprises are entitled to relaxation of some reporting requirements.

Tip: An employer who would be damaged by full compliance with OSHA requirements can petition the Secretary of Labor for a temporary or permanent "variance" that protects the company against noncompliance penalties. Variances are effective only for the company that applies for them. It is no defense against a charge of noncompliance that a variance was granted to a different company in a similar situation.

The OSH Act interacts with various other statutes. It is probably a violation of public policy to discharge a worker because he or she filed a Worker's Compensation claim after suffering an occupational injury; to retaliate against a whistle-blower who reported unsafe conditions to OSHA; or to take steps against someone who cooperated in an OSHA investigation.

Federal labor law says that a walkout premised on unsafe working conditions will not be treated as a strike. Furthermore, it is a protected concerted activity for workers to complain about safety conditions in the workplace, and therefore the employer cannot use this as a premise for employee discipline.

However, state courts will not necessarily consider an OSHA violation relevant evidence of neglect if the employer is sued. A 1997 case says that, under the law of that particular state, OSHA regulations do not have the "compulsory force" under state law that would prove that the employer was negligent. [*Sumrall v. Mississippi Power Co.*, 639 So. 2d 359 (Miss. 1997)]

§ 31.03   OSHA REGULATIONS

The main authority for federal regulation of workplace safety comes from the OSH Act itself. OSHA's agency rules appear in the Code of Federal Regulations. In addition to the General Duty Clause, OSHA enforces more specific guidance in the form of the General Industry Standards that cover most industrial workplaces, and the Construction Standards.

The General Industry Standards deal with topics such as:

- Condition of floors (this is called the "walking/working" standard);
- Number and design of entrances and exits;
- Noise control;
- Radiation safety;
- Proper handling of hazardous materials (known as "hazmats")—toxic chemicals and toxic wastes;
- Personal Protective Equipment (PPE) such as respirators, hard hats, steel-toed shoes, work gloves, etc.;
- Fire prevention and safety;
- On-site first aid and medical treatment;
- Requirements for guards on machinery;
- Proper use of tools and other hand-held equipment;
- Welding and cutting;
- Control of electrical hazards;
- Design and maintenance of lifts and powered platforms;
- Access to employees' health records.

The Construction Industry Standards overlap with the General Industry Standards. The two rules sometimes treat the same topics, but the construction rules tend to be more stringent in this case. The construction standards also cover control of asbestos, welding and cutting, scaffolding, steel construction, and the use of masonry and concrete in construction. In 1994, OSHA proposed an "indoor air quality standard" that would have banned smoking in nearly all workplaces. This was a very controversial rule (more than 100,000 comments were received!), and at the end of 2001, OSHA finally withdrew the proposal, stating that it would focus its attention on other safety and health problems. [*See* 66 Fed. Reg. 64946 (Dec. 17, 2001)]

See also CPL-02-00-135, *Recordkeeping Policies and Procedures Manual*, <http://www.osha.gov/pls/oshaweb/owadisp.show_document . . . > (Dec. 30, 2004) for the employer's obligations for maintaining OSHA records.

§ 31.04   CONTROLLING PHYSICAL HAZARDS

[A]   Personal Protective Equipment

An important part of the employer's duty of providing a safe workplace is to furnish protective equipment and to make sure that machinery is guarded and that, where appropriate, moving parts will stop before employees are injured.

The legal system treats PPE (Personal Protective Equipment) as essential to workplace safety. Wherever possible, employers should eliminate hazards directly, by reducing the likelihood of falls, falling objects, burns, chemical exposure, etc. But it is not always possible to remove the hazard, and even when it is physically possible, the cost may be prohibitive.

In such situations, the employer has a duty to provide PPE, and the employee has a complementary duty to use it. The employer must provide suitable equipment, in sizes that fit the workers, and must train them in how to use the equipment. The obligation exists whenever a reasonable person, familiar with workplace conditions and industry practices, would require PPE. The industry standard is not a defense, however, if the employer knew or should have known that dangerous conditions were present—for instance, if injuries had occurred in the past under similar circumstances.

A respiratory protection rule took effect October 5, 1998. The standard, known as 1910.134, covers respirator use in general industry, shipyards, longshore work, and construction, but not in agriculture. For guidance to employers, OSHA issued compliance directive CPL 2-0.120, explaining how to analyze workplace hazards, select respirators, when to change the chemical cartridges in respirators, and how to make sure respirators fit properly. [*See* <http://www.osha.gov>]

Over five years after initial publication of a Notice of Proposed Rulemaking, OSHA reopened it, saying that additional information was needed as to whether some equipment should be exempted from the requirement that the employer provide and pay for PPE. Although unions objected, contractors took the position that hard hats and safety glasses are tools of the trade that employees should supply for themselves. [64 Fed. Reg. 15401 (Mar. 31, 1999); 69 Fed. Reg. 41221 (July 8, 2004); *see* 73 LW 2124]

[B]   Lockout/Tagout

OSHA's lockout/tagout rule (29 C.F.R. § 1910.147) applies in nonconstruction workplaces where the machinery has potentially dangerous moving parts. The rule imposes obligations on employers to immobilize machinery while it is being serviced, cleaned, repaired, etc. The rule does not apply to normal operation of the machinery, because in those situations the equipment and work routines are supposed to prevent injuries due to moving parts.

To comply with the lockout/tagout rule, machinery could be equipped with a trip control ("panic button") so it can be shut down quickly in an emergency.

Blades and other dangerous parts can be protected with guards that protect workers' bodies from contact and prevent scrap materials from becoming projectiles. If guards are impractical, machinery could be equipped with sensing devices that turn off the machine if a body part goes beyond the safe point. Machinery can also be designed to require two hands to operate, so that it will not work when a hand is within reach of moving parts.

[C]   Bathroom Breaks

The OSHA general industry sanitation standard [29 C.F.R. § 1910.141] requires the presence of toilet facilities in the workplace. An April 6, 1998, letter from OSHA forbids employers to impose unreasonable restrictions on bathroom use. OSHA inspectors who receive complaints on this issue are directed to investigate the reasonableness of the employer's policy.

Female workers (especially pregnant women) need more bathroom breaks than male workers, although older male workers may need to use the restroom more often because of prostate enlargement.

If increased need for elimination is due to a health condition, it may be necessary to provide reasonable accommodation under the Americans with Disabilities Act. For instance, the worker might be allowed more breaks during the day—but short breaks, just long enough to visit the restroom. Or the employee might be assigned the workstation closest to the restroom, so he or she can return to work more quickly. [*See* 66 L.W. 2579 (March 31, 1998), and 2636 (April 21, 1998), and Mary Williams Walsh, *Blue-Collar Urgency: Bathroom Rights,* New York Times, Nov. 22, 2000, at p. G1]

§ 31.05   CONTROLLING EXPOSURE TO HAZARDOUS CONDITIONS

[A]   Generally

The employer must limit employees' exposure to hazardous materials (e.g., asbestos, lead) and conditions (e.g., potentially damaging noise levels). Hazardous substances must be stored properly. Employees must be warned about their presence and taught how to handle the materials safely.

Other laws, such as environmental laws and laws requiring notification to the community of the presence or accidental release of hazardous substances, are also triggered when dangerous materials are used in a workplace. The company must have an emergency-response plan that involves coordination with fire departments and other community resources.

OSHA planned to require hospitals to set up facilities and procedures to limit the spread of tuberculosis, SARS, and other infectious respiratory diseases. Hospitals charged that the required isolation facilities were too expensive, and they had already brought workplace tuberculosis risks under control. OSHA dropped the plan in mid-2003, and the agency removed its tuberculosis rule from its semiannual regulatory agenda. The announcement angered union leaders who expressed concern about the possibility for epidemics and biological warfare. OSHA administrator John Henshaw replied that reported cases of tuberculosis declined 43% since 1993, and many workplaces already implement the Centers for Disease Control's tuberculosis guidelines. According to the CDC, however, there were 20 states in which the number of tuberculosis cases rose between 2000 and 2001. [Marjorie Valburn, *OSHA Drops Plans for Rule Aimed at Tuberculosis, Angering Unions,* Wall Street Journal, May 28, 2003, at p. D5]

With respect to another workplace infection issue, a New York court ruled that employer liability for emotional damages from HIV exposure, like the AIDS-phobia cause of action, is limited to six months (the time frame during which it could be determined if exposure resulted in infection). The plaintiff had several AIDS tests since the exposure—all negative—but claimed that she suffered post-traumatic stress disorder (PTSD) and panic attacks that prevented her from working. The court treated the plaintiff's allegation that she had suffered PTSD unrelated to AIDS-phobia as an attempt to avoid the applicable statute of limitations and bring a stale claim. [*Ornstein v. New York City Health and Hosps. Corp.* No. 5331 (N.Y.A.D. 2006); *see* Rebecca Moore, *Employer's Liability Limited in Case Involving HIV Exposure,* PlanSponsor.com (Mar. 8, 2006)]

A construction company was cited for eight safety violations when a worker died in a fall during demolition. The D.C. Circuit affirmed the Occupational Safety and Health Review Commission's (OSHRC) confirmation of the violations, but found it troubling that the company was cited only for failure to train and failure to ensure integrity of the surface but not for use of improper demolition techniques. The D.C. Circuit agreed that it was obviously dangerous to drill holes in concrete slabs while standing on the slabs, so the citation for failure to warn was properly upheld. The Court of Appeals upheld OSHRC in its ruling that the obligation to provide a safe walking/working surface extends throughout the process and is not limited to the time before demolition begins. Although six slabs were demolished without incident, the ALJ could nevertheless consider expert testimony that drilling holes weakens the structural integrity of concrete. In a multi-employer workplace, one of the employers can assert a defense only if it proves, by a preponderance of the evidence, that it did not create the hazardous condition; did not control the condition to the point that it could have abated it; and either did not or could not have known that the condition was hazardous, or that it took reasonable steps to protect its employees. In this instance, the violation was in plain view, and steps were not taken to protect employees: some workers did not get any safety training, and the worker who died was not trained on specific hazards. The company's instructions to stop demolition if anything looked wrong were inadequate because of the lack of guidance as to what conditions were hazardous. [*Fabi Constr. Co. v. Secretary of Labor*, 370 F.3d 29 (D.C. Cir. 2004)]

[B] PELs

A PEL, or Permissible Exposure Limit, is set for certain hazardous substances such as asbestos and lead. A PEL is a level of contact with the substance that employees can encounter without becoming endangered. The employer has an obligation to monitor the plant environment to determine the level of the regulated substance, to provide appropriate safety equipment (e.g., face masks and respirators) and to train employees in safety techniques.

OSHA rules require that employees have access to showers, changing rooms, eye baths, first aid, and other measures for preventing long-term contamination. Where necessary, the employer must provide protective clothing and appropriate containers for collecting contaminated clothing for treatment or disposal. Employees must not be permitted to smoke or eat in any environment where asbestos, lead, etc., are present. Warning signs must be posted in danger areas.

The employer's basic job is to keep employee exposure below the PEL. In some instances, this is impossible. When exposure reaches the "action level" defined by OSHA, the employer must take additional steps, such as periodic medical testing of employees to see if they have suffered environmental injury or illness.

For years, the Public Citizen Health Research Group has been trying to get OSHA to reduce the PEL for hexavalent chromium, which is a well known carcinogen. In 1998, the Third Circuit refused to issue an order compelling OSHA to lower the PEL [*Oil, Chemical & Atomic Workers Union v. OSHA*, 145 F.3d 120 (3d Cir. 1998)] in part because OSHA said that it was going to issue a Proposed Rule by September 1999. OSHA failed to issue the rule. In late 2002, the Third Circuit decided to grant Public Citizen's request and order OSHA to set a new, lower standard. OSHA announced that it had begun the rulemaking process. The court said that the OSHA announcement did not make the case moot, because it didn't guarantee that rules would ever be issued (OSHA missed ten of its own deadlines for issuing new hexavalant chromium standards) or provide court supervision. The Third Circuit ordered both sides to submit to mediation to work out a timetable for rulemaking. If they can't agree, the mediation panel will set the schedule. [*Public Citizen Health Research Group v. Chao*, 314 F.3d 143 (3d Cir. 2002)]

The Third Circuit held that it was not arbitrary or capricious for the Secretary of Labor to turn down a union request to regulate fluids used in metalworking. Despite the ten-year pendency of regulations on this subject, the court found that it was rational for OSHA to use its scarce enforcement resources to police substances that posed greater risks to workers. [*UAAAW v. Chao*, 361 F.3d 249 (3d Cir. 2004)]

A company received multiple sanctions for occupational safety and health violations. OSHRC rejected four of the charges. DOL sought review, and the Seventh Circuit affirmed the citations on the grounds that OSHRC lacked substantial evidence on the record to reject the charges. The company makes truck brakes and wheels, releasing a great deal of dangerous silica dust that is subject to a PEL. The problem was exacerbated by the installation of a new conveyor belt system in 1989. In 1996, the company's insurer recommended that the employees be required to wear respirators until the problem was solved. However, 29 C.F.R. § 1910.1000(e) says that, because employees are often inconsistent about using equipment, a personal protective equipment (PPE) requirement is proper only if there are no feasible engineering or administrative controls to bring the levels of hazardous substances within the PEL. When inspection showed silica exposures 1.6 times the PEL, OSHA assigned a health response team, which recommended blowing in fresh air, adding physical barriers to block the dust, and improving housekeeping within the plant. Three citations were issued. The employer appealed, noting that it was installing a new system to improve conditions and that individual respirators were available. OSHRC vacated the citations on the grounds that DOL failed to prove that the proposed engineering and administrative controls would significantly reduce silica levels, and that employees could protect themselves with individual respirators. The Seventh Circuit reinstated the citations, finding that the record as a whole showed that DOL's suggested measures were feasible. The employer said that its planned improvements should have been taken into account. The Seventh Circuit said that they had received proper consideration, which had resulted in the violation's reduction from "willful" to "serious." [*Chao v. Gunite Corp.*, 442 F.3d 550 (7th Cir. 2006)]

[C] Noise Levels

In workplaces where the noise level routinely exceeds 85 decibels per eight-hour shift, the employer has an obligation to create and maintain a comprehensive program for hearing conservation. The environmental noise level must be monitored; employees' hearing must be tested (with a baseline reading within six months of initial exposure to high occupational noise levels, and an annual checkup after that), and they must be trained to protect themselves against hearing loss. If any audiometric test shows that an employee's hearing has deteriorated, the employer's obligation is to notify that worker within 21 days and then make sure that the worker uses hearing protection devices in the future.

[D] Workplace Violence

More than 40% of employees reported that they had been the victim of psychological aggression (including threats of physical violence) within the workplace. Six percent said they had been slapped, kicked, or attacked with a weapon, and 96% of those reporting physical violence also said they were the victims of psychological abuse. One quarter of those reporting abuse said they were attacked by customers, clients, or patients; 15% said they were victimized by co-workers; and 13% alleged that bosses or supervisors were responsible. The balance of the incidents involved outsiders (e.g., a spouse going to the workplace to threaten or attack an employee). [News Articles, *Survey: Outsider Most Often Workplace Violence Perpetrators*, PlanSponsor.com (Jan. 27, 2005)]

The FBI's early 2004 report on workplace violence suggested that OSHA should make this problem a priority—for example, by better data collection about violent incidents, training programs, and creating and disseminating model policies and anti-violence plans. The FBI's recommendation when an employee is being stalked or harassed by a partner or former partner is that the employer should assist the victim, help the victim obtain police protection, and give time off to get medical treatment and pursue legal remedies. The FBI warned that although some employers "solve" the problem by firing the victim, this is not an appropriate response. [FBI report on workplace violence, <http://www.fbi.gov/page2/march04/violence030104.htm>, discussed at 72 LW 2547]

Late in 2004, the U.S. Supreme Court applied the intentional infliction of emotional distress cause of action against an employer who failed to provide a safe workplace. The plaintiff sued after she was kidnapped from work and raped by her former lover. She informed her employer that she had an order of protection against him and asked not to be assigned to remote locations where she was vulnerable. Her supervisor ignored her concerns and tried to reconcile the couple. After the attack, the plaintiff complained to the employer about the supervisor's facilitation of the attack. She was required to continue reporting to him. The Supreme Court dismissed her constitutional claims but upheld the intentional infliction of emotional distress element of the case because the employer's actions (granting access to the attacker; refusing to let her work in a safer location) inflicted distress over and above that suffered directly from the incident. Worker's Compensation exclusivity did not apply, because the employer's conduct was intentional rather than negligent. Furthermore, most states do not cap damages for intentional infliction of emotional distress. [*Gantt v. Security USA, Inc.*, 543 U.S. 814 (2004)]

§ 31.06   ERGONOMICS

Ergonomics is the study of the mutual adaptation between tools and the human body. Ergonomically efficient tools will reduce the number, or at least the degree, of injuries associated with tool use.

OSHA has made several attempts to impose ergonomic requirements on industry. This has been an extremely controversial quest. Congress's appropriation bills for OSHA between 1996 and 1998 actually forbade the agency to adopt ergonomics standards.

The Occupational Safety and Health Review Commission (OSHRC) issued an April 1997 decision that was the first declaration that the Secretary of Labor can properly cite ergonomic hazards under the general duty clause. [*Secretary of Labor v. Pepperidge Farm Inc.*, 65 L.W. 2725 (OSHRC April 26, 1997). *See also Reich v. Arcadian Corp.*, 110 F.3d 1192 (5th Cir. 1997)]

In July 1997, NIOSH released a study indicating a strong correlation between job activities and injury to the musculoskeletal system of the back, neck, and upper arms—a subject that was to become highly controversial. [NIOSH, *Musculoskeletal Disorders and Workplace Factors,* July 1997]

OSHA published a draft ergonomics regulation on January 6, 1999. A revised Working Draft of March 12, 1999, was placed on the OSHA Web site but marked "do not cite or quote."

OSHA issued proposed regulations on ergonomics on November 2, 1999, calling for comments by February 1, 2000. Under the proposal, about 1.6 million employers would have to set up a basic ergonomics program of education and reporting. If at least one musculoskeletal disorder (MSD) occurred in the workplace at any time, a full program of prevention would be required.

Informal public hearings were scheduled to begin on February 2, 2000. The proposal said that regulations would become effective 60 days after OSHA's publication of a final standard reflecting the comments received. However, on January 27, 2000, then-Secretary of Labor Alexis Herman extended the comment period to March 2 and re-scheduled the hearings for March 13.

In June 2000, the House of Representatives voted 220–203 to prevent the Department of Labor from implementing new ergonomics standards at least until October 2001. However, OSHA published a very lengthy Final Rule in the November 14, 2000 Federal Register.

The rule, as a general industry standard, was supposed to cover approximately 6.1 million worksites with 102 million workers. The final rule provides a two-page checklist of MSD situations and risk factors, including use of a computer keyboard or mouse for more than four hours a day, kneeling or squatting for over two hours a day, or repeatedly lifting heavy packages during the work shift. The rule requires implementation of a program for managing MSDs within seven days of the occurrence of such an injury. Under this rule, employees suffering work-related MSDs are entitled to receive paid leave and benefits when off work or returned to a light-duty job.

The Final Rule was immediately challenged in court by organizations including the Society for Human Resource Management, U.S. Chamber of Commerce, and the National Association of Manufacturers. [*See* Yochi J. Dreazen, *Ergonomics Rules Are First in a Wave of Late Regulations,* Wall Street Journal, Nov. 14, 2000, at p. A4; Darryl Van Duch, *Ergonomics Rules Draw Attacks,* National Law Journal, Dec. 5, 2000 (law.com)]

In March 2001, both Houses of Congress used a little-known federal statute called the Congressional Review Act of 1996 (CRA) to repeal the ergonomics regulations. It was the first time the CRA had actually been put into practice. Under the CRA, as long as 30 Senators agree, a vote can be taken directly on the floor of Congress, without committee discussions, to overturn Regulations promulgated during the preceding 60 days. Furthermore, if the CRA is invoked, the agency that issued the regulations struck down by Congress will never be permitted to enact "substantially similar" rules in the future.

Senate Joint Resolution 6, dealing with the ergonomics rules, was introduced on March 1, 2001. The Senate voted 56–44 to overturn the ergonomics rules.

The House vote was 223–206 to overturn the regulations. By and large, the Republicans voted against the rules, the Democrats in favor of them. [*See* Steven Greenhouse, *House Joins Senate in Repealing Rules on Workplace Injuries,* New York Times, March 8, 2001 at p. A19]

In April 2002, the Bush administration announced its policy for reducing repetitive stress injuries through the adoption of voluntary industry safety guidelines. The DOL did not get any additional funding to supervise adherence to the guidelines. The plan calls for OSHA to work with industries with unusually high rates of RSIs to develop industry-specific guidelines for reducing injuries, and for OSHA to take action against companies that do not take adequate steps to reduce their injury rates. [Steven Greenhouse, *Bush Plan to Avert Work Injuries Seeks Voluntary Steps by Industry,* New York Times Apr. 6, 2002, at p. A1; Kathy Chen, *Bush Proposal on Repetitive Stress Injuries Relies on Voluntary Industry Guidelines,* Wall Street Journal Apr. 8, 2002, at p. A28.]

OSHA issued only 12 citations for ergonomic injuries in 1997, 2 in 1998, 4 in 1999, 5 in 2000, and none at all in 2001 or 2002. Although it is credible that industry is by and large successful in maintaining safe workplaces, it is hard to believe that there were no violations worthy of enforcement action in an entire nation over a two-year period. During the first Bush presidency, there were 251 inspections for ergonomic issues, resulting in 935 citations—although 608 of those citations were written for only five companies. During the Clinton administration, there were 85 ergonomic inspections and 120 citations. The current Bush administration had 11 ergonomic inspections and 11 citations, issued after a two-year enforcement hiatus. OSHA planned inspections of 3,200 high-hazard inspections by the end of 2003, using the general duty clause rather than specialized ergonomics guidelines. [Albert R. Karr, *Business Groups Sound Ergonomics Alarm,* Wall Street Journal, Sept. 8, 2003, at p. A4; *see also* Albert R. Karr, *Employers Win Ergonomics Duel by Achieving Delay in Guidelines,* Wall Street Journal, Nov. 13, 2003, at p. A3 ER]

At the end of April, OSHA announced the formation of a 15-member National Advisory Committee on Ergonomics to advise on gaps in existing research and how to perform the needed research and communicate research results to industry and the public. The first industry-specific guidelines to be developed were in the nursing home industry, because workers in this industry have a very high injury rate (resulting, e.g., from lifting patients, moving equipment, and assaults by patients). In June 2002, OSHA announced an initiative to develop guidelines in the retail grocery and poultry processing industries. It was expected that the three sets of draft guidelines would be published for public comment late in 2002. [For OSHA actions, *see* OSHA Trade News Releases, *OSHA Announces Formation of National Advisory Committee on Ergonomics,* <http://www.osha.gov/media/oshnews/apr02/trade-20020430.html> and *OSHA to Develop Ergonomics Guidelines for Retail Grocery Stores, Poultry Processing,* <http://www.osha.gov/media/oshnews/june02/trade-20020610.html>] The retail grocery store ergonomics guidelines were published in May 2003. [68 Fed. Reg. 25,068 (May 9, 2003)]

§ 31.07   VARIANCES

The OSH Act permits employers to petition for variances that will excuse them from having to comply with requirements that are particularly onerous. A variance can only be granted if employees will not be exposed to undue risk or danger.

The CFR includes rules for "national security variances" and "experimental variances," but most of the variances granted are classified as either "temporary" or "permanent."

Grounds for a temporary variance are that the company will eventually comply with a new regulation, but cannot do so by its scheduled effective date because of a shortage of staff, materials, or equipment. (Being unable to afford to comply is not considered good cause for a variance.) A temporary variance lasts up to one year. It can be renewed twice, for up to 180 days at a time. The application must demonstrate that the employer is doing everything it can to comply as soon as possible, and that employees are being protected from undue hazards in the meantime.

A permanent variance is granted to an employer whose work methods are unconventional but still provide at least as much protection for employees as the OSHA regulations do. A company asking for a permanent variance can also apply for an interim variance.

The original plus six copies of the variance application and supporting documents must be filed. The documents must be signed by an authorized representative of the company, such as a corporate officer or the corporation's attorney.

Employees are entitled to notice of the variance application. They can ask that a hearing examiner conduct a hearing on the application.

Variance applications are reviewed, and then granted or denied, by the Assistant Secretary of Labor of Occupational Health and Safety in Washington. Anyone affected by a variance after it is granted can petition for modification or revocation of the order granting the variance. After a temporary variance ends, the employer can petition to have it renewed or extended.

§ 31.08   DIVISION OF RESPONSIBILITY

For OSHA purposes, companies are responsible for the safety of their "employees." A company that has all its work done by leased employees or independent contractors will not be subject to OSHA unless the arrangements are only a subterfuge to avoid liability. What counts is the economic reality of the work relationship, including the degree of control over the work, who signs the paycheck, and whether payment is a regular salary or a per-project amount. The power to change working conditions or fire the employee is considered especially significant.

If several employers are involved (e.g., a temporary employment agency and its clients), OSHA responsibilities will be allocated based on actual job performance and working conditions. The basic rule is that the general contractor has primary OSHA responsibility for a construction worksite.

OSHA liability of general contractors can derive from several theories:

- A construction contract provision under which the general contractor agrees to provide safety equipment;
- The general contractor's role of controlling conditions because it is in charge of the site;
- The general contractor is the only party involved with the specialized knowledge to abate the hazards;
- The general contractor's actual knowledge of the hazards (by observation or by notice from a subcontractor), creating a duty to cope with the hazards.

In doubtful cases, OSHA cites all possibly responsible parties and then allows them to make arguments why they are not liable. However, both a company that creates a hazard and the actual employer of the employees exposed to the hazard (and who were not protected by their employer) can be found liable.

OSHA's internal directive, CPL 02-00-124 [*see* <http://www.osha.gov/pls/oshaweb/owadisp.show_document?p_table=DIRECTIVES&p_id=2024>] explains how the agency will issue citations to multi-employer workplaces. If a particular employer is in a position to create, control, or correct hazards, or if it exposes employees to danger, OSHA will check the employer's conduct. If it failed to satisfy all its occupational safety and health obligations, citations can be issued.

OSHA uses a two-step test to see whether the Construction Standard should be applied to nonconstruction companies. The tests are ability to direct or control trade contractors, and a degree of involvement in the multiple activities that are needed to complete a construction project. The Seventh Circuit found that an engineering firm that consulted on a sewer project where a fatal accident occurred, did not become subject to the Construction Standard. [*CH2M Hill Inc. v. Herman*, 192 F.3d 711 (7th Cir. 1999)] The court found that the engineering firm did not exercise substantial supervision over actual construction, and therefore did not have enough control for liability to be imposed.

Under the "peculiar risk" doctrine, someone who hires an independent contractor to perform inherently dangerous work is liable for any torts committed by the independent contractor against others in the course of doing the work. However, in California, this doctrine cannot be used by employees of a subcontractor who are injured by the subcontractor's negligence, to sue the general contractor. [*Toland v. Sunland Hous. Group Inc.*, 18 Cal. 4th 253, 74 Cal. Rptr. 2d 504, 955 P.2d 504 (1998)]

Secretary of Labor v. Yandell [OSHRC No. 94-3080 (March 12, 1999)] permits an individual or corporate employer to be cited for violating OSHA regulations even after it has gone out of business.

The Seventh Circuit vigorously affirmed the dismissal of the indictment charging the defendant with a violation of OSH Act § 17(e) after the electrocution death of two employees of the defendant's wholly owned subsidary. OSHA asserted that the defendant was culpable because it oversaw its subsidiaries' safety programs and provided safety training to employees of the subsidiaries. However, notwithstanding the corporate affiliation, the Seventh Circuit ruled that unless it would be possible to pierce the corporate veil, the parent corporation should not be deemed culpable for deaths of persons employed by another entity. [*United States v. MYR Group, Inc.*, 361 F.3d 364 (7th Cir. 2004)]

Another "division of responsibility" question is how liability should be allocated between employers and the manufacturers of allegedly dangerous products used in the workplace. New Jersey held that the OSH Act preempted a products liability suit by an injured worker against the manufacturer of the forklift that struck him. (The plaintiff charged that additional warning devices should have been designed into the product.) The concept of "conflict preemption" applied because manufacturers could not comply with both federal and state requirements, so only the federal requirement applied. [*Gonzalez v. Ideal Title Importing Co.*, 74 L.W. 1076 (N.J. July 27, 2005)]

A federal court in Cleveland permitted plaintiffs' lawyers to allege that manganese fumes from welding caused Parkinson's disease, a ruling that could affect arguments in thousands of cases nationwide. About 4,500 cases have been consolidated in Cleveland for MDL, and perhaps another 5,000 are in state courts. In addition to up to 500,000 welders, many other factory workers are exposed to manganese fumes. The theory of most of the suits is that manufacturers of welding materials gave inadequate warnings about known dangers. [Timothy Aeppel, *Plaintiffs in Welding-Fumes Case Win a Skirmish in Federal Court*, Wall Street Journal, July 26, 2005, at p. D4]

§ 31.09   OSHA ENFORCEMENT

[A]   Generally

Unlike ERISA enforcement (where federal jurisdiction preempts the state role), OSHA enforcement is coordinated between the states and the federal government. States have discretion to shape the degree of their occupational safety enforcement involvement. They can draft regulatory plans; if the Department of Labor believes the plan does enough to protect worker safety, it becomes an "approved state plan."

About half the states have approved state plans: Alaska, Arizona, California, Connecticut, Hawaii, Indiana, Iowa, Kentucky Maryland, Michigan, Minnesota, Nevada, New Jersey, New Mexico, New York, North Carolina, Oregon, South Carolina, Tennessee, Utah, Vermont, Virginia, Washington, and Wyoming. However, the Connecticut and New York plans are limited to coverage of state employees, not private-sector workers.

In states that do not have an approved state plan, OSHA has primary responsibility for safety enforcement. State governments, however, are allowed to regulate issues that the OSH Act does not cover (such as boiler and elevator safety) as well as broader safety issues (such as fire protection in buildings that are open to the public).

One important function of state OSH agencies is offering free on-site consultations about how to maintain a safer workplace. The consultation is a simulated inspection, but the inspector is only authorized to point out problem areas and suggest solutions, not to issue citations or penalize the company. The consultation begins with an opening conference with the employer, proceeds to a walk-through and identification of safety problems, and ends with a closing conference about how to solve those problems.

This program has been criticized by the GAO, which says that the consultation program does not collect the right information to actually help reduce workplace injuries. The GAO says that although the number of consultations is going up, the number of workplace hazards identified has been declining. [Jeff Bailey, *GAO Criticizes OSHA's Program for Small Businesses*, Wall Street Journal, Oct. 30, 2001, at p. B2]

In July 2001, the Department of Labor announced that it would relax its OSHA enforcement but would add staff to help companies achieve initial compliance and avoid violating OSHA. DOL said that most of its oversight would go to the 5% of companies with the worst health and safety record (e.g., certain construction companies). [Kathy Chen, *Labor Department to Ease Workplace Enforcement*, Wall Street Journal, July 3, 2001, at p. A2]

In August 2004, Judge Schira Scheindlin of the Southern District of New York approved a FOIA request made by the *New York Times* and ordered OSHA to release injury and illness rates for 13,000 work sites that received OSHA warnings about egregious conditions (although workplace injuries and safety data are collected, OSHA does not formally disclose injury/illness rates for particular sites). The judge was not persuaded by the agency's argument that because certain of the information used to rank companies by accident rate, such as the number of employee hours worked, is confidential, the end product should also be confidential. [Nicholas Zamiska, *Judge Orders OSHA to Release Safety Data for U.S. Companies*, Wall Street Journal, Aug. 4, 2004, at p. D2]

In March 2003, the Bush administration issued a memo to OSHA officials to crack down on repeat violators by doing additional follow-up inspections of companies with serious violations, with possible contempt of court sanctions if the violations are not corrected. OSHA inspectors were also directed to improve their coordination of enforcement of occupational safety rules at different worksites owned by the same corporate entity. [David Barstow and Lowell Bergman, *OSHA to Address Persistent Violators of Job Safety Rules*, New York Times, Mar. 11, 2003, at p. A1] Margaret Seminario, AFL/CIO director of safety & health, says focusing on repeat offenders isn't a bad idea, but enhanced enforcement "seems to be missing." She says that the average fine for a willful safety violation declined 26% during the Bush administration, from $36,487 in 2000 to $26,888 in 2002. Average fines for failure to correct violations fell 68%, from $7,687 in 2000 to $2,448 in 2002.

[B] Inspections

Inspections are a central part of OSHA's enforcement function, because direct evidence about workplace conditions is necessary.

In fiscal 2003, OSHA performed 12,263 inspections, resulting in the issuance of 25,532 violations. In fiscal 2004, 26,318 violations were issued in the course of 11,728 inspections. Seventy-five percent of the violations were willful, repeat, or failure to abate violations. [(no by-line) *OSHA Official Says Agency Targeting 55 Employers for Enhanced Enforcement*, 73 LW 2551 (Mar. 16, 2004)]

In 2004, OSHA's staff of about 1,000 inspectors conducted about 38,000 inspections, mostly of workplaces with 250 or fewer employees. In that year, the average penalty was $955. [Elizabeth Olson, *A Move to Ease Safety Rules for Some Employers*, New York Times, Jan. 26, 2006, at p. C6]

A "programmed inspection" takes place on a routine basis, when workplaces are chosen at random from a list of sites with above-average injury rates.

Inspections can also be made based on written complaints from employees, former employees, or their representatives, such as attorneys and union staff. Complaints are made to OSHA's area director or Compliance Officer (CO). OSHA investigates the complaint and sends a copy of the complaint to the employer. (The complainant can request that his or her name be suppressed on the employer's copy.) Depending on the nature of the complaint, OSHA will either send the employer a letter describing the hazard that has been charged and giving a date for abatement, or schedule an inspection. The inspection probably will be scheduled if the employer ignores a letter from OSHA or if there is evidence of other safety problems.

OSHA is supposed to respond to a complaint of imminent danger within one day, to an allegation of a serious hazard within five working days, or within 30 working days if the complaint is less serious. A serious hazard is one that creates a reasonable expectation that it could cause death or irreversible bodily injury.

Generally speaking, OSHA inspections are made on an unannounced basis. However, the employer is entitled to notice if an imminently dangerous situation is alleged (because abatement is more important than detecting violations), if special arrangements are needed for the inspection, or if the inspection will be made outside normal business hours.

The CO shows credentials at the workplace and asks for permission to inspect. If permission is refused, the CO cannot perform a search without an administrative search warrant granted by a court, based on OSHA's showing that it has reason to believe that violations of the General Duty Clause or a more specific standard have occurred. However, courts need far less proof to authorize an administrative search than a search in a criminal case.

Most employers grant permission, so the CO explains the procedure in the opening conference with the employer. Next is the "walk-through" (employer and employee representatives are allowed to comment). At this stage, the CO makes notes on any hazardous or noncompliant conditions prevailing in the workplace. At this point, the inspector often points out trivial violations that can be corrected on the spot: mopping up a pool of water that could cause a slip, for instance. At this stage, the CO usually asks to see the business's logs, summary reports, exposure records, training records, and other safety-related paperwork.

If the inspection is based on a complaint, the employer has the right to review the complaint, and can instruct the CO to limit the inspection to the issues raised by the complaint. Employers who take this option should make a written record of the scope of authorization, give a copy to the inspector, and retain a copy for their records.

The last part of the inspection is the "closing conference" when the CO reveals findings about potential OSHA violations.

COs do not have the power to issue citations during an inspection. The CO must return to the OSHA office and confer with the Area Director about the level of citation (if any) that should be issued in response to each perceived deficiency.

The procedure is slightly different in the construction industry. A "targeted inspection" is a short-form inspection that concentrates on the major hazards to construction workers' safety: falls, falling objects, electrical hazards, and vehicle accidents. The CO decides whether to do a focused or a full inspection during the opening conference. At sites where the general or prime contractor has a workable safety plan and designates a representative to work with OSHA, only a focused inspection will be performed. In contrast to a nonconstruction inspection, citations can be issued during a focused inspection if there are serious violations, or non-serious violations that are not abated immediately.

Employers are forbidden to retaliate against employees who inform OSHA of workplace violations. OSHA issued a compliance directive updating its Whistleblower Investigation Manual in light of enhanced protection for whistle-blowers under the Sarbanes-Oxley Act and the 2002 Pipeline Safety Improvement Act. OSHA's compliance safety and health officers are responsible for interpreting the worker protections under various state and federal statutes. The compliance officers are directed to advise employers and workers of their rights and responsibilities, to take complaints, and to notify the OSHA Area Director if an employee claims that he or she was punished for being a whistleblower. [Final Rules, 69 Fed. Reg. 52,103 (Aug. 24, 2004); Ellen Byerrum, *Protections for Job Safety Whistleblowers Among Weakest of Those Overseen by OSHA*, 72 L.W. 2211 (Oct. 21, 2003), noting that OSHA is responsible for enforcing whistleblower protection in 14 varied statutes, most of them concerned with the environment, transport, and energy]

[C] Tips for Easier Inspections

For advice about how to sail through an inspection with the minimum of trauma, *see* the informative article by Robert J. Grossman [Robert J. Grossman, *Handling Inspections: Tips From Insiders,* HR Magazine, Oct. 1999, at p. 40] including these tips:

- Check the credentials of anyone claiming to be an OSHA inspector. (The OSHA photo IDs have the Department of Labor seal on the back). An environmental activist, labor organizer, or industrial spy could be trying to gain behind-the-scenes access to your operation by impersonating an OSHA inspector;
- Ask if the inspection is programmed; is based on a complaint; or is a follow-up after an accident;
- Find out if the complainant is a current employee. (The inspector will not give you the name, but will tell you if the complainant falls into this category);
- Have your lawyer review all requests for documents and information, and review what you turn over;
- The inspector may quit after a record review, if the records are complete and up to date;
- At the opening conference, get the inspector to agree to protect your trade secrets;
- If the inspector takes photographs or makes a video during the walk-around stage, take your own confirming photos and videos and keep them for comparison;
- Get duplicates of physical samples taken by the inspector, and ask for copies of OSHA's test reports;
- Make sure that someone within the organization has ongoing OSHA responsibility (HR often takes this role). Train employees how to respond to questions from an OSHA inspector;
- Take the inspector to the area he or she wants to see by the shortest, most direct route and not the long way around—in case the inspector sees something else that raises questions;
- Get to know the personnel in the OSHA area office and develop a cooperative working relationship with them.

§ 31.10 OSHA CITATIONS

[A] Categories of Violations

The CO's comments during an inspection are not official OSHA pronouncements, and the employer cannot be penalized for failing to respond to them. However, penalties can be imposed for failure to respond to a written citation from the OSHA Area Director that is sent within six months after the date of the alleged violation that is cited. The citation form lists the violations, classified by seriousness, imposes penalties, and sets a date for abating each violation. Usually, the citation will be Form OSHA-2, sent by certified mail, although other forms can be used.

OSHA violations are generally divided into four categories: de minimis (trivial), nonserious, serious, and other. Penalties are heavier on willful violations or repeat violations within a three-year period. Criminal penalties might be imposed in the very worst cases, such as the preventable death of an employee.

[B]   Penalties

Penalties are set under OSHA § 17 (294 U.S.C. § 666). [For OSHA's Field Inspection Reference Manual, CPL 2.103, Section 8-Chapter IV Post Inspection Procedures, *see* <http://www.osha.gov>]

It's hard to predict what penalty will be imposed for any particular OSHA violation. There are many factors involved, primarily the gravity of the violation. However, the size of the business, the employer's past history of violations, and whether or not the employer acted in good faith are all important considerations.

The civil penalty for a violation, including a violation that consists of failure to post the mandatory notice, can go up to $7,000 per violation. If a violation is not serious, and the penalty would be less than $100, then no penalty is assessed; there is a $100 minimum penalty for serious violations. Furthermore, if a violation is willful, the minimum penalty is $5,000 for a nonserious or posting violation—and this minimum amount cannot be reduced by administrative discretion. The minimum penalty for a willful serious violation is $25,000.

The gravity of a violation depends on two factors: the severity of the damage that the violation could cause and how probable it is that the violation will result in occupational injury or illness.

The multifactorial penalty analysis also reflects factors such as the number of workers exposed, how close they were to the danger, how frequently they were exposed, and how long exposure continued, whether appropriate PPE was used to reduce the risk, and other working conditions.

OSHA has the discretion to reduce penalties greatly, to reflect good faith, small business size (no reduction can be made on this basis if the enterprise has more than 250 employees), and previous acceptable history with regard to occupational safety and health violations.

In fiscal 2003, for example, Assistant Secretary of Labor Patrick Pizzella testified before the House Government Reform Subcommittee on January 28, 2004, that there were 24,583 OSHA enforcement actions involving penalties. Most of them (20,780) involved companies with fewer than 250 employees, and in fact more than half (12,366) involved very small employers—25 or fewer employees. Penalties were reduced in approximately three-quarters of all cases (17,699 out of the 24,583). Of the $75 million in penalties originally assessed, a

$40 million reduction was granted. Of the employers of 250 or fewer workers, 14,738 obtained a reduction in penalties, as did 8,270 of those with fewer than 25 employees. [72 L.W. 2447]

Failure-to-abate penalties are applied when a cited violation becomes a final order, and the employer fails to correct the violation. Normally, the maximum failure-to-abate penalty will be limited to 30 times the daily proposed penalty for that violation.

An employer who repeatedly violates OSHA is subject to much harsher penalties: up to $70,000 per violation. If the employer has fewer than 250 employees, the penalty based on the gravity of the violation (GBP) is doubled for the first repeated violation, and quintupled if a violation was previously cited twice. For employers of over 250, the GBP is multiplied by five for a first repeated violation, by 10 for a second repeated violation. (The overall potential for harm is greater in a larger workplace, which explains the difference.)

The civil penalty for failure to maintain the proper records can be as high as $7,000 per violation: *see* OSHA § 17(c). Failure to post the annual record in February each year, so employees can review it, can be penalized by a $1,000 fine. (Starting in 2003, the annual summary will have to remain posted throughout February, March, and April of each year.)

Failure to post OSHA citations as required by 29 C.F.R. § 1903.16 is punishable by a fine of $3,000. Failure to report a fatal accident is penalized by $5,000 to $7,000. Refusing to provide records to employees or their representatives to examine or copy is subject to a fine of $1,000 per form per year that is denied to employees. A penalty of $2,000 can be imposed if the employer has advance notice of an inspection but fails to inform the employee representative (thus preventing the representative from participating in the inspection).

29 U.S.C. § 666(e) imposes penalties whenever a willful violation of an OSHA standard leads to the death of any employee. This penalty can be assessed against the culpable employer on a multiemployer worksite, even though the deceased worker was employed by one of the other companies at the site. [*United States v. Pitt-Des Moines Inc.,* 168 F.3d 976 (7th Cir. 1999)]

Criminal prosecutions are extremely rare, even in cases of obvious disregard of worker safety. About a hundred companies are cited each year for fatal accidents involving workers, but there are never more than a dozen prosecutions in any year. Between 1982 and 2002, according to the *New York Times*, there were over 170,000 occupational deaths. OSHA investigated 1,242 "horror stories": workplaces where willful violations resulted in preventable deaths. Yet even in these worst-case scenarios, OSHA tried to prosecute only 7% of the cases. OSHA staffers say that the agency never rewards—and sometimes punishes—zealous attempts to evoke criminal penalties. The *Times* examined records for 2,197 workplace deaths, finding that 1,798 incidents involved violation of rules that could have led to prosecution. Only 196 cases were referred to prosecutors; the prosecutors rejected 92 cases. Overall, there were 104 prosecutions, 81 convictions, but only 16 jail sentences.

Nor has financial enforcement been strictly pursued. In 2001, about 60% of cases were downgraded to remove allegations of willfulness. Even in willful cases, fines are typically reduced after negotiations with the employer. Since 1991, the median fine initially proposed was $54,600, reduced to $25,000, and in even in cases where there was a fatality, the average fine went down from $62,500 to $8,000 after negotiations removed the element of willfulness. [David Barstow, *U.S. Rarely Seeks Charges for Deaths in Workplace*, New York Times, Dec. 12, 2003, at p. A1]

However, quiet efforts are under way to improve this state of affairs. OSHA, the EPA, and a group of Justice Department prosecutors began to work together to prosecute the worst violators, especially in cases of injury or death. In March 2005, oil refiner Motiva Enterprises was sentenced to three years' probation and a $10 million fine for the negligent endangerment of workers and environmental damage. The initiative represented a change in OSHA policy, which previously refrained from referring even the most serious violations to prosecutors. Between 1982 and 2002, there were about 1,200 worker deaths that were deemed related to employer safety violations, but fewer than 7% of those cases resulted in prosecutions. OSHA does not have experienced criminal investigators on staff, but the EPA does, so interagency cooperation could lead to a larger number of investigations and perhaps prosecutions. [David Barstow and Lowell Bergman, *With Little Fanfare, A New Effort to Prosecute Employers That Flout Safety Laws*, New York Times, May 2, 2005, at p. A17]

A 1990 OSHA compliance directive sets out an egregious penalty policy, under which employers are cited for each instance of a violation of standards, rather than grouping the violations. The result is that penalties can be much higher. In the agency's 2000 fiscal year, six egregious cases were brought, versus eight in 2001, three in 2002 and only two in 2003.

However, in late 2003 OSHRC reduced the penalties imposed on a building owner who hired undocumented aliens to remove asbestos, giving them only face masks as protection. OSHA imposed penalties of $1.14 million, but OSHRC reduced this amount to $658,000. An explosion, seriously injuring three workers, occurred when a worker opened what he thought was a water line but actually was a gas line; the gas ignited when another worker started his car engine. OSHA cited the employer for 11 willful violations of the respirator standard and 11 violations of the asbestos training standard, calling for $1.48 million in penalties. The ALJ upheld the violations but reduced the fine to $1.14 million. OSHRC affirmed only one of each of the violations, further cutting the penalties to $658,000. The OSHRC position was that the standards did not support issuing a separate citation per employee affected. [*Secretary of Labor v. Ho*, OSHRC No. 98-1645 (Sept. 29, 2003), discussed in *Industry Observers Split Over Effect of Recent Decision Involving Egregious Policy*, 72 L.W. 2219 (Oct. 21, 2003)]

Criminal penalties (imposed by courts, not directly by OSHA) can be imposed, under OSHA § 17(f)-(h), for giving advance notice of an inspection that is supposed to be made unannounced, for giving false information, or assaulting or interfering with the work of a CO.

It does not constitute double jeopardy to impose administrative penalties on an employer after it has been convicted of criminal OSHA violations, because the administrative penalties are clearly civil and cannot result in imprisonment. [*S.A. Healy Co. v. OSHRC*, 138 F.3d 686 (7th Cir. 1998)]

§ 31.11   OSHA APPEALS

Employers don't have to agree with an OSHA citation. There are several administrative steps that can be taken to protest—although these administrative remedies do have to be exhausted before filing suit.

If an employer challenges a citation, OSHA has to prove that the employer failed to live up to some applicable standard. The agency also has to prove that feasible corrective measures existed that could have brought the employer into compliance. If the standard has a time element (for example, the noise exposure standard does), then OSHA also has to prove that the condition existed long enough and intensely enough to constitute a violation.

OSHA has to prove that the employer knew about the condition or could have become aware by exercising due diligence. It is not necessary to prove that the employer was aware of the standard and deliberately chose to violate it. A supervisor's or foreman's knowledge will be attributed to the employer, unless the employer maintained work rules that satisfied the OSHA standard, communicated those rules to employees, and enforced the work rules.

OSHA is entitled to prove the employer's knowledge (and therefore does not have to prove actual knowledge) in some situations:

* Another employee has already been injured by the same hazardous conditions;
* Several written employee complaints have already been made to OSHA;
* The employer knows that employees habitually omit safety equipment, or otherwise allow hazardous conditions to be present in the workplace;
* The employer doesn't provide enough training;
* The employer doesn't enforce its own safety rules;
* The hazards would easily have been discovered if the employer had performed an adequate inspection.

An employer that receives an OSHA citation has 15 days to file a Notice of Contest, disputing that there was a violation, demanding a fair period of time to abate the violation, or challenging the size of the penalty. If the employer is not sure whether or not to contest, it can schedule an informal conference with the OSHA area director to discuss OSHA's position on workplace conditions and how to improve them. The 15-day limit is strictly applied: OSHRC does not have jurisdiction to review a notice of contest filed after the 15-day period expires. [*Chao v. Russell P. LeFrois Builder, Inc.*, 291 F.3d 219 (2d Cir. 2002); *see also* 71 L.W. 2237]

There is no official form for the Notice of Contest; it is simply a letter stating in plain English that the employer disagrees with the citation and wants to contest some or all of the violations, to ask for a smaller penalty, and/or ask for more time to comply. If the Notice of Contest is not filed within the required 15 days, the citation becomes final, and no court has the power to reverse it or even to review it.

Tip: If an employer appeals in bad faith, knowing that the citation is valid, the whole period of time until the challenge is resolved is treated as a period of noncompliance, with additional penalties for each day.

Another factor is whether the citation will affect other cases. For instance, some courts allow an OSHA citation, especially an uncontested one, to be introduced as evidence of dangerous conditions (e.g., in a Worker's Compensation hearing). Contesting the violation can help clear the employer's name.

When a notice is filed, an OSHA Administrative Law Judge (ALJ) will set a date for a hearing. Although the hearing is informal, it is still governed by the Federal Rules of Evidence. The ALJ's decision becomes final 30 days after it is rendered, unless it is contested.

All Notices of Contest, and all ALJ decisions, are automatically passed along to the Occupational Safety and Health Review Commission (OSHRC). OSHRC has the power to order review of part or all of an ALJ decision. The employer, or any other party adversely affected by the decision, can file a Petition for Discretionary Review. Although it has the power to raise the level of a violation, OSHRC usually doesn't do so.

The employer can raise many arguments to OSHRC:

- The CO got the facts wrong;
- The employer did not know, and had no duty to know, that the violation had occurred;
- The inspection itself was improper—for example, the inspection was really a search, requiring a warrant that had not been obtained;
- OSHA applied the wrong standard;
- The standard itself was invalid, because it was not properly promulgated, or was so vague that employers could not reasonably be expected to understand and comply with it;
- The real cause of the violation was misconduct by employees, beyond the employer's control; this misconduct is unlikely to recur;
- Complying with the OSHA requirement actually increased the hazards to employees rather than decreasing them, but the employer was unable to get a variance.

OSHRC issues an order after considering the employer's arguments and defenses. The employer has 60 days from the date of the OSHRC order to file a further appeal. The employer can now go to federal court, because administrative remedies have been appealed. In fact, the employer can bypass the District Court (the lowest tier in the federal court system, where federal cases normally begin) and appeal either to the Court of Appeals for the Circuit where the violation is alleged to have occurred, or to the District of Columbia Circuit.

Early in 2003, the Sixth Circuit ruled on an appeal of an OSHRC decision about a worksite drowning accident. OSHRC found that the employer violated two sections of the OSH Act: Employees were not instructed about the hazards of a basin filled with accumulated water, nor were they required to use Personal Protective Equipment in a hazardous situation. The company appealed on the grounds that OSHRC acted arbitrarily and capriciously and abused its discretion. However, the Sixth Circuit affirmed OSHRC, because the company's safety policy failed to warn employees strongly enough about the potential risks, and because PPE was not mandated in a situation in which it should have been. The company asserted the defense of unpreventable misconduct by the employees, but the Sixth Circuit limits that defense to situations in which the employer has a thorough safety program, which is properly communicated and enforced; the employee's conduct could not have been foreseen; and the safety program has been effective in practice. Those factors were not present in this case. [*Danis-Shook Joint Venture XXV v. Secretary of Labor*, 319 F.3d 805 (6th Cir. 2003)] Similarly, in 2004, the District of Columbia Circuit upheld OSHRC, which affirmed several citations issued for fall protection violations after an employee died in a fall. The death occurred after OSHA had received a hot-line call about falls and other safety hazards, and an investigation was underway. The company said that it did not have the requisite level of knowledge to support the violation, and it was not willful.

The D.C. Circuit confirmed the decisions of an ALJ and the OSHRC to uphold an OSHA citation for blocking the exit in a workplace (29 C.F.R. § 1910.37(k)(2) sets the rules for "means of egress"). A Wal-Mart stockroom had mobile conveyor rails that blocked access to the emergency exit. A $5,000 penalty was assessed, based on the size of the business, the seriousness of the violation (any delay in an emergency could cause injury or death), and whether it was a repeat violation (it was held to be substantially similar to an earlier citation for putting shopping carts in the path to the exit). The court rejected the employer's argument that employees could exit through the truck bay doors because those doors not only were 4 feet above ground level, but were frequently blocked by trucks. The court also did not accept Wal-Mart's contention that individual Wal-Mart stores should be considered to be separate employers for OSHA purposes. [*Wal-Mart Stores, Inc. v. Secretary of Labor*, 406 F.3d 731 (D.C. Cir. 2005)]

As the District of Columbia Circuit pointed out, ALJ determinations must be accepted unless they are patently unsupportable, which was not true in this case. The company either knew or could have known with reasonable diligence that there were deficiencies in the fall protection plan. The company was plainly indifferent to OSHA requirements, which will support the characterization of a violation as willful—and in this instance, there had been six previous inspections that reported multiple fall-protection violations. The Court of Appeals rejected the company's argument that the regulations did not give proper notice of what was required, because the regulations were specific and detailed enough (covering 26 different types of scaffolding) to inform construction companies of the expectations they must meet. [*AJP Construction Inc. v. Secretary of Labor*, 357 F.3d 70 (D.C. Cir. 2004)]

Although Model Rule 4.2 (of the rules of legal ethics) prohibits lawyers from contacting their clients' opponents directly rather than through the opponents' counsel, communications are barred only with supervisors or other employees whose actions may be imputed to the employer. Therefore, it was not unethical for a DOL attorney to discuss a matter with a construction company without first getting the approval of the construction company's attorney. In turn, OSHRC held that it was therefore correct for the ALJ to refuse to dismiss the case. [*Secretary of Labor v. Lanzo Construction Co.*, OSHRC 97-1821 (Feb. 27, 2004), 72 LW 2534]

§ 31.12   ABATEMENT

Abatement—removal of hazardous conditions—is the rationale for the whole OSHA process. An uncontested citation, a citation for which the contest period has expired, and a citation where the employer's challenge was partially or wholly unsuccessful, all give rise to abatement responsibilities.

Employers are required to abate violations within the shortest reasonable interval for correction. The CO orders an abatement date. Ordinarily, this will not be more than 30 days, although the initial abatement date could be more than 30 days from the date of the inspection if structural changes are needed, or if abatement relies on components that take a long time to deliver. [*See* OSHA Field Inspection Reference Manual CPL 2.103, at <http://www.osha.gov>]

Tip: If a citation notes several violations, only some of which are contested, the appropriate action is to correct the uncontested violations, notify the OSHA area director that correction has occurred, and pay the penalties for the uncontested violations. With respect to contested citations, abatement and payment of fines will be suspended until there is an OSHRC final order.

OSHA reinspects the premises. If the same conditions are detected, penalties of up to $1,000 a day can be imposed. The employer, however, can contest penalties in the same way as an original citation.

The employer is entitled to file a Petition for Modification of Abatement (PMA) with the OSHA Area Director, no later than the scheduled abatement date, if factors beyond the employer's control prevent abatement. The PMA explains what the employer has done to cure the problem, how much additional time is required and why, and what the employer will do to protect employees until full abatement is achieved. The PMA must be posted and served on the employer's workforce, because they have the right to contest it.

If the PMA is uncontested, the Secretary of Labor has the power to approve it. OSHRC holds a hearing on contested PMAs, to determine if the employer did in fact act in good faith and was really unable to achieve full compliance. The employer does not have to comply with the underlying citation during the time that the PMA is under consideration.

§ 31.13   OSHA CONSULTATION

State OSH agencies, working under grants from the federal OSHA, offer free on-site consultation services to identify and eliminate potential safety problems before they become real ones. The consultants are also available by telephone for advice and discussion. On-site visits are followed up by a written analysis of workplace hazards and suggestions for correction.

The consultants do not have the authority to impose penalties, but participating employers must agree to take steps to correct whatever problems the program uncovered.

Consultations cannot take place while an OSHA inspection is already underway, but if a consultation is scheduled, there is a good chance that OSHA will cancel a scheduled inspection, unless it is investigating a fatality or serious accident, or it is suspected that employees are in imminent danger.

An employer that has completed a consultation, made corrections based on the recommendations, and who posts a notice of correction where employees can see it, is entitled to request one year's immunity from scheduled OSHA inspections.

OSHA gives priority to scheduling consultation in industries with high hazards. The names of companies engaging in consultation will not be disclosed to state or federal enforcers unless the employer refuses to correct imminent hazards that are discovered during the process. [See 29 C.F.R. § 1908.5; for a map of locations, see <http://www.osha.gov/dcsp/smallbusiness/consult_directory.html>]

§ 31.14   VOLUNTARY PROGRAMS

Under the title of Voluntary Protection Programs (VPP), OSHA has three incentive programs (Star, Merit, and Demonstration) for employers with good safety records, who are supposed to serve as examples for other companies. Participants qualify for participation by proving that they maintain safe workplace and provide ongoing safety training for workers. OSHA and state authorities do not do programmed inspections at participating companies, although inspections will still be made if a complaint is registered.

Employers can apply to OSHA for VPP certification. They must complete applications that demonstrate their qualifications for participation. OSHA sends an inspector to check the company's safety records and site conditions.

Also see the OSHA Strategic Partnership page <http://www.osha.gov/dcsp/partnerships/index.html>, explaining the Partnership program, "an extended, voluntary, cooperative relationship with groups of employers, employees, and employee representatives" to improve safety and health.

OSHA launched two VPP pilot projects in May 2004. Fifteen companies and organizations participated in a one-year test. The OSHA Challenge program provides a phased entry for work sites that want suggestions for improving their VPP status. All employers, whatever their current safety status, are eligible for the Challenge program, which has industry and construction tracks offering mentoring by qualified volunteers. The VPP Corporate Program allows a streamlined application and on-site evaluation process for employers that have already made a significant VPP commitment. [(no by-line) *OSHA Offers New Compliance Programs Available on a Voluntary Basis, Industrywide*, 72 LW 2741 (June 8, 2004)]

CHAPTER 32

UNEMPLOYMENT INSURANCE

§ 32.01 INTRODUCTION

In the late 1990s, the subject of unemployment insurance was something of a backwater: a topic of limited interest in a booming, full-employment economy. However, starting in mid-2001, and accelerating after the September 11 attack, unemployment insurance, and especially the employer's experience rating and funding obligations, became far more interesting.

Unemployment compensation (UC) is a state-administered insurance system. Employers make contributions to a fund. The State Employment Security Agencies (SESAs) that administer the system receive federal funding. In exchange, they must perform investigations and other managerial tasks.

Each state creates an Unemployment Insurance Trust Fund from employer contributions. In a few states, employee contributions are also required. However, FICA tax imposes equal (and substantial) burdens on both employer and employee, but unemployment tax is almost exclusively a responsibility of the employer. The theory is that in good times, unemployment will be low, and the fund will accumulate a surplus that can be used in bad times to pay unemployment insurance claims.

The Department of Labor's unadjusted and seasonally adjusted data on the number of unemployment insurance claims can be found at <http://www.dol. gov>.

According to the GAO, 8.8 million workers received a total of $41.3 billion in unemployment benefits in 1994. [GAO, *Unemployment Insurance: Factors Associated with Benefit Receipt,* <http://www.gao.gov/cgi-bin/getrpt?GAO-06-341 (Mar. 2006)]

Sometimes employers cushion the effect of a layoff by providing supplemental unemployment benefits (SUB) as defined by Code § 3402(o): amounts paid to a person under a plan to which that person's employer is a party, made because of temporary or permanent separation from employment that results from a Reduction in Force or discontinuance of a plant or operation. SUB benefits are included in the recipient's gross income and are subject to income tax withholding, but are exempt from FICA and FUTA. [*See* § 2.03[A]]

Tip: The Medicare Prescription Drug Improvement and Modernization Act [P.L. 108-173] provides that one type of "qualified medical expense" that can be withdrawn from a Health Savings Account (HSA) without tax penalty is a premium paid for health insurance by a person receiving federal or state unemployment benefits.

---

§ 32.02 ELIGIBILITY FOR BENEFITS

[A] Generally

Two of the most important determinants in entitlement are whether the employee worked long enough before termination to qualify for benefits; and the reason for termination. The "base period" is the period of time used to analyze whether the job continued long enough.

In most states, the base period is the first four of the preceding five completed calendar quarters. Some states allow the four most recent quarters of employment to be counted. The difference is whether the most recent months of employment (which might have higher earnings) will be counted. Theoretically, only persons who earned at least a minimum amount during the base period can collect UI benefits. In practice, these limits are so low that nearly all employees meet them.

The rationale for the UI system is to provide benefits for employees who lose their jobs through "no fault of their own." But in this context, an employee will not be considered to be at fault even if the employer was justified in firing him or her—for instance, if an employee is fired for incompetence but there was no crime or wrongdoing. For example, in *Time Warner Cable,* Unempl. Ins. Rep. (CCH) ¶ 8314 (Miss. App. 2006), benefits were held to have been correctly paid to a claimant who was terminated for lack of knowledge and judgment needed in his job. Inefficiency, unsatisfactory conduct, and good-faith errors do not constitute misconduct.

In general, benefits will not be available to anyone who quit voluntarily without good cause. However, states vary as to whether employees who quit will be entirely denied UI benefits, or whether benefit eligibility will merely be delayed. If the employer's conduct has been so abusive as to constitute constructive discharge, then the employee will be deemed to have had good cause to resign. An employee was deemed to have had good cause to quit where the employer broke a verbal promise to give her a raise, in that breaking the promise was a substantial breach of the employment agreement [*Hayes,* Unempl. Ins. Rep. (CCH) ¶ 8556 (Minn. App. 2003)] or where a grocery department manager's demotion was a substantial adverse change, because his salary was cut and his working hours increased significantly. *Rootes* [Unempl. Ins. Rep. (CCH) ¶ 8559 (Minn. App. 2003); but *Korpics,* Unempl. Ins. Rep. (CCH) ¶ 12,443 (Pa. Commw. 2003)] holds that a demotion from day-shift supervisor to a similar night-shift job did not provide good cause to quit, both because the duties and pay were similar and because the demotion was justified by the claimant's poor work performance. The Missouri Court of Appeals ruled in 2006 that being told one's working hours would be reduced was not good cause to quit. No reasonable employee, especially one who did not have another job lined up, would have felt compelled to leave employment. [*Miller,* Unempl. Ins. Rep. (CCH) ¶ 8626 (Mo. App. 2006)] However, there are situations where the employee is considered to have acted with good cause, even if the employer was not at fault. Many states interpret quitting a job to follow a spouse who has gotten a job elsewhere to constitute good cause.

However, Pennsylvania ruled that a claimant quit work without good cause when her husband was relocated to Ohio. The claimant failed to show that the move to Ohio caused insuperable problems for commuting, or that maintaining two residences caused economic hardship. The Pennsylvania Commonwealth Court did not necessarily treat maintaining the family unit as good cause to quit. [*Sturpe,* Unempl. Ins. Rep. (CCH) ¶ 12,433 (Pa. Commw. 2003)]

In mid-2004, a New York intermediate-level court held that a woman who quit her job charging that she had been sexually harassed was not eligible for unemployment benefits because she had quit voluntarily. The $2,000 in benefits already received would probably have to be returned. The court held that she overreacted to personal animosity of a co-worker; personality conflict is not valid grounds for resignation as far as the unemployment compensation system is concerned. [*Gully v. Commissioner of Labor* (AD 3d Dept. 2004), discussed in John Caher, *No Benefits for Woman Who Left Job After Claiming Harassment,* New York Law Journal, June 15, 2004 (law.com); *but see Munro Holdings LLC,* Unempl. Ins. Rep. (CCH) ¶ 10,178 (Ohio App. 2005): A waitress who was sexually harassed by the owner of the restaurant was entitled to benefits; she had no reason to believe the harassment would end, and obviously the person committing the harassment was aware that it occurred.]

Pennsylvania's Commonwealth Court ruled that a group of former Verizon employees who accepted buyout packages were not entitled to unemployment benefits, because they had left their jobs voluntarily without compelling necessity. However, one claimant's case was remanded for further proceedings based on her allegations that she accepted the buyout because she had ceased to be assigned work and was afraid that she would lose her job if she didn't take the buyout package. A 2003 case also involving Verizon workers held that even though the workers didn't think they had a free choice, they nevertheless were not eligible for unemployment benefits once they accepted buyout compensation. The Pennsylvania rule is that the claimant who testifies that continuing work was not available can show necessitous and compelling cause to quit; the employer is not required to prove that work was available. [*Johnson v. Unemployment Compensation Board of Review* (Pa. Commonwealth 2005); the earlier case is *Renda v. UCBR* (Pa. 2003), discussed in Asher Hawkins, *Bought-Out Verizon Workers Denied Jobless Aid,* The Legal Intelligencer (Mar. 10, 2005) (law.com)]

Benefits are also denied to persons who are guilty of "misconduct detrimental to the best interests of the employer." This is interpreted in an industrial rather than moral light, so improper activities are likely to rule out UI benefit eligibility even if they are not criminal in nature. Poor job performance would not be treated as "misconduct," unless it demonstrated gross negligence or willful disregard of the employer's best interests.

Depending on the state, disqualifying misconduct might also have to be work-related. Excessive absence or insubordination might be treated as misconduct. Being intoxicated on business premises would almost certainly be considered misconduct. For example, Kansas denied benefits for disqualifying misconduct on the basis of the claimant's repeated insubordination to a supervisor in an open area where other workers could hear the interaction, which also involved an unprovoked barrage of vulgar and abusive language. [*Siler,* Unempl. Ins. Rep. (CCH) ¶ 8265 (Kan. App. 2003)] A truck driver whose blood alcohol concentration exceeded the legal limit was guilty of disqualifying misconduct, even though he was not convicted of driving under the influence and did not lose his license;

he should have known that duty to his employer precluded driving while impaired. [*Risk*, Unempl. Ins. Rep. (CCH) ¶ 8557 (Minn. App. 2003)] Benefits were denied to a veterinarian who was fired for failing to follow orders to get a state license. The Indiana Court of Appeals did not accept his argument that the employer let him work anyway, knowing that he lacked the license. The court found it reasonable to hire someone contingent on that person's satisfying obligations in the future. [*Nersessian*, Unempl. Ins. Rep. (CCH) ¶ 8599 (Ind. App. 2003)]

In contrast, Florida held that although it may have been proper to fire a truck driver for insubordination, he was not guilty of disqualifying misconduct because he was ordered to make day-shift deliveries—outside his regularly assigned night shift. [*Davidson*, Unempl. Ins. Rep. (CCH) ¶ 8936 (Fla. App. 2003)] Benefits were granted to an Arkansas claimant who was fired after a single failure to get advance approval from his supervisor to use his accrued vacation time for military leave. There had been no disqualifying misconduct, because employees were allowed to use vacation time for that purpose, and there was no written policy requiring permission from the supervisor. [*Maxfield*, Unempl. Ins. Rep. (CCH) ¶ 8518 (Ark. App. 2003)]

Continued eligibility requires the claimant to make a serious search for work. Benefits will be terminated if the claimant receives but rejects a legitimate job offer for suitable work. Benefits will not be paid in any week in which the claimant receives a pension, annuity, retirement pay, or any other private or government payment based on past work history. But benefits can be paid in a week in which the claimant receives a distribution from a profit-sharing plan, because that is not treated as compensation for work. According to the Florida Court of Appeals, a claimant who started his own business did not commit fraud by receiving UI benefits. He continued to look for employment, and the referee erred by saying that startup services for the business meant that the claimant was already employed when he received the benefits. [*Grover*, Unempl. Ins. Rep. (CCH) ¶ 8970 (Fla. App. 2005)]

Benefits can be paid based on job loss due to a material change in working conditions imposed by the employer, if the employee has a valid reason for being unable to work under the new conditions. (This is referred to as "voluntary with good cause attributable to the employer.") A published job description can be evidence of the original nature of the job, and therefore whether material change has occurred. If a job is described as a day-shift position, a change to a night or swing shift might well be considered material.

In mid-2003, the New York Court of Appeals ruled that the employee's physical presence is critical, not the location of the employer on whose behalf the work was done. So a worker who telecommuted from Florida could not collect New York unemployment benefits, even though her employer was located in Long Island and work was directed and controlled from New York. [*Allen v. Commissioner of Labor,* 72 L.W. 1023 (N.Y. 7/2/03); *see* John Caher, *N.Y. Court First to Rule on Telecommuting,* New York Law Journal, July 3, 2003

<http://www.law.com>; Al Baker, *Telecommuter Loses Case for Benefits,* New York Times, July 3, 2003, at p. B1]

In a Wisconsin case from 2001, for example, benefits were granted because it was not considered unreasonable for the employee to quit instead of accepting a transfer to a plant 25 miles away. Although the offered new job was similar to the old one, and paid the same hourly base rate, the employee would suffer an effective 19% reduction in net pay because of commuting costs, loss of lead worker pay, and lower incentive pay. [*Research Prods. Corp.,* Unempl. Ins. Rep. (CCH) ¶ 9507 (Wis. Cir. 2001)]

The employer's failure to investigate a claimant's repeated reports of sexual harassment made her resignation a voluntary quit with good cause attributable to the employer, so benefits were available. [*Yaeger,* Unempl. Ins. Rep. (CCH) ¶ 8915 (Fla. Dist. App. 2001)]

The Ohio Court of Appeals ruled that participants in a "Special Separation Program," receiving separation pay greater than the weekly benefit amount in addition to an unreduced retirement benefit, were not entitled to unemployment benefits because they received higher payments than the employer's normal severance policy provided. [*Stoll,* Unempl. Ins. Rep. (CCH) ¶ 10,135 (Ohio App. 2002)]

Strikers were held to be entitled to benefits after the date that permanent replacements were hired. (The employment relationship is severed when employees have been notified that they have been replaced, or their positions are permanently filled by someone else.) [*M. Conley Co.,* Unempl. Ins. Rep. (CCH) ¶ 10,186 (Ohio 2006)] School district employees were properly denied benefits during a work stoppage. When CBA negotiations reached an impasse, the employer implemented its best and final offer, which was not so unreasonable that employees would feel constrained to strike. Therefore, the work stoppage was a strike, not a lockout, and benefits were unavailable. [*Tietz,* Unempl. Ins. Rep. (CCH) ¶ 10,178 (Ohio App. 2005)] Laid-off union members who got a one-time special payment (representing holiday pay) under a strike settlement received "remuneration" and therefore were ineligible for benefits. They received a newsletter and a flyer from the union explaining that the payments could result in temporary ineligibility. [*Burns,* Unempl. Ins. Rep. (CCH) ¶ 10,181 (Ohio App. 2006); *Nicholas,* Unempl. Ins. Rep. (CCH) ¶ 10,172 (Ohio App. 2005)]

ERISA does not preempt a Texas law that forbids waivers of claims for unemployment compensation. [*Mitchell Energy & Dev. Corp. v. Fain,* 311 F.3d 685 (5th Cir. 2002) (former employees allegedly waived their right to receive unemployment benefits when they participated in a voluntary retirement program)] Benefits were granted to a part-time worker who took a leave of absence to complete the training required for his full-time apprenticeship. Leave was not voluntary because of the external persuasion applied. In any event, state law allowed benefits to continue during approved training programs. [*Voisin,* Unempl. Ins. Rep. (CCH) ¶ 9548 (Wis. Cir. Ct. 2005)]

[B] BAA-UC

The Department of Labor created a program called BAA-UC (BAA stands for Birth and Adoption) [20 C.F.R. Part 604], through a Notice of Proposed Rule-making at 64 Fed. Reg. 67972 (Dec. 3, 1999), finalized, without significant changes, at 65 Fed. Reg. 37209 (June 13, 2000). The program allowed new parents to receive unemployment benefits for a one-year period beginning with the week of birth or adoption, because they would be treated as being "able and available for work" during this time period. The DOL regulations gave states the ability to opt in to the program, but no state elected to do so.

A lawsuit [*LPA, Inc. v. Chao,* 211 F. Supp. 2d 160 (D.D.C. 2002)] challenged the BAA-UC program as inconsistent with federal law. Although the suit was dismissed on procedural grounds, it caused the DOL to re-think the program. After review, the DOL decided that the BAA-UC experiment was a bad decision and an invalid interpretation of the rules about availability for work. It would also put additional strain on already hard-pressed state unemployment insurance funds. Therefore, the DOL decided to terminate the experiment, publishing a Notice of Proposed Rulemaking for this purpose at 67 Fed. Reg. 72122 (Dec. 4, 2002).

[C] Disaster Unemployment and the JCWAA

One of the responses to the September 11, 2001, terrorist attack was a Department of Labor Interim Final Rule published in the Federal Register on November 13, 2001. [66 Fed. Reg. 56959-56962, taking effect as of that date]

A federal statute, 42 U.S.C. § 177(a), the Robert T. Stafford Disaster Relief and Emergency Assistance Act, establishes the Disaster Unemployment Assistance (DUA) program. Up to 26 weeks of benefits can be furnished after a major disaster declared by the President, for unemployment caused by that disaster for which no other benefits are available. DUA eligibility ceases when the state agency finds that unemployment is no longer directly traceable to the major disaster.

The DUA benefit is considered a UC benefit. It cannot exceed the maximum benefit payable under the state's UC law.

The November 2001 rule provides a definition of "unemployment as a direct result" of a major disaster [20 C.F.R. § 625.5(c)]—a term that was not previously defined. According to the Interim Final Rule, the DUA benefits are limited to the immediate result of the disaster itself, not more remote consequences of a chain of events that was started or made worse by the disaster. Examples of direct results are unemployment caused by damage to or destruction of the physical worksite, lack of access to the worksite because the government has ordered it closed, or lack of work and lost revenues caused to a business that got the majority of its income from the premises that were damaged, destroyed, or shut down. But "ripple effects" (for instance, if an office building is closed, workers who can't come in to work don't stop at a coffee shop for snacks) are not covered.

The Interim Final Rule gives, as an example of potential DUA beneficiaries, workers at airports (including restaurant and store employees and service personnel) closed by government orders. But workers at other airports would not be entitled, even if a decline in air travel resulted in job loss. DUA issues were prominent during the catastrophic hurricane season of 2005 (which will presumably set precedents for future natural disaster cases). *See* 70 Fed. Reg. 61,472 (Oct. 24, 2005) for extensions of the time to file for DUA benefits for persons affected by Hurricanes Katrina, Rita, and Wilma.

In addition to this federal law, some states have state "optional trigger" laws that let them provide a 13-week extended benefit period when the state unemployment rate hits 6.5%. Oregon and Washington were the only states that both had such a statute and had a high enough unemployment rate to kick it into operation. [Russell Gold, *Extending Benefits,* Wall Street Journal, March 13, 2001, at p. B8]

Part of the Job Creation and Worker Assistance Act of 2002 (JWCAA) [Pub. L. No. 107-147] is the Temporary Extended Unemployment Compensation Act. JCWAA § 202 gives the states the power to enter into an agreement with the U.S. Secretary of Labor under which the state provides temporary extended unemployment benefits to people who have used up their other unemployment benefits; for example, if they have received the maximum amount of benefits payable under state law, or their benefit year has expired. (The federal government reimburses the state for the temporary extended benefits that the state pays.)

A beneficiary's eligibility also requires having worked 20 weeks in the base year. The temporary extended unemployment benefit amount is the same as the unemployment benefit payable during the regular benefit year for a week of total unemployment. Temporary benefits can be paid starting in the week the state enters into the agreement with the Secretary of Labor. The program was originally scheduled to end as of January 1, 2003. It was extended to June 1, 2003 by P.L. 108-1 (which doesn't have a short title), and once again to December 31 by P.L. 108-26 (The Unemployment Compensation Amendments of 2003 Act"). However, that was the final extension, and the program ended December 2003. The Center for Budget and Policy Priorities estimated that in January 2004, 375,000 workers lost state benefits and did not qualify for additional federal benefits.

[D]   Case Law on Benefit Eligibility

The treasurer of a corporation (of which he was also a 25% shareholder) applied for UI benefits. The New Jersey Superior Court ruled that he was not unemployed at the point when the company stopped operating but had not yet dissolved or applied for bankruptcy protection. In this reading, UI benefits are not available to a 5% or greater stockholder as long as he or she holds corporate ownership or continues to own stock. [*Fernicola,* Unempl. Ins. Rep. (CCH) ¶ 8637 (N.J. Super. 2000)]

The question of who should be considered an employee arises in many contexts, including unemployment compensation. The UI system is for "employees," not independent contractors, so characterization is important. The Ohio Court of Appeals held that a delivery driver who subleased a truck from a trucking company was an employee and hence potentially entitled to benefits, because the company controlled his work schedule and maintained the truck, which had to be returned to a designated storage location at the end of the work shift. [*Toth,* Unempl. Ins. Rep. (CCH) ¶ 10,109 (Ohio App. 2001)]

The Illinois Supreme Court held in 2002 that installers who contracted with a carpet company were independent contractors, not employees. The installation was not performed in the usual course of the carpet company's business (purchasers could make their own arrangements for installation); the company did not supervise the installers at the worksite; the installers supervised employees of their own; and the installers were allowed to work for other companies, including competitors of the carpet company. [*Carpetland USA Inc.,* Unempl. Ins. Rep. (CCH) ¶ 8491 (Ill. Sup. 2002)] A nurse working under an intermittent employment contract was not entitled to benefits after the contract expired: A person who chooses to work under a fixed-term contract is not involuntarily unemployed when the contract ends. [*Brinkman,* Unempl. Ins. Rep. (CCH) ¶ 10,179 (Ohio App. 2005)]

Also note that, in *Economy Office Maintenance Inc.,* [Unempl. Ins. Rep. (CCH) ¶ 12,307 (N.Y. App. Div. 2002)] a company was held liable for additional unemployment insurance contributions, based on testimony from the company's president and secretary that in fact they had control over the workers, and agreements calling the workers independent contractors were not accurate.

In the view of the Arkansas Court of Appeals, benefits should have been granted to a person who was discharged for pleading "no contest" to a domestic violence felony. The charges did not harm the employer's interests, because they were not work-related. [*Baldor Elec. Co.,* Unempl. Ins. Rep. (CCH) ¶ 8501 (Ark. App. 2000)] According to Louisiana's District Court, providing a false Social Security number and false information about one's criminal record constitutes material misconduct. The job was coordinator of environmental health and safety, so the employer had the right to expect honesty and integrity, and the employer's work rules spelled out a zero-tolerance policy for document falsification. [*Sheppard,* Unempl. Ins. Rep. (CCH) ¶ 9043 (La. Dist. Ct. 2002)] Discharge for violation of the corporate e-mail policy (continuing to send e-mails with sexual content after a warning from the supervisor) is also based on disqualifying misconduct. [*Mercer,* Unempl. Ins. Rep. (CCH) ¶ 9042 (Iowa Dist. Ct. 2002)] Benefits were denied on the basis of disqualifying misconduct when a machinist used small amounts of scrap materials and a few minutes of time on the employer's machinery for a personal project without permission; the ALJ was wrong to say that the employer's interests were not substantially harmed. [*Doerfer Acquisition Co.,* Unempl. Ins. Rep. (CCH) ¶ 9051 (Iowa Dist. Ct. 2003)]

The Mississippi Court of Appeals denied benefits, on the grounds of disqualifying misconduct, to two claimants who participated in an unauthorized strike that violated the no-strike provision of their Collective Bargaining Agreement (CBA). [*Berry*, Unempl. Ins. Rep. (CCH) ¶ 8284 (Miss. App. 2001)] They were aware that the strike violated the CBA. They had used grievance procedures in the past; this time, they were too impatient to go through channels. A work stoppage that occurred after the employer told the union that it was changing the employees' health coverage was a lockout, not a strike, because the employer was the one who changed the status quo. It would have been futile for the union to request continued work, because there was no evidence that the employer would have allowed the union members to keep working. Therefore, the union members were entitled to unemployment benefits. [*Schott Glass Technologies Inc.*, Unempl. Ins. Rep. (CCH) ¶ 12,436 (Pa. Commw. 2003)]

A common finding is that a discharge for poor job performance does not constitute intentional misconduct; the mere fact that a worker's job performance can reasonably be described as negligent does not mean that the person was culpable, or intentionally disregarded the employer's interests. [*See, e.g., Harsco Corp.*, Unempl. Ins. Rep. (CCH) ¶ 8668 (La. App. 2002); *Kemper County Sch. Dist.*, Unempl. Ins. Rep. (CCH) ¶ 8289 (Miss. App. 2002)] The claimant's state of mind determines whether misconduct occurred: In a case in which a health care facility employee knew that the employer didn't want her to carry out a particular course of treatment on a patient, but she did so anyway, there was willful disregard of the employer's interests. [*South Central Rehabilitative Resources Inc.*, Unempl. Ins. Rep. ¶ 8479 (Mass. App. 2002)]

An individual who has a reasonable expectation of reemployment (absolute certainty is not required) will not be required to make a formal search for other work. [*Thomas*, Unempl. Ins. Rep. (CCH) ¶ 9510 (Wis. Cir. 2000)] The claimant, #2 on the seniority list of a unionized workplace where the Collective Bargaining Agreement stipulated recall on the basis of seniority, could reasonably expect to be called back to work when the workplace re-opened after it was purchased. So he could collect unemployment benefits in the interim, even if he didn't make a job search.

Benefits were denied to a person who quit to get a higher-paid job, then was laid off from that job: The offer of higher pay elsewhere is not good cause to leave a job, because the first employer is not at fault. [*Total Audio-Visual Systems, Inc.*, Unempl. Ins. Rep. (CCH) ¶ 8484 (Md. App. 2000)] But ending a relationship with a temporary placement agency in order to accept a full-time permanent job constitutes good cause for quitting temporary work. [*Duby*, Unempl. Ins. Rep. (CCH) ¶ 8896 (Fla. App. 2000)] Benefits could therefore be granted after the loss of the permanent job.

It was a voluntary quit when a claimant left her job after receiving a number of warning letters from a supervisor; the claimant failed to follow the employer's grievance procedure. Not getting along with one's supervisor is not considered good cause to leave a job. [*Petersen*, Unempl. Ins. Rep. (CCH) ¶ 12,301 (N.Y. App. Div. 2002)] Benefits were denied to a claimant who walked off the job without trying to resolve a dispute with his employer after the dealership where he worked was reorganized. He was not asked to resign and could have kept his job. The general principle is that an employee who has a working-conditions problem must make a reasonable attempt to resolve it before quitting. [*Fisher,* Unempl. Ins. Rep. (CCH) ¶ 10,187 (Ohio 2006)] West Virginia held that benefits should not have been awarded to city workers who claimed that they quit because of workplace violence and harassment. The record showed that the city took adequate measures to protect their safety, so their resignation was a voluntary termination. [*Adkins,* Unempl. Ins. Rep. (CCH) ¶ 8793 (W.Va. App. 2006)] Benefits were also denied when a bus driver's license was suspended for failure to pay child support; he did not quit with good cause for a compelling reason, in that his license problems were the result of his own misconduct. [*Pollard,* Unempl. Ins. Rep. (CCH) ¶ 12,425 (Pa. Comm. 2002)]

Ability to work is another important criterion. The claimant in *Daniels* [Unempl. Ins. Rep. (CCH) ¶ 9022 (Iowa Dist. Ct. 2000)] was seven months pregnant when her doctor told her to find a job she could do sitting down. She worked as a blackjack dealer, required to stand for her entire seven-hour shift. Her employer put her on medical leave; unemployment benefits were denied because of her medically based inability to work.

In contrast, a truck driver was granted benefits in another Iowa case. [*Priority Express Inc.,* Unempl. Ins. Rep. (CCH) ¶ 9026 (Iowa Dist. Ct. 2000)] Her work-related back injury required her to drive a vehicle with an automatic transmission. The employer transferred her from the only route that had a truck she could drive. The district court treated her leaving the job as justified by the employer's refusal to accommodate her disability-related needs.

As the ADA chapter shows, both parties must participate in the process of accommodation. The Washington Court of Appeals denied benefits to a claimant who developed sensitivity to the chemicals used in his job. The employer moved him to a job in an outside tunnel, but the problems continued. The company's HR director suggested that he seek accommodation under the ADA, but he quit instead. Benefits were denied because he failed to exhaust all reasonable alternatives before leaving the job. [*Woods,* Unempl. Ins. Rep. (CCH) ¶ 9022 (Wash. App. 2000)]

Even if there is no statutory bar to duplicate benefits, unemployment benefits cannot be paid at the same time as Worker's Compensation benefits—because one is premised on the ability to work, the other on *inability* to work. [*Ballard,* Unempl. Ins. Rep. (CCH) ¶ 8594 (Ind. App. 2000)]

Benefits were denied for misconduct in the case of an employee who, after three warnings for sleeping on the job, was found asleep in a parked truck. [*DeMaria,* Unempl. Ins. Rep. (CCH) ¶ 12,279 (N.Y. App. Div. 2001)]

[E] Cases Involving Drugs

In a 1998 Missouri appellate case, a truck driver was fired after failing a drug test. The employer said that benefits should be denied because he was fired for good cause. The truck driver's argument was that the report from the drug testing lab was hearsay and not admissible. The employer's contention was that the law of evidence provides a hearsay exception for documents kept in the course of business. But the trial court agreed with the fired employee, because the record was prepared in the course of the lab's business, not the trucking company's. But when the case was appealed, the employer prevailed: Anybody's business records can be introduced, as long as they were made in the normal course of business, they were made close enough to the event to be reliable, and there are other reasons to consider them reliable. [*Associated Wholesale Grocers v. Moncrief,* 970 S.W.2d 425 (Mo. App. 1998)]

An employer's policy called for termination of any employee found with a detectable level of alcohol or illegal drugs. The plaintiff of *Smith v. Zero Defects Inc.* [132 Idaho 881 (1999)] tested positive for amphetamines in a random test, although he did not appear to be impaired at that time. Several states (Idaho, Nebraska, Nevada, Oklahoma, and Utah) consider violation of an employer's zero-tolerance policy to be misconduct serious enough to rule out benefits. In these states, off-duty drug use can be serious enough to prevent the user from receiving unemployment benefits. But Arizona, Kansas, Oregon, and Washington require evidence of workplace impairment.

The Oregon Court of Appeals said that it was not disqualifying misconduct for an employee to refuse when the employer ordered him to take a drug test on his own time, without compensation, after being written up for insubordination. [*Andrews,* Unempl. Ins. Rep. (CCH) ¶ 8878 (Or. App. 2000)] The court held that the employer's policy of requiring a drug test after all reprimands was not reasonable in cases where there was no evidence of drug use.

In Pennsylvania, however, off-duty misconduct that does not affect job performance is not considered willful misconduct that will rule out unemployment benefits. [*Navickas v. UCRB,* 787 A.2d 284 (Pa. 2001)] Benefits were allowed for a worker who was fired from a nursing home for off-duty marijuana use. The Pennsylvania Supreme Court acknowledged that the dismissal was perfectly proper, but because the drug use did not affect the employee's work, it did not constitute willful misconduct. [*Burger v. UCRB,* 569 Pa. 139, 801 A.2d 487 (Pa. 2001) In 2006, however, the Idaho Supreme Court ruled that a claimant who failed a drug test was properly denied benefits after he was fired. He violated the employer's valid, and clearly communicated, expectation that there would be a drug-free workplace. [*Desilet,* Unempl. Ins. Rep. (CCH) ¶ 8499 (Idaho Sup. Ct. 2006)]]

§ 32.03   CALCULATION OF BENEFITS

[A]   Basic Calculation

The actual benefit depends either on the claimant's average weekly wage, or the wage earned in the quarter of the base period when wages were highest. For partial weeks of unemployment, a reduced benefit is available, although the various states use different calculation methods.

Individual claimants are usually assigned a 52-week "benefit year," beginning when the claim is filed, although some states use the same benefit year for all claimants. Usually, a one-week waiting period is imposed before benefits become payable. Most states limit the payment of basic benefits to 26 weeks, although a few states permit 30 weeks of payments. Once claimants use up the basic benefit, they must wait until the next benefit year before starting another base period and therefore qualifying for unemployment benefits all over again. So someone who receives benefits in a particular benefit year will have to be re-employed and work for at least a second base period before qualifying for a second benefit period.

Extensions to the basic benefits are available under appropriate circumstances. The Employment Security Amendments of 1970 created a program of Federal-State Extended Benefits, covering benefits during weeks 27–39 of a spell of unemployment. Some states (Alaska, California, Connecticut, Hawaii, Minnesota, Oregon) have state-funded extended benefits programs that do not receive federal funding.

[B] Benefit Offsets

Benefit offsets may be applied in two situations: if the unemployment benefit is reduced because other income is received, or if the UI benefits offset other amounts that the person would otherwise be entitled to receive.

As noted above, payments (e.g., pension, IRA) reduce entitlement to unemployment compensation if they can be traced to work done by the employee in the past. The offset is applied only to a plan maintained or contributed to by the company that was the employer during the base payment period, or the employer that is chargeable with the unemployment claim. So if the pension was earned at Company A, but the worker became unemployed while working for Company A, pension will not offset the unemployment insurance benefit.

States differ in their treatment of rollovers. Some states (e.g., New York and North Carolina) require a reduction of unemployment benefits because of rollovers; the other states do not. The Department of Labor's interpretation is that rollovers should not reduce unemployment benefits, but each state is permitted to set its own unemployment rules; this is not an exclusively federal area of regulation. [*See* Dori R. Perrucci, *When Pension and Unemployment Checks Don't Mix,* New York Times, Jan. 13, 2001, at p. Bus8] Furthermore, reduction is necessary only for amounts based on the claimant's own past work history, not when a person receiving benefits gets a distribution as a surviving spouse.

A New York case [*Sokolowski,* Unempl. Ins. Rep. (CCH) ¶ 12,280 (N.Y. App. Div. 2001)] holds that benefits should not have been reduced to zero on account of the pension paid by the employer. The pension was based on years of service and wages in the employee's high-five years, but that period occurred before his unemployment insurance base period. The employee did accrue service credit after being laid off, but that was not employment during the base period either. In contrast, the Florida Court of Appeals treated a back pay award from NLRB proceedings as "earned wages," so the claimant had to repay unemployment benefits that were previously awarded. [*Ching,* Unempl. Ins. Rep. (CCH) ¶ 8913 (Fla. App. 2001)]

In the view of the Illinois Court of Appeals, a claimant was unemployed and therefore entitled to receive benefits because the Incentive Stock Options he was entitled to receive from his employer did not constitute remuneration. Unexercised, unvested options have only a speculative value and are not wages. Furthermore, the option grant was dependent on approval from the corporation's Board of Directors, which was not granted. [*Hmelyar,* Unempl. Ins. Rep. (CCH) ¶ 8498 (Ill. App. 2003)]

About half the states deny unemployment benefits in weeks in which Worker's Compensation benefits are also received, or consider the Comp benefit income that reduces the benefit. (There is also a question of whether someone whose condition is bad enough to justify Comp benefits is "ready and able" to work even if he or she wants to work.)

Vacation pay also generally offsets unemployment benefits although an exception might be made if the claimant is deemed to be on vacation involuntarily rather than choosing to take time off.

Back pay awarded in a Title VII case generally is not reduced by UI. However, some courts, like the Second Circuit, say that courts that hear Title VII cases have discretion to reduce the award to account for UI received.

§ 32.04   EXPERIENCE RATING

[A]   Determination of Rating

The unemployment insurance rate that employers pay to help fund the system is partially based on their "experience" (the number of claims against them). The more claims, the higher the insurance rate. Seasonal businesses in particular often have a regular pattern of laying off workers who rely on UI until they are rehired.

For 2006, tax rates range from 0 (the minimum under the laws of many states, after all credits have been taken into account) to 10% or more in Massachusetts, Michigan, Pennsylvania, and Tennessee for employers with a large amount of unemployment claims. Maximum benefits vary greatly from state to state (e.g., $220/week in Alabama, $778/week in Massachusetts). [Table of 2006 All-State Tax Rates, Unempl. Inc. Rep. (CCH) ¶ 3000A; a chart of *Significant Provisions of State Unemployment Insurance Laws* as of January 2006 appears at ¶ 3001]

The standard rate is 5.4%, although many employers qualify for a more favorable experience rate because of their record of few discharges and layoffs.

The treatment of new employers varies from state to state. Some states impose a higher initial rate, until the employer can demonstrate its compliance with filing and payment requirements and its low experience of unemployment. On the other hand, some states have a special low rate for new employers until and unless they demonstrate bad claims experience. Some states even allow a zero rate (no tax at all) on employers with especially good claims experience. But all employers may become subject to the standard rate, and perhaps even additional "subsidiary contributions" if the state as a whole has a high unemployment rate and consequently has a low balance in its UI fund.

There are four basic methods of experience rating:

- Variations in payroll over time (showing whether the workforce has increased or decreased);
- Reserve ratio;
- Benefit ratio;
- Ratio of benefits to wages.

Some states use hybrid methods. States often permit joint filing and risk pooling: joint payment by a group of employers who get a combined experience rate for the group as a whole. A further refinement is a distinction between "charging" and "noncharging" claims. Some claims are not charged against the last employer's experience rating: for instance, claims for very brief periods of unemployment, or cases where the employee spent very little time working for the last employer. In some states, the employer is not charged for benefits paid after a period of disqualification based on voluntary quitting or misconduct, or when benefits are terminated because of the claimant's failure to seek suitable work. The rationale is that employers should not be penalized for circumstances beyond their control.

Another question is whether all employers in the base period, or only the last one in the series, will be charged with the claim. If more than one employer is charged, they might be charged with the most recent employer charged first, or the charge might be divided proportionate to the amount of wages they paid during the base period.

"SUTA dumping," to avoid the federal State Unemployment Tax Act, is the practice of transferring employees from a unit with high turnover (which increases unemployment tax liability) to one with low turnover, then eliminating the first unit and creating a new unit for further transfers. According to Kelly Services, the practice began in the mid-1990s, but was fairly rare then because the economy was booming; it gained attractiveness after the 2001 stock market crash. [Michael Schroeder, *Tax Dodge Faces Extinction*, Wall Street Journal, Aug. 4, 2004, at p. A4] Congress considered this practice such a threat to the soundness of the unemployment insurance system that it passed legislation, the SUTA Dumping Prevention Act of 2004, P.L. 108-295. To receive federal unemployment insurance grants, the states must pass laws that penalize SUTA dumping no later than mid-2006. By June 2005, all the states had submitted draft legislation to the Department of Labor. [*See* Congressional Research Service, *SUTA Dumping*, report RS 22069 (May 27, 2005)]

[B] Collateral Estoppel

Two related legal doctrines, collateral estoppel and res judicata, may come into play in contesting unemployment claims. An employer's unsuccessful contest of one worker's claim could harm the employer in later lawsuits. Legal advice is required as to the comparative risk of letting a claim go through without opposition (which will increase the employer's experience rating and therefore its rates) or contesting the claim but losing and being at a disadvantage when similar claims are made later.

The doctrine of res judicata refers to a matter that has already been tried. If one court has already dealt with a case, a higher court may handle an appeal of the matter, but a different court, which is not in the same line of authority, will not decide a matter that has already been decided. The doctrine of res judicata applies only to the same legal issues and the same or closely related parties. So if one employee sues his or her employer for race discrimination, the defense of res judicata will not be available if a different employee sues another employer for race discrimination. But Employee A's suit against Company B may have "collateral estoppel" effect on Employee C's suit against Company B, because Employee A's suit involves decisions on some basic issues about Company B's policies.

Either side can use collateral estoppel. In a later court case, the employer says that the administrative decision proves that the employee was guilty of misconduct, so terminating the employee was not wrongful. [*See* Chapter 39 for wrongful termination suits] The employee might assert that having received unemployment benefits proves that he or she did not quit and was not guilty of misconduct. Usually, administrative decisions in an unemployment matter will be granted collateral estoppel effect—but some states say that only a court decision can have that effect.

[C] Planning Steps to Reduce Unemployment Tax Liability

The unemployment insurance system is designed to stabilize employment, so it penalizes employers who dislocate workers unnecessarily. Terminated employees often find it much easier to get a new job if their employment record indicates that they quit instead of being fired. Agreeing to treat the termination as a resignation can benefit both employer and employee, if the employer's experience rate stays low. But employees must understand the effect that the characterization of the termination will have on their UI application.

Benefits were not available to an employee who took a severance package that provided substantial compensation in exchange for the employee's agreement to resign. The severance package was the result of extensive negotiations, in which the employee was represented by an attorney, so it was clear that the employee understood the implications of the deal. [*Operadelaware,* Unempl. Ins. Rep. (CCH) ¶ 8226 (Del. Sup. 2001); *but see Baldwin,* Unempl. Ins. Rep. (CCH) ¶ 8787 (W.Va. Cir. Ct. 2005), holding that UI benefits are available to someone who participates in a voluntary severance program initiated by the employer, if the employer sets up a workforce reduction plan, and the claimant's separation from service resulted from lack of work.]

Companies can take various steps to reduce their experience rating and therefore their liability for unemployment tax:

- Understanding the nature and interaction of the federal and state payroll taxes;
- Reducing FUTA payments appropriately to compensate for state tax payments;
- Making sure taxes are paid when due;
- Reviewing state experience records for correctness;
- Understanding the experience rating system and the claims appeal procedure;
- Transferring employees within the organization instead of terminating them, to reduce unemployment claims;
- Analyzing operations to see if they could be made more consistent, less seasonal (thus avoiding layoffs and terminations);
- Firing unsatisfactory employees quickly, before they become eligible for benefits;
- Holding exit interviews with employees who quit, with a view to resolving problems that lead to resignations;
- Scheduling layoffs for Fridays, not earlier in the week wherever possible, because all the states provide benefits for partial weeks of employment;
- Maintaining adequate documentation of misconduct (which will also be useful if the terminated employee makes discrimination or wrongful termination claims);
- Monitoring all benefit claims and appealing claims that the company believes to be unfounded (e.g., employees who quit asserting involuntary termination).

Employers should also take prompt action, applying their own rules fairly and objectively. The Texas Court of Appeals, for instance, allowed benefits to be paid to an employee who was placed on indefinite suspension without pay 18 months after the first violation of the employer's rules, and 9 months after the last violation, because the employer failed to prove that the delay in discharge was reasonable. [*Morris III,* Unempl. Ins. Rep. (CCH) ¶ 8457 (Tex. App. 2001)] In a West Virginia case, benefits were barred for a time, but only for the period for simple misconduct. The claimant, who had already received four warnings for various infractions, was fired after leaving the work area without permission of her supervisor. The court said that she was not guilty of gross misconduct, because none of the warnings said she was at risk of being fired. [*Williams,* Unempl. Ins. Rep. (CCH) ¶ 8774 (W. Va. Cir. Ct. 2001)]

The laws of a number of states (Arizona, Arkansas, California, Colorado, Georgia, Indiana, Kansas, Kentucky, Louisiana, Maine, Massachusetts, Michigan, Minnesota, Missouri, Nebraska, New Jersey, New Mexico, New York, North Carolina, North Dakota, Ohio, Pennsylvania, South Dakota, Texas, Washington, West Virginia, Wisconsin) allow employers to make intentional overpayments of unemployment insurance taxes, resulting in a lower tax rate for the next tax period; sometimes the numbers work out so that a small voluntary contribution produces a large reduction in future liabilities. [Unempl. Ins. Rep. (CCH) Newsletter No. 540 (Mar. 28, 2005)]

§ 32.05   ADMINISTRATION AND APPEALS

Traditionally, states required in-person application for unemployment benefits, but as of November 2004, only six states did not have mechanisms for filing a claim remotely. Most states (29) allowed both telephone and Internet applications; 10 were telephone-only, and five were Internet-only. [GAO, *Unemployment Insurance: Better Data Needed to Assess Reemployment Services to Claimants*, <http://www.gao/gov/cgi-bin/getrpt?GAO-05-413>]

If and when an ex-employee applies for UI benefits, the employer is asked for the reason for the termination. The employer is given a certain number of days to contest the claim. Once this period elapses, the employer can no longer protest the granting of benefits. If the employer objects to the grant of benefits, the state agency that administers unemployment benefits will assess the matter. The decision can be appealed to an Administrative Law Judge, an administrative board, and finally through the state court system (the federal courts are not appropriate for these questions).

If the employer fails to meet its burden of proof about the employee's disqualification at the administrative hearing, the case will not be remanded to give the employer another chance—and a remand will probably not be granted to submit additional evidence, [*Holmes,* Unempl. Ins. Rep. (CCH) ¶ 8664 (La. App. 2001)] so it's important to prepare well for the initial administrative hearing.

§ 32.06   FUTA COMPLIANCE

[A]   Generally

Employers (but not employees) have an obligation to make payments under the Federal Unemployment Tax Act (FUTA) to fund the federal program of unemployment insurance. The federal FUTA tax rate is 6.2%, but this tax is imposed only on the first $7,000 of wages. The states set their own taxable wage bases.

Most employers actually pay a rate lower than 6.2%, because they qualify for a 5.4% credit for state employment taxes they have already paid. This is sometimes referred to as the "normal credit" or "90% credit." Sometimes the company will qualify for an even lower FUTA rate if its experience rating is good. The additional credit equals the difference between the basic state rate of 5.4% and the employer's actual experience rate. However, the full credit can be claimed only in states that the Department of Labor certifies as compliant with federal requirements. To qualify for the full credit, the employer must make all state contributions by January 31 (the due date for Form 940).

The employer reports its FUTA liability on IRS Forms 940 or 940-EZ. The short form can be used by any employer (no matter how many workers it employs) that makes unemployment tax contributions to only one state, in which all wages subject to FUTA are also subject to the state tax, and the state taxes are paid no later than the due date for the federal form. However, some states exempt the pay of corporate officers from state unemployment tax—so, in those states, the short form cannot be used. *See* IRS Tax Topics Topic 759 for an explanation of depositing FUTA taxes and filing Form 940 or Form 940EZ. [<http://www.irs.gov/taxtopics/tc759.html>] If FUTA liability is greater than $500 for any of the first three quarters of the year, deposits have to be made quarterly. If the FUTA amount for the fourth quarter, plus undeposited amounts from earlier quarters, is more than $500, a deposit is required by January 31 of the following year; otherwise, the employer can either make the deposit or pay the amount with the Form 940 or 940-EZ by January 31. Deposits can be made either with Form 8109, the Federal Tax Deposit Coupon, or through the Electronic Federal Tax Payment System (EFTPS).

[B] Other Tax Issues

The Supreme Court decision, *United States v. Cleveland Indians Baseball Co.*, [532 U.S. 200 (2001)] holds that for FICA and FUTA purposes, if a case is settled through back pay payments to employees, the funds are taxed in the year the wages are actually paid—and if rates have increased over time, the later payment date means that higher rates apply.

Recipients of unemployment benefits can direct the state to withhold federal and/or state income tax from the benefits. [*See* Pub. L. No. 103-463, also known as GATT (General Agreement on Taxes and Tariffs) or the Uruguay Round Agreements Act]

IRS Private Letter Ruling 9525054 deals with a corporation's contributions to a trust that provided benefits linked to receipt of state UI benefits. The IRS ruled that the payments were not wages for FICA or FUTA purposes. Income tax withholding was not required. The tax treatment was the same even for employees who received benefits from the fund when they were ineligible for state unemployment benefits, e.g., before the waiting period had expired; because they didn't have enough wage credits; or they had exhausted the state benefits. Benefits from the trust became taxable wages if, when they added to all other remuneration including the state UI benefit, the total was greater than the worker's weekly pay earned during employment.

A SESA's claim for reimbursement of a bankrupt company's unemployment compensation liability gets priority as an "excise tax" in the company's Chapter 11 proceeding. Worker's Compensation, in contrast, is not treated as an excise tax, because the Comp system offers opportunities for private insurance that are absent in the UI context.

WORKER'S COMPENSATION

§ 33.01   INTRODUCTION

The states administer the Worker's Compensation (WC) system to provide income to individuals who are unable to work because of employment-related illnesses and injuries. WC benefits, like unemployment insurance benefits, are funded by insurance maintained by the employer.

In 2003, the cost of WC coverage accelerated. The Insurance Information Institute reported that the average cost was up 50% in three years. In California, the cost had approximately doubled. Special legislative sessions were convened in Florida, Washington State, and West Virginia to examine cost-saving mechanisms. The rapidly rising costs were blamed on the aftereffects of a price war, as insurers strove to make up for the effects of earlier rate cuts (as well as investment losses in the poor stock market climate in the early 2000s). The number of claims has declined significantly—down 36% in the past decade—but explosive increases in medical costs have led to near-doubling of average medical costs per claim, to an average of $15,300 nationwide, and $35,201 in California. The premiums paid to state pools, for those who cannot get private insurance, almost quadrupled between 1999 and 2003, reaching $1.2 billion in the later year. [Joseph B. Treaster, *Cost of Insurance for Work Injuries Soars Across U.S.*, New York Times, June 23, 2003, at p. A1]

Employers' costs (including premiums, deductibles, and administration costs) for WC went up 9.6% between 2002 and 2003, even though the number of covered employees actually declined, because insurance premiums rose. In 2003, employers' total WC-related costs were about $80.8 billion. Cash benefit payments to injured workers rose 3.2%, reaching $54.9 billion in 2003. Fewer compensable injuries were reported in 2003 than in 2002, although the injuries tended to be more costly. [News item, *Workers' Comp Costs Increase Nearly 10%*, Wall Street Journal, July 22, 2005, at p. A2]

The WC system balances the interests of employers and employees: the employees' need for continuing income; the employer's need to have claims resolved quickly, in an administrative system that is not prone to make large sympathy awards the way the jury system is. Employers have a duty to make a prompt report of all accidents to the agency that administers the WC system. If an employee claims job-related injury or illness, the claim is heard by a WC tribunal. Depending on the state, this may be referred to as a board or a commission. The tribunal decides if the claim is valid. If so, benefits are awarded: reimbursement of medical expenses, plus weekly income.

WC benefits do not begin until a waiting period (typically three–seven days) has elapsed. This serves to distinguish genuine temporary disability from minor incidents without lasting consequences. However, most state WC laws also provide that, if a disability continues for a period of time (set by the state at anywhere from five days to over seven weeks), retroactive payments dating back to the original date of the injury will be granted.

The weekly benefit is usually limited to half to two-thirds of the pre-accident wage, subject to fixed minimum and maximum payments (often keyed to the state's average income) and also subject to an overall limitation on payments. In some states, additional payments are available if the worker has dependent children—especially in cases where the work-related incident caused the death of the worker. A burial benefit is also paid in death cases. Depending on the state it ranges between $1,000 and $5,000.

The March 2005 New York case of *Valentine v. American Airlines* [17 A.D. 3d 38 (3d Dept. 2005)] denies Worker's Compensation death benefits to the registered domestic partner of a flight attendant who died at work in November of 2001. The partners owned a home, had joint accounts, and designated one another as executors and beneficiaries. The court upheld the Worker's Compensation Board's ruling that the survivor was not a surviving spouse because there was no legally valid marriage, finding that the restriction of Worker's Compensation survivor benefits to legal spouses was rationally related to the state interest in processing benefit payments efficiently.

In 1999, the Supreme Court decided a Worker's Compensation case, *American Manufacturers Mutual Insurance Co. v. Sullivan.* [526 U.S. 46 (1999)] Under Pennsylvania's WC Act, once liability is no longer contested, the employer (or its insurer) has an obligation to pay for all reasonable or necessary treatment. However, an insurer or a self-insured employer is permitted to withhold payment for disputed treatment pending utilization review by an independent third party. The plaintiffs in this case sued state officials, WC insurers and a self-insured school district for civil rights and Due Process violations charging that their benefits had been withheld without notice, depriving the employees of a property right.

The Supreme Court held for the defendants. In the court's analysis, private insurers carrying out utilization review are not "state actors" subject to the Due Process Clause of the Constitution. Employees only have a property right after the treatment has been found reasonable and necessary. Therefore, the insurer has no obligation to notify employees, or to hold a hearing, if it withholds benefits until review has been completed and a decision made in the employees' favor.

§ 33.02   CLASSIFICATION OF BENEFITS

[A]   Type and Degree of Disability

If the initial tribunal accepts the contention that the worker is genuinely disabled, and the disability is in fact work-related, benefits are awarded based on the type and degree of disability.

There are four categories:

- Permanent total disability;
- Permanent partial disability;
- Temporary total disability;
- Temporary partial disability.

Permanent disability payments can be based on wage loss, earning capacity, physical impairment, or some combination. A "schedule injury" is loss of a finger, toe, arm, eye, or leg. The schedule determines the number of weeks of benefits payable for such an injury. Death benefits are also available to the survivors of persons killed in work-related incidents. For injuries such as back strains related to lifting, the tribunal must make a case-by-case determination of the number of weeks of disability that can be anticipated, and the seriousness of the disability.

Benefits can be granted for either "disability" or "impairment." The difference is that disability is defined to mean loss of wages, whereas impairment is permanent partial disability that does not cause wage loss.

The concept of Maximum Medical Improvement (MMI) comes into play in the case of a temporary disability. MMI is a doctor's opinion that there is no reasonable medical probability of further improvement in function (as determined based on factors such as current and proposed treatment, history of improvement, and pre-existing conditions). Most states impose an obligation on the employer to notify the employee that MMI has been reached, and the employee is likely to lose benefits within 90 days unless he or she returns to work or finds other employment. Benefits can be extended past the MMI if the claimant makes an honest effort yet cannot find suitable work.

In addition to making wage-based payments, the employer must provide the employee with reasonable and necessary medical treatment, continued as long as the injured employee's medical condition requires. Most states include chiropractic in the definition of medical care. Many include home health attendants as well.

Tip: Sometimes, entitlement to WC is suspended during any period of time when the tribunal has ordered, or the employer has requested, a medical examination that the employee refuses. But protective state laws require confidentiality of information not related to the case. These laws also permit the employee to bring his or her own doctor to the examination, and permit the employee to see the examination report.

[B] Compensable Injuries

Whether an incident is covered by WC depends on several factors:

- Whether the injured person is a common-law employee rather than an independent contractor. Early in 2002, California ruled that even a hirer of an independent contractor can be liable to the contractor (or employees of the contractor) if, for example, the hirer provides unsafe equipment or makes another affirmative contribution to the injury—merely controlling safety conditions at the site is not enough to impose liability. [*McKown v. Wal-Mart*

Stores Inc., 27 Cal. 4th 219, 38 P.3d 1094, 115 Cal. Rptr. 2d 868 (2002); *Hooker v. DOT,* 27 Cal. 4th 198, 38 P.3d 1081, 115 Cal. Rptr. 2d 853 (2002)]

- Top managers may be denied benefits on the theory that they are the corporation's alter ego rather than ordinary employees. Under New York law, if a corporation has only one or two executive officers who are the sole stockholders and hold all the corporate offices, they are deemed to be included in the Worker's Compensation insurance contract unless they opt out. But if they do opt out, that also eliminates the corporation's coverage for third-party claims arising out of injuries to the officers, under the employer liability part of the Worker's Compensation policy. (One of the co-owners of the business was seriously injured while working as a subcontractor; he sued the hiring company, the general contractors, and the owners of the property where he was working.) [*Continental Insurance Co. v. New York,* 99 N.Y.2d 196, 782 N.E.2d 1145, 753 N.Y.S.2d 9 (2003)]

- Whether the injury arises out of employment (illness or damage that could have happened to anyone, employed or not, is not covered under WC);

- Whether the injury arose in the course of employment (not during the commute to work or during horseplay).

In an Illinois case, benefits were denied for an at-work ankle injury suffered by an employee who hitched a ride on a forklift. The injury was not deemed work-related (he was on his way to the break room to pick up his lunch). Furthermore, the employer had an adequately publicized policy against riding double on forklifts, because they are not designed to carry passengers safely. [*Saunders v. The Industrial Comm'n,* 189 Ill. 2d 623 (Ill. Sup. 2000)]

A plant operator died in a one-car accident when he was driving his personal vehicle to work. His job responsibilities included travel inside and outside the state and being on call to make repairs. He chose to get a monthly travel allowance and mileage payments for his own vehicle instead of driving a company truck. Although accidents during commuting are usually not compensable, an exception is made when the employer involves itself by providing transportation or reimbursing employee travel expenses. Therefore, the employee's widow was entitled to compensation, but only in the minor amount of $7,000. [*Phillips v. Epco Carbon Dioxide Prods. Inc.,* 810 So. 2d 1171 (La. App. 2002)]

The Washington Court of Appeals found that a "drive-through lane" between the roadway on the employer's property and the sidewalk next to the workplace was not a "parking area" (injuries occurring in parking areas are excluded by many state WC systems). It was a temporary loading zone, and picking up a paycheck is a work-related activity, so an employee was entitled to WC benefits when she slipped and fell on ice and snow in the loading zone. [*Madera v. J.R. Simplot,* 104 Wash. App. 93 (2001)]

Sometimes injuries occurring outside the workplace will be covered—e.g., if the employer sent the employee to make a delivery or perform an errand, and the injury occurred in that place or en route. Injuries occurring during employer-sponsored athletics, or at a company picnic or holiday party, are probably compensable. Injuries on company premises during scheduled breaks are probably compensable, but employees take unscheduled breaks at their own risk because such injuries are considered to occur outside working hours. If employees are engaged in work-related tasks, injuries occurring at home can be compensable. [*A.E. Clevite, Inc. v. Tjas,* 996 P.2d 1072 (Utah App. 2000) (worker who became a paraplegic when he slipped while salting down his driveway so it would be safe for the expected delivery of a work-related package)]

Whether an incident is covered by WC may also depend on:

- Whether the injury results from an "accident" (an unexpected occurrence that can be linked to a definite time, place and occasion);
- Whether there is any reason that removes the injury from statutory coverage (e.g., the employee's substance abuse was a significant causative factor). The Arkansas Supreme Court reversed the lower court, for instance, finding that testimony that a carpenter smelled of alcohol at the time of his fall from a roof was enough to trigger the statutory presumption that the accident was caused by substance abuse, even though the hospital staff did not perform a blood alcohol test that would yield results that could be introduced into the record. [*Flowers v. Norman Oaks Construction,* 341 Ark. 474 (2000)]

One of the most vital factors is the employer's degree of control over the employee's activities. A Missouri case [*Leslie v. School Servs. & Leasing Inc.,* 947 S.W.2d 97 (Mo. App. 1997)] holds that a job applicant injured during training had not become an "employee," and therefore was not covered by WC. In this case, the potential employer didn't require her to take the training, didn't control her activities during the training process, and in fact didn't even guarantee her a job if she completed the training successfully.

In 2004, the New Jersey Supreme Court ruled that injuries occurring during a recreational or social activity can come under WC provided that the employee believed that he or she was required to engage in the activity. (In this case, the plaintiff was injured after being urged by the employer to drive a go-cart, despite his statement that he did not know how to drive.) The court's ruling was motivated by a belief that otherwise the employee would be excluded from WC in situations where the employee refused the employer's direction (and therefore was insubordinate); the court noted that the employer holds most of the power in the situation. [*Lozano v. De Luca Construction Co.,* 178 N.J. 513; 842 A.2d 156 (N.J. Super. Ct. App. Mar. 2004). Note that N.J.S.A. § 34:15-7 allows payment of WC benefits for recreational injuries sustained through activities that are a regular incident of employment and produce benefit for the employer over and above improved employee fitness and morale]

At-work assaults raise difficult questions. The general rule is that injuries caused by assaults are compensable if the job increases the risk of encountering dangerous people (e.g., convenience store clerks are at risk of being robbed). But if the assault occurred for personal reasons, for instance if an abusive spouse commits an assault at the victim's workplace, the fact that the assault occurred at work will not necessarily render the injury a compensable one, if it is not work-related in any way. The WC system is essentially a no-fault system, so it will not be necessary to decide if the employer was at fault in not having a better security system.

Schmidt v. Smith [155 N.J. 44, 713 A.2d 1014 (1998)] says that bodily injury caused by sexual harassment is covered by the employer liability section of the Worker's Compensation insurance policy, because this section of the policy is designed to make funds available to compensate employees for their work-related injuries, even those for which Worker's Compensation payments are not available.

The Pennsylvania Supreme Court, without really exploring the policy issues, upheld a lower court's determination to uphold an award of Worker's Compensation benefits to an illegal alien, on the grounds that the employer did not show that the injured person failed to satisfy the requirements of a section of the Worker's Compensation Act. However, if the employer applies for suspension of such benefits, the employer does not have to make a showing of job availability. [*Reinforced Earth Co. v. WC Appeals Board (Astudillo),* 810 A.2d 99 (Pa. 2002)] However, compare this with *Granados v. Windson Development Corp.* [257 Va. 103, 509 S.E.2d 290 (1999)], which holds that an alien who was hired after submitting forged immigration documents could not become a lawful employee entitled to Worker's Compensation, because no employment contract could be formed.

In mid-2005, the Eleventh Circuit ruled that an allegation that an employer hired illegal workers as part of a conspiracy to reduce wages and cut the number of WC claims stated RICO and state-law claims. [*Williams v. Mohawk Indus. Inc.*, 411 F.3d 1252 (11th Cir. 2005). Certiorari was granted in December 2005, but the case was never heard: certiorari was dismissed as improvidently granted in June 2006, and the case was remanded to the Eleventh Circuit: No. 05-465 (June 5, 2006).

Although the federal immigration law IRCA (8 U.S.C. § 1101 et seq.) preempts state and local laws that impose criminal sanctions for employing ineligible aliens, it does not include preemption language covering state WC laws. The purpose of the WC Act is remedial and humanitarian, not penal. Because it does not impose penalties for employing aliens, there is no conflict with IRCA.

According to the California Court of Appeals, Congress has not occupied the field of WC law, so state laws are preempted only if there is an actual conflict created by the state law's impairment of enforcement of the federal law. California's response to *Hoffman* was to enact a law making immigration status relevant with respect to reinstatement of undocumented employees and denial of recovery of back pay to individuals ineligible for rehiring. It is also a crime to make knowingly false or fraudulent material representations to receive WC benefits. However, even a person who used fraudulent documents to obtain employment can receive WC as long as the person has not been convicted of document fraud and nexus ran between using the documents and being hired, not using the documents and the injury. [*Farmers Brothers Coffee v. Workers' Compensation Appeals Board and*

Ruiz, 133 Cal. App. 4th 533 (Cal. App. 2005). The principle that a person convicted of violating California Ins. Code § 1871.4 by making knowingly false or fraudulent material representations to get WC benefits is debarred from receiving WC comes from *Tensfeldt v. Workers' Comp. Appeals Bd.*, 66 Cal. App. 4th 116 (1998)]

If the incident is covered, the next question is whether WC exclusivity applies. [*See* § 33.03]

[C] Problems of Co-Employment

There are many reasons for employers to use temporary, contingent, part-time, or leased workers. In some cases, employee leasing results in lower WC costs. For employers who do not self-insure, the insurance rate has a lot to do with past experience. The smaller the workplace, the greater the impact that a few claims—especially a few very large claims—will have on its experience rating. That is one of the motivations for using leased workers to replace some or all of a company's common-law employees. [*See* § 1.09 for more about employee leasing]

Although a large leasing company will not qualify for small business dis-counted rates, a leasing company can offer the services of a broad range of workers, some in low-risk occupations such as office work.

In its initial years, a leasing company will probably qualify for low rates, because there has not been enough time for many accidents to happen. Abuses of the system are possible, if companies dissolve and re-form to manipulate their experience rates. Just for this reason, some states (e.g., Arizona, California, Colorado, Florida, Nevada, New Hampshire, New Mexico, Oregon, South Carolina, Texas, and Utah) disregard the presence of leasing companies, and still require the underlying employer to buy WC insurance and maintain its own experience rating.

Furthermore, state courts may decide that the leasing company or temporary agency's client is the actual employer, because it has real control over the worker's activities and therefore is legally responsible for compensation for injuries. Both companies might also be treated as co-employers.

Another possibility is that, if the underlying employer takes the position that the leasing company is the true employer, the underlying employer might be treated as a third party that can be sued for tort claims and cannot assert WC exclusivity. The underlying employer might be sued for negligence or for violating established safety rules, and might be forced to pay damages (including punitive damages). Nor would the employee's WC benefits be used to offset the underlying employer's liability in this situation.

The National Association of Insurance Commissioners (NAIC) has drafted an Employee Leasing Registration Model Act under which leasing firms must register with the state before they purchase WC insurance. At the time of registration, they must disclose their ownership and their past WC history. Registration will not be permitted if the company has had its insurance policies terminated in the past for failure to pay premiums.

A laborer who worked for Southern Personnel died after incurring injuries at Compression Coat, a pipe coating facility. Compression Coat paid weekly invoices to Southern Personnel for staffing costs, including WC insurance. Because another Southern Personnel employee died in a similar accident, Southern's WC insurer refused to provide insurance at the Compression Coat facility. Southern transferred all its employees to C.L. Management, which leased them back to Southern. C.L. got lower WC rates than Southern could have.

After the laborer's death, his family sued Southern and Compression Coat for wrongful death and survivor benefits. Compression Coat said that it was his special employer, Southern said it was immune from tort suit because it was his general employer. The plaintiffs identified C.L. Management as his employer. The Louisiana Court of Appeals dismissed the suit against Southern, because either it was his employer and immune from tort suit or it was not his employer and therefore owed him no duty. Compression Coat was also exempt, as a borrowing employer. [*Pradia v. Southern Personnel of Louisiana Inc.,* 776 So. 2d 474 (La. App. 2000)]

In a less drastic case, a worker was injured when he fell into an uncovered floor drain. He received comp benefits from his employer, the Stanley Jones Corporation, which was a subcontractor of Haskell Co. The injured person sued Haskell for personal injuries, based on a Kansas statute that relieves the principal contractor of responsibility for providing WC when the subcontractor obtains the coverage. The Kansas court said that the contractor is still the statutory employer, and therefore immune from tort suits. [*Robinett v. The Haskell Co.,* 12 P.3d 411 (Kan. 2000)]

Under the "last injurious exposure" rule, a claimant's last employer is fully responsible for a work-related injury that could have caused disability while working for that employer. In a 2002 Oregon case, the claimant was an equipment operator who had spent 15 years using jackhammers, chain saws, and grinders. Prior to that, he had been a combat soldier in Vietnam. He filed a comp claim for a hearing aid. The trial court ruled against him, attributing the hearing loss both to work and to military service—so he would only be entitled to benefits if the military service was considered employment. But, in a decision that will be very relevant as veterans who have served in Iraq return to the workforce, the Oregon Court of Appeals ruled that being a soldier is employment because the soldier is under the control of the military, subject to implied contracts about the rights of service members. Because both types of employment placed the claimant at risk of hearing loss, the civilian employer was required to provide the hearing aid under the last injurious exposure rule. [*In the Matter of Compensation of Fordice/Wallowa County v. Fordice,* 181 Or. App. 222, 45 P.3d 963 (Or. App. 2002)]

[D]   How the WC System Handles Disease Claims

WC benefits are also available if an employee develops a work-related disease. However, occupational diseases create some difficult problems of analysis. Disease is covered only if there is a close connection between onset of the disease and the work environment. This is fairly clear for "brown lung" disease and cotton mills, but more difficult if the claim is that nonsmoking employees have been harmed by cigarette smoke exhaled by customers and co-employees who smoke.

Depending on the state, benefits may also be available if workplace conditions aggravate a disease that the individual already had. In California, Florida, Kentucky, Maryland, Mississippi, North Dakota, and South Carolina, WC benefits will be available but will be reduced to compensate for the pre-existing condition. If, for instance, the worker's condition was 25% due to workplace factors, 75% due to the preexisting condition, only 25% of the full benefit will be payable.

Occupational disease creates difficult questions involving "long tail" claims: claims made on the basis that it took years, or even decades, for the symptoms caused by occupational exposure to hazardous substances to manifest themselves. During this long period of time, the employee could have held several jobs (involving exposure to different hazards) and/or engaged in behavior such as smoking that is hazardous or compounds other hazards.

The general rule under the legal system is that claims are timely if they are filed within a reasonable time after the individual first experiences disability or symptoms, and could reasonably be expected to draw a connection between work exposure and illness.

Another question is whether the employee's exposure was extensive enough to trigger the claimed symptoms. The epidemiology (disease pattern) for similar exposures should be studied to see if the employee's alleged experience is typical. Furthermore, one disease claim by an employee could trigger a wave of related claims from other employees who actually are ill, believe themselves to be ill because they have developed psychosomatic symptoms, or who just hope for easy money.

Asbestos-related disease is "bodily injury by disease" rather than "bodily injury by accident" under WC and employer liability insurance policies. Asbestos exposure is not an accident because it is not violent and because it develops over a latency period rather than right away. [*Riverwood Int'l Corp. v. Employers Ins. of Wausau,* 420 F.3d 378 (5th Cir. 2005)]

Repetitive stress injuries, such as carpal tunnel syndrome caused by use of computer keyboards, raise difficult issues. In a way, they have aspects of both disease and injury.

The Nebraska Supreme Court granted benefits to a secretary who claimed cumulative trauma injury to her neck and shoulder. The court ruled that three factors are required for compensability: an unexpected or unforeseen event; objective symptoms; and "sudden or violent" onset of the symptoms. The court said that onset can be sudden or violent even if the injury does not occur instantaneously and with force—as long as there is an identifiable point in time when it does occur, requiring cessation of work and medical treatment. The secretary did require medical treatment and did become unable to work, so her RSI claim was sustained. [*Fay v. Dowding, Dowding & Dowding,* 261 Neb. 216 (2001)]

The South Carolina Court of Appeals granted benefits in a carpal tunnel syndrome case, ruling that it was an "injury by accident" (and not, as the employer claimed, an occupational disease) even though it had a gradual rather than a distinct onset. [*Pee v. AVM, Inc.,* 344 S.C. 162 (S.C. App. 2001)]

After an insurance company acquired another company and computerized its offices, a claims representative's caseload went from 100 to 130 cases a month to 150 to 200 a month. He had to work 70- to 75-hour weeks, including extensive computer work that he found distasteful. He developed coronary artery disease. His treating physician identified the disease as stress-related, and said the claims representative should not work more than 40 to 45 hours a week. He sued his employer for medical expenses and disability benefits. Although the trial court awarded him benefits on the basis of 30% physical impairment of the body as a whole, the Court of Civil Appeals reversed in mid-2002, on the grounds that there was no proof that he suffered anything worse than ordinary job stress. Nor did he prove by clear and convincing evidence that his heart condition was caused by a materially excessive risk from employment. [*Safeco Ins. Cos. v. Blackmon,* 2002 Ala. Civ. App. LEXIS 496 (Ala. Civ. App. May 31, 2002)]

In 1975, a nurse's assistant suffered a needlestick. She did not discover until much later that she had been infected with hepatitis-C. Twenty-three years after the accident, she applied for Worker's Compensation, but was denied because the claim was far too late under the applicable two-year statute of limitations for occupational disease or infection. The injury was the initial needlestick, not the diagnosis. [*Young v. Cross County Hosp.,* No. CA01-1208 (Ark. App. May 1, 2002)]

[E] Psychological Injuries

By and large, the WC system deals with palpable physical injuries and diseases, although in some circumstances mental and emotional illnesses can be compensable. Emotional and mental injuries are analyzed in three categories:

- Mental-physical—physical impact of mental conditions, such as chest pains and high blood pressure;
- Physical-mental—such as suffering a phobia after being involved in an accident or developing "AIDS-phobia" after a needle-stick incident;
- Mental-mental—injuries with no physical component.

In all the states, mental-physical and physical-mental injuries are compensable as long as a causal connection between the two is established. Compensability of mental-mental injuries is less clear-cut. Some states, including Alabama, Florida, Georgia, Kansas, Minnesota, Montana, Nebraska, Ohio, Oklahoma, and South Dakota refuse to compensate cases where there is no demonstrated physical involvement. In the other states, it may be necessary to prove a connection to a severe, unpredictable event, and compensability may depend on whether the onset was gradual or sudden.

A Wyoming case holds that it is not a violation of the constitutional guarantee of equal protection for a WC system to impose a higher standard of proof for mental than for physical injuries. [*Frantz v. Campbell County Mem. Hosp.*, 932 P.2d 750 (Wyo. 1997)]

According to the New York Supreme Court, suicide can be compensable, even if the worker suffered from pre-existing depression, as long as a work-related injury was at least a contributing cause of the suicide. [*Altes v. Petrocelli Elec. Co.*, 270 A.D.2d 767 (N.Y. Sup. 2000)]

In the past few years, Pennsylvania has decided a number of interesting cases relating to mental-mental injuries. In early 1999, a mental injury award was upheld for an employee who was falsely blamed for theft because the employer's records were inaccurate. The plaintiff underwent so much stress that she was unable to work and was institutionalized in a mental hospital. [Danielle N. Rodier, *Mental Injury Wins Rare Comp*, National Law Journal, Mar. 1, 1999, at p. B2]

In May 2000, the Pennsylvania Supreme Court ruled that the burden of proof is the same for mental-mental as for mental-physical claims—the claimant must prove that the injury arose out of abnormal working conditions. Oppressive behavior by a supervisor, if extreme enough, can constitute abnormal working conditions. In one case, the claimant's pre-existing depression was exacerbated; in the other, the supervisor physically touched and pushed the employee who was being accused. [*See* Tracy Blitz Newman, *PA High Court Raises Bar on Workers' Comp. Mental/Physical Claims*, The Legal Intelligencer (May 22, 2000) (law.com); Danielle N. Rodier, *Run-Ins With Screaming Supervisors Can Be Abnormal Working Conditions*, The Legal Intelligencer (June 2, 2000) (law.com)]

Post-traumatic stress disorder can be either an accidental injury or an occupational disease for WC purposes. According to two New Jersey cases from 2003, the statute of limitations for filing a claim does not begin to run until the worker either knows or should have known that he or she sustained a compensable injury. Therefore, the two suits were permitted to proceed even though they were filed after the two-year statute of limitations for accident claims had run. If the facts of the case justify characterizing the worker's situation as both disease and injury, the worker can file both claims. In the unusual circumstance in which an unexpected traumatic event results in a latent or insidiously progressive injury, the "accident" does not occur for WC purposes until a reasonable person would be alerted that a compensable injury had occurred. [*Brunell v. Wildwood Crest Police Dep't*, 176 N.J. 225; 822 A.2d 576 (N.J. 2003); *Stango v. Lower TWP Police Dep't*, 172 N.J. 359; 798 A.2d 1272 (N.J. 2003)]

§ 33.03   WC EXCLUSIVITY

The WC system gives employers the protection of "worker's compensation exclusivity"; in other words, in the normal work-related injury or illness case, the employee's only remedy against the employer is to collect compensation benefits.

Tort lawsuits are not permitted. However, exclusivity applies only against the employer. If the employee is injured by a product manufactured by the employer, the employee can sue the employer in its capacity as manufacturer. Suits against other manufacturers, or non-employer parties responsible for hazardous conditions at the workplace, are also a possibility. The employer itself can sue the third party in order to recover the medical benefits that the employer provided on behalf of the employee.

WC is essentially a no-fault system, so negligence by any party is usually irrelevant. However, in some states, a worker's failure to use safety equipment can reduce (but not eliminate) the benefits that would otherwise be payable after an accident. Sometimes, the employer's wrongdoing will take the case out of WC exclusivity. Some (but not all) courts would allow an ordinary tort suit against an employer that deliberately concealed information about workplace hazards.

Compensation benefits will be granted only if the employee has medical evidence to prove the connection between the job and the disabling condition. Furthermore, the employee must be incapacitated by the condition, so benefits will not be awarded to a person who stoically continues to work despite pain. Courts have reached different conclusions as to whether a person is permanently and totally disabled only if there is absolutely no job he or she can perform, or whether "human factors" such as job availability within a reasonable commuting distance must be considered.

In a 1999 Pennsylvania case, one worker made a deliberate false claim that another worker threatened "to bring a gun in here and kill somebody." The police took the employee who was supposed to have made the threat to a mental hospital. After an interview with a psychiatrist, she was released. She sued the employer for defamation, claiming severe emotional distress. The employer claimed WC exclusivity because defamation is an intentional tort causing emotional distress. But the employee was permitted to maintain the defamation lawsuit, on the theory that WC deals with physical or mental injuries, whereas defamation deals with damage to reputation. [*Urban v. Dollar Bank,* 725 A.2d 815 (Pa. Super. 1999)]

For WC purposes, rape and robbery committed at a workplace by an unknown assailant are considered "accidental workplace injury." Therefore, according to *Melo v. Jewish Board of Family & Children's Servs. Inc.* [N.Y. L. J., Feb. 8, 2000, at p. 29, col. 3] WC exclusivity applies, and the victim does not have the right to bring tort claims against the employer.

Virginia denied WC exclusivity as to claims such as negligent hiring brought by an employee who was assaulted by a co-worker. The employer allegedly was aware at the time of hiring that the perpetrator had been convicted of rape; however, the assault did not arise out of employment, did not further the employer's business, and was directed against the victim personally. [*Butler v. Southern States Cooperative,* 270 Va. 459 (Va. 2005)]

An insurance agent charged she was subjected to 18 months of sexual harassment by her immediate supervisor. She quit her job and was treated for psychological injuries including depression, suicidal ideation, sleeping and eating disorders, and panic attacks. She sued her ex-employer for violations of state civil rights law and intentional infliction of emotional distress. Three months later, she applied for Worker's Compensation on the basis of psychological disability. She was awarded $415 a week temporary total disability and 425 weeks of permanent partial disability at $155 a week. The employer paid about $40,000, then applied for dismissal of the civil rights case on the grounds of exclusivity. The Kentucky Supreme Court ruled that, although there is a WC exception for injuries inflicted through the deliberate intention of the employer, so civil rights suits are not ruled out entirely, the plaintiff must elect between WC benefits and a discrimination suit. Therefore, accepting the WC benefits ruled out an attempt to seek redress of the same injuries in another forum. [*American Gen. Life & Accident Ins. Co.*, 74 S.W.3d 688 (Ky. Sup. 2002)]

In a Florida case [*Turner v. PCR, Inc.*, 754 So. 2d 683 (Fla. Sup. 2000)] one worker died and one was seriously injured in an explosion that occurred while they were mixing chemicals. The plaintiffs asserted the intentional tort exception to WC exclusivity. This requires proof either of the employer's deliberate intent to injure, or conduct that a reasonable fact-finder would consider substantially certain to result in injury or death. The case was allowed to go to trial, because the employer concealed the hazards of the mixing process, did not provide training or safety equipment, and was aware of the risks because there had been three similar explosions in the previous two years.

Two men were severely burned when flammable vapors were ignited. The injured persons and their families sued the parent company of the company that owned and operated the factory where they worked. In the plaintiffs' view, the parent company was a responsible third party because it caused the dangerous condition that led to the injuries. The First Circuit held that to sue a parent company, the employee must establish that the parent company (either expressly or by implication) assumed primary responsibility for workplace safety. The employee has the burden of presenting specific facts to show such an express or implied duty. In this case, the First Circuit ruled that the parent company did not assume the safety responsibility. [*Mendez-Laboy v. Abbott Laboratories Inc.*, 424 F.3d 35 (1st Cir. 2005)]

The Texas Supreme Court ruled that a worker can have more than one "employer" for WC exclusivity purposes. Therefore, a temporary staffing provider was entitled to summary judgment in a case where the temporary staffing provider sent the plaintiff to a factory job where she was injured while operating a stamping machine. The worker received WC benefits under the factory's WC coverage, and sued the service provider for negligence and failure to train and supervise her, warn her about the dangers, or provide a safe workplace. She also sued the factory. The trial court ruled that she was the factory's borrowed employee (because of its right to direct and control her work), and that WC exclusivity applied. At the first appeal, the Court of Appeals said that a person can have only one employer for WC purposes; but the appeal to the Supreme Court produced the ruling that both a leasing company and its client are entitled to assert WC exclusivity. Under the

Texas Labor Code's definition of co-employment, if a staff leasing company elects to provide WC for both itself and its client company, its policy covers both as to the leased employees. When the owner of premises secures WC coverage for its general contractor and the contractor's subcontractor, WC exclusivity prevents a negligence suit by the subcontractor's employees against the general contractor. [*Wingfoot Enters. v. Alvarado,* 111 S.W.3d 134 (Tex. 2003)]

The First Circuit tackled questions about WC exclusivity arising where the employer was involved in a series of mergers, but the employee's job status was unaffected. The plaintiff alleged that defects in a press before the merger caused his injuries, and his claim against the successor was based on its status as successor to the company that owned the allegedly defective press. He also alleged that the predecessor company knew that the press was defective, but did not repair or disclose the defects. The plaintiff's legal theory was that this products-related liability is independent of the WC obligation, and the changes in the employer's corporate structure eliminate the normal barriers to tort suits brought by injured employees. The First Circuit ruled that once the plaintiff had already been compensated under Massachusetts WC law, tort claims were barred. To the court, the key question was whether, without the mergers, the plaintiff's former employer would have been liable to the plaintiff. Because it would not be, the current employer was immune. A merger makes the surviving corporation liable for the obligations of the companies that merged into it—but also allows the surviving corporation to inherit WC immunity unless there is a separate duty to the claimant outside the employment relationship. [*Braga v. Genlyte Group Inc.*, 420 F.3d 35 (1st Cir. 2005)]

WC exclusivity was found in a California case. [*Gunnell v. Metrocolor Laboratories Inc.*, 112 Cal. Rptr. 2d 195 (Cal. App. 2001)] Employees were hurt when the employer removed warning labels, told employees that a hazardous chemical was safe and failed to provide safety equipment. A case of criminal battery would not have been WC exclusive, but here the employer did not use physical force or violence against employees.

The question in a 2003 Eighth Circuit case was whether the rubber mixer that injured the two plaintiffs who were trying to repair it was a fixture on the defendant's real property or a dangerous chattel. At first, the plaintiffs sued in state court on a products liability theory, claiming that the stop-pin in the machine was defective. The defendant asserted WC exclusivity. The plaintiffs refiled their suit, adding a claim that the defendant failed to warn them or remove or screen off the danger. The Eighth Circuit concluded that the mixer was a fixture, because it was so adapted to the place where it was used that it became a part of the land. Under (Missouri) state law, a landowner is not liable for injuries to employees of independent contractors working on the property, because the price charged to do work includes WC coverage for the contractor's employees. The employees were clearly covered by WC and were not entitled to use a premises liability theory to recover against the defendant. [*Mouser v. Caterpillar, Inc.,* 336 F.3d 656 (8th Cir. 2003)]

Claims brought by uranium plant workers against the plant's fuel supplier and three operators of the plant were dismissed. Although the workers were not informed about the dangerous radioactive substances they were exposed to (substances that are well known to cause cancer), the plaintiffs did not have any existing clinical symptoms of disease when they sued. The Sixth Circuit pointed to Worker's Compensation as the exclusive remedy. The exception did not apply, because although dangerous conditions were permitted to exist, there was no intent to harm the workers. [*Rainer v. Union Carbide Corp.*, No. 03-6032 (6th Cir. Mar. 8, 2005), file name: 05a0112p.06; *Moore v. Environmental Constr. Corp.*, 147 S.W.3d 13 (Ky. 2004) (even wanton negligence does not constitute intentional conduct)]

A TPA refused to authorize the patient's own doctor to operate on her to treat a work-related injury. She charged that the doctor they did authorize operated on the wrong part of her spine. She sued the TPA for medical malpractice, battery, and intentional infliction of emotional distress, but her claims were dismissed. The Florida Court of Appeals ruled that a TPA is entitled to the same WC immunity as an employer or insurer (that is, WC exclusivity applies), and there was no reason to rule out exclusivity, because the TPA had no intent to injure the plaintiff. [*Protegrity Services Inc. v. Brehm*, 2005 WL 320704, Fla. App. Feb. 11, 2005]

A New Jersey employee was sent to Minnesota by his employer to work in a call center. He and a co-worker were driving back to their hotel in the co-worker's rented car when they were involved in a crash with a UPS van. The injured employee sued UPS, the UPS driver, and his co-worker. New Jersey law says that someone is still in the "course of employment" when required to be away from the regular workplace when he or she is in direct performance of duties assigned or directed by the employer. In this case, the Eighth Circuit treated travel to and from the hotel as part of working away from the usual base of operations and thus a direct performance of job duties. [*Cahalan v. Rohan*, 423 F.3d 815 (8th Cir. 2005)]

Although, in general, injuries incurred when going to and returning from work are not covered by WC, the District of Columbia has a "traveling employee" exception that makes WC exclusive for injuries of a person for whom travel is integral to the job. However, relocating to accept a new assignment does not make a person a "traveling employee." For example, an employee who was sent to the Philippines for a two-year assignment, was kidnapped after eating dinner on a day off from work. After three weeks of imprisonment and torture, including having a portion of his ear cut off, the employer paid the ransom and he was released. Although he worked under an employment contract in which job-related injuries were only covered by WC, the DC Circuit ruled that his injuries were not work-related, nor were they a reasonable and foreseeable part of the work. He therefore could sue the employers for negligence and intentional infliction of emotional distress. [*Khan v. Parsons Global Servs. Ltd.*, 428 F.3d 1079 (D.C. Cir. 2005)]

A Texas man experienced a work-related back injury requiring surgery. His insurer denied coverage for the antibiotic prescribed to control post-surgical infection. Without the antibiotic, he developed an infection that required hospital-ization and two more operations. He sued the insurer for breach of contract and other wrongdoing. Although the insurer claimed that the plaintiff was required to exhaust his administrative remedies under the Worker's Compensation system, the Fifth Circuit disagreed. The insurer was wrong in refusing to provide a drug that was a necessary part of the treatment of what even the insurer admitted was a compensable injury. The plaintiff had no duty to exhaust administrative remedies after being denied a benefit that did not require pre-authorization under the terms of the plan. [*Gregson v. Zurich Am. Ins. Co.*, 322 F.3d 883 (5th Cir. 2003)]

A mentally disabled person was injured during an assignment on a church clean-up crew; his arm was broken when he attacked another disabled worker and was restrained by a supervisor. Rather than pressing a WC claim, he brought suit in tort against his employer, the Rocky Mountain Job Opportunity Brigade (RMJOB). (The tort claims involved misrepresentation that the job site was safe and appropriate for mentally disabled workers and violation of state standards for treatment of the developmentally disabled.) RMJOB's liability insurer settled with the injured worker. RMJOB tried to get its WC carrier to participate in the settlement negotiations; however, the WC carrier's position was that the injured person lacked the mental capacity to enter into an employment contract, and therefore could not be an "employee." The WC carrier obtained summary judgment at the trial level, and the Tenth Circuit affirmed, because the WC carrier owed no duty to defend RMJOB or contribute to its settlement; there is no duty to defend where there is no possibility of a judgment to be indemnified.

To avoid WC exclusivity, potential employee-plaintiffs often seek to assert that they were not employees at the time of the injury or that the injury occurred outside the course of employment. The question is significant to insurers if WC and general tort are covered by different policies, and one insurer tries to involve the other when liability is unclear.

In this case, the Tenth Circuit concluded that the disabled person could not seek WC benefits, so RMJOB could not have been held liable for WC benefits— the only thing that the WC insurer covered. The Tenth Circuit also concluded that the majority of courts have ruled that a WC insurer has no duty to defend a state-court tort suit where there is an allegation that a WC claim that should have been filed was not filed. [*Carolina Cas. Ins. Co. v. Pinnacol Assurance*, 425 F.3d 921 (10th Cir. 2005)]

§ 33.04   ALTERNATIVES FOR INSURING WC

[A]   Types of Available Insurance

Depending on state law and the employer's own financial status and risk category, there are several ways to cope with the obligation to provide benefits for injured employees.

- Buying insurance from a state-run fund that is the sole source of WC coverage within the state;
- Buying insurance from a commercial carrier. Nearly all privately purchased policies will follow the form of the "standard policy"—the Worker's Compensation and Employers' Liability Policy developed by the national Council on Compensation Insurance (NCCI);
- Buying insurance from a state fund that competes with commercial carriers;
- Self-insurance (most employers who take this option combine it with third-party administration, reinsurance, or both);
- Insurance through a captive insurer owned by the employer;
- Participating in an assigned risk pool (depending on circumstances, this can be either mandatory or voluntary).

The Supreme Court ruled in mid-2006 that in the context of Chapter 11 bankruptcy, premiums owed to a WC insurer are not unpaid contributions to an "employee benefit plan" and therefore are not accorded priority under 11 U.S.C. § 507(a)(5). [*Howard Delivery Serv. Inc. v. Zurich American Ins. Co.*, No. 05-128 (June 15, 2006) <http://laws.lp.findlaw.com/us/000/05128.html>]

[B]   State Funds

The states of North Dakota, Ohio, Washington, West Virginia, and Wyoming have monopolistic state funds, i.e., all covered employers have to buy their coverage from the fund. Until July 1, 1997, Nevada was in this category, but now it maintains a state fund but allows private coverage.

The states that have competitive state funds (i.e., the employer chooses whether to purchase coverage from the state funds or a private insurer) are Arizona, California, Colorado, Idaho, Louisiana, Maine, Maryland, Michigan, Minnesota, Montana, New Mexico, Nevada, New York, Oklahoma, Oregon, Pennsylvania, Rhode Island, Texas, and Utah. State funds set their own rates, which can be low because the fund has very low marketing expenses.

Texas allows employers to self-insure for WC, but they must be careful to provide benefits at least roughly comparable to the benefits that would be available under an insured plan. In *Reyes v. Storage & Processors Inc.* [995 S.W.2d 722 (Tex. App. 1999)], the court said that employers cannot require arbitration of claims for work-related injuries if the benefits they provide are substantially less generous than Comp benefits.

The employers involved in *Lawrence v. CDB Services, Inc.* [44 S.W.3d 544 (Tex. Sup. 2001)] and *Lambert v. Affiliated Foods* [20 S.W.3d 1 (Tex. Sup. 2001)] were nonsubscribers to the Texas WC Act. Employees were offered a plan of disability, dismemberment, and death benefits, but participants in the plan had to waive the right to bring either common-law or WC suits against the employer. Their only remedy was to pursue their benefits under the plan. The cases came to court when two employees who had signed waivers claimed the waivers were unenforceable because they were against public policy. The Texas Supreme Court said that the WC Act does not rule out pre-injury waivers like these; that the plan did not shift the risk of injury unfairly to workers—in fact, the plan provided immediate and certain benefits in exchange for the waiver of the right to sue in a case which might never arise. The court did not accept the public policy argument, because the WC statute does not explicitly ban such waivers.

[C] Assigned Risk Pools

In any situation in which people or organizations have a legal obligation to maintain insurance coverage, some of them will not be insurable under normal underwriting standards. Assigned risk pools are created to issue coverage. In the WC context, the NCCI administers the National Worker's Compensation Reassurance Pool. It covers about 25% of all employers, making it the largest single WC insurer in the United States.

This WC assigned risk pool has some unusual features. Commercial insurers have to support it by paying "residual market assessments" of approximately 14 cents on every premium dollar they receive. But because of this heavy assessment, commercial insurers are less willing to grant discounts to their insurable customers, thus driving more employers to see the assigned risk pool as an attractive alternative.

[D] Self-Insurance and Captive Companies

In all the states except North Dakota and Wyoming, employers who satisfy certain criteria (e.g., being financially capable of paying all WC claims that arise in the course of operations; posting bond or establishing an escrow) can elect to self-insure.

Tip: Self-insurance is considered a privilege. It can be revoked by the state if an employer fails to file the necessary reports, does not maintain the required amount of excess insurance, or otherwise fails to keep up its end of the bargain. A change in corporate ownership might also lead to revocation of the privilege, even if the corporate structure remains the same.

In practice, self-insurance is practical only for very large companies with six- or seven-figure WC premium obligations; about one-third of the WC market is now self-insured because some economic giants have taken this option.

More than half the states impose a requirement that self-insured companies maintain reinsurance (excess coverage). It is prudent for companies to do this even if it is not required. Self-insured employers generally must show that they have arranged for claims administration, employee communications, and safety programs. These functions are usually performed under a Third Party Administration (TPA) arrangement. An effective TPA should have 24-hour-a-day claims service;

low turnover (experienced representatives do a much better job than novices); a high proportion of employees who have obtained professional certification in loss control; quick settlement of claims; and a low average final cost per claim.

In a pure self-insurance arrangement, the employer sets up reserves and pays all WC claims from these reserves. In a group arrangement, several companies join forces. Each one is jointly and severally liable for all Comp claims within the group. Most of the states permit group self-insurance; nationwide, there are over 250 group self-insurance pools. In a limited self-insurance arrangement, the employer is responsible for the Self-Insured Retention (SIR), which is roughly equal to a deductible, and excess insurance pays the rest.

Excess coverage can be written on a per-occurrence or per-loss basis, covering an aggregate amount for the year or per accident per payment year. (The payment year is a relevant concept because the consequences of an injury might extend over several years.) Specific excess insurance limits the employer's liability for claims for any occurrence where the exposure exceeds the SIR. Aggregate excess insurance copes with the possibility of a bad year. The employer has to pay the amount in the aggregate retention or loss fund. This is usually expressed as a percentage, such as 125%, of the reinsurance premium for the year. Aggregate excess coverage usually stops at $1 million or $2 million, so the employer will be at risk once again if the exposure is greater. Specific excess insurance is both easier to obtain and less expensive than aggregate insurance.

To self-insure, the company must file an application with the state (this typically costs $100–$1,000). The employer may have to post a letter of credit as security, and the lending bank will impose fees. Excess insurance and TPA fees each costs about 8–13% of the amount that would otherwise be the WC premium. States also impose taxes on self-insurance arrangements—about 1–4% of the premium that would have been charged by an insurer, incurred losses, or paid losses.

Working through a captive insurance company (one that does business only with a company that is its sole shareholder, or a small group of cooperating companies) is another option. The advantage of this arrangement to the employer is the ability to keep the underwriting income (deposits that are the equivalent of premiums, plus investment income), but the company will also have to pay the expenses of the captive insurer.

[E] High-Deductible Plans

A high-deductible plan combines features of both insurance and self-insurance. To reduce its premiums, the employer agrees to accept a higher deductible. Usually, it falls between $100,000 and $1 million, but policies are available with deductibles up to $5 million. Any employer can purchase a high-deductible policy. Unlike self-insurance, there are no financial qualifications imposed by the state.

When a claim is made under a high-deductible plan, the insurer pays the full claim, then bills the policyholder for payments made that fell within the deductible. Bills are usually sent on a monthly basis. Employers who buy high-deductible policies are generally required to create an escrow fund equal to about three months' potential loss payments, and must submit a letter of credit in an amount equal to the deductible. At the end of the first year of high deductible coverage, the letter of credit is adjusted upward or downward to reflect experience. Paid losses are billed until all claims have been closed. The high-deductible insurer may require indemnification or a hold-harmless agreement offering remedies against the employer if, for instance, legislation is passed subjecting the insurer to increased losses that fall within the deductible.

§ 33.05   SETTING THE WC PREMIUM

There are 600 industry classifications, each identified by a four-digit number. An employer's basic WC premium is the "manual rate" for its industry classification. The manual rate is the average cost of WC coverage for the classification, based on the number of claims in the past three years for injuries serious enough to cause lost work time. The rate is sometimes expressed as a percentage of total payroll, but is usually defined as a number of dollars per $100 of payroll. Large employers may qualify for premium discounts, because the administrative expenses are fairly similar for policies of all sizes.

The manual rate is only one factor in setting an individual employer's rate. Experience rating (the employer's actual claims experience for the previous two years) can increase or decrease the base premium that will be imposed in the future. States can also adopt retrospective rating, under which past losses are used to adjust the premium already charged for a particular year, so that either the employer is entitled to a refund or will have to make additional payments.

WC policies have both general inclusions, which recur in many industries (for workers in employee cafeterias, and repair and maintenance crews, for instance) and general exclusions that are written out of ordinary industry classifications (for instance, construction activities performed by employees; running an employer-operated day care center).

§ 33.06   BAN ON RETALIATION

Nearly all the states have passed statutes making it illegal to retaliate against an employee, either specifically for filing a Worker's Compensation claim or for filing any "wage claim" or "wage complaint," a broad category that includes WC. The states are Alabama, Arizona, California, Connecticut, Delaware, Florida, Hawaii, Idaho, Illinois, Indiana, Kansas, Kentucky, Louisiana, Maine, Maryland, Mississippi, Michigan, Minnesota, Missouri, Montana, New Hampshire, New Jersey, New Mexico, New York, North Carolina, North Dakota, Ohio,

Oklahoma, Rhode Island, South Carolina, South Dakota, Texas, Vermont, Virginia, Washington, West Virginia, Wisconsin, and Wyoming.

Even in the minority of states that do not have a statute, it is very likely that courts will treat retaliatory discharge as an illegal violation of public policy.

Discharge is not the only employment action that can give rise to retaliation charges: A retaliatory demotion, that results in a pay cut, is also wrongful, and can give rise to a lawsuit. [*Brigham v. Dillon Cos. Inc.,* 935 P.2d 1054 (Kan. Sup. 1997)]

The Washington State case of *Warnek v. ABB Combustion Engineering* [137 Wash. 2d 450 (1999)] permits an employer to refuse to rehire employees who made WC claims against the same employer in another state. In this reading, the anti-retaliation statute applies only within a state, not inside it. The court also drew a distinction between refusing to rehire and discrimination during employment or discharge. Only discrimination is unlawful.

However, not all employees can use the state courts to bring claims of retaliatory discharge. According to the First Circuit, if the workplace is unionized, § 301 of the Labor-Management Relations Act preempts a claim that the employee was not rehired after a period of disability because the employer retaliated against her for filing a WC claim. The court deemed the claim preempted because the "management rights" clause in the collective bargaining agreement gave management the sole right to hire and fire. Therefore, assessing the validity of the retaliation claim requires interpretation of the CBA, and therefore § 301 comes into play. [*Martin v. Shaw's Supermarkets Inc.,* 105 F.3d 40 (1st Cir. 1997)]

In contrast, the Eighth Circuit's 1995 decision is that an employee's claim of unlawful retaliatory discharge cannot be removed from state to federal court, because state remedies are not preempted in that situation. The Eighth Circuit did not believe that deciding the case required interpretation of the CBA. [*Humphrey v. Sequentia Inc.,* 58 F.3d 1238 (8th Cir. 1995). *See* § 30.02[D] for further discussion of LMRA § 301]

Also see 28 U.S.C. § 1445(c), which says that civil actions "arising under" state WC laws cannot be removed to federal court. But there is an exception for suits alleging "deliberate injury," which can be removed to federal court. According to the District Court for the District of West Virginia, a retaliatory discharge case arises under WC and therefore belongs in state, not federal, court. [*Thorne v. Wampler Foods,* 111 F. Supp. 2d 744 (N.D.W.V. 2000)]

The Ninth Circuit ruled that it is not retaliation to fire a worker for lying about previous occupational injuries on a questionnaire. Although the state's Right to Privacy in the Workplace Act forbids employers to ask prospective employees if they have ever filed a Worker's Compensation claim, it is permissible to ask about previous occupational injuries, time lost from work because of work-related injuries, or medical treatment for those injuries, even though it wouldn't be difficult to extrapolate from those disclosures that a Comp claim had been filed. [*Carter v. Tennant Co.,* 383 F.3d 673 (9th Cir. 2004)]

The Eighth Circuit upheld summary judgment for the employer in the case of a plaintiff who charged that she was fired for exercising her rights under the state

Worker's Compensation Act and the FMLA. The plaintiff had carpal tunnel syndrome when she was hired as a sonographer, a job that required gripping the machine for 95% of the work day. Her doctor said that her symptoms were work-related, but did not place restrictions on her ability to function. After she filed a WC claim, the employer ordered that she be examined by the employer's doctor, who restricted her ability to work and suggested light gripping only and less than 15 minutes' gripping per hand per patient (which, the plaintiff said, was insufficient to do her job). The Eighth Circuit view is that the ban on WC retaliation exists in the context of at-will employment. If the employee's compensable condition prevents him or her from being capable of performing the job, then termination is based on the inability to work, not on having filed a WC claim. [*Bloom v. Metro Heart Group of St. Louis, Inc.*, 440 F.3d 1025 (8th Cir. 2006)]

§ 33.07   ADMINISTRATION OF WC

[A]   Generally

In most states, employers are required to participate in the WC system (although Texas and New Jersey allow private employers to opt out of the system entirely, as long as they notify the Compensation Commission and their employees that they have left the system). The tradeoff is that injured employees have the right to bring tort suits against employers who are outside the WC system, whereas in most cases workers who are injured in a WC-covered workplace will not be allowed to sue the employer.

Some states allow employees to opt out of WC coverage as long as they do so in writing, within a reasonable time after starting a new job, and before any accident or injury has occurred. Corporate officers are often given the option of leaving the WC system.

In about a third of the states, the state itself runs the WC fund. Those states give employers three choices for handling their responsibilities:

- Pay into the state fund;
- Buy insurance from a private carrier;
- Self-insure by maintaining a segregated fund that contains enough money to handle the expected compensation claims.

In states with no state fund, employers can either buy insurance or self-insure.

The insurance premium depends on the level of risk: A coal mine is much more likely to have occupational injury claims than a boutique. The nationwide average premium is about 2.5% of compensation.

The general rule is that employees are obligated to notify the employer within a short time (usually about five days) after an injury or the onset of an illness. Employers should encourage reporting, because such information is needed for WC and other purposes (OSHA reports, improving safety conditions).

Lack of prompt notice of claim can eliminate an injured person's chance of recovery. In a mid-2002 Alabama case, the injured person told her treating doctor that her injury was not work-related, and she was on non-WC disability leave for nearly six months. The employer notified her that she would be fired if she failed to return before the end of the six months. She did not return, was fired, and filed a WC suit. She said that she concealed the true work-related nature of the injury because she wanted to return to work and wanted to be able to choose her own doctor. Her case was dismissed—a person who chooses not to notify the employer and not to file a timely Comp claim (giving the employer the chance to manage the claim or raise any defenses it has) cannot collect benefits. [*Mid-South Elec. Co., Inc. v. Jones,* 2002 Ala. Civ. App. LEXIS 925 (Ala. Civ. App. June 7, 2002)]

In some WC systems, the employer notifies its WC insurer, which then files the report. In other systems, the employer (whether it has insurance or is self-insured) is responsible for notifying the compensation board. If the employer fails to make the necessary report, the employee will probably be given additional time to pursue his or her claim.

If the employer agrees that the injury or disease is work-related and accepts the employee's characterization of its seriousness, the claim is uncontested. Most states follow the "agreement system" under which a settlement is negotiated by the parties, or by the employee and the employer's WC insurer. In some states, the agency that administers WC claims must approve all settlements, even in uncontested cases. Most settlements involve payment of ongoing benefits at a continuing rate: either a percentage of the employee's pre-accident income, or a percentage of the state's average income. However, there is an increasing trend to settle WC cases for a lump sum.

However, some uncontested cases are treated as "direct payment" cases. Either the employer or the insurer initiates the process, by making the statutory initial installment payment to the employee. Under this option, the employee does not have to sign anything or agree to anything—unlike the agreement system, which results in a written agreement.

WC settlements cover only the matters specifically set out in the agreement, so agreements must be drafted carefully. Employers are allowed to settle claims that have already accrued, but not future claims (such as claims for future medical expenses), because employees cannot be required to give up future claims that are hard to quantify in advance.

Generally, any settlement between employer and employee will be final. However, there are grounds for which agreements can be set aside, such as fraud, mutual mistake of fact (both sides believe something about the employee's condition that turns out not to be accurate), or mistake of law (misinterpretation of the legal rules and their consequences). Usually, the mere fact that the employee did not have a lawyer is not enough to invalidate a settlement—unless, perhaps, the employer prevented the employee from seeking legal advice. Just to be on the safe side, employers should inform employees that they have the right to be represented by counsel.

Contested cases are heard and decided by the agency administering the system. However, there are comparatively few contested cases. In most cases, it is quite clear that there has been an injury. Because WC is a no-fault system, it is not necessary to apportion blame.

In some states, mediation is either an option that is available (but only if both sides agree); in other states, it is compulsory. In mediated cases, a neutral mediator has at least one informal meeting with the parties. Sometimes, the meeting is held off the record, so both sides can speak freely, without having to restrict what they say to things that would help their case in formal legal proceedings. If necessary, the mediator arranges more meetings, until the mediator is either able to facilitate a settlement, or it is clear that an impasse has been reached.

In some states, when mediation fails, binding arbitration can be applied; in other states, the case is sent to the Comp board for adjudication.

Appeal rights are granted to dissatisfied employers and employees. Usually, parties get 30 days to file for an appeal, although the requirements of different states range from 10 days to one year. Grounds for appeal include improprieties in the process and changed circumstances (such as unpredictable improvement or deterioration in the employee's condition) that were unknown at the time of the award.

After exhaustion of remedies (the process of going through all the administrative appeals), the case can be taken to court by a dissatisfied party.

Many state laws entitle the employee to an additional payment of 10–20% if the employer is late in making a required payment. Civil fines may also be imposed, and the unpaid amounts could operate as a lien on the employer's assets.

[B] Responding to an Accident

Even before there have been any accidents, your workplace should have an effective procedure in place, and should hold regular drills to make sure everyone can handle the procedure. Make sure that employees learn first aid and CPR. Keep plenty of first aid kits around, with fresh supplies, in convenient locations. It's important to provide first aid for all minor incidents, and immediate medical care in more serious cases.

Somebody must be designated to take charge of taking the injured worker to a doctor's office or hospital emergency room, or to call an ambulance. Someone must be in charge of filing the initial accident report (and an OSHA incident report if necessary). [See § 24.02[A]] Some insurers have 24-hour telephone lines that can be used for WC and OSHA reporting, and to assign a case manager to review utilization of care and the injured person's potential for rehabilitation. There is clear evidence that the earlier and more aggressively rehabilitation can be pursued, the more likely it is that the employee will be able to return to work (or at least to limited duties or a less strenuous job) instead of becoming permanently disabled.

In addition to immediate accident reports, some states require a yearly report of all workplace incidents, similar to the OSHA annual report. [See § 24.02[A]]

Follow-up status reports may also be required on individual accidents. Employers who fail to make mandatory reports can be subject to fines; there may even be criminal penalties.

As Chapter 18 shows, managed care dominates the U.S. health care system. It also plays a role in WC cases. Some states such as Connecticut, Florida, and Ohio make managed care involvement in WC cases compulsory. Many other states have laws authorizing managed care as an option in WC cases: Arkansas, California, Georgia, Kentucky, Massachusetts, Minnesota, Missouri, Montana, Nebraska, Nevada, New Hampshire, New Jersey, New York, North Carolina, North Dakota, Oregon, Pennsylvania, Rhode Island, South Dakota, Utah, and Washington.

Note that an Ohio court has struck down a provision of the state Comp law (Ohio Rev. Code Ann. §4123/54(A)(2)). This provision—found in many other states—requires drug and alcohol testing of all injured workers with no requirement of suspicion that the injured person was under the influence. It imposes a rebuttable presumption that refusing to take the test shows impairment. The court found that this is an unreasonable search that violates the Fourth Amendment, except in especially safety-sensitive industries, or if the injured person had a demonstrated history of substance abuse. [*State ex rel. Ohio AFL-CIO v. Ohio Bureau of WC,* 97 Ohio St. 3d 504, 2002 Ohio 6717, 780 N.E.2d 981 (Ohio 2002)]

§33.08   WC IN RELATION TO OTHER SYSTEMS

Usually, Comp cases involve only the injured person and the employer, or perhaps those parties plus an insurer, but sometimes third parties get involved as well. For example, under New York's Workers' Compensation Law, there are only two instances in which a property owner can bring a third-party claim against the employer of an injured worker. One of them is when the worker's injury is "grave"; the other is when the employer and owner have entered into a written contract to indemnify the property owner. In March 2005, New York's Court of Appeals ruled on the question of whether the written contract has to be a signed agreement. The third-party defendant, which had taken over as contractor and was a representative of the third-party defendant, sent a memo to the employer to clarify that under "this contract" the third-party defendant did not assume responsibility for work done by the previous general contractor. The third-party defendant did not sign the contract or an addendum to the contract, but it did the work and was paid under the contract.

The plaintiff, a laborer, suffered an eye injury in the course of demolition work on the project. He applied for and got Worker's Compensation benefits, and he also sued the building owner, which sued the third-party defendant for indemnification. The defendant admitted that there was a contract but denied that there was a binding obligation to indemnify the property owner, because the third-party defendant never signed the contract.

The Court of Appeals ruled that, when it passed the relevant provision of the Worker's Compensation law, the state legislature did not show its intent to change the common-law rule, under which a contract can be enforceable even if it has not been signed. In this case, the third-party defendant worked (and got paid) as if there had been a valid contract, so the indemnification provisions should also be given effect. [*Flores v. Procida Realty & Constr. Corp.*, 2005 WL 708381 (N.Y. Mar. 29, 2005)]

[A]   Taxation of WC Benefits

Generally speaking, WC insurance premiums paid by employers, or WC benefits received by employees, are not taxable income for the employee. Therefore, the employer does not have to perform tax withholding on these amounts, or withhold or pay FICA or FUTA tax on them. However, in a limited range of situations, WC benefits will be taxable: e.g. if they are paid to a person who has returned to work in a light-duty position; if they reduce Social Security benefits; or if state law calls for payment of non-occupational disability benefits. [*See* Chapter 20 for the related topic of disability benefits provided under a fringe benefit plan]

The amount that the employer pays in WC premiums is tax deductible. So are loss amounts paid by a self-insured employer. However, reserves maintained in order to satisfy the deductible under a WC policy are not tax-deductible.

[B]   ERISA

The general tenor of court decisions on this subject is that WC benefits can legitimately be used to offset accrued benefits that derive from the employer's contribution to a pension plan—but only if a statute specifically provides this, or if the plan has been drafted to include this specific provision. ERISA preempts state WC laws to the extent that they "relate" to an ERISA plan.

In 1992, the Supreme Court decided that a state law relates to an ERISA plan if it refers to or has a connection with the plan, even if the effect is indirect, and even if the law was not designed to affect the plan. Therefore, a law requiring employers to provide health insurance to employees who received or were eligible for WC was preempted. [*District of Columbia v. Greater Wash. Bd. of Trade*, 506 U.S. 125 (1992)]

[C]   The ADA

A person might claim disability discrimination and also claim eligibility for WC benefits, at the same time or at different times.

The right to get WC benefits is considered a privilege of employment for ADA purposes [*see, e.g., Harding v. Winn-Dixie Stores*, 907 F. Supp. 386 (M.D. Fla. 1995)], so a case can be brought premised on alleged discrimination in this area. However, the ADA does not have the strong preemptive power that ERISA does to rule out state-law claims. In 1998, for instance, a case was allowed to proceed even though the ADA's standard of proof is higher for employees with pre-existing conditions. [*Baley v. Reynolds Metals,* 153 Ore. App. 498, 959 P.2d 84 (Ore. App. 1998)]

A person injured at work might be entitled to benefits but still able to work with reasonable accommodation. A WC judge's determination that the injured person could not work even on a reduced schedule is proof that the person is not a "qualified individual with a disability." [*Dush v. Appleton Elec. Co.,* 124 F.3d 957 (8th Cir. 1997)] An employee who enters into an agreement stating that he or she needs a stress-free work environment is not qualified for a high-stress job like being a safety police officer. [*Jackson v. County of Los Angeles,* 60 Cal. App. 4th 171, 70 Cal. Rptr. 2d 96 (1998)]

The testimony or findings from an ADA case can have an important evidentiary effect in a WC case. Someone who sued under the ADA because of a past injury cannot deny that the injury was a preexisting disability when it comes to a later injury that becomes the subject of a WC case. [*Cobb v. Coyne Cylinder Co.,* 719 So. 2d 219 (Ala. App. 1998)]

Should the value of health insurance premiums paid by the employer be included in calculating the injured person's "weekly wage" for WC purposes? In 2000, the Georgia Court of Appeals said no, but early in 2001 the Washington Supreme Court said yes, on the grounds that wages includes the reasonable value of any "consideration of like nature" paid to a worker. [*Groover v. Johnson Controls World Wide Serv.,* 241 Ga. App. 791 (2000); *Cockle v. Department of Labor & Indus.,* 142 Wash. 2d 801 (2001)]

There are also problems in relating WC to the ADA if an employer interviews a job applicant who seems to have some physical limitations, which might have been caused by an earlier compensable injury.

Job interviews are not appropriate settings for discussing an employee's history of injuries—or health status in general. Inquiries about past WC claims are not allowed, because they are considered to be disability-related.

However, during the interview, it is permissible for the interviewer to discuss the essential duties of the job and tasks that are sometimes necessary. The interviewer can find out whether the applicant can perform the essential duties, with or without reasonable accommodation by the employer.

Once an employer is ready to extend a conditional job offer to an applicant, asking about past WC claims is allowed, but only if the question is posed to everyone who gets a conditional job offer, not just those who seem to have some impairment. Concern that hiring someone with a prior injury will increase the company's WC costs is not a legitimate reason for denying a job to a qualified applicant.

It probably violates the ADA to maintain a policy that injured employees cannot return to work until they are 100% fit to resume all their old duties. When an employee wants to return to work, the ADA requires the employer to offer a light-duty assignment if this would be a reasonable accommodation to disability. But the employer is not required to create new jobs just to help employees get back on their feet. Nor is it necessary to "bump" another employee to accommodate disability.

Referring an injured person to a vocational rehabilitation program is not considered a reasonable accommodation, if the employee could return to work with accommodations that do not constitute a hardship to the employer.

The ADA does not preempt state case law that denies WC to a person whose injuries are causally connected to an underlying physical condition (such as earlier injuries) and who lied about the existing condition before being hired.

The ADA does not preempt the state law because the ADA permits pre-employment inquiries that are related to the applicant's ability to do the job. Even if the employer asks improper questions, lying is not an appropriate response. [*Caldwell v. Aarlin/Holcombe Armature Co.,* 267 Ga. 613, 481 S.E.2d 196 (Ga. Sup. 1997)] So even if the employer should not have asked questions that violated the ADA, the employee's answers can still be legitimate evidence in a WC case. [*See Dureoun v. C&P Production Specialist,* 718 So. 2d 460 (La. App. 1998)]

In *Gutermuth v. Bedford* [43 S.W.3d 270 (Ky. Sup. 2001)], the employee could not collect WC benefits for a neck injury incurred when she drove a cherry-picker over a break in the concrete floor, because her job application concealed her six previous arm operations and medically imposed restrictions on lifting her arms. She also had work-related knee problems, and non-work-related back problems. She would not have been hired for the physically demanding jobs if she had disclosed these limitations, so WC benefits were unavailable.

The Seventh Circuit decided that it is not a violation of the ADA to reject a group of job applicants whose "nerve conduction tests" showed that they had neuropathy, and therefore were vulnerable to future repetitive stress injuries. [*EEOC v. Rockwell Int'l Corp.,* 243 F.3d 1012 (7th Cir. 2001)] In the Seventh Circuit's view, the employees were not currently disabled. The employer did not discriminate against them on the basis of perceived disability, because the employer did not regard them as potentially unable to perform a broad range of jobs.

[D] Second Injury Funds

Although they predate the ADA, in a way "second injury funds" serve the same purpose as the ADA: promoting the employment of people with disabilities. Second injury funds (which exist in, for example, California, Missouri, New Jersey, and Washington State) deal with the situation in which a permanent disability is compounded by a later injury to become either a permanent partial disability that is more serious than before, or a permanent total disability. In states that do not have these funds, an employer who hires someone whose pre-existing condition deteriorates because of occupational factors, would be responsible for all of the employee's WC benefits, even though the occupational factors may be comparatively less important than the pre-existing condition.

When there is a second injury fund in the picture, the employer is responsible only for the economic consequences of the later injury. The second injury fund, which is publicly funded, takes on the rest of the economic burden.

The first injury must have been serious enough to be compensable, but need not actually have come under the WC system. For instance, the second injury fund could get involved if a work-related injury aggravates an existing condition caused by a non-work-related automobile accident or a birth defect.

Tip: To collect from the fund, the employer may have to certify that it knew about the pre-existing condition at the time of hiring. This, in turn, requires asking questions in a way that does not violate the ADA.

[E] Social Security Disability Income

In many states, the Social Security Disability Income (SSDI) system is considered the primary payer whenever an employee is injured seriously enough to meet the Social Security Administration's stringent definition of total disability. The states in this category are Alaska, Arkansas, California, Colorado, Florida, Louisiana, Maine, Massachusetts, Michigan, Minnesota, Missouri, Montana, Nevada, New Jersey, New York, North Dakota, Ohio, Oregon, Utah, Washington, and Wisconsin.

When SSDI is involved, the payments from the federal agency reduce the WC benefit dollar-for-dollar, until the combination of SSDI and WC reaches the level of 80% of the worker's pre-accident earnings. However, SSDI reduces only the part of the benefit that represents lost income, not the part that goes to medical care or legal fees.

In states that coordinate with SSDI, employers sometimes hire lawyers to represent injured workers in their SSDI cases. That way, the employer's WC experience is charged with a much smaller claim. Self-insured employers, who would otherwise have to pay the whole claim themselves, have an even stronger reason for promoting the employee's claim.

§ 33.09   TECHNIQUES FOR LOWERING COMP COSTS

Employers can reduce their costs via good planning—sorting valid from invalid claims, and finding more economical ways to handle the valid claims. Companies have had some success by educating workers that everyone is responsible for reducing injuries and maintaining a safer workplace. Focusing on getting injured workers back to work as soon as possible also helps cut costs. Departments can be made responsible for their own injury rates, and be made responsible for keeping their rates at least as low as those for comparable operations.

HR policies that are associated with lower WC rates include:

- Increasing employee involvement (e.g., through the use of quality circles). The more employees get involved, the more careful they will be about identifying potentially dangerous conditions, finding ways to correct them—and the more motivation they will have to return to work quickly after an injury;
- Strengthening grievance and conflict resolution procedures if dangerous conditions are alleged, and to resolve claims;
- Reducing turnover: Experienced workers are less likely to get hurt than novices;
- Training workers better—especially in lifting and safe handling of hazardous materials;
- Using health maintenance and wellness programs.

The National Institute of Occupational Safety and Health (NIOSH) defines three areas in which employers can be proactive to cut Comp costs:

- Using engineering controls, such as workstation layout, choice of tools, work methods, to tailor the job to fit employee capabilities and limitations;
- Reducing risk exposure through administrative controls, such as more rest breaks, better training, task rotation;
- Supplying workers with Personal Protective Equipment (PPE), although scientific consensus has not been reached on which devices are effective.

An article in CCH's Worker's Compensation newsletter gives some useful tips for spotting claims that might be fraudulent:

- Delayed reporting of injury;
- Accidents of a type that might be staged;
- The worker claiming injury was on probation or has been identified as having a poor work record;
- The alleged injury is not consistent with the worker's assigned duties;
- The injury is reported just after a weekend or holiday—showing that the injury might have been incurred away from the workplace, or work might have exacerbated a non-work-based injury.

Sixteen states (Alaska, Arkansas, Colorado, Connecticut, Florida, Georgia, Iowa, Kansas, Maine, Michigan, Minnesota, Montana, Nevada, New Jersey, Oregon, and South Carolina) have adopted the National Crime Prevention and Privacy Compact. [42 U.S.C. § 14616 *et seq.*] The FBI and the participating states have databases that can be accessed together in a single query if you need to do criminal record background checks—not least to see if a job applicant has a fraud conviction. [No by-line, *Tips for Better Background Checks to Help Comp Costs*, CCH Worker's Compensation Newsletter #213 (Aug. 6, 2002)]

Sometimes, a WC insurance premium quote will be inaccurate, and the premium can be reduced simply by:

- Checking to see if payroll is stated accurately, because the higher the payroll, the higher the premium;
- Making sure that employees are assigned to the lowest risk classification that accurately reflects their duties;
- Having your insurance agent review the calculations.

PART VII

SUBSTANTIVE LAWS AGAINST DISCRIMINATION

TITLE VII

§ 34.01   INTRODUCTION

Title VII, passed as part of the Civil Rights Act of 1964, is the main federal civil rights statute that bans discrimination in employment. It has been enacted at 42 U.S.C. § 2000e *et seq.* (By the time Title VII came around, the United States Code was pretty much "full-up," leading to some very odd section numbers. Title VII starts with just plain § 2000e, which is divided into subsections running from § 2000e(a) to 2000e(n). The next section is § 2000e-1, with additional sections up to § 2000e-17.)

Title VII is supplemented by other civil rights statutes: Sometimes other parts of the United States Code (such as 42 U.S.C. §§ 1981, 1983, and 1985) are invoked in employment discrimination suits. Disability discrimination is barred by the Americans with Disabilities Act. [*See* Chapter 36] Age discrimination is barred by the Age Discrimination in Employment Act. [*See* Chapter 37]

In a sense, the Family and Medical Leave Act, [29 U.S.C. § 2601 *et seq.*] discussed in detail in Chapter 38, is also an antidiscrimination statute as well as an employee benefits statute, because it prevents discrimination against individuals who are ill or who must cope with illness as part of their family responsibilities. Note that any federal, state, or local law that creates special rights or preferences for veterans continues in force and is not repealed by Title VII, [42 U.S.C. § 2000e-11] a provision that is more prominent in the post-9/11 environment.

The areas of discrimination forbidden by Title VII are race, color, religion, sex, and national origin. These are known as "suspect classifications," because employers are not supposed to discriminate for reasons involving these classifications.

Also see 42 U.S.C. § 2000e-2(h), which says that it is not an unlawful employment practice for an employer to abide by FLSA § 6(d), [29 U.S.C. § 206(d)] which allows certain differences in the minimum wage.

Title VII enforcement has two aspects: public (governmental) and private (suits brought by employees, job applicants, ex-employees, or groups of people in these categories). Section 2000e-5 gives the Equal Employment Opportunities Commission (EEOC) the power "to prevent any person from engaging in any unlawful employment practice" that is banned by 42 U.S.C. §§ 2000e-2 or 2000e-3.

State laws still remain in force, although state laws are not permitted to require or even allow anything that is treated as an unlawful employment practice under Title VII. [42 U.S.C. § 2000e-7]

§ 34.02   TREATMENT/IMPACT

Discrimination claims are divided into two categories, each of which has its own requirements for drafting complaints and proving the case, and its own defenses that the employer can assert to win its case.

The two categories are disparate treatment and disparate impact. A disparate treatment case alleges that persons were singled out for inferior treatment because of the group they belong to. A disparate impact case alleges subtler forms of discrimination.

For instance, an allegation that a police department refused to hire Hispanics would be a disparate treatment claim. A disparate impact claim might challenge the police department's requirement that all newly hired officers be over 5′ 10″ tall, on the grounds that more Hispanics than people from other backgrounds are unable to meet this requirement, and therefore a requirement that seems at first glance to be acceptable actually discriminates against members of a protected group.

Under Title VII, a "mixed motive" case can be maintained. That is, if an employer has several motivations for making an employment decision or adopting an employment practice, Title VII forbids practices that are partially motivated by discrimination against a protected group, not just those where discrimination is the sole motivation. [*See* 42 U.S.C. § 2000e-2(m)]

Under the Supreme Court's June, 2003 decision [*Desert Palace, Inc. v. Costa*, 539 U.S. 90 (2003)], a Title VII plaintiff can obtain a mixed-motive jury instruction without necessarily showing direct evidence of discrimination, because the statute does not specifically require direct evidence. Therefore, the general rule of civil litigation—allowing proof by direct and/or circumstantial evidence—applies.

§ 34.03   TITLE VII COVERAGE

Title VII bans "unlawful employment practices." Unlawful employment practices discriminate against an employee or job applicant on the basis of the individual's race, color, religion, sex, or national origin. [42 U.S.C. § 2000e-2(a)] Note that Title VII does not ban sexual-orientation discrimination, but some applicable state and local statutes do.

Unlawful employment practices on the part of the employer are defined by 42 U.S.C. § 2000e-2(a) as:

- To fail or refuse to hire;
- To discharge;
- To discriminate with respect to compensation, terms, conditions, or privileges of employment;
- To limit, segregate, or classify employees or job applicants in a way that deprives or tends to deprive them of employment opportunities, or otherwise adversely affects their status as employees.

Title VII also bans discriminatory practices by employment agencies and labor unions, but their activities are outside the scope of this book.

In late 1998, the Fourth Circuit joined the Third, Fifth, Seventh, Eighth, Tenth, Eleventh, and D.C. Circuits in ruling that only employer companies, and not individuals, can be held liable under Title VII. [*Lissau v. Southern Food Serv.*, 159 F.3d 177 (4th Cir. 1998)]

So far, discrimination on the basis of obesity has been held not to constitute a cause of action under Title VII, although perhaps certain cases of morbid obesity (weight twice or more what is normal for the person's height) might be treated as a disability. Michigan and Washington have state laws, and San Francisco and Santa Cruz, California, have local laws banning discrimination on the basis of physical appearance. [Steven Greenhouse, *Overweight, but Ready to Fight,* New York Times, Aug. 4, 2003, at p. B1]

An important—and growing—part of the employment discrimination caseload is the "retaliation" case. Section 2000e-3(a) makes it unlawful for an employer to discriminate against anyone who has opposed an unlawful employment practice or who has "made a charge, testified, assisted, or participated in any manner in an investigation, proceeding, or hearing" under Title VII. [*See* § 34.08 for more about retaliation cases]

It is also an unlawful employment practice to indicate "any preference, limitation, specification, or discrimination" based on race, color, religion, sex, or national origin in a help-wanted ad, unless belonging to a particular group is a Bona Fide Occupational Qualification (BFOQ). [*See* 42 U.S.C. § 2000e-3(b)]

It might be a BFOQ to be male or female (e.g., because of authenticity, for an actor or actress; for privacy, for a restroom attendant); to be under 40 (in a job where public safety depends on youthful reactions) or even to belong to a particular religion (e.g., to work in a kosher slaughterhouse). In the disability context, it is a BFOQ not to pose a safety risk to oneself or others. Where safety or efficiency is involved, it may be possible to raise a "business necessity" defense for a discriminatory business practice.

Race is never a BFOQ. [*See Ferrill v. Parker Group, Inc.,* 168 F.3d 468 (11th Cir. 1999)] A black woman was hired to telemarket to black voters and then fired after the election. The employer failed in its claim that race is a BFOQ for telemarketers (on the theory that consumers are more responsive to persons of their own race).

In 2003, a Foreign Service applicant filed suit against the State Department when his Foreign Service application was rejected on medical grounds because he is HIV-positive. Plaintiff Lorenzo Taylor claims the criteria are discriminatory and outmoded. The State Department position is that new hires must be able to be stationed anywhere, no matter how isolated the post or how limited its medical facilities; Powell indicated that he was willing to accept any posting. [Christopher Marquis, *State Dept. Is Sued by Applicant With H.I.V.,* New York Times, Sept. 14, 2003, at p. A20]

§ 34.04 EXCEPTIONS TO TITLE VII COVERAGE

[A] Definition of Employer

Perhaps the most important exception is found in 42 U.S.C. § 2000e(b), which defines an "employer" as a natural person or business engaged in an industry affecting commerce—and having 15 or more employees for each work day in 20 or more weeks either in the year in question or the preceding calendar year. So a very small business will be exempt from Title VII. Possibly some businesses with even more than 15 employees will escape coverage because their business does not "affect commerce," but most businesses do sell or at least attempt to make interstate sales, so their business will be deemed to "affect commerce."

The 15-employee figure is calculated based on the number of people on the payroll, not the number of full-time employees. [*Walters v. Metropolitan Educ. Enters., Inc.,* 519 U.S. 202 (1997)]

Whether a company has 15 employees or not is a substantive element of the Title VII claim (in this case, a sexual harassment charge), not a jurisdictional prerequisite. The practical significance of this 2006 Supreme Court ruling is that the number of employees is an issue that can be waived if it is not raised on time, whereas questions of subject matter jurisdiction can be raised at any time. The Supreme Court decided that the 15-employee requirement is not jurisdictional because it is not found within the part of the Title VII statute that grants jurisdiction to the federal courts. [*Arbaugh v. Y&H Corp.,* 126 S. Ct. 1235 (U.S. 2006)]

Suit could be brought under Title VII against a U.S.-based parent corporation, even though it had only six employees, because its wholly owned Mexican subsidiary had at least 50 employees. Even though the Mexican employees would not be protected by Title VII, the Ninth Circuit ruled in 2002 that they should be included in the count. [*Kang v. U Lim America Inc.,* 296 F.3d 810 (9th Cir. 2002)]

Another exception is allowed under 42 U.S.C. § 2000e-2(e) if religion, sex, or national origin is a bona fide occupational qualification "reasonably necessary to the normal operation" of the business. Educational institutions sponsored by a religious organization, (e.g., Notre Dame or Yeshiva University) or institutions "directed toward the propagation of a particular religion" are permitted to base hiring and other employment decisions on religion—parochial schools can, but do not have to, employ staffers of other religions.

According to the Seventh and Eighth Circuits, Congress took a valid action in 1972 when it abrogated sovereign immunity and made the states subject to Title VII, so Title VII disparate impact suits can be brought against a state employer. [*Nanda v. Board of Trustees of the Univ. of Illinois,* 303 F.3d 817 (7th Cir. 2002); *Okruhlik v. University of Arkansas,* 255 F.3d 615 (8th Cir. 2001)]

[B] Aliens

Section 2000e-1 provides that Title VII does not apply to the employment of "aliens." In August 1998, the Fourth Circuit reversed its earlier ruling. Now *Egbuna v. Time-Life Libraries, Inc.* [153 F.3d 184 (4th Cir. 1998)] holds that it is necessary to be a U.S. citizen or an alien holding a valid work visa, to be a "qualified" individual. So an alien who does not have legal worker status in the United States cannot make out a Title VII prima facie case.

Furthermore, an employer does not violate Title VII if it (or a corporation it controls) takes an action with respect to an employee in a foreign country that is necessary to avoid violating that country's law—even if the action would be barred by Title VII if it were taken in the United States. The factors in whether an employer controls a corporation include whether there is common management, ownership, or financial control, and whether the two organizations have related operations.

Private social clubs such as country clubs are exempt from Title VII. However, the Eastern District of Virginia allows 42 U.S.C. § 1981 civil rights claims to be brought by employees and ex-employees of private clubs. In this reading, the Title VII exclusion is designed to protect freedom of association, but allowing § 1981 suits does not restrict freedom of association. [*Crawford v. Willow Oaks Country Club,* 66 F.3d 767 (E.D. Va. 1999)] *See also* § 23.11 on immigration and nationality issues in hiring.

[C] National Security

Another exception, that will probably become far more important after September 11, 2001, than before, is the 42 U.S.C. § 2000e-2(g) national security exception. It does not violate Title VII to fire or refuse to hire someone who has not met, or no longer meets, security clearance requirements "in effect pursuant to or administered under any statute of the United States or any Executive order of the President."

[D] Seniority Systems

Employers are permitted, under 42 U.S.C. § 2000e-2(h), to abide by "bona fide seniority or merit systems," or to base compensation on quantity or quality of production, or to pay different rates at different locations—even if the result is to provide different standards of compensation or different terms, conditions, or privileges of employment. However, employers are not allowed to impose such differences in treatment if they are "the result of an intention to discriminate" on the basis of race, color, religion, sex, or national origin.

Also see 42 U.S.C. § 2000e-5(e)(2), which says that the unlawful unemployment practice occurs, with respect to a seniority system that was adopted "for an intentionally discriminatory purpose," whether or not the purpose can be discerned from the face of the provision, either when the seniority system is adopted, when the potential plaintiff becomes subject to the seniority system, or when the seniority system is applied in a way that injures the potential plaintiff.

Section 2000e-2(h) also allows employers to use validated pre-employment tests of ability, as long as testing is not designed, intended or used to discriminate.

The subject of test scores is taken up again in 42 U.S.C. § 2000e-2(l), which states that it is an unlawful employment practice to adjust scores or use different cutoff scores in hiring or promotion tests, based on the race, color, religion, sex or national origin of the test taker.

§ 34.05   RACIAL DISCRIMINATION

[A]   Basic Protections

The first equal opportunity laws were bans on racial discrimination. The Civil Rights Act of 1866, enacted at 42 U.S.C. § 1981, was passed to give former slaves the same rights as "white citizens." There is no requirement of a minimum number of employees for a § 1981 suit, and the EEOC and state antidiscrimination procedures do not have to be invoked before bringing suit under this provision.

The Civil Rights Act of 1991 generally requires plaintiffs to proceed under § 1981 if they have claims of racial discrimination, before using Title VII. Compensatory and punitive damages are not available under Title VII for any plaintiff who can get such damages under § 1981.

There have been some major recent cases about race discrimination. The quest to have a completely race-neutral workplace is a difficult one, and claims have been raised both by majority and minority groups that their rights have been violated.

In *Johnson v. Zema Systems Corp.* [170 F.3d 734 (7th Cir. 1999)], a black manager said he was fired because he spent much of his time supervising white rather than black employees in a segregated and hostile environment. The employer relied on the "same actor" defense, i.e., if the manager who hired the plaintiff also fired him or her, the manager could not have been motivated by racial bigotry. The Seventh Circuit did not accept this as a valid defense, noting that the firing might occur because the hiree did not conform to the hirer's stereotypes about the group he or she belongs to.

A 2003 case from the Fourth Circuit was brought by a uniformed corrections officer who charged that he was disciplined for violating the employer's dress code and grooming policy by wearing dreadlocks. He alleged religious and racial discrimination under both state and federal law and asserted a state-law defamation claim. In the plaintiff's view, the policy burdened his religious expression because female officers were allowed to wear braided hair that was longer than his dreadlocks, and the policy was not enforced against 13 other dreadlock-wearing officers. Furthermore, an Orthodox Jew and a Sikh were granted religious exemptions from the dress code.

The Fourth Circuit ruled that a neutral law of general applicability does not have to be justified by a compelling government interest, even if it has an incidental effect of burdening a religious practice. However, the Fourth Circuit did not regard Title VII as the only way that a public employee could bring a Constitutional claim. The case was remanded to the District Court so he could pursue a 42 U.S.C. § 1983 claim. He was also entitled to a trial on his First Amendment claims. The Fourth Circuit upheld the dismissal of his 42 U.S.C. § 1981 charges (he claimed that he was subjected to inconsistent enforcement because he is black, but the court found that the employer did not discipline all black employees with hairstyles that violated the dress code). His defamation claims were also dismissed, because he violated the rules, whether or not the rules were valid, and therefore it was not defamatory to say that he did. [*Booth v. Maryland Dep't of Public Safety and Correctional Servs.*, 327 F.3d 377 (4th Cir. 2003)]

The Seventh Circuit ruled in mid-2001 that it is permissible to use date of birth as a tie-breaker for an eligibility list for promotions, where the candidates have the same test score and the same amount of seniority. (The plaintiff, a black woman, was younger than the white man who was competing for the promotion.) It was not sufficient for the plaintiff to show that there were possible alternative tie-breaking practices that the employer failed to adopt. [*Price v. Chicago*, 251 F.3d 656 (7th Cir. 2001)]

The Tenth Circuit has applied the *Faragher/Burlington* test [*see* § 35.02] to conduct that creates a racially hostile environment. Conduct is deemed to be within the scope of employment if it is motivated by intent to serve the employer. So the employer will be liable for discriminatory conduct by a supervisor reflecting prejudice within the labor force. [*Wright-Simmons v. City of Oklahoma City*, 155 F.3d 1264 (10th Cir. 1998)] Even a single racial slur by a supervisor in the presence of another supervisor can be severe enough to create a hostile work environment. [*Taylor v. Metzger*, 706 A.2d 685 (N.J. 1998). *Also see Swinton v. Potomac Corp.*, 270 F.3d 794 (9th Cir. 2001), denying the Faragher/Burlington affirmative defense, but requiring the plaintiff to prove that the employer knew or should have known of the harassment and failed to take appropriate corrective steps]

In the Ninth Circuit view, the District Court should not have discounted insults and hostile actions targeting a black employee because a white employee was similarly abused, if the white employee was harassed for associating with the black colleague. The Ninth Circuit ruled that a Title VII violation can be established based on pervasive hostility in the workplace even if the plaintiff is not the target. [*McGinest v. GTE Service Corp.*, 360 F.3d 1103 (9th Cir. 2004)]

Although in the early years of Title VII, it was often invoked in cases where black employees or applicants charged that they were disadvantaged vis-à-vis white comparators, cases are often brought today charging favorable treatment of Latinos and discrimination against black people. Pork processor Farmer John Meats settled with the EEOC for $110,000 on charges that it discriminated against black applicants by limiting hiring almost entirely to Hispanic workers. Zenith National Insurance Corp. settled with the EEOC for $180,000 on allegations that it hired a Hispanic applicant for a mailroom job, despite his lack of relevant experience, while discriminating against better-qualified black applicants. [Miriam Jordan, *Blacks v. Latinos at Work*, Wall Street Journal, Jan. 24, 2006, at p. B1]

The Eighth Circuit dismissed the Title VII portion of a racial harassment claim, because the employer's racial slurs against several groups, amounting to about one outburst per month over a two-year period, were not severe or pervasive enough to create a hostile work environment. However, the § 1981 claim (termination as retaliation for objecting to the slurs) was permitted to go to trial. [*Bainbridge v. Loffredo Gardens Inc.*, 378 F.3d 756 (8th Cir. 2004)]

The Eleventh Circuit dismissed a racially hostile work environment claim. The plaintiff charged that the vice president of HR said she wanted to change the "complexion" of the department; that she called a black worker a "dunce"; and that she e-mailed a complaint about the plaintiff's management style. The court found this evidence insufficient. It was not proven that "complexion" was intended literally rather than figuratively. Not all of the statements alleged to create a hostile environment related to the plaintiff; and taken as a whole, they were not severe, pervasive, humiliating, or physically threatening. [*Luckie v. Ameritech Corp.*, 389 F.3d 708 (7th Cir. 2004)]

The often-cited case of *Herrnreiter v. Chicago Housing Auth.* [315 F.3d 742 (7th Cir. 2002)] was brought by a white auditor who was transferred by his black supervisor from the agency's investigation division to its auditing division. The Seventh Circuit held that there was no actionable racial discrimination (even though the plaintiff preferred the investigator's job) because he was not demoted to an objectively inferior position or prevented from exercising his professional skills.

In 2003, the Seventh Circuit pursued a theme that arose in several contemporary cases by ruling that not every genuine difficulty on the job rises to the level of adverse employment action, and therefore affirming the District Court's dismissal of a black male worker's claims of race discrimination and retaliation (for complaining about racist remarks). The plaintiff alleged that he was offered a promotion to team leader at the same time as a white employee; that he was told that the team leader position had been abolished (although it was later restored—and offered to the white employee but not to the plaintiff); and that after a back injury, he was assigned tasks that aggravated his injuries, was not allowed to work while taking prescription medication, and the company delayed in giving him the back brace he needed and that was supposed to be provided by a corporate plan. The Seventh Circuit held that there was a legitimate non-discriminatory reason for withdrawing the team leader position. As for allegations that the plaintiff was given harder jobs and made to work alone while whites worked in teams, these are not adverse job actions because they did not qualitatively or quantitatively change the terms or conditions of employment; neither are denial of a back brace or bans on prescription medication use. [*Johnson v. Cambridge Indus.*, 325 F.3d 892 (7th Cir. 2003)]

[B] Reverse Discrimination

A white male plaintiff claimed that he was denied a promotion because of reverse discrimination, and the woman who got the promotion was less qualified. Because a white male is not a member of a protected class, the Seventh Circuit defined the prima face case as showing "background circumstances" (e.g., a pattern of not promoting white males; the choice of a significantly weaker candidate) evidencing reverse discrimination. The Seventh Circuit held that the plaintiff did produce a prima facie case by showing that most of the promotions went to women. But he did not win at trial: the plaintiff failed to show that the employer's defense, that it believed the woman was better qualified for the promotion—was false or pretextual. [*Mills v. Health Care Serv. Corp.*, 171 F.3d 450 (7th Cir. 1999)]

The Southern District of New York does not require "special circumstances" for a white male to bring a reverse bias claim; he is not required to meet a higher pleading standard for white males than for minorities or women who charge violations of Title VII. [*Tappe v. Alliance Capital Mgmt.*, 198 F. Supp. 2d 368 (S.D.N.Y. 2001)]

Note, however, that the Seventh Circuit granted summary judgment for the defense on a male ex-employee's allegations that the female executive director belittled male employees and made anti-male comments. The evidence showed a generalized misanthropy rather than anti-male bias; and the executive director was the person who hired the plaintiff, and who replaced him with another male. [*Steinauer v. DeGolier*, 359 F.3d 481 (7th Cir. 2004)]

A white female plaintiff was allowed to pursue a Title VII reverse discrimination claim when her employer gave her a rating of "excellent" rather than "outstanding," with the result that she received a smaller bonus than a similarly situated black employee. [*Russell v. Principi*, 257 F.3d 815 (D.C. Cir. 2001)]

Eight white female librarians were awarded $25 million in compensatory and punitive damages against members of the library board and the director of the board for racially motivated demotions and transfers to less desirable branch locations. But the jury did not award any damages against the library system itself, finding that discrimination against white employees was not official policy. [*Bogle v. McClure*, No. 1:00-CV-2071 (N.D. Ga. Jan. 7, 2002). *See* R. Robin McDonald, *Georgia Jury Awards Librarians $25M for Race Bias*, Fulton County Daily Report (Jan. 17, 2002) (law.com)]

In 2006, the Eastern District of Pennsylvania denied a new trial in a case in which the jury awarded more than $2.9 million in damages to four white male plaintiffs who charged that a black woman fired them because she thought there were too many white male managers in the department. However, the compensatory damage awards were reduced from $757,271 for all of the plaintiffs to $417,530 because the judge deemed that back pay had been calculated incorrectly. The award of $500,000 to each of the four plaintiffs for mental anguish, pain and suffering, and humiliation was upheld. The judge did not see any impropriety in awarding the same amount to each of the plaintiffs. Reinstatement was ordered for three of the plaintiffs. (The fourth had moved to Florida and had taken a new job, so he was awarded $243,000 in front pay in lieu of reinstatement.) [*Johnston v. School Dist. of Phila.* (E.D. Pa. 2006); *see* Shannon P. Duffy, *Bulk of $2.9M Verdict Upheld in Reverse Discrimination Case*, The Legal Intelligencer, Apr. 17, 2006 (law.com)]

[C] Affirmative Action and Quotas

A very important question in employment law is how to balance the rights of current employees and applicants against the desire to have a workplace that is truly representative and does not reflect past discrimination.

According to 42 U.S.C. § 2000e-2(j), Title VII does not require employers to grant preferential treatment to any individual or any group because the workforce is imbalanced in terms of the number or percentage of workers from groups that have been discriminated against in the past. In other words, employers do not have to use quotas in hiring, promotion, etc.

In 1977, the Supreme Court decided that it is unlawful to perpetuate the present effects of past discrimination, although bona fide seniority systems can be left in operation. [*Teamsters v. U.S.,* 431 U.S. 324 (1977)] Under this approach, preferential hiring of women and minorities might be acceptable to correct an imbalance in the workforce that results from past discrimination. It might also be acceptable to set goals to remove past discrimination and to remove the barriers that existed in the past to prevent racially neutral hiring, but the hiring system must not exclude white applicants.

Cases in the late 1990s say that employers should not set up affirmative action programs merely to enhance diversity within the workplace, but an affirmative action program might be an appropriate corrective measure if there is a history of racism in a particular industry. [*Johnson v. Transportation Agency of Santa Clara County,* 480 U.S. 616 (1987); *Eldredge v. Carpenters Joint Apprenticeship and Training Committee,* 94 F.3d 1366 (9th Cir. 1996); *Schurr v. Resorts Int'l Hotel,* 196 F.3d 486 (3d Cir. 1999)]

The Supreme Court agreed to hear the case of *Piscataway Township Board of Education v. Taxman* [#96-679, *cert. dismissed,* 522 U.S. 1010 (1997)] involving the important issue of whether a well-qualified employee can be laid off to promote the goal of diversity in the workplace. However, the case was settled out of court in late November, 1997, so the Supreme Court did not issue a decision.

On December 14, 1998, the EEOC and the Department of Labor proposed a new work-sharing plan, under which the DOL can sue federal contractors for remedies (including punitive damages) if the contractors are guilty of race, sex, or religious discrimination. Employees of federal contractors have the option of filing discrimination charges with either the EEOC or the DOL.

In the past two decades or so, affirmative action has been most prominent in the context of government contracts. In 1995, the U.S. Supreme Court decided that race-based preferences in government contracting are permissible only if the actual contractor has been the victim of discrimination—not merely that he or she belongs to a group that has historically been economically disadvantaged. [*Adarand Constructors Inc. v. Pena,* 513 U.S. 1108, and 515 U.S. 200 (1995)] The case continued to bounce up and down the court system with various decisions that had more to do with technical legal issues than with the rights and wrongs of affirmative action. The case was supposed to be reheard by the Supreme Court, but in November 2001, the Supreme Court dismissed certiorari as having been improvidently granted. [*Adarand Constructors v. Mineta*, 534 U.S. 103 (2001)]

[D] Executive Order 11246

Executive Order 11246 requires government contractors and contractors on federally assisted construction projects worth over $10,000 to have a policy of furthering equal employment opportunity. If the contractor or subcontractor has more than 50 employees, and the contract is worth over $50,000, the company must have a formal affirmative action program, which must be submitted to the Office of Federal Contract Compliance Programs (OFCCP) within 30 days of the OFCCP's request to *see* the program.

Contracts over $1 million require a pre-award audit of the affirmative action program. [*See* 41 C.F.R. Part 60] There are separate, slightly different, rules for construction contractors.

A company charged with reverse discrimination because of its affirmative action program can cite as a defense that it followed the EEOC's Guidelines on Affirmative Action. To qualify for this defense, the employer must have a written plan. It must act reasonably, taking actions based on self-analysis that leads to a reasonable conclusion that there are actual problems of job bias that require correction. The plan of action must be tailored to eliminate inequality. It must last only as long as it takes to eliminate the effects of past discrimination.

[E] National Origin Discrimination

Since the September 11 attack, there has been an increase in attention to the related problems of national origin discrimination against people of Middle Eastern and South Asian origin and religious discrimination against Muslims. As the EEOC points out, immigrants are now a substantial part of the workforce.

The EEOC responded to the increasing threat of national origin discrimination by issuing guidance on national origin discrimination.

According to the guidance document [EEOC, National Origin Discrimination, <http://www.eeoc.gov/origin/index.html> (modified Mar. 29, 2006); the EEOC also issued a new § 13, "National Origin Discrimination," as part of the agency's manual, replacing transmittals 622 on Citizenship, Residency Requirements, Aliens and Undocumented Workers, and 623, Speak-English-Only Rules and Other Language Policies], national origin discrimination means less-favorable treatment imposed because of someone's country of origin, ethnicity, or accent, or belief that someone has a particular ethnic background. Discrimination on the basis of marriage or other association with people of a disfavored nationality is also covered.

The EEOC position is that employers have a responsibility to prevent or at least correct ethnic slurs that create a hostile work environment. Employment decisions may be made on the basis of accent only if a person's accent materially interferes with job performance. Fluency in English can be imposed as a job requirement only if it is required to do the job; English-only rules are permissible only if they are adopted for non-discriminatory reasons such as promoting the safe or efficient conduct of the business. The agency's stance is that all antidiscrimination laws apply whether or not the discriminatee is a citizen, although remedies are limited for those who do not have authorization to work in this country.

The EEOC has discussed harassment and discrimination against Asians. [EEOC, *Questions and Answers About Employer Responsibilities Concerning the Employment of Muslims, Arabs, South Asians, and Sikhs* (July 16, 2002) <http://www.eeoc.gov/facts/backlash-employer.html> (modified Mar. 21, 2005)] The agency position is that it is impermissible to deny employment (e.g., to people who wear turbans, headscarves, or other religious dress) even if the employer believes that customers will be hostile to such workers. A manager or supervisor who learns about ethnic slurs or harassment in the workplace should tell the harassers to stop doing this, and discipline anyone who is found to have committed harassment. If employees ask for the use of space for prayer, the employer can turn down the request only if the space is legitimately required for business needs. (Employers have a duty of reasonable accommodation to religious practice, whereas they merely need to avoid discrimination on the basis of national origin.) Nor can background checks be made more stringent based on an applicant's country of origin.

The relevant factors in determining whether national origin harassment has occurred include whether physical threats were made or workers were intimidated; whether the conduct was hostile and patently offensive; the frequency of the conduct; the context in which it occurred; and whether management acted appropriately after learning of the conduct.

A Lebanese-American citizen, a Muslim, says she was subjected to national origin discrimination because she was not offered a permanent teaching job after three terms of work as a substitute teacher. She was suspended for a year after trying to see the District Superintendent; she said it was "a matter of life and death," and she wanted to resolve her job situation before she became so angry that she would "blow up." This was treated as a bomb threat, and the police were summoned.

She sued the school district. The District Court granted summary judgment for the employer on her claims of national origin and religious discrimination and retaliation. However, the Ninth Circuit ruled that the case should have gone to trial, because the plaintiff raised genuine issues of material fact. It was unclear whether her accent impaired her effectiveness as a teacher, and whether one school's failure to hire her (on the grounds that they needed a biology teacher who could also coach the ski team) was pretextual. However, the Ninth Circuit ruled that claims with respect to only one year were valid; claims about the earlier years were filed too late, and were time-barred. [*Raad v. Fairbanks North Star Borough Sch. Dist.*, 323 F.3d 1185 (9th Cir. 2003)]

In September 2003, the jury ruled for the defense in a wrongful termination suit brought by a Lebanese-American executive. He alleged that he was pressured into quitting after being questioned about being a Muslim of Arab origin at a company dinner party. The jury, however, did not accept that he was forced to resign; the jury believed the defense argument that he resigned (after some past instances of threatening to quit as a tactic of office politics) because he failed to achieve a spinoff and IPO of the division he headed. [*Maghribi v. Advanced Micro Devices*, discussed in Shannon Lafferty, *Jury Rejects Bias Suit by Muslim Executive*. The Recorder, Sept. 15, 2003 (law.com)] The Ninth Circuit ruled that a CEO's insistence on calling an employee "Manny" or "Hank" rather than his Arabic name, Mamdouh el-Hakem, constituted intentional hostile work environment discrimination forbidden by 42 U.S.C. § 1981, even in the absence of racial epithets. [*El-Hakem v. BJY Inc.*, 415 F.3d 1068 (9th Cir. 2005)]

The Tenth Circuit permitted Hispanic employees who said that an English-only policy caused them to be taunted by native English speakers to maintain hostile environment discriminatory impact claims. In the court's view, the employer anticipated that this would happen and had no justification for imposing the policy. [*Maldonado v. Altus*, 433 F.3d 1294 (10th Cir. 2006)]

A Hispanic female charged that she was subjected to a hostile work environment because of her sex and national origin, and that national origin discrimination was the reason why she did not receive a timely raise and why she was eventually terminated. The District Court granted summary judgment on her national-origin hostile environment charge, but the Eighth Circuit reversed because she raised triable issues as to bigoted remarks from co-workers and supervisory unwillingness to listen to, much less correct, complaints. The Eighth Circuit found that a reasonable fact-finder could conclude that the plaintiff was forced to work in close proximity to persons who subjected her to many demeaning comments and acts. There was also a fact question as to whether the employer had notice of the alleged harassment. However, claims relative to her termination were dismissed, because the Eighth Circuit accepted the defendant's contention that, after the plaintiff was involved in two separate altercations with other employees, there was a legitimate non-discriminatory reason to discharge her. [*Diaz v. Swift-Eckrich, Inc.*, 318 F.3d 796 (8th Cir. 2003)]

Summary judgment for the defense was granted in a Title VII suit brought by a Brazilian national who charged national-origin wage discrimination. The plaintiff was hired in Brazil by the Brazilian subsidiary of a U.S. corporation. He was transferred to Indiana for a two-year training assignment. He continued to be employed by the Brazilian subsidiary and earned his Brazilian salary plus a $20,000 stipend limited to the term of the U.S. assignment. After two years, his request for a permanent transfer to the United States was granted and he was paid on a par with current employees in the same position. Senior buyers, hired from outside the company, earned more than the plaintiff did. The Seventh Circuit was not persuaded by a statement allegedly made by the plaintiff's supervisor (that the plaintiff earned less because he was a Brazilian) because the supervisor did not set salaries or have hiring authority. The Seventh Circuit also accepted the defense argument that the higher-paid senior buyers had greater responsibilities and higher qualifications than the plaintiff, which justified the salary differential. [*Cardoso v. Robert Bosch Corp.*, 427 F.3d 429 (7th Cir. 2005)]

After an HR administrator was fired in 1999, she sued her former employer under Title VII, charging race and national-origin discrimination, plus a state-law charge alleging that she was fired in retaliation for her compliance with immigration law. The District Court granted summary judgment for the employer, and the plaintiff gave up on the federal claims, but continued to maintain that Illinois state law prevents firing someone who attempts to keep undocumented workers off the payroll. (After the Social Security Administration notified the ex-employer that some of its W-2 forms did not have valid Social Security numbers, the plaintiff investigated and found that the workers had provided invalid numbers. She was told to send letters to the employees, but she refused, saying this was illegal, and she refused to process the information the employees sent; she charged she was discharged in retaliation for this.)

The District Court ruled that the plaintiff had a federal remedy under 8 U.S.C. § 1324b(a)(5), and therefore her state retaliatory-discharge claim was preempted. The Seventh Circuit said the District Court was wrong. The federal remedy doesn't necessarily preclude the state one. Anyway, § 1324b(a)(5) applies only to retaliation for protesting discrimination on the basis of citizenship or national origin. The plaintiff said she was trying to prevent the employment of illegal aliens, a different situation altogether. But the Seventh Circuit ruled that the plaintiff did not have a valid claim, because the employer merely followed a suggestion from the Social Security Act that the validity of the Social Security Numbers be confirmed; the plaintiff was not entitled to enforce her own interpretation of the law. [*Arres v. IMI Cornelius Remcor, Inc.*, 333 F.3d 812 (7th Cir. 2003)]

§ 34.06   SEX DISCRIMINATION

[A]   Generally

Discrimination on account of sex is unlawful, except if there is a gender-based (bona fide occupational qualification) BFOQ. The Sixth Circuit held that being female is a BFOQ for working as a correctional officer in a women's prison. [*Everson v. Michigan Dep't of Corrections*, 391 F.3d 737 (6th Cir. 2004)] In 1983, the Supreme Court decided that it constitutes sex discrimination for a health plan to provide less comprehensive benefits to male employees and their wives than to female employees and their husbands. [*Newport News Shipbuilding v. EEOC*, 462 U.S. 669 (1983)]

A running test that requires an applicant for the Police Department to run 1.5 miles in 12 minutes or less measures the minimum aerobic capacity needed to perform the job. The test is job-related and reflects business necessity, and therefore does not violate Title VII even though it excludes 90% of the female applicants. [*Lanning v. Southeastern Pa. Transp. Auth.,* 308 F.3d 286 (3d Cir. 2002)]

On a showing of enough circumstantial evidence that women suffer more bullying and harassment than men, female employees can maintain a Title VII gender-based discrimination action, even if the harassment takes the form of shouting, screaming, foul language, and invading employees' personal space rather than a direct solicitation of sexual activity. [*EEOC v. National Educ. Ass'n Alaska,* 422 F.3d 840 (9th Cir. 2005)]

A male social worker's sex-discrimination claim, challenging the employer's subjective interview practices, failed in *Scott v. Parkview Memorial Hospital.* [175 F.3d 523 (7th Cir. 1999)] The plaintiff claimed that the interview process unfairly favored women because it privileged traditional feminine qualities such as warmth and empathy. However, the Seventh Circuit viewed subjective interviews as a necessary part of professional recruitment, and furthermore that the qualities useful in the interview were also useful in performing the job, so the interview practice was valid and job-related.

It violates the Fourteenth Amendment's guarantee of Equal Protection to apply a facially neutral state law in a way that reflects sexual stereotyping. Therefore, a male state trooper should have been granted a 30-day parental leave when his child was born. (Leave was denied on the basis that only women can be primary caregivers for infants.) However, *Knussman v. Maryland* [272 F.3d 625 (4th Cir. 2001)] holds that an award of $375,000 in emotional distress damages was disproportionate to the actual damages that the trooper suffered.

A Ninth Circuit decision holds that it is illegal sex discrimination for an airline to set its weight limits for female flight attendants based on tables for persons with a medium frame, while using tables for a large frame to set limits for male flight attendants. The court treated this as disparate impact discrimination not qualifying for a BFOQ defense. The airline called it a grooming standard (which can permissibly differ by sex), but the court said that requiring woman flight attendants to be thinner than males of the same height did not improve their ability to do their jobs. [*Frank v. United Airlines,* 216 F.3d 845 (9th Cir. 2000)]

A woman manager's refusal to follow her male boss' order to fire an "unattractive" woman sales associate was held to be protected activity under California anti-discrimination law. Retaliation against the manager was sex discrimination, because men were not subject to standards of attractiveness. The text of whether a retaliatory activity constitutes adverse employment action is whether it is likely to prevent employees from engaging in protected activity, and not whether the action materially affects the terms or conditions of employment. [*Yanowitz v. L'Oreal USA Inc.,* 131 Cal. Rptr. 2d 575 (Cal. App. 2003)]

The First Circuit ruled that the plaintiff failed to make out the prima facie case in her pay equity and failure-to-promote suit. Although she applied for a number of promotions, and men were hired for those jobs, the employer provided legitimate non-discriminatory rationales based on superior qualifications. She was not able to demonstrate that these rationales were pretextual, given the credence that courts award to management discretion in hiring. The plaintiff alleged that men achieved comparable promotions more rapidly, but the court did not consider the promotions truly comparable, because they occurred at times when different market conditions prevailed. As for the alleged pay disparity, all of the individuals in question received pay within the ranges given in corporate guidelines. The men who were promoted later gained the advantage of a higher general wage scale, as well as having the superior qualifications noted by the employer in its defense. [*Rathbun v. Autozone Inc.*, 361 F.3d 62 (1st Cir. 2004) (note that on another issue, the First Circuit held that employment discrimination claims in Rhode Island are subject to the three-year statute of limitations for personal injury rather than a one-year statute of limitations under the Rhode Island Fair Employment Practices Act)]

A city planner sued the municipal government and two individuals under Title VII, the ADEA, and the state (Missouri) Civil Rights Act. The plaintiff was hired at a starting salary above the minimum for the job, and was told she was in competition with one co-worker for a senior position that would be opening up. The co-worker (who had obtained a Master's degree) got the position. At that point, the plaintiff perceived that she was getting inferior assignments because of the sexist working environment; she resigned and brought suit. The Eighth Circuit accepted the argument that the male co-worker was better qualified, taking the position that employers are in a better position than courts to assess employee qualifications. The plaintiff charged that she was underpaid because she was a woman, although she made this claim on Equal Protection rather than EPA grounds. The Eighth Circuit (like the Tenth and Eleventh Circuits) required her to prove that the pay disparity was motivated by discriminatory animus. When a plaintiff makes out a prima facie case, it is an adequate defense for the employer merely to proffer non-gender-based reasons for the disparity; the employer is not required to prove them. The Eighth Circuit rejected the claims against the individuals. The mere fact that they worked for a state agency was not enough to convert them into state actors, so they could not be held liable under 42 USC § 1983 for harassment, because the harassment as alleged by the plaintiff did not involve the use of state authority or official position. [*Ottman v. City of Independence, Missouri*, 341 F.3d 751 (8th Cir. 2003)]

The Seventh Circuit held that a letter from a university's president to the Director of the Office of Women, expressing concern over denial of tenure to a woman faculty member, was not an admission of discriminatory intent. It should not be cited as direct evidence of sex discrimination. [*Lim v. Trustees of Indiana Univ.*, 297 F.3d 575 (7th Cir. 2002)]

According to the Sixth Circuit, a company's antinepotism policy (requiring one spouse to resign when two employees marry) was rational. However, firing someone for criticizing the policy could be a violation of the employee's right of freedom of thought. In *Vaughn v. Lawrenceburg Power System* [269 F.3d 703 (6th Cir. 2001)], the bride agreed to resign, then the groom was fired for agreeing with the statement, "I take it you do not fully agree with our policy." The Sixth Circuit said that antinepotism rules get heightened scrutiny under the First Amendment right of freedom of association if, but only if, they place a direct and substantial burden on the right to marry. [*See also Montgomery v. Carr,* 101 F.3d 1124 (6th Cir. 1996)]

The Seventh Circuit did not agree with a female supervisor that she was constructively discharged when she was transferred to an evening schedule. She claimed that these "intolerable" working conditions violated her "wifely instincts" that would force her to quit her job in order to take care of her husband's needs in the evening. The court was not impressed by these arguments. [*Grube v. Lau Indus. Inc.,* 257 F.3d 723 (7th Cir. 2001)]

[B]   The Pregnancy Discrimination Act (PDA)

Section 2000e contains vital definitions for understanding federal antidiscrimination law. Sex discrimination includes, but is not limited to, discrimination "because or on the basis of pregnancy, childbirth, or related medical conditions." [42 U.S.C. § 2000e(k)]

This part of Title VII is referred to as the Pregnancy Discrimination Act (PDA). Under the PDA, women "affected by pregnancy, childbirth, or related medical conditions" have to be treated the same way as "other persons" who are not affected by such conditions, but who are comparable in their ability or inability to work. In other words, the PDA does not treat pregnancy itself as a disability, but to the extent that a particular pregnant worker does encounter disability, the employer must treat it the same way as other non-occupationally-related disability.

The PDA requires equal treatment for "all employment-related purposes," including fringe benefits—a category that includes the all-important health benefits. However, employers do not have to provide health coverage if they would not otherwise. Employers have the discretion to provide abortion benefits, and are required to cover medical complications of abortion, but do not have to cover elective abortions, only abortions in situations where the mother's life would be endangered by carrying the fetus to term.

According to the EEOC, the number of pregnancy discrimination lawsuits rose 31% between 1992 and 2005 (going from 3,385 to 4,449), and the amount of pre-litigation settlement relief tripled during that time period ($3.7 million in 1992 to $11.6 million in 2005). The EEOC also took more pregnancy discrimination cases to trial: six or fewer per year in the mid-1990s, but 30 in 2005 alone. The EEOC suggests that there are far more instances of pregnancy discrimination than there are charges, either because the victims are afraid of retaliation or because they don't have the energy to have a job, a baby, and a discrimination suit! [Tresa Baldas, *Pregnancy Discrimination Suits on the Rise,* National Law Journal, Apr. 14, 2006 (law.com) (the article notes the filing of lawsuits by a national marketing manager charging demotion and unfair treatment); *Babb v. Merisant,*

No. 06 C 1383 (N.D. Ill.) (demotion and termination for pregnancy complications involved in carrying quadruplets); *Elwell v. Google*, No. 05 CV 6487 (S.D.N.Y.)]

As a threshold question, to succeed, the plaintiff must be a common-law employee. A recent case was dismissed on the basis that the host of a television program was an independent contractor, who entered into arrangements with the station for each separate episode. She received a flat fee for each episode; no taxes were withheld, no benefits were provided, and she was free to undertake other television work. Although she received unemployment benefits, the First Circuit did not deem this local determination controlling on the issue of her status under Title VII—a federal law. [*Alberty-Velez v. Corporacion de Puerto Rico Para La Difusion Publica*, 242 F.3d 418 (1st Cir. 2003)]

The District Court awarded $150,000 for lost earnings and $1.85 million for emotional distress and damage to career and reputation to an Oakland, Calif., police officer who was passed over for promotion after becoming pregnant. The plaintiff was the highest-ranking woman on the force and had passed the Captain's examination, but was denied the promotion she was promised when a vacancy was posted during her maternity leave. The promotion list including the plaintiff had expired, so a man with less experience was promoted to Captain. In 2003, the suit was dismissed, based on statements by police officials that promotions were frozen at the time when the plaintiff was eligible; however, the Ninth Circuit reinstated the suit in 2005, relying on a ruling in another case establishing the principle that employers cannot use undocumented oral claims of a hiring or promotion freeze to avoid trial of discrimination claims. [*Glenn-Davis v. Oakland* (Cal. App. 2006); *see* Rebecca Moore, *Police Officer Wins $2M in Pregnancy Discrimination Suit*, PlanSponsor.com (Feb. 28, 2006)]

If pregnant employees are covered by the plan, the pregnant wives of employees must be covered (in a plan with dependent coverage), and vice versa. However, it is permissible to exclude the pregnancy-related conditions of dependents other than the spouses of employees, as long as the exclusion is applied equally for male and female employees and their dependents.

29 C.F.R. Part 1604, Question 17 says that if an employer has a policy of continuing benefits for employees who are on leave (e.g., when they are injured; when they are on military leave), then benefits must be continued for pregnancy-related leave to the same extent.

Note, however, the 2005 ruling that it was not a violation of New Jersey's anti-discrimination law for an employer to refuse to grant extended medical leave for pregnancy complications. The employer already had a gender-neutral leave policy that was more generous than either state or federal law required. [*Gerety v. Atlantic City Hilton Casino Resort*, 877 A.2d 1233 (N.J. 2005)]

A parental leave policy that allows biological mothers and adoptive mothers and fathers—but not biological fathers—to use accrued paid sick leave does not violate Title VII or the guarantee of equal protection. The Eighth Circuit reads the PDA to require biological mothers to treat pregnancy-related disability leave on a par with other disabilities, and it is not unreasonable to assume that the period of disability will last six weeks. Letting adoptive parents use one week of paid sick leave is reasonable because biological parents are offered health benefits to offset childbirth costs, and the leave provides financial support for adoption. [*Johnson v. University of Iowa*, 431 F.3d 325 (8th Cir. 2005)]

Peralta v. Chromium Plating & Polishing Corp. [2000 U.S. Dist. LEXIS 17416 (E.D.N.Y. Sept. 15, 2000), N.Y.L.J., Oct. 18, 2000, at p. 38 col. 4] makes it clear that it was improper to fire a pregnant employee whose doctor said she should be placed on light duty. The employer said that she was placed on unpaid leave, but in either case she was treated differently from nonpregnant employees. The Eastern District would not allow the employer to treat protecting the unborn baby as a reason to impose a BFOQ of not being pregnant (even though the employee had miscarried an earlier pregnancy while working there).

The Southern District says that the BFOQ exception only comes into play when the employer seeks to protect third parties whose safety is part of the company's central mission. Customers are in that category, but employees' unborn children are not. In this analysis, potential tort liability is not a BFOQ either. The way to handle potential liability risk is to get a waiver from an employee who wants to keep working, rather than to fire her.

The Fifth Circuit upheld an employer's policy of limiting light-duty assignments to workers injured on the job. As long as pregnancy-related disability is treated on a par with other nonoccupational disability, there has been no PDA violation, even if pregnant workers have to stop work earlier than they would have preferred. [*Urbano v. Continental Airlines,* 138 F.3d 204 (5th Cir. 1998)]

In a case where the discharge occurs significantly after pregnancy and delivery, the plaintiff must show that she was affected by pregnancy, childbirth, or a related medical condition at the time of the adverse job action. A case where the plaintiff was fired eight months after her return from maternity leave (11 months after the baby's birth) was dismissed for lack of evidence. Alleged harassing comments before the baby's birth were not sufficient to demonstrate discrimination nearly a year later. [*Solomen v. Redwood Advisory Co.,* 183 F. Supp. 2d 748 (E.D. Pa. 2002)]

In contrast, the Fourth Circuit permitted a plaintiff to maintain a suit charging that she was fired for being pregnant, even though she was replaced by another woman—as long as the person who fired her did not choose her replacement and the replacement was a non-pregnant woman. The employer claimed that it could not have committed pregnancy discrimination because almost one year elapsed before the plaintiff was fired; however, the plaintiff's supervisor had tried to fire her while she was pregnant and replace her with a man, but was overruled. The Fourth Circuit also held that a jury could conclude that the plaintiff's sales territory was reduced and her quotas were increased while she was pregnant to prevent her from performing satisfactorily. [*Miles v. Dell Inc.*, 429 F.3d 480 (4th Cir. 2005)]

According to the Second Circuit early in 2003, the Pregnancy Discrimination Act's ban on discrimination on the basis of pregnancy or related conditions does not cover alleged discrimination on the basis of infertility, because both men and women can be infertile, and both sexes have reproductive organs. [*Saks v. Franklin Covey Co.,* 316 F.3d 337 (2d Cir. 2003)]

According to the Seventh Circuit, it was not a violation of the PDA for an employer to offer full-time work to a temporary employee, beginning some time after the baby was born. In this view, a manager's detailed discussions about pregnancy and workers not returning after childbirth were not found to be evidence of discrimination—just a tactless way of saying that the job would be held open for the temporary worker's return. [*Venturelli v. ARC Community Services Inc.,* 336 F.3d 606 (7th Cir. 2003)]

A mid-2003 Ninth Circuit case involved a six-months-pregnant job applicant who was told that jobs were available. She was offered and accepted a shift in a hotel's delicatessen. The next day, she was told that the food and beverage director wanted her to work six days a week as a floater waitress. She accepted, and quit another job she held. Then she was offered a job as a supervisor. When she arrived at the scheduled start date, she was told that the offers to her were reversed because she was pregnant. She sued, and the District Court ruled that she failed to satisfy all the *McDonnell-Douglas* tests because she did not prove that the waitress and supervisor positions remained open after she was rejected, or that the defendant continued to advertise those jobs. But the Ninth Circuit revived the case, ruling that the plaintiff's claim that the supervisor would not let her work while she was pregnant was direct evidence raising a question of material fact. Therefore, it was improper to grant summary judgment on the waitress and supervisor claims. [*Palmer v. Pioneer Inn Associates Ltd.,* 338 F.3d 981 (9th Cir. 2003)]

[C] The Equal Pay Act (EPA)

The Equal Pay Act [29 U.S.C. § 206] is related to the Title VII provisions that forbid sex discrimination, but it is not a part of Title VII. The EPA covers all employers with *two* or more employees. It forbids discrimination in compensation, including all forms of benefits, on the basis of sex—if the two jobs are of equal skill, effort, and responsibility and are performed under similar working conditions. In other words, the statute does not apply to "comparable worth" claims under which women claim that a typically female job is of greater value to society than a higher-paid but different job typically performed by men (e.g., child care workers and parking lot attendants).

Cost-based defenses are not allowed under the EPA, [*see* 29 C.F.R. § 216(b)] which says that even if it costs more to provide benefits to women than to men, the employer must either eliminate the benefit or provide it to everyone.

The EPA imposes civil penalties on employers who violate it; even criminal penalties, as prescribed by Fair Labor Standards Act § 216(a), are a possibility. Punitive damages are not allowed, but double back pay is. A winning plaintiff can get costs and attorney's fees.

An EPA suit by female professors against a state university was vacated and remanded by the Supreme Court. On remand, the Seventh Circuit upheld the EPA as a valid exercise of congressional authority, which meant that it was also legitimate for Congress to take away the state's Eleventh Amendment immunity from being sued. [*Varner v. Illinois State U.,* 226 F.3d 927 (7th Cir. 2000)]

In a Seventh Circuit Title VII and EPA case, the plaintiff was hired as an associate professor, earning $45,000; her male predecessor earned about $37,000. In 1997 her pay was raised from $58,000 to $62,000 so that she would earn more than a male professor under her supervision. Between 1991 and 1998, her average annual salary increase was 4.37% a year, versus 3.25% a year for the faculty as a whole. In 1998, a male associate professor was hired for $90,000, replacing a woman who had earned $86,000. The male professor also directed the university's Physical Therapy program, which needed a great deal of improvement to retain its certification.

The university did two pay equity studies, both of which showed a statistically significant gap between male and female salaries. One study identified the plaintiff as underpaid; her salary was therefore raised.

According to the District Court, the plaintiff failed to make out a prima facie case, because the male professor had important extra duties for the Physical Therapy program. He also supervised more students and teachers than the plaintiff did, and they had different educational backgrounds, and his department produced far more tuition revenue than hers did. That prevented him from serving as a specific comparator, leaving the plaintiff reliant on statistics to prove her case. The Seventh Circuit treated the salary studies as just part of a process, not proof of appropriate salary levels. Furthermore, because of the differences between their qualifications and job duties, he was not a similarly situated male who received preferential treatment, so her Title VII case was also dismissed. [*Cullen v. Indiana U. Bd. of Trustees,* 338 F. 3d 693 (7th Cir. 2003)]

The Eighth Circuit decided in 2003 that the Army's salary retention policy for civilian employees was entitled to the EPA exception for "factors other than sex," even though the plaintiff earned less than her male co-workers. Although she asserted that her salary was affected by past injustices, the court ruled that this argument merely requires a careful examination of the record to *see* if the employer improperly asserted a market-forces theory to justify the pay disparity. [*Taylor v. White,* 321 F.3d 710 (8th Cir. 2003)]

A state agency gave lateral hires a salary at least as high as they had earned in the past, plus a raise if the salary scale under the new job permitted it. A female worker brought suit, charging that this practice discriminated against women. The plaintiff alleged that she and a man with a different title did the same work, but he earned more because the process of setting initial salaries favored him, and the agency's practices maintained the salary gap. Seventh Circuit precedent is that past wages are a "factor other than sex" that will justify pay differentials because federal courts are not entitled to set standards for business practices. As long as an employer has a reason other than sex, it is not up to the court to inquire whether the reason is a good one. In the Seventh Circuit view, men's higher wages reflect the greater amount of time women spend on child-rearing, something that the

Seventh Circuit did not interpret as discrimination. In the case at bar, the plaintiff failed to introduce expert testimony showing that the previous employers' salary scales were discriminatory. [*Wernsing v. DHS, State of Illinois*, 427 F.3d 466 (7th Cir. 2005), citing, e.g., *Covington v. Southern Illinois Univ.*, 816 F.2d 317 (7th Cir. 1987). Other circuits, however, have held that past wages constitute a "factor other than sex" only if the employer has an acceptable business reason for using past wages to set starting pay for new hires: *Aldrich v. Randolph Central School District*, 963 F.2d 520 (2d Cir.), *cert. denied*, 506 U.S. 965 (1992); *EEOC v. J.C. Penney Co.*, 843 F.2d 249 (6th Cir. 1992); *Kouba v. Allstate Ins. Co.*, 691 F.2d 873 (9th Cir. 1982); *Glenn v. General Motors Corp.*, 841 F.2d 1567 (11th Cir. 1988)]

A contrary result was reached in a 2006 Sixth Circuit Case. Nurse practitioners working for the federal Department of Veterans' Affairs (DVA) brought suit under the EPA and Title VII, alleging they (95% of whom are female) are paid less than physician's assistants (most of whom are male) for performing jobs of equal skill, effort, and responsibility under similar working conditions. The District Court granted summary judgment to the agency, accepting the affirmative defense that it was merely following the two separate statutes that set pay for the two types of health practitioners. The nurse practitioners were required to have Master's degrees, whereas the physician's assistants didn't even have to have a bachelor's degree. (In fact, one woman who was qualified as both an NP and a PA worked as a PA because it paid more.) The Sixth Circuit reinstated the suit, noting that the DVA advertised for either an NP or a PA for certain jobs, and the two kinds of workers often filled in for one another. Both statutes allowed the DVA to increase salaries to cope with recruitment problems. The DVA chose to do so for PAs but not for NPs, even though recruitment problems were equally severe. [*Beck-Wilson v. Principi*, 441 F.3d 353 (6th Cir. 2006)]

A plaintiff, a bank vice president, received a negative performance review and was placed on six months' probation. A few months later, she quit and took a higher-paying job, and brought suit under the Equal Pay Act, Title VII, and the Missouri Human Rights Act. However, the Eighth Circuit dismissed her case. The court accepted the defense argument that she (and two other female vice presidents) earned $10,000 a year less than male vice presidents but despite the same job title, the differences reflected differences in duties, skills, and experience and therefore were not discriminatory. Nor did the court believe that she suffered retaliation for complaining about discrimination; she had had previous negative reviews, and auditors independently raised concerns about her supervision of the accounting department. Because she quit before the probation period ended, her constructive discharge claim failed, because it was unclear whether the problems with the ex-employer could have been resolved, and because there was no proof that the employer had violated any of the anti-discrimination laws. [*Tenkku v. Normandy Bank*, 348 F.3d 737 (8th Cir. 2003). For the proposition that actual duties, not just the job title, must be considered in salary comparisons, *see Hunt v. Neb. Pub. Power Dist.*, 282 F.3d 1021 (8th Cir. 2002)]

A female part-time clerical worker got an inside sales job with the same company, then was promoted to an outside sales job. A male clerical worker took over her inside sales job. She was offered a new job; if she took it, she would not get a raise, would have fewer accounts, but would lose her company car. If she did not take the so-called promotion, she could keep the car but would have to take on more accounts. She took the job, and earned $756 a week. When she left, the man who had taken her old inside sales job replaced her, earning $900 a week plus a company car. She sued under the EPA, charging that she was paid less than the man who replaced her, and was denied the benefit of the company car. She won at trial, and the jury awarded $10,000 in lost wages and benefits, $125,000 in nonpecuniary damages, and $1 million in punitive damages in a sex discrimination/EPA case. The District Court reduced the damages to $9,462, $30,000, and $200,000 respectively. The defendant appealed, claiming that the man earned more but in effect covered two sales positions, and therefore the pay disparity was based on factors other than sex. The Eighth Circuit held that it was not unreasonable for the jury to find that the plaintiff and her successor did equal jobs. Although the man had more accounts, he also had an assistant. The Eighth Circuit therefore upheld the jury's finding that the defendant was liable. But, because the evidence did not show malice or reckless indifference to federally protected rights, the court set aside the punitive damage award. [*Lawrence v. CNF Transportation, Inc.,* 340 F.3d 486 (8th Cir. 2003)]

For pay equity resources, *see* the DOL Women's Bureau [<http://www.dol.gov/wb/welcome.html>] and the Equal Employment Advisory Council. [<http://www.eeac.org>] Federal contractors can access the audit manual for OFCCP compliance at <http://www.dol.gov/esa/regs/compliance/ofccp/fccm/fccmanul.htm>.

[D] Sexual Orientation and Gender Behavior Discrimination

Although there are a number of state and local laws banning discrimination in the workplace on the grounds of sexual orientation, Title VII does not forbid discrimination on the basis of actual or perceived homosexuality or bisexuality. As the debate over gay marriage continues, it will be interesting to *see* if, for example, courts will uphold or overthrow dismissals based on an employee's having gone through a civil union or marriage ceremony with a same-sex partner. [*See also* § 18.06 for health plan issues]

The National Center for Transgender Equality reported in 2005 that 28% of the U.S. population (versus only 5% in 2001) was covered by the laws in six states and 74 localities prohibiting discrimination against transgendered persons (cross-dressers and transsexuals). Surgeons usually wait to perform sex-change surgery until the person has dressed and lived as a member of the sex he or she is transitioning into for at least one year. The Human Rights Campaign said that number of Fortune 500 companies with anti-discrimination policies covering transsexuals doubled between 2003 and 2004. [Kelly Pate Dwyer, *An Employee, Hired as a Man, Becomes a Woman. Now What?* New York Times, July 31, 2005, at § 10 p. 1]

In some instances, the case revolves around whether a person suffered adverse employment action not because of sexual activities or sexual orientation, but because a male employee was perceived to lack masculinity or a female employee to be unfeminine. (As discussed below at § 34.06[E], however, the highly feminine behavior of a woman becoming a mother also gives rise to workplace litigation.)

Employee plaintiffs have asserted theories of gender non-conformity bias that derive from the discussion of sex stereotyping in *Price Waterhouse*. [*Nichols v. Azteca Restaurant Enterprises Inc.*, 256 F.3d 864 (9th Cir. 2001); *Higgins v. New Balance Athletic Shoe Inc.*, 194 F.3d 252 (1st Cir. 1999)] Although Title VII does not cover transsexuality, transsexual plaintiffs now raise claims that they are discriminated against because they present themselves as the "other" sex and do not conform to gender stereotypes. [*See, e.g., Tronetti v. TLC Healthnet Lakeshore Hosp.*, 2003 WL 22757935 (W.D.N.Y. Sept. 26, 2003) This issue is discussed in *Price Waterhouse, Sex Stereotyping, and Gender Non-Conformity Bias*, 73 LW 2211 (Oct. 19, 2004)]

The Second Circuit decided a case brought by a lesbian who charged her employer with discriminating against her for failing to satisfy stereotyped expectations of femininity. She was hired as an assistant and trainee at a hair salon. Only about 10 to 15% of the assistants complete the training program, which takes two to three years. The plaintiff alleged that few women got that far. The plaintiff said that she was continually harassed for not being feminine; the defendant said that her performance as a hairdresser was inconsistent, and clients didn't like her hostile attitude. The Second Circuit said that it was difficult to disentangle the plaintiff's charges of sex stereotyping from those of sexual orientation stereotyping. In any event, the Second Circuit did not believe that the plaintiff proved that she had suffered discrimination on the basis of her masculine appearance. District courts in the Second Circuit have held that Title VII claims cannot be premised on being an effeminate male or masculine female. The employer said that it maintained a policy of requiring haircutters to have their hair cut at the shop, so they could serve as an advertisement. There were no objections raised when the plaintiff got a Mohawk cut in-house; she was, however, censured for getting a bad haircut at a barbershop. Although the plaintiff stated that she was penalized for getting a masculine hairstyle, the defendant said that the objection was the poor quality of the cut; a well-styled crewcut would have been acceptable. [*Dawson v. Bumble & Bumble*, 398 F.3d 211 (2d Cir. 2005); *see also Howell v. North Central College*, 320 F.Supp.2d 717 (N.D. Ill. 2004)]

The Ninth Circuit upheld the termination of a casino bartender for refusing to wear makeup. She was fired after close to 20 years of working there and garnering excellent ratings. (She objected to makeup as demeaning and personally offensive.) The Ninth Circuit held that the plaintiff did not have a cause of action under Title VII: she failed to show that the grooming policy imposed greater burdens on female than on male bartenders. For example, she failed to prove the amount of time and money women had to invest to comply with the policy.

In the Ninth Circuit, the rule is that employers can impose different grooming standards on men and women, as long as one sex is not burdened more than the other. [*Jespersen v. Harrah's Operating Co.,* 392 F.3d 1076 (9th Cir. 2004)] The case was reheard en banc (i.e., by all the judges of the Ninth Circuit). [444 F.3d 1104 (9th Cir. 2006)] The full court affirmed the three-judge panel's decision, agreeing that the plaintiff failed to show that the company's appearance policy imposed a greater burden on women. Although the en banc panel left the door open for claims that makeup requirements and other appearance standards can be unlawful sexual stereotyping, in this case it was held that the plaintiff failed to create any triable issues of fact.

The plaintiff achieved far greater success in a 2005 Sixth Circuit case. The plaintiff was a pre-operative male to female transsexual police officer when he passed the sergeant's exam for the Cincinnati Police Department. He scored 18th on the exam out of 105 candidates. However, he was not appointed as a sergeant because he failed the mandatory probation period. The jury awarded him $320,000 in damages, and the district court added $527,888 in attorneys' fees and $25,837 in costs. The Sixth Circuit affirmed the district court. Probationary sergeants were rated on an 18-point scale, with "judgment" considered the most important. "Command presence" was also important, although most of the witnesses in the case defined it differently; the plaintiff contended that because he was known to wear women's clothes and makeup off-duty, he was perceived as being unable to get his co-workers to respect him.

The Sixth Circuit has precedent that transsexuals are a protected class under Title VII, because sex stereotyping based on gender nonconformity is impermissible discrimination whether the person is transsexual or merely acts in an "unfeminine" or "unmasculine" manner. In this case, the Sixth Circuit ruled that a reasonable jury could conclude that there had been intentional discrimination because, although the plaintiff's scores during probation were not good, they were better than those of another person who became a sergeant. It was not necessary to show that another transsexual officer was favored over the plaintiff, only that he was the only person not to become a sergeant after the probationary period in seven years; that the other police officers knew that the plaintiff was in the process of transitioning to being a woman; and that he was often criticized for lacking command presence, which could reasonably be interpreted to mean that he was not masculine. [*Barnes v. City of Cincinnati,* 401 F.3d 729 (6th Cir. 2005)] The Supreme Court denied certiorari (126 S. Ct. 624), so the jury verdict ($320,000 in damages plus $550,000 in attorneys' fees), affirmed by the Sixth Circuit, became final. [Gina Holland (AP), *Supreme Court Avoids Transsexual Police Officer Case,* Nov. 8, 2005 (law.com)] The Sixth Circuit rule is that after a full trial on the merits, the Court of Appeals must focus on the ultimate question of discrimination, not whether the plaintiff presented a prima facie case: *Noble v. Brinker Int'l Inc.,* 391 F.3d 715 (6th Cir. 2004). On transsexuals as a protected class, *see Smith v. City of Salem, Ohio,* 378 F.3d 566 (6th Cir. 2004).

Additional issues are raised by persons who have had sex-change operations, those who are preparing for such operations, cross-dressers, and other people who violate gender-based norms of conduct.

A 2001 Minnesota case holds that it does not constitute sexual orientation discrimination to require a transsexual employee to use the rest room on the basis of biological rather than perceived gender. [*Goins v. West Group,* 635 N.W.2d 717 (Minn. 2001)]

[E] "Sex-Plus" Discrimination

The sex-plus cause of action asserts that the plaintiff suffered discrimination on the ground of sex and other factors—e.g., motherhood. Title VII does not list parenthood as a protected category. The Pregnancy Discrimination Act and Family and Medical Leave Act are limited to pregnancy and childbirth, and do not forbid bias against women who act as primary caregivers of their children. In 2004, the District Court for the District of Connecticut ruled that child care is gender-neutral and hence not protected under Title VII. [*Guglietta v. Meredith Corp.,* 301 F. Supp. 2d 209 (D. Conn. 2004). However, in a failure to hire/failure to promote case, the same district treated interview questions about child care arrangments as evidence of bias: *Senuta v. Groton, Connecticut,* 2002 U.S. Dist. LEXIS 10792 (D. Conn. Mar. 5, 2002)]

In the Second Circuit view, *Price Waterhouse* applies to assumptions that a woman will conform to a stereotype as well as penalizing women who do not conform, so comments that motherhood cannot be combined with a career can be evidence of an impermissible sex-based motive. Therefore, an employee who was denied tenure because she was the mother of young children had enough evidence to support a sex discrimination case. [*Back v. Hastings on Hudson Free School Dist.,* 365 F.3d 107 (2d Cir. 2004)]

Two state agency employees were mothers of infants. They were terminated for failure to attend a three-week training session in another city. The Supreme Court of West Virginia held that they failed to make out a *prima facie* case of disparate impact sex discrimination under the state human rights law. Although they cited the greater role that women play in child care, they did not provide statistical evidence of the specific disparate impact of this role on female versus male consumer service representatives. [*Pittsnogle v. West Va. Dep't of Transp.,* 605 S.E.2d 796 (W. Va. 2004)]

§ 34.07   RELIGIOUS DISCRIMINATION AND REASONABLE ACCOMMODATION

[A] Employer's Duties and Obligations

According to the EEOC, charges of religious discrimination, although few in number, are increasing. Recently, there have been many more claims involving

Muslims or persons perceived as Muslims even though they belong to other faiths (e.g., Sikhs or Hindus). In March 2003, the EEOC announced a $1.1 million settlement against Stockton Steel, benefiting four Pakistani machine operators who alleged that they were given the worst assignments, ridiculed during daily prayers, and subjected to ethnic slurs. A group of New York City bus drivers who wear veils brought suit because they were transferred from bus driving (i.e., a job in contact with the public) to washing buses and other non-public-contact positions. A 2006 New York Times article points out that converts are the group most likely to litigate, because typically they are U.S.-born citizens with no immigration issues. [Andrea Elliott, *In a Suspicious U.S., Muslim Converts Find Discrimination,* New York Times, Apr. 30, 2006, at p. B1.

A Muslim convert was fired after she began to wear a robe and head scarf to work. The defendant said she was fired for missing a scheduled shift. The Eastern District of Pennsylvania denied summary judgment for the employer on the grounds that the plaintiff proved that other violations of the dress code (which requires employees to wear the seasonal fashions displayed in the store) had been tolerated. The Eastern District accepted the plaintiff's argument that the alleged reason for her termination was pretextual. The employer said that as soon as it learned that the plaintiff was a Muslim, she was allowed to wear overgarments at work; the plaintiff said that she was treated rudely when she did this. The company claimed that it believed that the plaintiff was a Mormon—a claim that the Eastern District did not find very credible—but the court ruled that proof of religious discrimination does not require showing that the defendant correctly identified the religion against which it discriminated. [*Davis v. Mothers Work Inc.* (E.D. Pa. 2005); *see* Shannon P. Duffy, *Judge OKs Muslim Woman's Lawsuit,* The Legal Intelligencer, Aug. 9, 2005 (law.com)]

Religion includes belief and all forms of religious observance and practice. Two recent cases tackle the question of what constitutes a religious belief. The Eastern District of Wisconsin held that a sincerely held belief that takes the place of religion in the employee's worldview could constitute a religion, whether or not it involves concepts of God or an afterlife. Therefore, it was a violation of Title VII to demote a supervisor for expressing his sincere religious views in favor of white supremacy in a non-work-related newspaper article. The concept of reasonable accommodation applies only to religious observance or practice, not religious ideas. [*Peterson v. Wilmur Communications Inc.,* 205 F. Supp. 2d 1014 (E.D. Wis. 2002)] However, the California Court of Appeals held that it does not constitute religious discrimination to refuse to hire a vegan who refused to be vaccinated with a vaccine grown in chicken embryos, because beliefs about harming animals are secular, not a religious philosophy, because they were deemed to lack a spiritual or otherworldly component. [*Friedman v. Southern California Permanente Med. Group,* 125 Cal. Rptr. 2d 663 (Cal. App. 2002)]

Employers do not have an obligation to incur "undue hardship on the conduct" of their business if they can demonstrate that they are unable to make reasonable accommodation to an employee's or applicant's religious observance or practice. [42 U.S.C. § 2000e(j)] In fact, a 1977 Supreme Court case holds that investing more than a minimal amount in accommodation can actually represent an illegal preference in favor of the employee who receives the accommodation. [*TWA v. Hardison,* 432 U.S. 63 (1977)]

Except in very limited cases (being a priest or minister, for example) religious beliefs are irrelevant to employment and cannot be used as a hiring criterion. Employers are not supposed to prefer one religion over another, or even to prefer organized religion over atheism or agnosticism.

The duty of reasonable accommodation requires employers to try to fit in with employees' beliefs and religious duties. Under EEOC guidelines, all sincerely held moral and ethical beliefs are entitled to the same protection as religious beliefs. But note the Seventh Circuit's 2005 holding that as long as an employer refuses to recognize employee affinity groups for any religion, it is not religious discrimination for the company to refuse to recognize affinity groups for particular religions, even if affinity groups for other Title VII suspect categories (e.g., ethnic groups) are recognized. [*Moranski v. GM Corp.,* 433 F.3d 537 (7th Cir. 2005)]

The Ninth Circuit found that an Evangelical Christian supervisor who was fired for hostile treatment of a lesbian subordinate did not show that her discharge was occasioned by hostility to her religion. The court refused to infer discriminatory animus from the employer's failure to take the steps that usually preceded a firing for violation of the anti-harassment policy. [*Bodett v. Cox Com. Inc.,* 366 F.3d 736 (9th Cir. 2004)]

In contrast, however, AT&T Broadband maintained a diversity policy requiring all employees to "recognize, respect, and value differences." A fundamentalist Christian employee refused to sign the certificate, because his religion teaches that some differences are sinful and do not deserve to be valued. The District of Colorado found that he put the employer on notice of his religious objection to the policy, requiring the employer to start the interactive process of accommodation; not doing so violated the employee's right to religious accommodation. [*Buonanno v. AT&T Broadband LLC*, 313 F. Supp. 2d 1069 (D. Colo. 2004)]

In 1986, the Supreme Court held that employers are not obligated to accept the employee's characterization of what would be a reasonable religious accommodation. The employer can make its own reasonable suggestion of how to accommodate the employee's belief. [*Ansonia Bd. of Educ. v. Philbrook,* 479 U.S. 60 (1986)]

Employees will probably have to be permitted to wear forms of dress, jewelry, and hairstyles required by their religion. The exception might be a situation in which the employer can show a genuine safety hazard that cannot be accommodated in another way. For example, a "no-beard" policy could not be enforced against an employee whose religion requires him to grow a beard, unless the beard is unsanitary or creates a hazard of getting caught in machinery—and there is no method of securing the beard that would preserve safety and cleanliness.

Probably the most common religious accommodation issue involves work assignments when the employee is supposed to observe a Sabbath, attend religious services, study the scriptures, teach in a religious school, or the like. The consensus is that the employer has to accommodate activities (or non-activities, like avoiding work on the Sabbath) that are mandated by an organized religion, but not employee's personal wishes about religious observance.

The EEOC considers it unlawful discrimination to set overtime rates in a way that disadvantages employees who observe a Sabbath other than Sunday. [*See* Guidelines, 29 C.F.R. Part 1605] The EEOC considers acceptable accommodations to include voluntary substitution of one employee for another, swapping shifts, lateral transfers, changes of job assignment, and flextime (i.e., the employee makes up the time devoted to religious observance).

However, employers are not required to accommodate religious observance by violating the seniority rights of a nonobservant employee. In the view of the EEOC, it would be undue hardship for the employer to have to pay overtime to other employees to cover for the religious employee or to have an untrained or inexperienced person covering for the religious employee.

When it comes to union security, the National Labor Relations Act, at 29 U.S.C. § 169, provides that if an employee belongs to a religion that has traditionally objected to unions, then the employer cannot require the employee to join or support a union, even if the operation is an agency shop or participates in another union security arrangement. However, the employee's religious objection can be accommodated by requiring him or her to contribute an amount equivalent to the union initiation fee and dues to a charitable organization that is neither a union nor religious in nature. That way the employee does not benefit financially from the antiunion belief, but is not required to perform a religiously repugnant act.

States are not allowed to pass laws that give employees an absolute right to get their Sabbath day as a day off—that would be an unconstitutional establishment of religion. [*Estate of Thornton v. Caldor, Inc.,* 472 U.S. 703 (1985)] However, an employee who is fired for refusing to work on the Sabbath is entitled to collect unemployment benefits. [*Hobbie v. Unemployment Appeals Comm'n of Florida,* 480 U.S. 136 (1987)] Some state laws, including New York's Human Rights Law, make it clear that employees who get time off for religious observances must make up the time at another time that is religiously acceptable.

Employers may have to become umpires if an employee claims that his or her own faith requires preaching and seeking converts at work, but co-workers aren't interested or are actively hostile. A 1997 case [*Venters v. City of Delphi,* 123 F.3d 956 (7th Cir. 1997)] involves a police dispatcher who alleged that she was fired because her born-again boss insisted she share his religious views. The decision suggests that unwanted proselytizing could create a "hostile religious environment" in the workplace, similar to a climate of racial hostility or sexual harassment.

It should be noted that employees who are not allowed to preach in the workplace can invite co-workers to a church service, prayer meeting, Bible study group, etc., that meets outside the workplace, so their religious expression can be continued elsewhere.

The plaintiff's claim of a religiously hostile workplace was rejected in *Hernandez-Torres v. Intercontinental Trading Co.* [158 F.3d 43 (1st Cir. 1998)] Although he received a number of e-mails urging greater productivity, he was not singled out: Nonreligious employees received similar messages. He continued to receive favorable assessments, so he did not suffer job detriment because of his religious convictions. When his claim of religious discrimination failed, his retaliation claim also had to be dismissed.

[B] Steps Toward Religious Accommodation

Employers should extend at least the same tolerance to religious garb as to "fashion statements." Where there are actual risks (such as robes getting caught in machinery), document the risk, and work with religious leaders to find out what kinds of safety garments are compatible with religious needs.

Bulletin board postings or the corporate intranets can be used to get volunteers to cover for workers taking prayer time or observing religious holidays. A diverse workforce really helps here—Christian employees can cover the holidays of non-Christian religions, and vice versa. Optional or floating personal days can be used for religious observance.

Because Islam requires five daily prayers, several occurring during the normal work day, it can be difficult to accommodate Muslim employees in a production line environment. Part of the prayer obligation is keyed to sundown, so it does not occur at the same time every day, making it harder to schedule prayers. The need for Muslims to wash their hands and feet before prayer can cause hazardous wet conditions in the washrooms (or hallways, if water is tracked). One simple solution is to install a special self-draining basin, or arrange to have the floors mopped more often.

Although it is often impossible to arrange the menu in the employee cafeteria to conform to all dietary requirements, it is a reasonable gesture to provide some vegetarian alternatives, and to make sure that people whose religion bans the consumption of pork or beef will have other menu choices available.

A growing concern for many employers is how to balance some employees' desire to evangelize for their faith against the desire of other employees to maintain their existing religion (or lack thereof) and lifestyle. Cases have been brought alleging a religiously hostile environment caused by unwanted attempts at religious conversion.

In some instances, the employer company itself wants to make faith-based principles and practices a part of work life. It should be noted, however, that Colorado's Universal Traffic Service was required to pay damages of $750,000 (mostly in punitive damages) plus $15,000 back pay for one employee, plus costs and fees of over $160,000 for requiring employees to listen to sermons from the owner and to sign a company prayer. (The award was subsequently reduced to $50,000 per employee because of the operation of the damage caps.) A jury awarded $40,000 in religious discrimination damages to a woman who was expected to attend her employers' church and was insulted as a "Jezebel" when she wore a short-sleeved dress to services. [Helen Irvin, *Proselytizing in the Workplace: The Risk of Religious Harassment*, 73 LW 2131 (Sept. 14, 2004). The "Jezebel" case is *Robinson v. Healthworks Int'l LLC*, 837 So. 2d 714 (La. App. 2003)]

[C]   Case Law on Reasonable Accommodation

The Second Circuit ruled in 2003 that an employer's rejection of an employee's proposed accommodation of religious needs is a discrete act. Therefore, the statute of limitations is 300 days from the occurrence of the act; the statute of limitations does not restart with every scheduled prayer time that the employee was forced to work. Once an employer rejects a proposed accommodation, the facts to make the case are in existence; the decision is not re-implemented periodically. [*Elmenayer v. ABF Freight Sys. Inc.*, 318 F.3d 120 (2d Cir. 2003)]

According to *Weber v. Roadway Express Inc.*, [199 F.3d 270 (5th Cir. 2000)] the employer had no obligation to accommodate a Jehovah's Witness truck driver who wanted to be assigned only male driving partners, because his religion forbade him to take overnight trips with any woman other than his wife. The employer would have encountered a serious burden to reconfigure the schedules. Although the employer had accommodated nonreligious requests in the past, it did so only consistent with business needs and did not have an obligation to encounter undue hardship to accommodate the truck driver.

In *Shelton v. University of Medicine & Dentistry of New Jersey*, [223 F.3d 220 (3rd Cir. 2000)] a nurse alleged that she was not offered reasonable accommodation to her religious objection to performing tasks that would allow infants to die. The hospital did not perform elective abortions, but sometimes the labor and delivery staff had to assist in abortions performed for reasons of the mother's health. Therefore, the hospital offered her a transfer from the labor ward to the neonatal ICU. She refused to discuss open nursing positions with the hospital's HR department.

In the Third Circuit view, the plaintiff satisfied her prima facie case of religious discrimination, in that she did hold sincere religious views, and she did lose her job. But the court still ruled for the employer, on the theory that the employer's duty is satisfied by offering any reasonable accommodation, even one that is not accepted by the employee. In this case, the employee forfeited her cause of action by refusing to discuss alternatives, so she would have lost even if the proposed accommodation had not been reasonable.

Late in 2003, the Seventh Circuit granted a rehearing in a case holding that a social service agency was not required to accommodate the employee's desire to wear a head covering for religious reasons. [*Holmes v. Morton County Office of Family & Children*, 349 F.3d 914 (7th Cir. 2003)] However, the court denied rehearing (thus allowing the decision to stand) in a case holding that the state police do not have an obligation to re-assign a police officer who has a religious objection to being assigned to enforcement duties at a casino. [*Endres v. Indiana State Police,* 334 F.3d 618 (7th Cir. 2003)]

The Church of Body Modification was established in 1999, and has about 1,000 members. One of them sued her employer, charging that the multiple facial piercings that violated the employer's ban on facial jewelry were required by her religion. At first, she offered to wear plastic retainers or bandages over the piercings and jewelry. The employer initially rejected this offer. When the employer changed its mind, the employee had changed hers and said that her religion required her to be a confident role model. The First Circuit ruled for the employer, stating that it had a right to control its public image, and there was no reasonable accommodation it could make without abandoning its grooming standards. [*Cloutier v. Costco Wholesale Corp.*, 390 F.3d 126 (1st Cir. 2004)]

§ 34.08   RETALIATION

Section 8 of the EEOC Compliance Manual (used by EEOC offices), EEOC Directives Transmittal 915.003 (May 20, 1998), covers retaliation. There are three essential elements in a retaliation claim that the EEOC will pursue:

- The charging party engaged in protected activity, such as opposing discrimination or participating in the Title VII complaint process;
- The employer took adverse action against the charging party;
- There was a causal connection between the protected activity and the employer's adverse action.

A retaliation complaint might be proper if the charging party had a reasonable good-faith belief that the employer committed discrimination (even if this belief was incorrect), and the charging party used a reasonable means to protest this to the employer.

It is illegal to retaliate against a charging party if he or she, or someone closely associated with him or her, participated in any statutory enforcement proceeding. This includes any investigation, proceeding, hearing, or suit under any of the statutes enforced by the EEOC. It is unlawful for one employer to retaliate on the basis of a complaint against another employer.

The Supreme Court resolved several questions about the retaliation cause of action in its June 22, 2006, decision in *Burlington Northern & Santa Fe Railway Co. v. White.* [No. 05-259, <http://caselaw.lp.findlaw.com/us/000/05-259>] The Supreme Court ruled that retaliation against employees who engage in protected concerted activity is unlawful, whether or not the form the retaliation takes is employment-related. The Supreme Court reached this conclusion based on differences in the statutory language covering the substantive ban on discrimination and the anti-retaliation provision. However, to be actionable, the retaliatory measures must be severe enough that a reasonable employee might have been deterred from pursuing discrimination charges. In the case at bar, there was actionable retaliation because even though the petitioner's job classification did not change, she was assigned less attractive work (more arduous, dirtier, more strenuous) to punish her for complaining about workplace sexual harassment.

An employee who volunteered to testify at another employee's sexual harassment suit, but was not called, has participated in the proceeding and is protected by the Title VII anti-retaliation provision, which covers all forms of participation in discrimination charges. [*Brown v. Astro Holdings Inc.*, 385 F. Supp. 2d 519 (E.D. Pa. 2005)]

The EEOC might seek temporary or preliminary relief such as injunction if the retaliation places the charging party at risk of irreparable injury and there is a substantial likelihood that the retaliation claim will succeed. The compliance manual notes that all of the statutes enforced by the EEOC make both compensatory and punitive damages available to victims of retaliation.

Although Title VII retaliation damages are subject to the statutory cap, there is no cap on ADEA or EPA damages.

In a mid-2003 Sixth Circuit case, the plaintiff, a black female surgical technician, sued her employer for denying her a promotion on the basis of race and in retaliation for her complaints about discriminatory hiring policies. The jury found in her favor, awarding $40,000 in back pay, $50,000 in compensatory damages for emotional distress, and $210,000 in punitive damages. The Fourth Circuit agreed that the employer was liable, and upheld the damage award except for the punitive damages. The plaintiff worked part-time for the defendant hospital when she was called up for a military reserve commitment. After serving her military commitment, she applied for a full-time job with the defendant. She was told that there were no jobs for surgical technicians, but she was offered a lower-paid, less-skilled job which she accepted in the hope of getting a promotion. She also went to nursing school and continued applying for surgical technician jobs which were consistently denied. She made an internal complaint about racial discrimination, but was ignored and suffered a hostile work environment. After graduation from nursing school, she was denied employment as a nurse despite a large number of job openings and her excellent school and work record. Eventually she went to work as a nurse at another hospital that paid less.

The Fourth Circuit ruled that the plaintiff clearly engaged in protected activity (complaining about Title VII violations), and failure to promote is an adverse employment action. The jury could reasonably have concluded that she suffered retaliation. The court agreed that an award of emotional distress damages can be supported by the plaintiff's testimony standing alone. The defendant's argument that the physical consequences of emotional distress should be disregarded because the plaintiff did not seek medical attention was not accepted by the court, which found that the defendant preferred to rely on prayer and support from her family to cope with distress. However, the Fourth Circuit overturned the award of punitive damages, finding that the employer made a good-faith effort to comply with

Title VII, and therefore should not be held vicariously liable for discrimination committed by its employees. [*Bryant v. Aiken Regional Medical Centers Inc.*, 333 F.3d 536 (4th Cir. 2003)]

According to the Eleventh Circuit, protection against retaliation for participation in an investigation is limited to the EEOC investigation. An employer is not liable for retaliation on the basis of participation in the employer's own internal investigation. [*Clover v. Total Sys. Servs. Inc.*, 157 F.3d 824 (11th Cir. 1998)] It is not unlawful retaliation to discharge an employee based on the employer's good-faith belief that she lied during such an internal investigation, because the retaliation provision is not triggered until there has been an EEOC filing. [*EEOC v. Total Sys. Servs. Inc.*, 221 F.3d 1171 (11th Cir. 2000)]

An employee who was accused of sexual harassment was permitted to maintain a retaliation claim with respect to denial of promotion, on the grounds that defending oneself against sexual harassment charges is protected concerted activity. [*Deravin v. Kerick*, 335 F.3d 195 (2d Cir. 2003)]

An IRS employee tried unsuccessfully to assert a unique argument in a retaliation case. The plaintiff, Twisdale, who is white, claims that black supervisors harassed him and retaliated against him because of his actions vis-à-vis a black employee whom he supervised. That employee (Ms. Barry Madison) filed charges with the IRS EEO office; the plaintiff was ordered to investigate these charges. He reprimanded Madison for a minor ethical violation. Madison then charged Twisdale with discrimination; Twisdale claims that this is the reason why he himself became a target for harassment and retaliation. Eventually, Madison prevailed on her complaint (although there was no finding that Twisdale discriminated against her), and the reprimand was removed from her file.

The Seventh Circuit held that Twisdale could not be said to have suffered retaliation, because he got good assignments (although not necessarily his first choice) and performance bonuses; a year later, he was promoted a grade, although this did involve a transfer to a city other than one of the ones requested by Twisdale.

Twisdale claimed the equivalent of prosecutorial immunity for his participation in the investigation of Madison's charges. However, the Seventh Circuit declined to interpret the concept of participation in a discrimination charge to include taking a position contrary to the alleged discriminatee, because the court did not think such an extension would further the objectives of Title VII. [*Twisdale v. Snow*, 325 F.3d 950 (7th Cir. 2003)]

CHAPTER 35

SEXUAL HARASSMENT

§ 35.01 INTRODUCTION

Sexual harassment is the subjection of an employee to unwanted sexual contact, propositions, or innuendoes. Sexual harassment occurs in two forms: either "quid pro quo" harassment, where an employee is threatened with job detriment for not complying with a sexual proposition or offered job benefits for compliance, or "hostile environment" harassment, where the atmosphere in the workplace is offensive

Although it may be unprofessional, it is not unlawful for a supervisor to date or have sexual relations with a subordinate. The essence of harassment is continued pressing of unwanted sexual attentions. Sexual harassment can also occur if a supervisor penalizes a subordinate who terminates or wishes to terminate a sexual relationship that was consensual at the outset. Some companies, trying to cope with the difficulty of forbidding interoffice romances but also wishing to avoid liability for sexual harassment, are asking for employees to sign "love contracts" confirming that a relationship is consensual and not the product of undue influence by a supervisor, and setting guidelines for appropriate behavior in the office. Transferring one romantic partner to another department is sometimes done (although this can be interpreted as retaliatory if litigation does ensue). [Lindsay Fortado, *Workplace "Love Contracts" on the Rise*, National Law Journal, Mar. 3, 2005 (law.com)]

Sexual harassment is considered a form of sex discrimination and therefore is forbidden by Title VII. The EEOC has adopted a two-part test. Conduct is unwanted if the employee did not solicit or initiate the conduct, and the employee finds it undesirable or offensive.

However, the Eleventh Circuit did not permit a "reverse-discrimination" sexual harassment suit, brought by a plaintiff who was denied the promotion that went to the employee who had a consensual sexual relationship with the boss. The holding of *Womack v. Runyon* [147 F.3d 1298 (11th Cir. 1998)] is that an isolated instance of favoring a sexual partner cannot constitute sex discrimination, because the plaintiff class would consist of all of the company's employees (male and female), because they were all equally disadvantaged by such favoritism.

The Fourth Circuit refused to apply disparate impact analysis in sexual harassment cases, and ruled late in 2002 that the alleged sexual harassment was not actionable because co-workers would have subjected the plaintiff to the same offensive behavior and vulgar language if she had been male. [*Ocheltree v. Scollon Prods. Inc.*, 308 F.3d 351 (4th Cir. 2002)] The Fourth Circuit re-heard the case. Its July, 2003 opinion (335 F.3d 325) revised the earlier opinion. The 2003 version took the position that a reasonable jury could have found that the conduct was indeed sexually discriminatory, because male co-workers repeatedly attempted to embarrass the plaintiff and make her uncomfortable because she was the only female worker. The revised opinion also said that a reasonable jury could find that the frequency with which the plaintiff was subjected to vulgar talk and gestures created a pervasively abusive work environment. The July, 2003 opinion finds the employer failed to provide an adequate complaint procedure, and the plaintiff tried to complain about the harassment but management refused to discuss the matter with her. Therefore, the July 2003 Fourth Circuit opinion reinstates the jury verdict in the plaintiff's favor with respect to compensatory damages. However, the revised opinion denies punitive damages to the plaintiff, because the evidence was not legally sufficient to prove that the employer had the degree of knowledge of the harassment that would be required to impose punitive damages. The Ninth Circuit also permitted a gender-based harassment action to be maintained based on a showing that women were subjected to a greater degree of bullying, shouting, cursing, and invasion of personal space, even though the perpetrator was not attempting to solicit sexual activity from employees. [*EEOC v. National Educ. Ass'n Alaska,* 422 F.3d 840 (9th Cir. 2005)]

The sexual harassment cause of action requires that the victim suffer tangible job action, not merely lack of friendliness or exclusions from workplace social activities. It was not a tangible job action when the plaintiff was fired, but immediately rehired the next day. However, a lateral transfer that did not affect pay or responsibilities was a tangible job action because it forced the plaintiff into the negative situation of having to decide between a long commute and relocating. (The plaintiff charged that his supervisor retaliated against him for rejecting sexual advances.) [*Keeton v. Flying J Inc.,* 429 F.3d 259 (6th Cir. 2005). *See Birch v. Cuyahoga County Probate Court,* 392 F.3d 151 (6th Cir. 2004), holding that decisions that are rescinded before the employee has time to suffer tangible harm are not adverse job actions] In a 2006 sexual harassment retaliation case, *Burlington Northern & Santa Fe Railway Co. v. White,* the Supreme Court ruled that retaliation liability is broader than liability for workplace discrimination: retaliation can be actionable even if the employee's job classification and compensation do not change, as long as the retaliatory measures are severe enough to be daunting to a reasonable employee. [No. 05-259, <http://caselaw.lp.findlaw.com/us/000/05-259>]

Although one or more individuals may commit sexual harassment, it is the employer company that has the legal liability. The only way the employer can avoid liability is by carrying out appropriate investigations of allegations of harassment and by taking appropriate steps to deal with harassment accusations that are well founded.

Under a commercial general liability (CGL) or umbrella liability policy, insurers have no duty to defend against an EEOC suit for intentional sexual harassment. [*American States Insurance Co. v. Natchez Steam Laundry,* 131 F.3d 551 (5th Cir. 1998)] Therefore, the insurance company did not act in bad faith by not providing a defense or insurance benefits. The agency's allegations came under the intentional-acts exception of the policy, and the insurer made an adequate investigation before denying the claim.

The Ninth Circuit has upheld the application of the CRA '91 cap on damages to hostile work environment cases, on the grounds that it is a rational exercise of government power; does not violate the Due Process rights of plaintiffs; and serves the legitimate purpose of discouraging frivolous suits and protecting employers from cripplingly high awards. [*Lansdale v. Hi-Health Supermarket Corp.*, 54 Fed. Appx. 268 (9th Cir. 2002)]

§ 35.02   THE EMPLOYER'S BURDEN

In this context, two of the key cases are *Burlington Industries, Inc. v. Ellerth* [524 U.S. 742 (1998)] and *Faragher v. City of Boca Raton.* [524 U.S. 775 (1998)] If the action that the plaintiff complains of had adverse employment effect on the victim, the employer is absolutely liable. The employer is still liable even if no adverse employment effect occurred—unless the employer can assert as a defense that it maintained proper antiharassment and grievance policies.

The *Ellerth* case involved a sales representative who felt threatened by repeated remarks and gestures from a manager (not her immediate supervisor). She was not deprived of job benefits. Although she knew the company had an antiharassment policy, she did not complain about the harassment while it was occurring. She quit her job but did not attribute her resignation to harassment. Three weeks later, she sent a letter to the company explaining why she resigned.

The Supreme Court's decision was that the supervisor's threats of adverse job action created a hostile work environment. In such a situation, the employer becomes vicariously liable for the supervisor's conduct by:

- Failing to stop it after learning about it;
- Giving the supervisor apparent authority over the victim, thus making harassment possible;
- Allowing the supervisor to actually take adverse job action against the victim.

However, the other side of the coin is that the employer can be free of liability by taking reasonable care to maintain a workable complaint procedure, if the plaintiff fails to use the procedure.

In the *Faragher* case, a lifeguard sued her municipal employer and two supervisors for creating a hostile environment (including lewd touching of female employees). The employer did have an antiharassment policy, but it was not publicized to the employees. The employer didn't supervise the conduct of the supervisors themselves, and didn't create a procedure for reporting to someone other than the supervisor who committed the harassment. Therefore, the Supreme Court held that the employer was legally responsible for the hostile environment, because it failed to communicate the antiharassment policy and didn't track the conduct of supervisors.

In 2003, the Third Circuit (contrary to holdings in the Second and Sixth Circuits) held that the *Ellerth/Faragher* affirmative defense would not be available to employers in situations where the employee was able to prove constructive discharge. The Supreme Court reversed the Third Circuit in mid-2004.

The Supreme Court settled a contentious point by holding that the test of constructive discharge is objective (whether a reasonable person would feel compelled to resign) rather than subjective (the individual employee's personal reaction to the situation). The Supreme Court also noted that, although firing an employee is always an official act (and therefore the affirmative defense is not available), constructive discharge is not always an official act of the employer company. Therefore, the company should be given the chance to assert and prove the affirmative defense. [*Suders v. Easton*, 325 F.3d 432 (3d Cir. 2003), *rev'd sub nom. Pennsylvania State Police v. Suders*, 542 U.S. 129 (2004)]

It is not always simple to determine whether an individual accused of harassing conduct is a supervisor or not. In 2003, the Second Circuit refused to draw a bright-line test, instead preferring a broader inquiry into the facts of the case. The plaintiff was assigned to work as helper to six elevator mechanics. The union contract designated one of the mechanics as mechanic in charge—able to assign work and direct the work force, even though this person was not a supervisor. The plaintiff claimed that the mechanic-in-charge harassed her, and that her complaints to the shop steward and her supervisor were ignored. At first, the District Court ruled that the mechanic-in-charge was not a supervisor because his only power was to distribute assignments. The Second Circuit reversed, finding that the senior employee had special dominance over his co-workers, and the official supervisor was seldom around to control him. [*Mack v. Otis Elevator*, 326 F.3d 116 (2d Cir. 2003). According to the Fourth and Seventh Circuits, to be a supervisor, a person must have economic (hiring and firing) authority over the plaintiff worker—*see, e.g., Parkins v. Civil Constructors of Illinois Inc.*, 163 F.3d 1027 (7th Cir. 1999)]

A 2005 Eastern District of Pennsylvania case suggests that it may be more difficult for employers to get summary judgment than they expect, because many cases involve fact issues that require a full trial. In the case at bar, the alleged harasser was a low-level manager, whose ability to harass was more or less on a par with any co-worker. The plaintiff, a teenage part-time employee, charged at least 50 incidents of offensive touching, but did not complain until the day she quit her job. The defense argued that the plaintiff's failure to report the harassment prevented the employer from investigating or taking measures. However, the judge refused to grant summary judgment, stating that it was a jury issue as to whether the employer maintained an effective anti-harassment policy and whether the plaintiff was notified of it. There was no employee handbook; there was no anti-harassment policy; and although the required poster was on the bulletin board, it was not clear whether any of the employees ever saw it. Whether the plaintiff quit voluntarily or was constructively discharged also was a jury issue. [*Wells v. Happy Tymes Family Fun Center Inc.* (E.D. Pa. 2005), discussed in Shannon P. Duffy, *Sexual-Harassment Defense May Be Weaker Than Thought*, The Legal Intelligencer, Dec. 2, 2005 (law.com)]

Although many cases involve the conduct of supervisors (because of their ability to affect working conditions), employers have also been held liable, in appropriate cases, for harassment committed by nonsupervisory, fellow employees, and by customers.

In a 2004 case, a person described as a "foreman" was treated as a co-employee because he did not have direct authority over the employee he harassed; therefore, liability was not imposed under *Ellerth/Faragher*. [*Joens v. John Morrell & Co.*, 354 F.3d 938 (8th Cir. 2004)]

The Seventh Circuit permitted a hospital nurse who was harassed by an independent contractor doctor to sue the hospital under Title VII, but not to maintain equal protection and retaliation claims. If the hospital intentionally created or tolerated hostile working conditions, the Seventh Circuit ruled that it didn't matter whether the harasser was a supervisor, independent contractor, or patient. However, the other claims were dismissed for lack of evidence of adverse action or intentional discrimination against the plaintiff. The Seventh Circuit ruled that tort concepts about a principal's liability for the actions of an independent contractor do not apply to Title VII. [*Dunn v. Washington County Hosp.*, 429 F.3d 689 (7th Cir. 2005)]

In a quid pro quo case, a series of minor effects that would not be actionable by themselves can be joined together to prove tangible job detriment, and therefore make out the case. [*Reinhold v. Virginia*, 151 F.3d 920 (4th Cir. 1998)]

The employer's burden rests with the employer—harassed employees can't sue their unions for involvement in the employer's failure to redress sexual harassment. If one union member accuses another of harassment, the union has a duty to give both of them fair representation at the disciplinary hearing—but the union does not have an obligation to investigate or remedy discrimination. [*Thorn v. Amalgamated Transit Union*, 305 F.3d 826 (8th Cir. 2002)]

§ 35.03   APPROPRIATE EMPLOYER RESPONSES

[A]   Statutory and Case Law

Most companies are aware of the potential risk of sexual harassment litigation. After the landmark *Ellerth* and *Faragher* cases, the employer must prevent severe, pervasive unwelcome physical and verbal conduct to prevent the development of a hostile, intimidating, or offensive environment. Supervisors and managers must be trained to recognize and report harassment. There must be a chain of command that can bypass an alleged harasser. Employees must believe that their complaints will be taken seriously. Top management must be involved, to prove that the company takes these matters seriously.

If customers commit the harassment, the Tenth Circuit analyzes the situation as if the harassers were co-employees (not supervisors). So the employer will not be strictly liable for the actions of customers, but will be liable if its negligence permitted the harassment to continue. [*Lockard v. Pizza Hut Inc.*, 162 F.3d 1062 (10th Cir. 1998)]

These cases rely on agency law concepts such as the apparent authority of the supervisor. Therefore, the employer should not only limit the extent to which harassers can take action against employees, it should make sure that all disciplinary actions are legitimate. It is important to look behind supervisors' write-ups to make sure that the lateness, poor work habits, etc., actually occurred—and that one subordinate was not singled out for conduct that was not punished in employees who did not become sexual targets.

A parent corporation can be directly as well as vicariously liable (as part of an "integrated enterprise") when its wholly owned subsidiary retaliates against an employee who complained of sexual harassment, if the parent company set the policy, employed the person who received the complaint, and issued the layoff notice. [*Ferrell v. Harvard Indus. Inc.*, 70 L.W. 1304 (E.D. Pa. Oct. 23, 2001)]

In *Corcoran v. Shoney's Colonial Inc.*, [24 F. Supp. 2d 601 (W.D. Va. 1998)] the employer was held vicariously liable on the plaintiff's hostile environment claim, despite the employer's prompt investigation and separation of harasser from victim. The court read *Faragher/Burlington* to impose vicarious liability, even if prompt remedial action is taken, unless the employee failed to take advantage of the employer's corrective mechanism.

For an example of how an employer met its burden, *see Montero v. AGCO Corp.* [192 F.3d 856 (9th Cir. 1999)] The employee's claim was dismissed because the employer promptly investigated and resolved an allegation of sexual harassment (within 11 days of the complaint). Furthermore, because the employee had taken two years to complain, she was also at fault for failing to make use of the complaint mechanism.

As long as the employer performs an adequate investigation, the fact that the investigation is not performed quickly will not rule out the Faragher/Ellerth defense. [*Tatum v. Arkansas Dep't of Health*, 411 F.3d 955 (8th Cir. 2005)] The Ninth Circuit ruled that a male sales executive who alleged that his female supervisor at a TV station sexually harassed him should not be allowed to proceed with his case. He insisted on trying to solve the problem by himself, without using the employer's complaint process. Without the alleged victim's cooperation, the employer could not investigate or take steps to prevent or correct harassment. [*Hardage v. CBS Broad.*, 436 F.3d 1050 (9th Cir. 2005)]

In fact, a recent Eighth Circuit case finds not only that the employer met its burden (by investigating, suspending the perpetrator for seven days, ordering him to take an antiharassment training class, and warning him he would be terminated if there were any further incidents) but was entitled to have the plaintiff pay its attorneys' fees. [*Meriwether v. Caraustar Packaging Co.*, 326 F.3d 990 (9th Cir. 2003)] In this case, the plaintiff pursued the case against the employer in federal court, but both the District Court and Eighth Circuit ruled that the alleged single incident in which a co-worker grabbed the plaintiff's buttock could not be treated as creating a hostile working environment.

An employer refused to reinstate a worker returning from medical leave. The employer said that she was totally disabled by paranoid schizophrenia, whereas the employee charged that the employer retaliated against her for complaining about on-the-job sexual harassment. During the leave, the employee had applied for, and been granted, Social Security Disability Income (SSDI) benefits. The Seventh Circuit ruled in *Wilson v. Chrysler Corp.* [172 F.3d 500 (7th Cir. 1999)] that applying for disability benefits rules out a sexual harassment claim, because in a Title VII case (a category that includes sexual harassment), there is no obligation of reasonable accommodation.

In 2003, the Eleventh Circuit reversed summary judgment for the employer, finding that a reasonable jury could conclude that the employer failed to respond to the plaintiff's sexual harassment complaint. [*Watson v. Blue Circle Inc.*, 324 F.3d 1252 (11th Cir. 2003)]

Later that year, the Eighth Circuit also reversed summary judgment for the defense, because the plaintiff presented evidence of a prolonged series of incidents of touching and innuendo extending over seven years. Because the conduct was ongoing and daily, it was sufficient to create a hostile work environment. [Compare *Eich v. Board of Regents for Central Missouri State University*, 350 F.3d 752 (8th Cir. 2003) with *Duncan v. General Motors*, 300 F.3d 928 (8th Cir. 2002) where the conduct was "offensive and disrespectful" but not tantamount to a hostile work environment]

Two UPS employees brought a Kentucky Civil Rights Act case against the company and the employee accused of harassing them. The case was removed to federal court. Although the trial court granted summary judgment for the defendants, ruling that UPS did not have notice of the harassment, that it did not arise to the level of creating a hostile work environment, and that the individual was not personally liable, the Sixth Circuit reversed and remanded in part. (The accused harasser was allowed to resign in lieu of termination after UPS investigated the complaints.) The Sixth Circuit implied that it was likely that the plaintiff would lose once a full trial was held, but nevertheless it concluded that UPS was not entitled to use the affirmative defense at the summary judgment level. Whether or not the victim of harassment complains, an employer cannot avoid liability if it failed to prevent harassment or correct harassment of which it was aware. Just having an anti-harassment policy isn't enough unless the policy is actually effective as implemented. One plaintiff failed to allege enough incidents or severe enough incidents to create a hostile work environment, but the other plaintiff alleged 17 incidents—enough to get a jury trial. [*Clark v. UPS*, 400 F.3d 341 (6th Cir. 2005); *McCombs v. Meijer, Inc.*, 395 F.3d 346, 355 (6th Cir. 2005) (there must be a jury trial if the employer's response is indifference or unreasonable)]

The employer's failure to investigate a claimant's repeated reports of sexual harassment made her resignation a voluntary quit with good cause attributable to the employer, so benefits were available. [*Yaeger*, Unempl. Ins. Rep. (CCH) ¶ 8915 (Fla. Dist. App. 2001)]

In April 2003, the largest sexual harassment settlement in New York State history was announced: The Lutheran Medical Center agreed to pay close to $5.5 million to settle a sexual harassment case involving a doctor who subjected more than 50 female employees to invasive touching and improper questions about their sex lives during mandatory pre-employment physical examinations. He also threatened to deny or delay their employment if they refused to cooperate with this conduct. He was fired in January 2000 after numerous protests had been made, but the plaintiffs' complaint alleged that the hospital knew or should have known when the doctor was hired in 1996 that he had a history of harassing female employees—he had been the subject of a California case in 1988. The proposed consent decree before the Southern District of New York calls for the payment of damages, creation of a training program, and a promise never to rehire the doctor. [Tamara Loomis, *Record $5.5M Accord Reached in Doctor Harass Case* [sic], N.Y.L.J. (Apr. 10, 2003) (law.com)]

[B] EEOC Enforcement Guidance

The EEOC's position about what employers should do is summed up in its 20-page guidance available online. [*Enforcement Guidance: Vicarious Employer Liability for Unlawful Harassment by Supervisors,* Number 915.002, (June 18, 1999) <http://www.eeoc.gov/policy/docs/harassment.html>]

The Guidance makes employers responsible for preventing harassment of all kinds—harassment based on sex (including derogation of women or men because they are women or men, even if the harasser is not seeking sexual gratification); race, color, religion, national origin, age, disability, or protected activity such as enforcing legal rights.

Under this Guidance, the employer will not be liable if harassment does not subject the employee to tangible disadvantages, as long as the employer uses reasonable care to prevent harassment. The employer is also free of liability if it takes reasonable steps to correct harassment that has already occurred, provided that the employee is also at fault by failing to take advantage of the policies and procedures in place.

The actions of "supervisors" can subject the employer to liability—but this term is not defined in Title VII. The key test is whether, based on the real situation in the workplace, the alleged harasser had enough authority over the alleged victim to make it easier to harass and harder for the victim to resist.

The EEOC uses a two-part test. Either a supervisor has authority to direct someone else's daily work activities, or has authority to implement or at least recommend tangible employment decisions such as awarding a raise or bonus, promoting or firing the employee. The employer can also be liable for harassment by someone whom the victim reasonably thought was a supervisor, even if this was not the case.

Merely having a policy isn't enough: It must really be enforced. The EEOC encourages employers to terminate harassment even before it reaches the severe, protracted level that would justify a lawsuit.

Under the EEOC interpretation, the employer is always liable when a harassing supervisor subjects an employee to tangible employment action. A tangible employment action means a significant change in employment status such as firing, denial of a promotion, reassignment, an undesirable work assignment. An unfulfilled threat, a trivial effect, or causing hurt feelings doesn't count.

This is the minimum that the EEOC will accept as a satisfactory corporate antiharassment policy:

- Clear explanations of what constitutes prohibited harassment;
- Assurances that employees who report harassment will not suffer retaliation;
- A clear explanation of a workable procedure for investigating complaints promptly, fairly, and thoroughly (with alternatives so that no one will be expected to report harassment to the person who committed it);
- A confidentiality procedure for complaints;
- Assurance of fast, appropriate response when the investigation shows that harassment has occurred.

Adequate responses to confirmation of a harassment allegation include:

- A warning or an oral or written reprimand to the harasser;
- Training and counseling the harasser about why the conduct violated the employer's policy;
- Transferring, reassigning, demoting, suspending, or, in appropriate cases, firing the harasser;
- Monitoring to make sure harassment has ended;
- Allowing the victim to take leave to get out of the range of harassment;
- Correcting the victim's file to remove unfair evaluations;
- Having the harasser apologize to the victim;
- Checking to make sure that there is no retaliation for reporting the harassment.

Sexual harassment charges are subject to the same timing rules as other Title VII cases. Early in 2003, for instance, the Eighth Circuit ruled that an employee's sexual harassment claims were time-barred. Her deposition said that the last act of sexual harassment occurred in the winter of 1998–1999. She filed with the EEOC in January 2000, i.e., more than 180 days after the last alleged act of harassment. She was discharged in December 1999, but there was no evidence connecting the discharge and the alleged sexual harassment, so this date could not be used as the starting point for a sexual harassment claim. [*Diaz v. Swift-Eckrich, Inc.,* 318 F.3d 796 (8th Cir. 2003)]

[C] Internal Investigations of Harassment Allegations

An article by two Winston & Strawn attorneys [Susan Schenkel-Savitt and Jill H. Turner, *Effective Investigation of Sexual Harassment Claims,* archived at <http://www.lawnewsnetwork.com>] gives some insights into appropriate investigation of sexual harassment charges. [For more how-tos for internal investigations, see Jonathan A. Segal, *HR as Judge, Jury, Prosecutor, and Defender,* HR Magazine, October 2001, at p. 141]

Employers can't just summarily fire everyone accused of harassment, because some of those charges could be fabricated; the result of honest misunderstanding; or the accused person's misconduct might not have been serious enough to justify termination. Overreaction on the employer's part could constitute wrongful termination. [*See* Chapter 39] A mechanism for unbiased internal investigations is necessary, to strike the proper balance between the rights of accusers and accused persons.

Whoever conducts the investigation may have to testify later on, so an in-house or outside attorney who normally represents the corporation could be a poor choice. Attorneys are not allowed to serve as witnesses in cases where they are also representing a party.

However, choosing an attorney rather than someone else can be a good choice, because communications between attorney and client are privileged (opposing parties in litigation can't get hold of them). An attorney's "work product"—the materials drafted by the attorney while preparing the case—is also protected. Similar privileges are not extended to other professionals. If the company will want to assert confidentiality at the pretrial and trial stages, it will have to be sure to keep the materials confidential. Access must be limited to the people involved in the investigation; there must be no general distribution.

The investigator must determine:

- Who claims to have been the victim of harassment (in many cases, harassment involves a number of people);
- Everyone who is accused of committing harassment, contributing to a hostile work environment, or participating in a cover-up;
- Everyone who is claimed to be a witness—and the extent to which their recollection tallies with the complainant's;
- Detailed information about the alleged acts of harassment or the duration and nature of the hostile environment;
- Whether the acts occurred on company property, at company functions, or elsewhere;
- Did the complainant make a prompt report of the alleged harassment? To whom was it made? If there was no report, was there any justification for failing to report at or close to the time of the incident?

The investigator should follow up by contacting witnesses and checking matters of fact. For instance, if an incident is charged on a particular date, the investigator should verify whether the alleged harasser was out of town at the time.

The interview with the alleged harasser is very important. It is up to the employer whether or not to reveal the name of the person making the allegation. To protect the employer against later claims by the alleged harasser, the investigator should make it clear that an investigation is underway, and no conclusions have yet been reached as to the validity of the accusation. The accused person must be given a full, fair chance to get his or her own story on the record.

Additional rounds of interviews may be needed to follow new lines of investigation or confirm disputed facts. The end product of the investigation should be a confidential written report to the person with corporate-level HR responsibility.

Whenever it is determined that an allegation is well founded, the company has a responsibility to take action. The appropriate action is proportionate to the seriousness of the conduct and serves to deter future harassment. The action should also be proportionate to steps the employer has taken in similar cases in the past. The harasser's employment record may provide either mitigation factors (such as a long history of good performance) or aggravating factors (past instances of discipline, especially prior instances of harassment).

If the employer determines that a sanction short of dismissal is appropriate, steps should be taken to keep the harasser and victim apart, but without retaliating against the victim for having complained! The employer should also follow up (and keep written records) to make sure that the disciplinary action has served to prevent future harassment incidents.

§ 35.04   HOSTILE WORK ENVIRONMENT HARASSMENT

[A]   Generally

A hostile work environment is one where actions are taken to make an employee feel unwelcome. Harassment cases have been recognized dealing with race, religion, disability, and age, as well as cases in which women are made uncomfortable by, e.g., unwanted touching, crude propositions, dirty jokes, pin-ups, etc. Hostile work environment sexual harassment cases have been recognized for many years, dating back to the Supreme Court case of *Meritor Savings Bank v. Vinson.* [477 U.S. 57 (1986)]

It can be difficult to predict what conduct will be considered sufficiently outrageous to create a hostile environment, because different courts have reached very different conclusions. There is often disagreement about the seriousness of conduct that constitutes harassment, how severe and prolonged it must be, and the extent of injuries that the complainant must suffer before having a sustainable case.

According to *Howley v. Town of Stratford* [217 F.3d 141 (2d Cir. 2000)], one incident of verbal harassment of a female fire lieutenant by a male subordinate, at a union meeting, can be deemed to constitute an intolerable alteration of the work environment. The theory was that it diminished subordinates' respect for the commanding officer, which in turn impaired the fire department's basic public safety mission.

In contrast, one incident in which a male employee touched a female co-worker's breast and stomach was held not to create a hostile environment. No physical injury occurred, and the employer promptly removed the harasser from the workplace. According to *Brooks v. San Mateo, California,* [229 F.3d 917 (9th Cir. 2000)] although similar incidents had occurred in the past (but were not reported), the Ninth Circuit did not believe that a reasonable employee would have believed that the terms and conditions of employment were altered for the worse. Ostracism suffered by the female employee from co-workers, because she reported the incident, cannot be considered adverse employment action.

In *Quantock v. Shared Marketing Servs. Inc.*, [312 F.3d 899 (7th Cir. 2002)] the company president asked the plaintiff for three different types of sexual activity; all three propositions occurred in a single incident. The District Court granted summary judgment for the defendant because of the brevity of the incident, but the Seventh Circuit held that a reasonable jury could have found that a hostile work environment was created because of the severity of the incident.

In the case of *Breda v. Wolf Camera*, [222 F.3d 890 (11th Cir.); *on remand*, 148 F. Supp. 2d 1371 (S.D. Ga. 2001)] first the defendant succeeded in getting summary judgment. However, the Eleventh Circuit remanded the case for a new trial. The new trial, in July 2001, resulted in another dismissal. The Southern District of Georgia judge held that, given the crudity and vulgarity of modern culture, a certain amount of vulgarity, even boorish behavior, must be tolerated in the workplace. The judge characterized the conduct at the workplace that impelled the plaintiff to resign as "juvenile, offensive, and at times even mean-spirited" but also said that the tally of sexualized comments and gestures did not add up to enough for a Title VII cause of action.

Suggestive male nude pictures posted on an office bulletin board by a male co-worker did not create a hostile sexual environment for the female plaintiff because the court did not believe that a rational jury could find that the terms of the plaintiff's employment were altered to create a pervasive atmosphere of intimidation, ridicule, and insult. [*Brennan v. Metropolitan Opera Ass'n Inc.*, 192 F.3d 310 (2d Cir. 1999)]

The Sixth Circuit held that, in an all-male workforce, the employer is not liable for vulgar horseplay by co-workers. Because all the workers were male, there was no element of sex discrimination and therefore no case against the employer. [*EEOC v. Harbert-Yeargin Inc.*, 266 F.3d 498 (6th Cir. 2001)]

[B] Retaliation

As Chapter 34 discusses, allegations of retaliation for filing discrimination claims are in themselves a major litigation area. In *Rogers v. City of Chicago*, [320 F.3d 748 (7th Cir. 2003)] a Chicago police officer filed a two-count complaint charging both hostile work environment sexual harassment and retaliation, but she was unsuccessful. It was held that the conduct she alleged did not rise to the level of harassment; occasional vulgar banter or innuendo is not deemed actionable. There was no showing that the workplace was objectively offensive, i.e., that a reasonable person would find it hostile or abusive.

As for retaliation, the plaintiff could not provide direct evidence of retaliation; there was no admission by a decision maker that he took action against Rogers because she complained of discrimination. In the Seventh Circuit, the rules for proving retaliation through indirect evidence come from *Stone v. City of Indianapolis*. [281 F.3d 640 (7th Cir. 2002)] The plaintiff must show that after filing the complaint, only the plaintiff, and not any similarly situated employee, who did not file a charge, was subjected to adverse employment action despite satisfactory job performance. But the employer will be able to get summary judgment by providing unrebutted evidence of a non-discriminatory reason for taking action against the plaintiff. The plaintiff does not have to prove a causal link between the protected action (the discrimination complaint) and the adverse employment action. *Also see Deravin v. Kerick.* [335 F.3d 195 (2d Cir. 2003)] The plaintiff, an employee of the New York City Department of Corrections, was accused of sexual harassment. He was permitted to maintain a retaliation claim when he charged he was denied a promotion, because defending one's self against sexual harassment charges is deemed to be protected concerted activity.

Although the jury awarded over $353,000 to a female professor for hostile work environment, sexual harassment, and retaliation claims, the district court granted judgment as a matter of law to the defense, and the Eighth Circuit affirmed. The courts found that, although denial of tenure would constitute adverse employment action, it was not true that the plaintiff was formally denied tenure—she quit partway through the review process. When there was no official action, the retaliation claim had to fail. The Eighth Circuit also granted deference to the tenure determination process, and ruled that faculty members cannot challenge a tenure decision before they have completed the university's internal review process. [*Okruhlik v. University of Arkansas*, 395 F.3d 872 (8th Cir. 2005)]

§ 35.05   SAME-SEX HARASSMENT

For several years, courts were divided about whether sexual harassment of a male employee by a male supervisor, or a female employee by a female supervisor, was barred by Title VII. Perhaps this reflects a stereotype of sexual harassment as only something that is perpetrated by males against females. Questions were raised as to whether same-sex harassment could be described as occurring "on account of sex," because the harasser is of the same sex as the victim.

The uncertainty was resolved by the Supreme Court in *Oncale v. Offshore Services Inc.*, [523 U.S. 45 (1998)] which brought same-sex harassment into the ambit of Title VII.

Surprisingly, however, the Seventh Circuit ruled that neither male nor female state-government employees could sue for sexual harassment, on the grounds that a supervisor who propositioned both male and female employees could not have been committing discrimination on account of sex. [*Holman v. State of Indiana*, 211 F.3d 399 (7th Cir. 2000)]

Early in 2003, the Eleventh Circuit decided that a state university did not have Eleventh Amendment immunity in a suit brought by an employee charging a supervisor with sexual harassment; it made no difference that in this case the allegation was of same-sex harassment. [*Downing v. Board of Trustees of the Univ. of Ala.,* 321 F.3d 1017 (11th Cir. 2003)]

In a suit for hostile work environment, same-sex discrimination, and retaliation, the district court granted summary judgment for the employer, finding that no adverse employment action occurred and she was not discriminated against on account of sex. However, the Tenth Circuit affirmed in part and reversed in part, finding genuine issues of material fact. The plaintiff alleged that, although her job performance was not affected, she was subjected to an environment of lewd jokes, gestures and banter, and offensive touching and gestures. She also alleged that the supervisor tended to disappear into locked rooms with a consenting female employee. The unusual twist to this case was that the plaintiff was a heterosexual female who charged that the hostile environment was created by indiscreet and obstreperous lesbians. The plaintiff alleged that she suffered retaliation in the form of increased hostility, being written up for a disagreement with a co-worker, and the circulation of a memo telling employees to stop using foul language and to refrain from obnoxious behavior. The plaintiff also said that she was threatened with termination if she continued to complain, but the threat was not carried out.

The district court said that women could not create an anti-woman hostile environment. But the Tenth Circuit reads one part of the *Oncale* test to mean that "because of sex" depends on whether the harasser's conduct was motivated by sexual desire toward persons of the victim's sex. The district court treated the incidents as aggression toward a person the harassers disliked, not sexual overtures. The Tenth Circuit, however, found that there was enough evidence in the record (e.g., intimate touching; possible voluntary sexual conduct among other workers) to conclude that sexual desire played a part. The Tenth Circuit remanded for consideration of whether there was an objectively hostile or abusive work environment. But the Tenth Circuit dismissed the retaliation claims, finding that at worst the plaintiff suffered one instance of discipline, which did not add up to retaliation. The memorandum, cited by the plaintiff as evidence, could more reasonably be interpreted as management's attempt to satisfy its burden by preventing further incidents of harassment. [*Dick v. Phone Directories Company,* 397 F.3d 1256 (10th Cir. 2005)]

§ 35.06   ORIENTATION AND PERCEIVED ORIENTATION

Although a number of states and cities have their own laws against sexual-orientation discrimination, Title VII itself does not forbid discrimination on the basis of homosexual or bisexual orientation. [*Higgins v. New Balance Athletic Shoes Inc.,* 194 F.3d 252 (1st Cir. 1999); *Bibby v. Philadelphia Coca-Cola Bottling Co.,* 260 F.3d 257 (3d Cir. 2001)] The *Bibby* case says that three kinds of same-sex harassment are illegal: unwanted sexual advances made toward an employee of the same sex; harassment because the harasser believes that women or men do not belong in that type of workplace; or harassment for failure to behave with appropriate masculinity or femininity.

Although Title VII does not cover transsexuality, some transsexual plaintiffs now raise claims that they are discriminated against because they present themselves as the "other" sex and do not conform to gender stereotypes. [*See, e.g., Tronetti v. TLC Healthnet Lakeshore Hosp.*, 2003 WL 22757935 (W.D.N.Y. Sept. 26, 2003); *Barnes v. Cincinnati*, 401 F.3d 729 (6th Cir. 2005), *cert. denied* 126 S. Ct. 624; *Price Waterhouse, Sex Stereotyping, and Gender Non-Conformity Bias*, 73 LW 2211 (Oct. 19, 2004)]

The Eastern District of Pennsylvania granted summary judgment for the employer in *Bianchi v. City of Philadelphia.* [183 F. Supp. 2d 726 (E.D. Pa. 2002)] The plaintiff claimed that, although he was not homosexual, his co-workers believed he was and harassed him on that account. The opinion says that plaintiffs who bring claims of this type can get past a motion for summary judgment only by proving that the alleged discrimination resulted from failure to satisfy social ideas about appropriate gender behavior: about conformity to ideas about masculinity for men and femininity for women. [*See* Shannon Duffy, *Lack of Evidence Ends Same-Sex Harassment Title VII Claim,* The Legal Intelligencer, (Jan. 10, 2002) (law.com)]

The Western District of New York ruled in 2004 that a gay male employee's allegation that co-workers harassed him because he did not meet stereotypes of masculinity could be brought under Title VII, because sex stereotyping violates Title VII in that it is done on the basis of one sex: *EEOC v. Grief Brothers Corp.*, 2004 WL 2202641 (W.D.N.Y. Sept. 30, 2004).

For example, the Seventh Circuit allowed a young man to litigate a sexual harassment claim based on alleged harassment targeting him as effeminate because he wore an earring. [*Doe v. City of Belleville,* 119 F.3d 563 (7th Cir. 2001)] A claim of harassment on the basis of perceived effeminacy was upheld in *Nichols v. Azteca Restaurant Enterprises Inc.* [256 F.3d 864 (9th Cir. 2001)] In contrast, in deciding *Bibby* the Third Circuit treated the *Bianchi* case as an allegation of harassment on the basis of a false perception of homosexuality—a ground that is not covered by Title VII.

Two mid-2002 cases reached opposite conclusions. The Ohio Court of Appeals agreed that a gay male worker stated a cause of action for severe emotional distress and depression affecting his work performance as a result of continuous harassment, graffiti, and unwelcome sexual remarks. [*Tenney v. GE Corp.,* 2002 Ohio 2975 (Ohio App. 2002)] But, in the Florida Court of District Appeals view, a lesbian did not state an emotional distress claim by alleging a severe and pervasive pattern of harassment by supervisors, including derogatory comments about homosexuality and abusive conduct directed to her as a lesbian, because the court did not find the conduct sufficiently outrageous to be actionable. [*DeLaCampa v. Grifola Am. Inc.,* 819 So. 2d 940 (Fla. Dist. App. 2002)]

Hamner v. St. Vincent Hospital and Health Care Center Inc. [224 F.3d 701 (7th Cir. 2000)] holds that sexual-orientation discrimination and harassment by a supervisor premised on the plaintiff's perceived effeminacy is not covered by

Title VII, because it is not "specifically intimidating to men and their manhood" or premised on "general hostility to men."

The Seventh Circuit ruled that a sexual harassment claim cannot be based on sexual orientation. The plaintiff charged that he was harassed because his friendship with a co-worker did not conform to co-workers' stereotypes about masculinity. However, the Seventh Circuit viewed the plaintiff's evidence as showing only disapproval of his work performance or perceptions about his sexual orientation. Furthermore, it was difficult to separate the alleged harassing conduct from the level of vulgar horseplay that was an ongoing characteristic of the work environment. Although there was a dispute about whether the plaintiff quit or was terminated, his retaliation claim still had to fail when the underlying sexual harassment claim was dismissed. [*Hamm v. Weyauwega Milk Prods. Inc.*, 332 F.3d 1058 (7th Cir. 2003)]

In contrast, the District Court for the Eastern District of Pennsylvania ruled that a gay male plaintiff who charged that he suffered discrimination for failure to live up to perceptions about masculinity and male behavior raised a valid theory. Despite the differing theoretical approaches, the result was the same: the case was nevertheless dismissed for failure to show that the alleged harassment by co-workers was severe or pervasive enough to be cognizable. Nor, in the court's view, did the plaintiff prove that management failed to respond to complaints. The court rejected the defense argument that abusing the plaintiff as "gay," "queer," or "faggot" invalidated the case by making it a claim of sexual orientation discrimination that is outside the scope of Title VII. But the court found it more compelling that harassment was sporadic, and ceased for long periods, and the conduct was limited to offensive utterances. Furthermore, the employer investigated the charges and reprimanded some co-workers, causing them to alter their behavior. [*Kay v. Independence Blue Cross*, 2003 U.S. Dist. LEXIS 8521 (E.D. Pa. May 16, 2003)]

In July 2001, a New Jersey state court allowed a transsexual doctor to sue the ex-employer who discharged her from the job once held (as a man) as a medical director, because the state antidiscrimination law deals with transsexualism as a disability. However, the court dismissed the doctor's claim of sexual-orientation discrimination, on the grounds that the plaintiff was not, and was not perceived as, homosexual or bisexual. [*Enriquez v. West Jersey Health Sys.*, 342 N.J. Super. 501 (2001)]

§ 35.07   WRONGFUL DISCHARGE CLAIMS

Employers often fear that they may be caught between two fires. If they do not respond to allegations, they face EEOC charges and/or lawsuits. But if they fire an alleged harasser, he or she may sue for wrongful termination. It is a delicate balance, but the employer can avoid liability by carrying out a thorough investigation in each case and taking proportionate steps against anyone found to have committed harassment. A complete "paper trail" is very important here (as in many other contexts).

A company with a no-tolerance policy fired an employee after investigation showed that he had sexually harassed another worker. The discharged employee went to arbitration. The arbitrator held that discharge was too severe a punishment. Reinstatement (although without back pay) was ordered. The practical effect was a nine-month unpaid suspension.

The employer sued the harasser's union under Labor-Management Relations Act § 301 claiming that reinstating the harasser would violate public policy. The Fourth Circuit disagreed, agreeing with the arbitrator that the loss of nine months' pay was adequate punishment. [*Westvaco Corp. v. United Paperworkers Int'l Union*, 171 F.3d 971 (4th Cir. 1999)]

In *Ribando v. United Airlines Inc.*, [200 F.3d 507 (7th Cir. 1999)] a male worker accused a female co-worker of making harassing or derogatory remarks about him. The employer went through union-managed mediation, questioned several people, put a letter of concern in the female worker's file, but took no other action. The Seventh Circuit held that the woman could not maintain that the employer had engaged in severe or pervasive gender-based harassment against her: In fact, it had fulfilled its obligation to investigate the harassment charge.

When discriminatory discipline is charged, the question is whether different discipline is imposed for the same offense. A black female employee did not have a discrimination claim when she was fired for groping the genitals of male co-workers, when a white female was not fired for exposing her breasts on request, because the black female had engaged in conduct contrary to the wishes of its recipients, justifying a higher level of discipline. [*Wheeler v. Aventis Pharmaceuticals*, 360 F.3d 853 (8th Cir. 2004)]

Another implication of wrongful termination law is that in Maryland, an employee discharged for refusing to have sexual intercourse with a harasser can pursue a tort claim for abusive discharge in addition to the sexual harassment charges. The additional tort claim can be pursued because the state has a public policy against prostitution—and having sex to keep a job is, in effect, prostitution. [*Insignia Residential Corp. v. Ashton, Maryland*, 755 A.2d 1080 (Md. 2000)]

§ 35.08 DAMAGE ISSUES

The Seventh Circuit allows a sexual harassment plaintiff to get punitive damages in cases in which there were no compensatory damages. [*See Timm v. Progressive Steel Treating Inc.*, 137 F.3d 1008 (7th Cir. 1998)] This might occur, for instance, where a company fails to establish a complaint procedure and then blames the plaintiff for failure to go through channels. In this case, the plaintiff mitigated her damages so effectively that she got a higher-paying job, and therefore could not collect a back pay award.

The First Circuit upheld the District Court's award of $160,000 in punitive damages against Wal-Mart of Puerto Rico in a hostile work environment case. (The plaintiff eventually quit his job because of never-ending jokes about the penile implant he had to correct impotence caused by his medical condition.) On appeal, Wal-Mart's position was that the jury was not properly instructed on the company's open-door policy for employee complaints—a policy that it said the plaintiff could have used to mitigate damages. The District Court jury found that the plaintiff did complain several times, but his supervisors and managers refused to take any action to terminate the harassment. [*Arrieta-Colon v. Wal-Mart Puerto Rico Inc.*, 434 F.3d 75 (1st Cir. 2006)]

Using the California state antidiscrimination law rather than federal law, the California Court of Appeals ruled that a law firm is directly, not just vicariously, liable for failing to protect a staff member against harassment by a partner. The ruling of *Weeks v. Baker & McKenzie* [74 Cal. Rptr. 2d 510 (Cal. App. 1998)] is that the firm employed the partner in conscious disregard of the safety and rights of vulnerable employees. Therefore, the firm's liability was not limited to the $225,000 punitive damage award against the harassing partner—$3.5 million in punitive damages could be awarded against the firm.

Late in 2003, the District of Columbia Court of Appeals struck down an award of $4.8 million in punitive damages in a sexual harassment retaliation case, finding it to be unconstitutionally excessive. The ratio of 26:1 between punitive and compensatory damages exceeded the then-current Supreme Court limitation of punitive damages to a single-digit ratio. The award was also improper because it reflected the defendant's nationwide conduct, not just its treatment of the individual plaintiff. Furthermore, the most relevant civil penalty under the local Human Rights Act was only $50,000 for multiple offenses. [*Daka Inc. v. McCrae*, 839 A.2d 682 (D.C. App. Dec. 24, 2003)]

A Pennsylvania jury award of over $3.2 million, including $2.5 million in punitive damages, raised issues of how to apply the cap—particularly because punitive damages are not available under the state anti-discrimination law. The plaintiff, a one-time Federal Express driver, charged that supervisors and co-workers harassed her, even tampering with the brakes on her truck. The award called for about $100,000 in back pay, $290,000 in front pay, $350,000 in compensatory damages for emotional suffering, plus the punitive damages. The jury also allocated 60% of the compensatory damages to the discrimination cause of action, the other 40% for infliction of emotional distress, with the punitive damages equally divided between the two. FedEx announced that it would appeal, and clearly one issue on appeal would be how to apply the $300,000 cap to the case. [*Shaub v. Federal Express*, No. 02-1194 (E.D. Pa. 2004) discussed in Shannon P. Duffy, *$3.2M Verdict Against FedEx for Sex Harassment*, The Legal Intelligencer (Feb. 27, 2004) (law.com). In February 2003, there was a $2.3 million jury verdict in another Pennsylvania FedEx case—this time for retaliation; the case was settled on confidential terms]

In *State Dep't of Health Services v. Superior Court of Sacramento County*, [31 Cal. 4th 1026 (Cal. 2003)] decided by the California Supreme Court on November 24, 2003, the court applied the common-law doctrine of avoidable consequences. Under this principle, damages can be reduced or even eliminated if the victim could have prevented some or all of the harassment by complaining earlier. The plaintiff alleged that her supervisor physically and verbally harassed her for close to two years but she did not complain to management until the end of that time. Once she complained, her employer investigated and disciplined the harasser. Although the relevant statute imposes strict liability on employers where the harasser is a supervisor, nevertheless damages are not available with respect to anything the plaintiff could have avoided by reasonable effort and without undue risk, expense, or humiliation.

Similar issues arose in the Seventh Circuit case, where the question was whether the plaintiff unreasonably failed to avail herself of the procedure the employer set up for reporting complaints of harassment. The plaintiff's account was that she didn't complain right away about harassment from her supervisor because she thought that her supervisor would stop if she told him to. Eventually she went to her supervisor's supervisor, who testified that the plaintiff complained about "differences" but did not mention sexual harassment. The plaintiff later went to the employer's Office for Access and Equity but was not willing to give details; she went on medical leave the next month and did not submit the Request for Further Action form for another month after that. The Seventh Circuit held that there was a triable issue of constructive discharge (the plaintiff resigned while she was on medical leave). Her written report was filed three months after the first alleged act of harassment—but only eight days after the last. The Seventh Circuit ruled that employees may need time to check the facts, which influences the decision of whether a report is timely or untimely. [*Hardy v. University of Illinois at Chicago,* 328 F.3d 361 (7th Cir. 2003)]

After constant harassment (including assault) and many complaints that went unanswered, the harassment victim herself was fired. She suffered from breathing difficulties and anxiety and took a prescription anti-depressant. She was offered reinstatement, but was afraid to return because she suffered insomnia, shortness of breath, crying spells, and chronic chest pain as a result of these incidents. Eventually she returned to work; the harassment continued, and her complaints also continued to be ignored. The harasser retaliated against her; the victim took a drug overdose that was diagnosed as a suicide attempt; and eventually she quit. There had never been a corporate investigation of any of her charges, despite union intervention. At trial, the jury awarded $839,470 in compensatory damages, $33,314 back pay, and $650,000 in punitive damages. The district court awarded $174,927 in attorneys' fees plus $38,921 front pay. The Eighth Circuit affirmed the district court, given the extent of the harassment, its extremely deleterious effects on the plaintiff, and management's refusal to respond to multiple complaints. However, the damages were subject to the Civil Rights Act (CRA) '91 caps. The district court allocated all of the compensatory damages to the state law claim, reduced the punitive damages to $300,000 (the cap amount), and allocated them to the Title VII claim. [*Baker v. John Morrell & Co.,* 382 F.3d 816 (8th Cir. 2004). In the Eighth Circuit, a hostile environment claim can be proved by demonstration of pervasive sexual innuendo and repetitive offensive touching: *Eich v. Board of Regents*, 350 F.3d 752 (8th Cir. 2003)]

On the basis that there was a sexually hostile work environment that the employer failed to remedy despite its knowledge, a jury awarded $500,000 in emotional distress damages and $1 million in punitive damages. The district court denied the defendant's motion for judgment as a matter of law and refused to reduce the damages. The Eighth Circuit upheld the district court. A co-worker engaged in an ongoing campaign of harassment including offensive comments, unwanted touching, and even threats of rape and murder. The plaintiff filed a complaint with the EEOC on June 7, 2000, so the 300 days during which acts could be counted began on August 12, 1999. Insofar as this was a hostile environment claim, it was timely if there was any act contributing to the claim within the 300-day period. Although the harassment stopped for a while and then resumed (and, in fact, got worse), the Eighth Circuit deemed all the acts to contribute to the creation of an actionable hostile environment: the same harasser committed the same kind of acts before and after the trigger date in 1999. There was no evidence that any intervening actions by the employer severed the connection between acts before and after this date. The Eighth Circuit rule is that, as long as any actionable act of harassment occurs during the limitations period, the entire hostile environment is treated as a unit. The Court of Appeals found that the compensatory damages award was large, but not monstrous or shocking enough to justify remittitur. The court pointed out that the plaintiff suffered constant fear, panic attacks, moved to a new home to avoid the harasser, and got mace and a gun permit. Her therapist reported that the prognosis for her anxiety disorder was poor. The Eighth Circuit ruled that punitive damages were sustainable, because the jury was entitled to find that the supervisor knew of and allowed the abusive and degrading environment to continue. The Title VII punitive damages were subject to a cap of $300,000, but the Eighth Circuit deemed the balance of the punitive damage award to qualify for confirmation under state law, which was not capped. [*Rowe v. Hussmann Corporation*, 381 F.3d 775 (8th Cir. 2004)]

§ 35.09   LIABILITY OF INDIVIDUALS

Sexual harassment charges are not really very similar to charges of, say, environmental pollution, commercial fraud, or tax evasion. Although a corporation is only an artificial person, so individuals must commit its wrongful acts, in some cases individuals who commit a tort or a crime are doing so on behalf of the corporation. People who commit sexual harassment may be echoing a corporate culture that tolerates such things, but they are not benefiting the corporation!

Nevertheless, the language of Title VII, like most antidiscrimination statutes, refers only to "employers," and with few exceptions, courts have ruled that only the employer corporation, and not the individual, is liable for harassment. [No individual liability: *Carrisales v. Department of Corrections*, 90 Cal. Rptr. 2d

804 (Cal. 1999). *But see Speight v. Albano Cleaners,* 21 F. Supp. 2d 560 (E.D. Va. 1998), where the individual supervisor was held liable, but the corporation was not held liable]

Reno v. Baird [957 P.2d 1333 (Cal. 1998)] holds that an individual manager, although potentially liable for harassment, is not an "employer" under California's antidiscrimination statute. Although the state's Fair Employment and Housing Act defines "employer" to include "any person acting as an agent of an employer, directly or indirectly" the *Baird* court interpreted this language to make employers liable for the action of their agents, not to make agents personally liable.

A group of former employees of a television station charged a pattern of sexual harassment by the station's former president and general manager. The plaintiffs' claims against the President as an individual were dismissed because individuals are not liable. The District Court granted summary judgment for the defendant, but the Fifth Circuit affirmed the dismissal as to one of the plaintiffs but vacated it for the other three. There were triable issues as to whether the president, who was known to have a history of making repeated inappropriate advances to female employees, was the station's proxy so that his actions should be imputed to the employer. The Fifth Circuit dismissed claims that the president favored his girlfriend over other employees, on the grounds that all employees, male and female, are placed at an equal disadvantage by such conduct. In the District Court's view, the president could not be the corporation's proxy because he owned only two percent of its stock. The Fifth Circuit, however, held that the relevant issue is whether he held a high enough position in the management hierarchy to be able to speak for the corporation. [*Ackel v. National Communications, Inc.,* 339 F.3d 376 (5th Cir. 2003). The Fifth Circuit does not impose sexual harassment liability on individuals. *Smith v. Amedisys Inc.,* 298 F.3d 434 (5th Cir. 2002). For the issue of favoritism toward a lover, *see Green v. Administrators of the Tulane Educational Fund,* 284 F.3d 642 (5th Cir. 2002)]

In a late 2003 Eighth Circuit case, the plaintiff sued her former employer, a state agency, for sexual harassment, disparate-treatment sex discrimination, retaliation, and violation of the Equal Pay Act. She also sued her supervisor as an individual under 42 U.S.C. § 1983 and for retaliation. The Eighth Circuit ruled that the supervisor was entitled to qualified immunity. The plaintiff charged that the supervisor made many disparaging comments about women and said she should be more feminine and should do more clerical work.

Although the District Court refused to grant qualified immunity because it stated that intentional sexual harassment by a person acting under color of state law violates the Fourteenth Amendment, the Eighth Circuit ruled that, on the contrary, even interpreting the evidence in the light most favorable to the plaintiff, there were only a few isolated and not very severe incidents—nothing rising to the status of a violation of Constitutional rights. [*Tuggle v. Mangan,* 348 F.3d 714 (8th Cir. 2003)]

Similarly, *Henthorn v. Capitol Communications, Inc.* [359 F.3d 1021 (8th Cir. 2004)] dismisses a sexual harassment/retaliation case because the repeated unwelcome sexual advances represented wrongful conduct on the supervisor's part and were unprofessional and offensive—but did not rise to a level so extreme as to render the work environment hostile and offensive. The retaliation claim also failed because the Eighth Circuit did not deem the plaintiff's terms and conditions of employment to have changed after she rejected her manager's advances or after she filed a complaint. She continued to do the same job for the same salary; the employer produced evidence of a legitimate, nondiscriminatory reason for denying her a promotion she wanted.

§ 35.10   INTERACTION WITH OTHER STATUTES

It is a familiar theme throughout this book that legal concepts do not exist in isolation, and a single case may trigger many statutes and regulations.

In *Wilson v. Chrysler Corp.*, [172 F.3d 500 (7th Cir. 1999)] the employer refused to reinstate a worker returning from medical leave. The employer's position was that she was totally disabled by paranoid schizophrenia, whereas the employee charged that the employer was retaliating against her for complaining about on-the-job sexual harassment. During the leave, the employee had applied for, and was granted, Social Security Disability Income (SSDI) benefits.

The Seventh Circuit ruled that applying for disability benefits rules out a sexual harassment claim. This is not necessarily true of an ADA claim: The Seventh Circuit view is that in ADA cases, a qualified disabled person may be able to work if reasonable accommodation is provided, but reasonable accommodation is not an issue in sexual harassment and other Title VII cases.

According to the Kentucky Supreme Court, there is an exception to Worker's Compensation exclusivity for injuries occurring through the "deliberate intention" of the employer. Therefore, although a suit against the employer for the physical and psychological consequences of sexual harassment would not necessarily be barred by WC exclusivity, nevertheless plaintiffs must make a choice. Either they can bring a tort suit (for instance, for intentional or negligent infliction of emotional distress; battery) or file for Worker's Compensation benefits. Acceptance of the Comp benefits rules out a suit involving the same injuries. [*American General Life & Accident Ins. Co. v. Hall*, 74 S.W.3d 688 (Ky. Sup. 2002)]

In another context requiring determination of the willful nature of acts, the Northern District of New York permitted a Chapter 7 debtor to discharge over $430,000 in damages for sexual harassment of an employee. The court ruled that although the conduct was reprehensible, there was no proof of intention to inflict emotional or economic harm on the harassment victim: malice is inherent in sexual harassment, but intent to injure is not. However, several other cases have treated sexual harassment as willful and malicious conduct precluding discharge of the damages in bankruptcy. [*In re Busch*, 311 B.R. 657 (N.D.N.Y. 2004); contra, *In re Clifford F. Smith*, 270 B.R. 544 (Bank. D. Mass 2001); *In re Kelly*, 238 B.R. 156 (Bank. E.D. Mo. 1999); *see* John Caher, *Bankruptcy Wipes Out Debt From*

Sexual Harassment Suit, New York Law Journal, Sept. 7, 2004 (law.com)] The Bankruptcy Abuse Prevention and Consumer Protection Act of 2005 (BAPCA; P.L. 109-8) denies a discharge in a Chapter 13 case for civil damages awarded against the debtor when the debtor's willful or malicious injury resulted in personal injury or death to a plaintiff.

A "top-hat" (executive benefit) plan called for payment of benefits on termination, with no qualifications. Because the plan did not mandate forfeiture when an employee was fired for cause, someone who was fired for sexually harassing employees was eligible for the benefits. [*Fields v. Thompson Printing Co.*, 363 F.3d 259 (3d Cir. 2004)]

CHAPTER 36

AMERICANS WITH DISABILITIES ACT (ADA)

§ 36.01   INTRODUCTION

Since its passage in 1990, the Americans With Disabilities Act (ADA) has been contentious and controversial. In recent years, the Supreme Court and the lower courts have greatly limited the scope of this Act, especially in the employment arena.

The ADA starts at 42 U.S.C. § 12101 (regulations at 29 C.F.R. § 1630.1). Title I is the employment title; Title II deals with public services (i.e., provided by government agencies), Title III with public accommodations, and Title IV with miscellaneous issues, some of which relate to employment.

A 2000 study, by the National Organization on Disability, showed that only 30% of disabled people aged 18–64 were employed—versus 80% of non-disabled persons in the same age range. Of the disabled population who say they are able to work, only 56% are employed. About one-third of employed people with disabilities (36%) say they have suffered workplace discrimination, and half say that they were denied a job at some point because of their disability. However, disabled workers are not laid off at a higher rate than their non-disabled co-workers. In 2002, 50% of the hiring managers surveyed told Beta Research Corporation that they were actively recruiting disabled workers. [Steven Greenhouse, *Pursuing a Chance in a Hard Job Market*, New York Times, June 15, 2003, at p. 1]

According to the ABA's Commission on Mental and Physical Disability, for 2002, there were 442 ADA Title I reported or unreported cases available online or through EEOC statistics. The employer won 94.5% of the time, the employee only 5.5% of the time. The circuit in which the employees had the highest percentage of victories was the Fifth, but only 14.5% of the plaintiffs succeeded there; in the other circuits, the percentage fell somewhere in the range of zero to 7.7%. (In 2000, 2001, and 2002, there were no plaintiff verdicts in any ADA case in the Eleventh or D.C. Circuits.) Generally speaking, employers won their cases by achieving summary judgment; only 3.9% of the cases in which the employer prevailed were resolved on the merits. At the EEOC level, employees prevailed in 21.9% of the cases, down from 26.7% in 2001. [Commission on Mental and Physical Disability Law Reporter, *2002 Employment Decisions Under the ADA Title I—Survey Update* <http://www.abanet.org/disability/reporter/feature.html>]

In August 2002, the EEOC issued an ADA handbook for small businesses, which can be downloaded from the EEOC Web site (<http://www.eeoc.gov/ada/adahandbook.html>).

§ 36.02   REACH AND RANGE OF ADA TITLE I

According to 42 U.S.C. § 12101, Congress went on record that the over 43 million employees with disabilities (a number that is increasing as the population ages) have a history of social alienation and discrimination in important areas such as work, housing, public accommodations, health services, and education. Congress declared that people with disabilities are a minority group that has suffered discrimination—and that our national goal in dealing with people with disabilities should be "to assure equality of opportunity, full participation, independent living, and economic selfsufficiency." The legislative purpose is given as providing "clear, strong, consistent, enforceable standards addressing discrimination against individuals with disabilities."

A "covered entity," as defined by 42 U.S.C. § 12111(2), means an employer, an employment agency, a union, or a joint labor-management committee.

Only employers who have at least 15 employees in each working day in each of 20 or more weeks in the current or preceding year are subject to the ADA. [42 U.S.C. § 12111(5)]

In an April 22, 2003, decision, the Supreme Court ruled that four physicians who were shareholders and directors of a medical PC were probably not "employees," using the economic reality test. The doctors controlled business operations; they were not subject to the control of others. If so, the professional corporation had fewer than 15 "employees," and the PC's bookkeeper could not bring suit under the ADA, whether or not it was true that she was terminated because of disability. [*Clackamas Gastroenterology Assocs., PC v. Wells*, 538 U.S. 440 (2003)]

Tip: In an ADA case (or an ADEA case), several closely related small affiliates of a larger corporation can have their workforces aggregated to determine if the 15-worker test has been met. Aggregation is proper if the corporate veil can be pierced (i.e., if practical realities justify disregarding the formal organization) and the parent company is liable for the debts, torts, and breaches of contract of its subsidiaries; if the business was divided up to avoid having to comply with employment laws; or if the parent company directed the discriminatory act or policy. [*Papa v. Katy Indus. Inc.*, 166 F.3d 937 (7th Cir. 1999)]

An employer with fewer than 15 employees, although exempt under the ADA, can be sued under the Rehabilitation Act. [*Schrader v. Fred A. Ray MD PC*, 296 F.3d 968 (10th Cir. 2002)]

Individuals are nearly always exempt from being sued under antidiscrimination suits (only the employer company is liable). *Alberte v. Anew Health Care Services* [588 N.W.2d 298 (Wis. App. 1998)] permits an ADA suit against an individual who was president, administrator, and 47.5% shareholder in a company accused of disability discrimination. In this reading, the president was the company's agent and personally liable for both compensatory and punitive damages.

Neither a doctor nor a medical services firm employing the doctor can be sued under ADA Title I for finding an employee unable to do his or her job. Neither of them is a covered entity subject to the ADA's ban on discrimination, because they do not have significant control over the employee's job performance, and the employer did not delegate employment decision-making to them. [*Satterfield v. Tennessee*, 295 F.3d 611 (6th Cir. 2002)]

A U.S. citizen who works outside the United States can count as an employee entitled to protection under the ADA. [42 U.S.C. § 12111(4)] However, it is not unlawful for a workplace outside the United States to comply with local law, even if the result is discrimination. Foreign operations of a foreign company that is not controlled by an American employer are exempt from the ADA. [42 U.S.C. § 12112(c)]

Section 12115 requires employers to post notices of ADA rights "in an accessible format" in the workplace.

The ADA does not invalidate or limit the remedies, rights, and procedures of any state or federal law that provides additional protection of the rights of individuals with disabilities. [42 U.S.C. § 12201]

"Mixed-motive" cases (where disability discrimination is alleged to be only one factor in the employer's decision) can be brought in some circuits, where it is not necessary for the plaintiff to allege that the employer was solely motivated by disability discrimination. [*McNely v. Ocala Star-Banner Corp.*, 99 F.3d 1068 (11th Cir. 1996)]. However, the Sixth Circuit does not allow mixed-motive cases: to sue there, the plaintiff must allege that disability must have been the sole cause for the employment decision. [*Hedrick v. Western Reserve Care System*, 355 F.3d 444 (6th Cir. 2004); *McLeod v. Parsons Corp.*, 73 Fed. Appx. 846 (6th Cir. 2003)] On the other hand, the Ninth Circuit does permit mixed-motive ADA cases. [*Head v. Glacier Northwest*, 413 F.3d 1053 (9th Cir. 2005)]

Most of the circuits allow hostile environment claims in the ADA context, because the ADA uses the same language as Title VII ("terms, conditions and privileges of employment) so the concept of the hostile work environment has been extended to cover the ADA as well as Title VII. [*Shaver v. Independent Stave Co.*, 350 F.3d 716 (8th Cir. 2003); *Flowers v. Southern Regional Physician Services Inc.*, 247 F.3d 229 (5th Cir. 2001); *Fox v. General Motors Corp.*, 247 F.3d 169 (4th Cir. 2001)] To win a hostile environment suit, the plaintiff must show that he or she is a member of the protected group; that unwelcome harassment occurred; that it resulted from membership in the protected class; and it was severe enough to affect the terms, conditions, or privileges of employment. [*Reedy v. Quebecor Printing Eagle, Inc.*, 333 F.3d 906 (8th Cir. 2003)] In the *Shaver* case, the plaintiff had severe epileptic seizures, and at least some of his colleagues treated him as stupid or mentally ill for that reason or because he had had brain surgery resulting in removal of part of his skull. There is evidence that he was taunted, but the Eighth Circuit concluded that the verbal harassment was not severe enough to rise to the level of an objectively hostile work environment. The plaintiff was upset, but not threatened or traumatized.

In contrast, the Northern District of Illinois found that summary judgment was inappropriate where a plaintiff who had cerebral palsy alleged enough name-calling, insulting graffiti, and physical intimidation to get a full trial on the issue of hostile work environment. [*Luttrell v. Certified Grocers Midwest Inc.*, 2003 U.S. Dist. LEXIS 21520 (N.D. Ill. 2003)]

Although Congress specifically stated in 42 U.S.C. § 12202 that states are NOT immune from ADA suits, the Supreme Court held in 2001 that Congress had no right to abrogate the states' "sovereign immunity" (freedom from being sued) with respect to ADA Title I cases that seek money damages rather than injunctions, because there was no documentation of a past history of disability discrimination perpetrated by the states themselves. [*See Board of Trustees of the Univ. of Ala. v. Garrett*, 531 U.S. 356 (2001)] In 2002, the Supreme Court held that punitive damages are not available in a suit for discrimination against disability discrimination committed by a public body, or by an agency that receives federal funding. [*Barnes v. Gorman*, 536 U.S. 181 (2002)] Although this is not directly relevant to private employment, it is another indication of the Supreme Court's attitude toward the ADA.

The Fifth Circuit later ruled that Congress did not properly abrogate the states' sovereign immunity with respect to ADA Title II either [*Reickenbacker v. Foster*, 274 F.3d 974 (5th Cir. 2001)], and the Second Circuit agrees. [*Garcia v. SUNY Health Sciences Ctr.*, 280 F.3d 98 (2d Cir. 2001)] *Gibson v. Arkansas Dep't of Corrections* [265 F.3d 718 (8th Cir. 2001)] says that although the states themselves are immune from suits for damages under the ADA, state officials can be sued to get prospective injunctive relief. It has also been held that states can be held liable for retaliation against employees who exercise ADA rights. [*Roberts v. Pennsylvania Dep't of Pub. Welfare*, 199 F. Supp. 2d 249 (E.D. Pa. 2002). *See* Shannon P. Duffy, *States Not Immune From ADA Retaliation Suits*, The Legal Intelligencer (Feb. 27, 2002) (law.com)]

However, the Fifth Circuit ruled that the Eleventh Amendment does not give the states immunity against ADA suits brought by the United States itself seeking victim-specific relief for individuals. In this situation, the individuals themselves would not be able to sue—but one consequence of a state ratifying the U.S. Constitution is consent to being sued by the United States itself and by other states. [*United States v. Mississippi Dep't of Pub. Safety*, 321 F.3d 495 (5th Cir. 2003)] The Georgia Court of Appeals held that the Eleventh Amendment does not bar a former employee's suit against the Georgia Department of Human Resources. In this interpretation, the Georgia Fair Employment Practices Act creates a right of action against the state for disability discrimination, waiving sovereign immunity—and sovereign immunity can't be asserted against the federal statute if it has been waived for the state counterpart. [*Williamson v. Department of Human Resources*, 258 Ga. App. 113, 572 S.E.2d 678 (Ga. App. 2002)]

On a related issue, early in 2003 the Sixth Circuit ruled that health plans did not violate the ADA by refusing to reimburse health plan participants for speech therapy services for their children. ADA Title III (public accommodations) does not cover the content of insurance policies, and a benefit plan sponsored by an employer cannot properly be characterized as goods offered by a place of public accommodation. In this reading, a public accommodation must be a physical place such as a store or office. [*Kolling v. Blue Cross & Blue Shield of Mich.*, 318 F.3d 715 (6th Cir. 2003)]

The Eleventh Circuit allowed a former employee to sue under Title I to challenge the different caps in the employer's long-term disability plan for physical and mental disabilities—Title I suits are not restricted to current employees. [*Johnson v. KMart Corp.*, 281 F.3d 1368 (11th Cir. 2001)]

§ 36.03   FORBIDDEN DISCRIMINATION

It is unlawful to discriminate against a qualified individual with a disability (QIWD) because of that person's disability, with respect to the terms, conditions, and privileges of employment: e.g., job application, hiring, promotion, discharge, compensation, and training. [*See* 42 U.S.C. § 12112]

Section 12112 goes on to enumerate seven types of action that constitute disability discrimination:

- Limiting, segregating, or classifying applicants or employees in ways that affect their opportunities, because of disability;
- Entering into a relationship (for instance, with an employment agency) that results in disability discrimination;
- Using standards, criteria, or methods of administration that either discriminate or perpetuate discrimination by another party under the same administrative control (e.g., another division in the same company);
- Denying jobs or benefits to a qualified person who has a relationship or association with someone else who has a disability (e.g., refusing to hire someone merely because he or she is married to a person with a disability who has high medical bills that might result in higher EGHP premiums);
- Failing to make a reasonable accommodation to known physical or mental limitations of an employee or applicant who is a QIWD—unless the accommodation would work undue hardship on the employer; or denying employment opportunities to QIWDs if the denial is based on the need to accommodate;
- Using employment tests or other standards or criteria that screen out people with disabilities—but a defense is available for job-related measures that are consistent with business necessity;
- Using tests that are biased by an applicant's or employee's impairment (speech difficulties, for instance) and therefore fail to reflect the job aptitudes that the test is supposed to assess.

It is also unlawful to retaliate against anyone who opposed any act of disability discrimination, or who made a charge, testified, assisted, or participated in an investigation, administrative proceeding, or court case. It is unlawful to interfere with the ADA investigation process, or to "coerce, intimidate, threaten, or interfere with" anyone because of enforcement of ADA rights. [42 U.S.C. § 12203]

Although it is not an employment case (it deals with discrimination by a dentist against an HIV-positive patient), *Bragdon v. Abbott* [524 U.S. 624 (1998)] has some interesting things to say about the ADA. *Bragdon* sets up a three-step test for ADA cases:

- Does the plaintiff have an impairment?
- Is the major life activity that is impaired covered by the ADA?
- Does the plaintiff's impairment substantially limit that major life activity?

Looking specifically at HIV in the employment context, the Fifth Circuit ruled in 2002 that a telephone company service representative, who was diagnosed as HIV-positive when on medical leave for stress, was not disabled. He was not restricted in any of his major life activities, even working, although his doctor advised him not to return to the same stressful job after his leave. The employer also tried to find alternative positions for him, showing that he was not perceived as disabled with respect to a broad range of jobs. [*Blanks v. Southwestern Bell Communications Inc.*, 310 F.3d 398 (5th Cir. 2002)]

In May 2004, the Seventh Circuit held that it was not a violation of the ADA (or the FMLA) to fire an employee with AIDS who had a confrontation with a supervisor in which he uttered racial slurs, and an altercation in which he threatened to "get" another employee. (He was arrested and found guilty of disorderly conduct for threatening that employee.) He was on final warning for absenteeism when he informed his employer that his AIDS condition caused him to be absent so frequently. The employee service manager informed him that he could apply for FMLA leave for some of his absences. However, a few weeks later he was given a last-chance agreement because he still had 14 unexcused absences in the previous 11 months, including six no-shows for which he had not called in. The Seventh Circuit did not accept that the short duration between his disclosure that he had AIDS and his termination was proof of discrimination, because his disciplinary status was already very poor. Furthermore, there was nothing about having AIDS that impelled him to threaten supervisors or co-workers. [*Buie v. Quad/Graphics Inc.*, 366 F.3d 496 (7th Cir. 2004)]

Similarly, it was held that it did not violate the ADA to fire a person legally blind as a result of glaucoma because, for reasons related both to his physical condition and his attitude, the plaintiff frequently damaged product, slowed down the production line, drove a forklift into the wall, and generally did a bad job. The company relaxed its usual practice of rotating tasks in the effort to find work he could do. However, the ADA does not require employers to provide special training to persons with disabilities, nor was assigning another employee to check his or her work a reasonable accommodation. [*Hammel v. Eau Galle Cheese Factory*, 407 F.3d 852 (7th Cir. 2005)]

A plaintiff who can show directly that the employer refused to train her to use a specific piece of machinery (in this case, a high-speed scanner) because of her disability (she had only one hand) can pursue a disparate treatment ADA claim without having to prove that the refusal was an adverse job action. Unlike other antidiscrimination statutes, the ADA specifically refers to denial of training. In the case of *Hoffman v. Caterpillar Inc.* [256 F.3d 568 (7th Cir. 2001)], the plaintiff said that knowing how to use the high-speed scanner was essential to eligibility for promotion. However, the Seventh Circuit ruled that, to get damages, she would have to prove that she was physically capable of running the scanner. Because using the scanner was not an essential function of her job, the employer did not have a duty to reasonably accommodate her in this regard.

[A]   Association

The ADA also forbids discrimination in fringe benefits on the basis of an employee's relationship to or association with a person who has a disability. In October 2005, the EEOC issued a series of questions and answers about this part of the ADA. An employer that provides dependent coverage cannot refuse to cover a disabled family member. The Q&A says that refusing to hire an applicant because a disabled family member will raise insurance costs violates the ADA. It also is a violation to offer the job, but deny dependent health coverage if it would otherwise be available to a nondisabled dependent. However, it is not necessary to provide additional coverage because the dependent with a disability requires more health care than most people. [*See* <http://www.eeoc.gov/facts/association_ ada.html> and the press release at <http://www.eeoc.gov/press/10-17-05.html>]

The Eighth Circuit ruled that summary judgment should not have been granted for the employer where a former employee alleged that she was terminated because of her association with a person with a disability (her newborn child with Down syndrome). The employer's defense was that her position had been eliminated while she was on maternity leave. The Eighth Circuit found that the job was eliminated two months after the child was born and the employer became aware of the child's disability and that the plaintiff's work record prior to her pregnancy had been excellent, so there were issues of material fact to be resolved at trial. [*Strate v. Midwest Bankcentre, Inc.,* 398 F.3d 1011 (8th Cir. 2005)]

A person fired only a few weeks after being hired brought an ADA and ERISA suit. He alleged that he was fired because his wife was mentally ill or, in the alternative, because he tried to get the EGHP to cover treatment for her. The employer said that he was fired for poor job performance. To prove the ADA case, the employee would have to show that the circumstances raised a reasonable inference that his wife's disability was a determining factor in his termination. He would have to establish discriminatory motivation, including that the wife's disability was costly to the health plan; the condition was transmissible to the employee; or the employee was unable to concentrate at work because of the disability. The Southern District of Indiana found that none of these factors were present. He did not show that the EGHP would have covered his wife's treatment and he did not elect COBRA coverage after his termination, which showed that he was not strongly concerned with health care coverage. In addition, his litigating position was that his work was satisfactory, so he did not show that his wife's condition affected his ability to work. [*Tracy v. Financial Ins. Mgmt. Corp.*, 2006 U.S. Dist. LEXIS 1949, <http://www.insd.uscourts.gov/opinions/AN619002.PDF> (S.D. Inc. 2006)]

§ 36.04   DEFINING "DISABILITY"

[A]   Generally

According to 42 U.S.C. § 12102, there are three forms of disability:

- A physical or mental impairment that substantially limits one or more of the major life activities of such individual;
- A record of such an impairment;
- Being regarded as having such an impairment (even if the impairment is only perceived and does not exist).

According to the statute, transvestism is not a disability, [42 U.S.C. § 12209] nor are homosexuality, bisexuality, transsexualism, pedophilia, exhibitionism, gender identity disorders, compulsive gambling, kleptomania, pyromania, or current use of illegal drugs. [42 U.S.C. § 12211]

The Ninth Circuit reversed a District Court ruling that applicants for driving jobs who only had the use of one eye were not disabled. The applicants *were* limited in the major life activity of seeing. However, the Ninth Circuit held that there was a valid defense based on the safety of others because there was evidence that drivers with monocular vision had more accidents than drivers with binocular vision. [*EEOC v. UPS, Inc.*, 424 F.3d 1060 (9th Cir. 2005)]

However, state laws may impose requirements differing from those of federal law. For instance, a 2001 New Jersey case says that transsexuals are protected against gender and disability discrimination under the state Law Against Discrimination. The plaintiff's sexual orientation discrimination claim was dismissed on the grounds that the male-to-female transsexual plaintiff neither was nor was perceived to be homosexual or bisexual. [*Enriquez v. West Jersey Health Sys.*, 342 N.J. Super. 501 (2001)]

A QIWD is defined by 42 U.S.C. § 12111(8) as one who can perform the essential functions of the job (with or without accommodation). The employer's determination about which functions of a job are essential is entitled to consideration. Written job descriptions used in advertising or job interviews are considered evidence of the essential functions of the job. In other words, these descriptions must be drafted with care!

The EEOC's position is that determining which functions are essential to a job is a complex process involving several factors, e.g.:

- Expertise or skill needed to do that task;
- Other employees available to perform that function (as individuals or as a team);

- If that function is the entire rationale of the job;
- Time spent on that particular function;
- Qualifications of people who held the same job in the past;
- What would happen if the individual did not perform the function in question;
- What the Collective Bargaining Agreement (if there is one) says about the function as it relates to the job.

In June 1999, the Supreme Court decided three major employment-related cases, concluding that an individual is not disabled if the condition has been corrected, e.g., through medication or an assistive device. [*Murphy v. United Parcel Serv.*, 527 U.S. 516 (1999); *Sutton v. United Air Lines*, 527 U.S. 471 (1999); *Albertsons v. Kirkingburg*, 527 U.S. 555 (1999). *See* 65 Fed. Reg. 36327 (June 8, 2000) for the EEOC's Final Rule drafted to conform to these rulings]

A late 2001 decision by the Tenth Circuit says that a truck driver who took medication to control seizures was not a QIWD even though his doctor certified him as fit to drive, because the need for medication made him unable to meet job-related Department of Transportation standards. [*Tate v. Farmland Indus. Inc.*, 268 F.3d 989 (10th Cir. 2001)]

The Seventh Circuit held that "liver function" is not a major life activity under the ADA, so firing someone for having cirrhosis does not violate the ADA, a statute that focuses on the activities that are limited by an impairment, not on the characterization of the impairment. [*Furnish v. SVI Sys. Inc.*, 270 F.3d 445 (7th Cir. 2001)] In contrast, given the limitations on the major life activities of cleansing blood and eliminating body wastes, the Third Circuit ruled that the district court erred in finding that a person with end-stage renal disease did not have an ADA disability. [*Fiscus v. Wal-Mart Stores Inc.*, 385 F.3d 378 (3d Cir. 2004)] The Fourth Circuit also has ruled that elimination of body waste by the kidneys is a major life activity, so a dialysis patient's ADA claims could go to trial. [*Heiko v. Colombo Sav. Bank FSB*, 434 F.3d 249 (4th Cir. 2006)]

Two recent cases involve multiple sclerosis. In late 2003, the Tenth Circuit ruled that an employee with multiple sclerosis, who claimed that she needed frequent unpredictable leave time, could not exert herself on a sustained basis, could not lift heavy objects, do housework, or care for her children, did not raise a factual issue of substantial limitation in any major life activity. The court ruled that she did not show that her limitations prevented her from completing her job or made her totally unable to perform major life activities. [*Croy v. COBE Labs Inc.*, 345 F.3d 1199 (10th Cir. 2003)] Early in 2004, an employee who was fired shortly after telling his employer that he had early-stage multiple sclerosis was not permitted to use the timing to prove discrimination. (He had a documented history of poor work performance.) The District Court ruled that early MS with annual flare-ups is only an ADA disability if the plaintiff can prove that it substantially impairs a major life activity. About once a year there is a period of a week to a month during which the plaintiff gets dizzy, can't control one side of his body, and has trouble climbing stairs; he has mobility problems at other times. But the court said that he did not offer evidence of more than moderate impairment in the major life activity of walking. [*Yudkovitz v. Bell Atlantic Corp.*, 2004 U.S. Dist. LEXIS 1165 (E.D. Pa. Jan. 12, 2004), discussed in Shannon P. Duffy, *Early-Stage MS Ruled Not a Disability*, The Legal Intelligencer (Jan. 14, 2004)]

Although the Fifth Circuit has ruled that chronic pancreatitis is an impairment that substantially affects the major life activity of eating, [*Holtzclaw v. DSC Communications Corp.*, 255 F.3d 254 (5th Cir. 2001)] in a 2003 case, the Fifth Circuit ruled that a factory worker with chronic pancreatitis was not disabled for ADA purposes. He was discharged, and claimed that this was because of the pain medication he had to take (operators of heavy machinery must stay alert). The Fifth Circuit ruled that he did not provide evidence that his pancreatitis substantially limited the major life activity of eating, thus making it severe enough to be an ADA disability. Nor did he prove that the employer incorrectly perceived his impairment to be substantially limiting; in fact, they gave him sick leave when he required it. [*Waldrip v. GE*, 325 F.3d 652 (5th Cir. 2003)]

The Eighth Circuit ruled that a diabetic pharmacist who was fired for closing the pharmacy during his lunch breaks was not disabled for ADA purposes. The disability analysis cannot be triggered by what would happen if mitigating measures were not applied (i.e., what would happen if the diabetic condition were not treated). [*Orr v. Wal-Mart Stores Inc.*, 297 F.3d 720 (8th Cir. 2002)]

Later, however, the Ninth Circuit permitted a diabetic banker to go to trial on her claim that not letting her eat at her desk was a refusal to accommodate her substantial limitations in the major life activity of eating. The plaintiff's need for continual blood sugar monitoring and diabetic care raised triable issues. [*Fraser v. Goodale*, 342 F.3d 1032 (9th Cir. 2003)]

UPS should have made an individual determination as to whether a deaf applicant could safely drive vehicles smaller than those covered by DOT hearing standards—particularly because the company allows insulin-dependent diabetics to drive small UPS vehicles (although they cannot satisfy DOT standards for large-vehicle operation), and because UPS never analyzed the hearing requirements for safe driving. [*Bates v. UPS*, 73 LW 1264 (N.D. Cal. Oct. 21, 2004)]

The trial court dismissed a Texas Labor Code discrimination case brought by a woman whose leg was amputated at the knee, on the ground that she could walk with a prosthesis (although slowly and with a limp). On appeal, it was held that she was in fact disabled because it did not concentrate on the effect of the mitigating measure but on the extent of her limitations in walking when compared to the general population. [*Little v. Texas Dep't of Criminal Justice*, 145 S.W. 3rd 324 (Tex. 2004)]

A custodian with cerebral palsy sued his employer of 27 years for failure to promote (he made 10 applications over a 12-year period) and failure to provide reasonable accommodation. The district court granted summary judgment for the employer on the grounds that the plaintiff did not have an ADA disability, but the Third Circuit reversed and remanded, finding at least a genuine issue of fact as to the effect of the plaintiff's impairment on his ability to perform manual tasks and learn. The plaintiff was partially paralyzed on the right side and in his right hand, and has a deformed arm and leg. He cannot lift anything heavy or grip with his right hand. His IQ has been tested in the 72 to 88 range. He cannot read test questions himself, and can only take tests by having the questions read to him. The district court ruled that, because the plaintiff graduated from high school and received computer training, his learning impairments are not substantially limiting. The Third Circuit noted that the plaintiff was in special education classes, and read at a second-grade level. In the Third Circuit view, the measure of substantial limitation is the extent of difficulties encountered by the plaintiff, not what he or she is able to overcome. [*Emory v. Astrazeneca Pharmaceuticals LP.*, 401 F.3d 174 (3d Cir. 2005). *But see Luttrell v. Certified Grocers Midwest, Inc.*, 2003 WL22844239 (N.D. Ill. Dec. 1, 2003) (finding that a genuine issue of material fact exists as to whether plaintiff with "mild" cerebral palsy resulting in a deformed left hand is disabled under the ADA)]

In a case that went to the Eighth Circuit, the district court jury rendered a verdict in favor of the plaintiff, granting back pay and punitive damages. The plaintiff cross-appealed the denial of front pay. The Eighth Circuit, however, reversed and directed judgment in favor of the defendant. The plaintiff was a boiler operator. After shoulder surgery, he returned to work with limitations, including limitations on lifting. He got into trouble for videotaping inside the plant without permission. He went on leave for back surgery, then was fired for violating the plant's security rules. He charged that he was terminated because he was regarded as disabled. The Eighth Circuit ruled that when the major life activity involved in an ADA case is working, substantial limitation means that the plaintiff must allege inability to work in a broad class of jobs, not just one particular job. The Eighth Circuit has also ruled that demotion is not actionable in the regarded-as context, because continued employment (even in a lesser capacity) demonstrates the employer's belief that the plaintiff is not unemployable in general. [*Knutson v. Ag Processing, Inc.*, 394 F.3d 1047 (8th Cir. 2005); *see also Schuler v. SuperValu, Inc.*, 336 F.3d 702 (8th Cir. 2003), and *Epps v. City of Pine Lawn*, 353 F.3d 588, 593 (8th Cir. 2003), on the question of being disabled for a broad range of jobs]

[B] Attendance

The question is often raised whether predictable, regular attendance is a fundamental job qualification. If it is, then it does not violate the ADA to fire, refuse to hire, etc., a person who cannot satisfy attendance requirements because of disability. [*See, e.g., EEOC v. Yellow Freight Sys., Inc.*, 253 F.3d 943 (7th Cir. 2001) (granting an unlimited number of sick days is not a reasonable accommodation); *Carlson v. Inacom Corp.*, 885 F. Supp. 1314 (E.D. Mich. 1996); *Fritz v. Mascotech Automotive Sys. Group. Inc.*, 914 F. Supp. 1481 (E.D. Mich. 1996); *Vorhies v. Pioneer Mfg.*, 906 F. Supp. 578 (D. Colo. 1995)] *Cehrs v. Northeast Ohio Alzheimer's Research Center* [155 F.3d 775 (6th Cir. 1998)] does not permit employers to rely on a presumption that regular attendance is an essential job function: They must provide evidence about the need for predictability in that particular job as distinct from employment in general.

A person whose physical or mental condition precludes working more than 40 hours a week has been held not to be ADA disabled, [*Tardie v. Rehabilitation Hosp. of R.I.*, 168 F.3d 538 (1st Cir. 1999)] given that there are many jobs available that do not require a commitment of over 40 hours a week. *Also see Davis v. Florida Power & Light*, [205 F.3d 1301 (11th Cir. 2000)] finding that mandatory overtime was an essential function of the job, and it would violate the collective bargaining agreement to provide a no-overtime or selective-overtime arrangement for a disabled worker.

However, in *Alifano v. Merck & Co. Inc.* [175 F. Supp. 2d 792 (E.D. Pa. 2001)], the Eastern District of Pennsylvania held that fibromyalgia/chronic fatigue syndrome could result in substantial impairment of major life activities, including working, even though the plaintiff claimed only that she could not travel on business or work more than an eight-hour day. Later, the District Court for the District of Massachusetts ruled that a former employee with fibromyalgia provided extensive medical documentation of her inability to sit; even though most of the evidence came from the time after her resignation, the court accepted it as probative of her inability to sit before her resignation. [*Labrecque v. Sodexho USA Inc.*, 287 F. Supp. 2d 100 (D. Mass. 2003)]

An employee of the court system suffered cluster headaches for many years. By 1985, he was missing work frequently and not doing a substantial portion of his duties. To accommodate his absences, the Clerk's Office created a new position for him that he would be able to handle. He was also routinely granted discretionary leave after using up his medical leave and vacation time. He was permitted discretionary leave without pay starting at the end of 1999, with no end date, but was fired at the beginning of 2000. He sued under both the ADA and the FMLA. At the trial court level, he lost on the FMLA claim but prevailed on the ADA claim and was awarded back pay and reinstatement. However, the Eleventh Circuit reversed the trial court. The Eleventh Circuit found that the plaintiff was not a QIWD, because he was asking for indefinite leave, which is not a reasonable accommodation—a concept that refers to the employee's current ability to work, not projected ability to work in the future after a period of recovery. [*Wood v. Green*, 323 F.3d 1309 (11th Cir. 2003)]

But, at the other end of the scale, evidence that the plaintiff never missed work precluded a determination that he was substantially limited in the major life activities of standing and sitting. [*Pegram v. Honeywell Inc.*, 361 F.3d 272 (5th Cir. 2004)]

Early in 2002, the Eighth Circuit took the view that an engineer who suffered brain damage was disabled for ADA purposes. He had long-term impairments that prevented him from working full-time, and his condition affected more than a single aspect of a single job; he was severely restricted in the kinds of work he could do. [*Moysis v. DTG Datanet*, 278 F.3d 819 (8th Cir. 2002)] *But see Whitlock v. Mac-Gray Inc.*, [345 F.3d 44 (1st Cir. 2003)] holding that a physician's statement that the plaintiff was totally disabled by attention deficit hyperactivity disorder (ADHD) did not make him disabled for ADA purposes. A diagnosis of impairment and a conclusory allegation of disability is not enough. The plaintiff claimed that he was unable to work, but this claim was invalidated by his admission that he could do his job and had taught himself to use a computer.

[C] Infertility

A 1996 case says that reproduction is not a major life activity, but in 1997, the Northern District of Illinois disagreed, even though reproduction does not directly affect employment. [*Compare Krauel v. Iowa Methodist Med. Ctr.*, 95 F.3d 674 (8th Cir. 1996), *with Erickson v. Board of Governors, Northeastern Ill. Univ.*, 911 F. Supp. 316 (N.D. Ill. 1997, *later proceedings*, 207 F.3d 945 (7th Cir. 2000)]

The plaintiff in *Saks v. Franklin Covey Co.* [117 F. Supp. 2d 318 (S.D.N.Y. 2000)] was covered by a self-insured health plan that excluded "surgical impregnation procedures." She sued under Title VII, the ADA, and the Pregnancy Discrimination Act. The court ruled that infertility might be a disability, because it interferes with the major life activity of procreation.

However, the ADA claim was dismissed because all employees got the same coverage; infertile employees were not singled out for inferior coverage of reproductive services. The plan also qualified for the safe harbor for bona fide employee benefit plans. The Title VII claim failed because both male and female infertility were excluded. Surgical procedures were excluded for both female employees and wives of male employees. The PDA claim failed because infertility treatments were equally unavailable to pregnant and nonpregnant employees and beneficiaries.

The Second Circuit affirmed the dismissal in 2003, [*Saks v. Franklin Covey Co.*, 316 F.3d 337 (2d Cir. 2003)] although using a slightly different rationale. The District Court looked at the question of whether all employees have equal access to plan benefits. The Second Circuit said that this standard, often used in ADA cases, was wrong because this was really a Title VII case. Therefore, the correct standard is whether sex-specific conditions exist. If they do, the question becomes whether excluding coverage for those conditions results in a plan with inferior coverage for one sex.

According to the Northern District of Illinois, it did not violate the ADA to refuse to pay for infertility treatment for an employee's spouse, because the law does not extend to dependents of an employee if the dependents do not perform services for the employer. [*Niemeier v. Tri-State Fire Protection Dist.*, 2000 U.S. Dist. LEXIS 12621 (N.D. Ill. Aug. 24, 2000)] Furthermore, non-employees can't sue the employer under Title VII or the PDA. The employee had standing (the legal right to pursue the PDA claim), but the claim itself was invalid, because the plan did not cover fertility treatment for either sex.

[D] Psychiatric Disability

ADA regulations [29 C.F.R. § 1630.2(h)(2)] define mental impairment to include developmental disability, learning disabilities, organic brain syndrome, and neurological disease, as well as mental or psychological disorders. The examples given by the EEOC are major depression, bipolar disorder, panic disorder, obsessive-compulsive disorder, post-traumatic stress disorder, schizophrenia, and personality disorders.

The psychiatric profession's official compendium, the Diagnostic and Statistical Manual of Mental Disorders (DSM), is the first step in identifying mental disorders. However, certain disorders are included in the DSM but excluded from ADA coverage—for instance, current drug and alcohol abuse, compulsive gambling, certain sexual disorders, and kleptomania.

Furthermore, persons who are troubled but not classically mentally ill may seek treatment such as family therapy. Such individuals are not impaired for ADA purposes. A mental illness impairment may be present yet not covered by the ADA, if it is mild enough not to substantially limit the impaired person's ability to work and carry out other major life activities.

The EEOC Guidance on mental disability deals with impairment of the major life activity of interacting with others. The test is whether, compared to an average person in the general population, the employee is significantly restricted in human interactions because of severe problems such as "consistently high levels of hostility, social withdrawal, or failure to communicate where necessary," with a long-term or potential long-term duration. Similar considerations are used to assess alleged limitations in the ability to concentrate, or the ability to get adequate sleep or care for one's self.

The EEOC Guidance on mental disability [EEOC Guidance No. 915.002 (March 25, 1997)] says that an individual poses a direct risk if an individualized assessment is made based on reasonable medical judgment, the most current medical knowledge, and/or the best objective evidence available. More specifically, the fact that a person has a history of psychiatric disability, or is currently under psychiatric treatment, is not enough to render that person a direct risk.

Issues may arise as to whether an employee who is difficult to work with because of an aggressive attitude or combative personality has a psychiatric disability that requires accommodation. The World Health Organization's estimate is that mental health problems cost six lost work days per 100 workers in the United States, account for 35% to 45% of absenteeism, and 59% of the productivity lost to injury and illness. The EEOC says that, at 20%, mental/psychiatric disability is its largest category of ADA cases. Anxiety disorder and depression are the most common diagnoses involved. According to management-side attorney

Jonathan Mook, the ADA becomes involved only if the employer is on notice that the employee receives treatment for a recognized medical condition; otherwise, the employer should react just as it would to any other instance of disruptive behavior. The First Circuit has ruled that "getting along with other people" is not a major life activity for ADA purposes. The Second Circuit overturned a jury award to an employee with bipolar syndrome, because of lack of proof of severe limitation in the plaintiff's ability to communicate or deal with others, ruling that employers should not be at the mercy of impossible employees. [*Jacques v. DiMarzio Inc.*, 386 F.3d 192 (2d Cir. 2004); the Ninth Circuit treated panic and anxiety disorder as a substantial limitation in interaction with others: (*McAlindin v. County of San Diego*, 192 F.3d 1226 (9th Cir. 1999)] The EEOC announced that it has no plans to update its 1997 guidance on psychiatric disabilities. [For discussion of these issues, *see* Lyda Phillips, *Accommodating the Problem Employee: No Easy Answers, Experts and Courts Agree*, 73 LW 2275 (Nov. 16, 2004)]

An epileptic who was fired after several incidents of aggressive and threatening behavior was neither disabled nor regarded as disabled. The Eighth Circuit held that he did not show that epilepsy substantially limited major non-work life activities. Although the plaintiff's former employer told him to get anger-management therapy, the Eighth Circuit did not deem this to mean that the employer regarded him as having an emotional condition that was substantially limiting. [*Brunke v. Goodyear Tire & Rubber Co.*, 344 F.3d 819 (8th Cir. 2003)]

The First Circuit reversed the District Court's grant of summary judgment for the employer. There was a factual issue as to whether the employer failed to accommodate an employee suffering from major depression. The employee asked at least six times for a temporary transfer to another office. The transfer appeared to be feasible and not an undue hardship, and the court ruled that a reasonable finder of fact could have concluded that the employer failed to engage in the required interactive process. [*Calero-Arezo v. Department of Justice*, 355 F.3d 6 (1st Cir. 2004)]

Does providing a lower level of disability benefits for mental illnesses than for physical ailments violate the ADA? *Kimber v. Thiokol Corp.* [196 F.3d 1092 (10th Cir. 1999)] says no. *Rogers v. Department of Health and Environmental Control* [174 F.3d 431 (4th Cir. 1999)] says that neither the ADA nor Title VII requires plans for state employees to furnish the same benefit levels for physical and mental ailments. *Morrill v. Lorillard Tobacco Co.* [2000 U.S. Dist. LEXIS 18810 (D.N.H. Dec. 7, 2000)] finds that ADA Title I was not violated by imposing a 50% copayment and 20-visit limit on mental health benefits, versus a 15–20% copayment for an unlimited number of visits for other claims.

Although ADA Title IV [42 U.S.C. § 12201(c) *et seq.*] provides a safe harbor for insurers and employee benefit plans that underwrite, classify, and administer risk in a way that is not a subterfuge to avoid the ADA, *Lewis v. Aetna Life Ins. Co.* [7 F. Supp. 2d 743 (E.D. Va. 1998)] says that the plan's distinction between physical and mental disabilities violated the ADA because the insurer was unable to furnish actuarial support for the distinction.

[E] *Williams* and "Impairment"

Early in 2002, the Supreme Court decided *Toyota Motor Manufacturing, Kentucky, Inc. v. Williams.* [534 U.S. 184 (2002)] The court held that the plaintiff, who had carpal tunnel syndrome, was not disabled for ADA purposes. She was able to care for herself and perform ordinary daily tasks.

In this view, merely having an impairment does not make a person disabled, nor does being unable to perform the tasks associated with that person's specific job, as long as the person can perform other tasks. Many courts have interpreted *Williams* to define when an impairment alleged by an ADA plaintiff rises to the status of a disability. The Tenth Circuit limited the *Williams* analysis to the major life activity of performing manual tasks, using other analytical factors to analyze the major life activity of working. [*Rakity v. Dillon Cos Inc.*, 302 F.3d 1142 (10th Cir. 2002)] The Seventh and Ninth Circuits use *Williams* to analyze all major life activities except working. [*Mack v. Great Dane Trailers*, 308 F.3d 776 (7th Cir. 2002); *EEOC v. UPS*, 306 F.3d 794 (9th Cir. 2002)] In 2005, the Seventh Circuit held that 29 C.F.R. § 1630.2(j)'s definition of "substantial limitation" remains valid even after the *Williams* decision, and the regulation can be considered in determining whether a department store employee's difficulties in walking substantially limited her in major life activities. [*EEOC v. Sears, Roebuck & Co.*, 417 F.3d 789 (7th Cir. 2005)]

The Eighth Circuit ruled that an ADA case was properly dismissed where the plaintiff, who developed work-related back pain and hand discomfort, did not show the effect of his limitations on his ability to perform the variety of tasks central to daily life. In fact, his evidence showed that although he had problems with lifting and using vibrating tools, he coped fairly well in daily life. The Eighth Circuit conceded that he had an impairment, but did not show disability. Although his evidence was restricted to work-related matters, he failed to claim a limitation in the life activity of working. [*Philip v. Ford Motor Co.*, 328 F.3d 1020 (8th Cir. 2003)] In another case, a constructive discharge claim could not be maintained by a worker who was in pain when engaging in many normal tasks before he had back surgery. After the surgery, however, his mobility was restored and he could perform tasks central to most people's lives, so he was not disabled for ADA purposes. [*See also Rooney v. Koch Air LLC*, 410 F.3d 376 (7th Cir. 2005)]

The Eighth Circuit reversed a grant of summary judgment for the employer in a case where accommodation was denied. A railroad engineer whose right hand and arm were mutilated in an accident took a job as an on-call engineer, who can be called to report to work at any time on one-and-a-half-hour's notice. Before 1997, the plaintiff was usually given additional notice, so he had enough time to bathe, shave, dress, and drive to work (all of which took him longer than an employee who had full use of both arms). In 1997, the policy was changed, and all employees were given a uniform two-hour call. The plaintiff's request for additional notice was refused. Because employees were vulnerable to termination for lateness, the plaintiff then asked for a different job with regular hours. The only regularly scheduled job that he could get with his seniority was a demotion to weekend conductor, at lower pay. He accepted the demotion and filed disability discrimination charges with the EEOC.

In the Eighth Circuit's view, his ability to care for himself was limited by an impairment that prevented or severely restricted him in carrying out activities that are of central importance to most people's daily life.

The Eighth Circuit noted that some other circuits recognize a cause of action for constructive demotion, using the same standards as constructive discharge: whether a reasonable person would have found the conditions intolerable. [*Fenney v. Dakota, Minnesota & Eastern Railroad Co.*, 327 F.3d 707 (8th Cir. 2003). On constructive demotion, *see Brown v. Lester E. Cox Med. Ctrs.*, 286 F.3d 1040 (8th Cir. 2002); *Simpson v. Borg-Warner Automotive, Inc.*, 196 F.3d 873 (7th Cir. 1999); *Sharp v. City of Houston*, 164 F.3d 923 (5th Cir. 1999)]

The Fourth Circuit ruled that a courier who was fired after a work-related back injury was not substantially limited in his ability to work despite his 30-lb. lifting limitation. Although the vocational expert estimated that he could not perform 57% of the job titles in his geographical area, the expert testified that there were 100,000 actual jobs in the region that he could perform. [*Taylor v. Federal Express*, 429 F.3d 461 (8th Cir. 2005); *Nuzum v. Ozark Automotive Distribs. Inc.*, 432 F.3d 461 (8th Cir. 2005) also says that a lifting restriction is not a disability (particularly since the plaintiff got another reasonably similar job, although it paid less), and the plaintiff failed to show substantial limitation in any major life activity]

Under *Williams*, an impairment must be permanent or long-term, so the First Circuit did not deem ovarian cysts that caused only temporary impairment (until they were removed and the plaintiff recovered) to be an ADA disability. Although the plaintiff's retaliation claim was not directly dependent on the success of her disability claim, she never directly requested an accommodation. She did not go to the state anti-discrimination agency or bring suit until after she had been discharged, so her discharge could not have been retaliatory. She was fired for theft of company time (making unauthorized phone calls during working hours) and reinstated at arbitration because the company had not described the calls as theft, and the evidence against her was weak. Her regarded-as-disabled claim was also dismissed because it was not raised before the district court and therefore could not be presented for the first time at the court of appeals level. [*Guzman-Rosario v. UPS Inc.*, 397 F.3d 6 (1st Cir. 2005)]

The Second Circuit affirmed summary judgment for the employer in a case where an employee was traumatized and developed insomnia after a close call in a firebomb incident in the New York City subway system. She asked to be assigned to work away from the subways. The Transit Authority refused. She filed an ADA claim based on substantial limitation in sleeping. But the employer prevailed in court, because the requested accommodation was not related to her disability. [*Felix v. NYC Transit Authority*, 324 F.3d 102 (2d Cir. 2003)]

An employee with attention deficit syndrome was initially permitted to put partitions around his workspace and use a radio to block background noise as an accommodation to his condition. Then he was moved to another work area where these tactics could not be used. He took short-term disability leave; returned, and once again was allowed to use the radio and partitions and work a shortened schedule. Then he took another leave, and his doctor said he was totally disabled and unable to return to work. In the First Circuit view, the plaintiff's evidence merely showed impairment, not disability; *Williams* holds that a medical diagnosis of impairment is not probative of disability. The plaintiff did not show his inability to work at a broad range of jobs; in fact, his testimony showed that he thought he was performing adequately at the job he held. [*Whitlock v. Mac-Gray Inc.*, 345 F.3d 44 (1st Cir. 2003). *Also see Gonzalez v. El Dia, Inc.*, 304 F.3d 63 (1st Cir. 2002) (conclusory medical testimony about ability to work does not prove disability)]

§ 36.05   REASONABLE ACCOMMODATION

[A]   Employer's Obligation

Employers have an obligation to engage in an interactive process of reasonable accommodation, to permit employment or continued employment of qualified individuals with disabilities. However, it is not required that employers undergo undue hardship in making such accommodations.

Section 12111(9) says that the category of reasonable accommodation may include making existing facilities readily accessible and usable by QIWDs. It can also include job restructuring, part-time or other altered work schedules, reassignment to a *vacant* position (in April 2002, the Supreme Court ruled that it is not in general "reasonable" to reassign an employee if the reassignment violated an established seniority system—but the employee can demonstrate that an exception should be made in his or her individual case: *U.S. Airways v. Barnett*, 535 U.S. 391 (2002)). Other possible reasonable accommodations include acquiring or modifying equipment, providing training, making readers or interpreters available, etc.

It is an established principle that employers are not required to provide indefinite leaves of absence or unlimited sick days as a reasonable accommodation to disability. [*See, e.g., Wood v. Green*, 323 F.3d 1309 (11th Cir. 2002), *cert. denied* 540 U.S. 982 (2003); *EEOC v. Yellow Freight Sys., Inc.*, 253 F.3d 943 (7th Cir. 2001); *Nowak v. St. Rita High Sch.*, 142 F.3d 999, 1004 (7th Cir. 1998)]

According to the First Circuit, ability to lift more than 50 pounds is an essential function of nursing. Therefore, the employer does not have to accommodate a nurse with a back injury, either by assigning other employees to help her lift, or by reinstating the position of "medicine nurse" (which did not involve lifting) after the position had been abolished. [*Phelps v. Optima Health Inc.*, 251 F.3d 21 (1st Cir. 2001)]

A boiler mechanic suffered an on-the-job knee injury. He was assigned to light duty, but went on medical leave of absence after a month; he returned to light duty, took another medical leave, but did not return to work. The following year, he asked to return to work, saying that he could operate the boiler with some help, repair sewing machines, and do trouble-shooting. His request to return was rejected on the ground that he had too many limitations to work effectively and could not be accommodated; the amount of sewing machine repair and trouble-shooting required would not justify a full-time position. He was terminated under a collective bargaining agreement provision permitting termination of employees absent for over 18 months. The district court granted summary judgment for the employer, finding that the plaintiff could not perform the essential functions of the job with or without accommodation. The Seventh Circuit affirmed, finding that the job involved heavy exertion and frequent lifting of up to 100 pounds—far in excess of the plaintiff's medical limitations. The suggested accommodations were not reasonable because they would significantly change the essential functions of the job. The Seventh Circuit also held that the duty to engage in the interactive process does not necessarily require meeting with the employee's attorney and a vocational counselor; a face-to-face meeting with the employee him- or herself can be adequate. [*Ammons v. Aramark Uniform Services Inc.*, 368 F.3d 809 (7th Cir. 2004)]

"Auxiliary aids and services" is defined by § 12102 to mean interpreters or other effective methods of communicating with hearing-impaired people, readers, taped texts, and other ways to deliver texts to the visually impaired, acquiring or modifying adaptive equipment or devices, or "other similar services and actions." About 120,000 disabled individual workers nationwide are assisted by nondisabled job coaches (trainers or monitors assigned to help them). Home Depot agreed to a $75,000 settlement when it terminated a mentally disabled worked without first consulting her job coach. In this case, the worker was fired after missing two days of work; she said that she was contacted by someone who either was or claimed to be a supervisor who told her she was not scheduled for work on those days. [Paul Vitello, *Home Depot Pays a Disabled Ex-Worker*, New York Times, Oct. 25, 2005, at p. B7]

An undue hardship is an action that requires significant difficulty or expense. [42 U.S.C. § 12111(10)] This determination is made based on factors such as the cost of the accommodation and how it compares to the employer's budget.

The employer must retain records about requests for accommodation for one year after the request or personnel action, whichever is later. [29 C.F.R. § 1602.14]

The Ticket To Work and Work Incentives Improvement Act of 1999 [Pub. L. No. 106-170] allows disabled persons to retain Medicare and/or Medicaid coverage for their health needs after they return to the workforce.

There is evidence that modest investments in accommodation can be very productive. The Job Accommodation Network, part of the Department of Labor's Office of Disability Employment Policy, has a series of worksheets online, including one about the favorable cost-benefit status of disability accommodations. The Job Accommodation Network retained the University of Iowa's Law, Health Policy, and Disability Center to research the cost of accommodations. The research showed that more than half of accommodations didn't cost the employer anything, and the average expense for those that did had a cost of about $600.

Accommodations for disability resembled those sought by employees looking for work-family balance (e.g., flexible work schedules, better computer software, ergonomic workstations, and the availability of telecommuting). Among employers who asked the Job Accommodation Network for advice, 84% said they wanted to retain a current employee and 2% wanted to be able to promote a current employee. On average, the employees in questions had seven years' tenure and earned $48,000 a year. Close to half (43%) of the employees the companies sought to retain had at least a college degree. In short, these were valuable employees who would have been costly to replace.

Three quarters of the respondents said that the accommodations they made were very effective or extremely effective. In 87% of the cases, the company retained a valuable employee; 12% promoted a valued employee, 17% hired a qualified person with a disability; 74% increased the productivity of a current employee; 51% experienced better attendance from the employee who received the accommodation; and 42% cut their Worker's Compensation or other insurance costs. Indirect benefit, such as increased diversity, better morale within the company, better interactions among co-workers, and a safer workplace, also were attributed to their accommodation efforts. [Fact Sheet Series, *Workplace Accommodations: Low Cost, High Impact*, <http://www.jan.wvu.edu/media/LowCostHighImpact.pdf>. The full survey is discussed in D.J. Hendricks, et al., *Cost and Effectiveness of Accommodations in the Workplace: Preliminary Results of a Nationwide Study*, Disability Studies Quarterly (2005), <http://www.dsq-sds.org/index.html>]

[B] EEOC Enforcement Guidance

On October 17, 2002, the EEOC released a major enforcement guidance. [*Enforcement Guidance: Reasonable Accommodation and Undue Hardship Under the Americans With Disabilities Act*, <http://www.eeoc.gov/policy/docs/accommodation.html>] Compliance with these guidelines will assure that the corporation will not become the target of EEOC enforcement activities—although it is quite likely that courts will not require employers to satisfy all of the EEOC's concerns.

Under the Guidelines, employers need not eliminate essential job functions. Employers do not have to provide items used for both work and nonwork tasks; employees are responsible for furnishing their own prostheses, eyeglasses, and hearing aids.

Employees who want accommodation must make a clear request but need not use the term "reasonable accommodation," as long as it is clear what they mean. Employers must act on reasonable verbal requests but can ask to have them confirmed by a written memorandum.

The employer can demand reasonable documentation of, for instance, the nature, severity, and duration of the impairment, which activities are impaired, and the extent to which the employee's functional ability is limited. But documentation cannot be required if the disability and accommodation are obvious, or if the employee has already furnished adequate information. The employer can choose its preferred (usually the most cost-effective) reasonable accommodation, and need not follow the employee's suggestion.

Using accrued paid leave, or unpaid leave, is a reasonable accommodation, but employers do not have to offer additional paid leave to employees with a disability. Employees should be allowed to exhaust paid leave before taking unpaid leave. Unless it is an undue hardship, the employer must keep the job open during leave. A leave request need not be granted if the employer can keep the employee at work via a reasonable alternative accommodation.

The EEOC position is that employers should consider ADA and FMLA entitlement separately and then determine whether the two statutes overlap. The EEOC's example is an ADA-disabled person who needs 13 weeks of leave. The FMLA requires only 12 weeks of leave, but the EEOC says the ADA requires the employer to provide the 13th week unless that would be an undue hardship.

If there is a vacant position available for transfer, the employer does not have to train the person with a disability as an accommodation, unless training would be offered to a nondisabled employee. The EEOC position is that a transfer is a reasonable accommodation, so it must be offered even if the employer does not normally provide transfers. It is not enough to allow the disabled employee to compete for a vacant position; it should be offered to any QIWD who wants the transfer as an accommodation.

> **Tip:** See the EEOC's worksheet, <http://www.eeoc.gov/facts/telework.html>, for the agency's position on the extent to which telecommuting constitutes reasonable accommodation. The ADA does not require all employers to make telecommuting available. In the individual case, EEOC attorney Sharon Rennert said that the key is whether the employee would clearly be unable to handle the job without telecommuting, and whether the job was conducive to being performed from the employee's home. If so, the EEOC recommends allowing telework even if the employer does not have a formal program.

Even the EEOC sometimes concedes that affirmative action is inappropriate. A January 31, 2000, Opinion Letter says that if there is only one vacant position, it should be used to provide reasonable accommodation to a disabled current employee rather than hiring a black female applicant or promoting a black female employee to take the position—in fact, reasonable accommodation might justify assigning an employee with a disability rather than a more qualified candidate. [*EEOC Says*

Accommodation Takes Priority Over Affirmative Action, archived at <http://www.lawnewsnetwork.com>]

A late 2004 informal guidance letter from the EEOC says that a commercial airline was not justified in requesting all of a pilot's medical records when the request was made after the employee returned to duty, and more than a year after sick leave was taken. The EEOC treated the request as a fishing expedition for medical information unrelated to the sick leave. The EEOC reiterated its interpretation of the ADA: that health questions and medical certification can be obtained only on the basis of a reasonable belief, supported by objective evidence, that the employee's medical condition impairs the ability to perform the essential functions of the job, or the medical condition renders the employee a direct threat. [EEOC Advisory Letter (Oct. 5, 2004), <http://www.eeoc.gov>; *see* 73 LW 2393]

[C] Case Law

Some courts say that the employee must take the first step by requesting accommodation. [*Gaston v. Bellingrath Gardens & Home Inc.*, 167 F.3d 1361 (11th Cir. 1999); *Mole v. Buckhorn Rubber Prods. Inc.*, 165 F.3d 1212 (8th Cir. 1999)]

Taylor v. Phoenixville School District [174 F.3d 142 (3d Cir. 1999)] adopts the EEOC position that, as soon as an employee asks for reasonable accommodation, the employer has a duty to engage in an interactive process with the employee and must cooperate with the employee to find out if the employee really is ADA-disabled, finding out what accommodations the employee wants, and determining if they are practical.

The employer can decide which reasonable accommodation to offer; it is not obligated to accept the employee's suggestions. [*Keever v. City of Middletown*, 145 F.3d 809 (6th Cir. 1998); *Rehling v. City of Chicago*, 207 F.3d 1009 (7th Cir. 2000)] Finding a job free of stress caused by fellow-employees is not a reasonable accommodation to which a clinically depressed employee is entitled. [*Gaul v. Lucent Techs., Inc.*, 134 F.3d 576 (3d Cir. 1998)]

A truck driver with polycystic kidney disease sought accommodation to his dialysis schedule and 40-pound lifting restrictions. The Eighth Circuit found that, because he had performed all the essential job functions for several months, returning him to that job was at least potentially a reasonable accommodation, despite the employer's claim of undue hardship. Although reallocation of essential job functions is not required, the Eighth Circuit noted that the relevant state human rights law explicitly defines schedule modifications and job restructuring as means of reasonable accommodation. [*Kammueller v. Loomis Fargo & Co.*, 383 F.3d 779 (8th Cir. 2004)]

A nurse who had arthritis in both knees later broke her leg and needed surgery and a leave of absence. A functional capacity evaluation found that the condition of her knees prevented her from working as a general duty staff nurse. She asked to be placed on an "ADA list" of employees with permanent work restrictions. She was offered a lower-paid desk job; applied for but was turned down for administrative posts; and eventually was hired as an admissions nurse with no loss of earnings or benefits. She brought ADA (and ADEA) claims that she was refused reasonable accommodation of disability.

The Sixth Circuit rejected her claims, finding insufficient direct evidence of disability discrimination, and rejecting the applicability of mixed-motive analysis to ADA cases. In the Sixth Circuit view, the initial job offer was a reasonable accommodation although it paid less. By rejecting this accommodation, the plaintiff ceased to be a QWID. [*See* 29 C.F.R. § 1630.9(d)] The jobs that the plaintiff applied for would have been promotions—and the ADA does not obligate employers to offer promotions to disabled employees. [*Hedrick v. Western Reserve Care System*, 355 F.3d 444 (6th Cir. 2004). For the proposition that reassignment to a lower-paid job is a reasonable accommodation, *see McLeod v. Parsons Corp.*, 73 Fed. Appx. 846 (6th Cir. 2003)]

The Seventh Circuit decided that it does not violate the ADA to refuse a software engineer's request to work at home as an accommodation to the fatigue and pain caused by treatment for cancer. In fact, in the Seventh Circuit view, most jobs require supervision, teamwork, and interaction with others, so working at home will rarely constitute a reasonable accommodation. [*Rauen v. United States Tobacco Mfg. Ltd.*, 319 F.3d 891 (7th Cir. 2003)]

The Tenth Circuit found regular presence at the workplace was essential for the job of service coordinator (arranging appointments for communication system technicians). The work was held to be low-level and to require supervision that would not be possible if the employee worked at home. Therefore, working at home was not a reasonable accommodation for an employee who suffered post-traumatic stress disorder after witnessing a workplace shooting incident that killed several coworkers. [*Mason v. Avaya Communications, Inc.*, 357 F.3d 1114 (10th Cir. 2004)]

The Third Circuit obligates the employer to think creatively to create accommodation. In *Skerski v. Time Warner Cable Co.*, [257 F.3d 273 (3d Cir. 2001)] the plaintiff was a cable installer who couldn't climb as a result of panic attacks. The employee wanted the employer to provide him with a bucket truck, which he could use to perform his job even if he did have an attack. The employer had a bucket truck available, but demoted him to a lower-paying job. The Western District of Pennsylvania dismissed the case, calling climbing an essential function of the installer's job. The Third Circuit reversed and remanded the case to see if climbing really was essential; inconvenience to the employer is not undue hardship. Courts usually do not require as much of employers as the EEOC Regulations; this is an unusual case in which the court ordered even more than the EEOC would have demanded.

According to *Donahue v. Consolidated Rail Corp.*, [224 F.3d 226 (3d Cir. 2000)] the employer need not engage in the interactive process if the employee failed to show that there were any available jobs he or she could have done with reasonable accommodation.

Furthermore, a person who claims that his or her injury prevents full-time work, and therefore is allowed to work a part-time schedule, is estopped from claiming that the employer refused accommodation, because the person is unable to work full-time even with accommodation. [*DeVito v. Chicago Park Dist.*, 270 F.3d 532 (7th Cir. 2001)]

The EEOC position, [29 C.F.R. § 1630.2(o)] echoed by several appellate cases, is that reassignment to a job that the employee can handle constitutes a reasonable accommodation. [*Dalton v. Subaru-Isuzu Automotive, Inc.*, 141 F.3d 667 (7th Cir. 1998); *Cravens v. Blue Cross/Blue Shield*, 214 F.3d 1011 (8th Cir. 2000); *Aka v. Washington Hosp. Ctr.*, 156 F.3d 1284 (D.C. Cir. 1998)] The disabled person in search of accommodation must be able to prove his or her ability to handle the new job. [*DePaoli v. Abbott Labs.*, 140 F.3d 668 (7th Cir. 1998)] The Second Circuit said that as long as a comparable job is available, it is not a reasonable accommodation to offer an ADA plaintiff reassignment to a part-time job (with much lower compensation and benefits) or to another location (resulting in loss of seniority). [*Norville v. Staten Island Univ. Hosp.*, 196 F.3d 89 (2d Cir. 1999)]

Yet other courts say that if the employee is not able to perform the tasks of the current job, he or she is not qualified, and therefore the employer is not obligated to offer another job assignment. [*Smith v. Midland Brake Inc.*, 138 F.3d 1304 (10th Cir. 1998); *Malabarba v. Chicago Tribune Co.*, 149 F.3d 690 (7th Cir. 1998)]

It was a reasonable accommodation to assign a federal worker who could no longer work as a custodian because of her asthma to a position driving a subway train. Offering her that position, at her original salary (rather than the higher salary normally paid to subway drivers), did not require a promotion, did not create a new position, and did not unduly burden the employer. (In fact, it made it possible to save money by using a low-paid employee, when higher-paid mechanics had often been assigned to do the work.) The employer was not required to create a new position, and indeed was helped to fill a job that had often been vacant. There had been many instances in which jobs were reassigned across grades, so the employer was not required to alter its personnel policies just to assist the plaintiff. The federal government employer said that the plaintiff forfeited her right to reasonable accommodation by turning down an offer of a job as an elevator operator—but that job would have violated her medical restrictions, whereas she was able to perform the subway driver's job adequately and without exacerbating her asthma. Therefore, the Federal Circuit affirmed the Office of Compliance's award of about $4,000 in back pay, $10,000 for pain and suffering, and fees and costs of close to $50,000. [*Office of the Architect of the Capitol v. Office of Compliance*, 361 F.3d 633 (Fed. Cir. 2004)]

The Seventh Circuit ruled that it was not a reasonable accommodation to hire someone to perform lifting tasks for a construction worker who was under permanent lifting restrictions because of his shoulder injury. The court refused to second-guess the employer's determination that lifting was an essential part of the job. Nor was the employer obligated to offer a trial period to see if the plaintiff could do an adequate job despite his limitations. [*Peters v. City of Mauston*, 311 F.3d 835 (7th Cir. 2002)]

The Eighth Circuit also refused to second-guess an employer's determination that vacuuming was an essential function of the job of a hotel housekeeping supervisor. Therefore, after a non-work-related automobile accident exacerbated the plaintiff's previous neck and back injuries, causing chronic pain and lifting restrictions, she was unable to function as a "working supervisor." It would not have been a reasonable accommodation for the hotel to allow her to assign someone else to vacuum for her for an indefinite period. In the Eighth Circuit view, the employer was not liable for failure to engage in an interactive process of accommodation, because the plaintiff did not make a timely request, and could not propose any reasonable accommodation that would not have been an undue hardship on the employer. [*Alexander v. The Northland Inn*, 321 F.3d 723 (8th Cir. 2003)]

The Ninth Circuit ruled that a police detective, whose depression was accommodated by not assigning her to on-call duty on the night shift, stated a claim that her supervisor interfered with her ADA rights by telling her to give up the accommodation or take a demotion or forced retirement. [*Brown v. Tucson*, 336 F.3d 1181 (9th Cir. 2003)]

Employers can legitimately stipulate that light-duty assignments are temporary. However, if no end date is given for the assignment, a court might treat the light-duty job as a permanent accommodation that cannot be withdrawn without violating the ADA. [*Hendricks-Robinson v. Excel Corp.*, 154 F.3d 685 (7th Cir. 1998)]

The California Court of Appeals ruled in 2006 that neither the federal ADA nor the California FEHA requires an employer to make a light-duty assignment permanently available to an injured employee once it becomes evident that the employee's disability will be permanent. Neither statute requires the employer to create a new position to accommodate employee needs. (In this case, the plaintiff was a police officer injured on duty who sought a permanent desk job; the police department's position was that the permanent desk jobs are held by civilian technicians who are paid less and get fewer benefits than sworn police officers.) [*Raine v. Burbank*, 135 Cal. App. 4th 1215 (Cal. App. 2006)]

The Eighth Circuit ruled than even an employer who engages in the interactive process can be liable for failure to implement the accommodations with reasonable promptness. A manager who suffered badly from stress, had a nervous breakdown after persistent badgering from his manager, and took FMLA leave asked for a summary of meeting discussion topics in advance so he could prepare for meetings with the manager. The employee said that he could perform his job if he had the information in advance so he could be ready to answer questions about operations data. The First Circuit upheld the District Court's ruling that the defendant failed to act in good faith when it did not implement the accommodation. [*Battle v. UPS, Inc.*, 438 F.3d 856 (8th Cir. 2006)]

The Tenth Circuit says that the employer has the burden of persuasion as to whether a proposed accommodation would be an undue hardship, but other courts have disagreed. [*Colorado Cross Disability Coalition v. Hermanson Family Ltd. Partnership*, 264 F.3d 999 (10th Cir. 2001)]

The employee as well as the employer must participate in the process. A $1.5 million verdict for the plaintiff was vacated because the plaintiff rejected the proposed accommodation without discussion or counter-offer, and applied for long-term disability instead. [*Davis v. Guardian Life Ins. Co. of Am.*, discussed in Shannon P. Duffy, *Judge Vacates $1.5 Million Verdict in ADA Case*, The Legal Intelligencer (Dec. 20, 2000) (law.com)]

§ 36.06   DEFENSES

[A]   Primary Defense

The primary defense, under 42 U.S.C. § 12113, is that the employer's criterion, standards, or tests may screen out individuals with a disability, but are nevertheless appropriate because they are job-related and consistent with business necessity, and the employer cannot achieve the same goals via reasonable accommodation. Qualification standards can lawfully rule out employment of anyone who poses a direct threat to the health or safety of others. According to 42 U.S.C. § 12111(3), a "direct threat" is a significant risk to the health or safety of others that cannot be eliminated by reasonable accommodation.

Furthermore, the Secretary of Health and Human Services publishes a list of infectious and communicable diseases that can be transmitted by food handling. If the risk cannot be eliminated by reasonable accommodation, then an employer can legitimately refuse to assign or continue to assign someone who suffers from such a disease to a food handling position. This provision does not preempt state public health laws about food safety. The Supreme court greatly increased the applicability of this exception in a June 2002 decision [*Chevron USA Inc. v. Echazabal*, 536 U.S. 73 (2002)] by allowing employers to use it in the context of danger to a job applicant or employee whose own physical condition would be endangered by workplace conditions. In July, 2003, the Ninth Circuit decided that summary judgment for the employer should not have been granted, so the case was sent back to the District Court once again to determine whether the direct threat defense applied to the plaintiff's individual factual situation. [336 F.3d 1023 (9th Cir. 2003)]

The Eleventh Circuit held in late 2001 that an HIV positive dental technician poses a direct threat to others and therefore is not a QIWD. [*Waddell v. Valley Forge Dental Assoc.*, 276 F.3d 1275 (11th Cir. 2001)]

A Wyoming state case says that it was not a violation of the ADA for the state medical board to revoke the license of a doctor suffering from bipolar disorder, even without granting him the treatment options offered to substance-abusing doctors. He was not a "qualified individual" because of the severe health and safety risk he posed to others. He had performed unnecessary and inappropriate surgery, and at least one patient had died. [*Kirbens v. Wyoming State Bd. of Medicine*, 992 P.2d 1056 (Wyo. 1999)]

The plaintiff, who was already under a final warning, was fired after an altercation at the workplace. Co-workers and supervisors feared for their safety. After the final warning, the plaintiff refused counseling from the EAP, but did begin therapy with a psychologist who diagnosed Attention Deficit Hyperactivity Disorder. He got a prescription for Ritalin, which significantly reduced the ADHD symptoms. He was also given more than 40 days FMLA leave, based on a medical certificate from the psychologist. The plaintiff's testimony, corroborated by the psychologist, is that ADHD does not cause anger, but may make it hard for a person to focus in a stressful situation. The plaintiff claimed that assigning him to a new machine at work caused stress. The psychologist sent a note to the medical department requesting a transfer back to the old machine to reduce job stress. However, ADHD was not mentioned, and the letter did not request accommodation to a disability. He was hospitalized for depression for two weeks, and then cleared to return to work.

After being discharged, the plaintiff brought suit under the ADA, claiming failure of reasonable accommodation, plus a state claim of wrongful discharge contrary to public policy. The plaintiff has held various jobs in the interim, and has never asked for accommodation. The case was dismissed, for failure to prove that he was disabled or that he was otherwise qualified. He did not show an impairment limiting major life activities. Furthermore, even if behavior stems from a mental disability, employers are not required to continue to employ someone whose behavior is beyond acceptable limits, and who threatens the safety of others. [*Calef v. Gillette Co.*, 322 F.3d 75 (1st Cir. 2003)]

The Tenth Circuit found that it was proper to give a jury instruction that the plaintiff, a one-time deputy sheriff suffering from post-traumatic stress syndrome, had the burden of proving she did not pose a direct threat to others. Although "direct threat" is a defense, the qualification standards for a job can include not being dangerous to others, and it was not error to give an instruction requiring the plaintiff to prove that she could perform the essential function of not endangering other persons. [*McKenzie v. Benton*, 388 F.3d 1342 (10th Cir. 2004)] As for the other circuits, the Ninth Circuit treats "direct threat" as an affirmative defense, and therefore the employer must prove it: *Hutton v. Elf Atochem North America, Inc.*, 273 F.3d 884 (9th Cir. 2001). The plaintiff has the burden of proof on this issue in the First and Eleventh Circuits: *EEOC v. Amego, Inc.*, 110 F.3d 135 (1st Cir. 1997); *Moses v. American Non-Wovens, Inc.*, 97 F.3d 446, 447 (11th Cir. 1996). In the Fifth Circuit, first the plaintiff must prove that he or she is qualified, including not being a direct threat—but a court's finding that the employer's safety requirements tend to screen out disabled persons then causes a shift, so that the employer must prove that the employee poses a direct threat: *Rizzo v. Children's World Learning Ctrs., Inc.*, 173 F.3d 254, 259-60 (5th Cir. 1999), *aff'd en banc*, 213 F.3d 209 (5th Cir. 2000*), cert. denied*, 531 U.S. 958 (2000).

However, in mid-2002 the Tenth Circuit ruled that the District Court should not have granted summary judgment to a school district that fired a teacher who had been diagnosed with depression. Even though there had been substantiated reports that the teacher had committed child abuse, the case should have been tried so that a jury could have decided the direct-threat defense. [*Whitney v. Board of Educ. of Grand County*, 292 F.3d 1280 (10th Cir. 2002)]

[B] Drug and Alcohol Exception

Congress must have been concerned about the potential for claims of disability on the basis of substance abuse, because there are several statutory references. According to 42 U.S.C. § 12111(6), a "drug" is a controlled substance as defined by federal law, and "illegal use of drugs" means using controlled substances, but does not include drugs taken under the supervision of a licensed health professional.

Section 12114 says that an employee or job applicant who is currently engaging in the illegal use of drugs is not a qualified individual with a disability. However, a person who is in rehab, has completed a rehab program, or otherwise stopped using drugs can be considered a qualified individual with a disability. So can a person who is not in fact using illegal drugs, but who is incorrectly perceived to be.

The plaintiff in the Supreme Court case of *Raytheon v. Hernandez* [540 U.S. 44 (2003)] was forced to resign after he tested positive for cocaine, thus violating a workplace conduct rule. More than two years later, after he said he had stopped using drugs, he applied to be rehired. Rehiring was denied, on the basis of a corporate policy against rehiring anyone who had been terminated for misconduct. The employee who rejected his application said that she did not know he was a former addict when she denied the application.

The plaintiff sued, charging that he was discriminated against as an ex-addict or because he was perceived to be a drug user. Later, he added a claim that even if the no-rehire policy was facially neutral, it had disparate impact on ex-addicts. The Ninth Circuit dismissed the disparate impact claim, but said that the plaintiff proved a prima facie case of disparate treatment, and the employer did not give a legitimate nondiscriminatory reason for its no-rehire policy. The Supreme Court reversed the Ninth Circuit, holding that the lower court improperly applied disparate impact analysis to the disparate treatment claim. Although both kinds of claims can be brought under the ADA, they must be applied properly. In the Supreme Court view, the no-rehire policy was neutral and satisfied the *McDonnell-Douglas* requirements. On remand, the Ninth Circuit found that there was a genuine issue of material fact as to whether the decision to refrain from rehiring him was disability-based, and therefore the Ninth Circuit reversed the grant of summary judgment for the defense. [362 F.3d 564 (9th Cir. 2004)]

Employers are allowed to forbid the use of alcohol or illegal drugs at the workplace, can enforce the requirements of the Drug-Free Workplace Act, can make a rule that employees not be under the influence of alcohol or drugs when they are at work (even if they used the substances outside the workplace), and can adopt reasonable procedures (including drug testing) to make sure employees are not currently abusing substances. Drug testing is not considered a "medical examination" for ADA purposes. Many of these provisions are repeated in 42 U.S.C. § 12210.

According to the Fifth Circuit, a hospital did not violate the ADA by firing a hospital pharmacist who voluntarily reported his cocaine addiction and entered a rehab program. [*Zenor v. El Paso Healthcare Sys. Ltd.*, 176 F.3d 847 (5th Cir. 1999)] He was considered to be a "current user" because of the risk of relapse, so the "rehab program" safe harbor did not apply in his case. Furthermore, his job gave him access to pharmaceutical cocaine, greatly increasing the risk of future drug abuse. Although he might have been qualified for many other jobs, the contact with controlled substances meant that, as a substance abuser, he was not a QIWD for the specific job of hospital pharmacist.

Several courts have concluded that employers can apply the same standards of conduct to all employees—whether or not they have a substance abuse problem. [*Mercado v. N.Y.C. Hous. Auth.*, 1998 WL 151039 (S.D.N.Y. March 31, 1998); *Williams v. Widnall*, 79 F.3d 1003 (10th Cir. 1996); *Rollison v. Gwinnett County*, 865 F. Supp. 1564 (N.D. Ga. 1994)]

A salesman who had ongoing alcohol problems was fired. He said that he was fired because he had been observed drinking at work, and an empty bottle was found in his desk. The plaintiff went back into rehab. His manager said he could have time off to enter a treatment program, and told him to call when he completed the program. After his discharge, he called the manager and was informed he had been terminated. He filed ADA charges with the EEOC, charging failure to make reasonable accommodation or, in the alternative, disability discrimination. The First Circuit treated alcoholism as an ADA impairment—but that does not prove that the impairment substantially limits one or more major life activities. The First Circuit found for the defense, because employees can be held to the same standards whether or not they are alcoholics. The plaintiff failed to prove that he was excluded from a class of jobs, or a broad range of jobs in various classes, or that the defendant perceived him as having an ADA impairment. [*Sullivan v. Neiman Marcus Group, Inc.*, 358 F.3d 110 (1st Cir. 2004)]

A "last chance" agreement, where reinstatement after rehab is conditional on continued good performance (and perhaps on passing periodic drug tests) has been upheld as a reasonable accommodation to the disability of alcoholism. [*See, e.g., Longen v. Waterous Co.*, 347 F.3d 685 (8th Cir. 2003); *Marrari v. WCI Steel Inc.*, 130 F.3d 1180 (6th Cir. 1997)]

> **Tip:** A typical agreement of this type is signed by an employee who has completed a rehab program. The employee agrees to get clearance from the Employee Assistance Program before returning to work. The employee agrees to stay clean and sober and abide by the program requirements of Alcoholics Anonymous, Narcotics Anonymous, or other program. In a drug rehab situation, the employee agrees to periodic unannounced drug tests for a period of a year and agrees to automatic termination for failing a test—or refusing to take a test. The employee agrees that this is a last chance, and that he or she must comply with all of the employer's normal disciplinary rules (e.g., attendance and promptness) despite the substance problem.

The Fifth Circuit allowed Exxon to defend its policy of permanently refusing employees who have been treated for substance abuse from safety-sensitive positions with little supervision. [*EEOC v. Exxon*, 203 F.3d 871 (5th Cir. 2000)] As long as the standard is applied equally to all employees within a class, the employer can assert business necessity without proving that former substance abusers constitute a direct threat to safety.

> **Tip:** A substance abuser entering a rehab program (at least if it is an inpatient program) may be entitled to FMLA leave. Reasonable ADA accommodation may require providing additional leave after the 12 weeks of FMLA leave have been used up.

§ 36.07   "REGARDED AS" LIABILITY

The ADA covers qualified individuals who actually do not have a disability, but who are discriminated against because of the perception that they do. According to *EEOC v. R.J. Gallagher Co.*, [181 F.3d 645 (5th Cir. 1999)] the relevant evidence is what the employer believed—not medical testimony about the true state of the employee's health and abilities.

An employer can be liable on a "regarded as disabled" claim based on an innocent misunderstanding (or stereotypes) about the employee's capacity. But if the employee is responsible for the error, or unreasonably fails to correct the employer's misconceptions, then the employer cannot be held liable. [*Taylor v. Pathmark*, 177 F.3d 180 (3d Cir. 1999)].

The circuits are split as to whether reasonable accommodation is required in "regarded-as" cases. The Eleventh Circuit ruled in 2005 that it is. [*D'Angelo v. Conagra Foods, Inc.*, 422 F.3d 1220 (11th Cir. Aug. 30, 2005)] The Fifth, Sixth, Eighth, and Ninth Circuits have ruled it is not. [*See Kaplan v. North Las Vegas*, 323 F.3d 1226, 1233 (9th Cir. 2003); *Weber v. Strippit, Inc.,* 186 F.3d 907 (8th Cir. 1999); *Workman v. Frito Lay, Inc.,* 165 F.3d 460, 467 (6th Cir. 1999); *Newberry v. East Texas State Univ.*, 161 F.3d 276, 280 (5th Cir. 1998)] However, the Third

Circuit does. [*Williams v. Philadelphia Housing Auth. Police Dept.*, 380 F.3d 751, 772–76 (3d Cir. 2004)] The First Circuit has implied this without directly stating it. [*Katz v. City Metal Co.*, 87 F.3d 26, 32–34 (1st Cir. 1996)] The Seventh Circuit ruled that a plaintiff was not regarded as disabled and therefore avoided the issue of whether accommodation was required. [*Cigan v. Chippewa Falls Sch. Dist.*, 338 F.3d 331 (7th Cir. 2004)]

In *Hilburn v. Murata Electronics*, [181 F.3d 1220 (11th Cir. 1999)] the employee had two problems: her own heart disease, and the serious illness of family members, requiring substantial time off. After she had a heart attack, she had some limitations in lifting, but could walk, run, and carry out all other normal activities. Her "regarded-as" claim failed, because the Eleventh Circuit ruled that the major life activity of working was substantially unimpaired.

According to the Second Circuit, a trucking company did not violate the ADA by refusing to hire drivers who used prescription drugs with side effects that could impair their driving ability. According to the Second Circuit, the trucking company did not perceive such persons as disabled. Furthermore, the EEOC's regulation, 29 C.F.R. § 1630.2(j)(3)(i) says that inability to perform a particular job is not the equivalent of a substantial limitation in the activity of working; being a truck driver is not a class of job or a broad range of jobs. The fact that the defendant company did not have any less demanding driving jobs to offer (that might have been performed safely by prescription medication users) does not prove that the defendant regarded the applicants as unfit for any driving position at all. [*EEOC v. JB Hunt Transport*, 321 F.3d 69 (2d Cir. 2003)]

The "regarded-as" claim was also unsuccessful in *Shipley v. City of University City* [195 F.3d 1020 (8th Cir. 1999)] because the refusal to reinstate him after an injury-related absence was caused by the employer's belief that he could no longer perform that particular job, not that he was incapable of working at all.

The Eighth Circuit upheld the district court's dismissal of a refusal-to-promote claim brought by a factory worker with the connective tissue disorder Marfan's syndrome. The plaintiff disclosed his heart condition during the job interview and the evaluation believed he was legally blind, but the employee did not show that he was regarded as having an impairment limiting a major life activity. There was no evidence that his health was considered, and the person who actually was promoted had more experience, so it would not be reasonable for the trier of fact to infer discrimination. [*Genthe v. Quebecor World Lincoln*, 383 F.3d 713 (8th Cir. 2004)]

Earlier, the Seventh Circuit ruled that an employer's acting on an incorrect belief about the plaintiff's health status violates the ADA only if the employer believed that the employee suffered from an ADA disability [*Tockes v. Air-Land Transport Serv. Inc.*, 343 F.3d 895 (7th Cir. 2003)] and applied *Williams* to regarded-as claims, because the terms "substantially limited" and "major life activity" are defined the same way whether or not the plaintiff actually has or is merely regarded as having a disability. [*Mack v. Great Dane Trailers*, 308 F.3d 776 (7th Cir. 2002)]

A sanitation worker was fired after it was determined that he had uncorrectable night blindness. (He could drive safely during the day.) The District Court found that no reasonable jury could find him to be either disabled or regarded as disabled, but the Second Circuit reversed and remanded, based on the effects of night blindness on the major life activity of seeing. The record showed that the sanitation department incorrectly believed that the plaintiff suffered from macular degeneration and that his disease prevented him from carrying out his duties. In fact, he was doing a good job; his condition was stable, not deteriorating; and he could do anything the job called for other than driving at night. [*Capobianco v. New York*, 422 F.3d 47 (2d Cir. 2005)]

The Fifth Circuit held that a Type II diabetic (who never has any health-related problems in working) made out an ADA case by charging that a job offer was withdrawn because he was regarded as disabled. The employer said that he was rejected not because he had the disease but because (on the basis of misinterpretation of the plaintiff's answer to one question during his preemployment physical) the company believed that he failed to control his diabetes. The Fifth Circuit said that control is an issue only in a case of actual disability, not a regarded-as case because in a regarded-as case, there is nothing for the plaintiff to control. The Fifth Circuit ruled that even if plaintiffs who fail to control their condition are disqualified from bringing ADA cases, in this case the defendant violated the ADA by instituting a blanket rule against hiring "uncontrolled" diabetics, failing to give individualized consideration to the plaintiff's ability to work. However, the court later withdrew its opinion after granting a rehearing. [*Rodriguez v. ConAgra Grocery Prods. Co.*, 431 F.3d 204 (5th Cir. 2005), rehearing granted 436 F.3d 468. The issue of failure to mitigate has arisen frequently, but nearly always in the context of disability rather than perceived-as disabled cases. *See, e.g., Winters v. Pasadena Indep. Sch. Dist.*, 124 Fed. Appx. 822 (5th Cir. 2005); *Gowesky v. Singing River Hosp. Sys.*, 321 F.3d 503, 507 (5th Cir. 2003)]

§ 36.08   DISABILITY AND THE BENEFIT PLAN

[A]   Employer's Obligations and Challenges

Under the ADA, employers are permitted to make benefit plan decisions that are consistent with underwriting, reasonable risk classifications, or actual or reasonably anticipated experience. If the employer does not normally provide health benefits, it has no obligation to provide special insurance coverage for the disabled or to adopt a plan that covers both disabled and nondisabled employees.

A health plan participant can maintain a cause of action charging that he was the victim of retaliation because his health condition increased the employer's health insurance premium. The Eastern District of Tennessee ruled that a reasonable jury could conclude that Crohn's disease was a disability. There was evidence that the HR manager said that it could not afford rising health premiums, and the manager who said this participated in the decision to fire the plaintiff, who was terminated shortly after the conversation. [*Boles v. Polyloom Corp. of Am.*, No. 1:04-CV-147 (E.D. Tenn. Mar. 6, 2006); *see* Rebecca Moore, *Court Allows Retaliation Charge of Health Plan Participant*, PlanSponsor.com (Mar. 10, 2006)]

In several cases, employees have been unsuccessful in using ERISA to challenge a "cap" (maximum amount that will be paid, e.g., $100,000 or $1 million) imposed on health benefits payable for treatment of AIDS-related illnesses. Courts have found that there was no ERISA violation in imposing a cap only on HIV-related health care, or on capping HIV-related treatment at a lower level than treatment of other expensive illnesses. [*McGann v. H&H Music Co.*, 946 F.2d 401 (5th Cir. 1991); *Owens v. Storehouse Inc.*, 948 F.2d 394 (11th Cir. 1993)]

The Western District of Michigan dismissed an ADA case brought by a plan participant who had hearing and mobility limitations and who asserted that the plan's lifetime plan cap for employees with hearing problems was discriminatory because benefits for other disabilities were not capped. But, to the court, the ADA only mandates equality between the disabled and the nondisabled, not among all forms of disability. If all employees have access to the plan, it is permissible to provide lower benefits for a specific type of disability. [*Schultz v. Alticor/Amway Corp.*, 177 F. Supp. 2d 674 (W.D. Mich. 2001)]

The Supreme Court's denial of rehearing had the effect of affirming the Seventh Circuit (although without opinion) in *Doe v. Mutual of Omaha* [528 U.S. 1106 (2000)]: Title II of the ADA (the title dealing with public programs) is not violated by a health insurance policy or self-funded health plan that puts a much lower limitation on AIDS-related health care than other illnesses. The Seventh Circuit's rationale is that the insurer did not refuse to sell insurance to persons with AIDS, although the policy was less valuable to them than to people with other health problems.

Three Circuit Courts (the Sixth, Seventh, and Eleventh) have ruled that a totally disabled retiree or ex-employee is not "qualified" (because he or she is unable to perform job functions) and therefore cannot sue for fringe-benefit discrimination. [*Morgan v. Joint Admin. Bd. Retirement Plan*, 268 F.3d 456 (7th Cir. 2001); *EEOC v. CAN Ins. Cos.*, 96 F.3d 1038 (7th Cir. 1997); *Parker v. Metropolitan Life Ins. Co.*, 99 F.3d 181, *aff'd*, 121 F.3d 1006 (6th Cir. 1997); *Gonzalez v. Garner Food Servs., Inc.*, 89 F.3d 1523 (11th Cir. 1996)]

Those cases were brought under Title I, the employment discrimination part of the statute. Employers may also be sued under Title III, the public accommodations title. If an employee benefits plan is considered a public accommodation (this is not settled law), then excluding a disabled person from it could violate the ADA, even if the person with a disability is no longer a qualified employee. Most courts limit "place of public accommodations" to a physical place like an office or shopping mall, e.g., *Ford v. Schering-Plough Corp.* [145 F.3d 601 (3d Cir. 1998)]

[B]   EEOC Compliance Manual

In 2000, the EEOC redrafted its Compliance Manual Section 3, which can be found at <http://www.eeoc.gov/policy/docs/benefits.html>. (However, the viability of the EEOC's position may be questionable in light of later Supreme Court decisions.) The employer must provide "equal" benefits for all employees, irrespective of disability. However, benefits can be "equal" even if there are certain distinctions drawn on the basis of disability. The employer is entitled to employ practices that reflect sound actuarial principles or are related to actual or reasonably anticipated experience.

The first question is whether benefits for the employee who has a disability are the same (same types of benefits, same payment options, same coverage for the same costs). If the benefits are unequal, the question is whether the difference is based on the disability. If benefits are unequal because of disability, the employer has violated the ADA unless it can show that the difference is not a subterfuge to avoid the purposes of the ADA. (A practice can be a subterfuge even if it was adopted before the ADA became effective—and even if the employer does not have intent to discriminate.)

The "same coverage" for all employees means the same as to premiums, deductibles, waiting periods, and coverage caps. A distinction is based on disability if it singles out a particular disability, a discrete group of disabilities, or disability in general. Therefore, a distinction is not disability-based if it applies to many dissimilar conditions, and imposes limitations on individuals with and without disabilities.

The employer can rebut charges of disability discrimination by proving that disparate treatment is necessary to maintain the solvency of the plan, because covering the disabilities at issue would cost enough to threaten the fiscal soundness of the plan, and there is no way to change the plan without affecting disabilities.

The EEOC position is that, because employers are not required to maintain plans at all, the ADA is not violated by offering service retirement benefits (based on length of service for the employer) but not disability retirement benefits. But if the employer offers both types of retirement plan, disability discrimination is forbidden.

In the EEOC view, it violates the ADA to:

- Exclude an employee from participation in a service or disability retirement plan because of disabilities;
- Have a different length of participation requirement in the same plan because of disability;
- Provide different levels of types of coverage within a plan (although coverage levels can be lower in disability than in service retirement plans).

Service retirement benefits can legitimately be denied to any employee who voluntarily took disability retirement.

§ 36.09   QUESTIONS AND MEDICAL TESTS

The general ADA rule is that employers are not permitted to ask job applicants or do medical exams to find out if the applicant has a disability or to discover the nature and severity of the disability. However, it is permissible to tell the applicant what the job entails and ask about ability to perform these tasks. So "have you ever had any back problems?" is not a legitimate question, but "This job involves lifting 25-pound weights several times an hour, and sometimes involves lifting up to 100 pounds—can you handle that?" is acceptable.

In late 2005, the EEOC issued an Advisory Letter stating that there is an exception to the ADA's ban on disability-related inquiries before making a job offer if the employer has an affirmative action program for people with disabilities. To qualify, the employer's program must include an interview that gives a person with a disability a real opportunity to compete for a job; the information sought must not be greater than what is needed to determine his or her eligibility for the interview; and the applicant must voluntarily provide the information. [EEOC Advisory Letter, <http://www.eeoc.gov/policy/docs/preemp.html> (Nov. 8, 2005)]

Once the company decides to extend a job offer, then it is permissible to require a medical examination, as long as all employees (whether or not they have a disability) are subject to this requirement, and the results of the examination are kept in separate medical files and kept confidential, disclosed only to persons with a genuine work-related need to know.

Furthermore, any medical examination or inquiries must be job-related and consistent with business necessity. Voluntary medical examinations (including taking medical histories) are allowable if they are part of a program available to all employees at a work site, and an employer can ask about an employee's ability to perform job-related functions. [42 U.S.C. § 12112(d)]

Use of the Minnesota Multiphasic Personality Inventory (MMPI) as part of a battery of tests required for promotion violated the ADA. The test results were not interpreted by psychologists. The company claimed the tests were scored to determine personality traits, but the practical result was that employees with mental health disorders were denied consideration for promotion. The Seventh Circuit ruled that the MMPI is considered a medical examination because it was designated to diagnose mental illness and, as applied in practice, it impaired the job opportunities for persons with mental illnesses. [*Karraker v. Rent-a-Center, Inc.*, 411 F.3d 831 (7th Cir. 2005)]

EEOC advisory letters from December 2002 (*see* 71 L.W. 2536) reiterate that it is improper for an employer to ask disability-related questions before making a conditional job offer. Some of the examples cited by the EEOC are whether an applicant is diabetic, uses prescription drugs, or has used illegal drugs or been in a rehab program in the past. The EEOC also said that tests of physical agility are permissible after a conditional job offer has been extended, but tests used to screen for disability must be job-related and must reflect business necessity.

Physical agility and fitness tests are not considered medical tests if they do not include any criteria such as measuring heart rate or blood pressure.

If the employer wants to impose a requirement of HIV testing, it must be applied uniformly to everyone who applies within a particular job category. It is not permissible to identify some applicants as appearing to be at risk of AIDS, and single them out for HIV testing. Even if an applicant tests positive, the employer is not allowed to withdraw its conditional job offer on this basis, unless being HIV positive renders the applicant unable to perform the central functions of the job.

Section 12112 also requires employers to maintain the confidentiality of HIV test results, which must be kept separate from other employee records and even from other medical records. Access must be restricted to individuals with a real need to know, such as supervisors who may have to offer reasonable accommodation, first aid personnel, and government officials who are assessing the employer's ADA compliance.

Three HIV positive persons applied for flight attendant positions with American Airlines. They were given conditional offers of employment, contingent on passing medical exams and background checks. At this point, they were required to fill out medical histories and provide blood samples. None of them disclosed their HIV positive status or the medications they took, although the job application stated that false or fraudulent information, or failure to disclose medical conditions or medication use, would be grounds for termination. When the blood samples were processed, the airline rescinded the job offers on the basis of failure to disclose their HIV status.

The three brought suit on privacy and ADA and California FEHA grounds. The district court granted summary judgment for the airline, but the Ninth Circuit allowed the suit to proceed (except with respect to one plaintiff's claim of intentional infliction of emotional distress). The plaintiffs alleged that they were not told what the medical examination would entail. They were notified about, and gave their consent only to, urine testing. The plaintiffs asked for an explanation of why blood samples were taken, and were told that they were being checked for anemia. In the Ninth Circuit view, for a job offer to satisfy the requirements of the ADA and California law, the employer either must have completed all non-medical parts of the application process or be able to prove that it could reasonably have done so before making the offer. The ADA requires medical examinations (if given at all) to be a separate, second step of the selection process occurring only after all other selection issues have been resolved. The Ninth Circuit held that job applicants can keep their medical condition private until the last stage of the hiring process; at that point, they can decide whether or not to disclose the condition. Therefore, the Ninth Circuit held that the so-called conditional job offers were not real, because the applicants were required to undergo an immediate medical examination prematurely, while both medical and nonmedical conditions on hiring remained. Although the airline testified that it had to streamline the application process to remain competitive with other airlines for applicants, the Ninth Circuit held that the airline failed to prove that there were no reasonable alternatives that would put the medical examination in its proper place—at the end of the selection process.

The California Constitution's right of privacy is broader than the federal one, because it imposes obligations on private parties as well as state actors. The appellants charged that the airline violated their privacy rights by performing blood tests without notice or consent. The court found that the blood tests implicated a protected privacy interest. Whether an expectation of privacy is reasonable is a fact question that can't be determined without a full trial, so summary judgment was inappropriate. Although the applicants consented to blood testing, they did not consent to any and all use that might be made of their blood samples, or to blood tests outside the ordinary and accepted range of pre-employment testing. However, claims of intentional infliction of emotional distress were dismissed, because there was no proof that the blood tests, even if illegal, were extreme or outrageous enough to violate norms of decency. [*Leonel v. American Airlines, Inc.*, 400 F.3d 702 (9th Cir. 2005)]

An employer's requirement that a worker who claims to be disabled must have an independent medical exam is not enough to prove that the employer regarded that employee as disabled. The employer can demand an independent examination as long as it is job-related and there is a business necessity for it. [*Tice v. Centre Area Transp. Auth.*, 247 F.3d 506 (3d Cir. 2001)]

The Sixth Circuit agreed that a grocery store was justified in firing a produce clerk who said he was HIV positive but neither verified his condition nor took the medical examination requested by the employer. The examination was job-related and consistent with business necessity, because minor injuries at work could endanger an HIV positive employee or other people. [*EEOC v. Prevo's Family Market Inc.*, 135 F.3d 1089 (6th Cir. 1998)]

For more about workplace HIV issues, including a sample business case and sample workplace policies and training manuals, *see* HIV/AIDS Workplace Toolkit available at <http://www.shrm.org/diversity/aidsguide/policy.asp>, explaining Business Response to AIDS, a joint venture between business groups and the Centers for Disease Control.

Tip: After the September 11 attack, the EEOC announced that it is not a violation of the ADA for an employer to ask employees about their medical condition in case they need help in an emergency evacuation, Nor is it a violation of employee privacy to share such information with safety and first aid workers. The Fact Sheet on obtaining and using emergency evacuation information was published at <http://www.eeoc.gov/facts/evacuation.html>.

It has been held that it does not violate the ADA for a factory to reject job applicants if pre-employment testing shows that they are prone to develop carpal tunnel syndrome. [*EEOC v. Woodbridge Co.*, 263 F.3d 812 (8th Cir. 2000); *EEOC v. Rockwell Int'l Corp.*, 243 F.3d 1012 (7th Cir. 2001)] The courts held that these were not sustainable "regarded-as" cases, because the employer did not view the applicants as limited in their ability to hold a broad variety of jobs-only as unsuitable for the particular job.

A job applicant is not entitled to damages when an employer makes inappropriate prehiring inquiries if there were other reasons not to hire that person (here, lack of experience and availability of a laid-off employee to fill the job). [*Griffin v. Steeltek Inc.*, 261 F.3d 1026 (10th Cir. 2001)]

§ 36.10   INTERACTION WITH OTHER STATUTES

In 2003, the Supreme Court held that, in a suit under the Federal Employers Liability Act (FELA), damages for mental anguish (fear of developing cancer after exposure to asbestos) can be recovered if the plaintiff has already suffered another actionable injury (e.g., asbestosis). Pain and suffering associated with physical injury is actionable, even though independent claims for negligent infliction of intentional distress often are not. Here, the plaintiffs did not seek damages for the increased risk of future cancer. Instead, they sought compensation for their current injuries, which include experiencing fear. However, to win a case of this type, the plaintiff must prove that the alleged fear is genuine and serious. Although this case deals specifically with a federal employment statute, it's an important indication of the Court's thinking on these topics. [*Norfolk & Western Railway Co. v. Ayers*, 538 U.S. 135 (2003)]

Tip: California's Poppink Act defines disability more broadly than the federal ADA. Under California law, a disability is a physiological condition that limits a major life activity; the federal law requires a substantial limitation. So California employers may be subject to liability in some cases that would not be covered under the federal law. [*See Colmenares v. Braemar Country Club Inc.*, 29 Cal. 4th 1019, 63 P.3d 220, 130 Cal. Rptr. 2d 662 (Cal. Sup. 2003)]

[A] The Rehabilitation Act

The ADA is a successor statute to the Rehabilitation Act. There are many circumstances in which the HR department will have to apply the ADA in conjunction with other laws—typically, the FMLA and ERISA.

The ADA was preceded by the Rehabilitation Act of 1973 (Rehab Act). [29 U.S.C. § 793 *et seq.*] The Rehab Act applies to federal contractors and subcontractors whose government contract involves more than $2,500, and to federal programs and federal grantees. It does not apply to businesses that are not involved in government contracting.

Rehab Act § 503 protects qualified handicapped applicants against discrimination in employment practices. However, one reason that the ADA was passed is that the Rehab Act does not contain a private right of action. In other words, handicapped persons who charge that they were victims of discrimination cannot sue the alleged discriminators. Another section, § 504, does carry a private right of action, but only for discrimination solely on account of handicap in a federally financed program or activity.

Rehab Act § 503 imposes an affirmative action requirement. Federal contractors must have goals for hiring and promotion of qualified handicapped individuals. However, the Department of Labor does not have the power to enforce this requirement by bringing administrative prosecutions against companies that violate it.

In the case of *Hiler v. Brown*, [177 F.3d 542 (6th Cir. 1999)] a brain-injured Vietnam veteran claimed that he was denied a promotion because of war-related inability to communicate quickly in writing. He sued his supervisors as individual defendants under the Rehab Act. The Sixth Circuit held that the Rehab Act's language tracks the Title VII language, and only the employer company, not individuals, can be sued under Title VII.

In an early 2003 Rehab Act case, the Second Circuit concluded that the plaintiff submitted enough evidence to go to trial on his unlawful termination claim, but that his failure-to-promote claim was properly dismissed. [*Kinsella v. Rumsfeld*, 320 F.3d 309 (2d Cir. 2003)] The plaintiff is legally blind; with correction, his vision is 20/200 in each eye, and he is unable to drive, shop, or travel alone, or read without a magnifying glass. He was hired by the Air Force to work as a copier operator in its print shop. He claims that he was actually working as a Bindery Machine Operator, and repeatedly requested reclassification in that job, which would mean a promotion and a pay raise. In 1993, two print shops were consolidated. There was a Reduction in Force, and the plaintiff was told that he did not qualify for any of the remaining positions. All the other print shop employees were offered jobs of some kind. He remained unemployed for about two years, when he found a part-time job with lower pay and fewer benefits. Although the plaintiff admitted that the RIF was legitimate, he claimed that in his case it was applied as a pretext to fire him—a contention that the Second Circuit felt entitled the plaintiff to get a full trial. However, the Second Circuit ruled that his failure-to-promote claim was properly dismissed because he failed to apply for specific positions that then went to other workers.

The district court granted summary judgment for the employer in a Rehab Act case brought by an insulin-dependent diabetic seeking a transfer to the job of Criminal Investigator. The district court held that the plaintiff was not disabled for Rehab Act purposes, but the Seventh Circuit reversed and remanded. The job standards specified good health and specifically ruled out applicants with chronic endocrine conditions on the ground that they might suffer a blood sugar crisis endangering themselves and others during their irregular working hours. The Seventh Circuit rejected determinations that everyone with a specific condition is disabled. Individual determinations must be made.

The Seventh Circuit required consideration of the plaintiff's condition after corrective or mitigating measures—including the side effects of those measures. The Seventh Circuit ruled that a rational trier of fact could find a limitation in the major life activity of eating because the plaintiff is restricted in his diet, must check his blood sugar four times a day, and his blood sugar readings may force him to eat right away or delay eating. The Seventh Circuit ruled that there was a genuine issue of material fact as to whether he can do the job (a reasonable jury could conclude that he could manage his blood sugar safely), so a full trial is required. However, the Seventh Circuit upheld the district court's grant of summary judgment for the employer on the "regarded as" issue, because the Seventh Circuit rule is that stating that a person is incapable of performing a particular job is not tantamount to regarding the person as disabled in any general sense. [*Branham v. Snow*, 392 F.3d 896 (7th Cir. 2004)]

It is inappropriate to give a jury instruction in a Rehab Act case that the plaintiff only has to prove that discrimination was a motivating factor for the employer's action. Although that would be correct in an ADA case, the Rehab Act requires proof that disability discrimination was the employer's sole motivation. [*Soledad v. Department of Treasury*, 304 F.3d 500 (5th Cir. 2002)]

[B] The ADA and Disability Benefits

Although independent contractors are not covered by the ADA, the Seventh Circuit allowed ADA (and ADEA) claims to proceed when brought by a terminated employee who was promised consulting work and charged that he was denied the promised work in retaliation for pressing discrimination charges. The consulting arrangement grew out of the employment relationship, and loss of access to consulting could deter other employees from pursuing discrimination charges. [*Flannery v. Recording Industry Ass'n of America*, 354 F.3d 632 (7th Cir. 2004)]

A February 12, 1997, EEOC Notice No. 915.002, sets out the EEOC's position that employees can legitimately make ADA claims (based on the assertion that they are qualified to perform essential job functions) at the same time that they apply for disability benefits (which are premised on inability to do gainful work). The EEOC's view is that the two positions are not necessarily contradictory. The ADA assumes that people with disabilities can work; disability programs assume that they can't. Worker's Compensation, Social Security Disability, and other disability programs concentrate on classes of disabled people (e.g., by drafting schedules of impairments). The concept of accommodation is not involved. Nor do the disability-related programs distinguish between essential and marginal job tasks.

The EEOC's position is that even representations of disability made in a Worker's Compensation or disability hearing will not necessarily prevent the person from filing an ADA claim, because the questions posed at the hearing may be imprecise or may focus on disability rather than employability.

The EEOC wants to prevent situations in which someone is in effect driven out of the workforce by outright discrimination or by the employer's refusal to make the reasonable accommodations that would have made the person employable. Another possibility is that the person might have been unable to work when he or she applied for disability benefits, but at the earlier or later time referenced in the ADA claim, he or she could have worked if he or she had not been subjected to disability-based discrimination.

This position was adopted by the Supreme Court. [*Cleveland v. Policy Mgmt. Sys. Corp.*, 526 U.S. 795 (1999)] According to *King v. Herbert J. Thomas Memorial Hospital*, [159 F.3d 192 (4th Cir. 1998)] actually receiving disability benefits (as distinct from just applying for them) prevents an age-discrimination plaintiff from claiming she was able to perform the job at the time of her discharge.

According to *EEOC v. Stowe-Pharr Mills Inc.* [216 F.3d 373 (4th Cir. 2000)], the employer is not entitled to summary judgment just because the plaintiff applied for Social Security Disability Income benefits—the employee must be given a chance at trial to explain the apparent contradictions. However, information provided in the benefits application is admissible as evidence in the ADA case, because it proves whether or not the plaintiff previously requested accommodation. [*Whitbeck v. Vital Signs Inc.*, 159 F.3d 1369 (D.C. Cir. 1998)] A Social Security Disability determination can affect the plaintiff's damages, by proving the periods of time during which the plaintiff would not have been able to perform the essential job functions even with accommodation. [*Flowers v. Komatsu Mining Sys.*, 165 F.3d 554 (7th Cir. 1999)]

In a very complex case (also involving claims of racial, religious, and hostile work environment discrimination), the plaintiff was dismissed from her job as a telemarketing representative after a series of attendance violations. [*Gilmore v. AT&T*, 319 F.3d 1042 (8th Cir. 2003)] The plaintiff applied for SSDI benefits. Citing *Lane v. BFI Waste System of North America*, [257 F.3d 766 (8th Cir. 2001)] the court said that even though applying for SSDI does not automatically preclude an ADA suit, a plaintiff who has sworn to his or her inability to work will be required to reconcile that with the position taken in the ADA suit that he or she is qualified to work.

On a related issue, late in 2003 the Supreme Court decided that it was reasonable for the Commissioner of Social Security to use that agency's definition of "disability" to deny benefits to a claimant who had recovered to the point of being healthy enough to do her former job—as an elevator operator—even though that job no longer exists in significant numbers within the national economy. [*Barnhart v. Thomas*, 540 U.S. 20 (2003)]

[C] The FMLA

A person with a "serious health condition" (as defined by the FMLA) may also be a QIWD. FMLA leave, although unpaid, is easier to obtain than medical leave as a reasonable ADA accommodation, because employers with 50 or more employees have to grant FMLA leave to eligible employees. Reinstatement after FMLA leave is automatic, but ADA reinstatement requires showing of ability to perform essential work tasks (with or without reasonable accommodation).

A night-shift engineer was found to spend most of his shift sleeping on the job. One night, he left work early, saying that he didn't feel well and would take the rest of the week off. His sister said that he was very sick. His supervisor telephoned (the employee sounded "weird") and scheduled a meeting. The employee failed to appear at the meeting, and was fired for that non-appearance and for sleeping on the job. By that time, he was hallucinating and had made several suicide attempts. After a few months of treatment, his mental condition had stabilized. He wanted to return to work, but his employer wouldn't take him back. He sued under the ADA and the FMLA.

The plaintiff admitted that he was in bad shape mentally and could not work at that point, but claimed that the ADA requires accommodation. In the Seventh Circuit view, however, not working at all is not a reasonable accommodation, and a person who is not able to do the job at all is not a QWID. Part-time work may be acceptable as an accommodation for someone recovering from an illness, but not working at all for an extended time is not a reasonable accommodation; prolonged inability to work removes a person from the ADA-protected class.

On the FMLA front, however, the Seventh Circuit remanded the case to see if a reasonable employer would have been on notice from his erratic behavior that he had a serious health condition, and to determine the question of whether a mentally ill person is capable of giving notice that he or she requires FMLA leave. The Seventh Circuit left open the possibility that his last two unsatisfactory weeks at work could be reclassified as unpaid FMLA leave, opening up the possibility of reinstatement. [*Byrne v. Avon Products, Inc.*, 328 F.3d 380 (7th Cir. 2003)]

[D] HIPAA and Wellness Programs

Under HIPAA, a plan may not discriminate among similarly situated persons based on their health status, so differences in costs or premiums are forbidden. However, "adherence to programs of health promotion and disease prevention" (i.e., wellness programs) can lawfully give rise to premium discounts or reduced payment responsibilities. Wellness programs can include, for example, assessment of the health risks affecting individual employees, health screening, integration with the corporate attendance program, and diet or exercise plans.

Health assessments (often performed by outside contractors) usually ask employees questions about health and lifestyle issues and make recommendations for improvement. Assessments also can be used to channel employees into more intensive counseling or disease management programs. High-risk employees account for the majority of employer health costs and have the highest level of health-related absences and disability claims. However, high-risk employees might also have an ADA disability, making the wellness program arguably a disability-based benefit. Under the ADA voluntary medical examinations are permissible as part of a voluntary health program for which disabled employees are not penalized if they choose not to participate. HIPAA allows employers to provide incentives for health improvement; however, the ADA forbids penalties based on disability, and it is possible that a major incentive could be construed as a penalty for nonparticipants. In addition, requiring a certain degree of improvement in health scores could reflect a discriminatory assumption that everyone's health is capable of being improved.

Again, the program should be voluntary, and employees whose tests reveal abnormalities should be told to consult their own doctors. HIPAA requires wellness programs to provide a reasonable alternative standard for employees whose conditions make it impossible or contraindicated for them to meet the program's ordinary health standards, and the alternative must not pose undue hardship to older or disabled employees. HIPAA's privacy rules also apply to health care providers who treat employees, so information should be released to the employer only on an aggregate basis, not in an individually indentifiable form.

It is not clear how the ADA affects wellness programs. Under the ADA, differences in benefits are permitted as long as the employer can show that no disability-related distinction was drawn, or that the wellness program is a bona fide plan that is not a subterfuge to evade the purposes of the ADA.

Because older employees tend to do worse on health assessments, ADEA problems also could arise. However, wellness programs probably will survive an ADEA challenge because the employer will probably spend more for older than for younger employees, and the ADEA permits a higher spending level for older employees. [Chicago Consulting Actuaries, *Impact of ADA and ADEA on Wellness Program Design*, archived at <htpp://www.ccastrategies.com> (Oct. 7, 2005)]

§36.11 ADA ENFORCEMENT

The EEOC has enforcement power over the ADA. [42 U.S.C. § 12111(1)] The remedies available for disability discrimination are also available in retaliation cases. [42 U.S.C. § 12203(c)] ADA charges must be filed with the EEOC or the state agency. [*See* § 41.03 for an explanation of the process] The charge must be filed within 180 days of the last discriminatory act (in nondeferral states) or within 300 days of the last act (in deferral states). The Title VII investigation and conciliation procedures will be followed, and the ADA remedies are equivalent to Title VII remedies, with the distinction that reasonable accommodation can be ordered as an ADA remedy.

The EEOC and the federal courts have discretion to make an attorneys' fee award to the prevailing party. If the United States loses a case, it can be required to pay attorneys' fees—but if the United States wins, the other party cannot be required to compensate the government for the costs of the case. [*See* 42 U.S.C. § 12205]

A mid-2003 Tenth Circuit case examines some critical timing issues for ADA cases. The plaintiff, who is deaf, charges that America OnLine refused to consider him for employment because of his deafness. Most of the AOL call center work is done by "technical consultants" on the phone. The call center has both voicephone and non-voicephone jobs; the pay, benefits, and seniority are the same for both. In 1996, seven deaf people were hired for non-voicephone jobs; after the company opened a call center in the Philippines in 1997, it stopped hiring in the United States for non-voicephone jobs. The plaintiff applied twice and was turned down because he couldn't use a voicephone.

He brought suit January 7, 1997, based on job applications made in September 1997 and November 1998. The plaintiff asserted the "continuing violation" doctrine, i.e., that the two refusals to hire were part of a series of related acts. The Tenth Circuit rejected the application of this doctrine to separate acts (as opposed to a truly ongoing situation such as a hostile environment). The Tenth Circuit ruled that refusal to hire must be viewed as a discrete act, even if it was undertaken under a company-wide policy. Therefore, the claim about the 1997 rejection was time-barred.

However, the Tenth Circuit ruled that the plaintiff was entitled to a trial on the issue of whether voicephone experience was a legitimate requirement for working in the call center (where deaf employees were already performing satisfactorily). The Tenth Circuit interpreted "hiring" to mean all of the processes for filling a specific job, including lateral transfers and promotions as well as new hires. Therefore, the plaintiff would have to be considered a QWID if he was able to perform the essential functions of the job he applied for. In this view, although the court must give consideration to the employer's determination of what is essential to a job—as long as the job specification is job-related, uniformly enforced, and reflects business necessity—the employer's decision is not conclusive. The case was remanded, because the plaintiff was not asking for a reassignment (which would not be required by the ADA), only a restructuring of the non-essential requirements of the job that the plaintiff wanted. [*Davidson v. AOL*, 337 F.3d 1179 (10th Cir. 2003)]

§ 36.12   THE ADA PRIMA FACIE CASE

Once a disabled employee makes out a prima facie case, the burden then shifts to the employer to prove, by a preponderance of the evidence, that it either offered the plaintiff reasonable accommodation or was unable to do so because of undue hardship. [*Community Hospital v. Fail*, 969 P.2d 667 (Colo. Sup. 1998)] The court's theory is that the employer has more information about the availability of accommodation, so it is up to the employer to prove this issue.

The Ninth Circuit ruled that medical or comparative evidence about the plaintiff's claims of substantial impairment in major life activities is not required at the summary judgment stage; it is a matter to be raised at the actual trial when the plaintiff's testimony can establish whether there is a genuine issue of material fact. The Ninth Circuit also ruled that in a case where discrimination could have been one of several factors in the employer's decision, the jury should have been given a "motivating factor" instruction. This decision also identifies reading as a major life activity. [*Head v. Glacier Northwest*, 413 F.3d 1053 (9th Cir. 2005)]

An employer can move for and obtain Judgment as a Matter of Law after a jury finding if there was inadequate evidence to support the finding that the plaintiff was disabled. The issue of disability refers to the elements of the claim, so it can be reconsidered even after the case has gone to the jury. [*Collado v. UPS, Inc.*, 419 F.3d 1143 (11th Cir. 2005)]

§ 36.13   DAMAGES

Under *EEOC v. Wal-Mart Stores*, [187 F.3d 1241 (10th Cir. 1999)] a written antidiscrimination policy, taken by itself, is not the equivalent of a good-faith effort to comply with the ADA. That made the employer vicariously liable and subject to punitive damages when a supervisor discriminated against a hearing-impaired employee. Failure to provide ADA training for supervisors meant that the policy was not really implemented. The Eighth Circuit upheld the jury's $75,000 punitive damage award, finding that it was not high enough to shock the conscience.

A jury awarded $2.5 million to a plaintiff, finding that her termination violated the ADA and Pennsylvania's state antidiscrimination law. Late in 2002, the Third Circuit upheld the jury verdict. The plaintiff, who suffered from multiple sclerosis, was denied a reasonable accommodation (changing her work assignment to remove the most stressful tasks). The jury verdict was divided into $2 million compensatory and $500,000 in punitive damages, but was not allocated between federal and state damages. The ADA damage cap was $300,000; the state law does not include a damage cap. The District Court applied the cap amount only to the punitive damages, thus lowering them from $500,000 to $300,000, and apportioned all the compensatory damages to the state-law claim. (The state law doesn't allow punitive damages, so the court didn't allocate any of the punitive damages to the state claim.) In this view, the CRA '91 damage cap limits only the federal damages, not damages received under a state claim—even one that is virtually identical to a federal claim that is subject to the cap. The Third Circuit refused to impose any further restrictions on the jury verdict, because it did not believe that the verdict was excessive enough to shock the conscience. [*Gagliardo v. Connaught Labs. Inc.*, 311 F.3d 565 (3d Cir. 2002)]

The plaintiff, who suffered from the ADA disability of depression, was a respiratory therapist. He applied for a transfer, claiming that his boss would not follow the already agreed-upon accommodations to his disability. The hospital where he worked demanded a full psychiatric evaluation, which was not required of other persons seeking a transfer. Then he was put on paid administrative leave of absence and then unpaid suspension during investigations of improper patient care;

a number of doctors and patients had also complained about his unprofessional conduct. After the investigation, he was fired for misconduct. He grieved his termination, the arbitrator found in his favor, and the case was settled for six-figure damages. The plaintiff agreed to resign from his job. In the interim, his termination had been reported to the Respiratory Care Board, pursuant to California law (although the employer did not make the mandated reports in other cases of termination for cause). There was evidence that the defendant turned over damaging records but not those in the plaintiff's favor, and the plaintiff's win at arbitration was not disclosed. The Respiratory Care Board temporarily suspended the plaintiff's credentials, then restored them after a psychological examination. The plaintiff sued the hospital, claiming that defendant's refusal to confirm his past employment prevented him from getting jobs. (The defendant claimed that there were no inquiries about the plaintiff's employment history.) The Ninth Circuit said that the settlement barred ADA and state law claims for acts prior to the settlement. However, a reasonable trier of fact might find that it was a breach of contract for the defendant to fail to update its records to show the plaintiff's resignation rather than termination. Retaliation claims dating before the settlement were barred by the settlement, but post-settlement retaliation claims could be litigated. The claim of intentional interference with prospective economic advantage was dismissed as too speculative, because the plaintiff could not prove that he would have gotten the jobs he applied for if the defendant had confirmed his employment and stated that he resigned. [*Pardi v. Kaiser Permanente Hosp. Inc.*, 389 F.3d 840 (9th Cir. 2004)]

At the beginning of 2004, the Seventh Circuit confronted the question of whether compensatory and punitive damages are appropriate remedies in ADA retaliation cases. It affirmed the District Court's determination that those remedies are not available, and to conduct the trial without a jury. (The plaintiff, who had multiple sclerosis, was demoted, and then fired shortly after protesting her demotion and filing EEOC charges of disability discrimination and retaliation.) She brought suit for ADA discrimination, retaliation, and under the state law against intentional infliction of emotional distress. She asked for front pay, back pay, compensatory and punitive damages, reinstatement, attorneys' fees, and costs. She filed a second discrimination charge with the EEOC, covering retaliatory discharge, got another Right to Sue letter, and amended her complaint, withdrawing the state-law claim but demanding a jury trial.

The District Court agreed with the defendant that jury trial was not available, and the Seventh Circuit upheld the District Court. Although the Second, Eighth, and Tenth Circuits have upheld jury verdicts granting compensatory and punitive damages, the Seventh Circuit interpreted the Civil Rights Act of 1991 to allow compensatory and punitive damages for ADA claims only if they fall under Sections 12112 or 12112(b)(5). Retaliation claims are provided for by § 12203—and therefore the remedies are limited to the equitable relief provided by 42 U.S.C. § 2000e-5(g)(1). Because the plaintiff was only entitled to equitable remedies, she had no right to a jury trial. [*Kramer v. Banc of America Securities, LLC*, 355 F.3d 961 (7th Cir. 2004)]

A jury awarded $32,000 in back pay and $18,000 in punitive damages for failure-to-hire discrimination on the basis of actual and perceived disability. The plaintiff eventually took another job for $10.25 an hour. He testified that if the defendant had hired him, he would have earned $13.60–$14.30 an hour, whereas the defendant said that he would have been hired at a rate of $9 an hour with the potential for a raise to $11 an hour.

The defendant appealed, claiming that the District Court abused its discretion by awarding two years of front pay at an unrealistically high hourly rate. (The District Court dismissed the punitive damage award, finding that there was no evidence of malice or reckless indifference to the plaintiff's rights.) On appeal, the Eighth Circuit found that the front pay award was appropriate; the two-year term was proper (rather than the eight years the plaintiff asked for) because he was young enough to have many years in the workforce to make up for the loss of income. [*Ollie v. Titan Tire Corp.*, 336 F.3d 680 (8th Cir. 2003)]

§ 36.14   ARBITRATION OF ADA CLAIMS

Wright v. Universal Maritime Service Corp. [525 U.S. 70 (1998)] involves an injured stevedore who was denied employment because potential employers deemed him to be permanently disabled. The plaintiff sued under the ADA without first filing a grievance or going through arbitration under the collective bargaining agreement.

The lower federal courts dismissed his case because of his failure to exhaust grievance remedies, but the Supreme Court unanimously reversed. Although ADA claims are subject to compulsory arbitration under the U-4 (securities industry employment agreement), the Supreme Court treated this case differently because Wright's claims arose under a statute, not a contract. Contract claims are presumed to be subject to arbitration, but statutory claims are not.

For a CBA to rule out litigation of a claim under an antidiscrimination statute, *Wright* says that the CBA must be very clear on that point. A generalized arbitration clause that fails to specify the antidiscrimination statutes that it covers will not be enough to keep disgruntled employees out of the court system.

According to *EEOC v. Waffle House Inc.,* [534 U.S. 279 (2002)] the EEOC can pursue an ADA case, including victim-specific relief, even though the employee him- or herself was covered by a mandatory predispute arbitration requirement and would not have been able to sue the employer because of this requirement. [*See* Chapter 40 for fuller discussion of arbitration and ADR]

CHAPTER 37

AGE DISCRIMINATION IN EMPLOYMENT ACT

§ 37.01   INTRODUCTION

The Age Discrimination in Employment Act (ADEA), unlike Title VII and the ADA, is found in Title 29 of the United States Code starting at Section 621. (Title VII and the ADEA are in Title 42). In other words, Congress considered the ADEA to be labor law instead of civil rights law. [*See* § 41.06[A] for a discussion of EEOC procedure for filing discrimination charges, and § 42.11 for a discussion of procedural issues arising in private ADEA lawsuits filed by an employee or class of employees]

Congress defined its purpose in passing the ADEA as protecting older people who want to stay in the workforce and are still capable of working from discrimination involving "arbitrary age limits." The ADEA's aim is to "promote employment of older persons based on their ability rather than age; to prohibit arbitrary age discrimination in employment; to help employers and workers find ways of meeting problems arising from the impact of age on employment." [29 U.S.C. § 621]

The basic rule is that anyone over age 40 is protected by the ADEA [29 U.S.C. § 631], so the protected group is not restricted to senior citizens. In a limited range of situations, being under 40 is a bona fide occupational qualification (BFOQ). In other cases, adverse employment action against an older person could be legally justified by a Reasonable Factor Other than Age (RFOA). State age discrimination suits have been upheld when young people are deprived of employment opportunities because of their youth because this, too, is discrimination "on account of age." [*Bergen Commercial Bank v. Sisler,* 157 N.J. 188 (N.J. 1999); *Zanni v. Medaphis Physician Servs. Corp.,* 240 Mich. App. 472 (2000)]

A Collective Bargaining Agreement (CBA) provision mandating that one fifth of the bargaining unit's employees to be over 50 could not be enforced because it violates state law that forbids age to be used as a basis for decisions as long as the person concerned is an adult. [*Ace Electrical Contractors Inc. v. IBEW,* 414 F.3d 896 (8th Cir. 2005)]

The Center for Retirement Research at Boston College tackled the question of whether age discrimination is still prevalent in the workforce in a 2005 study. Discrimination is only one explanation that could be given for greater difficulties older workers find in getting new jobs. For example, they could have earned high salaries based on having specific skills suited to their old job, but which are less valuable to potential employers, who are unwilling to match the past salary. Psychological studies have shown that identical resumes are more appealing if they are said to come from younger workers, although it is possible that real-world hiring offers additional opportunities to older workers to avoid age discrimination charges. (It is harder to prove that a failure to hire was discriminatory than that reasons given for firing or refusing to promote an actual employee with a good work record were pretextual.) The study found that younger workers were 40% more likely to be called for interviews than over-50 workers, so that an older worker might need to send out 27 resumes (versus 19 for a younger worker) to get an interview. [Joanna N. Lahey, *Do Older Workers Face Discrimination?* (July 2005) <http://www.bc.edu/centers/crr/issues/ib_33.pdf>]

§ 37.02   ADEA EXCEPTIONS

The ADEA bars job discrimination, so a discharge for good cause will not violate the ADEA. As is true of many other labor and anti-discrimination laws, the ADEA exempts very small businesses. The definition of "employer" is limited to industrics affecting commerce and having 20 or more employees for each workday in each of 20 or more weeks in the current or previous year. [29 U.S.C. § 630(b)]

The ADEA applies to employees of the United States branch of a foreign corporation that has 20 or more employees worldwide; there need not be 20 employees at the U.S. branch. [*Morelli v. Cedel,* 141 F.3d 39 (2d Cir. 1998)] The number of employees at several small affiliates of a larger corporation can be aggregated for the 20-employee test if the parent company directed the discriminatory act or policy; the original larger enterprise was split up to avoid liability; and the corporate veil can be pierced (i.e., the parent can be held liable for the subsidiaries' debts, torts, and breaches of contract). [*Papa v. Katy Industries Inc.,* 166 F.3d 937 (7th Cir. 1999)]

Although the general rule under the ADEA is that no one can be compelled to retire simply because of that person's age, there is an important exception. Under 29 U.S.C. § 631, a person who has been a "bona fide executive or high policy maker" for two years just before retirement, can lawfully be compelled to retire at 65, as long as he or she is entitled to aggregate retirement benefits that are the equivalent of an annuity of $44,000 a year or more.

The Higher Education Amendments of 1998 [H.R. 6 (Oct. 7, 1998)] reinstate a traditional ADEA exception. Under the Amendments, it is lawful to require tenured faculty members to retire solely on the basis of age. Although this act affects a small group of individuals, it is significant in showing a possible trend toward restricting the scope of the ADEA and other civil rights legislation.

EEOC Guidelines [29 C.F.R. § 1625.12(d)] define a bona fide policymaker as the manager of an entire enterprise, or at least a customarily recognized department or subdivision. He or she must direct the work of at least two employees, and must hold a job that regularly involves the exercise of discretionary power. At least 80% of work time (or at least 60% in a retail or service business) must be spent on managing the business rather than on routine tasks.

A school district's early retirement program offered cash to teachers retiring at ages 55–65. An ADEA suit was brought. The school district claimed the safe harbor for voluntary early retirement programs consistent with the objectives of the ADEA. The Eighth Circuit, however, said that the plan did not qualify for the safe harbor because the purpose of the ADEA is to eliminate arbitrary age-based distinctions. Perhaps a program conditioned on years of service, not age, would qualify. [*Jankovitz v. Des Moines Independent Community Sch. Dist.,* 421 F.3d 649

(8th Cir. 2005), discussed in Faegre & Benson LLP, *Employers Should Take Care in Designing Early Retirement Incentive Programs* (Oct. 15, 2005) (benefitslink. com)]

The Seventh Circuit refused to reach the merits of an age discrimination suit brought by a church organist who was fired after a dispute about the Easter music for the cathedral and replaced by someone much younger. The Seventh Circuit ruled that, for First Amendment reasons, the federal courts do not have jurisdiction over cases involving the internal affairs of a religious organization; however, the court deemed it necessary to get involved in doctrinal matters to resolve this case. [*Tomic v. Catholic Diocese of Peoria,* 442 F.3d 1036 (7th Cir. 2006)]

Although the federal National Bank Act allows the dismissal of bank officers at the bank's pleasure, it does not contain an ADEA exemption. Therefore, the Ninth Circuit allowed a bank officer to maintain a claim under a similar state law. [*Kroske v. U.S. Bank Corp.,* 432 F.3d 976 (9th Cir. 2005)]

§ 37.03 FORBIDDEN PRACTICES

[A] Statutory Prohibitions

Under 29 U.S.C. § 623, employers are forbidden to:

- Discriminate because of age (by firing or failing or refusing to hire, or in any other way) against anyone in connection with "compensation, terms, conditions, or privileges of employment";
- Use age to "limit, segregate, or classify" employees that reduce employment opportunities or "otherwise adversely affect" status as an employee;
- Reduce any employee's wage rate to comply with the ADEA;
- Discriminate against an employee or job applicant because of that person's protests about age discrimination, or in retaliation for that person's bringing an ADEA charge or involvement in someone else's ADEA charge;
- Publish Help Wanted ads that indicate "any preference, limitation, specification, or discrimination, based on age."

Section 623 also forbids age discrimination perpetrated by employment agencies and unions, but those provisions are outside the scope of this book.

However, in late 1998, the Eighth Circuit joined the Fifth, Sixth, and Seventh Circuits in ruling that it does not constitute age discrimination for an employer to make reasonable inquiries about an older person's retirement plans. [*Watkins v. J&S Oil Co.,* 164 F.3d 55 (8th Cir. 1998)]

A group of ex-employees brought suit under the ADEA, ERISA, and Title VII after their jobs were outsourced. They charged an intention to interfere with their pension benefits (ERISA § 510). The District Court, affirmed by the Eighth Circuit, dismissed their claims. The employer had a defined benefit plan allowing normal retirement at 65, early retirement at 55, or when the participant's age and years of service added up to at least 80. When it set up the outsourcing plan, the employer amended its plan to allow unpaid "bridge" leaves of absence so workers could qualify for early retirement. A number of employees were rehired by the firm to which the jobs were outsourced. Initially, the value of the benefit packages for the rehired employees was calculated at 90% of the value of the employer's benefit package. The package was then enhanced, to 95% of the original value—or 105%, if the potential for receiving bonuses was taken into account. The Eighth Circuit concluded that there was a legitimate, nondiscriminatory reason to outsource—to improve management in order to keep an important government contract—and improvements in the benefit package showed an intent to respect employees' financial needs. [*Register v. Honeywell Fed. Mfg. & Tech. LLC,* 397 F.3d 1130 (8th Cir. 2005)]

The EEOC has ruled that the ADEA applies to apprenticeship programs. Early in 2005, the Fourth Circuit upheld this rule as valid and not contrary to the Congressional intent in passing the ADEA. [*EEOC v. Seafarers Int'l Union,* 394 F.3d 197 (4th Cir. 2005)]

In a mid-2004 case, the Second Circuit upheld a jury verdict for plaintiffs who had been laid off under a facially neutral policy that had disparate impact on older workers, when the corporate goals could have been achieved in a non-discriminatory manner. (Initially, there were 26 plaintiffs; nine settled before the end of the trial.) The jury awarded $4.2 million to the 17 remaining plaintiffs, and the district court awarded close to a million dollars in fees and costs. [*Meacham v. Knolls Atomic Power Laboratory,* 381 F.3d 56 (2d Cir. 2004)]

Even though there was a reduction in force (RIF) going on, the Third Circuit denied summary judgment for the employer. The employer offered age-neutral reasons for the decision, but a full trial was ordered based on the plaintiff's showing that those reasons were implausible and conflicting. The Third Circuit applied *McDonnell-Douglas* burden-shifting analysis even though the RIF affected adequate employees as well as those performing poorly because illegal motivations could be used to select employees for RIF. In this case, there were 43 employees— seven employees over 40 and no employees under 40—who were chosen for RIF. [*Tomasso v. Boeing,* 445 F.3d 702 (3d Cir. 2006)]

Furthermore, to be justiciable the employment actions must be significant. The Tenth Circuit affirmed the District Court's grant of summary judgment for the employer in a case in which a 64-year-old clerk/receptionist at an AIDS clinic alleged denial of promotion and constructive termination. The younger employees claimed as comparators by the plaintiff were not comparable because they were far less rude and abrasive to clinic patients. The failure to promote claim failed because the defendant had legitimate reasons (more recent and relevant experience) for promoting the younger person. The adverse actions claimed by the plaintiff, such as rearranging her furniture and manipulating her scheduled time off at Christmas, were trivial and remote in time from her grievance filings. The Tenth Circuit ruled out the claim of constructive discharge, finding that the plaintiff was appropriately disciplined for her harsh demeanor toward clinic patients. To the court, the hostile environment that she alleged represented the "ordinary tribulations of the workplace" that, under *Faragher/Ellerth*, must be filtered out of a discrimination case. According to the Tenth Circuit, isolated incidents (unless they are very serious) and offhand comments are not actionable, and in any case the employer responded promptly and appropriately to the plaintiff's grievances. [*MacKenzie v. Denver*, 414 F.3d 1266 (10th Cir. 2005)]

The Eighth Circuit affirmed dismissal of an ADEA suit, finding that a small reduction in hours, negative performance reviews, and allegations of differential treatment as compared to younger employees (e.g., he claimed that younger workers were given advance notice of inspections) were inadequate to constitute adverse employment actions. The court found that the plaintiff's working hours—as is typical for retail employees—fluctuated, even before the alleged discrimination. The plaintiff also had a number of medical absences that reduced his hours. The plaintiff pointed to his negative performance reviews as adverse actions, but the court noted that performance reviews are only adverse actions if they result in detrimental changes in the terms or conditions of employment. [*Baucom v. Holiday Cos. Inc.*, 428 F.3d 764 (8th Cir. 2005)]

[B] Supreme Court Precedents

A Supreme Court case, *Public Employees Retirement System of Ohio v. Betts* [492 U.S. 158 (1989)] held that the ADEA did not apply to employee benefits. In 1990, Congress amended the statute, adding a new § 630(l), extending the ADEA ban on age discrimination in "compensation, terms, conditions, or privileges of employment" to cover "benefits provided pursuant to a bona fide employee benefit plan."

To win, the ADEA plaintiff does not have to show that he or she was replaced by someone under 40; it may even be possible to win by showing age-motivated replacement by another person over 40 (for instance, choosing someone who will retire soon, thus removing two older workers from the workplace). [*O'Connor v. Consolidated Coin Caterers Corp.*, 517 U.S. 308 (1997)]

The Tenth Circuit refused to impose a bright-line test (where an age difference of five years or less would rule out age discrimination), and permitted an ADEA action to proceed when a 62-year-old was replaced by a 57-year-old. The small gap in ages would make it harder for the plaintiff to prevail, but it was only one factor for the jury to consider. [*Whittington v. Nordam Group Inc.*, 429 F.3d 986 (10th Cir. 2005)]

In 2004, the Supreme Court ruled that one group of over-40 workers could not use the ADEA to charge they were the victims of discrimination in favor of another group of over-40 workers who were older than they were. (This was a retiree health benefits case about grandfathered benefits.) The Supreme Court concluded that the ADEA permits employers to favor their oldest group of workers, even at the expense of younger workers who are nevertheless over 40 and covered by the ADEA. [*General Dynamics Land Systems, Inc. v. Cline,* 540 U.S. 581 (2004); *see also Lawrence v. Town of Irondequoit,* 246 F. Supp. 2d 150 (W.D.N.Y. 2002), permitting employers to enhance retiree health benefits for persons over 80]

Normally, however, to win an ADEA case, the plaintiff must show replacement by someone significantly younger than him- or herself. Where a yard supervisor was demoted but not replaced by a person significantly younger than himself, the Sixth Circuit ruled that there was no ADEA violation. The plaintiff started out as a laborer, then was promoted to management, eventually reaching the rank of yard supervisor. When he was 54, he got a performance rating of "does not meet expectations," and was reassigned to the newly created, non-supervisory position of "planner." His salary and benefits remained the same, but his duties were reduced. The Sixth Circuit upheld the District Court's dismissal of the claims, holding that in an ADEA case, the prima facie case includes proof that the plaintiff was replaced by someone substantially younger. The case can still be proved if the replacement is over 40 (and therefore within the protected group himself). Unless there is direct evidence that the employer considered age to be significant, a six-year age difference is not enough; eight years might be, and 10 years probably would be. [*Grosjean v. First Energy Corp.,* 349 F.3d 332 (6th Cir. 2003)]

Furthermore, ADEA cases can turn on "age-related factors" rather than the mere fact of age. A 30-year-old can't have 30 years of employment experience. However, an employee with 20 years' seniority might be only 38, and could have more seniority than an older person who joined the company later. *Hazen Paper Co. v. Biggins* [507 U.S. 604 (1993)] requires ADEA plaintiffs to prove that age, and not just age-related factors, influenced the employer's decision.

In mixed-motive cases, *Price Waterhouse v. Hopkins* [490 U.S. 228 (1989)] says that the plaintiff must show that age is a substantial factor in the employment decision—it doesn't have to be the only factor or even the most important one. But if the employer can offer a defense (by a preponderance of the evidence, not proof beyond a reasonable doubt) that it would have made the same decision even if age had not been used as a criterion, the defendant will win the case. The Civil Rights Act of 1991 overruled this decision for Title VII cases—but not for ADEA cases.

St. Mary's Honor Center v. Hicks [509 U.S. 502 (1993)] says that the plaintiff always has the "ultimate burden of persuasion." So if the judge or jury (whichever is responsible for determining the facts of the case) does not believe the employer's explanation of the reasons behind its conduct, the plaintiff could still lose—if he or she fails to provide adequate evidence. The *Hicks* standard is sometimes called "pretext-plus": The plaintiff has to do more than show the defendant's excuses are a mere pretext for discrimination.

Although the ADEA statute explicitly waives sovereign immunity, permitting suits by state employees, the Supreme Court ruled that Congress violated the Eleventh Amendment by abrogating sovereign immunity without demonstrating a history of violations of this type committed by state employers. [*Kimel v. Florida Board of Regents*, 528 U.S. 62 (1999)]

Late in 2000, the Second Circuit found that if there is enough evidence of the plaintiff's poor work performance, then the jury cannot accept the plaintiff's pre-textuality argument. Therefore, summary judgment can validly be granted for the employer. [*Schnabel v. Abramson*, 232 F.3d 83 (2d Cir. 2000)]

The Supreme Court's June 2000 decision in *Reeves v. Sanderson Plumbing Products Inc.* [530 U.S. 133 (2000)] is a narrow procedural one. It holds that an ADEA plaintiff can defeat a motion for judgment as a matter of law (a procedural technique for terminating a lawsuit without a full trial) by establishing a prima facie case plus enough evidence for a reasonable court or jury to find that the employer's defense is merely pretextual. It is not required that the plaintiff intro-duce any further evidence at this stage, unless a rational finder of fact would not be able to find the defendant's conduct discriminatory. However, *Reeves* had little practical impact on the litigation climate [*see* 69 L.W. 2185 (Oct. 3, 2000)]; it certainly didn't issue in a new pro-plaintiff era.

In 2002, certiorari was granted in *Adams v. Florida Power*, No. 01-584, on the issue of whether ADEA disparate impact claims are cognizable, but later that year, certiorari was dismissed as improvidently granted: 535 U.S. 228 (2002). The Supreme Court finally resolved the issue in 2005, ruling, in *Smith v. Jackson*, 544 U.S. 228, that disparate impact claims are cognizable.

[C] Employee Status

ADEA cases are limited to the employment context, not all aspects of eco-nomic life. Therefore, it could not be an ADEA violation to use age to refuse an automobile dealership to an applicant; dealers are contractors, not employees. [*Mangram v. GM Corp.*, 108 F.3d 61 (4th Cir. 1997)]

Salespersons who are independent contractors are not covered by the ADEA. [*Oestman v. National Farmers Unions Inc.*, 958 F.2d 303 (10th Cir. 1992)] However, the Second Circuit has ruled that members of a corporation's Board of Directors are entitled to the protections of the ADEA if they work full time as corporate managers or officers, and report to senior board members. [*Caruso v. Peat, Marwick Mitchell & Co.*, 664 F. Supp. 144 (S.D.N.Y. 1987)]

The critical test of employee status is whether the economic realities of that person's situation are more like employment or more like another relationship (such as being a partner in a partnership). [*EEOC v. Sidley Austin Brown & Wood*, 315 F.3d 696 (7th Cir. 2002)] The shareholders in a professional corporation are not counted in determining if the PC has 20 "employees" for business pur-poses. According to the Seventh Circuit, a doctor who was a shareholder-director in a professional corporation was not an employee and therefore could not bring an ADEA suit against the PC. (He wanted to bring suit because, under the PC's latest profit-sharing plan, he would receive only a modest base salary and would not receive a profit-sharing distribution because his practice income was not large enough.) The court reached this conclusion, not merely because he held shares in the PC, but because he was not subject to control over his work and had always exercised a high degree of independence in his medical practice. [*Schmidt v. Ottawa Med. Ctr. PC*, 322 F.3d 461 (7th Cir. 2003)]

Tip: In April 2003, the Supreme Court ruled (although in an ADA rather than an ADEA case, and a case brought by someone who was an ordinary employee rather than by a shareholder-director) that doctors-shareholders in medical PCs are NOT employees, and are not counted in determining if the business has enough employees to be subject to an antidiscrimination statute. [*Clackamas Gastroenterology Assocs., PC v. Wells*, 538 U.S. 440 (2003).

A 59-year-old insurance agency manager had been working for the company for close to 35 years when he was informed he would be terminated unless he resigned. He did resign, and then filed an ADEA charge with the EEOC and got a right-to-sue letter. The District Court granted summary judgment for the employer, on the grounds that the plaintiff was an independent contractor. However, the Eighth Circuit reinstated the suit and allowed the plaintiff at least to make his arguments to a jury. In applying the economic reality test, some of the factors favored each interpretation. The plaintiff worked under a contract that described him as an independent contractor; he was paid on a commission basis, with independent judgment about who to approach as a customer; and paid taxes as an independent contractor. However, length of tenure is an important factor, and he had been working there for more than three decades; he was told where to work and on what schedule; the company provided him with insurance; underwriting decisions were up to the insurer and not the plaintiff; and the plaintiff was subject to the insurer's corporate anti-harassment policy. [*Jenkins v. Southern Farm Bureau Casualty*, 307 F.3d 741 (8th Cir. 2002)]

The Seventh Circuit upheld the dismissal of age discrimination claims by a group of 6,400 Allstate insurance agents, on the grounds that the shift from employees to independent contractors selling policies was implemented in an age-neutral fashion. The Supreme Court denied certiorari in March 2006. [*Isbell v. Allstate Ins. Co.*, 418 F.3d 788, *cert. denied*, 126 S. Ct. 1590 Mar. 20, 2006; *see* Fred Schneyer, *U.S. Supreme Court Turns Away Allstate ADEA Case*, PlanSponsor.com (Mar. 22, 2006)]

Although the ADEA statute refers to "employees," coverage is not limited to current active employees. Retirees have standing to sue their union for ADEA violations in connection with health plan amendments that excluded Medicare-eligible retirees. [*McKeever v. Ironworkers' Dist. Council*, 65 L.W. 2608 (E.D. Pa. March 7, 1997)] The D.C. Circuit also allowed federal employees to bring ADEA retaliation suits after their discharge or resignation. [*Forman v. Small*, 271 F.3d 285 (D.C. Cir. 2001)]

[D] Occupational Qualifications and RFOAs

Being under 40 can be a bona fide occupational qualification (BFOQ) for a narrow range of jobs, usually involving public safety (e.g., the strength, agility, and quick reaction time required of police officers and firefighters), [see 29 U.S.C. § 623(f)(1)] but most ordinary private sector jobs will not give rise to a BFOQ defense.

Reasonable factors other than age (RFOA) can offer a defense, as long as the employer used objective, job-related criteria to make the employment decision, and applied those criteria uniformly. Courts have often accepted arguments that the employer's decision was not really age-based, but was inspired by factors that merely tend to go along with age: for instance, the tendency of salaries to rise with experience. Employers in search of cost cutting might discharge higher-paid older workers in order to replace them with lower-paid workers. The EEOC Regulations say that, if the RFOA has a disparate impact on over-40 workers, the employer must prove that it has a business necessity for the action.

It is a defense to an age discrimination charge if an employer follows the provisions of "a bona fide seniority system that is not intended to evade" the ADEA's purposes. [29 U.S.C. § 623(f); 29 C.F.R. § 1625.8] However, even a valid seniority system cannot be used to impose involuntary retirement on an employee who is capable of working and wants to continue. Furthermore, older seniority systems (and retirement plans) are not "grandfathered in." Section 623(k) requires all seniority systems and benefit plans to comply with the ADEA, no matter when they were adopted.

§ 37.04 IMPLICATIONS FOR BENEFIT PLANS

[A] Generally

At one time, it would have been accurate to say that the ADEA covered only hiring, firing, and salary, but not employee benefits, based on a Supreme Court decision, *Public Employees Retirement System of Ohio v. Betts* [492 U.S. 158 (1989)] In 1990, however, Congress passed a statute, the Older Workers Benefit Protection Act (OWBPA) to make it clear that the ADEA covers all of the terms and conditions of employment, including the full compensation package. Therefore, in the current legal environment, it is important to discover how the ADEA interacts with ERISA, insurance laws, and other laws affecting compensation and benefits.

Section 623(i) takes up the question of how the ADEA interacts with employee benefit plans. Employers are forbidden to "establish or maintain" a pension plan that requires or even permits age-based termination or reduction of pension credits. In a defined benefit plan, benefits must continue to accrue at the same rate. In a defined contribution plan, the employer's allocations must be made to all employees' accounts on the same basis, irrespective of their ages. [29 U.S.C. § 623(i)(1)] People who count as "highly compensated employees" for tax purposes are not entitled to this protection. [See 29 U.S.C. § 623(i)(5)]

The ADEA provides various defenses and safe harbors for employers. Voluntary early retirement plans are allowable as long as they are consistent with the ADEA's purpose of protecting employment rights for older workers. [29 U.S.C. § 623(f)(B)(2)]

It is permissible for a plan to put an upper limit on the amount of benefits a plan can provide to anyone, or to limit the number of years of employment that can be taken into account, as long as these provisions are imposed without regard to age. [29 U.S.C. § 623(i)(2)] For instance, if the plan does not permit crediting of more than 30 years of service, this is an allowable age-neutral provision because it applies to employees with more than 30 years' tenure whether they started working for the company at age 18 or age 40.

Once an employee has reached the plan's Normal Retirement Age (NRA) and has started to receive a pension, then the employer's obligation to continue accruing benefits is satisfied by the actuarial equivalent of the pension benefits themselves. [29 U.S.C. § 623(i)(3)(A)]

Section 623(i)(3)(B) says that, for employees who have reached NRA but have not started to draw a pension (typically, employees who defer their retirement and are still working), and whose benefits have not been suspended pursuant to ERISA § 203(a)(3)(B) or I.R.C. § 411(a)(3)(B), the employer's obligation to keep accruing benefits is satisfied by making an actuarial adjustment to the pension that the employee eventually receives, so that he or she gets a larger pension because of deferred retirement.

Because the ADEA covers persons over age 40, the protected group includes many people who will voluntarily elect early retirement. Section 623(l) says that it does not constitute age discrimination for a pension plan to set a minimum retirement age as a condition for being eligible for either early or normal retirement.

A defined benefit plan can lawfully provide early retirement subsidies, or supplement the Social Security benefits of retirees who get a reduced benefit because they retire before the plan's NRA. [29 U.S.C. § 623(l)(1)(B). With respect to retiree health benefits, also *see* 29 U.S.C. § 623(l)(2)(D)]

There is no ADEA violation if a departing employee's severance pay is reduced to account for the value of retiree health benefits, and/or the value of additional pension benefits that are made available because of a contingency that is not based on age to a person who is already eligible for a full retirement benefit. [29 U.S.C. § 623(l)(2)] For this purpose, severance pay is defined to include certain supplemental unemployment insurance benefits. [*See* 29 U.S.C. § 613(l)(2)(C) and I.R.C. § 501(c)(17)]

Tip: If the employer says that retiree health benefits will be provided, and reduces severance pay accordingly, but fails to provide retiree health benefits, 29 U.S.C. § 623(l)(2)(F) lets employees sue for "specific performance" (i.e., to make the employer provide the benefits). This is an additional right, over and above any other remedies the individual has.

However, according to the Eleventh Circuit, Social Security benefits should not be used to reduce back pay under the ADEA; neither should unemployment compensation. However, if the employee applies for Social Security benefits, that could be evidence that the employee didn't try hard enough to get another job—which could be grounds for reducing the back pay award. [*Dominguez v. Tom James Co.,* 113 F.3d 1188 (11th Cir. 1997); *Brown v. A.J. Gerrard Mfg. Co.,* 715 F.2d 1549 (11th Cir. 1983)]

In mid-2003, the EEOC reversed its earlier position and proposed Regulations under which employers would be allowed to coordinate retiree health benefits with Medicare: i.e., it would not be considered an ADEA violation to reduce or even eliminate retiree health benefits at the point at which the ex-employees become eligible for Medicare. [68 Fed. Reg. 41542 (July 14, 2003)]

On April 22, 2004, the EEOC approved a Final Rule permitting employers to coordinate their coverage with Medicare, i.e., ruling that coordination qualified for the exemption from the ADEA. On February 4, 2005, the AARP brought suit in the Eastern District of Pennsylvania, seeking a preliminary injunction against implementation of the Final Rule. On February 7, 2005, the Department of Justice, on behalf of the EEOC, agreed to delay publication of the rule for 60 days to give the District Court time to make a ruling. On March 30, 2005, the court enjoined publication of the regulation, accepting the EEOC's argument that although employers might terminate their retiree health programs if they were unable to coordinate with Medicare, nevertheless the *Erie* decision made the Final Rule untenable. However, on June 29, 2005, the decision in *National Cable & Telecom* was handed down, requiring federal courts to defer to an agency's interpretation of an ambiguous statute (as long as the statute is within the agency's scope of operations, and the construction is reasonable). On September 27, 2005, the Pennsylvania court granted summary judgment to the EEOC, allowing the exemption but keeping the injunction in place until AARP exhausted its appeals. [ERISA Industry Committee, *ADEA Timeline,* <http://www.eric.org/481100000032.filename. AARP_v._EEOC_Timeline>]

More than a dozen business groups filed amicus briefs in an appeal to the Third Circuit. Their position was that before the original *Erie* decision in 2000, coordination of retiree benefits with Medicare was a long-standing tradition that was crucial to an employer's ability to afford to offer retiree health benefits at all. [Fred Schneyer, *Business Groups Lobby to Uphold Erie County Decision,* PlanSponsor.com, Apr. 17, 2006]

[B] Case Law on Pension and Benefit Issues

The Ninth Circuit decided in 1999 that it violates the ADEA to calculate disability retirement benefits based on the age at the time of hiring. [*Arnett v. California Pub. Employees Retirement Sys.,* 207 F.3d 565 (9th Cir. 1999)] Under *Hazen,* calculations based on actual years of service are acceptable, because a younger person might have more years of service than an older person who was hired at a later age. However, age at hire raises different issues because it had a strong effect on the potential disability benefit. The Ninth Circuit remanded the case to the District Court for disposition. A much later case holds that the ADEA permits the calculation of disability retirement benefits based on the number of years someone would have worked absent disability—even though this method puts older workers at a disadvantage. (Persons disabled after they become eligible for retirement receive only the normal retirement benefits.) The method was adopted to compensate younger workers for lost years of earnings opportunities, not to discriminate against older workers. [*EEOC v. Jefferson County Sheriff's Dep't,* 414 F.3d 467 (6th Cir. 2005)]

Unlike the ADA, the ADEA does not contain a concept of reasonable accommodation. In late 2003, the Third Circuit tackled the difficult question of what happens when a person asserts claims of both disability and age discrimination. The plaintiff in this case was injured at the end of 1994, suffering permanent nerve damage and weakness. He could not return to his old job, which required heavy lifting and the use of both hands. He took a light duty assignment and eventually lost his job at the end of 1997. He applied for and was awarded Social Security Disability Income (SSDI) benefits—in other words, the Social Security Administration agreed with his statement that he was totally and permanently disabled. Several years later, he sued his ex-employer under the ADEA, charging that he was terminated at age 59 and replaced by a person under 40.

The Third Circuit upheld the District Court's dismissal of his ADEA case, because he espoused two mutually contradictory positions. There have been some ADA cases where applying for or even receiving SSDI did not prevent the ADA case from going forward, because SSDI is an assertion of total disability, whereas it is possible that there could be a valid ADA case if the person could work with reasonable accommodation, but accommodation was denied. There is no reasonable accommodation requirement under the ADA, so it is a direct contradiction to claim that the plaintiff was able to work but was terminated because of age discrimination, and also to claim that the plaintiff was totally disabled. [*Detz v. Greiner Industries, Inc.,* 346 F.3d 109 (3rd Cir. 2003)]

In a case in which the plaintiff alleged both ERISA and ADEA violations in connection with the employer's severance pay plan and cash balance conversion, the First Circuit held that the plaintiff waived the ADEA claim by failing to raise it at the District Court level. Furthermore, the plaintiff knew that the plan had been amended, reducing his pension entitlement, on October 14, 1998. Therefore, the EEOC charge filed in December 1999 was untimely, because it was made more than 300 days after the alleged act of discrimination. The statute of limitations started when the decision to reduce pension benefits was made and communicated to the plaintiff. The court refused to apply the concept that a claim is timely as long as there is one act in an ongoing pattern of discrimination during the 300-day period, because that concept comes from a Title VII hostile work environment case and is not applicable to ADEA cases. [*Campbell v. BankBoston, N.A.,* 327 F.3d 1 (1st Cir. 2003)]

A 56-year-old employee got education assistance from his employer for a bachelor's degree, but was turned down for additional assistance toward his master's degree on the grounds that he was too old for the employer to invest any more in him. The California Supreme Court ruled in mid-2002 that it is permissible to provide lower benefits for employees over 40 than for younger employees, and also rejected his common-law tort claims. [*Esberg v. Union Oil Co. of California,* 28 Cal. 4th 262, 47 P.3d 1069, 121 Cal. Rptr. 2d 203 (2002), discussed in Mike McKee, *California Justices OK Age Discrimination in Job Benefits,* The Recorder (June 26, 2002) (law.com)]

§ 37.05   HEALTH BENEFITS

If the employer maintains a group health plan, the plan must cover over-65 employees on equal terms with younger employees. Either the cost per employee must be the same, irrespective of age, or the employer must offer equal benefits.

Under ADEA § 3(f)(2), an employer can abide by the terms of a bona fide employee benefit plan without violating the ADEA or the OWBPA. A bona fide plan is one which:

- Existed before the challenged employment action occurred;
- The terms of the plan are observed;
- The plan is not used to force anyone into involuntary retirement;
- (Except for voluntary early retirement plans) the costs incurred, or the benefits paid, are equivalent for older and younger employees.

For EEOC regulations on this subject, see 29 C.F.R. § 1625.10.

Under ADEA § 4(f)(2), the employer is allowed to compare costs quoted on the basis of five-year age brackets (e.g., employees aged 30–35). Comparisons must be made using adjacent age brackets: not the costs of employees 65–70 versus those of employees aged 20–25, for instance.

ADEA § 4(l)(3)(B) allows long-term disability benefits to be reduced by pension benefits for which the individual is eligible at age 62 or normal retirement age. Also see Regulations at 29 C.F.R. § 1625.10(f)(1)(ii). The EEOC says it will not pursue an ADEA claim in situations where disability benefits stop at 65 for disabilities occurring before 60, or stop five years after a disability that occurred after age 60.

§ 37.06   PROVING THE ADEA CASE

The Tenth Circuit ruled that in order to exhaust their administrative remedies, private-sector employees have a duty to cooperate with the EEOC's investigation of their age bias charges before they file suit. [*Shikles v. Sprint/United Management Co.*, 426 F.3d 1304 (10th Cir. 2005)]

The Fifth Circuit ruled that summary judgment should not have been granted for the employer. The plaintiff, a sales associate, did not have to show that a younger employee received preferential treatment. The plaintiff's prima facie case casting doubt on the employer's claim that he resigned voluntarily was adequate to justify liability. In this case, direct evidence of discrimination was also present in the form of a "smoking gun" memorandum suggesting awarding severance pay to 14 over-50 employees to give the company flexibility to bring in "new players." This was direct evidence because the memo was written by an executive who had the power to terminate employees and grant them severance. [*Palasota v. Haggar Clothing Co.*, 342 F.3d 569 (5th Cir. 2003)]

The First Circuit ruled in 2004 that a corporation can be liable for age discrimination if a neutral decisionmaker relied on manipulated information provided by a biased employee who wanted to get the plaintiff fired. (The Fifth, Seventh, Eighth, and D.C. Circuits have also imposed corporate liability when the final decision was made by a neutral party but the process was tainted by animus from elsewhere.) [*Cariglia v. Hertz Equipment Rental Corp.*, 363 F.3d 77 (1st Cir. 2004)]

The Second Circuit held that age discrimination claims brought by a person terminated in a merger were correctly dismissed. Although there was a substantial age disparity between the plaintiff (61 years old) and her replacement (43 years old), the plaintiff failed to show as part of her prima facie case that the acquiror knew of the age difference. The person who fired the plaintiff had never seen her or spoken to her; the fact that she had 16 years' experience did not indicate her age; and the seller of the TV station did not give employees' age information to the buyer. [*Woodman v. WWOR-TV*, 411 F.3d 69 (2d Cir. 2005)]

In an October 2000 case, summary judgment was granted for the employer. The plaintiff failed to rebut testimony that he was not hired because of his poor interview performance. He didn't ask any questions about the position; he didn't give a good explanation for having held so many jobs in the past; and he rambled instead of giving concise answers to the interviewer's questions. [*Chapman v. AI Transport Inc.*, 229 F.3d 1012 (11th Cir. 2000)]

A 60-year-old employee was terminated when his employer lost government contracts. At his exit interview, he asked if he was being fired for poor performance. He was told "absolutely not." When he filed suit under the ADEA, the employer claimed that he was terminated because he was impossible to get along with. The jury (as upheld by the Seventh Circuit) didn't believe this, particularly since there was no documentation of the alleged personality problems in his generally good evaluations. [*Wilson v. AMGen Corp.*, 167 F.3d 1114 (7th Cir. 1999)]

According to the Fourth Circuit, disparaging comments about age are weaker evidence of discrimination than similar comments about race or sex. Racist or sexist remarks can be made by "outsiders," whereas everyone ages. [*Dockins v.*

Benchmark Communications, 176 F.3d 745 (4th Cir. 1999). *See* § 42.08 for a discussion of technical rules of proof]

In a suit brought by a group of RIF-ed (reduction in force) over-40 employees, statements by managers about the general need to reduce the average age of the workforce did not constitute direct evidence of discrimination. According to the Sixth Circuit, the statements responded to concerns about the impending retirement of many skilled workers. The court said that employers can maintain a reasonable age balance without violating the ADEA, and concern about the nationwide phenomenon of the aging workforce is not proof of age bias. [*Rowan v. Lockheed Martin Energy Sys. Inc.,* 360 F.3d 544 (6th Cir. 2004)]

The EEOC proposed significant changes in the way that ADEA charges would be handled, in a Notice of Proposed Rulemaking (NPRM) published at 67 Fed. Reg. 52431 (Aug. 12, 2002); finalized, effective January 16, 2004, at 68 Fed. Reg. 70150 (Dec. 17, 2003). [*See* § 41.05 for more details about the charging process in ADEA cases]

In an age discrimination case alleging improper termination, the jury found for the plaintiff, and also found that the defendant's violation was willful, and therefore awarded $238,000 in back pay, $247,000 front pay, and attorneys' fees of $65,000. The Eighth Circuit affirmed these awards. The employer's position was that a 32-year-old replaced the 64-year-old plaintiff, but this was justified by declining sales and the plaintiff's failure to meet corporate goals. However, the plaintiff produced evidence of a nationwide decline in sales; co-workers testified that age was a factor in the termination; and younger managers who failed to meet sales goals were not terminated.

Early in 2004, Magistrate Judge Jacob P. Hart dismissed a case, finding that the only remaining claim (Title VII race claims had previously been dismissed) was an ADEA claim that did not allege lost wages. The plaintiff was a kitchen worker who said that he was denied a promotion to busman on the grounds that he was too old. Although the busman earned a lower salary than the kitchen staff, the plaintiff felt that the job change would be a promotion because it offered more prestige, better working conditions, and a chance to seek further promotion to a better-paid job as a waiter. In Hart's view, however, the ADEA does not allow compensatory or nominal damages, and even if a violation is willful, a liquidated damages award is impossible without wage loss. [*Beverly v. Desmond Hotel & Conference Center* 2004 U.S. Dist. LEXIS 2640 (E.D. Pa. 2004), discussed in Shannon P. Duffy, *No Nominal Damages Under ADEA,* The Legal Intelligencer (Jan. 29, 2004) (law.com)]

A similar case, also involving an older manager punished for declining sales (but in this case, by demotion rather than termination), was decided by the Sixth Circuit early in 2003. [*Wexler v. White's Fine Furniture Inc.,* 317 F.3d 564 (6th Cir. 2003)] The plaintiff was 55 when he was hired as a sales representative, promoted to manager two years later, and then demoted. This case raises the question of the applicability of the "same actor inference": the inference that if someone was hired and fired by the same person, discrimination was not involved, because the hirer was aware of the characteristic which later was allegedly the basis for discrimination. (The inference comes from the case of *Buhrmaster v. Overnite Transportation Co.* [61 F.3d 461 (6th Cir. 1995)].) However, the Sixth Circuit ruled that the case should not have been dismissed, because a reasonable fact-finder could interpret the plaintiff's evidence as showing that his demotion had a mixed motive, including improper use of stereotypes about older workers.

An important question in evidence law is when other alleged "bad acts" by the same party are admissible. A late-2003 Third Circuit case looks at the other side of the coin: alleged "good acts" to rebut charges. A defendant was allowed to present evidence that it hired another older worker 20 months after the plaintiff's termination. This was relevant as a subsequent good act, and therefore admissible under Federal Rules of Evidence 404(b) on the issue of discriminatory intent. To the Third Circuit, subsequent hiring practices can be used to rebut the plaintiff's evidence of discrimination. The Third Circuit ruled that the defendant asserted a legitimate reason (insubordination) for firing the plaintiff, and did not think that the later hiring decision was too remote in time to be introduced in evidence. [*Ansell v. Green Acres Contracting Co.*, 347 F.3d 515 (3d Cir. 2003)]

On questions of evidence of age discrimination, *Fakete v. Aetna Inc.* [308 F.3d 335 (3d Cir. 2002)] holds that a reasonable jury could find that a manager's statement that he was looking for younger single people as employees, and that the plaintiff would not be happy at the defendant company in the future, proved that it was more likely than not that age was a substantial factor in the termination decision. There are cases that find that remarks about age did not furnish direct evidence—but here, the speaker was someone who had the power to make employment decisions (not just any co-worker), and the context was the plaintiff's direct question about his future at the company, not just a random conversation.

However, the First Circuit did not find that the company president's remark (that after his discharge, the plaintiff would probably sue for age discrimination) precluded the company's defense that it had valid non-discriminatory reasons for the termination—because litigation is a common phenomenon in our society, and acknowledgment of the risk of being sued is not an admission that discrimination occurred. [*Wallace v. O.C. Tanner Recognition Co.*, 299 F.3d 96 (1st Cir. 2002)]

A safety training coordinator with over 30 years of service brought an ADEA/wrongful termination suit, claiming that he was fired for his open opposition to corporate policies that he said were unsafe. The district court granted summary judgment for the employer on the ADEA claim. The wrongful discharge claim was tried, resulting in a jury verdict of $720,000. The defendant's motion for a new trial was granted, resulting in a verdict of $920,000. On appeal, the Eighth Circuit upheld summary judgment on the ADEA count, holding that the plaintiff's evidence did not give rise to a reasonable inference that age was a determinative factor in the decision not to rehire him. He did not have valid recent experience as a lineman, and the successful applicants did, so the employer had a valid, non-discriminatory reason for its decision. [*Kohrt v. MidAmerican Energy Co.*, 364 F.3d 894 (8th Cir. 2004)]

A group of 27 older employees brought suit under the ADEA after the acquiring corporation failed to rehire them after buying the plant where they worked. Although the district court granted summary judgment for the defense, holding that the plaintiffs were never employed by, and therefore could not have been wrongfully terminated by, the defendant, the Tenth Circuit affirmed dismissal as to wrongful termination claims but not as to refusal to hire claims. The plaintiffs' state and EEOC charges alleged that they were over 40, doing satisfactory work, and age-based factors were significant as shown by the terminated workers predominantly being older than the rehired workers. The court did not accept the defendant's argument that the plaintiffs did not exhaust their administrative remedies because they did not raise "failure to hire" charges before the EEOC. The Tenth Circuit held that charges are construed liberally, and the charges were sufficient to place the defendant on notice of what it was alleged to have done. It was understandable that the plaintiffs would think of the two corporations as a unit and consider themselves terminated rather than denied hiring. [*Foster v. Ruhrpumpen, Inc.*, 365 F.3d 1191 (10th Cir. 2004)]

According to the Eleventh Circuit, it is not mandatory for the trial court to instruct the jury on the question of whether an employer's asserted nondiscriminatory rationale is a pretext. (Some circuits do require a pretext instruction, however.) Therefore, failure to give the instruction was not error where the pattern instruction already covered the topic and the plaintiff's desired instruction could be confusing to the jury. [*Conroy v. Abraham Chevrolet-Tampa Inc.*, 375 F.3d 1228 (11th Cir. 2004)]

A group of Mississippi police officers objected to a plan that gave higher percentage raises to police officers with *fewer* than five years' service. Because the veteran officers tended to be older than those with shorter tenure, they alleged that the practice had a disparate impact on older officers, even though it did not explicitly categorize them on the basis of age. The U.S. Supreme Court ruled in the spring of 2005 that the plaintiffs did not have a valid claim—but the Court clarified that, in the right circumstances, disparate-impact ADEA cases can be valid, because the ADEA's statutory language is very close to that of Title VII. However, employers who are charged with disparate impact age discrimination can raise a defense that the disputed practice is based on reasonable factors other than age (RFOA), whereas there is no similar defense in race or sex discrimination cases.

The plaintiffs in this case were unsuccessful because they failed to identify the specific aspect of the pay plan that harmed the interests of older workers. The defendant, on the other hand, had a reasonable explanation for its adoption of the practice: to retain the newer officers, their compensation had to be brought closer to market norms. [*Smith v. City of Jackson, Mississippi*, 544 U.S. 228 (2005)]

The plaintiff in a First Circuit case charged the U.S. Postal Service with a pattern of discriminatory harassment on the basis of his age, his refusal to retire, and his exercise of First Amendment rights. His constitutional claim was dismissed, on the grounds that the ADEA is the only remedy for age discrimination. The plaintiff, a mechanic and union member, was ordered to show cause why his

ADEA claim should not be dismissed for failure to exhaust his administrative remedies (the grievance procedure under his collective bargaining agreement). The First Circuit ruled that the District Court was correct to dismiss the ADEA claim, because the plaintiff failed to provide a plausible explanation why he should be exempted from the procedural requirements. [*Tapia-Tapia v. Potter,* 322 F.3d 742 (1st Cir. 2003)]

Also on issues of timing *see Wright v. AmSouth Bancorporation.* [320 F.3d 1198 (11th Cir. 2003)] The question was when the 180-day limitations period began: When he received an evaluation stating that his work needed significant improvement? When he was turned down for a raise and bonus because of poor performance (but was told that he was not at risk of being fired)? When a 29-year-old woman was hired to replace him? When he was told that his employment was being terminated, and he should meet with the HR department to set his last date at work?

The District Court ruled that he should have been aware of his impending termination when his replacement was hired. However, the Eleventh Circuit ruled that the plaintiff was not told until December 1999 that his employment was at an end, so that was the date on which the limitations period began. A final decision that has not been communicated to the employee cannot start the limitations period.

Federal employees are subject to some special rules. They can go straight to the District Court to assert ADEA claims without going through the normal administrative process. According to the First Circuit, when they do so, the appropriate statute of limitations is the one found in the Fair Labor Standards Act, not Title VII. [*Rossiter v. Potter,* 357 F.3d 26 (1st Cir. 2004)]

However, under 29 C.F.R. § 1614.407(a), suit must be brought within 90 days of the final agency action. A plaintiff's final agency action occurred on June 15, 2001, making the last day to file September 13, 2001. His attorney filed the complaint on the 12th, expecting it to be delivered the next day. However, it was not actually delivered until the 18th. The District Court dismissed the case as untimely, and the Eighth Circuit affirmed. Nor was equitable tolling granted: the plaintiff was deemed to have had adequate notice of the filing requirements, he had a lawyer, and the delay was not the fault of the clerk's office; it was not reasonable to expect next-day delivery from 450 miles away. The Eighth Circuit's decision didn't refer to the disruption right after the 911 attack. [*Hallgren v. U.S. Dep't of Energy,* 331 F.3d 588 (8th Cir. 2003)]

[A] Damage Issues

In a 2002 case, the Eighth Circuit ruled that fringe benefits were properly included in the back pay award, and upheld an award of front pay lasting until the plaintiff would be 68, based on the plaintiff's testimony that that was the age at which he planned to retire. [*Hartley v. Dillard's, Inc.,* 310 F.2d 1054 (8th Cir. 2002)]

The Third Circuit tackled ADEA damage issues in early 2004. The plaintiff, a veteran plumber, was not hired for a job teaching at a trade school. The school district gave varying explanations of why he was not hired, including his lack of certification in refrigerant recapturing. The plaintiff pointed out that this was not listed as a necessary qualification in the advertisement and was irrelevant to performing the job. The school superintendent said that he didn't want any more "old plumbers" hired and told the plaintiff that "a fine young man" got the job instead.

The jury awarded $254,000 in damages. The District Court reduced this to $81,750 in light of the plaintiff's interim earnings, then doubled this figure as liquidated damages. The Third Circuit rejected the school district's argument that, as a municipality, it was immune from liquidated damages because they are punitive, and punitive damages can be imposed on a municipality only if the governing statute expressly authorizes it. The Third Circuit conceded that there are Supreme Court cases treating liquidated damages as punitive. However, the Fair Labor Standards Act provisions that have been incorporated into the ADEA specifically permit liquidated damages to be awarded against any employer, explicitly including states and their political subdivisions.

The school district also sought to have the damage award reduced because the back pay award included retirement benefits that, in the district's interpretation, constituted front pay. The Third Circuit did not accept this argument, ruling instead that retirement benefits are not necessarily front pay rather than back pay, and it was reasonable for the jury to award the retirement benefits that would have accrued as the plaintiff worked until retirement age. The Third Circuit also found the award of attorneys' fees ($150-$200/hour, depending on the attorney's level of experience) to be reasonable in light of comparable fees charged in the region. A fee of $85/hour for paralegals was not unreasonable given the broad range of complex trial preparation work that they did. [*Potence v. Hazleton Area Sch. Dist.*, 357 F.3d 366 (3rd Cir. 2004)]

In a mid-2003 Fifth Circuit case, the plaintiff was 60 years old when he was fired and replaced by a 38-year-old. The defendant claimed that he was fired for refusing an order to report for work. The jury found that his discharge represented a willful ADEA violation. The jury did not award front pay, but awarded $115,000 in back pay, doubled as liquidated damages, plus $67,000 in attorneys' fees and $6,000 in costs and interest.

The plaintiff introduced evidence that the company had a choice between laying him off and laying off a younger person, and chose to retain the younger worker. In the court's view, the evidence was sufficient for the jury to find the employer's explanation was pretextual. There was no direct evidence of discrimination, so the *McDonnell-Douglas* analysis applied. After *Reeves v. Sanderson*, however, once a case is fully tried on its merits, the focus shifts to whether there is enough evidence in the record to support the jury's findings.

The Fifth Circuit does not require outrageous conduct to find that the employer acted willfully. Here, the jury found that the plaintiff was terminated because of his age, and his supervisor could not have held a good-faith but mistaken belief that his conduct was acceptable under the ADEA. But the Fifth Circuit disapproved of what the plaintiff did, or rather failed to do—he did not continue the search for a substantially equivalent new job, although he did take a lower-level job. A plaintiff's attempt to mitigate damages does not have to be successful, but must constitute an honest attempt to find comparable work.

The Fifth Circuit therefore strictly limited the amount of back pay that the plaintiff could receive, which also reduced the liquidated damages, and reversed the attorneys' fee award, because the size of the damage award is a significant factor in setting the fee level. [*West v. Nabors Drilling USA, Inc.*, 330 F.3d 379 (5th Cir. 2003) (the standard for mitigation of damages comes from *Hartley v. Dillard's Inc.*, 310 F.3d 1054 (8th Cir. 2002))]

A patent lawyer was awarded more than $500,000 in back pay, which was doubled on the grounds that willful discrimination had occurred. The District Court refused to award front pay, so both the plaintiff and defendant appealed to the Seventh Circuit. The plaintiff was fired at age 51 with 14 years' tenure. He said that he was fired 10 days before early retirement benefits would have vested. The defense claimed he quit voluntarily, but that his work performance was poor enough to justify terminating him. The Seventh Circuit said that the District Court erred in excluding (as too remote) evidence of a corrective plan the plaintiff had been placed on earlier. The Court of Appeals found that it was relevant to the quality of the plaintiff's work performance. Nor should the jury have been instructed that proof of pretext compels an inference of discriminatory intent; the Seventh Circuit said that it merely allows it.

The defendant protested the admission of two types of evidence: the plaintiff's testimony about emotional distress as a result of termination and testimony about discrimination against other over-40 employees. Usually, emotional distress is not relevant in ADEA cases because it is not an element of damages. But in this case, the Seventh Circuit said that the employer opened the door to such testimony by raising the defense that the plaintiff quit his job. The plaintiff testified that he would not have quit because of the emotional toll on him and his family. Although testimony about the other employees was not sufficient to establish a pervasive corporate culture of discrimination, the Seventh Circuit ruled that admitting it was not harmful error. Front pay compensates for the loss of earnings resulting from a discharge, but the plaintiff has a duty to mitigate damages by seeking comparable employment. In this case, the plaintiff contended that he applied for a number of jobs but received no job offers, so his expert witness calculated front pay based on his never finding another job. The Seventh Circuit ruled that the plaintiff's skills and experience were such that some kind of employment could be found, so a front pay award was improper.

The Seventh Circuit ordered a new trial limited to the issue of liability; damages would be doubled only if the second jury found a willful violation. [*Mattenson v. Baxter Healthcare Corp.*, 438 F.3d 763 (7th Cir. 2006). *See Rodriguez-Torres v. Caribbean Forms Manufacturer, Inc.*, 399 F.3d 52, 67 (1st Cir. 2005) on the duty to mitigate]

In a late-2003 Tenth Circuit case, the plaintiff, of Hispanic and Filipino heritage and also over 50, sued under Title VII (for national origin discrimination and retaliation) and the ADEA after receiving a negative performance review, being demoted, getting a smaller raise and bonus than usual, and being turned down for a lateral transfer. The jury found in his favor and awarded $300,000 in back pay, $5 million in compensatory damages and another $5 million in punitive damages, finding the employer to be guilty of willful discrimination. The District Court reduced the awards of back pay and damages, finding them to be against the weight of the evidence, but awarded two years of front pay (starting when the plaintiff was laid off), for a total of $412,504 plus two years of front pay (close to $250,000). One of the issues the defendant raised on appeal was whether the plaintiff was precluded from receiving front pay because, after the trial, the defendant offered him a position substantially equivalent to the one he applied for but was turned down for.

The Tenth Circuit affirmed the District Court in part, but reversed in part, and remanded the case for reconsideration. The Tenth Circuit allows a plaintiff in a race/age discrimination case to receive the statutory maximum damages on a Title VII compensatory damage claim (*see* § 42.12[B] for discussion of the CRA '91 damage cap), plus ADEA back pay and liquidated damages. On the issue of front pay, both Title VII and the ADEA make this available as a remedy. Reinstatement is the preferred remedy, but this is not always practical—particularly since in this case, the defendant corporation's financial condition was deteriorating, so any job might be short-lived. Furthermore, where there is a hostile environment that renders reinstatement inappropriate, even an unconditional offer of reinstatement in a comparable job does not prevent an award of front pay as an alternative to reinstatement. [*Abuan v. Level 3 Communications, Inc.*, 353 F.3d 1158 (10th Cir. 2003)]

As Chapter 40 shows, arbitration is involved for an ever-increasing proportion of employment disputes—although the court's caseload continues to be increased by cases examining the question of whether a particular dispute should be litigated or arbitrated.

ADEA and state claims for unlawful retaliation, invasion of privacy, promissory estoppel, and violation of state public policy were brought in state court by a television news anchor. The defendant removed the case to federal court and moved to dismiss or, in the alternative, stay the case pending arbitration (because the plaintiff had signed an arbitration agreement). The District Court ruled that the arbitration agreement was enforceable, but severed three of its provisions. The Sixth Circuit affirmed the severance of the cost-shifting and remedies provisions and left the evidentiary provision to be interpreted by the arbitrator. The Sixth Circuit upheld the validity of the arbitration agreement because there was no extreme disparity in bargaining power that would make the agreement unconscionable: The news anchor was educated, experienced in media, and had already worked under an employment agreement containing a similar arbitration clause. The employer had discretion to determine if the plaintiff's performance was adequate. Under the terms of the arbitration agreement, the arbitrator was bound by the employer's determination if the arbitrator concluded that the employee engaged in the conduct complained of—or if the employer reasonably believed that the employee engaged in that conduct. The District Court found this provision invalid and unenforceable because it changed the *McDonnell-Douglas* evidentiary standard by preventing the employee from showing that the employer's asserted non-discriminatory reason was pretextual. The Sixth Circuit reversed on this point, holding that the arbitration agreement did not prevent employees from making out a prima facie case. However, the Sixth Circuit agreed with the District Court that the arbitration agreement's cost-shifting provision should be severed because, by making losing plaintiffs pay the full cost of arbitration, it could have the effect of discouraging a substantial number of employees from pursuing discrimination claims. [*Scovill v. WSYX/ABC*, 425 F.3d 1012 (6th Cir. 2005)]

§ 37.07   WAIVERS OF ADEA RIGHTS

[A]   Requirements for Valid Waiver

It makes sense for employers to make it part of the severance process to request that terminating employees sign a waiver of their rights to bring suit for discrimination allegedly occurring in the course of the employment relationship. However, in order to be valid and enforceable, a waiver of ADEA rights must be strictly tailored to satisfy the requirements of the Older Workers Benefits Protection Act, a 1990 statute that has been enacted as 29 U.S.C. § 626(f)(1). Furthermore, waivers do not prevent the EEOC from carrying out an age discrimination investigation or bringing suit against the employer. It is unlawful for ADEA waivers to prohibit employees from filing charges with the EEOC or participating in EEOC investigations.

A waiver is not valid if it is not "knowing and voluntary" on the part of the employee. No one can surrender legal rights without receiving full disclosure of the implications of the document he or she signs. The ADEA provides a definition of what is required before a waiver will be considered knowing and voluntary:

- The agreement that contains the waiver must be written in understandable terms;
- The waiver specifically mentions ADEA rights or claims;
- Only claims that have already arisen are waived—not claims that might arise in the future;
- The employee receives something in return for the waiver; it is not enough that the employee receives severance or other benefits that would be provided even if there had been no waiver;
- The document includes a written warning that the employee should consult a lawyer before signing the agreement;
- The employee gets at least 21 days to think over the employer's severance offer. If the agreement is offered to an entire group (e.g., in connection with a layoff or incentives for voluntary departure) then the offer must remain open for at least 45 days;

- When incentives are offered to a group, everyone in the group must get an understandable notification of the features of the program: who can participate; eligibility factors; time limits; and the ages and job titles of everyone eligible or chosen for the program, vis-à-vis the ages of workers in the organizational unit or job classification who were not eligible or selected. (This was included in the law to make it easier for potential plaintiffs to decide if age was an improper factor in selecting employees for the program.)

Waivers are also used when charges have been filed, and then the employer and employee agree on a settlement. In this case, the waiver is only considered knowing and voluntary if all the rules noted above have been observed, and the employee has been given a reasonable time to consider the offer.

Getting a waiver does not provide complete protection for the employer. Sometimes the employee will go to court and sue anyway, claiming that the lawsuit is permissible because the waiver was defective in some way. Section 626(f)(3) provides that it is up to the employer to prove that the waiver satisfied the various requirements and therefore was knowing and voluntary. The employee is not required to prove that the waiver was invalid.

The EEOC's response to widespread layoffs in 2001 was that waivers from laid-off employees can offer an affirmative defense—but that the employer must be ready to prove the validity of the waivers. [Darryl Van Duch, *New EEOC Rule Targets 'Won't Sue' Severance Pledges,* National Law Journal, (March 5, 2001) (law.com)] A little later, Ida L. Castro (who was then the Chair of the EEOC) said "unlawful waivers that strip older workers of their rights under the ADEA will be pursued by the EEOC to the fullest extent of the law." [*See EEOC Scores Victory in Age Bias Suit Against Major Information Technology Company,* <http://eeoc. gov/press/6-12-01.html>]

[B] EEOC Rules

The EEOC's rule on waivers, effective July 6, 1998, can be found at 29 C.F.R. § 1625.22. A valid ADEA waiver must:

- Be embodied in a written document that contains the entire agreement (the agreement cannot be written but supplemented by oral discussion);
- Be written in plain English, appropriate to the signer's educational level;
- Information about exit incentives must also be understandable;
- Be honest and accurate, not misleading;
- Specify that it relates to ADEA claims;
- Advise the employee to consult an attorney before signing.

In general, waivers can release existing claims but not those that might arise in the future. However, the Final Rule allows an otherwise valid waiver to include the signer's agreement to retire, or otherwise terminate employment at a specified future date.

For the waiver to be valid, the signer must receive consideration specific to the waiver, which he or she would not receive otherwise. Therefore, normal severance pay is not adequate to support a waiver. Nor does it constitute valuable consideration if the employer restores a benefit that was wrongfully terminated in the past. However, the Final Rule says that it is not necessary to give greater consideration to over-40 employees who sign waivers than to under-40 employees, even though the older employees waive an additional range of claims (those arising under the ADEA).

Despite the existence of waivers, a certain number of employees will nevertheless bring age discrimination claims against the employer, claiming that the waivers were invalid and therefore did not constitute a knowing and voluntary waiver of the right to sue.

The Supreme Court's decision in *Oubre v. Entergy Operations Inc.* [522 U.S. 422 (1988)] says that such a person can bring suit under the ADEA even without tendering back (returning) the severance pay received under the agreement that included the allegedly invalid waiver. The rationale is that the defective waiver does not qualify for ratification by the ex-employee, so it is not necessary to return the consideration to avoid ratification.

The EEOC published Final Regulations to implement *Oubre.* [*See* 29 C.F.R. Part 1625 as amended by 65 Fed. Reg. 77438 (Dec. 11, 2000), effective January 1, 2001] The EEOC's position is that the existence of a valid waiver is an affirmative defense for the employer. That means that the employer has the burden of proving the validity, but the employee can produce evidence that the waiver was not knowing and voluntary. The EEOC analyzes covenants not to sue in the same way as waivers, and in fact believes they may be even more damaging to employee rights because employees might be deterred from bringing suit with respect to wrongdoing occurring after the covenant was signed.

According to the agency, ordinary contract principles about ratification and tender-back do not apply to employment waivers, because ex-employees might not be able to afford to give back the consideration even if they have a valid claim against the former employer.

Tender-back is not required even if the waiver seems to be lawful, and even if the employee does not allege fraud or duress. Once the case is resolved, the trial court may have to determine the employer's entitlement to restitution, recoupment or sell-off. However, the employer can only recover the amount of consideration paid for the waiver, or the amount the plaintiff is awarded for winning the case— whichever is lower. Employees who file suit in bad faith can also be required to pay the employers' attorneys' fees.

[C]   Case Law on ADEA Waivers

Note that, although the OWBPA requires employers to give employees 21 days to consider an early retirement offer, the employer retains the power to withdraw the offer; it does not become irrevocable for the 21-day period. [*Ellison v. Premier Salons Int'l Inc.,* 164 F.3d 111 (8th Cir. 1999)]

As a result of *Wright v. Universal Maritime Service Corp.,* [525 U.S. 70 (1998)] a general arbitration clause in a collective bargaining agreement will not preclude litigation of claims under the ADEA or other federal antidiscrimination statutes. Only a detailed clause that specifically refers to a particular antidiscrimination statute can prevent employees from litigating such claims if they prefer not to arbitrate them.

The most important issue is OWBPA compliance, which in turn depends on the terms of the waiver and the circumstances of its signing. The Seventh Circuit enforced a clear, unambiguous waiver signed by a lawyer (of all people!) who worked for a corporation. Presumably, he was able to understand the document. Even though he believed he was forced into a choice between resigning and being terminated on account of age, he was still bound by the waiver he signed. [*Lloyd v. Brunswick Corp.,* 180 F.3d 893 (7th Cir. 1999)] In another case, however, given the possibility that the company used fraud to induce employees to sign waivers, the Tenth Circuit refused to give effect to the waivers. [*Bennett v. Coors Brewing Co.,* 189 F.3d 1221 (10th Cir. 1999)]

A worker's signature on a release of lawsuits against the former employer was held by the Third Circuit to be a valid waiver of rights, even though it also waives the right to bring EEOC charges. It's true that the ADEA protects the right to bring EEOC charges, but the Third Circuit did not accept the agency's argument that including this invalid provision in a release makes the whole release invalid. As long as the release was entered into knowingly and is otherwise valid, the invalid provision will be severed and the rest will be enforced. [*Wastak v. Lehigh Valley Health Network,* 342 F.3d 281 (3rd Cir. 2003)]

The Tenth Circuit reads the OWBPA to require an employer who seeks releases from laid-off employees to explain not only who has been selected for layoff but why those selections were made. Thus, the Tenth Circuit found the release in the case at bar invalid because it failed to give employees sufficiently personalized notice about why they were selected for layoff. The ex-employees could therefore proceed with ADEA claims despite the release because the OWBPA requires a release to disclose eligibility factors so employees can decide whether they have viable employment discrimination claims. [*Kruchowski v. Weyerhaeuser,* 423 F.3d 1139 (10th Cir. 2005), discussed in Nancy N. Delogu and Gary D. Shapiro, *I Don't Know Why They Picked Me: 10th Circuit Broadens Requirements for Waiving Age Discrimination Claims,* <http://www.littler.com> (Sept. 2005)]

CHAPTER 38

THE FAMILY AND MEDICAL LEAVE ACT (FMLA)

§38.01 INTRODUCTION

The Family and Medical Leave Act (FMLA) was enacted on February 3, 1993, as 29 U.S.C. §2601–2654. Congress stated an intention to aid families in which both parents, or the single parent, work outside the home, and to minimize sex discrimination by making leave available in a gender-neutral manner.

The FMLA focuses on two subjects: health care (whether for the employee's own serious health condition or for a family member for whom the employee is a caregiver) and parenting a newborn or newly adopted child. 29 U.S.C. §2601(a)(2) says that "it is important for the development of children and the family unit that fathers and mothers be able to participate in early childrearing and the care of family members who have serious health conditions."

Under appropriate circumstances, qualifying employees can take up to 12 weeks of leave a year, whether the leave is taken all at once, in several blocks, or intermittently in small units. FMLA leave can be important for preserving the job (and benefits) of someone who has used up all of his or her sick days and is too sick to maintain a normal work schedule, but not sick enough to obtain disability benefits or file for disability retirement.

Employers have the option of providing paid leave under these circumstances, but it does not violate the federal statute for the employer to provide only unpaid FMLA leave. [*See* §38.06[G] for state-law developments]

Tip: Providing unpaid leave to an employee who is exempt from the Fair Labor Standards overtime requirements does not convert the employee from exempt to nonexempt. [29 U.S.C. §2612(c)]

Leave can be taken, under 29 U.S.C. §2612, for a total of 12 weeks in any 12-month period (not necessarily a calendar year), when the employee has or adopts or fosters a child (but this leave can only be taken during the first year after the child's birth or after the adoption or foster care placement) or for a serious health condition suffered by the employee or his or her spouse, parent, or child. If the employee is the sick person, the serious health condition must prevent the employee from performing the functions of the job.

The employer must give employees at least 60 days' notice of changes in the method of calculating the leave year. [29 C.F.R. §825.200(d)] The 12-week limit applies per year, not per illness. Therefore, an employee who uses up the allowance is not entitled to additional leave based on events later in the same leave year.

As defined by 29 U.S.C. §2611(9), a reduced leave schedule is a partial leave under which the employee does work, but for less than the usual number of hours per workday or workweek.

It is unlawful for employers to interfere with employees' exercise of FMLA right or to discriminate or retaliate against them for exercising such rights, charging the employer with FMLA violations, or participating in an investigation. [29 U.S.C. § 2615]

In the Ninth Circuit's view, it was an interference with FMLA rights for a supervisor to try to reduce the time off an employee needed after maternity leave to recover from childbirth and bond with her baby. Under 29 C.F.R. § 825.220, discouraging use of leave—for instance, by discouraging continuation of leave or imposing conditions that prevent use of the full 12-week entitlement—is a violation of the FMLA. Inappropriately characterizing FMLA leave as personal leave also interfered with the plaintiff's FMLA rights because it created the impression that the availability of FMLA leave was entirely within her supervisor's discretion. [*Liu v. Amway Corp.,* 347 F.3d 1125 (9th Cir. 2003)]

It is a violation of federal labor law to fire a worker who tried to get family leave when his pregnant wife was hospitalized. Even though this particular employee was not eligible for FMLA leave (he hadn't worked there long enough), talking to a manager and a co-worker about federal and state leave provisions is concerted activity protected by the National Labor Relations Act. Although the employer claimed a legitimate reason for the termination (three minor incidents during training six months earlier), the NLRB was not persuaded—the employee was not disciplined for those infractions at the time. The agency ordered his reinstatement, with back pay. [*Phillips Petroleum Co.,* 339 N.L.R.B. No. 111 (July 31, 2003)]

The FMLA does not modify federal or state antidiscrimination laws. [*See* 29 U.S.C. § 2651(a)] Employers always have a legal right to set up their own policies that are *more* generous than the FMLA: § 2653, and the federal statute does not preempt state and local laws that require employees to offer even more leave than the FMLA does. [29 U.S.C. § 2651(b)] In mid-2005, the DOL issued an opinion that says that state family leave laws are not preempted by the FMLA if they offer more generous benefits than the federal law. The opinion was requested specifically in connection with the Washington State Family Care Act. The Washington law allows employees to substitute paid sick leave for unpaid FMLA leave whether or not the employee or family member has a "serious health condition," whereas the federal law requires a serious health condition for the substitution. In general ERISA preempts state laws about employee benefits, but there is an exception where preemption would impair the enforcement of a federal law. The DOL concluded that allowing ERISA to preempt the Washington State law would interfere with Congress' intention that the FMLA provide a minimum level of protection, not an upper limit on leave rights. [DOL Advisory Opinion 2005-13A, <http://www.dol.gov/ebsa/regs/aos/ao2005-13a.html> (May 31, 2005)]

Employers do not have the power to draft their benefit plans or programs to limit FMLA rights, nor can a Collective Bargaining Agreement be used to cut back FMLA rights. [*See* 29 U.S.C. § 2652(b)]

The DOL's interpretation is that it violates the FMLA to deny awards or bonuses for perfect attendance to employees who take FMLA leave but have no other absences. However, the DOL permits productivity awards, and presumably workers who do not take FMLA leave are present on more days and therefore more productive. [*See* Kathryn Tyler, *All Present and Accounted For?* HR Magazine, Oct. 2001, at p. 101] According to the Northern District of Illinois, it violates the FMLA to deny a "stay bonus" of 50% of the base salary paid to those who remained with the employer through its transition to a new owner, to an employee who took 12 weeks of adoption leave. The court treated the program as the equivalent of an attendance bonus, which cannot be denied because of FMLA leave. [29 C.F.R. § 825.215(c)(2); *Dierlam v. Wesley Jessen Corp.,* 71 L.W. 1211 (N.D. Ill. Sept. 23, 2002)]

Tip: In a case in which the employer moves to dismiss an FMLA suit on the grounds that the plaintiff is not an eligible employee, the court should use Federal Rules of Civil Procedure Rule 56 to review the motion, and not Rule 12(b)(1)—Rule 56 is more favorable to plaintiffs, so it may be impossible to have the case dismissed at that stage; a full trial may be required. [*Morrison v. Amway Corp.,* 323 F.3d 920 (11th Cir. 2003)]

FMLA Title I covers private employment. The statute also has a Title II, covering federal employees. However, there is no private right of action under FMLA Title II, and the federal government never expressly waived sovereign immunity. [*Russell v. Department of the Army,* 191 F.3d 1016 (9th Cir. 1999)] Although the Supreme Court has ruled that Congress exceeded its power when it made state government employers subject to the ADA and ADEA, the Supreme Court reached the opposite conclusion with respect to the FMLA, finding that Congress validly abrogated state sovereign immunity when it comes to family leave. [*Nevada Dep't of Human Resources v. Hibbs,* 538 U.S. 721 (2003)] A few months later, however, the Tenth Circuit dismissed a state employee's claim, ruling that state employers can only be sued in connection with leave taken to care for a family member, not leave that an employee uses when he or she has a serious illness. [*Brockman v. Wyoming Dep't of Family Services,* 342 F.3d 1159 (10th Cir. 2003)]

The Sixth Circuit held that sovereign immunity bars a suit by an employee who sought FMLA leave when she had a serious health condition that prevented her from doing her job. The Supreme Court's 2003 *Hibbs* decision upholds the abrogation of sovereign immunity for the FMLA claims of employees caring for sick family members; however, the Sixth Circuit held that the Supreme Court's rationale was that women are much more likely to be caregivers than men, so abrogation was needed to prevent sex discrimination. The Sixth Circuit refused to abrogate sovereign immunity for employees' own illnesses, because there was no evidence of a history of discrimination against sick employees. [*Touvell v. Ohio Dep't of Mental Retardation & Developmental Disabilities,* 422 F.3d 392 (6th Cir. 2005)]

An advocacy organization noted that although in 78% of families both parents have jobs, the FMLA covers only about 60% of U.S. workers, and many of the workers entitled to leave cannot afford to take it. The study cites a survey showing only 12% of employers provided paid maternity leave and only 7% paid paternity leave. About 40% of low-income working parents do not have any paid leave (including sick days or vacation days) that can be used for child care needs. The report rates California as the best state in the nation for providing benefits for new parents, with Hawaii, Oregon, and the District of Columbia ranking next. Nineteen states, including Alabama, Idaho, Missouri, Pennsylvania, and Texas, got an "F" on the report card for lacking any benefit programs for new parents. The organization recommends paid parental leave for parents of newborns or newly adopted children; paid leave for prenatal bed rest; allowing employees to use their sick days to care for a sick family member; and job protection for parents broader than the federal FMLA requirements. [Jodi Grant, Taylor Hatcher, and Nirali Patel (National Partnership for Women and Families), *Expecting Better: A State-by-State Analysis of Parental Leave Programs,* <http://www.nationalpartnership.org/portals/p3/library/PaidLeave/ParentalLeaveReportMay05.pdf> (May 2005)]

The Employment Policy Foundation (EPF) conducted a survey in 2004, looking at the FMLA from the employer's perspective. EPF's research showed that an average of 14.5% of employees took FMLA leave, although telecommunications, manufacturing, and health care workers were much more likely to take leave than workers in other industries. EPF's figures showed a much higher rate of FMLA leave utilization than the DOL found in 2005. According to EPF, 35% of employees who took FMLA leave did so more than once, and close to 15% of the FMLA leave was taken by employees who were absent on leave six or more times a year. The EPF found that usage of FMLA intermittent leave was very common— 20% of leave was for one day or less, 30% for less than five days.

The EPF said that employers can find it difficult to track intermittent leave, which can also cause scheduling problems for the employer (especially because they found that in almost 50% of cases, employees did not provide notice before the day leave began, and in 11% more cases, employees gave notice when leave began or right afterward). Overall, EPF found that 27% of FMLA leave was taken for chronic conditions, although this too varied by industry—transportation and telecommunications workers took the most intermittent leave. The average length of all FMLA leave was 10.1 days, but telecommunications and utilities workers tended to take much shorter leaves than health care, financial services, or transportation workers. EPF estimated that in 2004, employers lost $4.8 billion in productivity through FMLA leaves, 0.6% of before-tax profits, with a further $10.3 billion spent on replacement workers to cover for employees on FMLA leave. Continuing health benefits for employees on FMLA leave cost another $5.9 billion, or close to 2% of all health care expenses. [Janemarie Mulvey (Employment Policy Foundation), *The Cost and Characteristics of Family and Medical Leave,* <http://www.epf.org/pubs/newsletters/2005/pb20050419.pdf> (Apr. 19, 2005)]

§38.02   FMLA ELIGIBILITY ISSUES

Like most federal employment discrimination laws, the FMLA exempts very small employers. The FMLA applies only to employers engaged in interstate commerce or activities affecting commerce (but most employers fit into this category)—and only if, in the current year or the previous calendar year, there were at least 50 employees on each workday of 20 or more work weeks. Furthermore, the FMLA does not apply when there are fewer than 50 people at that worksite and the total number of employees at all of the employer's sites within a 75-mile radius is less than 50. Anyone who acts on behalf of the employer, whether directly or indirectly, also counts as an employer. So does the successor in interest of a past employer. [29 U.S.C. §2611(4)]

A group of automobile service companies that shared a majority shareholder lacked common management and therefore could not be treated as a single integrated employer, even though they had some interrelated operations. Therefore, an FMLA claim had to be dismissed because the particular unit where the plaintiff worked had fewer than 50 employees and aggregation with the other units was denied. [*Hukill v. Auto Care Inc.*, 192 F.3d 437 (4th Cir. 1999)]

The defendant in a Tenth Circuit case provides outsourced housekeeping and laundry services in long-term care facilities. The company has about 17,000 employees and 1,300 clients in 42 states. The plaintiff worked in Colorado, more than 75 miles from the district and regional headquarters. The district court found for the plaintiff, defining the worksite as the defendant's regional office; the defendant had more than 50 employees within a 75-mile radius of that location. However, the Tenth Circuit reversed and remanded, finding the relevant regulations (825.111(a)(3)) invalid as applied to an employee with a fixed place of work. The Tenth Circuit found that deference was not required because it violated the normal meaning of the term "worksite" and thus was arbitrary, capricious, and manifestly counter to the FMLA's statutory intent. In the Tenth Circuit reading, the intent of the regulation is to determine whether the employer will have difficulty in finding a temporary replacement for a worker on leave; there were very few fellow-employees within the 75-mile radius of the nursing home where the plaintiff worked. [*Harbert v. Healthcare Services Group Inc.*, 391 F.3d 1140 (10th Cir. 2004). The case also says that, in the case of an employee of a temporary help agency, the "worksite" is the agency's office and not the various places where the worker is sent on assignments]

A contract service worker was terminated after taking leave to care for her sick father. She sued Air France and the ground handling company that provided outsourced services to Air France. Air France was not covered by the FMLA because it had fewer than 50 employees, so the question became whether Air France was liable as a "joint employer." [*See* 29 C.F.R. §825.106] If a company is a joint employer, the employees are counted toward coverage of both employers, no matter which company issues the paychecks.

The Ninth Circuit couldn't find any relevant FMLA joint-employment cases, so it looked at FLSA cases and decided that Air France did not have enough control to be a joint employer. Air France didn't hire or fire employees of the ground handling company; didn't set their pay or work schedules, and the service company used significant amounts of its own capital and equipment to provide the services.

Another factor was that the plaintiff was an at-will employee. Possibly the plaintiff would have been able to claim that there was an implied contract—but the employee handbook warned that insubordination and unexcused absences were cause for termination without progressive discipline, which would rule out a breach of contract claim. [*Moreau v. Air France,* 343 F.3d 1179 (9th Cir. 2003)]

A 2004 opinion letter issued by the DOL's Wage and Hour Division states that whether day laborers referred by an agency count toward the 50-employee minimum depends on factors such as the existence of an ongoing business relationship between employer and agency. The Wage and Hour Division holds that joint employment is usually present when an agency supplies employees; if there is joint employment, each worker counts toward the 50-employee minimum for both employers, even if the worker is on only one payroll. Both routine temporaries supplied by an employment agency and day laborers used from time to time will count toward the 50-worker limit if the relevant factors are present. [DOL Wage and Hour Div. opinion letter (Apr. 5, 2004, released July 26, 2004); *see* 73 LW 2077]

Even after it is established that an employer is covered, not all employees are entitled to take FMLA leave. Comparatively veteran employees have FMLA rights, but new hires do not. Eligibility is limited to an employee who not only has worked for the employer for at least 12 months, but put in at least 1,250 hours for that employer in the preceding year. [*See* 29 U.S.C. § 2611(2)(A)]

Vacation days, personal days, sick days, suspensions, and holidays do not count toward the required 1,250 hours. [*Clark v. Allegheny Univ. Hosp.,* 1998 WL 94803 (E.D. Pa. 1998)] The 1,250 hours are counted back from the time the employee went on FMLA leave, not from the time the employer fired the employee or took other adverse action. Therefore, a plaintiff who took three leaves that she claimed satisfied FMLA requirements, and therefore did not work 1,250 hours during the year before her discharge, was still entitled to bring an FMLA suit. [*Butler v. Owens-Brockway Plastic Prods. Inc.,* 199 F.3d 314 (6th Cir. 1999)]

A teacher in her first year of employment, who told her principal that she was pregnant and planned to take FMLA leave, did not have a valid claim against the school board when her contract was not renewed. She would not have been eligible for FMLA leave at the time she wanted her leave to start (because she had not worked for 12 months and 1,250 hours). Thus, there was no protected right which she could have suffered retaliation for attempting to exercise. [*Walker v. Elmore County Bd. of Ed.*, 379 F.3d 1249 (11th Cir. 2004)]

In 2002, the First Circuit ruled that six months of back pay granted to a plaintiff who successfully grieved the discharge did not count toward the 1,250 hour requirement, because it did not represent hours actually worked. But in mid-2004, the Sixth Circuit disagreed, ruling that when an employee is unlawfully terminated, the remedies can include credit toward FMLA eligibility. The Sixth Circuit's rationale was that unlawful termination deprives the employee of the opportunity to work, and that employers should not be rewarded for unlawful conduct by being permitted to interfere with FMLA rights after the reinstatement of an unjustly terminated person. [*Compare Riccio v. Potter*, 377 F.3d 599 (6th Cir. 2004), with *Plumley v. Southern Container Inc.*, 303 F.3d 364 (1st Cir. 2002)]

Even if an employer's own policies are more generous than the FMLA, FMLA leave is not available to persons who have worked for the employer for less than 12 months. DOL regulations require employers to live up to their own policies—but only with respect to extended periods of leave, not basic eligibility. [*Dolese v. Office Depot Inc.*, 231 F.3d 202 (5th Cir. 2000)]

In *Ragsdale v. Wolverine Worldwide*, [535 U.S. 81 (2002)] the Supreme Court ruled that the DOL regulation [29 C.F.R. § 825.700(a)] is invalid to the extent that it requires employers to disclose the relationship between FMLA leave and the employer's own leave policies.

§ 38.03   WHEN LEAVE IS AVAILABLE

An eligible employee can take FMLA leave for his or her own serious health condition or the serious health condition of an eligible family member.

The statute itself defines "serious health condition" as an "illness, injury, impairment, or physical or mental condition" that requires either inpatient care (in a hospital, nursing home or hospice) or at least continuing treatment by a health care provider. [29 U.S.C. §§ 2611(6) and (11)]

According to 29 C.F.R. § 825.114(c), the flu is ordinarily not a serious illness unless complications ensue. According to the Fourth Circuit, the flu was a serious health condition where the employee was incapacitated for a period of time, and needed three visits to the doctor. [*Miller v. AT&T Corp.*, 250 F.3d 820 (4th Cir. 2001)]

The Eighth Circuit found that a serious health condition justifying FMLA leave was present where the employee was off work for a week with what a nurse practitioner diagnosed as a viral infection, and there was continuing treatment (two visits). [*Rankin v. Seagate Techs. Inc.*, 246 F.3d 1145 (8th Cir. 2001)]

A UPS driver fired for poor attendance did not prevail on his FMLA claim. [*Haefling v. UPS*, 169 F.3d 494 (7th Cir. 1999)] Although he saw a doctor and got physical therapy for a neck injury, he did not prove that he had a period of incapacity lasting at least three days, or even that medical treatment was really necessary. Therefore, he did not prove that he had suffered a serious medical condition.

Qualifying family members are spouse (husband or wife only—not cohabitant), child (including adopted or foster child) who is either under 18 years old or mentally or physically disabled, or parent (biological parent or someone who played a parental role—but NOT a mother- or father-in-law, even though many individuals become caregivers for their in-laws). [*See* 29 U.S.C. §§ 2611(7) and (12)]

In a Southern District of Indiana case, the court decided that the plaintiff's daughter, who had a Caesarean delivery, had a serious health condition for FMLA purposes, and therefore her mother should have been given leave to take care of her. However, the court accepted the employer's argument that the plaintiff was fired because of her long-standing pattern of absenteeism, not because she exercised her FMLA rights. [*Blackburn v. Potter,* 2003 U.S. Dist. LEXIS 5269 (S.D. Ind. Mar. 31, 2003)] The Eleventh Circuit held that it was permissible to fire an employee who was out of work for four weeks (after being given two weeks' leave) to assist her daughter, who was having a baby. The leave request did not mention either the FMLA or pregnancy complications. Pregnancy in and of itself is not a serious health condition, so a valid FMLA request must assert the need for a caregiver as a result of complications. [*Cruz v. Publix Super Markets Inc.*, 428 F.3d 1379 (11th Cir. 2005). *See also Mauder v. Metropolitan Transit Auth.*, 446 F.3d 574 (5th Cir. 2006): termination of an employee who was already on a corrective action plan was not retaliation for his tardy request of FMLA leave; type II diabetes and medication side effects causing uncontrollable diarrhea was not a "serious health condition," and the employee did not provide timely or adequate medical information about the reason for his frequent absences from his desk] As a general rule, pregnancy will not be considered a serious medical condition, but in this case there were complications requiring major surgery and hence a serious medical condition was present. [*Aubuchon v. Knauf Fiberglas, GMBH,* 240 F. Supp. 2d 859 (S.D. Ind. 2003)]

The Western District of Wisconsin ruled that an employee can get FMLA leave for treatment of acute physical symptoms caused by substance abuse. [*Domnick v. Ver Halen Inc.,* 71 L.W. 1597 (W.D. Wis. Mar. 10, 2003); *but see* 29 C.F.R. § 824-114(d)—being too intoxicated to come to work is not grounds for FMLA leave]

Late in 2003, the Eleventh Circuit grappled with the question of whether a "day of incapacity" can be counted toward the "more than three consecutive calendar days of incapacity" (§ 825.114) if the employee is incapacitated for less than the entire day. The court concluded that the employee must be incapacitated for the whole day for the day to count. A partial day can be counted at the beginning or end of the period, to show that "more than" three days were involved, but there must be at least three full days within the period. [*Russell v. North Broward Hospital,* 346 F.3d 1335 (11th Cir. 2003)]

An employee who had one treatment for back pain while he was on sick leave was not covered by the FMLA because he did not have a "serious health condition," which requires multiple treatments or a continuing series of treatments. Another treatment post-leave did not add up to an ongoing treatment regimen. [*Jones v. Denver Public Sch.*, 427 F.3d 1315 (10th Cir. 2005)]

The EEOC's Interpretive Guidelines on defining ADA disability cannot be used to decide whether an employee's adult child is disabled in the context of deciding whether the employee is entitled to FMLA leave to care for the son or daughter. [*Navarro v. Pfizer Corp.*, 261 F.3d 90 (1st Cir. 2001)]

> **Tip:** If both spouses work for different employers, each one is entitled to 12 weeks of leave when a child is born or adopted, but if they work for the same employer, the employer can legally require them to split a single 12-week leave period, or to share the 12 weeks when they are caring for the same sick parent. [*See* 29 U.S.C. § 2612(f)]

§ 38.04   THE EMPLOYER'S OBLIGATION

[A]   Benefits

The employer must reinstate the employee after leave, and must maintain all employee benefits during leave. [*See* 29 U.S.C. § 2615(c) for health coverage requirements] However, the employee does not accrue seniority or additional benefits. FMLA leave is not considered a break in service when pension eligibility is determined.

"Benefits" means all of the employer's benefits (not just those offered under ERISA plans), e.g., "group life insurance, health insurance, disability insurance, sick leave, annual leave, educational benefits, and pensions." [29 U.S.C. § 2611(5)]

DOL Opinion Letters issued in 2006 require employers who have cafeteria plans to maintain the same level of coverage when employees are on FMLA leave. The employee must not be required to pay more for coverage than if he or she had not taken leave. When employees return to work post-leave, the employer cannot recover payments for the group health coverage. Ongoing contributions to multi-employer plans must also continue while the employee is on FMLA leave. [DOL Op. Letters 2006-2 (Jan. 20, 2006), 2006-3-A (Jan. 31, 2006), <http://dol.gov/esa/whd/opinion/flsa.htm> (no www); *see* Fred Schneyer, *DoL: Health Payments Must Be Maintained for Workers on FMLA Leave*, PlanSponsor.com (Mar. 3, 2006)]

An Omaha police officer sued, charging that he was improperly denied bonus annual leave subsequent to his FMLA leave. Police officers like the plaintiff are given two hours of additional leave for every pay period in years in which they take less than 40 hours of sick leave in a year and their sick leave accrual is 1,000 hours or more. The plaintiff did have 1,000 hours of accrued sick leave, but took three weeks of medical leave and substituted accrued sick leave (paid leave) for unpaid FMLA leave. The employer denied him the annual leave bonus because he took more than 40 hours of paid sick leave. The plaintiff claimed that denying him the bonus was tantamount to refusing to return him to an equivalent position with equivalent benefits, as required by 29 U.S.C. § 2614(a)(1)(B) and its regulations, especially 29 C.F.R. § 825.215(c)(2), which requires employees to have access to bonuses, including attendance bonuses, when they return to work after leave. The

Eighth Circuit ruled for the employer, construing bonuses as benefits rather than pay, and pointing out that the FMLA does not require accrual of benefits during the period of FMLA leave. His employer permitted him to take either paid sick leave or paid annual leave running concurrently with his FMLA leave. He could have chosen annual leave rather than sick leave, in which case he still would have qualified for the bonus; he forfeited the bonus by choosing sick leave. [*Chubb v. City of Omaha,* 424 F.3d 831 (8th Cir. 2005)]

When employees are on FMLA leave, the EGHP must maintain their coverage at the original level. If employees are required to pay part of the EGHP premium under normal circumstances, the plan can require them to continue contributing during FMLA leave. Furthermore, if the employee is more than 30 days late paying the premium, health insurance coverage can legitimately be terminated. If coverage is terminated in this manner, but the employee returns to work and is reinstated, then he or she is entitled to immediate reinstatement in the EGHP, with no need to satisfy plan requirements a second time.

If the employee quits instead of returning from leave, the employer is entitled to recover the health premiums expended on the employee's behalf during the leave period. But if the employee files a health claim for treatment during the leave period, a claim that would otherwise be allowable cannot be denied because the employee later terminates employment.

An employee was given time off to treat a kidney stone. The employee didn't request FMLA leave, and the employer didn't raise the possibility when leave was granted. Once the employee had been on leave for a month, he contacted the employer to arrange for payment of his health insurance premiums. He signed a payroll authorization form allowing the next month's premium to be deducted from his paycheck, but he did not make a direct payment.

When his leave expired, he resigned his job. He asked about paying the health insurance premium and was told he had 30 days to make the payment. Two weeks later, the employer canceled his health coverage without notice, retroactive to the beginning of the leave—a fact that the employee discovered only after health care providers called to say that his claims had been rejected. The Eastern District of Michigan held that the employer violated the FMLA in several respects: first, by requiring the plaintiff to pay the entire health premium while he was on leave, not the part paid by active employees; second, by failing to disclose even this improper rule; and third, by canceling the coverage retroactively without notice. Although in appropriate circumstances the employer will be able to recoup premiums laid out for employees who fail to return from FMLA leave, that does not alter the obligation to provide health coverage—particularly where, as here, the ex-employee showed a clear intention to retain coverage. [*Tornberg v. Business Interlink Servs., Inc.,* 237 F. Supp. 2d 778 (E.D. Mich. 2002)]

Early in 2003, the D.C. Circuit held that an employee has a cause of action (under the Privacy Act and the Rehab Act) against the employer for improper disclosure to co-workers of information from the employee's FMLA medical certification. (In this case, the plaintiff was an HIV-positive postal worker who claims that his status became common knowledge after he returned from FMLA leave.) [*Doe v. U.S. Postal Serv.,* 317 F.3d 339 (D.C. Cir. 2003)]

[B] Reinstatement

Section 2614 takes up the subject of reinstatement in more detail. It provides that an employee who returns from leave not only must not lose any benefits because of taking leave, but must be reinstated either in the old job or an equivalent new one. The second job is equivalent to the first if it provides equivalent terms and conditions of employment (benefits, pay, etc.)

The FMLA creates an exception for employees earning in the top 10% of the employer's workforce. It is not necessary to reinstate them after leave if reinstatement would cause "substantial and grievous economic injury" to the employer, and the employer promptly notifies the employee that reinstatement will be denied.

However, taking FMLA leave does not entitle any employee to anything he or she would not have been entitled to by remaining at work without taking leave, and seniority and employment benefits do not have to accrue during the leave.

If the employee never does return from leave (for instance, the mother of a newborn decides to stay at home with the baby), the employer is entitled to recoup health insurance premiums paid during the leave, as long as the failure to return is not caused by ill health or other factors beyond the control of the employee.

When an employee has been pronounced fit for work by his or her doctor and returns to work, the employer can require another medical examination only if the employee's behavior justifies an inference of ongoing limitations that interfere with the ability to work. [*Albert v. Runyon,* 6 F. Supp. 2d 57 (D. Mass. 1998)] According to *Underhill v. Willamina Lumber Co.,* [1999 WL 421596 (D. Or. June 17, 1999)] the employer's duty is to reinstate the worker; if there is a reasonable doubt about ability to return to work, the employer can then ask for an independent examination of fitness for duty. It is not acceptable to delay reinstatement until the examination has been completed to the satisfaction of the employer.

An employee who returns from FMLA leave and is ready to work is entitled, in the Sixth Circuit view, to immediate reinstatement, not reinstatement a month later. The statute does not provide the employer with additional time to adjust to the employee's return. Therefore, insisting that an employee take a longer leave than the employee could certify to be medically necessary could be treated as interference with FMLA rights. [*Hoge v. Honda of America Mfg. Inc.,* 384 F.3d 238 (6th Cir. 2004)]

In the First Circuit view, there is no duty of reasonable accommodation under the FMLA—so it is not unlawful to fire an employee who is on medical leave. Anyone who is on FMLA leave can be laid off during a RIF, if he or she would have been laid off anyway. [*O'Connor v. PLA Family Health Plan Inc.,* 200 F.3d 1349 (11th Cir. 2000)]

Heady v. U.S. Enrichment Corp., 146 Fed. Appx. 766 (6th Cir. 2005) also permits the termination of an employee who used extensive FMLA leave as part of a RIF. The plaintiff in this case was the lowest-rated of three office managers, and the employer wanted to eliminate one position. The Sixth Circuit held that the plaintiff made a prima facie case of retaliation, but the employer satisfied its burden of proving a legitimate, non-discriminatory reason for terminating her.

If a person's work performance is bad enough to justify termination anyway, it does not violate the FMLA to terminate that person while he or she is on FMLA leave. [*Hubbard v. Blue Cross/Blue Shield Ass'n*, 1 F. Supp. 2d 867 (N.D. Ill. 1998)] Nor is it a violation of the FMLA (or the PDA) to demote an employee after her return from maternity leave, if the demotion was caused by performance problems and the employee was treated no worse than male or female employees who did not do well at work but who were not pregnant. [*Armstrong v. Systems Unlimited, Inc.*, 2003 U.S. Dist. LEXIS 18485 (8th Cir. Sept. 8, 2003)]

The Sixth Circuit has ruled that it does not violate the FMLA to fire an employee after his return from leave, if during the leave he engaged in unauthorized employment contrary to the terms of the employee handbook. (The employee said that he needed to take leave to care for his wife and newborn child and to help manage his wife's restaurant.) There was no violation, because the employee was discharged for violating the employer's work rules, not for taking FMLA leave. [*Pharakhone v. Nissan N. Am. Inc.*, 324 F.3d 405 (6th Cir. 2003)]

When there is no reason to believe that the individual will be able to return to work and perform the essential functions of the job within the 12-week leave period, the individual is not protected by the FMLA. [*Reynolds v. Phillips & Temro Indus. Inc.*, 195 F.3d 411 (8th Cir. 1999)] Here, the plaintiff applied for no-fault insurance economic loss benefits, which included a doctor's certification of continuing disability that would preclude his return to his normal occupation.

After returning from leave, an employee suffering from multiple sclerosis was able to work only a four-day week. Instead of reinstating her to her old job as purchasing agent, the employer placed her as a payroll clerk until her intermittent leave allowance was used up. She was told she would be placed on unpaid leave until a suitable job opened up. The plaintiff quit and sued, claiming that the FMLA entitled her to reinstatement in her former position. But the court in *Covey v. Methodist Hospital of Dyersburg* [56 F. Supp. 2d 965 (W.D. Tenn. 1999)] disagreed. The court read 29 C.F.R. § 825.204(a) to mean that reinstatement is required if—but only if—the employee is able to work a full normal schedule. Employees on intermittent leave can be transferred to any available position that satisfies the employee's need for time off.

There was another issue in this case. The plaintiff said that, while the FMLA permitted the employer to put her on unpaid leave, the employer's own policy was more generous. The employer prevailed on this issue too. The court said that employees cannot sue under the FMLA to enforce the employer's own policies. The remedy, if any, is a suit for breach of contract.

There were two major issues in *Hunt v. Rapides Healthcare System Inc.* [277 F.3d 757 (5th Cir. 2001)] The first was whether the plaintiff made a reinstatement request before or after her FMLA leave expired. The second was whether the job she received (part-time, as-needed shifts in the unit she preferred, at lower pay and without health, retirement, or leave benefits) was equivalent to her preleave position, or whether it was adverse job action taken in retaliation against her use of FMLA leave. The plaintiff, a critical care nurse, turned down the offer of a full-time night shift job because she was a single mother who needed to be home at night; her day-shift job had been assigned to another worker, so it was not vacant or available for her to return to.

The FMLA Regulations say, at 29 C.F.R. § 825.216(a)(2), that the basic rule is that an employee returning from FMLA leave is entitled to return to the same shift on an equivalent work schedule. The exception is if the worker's job has been eliminated, but this exception is not available if the job has simply been assigned to another employee.

The issue in this case was whether summary judgment should have been granted for the employer. The plaintiff was allowed to continue her case with respect to whether she was entitled to reinstatement and, if so, whether the employer satisfied its duty to reinstate her. But her claims of retaliation and constructive discharge were dismissed. The Fifth Circuit's position is that a shift change by itself is not an adverse employment action that will support a retaliation claim. [*Serna v. City of San Antonio,* 244 F.3d 479 (5th Cir. 2001); *Benningfield v. City of Houston,* 157 F.3d 369 (5th Cir. 1998)] Therefore, the plaintiff did not have a viable retaliation claim, because she could have accepted the night shift job without losing pay or benefits.

She lost her claim that she was constructively discharged when she took the part-time job with lower pay and fewer benefits because she could not take the full-time night shift position. In the Fifth Circuit, the test of constructive discharge is not whether the plaintiff felt compelled to resign, but whether a reasonable employee would have felt that way in the same situation.

The Seventh Circuit ruled that the plaintiff failed to prove that her termination after return from leave violated the FMLA. She took about two months' leave for depression and anxiety. In the interim, two production lines had been combined and some workers reassigned. She was assigned to her old department, at the same pay and benefits, but now had to use hand tools in addition to her previous cleaning tasks. She hurt her wrist using the screw gun. After treatment, she was told that she could stop using the screw gun but had to continue caulking. She walked off the job and didn't return. A week later, the HR director offered to accommodate her new health restriction, but warning her that failure to return would be treated as a voluntary quit. She did not return, and brought an FMLA suit about two years later. The Seventh Circuit ruled in favor of the employer, finding that post-leave, her duties were substantially similar. Using the tools took up only a small part of the day and was not physically demanding. [*Mitchell v. Dutchmen Manufacturing Inc.,* 389 F.3d 746 (7th Cir. 2004)]

The defendant obtained summary judgment in an FMLA case brought by the night manager of a garage. When he had surgery, his wife telephoned the workplace and said he would be in the hospital for two to three days and then at home for six weeks. As a result of complications, he spent several weeks in the hospital. Almost three months after the surgery, he returned and tried to resume work. He was told that the person who had substituted for him when he was out sick had been given the job permanently, but he could take a new job as Quality Control Supervisor, at the same pay and benefits as the former Night Service Manager job. He took the Quality Control job, but he hated it and showed symptoms of depression, fatigue, and anxiety. Eventually the Quality Control job was eliminated. The only job open to him was a day-shift job as a service advisor. He didn't want the job, but accepted it nonetheless. He found that the workweeks of 55 to 68 hours (versus 40 hours at his former job) stressful. His salary was reduced, but he had the potential to earn more money overall because he could earn commissions. He had a nervous breakdown. His psychiatrist said the job change exacerbated his ongoing mental problems. He was placed on FMLA leave for 12 weeks, and did not return; he was fired.

He sued under the FMLA, charging that the defendant's failure to reinstate him to the Night Service Manager or equivalent position caused him to become mentally incapacitated to the point of becoming unable to work. He sought front pay, but this issue was raised for the first time on appeal. Furthermore, during discovery he said that he was not seeking front pay. In the Eighth Circuit view, when he returned as Quality Control Supervisor, he received the same pay and benefits as in his previous job, so his entire damage claim was based on entitlement to front pay—a claim that he had already waived. His contention that he was too disabled to work precluded reinstatement as a remedy. The defense was granted summary judgment on the claim that he was transferred to the Service Advisor job in retaliation for his use of FMLA leave, because the plaintiff failed to prove a causal connection. The transfer occurred six months after his return from leave, and even a two-month interval has been held to be too distant in time to justify a claim. The Eighth Circuit did not believe that a retaliation case had been made out—he was not terminated, he got a lateral transfer; and he had the potential to earn more as a result of the transfer, so the action was not punitive. [*McBurney v. Stew Hansen's Dodge City Inc.*, 398 F.3d 998 (8th Cir. 2005). The two-month rule comes from *Kipp v. Missouri Highway and Trans. Comm'n*, 280 F.3d 893 (8th Cir. 2002)]

§ 38.05   INTERMITTENT LEAVE

Section 2612(b) governs intermittent leave and leave that produces a reduced work schedule. The FMLA provides the equivalent of 12 weeks of work: up to 480 hours a year for full-time workers, and an equivalent prorated amount for part-time workers, such as 240 hours a year for someone who works a half-time schedule.

The FMLA regulations [*see* 29 C.F.R. § 825.205(b)] refer to the actual number of hours the employee usually works in a week; or in an average week, if the schedule varies. Therefore, a person who is exempt from receiving overtime benefits but who typically works longer than 40 hours a week can get additional intermittent leave because of this work history.

Employers are not obligated to grant intermittent leave for cosmetic procedures. The general rule is that leave to care for a newly born or adopted child must be taken in a block of time off, and not on an intermittent or reduced schedule—unless the employer agrees to the special schedule. Intermittent leave for parents can be denied unless the child has a serious health condition, or unless a pregnant employee has severe morning sickness or needs time off for prenatal care. Leave premised on a serious health condition can be taken intermittently or on a reduced schedule when it is medically necessary.

It is permitted for the employer to use health-related intermittent/reduced leave to offset birth or adoption leave taken by the employee in the same year, but only to the actual extent of intermittent or reduced leave that was taken.

When a health-related intermittent leave can be predicted, based on scheduled medical treatment, the employer can lawfully transfer the employee to an available alternative position—as long as:

- The employee is qualified for the position;
- The two jobs are equivalent in pay and benefits;
- The second job provides a better accommodation to the changed work schedule than the first job did. [*See* 29 C.F.R. § 825.205]

Once the need for intermittent leave ends, the transferred employee must be offered reinstatement in the former job or a comparable job. It violates the FMLA for employers to use transfers deliberately to discourage the use of FMLA leave or to retaliate against employees who take or request leave.

Tip: The employer is allowed to set the minimum span of intermittent leave as the shortest period that the payroll system can accommodate. If the payroll system can only handle full days, then intermittent leave periods can be added up until they total a full day, at which point a day's pay can be deducted from the worker's paycheck. The employees should be given advance written notice if this is the policy, and they should be asked to sign the notice showing that they are aware of the policy.

The District Court for the District of Maine ruled that an employer did not interfere with the FMLA rights of an employee who was not reinstated after he took FMLA leave. It's true that when he returned, his duties were more limited (and eventually his job was eliminated), because a more experienced person had been hired to run the HR department when he was gone. But the court did not believe the plaintiff's contention that the employer retaliated against him for taking leave to care for his wife, a cancer patient. The defendant, an Internet company, laid off 45 employees as part of a desperate financial struggle to stay in business.

The court also ruled that because the plaintiff took intermittent leave, he didn't really "return" to work because he hadn't left. The correct cause of action would have been a retaliation claim, which would require proof that an adverse employment action was taken because he asserted rights under the FMLA. [*Dressler v. Community Service Communications Inc.*, 275 F.2d 17 (D. Me. 2003)]

§ 38.06   RELATING FMLA LEAVE TO OTHER LEAVE

[A]   Generally

Because the employer can legally provide all FMLA leave on an unpaid basis, it is logical to allow the employer to provide paid leave for only part of the required FMLA leave period. Under § 2612(d), if the employer provides paid leave for part of the time, the balance of the 12 weeks can be unpaid. The employer can also require the employee (and the employee can elect) to receive payment for any part of the 12 FMLA weeks for which the employee has accrued vacation, personal, or family leave.

The same is true of substituting accrued paid vacation, personal, medical, or sick leave for unpaid FMLA leave based on a serious health condition. However, the FMLA does not require employers to adopt a policy of offering paid medical or sick leave if they did not already have such a policy.

Title 29 C.F.R. § 825.22(d) says that light-duty work is counted toward the 12-week allowance. In 2004, the Southern District of Indiana and the Northern District of Illinois decided two cases on the light-duty issue. In the Indiana case, the issue was whether failing to tell an injured worker that light duty was subject to the FMLA constituted interference with her FMLA rights. The court held that she was not prejudiced because she was on light duty for 13 weeks, so she received all the benefits she would have received by knowingly exercising FMLA rights. (Nevertheless, she was reinstated and her employer paid injury-related expenses.)

The Northern District of Illinois ruled that the FMLA is satisfied as long as an employee accepts a light-duty assignment voluntarily and without coercion, and his or her job is kept open for 12 weeks, whether the employee spends those weeks on unpaid leave or light duty. The plaintiff charged that she was coerced into doing light-duty work rather than taking a leave of absence, but the Northern District ruled that an ill or injured person is merely entitled to 12 weeks of job protection, not to receiving it in the mode he or she prefers.

An important factor in both these cases was that the plaintiffs failed to request FMLA leave; if they had, their serious health conditions would have mandated that the leave be provided. [*Roberts v. Owens-Illinois, Inc.*, 2004 WL 1087355 (S.D. Ind. May 14, 2004); *Artis v. Palos Community Hosp.*, 2004 WL 2125414 (N.D. Ill. Sept. 22, 2004)]

A 2003 case from the Eleventh Circuit looks at the interaction between FMLA leave and paid leave. The plaintiff claimed that he was terminated after he left the job site during a diabetic attack, and therefore he took FMLA leave and was entitled to reinstatement and damages. The District Court found for the defendant on the grounds that the plaintiff failed to use up his available paid sick leave—but the Court of Appeals ruled that the availability of paid leave is irrelevant in the FMLA context. The Eleventh Circuit also held that the plaintiff stated a claim of interference with his FMLA rights that was strong enough to get to trial, because of issues of material fact as to why he left the job site.

In the Eleventh Circuit view, an employer who offers paid sick leave has two options for leave that qualifies both as paid leave and under the FMLA. The employer can allow the employee to use the two leaves sequentially, or can require them to be concurrent. But offering sick leave and then firing the employee is not acceptable under the FMLA. The plaintiff could not prove his retaliation claim, because there was not enough evidence that he was fired for engaging in protected activity. However, the employer's motives are irrelevant to a claim of interference with FMLA rights, so the issue should have been tried. A reasonable jury could have accepted the plaintiff's version of events: that he was not insubordinate, he suffered a diabetic attack that impaired his vision and prevented him from performing the inspection he was ordered to do, and that he explained the situation to his supervisor. [*Strickland v. Water Works*, 239 F.3d 1199 (11th Cir. 2003)]

The Ninth Circuit case of *Rowe v. Laidlaw Transit, Inc.* [244 F.3d 1115 (9th Cir. 2001)] explains that qualifying unpaid leave is protected under the FMLA, even if it is not specifically designated as such by the employee. The plaintiff in this case suffered a serious ankle injury. She used up her sick leave and vacation days. Her doctor said she could only work five hours a day, subject to restrictions. She asked for a part-time schedule. The employer agreed to a reduced schedule, and paid her on an hourly basis. The plaintiff did not ask for FMLA leave; the employer did not discuss the matter with her. When she could resume full-time work, the employer resumed paying her based on her salary before the injury. The employee quit the year after the injury and sued the employer for failure to pay overtime. The employer said that she was a supervisor, exempt from overtime payment.

The Ninth Circuit upheld the District Court, which said that the employee was entitled to FMLA leave because of the nature of her serious health condition, and under 29 C.F.R. § 825.208(c), employees are entitled to FMLA protection if the employer fails to notify an employee that his or her paid leave satisfies FMLA conditions after the employee has provided a reason for the leave that qualifies under the FMLA. Unpaid leave must be treated like paid leave for this purpose.

State law may require employers to provide intermittent leave on more generous terms than the FMLA does. If the employee is also a qualified person with a disability as defined by the ADA, then it may be necessary to grant even more than the equivalent of 12 weeks' intermittent leave as a reasonable accommodation.

Sometimes it is hard to distinguish between leave taken because of complications of pregnancy and leave taken to prepare for parenting. Under Wage and Hour

Division regulations, FMLA leave is not available after the employee has taken a disability leave for pregnancy-related complications. However, if there is a post-delivery period when the mother is physically unable to work, that period can be counted as a leave for serious illness, even though it also represents parenting leave. This is especially significant if both parents work for the same employer and would otherwise have to split a single 12-week leave period.

If the state has a law obligating employers to provide paid or partially paid maternity leave, employees are entitled to unpaid FMLA law in addition to the paid leave required by state law. Furthermore, if the state has an FMLA-type law that extends coverage in circumstances that the federal law does not provide for (e.g., taking care of a friend or parent-in-law), the state-required leave is treated as if it were taken for non-FMLA purposes and therefore does not reduce the 12-week FMLA allowance.

The Tenth Circuit ruled that the City of Albuquerque may have committed sex discrimination by permitting male police officers to use comp time under the FMLA, while forcing female officers to use sick days for post-pregnancy time off. Under the city's program, accrued sick leave counts toward early retirement, but other kinds of leave do not. The plaintiffs said that they were prevented from using their comp time, which must fall below a "cap" before they will be permitted to work additional overtime. The case was remanded to the District Court because the plaintiffs adduced admissible evidence that the city granted more favorable treatment to at least one non-pregnant employee. [*Orr v. City of Albuquerque,* 417 F.3d 1144 (10th Cir. 2005)]

Taking a cross-country trip to fetch a more reliable family car during his wife's pregnancy, and his regular phone calls to her during the trip, did not constitute caring for her, so the employee was not entitled to FMLA leave for the trip. [*Tellis v. Alaska Airlines*, 414 F.3d 1045 (9th Cir. July 12, 2005)]

Statutes governing medical leave typically define the amount of medical leave that must be granted. Conditions that require long-term absences are often severe enough to trigger protection against disability discrimination. Worker's Compensation might also be involved if the illness or injury is work-related.

Many companies maintain a formal policy that sets a maximum length of available medical leave (e.g., six months or a year), with termination for employees who are unable to return to work after exhausting their leave allowance. Multi-state companies must make sure that the policy is acceptable under the laws of all the states in which they do business. Calendar-year employers might face situations in which an employee succeeds in taking 12 weeks' leave in each of two calendar years.

It is common for state medical leave laws to use the FMLA definitions and to provide that leave under the state law runs concurrently with the federal FMLA leave. However, Connecticut and the District of Columbia require access to 16 weeks of leave over a two-year period. California requires up to 12 weeks leave in a 12-month period, with a separate four-month leave requirement for disability related to pregnancy and childbirth. Both the ADA regulations and case law have recognized leave as an effective accommodation to disability. However, employers are not required to provide an infinite amount of leave; there must be a reasonable expectation that granting leave will permit the employee to recover to the point that the employee can perform the essential functions of the job (or perhaps of another available job). Some cases require leave only if there is a determinable date for return to work. [Chuck Rice and James H. Coil III, *Limits on Limited Medical-Leave Policies*, Kilpatrick Stockton LLP Employment Relations Today (Autumn 2005)]

[B] ADA Interface

See 29 C.F.R. §§ 825.701 and .702 for a discussion of the relationship between the FMLA and the ADA. An employer can satisfy both statutes by offering a reduced work schedule to a disabled employee until he or she has used the 12 weeks of FMLA leave. After FMLA leave, employees are entitled to reinstatement in a job equivalent to the original job. The FMLA permits the employer to demand a physical exam to determine if a worker can be reinstated after a health-related FMLA leave. To satisfy the ADA as well, the examination must be job-related, not a comprehensive inventory of all physical conditions.

Although the two statutes were designed to accomplish different goals, workers sometimes find that FMLA leave is more accessible than taking time off as an ADA reasonable accommodation. Remember, FMLA leave is available when the employee is the sick person—not just when the employee is a caregiver.

Furthermore, if the company employs at least 50 people and the employee has put in the necessary 1,250 hours in the previous 12 months, entitlement to FMLA leave is automatic. The employer's discretion as to what constitutes a reasonable accommodation is not a factor. The right to reinstatement is also automatic. Employers can raise a defense of unreasonable hardship in ADA cases—but not in FMLA cases.

Some other differences [as discussed in Holly H. Weiss and Jennifer L. Howard, *The Leave of Absence Triple-Header: ADA, FMLA and Workers' Compensation*, NY Employment Law & Practice Newsletter Vol. 3 #9 (June 2002) and Vol. 3 #10 (July 2002)]:

- The FMLA and ADA overlap only if someone is covered by both, and has both a serious health condition and a disability—a broken hip is a serious health condition but probably not a disability; normal pregnancy is a serious health condition but not a disability; blindness is a disability but not a serious health condition.
- FMLA leave cannot be denied even if the employee's condition is so bad that the employee's doctor will not certify his or her ability to return to work after the end of the leave period. However, the ADA does not require accommodations that will not be effective (will not assist the employee to perform essential job functions).

- Under the FMLA, the employer does not have the right to reject a leave request by offering transfer to another position, but an employee on a reduced schedule or intermittent leave can be transferred to a different job that fits that schedule and offers the same pay and benefits as the previous job. The ADA permits a temporary transfer if that is a less burdensome way to enable the employee to perform the essential functions of the job, but permanent reassignment is permitted only if any other accommodation would unduly burden the employer.
- As for light duty assignment, the FMLA permits an employee to insist on taking leave even if there are available light duty jobs that he or she can perform. Under the ADA, the employer can be required to assign the employee to a vacant light duty job as a reasonable accommodation, but there is no obligation to create a light duty job to suit the employee's needs.

These articles also look at Worker's Compensation (more about which at Chapter 33). Worker's Compensation defines disability in terms of specific injuries, such as the loss of hands or feet. The Worker's Compensation laws do not make explicit provision for leaves of absence, but denying reasonable time off could be interpreted as illegal retaliation for filing a Comp claim. However, it is lawful to fire someone who receives Worker's Compensation benefits as long as there is a legitimate non-retaliatory reason for the termination. Recipients of Worker's Compensation benefits are not guaranteed reinstatement if they recover from their injuries. If a work-related injury is also a disability, reasonable accommodation may be required under the ADA.

The Western District of Pennsylvania granted summary judgment for a clinically depressed nurse, finding that firing her violated the FMLA and the ADA. [*Wilson v. Lemington Home for the Aged*, 159 F. Supp. 2d 186 (W.D. Pa. 2001)] The employer said that FMLA leave was not provided because she did not ask for it specifically and did not disclose her doctor's diagnosis when she said she needed a month off (although she did say that she had suffered diarrhea, vomiting, and chest pains). But the District Court held that, when an employer knows that an employee has requested leave, it has an obligation to provide written notice of FMLA rights and responsibilities. The employer asked the employee for certification on December 19 and December 26. The employee responded that her doctor was out of the office until December 30. She was fired on December 19, and the employer treated her December 13 visit to the office to pick up personal items as a voluntary quit.

The Western District of Pennsylvania found direct evidence that the plaintiff was fired for exercising her FMLA rights. She was not properly notified of the certification requirements, so she could not legitimately be punished for not offering certification. It was improper to treat retrieval of personal items as resignation; in fact, the employer continued to ask for certification after the alleged resignation.

A December 2001 case dismisses claims that the plaintiff's FMLA rights were "interfered with," because there was no actual violation of her FMLA rights. The plaintiff, who suffered from fibromyalgia and chronic fatigue syndrome, was allowed to pursue ADA claims (because her symptoms could substantially impair major life activities, in that she could not work overtime hours or travel on business). However, although she charged that the employer fired her because she was disabled and because she tried to exercise her FMLA rights (despite the employer's failure to provide required disclosure about the FMLA), the court did not accept this argument. The Eastern District of Pennsylvania's decision in *Alifano v. Merck & Co.* [175 F. Supp. 2d 792] says that the FMLA (unlike the ADA) does not impose a duty on employers to offer reasonable accommodation to employees who return from leave. It does not violate the FMLA to terminate an employee who has taken FMLA leave—if the reason for the termination is that the employee is no longer capable of performing the essential functions of the job.

[C] COBRA and HIPAA

An IRS Final Rule, published starting at 64 Fed. Reg. 5160 (Feb. 3, 1999), provides that merely taking FMLA leave is not a COBRA qualifying event. However, a qualifying event does occur with respect to an employee (and any dependents of the employee who are at risk of losing health coverage) who fails to return to work at the end of the FMLA leave. The typical example is a new mother who does not return to work after the end of maternity leave.

Under the Final Rule, the COBRA qualifying event occurs on the last day of the FMLA leave. The employer is not allowed to condition the COBRA election on the employee paying the EGHP back for premiums paid on his or her behalf during the leave. However, if the employer has actually terminated coverage under the group plan for the whole class of employees that the employee belonged to before the FMLA leave, continuation coverage does not have to be offered to employees who do not return from leave. The HIPAA rules jointly released in late 2004 by the Treasury, DOL, and HHS (69 Fed. Reg. 78800, Dec. 30, 2004, amending 26 C.F.R. §§ 54.9801 to -9807, 29 C.F.R. §§ 701-708, and 45 C.F.R. § 146.20) provide important new guidance on the relationship between the FMLA and HIPAA's portability rules. HIPAA's protection ends if the individual goes for 63 days or more without "creditable coverage." The 2004 rule holds that a period of FMLA leave when the person on leave has not continued group health coverage does not count toward the 63-day period for the person on leave or his or her dependents.

The rule requires employers to issue HIPAA certificates of creditable coverage automatically when a person takes FMLA leave but does not elect continuation coverage. The agencies acknowledged that many people who go on FMLA leave will return to their original jobs post-leave, so certificates will be issued unnecessarily; but the agencies considered this small effort worthwhile to make sure proper certificates were issued when needed. A person who goes on leave, or a dependent of a person who goes on leave, is entitled to a special enrollment period if the employee does not return to work after the leave ends, and the special enrollment period continues until a certificate of creditable coverage is issued.

[D] Cafeteria Plans

The IRS published Final Regulations, effective October 17, 2001, applicable for cafeteria plan years beginning on or after January 1, 2002, explicating the FMLA obligations of cafeteria plans. [*See* T.D. 8966, R.I.N. 1545-AT47, 66 Fed. Reg. 52676]

The Final Regulations are based, with some significant changes, on a set of 1995 Proposed Regulations. The Final Rule states that the basic FMLA obligation is to offer coverage under any group health plan as long as the employee is on paid or unpaid leave, on the same conditions as coverage would have been provided if the employee had continued to work during the leave period.

When the employee is on unpaid FMLA leave, the employer must either allow the employee to revoke the coverage or continue coverage but stop contributing premiums to the plan. The employer can then maintain the coverage by taking over both the employer and the employee share of the premium. The employer can recover the employee share of contributions when the employee returns from the leave. If the employee does not return, 29 C.F.R. § 825.213(a) permits the employer to recover both the employer and the employee shares of the premium from the employee. However, an employee who directed that premium payments be discontinued cannot be required to make contributions until after the end of unpaid leave.

One difference between the Final Rule and the Proposed Regulations is that, under the Final Rule, employers can require employees who return from unpaid FMLA leave to resume participation in the plan, if the employer imposes the same requirement on employees returning from non-FMLA leave.

When an employee is not covered under an FSA (Flexible Spending Account) during leave either because the employee revoked coverage or because he or she failed to pay premiums, the employer must provide a choice between resuming the original level of coverage by making up for the missed premium payments, or resuming coverage at a prorated reduced level and resuming the original level of premium payments.

On the other hand, if FSA coverage continued during the FMLA leave, there is no proration. Employees on FMLA leave have the same rights during the leave period as cafeteria plan participants who are not on leave—including the same rights to enroll or change elections as any active employee. [*See* Treas. Reg. § 1.125-4(g)] This Final Rule supplements T.D. 8878 [65 Fed. Reg. 15548 (March 2000)] and T.D. 8921 [66 Fed. Reg. 1837 (Jan. 2001)] with respect to changes in cafeteria plan elections made during a plan year.

[E] Fair Labor Standards Act

A 1998 Opinion Letter from the Department of Labor [Opinion Letter #89 (1998)] says that salaried workers who are exempt from the FLSA (and therefore are not entitled to overtime pay) are not entitled to FLSA protection merely because their employer docks their paychecks to reflect unpaid FMLA leave, even though pay deductions for absence are more characteristic of FLSA-covered wage workers than of "exempts."

[F] USERRA

Under the Uniformed Services Employment and Reemployment Rights Act [38 U.S.C. § 4301 *et seq.*] (USERRA), the Department of Labor indicated in mid-2002 that National Guard members and reservists who are called to active duty, and then released from active duty and return to their civilian jobs, are entitled to count their active duty service toward the 1,250 hour "work" requirement for FMLA eligibility. *See* § 1.18[A].

[G] California Legislation

On September 23, 2002, California enacted an innovative law, S.B. 1661, requiring employers in that state to provide up to six weeks' paid leave per twelve-month period, under the Family Temporary Disability Insurance (FTDI) program. Eligible employees are those caring for a newborn or newly adopted child or a family member suffering from a serious health condition (an illness, injury, impairment, physical or mental condition requiring inpatient hospital or hospice care, treatment in a residential health care facility, or continuing treatment by a health care provider). The leave must be taken concurrently with FMLA leave and its California equivalent—in other words, the measure does not entitle employees to an additional amount of leave, it just means that in some circumstances they will receive paid rather than unpaid leave for caregiver time.

The definition of family member includes not only a husband or wife but also a domestic partner, as defined by California Family Code § 297 (a same-sex partner, or persons over 62 satisfying certain Social Security-related criteria; both partners must file a Declaration of Domestic Partnership). Benefits are not available for any day that another family member is able and available to provide care for the sick person.

The program takes effect on January 1, 2004, with benefits payable for leaves beginning on or after July 1, 2004. The program covers all employers. There is no exemption for very small businesses.

The program is entirely funded by mandatory employee contributions (i.e., the employer does not contribute). Employers must begin to take the deductions starting January 1, 2004. For calendar years 2004 and 2005, the contribution rate is .08% of salary, up to a wage limit ($68,829 for 2004; $79,418 for 2005). Benefits become payable after a seven-day waiting period, imposed to screen out everyday minor illnesses. Eligible workers can receive 55% of their wages, with benefits ranging between $50 and $728 a week (for claims beginning within the period July 1, 2004–December 31, 2004) and $50–$840 for the following year. Employees claiming the benefit must provide medical evidence to back up the claim.

The employer can require the employee to take up to two weeks of earned but unused vacation time before accessing FTDI benefits—but if this is done, up to one week of vacation must be applied toward the waiting period.

Washington State also has a 2002 statute requiring employers to allow employees to use their own sick days or other paid time off to care for their children, spouses, parents, in-laws, grandparents, and disabled adult children. (Most of the states permit public employees to do this, but it is unusual in the private sector.) [*See* Rebecca Cook (Associated Press) <http://www.lni.wa.gov/rules/wage-hour-familycare/proposal.htm>]

§ 38.07   NOTIFYING THE EMPLOYER

No one schedules an emergency, of course. However, treatment for some serious health conditions is scheduled in advance (e.g., elective surgery). Section 2612(e) requires the employee to give at least 30 days' notice before leave based on the expected due date of a baby, or the expected placement date for adoption or foster care. If the date of birth or placement is less than 30 days from the time the employee decides to apply for FMLA leave, the employee must give as much notice as is practicable.

The FMLA imposes a duty on employees taking leave based on planned medical treatment to make reasonable efforts to schedule the treatment in the way that causes the least disruption to the employer (as long as this does not endanger the sick person's health). The employee should provide at least 30 days' notice before the leave is scheduled to begin—but if the need for the treatment becomes known less than 30 days in advance, the employee must provide as much notice as is practicable.

The case of *Satterfield v. Wal-Mart Stores Inc.* [135 F.3d 973 (5th Cir. 1998)] involved an employee who did not have a telephone. She sent a note telling the employer she could not come in to work because of a pain in her side. She did not communicate with the employer at all for 12 days, after she had been operated on. This was her fourth unexcused absence in three weeks, so she was fired. The Fifth Circuit ruled that she did not even give the employer enough notice to trigger a duty to investigate her need for FMLA leave. Her prior unexcused absences made it reasonable for the employer to conclude that she was merely being irresponsible, not in need of medical leave.

The Sixth Circuit affirmed summary judgment for the defendant in a case in which a plaintiff was not allowed to return to work after taking leave to care for his 13-year-old learning-disabled son. The plaintiff submitted a request for two-and-a-half months off for child care. He didn't cite the FMLA or the child's special needs and didn't provide medical certification, although he said he orally requested and was granted FMLA leave. After the plaintiff had been on leave for about two weeks, the office manager sent him a letter saying that his leave was not deemed to fall under the FMLA; he was on leave of absence. When his son went back to school in the fall, the plaintiff asked about coming back to work and was told his job was filled and no other job was available.

In the Sixth Circuit view, notice was adequate to inform the employer of the need for FMLA leave—and the employer mentioned the FMLA in the denial letter, so it must have been aware that this was an issue. Under the Regulations, it's up to the employer to demand medical certification; it's not the employee's responsibility to volunteer it. However, the Sixth Circuit still ruled for the employer, on the grounds that the plaintiff's son did not have a serious health condition. Although the child had learning disabilities and did very poorly in school, he was still able to engage in normal daily activities. [*Perry v. Jaguar of Troy,* 353 F.3d 510 (6th Cir. 2003)]

An employee's wife went into false labor a month before the baby's due date. The employee asked for FMLA leave to stay home with his wife until the baby was born. The Seventh Circuit said that this was not an adequate FMLA request because it did not reference a serious health condition. The employee did have a doctor's note about pregnancy complications, but did not submit it until after the leave request was denied. The Seventh Circuit said employees should not be allowed to "mousetrap" employers by making inadequate leave requests and then producing the evidence later. In this case, the employee did not engage in deliberate deception, but crucial evidence about the need for leave was withheld, and employers do not have a duty to investigate to search out possible valid reasons for FMLA leave. [*Aubuchon v. Knauf Fiberglass, GMBH,* 359 F.3d 950 (7th Cir. 2004)]

Employers cannot fire employees merely for failing to comply with internal policies about sick leave, but the Sixth Circuit ruled that no reasonable jury could have concluded that the plaintiff gave adequate notice of intent to take FMLA leave when he repeatedly failed to explain his absences or provide documentation. The employer sent a registered letter giving him five days to contact the labor relations department. If he demonstrated the need, he would be granted sick leave; otherwise he would be fired. The cause of action for FMLA interference was unsustainable where the employee never gave notice of his need for FMLA leave, did not inform his employer that he had a serious health condition, did not respond to the five-day warning letter, and did not provide medical documentation until two weeks after his termination. [*Walton v. Ford Motor Co.,* 424 F.3d 481 (6th Cir. 2005)]

An employee who was fired for excessive absences was not protected by the FMLA because he failed to submit the required documentation and failed to indicate the need for FMLA leave. The employee did not disclose his diagnosis of anxiety and depression, and did not comply with the employer's request for substantiation of the request for leave. He was offered a chance to convert termination to an involuntary layoff with benefits, but did not provide the necessary documentation. Claiming a need for time off due to stress (without indicating a date of return) does not state an FMLA claim. [*Woods v. Daimler Chrysler,* 409 F.3d 984 (8th Cir. 2005); *see also Collins v. NTN-Bower Corp.,* 272 F.3d 1006 (7th Cir. 2001)]

§ 38.08   CERTIFICATION OF HEALTH CARE LEAVE

Employers have the right, under 29 U.S.C. § 2613, to require employees to prove that their request for medical leave is supported by a health care provider. This process is called certification. Employees have a duty to furnish the employer with a copy of the certification document, in a timely manner. (The best time for the employer to ask for certification is the time when the employee requests the leave, but the employer can defer the request for up to two days; the employee has 15 days to produce the certification.)

Appendix B to 29 C.F.R. Part 825 is an official form that can be used for certification. Employers and doctors can draft their own forms, but employers do not have the right to demand more information than the official form requires. An adequate certification provides at least this much information:

- The date when the serious health condition started;
- How long the health care provider predicts it will continue;
- The medical facts the health care provider has about the condition;
- Either a statement that the employee is too sick to carry out the functions of the job or that the employee is needed as a caregiver for an eligible family member (and how long the need for care is expected to continue);
- (If the employee wants intermittent leave or a reduced schedule for medical treatment such as cancer chemotherapy) how long the treatment is expected to last; the dates of the scheduled treatment;
- (For intermittent leave/reduced schedules in general) why the leave is medically necessary; how long it is expected to continue necessary.

If the employer has reason to doubt that the certification is valid, the employer has the right to demand (but will then have to pay for) a second opinion from a health care provider selected by the employer. The health care provider must be independent—not an employee of the employer company (i.e., the company physician is not allowed to take on this role). If the certification and the second opinion disagree about the need for the leave, then the employer can demand a third opinion from a health care provider agreed on by both the employer and the employee. The third opinion is final and binding on both employer and employee.

The Sixth Circuit treated a note on the doctor's prescription pad, saying the employee was able to return to work, as an adequate fitness-for-duty certificate entitling the employee to reinstatement. If the employer felt the note was not specific enough, the remedy would be to ask the doctor for additional information, not to deny reinstatement. [*Brumbalough v. Camelot Care Ctrs. Inc.*, 427 F.3d 996 (6th Cir. 2005)]

The Seventh Circuit ruled that a doctor's certificate giving a diagnosis of bronchitis was adequate to satisfy the FMLA notice requirement. Even though the certificate did not give the exact duration of incapacity, it put the employer on notice that the sick leave potentially qualified for FMLA status. [*Kauffman v. Federal Express*, 426 F.3d 880 (7th Cir. 2005)]

It did not violate the FMLA to enforce a "no call/no show" policy treating employees as having voluntarily quit if they missed work for a certain number of days without making contact to explain. In this case, the plaintiff failed to return to work after a scheduled vacation. She contacted her immediate supervisor, who authorized some additional days off but told the plaintiff that a doctor's note was necessary to justify the absences. Her daughter did contact the company for FMLA forms—but not until the day of the termination. The Tenth Circuit affirmed the grant of summary judgment for the employer because the employer did not interfere with the plaintiff's right to FMLA leave, and the employee violated an established policy of which she was aware (justifying her termination) and did not invoke the FMLA until a point at which her termination was already justified. [*Taylor v. Smith's Food & Drug Ctrs. Inc.*, 127 Fed. Appx. 394 (10th Cir. 2005)]

Now that the HIPAA privacy rules have taken effect (more discussion in Chapter 26), employers will have to be sensitive to the interaction between processing FMLA certifications and protecting private health data. Employers can avoid the HIPAA privacy requirements by getting information directly from employees, rather than accessing health plan files that are subject to the privacy rules. The employer should be sure to limit the information request to the information needed for the Form WH-380 (Medical Certification Statement). Under the HIPAA rules, the medical documentation submitted by the employee is considered an employment record and not a health care record, so the privacy rules are not triggered. But if the documentation of the serious health condition (or of an ADA disability) comes directly from the health plan, the privacy rules apply and the employee's authorization is needed for the employer to gain access to the data. In light of the privacy requirements, FMLA medical documentation should be kept separate from personnel files, and should also be isolated from the files used for health insurance purposes. [*FMLA Certification from Workers Avoids HIPAA Authorization* (Mar. 2003) <http://thompson.com/libraries/leave/gone/samplenews/gone0303.html? template=:templates:p>]

The employer can require further recertifications on a reasonable basis. Under 29 U.S.C. § 2613(a) and 29 C.F.R. § 825.308, demanding certification more often than once every 30 days will be considered unreasonable unless:

- The employee requested an extension of the leave;
- Circumstances have changed, making the original certification inaccurate;
- The employer has learned something that casts doubt on the original certification.

At the other end of the process, the employer is entitled to impose a policy (as long as it is uniformly applied) requiring employees returning from FMLA leave based on their own serious medical conditions to present written certification from their health care provider that they are fit to return to work. [29 U.S.C. § 2614(a)(4)]

When asked by the General Counsel of the Equal Employment Advisory Counsel for advice about recertification, DOL's Wage and Hour Division responded in May 2004. The query involved several scenarios: a health care provider certifies that the employee will have migraines indefinitely; diabetes is certified as a chronic serious health condition with no time frame; asthma is certified to last for an indefinite period with a three-month pollen season during which incapacity may occur; and certification of asthma where breathing tests and treatments are needed over a three-month period. The question was whether the employer can request recertification every 30 days. The DOL permitted recertification on a 30-day basis in connection with an absence. If there has been a change in circumstances, or the employer has reason to doubt the ongoing validity of the certificate, recertification can be required more often than every 30 days. For example, a pattern of Friday/Monday absences without medical reason could legitimately be grounds for suspicion. The letter says that although as a general rule employers should not have direct contact with employees' health providers, a query about the medical validity of Monday/Friday absence patterns can be added to the recertification form. (The Regulations, at § 825.307(a), require consent of the employee for the employer to contact the health care provider to clarify information in the certification.) [DOL Employment Standards Admin. Wage & Hour Division, letter to General Counsel of Equal Employment Advisory Council, <http://www.dol.gov/esa/whd/opinion/FMLA/2004_05_25_2A_FHLA.htm>]

If the employee's doctor reports that there is no need for leave, the employer is entitled to rely on that and deny the leave request. The plaintiff cannot claim that circumstances changed since the medical consultation. *Stoops v. One Call Communications, Inc.* [141 F.3d 309 (7th Cir. 1997)] says that the employee should have gotten an undated medical certificate instead.

It is improper for the employer to fire the employee for failure to provide adequate certification if the employer has not given the employee the amount of time provided by the FMLA (15 days for initial certification; recertification no more than every 30 days). As *LeGrand v. Village of McCook* [1998 WL 182462 (N.D. Ill. 1998)] points out, reducing the time frame makes it impossible to determine if the employee could have assembled the necessary proof in time.

An employer who doubts the accuracy of a medical certification (or questions whether the need for leave continues as long as the employee says it does) should be sure to ask for a second opinion right away. Failure to do so might prevent a courtroom challenge to the medical findings, although *Rhoads v. FDIC* [257 F.3d 373 (4th Cir. 2001)] says that it will not.

§ 38.09   DISCLOSURE TO EMPLOYEES

Employers have an obligation to post the standard EEOC notice to inform employees of their rights under the FMLA. Failure to do so can result in a civil penalty of up to $100 per offense. [29 U.S.C. § 2619] The notice, which must be at least 8½ × 11″, can be obtained from the local office of the DOL Wage and Hour Division, or can be enlarged and copied from 29 C.F.R. Part 825, Appendix C. Employers who employ a significant number of people who are literate in a language other than English must also post a translation of the notice into that language.

Companies that have employee handbooks must include FMLA information in the handbook. Even if there is no handbook, employees who actually request leave are entitled to a written explanation of their rights. Employers who have not satisfied the posting requirement can make up for this deficiency by providing adequate written notice at the time of a request for leave. [*Fry v. First Fidelity Bancorp.*, 67 EPD ¶ 43,943]

According to 29 C.F.R. § 825.301(b)(1), the employer's FMLA notice to employees must provide at least this much information:

- That the requested leave reduces the employee's "bank" of FMLA leave for the year;
- Whether the employer requires medical certification of the serious health condition; consequences if the certification is not provided;
- The fact that employees who are entitled to paid leave have a right to substitute paid leave for FMLA leave; the conditions under which the employer will substitute paid leave on its own initiative;
- The employee's right to be reinstated in a comparable job after returning from leave;
- The method for the employee to pay health premiums while he or she is on FMLA leave;
- Disclosure of the employee's obligation to reimburse the employer for premiums if the employee does not return to work after the leave;
- Any requirements for proving fitness for duty before returning to work;
- (For key employees) limitations on the right to reinstatement.

Tip: It is not a substitute for the required notice, but employees can be referred to the DOL's toll-free FMLA hotline, (800) 959-FMLA, for more information. FMLA information intended for employees can also be found at <http://www.dol.gov>.

A statement in the employee handbook that employees can take up to 12 weeks of FMLA leave in any 12-month period is inadequate because it fails to explain how the employer calculates the 12-month period. Therefore, the Ninth Circuit did not permit the employer to fire the plaintiff for taking too much sick leave. [*Bachelder v. America West Airlines, Inc.*, 259 F.3d 1112 (9th Cir. 2001)]

As noted above, in March 2002, the Supreme Court's decision in *Ragsdale v. Wolverine Worldwide, Inc.* struck down the DOL's regulation at 29 C.F.R. § 825.208 (saying that, where the employer fails to notify employees that FMLA leave will run concurrently with other leave—for example, paid sick leave—the two leave periods must be permitted to run consecutively, thereby increasing the amount of leave the employee can take.) The Supreme Court adopted the position of the Eighth and Eleventh Circuits, disagreeing with the Sixth Circuit, which found the rule to be valid. [*See Ragsdale v. Wolverine Worldwide Inc.*, 218 F.3d 933 (8th Cir. 2000); *McGregor v. AutoZone Inc.*, 180 F.3d 1305 (11th Cir. 1999); *Plant v. Morton International Inc.*, 212 F.3d 929 (6th Cir. 2000)]

Another regulation, 29 C.F.R. § 815.1100(d) says that employers that fail to respond promptly to FMLA leave requests may be compelled to provide leave that would otherwise be unavailable. Two Circuits—the Seventh and Eleventh—found this regulation invalid and unenforceable and are discussed below.

Dormeyer v. Comerica Bank-Illinois [223 F.3d 579 (7th Cir. 2000)] holds that the DOL did not have the authority to promulgate this regulation, which is unreasonable because it forces employers to provide benefits to which employees would not otherwise be entitled. The Eleventh Circuit held that the regulation is invalid because it alters the terms of the statute as passed by Congress. [*Brungart v. Bell South Telecommunications Inc.*, 231 F.3d 791 (11th Cir. 2000)]

Yet the District Court for the District of New Hampshire upheld another DOL regulation, 29 C.F.R. § 825.219(a), which requires the employer to reinstate a highly paid employee returning from FMLA leave, even if the job has been eliminated and the company undergoes substantial and grievous economic injury—if the employer failed to inform the employee of his key-employee status and discuss the implications of this status when he requested FMLA leave. [*Panza v. Grappone Co.*, 69 L.W. 1272 (D.N.H. Oct. 20, 2000)]

29 C.F.R. § 110(d) says that the employer is not allowed to challenge eligibility for leave once it has confirmed that the employee is entitled to it. But the court in *Seaman v. Downtown Partnership of Baltimore Inc.* [991 F. Supp. 751 (D. Md. 1998)] ruled that this regulation is invalid—it goes too far, because it usurps Congress' authority to set policy.

§ 38.10   ADMINISTRATIVE REQUIREMENTS

The Department of Labor's investigative authority under the FMLA is the same as its authority under FLSA § 11(a), including subpoena power. Employers have a duty to make and retain records showing FMLA compliance. The general rule is that the DOL can only require employers and employee plans to submit books and records once a year, unless the DOL is investigating a charge made by an employee, or has reason to believe that there has been an FMLA violation. [29 U.S.C. § 2616]

§ 38.11 FMLA ENFORCEMENT

[A] Litigation and Arbitration

Employees are allowed to sue employers for FMLA violations. As usual, the employer corporation or agency is the proper defendant. A supervisor at a public agency cannot be held personally liable under the FMLA for discriminating against an employee who took leave. [*Mitchell v. Chapman*, 343 F.3d 811 (6th Cir. 2003)] Employees can sue on their own behalf or on behalf of other similarly situated employees. FMLA suits (like Title VII, FLSA, ADEA, and NLRA suits) can be brought by ex-employees charging retaliation for exercising their FMLA rights; the cause of action is not limited to current employees. [*Smith v. Bellsouth Telecommunications, Inc.*, 273 F.3d 1303 (11th Cir. 2001)] *Duckworth v. Pratt & Whitney* [152 F.3d 1 (1st Cir. 1998)] also allows ex-employees to bring FMLA suits.

Implementing a staff restructuring was not a willful act triggering the three-year statute of limitations. Although a member of the HR department encouraged county officials to take advice of counsel as to whether the plaintiff's position could be restructured without violating the FMLA, failure to get legal advice is not tantamount to a willful violation of the statute. [*Hanger v. Lake County*, 390 F.3d 579 (8th Cir. 2004)]

According to *Petsche v. Home Federal Savings Bank*, [952 F. Supp. 536 (N.D. Ohio 1997)] the burden-shifting analysis used in Title VII cases also applies to the FMLA. Once the employee makes a prima facie case that the employer has violated the FMLA, the employer has to introduce evidence that the action taken against the employee did not constitute retaliation for exercising FMLA rights. However, *Diaz v. Fort Wayne Foundry Corp.* [131 F.3d 711 (7th Cir. 1997)] reaches precisely the opposite conclusion: that burden-shifting analysis doesn't apply. Instead, the FMLA plaintiff's obligation is to prove, by preponderance of the evidence, that his or her discharge violated FMLA rights.

The Fifth Circuit joined the Sixth Circuit in holding that an FMLA plaintiff can sustain a mixed-motive retaliation case by showing that the employer's action was at least partially motivated by retaliation for exercising FMLA rights, unless the employer can show that the same action would have been taken even absent the retaliatory motive. (The plaintiff still lost her case, because the Fifth Circuit determined that the employer satisfied its burden and would have fired her even if she had not sued the company for refusal to offer FMLA accommodation.) [*Richardson v. Monitronics Int'l*, 434 F.3d 327 (5th Cir. 2005)]

A Sixth Circuit case highlights the difficulties of integrating motherhood into corporate cultures that had never before had pregnant employees in senior positions. The plaintiff, the head of the company's finance division, announced her pregnancy. The company had no formal, official maternity leave policy. She attempted to discuss maternity leave on many occasions, but was rebuffed. She made a written request for four weeks of leave, working part-time at home during the leave. Soon after the announcement, she received a favorable performance review, a raise, and a bonus, although some concerns were raised about getting work done on time. Pregnancy complications made her start leave sooner than anticipated; she was authorized six weeks' paid leave and was told she could use vacation and personal time if additional leave was required. When she returned to work, she was given one day to choose among keeping her job, with a probable demotion; leaving with a severance package of four weeks' pay and medical benefits; or staying at work for 60–90 days while looking for another job. She felt compelled to resign and later sued under the FMLA and state anti-discrimination law for constructive discharge. The District Court granted summary judgment for the employer but the Sixth Circuit reversed, finding that material issues of fact remained to be resolved. The Sixth Circuit held that a threat of demotion, in and of itself, does not constitute constructive discharge—but it can be constructive discharge if other factors are involved as well. The company made it difficult for the plaintiff to negotiate maternity leave. The uncontested facts of the case showed that she was not informed of her eligibility for 12 weeks of FMLA leave; she received no response when she indicated the need for maternity leave; and she was required to produce a fitness-for-duty certificate under circumstances not permitted by the FMLA, all proving interference with her FMLA rights. [*Saroli v. Automation & Modular Components, Inc.*, 405 F.3d 446 (6th Cir. 2005)]

Working conditions, not just demotions or pay cuts, can support an FMLA retaliation claim. [*Hite v. Biomet Inc.*, 38 F. Supp. 2d 720 (N.D. Ind. 1999)]

Not only do employers face FMLA suits from employees or groups of employees; they can also be sued by the Department of Labor, which can sue on behalf of employees to recover the same kind of damages employees would get. If the DOL wins an FMLA case, the damages got to the employee, not to the government agency (unless it is impossible to locate the employees within three years). [*See* 29 U.S.C. § 2617(b)] The Secretary of Labor has the power to investigate and try to resolve complaints of FMLA violations, to the same degree as investigations and resolutions of violations of FLSA §§ 6 and 7. But employees are no longer allowed to bring FMLA suits once the DOL starts a suit. [29 U.S.C. § 2617(a)(4)]

A 42-year-old hotel employee took a six-week medical leave for an aneurysm. During his leave, another employee was promoted. When he returned, the plaintiff got a different title and a smaller office and reported to the newly reported employee. Initially, his responsibilities remained the same, and his pay and benefits remained the same. Then, tension arose over the plaintiff's failure to implement new hotel procedures. He was put on 30-day probation, fired, and replaced by a younger person. He brought suit for age and gender discrimination as well as for FMLA violations. He returned from leave in March of 1999 and brought suit in April of 2001. The District Court treated this as a timely filing, accepting the plaintiff's contention that he was fired in April 2000 in retaliation for leave taken about a year earlier. The First Circuit however, found that the claim was more than two years old, because it was based entirely on the alleged failure to reinstate him to his previous position when he returned from leave. Nor would the First Circuit extend the statute of limitations on the basis of willfulness. The First Circuit required a showing either that the employer knew or showed reckless disregard as to whether its conduct was prohibited under the FMLA. [*Hillstrom v. Best Western TLC Hotel*, 354 F.3d 27 (1st Cir. 2003)]

A worker who was fired after a private investigator videotaped him driving and shopping on days when he claimed he was out sick with a migraine could not show that his discharge was retaliation for using intermittent FMLA leave. In the First Circuit view, a retaliation claim can be pursued even if there is no claim of violation of substantive rights. In this case, no reasonable jury could have concluded that his discharge was retaliatory rather than a legitimate response to fabricating sick leave. [*Colburn v. Parker/Hannifin Inc.*, 429 F.3d 325 (1st Cir. 2005)]

FMLA claims can become the subject of arbitration as well as litigation. The Seventh Circuit found that where a Collective Bargaining Agreement included broad anti-discrimination language, the arbitrator did not exceed his powers by interpreting the FMLA as well as the CBA. [*Butler Mfg. Co. v. United Steelworkers*, 336 F.3d 629 (7th Cir. 2003)]

In a Third Circuit case, a former hospital pharmacist's arbitration agreement required her to arbitrate her claim that she was wrongfully terminated (violating the Pregnancy Discrimination Amendment; *see* § 34.06) and that she was denied reinstatement (violating the FMLA). The plaintiff took FMLA leave after her child was born. While she was on leave, her job was eliminated. The District Court denied the employer's motion to arbitrate, taking the position that the arbitration agreement ended when her job did. But the Third Circuit reversed and compelled arbitration, finding that the factual allegations of the complaint dealt with the same matters as the employment contract, and therefore arbitration was required. [*Varallo v. Elkins Park Hosp.*, 63 Fed. Appx. 601 (3d Cir. 2003)]

[B] Releases

An occupational health specialist was terminated from her job for poor performance, receiving two weeks' pay instead of notice. She was offered an extra month's salary in exchange for a release of rights to all other state, federal, or local claims. The FMLA was not specifically mentioned in the release form. She received a written memorandum saying she had 45 days to consider the release, and seven days to revoke it after signing it. She signed the release, accepted the extra month's pay, and didn't give it back. (*See* § 25.13 for a discussion of the concept of "tender-back" in connection with releases and lawsuits about the validity of the releases.)

The district court, citing 29 C.F.R. § 825.220(d), refused to enforce the release, because it says that "employees cannot waive, nor may employers induce employees to waive, their rights under the FMLA." However, the Fifth Circuit reversed, ruling that the regulation doesn't apply to post-dispute waivers of FMLA claims. The question is whether ex-employees count as employees for this purpose.

In 2002, the Eleventh Circuit ruled that because it is unclear what "employees" means in this context, courts should defer to the EEOC's interpretation to clarify the situation. But the Fifth Circuit noted that certain parts of the Regulation apply only to current employees, and this might also be true of the waiver situation.

The Fifth Circuit also interpreted "rights under the FMLA" to mean the right to take leave and be reinstated—not the cause of action for violation of the FMLA. In the Fifth Circuit view, public policy favors enforcement of waivers. Employees are not allowed to waive their substantive rights under the FMLA—but they are entitled to waive the right to money damages. The Fifth Circuit also said that keeping the money ratified the release; it isn't good enough to give back the money after the court case. [*Faris v. Williams WPC-I, Inc.* 332 F.3d 316 (5th Cir. 2003); *Smith v. BellSouth Telecomms Inc.,* 273 F.3d 1303 (11th Cir. 2001)] In contrast, the Fourth Circuit ruled in mid-2005 that 29 C.F.R. § 824.220(d) invalidates any release that is not approved by the DOL or by a court, and a severance package's general reference to all employment-related claims is subordinate to the specific FMLA principle of requiring approval for waivers. [*Taylor v. Progress Energy, Inc.,* 415 F.3d 364 (4th Cir. 2005)]

[C] Damages

If the employees win, 29 U.S.C. § 2617(a) provides that the court can order damages equal to the wages and benefits that the employee lost as a result of the violation. Even employees who have not lost compensation can receive damages to compensate them for financial losses (such as costs of hiring someone to care for sick relatives), but damages of this type are limited to 12 weeks' salary for the employee-plaintiff.

According to *Barrilleaux v. Thayer Lodging Groups Inc.* [1998 WL 61481 (E.D. La. 1998)], someone who sues for lost wages is not entitled to be compensated for care costs too.

Furthermore, winning FMLA plaintiffs can receive double damages: their damages (plus interest) and also an equal amount of liquidated damages. However, if the employer can prove that it acted in good faith and reasonably believed that it was in compliance with the FMLA, the court has discretion not to order double damages.

There is no statutory definition of "good faith," so the Western District of Missouri adopted the FLSA standard: whether the defendant made a good-faith effort to determine and observe the rights of the plaintiff. [*Morris v. VCW Inc.,* 1996 WL 740544 (W.D. Mo. 1996)]

An employee who has received an FMLA back pay award is not precluded from receiving liquidated damages for retaliation. The Tenth Circuit held that wages that are temporarily lost but restored after a significant delay must be treated as "lost or denied" for purposes of calculating FMLA liquidated damages. [*Jordan v. U.S. Postal Service,* 379 F.3d 1196 (10th Cir. 2004)]

A salesman told the supervisor of the facility where he worked three days a week (in addition to frequent business trips) that he had decided to retire. They discussed the potential for some form of post-retirement work, although it was clear that he was going to be replaced. He helped train his replacement. He filled out a retirement form and decided to move to Florida, for the good of his wife's health. However, the plaintiff's retirement decision was based on an incorrect belief that FMLA eligibility was limited to new parents. When he realized that he was eligible for leave to care for his wife's health needs, he decided that would be preferable to retirement. He was informed of the leave procedures, and was told that because it was close to Christmas, he could wait until after the first of the year to submit the forms. Leave was approved when he submitted the forms in January. In February the company prepared a personnel change notification form returning him to active status retroactive to his original date of employment. When his scheduled leave ended, he returned from Florida and said he was ready to resume work. His supervisor said that the company had implemented a hiring freeze and had no available jobs. Two weeks later, the plaintiff was offered a sales position involving a long commute and two to three nights on the road (which had not been true of his previous position). The plaintiff, who had been replaced in the interim, suggested a part-time arrangement, but was told that salespersons had to be available five days a week. He sued his employer for failure to reinstate. The Sixth Circuit reversed the district court's grant of summary judgment for the employer and remanded the case for consideration of the effect of the defendant's approval of FMLA leave on its ability to contest the plaintiff's entitlement to leave. The Sixth Circuit held that 29 C.F.R. § 825.305(d) requires that, if the defendant thought the medical certificate was incomplete, it had a duty to inform the plaintiff of that fact and give him a reasonable opportunity to cure the defect. [*Sorrell v. Rinker Materials Corp.*, 395 F.3d 332 (6th Cir. 2005); *Duty v. Norton-Alcoa Proppants*, 293 F.3d 481 (8th Cir. 2002), applies equitable estoppel in this situation]

Although most of the remedies are equitable ones, the Southern District of Georgia allows jury trials in FMLA cases, because they are allowed in Fair Labor Standards Act cases, and the two statutes contain many similar provisions. [*Helmly v. Stone Container Corp.*, 957 F. Supp. 1274 (S.D. Ga. 1997)] So does the Sixth Circuit. [*Frizzell v. Southwester Motor Freight*, 154 F.3d 641 (6th Cir. 1998)]

In one case, *McDonnell v. Miller Oil Co.*, [110 F.3d 60 (4th Cir. 1997)] the jury believed the plaintiff's claim that she was fired for exercising FMLA rights in connection with maternity leave. However, the jury did not award any damages, because the plaintiff failed to make a reasonable effort to get another job.

In addition to money damages, courts in FMLA cases can award the appropriate equitable relief for the case, including hiring, reinstatement, and promotion. FMLA winners are entitled to receive reasonable costs, defined to include attorneys' fees and expert witness fees. Section 2617(a)(3) makes this automatic for plaintiffs who win, not a matter of discretion for the court.

This is not true of all federal statutes. Some of them do not allow attorneys' fee awards at all, others allow a fee award to any prevailing party (plaintiff or defendant) or leave it up to the court whether an award should be made, or limit fee awards to cases in which the losing party's conduct has been outrageous.

It is not clear whether front pay is available under the FMLA, but several cases have treated it as an appropriate equitable remedy. [*See, e.g., Nichols v. Ashland Hosp. Corp.,* 251 F.3d 496 (4th Cir. 2001); *Churchill v. Star Enterprises,* 183 F.3d 184 (3d Cir. 1999)] In a recent Sixth Circuit case, a publishing sales representative was terminated when he was on medical leave. There was also evidence of interference with his FMLA rights because the defendant often asked him to perform work-related tasks when he was on leave. In this case, the plaintiff could not be reinstated, because he had another job, but that didn't necessarily mean he was entitled to front pay: the new job paid more than the old one, so he bettered his financial position by changing jobs. The Sixth Circuit stated that the test of availability of front pay is proof that it is required to completely make the plaintiff whole. Therefore, to get front pay, a plaintiff must give the court the data needed to calculate a front pay award with reasonable certainty; a purely speculative front pay award is inappropriate. However, the Sixth Circuit ruled that it was an error to deny liquidated damages, because the jury's ruling for the plaintiff implied a finding that the defendant did not act in good faith. [*Arban v. West Publishing Co.,* 345 F.3d 390 (6th Cir. 2003). For standards of proof for front pay, *see, e.g., Tyler v. Union Oil Co. of California,* 304 F.3d 379 (5th Cir. 2002); *Bruso v. United Airlines, Inc.,* 239 F.3d 848 (7th Cir. 2001)]

The plaintiff in a Sixth Circuit case was fired for violating the employer's leave policy (by failing to notify the Leave Coordination Department of the need for leave within the required time period; by failing to submit a timely medical certification form). The plaintiff charged the employer with interference with his FMLA rights, and with wrongful discharge contrary to public policy. The District Court dismissed both claims, but the Sixth Circuit revived the FMLA-interference claim and remanded the case for further proceedings.

The plaintiff was injured in a motorcycle accident, treated in a hospital emergency room, and was given a note telling him not to work for three days. He telephoned the employer to report the accident and give his return date. He expected the information to be passed along to the leave coordinator. The next day, the plaintiff went to another doctor, who gave him a note excusing four more days of absence. He was not scheduled to work the week after that, because of a plant shutdown. He returned to work and finally approached the Leave Coordination Department. At that point he was given a warning against further breaches of company policy. He completed the required paperwork and got medical certification of a serious health condition. Part of his leave request was denied, on the grounds that he had failed to notify the leave coordinator. Later, he missed work several times because of his injured shoulder. He submitted a timely leave request slip, but it was incomplete. He was ordered to submit a completed form, but could not do so by the deadline because his doctor didn't submit the form on time. Because this was the second time he violated leave policy, he was terminated.

The plaintiff received a copy of the employee handbook, which required the leave coordinator to be called in connection with all absences over one day; if the need for leave is unforeseeable, the request must be made no later than three consecutive workdays after the first missed day.

29 C.F.R. § 825.302 says that employers can require compliance with their usual and customary notice requirements—but failure to follow the internal procedure does not allow the employer to disallow or delay FMLA leave where the employee gave timely "verbal or other notice."

According to the Sixth Circuit, adequacy of notice by the employee is a mixed question of fact and law. The jury determines the facts as to when and how notice was given; the court determines whether that fact pattern was enough to put the employer on notice that FMLA leave was required. However, the Sixth Circuit dismissed the claim for wrongful discharge in violation of public policy, because the Ohio rule is that allowing such state claims is not necessary to the FMLA's enforcement scheme. [*Cavin v. Honda of America Mfg Inc.*, 346 F.3d 713 (6th Cir. 2003)]

PART VIII

PROCEDURE FOR HANDLING DISCRIMINATION CHARGES

Chapter 39

WRONGFUL TERMINATION AND AT-WILL EMPLOYMENT

§ 39.01   INTRODUCTION

Employees always have the right to quit their jobs, no matter how inconvenient their departure may be for the employer (although employment contracts can require a certain amount of notice, can obligate the employee to compensate the employer for economic loss caused by a resignation, and can impose reasonable restrictions on re-employment and use of the employer's proprietary information).

The employer's right to fire an employee is not so simple and clear-cut. Some employees have written contracts that specify the conditions under which they can be terminated. Unionized employees are covered by collective bargaining agreements (CBAs). In CBAs or individual employment contracts, if the agreement sets out a termination procedure (such as a warning, then a chance for the employee to respond to charges, a suspension, and then termination), then it is a breach of contract to terminate the employee without following the procedure.

Employers may also find that they are subject to responsibilities under implied contracts. The employer's written documents that it issues such as the employee handbook or even its oral statements are deemed to constitute a legally enforceable contract, then the employer will have to abide by that contract.

> **Tip:** Severance pay will probably not have to be given to an employee who is discharged for good cause—unless there is an implied contract to provide severance.

A supervisor is a representative of the employer when he or she is acting in the scope of his or her job, in a situation in which he or she is authorized to act. The supervisor's conduct will then have legal implications for the employer. A supervisor's negligence or outrageous conduct (such as abusive treatment of an employee that results in emotional distress) can be imputed to the employer. In many instances, the supervisor will *not* be personally liable, e.g., under federal and state antidiscrimination statutes or for inducing a breach of contract.

Even if termination is justifiable, however, it must be carried out in a reasonable manner, avoiding intentional infliction of emotional distress. The employer must also avoid both actionable defamation (destructive false statements) and depriving another employer of the accurate information needed to make a rational hiring decision.

"Constructive discharge" is the legal concept that an employee who responds to intolerable conditions by quitting is entitled to be treated as if he or she had been fired, because the employer's conduct was the equivalent of a discharge. To prove constructive discharge, the employee does not have to prove that the employer intended to force a resignation, only that it was reasonably foreseeable that a reasonable employee would quit under the same circumstances. The Supreme Court's mid-2004 decision, *Pennsylvania State Police v. Suders*, 542 U.S. 129 [(2004)] makes it clear that the test of constructive discharge is objective, not subjective, based on the behavior of the hypothetical reasonable employee rather than the personal reactions of the plaintiff. In a pregnancy discrimination/FMLA case, the Sixth Circuit ruled that a threat of demotion coupled with other factors can constitute constructive discharge. [*Saroli v. Automation & Modular Components, Inc.,* 405 F.3d 446 (6th Cir. 2005)]

The fact situation is not one that is likely to be repeated frequently, but it should be noted that at the end of 2004, the U.S. Supreme Court ruled that it did not violate a police officer's First Amendment or Fourteenth Amendment rights to fire him for selling videos (and police paraphernalia) on the Internet. The videos featured the officer in police-related pornographic scenarios. The Supreme Court held that he was not expressing himself on matters of public concern or commenting on police department operations. [*City of San Diego v. John Roe*, 543 U.S. 77 (2004)]

The vast majority of employees do not have a written contract. They are legally defined as "at-will" employees who work "at the will of the employer." However, at-will employers are not permitted to discharge employees for reasons that violate an antidiscrimination statute, or for reasons contrary to public policy.

Employees who want to bring suit under federal antidiscrimination laws (Title VII, the ADA, the ADEA, and the FMLA) have to satisfy elaborate procedural requirements. [*See* Chapters 40 and 41] Employees who charge the employer with wrongful termination merely have to go to state court and file a complaint. This is much easier to do, so employers may find themselves fighting on two fronts, or may be able to raise the argument that a wrongful termination case should be dismissed because the employee was required—but failed—to use the procedure for a discrimination suit.

§ 39.02   EMPLOYEE TENURE

The courts of some states (e.g., California) may treat the fact that an employee has worked for an employer for a long time as an implied promise of continuing employment. Especially if tenure has been very long (for instance, a decade or more), the state may impose an implied covenant of good faith and fair dealing. This has been done in Alabama, Alaska, Arizona, California, Connecticut, Delaware, Idaho, Massachusetts, Montana, Nevada, New Hampshire, New Jersey, New Mexico, South Carolina, Utah, and Wyoming.

This line of cases deems the employer to have implied a promise to treat the employee fairly and to avoid bad faith. This implied covenant has been held to invalidate the firing of some long-term workers, at least without the corporate equivalent of due process of law.

However, courts in other states, including Florida, Kansas, Michigan, Minnesota, Missouri, Nebraska, New York, Oklahoma, Texas, and Washington have rejected the implied covenant theory.

Nearly all of the states recognize a public policy exception (i.e., that it is illegal to fire even an at-will employee if the rationale for the firing violates public policy). The minority states that do not recognize this theory are Alabama, Florida, Georgia, Louisiana, Maine, Nebraska, New York, and Rhode Island. [*See* Charles J. Muhl, *The Employment-at-Will Doctrine: Three Major Exceptions,* Monthly Labor Review (Jan. 2001) <http://www.bls.gov/opub/mlr/2001/01/art1full.pdf>]

An ex-employee sued his former employer, charging that the wrongful termination of his employment cost him valuable unvested stock options and that some options were rescinded unlawfully and that the calculation of vested options was performed improperly. The First Circuit affirmed the District Court's grant of summary judgment for the employer. The employee handbook disclosed that employment was at will. The options vested periodically, contingent on continued employment, and therefore the company had the right to cancel the unvested stock options when he was terminated. The court also treated the rescission of a group of options (which happened when the employee was warned that his work was unsatisfactory) as a mutually agreed modification of the employment agreement. The fact that the employee continued to work furnished consideration for the contract modification.

The court rejected the plaintiff's argument that the option vesting schedule converted him into an employee for a term of years; the offer letter for the job specifically stated that he was an at-will employee who could be terminated at any time. Although Massachusetts permits an exception to the at-will rule when termination unjustly enriches the employer by depriving the employee of compensation for work already done, unvested options are not compensation for services already performed. Instead, they are contingent on continued employment. [*Cochran v. Quest Software Inc.*, 328 F.3d 1 (1st Cir. 2003); the exception for termination depriving a person of earned compensation comes from *Harrison v. NetCentric Corp.*, 744 N.E.2d 622 (Mass. 2001)]

§39.03 PROMISSORY ESTOPPEL

The theory of "promissory estoppel" is sometimes decisive in employment cases. The theory is that the employer's promise to the employee estops (precludes) the employer from disavowing that promise, often because the employee has "undergone detrimental reliance" (suffered in some way after relying on a statement or implication from the employer).

The classic example is a top executive recruited from another company, who gives up a high salary and stock options, has expenses of relocation, and then is fired shortly after taking up the new job.

In a 1994 Alabama case, the plaintiff won a claim for fraud in the inducement of contract because the employer lied about the facts she relied on in quitting her old job and going to work for the defendant company. A year later, another Alabama case imposed another requirement that plaintiffs must meet to prevail: the employer's promises must have been made with the intent to deceive. [*Kidder v. American South Bank,* 639 So. 2d 1361 (Ala. 1994); *National Security Ins. Co. v. Donaldson,* 664 So. 2d 871 (Ala. 1995)]

In a Colorado case, a company recruited one of its competitor's employees to open a new office. She was hesitant about leaving an established firm for a start-up, so they promised her that her new job would be much better in the long run than the old one. The new office closed in two months, and she was fired. The court decided that she was promised a "reasonable" term of employment, which the court interpreted to mean one year. [*Pickell v. Arizona Components Co.*, 931 P.2d 1184 (Colo. 1997)]

A Wisconsin case says that there is no breach of contract if an oral offer of at-will employment for an indefinite period is made and then withdrawn before the potential employee starts work [*Heinritz v. Lawrence Univ.*, 194 Wis. 2d 607, 535 N.W.2d 81 (Wis. App. 1995)]—a situation faced by many recent graduates.

An at-will employee in Michigan sued the company president for tortious interference with the employee's employment relationship with the corporation. The plaintiff says that she complained to the corporation's counsel about irregularities committed by the defendant, who retaliated against her and eventually got her fired. It's not clear whether Michigan state law permits such claims, but the Sixth Circuit allowed the case to proceed in federal court. [*Stanek v. Greco,* 323 F.3d 476 (6th Cir. 2003)] However, there are recent Michigan cases saying that in a suit against a supervisor, the plaintiff must prove that the supervisor acted solely for his or her own benefit, with no benefit to the corporation. [*Langrill v. Diversified Fabricators, Inc.*, 2002 WL 1375902 (Mich. App. June 25, 2002); *Diebolt v. Michigan State Univ.*, 2002 WL 1275502 (Mich. App. June 4, 2002)]

When an oral promise of continued employment was made to induce an employee to remain at her job during a merger so she could assist the transition team, her continued service with the company and surrender of the opportunity to look for another job were found to create an implied contract. [*Rinck v. Association of Reserve City Bankers,* 676 A.2d 12 (D.C. App. 1996)]

In contrast, Illinois says that an oral "contract" cannot be enforced because of a legal concept called the Statute of Frauds that requires all contracts lasting a year or more to be in writing in order to be enforceable. [*McInerney v. Chater Golf Inc.*, 176 Ill. 2d 482, 680 N.E.2d 1347 (1997)]

An employee may claim to have provided consideration for a promise of lifetime employment, by staying on the job and not pursuing other opportunities. But some courts say that a person can only hold one job at a time anyway, and therefore does not surrender any rights that would support a promise of lifetime employment. [*Bynum v. Boeing Co.*, 85 Wash. App. 1065 (1997)]

§ 39.04   PUBLIC POLICY

[A]   Generally

A whole line of cases permits employees to sue when they are fired for a reason contrary to the public policy of the state. In other words, it is unlawful to fire an employee for doing something that is acceptable or even admirable. For instance, no matter how inconvenient the timing is for the employer, it is not permitted to fire an employee for serving jury duty.

According to the Sixth Circuit, there are four elements in the cause of action for wrongful discharge that violates public policy. There must be a clear public policy, as manifested by the federal or a state Constitution, a statute, an administrative regulation, or the common law. The "jeopardy element" requires that the employee's termination jeopardizes this policy. The firing must have been motivated by conduct related to the public policy; and the termination cannot have been supported by an overriding legitimate business justification. In the Sixth Circuit view, although whistleblower plaintiffs don't have to be certain that the employer's conduct was illegal, the employee must at least give the employer clear notice that the employee believes that a governmental policy has been violated, to the extent that a reasonable employer would be aware that the complaint is based on that policy. The Sixth Circuit agreed that the district court properly dismissed a case in which the plaintiff failed to connect his air quality complaints to governmental policy. The Sixth Circuit also ruled that, because the decision to fire him was made on September 28, activities after that time could not prove retaliatory discharge. [*Jermer v. Siemens Energy & Automation, Inc.*, 395 F.3d 655 (6th Cir. 2005)]

The First Circuit ruled that for a safety engineer to inform his supervisors about potential overtime violations with respect to the security guards he supervised was part of his job duties. Doing so was not protected activity under the Fair Labor Standards Act, so firing him for raising the issue could not be retaliation in violation of the FLSA. [*Claudio-Gotay v. Becton Dickinson Caribe Ltd.*, 375 F.3d 99 (1st Cir. 2004)]

Under Pennsylvania state law, smaller businesses (manufacturers with fewer than 40 employees; service businesses with fewer than 15 employees) are exempt from criminal penalties for wrongful termination of employees for doing jury service. However, small business can still bring private suits for wrongful termination. The judge pointed out that in his home county, the majority of the workforce is employed by companies with fewer than 15 employees, which could make it very difficult ever to empanel a jury if employers were permitted to fire employees who carried out their civic duty. [*Sheeran v. Kubert Himmelstein & Associates* ___ Pa. D. & C. ___ (Pa. Common Pleas 2003), discussed in Melissa Nann, *Law Firm Manager Alleges Firing for Serving Jury Duty*, The Legal Intelligencer (Oct. 29, 2003) (law.com)]

It violates ERISA § 510 to fire an employee merely to prevent access to pension or welfare benefits. [*See* Chapter 15]

In 2005, the D.C. Circuit granted the NLRB's petition to enforce its decision. The court ruled that there was substantial evidence that the defendant violated NLRA § 8(a)(1) by firing a financial consultant who protested the reduction in compensation terms for the consultants associated with a corporate reorganization. The NLRB determined that the protest was protected concerted activity, so it was an unfair labor practice to fire him for that reason. The D.C. Circuit ruled that the

NLRB's determination that protected concerted activity occurred is entitled to considerable deference, as long as it is reasonable. In this case, the plaintiff engaged in individual acts to alert management to the concerns of the financial consultants, so even if he was not designated as a spokesperson, he was still engaging in concerted activity. [*Citizens Investment Servs. Corp. v. NLRB*, 430 F.3d 1195 (D.C. Cir. 2005)]

The First Amendment free speech rights of a welfare department investigator were not violated when she was fired for making a racist joke at an off-duty political dinner. According to the Massachusetts court, she was not making a speech on a matter of public concern (which would have been protected), and racism can undermine the agency's mission. [*Pereira v. Commissioner of Social Servs.*, 733 N.E.2d 112 (Mass. 2000)]

The rights of an arguably racist employee also had to be explicated in a mid-2003 Fourth Circuit case. A black co-worker complained about the two Confederate flag stickers on the plaintiff's toolbox. The employer asked him to remove the stickers. When he refused, he was fired under the corporate anti-harassment policy. The plaintiff sued in state court, and the case was removed to the federal system on the grounds that its resolution depended on a substantial question of federal law. The plaintiff's First Amendment and 42 U.S.C. § 1983 claims were quickly eliminated, because the employer was a private company, not a state actor. Nor could a 42 U.S.C. § 1981 claim succeed, because there was no allegation that he received differential treatment on the basis of race.

That concentrated the case on the issue of whether the First Amendment protects the plaintiff's right to display the Confederate flag, to the extent that it would violate a clear mandate of public policy to terminate him for doing so. The court accepted the defendant employer's argument that it had to provide a harassment-free workplace. On the main issue, the Fourth Circuit held that the workplace is not a Constitutionally protected forum for political discourse. The plaintiff did not have an enforceable right to display a Confederate flag within the employer's privately owned workplace, although once off the employer's premises he could display the flag on his own home or vehicle. [*Dixon v. Coburg Dairy, Inc.*, 330 F.3d 250 (4th Cir. 2003)]

A year later, however, the Fourth Circuit reheard the case and reversed its earlier opinion. The 2004 decision found that the District Court was not the proper forum for the case because there was no substantial question of federal law involved. Therefore, this time the Fourth Circuit sent the case back to the South Carolina state court. [*Dixon v. Coburg Dairy*, 369 F.3d 811 (4th Cir. 2004)]

The Sixth Circuit ruled that a former supervisor of labor relations who charges that he was fired for complaining about the corporate labor practices can sue for wrongful termination in violation of public policy despite his participation in those practices, which was held not to rule out such a suit. [*Himmel v. Ford Motor Co.*, 342 F.3d 593 (6th Cir. 2003)]

The Sixth Circuit upheld a policy under which a deputy court clerk was fired because of her "intimate association" with an attorney who litigated a number of cases in county court. The attorney happened to be married to, but separated from, another court employee when he proposed marriage to the plaintiff. The Sixth Circuit upheld the policy on the grounds that the relationship caused tension within the workplace; the plaintiff was not prevented from obtaining work elsewhere; and she was an at-will employee. The Sixth Circuit ruled that anti-nepotism policies are sustainable if they have a rational basis in a plausible policy motivation. [*Beecham v. Henderson County*, 422 F.3d 372 (6th Cir. 2005)]

In Maryland, an employee fired for refusing to have sex with a harasser can add a tort claim for abusive discharge to the sexual harassment suit, because the harasser's action violates the public policy against prostitution. (In effect, an employee who has sexual relations to keep a job is unlawfully engaging in sex for pay). [*Insignia Residential Corp. v. Ashton, Maryland*, 755 A.2d 1080 (Md. 2000)]

The employer claimed that the plaintiff in *Daley v. Aetna Life & Casualty* [249 Conn. 766 (1999)] was fired for incompetence. But even if her contention (that she was fired for asking for a family-friendly work schedule) was correct, she would not be able to assert a wrongful termination claim. Although it is meritorious of employers to offer a flexible work schedule, they are not obligated to do so, and not doing so is not a violation of public policy.

Bankruptcy Code § 525(b) prohibits employers from discriminating against anyone who is or has been a bankruptcy debtor. However, the Ninth Circuit recently ruled that this provision does not protect an employee from being fired after telling the employer of an intention to declare bankruptcy, but before the actual filing. According to the Ninth Circuit, the actual filing is significant because it triggers the automatic stay. [*Leonard v. St. Rose Dominican Hosp.*, 310 F.3d 653 (9th Cir. 2002)]

The public policy exception did not protect a plaintiff even if it was true that she was fired to retaliate against her husband's (a local policeman's) involvement in the drunk driving arrest of her boss' wife. Retaliation premised on the actions—lawful or otherwise—of a non-employee spouse is not a recognized ground for a suit. [*Bammert v. Don's Super Valu Inc.*, 254 Wis. 2d 347, 646 N.W.2d 365 (Wis. 2002)]

In an ADEA and wrongful discharge suit brought by a safety and training coordinator with over 30 years of service, the ADEA claim was dismissed (he was less qualified for rehiring than the younger candidates who actually were hired); the wrongful termination claim was tried. The plaintiff charged that he was fired in retaliation for criticizing unsafe corporate policies. The jury awarded him $720,000. The defendant moved for and was granted a new trial. This time, the second jury awarded $920,000. The Eighth Circuit affirmed the district court, holding that there is a clear public policy in favor of workplace safety, and state law forbids retaliation for a state occupational safety and health complaint. Some cases suggest that if there is an administrative complaint procedure, that rules out private suits, but the case law is not conclusive. Although the defense argued that the lack of a private federal cause of action for wrongful discharge under the OSH

Act forbids a similar suit under the Iowa OSH Act, the Eighth Circuit was not persuaded. Federal suits must be based on a specific statute, but common-law rights can be asserted for state-law claims. [*Kohrt v. MidAmerican Energy Co.*, 364 F.3d 894 (8th Cir. 2004)]

A married couple worked together as truck drivers. The husband was assigned to drive a truck that was so overweight that it could not legally be driven on the roads. He told the dispatcher that it was overweight. The couple was asked to drive a single-axle tractor that was also overweight. Then they were offered a different tractor to drive if they stayed overnight, which they did. In the morning, they were sent home for refusing a load, and then fired on the same grounds. They sued in state court for wrongful discharge. The employer removed the case to federal court, on the grounds that it was preempted by the National Labor Relations Act (see Chapter 30), because they were engaging in concerted activity as defined by 29 U.S.C. § 157. The couple moved to amend their complaint to add a count of fraud. The District Court would not allow the complaint to be amended, and dismissed their case. However, the Eighth Circuit reinstated the case and let them amend the complaint. They were acting on their own behalf, not engaging in concerted activity—they were hired as a team and worked together. The reason for rejecting the loads was that they violated legal weight restrictions, so they were following the applicable state law, not acting for their own benefit or the benefit of employees as a group. [*Williams v. Watkins Motor Lines, Inc.*, 310 F.3d 1070 (8th Cir. 2002)]

A recent New Jersey case holds that it violates public policy to discharge a supervisor who has been accused of sexual harassment without adequately investigating the charges first—and it also violates public policy to fire someone for having a consensual sexual relationship with someone at the workplace. [*Grasser v. United HealthCare*, 343 N.J. Super. 241, 778 A.2d 521 (2002), discussed in Henry Gottlieb, *Too Good at Purging the Workplace?* New Jersey Law Journal (Sept. 13, 2002) (law.com)] The Indiana Court of Appeals allowed a public policy wrongful discharge case to be maintained based on allegations that the plaintiff was fired for refusing to certify false financial and tax records, because if the plaintiff had complied with such demands he would have violated various laws and become personally liable individually or as part of a conspiracy. [*McGarrity v. Berlin Metals Inc.*, 774 N.E.2d 71 (Ind. App. 2002)]

The appellant in a California case worked for a company that was acquired. He was asked to sign a one-year covenant forbidding him to solicit the acquired company's customers or potential customers that he had dealt with under the former regime. He refused to sign, and was fired. His litigation theory was that it is a wrongful termination in violation of public policy to fire someone for refusing to sign an unenforceable covenant not to compete. The California Court of Appeals found that although the clause was less restrictive than a traditional covenant not to compete, it still had anti-competitive effect. In California, covenants not to compete are void unless they protect trade secrets or confidential or proprietary information, which were not involved here. The identity of the customers was not a trade secret and was not kept secret—in fact, the names were available on the corporate Web site. [*Thompson v. Impaxx, Inc.*, 113 Cal. App. 4th 1425 (2003)]

The Maryland Court of Appeals ruled in mid-2003 that it does not violate public policy to fire an employee after she tried to contact an attorney before signing off on her unfavorable performance appraisal. There is no real public policy that creates a "right to counsel" in the employment context, in the sense of the right to consult an attorney (although employees in a unionized workplace do have a right to bring a union representative to an investigatory interview that could result in discipline). [*Porterfield v. Mascari II Inc.*, 71 L.W. 1709 (Md. App. May 8, 2003)]

[B] Whistleblower Employees

The case of the "whistleblower" employee is more complex. Employees (often those who are dissatisfied for other reasons) go to the press, or file complaints with enforcement agencies, about some aspect of corporate conduct they find unsatisfactory. In some instances, firing (or taking other adverse employment action) against whistleblowers violates public policy, because in appropriate cases, whistleblowers are exposing violations of law or other improprieties.

The federal Sarbanes-Oxley Act [Pub. L. No. 107-204] (also discussed in this book in connection with 401(k) plans and corporate communications—notices to employees about "blackout" periods that restrict their abilities to trade their plan accounts) includes two provisions to protect whistleblowers.

In mid-2003, OSHA published an interim final rule providing procedures for employment discrimination complaints by employees who charge that they suffered retaliation for Sarbanes-Oxley whistleblowing (exposure of corporate fraud). [68 Fed. Reg. 31,859 (May 28, 2003)] OSHA issued a Compliance Directive and updated its Whistleblower Investigation Manual in light of Sarbanes-Oxley and the 2002 Pipeline Safety Improvement Act. Compliance safety and health officers are charged with understanding the protections for workers under the various statutes, and are required to take complaints and notify the area director when a whistleblower complaint is received. [<http://www.osha.gov/dep/oia/whistleblower/index.html>]

Under § 806 of the Act, 18 U.S.C. § 1514A is amended to provide that publicly traded companies are forbidden to "discharge, demote, suspend, threaten, harass, or in any other manner discriminate against an employee in the terms and conditions of employment" because the employee has engaged in any lawful act to provide information to the government or participate in an investigation of securities fraud or corporate wrongdoing. (The lawful acts condition is important—whistleblowers are not protected if they commit burglaries or hack computer systems to get this information, for example.)

Someone who believes that he or she has been discriminated against for whistleblowing can file a complaint with the Secretary of Labor; if, after 180 days, the Secretary has not issued a final decision, the whistleblower can sue in federal District Court (even if the amount in controversy is below the $75,000 usually required to get to federal court). The Sarbanes-Oxley Act provides for whatever relief is necessary to make a successful whistleblower claimant whole—i.e., compensatory damages, reinstatement with whatever seniority the person would have had without discrimination, back pay plus interest, and compensation for special damages such as attorneys' fees, expert witness fees, and costs.

Also see Sarbanes-Oxley Act § 1107, which provides for fines and/or up to 10 years' imprisonment, for knowing harmful actions, taken with intent to retaliate against someone who provided truthful information about Sarbanes-Oxley violations to any law enforcement officer. This provision covers all actions, including interference with any person's lawful employment or livelihood.

The first appellate ruling about the extraterritorial application of whistleblower protection under Sarbanes-Oxley came down in 2006. The First Circuit ruled that Sarbanes-Oxley does not apply to foreign citizens working outside the United States for a foreign subsidiary of a covered company. (The plaintiff was an Argentine employed by Latin American subsidiaries of a Massachusetts company; he charged that he suffered retaliation for informing his supervisors about forged invoices and inflated sales figures.) In the First Circuit view, Congress did not demonstrate an intention to have the statute apply extraterritorially; the statutory purpose was to protect shareholders and the integrity of the U.S. securities market. [*Carnero v. Boston Scientific Co.*, 443 F.3d 1 (1st Cir. 2006)]

In August 2004, the Department of Labor published Final Regulations, substantially similar to the Interim Final Regulations of May 28, 2003, covering procedures and schedules for handling employment discrimination claims brought by employees who claim whistleblower status under the Sarbanes-Oxley Act. (Although the regulations were promulgated by the DOL, administering the rules is delegated to OSHA.) A preliminary reinstatement order can be stayed, but only in an exceptional case, based on factors similar to those used to grant injunctive relief: for instance, irreparable injury, likelihood of success on the merits, and balance between the public interest and possible harm to the parties. [69 Fed. Reg. 52,103 (Aug. 24, 2004); *see* 73 LW 2119]

The Occupational Safety and Health Administration enforces ten federal whistleblower statutes, although the Sarbanes-Oxley Act is the only one that deals with financial wrongdoing rather than health and safety. In 2004, the vast majority of Sarbanes-Oxley cases were dismissed at the summary judgment stage; but of the few cases that actually went to trial, employees won about half. OSHA reported that by October of that year, 317 complaints had been filed by people claiming whistleblower status. One hundred seventy-six complaints were dismissed (many of the dismissals were appealed), 39 were withdrawn, 64 remained pending, and 38 ruled in the complainant's favor. OSHA stated that it had participated in arranging 13 settlements yielding more than $3 million for complainants, and an additional 17 employees settled for undisclosed amounts.

Many complainants were dissatisfied by the procedure (some weren't even interviewed by investigators). The procedure has also been criticized as one-sided because OSHA rules permit the accused company to meet with OSHA and contest its findings; whistleblowers do not get the same right. The investigator must give the company a copy of the complaint, but doesn't have to give the alleged whistleblower a copy of the employer's response. Corporate information disclosed to OSHA can be designated as confidential, keeping it away from the complainant. OSHA has made policy decisions that claims must be filed within 90 days of the alleged retaliation; that retaliation occurring outside the United States is not subject to Sarbanes-Oxley; and that harassment occurring before Sarbanes-Oxley was enacted is not actionable. [Deborah Solomon, *For Financial Whistle-Blowers, New Shield Is an Imperfect One,* Wall Street Journal, Oct. 4, 2004, at p. A1; Tamara Loomis, *Whistle While You Work,* Corporate Counsel, June 9, 2004 (law.com)]

At the end of 1998, the Supreme Court held that an action under 42 U.S.C. § 1985 (damage to person or property) can be maintained by an at-will employee who alleges that he was fired for assisting a federal criminal investigation of the employer company. [*Haddle v. Garrison,* 525 U.S. 121 (1998)]

Some states have statutes extending specific protection to whistle-blower employees. However, some of these statutes apply only to government workers, not employees of private-sector companies. The trend in the courts is to limit the number of situations in which employees will be considered protected whistleblowers.

For instance, the FDA regulations require reporting of research results that demonstrate a serious risk. A drug company director of research was fired for insisting that some test results be reported, when company officials did not think that the results were poor enough to be reported. The research director lost his wrongful discharge case. In the court's view, there had simply been a difference of opinion, and it is legitimate to fire someone for exercising poor judgment. [*Chelly v. Knoll Pharmaceuticals,* 295 N.J. Super. 478, 685 A.2d 498 (1996)]

The Third Circuit rejected a plaintiff's wrongful discharge claim alleging that he was fired in retaliation for complaining to state authorities, and lobbying for legislation to prevent insurance agents from being terminated without just cause. The court said that the whistleblower law that he cited protected public employees only. Under the relevant state (Pennsylvania) law it violates public policy to fire someone for refusing to commit a crime, or for exercising a statutory duty, or when a statute specifically protects the worker. But there is no general First Amendment protection for private-sector workers claiming that they are exercising free speech rights. [*Fraser v. Nationwide Mutual Ins. Co.,* 352 F.3d 107 (3d Cir. 2003)]

A Colorado employee was fired for sending a letter to a newspaper criticizing the employer's business practices. A Colorado statute makes it unlawful to fire anyone for lawful activity carried on outside the workplace, but that statute has an exception for bona fide occupational qualifications. The District Court for the

District of Colorado read this to mean that employers are entitled to an implied right of loyalty in public communications. The employee wasn't entitled to whistleblower protection. He failed to use the internal grievance procedure (which he probably would have done if he had a good-faith objective of solving the problem) and what was at issue was customer service quality, not public safety. [*Marsh v. Delta Air Lines Inc.*, 952 F. Supp. 1458 (D. Colo. Feb. 7, 1997)]

A Texas nurse reported a co-employee's apparent drug use at work and mishandling of prescription drugs. But it was not the alleged drug user who got fired—it was the reporting nurse. The nurse lost a whistleblower action in state court. Although the Texas Supreme Court agreed that protection of the safety of hospital patients is part of public policy, it also held that Texas legislators have limited whistleblower protection to specific context, but there is no general protection for employees discharged for reporting wrongdoing in the workplace. [*Austin v. Healthtrust, Inc.*, 967 S.W.2d 400 (Tex. 1998)]

In general, Wisconsin is not hospitable to whistleblower claims. Employees can be fired for complying with a law (but not for refusing to break one). Most whistleblower claims involve reporting of wrongdoing. However, in 1997, the state's Supreme Court created a special exemption, allowing wrongful discharge suits only by nursing home whistleblowers. [*Hausman v. St. Croix Care Ctr.*, 571 N.W.2d 393 (Wis. 1997)]

A quality control inspector said that she informed management about tainted meat, but was ignored. She contacted government inspectors, who found deficiencies in the plant. She was ordered not to contact the inspectors again. She was fired when the employer suspected her of "leaking" information to the inspectors. Her wrongful termination/whistleblower suit was unsuccessful. The court said that it was legitimate to fire her for disobeying an order to avoid further contact with inspectors. [*Dray v. New Market Poultry Prods. Inc.*, 518 S.E.2d 312 (Va. 1999)]

A fired whistleblower brought, and settled, a False Claims Act qui tam action against the ex-employer. (A qui tam action is brought to challenge alleged wrongdoing.) The Eleventh Circuit ruled that he could bring a later False Claims Act retaliation action. The qui tam and retaliation claims are based on the same facts, and the firing had already occurred, so both claims should have been resolved at the same time. The legal doctrine of res judicata ("matter already decided") prevented him from pursuing the retaliation claim.

A state whistleblower suit cannot be removed to federal court merely because the wrongdoing alleged by the whistleblower consisted of submitting false claims to the federal government. The Sixth Circuit ruled in 2006 that there was no private cause of action under the False Claims Act, so there was no substantial federal question that would justify removal under 28 U.S.C. § 1441(b). Alleging a federal law that has no private cause of action as an element of a state law cause of action does not state a claim "arising" under federal law. [*Eastman v. Marine Mechanical Corp.*, 438 F.3d 544 (6th Cir. 2006)]

Courts have said that "wrongful discharge" means just that: There is no cause of action for wrongful transfer if there is no loss of salary or benefits. In the case of

White v. State of Washington, [131 Wash. 2d 1 (Wash. 1997)] the plaintiff reported what she perceived to be patient abuse to the state nursing home regulators. In this analysis, she did not lose any money, so no legally enforceable rights had been violated.

In a 2002 California case, a plaintiff who claimed she was fired for testifying on behalf of one of her employees who had been sexually harassed was awarded a $1 million jury verdict in her whistleblower lawsuit. The Superior Court judge reduced the jury's verdict by $255,000—but awarded $714,000 to the plaintiff's lawyers (who were also entitled to one-third of the damages she received). The judge believed that the large fee was appropriate because of the lawyers' enthusiastic litigation of a case with complex layers of evidence. [*Kotla v. Regents of Univ. of Cal.*, No. V014799-8 (Cal. 2002), discussed in Jahna Berry, *Whistleblower's Counsel Awarded Hefty Fee*, The Recorder (Nov. 18, 2002) (law.com)]

OSHA has enforcement responsibility not just for OSH Act § 11(c), covering whistleblowers who make safety and health complaints, but for 13 other whistle-blower provisions under other statutes (e.g., the Asbestos Hazard Emergency Response Act, the Solid Waste Disposal Act, and the Sarbanes-Oxley Act). In fact, under OSH Act § 11(c) OSHA is the only possible enforcer; the statute does not include a private right of action under which employees can sue if they claim that they were fired because of their whistleblower roles. Between FY 1995 and 2002, OSHA had between 1,353 and 1,805 11(c) cases a year, most of which were dismissed or withdrawn. In each year, between 20–24% of the cases were settled, and OSHA found that about 300–400 cases had merit. [Ellen Byerrum, *Protections for Job Safety Whistleblowers Among Weakest of Those Overseen by OSHA*, 72 L.W. 2211 (Oct. 21, 2003)]

[C] WC Claimants

The Pennsylvania Worker's Compensation statute doesn't say in so many words that it is illegal for employers to retaliate against employees who file Worker's Compensation claims. Nevertheless, employees in this situation are allowed to bring wrongful discharge claims, on the grounds that the legislature did not rule out retaliation actions—it just failed to make explicit provisions for them. [*Shick v. Shirey*, 716 A.2d 1231 (Pa. 1998)]

Worker's Compensation was also involved in the case of *Lins v. Children's Discovery Center of America, Inc.* [95 Wash. App. 486 (1999)] The plaintiff was a manager with responsibility for six day care centers. She and five other employees were hurt in a work-related automobile accident. All six filed Worker's Compensation claims. The plaintiff's supervisor ordered her to fire the other five employees because the supervisor expected them to sue the employer.

The plaintiff refused to do this because she knew that the Washington State statute (unlike its Pennsylvania counterpart) explicitly bans retaliation for filing a WC claim. The plaintiff, who previously had received good performance ratings, got a bad performance rating and was put on probation, then was fired for neglect of duty and poor performance.

She sued for wrongful discharge in violation of public policy, claiming that she was fired for refusing to perform an act of illegal retaliation. The employer's contention was that it is not illegal to fire an employee for insubordination, even if the employee refused to obey an illegal order. The Washington Court of Appeals favored the plaintiff's argument, extending the public policy cause of action to protect employees who refuse to violate the law. The public interest favors law enforcement, and employees who are not afraid of losing their jobs will be more likely to refuse illegal orders.

§ 39.05   PREEMPTION ARGUMENTS

Preemption is the legal doctrine under which passage of a federal law limits or eliminates the state's power to regulate that subject. ERISA preempts state wrongful termination claims based on alleged termination to avoid paying pension benefits. All such claims must be brought in federal court, under ERISA § 510, and not in state court.

According to the plaintiff in *Group Dekko Services LLC v. Miller*, [717 N.E.2d 967 (Ind. App. 1999)] she was fired for protesting the mishandling of an employee's benefit claim. (The plaintiff was a benefits administrator, afraid that she would be held liable as a fiduciary for the way the claim was handled.) The court held that state wrongful discharge claims were preempted by ERISA, because determining whether she was a fiduciary would require interpretation of the plan.

The Family and Medical Leave Act preempts common-law claims of retaliatory discharge when an employee says he or she was fired as punishment for taking FMLA leave. [*Hamros v. Bethany Homes,* 894 F. Supp. 1176 (N.D. Ill. 1995)]

According to the Massachusetts Superior Court, because OSHA has no private right of action, it does not preempt state claims that an employee was wrongfully discharged for reporting safety violations. [*Antlitz v. CMJ Mgmt. Co.*, 1997 WL 42396 (Mass. Super. Jan. 30, 1997)] Kansas took a similar position in 1998. [*Flenker v. Willamette Indus. Inc.,* 266 Kan. 198, 967 P.2d 295 (1998)]

National Labor Relations Act §§ 7 and 8 do not so completely preempt state wrongful discharge claims that the state claims can be removed to federal court. In 2005 the Fourth Circuit held that preemption depends on a preexisting federal cause of action, and the wrongful discharge case was not based on the right to bargain collectively or the ban on unfair labor practices. [*Lontz v. Tharp*, 413 F.3d 435 (4th Cir. 2005)]

Preemption arguments can also be used in state court. If the employee is covered by a state antidiscrimination law that is not preempted by federal law, the employer may be able to get a wrongful termination suit dismissed, because the employee should have sued for discrimination. From the employer's viewpoint, the best-case scenario is that the employee waited too long, so the discrimination charges must be dismissed.

Chapter 40

ARBITRATION AND ADR

§ 40.01   INTRODUCTION

Taking a case to the court system is time-consuming, expensive, and often frustrating. Therefore, companies encounter nonlitigation means of dispute resolution in many contexts. In addition to commercial arbitration, which is beyond the scope of this book, unionized companies will often wind up arbitrating labor disputes.

Alternative Dispute Resolution (ADR) methods are supposed to be informal, governed more by justice and fairness than by strict rules of legal procedure. Depending on the ADR method, either one person or a panel of people will either assist the parties to work out their own solution (mediation) or will make a decision (arbitration). It has been estimated that an employment lawsuit takes an average of a year and a half from the date the case is filed to resolve, versus only one year for arbitration. Once the case gets to the arbitrator, 90% of arbitration hearings are completed in two days or less.

Both unionized and nonunionized companies often find mediation or arbitration a superior alternative to litigation when employees make claims that they have suffered employment discrimination. In fact, employers often use various methods to make sure that all claims will have to go through arbitration. The question is when and how it is legitimate to impose an arbitration requirement on employees. If the employees freely choose arbitration over litigation, this problem does not arise, but nevertheless, the employer will still have to find a way to present its case effectively to the arbitrator.

The "first principles" of arbitration are that arbitration should be independent of the court system and should provide flexibility and respect the rights of the parties.

§ 40.02   GRIEVANCES AND DISCIPLINE

[A]   "Progressive Discipline"

The typical Collective Bargaining Agreement (CBA) for a unionized company spells out a system of "progressive discipline" under which employees whose work performance is unsatisfactory will be warned, offered guidance and training, and given a series of escalating penalties before being fired. Progressive discipline is sometimes used in nonunionized environment, although less frequently.

The system must make it clear to employees what the employer's expectations are and what the employer intends to do if the rules are violated. Once employees have been told what they are doing wrong, they should be given a reasonable amount of time to correct it. There should be a monitoring process to sort out the employees who have made adequate progress from those who have not. The time period should probably be between 30 and 90 days: Too long a period may make the arbitrator believe that the employer is stringing together isolated, unrelated incidents to make a case.

Employees who have been subject to discipline are likely to feel that they were unfairly singled out—and in some cases, this will result in discrimination or wrongful termination charges. An important HR function is creating a legally sustainable system of progressive discipline, and making sure that supervisors understand the system and apply it objectively.

A legally sustainable disciplinary system should be:

- Consistent—not only must discrimination be avoided but employees should not be subjected to supervisors' whims or penalized when the supervisor has a bad day;
- Well documented—an arbitrator or court should be able to see that each step reflects the employer's own rules;
- Clear—employees should know that if they fail to meet X goals in Y days, they will be put on probation, lose wages, or be terminated;
- Appropriate—the degree of the sanction should reflect the severity of the error or misconduct;
- Reciprocal—employees should get a chance to give their side of the story to an objective decision maker who isn't already committed to management's viewpoint.

Arbitrators will examine the "step formula" under the system and see if it was followed. For example, if the first step results in a determination that the employee was at fault, then he or she might be verbally admonished, whereas by the fourth step, dismissal could be appropriate. If the step formula is not followed, the arbitrator is likely to reverse the decision or substitute a lesser penalty, and there's a good chance that the courts will uphold the arbitrator.

Presenting grievances to the employer is one of the clearest cases of concerted activity protected by the NLRA, whether or not the employees are unionized. However, they must in fact act in concert, or one employee must present a shared grievance. One person pressing his or her own agenda is not protected under the NLRA. For NLRA purposes, a grievance must be something that relates directly to the terms and conditions of employment.

Once they have made a complaint, employees are required to return to work within a reasonable time. In fact, one of the bywords of labor arbitration is "obey now, grieve later."

Sometimes, the employer will want to investigate a situation or will give the employee a chance to put his or her interpretation of contested facts on the record. If there is a reasonable likelihood that the "investigatory interview" will lead to dismissal or lesser forms of employee discipline, the employee has the right to bring a representative to the meeting.

Traditionally, this was known as the Weingarten right (named after an NLRB case) and was limited to unionized employees; in fact, it was a major recruitment tool for unions that joining a union would imply this right of representation. However, the NLRB, affirmed by the D.C. Circuit, extended the right to nonunion employees. [*Epilepsy Foundation of Northeast Ohio v. NLRB*, 268 F.3d 1095 (D.C. Cir. 2001)]

There is no right of representation (for unionized or nonunionized employees) if the meeting is simply a review of work rules, or is used to provide training—in other words, if the employee can't get into any trouble. But in a *Weingarten* situation, it is an Unfair Labor Practice for the employer to refuse to allow the employee to choose the particular union representative who will accompany the employee to the interview. In the Fourth Circuit view, allowing the employee free choice helps redress the imbalance of power between employer and employee. [*Anheuser-Busch Inc. v. NLRB*, 338 F.3d 267 (4th Cir. 2003)]

[B]   Grievance Records

It makes sense to buy or design standard forms for keeping track of employee grievances, although there is no specific federal requirement for making such records or keeping them for a particular length of time. The grievance form should contain:

- Identification of the CBA that creates the grievance procedure and the specific clause of that contract that has to be interpreted;
- Date the grievance was submitted;
- Grievance case number;
- Name, department, shift, and job title of the employee who submits the grievance;
- What the employee says is wrong;
- Records of statements by witnesses;
- Documentary evidence relevant to the grievance;
- Whether the employee was represented (e.g., by the shop steward or a fellow employee);
- Written decisions by the first-level supervisor or others involved in processing the grievance;
- A signed statement by the union representative as to whether the union considers the grievance to be adequately resolved;
- Signatures of the employee and all decision makers.

It can be very helpful to analyze past grievances to see how patterns change over time.

> **Tip:** If the grievance could be construed as alleging a hostile work environment (e.g., pervasive sexual harassment or harassment on the basis of race, nationality, or diversity), be sure to investigate thoroughly; failure to do so can subject the employer to liability.

[C] NLRB Deference

Although the NLRB has the power, under the NLRA § 10(a), to prevent unfair labor practices, the NLRB will defer to grievance arbitration (i.e., will not interfere) if several criteria are satisfied:

- Understanding the meaning of the CBA is central to resolving the dispute;
- The dispute came up during an ongoing collective bargaining relationship;
- The employees do not claim that the employer prevented them from exercising all their rights under labor law;
- The employer has agreed to a broad-based arbitration clause—in fact, one broad enough to cover the existing dispute.

§ 40.03   MEDIATION

A mediator is a neutral third party who listens to both sides and helps the parties themselves work out a solution that is acceptable to both of them. The American Arbitration Association has a set of uniform Employment Mediation Rules. Parties can trigger this procedure by writing a request to the AAA for mediation, or by filing a Submission to Mediation form, also with the AAA.

One reason that the procedure for filing discrimination charges is so elaborate is that part of the EEOC's job is to attempt mediation of the charge. [*See* Chapter 41]

§ 40.04   ARBITRATION VS. LITIGATION

Many studies have been done comparing the experience of resolving discrimination charges by arbitration versus litigation. In 1997, the federal General Accounting Office (GAO) found that 19% of employers they surveyed were using arbitration to resolve employment disputes. By 1996, over 3 million employees were subject to arbitration using the rules of the American Arbitration Association (AAA).

Concerns have been expressed that arbitration is pro-employer. The average discrimination court case costs the employer $124,000 in defense costs, so reducing costs is a boon for the employer. The risk is that arbitrators will, consciously or unconsciously, favor employers, because an employer is much more likely to need to pick arbitrators in the future than is an individual employee.

Statistics showing the number of times employees win when they go to trial in the federal courts show only the tip of the iceberg. Sixty percent of cases brought in federal court become the subject of motions to dismiss the case before a full trial is held—and employers win 98% of those motions. Therefore, a tremendous number of employment cases wash out before they ever get to the jury stage.

Another important difference is that, although employees are much more likely to win at arbitration, the awards average much smaller than amounts awarded by judges or juries. In litigation, employers are always at risk of a headline-making, multimillion dollar damage award (although really high awards are often reduced by an appellate court or the plaintiff settles for less than the full amount). [This information comes from *Arbitration Now*, a book published by the American Bar Association Section of Dispute Resolution in 1999, edited by Paul H. Haagen]

§ 40.05 LABOR ARBITRATION

[A] Grievance Arbitration and Contract or Interest Arbitration

Arbitration and mediation have a long history as means to settle disputes between labor and management without a strike and without litigation. By agreeing to arbitrate an issue, in effect the union agrees not to strike over that issue. The employer agrees not to take unilateral action.

The two main types of labor arbitration are grievance arbitration (also known as rights arbitration), used when there is a disagreement about interpretation of an existing contract, and contract or interest arbitration, invoked when the parties are not sure which provisions should be included in a new, renewed, or reopened CBA. However, this promotes a somewhat different mind-set from the type of arbitration discussed later in this chapter, where the focus is not on avoiding a strike dealing with an entire bargaining unit, but a court case involving one person's discrimination charge.

Nearly all collective bargaining agreements allow for an in-house grievance procedure, but if that does not resolve the problem, then final, binding arbitration, resulting in a decree that can be enforced by the court system, is the last part of the procedure.

Organizations such as the American Arbitration Association and the Federal Mediation and Conciliation Service maintain lists of qualified arbitrators, who are familiar both with the conditions in a particular industry and with arbitration rules and practices. If there will be only one arbitrator, then both sides will have to agree on an acceptable arbitrator. If there are three arbitrators, usually each side selects one arbitrator, and the two arbitrators select the third.

As a preliminary step, the employer and union try to agree on a statement of the issues involved in the grievance. If they cannot even agree on that, the arbitrator may have to draft the statement.

> **Tip:** If the employer wants to discharge or discipline an employee, it will proceed first in arbitration; in other matters, the union usually proceeds first.

[B] Arbitrability

If it is not clear whether a company has agreed to submit a particular issue to arbitration, then the issue is arbitrable. This principle comes from "The Steelworkers' Trilogy," three cases decided by the Supreme Court in 1960. [*Steelworkers v. American Mfg. Co.,* 363 U.S. 564 (1960); *United Steelworkers of Am. v. Warrior Gulf Navigation Co.,* 363 U.S. 574 (1960); *United Steelworkers of Am. v. Enterprise Wheel and Car Corp.,* 363 U.S. 593 (1960)] If a CBA contains both an arbitration clause and a no-strike clause, any dispute that involves the application and interpretation of the CBA is arbitrable unless arbitration is specifically ruled out by the terms of the contract.

Under the Steelworkers' Trilogy, the language of the CBA is the first thing the arbitrators consult, but this is not the only factor in the analysis. The "law of the shop" (practices that have evolved in that particular operation) can be considered. Factors such as the effect of the arbitrator's decision on productivity, morale, and workplace tensions are also legitimate considerations. Courts can't review the merits of an arbitration decision or whether a different resolution would have been more sensible. All the court can do is decide whether the arbitration award "draws its essence" from the arbitration agreement.

However, because of a later Supreme Court case, [*First Options of Chicago, Inc. v. Kaplan,* 514 U.S. 938 (1995)] the court system rather than the arbitrator decides whether a party agreed to arbitrate a particular type of dispute, if there is no clear, unmistakable evidence of the parties' intentions. There is no right to re-arbitrate an issue already considered by the NLRB in an unfair labor practice proceeding.

A number of courts have ruled on the division of labor between judges and arbitrators:

- Courts decide whether the parties are bound by an arbitration clause and whether the arbitration clause applies to a particular type of controversy, but arbitrators handle the other issues: *Shaw's Supermarkets, Inc. v. United Food & Commercial Workers Union,* 321 F.3d 251 (1st Cir. 2003),
- Whether three separate grievances can properly be consolidated as a single arbitration: *Richard C. Young & Co. v. Leventhal,* 389 F.3d 1 (1st Cir. 2004),
- Whether the right to arbitrate has been waived is determined by the arbitrator, at least when the waiver is alleged to result from litigation activity: *National American Insurance Co. v. Transamerica Occidental Life Ins. Co.,* 328 F.3d 462 (8th Cir. 2003); *Bellevue Drug Co. v. Advance PCS,* 333 F. Supp. 2d 318 (E.D. Pa. 2004), but the Fifth Circuit says that it's up to the court system to determine if litigation before the district court waives the right to arbitrate: *Tristar Fin. Ins. Agency, Inc. v. Equicredit Corp. of America,* 97 Fed. Appx. 462 (5th Cir. 2004).

A union filed a grievance on behalf of its members, charging that unilateral changes in the health benefit plan (for both active workers and retirees) violated the

CBA. The company's argument was that the grievance was not arbitrable with respect to the retirees because they were not employees covered by the CBA. The arbitrator decided that the union had standing to seek arbitration on behalf of the retirees (even though they were no longer members of the union) because the benefits were included in the CBA. The company sued in federal court to have the arbitrator's decision vacated, alleging that it did not draw its essence from the CBA. The District Court held that the union could represent the retirees at the arbitration, but only if the retirees consented to be represented. The District Court's rationale was that active workers are always represented by the union and have no individual claims, and can be subjected to mandatory arbitration, whereas retirees do have individual claims so they cannot be forced to arbitrate without their consent. The Sixth Circuit affirmed the District Court. Consent is required both to protect the retirees (so they do not lose their individual claims) and the company (which could be faced with multiple claims from unhappy retirees who say they should not be bound by the arbitrator's decision because they did not consent to arbitration). [*Cleveland Electric Illuminating Co. v. Utility Workers Union of Am., Local 270*, 440 F.3d 809 (6th Cir. 2006)]

[C] Potentially Arbitrable Issues

Many issues have been found potentially arbitrable. In fact, because collective bargaining and arbitration are complementary processes, the list is similar to the list of issues that are mandatory bargaining subjects:

- Sale of a business;
- Relocation of operations;
- Contracting out bargaining unit work;
- Temporary shutdowns;
- Discharge of an individual employee;
- Layoffs;
- Recalls after a layoff;
- Disputes about work assignments (including assigning supervisors to bargaining unit work);
- Work schedules;
- Classification of work;
- Compensation, including bonuses, overtime pay, incentive pay, and severance;
- Vacation, sick leave, and holidays;
- Seniority systems;
- Safety disputes;
- No-strike clauses.

The CBA covering a newspaper was silent on the issue of the extent to which disputes have to be arbitrated if they arise after the expiration of the CBA containing the arbitration clause. The First Circuit held in 2002 that it remained proper to arbitrate disputes about union security and automatic dues check off that arose during the contract even if arbitration occurred after the CBA expired. [*Providence Journal Co. v. Providence Newspaper Guild,* 308 F.3d 129 (1st Cir. 2002)]

The federal courts have jurisdiction to compel an employer to arbitrate claims that its conduct during an organizing campaign violated an agreement with the union. Such a dispute comes under the Labor Management Relations Act (LMRA) § 301 because it is more contractual than representational: the agreement can be interpreted without going into the question of who the union represents. [*Service Employees' Int'l Union v. St. Vincent Medical Ctr.,* 344 F.3d 977 (9th Cir. 2003)]

[D] The Process of Labor Arbitration

In most instances, when management and union hit a deadlock over a grievance or dispute, resort to arbitration will be automatic. However, depending on needs and comparative bargaining power, the arbitration clause might be drafted to allow only the union to invoke arbitration. Employees might also be given the right to invoke arbitration in situations where the union declines to press an employee grievance.

> **Tip:** Even if the CBA does not include a formal arbitration clause, management and union can sign a "submission agreement" agreeing to be bound by the arbitration decision on a one-time basis.

Arbitration clauses usually call for the involvement of either the Federal Mediation and Conciliation Service (FMCS) or the American Arbitration Association (AAA). However, the parties can agree on other ways to resolve disputes if they so choose.

Arbitration begins with a "demand": Either side invokes the CBA arbitration clause and notifies the appropriate agency. The FMCS can be called in by either management or union to assist in the negotiating process. The FMCS can also offer its services, but cannot demand to be made part of the process. FMCS will not mediate a dispute that has only minor effect on interstate commerce if there are other conciliation services (e.g., state agencies) available. The FMCS can also refuse to intervene on behalf of parties who have a record of noncooperation with arbitration, including failure to pay arbitration fees.

Sometimes, before a matter can be arbitrated, it will be necessary to determine if all the prerequisites for arbitration (e.g., those set out in the CBA or the predispute arbitration agreement) have been satisfied. But, in that case, is it up to the arbitrator or a court to make this basic determination? The Eighth Circuit held in 2004 that such determinations fall within the power of the arbitrator. In other words, it is a procedural question, not a substantive question of arbitrability, which would require a court decision. [*International Ass'n of Bridge, Structural,*

Ornamental and Reinforcing Ironworkers v. EFCO Corp. and Constr. Prods., Inc., 359 F.3d 954 (8th Cir. 2004)]

The Eighth Circuit ruled that it was not a breach of a union's duty of fair representation for it to refuse to arbitrate a grievance sought by an employee who was fired for falsifying his time sheet. The court found that the union local performed an adequate investigation before making its decision. It was not irrational to reject the option of arbitrating, given doubts about the employee's credibility and the union's past history of losing arbitration cases involving employee dishonesty. [*Martin v. American Airlines*, 390 F.3d 601 (8th Cir. 2004)]

Once an arbitration award is rendered, it is usually final, binding, and not subject to judicial review by any court. In other words, agreeing to submit to arbitration is a very significant decision that cannot be undertaken casually. It will probably be impossible to get any kind of review or have the decision set aside. However, a serious irregularity in the process, such as proof that the arbitrator was not impartial, may justify setting aside the award.

The Sixth Circuit has been especially active in vacating arbitration awards— 17 out of 75 cases since 1986—whereas the Supreme Court has not vacated an arbitration decision since 1960. The Sixth Circuit uses a four-part test and rules that an award might depart from the essence of the CBA and therefore be subject to challenge if it conflicts with the terms of the contract; imposes new requirements that are not in the contract; lacks rational support; or is based on general fairness considerations rather than the actual terms of the contract. In 2006, the Sixth Circuit's Judge Jeffrey S. Sutton ruled that the Sixth Circuit should conform its rules to the Supreme Court's almost absolute deference to the discretion of arbitrators. [*Michigan Family Resources Inc. v. SEIU Local 517*, 438 F.3d 653 (6th Cir. 2006); *see* Pamela A. MacLean, *Federal Judge Raises Alarm Over Vacated Arbitration Awards*, Nat'l Law Journal, Mar. 2, 2006 (law.com)]

The mission of the Federal Mediation and Conciliation Service (FMCS) is to assist in contract negotiation disputes between employers and their unionized employees. The FMCS also assists in mediation of discrimination cases and grievances before they reach the arbitration stage. Parties can request an arbitrator online, at <http://www.fmcs.gov> or can download request forms from the site and then fax them or mail them to the FMCS. [The FMCS' FAQ is at <http://www.fmcs.gov/internet/faq.asp?categoryID=336>; the agency's policies and procedures are at <http://www.fmcs.gov/internet/itemDetail.asp?categoryID=197&itemID=16959>]

Before 2003, four Circuit courts (the First, Third, Ninth, and D.C. Circuits) had already held that the Norris-LaGuardia Act prevents a District Court from issuing an injunction to stop a labor dispute from being arbitrated. In 2003, the Seventh Circuit joined this group. [*AT&T Broadband, LLC v. International Brotherhood of Electrical Workers*, 317 F.3d 758 (7th Cir. 2003)] The Seventh Circuit found that AT&T Broadband and the union were involved in a labor dispute; because they were, it would be improper to issue an injunction before the parties had been through the arbitration process.

[E] Case Law on Labor Arbitration

In late 2000, the Supreme Court decided that, in a unionized workplace, an arbitrator's decision is enforceable by the court system as long as the arbitration award draws its essence from the Collective Bargaining Agreement (CBA). So, unless the arbitrator's decision actually violates a statute or regulation, it must be enforced—even if it violates public policy. [*Eastern Associated Coal Corp. v. UMW,* 531 U.S. 57 (2000)] For example, in March 2004 the Fifth Circuit refused to overturn an arbitration award where the arbitrator interpreted the contract's requirement of timely presentation of grievances to mean that the grievance must be pressed shortly after the event, even if the union does not learn the facts until much later. Whether or not this was the best way to interpret the CBA, the arbitrator did in fact interpret the CBA rather than making a radical departure from it; therefore, the award had to be upheld. [*Teamsters Local No. 5. v. Formosa Plastics Corp.,* 363 F.3d 368 (5th Cir. 2004)]

The Seventh Circuit held that a union's 18-month delay prevented arbitrability of grievances about alleged underpayment of wages under an expired CBA. The events would have been arbitrable if the union had acted promptly because they occurred while the contract was still in force. [*R.J. Corman Derailment Servs. v. International Union of Operating Engineers,* 422 F.3d 522 (7th Cir. 2005)]

According to the Seventh Circuit, an employer is only permitted to make unilateral alterations in the terms and conditions of employment when an overall impasse in negotiations has been reached. In this view, inability to resolve a particular issue is not sufficient. [*Duffy Tool & Stamping LLC v. NLRB,* 233 F.3d 995 (7th Cir. 2000)] The Fifth Circuit does allow unilateral changes after a single-issue impasse, but the First, Sixth, and D.C. Circuits had already adopted the NLRB position (that impasse must be total to justify unilateral alterations) before the *Duffy* case.

Ohmite Manufacturing Co. [290 N.L.R.B. 1036 (1988)] says that it is unlawful to restrict permission to attend another employee's NLRB hearing to employees who have a real need to attend. It is also unlawful for the employer to base a denial on an improper motivation. In the case of *Cadbury Beverages Inc. v. NLRB* [160 F.3d 24 (D.C. Cir. 1998)], the employer fired an employee who disobeyed an order forbidding him to change his lunch hour to attend a co-worker's arbitration hearing. The discharged employee helped his co-worker prepare for the arbitration hearing, and therefore had a legitimate reason to attend, even though the case did not fall under *Ohmite.* The D.C. Circuit decided that Cadbury Beverages acted out of improper antiunion animus.

LMRA § 301 permits a federal District Court to enforce a subpoena *duces tecum* (for production of documents) issued by a labor arbitrator to a person or entity that is not a party to the collective bargaining agreement. [*AFTRA v. WJBK-TV,* 164 F.3d 1004 (6th Cir. 1999)] However, the labor arbitrator cannot order nonparties to appear and testify, only to produce documents.

Arbitration awards are quite hard to overturn. For example, a court cannot overturn an award merely because it believes the arbitrator made the wrong decision, or misinterpreted the facts of the case. One of the rare cases in which an award was overturned involved a new zero-tolerance drug policy adopted by an oil refining company for all its facilities nationwide. The policy was challenged by the union, which claimed that it was impermissible to adopt such a policy unilaterally, without bargaining. One arbitrator upheld the policy. The other arbitrator upheld most of the policy, but disapproved of the potential for firing employees immediately, without a chance for rehabilitation. The employer sought to have the district court vacate the award, but the district court upheld. The Third Circuit reversed the district court, finding that the arbitrator exceeded his discretion by attempting to substitute his own discretion in an area of legitimate management prerogative. The Third Circuit held that the award did not draw its essence from the collective bargaining agreement. [*Citgo Asphalt Refining Co. v. Paper, Allied-Industrial Chemical, and Energy Workers Int'l Union Local No. 2-991*, 385 F.3d 809 (3d Cir. 2004)]

[F] Just Cause

One of the distinctive features of a collective bargaining agreement is that it means that employees no longer work at the will of the employer. Therefore, they cannot be discharged, or even subjected to lesser forms of discipline, without just cause. So the arbitrator's task becomes to determine whether the employer did, indeed, act with just cause. The arbitrator must determine if the employee really did whatever the employer claims he or she did; whether the employer offered the employee due process before imposing discipline; and whether the discipline was reasonable and not out of proportion to the offense. Usually, arbitrators divide offenses into very serious offenses such as assaulting someone at work, stealing, or creating a safety hazard (which will justify dismissal) and less serious rules, which are appropriate for progressive discipline such as admonition, notations in the permanent record, or suspension with or without pay.

[G] Contract Interpretation

When arbitrators interpret a contract, their job is to find out what the parties meant. If the language of the contract is plain, clear, and unambiguous, the arbitrator has to follow it—even if the arbitrator doesn't think that the contract as written is very sensible or fair. In fact, if the arbitrator doesn't follow this "plain meaning rule," a court is likely to decide that the arbitrator's award is invalid and not entitled to be enforced by the court system.

In fact, if a contract (any kind of contract, not just a CBA) is supposed to represent the whole agreement between the parties, a legal principle called the "parol evidence rule" says that evidence of anything said or written before or during the negotiations cannot be introduced to contradict the written contract or vary its terms. ("Parol" is an archaic term for "word" or "speech.") However, parol evidence can be used to explain terms that are unclear or ambiguous.

However, where the CBA included broad anti-discrimination language, the arbitrator did not exceed his powers by interpreting the Family and Medical Leave Act as well as the CBA in rendering a decision. [*Butler Mfg. Co. v. United Steelworkers,* 336 F.3d 629 (7th Cir. 2003)]

§ 40.06   ARBITRATION OF EMPLOYMENT DISCRIMINATION CLAIMS

[A]   Employer-Imposed Clauses

The reputation of arbitration has had its ups and downs. A Supreme Court case, *Alexander v. Gardner-Denver,* [415 U.S. 36 (1974)] allowed an employee to litigate after pursuing arbitration remedies, on the grounds that the arbitration provision in the plaintiff's CBA did not offer enough protection for statutory claims—i.e., claims that arise under Title VII, the Americans With Disabilities Act, or other antidiscrimination law.

In 1991, however, the Supreme Court took a different tack. The important case of *Gilmer v. Interstate/Johnson Lane Corp.* [500 U.S. 20 (1991)] allowed an employer to impose mandatory arbitration (under the U-4 securities industry employment agreement) for ADEA claims. The Supreme Court said that it wasn't really contradicting the earlier *Gardner-Denver* decision, because that involved a union contract that the plaintiff was subject to along with all the other union members, whereas Gilmer signed the U-4 agreement as an individual.

Under *Gilmer,* an arbitration clause can be valid as long as the process provides a written award rendered by a neutral arbitrator, and as long as discovery and adequate remedies are available under the arbitration process.

The *Gilmer* case was the "opening bell" for recognition of employers' right to impose predispute arbitration requirements: That is, employees would be covered by employment agreements, job handbooks, or other means of ensuring that they would have to arbitrate discrimination claims instead of litigating them. *Welles v. DeanWitter Reynolds Inc.* [948 F.2d 305 (6th Cir. 1991)] allows enforcement of a predispute mandatory arbitration requirement in Title VII cases. *Solomon v. Duke University* [850 F. Supp. 372 (M.D.N.C. 1993)] does the same for the ADA.

The Civil Rights Act of 1991 and the Americans with Disabilities Act (ADA) both include language favoring arbitration and other forms of Alternative Dispute Resolution (ADR) as means of handling discrimination charges. For the ADA provision, *see* 42 U.S.C. § 12212: Wherever it is lawful and appropriate, ADR (including settlement negotiations, conciliation, facilitation, mediation, factfinding, minitrials, and arbitration) is "encouraged" when ADA charges are asserted. Similarly, in 2004 the Fifth Circuit ruled that there is no reason why arbitration of

Fair Labor Standards Act claims cannot be compelled. [*Carter v. Countrywide Credit Industries, Inc.*, 362 F.3d 294 (5th Cir. 2004)] The Fifth Circuit agreed with the District Court that the contract provision requiring the employer and employee to split the costs of arbitration was invalid—but also agreed with the District Court that the proper remedy was to sever this invalid provision and enforce the rest of the agreement.

The two main ADR methods are arbitration (a trusted person or panel renders a decision) and mediation (a trusted person helps the parties reach a mutually acceptable decision).

Tip: If an employer offers to arbitrate, and the employee refuses, this could be treated as evidence of the employer's good faith—preventing the employee from collecting damages for breach of the covenant of good faith and fair dealing.

Then, in the early 1990s, the courts retrenched somewhat from their support of predispute arbitration requirements under at least some circumstances. For example, in *Prudential Insurance Co. v. Lai*, [42 F.3d 1299 (9th Cir. 1995)] the court refused to compel arbitration under the U-4 agreement, because the plaintiff had not been warned about, and did not understand, that she had surrendered her statutory rights under Title VII. *Ramirez v. Circuit City Stores Inc.* [90 Cal. Rptr. 2d 916 (Cal. App. 1999)] says that the ADR policy in an employer's standard contract was unenforceable because it was a contract of adhesion (a one-sided contract imposed with no opportunity for negotiation), was oppressive to employees, and imposed obligations on employees but not the employer.

According to the Sixth Circuit (although not every court agrees), hours for which an employee was paid as part of an arbitrator's award for unlawful termination count toward the 1,250 minimum hours that must be worked during a year for the employee to be entitled to FMLA leave. [*Ricco v. Potter*, 377 F.3d 599 (6th Cir. 2004)]

In a unionized workplace, *ALPA v. Northwest Airlines Inc.* [199 F.3d 477 (D.C. Cir. 1999)] holds that unions cannot agree to substitute litigation for arbitration for all statutory discrimination claims asserted by union members. That takes arbitration out of the category of mandatory bargaining subjects. And that, in turn, frees employers to require arbitration agreements as a condition of employment, without negotiating with the union first.

The Fourth Circuit says that it is a material breach of the collective bargaining agreement for an employer to adopt arbitration rules that are grossly in its own favor and too strict on the employee. The FAA will not require enforcement of arbitration rules that are unfair. Therefore, even though there is an arbitration agreement already in place, the employee will be able to bring suit. [*Hooters of America Inc. v. Phillips,* 173 F.3d 933 (4th Cir. 1999); *Gonzalez v. Hughes Aircraft Employees Federal Credit Union,* 70 Cal. App. 4th 468 (Cal. App. 1999)]

Issues of cost have arisen in several cases, as part of the determination of fairness. The Florida Court of Appeals did not require arbitration of a pregnancy-discrimination claim, on the grounds that requiring the employee to pay half the arbitration costs violates the successful Title VII plaintiff's statutory right to recover all attorneys' fees and costs. [*Flyer Printing Co. v. Hill,* 805 So. 2d 829 (Fla. App. 2001)] *See* § 40.07[C] for further discussion of arbitration costs.

It can be tough to enforce provisions contained in an employee handbook. [*See* Chapter 24] After all, it is typical for the handbook to say that its provisions do not create an enforceable employment contract.

What about situations in which the employee is covered by a written employment contract, and that contract imposes a predispute requirement of arbitration? The California Court of Appeals has decided that it is unconscionable (and therefore, the clause is unenforceable) to allow the employer to litigate certain types of cases while the employee was required to arbitrate all claims, to limit the size of the award the employee can receive, imposing an absolute one-year statute of limitations, and allowing the employee to be terminated before the employer's claims could be resolved. [*Stirlen v. Supercuts, Inc.,* 51 Cal. App. 4th 1519, 60 Cal. Rptr. 2d 138 (1997)]

Although it is certainly less complex and formal than litigation, arbitration is still a formal system with defined rules and an objective decision maker. An employer's internal grievance procedure is not equivalent to arbitration. Therefore, an employee can sue for wrongful termination based on race and sex discrimination, because an agreement to use the internal grievance procedure is not an agreement to arbitrate. [*Cheng-Canindin v. Renaissance Hotel Assocs.,* 50 Cal. App. 4th 676, 57 Cal. Rptr. 2d 867 (1996)]

[B] AAA Arbitration

The American Arbitration Association (AAA) has long been respected for its work in dispute resolution. The AAA's National Rules for the Resolution of Employment Disputes (promulgated in 1993; amended in 1995 to increase due process protection for employees) cover about three million workers.

The due process standards for fair arbitration require that:

- The employee's role in selecting the arbitrator(s) is equal to the employer's role;
- Each side has a right to counsel;
- The arbitrator can order whatever discovery he or she thinks is necessary;
- The parties are entitled to the same remedies in arbitration that they could get from the court system;
- The arbitrator will provide a written opinion explaining the reasons behind his or her decision;
- Attorneys' fees will be awarded in the interests of justice, so the employee does not have to be successful enough to be considered the "prevailing party" to get a fee award.

Tip: The employer can indicate in employment applications, the employee handbook, and/or employment contracts that employment disputes will be resolved under AAA rules.

Since 1996, AAA arbitrators have had the power to order discovery. Either employers or employees can be ordered to produce documents, answer written lists of questions, or appear and answer questions posed by an attorney. Under the 1996 rules, any party can be represented by an attorney. The arbitrator has a duty to make a decision and render a written award within 30 days of the end of the hearing. The arbitrator has the power to render whatever award he or she thinks is just, including ordering one side to pay the attorneys' fees and costs of the other side.

The arbitrator gets paid a fee for working on the case, and the AAA itself is entitled to an administration fee. The AAA fee depends on the size of the claim or counterclaim, determined at the time it is filed, not by any later amendments.

The AAA's general policy is that it will administer arbitration even if the employer unilaterally imposed the arbitration requirement as a condition of employment. However, the organization reserves the right to refuse to enforce unfair arbitration policies—policies that fail to provide basic due process protection to employees.

Generally—but not always—it is the employer that seeks arbitration and the employee who wants to litigate. The converse was true in the case of a corporate CFO entered into a severance agreement with his soon-to-be-ex-employer. The agreement called for binding arbitration of all disputes, but did not specify the arbitrator or the rules to be used. The day after the agreement was signed, the CFO was indicted for abusing his position for personal financial gain. The company demanded AAA arbitration, seeking $400 million in damages for the conduct upon which the indictment was based. The CFO refused to consent to AAA jurisdiction, so the AAA dismissed the corporation's demand. The corporation then brought suit against the ex-CFO, who tried to have the case dismissed because of the arbitration agreement. The District Court ruled that arbitration should be deferred until the completion of the CFO's criminal trial; by the time the case reached the First Circuit, the criminal trial was finished. The First Circuit ruled that although federal policy favors arbitration, it is not an absolute principle. For example, the option to arbitrate is lost if it is not invoked in a timely manner. Factors in the determination include whether the party seeking arbitration acted in a way inconsistent with the right to arbitrate (e.g., litigated the issues); whether litigation was under way before the intent to arbitrate was announced; the length of the delay in invoking the right to arbitrate; whether the other party was prejudiced by the delay; and whether important intervening steps that would not be available in arbitration (e.g., discovery) occurred. The First Circuit ruled that the CFO waived the right to arbitrate by objecting to AAA jurisdiction without proposing an alternative. His former employer was prejudiced by having to devote extensive money and time to resolving the issues. [*In re Tyco Int'l Ltd. Sec. Litig. v. Swartz,* 422 F.3d 41 (1st Cir. 2005)]

In a Ninth Circuit case, the employer unilaterally imposed an arbitration policy. An employee was terminated when the employer said she falsified her time sheet. The employee said this was a pretext to terminate her because she was moonlighting to pay for school. The ex-employee sought arbitration of her wrongful termination claim. The employer refused to respond to letters from the AAA and failed to pay its $400 share of the filing fee. The ex-employee sued in state court; the employer removed the case to federal court and moved to compel arbitration, but the Ninth Circuit refused to allow the employer to enforce the arbitration provision because the employer had not complied with its requirements. [*Brown v. Dillard's Inc.,* 430 F.3d 1004 (9th Cir. 2005)]

[C] Securities Industry Arbitration

Workers in the securities industry have to sign a standard employment agreement called the U-4 as a condition of working in the industry. It was the only industry to have a uniform mandatory arbitration requirement, so it served as a kind of "test bed" for studying legal issues about arbitration.

As of August 7, 1997, the National Association of Securities Dealers (NASD) voted to eliminate mandatory arbitration of employment discrimination claims brought by registered brokers under federal and state antidiscrimination statutes.

The Eighth Circuit upheld an $840,000 arbitration award, denying the defendant's motion to reduce it to $340,000. The plaintiff was recruited by an investment bank and offered a contract including compensation guarantees. The employer tried to renegotiate the contract, removing the guarantees, but the employee was not acquiescent. He was assigned to a new and more difficult territory, but was still ranked fourth out of 19 salespersons. He was later told to return his cash bonus and that he was not performing adequately. He was threatened with termination for cause, and eventually terminated. He sought NASD arbitration and received the $840,000 award, then sought confirmation of the award in state court. The Eighth Circuit agreed that the arbitrator was not bound by the termination provision of the employment agreement because the covenant of good faith and fair dealing prevents an employer from discharging an employee and then denying a bonus on the basis that the employee resigned. [*McGrann v. First Albany Corp.,* 424 F.3d 743 (8th Cir. 2005)]

The Ninth Circuit held that the arbitration clause and the investment management agreement between employee benefit plan trustees and the plan's investment adviser did not bind a plan participant (who did not sign the agreement) who wanted to sue the adviser for breach of fiduciary duty. The participant was not an intended third-party beneficiary of the agreement, nor did the beneficiary take advantage of the agreement in any way that would create equitable estoppel. [*Comer v. Micor Inc.,* 436 F.3d 1098 (9th Cir. 2006)]

[D] Getting Ready for Arbitration

To be prepared for arbitration, you should:

- Review how the dispute arose, and what has already been done to resolve it;
- Check all relevant work rules and policies and how they were applied, both to the grievant and the other employees;
- Makes copies of all relevant documents for your own file, for the employee, and for the arbitrator;
- Inform the employee of documents in the employee's possession that you want copies of, and that you want copies sent to the arbitrator;
- If necessary, ask the arbitrator to subpoena necessary documents that you have not been able to get by informal means;
- Make sure all the witnesses sound accurate and articulate, but not mechanical or coached;
- Anticipate questions that will be asked during cross-examination, and prepare the witnesses to answer them;
- Make a list of points that you want each witness's testimony to put into the record;
- Review collections of published arbitration decisions, because even though arbitrators don't absolutely have to follow past precedents, they will often be swayed by interpretations that other arbitrators have reached in similar cases.

The first stage in an arbitration hearing is the opening statement. Usually, in a case where the employer's termination or discipline is being challenged, the employer will present its case first, because the employer has to prove the justification for its actions. In other types of cases, the employee usually gives the first opening statement. Next comes the other opening statement, and then the side that goes first introduces the testimony of its witnesses; the other side has the right to cross-examine. Then, the parties sum up their cases, and it is up to the arbitrator to decide.

[E] Appeals

In general, the court system tries to get involved with arbitration as little as possible, although arbitration awards can be enforced by the court system, and sometimes disputes about arbitrability or arbitration process are litigated. Especially because employees are often required to arbitrate claims that they would prefer to litigate, there are many instances in which the parties to an arbitration will want to appeal the decision. A 2003 California case is a good introduction to the problems of arbitration appeals. [*Little v. Auto Stiegler, Inc.*, 29 Cal. 4th 1064, 63 P.3d 979, 130 Cal. Rptr. 2d 892 (2003)] This case involves four interlocking questions:

- Is a provision in an arbitration agreement allowing either party to have any award over $50,000 reviewed by a second arbitrator unconscionable?

- If it is unconscionable, can it be severed from the agreement and the rest of the agreement enforced—or does it make the whole agreement invalid and unenforceable?
- Do the California rules for arbitration due process in statutory discrimination claims also apply to claims that an employee was wrongfully terminated contrary to public policy? (The plaintiff was a service manager of an automobile dealership, who claimed that he was demoted, and then fired, for discovering and reporting warranty fraud.)
- If these rules do apply, is the agreement's requirement that the employer pay all the costs of arbitration if it mandates arbitration still valid?

The California rules come from *Armendariz v. Foundation Health Psychcare Servs., Inc.*, [24 Cal. 4th 83 (2000)] which imposes minimum due process requirements that cannot be waived. The arbitration agreement must not limit damages that would normally be available under the relevant statute; the parties to arbitration must be allowed enough discovery to pursue their claims (although this will probably be far less than the often very intrusive discovery process allowed in litigation); the arbitrator must issue a written decision that is subject to enough judicial review to keep arbitrators in compliance with the relevant laws; and the employer must pay all the costs that are unique to arbitration.

The court in the *Little* case decided that it violates public policy for an employment agreement to require employees to waive their claims of termination contrary to public policy. Therefore, the *Armendariz* requirements also apply to these wrongful termination claims. With that under its belt, the court decided that the "appeals" provision was unconscionable, but that the rest of the agreement should be enforced. The provision was held to be unconscionable, because it was part of a contract of adhesion (a one-sided contract, imposed by a party with much greater power). The appeals requirement was unfair because it was onesided—in practical terms, only employees are likely to get $50,000 arbitration awards, so the appeal would benefit only the employer.

At trial, a California court ruled that an arbitration award violated state public policy against covenants not to compete and wrongfully ordered the plaintiff to pay a part of the arbitration expenses. (The covenant barred the plaintiff from selling the defendant's product, or any competing product, for two years after termination of the agreement to the plaintiff's old accounts.) However, the California Court of Appeals confirmed the award on grounds of arbitral finality. The Court of Appeals did order correction of the way the expenses were divided (the arbitrator ordered each side to pay half), but ruled that the error was merely cause for correcting the award, not vacating it. [*Jones v. Humanscale Corp.*, 130 Cal. App. 4th 401 (Cal. App. 2005)]

Early in 2004, the Ninth Circuit tackled the question of whether the federal courts can hear appeals of arbitration awards in the employer's favor—in other words, whether an employee can challenge an award of $0. The Ninth Circuit said no: when it comes to deciding whether the amount in controversy is the $75,000 required for diversity jurisdiction (jurisdiction based on the parties being citizens of different states), the amount in controversy is the amount actually awarded in the arbitration proceeding, not the amount that the employee claimed he or she was entitled to. The Ninth Circuit did not accept the employee's argument that there was a federal question that should be heard in the federal courts (whether the arbitrator manifestly disregarded the applicable law). According to the Ninth Circuit, the issue was not manifest disregard, but whether the arbitrator misunderstood the standards set for ADA claims by *Toyota v. Williams* (*see* § 36.04[E]). Arbitration awards are final even if the arbitrator's decision was less than a monument of legal analysis. [*Luong v. Circuit City Stores Inc.,* 356 F.3d 1188 (9th Cir. 2004)] Later in the year, however, another panel of the Ninth Circuit allowed a $0 arbitration award to be judicially reviewed if the amount at stake in the underlying dispute satisfies the amount in controversy requirement. [*Theis Research Inc. v. Brown & Bain,* 386 F.3d 1180 (9th Cir. 2004, amended Feb. 18, 2005)]

Also in the Ninth Circuit and in 2004, an appeal was dismissed. When a District Court denies arbitration in the one of the forums requested by the appellant, but compels arbitration in another forum also requested by the appellant, federal arbitration law holds that the order is not appealable. [*See* 9 U.S.C. § 16 for appeals rules] Although arbitration was denied in one forum it was compelled in another, and orders compelling arbitration are not appealable. [*Bushley v. Credit Suisse First Boston,* 360 F.3d 1149 (9th Cir. 2004)]

The executive director of an organization had an employment contract requiring arbitration of disputes. The shareholders fired the director, who brought suit for wrongful termination and conversion of his preferred stock. The district court ordered him to arbitrate. The arbitrator found that the plaintiff acted in bad faith on at least three occasions, justifying his termination pursuant to the employment contract. Although the arbitrator found that the plaintiff was entitled to $41,000 in back pay and $13,000 in dividends, those damages were offset by excessive payments of wages and dividends that he directed before his termination. Therefore, he owed his former employer close to $29,000 against future dividends. The arbitrator required the plaintiff to pay some $224,000 in fees and costs, because the former employer was the prevailing party.

The plaintiff sued in district court, alleging that the arbitration proceedings were technically defective and should be vacated. A district court's findings of fact supporting the confirmation of an arbitration award are reviewed for clear error, but legal conclusions are reviewed de novo. The arbitration award itself gets an extremely high degree of deference. It can be vacated only if it is completely irrational or manifests a disregard for the law. [*Manion v. Boat Dealers' Alliance,* 392 F.3d 294 (8th Cir. 2004); *see Stark v. Standberg, Phoenix & von Gontard, P.C.,* 381 F.3d 793 (8th Cir. 2004) and *Hoffman v. Cargill Inc.,* 236 F.3d 458 (8th Cir. 2001) on the standard of review]

The Fifth Circuit reinstated an arbitrator's award of about $1.5 million in benefits that were lost by employees who lost their right to severance benefits when their welfare benefit plan was amended just before a merger. The court ruled that the arbitrator correctly held that the plan sponsor violated its fiduciary duties by denying severance claims. Furthermore, in the Fifth Circuit, an arbitration award cannot be overturned on the ground that the arbitrator misunderstood the law or misinterpreted the contract—only if the arbitrator showed manifest disregard for the law. [*Kergosien v. Ocean Energy Inc.*, 390 F.3d 346 (5th Cir. 2004)]

A long-term employee won at arbitration in a case alleging breach of contract, breach of the covenant of good faith and fair dealing, age discrimination, harassment, and wrongful termination contrary to public policy. The arbitrator decided that there was a breach of the contractual guarantee of termination for cause only, although the arbitrator did not find age discrimination or violation of public policy. The arbitrator awarded economic damages of $915,000 and general damages for emotional distress of $275,000. The defendant filed a request for correction of the arbitration award. The arbitrator amended the award to eliminate the emotional distress damages. The case ended up in court, and the Los Angeles County Superior Court ruled that the arbitrator did not exceed his authority in issuing the original award, because he had the authority to resolve the dispute via a damage award. Although he made an error of law as to what damages could properly be awarded, that error was not a basis for correcting the original award. An arbitrator's amended or supplemental award must be issued within the California state law time limit for corrections if a ruling on a submitted issue was inadvertently omitted, but the "amended" award was not issued in time. The court affirmed the arbitrator's original judgment. [*Landis v. Pinkertons, Inc.*, No. B163016 (L.A. County Super. Ct. 2004), <http://caselaw.lp.findlaw.com/data2/californiastatecases/b163016.pdf>]

A dispute between a union and a group of three related businesses resulted in two arbitration awards (one of about $77,000 in damages for doing over 2,000 hours of bargaining unit work contrary to the CBA; the second to enforce the first). The defendants sued in district court to vacate the awards. The union got summary judgment on statute of limitations grounds, because the employer's challenge to the first award was untimely. The employer took the position that the first award left open issues that were decided in the second award, so that the first award did not become a final, appealable decision until after the second award was rendered. Under this theory, the statute of limitations for both awards didn't start to run until the second award was entered, so both appeals were timely. The Seventh Circuit rule is that failure to challenge an arbitration award within 90 days makes the award final. The defendant said that the two awards were actually a single decision, but the Seventh Circuit rejected this argument. The award becomes final and appealable when the arbitrator thinks the matter is finished—even if the arbitrators were wrong in believing they had finished their task, or the award is so poorly drafted that the losing party can't figure out how to comply with it. [*McKinney Restoration Co., Inc. v. Illinois Dist. Council #1 of the Int'l Union of Bricklayers and Allied Craftworkers*, 392 F.3d 867 (7th Cir. 2004); the rule on finality comes *from Smart v. IBEW*, 315 F.3d 721 (7th Cir. 2002)]

§ 40.07 MANDATORY PREDISPUTE ARBITRATION CLAUSES

[A] "Predispute" vs. "Postdispute" Clauses

There are many ways to draft an arbitration provision. Predispute arbitration clauses specify in advance that future disputes, if they occur, will be arbitrable. Such a provision can be either voluntary or mandatory. If voluntary, arbitration is just one option available for resolving disputes. If mandatory, the employee is blocked from suing the employer. Postdispute arbitration clauses are an agreement between employer and employee after a claim has been raised, and the best way to handle it is via arbitration.

In 1998, the Supreme Court resolved some difficult issues in *Wright v. Universal Maritime Service Corp.* [525 U.S. 70 (1998)] In this case, an injured stevedore was denied employment because companies that might have employed him considered him permanently disabled. He sued under the ADA without filing a grievance or going through arbitration under the CBA. The district court dismissed his case because he did not exhaust his grievance remedies. The Fourth Circuit upheld the district court.

However, the Supreme Court reversed the Fourth Circuit. The *Gilmer* case permits compulsory arbitration of an ADA claim, but the Supreme Court ruled that a contract claim must be treated differently from a statutory claim. Contract claims are presumed arbitrable, but statutory claims are not. A CBA must be very explicit to prevent litigation of a claim under a civil rights statute. A general arbitration clause that does not list the civil rights statutes that are covered will not prevent litigation under those statutes.

According to the Eighth Circuit, the employer's adoption of a mandatory arbitration requirement shifts the operation away from strict at-will employment. Therefore, the employer must show "discernable cause" for discharging any employees. [*PaineWebber Inc. v. Agron,* 49 F.3d 347 (8th Cir. 1995)]

A 2001 case, *Circuit City v. Adams,* [532 U.S. 105 (2001)] allowed a company to enforce its predispute arbitration requirement to prevent an employee from suing in state court. The employee's argument was that the FAA excludes "contracts of employment of seamen, railroad employees, or any other class of workers engaged in foreign or interstate commerce," and that he, like nearly all workers, was engaged in interstate commerce so the FAA should not apply. The Supreme Court, however, said that the exclusion was limited to transportation workers, not everyone whose work affects interstate commerce. Otherwise, the FAA would hardly ever be applicable, and would serve no purpose—whereas Congress clearly intended to promote arbitration as a means of settling disputes.

However, the case was sent back to the lower courts, and the Ninth Circuit decided [279 F.3d 889 (9th Cir. 2002)] that the agreement itself is unenforceable, because even though the Supreme Court decided that it satisfied the requirements of the FAA, it was too unfair and one-sided to survive California law.

Although part of the plaintiff's job was to drive a truck interstate to make deliveries, the Eleventh Circuit ruled that he was not a transportation industry worker entitled to the FAA exemption. Therefore, the pre-dispute arbitration agreement was enforced. [*Hill v. Rent-A-Center Inc.*, 398 F.3d 1286 (11th Cir. 2005)]

A trucking firm customer service representative is not a "transportation worker" for purposes of the FAA exemption; therefore, a representative can be required to arbitrate employment-related claims. [*Lenz v. Yellow Transp. Inc.*, 431 F.3d 348 (8th Cir. 2005)]

A Title VII plaintiff alleged that the employer waived its conceded contractual right to compel arbitration by waiting until the employee had brought suit, rather than demanding arbitration when the employee filed charges with the EEOC. The First Circuit ruled that, even though compliance issues are within the arbitrator's competency, a court must decide whether the right to arbitrate has been waived. Examining the merits of the case, the First Circuit ruled that, after the *Waffle House* decision, the employer's delay did not forfeit its right to arbitrate. The effect of *Waffle House* is that the employer can't cite an arbitration agreement with employees to prevent the EEOC from bringing an enforcement action. Therefore, it would lead to wasteful duplication to require the employer to seek arbitration while the EEOC is still investigating. On the substantive question of whether the employer had waived the right to demand arbitration, the First Circuit found that it had not, because the defendant did not engage in undue delay that could prejudice the plaintiff's case. [*Marie v. Allied Home Mortgage Corp.*, 402 F.3d 1 (1st Cir. 2005)]

Cases about Circuit City's arbitration agreement continued to occupy the courts in later years. In May 2003, the Ninth Circuit upheld the District Court's refusal to compel arbitration under the Circuit City agreement. The Ninth Circuit deemed the arbitration agreement, as a contract, to be subject to all of the defenses under contract law, including unconscionability. The Ninth Circuit found the agreement to be unconscionable because it was oppressive and deprived the weaker party of meaningful opportunity to negotiate. The court also noted that under California law, it is unlawful to impose a filing fee on employees who seek arbitration if the fees would not be incurred by an employee who had a free choice between arbitration and litigation. [*Ingle v. Circuit City Stores Inc.*, 328 F.3d 1165 (9th Cir. 2003), *aff'd* 408 F.3d 592 (9th Cir. 2005). *But see Circuit City v. Najd*, 294 F.3d 1004 (9th Cir. 2002) and *Circuit City v. Ahmed*, 283 F.3d 1198 (9th Cir. 2002), which upheld another version of the Circuit City agreement on the grounds that it gave job applicants a meaningful opportunity to opt out of the arbitration program]

In July 2003, the Ninth Circuit reversed the District Court's decision to compel arbitration, once again based on a finding that the arbitration agreement was unconscionable. The plaintiff in this case was hired by Circuit City in 1992, before the company instituted its mandatory arbitration policy. The program began in 1995, but the plaintiff managed to avoid signing the agreement until 1998. He was terminated in 2000. About a year later, he sued the employer in state court.

To preserve his right to arbitrate if the court found the claims to be subject to arbitration, he also requested arbitration and paid the $75 fee. The Ninth Circuit decided the case strictly on the basis of California law about unconscionability. On this basis, the Ninth Circuit found that the agreement was unconscionable because the plaintiff had no meaningful chance to opt out; even though there was a form for opting out of arbitration, his job was threatened and he was pressured not to make use of this opportunity. The Ninth Circuit found that various of the provisions of the 2001 version of the arbitration agreement were unconscionable; the court found the entire agreement invalid and unenforceable and refused to sever the offending provisions and enforce the rest. [*Circuit City Stores v. Mantor,* 335 F.3d 1101 (9th Cir. 2003)]

Yet another Circuit City arbitration clause was found acceptable in early 2006. The class action waiver was acceptable because employees could opt out of the arbitration program. It was held that employees were given adequate time to make the choice to opt out, so the agreement was not an unlawful contract of adhesion. [*Gentry v. Superior Court of L.A.,* 135 Cal. App. 4th 944 (Cal. App. 2006)]

An ADEA suit, with state claims for retaliation, invasion of privacy, promissory estoppel, and violation of state public policy, was removed to federal court. The defendant moved to dismiss or, in the alternative, stay the action pending arbitration under the parties' arbitration agreement. The District Court severed three provisions, but otherwise upheld the agreement. The Sixth Circuit affirmed the severance of the cost-shifting and remedies provisions, but left it up to the arbitrator to interpret the evidentiary provision. To the Sixth Circuit, the agreement was not procedurally unconscionable because there was no serious disparity in bargaining power. The plaintiff was a television news anchor who was well-educated, was experienced in working in the media, and had previously worked under an employment contract containing an arbitration clause. The evidentiary provision gave the employer discretion to determine if the plaintiff's work performance was adequate, and required the arbitrator to uphold the employer's action if the arbitrator thought that either the employee was guilty of the conduct charged by the employer—or the employer reasonably believed that those charges were true. The Sixth Circuit held that the provision did not infringe upon the plaintiff's right to establish an ADEA prima facie case; it merely required the arbitrator to uphold the employer's actions under certain circumstances. The evidentiary provision was not unenforceable because it could be interpreted in a way that preserved the plaintiff's rights. The cost-shifting provision, however, was correctly severed because requiring unsuccessful claimants to pay the whole cost of arbitration could deter a substantial number of employees from arbitrating their claims. [*Scovill v. WSYX/ABC*, 425 F.3d 1012 (6th Cir. 2005)]

Early in 2002, the Supreme Court returned to the subject of predispute arbitration mandates. The ruling in *EEOC v. Waffle House Inc.* [534 U.S. 279 (2002)] is that the EEOC can pursue employment discrimination litigation (in this case, involving the Americans with Disabilities Act) even if the employees themselves would be required to submit their disputes to arbitration. The decision is very important as an indicator of legal thinking about arbitration, but it will not have much practical effect, because the EEOC doesn't take on many cases a year, and not all of them involve companies with mandatory arbitration requirements.

In mid-2002, the Fourth Circuit held that the Federal Arbitration Act applies to employment agreements to arbitrate statutory discrimination claims—but only if the dispute is arbitrable, and only if the arbitration forum provides a means of enforcing rights under the statute. The Fourth Circuit agreed with the plaintiff that the arbitration clause he worked under was biased and invalid (the single arbitrator was chosen from a list drawn up by the union—he was a union organizer, so the union was also his employer). This mechanism left room for the union to choose biased arbitrators or punish arbitrators for deciding in favor of employees. [*Murray v. United Food and Commercial Workers Int'l Union Local 400,* 289 F.3d 297 (4th Cir. 2002)]

In a Title VII case, the Fifth Circuit held that the pre-dispute arbitration agreement was valid and binding. The plaintiff admitted that she had signed an Acknowledgment Form, although it could not be found in her personnel file when she brought suit. The plaintiff said that her signature was just an acknowledgment that she received the documents, not that she consented to arbitration. The district court accepted this argument. The Fifth Circuit said that Congress's policy in favor of arbitration is so strong that even interim anti-arbitration decisions can be appealed, whereas pro-arbitration decisions generally can't be appealed until they become final. On the merits, the Fifth Circuit ruled that the plaintiff was on notice that continuing to work for the employer constituted her consent to arbitrate employment discrimination claims. [*May v. Higbee Co.,* 372 F.3d 757 (5th Cir. 2004)]

A group of employees sought to litigate various Title VII, ADEA, FLSA, and ERISA claims. The Eleventh Circuit agreed that the District Court was correct to grant the employer's motion to dismiss the claims and compel arbitration pursuant to the employer's dispute resolution policy (DRP). The employer unilaterally imposed the DRP as the exclusive method of resolving employment disputes under the FMLA, ADA, and tort claims (although ERISA, Worker's Compensation, and NLRA claims were not covered). The court's rationale was that the FAA has a writing requirement, and the DRP was written; there is no signature requirement. The Eleventh Circuit accepted the employer's argument that employees' continuing to work represented consideration for the adoption of the DRP. In that circuit, there is no heightened "knowing and voluntary" standard for jury trial waivers in Title VII cases, although in *Campbell v. General Dynamics Gov't Systems Corp.,* 407 F.3d 546 (1st Cir. 2005), the First Circuit held that a dispute resolution policy sent to employees via a link at the bottom of an e-mail was invalid and unenforceable. The Eleventh Circuit distinguished *Campbell* because, in this case, employees received adequate notice of the implementation of the DRP. The court did not find the agreement so one-sided or oppressive that it should be denied enforcement. [*Caley v. Gulfstream Aerospace Corp.,* 428 F.3d 1359 (11th Cir. 2005)]

The New Jersey rule is that the only way an employee can validly waive employment rights that derive from statutes is by making an explicit, affirmative agreement that shows an unmistakable intent to accept arbitration to resolve the claims. Merely continuing to work at a job where the employee handbook contains a waiver clause is not enough. [*Leodori v. CIGNA Corp.*, 175 N.J. 293, 814 A.2d 1098 (2003)]

In 1998, the Ninth Circuit made the controversial decision that it is unlawful to fire an employee for refusing to agree to mandatory predispute arbitration of discrimination claims. [*Duffield v. Robertson Stephens*, 144 F.3d 1182 (9th Cir. 1998)] However, in 2002 one panel of the Ninth Circuit overruled the *Duffield* decision, deciding that it was permissible for a law firm to rescind a legal secretary's job offer because he refused to sign a predispute arbitration agreement. [*Lagatree v. Luce, Forward, Hamilton & Scripps*, 303 F.3d 994 (9th Cir. 2002)] In September 2003, the Ninth Circuit struck down the *Duffield* ruling. According to the Ninth Circuit, it is not a violation of Title VII to impose pre-dispute arbitration as a condition of employment. The Ninth Circuit held that compulsory arbitration does not undercut the right to a jury trial enacted by CRA '91, because the requirement of arbitration affects only the forum and not substantive rights. The Ninth Circuit reading of *Circuit City v. Adams* is that mandatory pre-dispute arbitration agreements are consistent with Congress' anti-discriminatory enactments. [*EEOC v. Luce, Forward, Hamilton & Scripps*, 345 F.3d 742 (9th Cir. 2003)] In June 2004, the Central District of California approved a settlement between the EEOC and the law firm. The EEOC allowed the firm to maintain its mandatory arbitration plan, despite the EEOC's own 1997 policy statement. The EEOC statement (that mandatory arbitration clauses are unsound because they violate basic principles of employment law) has not been well-received lately by the courts, but the agency has not issued an updated rule. [The settlement is No. LA CV 00-1322 (C.D. Cal. June 18, 2004); *see* (no byline) *EEOC Contravenes Policy, Allows Law Firm to Continue Mandatory Arbitration Plan*, 73 L.W. 2043 (July 20, 2004)]

An employer's failure to give the employee a copy of the arbitration rules was not a "special circumstance" that would invalidate the mandatory predispute arbitration agreement. The Second Circuit held that it was up to the employee to ask any questions she had before signing the agreement. Once she signed it, she was conclusively presumed to know its contents. [*Gold v. Deutsche Aktiengesellschaft*, 365 F.3d 144 (2d Cir. 2004)]

[B]   Claims Other than Discrimination

Mandatory predispute arbitration clauses are not limited to use in connection with discrimination claims. Five of the federal Circuit Courts have ruled that arbitration can be a proper way to handle ERISA claims. [*Bird v. Shearson Lehman/American Express*, 926 F.2d 116 (2d Cir. 1991); *Pritzer v. Merrill Lynch*, 7 F.3d 1110 (3d Cir. 1993); *Kramer v. Smith Barney*, 80 F.3d 1080

(5th Cir. 1996); *Amulfo P. Sulit, Inc. v. Dean Witter Reynolds, Inc.,* 847 F.2d 475 (8th Cir. 1988); *Williams v. Imhoff,* 203 F.3d 758 (10th Cir. 2000)]

In 2002, the Fourth Circuit ruled that claims under the Fair Labor Standards Act can be subject to mandatory arbitration, because there is no inherent conflict between the FAA and the FLSA. The FLSA is similar to the ADEA, and *Gilmer* makes it clear that mandatory arbitration of ADEA claims is appropriate. [*Adkins v. Labor Ready Inc.,* 303 F.3d 496 (4th Cir. 2002)]

The Sixth Circuit denied the defendant's motion to dismiss the federal case and compel FAA arbitration of the plaintiffs' FLSA claims. The plaintiffs filed an FLSA collective action charging failure to pay minimum wage and/or time and a half for overtime. Once suit was filed, 18 additional plaintiffs filed their consent to opt in. Although the plaintiffs signed pre-dispute arbitration agreements, the Sixth Circuit found that there was inadequate consideration, the agreements were contracts of adhesion, and the plaintiffs did not knowingly and voluntarily waive the right to jury trial. As an additional ground, the pool of arbitrators was found to be biased, thus preventing the arbitral forum from effectively vindicating statutory rights.

This case was different from the usual pre-dispute arbitration case because the arbitration agreement was not between the plaintiffs and the defendant, but between the plaintiff and a third-party arbitration service retained by the employer. The employees did not receive a copy of the contract between the employer and the arbitration service. That contract allowed the employer to cancel the arrangement with the arbitration provider. Therefore, the Sixth Circuit did not interpret the employer's promise to consider the employment application to be adequate consideration for the applicant's surrender of the right to arbitrate disputes not related to the application process. The plaintiffs, who were sometimes given the agreement to sign before employment, and sometimes afterwards, had limited education and needed jobs very badly, so they were in no condition to negotiate. Although Tennessee state law presumes that people know what they're signing, in this case the defendant's managers either did not explain the agreements at all, or gave inaccurate information and failed to disclose that the agreements mandated waiver of the right to jury trial.

As a general rule, a biased arbitration panel is not a ground for refusing to arbitrate, because it is possible to use the bias to overturn the arbitrator's decision once it is rendered. However, the Sixth Circuit applied a different analysis to this situation in which the process of selecting the arbitrator was fundamentally unfair, because it prevented the arbitral forum from being an adequate substitute for the court system. In this instance, the fees paid by the defendant were a major source of revenue for the arbitration provider, causing an obvious conflict of interest. [*Walker v. Ryan's Family Steak Houses, Inc.,* 400 F.3d 370 (6th Cir. 2005)]

In a case about alleged improper refusal of, and interference with accrual of, severance benefits, the defendant's position was that the plan required arbitration of disputes, and that the plaintiff failed to exhaust his administrative remedies. The severance plan covered "activation events" (for example, constructive termination, or actual termination other than for just cause) that occurred within two years of a change in control. Constructive termination is further defined as a substantive change in job duties or reporting relationships. Near the end of the two-year period, the plaintiff was fired for accessing information on his manager's computer without authorization. He claimed that he was given access to the part of the corporate network containing organization charts he reviewed to determine whether his reporting relationships had changed, and therefore he was eligible for severance on the basis of changed reporting relationships.

The plan in question required submission of claims to the plan administrator, who performs a three-step review process. At the end of the process, the employee can seek binding arbitration for claims of constructive termination or actual termination not for just cause. The plaintiff brought suit before completion of the three-step process. The suit alleged wrongful termination, violation of ERISA § 510 (termination to prevent benefit accrual), breach of fiduciary duty, and COBRA violations. The Sixth Circuit held that the ERISA and COBRA claims were not arbitrable—the FAA does not exclude arbitration of claims of this type, but the plaintiff's employment contract required arbitration only of constructive termination or unjust termination. There is a presumption in favor of arbitrability, but if a clause covers only a specific type of dispute, then other disputes are not subject to mandatory arbitration. The Sixth Circuit therefore had to determine if the ERISA and COBRA claims were substantially identical to the types of claims subject to arbitration. The claims for benefits under the severance plan had to be arbitrated in accordance with the requirements of the severance plan. [*Simon v. Pfizer Inc.*, 398 F.3d 765 (6th Cir. 2005)] However, when an employee whose attempts to make a COBRA election were frustrated (he hand-delivered premium checks to the former employer, who did not submit them to the insurer, which resulted in his loss of health coverage), the Northern District of Illinois ruled that the suit was barred by an arbitration agreement that required "any differences, claims or matters in dispute" arising out of or connected with the employment agreement to be arbitrated. The court rejected the plaintiff's argument that the claim arose after termination and therefore was not subject to the arbitration clause. Because it was employment-related, arbitration was required. [*Maroney v. Triple "R" Steel, Inc.*, No. 05 C 1249 (N.D. Ill. Aug. 11, 2005)]

In *Strawn v. AFC Enterprises Inc.*, [70 F. Supp. 2d 717 (S.D. Tex. 1999)] all employees had to sign a "Value Deal Agreement" mandating arbitration of all injury claims. Texas allows employers to opt out of the Worker's Compensation system, as this employer did. It had its own benefit plan, providing much less for injured workers than the Compensation system. The case arose when an injured worker received about $50,000 in benefits in arbitration, but then sued for additional tort damages.

The employer moved to compel arbitration. The employee countered that the arbitration agreement was unenforceable, relying on *Reyes v. Storage & Processors Inc.* [995 S.W.2d 722 (Tex. App. 1999)] *Reyes* says that a waiver of common-law causes of action is void as against public policy if the employer provides benefits substantially less generous than the Worker's Comp system does. The court agreed with the employee that AFC Enterprises' "miserly" benefits were not good enough. However, the arbitration agreement was merely voidable, and not void—and the employee did not ratify the agreement by accepting benefits under the arbitration award.

Three FedEx package delivery contractors sued the company in state court for breach of contract, fraud, negligent misrepresentation, and deceptive trade practices, and sought to rescind their contracts with FedEx. They alleged that FedEx recruiters deceived them about the nature and earnings potential of the work. FedEx first removed the case to federal court and then moved to dismiss the cases and compel arbitration. The District Court held that the claims fell outside the scope of the arbitration clause (because they referred to oral representations made by recruiters, not to the written contract), and the Tenth Circuit affirmed. The arbitration clause was narrowly drawn, limited to FedEx's termination of the independent contractor relationship, and not a comprehensive one covering all disputes between the parties. The issues the plaintiffs raised fell outside the scope of the clause. [*Cummings v. Fedex Ground Package Sys. Inc.,* 404 F.3d 1258 (10th Cir. 2005)]

Under Maryland law, an employment arbitration agreement that the employer could amend or revoke at any time was not enforceable because there was no consideration to create a valid contract. The employer's promise to arbitrate its claims against employees was illusory. Therefore, a terminated employee was permitted to litigate rather than arbitrate his claims of breach of contract, negligent misrepresentation, and failure to pay compensation that he alleged he had earned. [*Cheek v. United Healthcare of the Mid-Atlantic Inc.,* 835 A.2d 656 (Md. Nov. 13, 2003)]

The Fifth Circuit separated collective bargaining act claims from claims involving the Fair Labor Standards Act, ruling that arbitration is inadequate for the latter because it does not give workers access to FLSA remedies such as liquidated damages and attorneys' fees. [*Bernard v. IPB, Inc. of Nebraska,* 154 F.3d 259 (5th Cir. 1998)]

A hospital pharmacist sued her ex-employer after she took FMLA leave for the birth of a child. While she was on leave, her job was eliminated, and she was not rehired when she wanted to return to work. She sued the hospital for interfering with her FMLA rights. The hospital moved to compel arbitration. Although the District Court refused to compel arbitration (on the grounds that the arbitration agreement ended when the job did), the Third Circuit ruled that arbitration was required, because the plaintiff's factual case depended on what happened while she was still employed. [*Varallo v. Elkins Park Hosp.,* 63 Fed. Appx. 601 (3d Cir. 2003)]

[C] Arbitration Costs

The court decided, in the *Little v. Auto Stiegler, Inc.* [29 Cal. 4th 1064, 63 P.3d 979, 130 Cal. Rptr. 2d 892 (2003)] case discussed above, that an arbitration agreement's failure to specify an allocation for the costs of the process doesn't make the agreement void or unenforceable—it places the responsibility for paying all the arbitration costs on the employer. The court in the *Little* case ruled that this does not conflict with the Supreme Court's decision in a non-employment arbitration case, [*Green Tree Financial Corp. v. Randolph*, 531 U.S. 79 (2000)] holding that failure to allocate arbitration costs does not mean that an agreement is unenforceable on the grounds of failing to protect parties from excessively high arbitration costs. The *Little* court interpreted *Green Tree* to mean that someone who claims that the risk of excessively high costs prevents him or her from exercising the right to arbitration has the burden of proof as to the likelihood that such costs will be incurred.

In 2002, the Eighth Circuit held that a pension plan's mandatory arbitration clause, requiring the employee to pay half the arbitration costs in a benefit determination dispute, was invalid. The clause violated ERISA § 503 by denying the employee a reasonable opportunity for full and fair review of the claim. [*Bond v. Twin Cities Carpenters Pension Fund*, 307 F.3d 704 (8th Cir. 2002)]

The Eleventh Circuit would not allow an employee to use the risk of prohibitive costs to challenge the "loser pays" aspect of the arbitration agreement before arbitration. The court's rationale was that the employee would have to pay only if the case was lost, a determination that would be too remote and speculative at the earliest stages of the case. [*Musnick v. King Motor Co. of Ft. Lauderdale*, 325 F.3d 1255 (11th Cir. 2003); *see also Bess v. Check Express*, 294 F.3d 1298 (11th Cir. 2002), holding that an arbitration agreement must be enforced unless the record shows that the plaintiff is likely to encounter prohibitive costs by pursuing arbitration]

Early in 2004, the California Court of Appeals ruled that costs that are unique to the arbitral forum (that is, would not be encountered in litigation) cannot be charged to an employee who asserts a claim that he or she was discriminated against contrary to public policy. The Court of Appeals found the employee's ability to pay irrelevant in this context. [*Abramson v. Juniper Networks Inc.*, 9 Cal.Rptr. 3d 422 (Cal. App. 2004)]

According to the D.C. Circuit and the Tenth Circuit, a requirement that employees advance arbitration costs automatically denies them the right to effect arbitration. In the Fourth Circuit, the test (under *Bradford v. Rockwell Semiconductor Systems Inc.* [238 F.3d 549 (4th Cir. 2001)]) is the effect on the individual claimant, but the Sixth Circuit looks at the effect not just on the individual but on other similarly situated employees. [*Morrison v. Circuit City Stores Inc.*, 317 F.3d 646 (6th Cir. 2003)] The Sixth Circuit said that when courts make this determination, they should also consider the possibility that the plaintiff will not have to pay the costs either because the arbitration agreement itself shifts the costs to the losing party, or because the arbitrator might impose the costs on the employer. In this case, the Sixth Circuit did find the fees excessive and possibly discouraging of the exercise of arbitration rights—the fees ranged from $1,125 to $3,000.

The Third Circuit found that certain provisions of an arbitration agreement were invalid. Employees had to pay an initial non-refundable $500 fee to the

American Arbitration Association, a filing fee of $2,750, a case-filing fee of $1,000, and a $150 charge for each day of arbitration, and half the arbitrator's fee (arbitrators in that area charged $250 an hour, with a minimum of $2,000 a day). However, the Third Circuit also held that it was appropriate to sever those provisions and enforce the rest of the agreement to compel arbitration. The court interpreted the overall purpose of the agreement to be settling disputes through arbitration, so the invalid provisions were a nonessential, severable part of the agreement. [*Spinetti v. Service Corp. Int'l,* 324 F.3d 212 (3d Cir. 2003)]

Late in 2003, the Ninth Circuit ruled that an employer who failed to pay for arbitration of an employee's claims of breach of the employment contract (the employee charged that payments, including stock options, were not made as promised) was in default under § 3 of the FAA. Therefore, the employer could not have the employee's suit stayed in order to get arbitration of the same claims, even though the employment contract that the employer allegedly violated contained an arbitration clause. [*Sink v. Aden Enterp. Inc.,* 352 F.3d 1197 (9th Cir. 2003)]

§ 40.08   FACTORS THAT PROMOTE ADR SUCCESS

Most successful ADR systems embody several steps, including in-house procedures for resolving grievances before outside parties get involved. In-house resolutions can be quick and inexpensive. Using a mediator or arbitrator always involves some degree of delay and expense, even if it is far less than the ruinous effort of litigation.

Any ADR system should specify whether the matter will be heard by one mediator or arbitrator or by a panel. Panels usually have three members; it's definitely better to have an odd number to prevent 2–2 or 3–3 splits.

The ADR policy should specify not only the number but the qualifications of the decision makers. It should be clear which employees will be allowed to use ADR to settle disputes—and which ones will be compelled to use it. The policy should clarify which disputes are involved: All employment-related disputes? All federal statutory discrimination claims? Only certain federal claims? Only claims that would otherwise go to state court?

An appropriate policy is fair to employees, providing them with as much due process protection as litigation would offer. They should have an adequate opportunity to assert claims, get evidence about what the employer did, and receive adequate remedies if the mediator or arbitrator decides in their favor.

The American Bar Association's "Due Process Protocol" sets out these standards for fairness in mandatory arbitration matters:

- The employee is aware of the arbitration requirement and accepts it voluntarily;
- The employee can be represented at arbitration (e.g., by a lawyer or union representative);
- The employee has access to a full range of remedies;

- The arbitrator has the power to make the employer pay the employee's arbitration-related costs. Some cases about arbitration take the position that, since the employer wanted arbitration in the first place, it should pay the full cost. The system could also be set up so that the employee never has to pay more than 50% of the cost of arbitration, or never has to pay more than one day's fee for the arbitrators.

An agreement to arbitrate employment disputes capped punitive damages at $5,000. The Eighth Circuit ruled [*Gannon v. Circuit City Stores Inc.*, 262 F.3d 677 (8th Cir. 2001)] that even if this provision was invalid, it did not render the entire agreement unenforceable; it could have been severed and the rest of the agreement left in place. The Eighth Circuit did not hold that the provision was necessarily invalid even though the punitive damage limitation was much lower than what would have been permitted under CRA '91.

CHAPTER 41

EEOC AND STATE ENFORCEMENT OF ANTIDISCRIMINATION LAWS

§ 41.01   INTRODUCTION

The Equal Employment Opportunity Commission (EEOC) is in charge of enforcing Title VII and the Americans with Disabilities Act (ADA). It also enforces the Equal Pay Act (EPA) and Age Discrimination in Employment Act (ADEA), although the enforcement provisions for these acts are slightly different because they reflect their derivation from the Fair Labor Standards Act. EPA complainants do not have to file an EEOC charge; the rules for ADEA charges are found in 29 C.F.R. § 1626.4.

The basic enforcement scheme is that people who believe they have been discriminated against file charges with the EEOC. The EEOC works with state antidiscrimination agencies, using methods ranging from informal persuasion to litigation to get employers to comply with the law and eliminate any discriminatory practices occurring in the workplace.

The EEOC can intervene in a suit brought by an employee or can bring its own lawsuits against employers. The EEOC has the power to collect data, investigate allegations of discrimination, view conditions in the workplace, and inspect records. It can also advise employers about how to comply with the law. The EEOC has the power to subpoena witnesses and documents, bring suits, and supervise the collection of damages that courts have ordered or that employers have agreed to pay under a settlement.

Therefore, the EEOC has a dual role. It investigates charges brought by employees, but it can also litigate as a plaintiff. The theory is that the EEOC acts as plaintiff to preserve the rights of all the employees within the workplace. The EEOC always has a right to investigate and, where it believes a cause of action exists, to litigate. So employees' waivers and releases, or their settlement of claims against the employer, can prevent those employees from suing their employers, but will not prevent a suit by the EEOC. Furthermore, waivers and releases are void as against public policy if they try to prevent employees from assisting in an EEOC investigation.

Similarly, the EEOC can pursue an ADA case (including seeking specific relief for an individual) even if the individual employee was covered by a mandatory predispute arbitration agreement [*see* § 40.07] and therefore could not sue the employer. [*EEOC v. Waffle House*, 534 U.S. 279 (2002)] In an Eleventh Circuit case, 36 black employees brought suit for harassment and racial discrimination. Subsequently, the EEOC brought a separate suit alleging that 200 black employees had been subjected to a racially hostile work environment. Nine of the named plaintiffs in the private suit settled, and 22 cases were dismissed. At the district court level, the employer got summary judgment in the EEOC case on the ground that it involved the same claims as the private suit. In 2004, however, the Eleventh Circuit reversed, holding that there were only two types of privity that might apply: virtual representation, and control over the previous litigation. In virtual representation, the interests of the parties are closely aligned and the party in the initial litigation adequately represents those common interests.

Virtual representation is found based on factors such as participation in the earlier case, whether the group consented to be bound by the result, the chosen litigation tactics, and whether the two groups had a close relationship (e.g., the relationship between administrator and beneficiaries of the estate; between a company and its president and sole stockholder). The Eleventh Circuit held that the EEOC and the plaintiffs were not closely aligned. In this instance, the EEOC and the private plaintiffs engaged in joint discovery. The EEOC was involved in mediation of the complaints but did not participate in the trial of the private plaintiffs' case. The EEOC did not agree to be bound, although it tried to join the earlier litigation but was prevented from doing so. Because the EEOC was not a party in the private suit, was not in privity with its plaintiffs and did not control the private litigation, the agency was able to bring suit to challenge what it identified as company-wide racial harassment. [*EEOC v. Pemco Aeroplex Inc.*, 383 F.3d 1280 (11th Cir. 2004)]

The number of discrimination charges filed with the EEOC fell 5% from 2004 to 2005. In 2005, there were 75,428 charges filed at EEOC field offices, and 77,352 private-sector discrimination charges were resolved. Only 21.5% of resolutions were favorable to the charging party. The average time to process a charge was 171 days. The National Mediation Program resolved 7,908 cases, with an average resolution time of 81 days.

There were 26,740 charges of race discrimination (35.5%); 23,094 charges of sex discrimination (30.6%); 22,278 charges of retaliation (29.5%); 16,585 charges of age discrimination (22%); 14,893 disability charges (19.7%); 8,035 national origin discrimination charges (10.7%).

The EEOC obtained close to $380 million in monetary relief for charging parties. In 2005, $271.6 million in relief was obtained at pre-litigation stages of the case, the highest ever. This included $115 million obtained through mediation. The EEOC filed 417 suits—383 of them on the merits of a charge, the rest actions for subpoenas or preliminary relief. Of those, 337 merits suits were resolved, with litigation recoveries of $107.7 million, nearly all ($101.3 million) in Title VII cases. Sexual harassment charges were filed with either the EEOC or state agencies in 12,679 cases (about one seventh brought by men) and 4,449 pregnancy discrimination charges were made. [EEOC charge statistics for fiscal years 1992–2005 can be found at <http://www.eeoc.gov/stats/charges. html>; litigation statistics for the same years at <http://www.eeoc.gov/stats/ litigation.html>]

In 2005, there were 22,278 retaliation charges, 30% of the total (versus 27% of the total in 2000). There is some feeling that retaliation charges are easier to prove than the underlying discrimination case (because it's a matter of public record that an employee has sued or made an EEOC or state agency complaint). [Sue Shellenbarger, *Supreme Court Takes on How Employers Handle Work Harassment Complaints*, Wall Street Journal, Apr. 13, 2006, at p. D1]

For recent examples of EEOC settlements, *see, e.g.*, the following:

- A $562,500 settlement was approved in a racial harassment case brought by three African-American employees of a car dealership. The dealership also entered into a consent decree providing injunctive relief, changes in company policies, and EEO training for staffers. [*EEOC v. Lithia Motors Inc.*, No. CIV 05-cv-01901-PSF-MJW (D. Colo. Mar. 15, 2006); *see* EEOC press release, <http://www.eeoc.gov/press/3-16-06.html> (Mar. 16, 2006)]
- Melrose Hotel and Berwind Property Group agreed to pay $800,000 to 13 ex-employees for national origin discrimination against Hispanic employees in the form of a workplace English-only policy, firing Hispanic employees, and retaliating against employees who exercised legal rights. The consent decree prohibits future use of English-only rules. [*EEOC v. Melrose Hotel New York*, No. CV-04-7514 S.D.N.Y. (Mar. 16, 2006); *see* <http://www.eeoc.gov/press/3-16-06a.html>]
- A $1 million settlement was obtained in a racial harassment lawsuit in which a black employee was not only subjected to racial epithets, but also assaulted by co-workers who placed his head in a noose. The employer was aware of the harassment, but did not move to stop it. [*EEOC v. Commercial Coating Serv., Inc.*, No. H-03-3984 (S.D. Tex. Mar. 21, 2006); *see* <http://www.eeoc.gov/press/3-21-06.html>]

As Jathan W. Janove explains, [Jathan W. Janove, *Soothing the EEOC Dragon,* HR Magazine, May 2001, at p. 137] the worst-case scenario for a company is for the EEOC to expand a complaint into a class action, because then not only will the agency examine the company's conduct in past years, it may start a media campaign to recruit new plaintiffs, creating significant bad publicity.

To head off this very negative possibility, it often helps to volunteer significant nonmonetary relief measures; to offer to donate part of the amount that might otherwise be assessed as damages to worthy causes; or permit the EEOC to issue a press release describing the remedial measures (rather than the alleged discrimination).

EEOC investigators assign cases to classifications of A (the most serious), B, and C. In an A-1 case, the EEOC itself may pursue the case as plaintiff. An A-2 case is likely to result in a finding of good cause, but no litigation by the EEOC itself. It's a bad sign if the EEOC sends out a questionnaire to potential plaintiffs; asks the defendant for a statement of its position; if the EEOC does not ask the employer to mediate; or if it's a deferral state (see below) but the first contact comes from the federal EEOC.

It is often helpful to demonstrate good faith by offering unconditional reinstatement to a charging party. There are many cases indicating that if the charging party rejects such an offer, he or she will not be eligible for various kinds of relief (back pay, front pay, possibly even court-ordered reinstatement).

The Department of Labor also has the right to sue federal contractors for remedies, including punitive damages, if the contractors are guilty of race, sex, or religious discrimination. Employees of federal contractors get a choice of filing their complaints with the EEOC or the DOL. The EEOC and DOL have a work-sharing plan.

In September 2004, the EEOC announced that, starting in 2005, most of the approximately 1 million unsolicited phone calls received by the agency would initially be processed by a center operated by a contractor, changing a policy under which calls went through a central toll-free EEOC number or were answered directly by employees at the agency's 51 field offices. One contractor would be selected for a two-year pilot project. The EEOC estimated the cost of having con-tractors operate the center at $2 million to $3 million a year, versus $12 million or more to develop the infrastructure for an in-house contact center. The customer service representatives employed by the contractor will not process charges, but will collect information from potential charging parties (using a Web-based inquiry assessment tool) and submit it to EEOC offices for assessment and follow-up. The EEOC estimates that only 40% of unsolicited calls to the agency come from individuals who contemplate filing a discrimination charge; the other 60% want general information. [(No by-line) *Contract Employees Will Field Queries for EEOC in Two-Year National Pilot Project*, 73 L.W. 2150 (Sept. 21, 2004)]

§ 41.02   EEOC ADR

At times, the EEOC itself will engage in ADR with employers and employees as an alternative to normal charge processing methods. The EEOC issued two policy statements on these subjects in 1997, although formal regulations were not issued at that time.

Under these policy statements, the EEOC said ADR was not appropriate in some cases. The agency did not treat ADR as fair or appropriate in important test cases where the EEOC wishes to establish policy or set a precedent; where the EEOC would have to maintain an ongoing presence to monitor compliance; or where the case has significant implications for people besides the parties to the individual charge—for instance, other employees and other companies in the same or different industries.

The EEOC took the position that ADR was fair and appropriate if:

- It is voluntarily elected, not compelled;
- The EEOC provides help to employees who are confused about the process;
- The decision maker (mediator or arbitrator) is truly neutral;
- The proceedings are confidential;
- The outcome of the process is an enforceable written agreement.

EEOC ADR began in 1997. In that year, 780 cases were settled for a total of $10.8 million. In 1998, there were 1,500 settlements for an aggregate of $17 million. [Steven A. Holmes, *Jobs Discrimination Agency Lightening Its Load*, New York Times, Feb. 22, 1999, at p. A1]

The Janove article discussed above quotes EEOC staffer David Grinberg, saying that in fiscal 2000, 81% of charging parties who were offered mediation accepted it (but only 31% of employers agreed). About two-thirds of claims that went to mediation were resolved, in an average of 96 days.

As for using mediation later in the process, mediator Hunter R. Hughes said at a September 2000 seminar that mediating class actions before the suit is filed, or just afterwards, reduces defense costs and gives plaintiffs the chance to make their employers implement systemic changes in their employment practices. Hughes said that the earlier mediation begins, the better—because litigating positions have not hardened yet, and there will be less unfavorable publicity and bad feeling. Plaintiff attorneys are less supportive of this option. They believe that it gives class representatives more than their fair share of the settlement, because the class has not really come together by the time the settlement is obtained. [No by-line, *Early Mediation of Class Actions Provides Advantages for Defendants and Plaintiffs*, 69 L.W. 2207 (Oct. 10, 2000)]

In 2002, the EEOC announced a pilot program to begin in the following year in four or five of the agency's District Offices. Under the pilot, a small number of companies would be given the chance to use their own established internal ADR programs to resolve discrimination charges raised by employees. If an employee of one of the companies in the pilot files with the EEOC, the charging party can authorize the agency to suspend the complaint for up to 60 days for access to the employer's dispute resolution program. However, the EEOC time limits are not tolled during the ADR process. An eligible ADR program is one that is voluntary; does not impose fees on the employee; has been in operation for at least one year; addresses claims that antidiscrimination statutes have been violated; and generates written settlements that can be enforced by the court system. [No by-line, *Pilot Program Will Refer EEOC Charges to Pre-Approved Employer ADR Programs*, 71 L.W. 2456]

In April 2003, the EEOC expanded the voluntary mediation program through cooperative agreements with the anti-discrimination agencies of Alaska, New York City, Florida, Indiana, Iowa, Kansas City, Ohio, New Mexico, and South Carolina. To participate, an agency had to field mediators with at least five years' experience, and must be able to satisfy the EEOC's 45-day time frame for finishing a mediation.

From 1999 to 2003, more than 44,000 mediations, resolving over 30,000 charges, were processed under 18 nationwide EEOC agreements and more than 300 local ones. [*See* 72 L.W. 2218 and 71 L.W. 2684]

However, although both employers and employees praised the voluntary mediation program, and 96% of employers who engaged in mediation said they'd do it again, there was a glitch in the system in terms of securing consent to mediate. Eighty percent of charging parties agreed to mediate, but slightly less than one-third of employers accepted the option of mediation. Of the employers who rejected mediation, 94% said that the merits of the case did not deserve mediation; 57% did not think that the EEOC would issue a reasonable causing finding in the matter; and half held the incorrect belief that the mediation program required monetary settlements in every case. [No by-line, *Employers Praise EEOC Mediation Program, But Opt Out on Perceived Meritless Claims* 72 L.W. 2328 (Dec. 9, 2003)]

§ 41.03   TITLE VII ENFORCEMENT

Both the EEOC and state antidiscrimination agencies have a role in investigating an employee's allegations of discrimination. Initial charges can be filed with either the EEOC or the state or local agency.

However, if the employee goes to the EEOC first, it generally "defers" to the state or local agency. That is, it sends the paperwork to the state or local agency, and gives it a 60-day deferral period to resolve the complaint. [*See* 29 C.F.R. § 1601.74 for a list of state and local agencies that are deemed to have enough enforcement power to handle a discrimination charge] Furthermore, some agencies (listed in 29 C.F.R. § 1601.80) are "certified" by the EEOC, based on a track record of at least four years as a deferral agency, during which time the EEOC found its work product to be acceptable.

Title VII and ADA charges must be filed within the EEOC within 180 days of the time of the alleged discrimination (if there is no deferral agency in the picture) or within 300 days of the alleged discrimination, or 30 days of the time the deferral agency terminates processing of the charge (if a deferral agency is involved).

However, these timing requirements are tricky and provide many opportunities for the employer to get cases dismissed. In a case involving a deferral agency, the filing period is really only 240 days, because of the 60-day period when the EEOC steps aside and lets the deferral agency handle the matter. However, most deferral agencies have what is called "work sharing" agreements with the EEOC. In the jurisdiction of those agencies, an employee's complaint is timely if it is made more than 240, but less than 300, days after the alleged discrimination occurred.

Once the EEOC gets a charge, it is required to notify the subject of the charge. Because nearly all discrimination charges are brought against the employer corporation, and not against individuals, this will nearly always be the corporation. The EEOC's job is to attempt conciliation—to get the parties to agree on a view of what happened in the past and how discrimination is to be avoided or remedied in the future.

According to the Eastern District of Louisiana, it was permissible for an employer to contact employees who had filled out an EEOC questionnaire. The EEOC was not permitted to assert attorney-client privilege or the rule of legal ethics that forbids direct contact with a party who is represented by an attorney in order to keep the employer from contacting employees who completed the questionnaire but had not filed EEOC charges. The questionnaires were subject to pretrial discovery, because they were not prepared by a party or the representative of a party in anticipation of litigation; they were prepared for the

EEOC to select potential claimants on whose behalf the agency would seek damages. [*EEOC v. TIC (The Industrial Co.)*, 2002 W.L. 31654977 (E.D. La. 2002)]

It can be hard to determine when alleged violations of the law occurred. The problem gets even harder if the employee charges that there was more than a single discriminatory act. If there was a continuing violation (one that lasts a long time), or a series of related violations, then the timing requirements probably run from the latest action in the series. There could also be two separate violations, each with its own timing requirements: for example, discriminatory refusal to promote, followed by retaliation against the employee for filing discrimination charges.

Where the employer is accused of adopting a seniority system for intentionally discriminatory reasons (e.g., a desire to limit opportunities for women or minorities entering the workforce), the time to file the EEOC charge is the time at which the employee is injured by application of the seniority system to his or her particular case. That sounds innocent enough, but it had to be added to Title VII by the Civil Rights Act of 1991, to reverse a 1989 Supreme Court case [*Lorance v. AT&T Techs. Inc.*, 490 U.S. 900 (1989)] that said that the time ran from the date the seniority system was adopted. In many cases, the system was adopted long before the would-be plaintiff was hired by the company—and possibly long before he or she was born.

According to the Fifth Circuit, procedural failures required that a judgment in favor of an employee had to be vacated and his age discrimination case had to be dismissed. He filed a complaint with the EEOC and failed to check the box on the form indicating that he wanted the charge filed with both the EEOC and the Texas Commission on Human Rights. Therefore, he failed to go through the mandatory step of filing a state charge—so his federal lawsuit was invalid.

Texas has a work-sharing arrangement with the EEOC, but that only means that a single filing can apply to both state and federal procedures—not that the state procedure can be ignored, even in a case like this one where only federal claims are asserted against the employer. [*Jones v. Grinnell Corp.*, 235 F.3d 972 (5th Cir. 2001)]

The Fourth Circuit ruled that a retaliation claim brought by the EEOC was not barred by laches. The claimant was a former supervisor who alleged that he was fired for opposing race discrimination in the workplace. The Fourth Circuit ruled that the delay was caused by the state agency. The laches defense is applied only against the party responsible for the delay—in this case, the EEOC was not responsible. Designating state agencies and the EEOC as agents for one another is purely for the convenience of the charging party and does not make the two distinct agencies responsible for the faults of the other. [*EEOC v. Navy Fed. Credit Union*, 424 F.3d 397 (4th Cir. 2005)]

Another Fifth Circuit case, *Villma v. Eureka Co.* [218 F.3d 458 (5th Cir. 2001)] says that because Texas is a deferral state, the EEOC has to hold off on its charge processing for at least 60 days to permit the state investigation to proceed. Although the only way to trigger the 90-day period for bringing a federal suit is to get an EEOC right-to-sue letter, the EEOC letter does not start the 60-day period for a suit in state court under the Texas Human Rights Act. Only a civil action letter from the Texas Commission on Human Rights will trigger the state time period.

§ 41.04   EEOC INVESTIGATION

If the EEOC can't settle a charge informally, its next step is to investigate the facts and determine if there is reasonable cause to believe that the employee's complaint is well-founded. If it makes such a "reasonable cause" determination, it has an obligation to attempt to conciliate: to get the employer to improve its equal opportunity policies, sign a compliance agreement, and compensate the employee for past discrimination. The EEOC can't close its case file until it has evidence of the employer's actual compliance with the conciliation agreement.

The EEOC announced plans in April 2006 for new methods of investigating charges of systemic discrimination (pattern or practice cases or class actions where it is charged that discrimination has a broad impact on an industry, company, or geographic area). Investigation and litigation will be shifted from headquarters to the field. Each field district will be required to set up plans for finding and investigating systemic discrimination, with each investigation staffed by employees with the relevant expertise. The EEOC's Office of Information Technology has been ordered to produce an action plan for meeting technical needs. [Rebecca Moore, *EEOC to Revamp Procedures for Handling Systemic Discrimination*, PlanSponsor.com (Apr. 11, 2006)]

As a general rule, an EEOC determination letter is admissible evidence in a suit later brought by the charging party. However, the determination letter is not automatically admissible: The court can keep it out, under Federal Rules of Evidence Rule 403, if the court determines that the probative value of the document is significantly outweighed by negative factors such as prejudice and risk of confusion. [*Coleman v. Home Depot Inc.,* 306 F.3d 1333 (3d Cir. 2002)]

If the EEOC believes that the employer is blocking the process, it sends a written notice demanding compliance. Title VII § 706(c) gives the EEOC discretion to sue the employer if an acceptable conciliation agreement cannot be reached within 30 days after the end of the period when the EEOC defers to state agency jurisdiction, or 30 days of the date a charge is filed with the EEOC. There is no statute of limitations for suits brought directly by the EEOC: They can sue even for events in the distant past.

The Fifth Circuit ruled in late 2001 that the district court was right to refuse to enforce the EEOC's subpoena seeking evidence of sex discrimination at a point 19 months into a race-discrimination investigation; the EEOC should have filed its own charge if it wanted to pursue potential sex discrimination. [*EEOC v. Southern Farm Bureau Cas. Ins. Co.,* 271 F.3d 209 (5th Cir. 2001)]

If and when the EEOC concludes that there is no reasonable cause to believe that the facts are as charged by the employee, the EEOC will inform the charging party of this determination. In Title VII and ADA cases (but not Equal Pay Act or ADEA cases), the charging party can still sue the employer in federal court, but must get a "right to sue" letter from the EEOC indicating that the case has been closed. Usually, the EEOC gets 180 days to attempt conciliation, but the employee can ask for earlier termination of the EEOC's involvement, and earlier issuance of the right-to-sue letter. However, the employee can't bypass the conciliation process entirely.

Once the right-to-sue letter is issued, the employee has only 90 days to file the federal suit. If the 90 days pass without commencement of a suit, the EEOC can still bring suit, on the theory that the potential private plaintiff's inaction has reinstated the agency's own powers.

Although the EEOC has reduced its backlog, it is still clear that the heavily burdened agency is not going to complete its investigation of every charge within 180 days. Courts differ on whether the EEOC can issue right-to-sue letters based on simple inability to resolve the charge on time. [*See* Helen D. Irvin, *Courts Differ on "Early" Right-to-Sue Letters*, 69 L.W. 2259 (Nov. 7, 2000)]

The EEOC's own regulations [29 C.F.R. § 1601.28(a)(2)] say that an early letter can be issued if the EEOC determines that it probably will not be able to complete the investigation on time. Various District Courts have agreed. However, some courts say that the EEOC must wait to issue the letter until the 180 days have elapsed, because issuing an early letter would permit the agency to avoid its obligation to investigate. *Martini v. FNMA* [179 F.3d 1336 (D.C. Cir. 1999)] says that Title VII requires complainants to wait the full 180 days, to encourage informal resolution of as many charges as possible.

The EEOC's investigative powers generally end as soon as a right-to-sue letter has been issued. [*EEOC v. Federal Home Loan Mortgage Co.*, 37 F. Supp. 2d 769 (E.D. Va. 1999)] The exception is the case in which the EEOC thinks its investigation goes beyond the litigation, in which case it can intervene in the employee's private suit or file its own charges. However, the EEOC will not intervene in a suit, or bring a suit, if it makes a "no reasonable cause" determination.

The Southern District of Indiana ruled in mid-2003 that the EEOC does not have the power to expand an investigation of a single restaurant into a pattern-or-practice charge accusing the entire restaurant chain of nationwide sex discrimination. [*EEOC v. Jillian's of Indianapolis*, 72 L.W.1006 (S.D. Ind. June 16, 2003)]

The Eleventh Circuit dismissed an EEOC action and also reversed an award of attorneys' fees to sanction the EEOC for failing to satisfy its duty to attempt conciliation. The court ruled that the EEOC ignored a prompt letter from the defendant's general counsel showing an intent to resolve the charges without litigation, and informed the company that conciliation was unsuccessful. [*EEOC v. Asplundh Tree Export Co.*, 340 F.3d 1256 (11th Cir. 2003)]

Suits with the EEOC as plaintiff are limited to matters investigated as a result of a charge, not matters outside the scope of the matter for which the EEOC attempted to conciliate. In other words, the EEOC's efforts to conciliate one charge won't make the employer vulnerable to a host of other charges. Furthermore, because of the burden of its workload, the EEOC files only a few hundred suits a year.

§ 41.05 ADEA ENFORCEMENT

The rules for ADEA cases are similar, but not identical, to those for Title VII cases, so you should check to see if ADEA plaintiffs have violated any of the requirements for that type of suit.

In addition to suits brought by employees who charge that they have been subjected to age discrimination, the ADEA statute provides for enforcement by the Secretary of Labor; 29 U.S.C. § 26 gives the Secretary the power to investigate ADEA charges, including subpoenaeing witnesses and inspecting employers' business records. (The DOL has delegated this power to the EEOC.)

Even criminal penalties can be imposed against anyone who "shall forcibly resist, oppose, impede, intimidate or interfere with" a DOL representative engaged in enforcing the ADEA. [*See* 29 U.S.C. § 629] The criminal penalty is a fine of up to $500 and/or up to one year's imprisonment, although imprisonment will be ordered only in the case of someone who has already been convicted of the same offense in the past.

Although the EEOC can become an ADEA plaintiff, it seldom does so. The cases it selects are usually large-scale, involving egregious practices, many employees, or a pattern or practice of discrimination. The EEOC can bring a suit even if no employee of the company has filed timely charges of age discrimination.

If the EEOC files suit after an employee has already sued based on the same conduct on the employer's part, the earlier individual suit can proceed. However, an individual who wants back pay or other monetary relief cannot file suit after the EEOC starts its own suit, because the EEOC litigates on behalf of all affected employees.

However, if the EEOC complaint covers a pattern or practice of discrimination lasting "up to the present time," this means the date when the EEOC filed its complaint, so an individual can file a private suit charging the employer with committing discrimination after the filing of the EEOC complaint.

The EEOC doesn't need written consent from employees to file a suit on their behalf. The EEOC can seek relief for all employees on the basis of a charge filed by one employee who only reported discrimination against him- or herself. The EEOC can also undertake a single conciliation effort for multiple charges, as long as the employer is notified that the charge involves more than one complainant.

No employee who has already sued the employer can get back pay or other individual relief as part of an EEOC suit involving the same facts. However, if an employee tried to sue, but the case was dismissed on the basis of untimely filing, then the EEOC can bring a suit to get an injunction against the employer, even if the EEOC's case is based on the same facts as the suit that was dismissed.

> **Tip:** The general rule is that a company that files for bankruptcy protection is entitled to an automatic stay—a period of time during which suits against the company cannot proceed. However, a suit by the EEOC is considered an exercise of the government's regulatory, policing function, and therefore can proceed even while the automatic stay is in place.

§ 41.06   THE FEDERAL-STATE RELATIONSHIP

[A]   ADEA Interaction

Unlike ERISA, which preempts whole classes of state laws dealing with certain retirement and employee benefit issues, the ADEA specifically provides for a joint working relationship between the federal government and state anti-discrimination agencies; 29 U.S.C. § 625(b) gives the Secretary of Labor the power to cooperate with state and local agencies to carry out the purposes of ADEA.

Section 633(a) provides that state agencies retain their jurisdiction ove age-discrimination claims. However, federal ADEA suits supersede state age-discrimination enforcement efforts. A potential age-discrimination plaintiff has to go through enforcement procedures at both the state and the federal level. However, if the federal charge is filed on time, the complainant doesn't have to complete the state enforcement process—only to file a charge within the state system.

The federal ADEA provides that, if a state has a statute against age discrimination and has an enforcement agency, then potential plaintiffs have to file charges within both systems. The federal-state enforcement relationship revolves around the concepts of "referral" and "deferral."

Referral means that a state has a work-sharing arrangement with the EEOC, as provided by 29 C.F.R. § 1616.9. When an age-discrimination complaint is made to the state agency, the state agency refers it to the EEOC. If the state charge is dismissed, the EEOC has the power to conduct an independent investigation. Originally, the EEOC Regulations listed states that were identified as "referral" states because they had age discrimination laws. However, in August 2002, the EEOC proposed a set of regulations for ADEA litigation procedures: *see* 67 Fed. Reg. 52431 (August 12, 2002), finalized at 68 Fed. Reg. 70150 (Dec. 17, 2003), effective January 16, 2004. The EEOC says that because most of the states now have laws to forbid age discrimination, it is no longer necessary to maintain these lists. The EEOC will simply make referrals to the state agencies as appropriate.

An additional group of states (Arizona, Colorado, Kansas, Maine, Ohio, Rhode Island, South Dakota, and Washington) are "conditional referral" states. They do have antidiscrimination statutes, but the terms of these state laws are quite different from the federal ADEA. This situation creates the possibility that employees will bring claims that are covered by the state law, but not by the federal law. In such instances, the state-only claims will not be referred to the EEOC. Claims that are covered only by federal law must be filed directly with the EEOC, within 180 days of the discriminatory act.

The deferral concept means that the EEOC defers to the state and does not process the charge for a period of 60 days after the referral, so that the state agency can take action.

Except in a deferral state, the charge must be filed no later than 180 days after the discriminatory act, or the latest act that forms part of a pattern. In a deferral state, the last permissible filing date is either 300 days after the discriminatory act (or last discriminatory act in a series) or 30 days after the state agency dismisses its charge and notifies the complainant of the dismissal—whichever comes earlier. Unlike Title VII plaintiffs, ADEA plaintiffs do not have to get a right-to-sue letter.

If a state has a law against age discrimination, 29 U.S.C. § 633(b) provides that employees may not bring ADEA suits in that state until they have waited 60 days for the state to resolve the charges. If state charges have been dismissed in less than 60 days, the employee doesn't have to wait for the full 60-day period to end. The 60-day period is imposed to allow for conciliation of the charge. [*See* 29 U.S.C. § 626(d)]

During this period, the EEOC's task is to decide if it has a "reasonable basis to conclude that a violation of the Act has occurred or will occur." If the answer is "yes," the EEOC makes a "good cause" or "reasonable cause" finding—i.e., that the employee had good cause to complain. Then the EEOC will probably issue a Letter of Violation. However, the mere fact that no letter is issued does not prove that the EEOC did not detect any violations.

Courts have reached different conclusions about what to do if the plaintiff does not wait 60 days as required. The Sixth Circuit says that the case should be dismissed (but without prejudice, so it can be refiled later). On the other hand, the Eighth Circuit says that the case should not be dismissed, only suspended pending the administrative disposition of the complaint. [*Compare Chapman v. City of Detroit,* 808 F.2d 459 (6th Cir. 1986), *with Wilson v. Westinghouse Elec. Co.,* 838 F.2d 286 (8th Cir. 1988)] The Final Rule calls for the EEOC to issue a Notice of Dismissal or Termination when the agency finishes processing a charge. A complainant can file suit in federal or state court at any time after 60 days have passed since the filing of the age discrimination charge—whether or not the EEOC has issued its Notice of Dismissal or Termination. But once the Notice is issued, the complainant has only 90 days from the date of the notice to bring suit; otherwise, the suit will be dismissed as untimely.

Next, the EEOC tries to get the company into compliance by informal persuasion. If the company and the EEOC reach an agreement that the agency believes will eliminate the discrimination, then the agreement will be written down and signed by the EEOC representative, a company representative, and the employee who charged the discrimination. If the charging party is not satisfied, he or she can withdraw the charge. The EEOC still has independent authority to settle on behalf of other employees affecting the discrimination.

On the other hand, if conciliation fails and no agreement is reached (possibly because there has been no discrimination, and therefore the employer is unwilling to admit culpability and "admit" discrimination that never occurred in the first place), the EEOC and/or the charging party can sue. The charging party's suit must be brought no later than 90 days after receipt of notice from the EEOC that conciliation has failed, but it is not necessary to get a right-to-sue letter.

See 67 Fed. Reg. 52431 (Aug. 12, 2002) and 68 Fed. Reg. 70150 (Dec. 17, 2003). The notices inform the charging party that he or she has a right to sue the alleged perpetrator of age discrimination, but the right expires 90 days after the issue date of the NDT. Each aggrieved person will receive an individual NDT, but for multi-person charges, the NDT will not issue until proceedings end as to all of them.

Despite similarities, the NDT does not work in exactly the same way as a Title VII Right to Sue letter. A potential ADEA plaintiff can file suit at any time once 60 days have passed since the filing of the charge with the administrative agency, whether or not the NDT has issued. However, suit is untimely once 90 days have passed since the NDT date. To prevent confusion, the EEOC amended 29 C.F.R. § 1626.12 to clarify the difference between the notice that is issued when an EEOC conciliation attempt fails and this new type of notice.

The EEOC can terminate further processing of a charge if it discovers that a suit has been filed against the respondent of the charge, unless the agency determines that continued charge processing furthers the aims of the ADEA. However, the EEOC has the authority to investigate age discrimination cases and bring suit even if there is no individual charge filed. This is not true in Title VII or ADA Title I cases. When several people are involved in a charge, the EEOC will not issue an NDT until all the charges have been processed. The agency concluded that issuing a separate NDT to each charging party as his or her case was finished would lead to inefficient multiplication of court proceedings.

[B] State Laws Against Age Discrimination

Most of the states have some kind of law prohibiting age discrimination in employment. However, Alabama does not. Missouri, Oklahoma, and Wyoming have general antidiscrimination laws that do not go into detail about age claims. In Arkansas, Mississippi, and South Dakota, state employees, but not private-sector employees, are covered by the state ADEA. North Carolina provides that age discrimination violates public policy, but there is no comprehensive antidiscrimination law.

Some of the state laws cover all employers, whereas others cover only companies that employ at least a certain number of workers (which can be anywhere from 4 to 25, depending on the state). In other words, some small companies are subject to state ADEAs but not to the federal law. The Indiana statute, however, applies only in circumstances outside the federal law.

> **Tip:** In Georgia, Nebraska, New Hampshire, and South Dakota, violation of state antidiscrimination law can be a criminal offense.

Although the procedure varies from state to state, usually a person who claims to be a victim of age discrimination begins the state enforcement process by filing a charge with the state human rights/equal employment opportunity agency, within the time frame set out by the statute. Depending on the statute, this could be anywhere from 30 days after the alleged discriminatory practice to one year plus 90 days of the time the complainant discovered the employer acted illegally.

Most of the states, like the federal government, have a dual system of agency enforcement and private litigation. The agency investigates the charge and issues either a finding of good cause or a no-cause finding. If the agency deems that the charge is well-founded, then it tries to conciliate or sues the employer. On the other hand, if it makes a no-cause finding, or cannot resolve the matter promptly, the employee has the right to bring suit in state court, under the state antidiscrimination law. However, in some states, there is no agency enforcement, so employers are only at risk of private suit.

Another group of states (Massachusetts, Michigan, New York, Ohio, Pennsylvania) have a different dual system. Complaining employees get a choice: either to file a state-court suit right away, without going to the antidiscrimination agency, or to file an administrative complaint. However, election of remedies is usually required. So once an employee files in state court, he or she cannot go back and initiate the administrative process. Complainants in these states are entitled to use the 300-day filing period available in deferral states.

CHAPTER **42**

DISCRIMINATION SUITS BY EMPLOYEES: PROCEDURAL ISSUES

§ 42.01 INTRODUCTION

When it comes to litigating discrimination claims, it's understandable that both employers and employees feel vulnerable. Employers often feel that, no matter how little substance there is to a charge of discrimination, the employer will still have to fight the charge (which can be time-consuming and expensive) and might be ordered to pay immense damages. Employees feel that they are at the mercy of employers—that the only means of redress is complex and takes many years, by which time memories will have faded.

§ 42.02 CAUSES OF ACTION

In legal parlance, a cause of action is something for which someone can be sued. Employees can charge employers with various kinds of wrongdoing, and the same suit can combine discrimination charges with other causes of action, such as:

- Violation of Title VII of the Civil Rights Act of 1964 (discrimination on the grounds of race, sex, nationality, or color—sexual harassment is considered a type of sex discrimination);
- Violation of the Pregnancy Discrimination Act (PDA), an addition to Title VII, which forbids treating a qualified pregnant employee on less favorable terms than a comparably situated, nonpregnant employee;
- Violation of the Age Discrimination Act (discriminating against an individual who is age 40 or over, in any term or condition of employment, including hiring, firing, promotion, and benefits);
- Violation of 42 U.S.C. § 1981, the Civil War-era statute that gives all citizens the same right to make contracts as "white citizens." Four Circuits allow § 1981 suits by at-will employees who claim they were discharged on the basis of racial prejudice—even though they had no written employment contracts. [*Lauture v. IBM*, 216 F.3d 238 (2d Cir. 2000); *Perry v. Woodward*, 199 F.3d 1126 (10th Cir. 1999); *Spriggs v. Diamond Auto Glass*, 165 F.3d 1015 (4th Cir. 1999); *Fadeyi v. Planned Parenthood*, 160 F.3d 1048 (5th Cir. 1998)];
- Wrongful refusal to re-employ a military veteran;
- Violation of the Equal Pay Act: paying women less than men for the same job. This law does not permit "comparable worth" claims that allege that a typically female job is more valuable than a different and higher-paid job that is typically performed by men;
- Retaliation against an employee who filed a discrimination claim (or exercised other legal rights, e.g., in connection with unemployment benefits or Worker's Compensation) or cooperated in an investigation;
- Any act of wrongful termination for other reasons (e.g., discharging someone who "blew the whistle" on corporate wrongdoing);

- Violation of labor law (e.g., retaliating against someone for protected activity such as supporting the union or asserting a grievance against the employer). Nearly all labor law claims must be brought in federal, not state, court, because the federal statute the Labor Management Relations Act (LMRA) preempts state regulation—in other words, this is considered purely a federal matter;
- Breach of contract (either an explicit, written contract such as an employment contract or a collective bargaining agreement, or an implied contract);
- Defamation (in the context of an unfavorable reference or unfavorable statements in the press, and if the employer cannot assert a defense of truth);
- Interference with contractual relations, e.g., the employer prevents an ex-employee from getting a new job or establishing a business;
- Infliction of emotional distress (either negligent or intentional).

However, the Southern District of New York did not permit a UPS driver who was fired for refusing to cover his dreadlocks with a cap to maintain a suit for racial and religious discrimination. In this reading, Title VII does not prohibit discrimination against a particular hairstyle (the plaintiff conceded that his religions did not require him to wear dreadlocks). An employer can legitimately discharge workers who refuse to comply with appearance guidelines—the managerial prerogative includes imposing reasonable grooming requirements on employees who deal with customers. UPS ordered 18 drivers in the New York area to wear caps because their hairstyles were not deemed acceptably businesslike; 17 of them were black. The plaintiff refused to wear a wool hat, saying that it was uncomfortable in the warm months and could damage his hair. [*Eatman v. UPS,* 194 F. Supp. 2d 256 (S.D.N.Y. 2002)]

Frequently, employees will engage in several different proceedings, involving different statutes. Then, it becomes important to determine if the results of one proceeding will affect other proceedings (or prevent potential claims from being pursued). Denial of a person's FMLA claim for being fired while on maternity leave is res judicata to Title VII, ADEA, and the Florida Civil Rights Act claims. That is, the negative FMLA ruling is considered to have determined the other claims, because all the claims involve the same facts, which have already been litigated. [*O'Connor v. PCA Family Health Plan,* 200 F.3d 1349 (11th Cir. 2000)]

A group of current and former employees brought various ADEA, FLSA, ERISA, and Title VII claims. The District Court granted the defendant's motion to dismiss and compel arbitration pursuant to a dispute resolution policy, which the employer adopted as the exclusive method of resolving disputes related to employment. The policy included a four-level process for resolving disputes, beginning with a review by the HR department, then review by a management panel, mediation, and arbitration. The policy did not cover ERISA or Worker's Compensation claims. The employer retained the right to amend the policy, and did so to rule out class claims. In the year of the amendment, a group of plaintiffs brought a class action, alleging misclassification of workers who were not exempt under the FLSA as exempt, plus ADEA and ERISA allegations. The Eleventh Circuit treated the dispute resolution policy as an "agreement in writing" as required by the FAA, even though the employees didn't sign it, because the FAA has a writing, but not a signature, requirement. The Eleventh Circuit did not consider the agreement to arbitration as waiver of any substantive statutory rights—merely a change in the way they are enforced. Continued employment constituted acceptance of the dispute resolution policy, creating adequate consideration under state law. The Eleventh Circuit rejected the procedural unconscionability argument on the grounds that the policy was clearly presented to employees and its terms were not oppressive. [*Caley v. Gulfstream Aerospace Corp.*, 428 F.3d 1359 (11th Cir. 2005)]

"Testers" are often used in housing discrimination litigation: Minority group members apply to rent or buy a property. If the property is offered to white people after the testers are told that the property is off the market, this is potent evidence of discrimination. The Seventh Circuit decided that employment testers play a valuable role in combating employment discrimination. Therefore, they have standing to sue under Title VII, even though they don't really want the job. But they don't have standing under 42 U.S.C. § 1981, which would require actual intent to form a contract. [*Kyles v. J.K. Guardian Security Servs. Inc.*, 222 F.3d 289 (7th Cir. 2000)]

§ 42.03 STATISTICS ABOUT CHARGES AND RESULTS

In mid-2001, the results of research by two Cornell law professors were released. They studied nine years of data from the Administrative Office of the United States Courts. There were 7,378 civil cases of all kinds that were tried and appealed between 1988 and 1997.

During that time period, there were about 58,000 civil trials in the District Courts. Overall, plaintiffs won 43% of the cases—but of the 7,575 employment discrimination cases that went to trial (don't forget that the vast majority of claims wash out long before there is a trial), the plaintiffs won only about 30%.

When a plaintiff appealed a victory by the defendant, 12% of District Court verdicts of all types were overturned by the Court of Appeals—but plaintiffs only succeeded in upsetting a defense victory in an employment discrimination case 5.8% of the time. Overall, defendants were able to overturn plaintiffs' verdicts 32.5% of the time, but they were able to do this 43.6% of the time when employment-discrimination plaintiffs won at the trial court level.

The professors concluded that, although there were some regional variations, employers had a "huge advantage" in all 12 of the federal Courts of Appeals, especially the Fifth Circuit (which covers Louisiana, Mississippi, and Texas), where 14 of the 23 wins by employees were reversed, and 95.7% of the verdicts for employers were affirmed. [*See* Jess Bravin, *U.S. Courts Are Tough on Job-Bias Suits,* Wall Street Journal, July 16, 2001, at p. A2]

The American Bar Foundation concluded that discrimination plaintiffs have an unfair reputation for receiving huge damage awards in meritless cases. The study analyzed 645 press reports of employment discrimination cases published between 1990 and 2000. Nearly all (85%) of the stories covered a plaintiff victory, whereas during that decade only 32% of cases that were tried to a conclusion produced plaintiffs' verdicts. The median reported jury award was $1.1 million, whereas the median award for all decided cases was much lower, at $150,000. Although only about 1% of plaintiffs were participants in class actions, 34% of media accounts dealt with class actions. [American Bar Foundation study, *Media Misrepresentation, Title VII, Print Media, and Public Perceptions of Discrimination Litigation*, <http://slpr.stamford.edu/15_2.html>]

§ 42.04   TITLE VII PROCEDURE

[A] Complaining Party

Federal antidiscrimination laws include extremely complicated procedures for bringing a complaint, and one of the employer's main lines of defense is that the potential plaintiff has failed to satisfy the procedural requirements.

42 U.S.C. § 2000e(1) defines "complaining party" in a Title VII case as either the private person who brings a case or the EEOC or the U.S. Attorney General.

[B] The Charging Process

Nearly every phrase or term in this section has already been extensively litigated. Individuals who think they have experienced an unlawful employment practice cannot simply go to the relevant federal court and file a complaint. Instead, they must file a written, sworn document called a "charge" with an administrative agency. Would-be plaintiffs cannot go to court until there has been an administrative investigation and attempts to settle the matter without getting the court system involved.

The EEOC notifies the employer of the charge within ten days, disclosing the date, place, and circumstances of the allegedly unlawful practices, and then starts an investigation to see if there is reasonable cause for the charge. The EEOC's duty is to complete the investigation as soon as possible—and within 120 days of the filing of the charge (or the referral date) "so far as practicable." (The EEOC has a big backlog and often misses the 120-day deadline.)

Grievance procedures under a CBA, or company-sponsored grievance procedures in a nonunion company, have no effect on Title VII suits. So the employee doesn't have to use those procedures before filing a charge with an antidiscrimination agency. On the other hand, ongoing grievances under the CBA won't prevent or delay a Title VII suit.

If the EEOC does not believe that the charge is supported by reasonable cause, it dismisses the charge, and the employee then has the right to sue. In fact, it is not even held against the employee that the EEOC made a "no-cause" finding. A no-cause determination does not prevent the employee from suing. It does not limit the suit, what the employee can try to prove, or even the remedies he or she can receive. The judge or jury makes its own independent inquiry into the facts and is not influenced by the EEOC investigation.

But if the EEOC does believe that the charge is supported, then the EEOC's job is to try to use "informal methods of conference, conciliation, and persuasion" to get the employer to change the employment practice. The conciliation process is confidential, and statements made during the process can only be publicized or used as evidence in litigation based on the written consent of the person making the statement. Violating this confidentiality can be punished by as much as $1,000 fine and/or a year in prison.

The EEOC's powers to investigate a charge include having access "at all reasonable times" to all evidence that is relevant to the charges, and the EEOC also is entitled to make copies. [42 U.S.C. § 2000e-8(a)]

Exhaustion of remedies is a requirement. The Tenth Circuit ruled that, in order to exhaust their administrative remedies, private sector employees have a duty to cooperate with the EEOC's investigation of their age bias charges before they file suit. (In this case, after filing a charge, the plaintiff and his attorney canceled three phone interviews scheduled with the EEOC investigator; wouldn't return the investigator's calls; and did not provide any information other than what was contained in the original charge.) Exhaustion of administrative remedies is a prerequisite to suing under the ADEA. Failure to exhaust administrative remedies does not justify summary judgment for the defendant but, according to the Tenth Circuit, will justify dismissal of the case for lack of jurisdiction. [*Shikles v. Sprint/ United Management Co.*, 426 F.3d 1304 (10th Cir. 2005); ADEA suits have also been dismissed for non-cooperation: e.g., *Rann v. Chao*, 346 F.3d 192 (D.C. Cir. 2003). It has been held, in the Title VII context, that failure to cooperate with the EEOC is failure to exhaust administrative remedies: *Brown v. Tomlinson*, 383 F. Supp. 2d 26, 29 (D.D.C. 2005); *Smith v. Koplan*, 362 F. Supp. 2d 266, 268 (D.D.C. 2005)]

A Title VII plaintiff has not exhausted administrative remedies if a suit refers to time frames, discriminatory conduct, or perpetrators different from the ones raised in the administrative charges. In this case, the Fourth Circuit held that evidence of derogatory racial epithets that was not raised until the summary judgment stage of trial was inadmissible; furthermore, the EEOC charges related to supervisors, whereas the epithets were allegedly used by co-workers. [*Chacko v. Patuxent Inst.*, 429 F.3d 505 (4th Cir. 2005)]

[C] State Agencies

In a Fifth Circuit case, procedural failures required dismissal of an age-discrimination judgment in favor of the plaintiff. He filed a complaint with the EEOC and did not check the box on the form indicating that he wanted the charge filed with both the EEOC and the Texas Commission on Human Rights. Therefore, he failed to go through the mandatory step of filing a state charge—and his federal lawsuit was invalid. [*Jones v. Grinnell Corp.*, 235 F.3d 972 (5th Cir. 2001)] Although Texas has a work-sharing agreement, this merely means that a single filing can cover both state and federal requirements—not that the state procedure can be ignored, even in a case where the charging party asserts only federal claims.

§ 42.05   TIMING REQUIREMENTS

[A]   Generally

Section 2000e-5(c) says that if the state where the alleged unlawful employment practice occurred has a state antidiscrimination law, then EEOC charges may not be filed until 60 days have passed since commencement of state antidiscrimination charges. If the EEOC itself files a charge, it has an obligation to notify the appropriate state authority and give it sixty days to enforce the local law and eliminate the unlawful employment practice.

The basic rule is that, to avoid being dismissed as untimely, EEOC charges must be filed within 180 days of the date of the wrongful action. Then papers must be served on the employer within ten days. However, if the state has an antidiscrimination agency, the employee has 300 days from the date of the wrongful action to file with the EEOC. There is an additional requirement that the employee not wait more than 30 days after the state or local agency has dismissed a state charge to file with the EEOC. [42 U.S.C. § 2000e-5(e)(1)]

The charge has to be verified (the charging party has to state under penalty of perjury that the statements in the charge are true). [42 U.S.C. § 2000e5(b)] In March, 2002, the U.S. Supreme Court upheld an EEOC regulation, 29 C.F.R. § 1601.12(b), that allows "relation back." That is, if a charge is made within the 300-day period but verified later, it will still be timely because the verification "relates back" to the timely charge. The Supreme Court ruled in *Edelman v. Lynchburg College* [535 U.S. 106 (2002)] that Title VII requires both filing within 300 days and verification, but the two need not occur at the same time.

A Fifth Circuit case from mid-2003 explores the availability of relating back. The plaintiff, a black male, applied for a promotion; there were two open positions, but he was not selected. The jobs went to a black woman and a white man. The plaintiff filed a race, gender, and retaliation charge with the EEOC, but didn't check the disability box. His lawyer observed his stutter and suggested amending the charge to include disability discrimination. The plaintiff amended the charge and brought suit.

The plaintiff was then notified he might be terminated as part of a merger-related reorganization. He applied for transfers to other company facilities but was not selected. He amended his complaint to allege disability discrimination and retaliation in connection with the failure to transfer. Like most of the laid-off employees, he was offered a $45,000 layoff package, but he did not accept it because it would have involved releasing all claims against the employer.

The District Court ruled that his disability claim was time-barred, and dismissed the race, gender, and retaliation claims for lack of evidence. The plaintiff's position was that the amended charge, including the disability claim, should be allowed to relate back to the timely original charge. However, the Fifth Circuit held that an amendment that adds a new legal theory of recovery does not relate back, because the original charge did not place the defendant on notice of the existence of this claim. An exception can be made if the facts are essentially the same, but in this case they were not. [*Manning v. Chevron Chemical Co.*, 332 F.3d 874 (5th Cir. 2003)]

The Supreme Court resolved another timing issue. If the plaintiff's claim is for only one act of discrimination or retaliation, or for several separate acts, then the claim must meet the 180-day or 300-day requirement to be timely. However, if the plaintiff charges a number of acts that he or she claims made up part of the same practice creating a hostile work environment, then the claim is timely as long as there was at least one act in the series that occurred during the 180-day or 300-day period. [*National Railroad Passenger Corp. v. Morgan*, 536 U.S. 101 (2002)]

After a black female plaintiff's hostile work environment case was dismissed as untimely, the Supreme Court decided *Morgan*, changing the standard of timeliness for hostile work environment claims. If the law changes while a case is under appeal, the Court of Appeals applies the law that is in effect at the time of its decision. In this matter, most of the alleged incidents of discrimination occurred more than 300 days before her filing with the state antidiscrimination agency. She was able to keep her case going because of the continuous violation doctrine: Several incidents of demeaning remarks and racist epithets during the 300 days before her filing were alleged, thus allowing litigation of earlier acts as part of a continuing pattern of discrimination. [*Boyer v. Cordant Technologies Inc.*, 316 F.3d 1137 (10th Cir. 2003)]

The Seventh Circuit accepted the plaintiff's argument that each paycheck he received, that allegedly was too small because he was denied a promised raise because he was black, was a continuing violation. The plaintiff said that it took three-and-a-half years for him to realize that he was denied a raise that white employees were given. However, although his case was not dismissed as untimely, nevertheless he could not recover with respect to any pay period that ended before the 300-day point. [*Reese v. Ice Cream Specialties, Inc.*, 347 F.3d 1008 (7th Cir. 2003)]

According to the Eighth Circuit, damages in a black firefighter's case for racial harassment were properly limited to acts occurring within one year of the filing of his state agency charge. The acts complained of were discrete, not part of a continuing violation, and hence could not be used to seek damages for acts outside the one-year period. [*Mems v. St. Paul, Minn.*, 327 F.3d 771 (8th Cir. 2003)]

A mid-2003 Ninth Circuit case considers the effect of the *Morgan* ruling on employment actions that occurred outside the limitations period, based on decisions made under an allegedly discriminatory policy that remained in effect during the limitations period. The case arose when Post Office employees who claimed that the mail sorting machines caused respiratory problems sought to use respirators at work. The request was denied, under a Post Office policy that allows respirators only when air contaminants exceed the limits allowed by OSHA. The employees' union filed grievances in 1994 and 1997. The plaintiffs thought the matter was moving too slowly, so they contacted the EEOC in August, 1997 and filed complaints in September and October of that year. More than a year later, they sued in District Court under the Rehab Act. The District Court dismissed the suit, finding that federal employees are required to exhaust their administrative remedies, including going to an EEOC counselor to attempt an informal resolution within 45 days of the effective date of the alleged discriminatory action. The plaintiffs didn't go to the counselor, and can't point to any discrete discriminatory acts during the vital 45-day period. The employees asserted that their claims were timely because of the Post Office's ongoing discriminatory policy. But, after *Morgan,* time-barred actions cannot form the premise for a court case, even if those actions are related to actions that are alleged in a timely charge. Each separate act of discrimination re-starts the clock for filing charges. *Morgan* allows an exception for hostile work environment claims, because by their very nature they involve repeated conduct, so such claims are not time-barred as long as all of the acts covered by the claim are part of the unlawful practice, and at least one act falls within the limitations period. In this case, the statute of limitations cannot be extended, because there were no discrete acts within the relevant period. [*Cherosky v. Henderson,* 330 F.3d 1243 (9th Cir. 2003)]

The Eleventh Circuit ruled in 2005 that an employee who charges sex discrimination in the employer's pay system (including annual salary reviews) can get relief only for the 180-day filing period or the last salary decision before the 180 days began that affected her compensation. She cannot assert a continuing violation covering all salary reviews because *Morgan* sets out two time frames, depending on the type of case. There can be no recovery for a discrete act (e.g., termination or refusal to promote) that occurs outside the limitations period. For a cumulative-effects claim (e.g., hostile environment), conduct before the limitations period can be used to establish liability, as long as at least some discriminatory acts occurred during the limitations period. The Eleventh Circuit treated pay discrimination claims as discrete-act claims because either the decision or receipt of the paycheck was an individual act. The Eleventh Circuit did not require granting damages back to the salary decision, but indicated that was the earliest point to which relief could be addressed. [*Ledbetter v. Goodyear Tire & Rubber Co.,* 421 F.3d 1169 (11th Cir. 2005)]

The City of Newark obtained summary judgment, affirmed by the Third Circuit, on § 1983 claims that a police officer suffered retaliation because of his assistance with a federal corruption probe. The courts found that there was insufficient proof of causal connection between participation in the investigation and the retaliatory acts alleged. The Third Circuit ruled that § 1983 actions are subject to the personal injury statute of limitations for the state in which the cause of action accrued; in New Jersey, that is two years. The Third Circuit said that after *Morgan,* there is a bright-line test for individually actionable discrete acts and acts that, linked together, form a pattern adding up to a hostile environment. Individually actionable claims can't be aggregated. In this case, nearly everything charged by the plaintiff was a discrete act (e.g., denial of promotion), so most of his allegations were untimely because they were made more than two years after the alleged retaliatory act. [*O'Connor v. City of Newark*, 440 F.3d 125 (3d Cir. 2006). *Morgan* has also been applied to § 1983 by three circuits: *Sharpe v. Cureton*, 319 F.3d 259, (6th Cir. 2003); *Hildebrandt v. Illinois Dep't of Natural Res.*, 347 F.3d 1014, 1036 (7th Cir. 2003); *RK Ventures, Inc. v. City of Seattle*, 307 F.3d 1045, 1061 (9th Cir. 2002) and several district courts, e.g., *Ruiz Casillas v. Camacho Morales*, No. 02-2640, 2004 U.S. Dist. LEXIS 28135 (D.P.R. 2004), *Turner v. District of Columbia*, 383 F. Supp. 2d 157, 168 (D.D.C. 2005)]

The Second Circuit considered the issue of whether the rejection of something proposed by employees as a reasonable accommodation is a continuing violation. A Muslim truck driver wanted changes in his schedule to accommodate the time he needed for prayers. The employer refused, but said he could bid on evening work assignments that would allow him to pray during the day. The employee did not file a charge within the statutory period. The Second Circuit rejected his continuing violation argument. Although the effect of the rejection continued to be felt, the rejection itself was a one-time act. Once an employer rejects a proposed accommodation, any discrimination violation has already occurred; there is no periodic implementation of the decision. [*Elmenayer v. ABF Freight Systems Inc.*, 318 F.3d 130 (2d Cir. 2003)]

For charges claiming that a seniority system was intentionally adopted to be discriminatory (whether or not the system is facially discriminatory), the date from which the time to file runs is either the date of adoption of the seniority system, when the claimant becomes subject to the system, or when the claimant suffers injury as a result of the application of the system. [42 U.S.C. § 2000e-5(e)(2)]

The EEOC has 30 days after filing of a charge, or 30 days after the expiration of the period for referring charges from state agencies, to negotiate with the employer to produce a conciliation agreement that ends the unlawful employment practice. If the 30-day period expires without a conciliation agreement, the EEOC has the power to sue the employer in federal court.

On the other hand, if the EEOC makes a "no-cause" finding about the charge, or 180 days have passed since the charge was filed with the EEOC or referred from the state agency, and the EEOC has not filed suit and there has been no conciliation agreement, then the EEOC will notify the charging party. This is known as a "right-to-sue letter," because it enables the charging party to bring a federal suit.

In a 2003 case, the plaintiff's ADA suit was dismissed as untimely by the District Court for the District of Delaware. The plaintiff appealed, and the EEOC joined in the appeal, asking that the court make it clear that the 90-day period doesn't start until the plaintiff actually receives the right-to-sue letter. (In this case, the EEOC either failed to send the initial right-to-sue letter or mailed it to her old address; first told her that it was going to reopen her case and then that her case had been dismissed; and then eventually she got a right-to-sue letter in October 2000 and sued in January 2001.) However, the Third Circuit refused to do this, on the grounds that the EEOC should not be given the power to control the circumstances under which the court system can dismiss a case. [*Ebbert v. DaimlerChrysler Corp.*, 319 F.3d 103 (3d Cir. 2003)] Based on the District Court's finding that the plaintiff was not diligent, and let the case lapse for a period of 10 months, the Third Circuit refused to apply equitable tolling of the statute of limitations. However, the case was sent back to the District Court because it was not clear whether the EEOC gave the plaintiff enough information to know how to pursue her claim.

An assistant professor's contract received three annual renewals, but in August of 1997 she was told that her contract would not be renewed for the next academic year. She spoke to the intake officer at the state antidiscrimination agency 295 days after she found out that the contract would not be renewed. She claimed that she was not rehired because she did not conform to the stereotypically feminine behavior that was expected of female faculty members. She hand-wrote her charge on office stationery and checked the "file with the EEOC" box. The state's own statute of limitations under its antidiscrimination law was six months, so the state agency didn't even issue a case number to her. The charge was forwarded to the EEOC. In July 1998, the EEOC issued a right-to-sue letter. The plaintiff filed suit October 27, 1998.

The District Court dismissed her case on the basis that her charge was filed too late, because it was only filed with the EEOC, not the state agency. However, the Sixth Circuit allowed the case to proceed, taking the position that whether or not the state agency takes any further action on a claim, the potential plaintiff has instituted initial proceedings with the agency. The Sixth Circuit interpreted this case as a situation in which the state agency failed to take action—in effect, it failed to refer the charge to itself. It's settled law that plaintiffs should not suffer if the EEOC fails to refer a case to the state agency; the Sixth Circuit extended this principle to protect the plaintiff. Even an untimely state filing can trigger the 300-day period. So, because the plaintiff just managed to file with the state agency within the 300-day limit, she would be able to maintain her suit in federal court. [*Nichols v. Muskingum College,* 318 F.3d 674 (6th Cir. 2003)]

Late in 2005, the Northern District of Illinois held that, after *Waffle House* (*see* § 40.07[A]), it is no longer accurate to say that the EEOC stands in the shoes of the employees. Therefore, even though law firm partners who accused their firm of age discrimination failed to file timely charges, the EEOC could still seek monetary relief for them. [*EEOC v. Sidley Austin Brown & Wood*, 74 L.W. 1389 (N.D. Ill. Dec. 20, 2005)]

A Sixth Circuit plaintiff raised claims of two separate incidents of workplace sexual harassment. When the plaintiff applied for the job, she signed an employment application shortening the statute of limitations to six months. The first incident was a co-worker's alleged unwanted touching. The plaintiff complained, but the employer's investigation did not find enough evidence to discipline the alleged harasser. The plaintiff filed charges with the state agency on September 29, alleging that the incident had occurred about three weeks previously. The plaintiff reported a second incident on October 2. This time, the alleged harasser was suspended for ten days. The plaintiff also filed a criminal complaint; the alleged harasser pleaded guilty to fourth degree criminal sexual conduct and aggravated assault. In June of the following year, the plaintiff brought suit under Title VII; she also raised state civil rights and tort claims.

About six months later, the suit was dismissed because of her attorney's repeated failure to participate in conferences ordered by the court. Instead of moving to reinstate the dismissed case, the plaintiff brought suit once again. First the suit was removed to the district court because of supplemental jurisdiction and because of the presence of federal questions. Then it was dismissed as untimely. The district court found the six-month limitation reasonable and therefore found her claims to be untimely. The application form stated that the application was good for 12 months; the plaintiff was not hired until 13 months after her initial application for the job. The plaintiff claimed that therefore the limitations period had expired, but the Sixth Circuit said that it had not, because the application became part of her employment record. The plaintiff was equally unsuccessful with several other arguments. She claimed that her collective bargaining agreement superseded the application, because waiver of a statute of limitations is a mandatory bargaining subject. The court of appeals, however, noted that the CBA did not forbid waiver of the statute of limitations. The plaintiff called the application a contract of adhesion, but under the applicable state (Michigan) law, a reasonable reduction in the statute of limitations will be upheld. [*Thurman v. DaimlerChrysler Inc.*, 116 Fed. Appx. 638 (6th Cir. 2004); *Timko v. Oakwood Custom Coating Inc.*, 625 N.W.2d 106 (Mich. App. 2001) (it is not inherently unreasonable to impose a six-month statute of limitations in an employment contract)]

The concept of "laches" refers to delays by the plaintiff that are so extreme that they cause severe and unjustifiable prejudice to the defense. The concept was applied by the Seventh Circuit to dismiss charges of sex discrimination and retaliation in connection with the plaintiff's conduct during her 60-day probationary period as a trainee. Shortly after termination, the plaintiff filed sex discrimination charges with her state agency; the charges were cross-filed with the EEOC. She pursued her remedies through the state administrative process. Then the plaintiff moved to dismiss her state claims, saying that she was going to get a Right to Sue letter and proceed in federal court. At this point, the plaintiff alleges that the EEOC failed to act on her claims. After a year, she submitted a second request and got her Right to Sue letter and sued in federal court. By this time, more than eight years had passed since the alleged incidents of discrimination. Even the plaintiff admitted that there was no excuse for delay to this extent, but stated that her case should be permitted to proceed because the defendant was not prejudiced by the delay. The Seventh Circuit, however, found that there was no good reason to grant indulgence to the plaintiff's failure to resolve the matter. [*Smith v. Caterpillar, Inc.*, 338 F.3d 730 (7th Cir. 2003)]

In nearly all cases, the appropriate defendant is the employer company—there are virtually no situations in which Title VII suits can appropriately be brought against an individual person who is alleged to have performed discriminatory acts. The charging party must file suit within 90 days of the date of the right-to-sue letter—otherwise, the case can be dismissed for being untimely. [*See* 42 U.S.C. § 2000e-5(f)(1)]

Section 2000e-5(f)(3) provides that the suit can be filed in any federal District Court in the state where the alleged unlawful employment practice occurred. (The number of federal judicial districts in a state ranges from one to four.) The suit can also be brought in the judicial district where the relevant employment records are kept, or in the district where the plaintiff would have worked if there had been no unlawful employment practice. Finally, if the defendant company can't be found in any of those districts, the plaintiff can sue the defendant company in the judicial district where the company's principal office is located.

There is no explicit statute of limitations in 42 U.S.C. § 1981 (the federal law guaranteeing all persons within the jurisdiction of the United States the same rights to make and enforce contracts that "white citizens" have). Therefore, there was a circuit split on the proper statute of limitations to apply in § 1981 wrongful discharge cases. The split was resolved by the Supreme Court's May 2004 ruling: the statute of limitations is four years, because the current version of § 1981 was enacted by the Civil Rights Act of 1991 (CRA '91). Under federal law, the statute of limitations for all federal laws enacted after December 1, 1990, is four years, so that applies to CRA '91. [*Jones v. R.R. Donnelley & Sons Co.*, 541 U.S. 401, 2004)]

[B] Tolling

In a limited group of circumstances, the statute of limitations can be tolled (suspended) when it would be unjust to insist on strict compliance. Tolling may be permitted if:

- The employer was guilty of deception or some other wrongdoing that prevented the employee from asserting Title VII rights;
- The employee tried to file a timely lawsuit, but the pleading was rejected as defective;
- The employee filed in time, but in the wrong court.

Tolling is usually considered a defense, which means that it is up to the plaintiff to prove that it was available, and not up to the defendant to prove that it was not.

The term "tolling" is sometimes used to cover two different but related concepts. "Equitable tolling" allows a delayed case to continue because, even though the plaintiff's excusable ignorance or oversight caused the delay, the defendant is not prejudiced (harmed) by the delay.

According to the Sixth Circuit, a Title VII case was properly dismissed because the plaintiff failed to exhaust administrative remedies. The plaintiff failed to file with the EEOC within 45 days of the alleged discriminatory occurrence, as required by 29 C.F.R. § 1615.105(a). The Sixth Circuit did not accept the plaintiff's argument that she was entitled to equitable tolling because she tried to resolve the problem within the company where she worked. The Sixth Circuit explained that there are usually five factors used to determine the availability of equitable tolling: the plaintiff's actual or constructive notice of the time limits; whether it was reasonable for the plaintiff not to be aware of the limits; diligence in pursuing rights; and the degree of prejudice to the plaintiff. In this case, the plaintiff was a manager and familiar with the 45-day limit, which was explained in a Manager's Guide she had been furnished. She was also represented by an attorney, who should have alerted her to the timing requirements. Furthermore, her diligence argument failed, because no one in the employer company prevented her from exercising her rights; she herself caused numerous delays. [*Steiner v. Henderson*, 354 F.3d 432 (6th Cir. 2003)]

"Equitable estoppel" prevents the defendant from complaining about a delay that was caused in whole or part by the defendant's deceit or other conduct prejudicial to the plaintiff's interests, e.g., if the employee is afraid to approach the EEOC and endanger the internal investigation and grievance procedure that was being carried out. [*Currier v. Radio Free Europe*, 159 F.3d 1363 (D.C. Cir. 1998)]

If a Title VII suit is dismissed for being untimely, but the employee can assert another charge based on other facts, he or she can file a suit based on the second charge—as long as that one is timely! [*Criales v. American Airlines Inc.*, 105 F.3d 93 (2d Cir. 1997)]

Two sexual harassment cases a few months apart reach different conclusions as to whether the 90-day filing period should have been tolled. The D.C. Circuit refused to grant equitable tolling to an employee who claimed that severe, continuing harassment rendered her *non compos mentis* and unable to protect her own interests by filing in time. To the court in *Smith-Haynie v. District of Columbia* [155 F.3d 575 (D.C. Cir. 1998)], the only evidence of the plaintiff's distraction was her own statement. But the Ninth Circuit did permit equitable tolling in *Stoll v. Runyon*, [165 F.3d 1238 (9th Cir. 1999)] where the plaintiff suffered psychiatric disability after repeated sexual abuse, assault, and rape.

§ 42.06   CLASS ACTIONS

Class actions are governed by Rule 23 of the Federal Rules of Civil Procedure, especially Rule 23(b). The various subsections of Rule 23 create several alternative methods of litigating a class action, but each method has its own procedural requirements that must be satisfied. The requirements relate to what the plaintiffs want (money damages, or just an injunction?) and how people become members of the class (are they automatically included unless they opt out, or do they have to opt in?). It can also be difficult and expensive for the potential plaintiffs to give the required notice to everyone who might want to join the class.

Discrimination cases focusing on monetary damages can be hard to certify as class actions. Rule 23(b)(2) requires not only a common injury but uniform remedies for the whole class. Would-be plaintiffs who can't use Rule 23(b)(2) may have to fall back on Rule 23(b)(3), which requires them to prove that class-wide issues are more important in the case than individual issues. They must also prove that a class action is better than other methods of resolving the dispute. In some cases, a "hybrid" class action will be allowed. First a class is certified under Rule 23(b)(2) to decide if the employer is liable. If it is, damages are determined under Rule 23(b)(2).

A class of female prison employees seeking both injunctive relief and compensatory damages for sex discrimination could not be certified as a (b)(2) [non-opt-out] class. The Sixth Circuit ruled early in 2006 that a (b)(2) class is inappropriate where individual compensatory damages are sought because the individual claims for money damages will always predominate over the declaratory or injunctive relief. To certify the class, the court must determine that the plaintiffs allege significant proof that the employer has a general policy of gender discrimination and that the gender discrimination manifests itself in the same general fashion as each of the kinds of discrimination supporting the pattern or practice class action. According to the Sixth Circuit, commonality cannot be found simply because the employer's decision making about a protected group manifests itself in the same general fashion because discrimination can affect many aspects of employment (e.g., hiring, firing, benefits, work assignments). In a (b)(2) case, the question is whether monetary relief can be granted as long as injunctive or declaratory relief is ordered. The Sixth Circuit has ruled that back pay is an appropriate remedy in an Equal Credit Opportunity Act case because it is less complex and involves fewer individual issues than compensatory damages, and it is an equitable remedy, whereas compensatory damages are legal. However, the Sixth Circuit has analyzed Title VII cases as requiring individual determination of whether the discriminatory practice actually was responsible for the harm to the individual class member, whether there were non-discriminatory motives or affirmative defenses, and whether asserted defenses were pretextual. The plaintiffs could have brought individual Title VII suits, so it was an abuse of discretion to certify a (b)(2) class. [*Reeb v. Ohio Dep't of Rehabilitation & Correction*, 435 F.3d 639 (6th Cir. 2006)]

Late in 2001, nationwide class certification was denied to a group of black hotel workers suing the Adams Mark hotel chain who charged racially motivated unfair discipline and discrimination in promotions. The judge ruled that the would-be class members were not all affected by a centralized decision-making process (as distinct from decisions made by the management of a particular hotel).

Therefore, they could not show that their own claims were typical of the claims of the class or that common interests outweighed individual ones. Under current litigation practice, it is not enough for would-be class action plaintiffs just to allege discrimination against an entire group. The potential plaintiffs have to show that the discriminatory practice was pervasive or reflected in other employment activities. They must also provide detailed allegations, affidavits, and other evidence that the claims raised by individuals on their own behalf share questions of law or fact with the class claim. They must show that the individual claims are typical of the class as a whole. [*Vinson v. Seven Seventeen HB Philadelphia Corp.*, discussed in Shannon P. Duffy, *Class Action Claims Fail in Race Bias Suit Against Hotel Chain,* The Legal Intelligencer (Nov. 7, 2001) (law.com)]

Tip: A mid-2002 Supreme Court case, although it involves pension plans rather than discrimination claims, is an indicator of Supreme Court thinking about class actions. *Devlin v. Scardelletti* [536 U.S. 1 (2002)] allows a retiree who was not a named class member to appeal the settlement of a class action brought to protest the elimination of a cost-of-living increase in a defined benefit plan.

---

§ 42.07   THE DISCRIMINATION COMPLAINT

Once the case is cleared for litigation in federal court, the plaintiff must draft a complaint to inform the defendant and the court system of the nature of the allegations against the defendant. However, because the complaint is the first stage in litigation, the plaintiff may not have all the information that he or she will need to prove the case at the trial level. Early in 2002, the Supreme Court held that a valid discrimination complaint merely has to include a "short and plain statement" of the plaintiff's claim. Although once the trial occurs, the plaintiff will have to prove a prima facie case (see below), it is not necessary to set out a complete prima facie case at the complaint stage. [*Swierkiewicz v. Sorema N.A.*, 534 U.S. 506 (2002)]

Late in 2001, the Eleventh Circuit adopted a position already held by the Third, Seventh, and Eighth Circuits: An EEOC intake questionnaire constitutes a "charge" if it is verified and has the information a charge would contain, and a reasonable person would consider the questionnaire to manifest an intent to seek Title VII remedies. [*Wilkerson v. Grinnell Corp.*, 270 F.3d 1314 (11th Cir. Oct. 22, 2001)]

§ 42.08   MEETING BURDENS

In legal parlance, "the burden of production" means having to provide evidence to prove a particular point, and "the burden of proof" is the standard used to determine if adequate evidence has been supplied.

Section 2000e(m) says that "demonstrates" means "meets the burdens of production and persuasion." This covers the extremely important legal issue of who has to provide evidence of what. It is always easier to wait for the other party to produce evidence and then show that this evidence is incorrect, incomplete, not technically satisfactory, or inadequate to prove the case, than to have to submit independent evidence of one's own viewpoint.

Section 2000e-2(k) explains what the plaintiff has to prove in order to win a disparate-impact case. The complaining party must show that the employer's challenged employment practice has a disparate impact on a protected group. At this stage, the employer has a chance to prove that the employment practice is valid because it is job-related and consistent with the needs of the employer's business. However, if the employer demonstrates that the employment practice does not cause disparate impact, it is not necessary to prove business necessity for that practice. On the other hand, business necessity is only a defense against disparate impact claims, not against claims of intentional discrimination.

Another route for proving disparate impact is for the complaining party to demonstrate disparate impact and also show that the employer refused to adopt an alternative employment practice that would eliminate the disparate impact.

According to the Ninth Circuit, the 1991 amendments to Title VII, allowing proof of violation when discrimination was a motivating factor for the employer (rather than the sole motivating factor) does not require proof of the impermissible factor by direct evidence, because the statutory language does not include the phrase "direct evidence." A year later, the Supreme Court affirmed. [*Costa v. Desert Palace Inc.*, 299 F.3d 838 (9th Cir. 2002, *aff'd* 539 U.S. 90 (2003))]

To the First Circuit, a supervisor's remarks to an employee (who was the ex-owner of the business; he had sold it and stayed on as an employee) that it was time to step back, mentor the next generation of executives, and let the "young stallions" run the business because he wouldn't be around much longer—were not direct evidence of age discrimination. The court held that the remarks could reasonably be interpreted in a benign, non-discriminatory sense. [*Vesprini v. Shaw Contract Flooring Servs. Inc.*, 315 F.3d 37 (1st Cir. 2002)]

In an ADA case, the employer can move for and obtain Judgment as a Matter of Law after a jury finding if there was inadequate evidence to support the finding that the plaintiff is disabled. The issue of disability refers to the elements of the claim, so it can be reconsidered even after the case goes to the jury. [*Collado v. UPS*, 419 F.3d 1143 (11th Cir. 2005)]

Tip: In mid-2002, the Eleventh Circuit issued a ruling that could make litigation tougher for plaintiffs, by requiring job candidates who claim that they were not hired because of discrimination to prove that the person who made the hiring decision was aware of their minority status. In this case, the Eleventh Circuit held that the corporation could not be held liable for disparate treatment, because the plaintiff couldn't prove that the recruiter who made, and then rescinded the job offer a few hours later, knew that the plaintiff was a Jew. (The department manager who ordered the recruiter to rescind the offer said that he had already met the plaintiff at a job fair, and didn't want him hired because of his offensive personality—not because of his ethnicity.) [*Lubetsky v. Applied Card Sys. Inc.*, 296 F.3d 1301 (11th Cir. 2002)]

---

§ 42.09   RETALIATION CHARGES

A postal worker charged the postal service with discriminating and retaliating against him because he filed OSHA complaints about his working conditions. OSHA ordered remediation, which did not occur. He continued to complain, and OSHA did a formal inspection resulting in citations for violations. The plaintiff alleged that, although the identity of informants is supposed to be kept confidential, his identity was disclosed, resulting in threats and adverse job action, including removal from his job, name-calling, bullying, slashing his car's tires, a one-week suspension, and several incidents of being sent home without pay with the excuse that there was no work for him. Eventually he quit, alleging constructive discharge.

Under a 2006 Supreme Court decision, liability for retaliation is broader than liability for underlying workplace discrimination, and a retaliation case can be sustained even if the employee is not demoted and his or her compensation remains the same—as long as the retaliation is severe enough that a reasonable employee would take it into consideration in deciding whether or not to pursue a discrimination complaint. [*Burlington Northern & Santa Fe Railway Co. v. White*, No. 05-259, <http://caselaw.lp.findlaw.com/us/000/05-259>]

In the First Circuit view, Title VII provides relief independent of remedies under a unionized worker's CBA, but workers who use Title VII must satisfy its requirements. For instance, in this case the plaintiff's Title VII cause of action would be limited to the allegations he made in his administrative complaints to the Post Office, and could not refer to alleged later incidents. [*Morales-Vallellanes v. Potter,* 339 F.3d 9 (1st Cir. 2003)] The anti-retaliation provisions of Title VII protect a person who is named as a voluntary witness in a Title VII case, even if he or she is not called to testify at the trial. [*Jute v. Hamilton Sundstrand Corp.*, 420 F.3d 166 (2d Cir. 2005)]

§ 42.10   TITLE VII LITIGATION

[A]   Three-Step Process

A Title VII case is very different from other civil cases, because so much revolves around questions of intentions and statistics, not just the proof of simple facts.

The basic Title VII case is a three-step process. The plaintiff establishes a prima facie case: the basic facts that are suggestive of discrimination. This is sometimes referred to as "*McDonnell-Douglas* burden-shifting analysis" after the Supreme Court case that established this technique.

After the plaintiff submits a prima facie case, the defendant can ask the court to dismiss the case at that stage (summary judgment), if the prima facie case would not be good enough for the plaintiff to win if the defendant did not submit a case of its own.

On the other hand, if the prima facie case is strong enough to keep the case going, the defendant employer gets a chance to rebut the plaintiff's charge of discrimination. The employer can do this by proving a legitimate, nondiscriminatory reason for the job action against the plaintiff. The employer can also prevail by proving that its action was impelled by business necessity. If summary judgment is not granted, then there will have to be a full trial. The jury (or the judge, if there is no jury in the case) will have to decide the facts.

The third step is the plaintiff's again. At this stage, the plaintiff gets to show "pretextuality": that the employer's allegedly nondiscriminatory reasons are fabricated to hide its discriminatory motive.

Whether a company actually has 15 employees is a substantive element of the Title VII case, not a jurisdictional prerequisite. Therefore, if the issue is not raised in a timely fashion, it is waived. The Supreme Court held early in 2006 that the 15-employee requirement is not jurisdictional because it does not appear in the part of the Title VII statute that grants jurisdiction to the federal courts. The court's lack of subject matter jurisdiction can be raised at any point in the case. [*Arbaugh v. Y&H Corp.*, 126 S. Ct. 1235 (Feb. 22, 2006); similarly, *Minard v. ITC Deltacom Communications Inc.*, 447 F.3d 352 (5th Cir. 2006) for the FMLA]

[B]   Elements of the Prima Facie Case

The kind and amount of evidence that the plaintiff has to introduce to make a prima facie case depends on the kind of case (sex discrimination, sexual harassment, age discrimination, racial discrimination, etc.) and whether the plaintiff charges disparate treatment or disparate impact. Disparate treatment is a practice of intentional discrimination against an individual or group, whereas disparate impact is a practice that seems to be neutral and nondiscriminatory, but that has a heavier negative impact on some groups than others.

Furthermore, if the plaintiff charges that an employment practice has a disparate impact, and the employer responds by showing business necessity for that practice, the plaintiff can nevertheless win by proving that there was an alternative practice that would also have satisfied business necessity, but the employer refused to adopt that practice.

If a workplace decision involves many factors (for instance, promotion could be based on educational attainment, objective measures such as sales performance or departmental productivity, written tests, interviews, and assessments from supervisors), and the plaintiff challenges more than one of those criteria, the plaintiff has to be able to prove that each of those factors had harmful disparate impact on the plaintiff. If the various elements can't be separated and analyzed individually, then the whole decision-making practice can be treated as a single employment practice.

The "mixed motive" case works somewhat differently. It arises out of the situation in which several motivations influence the employer's decision. Some of them are lawful, others are discriminatory. The plaintiff can win a mixed motive case by showing that the discriminatory motive was influential. It is not necessary to prove that there were no legitimate motives involved. However, if the employer would have done the same thing even without a discriminatory motive being present, then the remedies available to the plaintiff will be reduced.

To establish the prima facie case, the plaintiff must show the following:

- That he or she belonged to a protected group;
- He or she had the necessary qualifications for the job (allegation of discriminatory failure to hire);
- He or she was doing an adequate job (if the allegation is improper discharge or failure to promote).

While disparate treatment cases usually depend on direct or indirect evidence of explicit discrimination, disparate impact cases usually turn on statistics about matters such as job applications and the composition of the workforce.

In mid-2003, the Supreme Court's *Desert Palace Inc. v. Costa* decision [539 U.S. 90 (2003)] resolved a Circuit split. The First, Fourth, Eighth, and Eleventh Circuits had ruled that once the defendant meets its burden by articulating a legitimate non-discriminatory reason for the job action, the plaintiff can get a jury instruction on mixed motive only by showing direct evidence. But the Supreme Court sided with the Ninth Circuit and allowed the instruction to be given on the basis of circumstantial evidence. In this case, the plaintiff, a truck driver, said that the employer's stated reason for firing her (a fight with another employee) was another instance of being treated more harshly than male co-workers for the same conduct. She also alleged that she was discriminated against when overtime work was available, and that supervisors were aware of and tolerated sex-based slurs against her.

The jury accepted her position and awarded her $364,000 in back pay and punitive damages for a mixed-motive case. The Supreme Court agreed that a mixed-motive jury charge can be given whenever the amount of evidence (whether direct or circumstantial) is adequate. This ruling therefore means that more cases will be submitted to the jury, and more plaintiffs will have a chance of prevailing. [*See* Shannon P. Duffy, *High Court Paves Easier Road to Jury for Discrimination Plaintiffs*, The Legal Intelligencer (June 11, 2003) (law.com)]

The plaintiff's prima facie case in a Title VII failure-to-promote case requires the employee to identify specific positions that he or she applied for but was denied. Saying that he or she was qualified for numerous promotions is not sufficient. [*Brown v. Coach Stores Inc.*, 163 F.3d 706 (2d Cir. 1998)]

[C] Evidence

Not only can each side introduce evidence about the course of the plaintiff's employment with the defendant company; in appropriate cases, the employer can introduce evidence about the plaintiff that the employer did not have at the time of the employment action.

The basic case on the use of after-acquired evidence is *McKennon v. Nashville Banner Pub. Co.* [513 U.S. 352 (1995)] In this case, the employer was allowed to introduce, at the trial, negative evidence about the plaintiff that the defendant learned after the employment action. Although the after-acquired evidence couldn't have motivated the employer, it was still relevant to the plaintiff's qualifications and credibility, so it can be introduced at trial.

O'Day v. McDonnell-Douglas Helicopter Co. [959 P.2d 792 (Ariz. 1998)] explains how to apply *McKennon* in state courts. If an employee sues for breach of contract, seeking lost wages and benefits, the after-acquired evidence can provide a complete defense for the employer as long as the employer can prove that the after-acquired evidence was serious enough to justify firing the employee if the employer had known about it earlier. In a tort suit for wrongful termination, the after-acquired evidence is not a complete defense, but does have the effect of limiting the remedies available to the plaintiff.

The Michigan Court of Appeals applied the after-acquired-evidence doctrine to a case in which the plaintiff was not hired (as opposed to a case where someone was hired, fired, and sued for discrimination—at which point the defendant employer discovered misconduct such as resume fabrication). *Smith v. Charter Township of Union* [227 Mich. App. 358, 575 N.W.2d 290 (1998)] holds that, in failure-to-hire cases, the damage period can extend only from the date of the wrongful denial of hiring until the inevitable point at which the employer would have fired the employee based on the lack of minimum qualifications that were falsely stated on the fabricated resume.

In many cases, the plaintiff introduces statistics to show a pattern of discrimination by the employer. In *Malave v. Potter*, [320 F.3d 321 (2d Cir. 2003)] for example, the District Court dismissed a Hispanic postal worker's claim of disparate impact discrimination. The District Court did not deem the statistical analysis offered by the plaintiff's expert witness to be sufficient proof of the plaintiff's contention that the Post Office discriminated in promotion, and that Hispanics were significantly underrepresented in senior positions.

However, the Second Circuit reversed the District Court and remanded the case for further consideration. The District Court said that the plaintiff should have looked either at the pool of job applicants or the eligible labor pool for the jobs, and not the overall number of Hispanics in the Connecticut postal work force. But the Second Circuit said that it would be inappropriate to impose a per se rule, because data was not available as to the number of qualified Hispanic postal workers who applied for promotions.

According to the Second Circuit, there is no bright line test for which statistics raise an inference of discrimination. However, to succeed, a plaintiff must identify a specific employment practice that discriminates, not just rely on bottom-line numbers about the employer's work force. The plaintiff must present statistical evidence of a kind and degree adequate to show that the practice has caused denial of promotion because of the applicants' membership in a protected group. When read in conjunction with the other evidence, adequate statistics must be of a kind and degree that reveals a causal relationship between the allegedly discriminatory practice and the disparity between actual promotions of group members, and the promotions that could be expected if there had been no discrimination.

[D]   Admissible and Inadmissible Evidence

A defense expert witness should not have been allowed to testify about the plaintiff's psychiatric credibility. This was not a proper subject for testimony under Federal Rules of Evidence 702, in that it invaded the jury's role of deciding whether testimony is credible. Nor should the defendant have been allowed to introduce evidence of the plaintiff's abortion (a decade earlier), because such evidence is prejudicial and not probative. A new trial was ordered in *Nichols v. American National Insurance Co.* [154 F.3d 875 (8th Cir. 1998)] because of the improperly introduced evidence.

The Second Circuit ruled that racist comments by a white employee can be used to show that the work environment was hostile to black people, even if the remarks were made after the black plaintiff resigned. [*Whidbee v. Garzarelli Food Specialties,* 223 F.3d 62 (2d Cir. 2000)] But testimony by four of the plaintiff's co-workers (that a supervisor's treatment of the demoted black employee was racially motivated) should not have been admitted. [*Hester v. BIC Corp.,* 225 F.3d 178 (2d Cir. 2000)] The witnesses could testify about their observations, but because they didn't know how good or bad the plaintiff's work performance actually was, they couldn't testify about the supervisor's motivation.

In a college professor's suit charging racial discrimination, the university vice provost's statements about the racial composition of the faculty were within the scope of employment. [Federal Rules of Evidence § 801(d)(2)(D)] Therefore, the statements were not hearsay, and were admissible even though the vice provost was not directly involved in making the decision to take adverse employment action against the plaintiff. (According to the plaintiff, the vice provost said that racists in the school administration were trying to get rid of black professors; the vice provost denied saying this.) [*Carter v. University of Toledo,* 349 F.3d 269 (6th Cir. 2003)]

A 2002 Massachusetts decision says that a state law, giving joint tortfeasors a right of contribution (i.e., allowing them to recover some of the damages they had to pay from others who were involved in the same wrongdoing) does not give an employer a right of contribution against the employee whose conduct subjected the employer to liability. [*Thomas v. EDI Specialists Inc.,* 773 N.E.2d 415 (Mass. 2002)] The reason for the statute is to require employers (not anyone else) to eliminate discrimination in the workplace. However, employers can enter into contracts with employees in which the employees agree to indemnify the employer (to reimburse the employer after it has paid damages).

[E]   Other Litigation Issues

If the plaintiff files suit in state court, the employer often tries to get the case removed to federal court. State courts usually have less crowded calendars, so cases can be decided faster. Sometimes, state law permits the employee to assert additional causes of action, or to get remedies that would not be available in federal court. Sometimes, too, a particular action is subject to state but not federal law. For example, some states ban discrimination in workplaces that are too small to be covered by the federal law. Sexual-orientation discrimination is not covered by Title VII, but is covered by certain state or local laws.

In many cases, federal law preempts state law. In other words, certain matters, such as most of labor law and benefit law, is covered by federal law, and the states cannot interfere. Therefore, if a plaintiff's state-court claims operate in one of these preempted areas, the employer has a strong argument for getting the case removed to federal court, or even dismissed.

An employee of a newspaper owned by the Unification Church charged that she was denied a raise because she was not a church member. The District Court for the District of Columbia ordered an unusual method of discovery. The defendant's lawyer was ordered to name a designee to compile an anonymous chart comparing pay raises for church members and non-church members over a three-year period. The data would be given to the plaintiff—but only if a connection was found between compensation and church membership. [*Johnson v. Washington Times Corp.*, 208 F.R.D. 16 (D.D.C. 2002)]

According to the Seventh Circuit, it was not improper for an employer to exercise a peremptory challenge to remove the only black person from the jury pool in a race discrimination suit. The potential juror said that her sister had filed a Title VII suit, and it was an ordeal—so the defendant had a race-neutral reason to fear hostility from this potential juror. Asking jury candidates if they know any discrimination suit plaintiffs is not a proxy for race, because there are many kinds of lawsuits and many possible connections (e.g., a friend who was an ADA plaintiff). [*Tinner v. United Ins. Co. of Am.*, 308 F.3d 697 (7th Cir. 2002)]

The Tenth Circuit ordered a new trial in an insurance manager's race discrimination case, because the District Court did not give a jury instruction explaining when an employer's stated non-discriminatory reason for a job action is really a pretext for discrimination. (In this case, an 11-year veteran black manager was demoted, fired for poor performance, and replaced by a white female. The plaintiff claimed that his performance was actually better than that of a white manager who was not disciplined. The defendant, however, said that the plaintiff was fired because an executive vice president didn't like him.) According to the Tenth Circuit, if discrimination can be inferred by showing that the stated reasons are pretextual, an instruction must be given that the jury can infer a discriminatory motive if they do not believe the employer's explanation. [*Townsend v. Lumbermens Mut. Cas. Co.*, 294 F.3d 1232 (10th Cir. 2002)] This is a controversial issue: The Second and Third Circuits require the trial judge to instruct jurors on all of the issues of guiding law, including pretext, but cases from the Seventh and Eleventh Circuits say specifically that the pretext instruction is not required and cases from the First and Eighth Circuits imply that the instruction doesn't have to be given.

[F] Avoiding Litigation Mistakes

Trial lawyer Gilmore E. Diekmann, Jr., tackles the mistakes that employer defendants make. [*See The Top Three Mistakes Employers Make at Trial,* archived at <http://www.lawnewsnetwork.com>] Although the vast majority of claims of employment discrimination wash out long before trial, and employers can get summary judgment (i.e., dismissal of poorly supported claims without a full trial), the fact remains that of the cases that actually go to a jury, the employee-plaintiff wins about two out of three.

Some of these are cases in which the employer got caught doing something obviously wrong and has to take its medicine. But others are cases that the employer could have won with better trial tactics and a better job of showing its side of the story to the jury.

Diekmann suggests that some cases go to trial because the employer's lawyer got involved too late and failed to identify a losing case that should have been settled. Sometimes, the wrong lawyer handles the case: a business lawyer rather than an experienced employment law litigator, for instance.

It is especially important for the trial lawyer to be completely familiar with all the depositions in the case. Depositions not only reflect testimony that was given at a particular time (and can be used to challenge inconsistent trial testimony) but give insight into the witness's character and thought processes (and thus the best way to challenge the testimony).

Juries are predisposed to like and sympathize with employee plaintiffs. It is usually counterproductive for the defense lawyer to seem arrogant, hostile, or bullying. In Diekmann's analysis, the defense lawyer's job is to present a simple story that the jury can understand and accept. Juries have to learn to look at the facts and the legal strategies rather than maintaining their initial sympathy for the plaintiff in situations where, in fact, the employer has the stronger legal arguments and the facts on its side.

§ 42.11   ADEA SUITS

[A] Generally

It is clear that the ADEA creates a private right of action—i.e., individuals can bring suit if they claim to have been subjected to age discrimination in employment. [*See* 29 U.S.C. § 626(c)] The statute is not very detailed. It says only that individuals can sue for "such legal or equitable relief as will effectuate the purposes" of the ADEA. However, a suit brought by the Secretary will terminate the rights of individuals to bring their own lawsuits involving their ADEA claims.

Under 29 U.S.C. § 626(d), would-be ADEA plaintiffs have to file their charges within 180 days of the alleged unlawful practice. In a "referral" state (a state whose antidiscrimination agency has a work-sharing agreement) the charge has to be filed within 300 days of the alleged unlawful practice. If the state-law proceedings are terminated, the potential plaintiff must file the charge within 30 days of the termination of the state proceeding.

When a charge is filed, all potential defendants are notified. In both the Title VII and ADEA contexts, the Secretary's duty is to "promptly seek to eliminate any alleged unlawful practice by informal methods of conciliation, conference, and persuasion."

In the federal system, whether a case can be heard by a jury (instead of just a judge) depends on several factors, including the preferences of the litigants and the nature of the suit itself. The basic rule is that juries are more appropriate for cases seeking money damages than those asking for purely equitable remedies such as injunctions or reinstatement. However, ADEA plaintiffs can demand a jury trial whenever they seek money damages, even if there are also equitable claims in the same suit.

A group of 27 employees sued Ruhrpumpen, Inc., charging that it violated the ADEA by failing to retain them as employees after buying the plant in which they worked. The district court granted summary judgment for the defendant, holding that the plaintiffs were never employed by the defendant company and therefore could not have been wrongfully terminated by it; their failure-to-hire claim was not filed with the EEOC and therefore was not cognizable; and four of the plaintiffs, who did not file charges with the EEOC, could not piggyback their claims on the claims of the other plaintiffs who did file.

The Tenth Circuit affirmed the dismissal as to the wrongful termination claim, but not as to the refusal-to-hire claim. For the plaintiffs who did file EEOC charges, the Tenth Circuit ruled that administrative remedies were properly exhausted and the charges sufficiently identified the people and practices at issue, and that the four who failed to file could use the single-filing rule to piggyback their claims.

Before the acquisition, the union was told that 94 of 120 production and maintenance workers would be rehired by the acquiring company. Employees were retained on the strict basis of seniority within their classification. Twenty-six people were laid off and given severance. The other 94 workers reported for work, but only 57 were rehired. Thirty-seven people, including the plaintiffs, were not rehired. The Tenth Circuit held that they were terminated by the predecessor company, not by the defendant. However, the court did not accept the defense argument that the plaintiffs did not state a "failure to hire" claim before the EEOC and thus failed to exhaust their administrative remedies. The court's view is that charges are to be construed liberally. It was understandable that the plaintiffs would treat the two employers as a unit, and believe that they had been terminated rather than denied hiring. The charges disclosed to the defendant what it was accused of doing. In a non-class-action multi-plaintiff suit, piggy-backing is allowed as long as at least one timely EEOC complaint was filed as to an individual claim. [*Foster v. Ruhrpumpen, Inc.*, 365 F.3d 1191 (10th Cir. 2004)]

[B] Timing Issues for ADEA Suits

The EEOC proposed regulations (67 Fed. Reg. 52431, Aug. 12, 2003) and finalized them at the end of 2003 (68 Fed. Reg. 70150, Dec. 17, 2003; effective January 16, 2004), Under the now-applicable regulations, the EEOC will dismiss (as untimely) charges filed more than 180 days after the discriminatory act—or more than 300 days in a referral jurisdiction. Extra time may be available if the charging party has a valid claim to waiver, estoppel, or equitable tolling.

The EEOC has a statutory obligation to try to eliminate alleged unlawful practices by means of informal conciliation. If the EEOC tries to conciliate but fails, it will give the charging party a notice—but the notice will be clearly labeled to distinguish it from the Notice of Dismissal or Termination, which is issued in ADEA cases as a rough parallel to the Right to Sue letter in other discrimination cases.

An age discrimination charging party does not have to wait until the NDT is issued to sue—as long as he or she waits at least 60 days after the charge was filed. But once the NDT is issued, the complainant has only 90 days to file suit (which can be filed in either federal or state court), or the case will be dismissed as untimely.

Federal employees are subject to some special rules. They can go straight to the District Court to assert ADEA claims without going through the normal administrative process. According to the First Circuit, when they do so, the appropriate statute of limitations is the one found in the Fair Labor Standards Act, not Title VII. [*Rossiter v. Potter,* 357 F.3d 26 (1st Cir. 2004)]

However, under 29 C.F.R. § 1614.407(a), suit must be brought within 90 days of the final agency action. A plaintiff's final agency action occurred on June 15, 2001, making the last day to file September 13, 2001. His attorney filed the complaint on the 12th, expecting it to be delivered the next day. However, it was not actually delivered until the 18th. The District Court dismissed the case as untimely, and the Eighth Circuit affirmed. Nor was equitable tolling granted: the plaintiff was deemed to have had adequate notice of the filing requirements, he had a lawyer, and the delay was not the fault of the clerk's office; it was not reasonable to expect next-day delivery from 450 miles away. The Eighth Circuit's decision didn't refer to the disruption right after the 911 attack. [*Hallgren v. U.S. Dep't of Energy,* 331 F.3d 588 (8th Cir. 2003)]

The 90-day requirement was added by the Civil Rights Act of 1991. Earlier, the ADEA statute of limitations was two years from the last discriminatory act, or three years from the last willful discriminatory act. But given the EEOC's large workload and small staff, in many cases the statute of limitations has actually gotten longer rather than shorter, because many charges take far more than two years for resolution.

It is in the employer's best interest for the court to rule that the cause of action "accrued" earlier, i.e., that the clock started ticking when the employee had to file suit. The earlier the cause of action accrues, the more likely it is that a claim can be dismissed as untimely.

If the alleged discriminatory act is firing the employee, there is a single act of discrimination. Most cases hold that the discriminatory act occurs on the date the plaintiff is unambiguously informed that he or she will be fired. The important date is the date of this notice, and not the first warning the plaintiff receives of impending termination, and not the last day the employee works for the employer or the last date he or she is on the payroll. The notice does not have to be formal, or even written, but it must be a definite statement that a final decision has been made to terminate the employee.

It is harder to place other discriminatory acts on a time continuum. It has been held that a claim of failure to promote accrues when the employees know or should have known about the facts that support the claim—probably, that a younger individual received the promotion that the plaintiff wanted.

If there is only a single employment decision, there is only a single act that might be discriminatory. However, some courts allow a plaintiff to argue that there was a continuing violation lasting over a period of time—for example, that the plaintiff kept his or her job, but was denied promotions he or she deserved because of age discrimination. In a case where the court accepts the continuing violation theory, the cause of action accrues with the last discriminatory act in the series. A filing that is timely for one act of discrimination will be timely for all acts of discrimination in the same series.

A bad performance appraisal that makes an employee more vulnerable to being laid off or RIFed (but that is not an actual threat of dismissal unless performance improves) is not considered an employment action that could give rise to an ADEA claim.

For discriminatory layoff charges, courts reach different conclusions as to when the cause of action accrues. One theory is that accrual occurs on the actual date of layoff. The other is that the cause of action accrues later, when the possibility of reinstatement ends because the employer has filled the last job for which the plaintiff might have been recalled.

In Title VII cases, the Civil Rights Act of 1991 clearly provides that the statute of limitations for a seniority system accrues on the latest of three dates: when the system is adopted; when an employee becomes subject to it; or when the plaintiff is injured by it. But Congress did not enact a similar provision relating to the ADEA. Some courts continue to foreclose employee claims, on the grounds that the claim accrued when the plan was adopted, often many years before the employee became subject to the plan.

[C]   Tolling the ADEA Statute of Limitations

The statute of limitations can be tolled (suspended), giving employees additional time to litigate, in various circumstances—usually as a result of deception or other misconduct on the part of the employer. However, certain circumstances have been held not to be wrongful conduct, and will not toll the statute of limitations:

- Putting an employee on "special assignment" until termination takes effect;
- Offering a severance benefits package. However, offering a lavish severance package, but preventing employees from discussing it, was held to discourage employees from vindicating their legal rights, and therefore to toll the statute of limitations.

Tip: The statute of limitations is not tolled during the employer's in-house grievance procedure. However, a collective bargaining agreement provision is invalid if it terminates the employee's right to pursue a grievance once he or she files age discrimination charges with the EEOC or the local anti-discrimination agency. The clause is void because it punishes employees for exercising their legal rights.

Even if tolling occurs, it probably cannot last beyond the point at which an employee who took reasonable steps to investigate would have been aware of discrimination.

Do not forget that 29 U.S.C. § 627 requires the employer to post a notice of ADEA rights. The EEOC and Department of Labor distribute free copies of the mandatory notice; posters can also be purchased from many publishers. If the notice is duly posted, then the court will presume that the employee could have read the poster and become aware of at least basic ADEA rights.

However, if the information is not posted, the court may conclude that the employer deprived the employee of access to information about ADEA rights, thus tolling the statute of limitations. Yet some courts say that the real test is whether the employee actually was aware of what the ADEA says. Given actual knowledge, the court may decide that the absence of a poster in the workplace does not justify extending the time to bring suit.

[D]   The ADEA Plaintiff's Burden of Proof

The *McDonnell-Douglas* pattern applies in ADEA cases. That is, first the plaintiff introduces evidence of a prima facie case of discrimination. If the evidence (taken at face value) is inadequate, the defendant employer can get summary judgment—that is, can have the case dismissed because of this inadequacy.

If, however, the case is good enough to survive a motion for summary judgment, it is the employer's turn at bat. By and large, proof is up to the plaintiff, but a BFOQ is an affirmative defense, which means that the employer has the burden of proving it. [*Western Air Lines Inc. v. Criswell,* 472 U.S. 400 (1985)] In non-BFOQ cases, the employer can rebut the prima facie case by showing a legitimate, non-discriminatory reason for the conduct challenged by the employee. Then the employee gets another chance, to demonstrate that the employer's justification is actually a pretext for discrimination.

It is not necessary in all cases for the plaintiff to prove that he or she was replaced by someone under 40 (i.e., outside the protected group). [*O'Connor v. Consolidated Coin Caterers Corp.,* 517 U.S. 308 (1997)] It is possible, although difficult, for the plaintiff to win a case in which he or she was replaced by another person over 40, as long as improper age-related motives are shown.

In 1993, the Supreme Court set a new standard for proving ADEA cases based on age-related factors rather than on age itself. For instance, a 30-year-old cannot have 30 years' employment experience, but a 38-year-old employee might have worked for the company for 20 years, and therefore have more seniority than a 50-year-old hired only 10 years earlier. In that example, the allegedly age-related factors of higher salary and benefits would actually make the 38-year-old the more expensive employee.

The key case on this issue is *Hazen Paper Co. v. Biggins,* [507 U.S. 604 (1993)] which requires the plaintiff to prove that the employer's decision was influenced by age, not merely by age-related factors.

According to the Eleventh Circuit, laid-off older workers don't always have to be rehired or offered a transfer to a new job, but they must at least be considered for rehiring; the possibility must not be rejected on the basis of age. Therefore, a prima facie case is made out when a younger employee is hired or transferred to replace an older employee who was RIFed. [*Jameson v. Arrow Co.,* 75 F.3d 1528 (11th Cir. 1996)]

In a disparate-treatment age-discrimination case, the plaintiff can prevail by having an adequate amount of either direct or indirect evidence. However, the burden of proof, and the way it shifts, is applied differently for direct versus indirect evidence. Evidence is direct if its introduction does not require the judge or jury to use any presumptions or make any inferences. Indirect evidence requires interpretation of the employer's actions and statements. [*See Torrey v. Casio Inc.,* 42 F.3d 825 (3d Cir. 1994)]

Price Waterhouse v. Hopkins [490 U.S. 228 (1989)] says that plaintiffs who have direct evidence of discrimination can require employers to prove that they would have fired or otherwise acted against the plaintiff even without discrimination. But without direct evidence, the ordinary three-step *McDonnell-Douglas* pretextuality analysis applies. *Hopkins* also covers mixed-motive cases, those in which the employer had several motivations. (The text of the ADEA has been amended to make it clear that mixed-motivate cases are covered.)

Hopkins requires the plaintiff to show that age is a substantial factor in the decision, but not necessarily the only one or even the most salient one. The employer can offer a defense that it would have taken the same employment decision even if age had not been used as a criterion. The employer merely has to prove this by a preponderance of the evidence, not beyond a reasonable doubt. The Civil Rights Act of 1991 overrules *Hopkins* in Title VII cases, but it remains in effect for ADEA cases.

In 2003, the Sixth Circuit ruled that it was acceptable to instruct an ADEA jury on the McDonnell-Douglas burden-shifting analysis. The Sixth Circuit rejected the defendant's arguments that the instruction is too difficult for juries to understand, or that the burden-shifting analysis is no longer relevant once a case gets to the jury. [*Brown v. Packaging Corp. of America,* 338 F.3d 586 (6th Cir. 2003)]

In several circuits, it is not mandatory for the trial court to give a pretext instruction to the jury, so failure to do so is not an error. In one case, the trial court properly refused to give the plaintiff's suggested instruction in the ADEA case of an older salesman (the employer said he was terminated for poor performance) because the pattern instruction covered the topic adequately and the suggested instruction could be confusing for the jury. [*Conroy v. Abraham Chevrolet-Tampa Inc.,* 375 F.3d 1228 (11th Cir. 2004)]

Direct evidence of age discrimination is hard to find—especially since even employers who do practice discrimination usually have enough sophistication to conceal it. As a practical matter, then, most ADEA cases will be based on statistical evidence in support of the allegation, with or without evidence about statements made by executives and supervisors. Statistics are especially prominent in disparate impact cases.

However, the legal trend has been to reduce the credence given to statistics. In *St. Mary's Honor Center v. Hicks,* [509 U.S. 502 (1993)] the court held that the plaintiff always has the "ultimate burden of persuasion." So if the fact-finder (which will be the jury or the judge in a nonjury case) doesn't believe the employer's explanation of why its conduct was legitimate, the plaintiff can still lose—if the plaintiff simply fails to offer enough evidence. The *Hicks* standard is sometimes called "pretext-plus": The plaintiff has to do more than just show that the defendant's excuses are a mere pretext for discrimination.

[E] The ADEA Prima Facie Case

The basic prima facie (initial) case for an ADEA lawsuit is:

- The plaintiff belongs to the protected group—that is, is over 40;
- The plaintiff was qualified for the position he or she held or applied for;
- The plaintiff was not hired, discharged, demoted, deprived of a raise, or otherwise disfavored because of age;
- (In appropriate cases) The plaintiff was replaced—especially by someone under 40, although it is not absolutely required that the replacement come from outside the protected age group. If the charge is a discriminatory RIF, plaintiffs must show that age was a factor (although not necessarily the only factor) in targeting them for termination, or at least that the employer was not age-neutral in implementing the RIF program. Employers can defend against an accusation

of a discriminatory RIF by showing good economic reason for cutting back; it isn't necessary to show that the company would be at the brink of bankruptcy without the reductions.

Depending on the type of case, the court where it is heard and the individual facts, the plaintiff may have to prove that his or her own qualifications and/or job performance were satisfactory, or may have to prove that they were superior to those of the person who replaced him or her.

[F] ADEA Class Actions

Sometimes, an employee contends that he or she is the only person to suffer discrimination. Sometimes, however, it is alleged that the company engages in a pattern or practice of discrimination, affecting many people, and it becomes necessary to determine whether it is appropriate to certify a class action (i.e., to allow employees to combine their claims and present a single body of evidence).

The theory of "virtual representation" is sometimes used to prevent a second class action covering issues that have already been raised in another class action. However, *Tice v. American Airlines* [162 F.3d 966 (7th Cir. 1998)] rejects application of this theory to a challenge by a group of airline pilots to an airline's policies about over-60 pilots. The Seventh Circuit said that the litigants in that case were not adequately represented by the earlier class action dealing with pilots and copilots, who are subject to a Federal Aviation Administration (FAA) policy mandating retirement at 60.

The *Tice* case dealt with the job for first officer. FAA rules allow people over 60 to hold the position of first officer, but the airline refused to employ any first officer who could not be promoted to captain. The indirect effect of this policy was to deny the job opportunity to persons over 60.

In the Seventh Circuit view, the earlier class action did not resolve the current case. ADEA class actions are "opt-in" rather than "opt-out" (i.e., no one is covered without electing to be included). The earlier case dealt with potential employees denied employment because of age; *Tice* dealt with current employees seeking to remain employed by accepting a demotion. Therefore, the *Tice* case was allowed to proceed.

In April 2002, however, the Seventh Circuit took a new tack, finding that the dispute should not be in the courts at all, because it was subject to mandatory arbitration under the Federal Arbitration Act (61 Stat. 669). However, the Seventh Circuit did not dismiss the case—it stayed (suspended) the case until the arbitration was resolved—because of the possibility that plaintiffs might be entitled to additional remedies by combining arbitration and litigation. [*Tice v. American Airlines Inc.*, 288 F.3d 313 (7th Cir. 2002)]

The question of timing in class actions was also addressed in *Armstrong v. Martin Marietta Corp.* [138 F.3d 1374 (11th Cir. 1998)] Certain employees were dismissed as plaintiffs from a pending ADEA class action. They brought their own suits. The Eleventh Circuit held that the statute of limitations is tolled (suspended) while a class action is pending, but starts all over again as soon as the District Court issues an order denying class certification.

Would-be plaintiffs who are thrown out of a class action because they are not similarly situated to the proper plaintiffs must file their own suits within 90 days of being removed from the class. Equitable tolling (i.e., permitting an action that would otherwise be too late to continue, on the grounds of fairness) can be granted only if the EEOC actually misinformed the plaintiffs about the statute of limitations, not if the plaintiffs simply failed to consider this issue or made an incorrect determination of how long they had to bring suit.

§42.12   TITLE VII REMEDIES

[A]   Fundamental Remedies

Once the case gets to court and is tried to a conclusion (many cases are either settled along the way, or are dismissed before a full trial has occurred), and if the plaintiff wins (most employment discrimination cases are won by the employer), then the question becomes what remedies the court will order. Remedies are governed by 42 U.S.C. § 2000e-5(g).

The fundamental remedies under this section are equitable: hiring or reinstatement (plus up to two years' back pay for the time the plaintiff would have been working absent discrimination). Furthermore, the amount that the plaintiff earned in the meantime—or could have earned by making reasonable efforts—is offset against the back pay. In other words, plaintiffs have a duty to mitigate their damages. They have an obligation to use their best efforts to earn a living, instead of relying on the hope the defendant employer will eventually be ordered to pay up.

If the plaintiff further succeeds in proving disparate treatment (as distinct from facially neutral practices that have a disparate impact on the group the plaintiff belongs to), then compensatory damages can be awarded to the plaintiff as reimbursement for costs (such as job hunting or therapy) incurred directly as a result of the discrimination.

However, in cases of racial discrimination, the plaintiff must look to the Civil Rights Act of 1866, [42 U.S.C. § 1981] and not to Title VII, for compensatory and punitive damages. If the alleged discrimination consists of failing to accommodate a disability, the employer will not have to pay compensatory damages if it made a good-faith effort at reasonable accommodation, even if the offer of accommodation was later deemed inadequate.

If the court finds that the employer engaged in the unlawful employment practice that the plaintiff charged, it can enjoin the respondent from continuing that abusive practice. The court can order the defendant to take remedial steps, including but not limited to hiring an applicant or reinstating an ex-employee.

Employers cannot be ordered to hire, reinstate, or promote anyone, or pay back pay to him or her, if the employment action was taken "for any reason other than discrimination on account of race, color, religion, sex, or national origin" or unlawful retaliation. [42 U.S.C. § 2000e-5(g)(2)(A)]

In a mixed-motive case where the defendant demonstrates that, although a discriminatory motive was present, it would have taken the same action (e.g., fired or refused to promote the plaintiff) purely on the basis of the other motivations even if there had been no discrimination, then the court can grant a declaratory judgment (a declaration that the employment practice was unlawful), enjoin its continued use, or award attorneys' fees that can be traced directly to the mixed-motive claim. But, because the employer would have taken the same action even without discrimination, the court cannot award damages to the plaintiff or order the defendant to hire, rehire or promote the plaintiff. [42 U.S.C. § 2000e-5(g)(2)(B)]

The court has discretion, under 42 U.S.C. § 2000e-5(k), to order the loser—whether plaintiff or defendant—to pay the winner's attorneys' fees (including fees for expert witnesses, which can be very high) and court costs. However, losing defendants can't be ordered to pay fees to the EEOC. If the EEOC sues a company and loses, it can be ordered to reimburse the defendant for its fees and costs for the suit.

Also note that 42 U.S.C. § 2000e-2(n) provides that employees usually cannot challenge employment practices that were adopted based on a court order or to carry out a consent decree in an employment discrimination case, if the employees knew about the case and either had their interests represented or had a chance to voice their objections. However, employees who actually were parties in the case can enforce their rights under the order or settlement, and judgments and orders can be challenged on the grounds of fraud or the court's lack of jurisdiction over the case.

One important factor in analyzing employment cases is what claim(s) the employee raises. Some employment discrimination claims fit into the "breach of contract" category, but most of them are more like "tort" claims. The importance of the tort/contract distinction is that the remedies are different for the two categories. If a plaintiff proves breach of contract, the court's job is to put the plaintiff back in the position he, she, or it would have been in if the contract had been carried out. In the context of an employment contract, or implied employment contract, that probably means earnings and fringe benefits that were lost because of the breach, possibly plus out-of-pocket expenses for finding a new job. (The doctrine of mitigation of damages requires plaintiffs to do whatever they can to limit the amount of damages they suffer—which definitely includes finding a new job if at all possible, pending resolution of the claims against the former employer.)

Back pay is not limited to simple salary. It includes benefits, overtime, shift differentials, merit raises, and the like. However, if the employer can prove that the employee would have been laid off, or was unavailable for work, back pay will not be available for the time the employee would not have been working anyway.

Fringe benefits are valued at the cost the employee would have to pay to replace them, not the (probably lower) cost the employer incurred to offer them.

Amounts earned in the new job reduce what the ex-employer will have to pay in damages. On the other hand, to the extent that the plaintiff proves that the employer committed one or more torts, the successful plaintiff can be awarded back pay, front pay (moving from the end of the trial forward), lost earnings, medical expenses, and value of pain and anguish, and emotional distress. The plaintiff's spouse might be granted an award for loss of consortium (marital services that were not rendered because of the employer's wrongdoing). In most states, interest on the judgment, running from the time the case is decided, can also be ordered—which mounts up quickly if the award is in six or seven figures.

The Tenth Circuit ruled that to assure complete compensation in a Title VII case, prejudgment interest is an element of back pay awards. The calculation starts with the date of the adverse employment action, but does not accrue until actual monetary injury has been sustained (e.g., after severance pay runs out). The court ruled that the plaintiff (who alleged religious discrimination after being assigned to work on the Sabbath) was injured when he was terminated for failing to report to work as scheduled, but the injury did not occur all at once: It incurred as each pay period passed, so the interest should be calculated on each missed paycheck. [Reed v. Mineta, 438 F.3d 1063 (10th Cir. 2006)]

Sometimes, front pay and reinstatement can be combined, i.e., if the remedies don't overlap, chronologically or economically. Front pay can be awarded to get the plaintiff to the "point of employability," at which point he or she can be reinstated.

The equitable remedy of front pay can be denied to an employee whose conduct after termination renders her ineligible for reinstatement. This case involved a sexual harassment plaintiff who got another job at a bank, who was fired for attempting to process an unauthorized loan application. The case was remanded to determine if her misconduct in the second job would preclude reinstatement in the first job. [Sellers v. Mineta, 358 F.3d 1058 (8th Cir. 2004)]

The general rule is that unemployment benefits received will not reduce the amount of back pay available to a successful Title VII plaintiff. However, in the Second Circuit, courts have the discretion to offset unemployment compensation against the back pay award.

Litigation in a 2004 D.C. Circuit case began in 1975 when a class of black construction workers sued the Iron Workers union for denying them the benefits of union membership because of their race. The plaintiff in this case was found to be a member of the plaintiff class and was awarded $166,000 in back pay and $10,000 in compensatory damages. However, there was conflicting testimony as to whether he sought union membership during or after the liability period, so his claims were remanded for redetermination of his status as class member. He settled his claims for $150,000.

A year later, he applied for pension benefits. Benefits were calculated on the basis of reported hours. The plaintiff's position was that his pension should have reflected hours that he was precluded from working by discrimination. He brought suit under ERISA § 502(a)(1)(B): benefits due under the terms of a plan. The pension plan defined hours of service to include hours for which back pay is awarded or agreed to. But, in the D.C. Circuit's view, the plaintiff entered into a complete release without waiting for adjudication of his status. That made it impossible for him to get a back pay award. The settlement did not allocate the lump sum to hours of service. There was no evidence that any funds were received as back pay, so there were no back pay hours to be factored into his pension. [*Francis v. Rodman Local Union 201 Pension Fund*, 367 F.3d 937 (D.C. Cir. 2004)]

After the EEOC obtained a disability discrimination award, the recipient of the award sued under 42 U.S.C. § 2000e-16(c) to increase the amount of compensatory damages. The Third Circuit had to decide whether the District Court could grant a new trial solely on the amount of damages (set by the defendant, because the plaintiff was a federal employee), while being bound by the EEOC's finding of liability. The Third Circuit said that a partial new trial is inappropriate. If there is a final administrative disposition that finds discrimination and awards relief, the claimant can either accept the disposition and the award or bring a suit. But if the claimant opts for litigation, both liability and remedy are reviewed de novo; review of only the award is not available. [*Morris v. Rumsfeld*, 420 F.3d 287 (3d Cir. 2005)]

Many discrimination cases can be brought by the plaintiff in federal court, because there is a federal question (alleged violation of a federal statute). If the plaintiff chooses to sue in state court instead, the issue arises of whether the defendant can get the case removed to federal court. Further issues arise when the reason for going to federal court is "diversity" (the plaintiff and defendant are citizens of different states). Federal courts have jurisdiction in diversity cases if, and only if, the amount in controversy is at least $75,000. Early in 2004, the Ninth Circuit refused to hear an employee's challenge to an arbitration award ruling for the employer. In the Ninth Circuit view, the amount in controversy was the amount awarded in the arbitration proceeding—that is, nothing, because the arbitrator found for the defense. So there was no federal question jurisdiction. There was another problem: as Chapter 40 shows, courts are usually deferential to arbitration awards. To overturn an award, the challenger must prove manifest disregard (that the arbitrator recognized the relevant legal principles, but refused to apply them). It's not enough to claim that the arbitrator misinterpreted the legal precedents or made an unwise decision. [*Luong v. Circuit City Stores Inc.*, 356 F.3d 1188 (9th Cir. 2004)]

The Eleventh Circuit punished a plaintiff who sued for discriminatory demotion before she filed for bankruptcy, but omitted the cause of action from her asset statement, by preventing her from seeking money damages in the suit. She also deceived the bankruptcy trustee by pretending that her suit merely sought reinstatement, not damages. In the court's view, she should not be allowed to use deceptive conduct to collect damages and keep them away from her creditors. [*Barger v. Cartersville*, 348 F.3d 1289 (11th Cir. 2003); *see* Donald Potter and Eric Steinert, *Plaintiff's Bankruptcy and Judicial Estoppel of Employment*

Litigation, 72 L.W. 2491 (Feb. 24, 2004) for discussion of this and other cases, such as *DeLeon v. Comcar Industries Inc.,* 321 F.3d 1289 (11th Cir. 2003) and *Burnes v. Pemco Aeroplex Inc.,* 291 F.3d 1282 (11th Cir. 2002), in which bankruptcy misconduct by debtor-plaintiffs prevented them from recovering on employment discrimination claims. *But see Parker v. Wendy's International Inc.,* 365 F.3d 1268 (11th Cir. 2004), reversing the District Court's dismissal of an employment discrimination case. In the Eleventh Circuit's view, the plaintiff omitted the claims from her bankruptcy filing inadvertently, without deceptive intent, and the interests of justice favored permitting her to pursue her claims]

[B] CRA '91 Cap on Damages

The Civil Rights Act of 1991 (CRA '91) [Pub. L. No. 102-166] imposes a cap on total damages that can be awarded to a successful Title VII plaintiff: The amount depends on the size of the corporate defendant, not the number or seriousness of the charges. The cap applies to punitive damages and most compensatory damages (but not to medical bills or other monetary losses that the plaintiff incurred before the trial).

Companies with fewer than 15 employees are exempt from Title VII, so the cap calculation begins at the 15-employee level. The damage cap is $50,000 for a company with 15–100 employees. The cap is set at $100,000 for companies with 101–200 employees, $200,000 for 201–500 employees, and $300,000 for companies with over 500 workers.

Pollard v. DuPont, [532 U.S. 843 (2001)] a sex-discrimination and harassment case (not sexual harassment—the harassment was directed at the plaintiff because she was a woman, not because the co-workers who sabotaged her work were trying to obtain sexual gratification), did not apply the $300,000 damage cap to the plaintiff's front pay claim. This case treats front pay as "such affirmative action as may be appropriate" as relief, rather than as compensatory damages. Therefore, front pay is not capped and can be awarded in whatever amount is equitable.

Late in 2002, the Third Circuit issued a strongly pro-plaintiff decision in the case of *Gagliardo v. Connaught Labs. Inc.* [311 F.3d 565 (3d Cir. 2002)] The court ruled that the federal damage caps should be applied to maximize the plaintiff's recovery, by assigning as much of the jury award as possible to remedies under an uncapped state statute. The court's rationale was that the intent of CRA '91 was to permit states flexibility in setting remedies, even remedies in excess of those that can be awarded under federal law. The Ninth and D.C. Circuits have also held that the cap does not limit state damages.

In this case (involving a refusal to make reasonable accommodations to a multiple sclerosis sufferer's fatigue and difficulty in concentration) the jury awarded $2 million in compensatory damages and $500,000 in compensatory damages. It was necessary to make several decisions about how the damages should be apportioned. The trial judge allocated all of the punitive damages to the federal ADA claim, because Pennsylvania's state antidiscrimination statute does not allow punitive damages. Then, based on the size of the employer, the trial judge cut the punitive damages to $300,000—the cap amount. The trial judge apportioned all $2 million in compensatory damages to the state claim. Within this amount, based on testimony from the plaintiff's expert witness that the plaintiff suffered economic loss of $450,000, the trial court allocated the remaining $1.55 million to pain and suffering. The District Court (upheld by the Third Circuit) found that the prerequisite for awarding emotional distress damages was met: a reasonable probability (not just a mere possibility) that the emotional distress affected the plaintiff's quality of life. In this case, co-workers and family members testified that work stress had caused mental trauma that turned a happy and confident person into a withdrawn, indecisive one. In the Third Circuit view, punitive damages are available under the ADA based on a showing of malice or reckless indifference in a discriminatory practice. The Third Circuit agreed that the plaintiff had met this burden by showing that the employer was aware that she had multiple sclerosis; that she informed the company of her difficulties with fatigue and concentration; and that she requested but was denied reasonable accommodation (e.g., changing her work assignment to less stressful tasks) on many occasions.

In the Seventh Circuit, a Title VII plaintiff can get both front pay and lost future earnings. [*Williams v. Pharmacia Inc.*, 137 F.3d 944 (7th Cir. 1998)] The court found that the two remedies are not duplicative, because front pay substitutes for reinstatement and is ordered for a limited period. It is an equitable remedy, and the judge sets its amount. In contrast, lost future earnings, as authorized by CRA '91, represent the future pecuniary loss that can be traced to the effects of discrimination.

In mid-1999, the Supreme Court decided that compensatory damages, as defined by CRA '91, can be awarded against a federal agency defendant. [*West v. Gibson,* 527 U.S. 212 (1999)]

The cap on foreign employers who violate Title VII is based on their total number of employees throughout the world, not just those in the United States. [*Morelli v. Cedel,* 141 F.3d 39 (2d Cir. 1998); *Greenbaum v. Svenska Handelsbanken,* 26 F. Supp. 2d 649 (S.D.N.Y. 1998)] More employees means a higher damage cap, so these decisions increase the damage exposure of foreign corporations.

The Eleventh Circuit says that every employee who is represented by the EEOC in a Title VII action is entitled to recover the full cap amount without filing a separate action or even intervening in the EEOC's action. They are not required to divide a single cap amount among them. [*EEOC v. W&O Inc.*, 213 F.3d 600 (11th Cir. 2000)]

[C] Punitive Damages

One of the most controversial questions is the matter of punitive damages. In a few cases, judges or juries have awarded a small or fairly small sum in compensatory damages, to compensate the plaintiff for actual losses chargeable to the fault of the defendant, but accompanied the small compensatory damages with enormous punitive damage awards. [*See, e.g., Cush-Crawford v. Adchem Corp.*, 271 F.3d 352 (2d Cir. 2001)] Where punitive damages were granted, at the cap amount of $100,000, even though there were no compensatory damages, on the theory that compensatory and punitive damages serve very different purposes, and therefore punitive damages might be appropriate in a case where there were no compensatory damages.

According to the Fourth Circuit, it was permissible to award $100,000 to a wrongfully demoted employee who was not awarded any compensatory damages on her sex discrimination claim. The Fourth Circuit deemed the judge's award of $410,000 in back pay and interest to justify the punitive damage award, because the loss of income she suffered was actionable harm, the lost back pay was roughly equivalent to compensatory damages, and there is no explicit statutory condition under CRA '91 that punitive damages are dependent on compensatory damages. [*Corti v. Storage Tech Corp.*, 304 F.3d 336 (4th Cir. 2002)]

The District of Columbia Court of Appeals would not let a $4.8 million punitive damage award in a sexual harassment retaliation stand. It was 26 times the compensatory damages, clearly exceeding the single-digit limitation. Furthermore, the award impermissibly reflected nationwide conduct and not just the treatment of the plaintiff. [*Daka Inc. v. McCrae*, 839 A.2d 682 (D.C. App. Dec. 24, 2003)]

The Seventh Circuit ruled that punitive damages awarded to a woman who was denied a promotion were excessive at $273,000. Damages were deemed excessive because the employer promptly corrected the discrimination and promoted her to another managerial spot two months later. The court gave her a choice between remittitur (reduction of the award; the court said that $150,000 was the highest possible award that would be reasonable) and a new trial. However, the court did not accept the employer's argument that an award of punitive damages ten times the compensatory damages violated the Due Process clause, because now that Congress has imposed limits on damages, the issue is no longer one of Constitutional dimensions. [*Lust v. Sealy Inc.*, 383 F.3d 580 (7th Cir. 2004)]

A plaintiff suffered serious harassment both because she held a "man's job" and because she was white and married to a black man. Her supervisors were aware of the harassment but failed to stop it. She also suffered retaliation for her complaints and accepted constructive demotions to escape the hostile work environment. The jury awarded $266,750 for emotional distress, $77,000 for back pay and benefits, and more than $2 million in punitive damages. The District Court entered judgment for a total of $1.6 million. In June 2001 the Eighth Circuit ruled that the plaintiff proved continuing violations of her civil rights. Therefore, under Iowa law, she was entitled to compensatory damages of $266,750 ($110,000 for sex discrimination and harassment; $155,000 for racial discrimination; the balance for constructive demotion). The Eighth Circuit also affirmed the back pay award. Iowa law uses the concept of continuing violations—a plaintiff can recover for the entire period over which his or her rights are violated, but does not allow punitive damages in discrimination cases. Therefore, any punitive damages ordered would have to be ordered under federal law.

In the Eighth Circuit view, there was enough evidence that management acted with malice or reckless disregard of the plaintiff's civil rights to justify sending the issue of punitive damages to the jury. However, the Eighth Circuit found that the District Court's jury instructions focused on the wrong period of time, so it was possible that some damages were awarded for conduct that was actually time-barred.

The $300,000 cap (based on the size of the employer) was applied to the sexual harassment and sex discrimination claims, but not to the constructive demotion or retaliation claim, because those claims could be treated as 42 USC § 1981 claims. The Eighth Circuit sent the case back to the District Court for reconsideration, using the *Morgan* standards for timeliness. [*Madison v. IBP Inc.*, 330 F.3d 1051 (8th Cir. 2003)]

A jury awarded a plaintiff more than $2.6 million in his suit against Proctor & Gamble. He charged that the company had a pattern or practice of discrimination against black technicians, and that he was fired in retaliation for filing a race discrimination complaint with the EEOC. The damages consisted of $29,000 for lost medical insurance, approximately $81,000 in lost wages, $500,000 for emotional pain and mental anguish, and $2 million in punitive damages. [News Articles, *Proctor & Gamble Loses Wrongful Termination Suit*, PlanSponsor.com (Feb. 2, 2006)]

A Seventh Circuit plaintiff filed an EEOC charge alleging that he was denied a promotion because of racial discrimination. He was fired shortly thereafter. In his Title VII suit, the jury awarded only $1,000 in compensatory damages, plus $345,000 in compensatory and punitive retaliation damages ($75,000 compensatory, $275,000 punitive). The court reduced this to $300,000 pursuant to the cap, based on the size of the employer. The Seventh Circuit ruled that the grant of punitive damages was reasonable and was not inappropriate in amount—the plaintiff was told "we can't have anyone working here who complains to the EEOC," and he produced evidence to rebut the defendant's claim that his work was poor, showing that he surpassed the targets he was accused of not meeting. [*Lampley v. Onyx Acceptance Corp.*, 340 F.3d 478 (7th Cir. 2003)]

Theoretically, punitive damages are supposed to be quite rare, ordered only in those cases where the defendant's conduct has been worse than merely negligent or improper.

A defendant that has acted maliciously, or at least with reckless indifference to the plaintiff's rights, can be ordered to pay punitive damages. The employer's conduct need not be "egregious" for punitive damages to be available. [*Kolstad v. American Dental Ass'n,* 527 U.S. 526 (1999)]

Zimmerman v. Associates First Capital Corp. [70 L.W. 1016 (2d Cir. May 31, 2001)] says that it was proper to impose punitive damages against a company on the basis of the vice president's acknowledgment that he had received EEO training, showing that he acted with reckless indifference toward federally protected rights.

The New Jersey Law Against Discrimination makes employers liable for punitive damages based on actions of their "upper management." In *Cavuotti v. New Jersey Transit Corp.*, [735 A.2d 548 (N.J. 1999)] a case about an alleged age-based refusal to promote, the court held that the category "upper management" is not limited to major corporate officers. Instead, it includes all managers with broad supervisory powers over the plaintiff-employee, as well as all managers to whom the employer company has delegated the responsibility for maintaining a nondiscriminatory workplace.

There are not many instances in which very large punitive damages have actually been paid. Such awards are vulnerable to being reduced on appeal. Or the plaintiff may feel both emotionally vindicated and sick of litigating the case, and may settle the case post-trial for much less than the theoretical award. Nevertheless, even if the order is never carried out, it can be a real public relations disaster for a company to be ordered to pay millions of dollars as a punishment.

The EEOC's Compliance Manual lists appropriate factors for deciding whether the employer acted with malice or reckless indifference:

- Degree of unacceptability of the conduct;
- The nature, severity, and extent of the harm suffered by the complaining employee;
- The duration of the conduct: A practice that persists for years is more serious than one that is terminated after a short period of time;
- Whether there was an extensive pattern of past discrimination, or only a few isolated incidents;
- Whether the employer tried to remedy the situation, or exacerbated it by covering up or retaliating against complainants.

The First Circuit imposed punitive damages on both a parent company and a subsidiary company in a sex-discrimination case. [*Romano v. U-Haul Int'l,* 233 F.3d 655 (1st Cir. 2000)]

[D] Attorneys' Fees and Costs

The attorneys' fee award was the sticking point that prevented approval of a major ($14.2 million) settlement. [*See Staton v. Boeing Co.*, 313 F.3d 447 (9th Cir. 2002)] A class of black employees sued Boeing under both state and federal law, charging race discrimination in promotion, training, and transfers; discriminatory discharges; and tolerating a racially hostile environment in the workplace. The settlement would have provided $3.77 million for 264 current and former employees, $3.53 million for the rest of the class, plus changes in the company's promotion process and a $3.65 million equal opportunity and diversity training program. The named plaintiffs got a maximum of $50,000 each, with an average of $16,500. The 3,400 unnamed class members who filed claims got an average of $1,000 each.

The District Court also approved attorneys' fees of over $4 million. The attorneys for the plaintiffs took the position that the relevant measurement was a "putative fund" representing the value of all the benefits obtained for the plaintiffs, including the damages, fees, cost of notice, and the value of the injunctive relief). The fee was 28% of the value of this putative fund. However, the Ninth Circuit found that calculating the fee award on the basis of a common fund was tied too closely to the final amount of the settlement, and might not have been in the best interests of the plaintiffs. The Ninth Circuit pointed out that courts have a special duty to protect the interests of class members because of the inherent conflict in that a larger fee for the attorneys means a smaller recovery for the class members. To collect common-fund fees, lawyers generally must make a separate petition to the court after the settlement, rather than using the settlement to bypass court approval.

According to the Seventh Circuit, Chicago attorneys hired for a Title VII case in Southern Illinois are entitled to a fee award reflecting Chicago hourly rates, not the lower rates prevailing in Southern Illinois. The plaintiff had to go out of town to find counsel because the local lawyers either lacked the relevant expertise or had conflicts of interest that prevented them from representing the plaintiff against the defendant university. [*Mathur v. Board of Trustees of S. Ill. Univ.*, 317 F.3d 738 (7th Cir. 2003)]

The Fifth Circuit allowed an attorney who won a Title VII failure-to-promote case and an attorneys' fee award to enforce the retainer agreement under which the client agreed to pay the lawyer 35% of the recovery. [*Gobert v. Williams,* 323 F.3d 1099 (5th Cir. 2003), extending the Supreme Court's 1990 decision about the Civil Rights Attorney's Fee Awards Act to the context of Title VII. *Venegas v. Mitchell,* 495 U.S. 82 (1990)]

An employer-defendant that won its sexual harassment case was awarded costs (transcription, copying, and videotaping) when the plaintiff's case was weak enough for summary judgment to be granted to the employer. [*Cherry v. Champion Int'l Inc.*, 186 F.3d 442 (4th Cir. 1999)] In fact, the Fourth Circuit said that the district court, which did not award the costs, abused its discretion, and the lower court should not have considered factors such as the plaintiff's good faith, lack of economic power as compared with the defendant, or the public interest in the courts being used to bring Title VII claims.

A Florida court went even further, requiring a plaintiff whose frivolous suit was dismissed at the summary judgment stage to pay $160,000 of the employer's fees and costs. [*Bernard v. Air Express Int'l USA Inc.*, discussed in Susan R. Miller, *Judges Reversing Tide, Making Some Plaintiffs Pay Attorney Fees, Costs,* Miami Daily Business Review (Dec. 7, 2000) (law.com)]

Federal Rules of Civil Procedure Rule 68 provides that when the defendant makes a formal settlement offer before the trial; the plaintiff rejects the offer; and the plaintiff wins the case, but is awarded less than the offer, the defendant is entitled to reimbursement of litigation costs. However, the Third Circuit ruled that the defendant can never recover attorneys' fees under this provision, because the plaintiff's suit was not frivolous—the plaintiff merely made a bad strategic decision in a valid case. [*Tai Van Le v. University of Pennsylvania,* 321 F.3d 403 (3d Cir. 2003)]

District court jurisdiction to hear suits "brought under" Title VII doesn't extend to a suit in federal court brought purely to recover attorneys' fees after winning an administrative claim, because no substantive rights under the statute are involved. [*Chris v. Tenet,* 221 F.3d 648 (4th Cir. 2000)]

§ 42.13 SETTLEMENT OF A DISCRIMINATION SUIT

[A] Generally

Suits can be settled at any time before a verdict or judicial decision is rendered. In fact, they can even be settled after the judge and jury have spoken. As long as there are appeal rights that could be exercised, the case is still open for negotiation. The objective of any settlement is to provide something for both parties: for the defendant employer, the chance to dispose of the case expeditiously and to eliminate the risk of a huge jury verdict; for the plaintiff, the chance to get at least some money quickly instead of many years later.

At a very early stage, the matter might be resolved by an agreement to let the employee resign instead of being fired and receive severance pay, and perhaps some other benefits, in exchange for releasing the employer from all liability. Both sides must agree on how the matter will be treated for unemployment insurance purposes (based on counsel from a lawyer).

In a situation where the employer acknowledges that the plaintiff has a valid case, or at least that the claims have some validity, the employer may want to settle early to limit its possible liability exposure and bad publicity.

Even if the employer thinks the plaintiff's claims are fabricated, exaggerated, or legally invalid, it still might be prudent to settle the case because of the sheer cost and effort involved in litigating a major suit, even if the final result is victory for the employer.

Usually, cases are settled somewhere around halfway between the plaintiff's demand and the defendant's counter-offer. Of course, both sides know this, and it influences the amounts they suggest at the negotiating table. No one should ever engage in negotiations without authority actually to settle the case, and without a range of acceptable settlement figures.

Tip: Cases that are settled quickly are also often settled within the policy limits of the employer's liability insurance policy. Therefore, the insurer will assume the entire cost of settlement. Moreover, if the employer does a prompt investigation of the allegations, negotiates in good faith, and does not unduly delay the settlement, the employer has not acted outrageously and has not violated the norms of public policy. Therefore, there will probably be no grounds for assessing punitive damages against the employer.

There are statutes, such as California's Civil Procedure Code § 998, that penalize plaintiffs who reject fair settlement offers. If the judge or jury awards less than a settlement offer previously made, then the statute may require the plaintiff to pay the defendant's lawsuit costs, on the grounds that the suit could have been avoided by the plaintiff's acceptance of a reasonable settlement.

When a settlement is reached, there are two major legal documents to be prepared. The first is a court order dismissing the case with prejudice (i.e., in a way that prevents it from being refiled later) and a release containing the terms of the settlement. It is usually prudent to try to provide the text of the release, in order to control the basic form of its terms.

A settlement can be offered without admitting culpability. Also, under 29 C.F.R. § 1601.20(a), the EEOC has the power to dismiss an employee's discrimination charge if the employee rejects a written settlement offer from the employer that is a legitimate offer of "full relief" (i.e., adequate compensation for the discrimination suffered by the employee). The EEOC sends the employee a strongly worded form letter that gives him or her only two choices: to accept the settlement offer promptly, or have the EEOC charge dismissed. (This only means that the EEOC will not be involved in the case, not that the employee is prevented from suing.)

Full relief means that the employee gets full back pay, plus any out-of-pocket expenses related to discrimination (such as moving expenses after a wrongful termination, or psychological counseling for a stressed-out employee). Compensation must also be included for nonmonetary losses such as loss of sleep, anxiety, and indigestion.

However, the employer must be aware that settling with one employee is not necessarily the end of the problem. It is against public policy (and a court might issue an injunction forbidding this) to include a provision in a settlement agreement that forbids a current or former employee to cooperate with an EEOC investigation. A settlement can prevent a person from pursuing his or her own claims against the employer, but the EEOC's right to investigate workplace conditions, and pursue claims on its own behalf (and on behalf of other employees) continues.

A firefighter plaintiff was terminated for sleeping through a fire call, and possibly other infractions. The termination was upheld by an administrative appeal. Then he was offered a deal under which his termination could be converted to a one-year unpaid suspension with a final warning. He would be reinstated about a year later. However, the deal required him to waive all employment-related claims, including discrimination claims. The plaintiff accepted the deal (he claims he was under pressure). He did not report to work when the suspension ended. He brought suit, charging racial discrimination and duress. The Eighth Circuit upheld the dismissal of his suit: the test under Missouri law is whether a party was deprived of free will by threats or wrongful conduct, so that no valid contract could be created. In this case, the plaintiff was in a stressful situation and made a decision he later regretted, but he was not deprived of free will. [*Clark v. Riverview Fire Protection District,* 354 F.3d 752 (8th Cir. 2004)]

[B] Tax Factors in Settling Discrimination Cases

The plaintiff's objective is to wind up with the best after-tax result from pursuing or settling a case. In some instances, appropriate structuring of the settlement can produce a better after-tax result for the plaintiff while reducing the cash-flow impact on the defendant.

Damages for breach of contract are taxable income for the plaintiff, because they are treated as delayed payment of compensation that the employee would have received earlier if there had been no breach of contract.

The treatment of tort damages is more complex. Damages are not taxable if they are payable because of the plaintiff's "personal injury." The Supreme Court has ruled that Title VII damages and ADEA damages are not received for personal injury, because they are not similar enough to the damages received in traditional tort cases (car crashes, for instance). [*United States v. Burke*, 504 U.S. 229 (1992); *Commissioner of Internal Revenue v. Schleier*, 515 U.S. 323 (1995)]

The Small Business Job Protection Act of 1996 clarified the application of I.R.C. § 104(a)(2), the provision on taxation of damages. Starting August 21, 1996, damages received for "personal physical injuries" and physical illness are received free of tax—for instance, if the employer's wrongful conduct makes the employee physically ill. Damages for emotional distress are taxable except to the extent of medical expenses for their treatment.

Taxable damages that are wage replacements (under the FLSA, NLRA, Title VII, and ADEA, for example) may be FICA wages and may be subject to withholding. *But see Newhouse v. McCormack & Co.*, [157 F.3d 582 (8th Cir. 1998)] where front and back pay awarded under the ADEA to a job applicant who was not hired was not considered "wages" subject to tax withholding.

A longstanding circuit split was resolved by the U.S. Supreme Court's January 2005 decision in *Commissioner v. Banks*, 543 U.S. 426 (2005). A judgment or settlement paid to a winning plaintiff's attorney under a contingent fee agreement must be included in the plaintiff's gross income, irrespective of whether state law gives the attorney special rights (over and above normal contract law rights) over amounts awarded to prevailing plaintiffs.

Section 703 of the American Jobs Creation Act (P.L. 108-357) makes attorneys' fees in employment discrimination cases an above-the-line deduction, although this is not true of attorneys' fees in other types of cases. *Banks* was decided after the enactment of this legislation, but the law is not retroactive.

CHAPTER 43

INSURANCE COVERAGE FOR CLAIMS AGAINST THE EMPLOYER

§ 43.01   INTRODUCTION

It is only prudent for a company to maintain insurance against significant risks. However, although the potential risk exposure in a discrimination, harassment, or wrongful termination suit is quite large, it can be difficult to buy insurance that will fully cover these claims—or even cover them at all.

Between 1994 and 2000, for example, the number of comparatively small judgments in employment-related suits decreased. In 1994, 52% of plaintiff's judgments were under $100,000, versus 30% in 2000. (Of course, some of the difference was due to inflation as well as changes in the law and jury attitudes.) In 1994, a mere 7% of plaintiff's verdicts were $1 million or more, whereas this was true of 20% of the plaintiff's verdicts in 2000. In 1999, the median award was $151,000; only a year later, it was $218,000. [Reed Abelson, *Surge in Bias Cases Punishes Insurers and Premiums Rise*, New York Times, Jan. 9, 2002, at C1; the same data is also quoted in Michael Barrier, *EPCI Providers Turn Up the Heat*, HR Magazine, May 2002, at p. 46]

Liability insurers expected a heavy increase in the volume of litigation as a result of recession and lay-offs. Some insurers responded by doubling or even tripling the premiums for employment practices liability insurance (EPLI), whereas some stopped selling the coverage altogether. EPLI insureds, like health insureds, also faced higher deductibles and lower coverage limits.

In 2004, very unlike the situation for health insurance, many employers found that their business insurance premiums actually declined, and insurers were liberalizing the terms and conditions on policies. Probably what happened is that the first wave of corporate scandals in the twenty-first century caused premiums to rise; they are now declining for many companies. According to the Risk and Insurance Management Society, 50% of D&O liability policy premiums went down by an average of 16%, whereas 39% of premiums increased by an average of 21%. Half of general liability policy premiums decreased, an average of 11%, but 38% went up by an average of 8%. Forty-three percent of Worker's Compensation policy premiums declined an average of 13%, but 50% rose, by an average of 14%. [Theo Francis, *Companies' Insurance Bills Get Snipped*, Wall Street Journal, July 15, 2004, at p. C1]

At the ABA annual meeting held in August 2003, a panel of experts looked at the history of EPLI for employment claims. The early policies had narrow coverage and large retentions (similar to deductibles in other types of insurance), in the range of $200,000 or more. In response to market fluctuations, retentions went down to $25,000–$50,000 but have come back up. Another trend is that coverage tends to be offered now on the basis of claims made and reported in the relevant year, not merely claims made. The experts noted that insurers are seldom required to pay up under a punitive damages clause, because cases in which punitive damages seem to be a real possibility are usually settled at a much earlier stage. Some policies now include a "hammer clause," under which the employer is liable for any amount (or any percentage) awarded over and above the amount for which the employee plaintiff was willing to settle.

When evaluating an application for EPLI, insurers consider factors such as the geographic location; the industry (retail operations and restaurants are considered hard to insure because the potential for claims is high); whether the employer maintains and enforces written anti-discrimination practices and policies; the quality of EEO training given to its employees; the quality of handling of internal grievances; and whether the employer has or plans Reductions in Force (because RIF'ed employees might sue). [No byline, *Employment Liability Insurance Market Takes Toll on Equal Employment Claims*, 72 L.W. 2108]

§ 43.02   COMMERCIAL GENERAL LIABILITY

[A]   Use of the CGL Policy

Most businesses get their basic liability coverage under the Commercial General Liability (CGL) policy. In fact, for most companies, this is the only liability insurance.

The CGL has two basic aims. The first is to provide a defense (i.e., supply a lawyer who will investigate, negotiate, and settle or try the case). The second is to pay whatever settlement or judgment the defendant company would otherwise have to pay to a successful plaintiff. The insurer's obligation is subject to the insured's obligation to pay a deductible. The insurer is not required to pay more than the limits of the policy. CGL policies are not really uniform. The Insurance Standards Organization (ISO) has published a very influential model policy, but insurers have the option of tailoring the model as they see fit.

Furthermore, the insurer must only pay for covered claims, not excluded ones. ISO has drafted an "employment-related practices exclusion," and the trend is for recent policies to follow this and simply exclude all claims related to a plaintiff's employment by a defendant. Even this is not as simple as it seems. For instance, a court might rule that the real injury to the plaintiff occurred after he or she was fired and therefore ceased to be an employee.

Even if the policy doesn't exclude all employment-related claims, there may be other factors that prevent the employer from collecting benefits under the policy.

After the September 11 attack, and as the economy continued to decline, the major commercial insurers reduced the availability of business liability insurance—for example, a company that previously could purchase $50 million in coverage would probably only be able to get $25 million worth, $25 million would probably be scaled back to $10 or $15 million, and deductibles and other costs to be assumed by the insured increased as well. [Jonathan D. Glater and Joseph B. Treaster, *Insurers Scale Back Corporate Liability Policies*, New York Times, Sept. 7, 2002, at p. C1]

[B]   Bodily Injury and Personal Injury

Coverage A of the CGL provides liability insurance when the insured becomes liable to someone who has suffered "bodily injury." It's rare for employment plaintiffs to claim that they suffered physically. Usually, they assert that they lost economic benefits (such as salary and pension) because of the employer's wrongful conduct. CGL Coverage A will *not* apply to charges of breach of contract or other economic consequences.

For this and other reasons, plaintiffs often ask for damages based on their emotional suffering. Their complaints allege pain and suffering, intentional infliction of emotional distress, or negligent infliction of emotional distress. (The availability of these causes of action varies between the federal and state systems, and from state to state.)

Most courts that have dealt with this question say that there is no "bodily injury" in an emotional suffering case unless the plaintiff can prove that there was at least some physical consequence of the emotional injury: an ulcer or high blood pressure, for instance. Even if there are physical consequences, they could be considered basically economic and therefore outside the scope of Coverage A.

The CGL's Coverage B deals with liability that the insured encounters for "personal injury" (such as libel or slander) or advertising injury (such as defaming another company's products in your ads). Coverage B might get involved in an employment-related case if, for instance, the plaintiff claims that the employer not only fired him or her, but blacklisted him or her and used a campaign of lies to prevent the ex-employee from getting another job or establishing business relationships.

[C]   CGL Case Law

A church music director claimed that the pastor defamed her by spreading negative and untruthful explanations of why the music director was fired. The church had an insurance policy that covered defamation, but that included a separate exclusion of all kinds of employment-related liability. There was no coverage under the policy, because whatever the pastor said related to the rationale for the discharge, and therefore fell under the employment exclusion. [*Parish of Christ Church v. Church Ins. Co.*, 166 F.3d 419 (1st Cir. 1999)]

The CGL exclusion for "employment-related practices" does exclude direct coverage for sexual harassment liability, but not a claim against the employer for negligent retention of the supervisor who committed the harassment, on the theory that negligent retention is a negligence claim, not a claim of intentional injury. [*Mactown Inc. v. Continental Ins. Co.*, 716 So. 2d 289 (Fla. App. 1998)]

According to *SCI Liquidating Corp. v. Hartford Fire Ins. Co.*, [181 F.3d 1210 (11th Cir. 1999)] the CGL doesn't have to cover claims made by an employee who alleged sexual harassment (including assault and battery), retaliation, intentional infliction of emotional distress, and negligent hiring and retention of the perpetrator. In this reading, there was no CGL occurrence, because intentional harassment is not an accident. Because of the close relationship with the harassment, injury arising out of negligent hiring and retention didn't fit the definition of occurrence either. Although the CGL included discrimination in its category of covered personal injury, it excluded employment-related claims.

The employer also had an umbrella policy covering personal injury, specifically including injury related to discrimination. The Eleventh Circuit sent the case back to the Georgia Supreme Court to determine whether sexual harassment by a fellow employee "arises out of and in the course of employment." At least in the Worker's Compensation context, the Georgia law is that co-employee harassment does not arise out of employment. If this is so, the employer would be covered under the umbrella policy because the exclusion of employment-related claims would not come into play.

Under liability insurance and Worker's Compensation insurance policies, asbestos-related disease is "bodily injury by disease" and not "bodily injury by accident." Asbestos exposure is not an accident because of its non-violent nature and because injuries develop over a latency period rather than manifesting immediately. [*Riverwood Int'l Corp. v. Employers Ins. of Wausau*, 420 F.3d 378 (5th Cir. 2005)]

The Eighth Circuit held that there was no duty to defend under the CGL in a case where a hotel manager left her job. The manager was arrested after the hotel reported to the authorities that she had stolen some rent receipts. She sued the former employer for false arrest, false imprisonment, unjust enrichment, wrongful termination, slander, and FLSA violations. The insurer sought—and obtained—a declaratory judgment that the CGL policy excluded matters arising out of termination of employment or employment-related practices. The hotel claimed that it was covered because the events giving rise to the litigation arose after termination of employment. However, under Missouri law, the phrase "arising out of" is construed very broadly, and all the incidents motivating the lawsuit flowed directly from employment. Therefore, the exclusion applied, and the insurer had no duty to defend the hotel against these allegations. [*Capitol Indemnity Corp. v. 1405 Associates, Inc.*, 340 F.3d 547 (8th Cir. 2003)]

A California court tackled some complex issues of successor liability and insurance in the early-2003 case of *Henkel Corp. v. Hartford Accident & Indemnity Co.* [29 Cal. 4th 934, 62 P.3d 69, 129 Cal. Rptr. 2d 828 (2003)] The plaintiff, Henkel, bought Amchem's metallic products line and assumed all related liabilities. The question facing the court was whether Henkel also acquired the benefits of the insurance policies issued by Hartford to Amchem to cover lawsuits alleging injuries from exposure to chemicals during the policy period.

The trial court entered summary judgment for the insurer, finding that there was no specific assignment language in the policy. The court of appeals reversed the trial court's judgment, finding that unless the policy explicitly rules out assignment, the benefits of the policy automatically pass to the new business owner by operation of law. But the superior court reversed again, finding that insurance policies cannot be assigned without the consent of the insurer. (It goes to show that interpreting the results of a court case depends on the stage of the case when the analysis is made!)

According to the superior court, there are three situations in which the buyer of corporate assets can become liable for the torts of the predecessor company (even without explicitly assuming the liabilities by contract). The buyer of assets can become liable if the transaction is a merger or consolidation, the purchasing corporation is a continuation of the selling corporation, or the transfer is fraudulent or undertaken to escape liability. The second possibility is that the acquiror of a product line can become liable for injuries caused by the predecessor's defective products if the acquisition extinguishes remedies against the predecessor business. There are also some statutes (such as the environmental statute CERCLA) that impose successor liability no matter what the contract says.

§ 43.03   OCCURRENCES AND THE PROBLEM OF INTENTION

[A]   Nature of Employment Claims

Coverage under Coverage A depends on there being an "occurrence," which is defined as an accident that was neither intended nor expected by the insured. Coverage B does not have an occurrence requirement, but it does exclude coverage of personal injuries that stem from a willful violation of the law, committed by or with the consent of the insured company.

At first glance, it would seem that employment cases could never be covered under the CGL, because the plaintiff accuses someone of deliberately injuring him or her. There is no form of corporate Alzheimer's that makes companies fire or underpay their employees in a fit of absent-mindedness.

The picture is far more complex. Some discrimination charges allege "disparate treatment" (roughly speaking, intentional discrimination), while others claim "disparate impact," (subtle negative effects on a protected group of employees). An employer's actions in adopting a policy or publishing an employee manual could have unintended consequences, which could possibly be treated as CGL "occurrences."

However, intentional discrimination would not be. Courts often treat some conduct (e.g., sexual harassment) as being so likely to have bad consequences for their victims that the consequences are presumed to have been intended, or at least expected, by the insured company.

Employment discrimination plaintiffs usually want the insurance company to be involved, because they know that liability insurance is another potential source of payment if they settle or win the case. In this instance, they are on the same side as the employer. They both want the CGL to cover the employee's claim. One simple strategy is for plaintiffs to add claims of negligent supervision by the employer, or negligent infliction of emotional distress, in the hope that these charges of negligence will be classified as covered "occurrences."

The CGL exclusion of "intentional" conduct does not apply to conduct that is negligent, or even grossly negligent. However, this tactic usually fails because the negligence charges are treated as purely incidental to more important charges of intentional conduct.

In most instances, termination of an employee, even wrongful termination, does not involve the intention or expectation of harm, so the insurer will probably have a duty to defend. CGL personal injury coverage often excludes damage resulting from the willful violations of a penal statute or ordinance, committed by the insured or with the knowledge of the insured. Civil rights laws are not considered "penal statutes" for this purpose. Even if actions are "willful" for Title VII purposes, the criminal law exclusion will not be triggered.

Some CGL policies offer an endorsement or rider (at additional cost over the basic premium) that covers discrimination and harassment claims, often by broadening the underlying policy's definition of personal injury.

CGL policies typically exclude bodily injury to employees, arising out of and in the course of employment, whether the employer is liable as an employer or in other capacities. But that provision is probably included in the policy simply for coordination with Worker's Compensation. The employee could succeed in arguing that the tort claims they make do not arise out of or in the course of the employment relationship, because supervisors are not employed to commit discrimination or harassment. The insurer may have at least a duty to defend. Furthermore, occupational injuries could be treated as a known risk that employees are aware of, whereas discrimination and harassment are not risks of the same category.

In a case where a company was sued for negligent hiring and retention of a person who murdered the owner of a house where he was sent to work, the insurer sought a declaratory judgment that it had no duty to defend the employers. In the insurer's view, negligent hiring and retention is not an occurrence, and the policy excluded bodily injury that was expected or intended from the standpoint of the insured.

However, the Sixth Circuit found a duty to defend, in that under state (Kentucky) law, negligent hiring and retention probably would be considered an occurrence. (Because there is no Sixth Circuit ruling on the subject the court was required to decide as it believed the Kentucky Supreme Court would decide.)

The manager who hired the murderer admitted that he failed to perform a criminal background check, and continued to employ him even after receiving theft complaints against him. Some courts hold that the decision to hire or retain someone is an intentional business decision, so it cannot be accidental even if negligence is involved. However, other cases (e.g., *United Fire & Cas. Co. v. Shelly Funeral Home*, 642 N.W.2d 648 (Iowa 2002)) treat negligence and intention as opposites. Under this theory, the independent wrongful act committed by a criminal employee does not put the insured employer's negligence beyond the scope of the policy's definition of "occurrence." The Sixth Circuit ruled that there would be coverage—even if hiring and retaining that person was intentional and even if it could be foreseen that the victim would be harmed—unless the employer actually intended the injury to occur. Negligent hiring/retention is not inherently injurious, because it is not by its nature substantially certain to result in injury. [*Westfield Insurance Co. v. Tech Dry, Inc.*, 336 F.3d 503 (6th Cir. 2003)]

[B] Public Policy Issues

A basic principle of insurance law is that you can't buy insurance to protect yourself against the consequences of your own intentional wrongdoing.

The current interpretation of this rule is that it does not violate public policy for companies to buy insurance covering employment-related liability, because this enhances winning plaintiffs' chances to collect. This benefit is deemed to outweigh the risk that companies will be more willing to engage in improper employment practices if they know they are protected by insurance.

A related policy question is whether insurance can cover punitive damages. About two-thirds of the states that have decided cases about this say yes. However, punitive damages for intentional wrongdoing cannot be covered, and most punitive damages are imposed precisely because of the intentionality of the defendant's wrongful conduct.

§ 43.04   EMPLOYMENT PRACTICES LIABILITY INSURANCE

Because of the gaps in CGL coverage of employment matters, a separate form of policy, Employment Practices Liability Insurance (EPLI) evolved as of about 1990. The EPLI is designed to cover damages, judgments, settlements, defense costs, and attorneys' fee awards in the employment liability context (suits, proceedings, or written demands seeking to hold the employer civilly liable). Events included under the EPLI are discrimination, sexual harassment, and wrongful termination, but not "golden parachutes" (payments to top managers who lose their jobs because of corporate transitions) or contractual obligations to make payments to terminated employees. The EPLI policy generally excludes criminal charges, fines, punitive damages, retaliation, and any amounts that are uninsurable because of a relevant state law.

In 1994, only 10 carriers issued such coverage, but by 1999, there were over 100 insurers in the EPLI market, and the Insurance Services Organization (ISO) had published a standard EPLI form. [*See* Daniel C. Skinner, William T. Edwards, and Gregory L. Gravlee, *Selecting Employment Practices Liability Insurance*, HR Magazine, Sept. 1998, at p. 146; Simon J. Nadel, *Employment Practices Liability Insurance Makes Some Headway With Employers*, 66 L.W. 2275]

The usual coverage limit is $1 million–$5 million, but some insurers offer "jumbo" policies of up to $100 million in coverage.

EPLI owners can benefit even if they are never sued, because insurers require insured parties to audit their HR functions, improve their procedures, and add new procedures to minimize the risk of suit. The policy may offer access to valuable low-cost consulting services, and compliance advice that would otherwise carry a high price tag.

A claims-made policy is one that provides coverage when claims are made while the insured still has coverage, but not for claims made after coverage expires, even if the allegedly wrongful conduct occurred while the policy was still in force. The ISO EPLI form modifies this by covering claims made during the 30 days after policy expiration, unless another insurer is already in the picture. If the same employee makes multiple claims, they are all considered to have arisen on the date of the first claim, so coverage will be continuous, and it will not be necessary to figure out whether the initial or the later insurer is responsible. Sometimes, it is a false economy to replace a liability insurance policy if the new policy has a waiting period, creating a gap in coverage.

Two commentators suggest the following questions for evaluating an EPLI policy:

- Does it cover all employees? What about the liability consequences of actions of leased employees and independent contractors?
- Are former employees covered?
- Are claims for breach of explicit or implied employment contract covered by or excluded from the policy?
- Is any coverage available for employment-related claims such as defamation or infliction of emotional distress?
- Can you choose the lawyer or law firm that will defend you, or are you required to accept the insurer's choice of counsel? How much control can you exercise over the defense strategy for your case?
- Does the insurer have to provide you with a defense in administrative (e.g., EEOC and local antidiscrimination agencies) proceedings, or only at trial? (Only a small percentage of discrimination charges make it to the trial stage, but the investigative stage can be very unpleasant for the employer.)
- Are retaliation claims (including retaliation for filing Worker's Compensation claims) covered? (This is a large and growing part of the discrimination caseload.)
- Are injunctive and declaratory relief covered, or only money damages?
- Is the deductible imposed on a per-year or per-claimant basis? (If the latter is true, an insured employer might end up having to pay several deductibles a year.)
- Are punitive damages covered? (Some states do not allow insurance coverage of such damages.) [Stephanie E. Trudeau and William Edwards, Employment Law Letter, archived at <http://www.ulmer.com>]

§ 43.05   OTHER INSURANCE

Although small businesses told National Federation of Independent Business' surveyers in 2004 that health insurance was their most pressing problem, they identified the availability and cost of liability insurance as their number 2 problem. (It was only number 13 in 2000.) The costs of Worker's Compensation were the number 3 issue in 2004 and only number 7 in 2000. However, in 2000, income taxes were considered the number 2 problem—and had declined to the number 5 priority in 2004. Two-thirds of those surveyed considered health insurance costs to be a critical problem, whereas only 32.8% believed this of Worker's Compensation costs; 30.1% about the cost and availability of liability insurance; 26.1% with a pressing concern about energy costs; and 23.2% about federal taxes. [Richard Breeden, *Liability Insurance Becomes a Pressing Concern*, Wall Street Journal, Sept. 21, 2004, at p. B7]

[A] Excess Liability and Umbrella Coverage

Every CGL policy has limits: maximum amounts of coverage obtainable under particular circumstances. If your company already has maximum CGL coverage, but feels that more is necessary, there are two ways to supplement it.

The first is "follow-form" excess liability insurance, which increases the dollar amount of coverage available under your CGL, Worker's Compensation, and Business Automobile Liability coverage, but subject to the same terms and exclusions. For many companies, an "umbrella" policy is a better choice, because it is more broadly defined and may cover situations that were excluded by the underlying policy. This kind of "gap" coverage is generally subject to a "retained limit," another term for "deductible."

Umbrella policies offer coverage in more situations because their definition of "personal injury" is broader than Coverage A or Coverage B of the standard CGL. A typical provision includes both bodily injury and mental injury, mental anguish, shock, sickness, disease, discrimination, humiliation, libel, slander, defamation of character, and invasion of property. Therefore, many employment-related claims would be covered.

[B] Worker's Compensation

Specialized Worker's Compensation coverage is available to deal with the employer's obligation to pay benefits to employees who are injured in job-related situations. Of course, because of WC exclusivity, the employer does not have to worry about ordinary liability suits from injured workers, although there may be special situations in which suit can be brought (against the employer or another party, such as the manufacturer of unsafe factory machinery) even though Worker's Compensation is involved. In a WC employment liability policy, Worker's Compensation is Coverage A; the employment liability (e.g., bodily injury that is not subject to WC exclusivity) is Coverage B.

Schmidt v. Smith [155 N.J. 44, 713 A.2d 1014 (1998)] says that bodily injury that results from sexual harassment is covered by the employer liability section of the Worker's Compensation insurance policy, which is a "gap-filler" designed to come into play when a person suffers job-related injuries, even if that person is not covered by Worker's Compensation. The Insurance Standards Organization (ISO) has not drafted a form for these policies, so they vary widely from insurer to insurer.

Tip: If the charges you face involve an injured worker (for instance, one who alleges disability discrimination after an injury), your Worker's Compensation insurer may have a duty to defend you because of the possibility that you could dispose of the case by claiming WC exclusivity.

[C]   Directors' and Officers' Liability (D&O)

D&O insurance covers the situation in which a corporation' directors and officers get not only themselves but the corporation into trouble. Frequently, executives will not agree to serve as directors or officers unless the corporation first promises them indemnification, i.e., that the corporation will pay the executive whatever amount he or she has to pay because of liability incurred while acting as a director or officer.

D&O insurance, in turn, reimburses the corporation for whatever it spends on indemnification, subject to a deductible and up to the limit of the policy.

In 2002, after the attention given to corporate scandals and the enhanced liability potential under the Sarbanes-Oxley Act, many companies found that it became difficult to recruit or retain directors. Although it is traditional for companies to provide D&O insurance for their directors, the insurance is getting harder to obtain, more expensive (in 2002 deductibles went up 100–300%, and insurers require insured companies to pay up to 30% of settlement costs), and more restrictive even when it is available. In some industries such as telecommunications and other high-tech businesses, insurers are not writing policies at all. Defense costs will not be covered if a director or company is found criminally liable, or if the company lied about its business affairs. In a bankrupt company, the directors and officers may have to compete with creditors, or even the bankruptcy trustee, for amounts recovered under a D&O policy.

The wariness of insurers is understandable given that most class actions are settled—with the average settlement amount rising from $7 million in 1996 to over $17 million in 2001—and for cases involving accounting fraud, the average settlement was even higher, at $23 million.

With only a few insurers left in the market, the remaining competitors are able to offer tough terms, knowing that insureds have few other places to go.

Corporations will take major steps to avoid being indicted (e.g., for accounting irregularities). The Department of Justice set a policy in 2003 that, if a corporation follows the long-established policy of paying legal fees for its executives who have been involved in criminal investigations or have been indicted, the corporation may be treated as refusing to cooperate with law enforcement. That, in turn, makes the corporation more vulnerable to indictment. This policy has been criticized as putting undue pressure on corporations and impairing the defense of individual officers and directors who may need corporate help to pay for an expensive defense. In some federal cases, the judges have taken steps to encourage corporations to furnish defense costs. The guidelines are embodied in the "Thompson memorandum," so-called because of the DOJ Deputy Attorney General who drafted them. [*See* Lynnley Browning, *Judges Press Companies That Cut Off Legal Fees,* New York Times, Apr. 17, 2006, at p. C1; Nathan Koppel, *U.S. Pressures Firms Not to Pay Staff Legal Fees*, Wall Street Journal, Mar. 28, 2006, at p. B1]

In mid-2003, a year after the enactment of Sarbanes-Oxley, the Wall Street Journal reported that D&O insurance premiums were still rising, although the speed of the increase had slowed. In 2002, major companies faced doubled or even tripled premiums. In 2003, the increases were a "mere" 25–30%, although they were higher in litigation-prone industries such as health care, deregulated energy, and telecommunications. Some smaller companies saw smaller increases or even flat premiums.

Often, insurers responded to major corporate scandals by reducing the amount of coverage available to other corporations—e.g., offering policies limited to $10 million rather than the $25 million sought by a policy applicant. Policies that once had $1 million deductibles now have deductibles that could be as much as $100 million, and coinsurance of 10–30% is common.

"Severability" clauses—determining when an individual will lose coverage—are an important point of contention. In the 1990s, the particular director or officer charged with wrongdoing would lose coverage, but his or her colleagues would remain protected. Then, as the first financial scandals hit, insurers added clauses making an entire policy void if any covered director or officer was found guilty of complicity in financial wrongdoing. Insurers have retreated slightly from this drastic position, but have not returned to earlier norms. Rescission of coverage is usually permitted on the basis of misstatements in the application for the policy. However, if the person signing the application was not aware of the misstatements, then innocent directors and officers will probably continue to be covered by the policy.

In older D&O policies, removal triggers usually didn't apply until someone had been found guilty in court—which seldom happened, because so many cases were resolved by settlement or by accepting regulatory penalties. The later policies tend to have a broader threshold for removal, including some kinds of settlements and filing a plea of guilty. [Theo Francis, *It Still Costs Big to Insure Against a Boardroom Scandal,* Wall Street Journal, July 31, 2003, at p. C1]

In 2004, the Wall Street Journal reported that the rate of increase for D&O premiums dropped sharply, from a peak of 150% annual increases in the first quarter of 2003 to a 17% increase in the fourth quarter. Probably as a result of the mutual fund scandals, rates for fiduciary liability insurance averaged 67% higher in the fourth quarter of 2003 than in the fourth quarter of 2002. [Theo Francis, *Some Insurance Is Costing Less at U.S. Businesses*, Wall Street Journal, Mar. 9, 2004, at p. A2]

In March 2004, the Eastern District of Pennsylvania ruled that an insurer did not have the right to unilaterally rescind a D&O policy covering five former executives of the Adelphia Corporation. For one thing, the insurer failed to refund the premiums paid for coverage under the policy. Therefore, each of the executives was awarded $300,000 each toward the cost of defending themselves against civil suits (but not against the criminal charges). Adelphia is bankrupt, and four of its one-time top managers have been indicted for fraud and conspiracy. Three of the executives in this case face criminal charges; two have been sued civilly but not accused of crimes. [*Associated Elec. & Gas Ins. Servs. Ltd. v. Rigas*, 2004 U.S. Dist. LEXIS 4498 (E.D. Pa. March 17, 2004)]

[D]   Errors & Omissions (E&O)

Errors and Omissions insurance pays, on behalf of the insured, all loss for which the insured person is not indemnified by the insured organization if the person is liable because of any wrongful act he or she committed or attempted. In general, committing disparate treatment discrimination will be considered a wrongful act that can be covered under the policy, unless the policy definition covers only negligent, and not intentional, acts and omissions.

In many companies, E&O insurance is complemented by D&O insurance that covers the company for losses it incurs when it indemnifies directors and officers acting in that capacity.

An important issue is whether or not administrative actions (such as state agency and EEOC proceedings) are considered "claims or suits" for insurance purposes. The insurer is likely to make the argument that back pay awarded to a prevailing plaintiff is equitable relief and not "damages" that could be covered under the policy.

However, many courts have rejected this argument and required liability insurers to handle back-pay awards against their policyholders. E&O insurers may also resist paying back pay if the policy excludes amounts owed under a "contractual obligation," but here again, the insured will probably prevail if a back pay award is made.

Another insurance form covers plans, administrators, and trustees against allegations of impropriety. Many employment-related claims involve ERISA allegations, so the employer should at least consider adding this coverage to its insurance portfolio.

§ 43.06   DUTY OF THE INSURANCE CONTRACT

[A]   Duty to Defend

A lesser-known, but perhaps more important, part of the liability insurance policy is the insurer' duty to defend. That is, whenever a claim is made against the employer, the insurer has to provide a lawyer and take care of the case. However, usually the insurer is in control of the litigation, and decides how vigorously to defend the case and when to settle (although some policies return control of litigation to the insured). Most policies are drafted so that, if the insured company settles the case without consent and participation of the insurer, the insured company will not be able to recover any part of the settlement costs from the insurer.

The insurer' duty to indemnify is the duty to pay on the insured' behalf when the insured settles or loses a lawsuit. The duty to defend is much broader. If the allegations against an insured company are invalid, or can't be proved, then the liability insurer's role is to get the charge dismissed, even though there is no liability to indemnify. In general, if the charges combine claims that are covered by liability insurance with others that are not, the insurer has a duty to defend against all the charges, not just the covered ones.

Usually, the insurer's duty to defend is triggered by a "claim" made against the insured employer. This is usually interpreted as filing a complaint with a court. EEOC or local agency proceedings are not generally considered "claims," so an insured company is on its own for a significant part of the process before the duty to defend begins.

The Tenth Circuit examined the duty to defend in a 2005 case that arose when a mentally disabled person was hired by a charitable organization to work on a clean-up crew. He attacked a co-worker and his arm was broken when a supervisor restrained him. He brought a tort suit against RMJOB, the organization that employed him. The liability insurer settled the case, but attempted to involve RMJOB's Worker's Compensation carrier in the case. The Tenth Circuit ruled that the WC carrier did not owe RMJOB a duty to defend, and it had no right of contribution against the WC carrier. Because there was no duty, that insurer could not be sued for breach of contract or promissory estoppel, nor could it be charged with violating the ADA by retaliating against RMJOB for associating with persons with disabilities. There was no possibility of a WC judgment that the carrier would have to indemnify. Most courts that have considered the issue have ruled that an allegation that a tort suit should have been brought as a WC claim does not impose any duties on the WC carrier. Where the tort and WC systems interface, the tort system is supposed to bear primary responsibility for redress of injuries. [*Carolina Cas. Ins. Co. v. Pinnacol Assurance*, 425 F.3d 921 (10th Cir. 2005)]

[B]   Duties of the Insured

Insurance companies are relieved of their obligation to pay claims if the insured company fails to satisfy its obligations. The most obvious duty is paying premiums. Liability policies also require the insured to notify the insurer as soon as possible whenever a "claim" is made. Therefore, legal advice is necessary to determine which allegations have the legal status of a claim.

An Eighth Circuit case highlights these issues. The plaintiff, a cleaning service, was sued in 1997 in Hawaii state court for sexual harassment of a maintenance worker. The plaintiff (Interstate Cleaning Corporation—ICC) believed the case was just a nuisance suit, and didn't notify its insurer that it had been served with a complaint. The sexual harassment plaintiffs offered to settle the suit for $25,000, but ICC refused to settle. The jury ruled in favor of the sexual harassment plaintiffs. ICC was able to get the state court judgment amended to reduce the damages, and eventually the sexual harassment plaintiffs and ICC reached a settlement. In April 1999, ICC finally notified its insurer of the suit. The insurer refused to provide coverage on the grounds that the policy (a CGL policy with a self-insured endorsement, subject to a deductible of $50,000 per occurrence and $300,000 a year for multiple occurrences) did not cover the acts charged by the sexual harassment plaintiffs. ICC sued the insurer.

The Eighth Circuit found that, in general, insured parties have a duty to give immediate notice of claim to their insurers, although this requirement can be excused when it is not reasonably possible to provide notice. However, if an insurer is not prejudiced by the insured's failure to give notice, the insurer cannot use the notice failure as a reason not to defend or pay benefits. In this case, late notice did prejudice the insurer, because it was unable to investigate or participate in settlement negotiations. Therefore, it was not obligated to defend or indemnify the insureds. [*Interstate Cleaning Corp. v. Commercial Underwriters Ins. Co.*, 325 F.3d 1024 (8th Cir. 2003)]

§ 43.07   QUESTIONS OF TIMING

Liability policies are divided into "occurrence" and "claims-made" policies. If there is an "occurrence" covered by the policy (see above), all the occurrence policies in force at that time must make payments. But the insured doesn't get five times the amount of the liability. Coverage is coordinated (divided among them) to prevent windfalls.

A claims-made policy works differently. It covers only claims that are made during the policy term with respect to events that happened during the policy term. Because this can be a difficult standard to meet, claims-made policies are often extended to cover events after the policy's "retroactive date." There may also be an "extended reporting period" after the policy expires, where events are covered if they occurred while the policy was still in force, but were reported later.

An employer covered by a claims-made EPLI policy faced an ADEA suit. The policy covered claims first made while the policy was in force, reported to the company not later than 60 days after expiration of the policy. On November 7, the EEOC notified the employer of an ADEA charge. The employee filed suit on December 22, and the employer notified the insurer on January 21. The Eastern District of Louisiana found that timely notice was not given. [*Specialty Food Sys. Inc. v. Reliance Ins. Co.*, 45 F. Supp. 2d 541 (E.D. La. 1999), *aff'd without opinion*, 200 F.3d 816 (5th Cir. 1999)] The EEOC charge was a "written demand or notice" received by the insured from "any person or administrative agency," so notice was due within 60 days of November 7.

§ 43.08   FIDUCIARY LIABILITY INSURANCE

Where the policy covers the plan itself, the insurer can sue the fiduciary to recover the amount it had to pay out because of the fiduciary's conduct. Fiduciary liability insurance is usually available only in limited amounts, on a claims-made basis.

Fiduciary liability insurance is an asset of the plan, but also protects trustees' personal assets. Furthermore, a fiduciary who breaches his or her duty may not be able to afford to reimburse the plan for its full losses.

For the policy to be truly useful, the definition of the "insured" should include the plan and/or trust, all past, present and future trustees and employees, and their successors. Coverage for the spouse of an insured if named as an additional defendant should also be included. The general rule is that most fiduciary liability policies don't cover third-party administrators or service providers who act as fiduciaries, although it may be possible to add them to the policy under an endorsement.

The definition of "loss" should include defense costs (including costs for investigators and expert witnesses) settlements, judgments, and pre- and post-judgment interest. Although liability insurance typically excludes coverage of fines and penalties, IRS Employee Plans Compliance Resolution System (EPCRS) penalties and amounts paid to the DOL when it wins or settles an ERISA § 502(l) case are usually either included in the basic coverage or added by endorsement.

> **Tip:** The entire policy has to be examined to see if there are additional limitations—for instance, the definition of "loss" may exclude fines and penalties.

Most fiduciary liability policies are claims-made policies. At each anniversary date, the insured can evaluate and adjust the policy limits and scope of coverage, bearing affordability in mind. Once a policy is purchased, it is hard to change carriers, because the application requires a warranty that there are no known claims or circumstances that would be excluded by the new insurer if they were fully disclosed—and it's very common for companies to face claims of this type!

In this market, too, coverage has become scarcer and more expensive. According to the Segal Company, the median limit of liability purchased typically increases with the size of the plan. For a plan with $1 to $10 million in assets, $2 million in fiduciary liability insurance is typical, rising to $5 million for $10–$100 million in plan assets and $10 million for assets over $100 million. A combined policy covering two plans can increase the available coverage, even to levels higher than the plan assets. Appropriate coverage limits for a pension plan depend on many factors, such as the plan's current and anticipated future financial condition; if it is underfunded or overfunded; how its portfolio has performed; if its assets are adequately diversified. For welfare benefit plans, the relevant issues include the effect of cost increases on the plan's financial reserves and other metrics, and whether the plan has changed its benefit structure or plans to do so soon.

Segal found not only that premium increases are very predictable (perhaps 15–25% for small plans between 2001 and 2002, or even 100% or more if the plan had risk factors such as poor financial statements or outstanding or threatened litigation), but that premiums differ greatly—the highest premiums for plans with limits under $1 million were almost ten times as high as the smallest.

The basic rule under ERISA is that the insurer must have a right of recourse (the right to be reimbursed) against the insured if the entire premium for fiduciary liability insurance comes from plan assets. Therefore, the fiduciaries' personal assets will not be protected. To protect the fiduciaries' property, a Waiver of Recourse (WOR) waiver must be purchased—and, furthermore, the premiums for the waiver must not come from plan assets. The insurer charges the fiduciary a premium for the WOR waiver. [Segal Newsletter, *January 2003 Fiduciary Liability Insurance: What Limit, What Price and What's Next?* Jan. 2003, <http://www.segalco.com/publications/newsletters/jan2003.pdf>]

Attorney Stephen Saxon published some suggestions about obtaining fiduciary liability insurance in 2006:

- Buy a "nonrecourse rider" if the plan pays for the insurance. ERISA prohibits fiduciaries from using plan assets to pay for fiduciary liability insurance, unless the plan has recourse against the fiduciary. The rider prevents the insurer from proceeding against the fiduciary in case there is a covered loss.
- Find out if the policy limits include defense costs, because if they do, an expensive defense can exhaust the policy.
- Check to see if the deductible applies to all the claims within a policy period or whether each allegation is subject to a separate deductible. Waiving the deductible for claims against individual fiduciaries is a common provision.
- The policy application will ask the trustees if they are aware of any potential claims (and there will be no coverage for claims that the trustees knew about but did not disclose), so obtain legal advice on how to answer the question completely and accurately.
- If the policy covers attorneys' fees on a "pay on behalf of" basis (i.e., the insured can select counsel rather than having to be represented by the insurer's attorneys) the policy will be much more useful if the fees are reimbursed as they are incurred, instead of only at the end of the case. [Stephen M. Saxon, *Insurance Policies: Tips on Securing Fiduciary Liability Insurance,* PlanSponsor.com, <http://www.plansponsor.com/magazine_type1_print.jsp?RECORD_ID=31594> (Apr. 2, 2006)]

INDEX

References are to section numbers.

G

Garnishment, 1.17
Gatekeepers, 18.13[E]
Gay marriage, 34.06[D]
  benefits under EGHPs, 18.06[A]
Gender behavior discrimination, 34.06[D]
Gender reassignment, 18.03[F]
General Industry Standards, 31.03
Genetic testing, 26.05
Genuine job vacancy, 30.09[D]
Gissel bargaining order, 30.07[A]
Glass ceiling, 29.02
Golden parachutes, 3.03[D], 16.01, 16.07[B]
  final regulations, 3.03[D], 16.07[B]
Green cards, 23.11[D]
Grief management programs, 28.01
Grievance records in arbitration and ADR,
  40.02[B]
Gross misconduct and COBRA, 19.02[A]
"Group emergency pool," 1.16
Group-term life insurance, 21.02[D]
Gulf Opportunity Zone Act, 2.06, 6.06[B],
  8.01[B][3]
Gyms, 22.06

H

H-1B visas, 23.11[E]
Hacking, 27.06
Handbooks, employee. See Employee handbooks
Hardship distributions and 401(k) plans, 6.06[B]
Hazardous condition exposure, 31.05
H-CAP, 15.19[B]
Health Coverage Tax Credit (HCTC), 19.02[A]
Health Insurance Portability and Accessibility
  Act. See HIPAA
Health management organizations. See HMOs
Health plan claims, 13.03
  attorneys' fees, 13.05[E]
  case law, 13.05, 13.07
  custodial services, 13.05[C]
  exclusions, 13.05[C]
  experimental treatment, 13.05[B]
  FMLA and, 38.04[A]
  full and fair review, 13.05[E]
  HIPAA EDI standards, 13.04
  procedural issues, 13.07
  standard of review, 13.05[E], 13.06
  statutes of limitations and timing issues,
    13.05[D]

workers' compensation, 13.05[C]
Health plans
  ADEA, 37.05
    bona fide plans, 37.05
  cafeteria plans, 22.03[A]
  CDHP plans, 18.18[A]
  claims. See Health plan claims
  COBRA. See COBRA
  disability plans. See Disability plans
  EGHPs. See EGHPs
  enforcement and compliance for qualified
    plans, 15.03[D]
  ERISA, 22.09
  HIPAA. See HIPAA
  HRAs, 18.18[B]
  Massachusetts requirement of employer to
    provide if employing 11 or more
    employees, 18.03
  retirees. See Retiree health benefits
  SPD, 11.02[B]
  USERRA, 1.18
Health reimbursement arrangement (HRA)
  plans, 18.09[D], 18.18
  COBRA continuation coverage, 19.02[F]
  combination with FSA, 18.11[A]
  comparison to other plans, 18.09[D]
  post-death treatment of account funds,
    18.09[D]
Health-Related Arrangements (HRAs),
  18.18[B]
Health Savings Accounts (HSAs), 2.06,
  9.10[A], 18.09[B]
  advantages of, 18.09[D]
  COBRA, nonapplicability of, 18.09[C]
  comparison to other plans, 18.09[D]
  eligibility rules, 18.09[D]
  IRS guidance, 18.09[C]
  post-death treatment of account funds,
    18.09[D]
  qualified medical expenses, 18.09[B]
  state tax treatment, 18.09[B]
Health Savings and Affordability Act of 2003,
  18.09[B]
Health Savings Security Accounts (HSSAs),
  18.09[B]
  qualified individual, 18.09[B]
High policy maker exception to ADEA, 37.02
Highway transport expenses, 22.06
HIPAA (Health Insurance Portability and
  Accessibility Act), 19.01
  ADA interface, 36.10[D]
  cafeteria plans, 22.03[B]

I

S